Ann.
1922

GOD IN CONTEMPORARY THOUGHT

PHILOSOPHICAL QUESTIONS SERIES
Editor in Chief
Sebastian A. Matczak, Ph. D., Th. D.
Professor of Philosophy
St. John's University
New York

No. 1. S. A. Matczak. *Le problème de Dieu dans la pensée de Karl Barth.* Louvain: Editions Nauwelaerts, 1968.
No. 2. _____, *Research and Composition in Philosophy.* Louvain: Editions Nauwelaerts, 1968. 2nd ed., 1971.
No. 3. _____, *Philosophy: A Select, Classified Bibliography of Ethics, Economics, Law, Politics, Sociology.* Louvain: Editions Nauwelaerts, 1970. 2nd ed., 1974.
No. 4. _____, *Philosophy: Its Nature, Methods and Basic Sources.* Louvain: Editions Nauwelaerts, 1976.
No. 5. _____, *Philosophy: Its History and Branches.* In preparation.
No. 6. M. R. Barral, *Progressive Neutralism: A Philosophical Aspect of American Education.* Louvain: Editions Nauwelaerts, 1970.
No. 7. W. Smith, *Giovanni Gentile on the Existence of God.* Louvain: Editions Nauwelaerts, 1970.
No. 8 J. F. Mitros, *Religions: A Select, Classified Bibliography.* Louvain: Editions Nauwelaerts, 1973.
No. 9. G. J. Van Treese, *D'Alembert and Frederick the Great: A Study of Their Relationship.* Louvain: Editions Nauwelaerts, 1974.
No. 10. S. A. Matczak (ed.), *God in Contemporary Thought.* New York: Learned Publications, Inc., 1977.

Others will follow.

Library of Congress Catalog Card Number: 75-31391
ISBN 0912116-12-9

© 1977 by Learned Publications, Inc.
83-53 Manton Street
Jamaica, New York 11435, U.S.A.

PHILOSOPHICAL QUESTIONS SERIES
—— 10 ——

GOD
IN CONTEMPORARY
THOUGHT

A Philosophical Perspective

A Collective Study

Editor

SEBASTIAN A. MATCZAK

DOCTOR IN PHILOSOPHY, DOCTOR IN THEOLOGY,
PROFESSOR AT ST. JOHN'S UNIVERSITY, NEW YORK

LEARNED PUBLICATIONS, INC.
NEW YORK

EDITIONS NAUWELAERTS
10, MUNTSTRAAT
LOUVAIN

BEATRICE-NAUWELAERTS
4, RUE DE FLEURUS
PARIS

1977

BY THE SAME EDITOR

Stanislaus Cardinal Hosius on Sacraments in General. Rome: Pontifica Universitas Gregoriana, 1951.

Stanisluas Hosius on Sacraments. Paris: Libella, 1952.

Stanislaus Cardinal Hosius: Present State of Research — Results and Postulates. New York: The Polish Institute of Arts and Sciences, 1961.

An Archiepiscopal Election in the Middle Ages: Jacob Swinka of Gniezno. New York: The Polish Institute of Arts and Sciences, 1963.

Karl Barth on God: Our Knowledge of the Divine Existence. New York: Alba House, 1962.

Le Problème de Dieu dans la pensée de Karl Barth. Louvain: Editions Nauwelaerts, 1968.

Select and Classified Bibliography of David Hume, Saint Louis, Missouri: The Modern Schoolman, 1964.

Fideism, Traditionalism. New York: The New Catholic Encyclopedia, McGraw-Hill, 1967.

Research and Composition in Philosophy. Louvain: Editions Nauwelaerts, 1968. 2nd edition, 1971.

Philosophy: A Select, Classified Bibliography of Ethics, Economics, Law, Politics, Sociology. Louvain: Editions Nauwelaerts, 1970. 2nd ed. 1974.

God in Contemporary Thought. Editor of this collective study. New York: Learned Publications, 1977.

ABOUT THE SAME EDITOR

Contemporary Authors (Detroit, Michigan: Gale Research Co.), Vol IX-X, p. 322.

Directory of American Scholars (New York: R. R. Bowker), 4th ed., p. 129; 5th ed. Vol. IV, p. 241.

Who's Who in American Education (Nashville, Tennessee: Who's Who in American Education), Vol. XXII, p. 988; Vol. XXIII, p. 553.

Who's Who in the East (Chicago: Marquis), Vol. XI, p. 689; Vol. XII, p. 728; Vol. XIII, p. 468.

Directory of the Catholic Theological Society of America (Yonkers, New York) 1965, p. 80; 1969, p. 64; 1972, p. 53.

Community Leaders in America (Raleigh, North Carolina: News Publishing Co.), 1969, p. 173.

Directory of International Biography (London: Artillery Mansions), 1969-1970, p. 628; 1973, p. 840.

The Writers Directory, 1971-1973 (Chicago — London: St. James Press, 1971), p. 277.

International Scholars Directory (Strassbourg, France: International Scholarly Publishers), 1973, p. 166.

Who's Who in America, (Washington, D.C.: Honorary Society), 1975.

International Behavioral Scientist (Sadhna Prakeshan, India), Vol. VI, No. 1, p. 98.

PREFACE

With great satisfaction and justified joy we present this collective work on the problems concerning our knowledge of God's existence. It is not easy to find an enterprise more worthy of man than a search for the truth, especially for the Ultimate Truth, the Principal of the whole of reality. Questions concerning the nature of this Truth and the ways of knowing it are the most pertinent that men with a variety of insights have ever asked. No doubt man will continue to ask such questions as time goes on, since they emerge from the roots of his being. As a rational being, he cannot cease to be profoundly engaged in a scrutiny of his *raison d'être* and of his ultimate destiny. The permanent gravity of these questions is expressed in the fact of the continuous presence of religions among men. Religions supply man with answers to his vexing perennial questions, but their answers are authoritative rather than rationalistic. Some, especially the more intellectually developed, are not satisfied with an imposed answer but seek an explanation in line with their rational nature. Hence, their search for a rational answer is in agreement with the dignity of their nature. Both the rationalistic and the religious approaches toward the Ultimate Truth testify to the fact that man's interest in God lies deeply rooted in his nature and activity, although this interest is expressed in a wide variety of forms which forcefully indicate the infinite riches of their ultimate Cause.

Philosophers quite clearly reflect this fact. They scrutinize its meaning with specific interest, although not without a great variety of opinions. The justification of their opinions, notably their presuppositions, the logical consistency of their reasoning and the final formulations of their positions have been repeatedly examined. It seems however, that the problem itself and therefore its answer will never cease to be explored enough, since man's finite capability and the immense reality surrounding him are not commensurable, and in consequence not exhaustible to men.

In this issue (No. 10) of the *Philosophical Question Series* we advance some aspects of the unceasing problems concering our knowledge of God's existence. We do not assume responsibility for the contents of the articles presented in this volume. However, we are firmly convinced that our efforts to find one of the best qualified scholars for each particular question have been successful.

Yet we are open to further elaborations and deeper discussions of these perennial problems. Further studies of the relevant questions and problems involved in this volume are imperative and highly rewarding for each man in particular and for mankind in general. Only a cumulative and unbiased effort can successfully lead us to approach the Truth and its ultimate source, God.

Sebastian A. Matczak
Editor

New York, U.S.A.

TABLE OF CONTENTS

PART ONE

GOD IN ANCIENT CULTURES

PART THREE

SELECTED THINKERS ON GOD

PART FOUR

SPECIFIC PROBLEMS

ACKNOWLEDGMENT

The warmest thanks must be presented to Dr. Anna Teresa Tymieniecka whose encouragement and help in the collection of articles made the publication of this this book possible.

We also thank Dr. Robert A. Herrera of Seton Hall University and Dr. Raymond F. Bulman of St. John's University for their help in soliciting articles.

Special thanks must also be presented to Dr. Walter W. Artus for his help and advice. Here cannot be ommitted the assistance of Harold Pemberton, who helped in various ways in the preparation of the manuscript; our very warm thanks have to be directed to him.

We cannot omit the expression our gratitude to Lloyd Eby, Jean Henri Vanalderwelt, Pauline Pilote, Alice Fleischer, Diane Muxworthy, John A. Sonneborn and many others who very effectively helped to realize our project.

* * *

Grateful acknowledgment is made to the various publishers and authors who kindly granted permission to quote from the following works:

To the Columbia University Press for permission to quote from *The Complete Works of Chuang Tzu,* translated by Burton Watson; *Biographical Dictionary of Republican China,* Vol. II, edited by Howard L. Boorman and Richard C. Howard.

To Holt, Rinehart and Winston for permission to quote from *This People Israel* by Leo Baeck.

To the Central Conference of American Rabbis for permission to quote from "The greatness of the Eternal One . . ." by Chaim Stern in *Gates of Prayer for Weekdays.*

To the *International Philosophical Quarterly* for permission to quote from Kenneth Inada's "Some Basic Misconceptions of Buddhism."

To the Hokuseido Press, Tokyo for permission to quote from *Nagarjuna* by Kenneth Inada.

To the Charles E. Tuttle Co., Inc. for permission to quote from *Shinto: The Kami Way* by Sokyo Ono, and *Gods of Northern Buddhism* by A. Getty.

To Paragon Book Reprint Corp. for permission to quote from *The National Faith of Japan* by D.C. Holton.

To Houghton Mifflin Co. for permission to quote from *The Complete Poetical Works of Tennyson,* by Alfred Tennyson.

To Paul A. Schilpp, Editor of the Library of Living Philosophers, Inc., for permission to quote from the *Philosophy of Alfred North Whitehead.*

To Holy Cross Orthodox Press for permission to qoute from "The Doctrine of One Nature in the Syrian Rites" by Severius Zaka Iwas published in *The Greek Orthodox Theological Review,* Vol. XIII, No. 2, Fall 1968.

To the American Association for the Advancement of Science for permission to quote from *Science,* Vol. 179, March 16, 1973, copyright 1973 by the American Association for the Advancement of Science.

To the Oxford University Press for permission to quote from *African Worlds* edited by Daryll Forde, *Lugbara Religion* by John Middleton, *The Oxford Translation of Aristotle* edited by W.D. Ross, *The Correspondence of Gerard Manley Hopkins and Richard Weston Dixon* edited by Claude Colleer Abbot, *The Shaping Vision of Gerard Manley Hopkins* by Alan Heuser, *Hinduism* by R.C. Zaehner, *Concordant Discord* by R.C. Zaehner and *The Dialogues of Plato* translated by Benjamin Jowett.

To Cambridge University Press for permission to quote from *A History of Indian Philosophy* by S. Dasgupta, and *The Axioms of Projective Geometry* by Alfred North Whitehead.

To The Jewish Publication Society of America for permission to quote from *Legends of the Jews* by Louis Ginzberg, and *God in Search of Man* by Abraham J. Heschel.

To A. Watkins Inc. for permission to quote from *The Descent of the Dove* by Charles Williams, copyright 1939.

To Routledge and Kegan Paul Ltd., London (Humanities Press, Inc., Atlantic Highlands, New Jersey) for permission to quote from *Western Civilization and the Natives of South Africa* by Issac Schapera.

To Random House, Inc. and Alfred A. Knopf, Inc. for permission to quote from *The Devil and the Good Lord and Two Other Plays* by Jean-Paul Sartre, translated by Kitty Black and Sylvia and George Leeseon, copyright 1960; *Collected Poems* by W.H. Auden, edited by Edward Mendelson, copyright 1959.

To Dover Publications Inc. for permission to quote from *Buddhist Suttas* by Rhys Davids.

To Russell and Russell for permission to quote from *The Essence of Plato's Philosophy* by Constantin Ritter.

To the University of North Carolina Press for permission to quote from *Metaphor in Hopkins* by Rober Boyle.

To the Ramakrishna-Vivekananda Center for permission to quote from *The Gospel of Sri Ramakrishna* by Swami Nikhilanda.

To SCM Press Ltd. for permission to quote from *New Essays in Philosophical Theology* edited by Antony Flew and Alasdair MacIntyre.

To Doubleday for permission to quote from *African Religions and Philosophies* by John S. Mbiti.

To University of Chicago Press for permission to quote from *The Religion of Israel* by Y. Kaufman, copyright 1960; and *Systematic Theology* by Paul Tillich, copyright 1954.

To Walker and Company for permission to quote from *The Burning Brand: Diaries* by Cesare Pavese, translated by A.E. Murch and Geanne Molli.

To Chilmark Press Inc. for permission to quote from *In Parenthesis* and *The Anathemata* by David Jones.

To Yale University Press for permission to quote from *Gerard Manley Hopkins: A Study of Poetic Idiosyncrasy in Relation to Poetic Tradition* by W.H. Gardner; *The Courage To Be* by Paul Tillich; *The Goal of Creativity in Psychotherapy* by Edith Weigert.

To George Braziller, Inc. for permission to quote from *Saint Genet, Actor and Martyr* by Jean-Paul Sartre, translated by Bernard Frechtman.

To Martinus Nijhoff for permission to quote from *New Being* by B. Osborne.

To Princeton University Press for permission to quote from *A Source Book in Indian Philosophy,* edited by Sarvepalli Radhakrishnan and Charles A. Moore, copyright 1957 by Princeton University Press; *A Source Book in Chinese Philosophy,* translated and compiled by Wing-tsit Chan, copyright 1963 by Princeton University Press; *A History of Chinese Philosophy* by Fung Yu-Lan, translated by Derk Bodde; *The Collected Works of C.G. Jung,* ed. Herbert Read, Michael Fordham, Gerhard Adler, William McGuire, trans. R.F.C. Hull, Bollingen Series XX, Vol. 12, *Psychology and Alchemy,* 2d ed. copyright © 1953, 1968 by Princeton University Press.

To Harper and Row, Publisher, Inc. for permission to quote from *Spiritual Problems in Contemporary Literature* by Stanley Hooper; *A History of Christian Thought* by Paul Tillich, edited by C.E. Braaten; and *Dynamics of Faith* by Paul Tillich.

To Grove Press Inc. for permission to quote from *What the Buddha Taught* by Walpola Rodula.

To the Magnes Press for permission to quote from *Yehezkel Kaufman Jubilee Volume* edited by Menonohem Haron.

To George Allen and Unwin, Ltd. for permission to quote from *Mysticism and Logic* by Bertrand Russell; *Buddhist Wisdom Books* by Edward Conze; *The Principal Upanisads* edited by S. Radhakrishnan; *The Brahma Sutra* by S. Radhakrishnan; *Outlines of Indian Philosophy* by M. Hiriyana; *Contemporary Indian Philosophy* by J.H. Muirhead and S. Radhakrishnan; *Religion and Man* by Rabindranath Tagore; *Real Conversation* by William Archer; *Outlines of Hinduism* by M, Hiriyana.

To Abingdon Press for permission to quote from J. Muilenberg in Vol. V and R. Denton in Vol. VI of the *Interpreter's Bible* and G.E. Mendenhall in Vol. II of the *Interpreter's Dictionary of the Bible.*

To the Macmillan Publishing Co. for permission to quote from the *Collected Poems of Thomas Hardy,* copyright 1925; the *Selected Poems of Thomas Hardy* edited and with an Introduction by John Crowe Ransom (Introduction: copyright 1960, 1961): *The Quest of the Historical Jesus* by Albert Schweitzer; *The Great Asian Religions* by Wing-tsit Chan *et al; Religion in the Making* by Alfred North Whitehead, copyright 1926, renewed 1954 by Evelyn Whitehead; *Process and Reality* by Alfred North Whitehead, copyright 1929, renewed 1957 by Evelyn Whitehead; *A Short History of Chinese Philosophy* by Fung Yu-lan, copyright 1948, renewed 1976 by Chung Liao Feng and Derk Bodde.

To William B. Eerdmans Publishing Co. for permission to quote from G. Quell's article in *Theological Dictionary of the New Testament.*

To The Westminster Press for quotations from The *Theology of the Old Testament,* Vol. I, by Walter Eichrodt, translated by J.A. Baker, published in U.S.A. by The Westminster Press, 1961, copyright © 1961 S.C.M. Press Ltd., used by permission.

To the Athlone Press of The University of London for permission to quote from *The Poems of Thomas Hardy: A Critical Introduction* by Kenneth Mardsen.

To the Viking Press Inc., the publisher, for permission to quote from *The Masks of God: Oriental Mythology* by Joseph Campbell, copyright © 1962.

To Schocken Books, Inc. for quotations reprinted by permission of Schocken Books, Inc. from *Major Trends in Jewish Mysticism* by Gershom G. Scholem, copyright © 1946, © 1954 by Schocken Books, Inc.

To E.P. Dutton and Co. for permission to quote from *Mysticism* by Evelyn Underhill.

To the Open Court Publishing Co. for quotations reprinted from *The Logic of Perfection* by Charles Hartshorne by permission of the Open Court

Publishing Co., LaSalle, Illinois, copyright © 1962; and from *A Natural Theology for Our Time,* copyright © 1967.

To University of Chicago Press, the publisher, for permission to quote from *The Religion of Israel* by Yehezkel Kaufman, copyright © 1960; and *Systematic Theology* by Paul Tillich, copyright © 1954.

To Shambhala Publications, Inc. for quotations reprinted by special arrangement with Shambhala Publications Inc., 1123 Spruce Street, Boulder, Colorado 80302, from *Treasures on the Tibetan Middle Way* by Herbert V. Guenther, copyright 1976 by Herbert V. Guenther.

To the Ronald Press Company for permission to quote from *Islam: The Straight Path-Islam Interpreted by Muslims,* edited by Kenneth W. Morgan, copyright © 1958.

To the Diocese of the American Church of America for permission to quote from *The Divine Liturgy of the Armenian Apostolic Orthodox Church,* edited by Archbishop Tiran Nersoyan.

To Charles Scribner's Sons for quotations reprinted from *The Range of Reason* by Jacques Maritain with the permission of Charles Scribner's Sons; copyright 1952 Jacques Maritain.

To Harvard University Press, the publisher, for permission to quote from *Three Muslim Sages* by Seyyed Hossein Nasr, 1964: *Nietzsche: A Self-Portrait from His Letters* by Friedrich Nietzsche, translated and edited by Peter Fuss and Henry Shapiro, copyright © 1971 by the President and Fellows of Harvard College.

To Harcourt Brace Jovanovich, Inc. the publisher, for permission to quote from *Diaspora* by Werner Keller.

To the University Press, University of Pennsylvania for permission to quote from *Oriental and Biblical Studies* by A.E. Speiser, edited by J.J. Finkelstein and M. Greenberg, 1967.

To Kent State University Press, the original publisher, for permission to quote from *The Wreck of the Deutschland: An Essay and Commentary* by John E. Keating.

To George Braziller, Inc. for permission to quote from *Situations* by Jean-Paul Sartre, translated by Renita Eisler; *The Words* by Jean-Paul Sartre, translated by Bernard Frechtman.

INTRODUCTION

Sebastian A. Matczak *

1. The Problem

The question of God, His existence and nature, is one of the most important and puzzling challenges which humankind has ever faced. It persistently occupies men's minds, radically affects their behavior, and profoundly changes their existence. Yet this question presents a serious problem to man's purely theoretical understanding. For an endeavor to understand God's invisible existence and nature must involve some understanding of the whole of reality by man's limited, finite reason. There seems to exist a disproportion in this task, between the instrument, that is man's limited perceptivity and the object, namely, infinite reality. In order that the task be fulfilled the investigation requires a comprehension not only of all the branches of philosophy, but also of other fields of human knowledge. Such a breadth of knowledge, very difficult to obtain, might of itself explain the differences among scholars in their manner of inquiry as well as in their final results.

2. A Practical Solution

Yet the apparently unbridgeable abyss between our finite reason and its infinite object is spanned by a multitude of peoples who firmly accept the existence of the Divine and act in accordance with this belief. Such a conviction has been firmly expressed in the various religions widespread among the peoples of the world during all periods of human history. These religions,

*Editor, Professor of Philosophy at St. John's University, New York, U.S.A.

although they differ in their creeds and rites, contain some clearly discernable common elements, notably the worship of the Divine, a Superior Being, and a belief in man's responsibility before the Deity in the present, but more particularly in the future life. Such attitudes are forcefully expressed in prayers and rituals throughout life and in particular in the care and burial of the dead (graves).[1]

True, these beliefs are often connected with additional features ascribed to the Deities. These features constitute specific and quite obvious differences between religions. They are usually, but not necessarily always products of imagination and of an endeavor to make the Deity more understandable and accessible to man.

3. A Serious Difficulty

The question arises, however, whether these imaginative presentations contribute essentially to the concept of the Divine or whether they change it to the extent that the real God becomes an idol.

This is a very serious question integrally connected with the validity of religions. It might be expected, therefore, that the answers to it will differ. To reach correct conclusions, the scholar has to know not only the externally expressed beliefs, rites and behaviors of particular religions but also their very spirit. Moreover, he must be able to compare the external manifestations of religions with their internal meaning and their true spirit. This obviously is not an easy task. To carry it out properly he must be more than a good unbiased historian of religion, and often also an archaeologist, he must also be a theologian specializing in a particular religion, and a philosopher. The rarity of such a comprehensive expertise means that the descriptions and conclusions made by various scholars of religions still leave much room for further research and evaluation.

---

1 B. Malinowski, *Magic, Science and Religion* (Garden City, N.Y.: Doubleday Anchor Books, 1954), pp. 47-53. C.J. Ducasse, *A Critical Examination of the Belief in a Life after Death.* Springfield, Ill.: Ch.C. Thomas, 1961. J. Staudinger, *L'homme moderne devant le problème de l'au-delà,* tr. by Rene Guillaume. Paris: Casterman, 1950. K. Rahner, *On the Theology of Death.* New York: Herder and Herder, 1964.

Moreover, with regard to the question of a Supreme God, some religions, for example Shintoism and Buddhism, present specific problems. Nonetheless, even in Shintoism we witness a sort of hierarchy among the deities. Thus, there is in such a faith an implicit suggestion at least that a superior, indescribable Divinity exists.[2] Furthermore, honoring ancestors cannot be severed either from a belief in a future life or from a sense of responsibility for our deeds. The notions of responsibility and of the existence of a Superior Being may be quite rudimentary and unexplicit, yet they do not seem to be excluded, since they flow logically from explicitly professed beliefs.[3]

Also in Shintoism we notice a recognition of *Kami,* that is of a special power emanating from objects or persons; this is a recognition of superior powers, transcendent energies existing in the world and influencing man. Even if these qualities are considered as cosmic, we find in them a recognition of a transcendence, superior to man, which he has to take into account.[4]

Similar recognition of transcendent superiority influencing man we find in the idea of *Mana* in Polynesia, *Fetish* in West Africa, *Orenda, Waken, Manito* and *Yok* in North America. These remind us of Rudolf Otto's *Holy* or *Numinous* which man intuitively recognizes from the depth of his spirit.[5]

The idea of Nirvana in Buddhism reminds us also of a future life and of man's unity with the Divine.[6] Unity here takes the form of man's immersion in ultimate reality, where a reconciliation of all differences occurs; as man is united with it, he does not suffer any longer. This Buddhist view compares somewhat with the concept of God in Christianity, which includes a belief in man's everlasting contemplation of God in heaven where he is wholly taken by

---

2 See below, Chapter X.

3 *Ibid.*

4 See also A.C. Bouquet, *Comparative Religion.* 6th ed. (Baltimore, Maryland: Penguine Books, 1964), pp. 194-199.

5 Ch. Dawson, *Religion and Culture* (New York: Meridian Books, 1959), pp. 38-39.

6 See below, Chapters VI, XI.

God's perfections and thus somehow immersed in Him. Christianity, however, points out the positive aspect of unity with God, namely man's happiness in enjoying God, whereas Buddhism emphasizes the negative aspect, i.e. absence of suffering. There are grounds for seeing an analogy between Buddhism's concept of God and that of Judaism in this regard.[7]

4. Need of Revelation

The question arises at this point whether the idea of the Divine believed by the peoples as Superior Being may be considered as the idea of true God, and thus attainable by man's reason alone, not aided by supernatural revelation?

The notion of Superior Being, even more of one Superior is not only the basic tenet of many of the world's major religions, such as Judaism, Christianity and Islam, which base their belief on supernatural revelation, but also is a strong theme in natural religions, such as the tribal faiths of Africa, Hinduism and Buddhism. It is noticed that the concept of God in some branches of those religions has been interpreted either in the pantheistic sense, or as a revealed concept of God.[8]

Moreover, it seems that the idea of one God has not been precluded from polytheistic religions. The multiple gods can be interpreted as and compared with angels and devils in monotheistic religions, who are superior to man, but are not the supreme God. Similarly the gods of a polytheistic religion are not the supreme God, but are superior to man and in this wise can be called gods.

We may add that polytheistic religions use images in order to express their intuition of superior reality, whereas more cultured men use arguments and concepts. Thus in the primitive religion man recognizing superior reality combines it with the power which

---

7 "God," *Encyclopaedia Judaica* (16 vols. New York: The Macmillan Co., 1971-1972), Vol. VI, pp. 643, 650, cf. also pp. 674-684.

8 For an examination of whether the *Veda* contains the Word of God, see below, Chapter VII.

he finds in the world surrounding him, whereas cultured man conceives it in an abstract and discursive way.[9]

Nevertheless natural religions are often not clear both on the existence of one God and on His nature. The variety of concepts they espouse emphatically demonstrates a need for some intervention. Men would patently benefit from God's special instruction on Himself over and above His disclosure of Himself through the visible world; in other words man needs a positive revelation besides the evidence of His existence provided by natural things. This revelation, although not absolutely necessary, would supply man with greater clarity and certitude of God's existence and His nature. However revealed knowledge is an absolute necessity if man is to possess a more intimate insight into God's nature.[10] The reason, as stated previously, is that the finite human intellect, which forms ideas from visible things, cannot perceive the bosom of the invisible and infinite Supreme Being by its own power.

The religions which base themselves on revelation, such as Judaism, Christianity, Zoroastrianism and Islam, claim to have such an intimate revealed insight. Christianity derives it from the revelation brought by Jesus Christ and from its matrix, God's revelation in Judaism.

However, if man is to accept it, the fact of revelation must accord with reason. This requirement arises from human nature, which is rational; man must know why he believes. As St. Paul wrote, "I know whom I believe."[11] This need must not be identified with a need to understand the content of revelation, which is mysterious. God is an infinitely Superior Being to man. Thus, He surpasses man's capability of understanding Him. Yet, man's rational nature demands that there be no contradiction in

---

9 Dawson, *op. cit.,* pp. 40-41.
10 Ludovicus Lercher, *Institutiones theologiae dogmaticae* (4 vols. Barcelona: Herder, 1945), I, pp. 16-32.
11 St. Paul, *II Tim.* 1, 12. See also Thomas Aquinas, *Summa Theologiae,* II-II, q. 2, a. 10. Augustine, *De utilitate credendi,* XXIV, 45; *De praedestinatione Sanctorum,* II, 5; *De Ordine,* II, 926. See also E. Gilson, *Introduction à l'étude de Saint Augustin* (Paris, 1949), 1 p. 304-305; S.A. Matczak, *Karl Barth on God* (New York, 1962), pp. 161-162, 317-318.

the concepts or events involved, although he accepts them on the authority of the provider of the testimony.[12]

The revelation accepted by many thinkers has been rejected by others. The grounds of the denial range from the absolute rationalism advanced during the Enlightenment, including the deism of the 18th century[13] and Hegel's thought, to the opposite pole of the fideism and traditionalism developed particularly in the 19th century.[14] The followers of the first trend reject any mysterious truth which cannot be fully understood by human reason, while the adherents to the second are inclined to think that man is not capable of grasping truth unless he is taught it.

Contemporary thinkers defend similar positions, although with various modifications. A satisfactory explanation and solution of their arguments needs to be made to justify the conclusions they support. Compelled by his rational nature as noted before, man looks for this justification. It may be provided by consistent reasoning, thus by sound philosophy, and by a clarification of the position in the light of historical facts investigated as objectively as possible.

5. Philosophy and Some of Its Problems

Hence, the problem of God, His existence and nature, belongs on the one hand to the field of religions, on the other hand to the field of philosophy and history. It seems to be a matter of fact that an average religious man accepts God intuitively rather than discursively; very often he is supported by authority, hence by faith. Such a faith has its justification in the acceptance of the authority of the reporter, father, mother, teacher or whomever.

---

12 *Ibid.,* pp. 264-269, 318.
13 R.Z. Lauer, *The Mind of Voltaire: A Study of His "Constructive Deism."* Westminster, Maryland: Newman Press, 1961. "Deism," *New Catholic Encyclopedia* (16 vols. New York: McGraw-Hill 1967), Vol. IV, pp. 721-724. F. Copleston, *A History of Philosophy* (6 vols. Westminster, Maryland: Newman Press, 1959), Vol. V. pp. 161-169.
14 S.A. Matczak, "Traditionalism," *New Catholic Encyclopedia, op. cit.,* Vol. XIII, pp. 228-230, see also "Fideism," *op. cit.,* Vol. V, pp. 908-910.

This justification constitutes reasonableness of faith, the foundation of man's belief. To show evidence of this reasonableness is the task of philosophy and history. These disciplines generate scholarly proofs for religion. History has to provide the proofs for the fact itself; philosophy has to show the reasonableness of this fact and its acceptability for man.

While historians generally accept certain facts fundamental to religious belief, philosophers are more divided, even on the most basic issue of all, the existence of God.

The opinions of the philosophers concerning God's existence might be reduced to three basic groups. One group represents the opinion that man is unable to solve this problem; these are agnostics of various kinds. A second group simply denies God's existence; these are atheists. Finally there are the theists, who accept God's existence, although they have different methods of demonstrating His existence and describing His nature.[15]

The most fundamental reason for the disagreement among philosophers is, as mentioned above, the infinity (or indefiniteness) of the whole of reality on the one hand and the finiteness of the human intellect on the other. Due to this limitation man is incapable of penetrating the depth of reality whether the finite or the infinite, and hardly, if at all, can he scrutinize all the causes and effects of either.

With this basic difficulty is closely connected the problem of the origin of the world, namely the question whether or not the world be the source of its own existence. If the world is limitless, it is infinite and eternal; thus, it could produce itself by its own internal energy. This problem, articulated in various ways, has been discussed seriously through the centuries from numerous points of view.[16] Aquinas contended that the infinity and eternity

15 For further study of this subject see S.A. Matczak *Le Problèm de Dieu dans la pensée de Karl Barth* (Louvain: Nauwelaerts, 1968), pp. XI-XXV.

16 M. Gierens (ed.), *Controversia de aeternitate mundi* (Rome: Universitas Gregoriana, 1933).

of the world can be reconciled with its having been created.[17] St.
Bonaventure on the contrary, rejected such a possibility.[18] Kant
emphasized the irresolvable antinomy lying at the threshold of the
problem, the possibility of proving rationally two contradictory
theses, namely that the world is infinite and eternal and that it is
finite and temporal.[19]

A series of related problems concerns our personal capability of
acquiring valid knowledge or reality, especially of the nature of
things and their transcendence. These problems involve the issue
of the existence of the external world. This existence, questioned
by some prominent English empiricists of the 18th century,
particularly by Hume,[20] pushing to the extreme Berkeley's
position,[21] became very systematically and profoundly elaborated
by Kant.[22] His doubts about the validity of our knowing in this
respect has been persistently discussed down to the present day
provoking new solutions to his revolutionary views. In these
discussions not only the boundaries of our knowing are
questioned, but also our own justifiability of existence which
becomes reduced to the phenomenal awareness of consciousness,
is considered as just a stream of flux of appearances.[23]

The results of these problems on the contemporary scene are
quite striking and diversified. Some current philosophers contend

17 *Ibid.,* pp. 66-73. See also "De potentia," q. 3, a. 3 in *Questiones disputatae*
(Rome: Marietti, 1949), Vol. II.

18 Bernardino, Bonansea, "The Impossibility of Creation from Aeternity According
to St. Bonaventure," *Proceedings of the American Catholic Philosophical Association*
(Washington, D.C.: The Catholic University of America, 1974), pp. 121-135.
Bonaventure, *In IV Libros Sententiarum* II, d. 1, p. 1, a. 1, q. 2 *(Opera omnia,* Ad Claras
Aquas, 1885), Vol. II, pp. 19-35. See also "The Question of an Eternal World in the
Teaching of St. Bonaventure," *Franciscan Studies,* 1974.

19 Kant, *Kritik der reinen Vernunft* in his *Werke* (ed. by E. Cassirer, 10 vols. Berlin:
B. Cassirer, 1912-1921), Vol. III, pp. 306-312.

20 Hume, *A Treatise of Human Nature,* ed. by L.A. Selby-Bigge (Oxford: Clarendon
Press, 1958), pp. 66-68.

21 Berkeley, "Three Dialogues between Hylas and Philonous," *The Works of George
Berkeley* (ed. by L.C. Fraser, 4 vols. Oxford: Clarendon Press, 1901), Vol. I, 379-485.

22 Kant, *op. cit.,* particularly his *"Transzendentale Dialektik,"* Vol. I, pp. 247-477.

23 H. Bergson, *Matière et memoire.* Paris: F. Alcan, 1910. W. James, *The Principles
of Psychology* (2 vols. New York: Dover, 1950), Vol. I, pp. 65, 237, 251, 273-274, 300,
405, 488. *Essays in Radical Empiricism* (New York: Longmans, Green and Co., pp. 1-10,
25. J.P. Sartre, *L'être et néant* (Paris: Gallimard, 1943), pp. 115 ff.

that being itself[24] is absurd or that truth is paradoxical;[25] others support the position of the mystery of being,[26] or defend the transcendental and code (symbolic) character of immediate existence leading to its final Source.[27] This Source is grasped intuitively rather than discursively.[28] Some hold that accepting the Divine is a legitimate choice for the human will,[29] whereas other militantly reject His existence.

The complexity of philosophical issues has been increased even more by the growing interest in the validity of intuitive, mystical and emotional experiences.[30] This interest has led to a mounting investigation of para-normal phenomena (parapsychology). Such research raises new problems and presents new hopes of reaching solutions of paramount importance for our knowledge of reality, of man himself and especially of the ultimate sources of them. The results are important not only for philosophy but for religion as well. In our collective study we are attempting to anticipate some of the problems involved.[31]

Other issues relevant to our knowledge of the Divine concern causality,[32] the analogy of being, and universals. These are perennial problems and philosophers have been struggling with them for centuries. They are still vigorously discussed in order to reach a final solution.[33] The solutions have serious bearing on the

24 Sartre, *op. cit.,* pp. 30-34.

25 S. Kierkegaard, *Concluding Unscientific Postscript,* tr. by D.F. Swanson and W. Lowrie (Princeton, New Jersey: University Press, 1941), pp. 180-184, 345, 498-508, 512-515.

26 G. Marcel, *Position et approaches concretes du mystere ontologique.* Paris: Vrin, 1949.

27 K. Jaspers, *Truth and Symbol,* tr. by J.J. Wilde, W. Kluback and W. Kimmel. New York: Twayene, 1947.

28 *Ibid.* See also Ch. S. Peirce, *Collected Papers* (8 vols. Cambridge, Massachusetts: Harvard University Press, 1960), Vol. V, pp. 311-326, 388-398.

29 W. James, *The Will to Believe.* New York: Longmans, Green and Co., 1897.

30 Below, Chapters XX, XXV. James, *The Varieties of Religious Experience.* New York: The New American Library, 1958. Bergson, *Les deux Sources de la morale et de la religion.* Paris: Alcan, 1932.

31 Below, Part IV.

32 *Ibid.*

33 Among the other studies with a somehow similar purpose, we might draw attention to R.E. Whitson, *The Coming Convergence of World Religions.* Paramus, New Jersey: Paulist Press, 1971.

nature of our knowing and consequently on our own entity, spiritual or material, and thus on our justifiability of the acceptance of the transcendent reality which is God.

A particularly difficult subject of inquiry concerning God's existence constitutes the problem of evil, or more precisely speaking, the problem of suffering. This problem includes not only men, but also animals, and any other being experiencing pain. These issues are closely connected with the questions of freedom, particularly man's freedom, and also with the purpose of man's and animals' existence. Consequently, they lead to the problem of teleology in the world, a quite discussed and perennial issue.

6. The Purpose and Setting of This Study

Our collective work intends to contribute to a better understanding of the supreme subject of religions, more particularly the Divine, and to our way of knowing Him. Therefore, the studies by various scholars presented in the following pages are concentrated on the existence of the Divine, His nature and the way we know Him. We do not claim that these studies constitute final explorations and interpretations of the question of God. Yet, they are serious scholarly efforts in the right direction. They intend to penetrate and explain the sense and spirit of particular religions. They highlight mankind's conviction of the existence of a Superior Being, who in various ways affects the existence of man and to whom man in turn is responsible.

In this study we are not attempting to elaborate on all the problems which human beings have confronted in examining the question of God. We are trying to signal some of them, hoping that in subsequent works we shall be able to present other aspects and discussions. Our efforts now and in the future are meant as contributions to what must be an ongoing, multifaceted exploration of the existence and nature of God, and of how we know Him.

Part I of this collective study is devoted to the views on God of the followers of the ancient cultures which still exist and are wide-spread. Part II presents the Christian position from the standpoint of the major Christian denominations and includes a discussion of the most outstanding pre-Christian philosophers, Plato and Aristotle. The next Part surveys the opinions concerning God of some modern thinkers, mainly philosophers, but also some voices from the field of literature, psychology and the arts. The final Part introduces specific problems such as causality and suffering; these essays especially open the door to further discussions.

The study is closed by an index of the names of those mentioned in the text.

Part One
God in Ancient Cultures

PRELIMINARY REMARKS

Religions of ancient cultures are widely diffused in the world today. As a consequence they play an important role in the knowledge of God on the contemporary scene. The more important among them are the Asiatic Religions. Hinduism according to the statistics of 1974 is the religion of approximately 516 million people,[1] i.e. 83% of the whole population of India[2] which in 1973 was 575 million. Chinese Taoism and Confucianism are probably even more widely spread religions, although statistics are not available, particularly after the Cultural Revolution.[3] Buddhism which extends throughout all of Asia numbers about 224 million believers. It is the prevailing religion of North India; 90% of the population in China are also followers of Buddhism.[4] Cambodia, Laos and Tibet also are recognized as Buddhist countries although statistics are not available.[5] Buddhism in its various forms is also followed in North America (188,000), South America (148,000) and Europe (10,000).[6] Shintoism, a national religion of Japan, numbers about 64 million in a population of about 100 million; the other highly important religion in Japan is Buddhism (about 30% of the population).[7] In Africa, native religions dominate the continent in spite of the progress of Christianity — about 94 million Christians in 1974.[8] Islam occupies quite a large territory and has significant centers in the rest

---

1 *The World Almanac & The Books of Facts* (New York: Newspaper Enterprise Association, 1974), p. 322.
2 "India," *Encyclopedia Britannica,* 1970.
3 *The World Almanac,* p. 322.
4 "Buddhism," *Encyclopedia Britannica,* 1970.
5 *Ibid.*
6 *Ibid.*
7 "Japan," *Encyclopedia Britannica,* 1970.
8 *The World Almanac,* p. 322.

of the World, particularly in Asia and Europe. It is one of the largest religious bodies in the World. In 1974 it numbered about 514 million followers, out of which there are about 94 million in Africa, 415 million in Asia, 5 million in Europe, 205,000 in North America, and 185,000 in South America. Arabs, Turks, Persians, Pakistans and Malay-Indonesians also are Muslims.[9] Finally we should mention Judaism, which extends over all the continents and countries, and which plays a fundamental role for Christianity in its background and beginning. The official number of the followers of Judaism was 15 million in 1974,[10] out of which about 7 million are in North America, 4 million in Europe, 300,000 in Africa and 73,000 in Oceania.[11]

There are many other religions which began in ancient cultures still very active today, but we have chosen those which seem to be more prominent.[12]

We list the religions in alphabetical order as follows: Africa (Native Religions, Islam); then China (Taoism, Confucianism, Neo-Confucianism, Buddhism); India (Hinduism, Neo-Hinduism, Malkani); Japan (Shintoism) and we close with Judaism (Rabbinic Tradition, Election).

9 "Islam," *Encyclopedia Britannica,* 1970.
10 *The World Almanac,* p. 322.
11 *Ibid.*
12 For Christianity, see below, Part II.

Africa

AFRICAN CULTURES
ESPECIALLY CITED IN THIS ANALYSIS

AFRICAN CULTURES

Numbered in order of their **appearance** in the text.

1. Gwambe or Gamba
2. Thonga
3. Shona
4. Tswana
5. Kono
6. Tonga
7. Lugbara
8. Ashanti
9. Yoruba
10. Bushmen (Khoisan)
11. Pygmies
12. Unga of Bangweulu
13. Zulu
14. Nguni
15. Kalabari
16. Mende
17. Cewa
18. Bemba
19. Lovedu

CHAPTER I

GOD IN AFRICAN THOUGHT AND LIFE
Charles E. Fuller*

African Ideas of God was the title of a work edited by the eminent British anthropologist and missionary, Edwin W. Smith, whose scholarly activities won him many honors, including the presidency of the Royal Anthropological Society. Smith knew and respected the mind of the African, and in the inquiry which he organized he called upon first hand observers of African life and thought, themselves also sensitive to the African spirit. His guidance in a study of the ideas of God in twelve widely scattered African cultures south of the Sahara was aimed at giving answer to Emil Ludwig, Acting Governor of the Anglo-Egyptian Sudan, who thought Africans incapable of conceiving God. In the words of Ludwig, challenged by Smith, *"Deity is a philosophical concept which savages are incapable of framing."*[1]

Since 1950 much has appeared in print about African peoples, their societies and their cultures. John Middleton, Robert T. Parsons, and others have written about specific cultural religions in Africa. The Kenyan theologian, John S. Mbiti, has described *African Religions and Philosophies.*[2] These and holistic ethnographies, representative of various African peoples, provide rich sources for the serious scholar to explore in the interest of discovering the functioning of religion in African thought and life. Appreciative of these sources, and without disparagement for any of these observations and analyses, my own effort will be to seek to reveal some of the more or less universal characteristics of the way Africans regard God, and to make clear some of the more

*Professor Emeritus of Sociology, St. John's University, New York, U.S.A.

1   Edwin W. Smith (ed.), *African Ideas of God* (London:Edinburgh House Press, 1950), p. 1.
2   John S. Mbiti, *African Religions and Philosophies* (New York: Praeger, 1969).

significant variations of their thought and life with respect to God.

In agreement with Edwin W. Smith, and in contradiction of the opinion of Emil Ludwig, it will be seen that Africans are not only capable of abstract and philosophical thinking about God, but also profound in their thought. In a sense familiar to those aware of the nature of Hebrew theological attitudes toward God, most Africans avoid the pastime which preoccupies members of other cultures who try to define God, and are then snared into worshipping their definitions, losing sight of what they have defined. The ethnocentrism with which observers, even scholarly observers, are predisposed to expect inferiority in the religion of others has been pronounced. Oversimplified and often inept characterizations have been made of African religion as "animism" or "dynamism," and unjustified stress has been laid by many on the last syllables of "ancestrolatry," as if those dealing with their ancestors were engaged in worshipping them. Too often we have not bothered to seek penetration into the African mind and spirit since we have tried to interpret African thought as if it were but some corruption of our own, having no roots in and of itself. The reader is asked to purge away any preconceptions and is urged to attempt a truly open minded inquiry into African feelings and thoughts with respect to God.

One approach would be particularly appropriate in beginning this inquiry. Without abandoning the central subject of our investigation, God, it is recommended that we for a time remove those connotations of the term which are associated with so-called classical religions. Especially urgent is the need to free the term of its linkage with number. Monotheism, polytheism, pantheism, and henotheism are such concepts, loaded with preconceptions, and fraught with rationalizations which pile ambiguities upon ambiguities as we seek to explain such ideas as unity and diversity in the Trinity. Similarly weighted terms as omnipotence, omniscience, omnipresence, and eternality are likewise too interlaced with theological complexities of the traditions common to Jewish, Moslem, and Christian faiths to be used in any neutral sense when observing religions external to these. The suggestion is made here that, without building a preconceived construct for the term, we simply speak of "divinity" where reference is made to "god" or "gods." Furthermore, when referring to divine power and other attributes in an African context we will employ terms more expressive of actual indigenous thought.

In addition to employing a relatively neutral vocabulary in our descriptions, it is essential that we make clear the diversity of subject matter with which we deal. There is no "African Religion" which can be identified as representative of all the thousand or more cultures to be found in Africa. Even in similar societies, having relatively similar religious beliefs and practices, there is sufficient variety to raise suspicion when anyone attempts to speak of "the African mind," or "the African religion." No single volume on the subject can adequately compile and compare, let alone synthesize theological beliefs which are part of African thinking. In recognition of this limitation, data will be drawn from several representative cultures, and generalizations will be suggested with due moderation. Parsons has expressed misgiving about this type of effort in his sympathetic but frank criticism of Talbot's study of the religion of seventeen tribal groups of Southern Nigeria[3] and Meek's characterizations of the religion of twelve tribes in Northern Nigeria.[4] He says: *"The religion of no one culture stands out and the features in which one might be different from another are thereby lost."*[5] This hazard is multiplied as we seek to bring into short compass the ideas of God in *Africa,* not just one portion of one state.

One of the earliest reliable sources of information about African beliefs before European intrusion began to make its influence felt through acculturation is in the letters of Portuguese seamen, explorers, and priests. Among these is the correspondence of the first martyr in Southern Africa, a Jesuit missionary, Fr. Gonzalo da Silveira along with that of his colleague, Fr. Andre Fernandes. These pioneer missionaries to the Gamba (now known as the Gwambe) among the Thonga and Tonga (Khoka) southwest of

3 Robert T. Parsons, *Religion in an African Society* (Leiden: E.J. Brill, 1964).

4 C.K. Meek, *The Northern Tribes of Nigeria* (London:Oxford University Press, 1925).

5 Parsons, *op. cit.,* p. xvii.

Inhambane in Mozambique reported what they saw among these
people from 1560 through 1562, a people relatively untouched
by outside influences save through coastal trading ninety miles
away.

Fr. Fernandes wrote that he could discover nothing in the
religion of these people similar to Moslem customs except circumcision (6/24/1560). Most of his remarks describe them, from
king to peasant, eager to hear and to interpret ideas from the
Christian gospel. Fr. Gonzale, however, early assessed their religious ideas. "These people resemble children who like to act together and follow each other's lead as far as any intellectual
impediment in receiving the faith is concerned, none of them
have any kind of idol or form of worship resembling idolatry."
He continues, "They have a God whom they call Umbe; they
recognize a soul which lives after death and is punished or rewarded according as it is good or evil, and thus our beliefs and
commandments suit them very well" (8/9/1560).

Recognizing "a superstitious belief in sorcery and charms,"
amulets which they called "medicine, which is but superstition,"
and swearing oaths by "blowing in each other's faces," (8/9/
1560) the Jesuit priest passed these customs by without realizing
their deeper meanings. Fr. Andre Fernandes also, noting how the
people of Gamba "cast bones" to discover the cause of sickness
or some misfortune, and to learn what remedy to use, appears to
have missed the explanation of divination. Describing the manner
in which a diviner would "smell out" wanted information with a
whisp of hair from a gnu's tail, the missionary did not ask how
this operation was supposed to work. However, at another place
he mentions that the people "honour a god they call Muzimo . . .
which is the same as Luck or Fortune." This divinity, they claim,
"is the luck of their forefathers and favours them in their undertakings, namely that they may be well-liked and successful with
their merchandise." Using what undoubtedly is the collective
variant of this name, Fr. Andre says that "Mozimo comes at
night when they are asleep to ask for food, and they give him
food and drink by placing it at the foot of a great green tree."
The Mozimo, he adds, could be used to kill an enemy, though

the priest suggests that this is due to the power of fearful imagination (12/5/1562). The importance of these descriptions lies in
the fact that they accurately represent beliefs and customs lasting
into the present time among the descendents of these 16th
century people.

Most Bantu speaking Africans, particularly in patrilineal societies, but specifically among the Gwambe and their Thonga
neighbors, share the essentials revealed in these reports. Idolatry
in any form is rare if ever among them. They are not at all
individualistic in their religious life, but are inclined to "act
together and follow each other's lead." Twentieth century
Gwambe are no less open to hear and sympathize with religious
teachings which mention divine power. While the name Fr.
Gonzalo reported as the local term for god is not recognized
(Umbe) the sound he heard *(umba* or *umbe)* is the final part of
Kulunkhumba, a widespread name for God in this region. Few
Bantu would try to define the meaning of Kulunkhumba or any
other name applied to divinity, other than to indicate their
reverence for the same. One assumption which is implicit in all
that they say about any manifestation of divinity is that all
sacred power resides in some spiritual form near to, but nevertheless separate from all that is part of their mundane existence. The
spirits of the deceased ancestors are occupants of the same area,
and have more intimate access to the somewhat mysterious
divine spirit than do the living. In fact, the Thonga and others
sharing their beliefs think that the more remote the ancestor the
nearer he is to the power which is termed divine.

In view of this remoteness, ordinary people, including the
chief, seek information from the ancestors and the divine spirit
beyond them through divination. Casting the "bones," the
diviner (known as a *nganga*) says that he consults the ancestors to
learn the cause and cure of troubles. Amulets, charms, fetishes,
medicines, and other symbols of prophylactic or therapeutic
power are all believed to possess that power by virtue of spirits.
Usually those having a Shona background or relationship to the
Tswana people will speak of the spiritual power in several dimensions. The root term, *Zimo* or *Dimo* has one form, Muzimo, for

divinity in a somewhat diffuse and universal or at least national sense. A different singular form suggests any one of numbers of particular spirits or ghosts of specific persons who have deceased, and who continue to be involved in the ongoing affairs of their descendents. This term has its plural which usually connotes the conjunction of spirits who, more or less jointly provide answers to questions put to them by the diviners when they "throw the bones" or use the "smelling out" procedures with the switch made of a gnu's tail. Every *nganga* whom I have questioned in Mozambique, South Africa, Rhodesia, and Botswana about the manner in which divination is accomplished has given the same answers; through prayer and through the Bible, the indigenous diviner seeks and obtains answers to important questions from the spirits through the divining bones or blocks *(hakata)* or switch. Questioned about the way in which the ordeal operates (another detail described in the sixteenth century) the explanation invariably has been that the spirits act so that, when an accuser and an accused both drink from a cup of poison, the guilty will be killed or made sick, and the innocent will be spared. When the spirits (or some particular spirit) are hungry they make this known through disaster or divination, and their descendents or certain persons singled out for the responsibility, are expected to feed them under a live, green tree such as the sixteenth century priests described. No attempt is made to describe divinity, but as the informants told the pioneer missionaries, their conception of divinity has the connotation of fate or fortune.

Parsons, describing the Kono of Sierra Leone, notes that when these people greet each other and make their farewells it is commonly in terms which link their well-being with Yata, their term for divinity.[6] In discussing the faith of the Tonga of the Zambezi valley, Hopgood speaks of Mizimo as the Jesuit priests found Mizimo in the past. Referring to Leza, another name for divinity, he says that among the Tonga, "Whatever exists owes its exist-

6 *Ibid.*, pp. 6-7.

ence to Leza, and whatever happens is due to his activity . . ."[7]
He likewise shows the Mizimo as closer to Leza than the living,
and notes that they are intermediaries between their descendents
and this more remote divinity.[8]

The root *imo,* preceded by various consonants, is said by
Edwin Smith to have been a common designation of divinity
throughout Bantu tribes everywhere. It appears as Muzimu, Mu-
zhimo, Molimo, Umlimo, Edimo, Bodimo, Njimo, and in numerous other forms. Smith calls attention to reasonable but variant
explanations of the etymology of the root: *ima* "stand, stand
firm," *dima* "to penetrate or permeate," etc.[9] The Barolong
branch of the Tswana were said by Ellenberger to have considered Morimo the "Father" of their ancestors.[10] On the other
hand, some Tswana in the past, according to Smith, spoke of
Modimo as a "divine Mother." J. T. Brown is cited as stating that
the Tswana with whom he worked forty years or more had a
taboo against saying the name Modimo, using circumlocutions
to refer to divinity except on rare occasions by important person-
ages.[11]

Among the Lugbara, northwest of Lake Albert and the River
Nile, Middleton reports similar conditions as found to the south,
under different terms. These people likewise deal primarily with
the spirits of their dead ancestors, nevertheless, God is
"associated" with almost every relationship between living and
dead. In his remoteness God is beyond the spirits and ghosts, and
in an intimate and sometimes unpleasant sense, is in streams and
other natural phenomena.[12] The Lugbara distinguish between all

7 Cecil R. Hopgood, "Conceptions of God among the Tonga of Northern
Rhodesia," in Edwin W. Smith (ed.), *African Ideas of God,* p. 62.

8 *Ibid.,* p. 67.

9 Smith. *op. cit.,* p. 117 f.

10 D. F. Ellenberger, *History of the Basuto* (London: Caxton Publishing Co.,
1912), p. 239.

11 J. T. Brown, *Among the Bantu Nomads* (London: Seeley, Service and Co.,
1926), p. 114 f.

12 John Middleton, *Lugbara Religion* (London: Oxford University Press, 1960),
pp. 25, 27, 31.

of these, but at the same time there is an ambiguity in which there is an uncertainty as to whether one or the other is being referred to at any moment.

The Ashanti, according to Busia, consider the universe full of spirits. He says:

> There is the Great Spirit, the Supreme Being, who created all things, and who manifests his power through a pantheon of gods; below these are lesser spirits which animate trees, animals, or charms; and then there are the ever present spirits of the ancestors *(nasamanfa)*, whose constant contact with the life of man on the earth brings the world of the spirits so close to the land of the living.[13]

These people of Gold and Ivory Coast differ from the Bantu in having a more highly developed concept of deities as separate entities, but there is still common ground in their beliefs. As Bantu of various parts of Africa south of the Sahara, these West Africans are caught in the ambiguity of a concept of plurality and unity as they think of divinity. This appears to be one of the universal traits of African religious thinking.

Divinity, as it appears to be conceived among Africans, is ever both one and many. Some people, as the African theologian, John S. Mbiti, find it not too difficult to harmonize these paradoxical concepts. Mbiti says:

> Every African people recognizes God as One. According to some cosmologies, however, there are, besides Him, other divinities and spiritual beings, some of whom are closely associated with Him. These beings are generally the personification of God's activities, natural phenomena and objects, or deified national heroes, or spiritual beings created by God as such. In a few cases, such as among the Bari, Lugbara and Turu, dual aspects of the One God are recognized, as an explanation of

---

[13] K. A. Busia, "The Asanti of the Gold Coast," in Daryll Forde (ed.), *African Worlds* (London: Oxford University Press, 1963), p. 191.

the transcendence and immanence of God, and of the problem of good and evil.[14]

The Lugbara, mentioned by Mbiti above, and described by John Middleton, well illustrate not only the combination of the one and the many, the immanent and transcendent, and other paradoxes noted, but also the manner in which these Eastern Sudanic people perceive divinity in a multiplicity of ways. As Middleton says; God in the sky is the creator of men *('ba o'ba-pi̯ri̯)* and in his remoteness good *(onyiru)*. As near to man, in streams and various natural phenomena, God is bad *(onzi)*. The spirits of the ancestors and the ghosts are "people in the earth," which is a Lugbara way of designating an existence like that of "people of the world outside" (living *on* the earth) without involving themselves in explanations of this "spiritual existence." Middleton comments:

> God is, for the Lugbara, a concept that links together several activities that at first sight might appear quite unrelated. The relationship between God and the ancestors is difficult to discover. It is never made explicit. Every lineage has its own ancestors, but God is everywhere, in a relationship of equal intensity with all lineages . . . Mountains are both the abode of God and of the two hero-ancestors, who are common to all Lugbara also; they lived before the formation of Lugbara society and were near to God.[15]

Ancestors and ghosts, as God himself, maintain a dynamic relationship with the living; and the cultic behavior toward them, while differing in detail, shows them in a common classification with God.

West African religious beliefs and practices, far more sophisticated in their theology, much more elaborate in their ritual both as to form and content, and exceedingly more extensive in their

---

14 Mbiti. *op. cit.,* p. 46.
15 Middleton. *op. cit.,* p. 28.

mythologies, exemplify in a complicated way what in most parts of Africa is a simple identification of the divine with all aspects of experience. One example would be the Yoruba.

These people of Nigeria, in rich symbolism of ritual and mythology, express religious ideas which at once reveal their social and theological outlook. Our concern here is the latter. In many forms their myths tell of the supreme god, Olorun, who in the time of creation sent from the heavenly firmament across a watery medium, a canoe loaded with a bag of soil, a five toed chicken, and *one* known as Odudwa. Odudwa scattered the soil on the water, and the chicken scratched around, creating a land which became the possession and kingdom of Odudwa, whose royal successors, the kings of Ovo (known as *alafin*), were to be owners and rulers of the Yoruba world. Between Orolun (owner of the sky), Odudwa (owner of the earth), the Alafin of Oyo, the *ara orun* (sky-people) or *egbe orun* (sky band) and the *orisa* (spirits of the great in several hierarchies) are complicated lines of interrelationship over which there is controversy among interpreters. But no matter how organized, by the Yoruba themselves or by observers, they all represent different emanations of divinity. The easily applied term "pantheon," misses the point that each of these, with the possible (but not essential) exception of Olorun, is but a manifestation of super-human divine reality in special functional relationship with humans in their diverse situations and concerns. In common with many West Africans, the Yoruba not only distinguish between these major entities and categories but also between individuals (as different *orisa),* and popular practice makes as clear a distinction as common Christian lay thought makes between Yahwah, "the Mother of God," Jesus, "the Holy Spirit," and any of the Saints. Mythology, ritual, and other evidences, however, suggest that while functions and occasions for reference to the different "entities" differ, they all fall within a commonly accepted category, similar to the idea conveyed by the term "divinity."[16]

In sub-Saharan Africa, particularly among Bantu peoples, this diffuse character of the concept of divinity is found almost universally. The primitive economies of gathering people, or those of either hunting or fishing groups appear to be correlated with a simpler form of belief which reflects isolation from influences leading to a multiplicity of outlooks. Other economies tend to demonstrate something of the kind noted in societies just mentioned, though with less sophistication.

Theophilus Hahn, a century ago, studying the mythology and examining the etymology of theological terms among the Khoisan (Bushmen and Hottentots), made his interpretation of the way they saw divinity. He called attention to numerous names applied to what others called "God." But he did not suggest that each was a different being. Rather, as he unraveled the evidence, he discerned that the Bushmen and their relatives described their thoughts about the sacred in various picturesque ways. The red dawning, dark night, a mythical, nameless ancestor, the successful, the rain source, the thunderer, the same again (the dependable), and other terms are cited, along with the author's views of their symbolic meanings. Sun, moon, and other natural phenomena are called upon to refer to the mysterious.[17] Writing in 1871, John MacKenzie told of Bushmen who, having or using no term of their own for God, borrowed the term *Morimo* from Tswana to mention a "Presence" in their divination practices similar to sources of knowledge or power people of other societies gained from outside themselves.[18]

Contemporary Bushmen of the Botswana Kalahari, according to George B. Silberbauer, believe in two supernatural beings. He says:

[16] Peter Morton-Williams, "An Outline of the Cosmology and Cult Organization of the Oya Yoruba," in E. P. Skinner (ed.), *Peoples and Cultures of Africa* (Garden City, N.Y.: Natural History Press, 1973), pp. 654-677.

[17] Theophilus Hahn, *Tsuni-Goam, The Supreme Being of the Khoi-Khoi* (London: Trubner and Co., 1881), p. 114 f.

[18] John Mackenzie, *Ten Years North of the Orange River* (London: Frank Cass and Co., 1971), p. 137.

Nodima [the root *dima* certainly is a Bantu root for God C.E.F.] lives in the sky and has human shape. He is invulnerable and invisible, omniscient and omnipresent. Gawama has many forms and has no fixed abode . . . When Nodima created the world it was good and it was complete. Gawama has, ever since, done his best to disrupt Nodima's work and to wreak evil. He is responsible for most misfortunes, including disease, and inspires men to do wrong.[19]

Unlike the unadorned directness of Bushman belief are the systems of belief and practice of the Bantu who make up most of the population of Africa south of the Sahara. In contrast with the Bushmen, the Central African Pygmies, and a very few Bantu cultures which have not ventured into any form of domestication, but have relied on hunting, fishing, or gathering, or some combination, most Bantu have explored many creative economies. Indeed, with the exception of those already mentioned, Africans throughout the continent have been engaged in a multiplicity of creative pursuits which have been reflected in their religious belief. Not only is the variety demonstrated in economic activity, but also in social organization. In a few cases specialization and isolation account for our finding religious belief and practice largely confined to one basic concern, as it appears to be among the Unga of Bangwelu swamps, a fishing people described by W. V. Brelsford.[20] Comparative study of African concepts of divinity is constantly reflecting at one level interests in how the people get their food, and another at how they organize their social life. African cultures are characterized by extreme variety and versatility. With the possible exception of Egypt, and to some extent Ethiopia, because of their longer periods of involvement in technological advance on many fronts, all African societies have throughout the past millenium been intimately close to every primitive and intermediate level of coming to grips with their environment. Among their ecological adjustments to the

19 George B. Silberbauer, *Bushmen Survey Report* (Gaborones, Africa: Bechuanaland Government, 1965), p. 95.

20 W. V. Brelsford, *Fishermen of the Bangweula Swamps* (Northern Rhodesia: The Rhodes-Livingston Institute, 1946).

flora, fauna, and mineral composition of their surroundings, as well as to the climatic conditions, all have had to depend upon the possible bounty of the earth and water. If they somehow escaped the necessity of continuous dependence upon scavenging and foraging, as some societies have had to practice year by year, few African groups have been able to subsist without some resort to gathering food from wild vegetation or using the products of hunting or fishing in order to survive. The evidences of exposure to cultural diversity is everywhere to be noted in Africa, so that the society most exclusively devoted to animal husbandry, and most disdainful of cultivators, must concede its having now or in its recent past need for dependence upon some form of agriculture. On the other hand, characteristically horticultural and agronomic peoples in Africa cannot claim independence of the pastoral. To an even greater degree, those who have culturally developed trading patterns presumably separate from gathering, hunting, fishing, cultivating, or herding, reveal their constant interrelatedness with these pursuits. Those who have to some extent specialized in the mining or processing of metals have likewise been too dependent upon the products of plant and animal to escape an involvement with their acquisition and use. All types of symbiotic adjustments between peoples of differing economic bases testify to this wide exposure of the African people to needs and advantages associated with all the basic ways of securing a living. The one possible exception is that of the most primitive forager or hunter/fisher and gatherer, whose real or relative isolation may have spared him knowledge of what is involved in cultivation, husbandry, trade, or mineral exploitation.

This apparent digression from theology purposely points to the diversity of economics involved in African culture to indicate that the religious correlates of all these give rise to the broad variety of ways in which divinity is conceptualized not only throughout Africa, but often within any one African culture. Theological concepts derived from life necessitating a hunter's adjustment to wild beasts and the forest, a fisher's relationship with bodies of water and their contents, a cultivator's dependence upon the elements, a herder's concern with animals and their fertility, a miner's apprehension about the mysterious processes involved in producing metal products, and the trader's problems of dealing with a variety of people, find their way into many African cultures, sometimes with seeming incongruity.

Audrey Richards long ago noted this as she observed the Zulu, a pastoral people, the interest of whose men is "entirely centered in their herds of cattle." These, who even today will categorize cultivation and witchcraft under a common denunciation, made their most important national rites those associated "with the agricultural year rather than the pastoral." Such include first-fruits and harvest ceremonies, in which men, pastoralists, took "a prominent part."[21]

Many investigators of African culture have called attention to such apparent incongruities. Finding that an agricultural or a pastoral society was delegating to an aboriginal subject the responsibility to placate the spirits of a mountain or spring, some observers have caught this snap-shot of diffusion in process. Schapera once capsulated much in his observation:

Apart from the major deities, the Bantu believed in local spirits of various kinds, whose sinister presence was generally greatly feared. There are the sacred woods or mountains inhabited by the spirits of dead chiefs or by dissociated spirits, often vague and shadowy in character, but none the less terrifying and dangerous to the traveler; . . . spirits of streams and pools, animal spirits, dangerous reincarnations of famous old chiefs and warriors; . . . caves inhabited by large pythons, sight of whom was fatal to the commoner, but who assisted the chief in his rain making; . . . spirits of trees and many more objects and places of similar kind.[22]

21 Audrey Richards, *Hunger and Work in a Savage Tribe* (London: Routledge, 1932), p. 102.
22 Isaac Schapera, *Western Civilization and the Natives of South Africa* (London: Routledge, 1934), p. 32.

Divine nature or power, sometimes characterized under the title of spirit, sometimes as god, and under varied names and descriptions, is related in African thought to what is of ultimate importance within the entire range of functional adjustment. It is not surprising that this includes natural phenomena important to the gatherer, hunter, and fisher, anything essential to the welfare of the cultivator of the soil, all that looms large in the mind of the pastoral peoples breeding, herding, and utilizing their animals, whatever the miner or smith sees as indispensible to his success with metals, and that which the trader values as affecting his commerce. But beyond this, African regard for the sacred includes beside these economic concerns others that are patent.

In Bantu thought in particular, but in African thinking in general, the sacred is involved in life itself, in its entirety. Nowhere do we find better illustrated the whole conceptualization underlying *rites of passage* as described by Van Gennep[2][3] than in Africa where these social rituals stepping persons up from one position in society to another involve the idea of some kind of divine spirit identified with each transitional movement. When the strength of the social or political unit is under fire, the African society implicates divinity in the prophylactic or therapeutic processes invoked. If there is need for understanding of what to do in certain crises, divination calls divinity into question. Should a decision be so momentous that the judgment and pronouncement may be too heavy for the shoulders of the human rulers, ordeals and other forms call upon the extra-human to take responsibility for the verdict and its implementation. Secret societies, age sets, special regiments, and other groupings, whatever their function (or dysfunction) tend to authenticate themselves with some reference to the divine. Diagnosis and healing seldom, in African practice, proceed very far without implication of the divine in some sense. Victor W. Turner, in an assessment of universals in the symbols used in African ritual, notes

23 Arnald Van Gennep, *The Rites of Passage* (Chicago: University of Chicago Press, 1908).

this broad gamut of objectives to which religious ritual is dedicated as he pursues his argument that sub-Saharan Africa shows a
remarkable similarity among the vast variety of symbols used in
ritual. He says:

> . . . The needs and dangers of social and personal survival pro-
> vided suitable conditions for the development of rituals as
> pragmatic instruments (from the standpoint of the actors) for
> coping with biological change, disease, and natural hazards of
> all kinds. Social action in response to material pressures was
> the systematic and symstematizing factor.[24]

To the observation of Turner with regard to ritual may be
added the comment that throughout all African cultures of
which we have knowledge there appears to be the tendency to
conceptualize in sacred form *the source of fulfillment of human
need as it is comprised in that culture to be of high value.* Although African efforts seem to relate divinity with what Tillich
might call "false ultimates," their varied evaluations of concerns
with which they identify their conception of the divine have
much that suggests a "quest for the ultimate ground of being."
Africans' faith may not speak the language of Tillich, but their
seeing the presence of divinity at every point where their cultural
values indicate needs approaching ultimacy suggests that their
thought and his are not strangers. It would seem that in their
search for the ultimate ground of being they find evidence that
God touches their finiteness at places mattering most to them
at their level of experience. Characteristically, African religious
thought does not relegate the experience of the divine to some
narrowly defined aspect of their being, but to the whole of their
personal and corporate life.

Reducing this to the level of specifics, the Kalabari, as Robin
Horton reports, deal with *owuamapu,* spirits of streams, etc.,
am'oru, spirits of their heros, and *duen,* spirits of the dead. Each

---

24 V. W. Turner, *Schism and Continuity in an African Society* (Manchester:
Manchester University Press, 1959).

Kalabari person may have one's own *so,* each household its *polo teme so* (house god), and each community its *ama temo so* (community god), a *so* sacred being dealing with customs and behavior, etc. *So,* as "heaven," created people's ways for particular people. But *Tamuno* created the world of mud, and as female creator of all, being everywhere, made each kind of people (or races) as they are.[25] The Kalabari *Ekine* Men's Society known as *Sekiapu,* "the dancing people," deals dramatically with socially significant ideas in dramatic masquerades, and before the performers act they invite the spirits to be in attendance. They also offer a sacrifice to a patron goddess to secure the success of what they say is *her* play. The diffuse way in which divinity is expressed in Kalabari belief and ritual is not unlike the manner in which other African cultures demonstrate their belief that the divine is manifested in countless ways in every part of their life.

It is this diffuse character of African conceptualization of the divine which makes one hesitate to use the word god or deity to express what they are thinking. In most Bantu languages one looks in vain for a generic term for "god." The anthropologist, missionary, or other supplies from some European language the word god, deity, or other designation, and sometimes one of these is equated with an African term. But the African word is a special designation for a concept which is usually dynamic, or somewhat descriptive. Thus the Zulu speak of *Nkulunkulu,* "the great great." Other names, such as the Tonga word, Leza, take action from associated verbs: *Leza* falls (it rains), *Leza* surpasses (it is very hot), *Leza* blows (it is windy), *Leza* shines (lightning flashes). But *Leza* is also dominant over the ancestral spirits, *mizimu,* with which the people commonly deal when seeking help. Among some Thonga (southern) the word *psikwembu,* ancestral spirits, is used collectively as though meaning "the personification of a unity of our common ancestral spirits." *Mozimo* is so used among many Shona as a unit comprising the

25 Robin Horton, "A Hundred Years of Change in Kalabari Religion," in J. Middleton (ed.), *Black Africa,* p. 192 ff.

collectively of *mizimo* which are ancestral spirits. *Xu,* roughly translated as Creator, was the Bushman's word to express what is comprised in the idea of cosmic creativity, and it finds its way into Xhoso (like the Zulu, a Nguni culture), rivaling indigenous names for the sacred.

Except for the west coast of Africa, north of the Equator, it is rare for Africans to have unambiguously permitted themselves to confine the idea of "godness" to any single deity or pantheon of gods. Furthermore, one common characteristic of most references which go beyond "spirit" to indicate divinity is the unwillingness of Africans in the traditional frame of mind to tie "god" down to a definition. W. T. Harris, in discussing the Mende of Sierra Leone, says that while they were willing to speak of themselves as "children of *Ngewo,*" they did not wish to call him either "father," "mother," "uncle," or other term of designation. Furthermore, according to Harris, it did not matter what name they applied to the idea of divinity, they had one common concept, that is of being subject to god.[26] Many observers have had the answer I have frequently had among southeast African people (Nguni, Thonga, Shona, Sotho, and Tswana), namely that whatever we call God is at once both too remote and too important to be characterized by some binding restriction such as location, sex, form, or other definition. "Nungungulu is and does," "Tuixo brings this," "Mwari refuses," "God will decide." These are phrases which best denote how Africans think of divinity. In most cases, if a pronoun is used it is one which is personal (singular or plural, but usually the former). But Bantu languages do not use sex designation in their pronouns, so the African is better off than the English speaking person who wishes to avoid making God a masculine word, but also prefers not to use in neuter or non-personal forms.

The personal qualities of divinity, both in singular and plural number, are particularly obvious in the many Bantu societies

26 W. T. Harris, "The Idea of God among the Mende," in *African Ideas of God,* p. 280 f.

which have patrilineal extended families or strong sib relationship. My own observations of this among the Nguni, Tswana,
Shona, and Thonga are such that I would not hesitate to use
illustrations from any one. Although none of these would seek
voluntarily to relate to divinity by way of the spiritual manifestations in the other, they would all be quick to recognize the validity of the others' beliefs. Members of any family, sib, or tribe
find relationship with divine power through "spirits" which are
believed to have personality. Whether "God," an ancestor, a
disembodied spirit, or even the spirit of a stream or hill, each
manifestation is treated as one would an individual person.
Taboo (*ku yila* in Thonga) is a possible exception, though there is
evidence that even in taboo there are essentially familial and sib
elements which prevent this from being without a characteristic
in some sense personal. Certainly in the interpretation of *mangatsila* (wonder working power) which the Thonga and their neighbors (in other terminology) describe as becoming associated with
certain individuals so that they can perform great feats, they
approach an abstraction suggestive of *mana*, but when they describe its actions they use anthropopsychic terms. For example,
mangatsila is used by a man to protect his fields, and when a
thief approaches he is seen, and his hand is caught and held by
mangatsila so that he cannot move until the owner comes and
takes proper action, informed and brought to the spot by *mangatsila*. Apart from the anomaly of taboo and *mangatsila,* one
could scarcely question the personal quality of any Thonga manifestation of divinity.

The Thonga approaching his ancestors calls them, one by one,
in proper order from the most recent to the oldest, and often
interjects a proverb or epitaph appropriate to individuals in the
line. Before terminating his opening remarks the one offering the
prayer will invariably ask the last named to pass on the message
and greeting to "all those whose names have been forgotten."
This postscript includes, according to many informants, the
Creator and any other individual roles which divinity may assume, for the African admits that he does not know all about the
remote mysteries. When a diviner (*nanga wa timsolo*) takes his

divining bones from the basket he treats them as if they were persons, for they represent people in his audience and community. But he treats them with special respect for another reason, when he asks them questions, and then throws them on the mat before him, they will become the very medium through which the living ancestral spirits will speak to him about the problem on which he is making inquiry. The whole ritual is couched in personal terms, the nature of which could be misrepresented were one to speak of this as "casting lots," or depending on the luck of the throw. It is "the ancestors" who are speaking. Among other people, as the Bushmen, and occasionally among the Thonga, diviners often speak of their equipment as being the voice of one or more whom they call "God."

No simple magical explanation satisfies the Thonga when they refer to charms, amulets, and other symbolic objects used in healing. These people, as other Southeast African Bantu, tend to regard these as tokens of the presence of the spirits which they are trusting to accomplish some good in or for them. Thonga spirit possession mediums, describing the costumes they wear, the dances they perform, the songs that are played and sung, and other parts of their so-called "magical routine" as prescribed by the appropriate spirits because of their preference for these particulars.

As do most African societies, the Thonga practice many rites of passage in one form or another. Differing in form and occasion, they all conform to one basic set of meanings. They represent some important step in the life of the individual in social status, and at the same time are practiced in such a manner as to involve the divine in these significant changes, relating the individual at once with society and the supportive divine.

For the Thonga one of these crisis ceremonies is at birth; another at the time the child begins crawling, when a string tied about its waist (puri) denoting its becoming a member of the community above and beyond the nuclear family, and another at puberty. Marriage and funeral rites likewise fit into this category. Among many of the tribes certain commonalities of the rites, as, for example, prescribed sexual continence at certain

times, and specified ritual intercourse at others, connote the
sacredness of the occasion, and call for practices stressing the
presence and concern of ancestral spirits.

Among the Thonga, some Shona, and as remotely as among
the Cewa of Malawi, the female puberty rites bear a name which
is only understandable among the Shona. The rite varies in detail,
but symbolizes the entry of a girl into sexual relationship with
males. What the Cewa call *cidamwari* the Thonga call *xikundlan-
amwari*. Shona provides translation for the latter term: "rendez-
vous with God (Mwari)." Both Cewa and Thonga rites suggest
that the whole ceremony has sacred relationships, but only the
Shona use that particular word, *Mwari*, for God. The Thonga,
however, when the girl successfully uses her specially carved,
doll-like wooden peg in the simulation of intercourse, sing and
shout their jubilation that she has entered relationship with God.
Data in many African cultures suggest that initiation rites generally have this assumption, that the divine is in fact a part of the
act.

Among matrilineages some of the ancestral rites indigenous
with patrilineal people have their parallel in rites honoring the
heroes of their matrilines. M. G. Marwick suggests that the Cewa,
while they honor a creator (Mlengi), and speak of one Ciuta or
Cauta as the Source of rain, who is approached through a special
cult, are most interested in cults dedicated to certain important
men within their matrilines.[27] Their divination is said to come
by way of the spirits.

Matrilineal Bemba, according to Audrey Richards, center their
religion about "the worship of spirits *(mipashi),*" particularly
those of the deceased chiefs *(citimukulu)*. Only the paramounts
were so singled out. The *mipashi,* say the Bemba, guard the descendents of the matrilineal ancestress. The spirit or spirits are
present in the chiefly stool and other sacred symbols of the office. Cultic rites for the favored ancestors or the founding ances-

---

27 M. G. Marwick, *Sorcery in its Social Setting* (Manchester: Manchester University
Press, 1965), p. 64 f.

tress take place either in a traditional shrine or near the sacred symbols of the chief, for these are believed to be silent witness to the presence of the sacred power authenticating the chieftainship.[28] But the *mipashi* were also believed to be present and to make this known when one of the women in the line was pregnant long enough to feel life in her womb. This was believed to be a sign of the protection assured by the ancestress to her descendents.

Reminiscent of earlier times, of which mythology has longer memory than everyday thought, the Bemba continue to have shrines for a hunting deity, *Mulenga*, together with his wife and mother. The matrilineal undertones of this fit well into the present social organization whether or not they represent what existed when and where Mulenga was a hunter. Oddly enough, the Cewa, according to Marwick, retain Mlengi (M'lengi or Mulengi) as the Creator in the distant past.[29]

In all parts of Africa, particularly in agriculturally based cultures, rain making rites are to be found. The Kriges (1943) wrote of *The Realm of the Rain Queen*, whose name, Mujaji, revered among the Lovedu of Transvaal, and applied by them and some of their neighbors to great rain making royal figures in the past, is an ordinary word for rain in some societies, as the Khoka on the Inhambane coast. In writing about the Plateau Tonga of Northern Rhodesia (now Zambia), Elizabeth Colson shows how these cultivators of the soil depend upon the rain cults which combine with the efforts to secure rain an attempt to purge the matrilineal kinship group and its neighborhood of wrongdoing. A shaman, under some feeling of compulsion, either founds or revives the cult, calling for rites near an already existent or a newly made shrine in the neighborhood. All the residents are urged to take part. They are berated for failure to maintain the established customs, and called upon to repent. Food offerings are brought, people eat, drink, dance, and pray for rain. The

---

28 Richards. *op. cit.*, pp. 169 f., 184 f.
29 Marwick. *op. cit.*, p. 64.

Thonga believe that the spirits in their matrilineage honor these cultic rites by bringing rain.[30]

Akin to divination, which has been mentioned, is the ordeal by which a defendent and his accuser, in a case which cannot be settled on the basis of objective evidence, each drink a poison or otherwise test their case by dependence upon a divine power to save the innocent and kill or sicken the guilty. The sixteenth century Gwambe practiced this, as do their modern descendents and people in many parts of Africa. As in divination, it is believed that the spirits or other powers intervene, revealing the truth through the magic of differential treatment of the two concerned. By this means the living judges need to take no responsibility for error in judgment. The divine judgment is declared through the ordeal.

It would be possible to multiply descriptions of rites, myths, and other elements in various African religious beliefs and practices endlessly. No two African societies would yield identical descriptions of their religious thought and behavior. In each culture it would be appropriate, for an adequate understanding of what they believe and do in the name of religion, to observe this within the context of their whole culture, not in isolation. Each would be in some sense unique from all others. Were one to view, in order, all the societies having a common economic base, as hunting and gathering, fishing and gathering, slash and burn cultivation, some form of animal husbandry, advanced agriculture, mineral handling, trading, or other, again it would be possible to conceive of classes of religious belief and practice correlated with different economies. Similar expectations might be had were we to bring together descriptions of all the religious behavior of people in specified types of social organization. But as has already been indicated above, diffusion has taken place across all the societies of Africa save a very few. The variety of religious ways have criss-crossed the continent as different

30 Elizabeth Colson, *Seven Tribes of Central Africa* (Manchester: Manchester University Press, 1959), pp. 153-161.

peoples migrated, sometimes merged with each other, and made various kinds of adjustments to each other over thousands of years. Controversy often springs up over claims regarding the influence of Hebrew, Moslem, and Christian ideas on African religion. Oddly enough, little has been said of the influence of Asiatic religions during the centuries when there was much commerce between East Africa and Southeast Asia. Religion in Africa has many roots. It remains to be seen whether, after looking at the numerous examples of African faith and ritual, some kind of unity can be seen.

Conclusion

Drawing from African religious mythology, ritual, and popular expression, the ethnologist or other comparative analyst derives a collection of diverse religious data. The names and characterizations of gods, demons, minor deities, spirits, powers, and other reifications of divinity are countless. The types of ritual vary from place to place and from time to time. Concerns to which religious belief and practice are related cover the gamut of African day-by-day experience. At first sight or after prolonged preoccupation with the never ending diversity, the observer may see only a Babel of mutually unintelligible particularisms. But this is an illusion based upon greater interest in form than in meaning.

Africans throughout the continent have traditionally had the persuasion that divine power is present and accessible to man. In a variety of creation accounts from the simplest picture of the turning over of a rock and releasing a world of creatures to the most elaborate myth dealing with hierarchies of personified agents of creation or birth, Africans assert their faith in a mysterious creative force responsible for the world and its living beings. Numerous forms of divination bear witness to the belief (as old in Hebrew, Christian and Moslem faith as it is in Africa) that man can find divine revelation in ways meaningful to each in one's own culture. The almost continent-wide use of the ordeal in Africa rests on the conviction that vengeance belongs to God, and that divinity can and should have the last word in the judgment of persons whose guilt is not readily proven or disproven by first-hand witnesses. Every sacrifice, large or small, voluntary or coerced by some disaster or the threats of priest or shaman, tells of the belief that the propitiation of divinity is efficacious. Evidences of taboo on one hand, sanctions leveled by spirits on another, and similar ideas suggest that Africans see a relationship between morality and the divine powers. This concern, at points, extends not only to more significant mores, but also to the seemingly trivial details of folkways. While many societies include ideas of divinity taking on anthropomorphic features, or even the form of animals, there is a persistent belief that divinity is essentially spiritual, and that the forms it takes are transitory. Many of the manifestations reported by Africans are similar to theophanies described in the Bible and the Koran, and some concepts could well be compared with either transubstantiation or consubstantiation as Christianity has explained the Eucharist.

Although no African statement of tradition has been reported to assert such doctrines as omniscience, omnipotence, omnipresence, or eternality, countless inferences of the kind protrude from mythology, suggesting that divinity is capable of knowing anything, being anywhere, doing almost anything, having been before any time humanly imaginable, and probably continuing into or after any time in the future which we can conceive.

Almost universal in African thought, if not wholly so, is the conviction that divinity is related to all natural phenomena. While those engaged in hunting, fishing, and gathering may be more apt to identify divinity with luck or success in these pursuits, the belief is far more widespread than among these primitive economies. Growing out of (but not confined to) the responsibility for cultivation are ideas about divinity controlling the rain, influencing the growing of plants, and producing harvests. Overlapping into other cultures of Africa is the idea that divinity is somehow involved in the responsibility for land tenure. Pastoral people of Africa have had the idea that divinity has a partiality for animals, and is especially influenced by animal sacrifice. This

belief, not unknown in the Bible, laps over in Africa into societies not engaged in animal husbandry at all. The intimate
relationship between divinity and the fertility of both man,
plant, and animal is widely believed. So, too, is the idea that the
divine is related to every fundamental stage of human development from conception through death.

Although different social systems affect the terminology and
symbolism of religious faith, it is clear that divinity is identified
with the social organization as it exists in any society. Patrilineal
societies with extended families and strong sib organization tend
to see divinity in the past, present, and future of the lineage even
as in Hebrew faith Jahweh was the God of Abraham, Isaac,
Jacob, and their progeny. The African and the Jew understand
equally well the idea that divinity is more readily understood,
received, and approached through one's own lineage than by
means of alien intermediaries. Matrilineages share many of the
same ideas, although preference for important male heroes or
royal figures tends to be found here rather than female figures
between the original ancestress and the present generation. Those
who have developed kingdoms and a concept of royal dynasties
have invariably equated these with divinity to some degree, holding that kings and kingly paraphernalia share something of the
divine nature. Ideas such as the divine right of kings, tempered
with some view of the rights of people to judge the responsible
behavior of their king, have been enunciated in African mon-
archies.

As far as the mining and use of ores in Africa reached, and in
some cases of accompaniment to other crafts depending upon
processes believed somehow beyond the direct control of the
human in charge, special concepts of divine power over these
processes persisted. Perhaps it was the mystery of the energy of
heat which most bewildered the smith, potter, and others who
used it. Divine involvement in the process was invariably a part
of these crafts.

To some extent, if only in the ritual of bargaining, the oaths
of agreement, etc., divinity was involved and believed to be present in trading and commerce. However, if at any place the

religious regard for divinity is tenuous, it is here just as much in Africa as in other parts of the world. "In God we trust" may be a word in commerce which accompanies a most meticulous effort to use human talents and cleverness to succeed in dealings with others having the same values.

African belief associates divinity with every level of human existence and experience. This broad application of faith has affected congregations of converts to Christianity or Islam. Missionaries often remark on the broader concept of divine involvement among the Africans than among their members in other lands.

A problem reported by numerous Christian missions relates to less than satisfactory regulation of sexual morality and a deterioration of outward respect for parents and other elders. A possible explanation lies in the effectiveness of European education in destroying the faith of young Africans in the validity of taboo, without any success in establishing confidence in some substitute for what was the indigenous control of this behavior by divine influence. In the African religion, kings, heroes, ancestors, and other manifestations of deity paid little attention to these matters which were automatically the sphere of taboo.

Similarly, problems have arisen in other quarters. When European influence challenged and denied the idea of reverence for the ancestors it destroyed the keystone upon which filial piety rested in African society. Once an individual moved in the confidence that each person progresses closer and closer to that point where, in old age, one has strong influence on the ancestors, and that after death one moves into the realm of the ancestors who share some of the divine power. Africans looked up the line, through this progression, to the apex of divine power in the more remote deity or deities. This defined the lines of authority and obedience.

In this African view, now being challenged by western thought, one central theme persisted which struggles for expression even in the Christian African congregations. It is that humans have a close affinity with the divine, that in some sense there is a divine spirit in man which through time, and by means of development, increases. As the individual in conception, birth, attainment of childhood, puberty, marriage, and any other point in his lifetime steps out of one status into one just above, so in death he steps up into a spiritual status which itself might be the beginning of a whole new series of steps upward. In some sense African faith sees these steps in the direction of more and more identification with divinity. Those embracing Christian teachings did not find the concept of "being born again" alien. Nor do they find difficulty in understanding and appropriating what some call "possession by the Holy Spirit." Their idea of immortality and future life may vary as much as do those in the western world, but they tend to visualize in that event something akin to becoming themselves a real part of the divine world which their own ancestors have already experienced. It is a world of the Spirit.

A SELECT BIBLIOGRAPHY

Brelsford, W.V., *Fishermen of the Bangweulu Swamps*. Livingston, Northern Rhodesia: The Rhodes-Livingston Institute, 1946.

Brown, J.T., *Among the Bantu Nomads*. London: Seeley, Service and Co., 1926.

Busia, K.A., "The Asanti of the Gold Coast," in *African Worlds*. Ed. Daryll Forde, London: Oxford University Press, 1963.

Colson, Elizabeth, "The Plateau Tonga of Northern Rhodesia," in *Seven Tribes of Central Africa*. Ed. Elizabeth Colson and Max Gluckman. Manchester, England: Manchester University Press, 1959.

Ellenberger, D.F., *History of the Basuto*. London: Caxton Publishing Co., 1912.

Hahn, Theophilus, *Tsuni-Goam, The Supreme Being of the Khoi-Khoi*. London: Trubner and Co., 1881.

Harris, W.T., "The Idea of God among the Mende," in Edwin W. Smith, *African Ideas of God*, 1950, - see Smith, E.W. below.

Hopgood, Cecil R., "Conceptions of God amongst the Tonga of Northern Rhodesia," in Edwin W. Smith, *African Ideas of God*, 1950, - see Smith, E.W. below.

Horton, Robin, "A Hundred Years of Change in Kalabari Religion," in John Middleton, *Black Africa*, 1970 - see Middleton, J.

———, "The Kalabari Ekine Society: A Boderland of Religion and Art," in Elliott P. Skinner, *Peoples and Cultures of Africa*, 1973, - see Skinner, E.P. below.

Krige, E.J. and J.D., *The Realm of a Rain Queen.* London: Oxford University Press, 1943.

Mackenzie, John, *Ten Years North of the Orange River.* 2nd edition. London: Frank Cass and Co., 1971.

Marwick, M.G., *Sorcery in its Social Setting.* Manchester, England: Manchester University Press, 1965.

Mbiti, John S., *African Religions and Philosophies.* New York: Praeger, 1969; Anchor Books, 1970.

Meek, C.K., *The Northern Tribes of Nigeria.* London: Oxford University Press, 1925.

Middleton, John, *Lugbara Religion.* London: Oxford University Press, 1960.
——— (ed.), *Black Africa: Its People and their Cultures Today.* New York: The Macmillan Co., 1970.

Morton-Williams, Peter, "An Outline of the Cosmology and Cult Organization of the Oyo Yoruba," in Elliott P. Skinner, *Peoples and Cultures of Africa,* 1973, - see Skinner, E.P. below.

Parsons, Robert T., *Religion in an African Society.* Leiden: E.J. Brill, 1964,

Richards, Audrey, *Hunger and Work in a Savage Tribe.* London: Routledge, 1932.

Schapera, Isaac, *Western Civilization and the Natives of South Africa.* London: Routledge, 1934.

Silberbauer, George B., *Bushman Survey Report.* Gaberones, Africa: Bechuanaland Government, 1965.

Skinner, Elliott P., *Peoples and Cultures of Africa.* Garden City, New York: Natural History Press, 1973.

Smith, Edwin W., *The Secret of Africa.* Lectures on African Religion. London: Student Christian Movement, 1929.
——— (ed.), *African Ideas of God.* London: Edinburgh House Press, 1950.

Talbot, P.A., *The Peoples of Southern Nigeria.* London: Oxford University Press, 1926.

Theal, George McCall, *Records of South-Eastern Africa* (9 vols.). Facsimile Reprint, Cape Town: C. Dtruik (Pty), 1898-1903.

Turner, V.W., *Schism and Continuity in an African Society.* Manchester, England: Manchester University Press, 1959.
———, "Symbols in African Ritual," in *Science,* Vol. 179, March 16, 1973. pp. 1098-1105.

Van Gennep, Arnald, *The Rites of Passage.* Translated from the French by Monika B. Vizedom and Gabrielle L. Caffee. Chicago: University of Chicago Press, 1908. Reprint in 1960.

CHAPTER II

KNOWLEDGE OF GOD IN ISLAM

*Robert E. Carter**

The uncompromising emphasis on the unity and majesty of God (Allah) in Islam has prompted one modern interpreter to remark that the religion might properly be called 'Allahism'.[1] It is perfectly clear that the designation 'Muhammadanism' is inappropriate and fallacious. Adherents of Islam worship the one God, Allah, and not Muhammad. Muhammad is a prophet of Allah, in fact the last of the great prophets according to Islamic doctrine,[2] but he is not God incarnate. While it is believed that Muhammad's prophecy both restored and *completed* the religion of the earlier prophets, it is not in keeping with Islam to assert, therefore, that Muhammad is the greatest of the prophets, for this suggests discontinuity. However much Muslims have stressed the importance of Muhammad in times past, they have never lost sight of the unity and transcendence of Allah. The term 'Islam' means peaceful submission to Allah's will, and so properly designates the supremacy of Allah, although it also may be taken to signify the importance of submission and careful adherence to religious duties. Since Islam emphasizes the absoluteness of God

*Associate Professor at Otonabee College, Trent University, Peterborough, Ontario, Canada.

1 Seyyed Hossein Nasr, *Ideals and Realities of Islam* (New York: Frederick A. Praeger, 1967), pp. 17-18.

2 The Islamic revelation is held to be in accord with other undistorted revelations from *the* One God: The Quran states that Allah "hath ordained for you that religion which He commended unto Noah, and that which We inspire in thee (Muhammad), and that which We commended unto Abraham and Moses and Jesus, saying: Establish the religion, and be not divided therein" (42:13). [More often than not, specified translations of passages from the Quran will be taken from Mohammed Marmaduke Pickthall's *The Meaning of the Glorious Koran* (New York: The New American Library of World Literature, Inc., Mentor paperback, 1956)].

and the relativity of all else,[3] 'Allahism' is the one designation which unequivocally catches this emphasis.

1. Ways of Knowing Allah

Allah is *the* God. The Quran states in many places that "there is no God save Allah,"[4] and "Muhammad is the Apostle of Allah." These two statements have been referred to as the short creed of Islam, and together they require that knowledge of Allah be gained through His revealed book and through Muhammad, His vehicle of revelation.

(a) The Quran

Islam is a revealed religion. God chose to reveal Himself to man through words. The Quran is the result, and must be viewed as the "perfection of language."[5] Coming directly from God to a man chosen for his purity and acceptability as a vehicle of Divine transmission, the Quran has God's guarantee of veracity if properly interpreted. It is precisely here that revealed religions encounter their greatest difficulties, for the slightest differences in interpretation of the many words, phrases and synonyms used may generate exegetical and theological debate without end. If Allah "is the sole reason for its [Islam's] existence,"[6] then it is hardly to be wondered at that the ambiguities surrounding the naming and describing of Allah in the Quran, which resulted in widely

---

3 *Ibid.,* pp. 15-16.

4 Titus Burckhardt in *An Introduction to Sufi Doctrine,* translated by D.M. Matheson (Lahore: Ashraf, 1959), p. 58 insists that "there is no God save Allah;" it is only adequately translated into English as, "there is no divinity if it be not the Divinity." The Divinity is a unique class of one member, and not simply the highest or greatest member of a generic class of many members.

5 Frithjof Schuon, *Understanding Islam* (London: George Allen & Unwin Ltd., 1963), p. 44.

6 *The Encyclopaedia of Islam,* Vol. I (New Edition, Leiden, Holland: E. J. Brill, 1960), p. 406.

divergent interpretations of His nature, proved central in the early debates of Islam.

Allah is mentioned in the Quran more than six thousand times, and since Allah is author as well as main subject of this holy book, what is said by Him of Himself must be seen as the basic source of information concerning His nature. Tradition has sorted these references to Allah, and the ninety-nine most Beautiful Names have been selected and committed to memory by the pious. Among the ninety-nine are the following: the One, the Unique, the Truth, the Real, the High and Great, the Creator, He Who is unlike all creation, He who does not cease to create, the Omniscient, the Omnipotent, the Bountiful, the Protector, the Generous, the Merciful, the Forgiver, the Compassionate, the supreme Judge, the just Punisher, and the Sage.[7] Some of these designations required commentary to show that those names which were commonly used to signify *human* traits were used in the Quran with quantitative and/or qualitative difference to characterize the Divine. For in addition to the use of the more abstract qualities of Mercy, Generosity or Wisdom, God is also spoken of in the Quran as having hands ("The Jews say: Allah's hand is fettered" 5:64), eyes which see and a face ("... whither soever ye turn, there is Allah's countenance" 2:115), and sits on a great throne (10:4). A.J. Arberry attributes this anthropomorphism to the still strong animistic tendencies of the early Muslims, and refers to one of the most literal anthropomorphists:[8] "Hishām ibn al-Hakam (d. *ca.* 200/816), is credited with having stated that God 'has a body, defined, broad, high and long, of equal dimensions, radiating with light, of a fixed measure in three dimensions, in a place beyond place, like a bar of pure metal,

---

7 *Ibid.*, p. 408. See also listing under *Al-Asmā' Al-Husnā, ibid.* Burckhardt, *op. cit.*, p. 63: "The Divine Qualities, each of which is unique, are indefinite in number. As for the Divine Names, they are necessarily limited in number, being nothing other than the Qualities summarized in certain fundamental types and 'promulgated' by Sacred Scriptures as 'means of grace' which can be 'invoked'."

8 A. J. Arberry, *Revelation and Reason in Islam* (London: George Allen & Unwin Ltd., 1957) pp. 20 ff.

shining as a round pearl on all sides, provided with colour, taste, smell and touch."[9]

It was the Mu'tazilites[10] who took strongest exception to this anthropomorphism. From the vantage point of today, it is clear that their rejection of the anthropomorphic interpretation was one of the reasons which led them to the opposite extreme of the unknowability of Allah, and so cost them the support of those who, while finding the attribution of human qualities to Allah dangerous, also found danger (and little of personal religious interest) in a rationalism which denied that any human attribution whatever could prove revelatory of God's nature. In fact, the traditionalists believed that the Mu'tazilites had removed all significant content from the conception of God, since they eventually denied not only human attribution (anthropomorphic or metaphorical), but all attribution whatsoever except that of eternality,[11] or of God as Creator of the world.[12] Otherwise, the negative path was chosen, and Allah is described as being without body, without substance, without parts, in no place, not in time, nor can He be described in any way which relates to things of this world. He is not this, not that. Ash'arism was, in part, a response to the crisis precipitated by the Mu'tazilite criticism of the naive traditionalism of the Sunnite anthropomorphism. The Ash'arites retained concern for the traditional Divine qualities, but viewed such characterizations as being somehow metaphorical. By not taking them literally they lost precision, but by rendering them metaphorical they avoided the charge of anthropomorphism.

Without attempting a history of the concept of Allah in Islam, it should be apparent that the Quran itself gives no univocal

9 A. J. Wensinck, *The Muslim Creed* (London: Frank Cass & Co. Ltd., 1965), pp. 67-68. Quoted in Arberry, *op. cit.*, p. 21.

10 A school of rational theologians in Islam who were the modernists of their time, and who began systematic discussion of Islamic doctrines in terms of Greek philosophical conceptions.

11 *Ibid.*, p. 75.

12 T. J. De Boer, *The History of Philosophy in Islam*, translated by Edward R. Jones (New York: Dover Publications, Inc. 1967), p. 47.

concept of God, but rather provides a rich and often poetic account of Him in His various manifestations. Mahmud Shaltout sums up the problem when he writes that the "Qur'an makes clear that Allah can be described, His qualities can be partially known, but His essence cannot be conceived of by man."[13] Nevertheless, the difficulties of interpretation notwithstanding, and the vagaries of Islam's history noted in brief, it remains important and true to recognize the Quran as the basic path to Islamic conception of God.

(b) The Prophet and the Prophets

Muhammad is referred to as the last of the prophets of God. This implies that there were others, and indeed the first of the prophets was Adam.[14] Abraham, Moses, Jesus and others are all accepted as genuine prophets, but the final and only pure revelation is that received by Muhammad. Nasr notes that to this end the prophet must be uneducated and otherwise unspoiled intellectually "for the same reason that the Virgin Mary must be virgin. The human vehicle of a Divine Message must be pure and untainted."[15] Just as philosophers have long known that the awareness of anything may be termed accurate and veridical if and only if the human organs of sensation and the intellectual faculty do not distort what is presented to them, or even create from their own resources what otherwise appears to come from outside these faculties, so the prophet is viewed in Islam as one who does not add to the revelation of which he is the vehicle, nor does he do more than perfectly mirror what is directly given *through* him. Nasr continues, "The soul of the Prophet was a *tabula rasa* before the Divine Pen and on the human level his

13 Mahmud Shaltout, "Islamic Beliefs and Code of Laws", in Kenneth W. Morgan, *Islam – The Straight Path* (New York: The Ronald Press Company, 1958), p. 98.
14 Kenneth Cragg, *The Call of the Minaret* (Oxford University Press, 1956), p. 47.
15 Nasr, *op. cit.*, p. 43.

quality of 'unletteredness' marks that supreme virtue of realizing the Truth through the contemplation of it which marks an 'extinction' in the metaphysical sense before the Truth."[16] But in addition to the special guarantee which God provides through the revelation which Muhammad received, the very *life* of Muhammad may serve to make us aware of our own essential nature, or clarify some aspect of the religious life or Quranic teaching.

Muhammad is the perfect man, the chosen one of Allah. He is the symbol of that perfection which a human being can achieve if he is an unfailing follower of Allah. Nasr, Schuon and others have observed that Islam views man as a theomorphic being. It is because we are *of divine form* that we will benefit from the revelation which Allah sent in the form of the Quran and through Muhammad. We have an intelligence capable of conceiving of the Absolute, and we have a will which is capable of choosing that which Allah wills us to choose and which leads to our salvation. Through the special revelation of the Quran, "God does no more than fill the receptacles man had emptied but not destroyed."[17] This does not mean that man is a fallen being, but only that he is "by nature negligent and forgetful; he is by nature imperfect."[18] Therefore, even Adam was both a theomorphic being and an imperfect being -- in short, like all other men, one in need of prophecy, requiring something to remind him of his own divine nature and the proper use of intelligence which leads to knowledge of God and the correct direction of will.

Precisely because each man needs a prophet (unless he is himself a Prophet) in order to be reminded of his nature and capacity for knowing the Divine and choosing His way, it is important in Islam to *observe* the prophets, and particularly the last of the prophets, in an attempt to lead a truly religious life. Thus it is that some of the ninety-nine Beautiful Names of Allah are based

16 Nasr, *op. cit.*, p. 77.
17 Schuon, *op. cit.*, p. 14.
18 Nasr, *op. cit.*, p. 22.

on the tradition connected with the sayings and actions of Muhammad himself. The *hadīth*, tradition based on Muhammad's words and actions, is the result of interest in living a religious life as externally appropriate and worthy as that lived by the prophet of Allah himself. Insofar as such living may remind a man of his innate and indestructible theomorphic nature, to that extent the prophet himself may be seen as a way of coming to know God. Indirectly, then, we have a way of knowing of God, but the method is dependent on a specific doctrine of *human nature.*

(c) The Nature of Man

(aa) The Intellect[19]

Even though it be admitted that all knowledge of the concept of God is contained explicitly or implicitly in the Quran, it remains a clear fact that for many Muslims it is through the proper use of the intellect that man may come to realization of this knowledge. Human intelligence is a gift from Allah, a part of our theomorphic design. But man can be led to the knowledge and affirmation of the one God only if he is set again and again on the correct path. Man needs to be reminded, as did the first man who was also the first prophet. Only by proper use of the intellect is man led to knowledge of Allah, "and it is precisely revelation, this objective manifestation of the Intellect, that

---

19 The reader should be warned that it is not intellect in the simple sense of 'reason' that is being discussed. Reason, by itself, has no way of distinguishing the path which is worth following for religious gains from one which is worth following for other purposes. The intellect here discussed is a 'reason' which includes the theomorphic recollection, which gives it an innate Divine direction. That which is more than intellect, and which is also sometimes termed intellect in studies of Islam, is that intuitive or contemplative or mystical identification which is as much a being as a knowing. Thus there is reason, 'reason' (which is theomorphically informed and directed) or intellect, and Intellect or mystical awareness. Please see section I.4 *(The Cosmos)* of this essay for an important further discussion of intellect.

guarantees this wholesomeness and permits the Intelligence to function correctly and not be impeded by the passions."[20] The Muslim accepts revelation because it is directly from God, but also because it awakens in him the latent memory of his own awareness of the Divine Unity. Our own intellect confirms what we knew all along. It is in this spirit that Schuon writes that certitude springs from intelligence "because through its fundamental nature it is already there."[21] This "spiritual subconscious," as Schuon terms it,[22] like Plato's doctrine of recollection serves as the immanent standard whereby certainty may be secured and truth recognized. Unless the mind in some sense already knows what it seeks to discover, it will be incapable of the discrimination required to select an instance of anything whatever, particularly an instance of certainty of judgment. The transcendent standard for Plato was supplied by his theory of forms, crowned by the Good: Allah is the metaphysical or absolute guarantee of Islam, and this guarantee is made available to men through the Quran. Man is not a fallen being, but a being who continually falls. He does not require revelation in order to make him aware of what he has inevitably forgotten, but to remind him of what he periodically forgets and to point him in the right direction for utilization of his natural faculties which are of God and can lead to knowledge of Him.

(bb) The Heart

The importance of Sufism, the mystical tradition within Islam, is being increasingly recognized both within and without Islam. Islamic mystics have been as varied in their doctrines as have Islamic theologians, but they are agreed that there is a direct path to God which leads beyond the intellect, and beyond knowledge about God, to knowledge of God through immediate acquaint-

20 *Ibid.*, p. 23.
21 Schuon, *op. cit.*, p. 144.
22 *Ibid.*, p. 152.

ance. Emphasis is placed on the heart partly in order to indicate that the knowledge which the mystic claims is of a different order from that gained through the use of the intellect, and partly to suggest the depth of personal involvement required to move from the source within the individual to the universal Source.[23] The heart is of divine origin, the divine spark within, and if nurtured and listened to can lead to a direct seeing of or even a union with God himself. Mystical knowledge is qualitatively different from knowledge of any other kind, and its goal is not intellectual awareness but immediate 'perception' of God or an aspect of God. Whether it is true of all mysticism, as Evelyn Underhill suggests, that there be "union between God and the soul,"[24] it is undoubtedly true of Sufism.

(d) The Cosmos

Allah is the Creator (29:24), and all that He has created bears his stamp of order. Nothing exists save that which Allah has created, and Allah Himself. The worldly harmony is so great that man must take care to view it as a significant *natural* revelation of God, and not as an end in itself. The Quran frequently affirms that the splendid orderliness of the cosmos is a "sign", for men of understanding (3:190), of God's sovereignty. The "Cleavor of the Daybreak" (6:97), the positioner of the sun, the moon, the stars, has provided natural revelation "for a people who have understanding" (6:98). Nature then is an open book, and it provides a way whereby man may come to an understanding of Allah and His nature ("He detaileth the revelations, that haply ye may be certain of the meeting with your Lord" 13:2).

---

23 Evelyn Underhill, *Mysticism* (New York: Meridian Books, 1955), p. 71: "We here mean not merely 'the seat of the affections,' 'the organ of tender emotion,' and the like: but rather the inmost sanctuary of personal being, the deep root of its love and will, the very source of its energy and like."

24 Evelyn Underhill, *The Essentials of Mysticism and Other Essays* (New York: Dutton Paperback ed., E. P. Dutton & Co., Inc., 1960), p. 6, observes that "the one essential of mysticism" is "union between God and the soul."

It need hardly be stressed that the order and harmony of the universe will not convince the nonbeliever of Allah's existence and provide him a way to knowledge of His unity. Natural revelation is successful only if man already has a latent knowledge of God. Man, as theomorphic being, has such inborn knowledge, and so is able to re-discover or confirm the Creator of the ordered universe as One, Wise, etc.[25] Fazlur Rahman has gone so far as to contend that "one of the main functions of the idea of God is to vindicate the orderliness of the universe -- that there is no lawlessness in nature, that the whole cosmos is an organic unity. This is the reason behind the insistent emphasis on the unity of God.[26] Actually, it would seem that the case could more realistically be made the other way around: that the all important conception of Divine Unity led inevitably to those studies which showed that the universe, too, was reflective of God's order. Hence, one of the main functions of the idea of cosmos is to vindicate the unity of Allah which is *nowhere* absent.

However that may be, it is more than apparent from a brief look at the Quran and later Islamic theology that man may be led to knowledge of God through attention paid to the order of nature. Man is capable of learning from nature, of discerning what nature reveals of the Divine, because of his own "spiritual subconscious."[27] The cosmos is a primordial symbol of Allah.

25 Mahmud Shaltout, *op. cit.*, p. 94: "The rational evidence for belief in Allah is based on Islam's call to ponder on the nature of the universe -- the earth, the heavens, the mysteries, the natural laws, the harmony and unity of the universe. Thus one comes to see that it is impossible that the universe could be self-created, or created by opposed or contradictory forces, or purposeless."

26 Fazlur Rahman, "The Qur'anic Concept of God, the Universe and Man," *Islamic Studies*, VI, March, 1967, p. 2.

27 Schuon, *op. cit.*, p. 152: "This spiritual subconscious, as here understood, is formed of all that the intellect contains in a latent and implicit fashion; now the

The intellect, through sense experience, may gain knowledge of the Divine.

2. The Nature of Allah

Religious observances such as prayer, fasting, the pilgrimage and almsgiving may be methodologically significant in preparing the individual to accept revelation or to properly exercise his reason in coming to learn of Allah, but it does not seem that they are themselves sources of knowledge, but only occasions for it, or preparation and even necessary conditions for it. An outline of the ways of knowing Allah has been suggested, and it is now required that a more detailed analysis be given of the nature of Allah.

(a) The Science of Unification

Muslim theology has been called "the science of unification"[28] because of its fundamental insistence on God's unity. The Quran

---

intellect 'knows' through its very substance all that is capable of being known and, like the blood flowing through even the tiniest arteries of the body, it traverses all the egos of which the universe is woven and opens out 'vertically' on the Infinite. In other words, the intellective centre of man, which is in practice 'subconscious' has knowledge, not only of God, but also of man's nature and his destiny; and this enables us to present Revelation as a 'supernaturally natural' manifestation of that which the human species 'knows' in its virtual and submerged omniscience, both about itself and about God. Thus the Prophetic phenomenon appears as a kind of awakening, on the human plane, of the universal consciousness that is present everywhere in the cosmos in varying degrees of opening up or slumber."

28 A. E. Affifi, "The Rational and Mystical Interpretations of Islam," in Kenneth W. Morgan, *Islam   The Straight Path* (New York: The Ronald Press Company, 1958), p. 145, Professor Nabil Shehaby of the Institute of Islamic Studies at McGill University suggested to me during a conversation that 'one-ification' would be the more accurate term in this context. 'Unification' implies the gathering together of multiplicity which the resulting unity *includes,* whereas Islam attempts to *eliminate* multiplicity altogether. Thus, aside from the cumbersomeness of the expression, Islam ought to be termed "The Science of One-ification."

describes the entire universe as pointing to the unity of Allah, *the* God. The first awareness which a Muslim must have is the knowledge of the One without another, and the greatest of all heresies is the upgrading of any other being, principle or person as competitor to this absolute and *unqualified* unity. Linguistically, it is clearly difficult to stress this Oneness which is unique, and yet give information about God's qualities, His creation and His law without adding qualities to Him which serve not merely to illuminate but to destroy this unity. Yet it is not enough to affirm that Allah is Allah, that He is the one God and that there is no other, and that He is essentially unified. The problem is, then, to say something of God's nature while at the same time preserving His unity.

The Quranic passages which anthropomorphize God by attributing to him hands, a face and eyes, etc., were soon interpreted as metaphorical. In a manner of speaking, for finite human consumption, it is as though God sees, creates with His hands and cares for men as we care for each other. As a matter of fact, God transcends all our categories of thought, imagination and language. He is Absolute and we relative. The relative can describe the Absolute either in relative terms or in negative terms, thereby indicating that the Absolute is not confined by any relative characteristic but *transcends* them all. The Beautiful Names do not describe God's essence: the relative cannot conceive of the Absolute, nor can the relative speak of the Absolute. The lasting influence of the Mu'tazilites on Islam may be their insistence that Allah possesses no eternal quality save eternity, leaving His unity untouched. Approaching the matter through negation, some Mu'tazilites spoke of God as Creator, for example, by stating that it is forbidden both to say that God has not ceased creating, and that He has not ceased non-creating, or that He has not ceased sustaining, or that He has not ceased not-sustaining.[29]

The question of the status of the creation may be viewed as exemplary of the difficulties of affirming the unity of God while

29 Wensinck, *op. cit.*, p. 75.

attributing to Him additional qualities. If God is Creator of the universe, then is the universe a second in addition to God, or is the universe but a part of God? If the former, then we have lost unity with the Creator, and if the latter, then we have lost the clear meaning of Creator as well as the theological significance of trying to know what already is known. Is the universe an illusion, and the attempt to unite with the Absolute the result of ignorance? What is to be done with the status of the illusion and the significance of the ignorance? The solution seems to be the acceptance of the paradox. The creation is not other than Allah, nor is it the same as Allah. Furthermore, it is not merely that it is a part of Allah while Allah Himself is more than that part, for such talk would destroy the unity of Allah and introduce the language of parts. Rather, it is the case that Allah is not the creation at all, and yet that it is not other than He. The view is one which denies both the existence of a universe separate from God, and denies that the universe is God (pantheism). What remains is the paradox which retains the tremendous force of the doctrine of unity of Allah, and yet also retains the immanence of a God who remains "closer to man than his own neck-vein."

Professor H.A.R. Gibb has noted that the transcendence of Allah has been affirmed again and again in the Quran "with an absoluteness which seems to leave no possible loophole for a doctrine of immanence."[30] He goes on to remark that the attributes of a loving God also recur in the Quran, demanding the immanent view of Allah. Whether the Absolute is transcendent or immanent, or whether these concepts simply suffer from the limitations of the relative, the paradox remains. The Mu'tazilites represent the extreme of transcendence and the rational requirements of such a view, while the anthropomorphists represent the extreme of immanence which offers a God so personal that one can reach out for His hand and look into His eyes at the day of judgment. The middle ground may be the recognition that the

---

30 H. A. R. Gibb, *Modern Trends in Islam* (Chicago, Ill.: The University of Chicago Press, 1947), p. 17.

paradox of Islam requires the acceptance of both positions (although perhaps not in the extreme forms), if only because man is a finite or relative being. The *Allāhu akbar,* used as the call to prayer, is in the superlative form, and implies that God is not only greater but greatest.[31] As such, it implies that "whatever one says of God he [sic] transcends it and is greater than it. It is thus a way of asserting the Infinite nature of God that transcends all limited descriptions and formulations of Him."[32]

The theological debates over creation and Creator, immanence and transcendence were of considerably greater significance to the theologians than to the rank and file believer. A different solution was offered by the Sufis who taught that man had access to personal communion with God. Yet it is hardly to be expected that the relative, even if in direct communion with the Absolute, will be any more able to communicate his intuition to others in relative language expressing relative concepts than were his more speculative theological brethren. The greatest contribution of the mystics has not been their attempts at describing the indescribable, but at calling to men's attention the possibility of direct access to that which is beyond conception, language and imagination.

(b) The Art of Union with God

The direct knowledge, intuition, or 'perception' of the Divine which Sufis (and perhaps all mystics) lay claim to is a *union* (variously described and delimited) with the Divine. Such knowledge is more akin to a state of *being* than it is of *having* knowledge. The mystical experience is *noetic,* as nearly all mystical commentators have noted, but it is noetic non-discursively (even though it may be discursively pointed to or symbolized); that is, the noesis affects the totality of the knower such that he becomes identified *(not necessarily substantially)* with the Known.

31 Nasr, *op. cit.,* p. 64.
32 *Ibid.*

The distinction between knower and Known, subject and Object is removed.

Sufism[33] is referred to as the esoteric or inward aspect of Islam, or the heart of Islam. The direct awareness of God to which the Sufi saints claim access is said by Sufism to be in accord with the Quran, and Islamic tradition generally. And while it is apparent from a brief reading of the history of Sufism that it has frequently been deemed suspect in terms of its relation to Islamic orthodoxy, sometimes heretical, and during one period the virtual orthodoxy of Islam, it remains a strong influence within Islam. Throughout, one constant charge made against Sufism has been that it was and is a *pantheism* to a rigorous monotheism stressing that Divine Unity is the identification of the natural world, including man, with the Divine who is thought of as transcendent and unique. Furthermore, when the Divine is viewed as the natural universe *including* man, then it is but a short step to the conclusion that all men are Divine. The mystic utterance, "I am God," is then to be taken literally, and has been recognized as a heresy in Islam and Christianity often enough to be seen as a problem which the mystics must deal with. The most direct approach to a solution of the problem may well be to precisely define pantheism.

Pantheism, if taken to mean the identification of God and the phenomenal universe as a whole, does not apply to most Sufi doctrine. It is true that the Sufi denies "a fundamental and irreducible separation between the Divinity and himself",[34] but

---

33 Reynold A. Nicholson in *The Mystics of Islam* (London: G. Bell and Sons, Ltd., 1941), pp. 18-27, offers a variety of definitions of Sufism from a variety of sources indicating the many tendencies included under this single term: (1) "Sufism is this: that actions should be passing over the Sufi (i.e., being done upon him) which are known to God only, and that he should always be with God in a way that is known to God only." (2) "Sufism is wholly self-discipline." (3) "Sufism is, to possess nothing and to be possessed by nothing." (4) "A Sufi is one who seeks to know God directly." (5) "Sufism is freedom and generosity and absence of self-constraint." (6) "Sufism is control of the faculties and observance of the breaths." (7) "To behold the imperfection of the phenomenal world, nay, to close the eye to everything imperfect in contemplation of Him who is remote from all imperfection — this is Sufism."

34 Burckhardt, *op. cit.,* p. 16.

only so that he may emphasize that nothing may exist truly separate from God. While the point is clear, its logical defence is less than apparent. For example, Burckhardt writes that "all beings are God, if considered in their essential reality, but God is not these beings and this, not in the sense that His reality excludes them, but because in face of His infinity their reality is nil."[35] This leaves open the possibility of either (a) the distinction between God and all else as being but an illusion without existence, or (b) an illusion with a lesser existence, or (c) a reality with existence, but lesser in quality and/or quantity than the Divine. There may be other possibilities. The defence does not make clear whether anything can exist separate from God, and allows the possibility that something does exist apart from God, but with lesser reality. Burckhardt is much more to the point when he concludes that the solution of what appears to be a paradox is not to be gained rationally, "but by an intuitive integration of paradox."[36] This point has been elaborated by W.T. Stace, who also argues that pantheism is not correctly understood as the simple identity of God and the World,[37] but rather includes both the propositions, "The world is identical with God" and "The world is distinct from, that is to say, *not* identical with, God."[38] This paradox is one of several paradoxes which Stace isolates, remarking that "paradoxicality is one of the universal characteristics of all mysticism."[39] He sees this pantheism which preserves paradox as the proper answer to the question whether the correct view of the relationship between man and nature, and the Divine, is monistic or dualistic; it is both. It is monistic in stressing the identity of the world and God (usually

35 *Ibid.*, p. 24.

36 *Ibid.*, p. 25.

37 W. T. Stace, *Mysticism and Philosophy* (New York: Macmillan and Co., Ltd., 1960), p. 211: "...if pantheism means nothing but the identity of God and the world, this is the same as saying that the pantheist means that 'God' is just another name which some people choose to use – for some very odd reason -- for what most people call the world."

38 Stace, *op. cit.*, p. 212.

39 *Ibid.*

directly experienced by the mystic), and dualistic in stressing the otherness of God (even allowing us to establish "the gulf as wide as we like in our imaginations and still remain pantheists"[40]). The "logic of opposites"[41] is the logic of mysticism. The Sufi who reports that the universe is like a great mirror which reflects God, and concludes that while the reflection (including the mirror) is God, God is also distinct from the mirror, appears to strengthen Stace's position. "A is B, but B is not A," is a common expression of the problem, but not of the paradox. A man is an animal, but not all animals are men. The point of the paradox, to continue the analogy, would require that the only animals be men, and that men both be animals and not be animals at the same time and in the same respects. A is B and A is not B: that is the correct formulation of the paradox. Burckhardt and Schuon[42] seem to argue against this paradox when they suggest that the resolution of the problem is the realization that pantheism has generally been associated with "naturalism and then materialism," and the question of the continuity of God and the universe has come to be limited to a discussion of substance, whereas there are other "levels or degrees of existence"[43] where the continuity is evidently absent due to the great differences pertaining to the Absolute and the relative.

If Stace's position is correct with respect to the mystical "logic of paradox," it would not be surprising to find alternative attempts to describe the relationship of God and man and/or nature which were monistic, dualistic, and "paradoxically pantheistic" *within a single tradition* or even in the writings of a *single* mystic trying to express the paradoxical within the confines of the logic of identity, where A is A, and cannot be *both*

40 *Ibid.,* p. 250.

41 *Ibid.,* Chapter 5, "Mysticism and Logic."

42 Burckhardt, *op. cit.,* pp. 22-25. Frithjof Schuon, *The Transcendent Unity of Religions* (London: Faber & Faber, 1954), Chapter 3, "Transcendence and Universality of Esotericism."

43 *Ibid.,* p. 25.

B and not B. It is not difficult, in fact, to find examples dealing with the relationship between man, nature and God in the writings of Sufis which run the gamut from monism, to dualism, to monist/dualist positions.

A representative of the monistic view is Farid ed-Din 'Attar, born sometime before 1150 A.D. He taught that the soul of man is Divine, and on the principle that like can know like, concluded that man can apprehend God.[44] The Divine is beyond human conception and experience, but through the heart God may reveal himself to man.[45] The result of this higher experience is the total annihilation of the self in God (fanā): "By Union, I have been merged in the Unity, I am become altogether apart from all else, I am Thou and Thou art I -- nay, not I, all is altogether Thou. I have become annihilated, 'I' and 'Thou' no more exist. We have become one, and I have become altogether Thou."[46] A similar monistic position is attributed to Ibn Arabi (1165-1240 A.D.). Affifi remarks that it was Ibn Arabi who first developed a consistent pantheism.[47] Ibn Arabi, as Affifi interprets him, emphasizes the Unity of all Being, reduces the phenomenal world to a shadow of reality, and sees perceived duality of God and universe as the astigmatism of the unaided intellect "which is incapable of comprehending the essential unity of the whole."[48] Nasr, by contrast, emphasizes Ibn Arabi's statement of the discontinuity of substance in God and the universe, while at the same time noting that a "trace" of God can be found in all natural things.[49] Both parts of the paradox are affirmed, and it is

44 Margaret Smith, *Readings from the Mystics of Islam* (London: Luzac and Co., 1950), p. 19.

45 Burckhardt, *op. cit.*, p. 18: "Those who stand 'outside' often attribute to Sufis the pretention of being able to attain to God by the sole means of their own will... Although its development [the contemplative capacity]...does include a certain logical process, knowledge is none the less a divine gift which man could not take to himself by his own initiative."

46 Smith, *op. cit.*, p. 103.

47 Affifi, *op. cit.*, p. 177.

48 *Ibid.*

49 Seyyed Hossein Nasr, *Three Muslim Sages* (Cambridge, Mass.: Harvard University Press, 1964), pp. 104-108.

concluded that "God is absolutely transcendent with respect to the Universe, but the Universe is not completely separated from Him."[50] Mystical union does not imply annihilation of the individual, but realization "that our existence from the beginning belonged to God."[51]

The great Jalāl-al-Dīn Rūmī, born in 1207 A.D., met 'Attar, who is said to have recognized that Rūmī was destined to become a religious genius. If 'Attar is representative of monism, then Rūmī is the monist/dualist, for he seems to fluctuate in his account of mystical union. The mystic goal of union with God is clearly affirmed, but the issue of annihilation of self in God is ambiguously stated. In some of his poems, Rūmī writes of the annihilation of the self, while in others he clings to a belief in the survival of personality. On the side of annihilation:

When a fly is plunged in honey, all the members of its body are reduced to the same condition, and it does not move. Similarly the term *istighrāq* (absorption of God) is applied to one who has no conscious existence or initiative or movement. Any action that proceeds from him is not his own. If he is still struggling in the water, or if he cries out, "Oh, I am drowning," he is not said to be in the state of absorption.[52]

In another poem ("The Life Everlasting") in which he treats of death and the day of resurrection, he writes that "...the light of the senses and spirits of our fathers is not wholly perishable, like the grass. Those who have passed from the world are not non-existent: they are steeped in the Divine Attributes."[53] Being bathed in the Divine Attributes does not rule out individual characteristics, but illuminates them or changes their appearance and nature. The universe, too is "created...in order that all things

50 *Ibid.*, p. 106.
51 *Ibid.*, p. 114.
52 *Ibid.*, p. 179.
53 Reynold A. Nicholson, *Rumi: Poet and Mystic* (London: George Allen & Unwin Ltd., 1956), p. 184.

in His knowledge should be revealed."[54] In short, it is less apparent that Rumi takes a clear position on the relation of man and universe to Divine than that he vacillates paradoxically from apparent monism to apparent dualism.

The dualist position is apparent in the writings of Muhammad Iqbal, born in 1873, and a reformer of Islamic doctrine. Iqbal was greatly influenced by Rūmī, and he wrote that his "life depends on his [Rūmī's] breath." The concept of ego or self is central in Iqbal, and even God is conceived of as the Supreme or Ultimate Ego. The goal of the mystic is not annihilation of the self, but communion of human self with Divine Self. If the self becomes spiritual enough, it will endure forever as a co-creator with God, its task being the continuation of the creative movement in the path of an ever increasing perfection.[55] God and man are co-workers. Man is not thoroughly independent of God, however, for God, of His own accord, chooses finite egos as participators in His work and as organic to His being.[56] Even in Iqbal something of the paradox can be found. In his famous *The Reconstruction of Religious Thought in Islam,* he wrote these two passages which seem to be somewhat at odds:

> I have conceived the Ultimate Reality as an Ego; and I must add now that from the Ultimate Ego only egos proceed. The creative energy of the Ultimate Ego, in whom deed and thought are identical, functions as ego-entities. The world in all its details, from the mechanical movement of what we call the atom of matter to the free-movement of thought in the human-ego is the self-revelation of the "Great I am."[57]

54 *Ibid.,* p. 111.

55 Muhammad Iqbal, *The Reconstruction of Religious Thought in Islam* (Lahore: Sh. Muhammad Ashraf, 1962), pp. 64, 123.

56 Muhammad Iqbal, *The Secrets of the Self,* translated with notes by Reynold A. Nicholson (New York: Macmillan and Co., Ltd., 1920), p. xviii. Cf. Ishrat Hasan Enver, *The Metaphysics of Iqbal* (Lahore: Sh. Muhammad Ashraf, 1948), p. 83.

57 Iqbal, *Reconstruction,* p. 71.

It is only when we look at the act of creation as a specific event in the life-history of God that the universe appears as an independent other.[58]

The paradox of God and self as well as that of the universe and the Divine appears to be part of the conception of God in Sufi thought. Whether the thesis propounded by Stace is correct or not, it is illuminating as an accurate account of the ambiguities connected with the mystical notion of God in Sufism, and perhaps in general.

What has not yet been indicated is why Iqbal is considered a mystic. But perhaps it is well to include an answer to this question in the concluding section dealing with modern Islam and the concept of God.

3. The Modern Period

Whatever may be said of modern developments in Islamic theology, Kenneth Cragg's remark that "theology in Islam is far behind all other academic disciplines in hospitality to new attitudes"[59] seems appropriate. The Egyptian Muhammad Abduh (1849-1905), whose efforts resulted in "the first 'modernistic' work of theology,"[60] is said to have achieved little else than the making of a small contribution to the modernisms which followed him. He stressed the pursuit of modern thought, "confident that in the last resort it could not undermine but only confirm the religious truth of Islam."[61] Sir Sayyid Ahmad Kham (1817-98) emphasized the acceptability and importance of reason in interpreting Islam in general, and even the Quran.[62] He

58 *Ibid.*, p. 77.

59 Cragg, *op. cit.*, p. 25.

60 W. Montgomery Watt, *Islamic Philosophy and Theology* (Edinburgh: Edinburgh University Press, 1962), p. 176.

61 H. A. R. Gibb, *Mohammedanism: An Historical Survey* (London: Oxford University Press, 2nd edition, 1961), p. 176.

62 Aziz Ahmad, *Islamic Modernism in India and Pakistan*, 1857-1964 (London: Oxford University Press, 1967), p. 41.

sought to utilize the development of scientific thought in the West, and his writings are said to show "the unmistakable influence of Unitarianism." Thus, his contributions to modernism in Islam include the introduction of Western scientific thought into Muslim theological interpretation, and the re-introduction of a rationalism with some of the boldness reminiscent of the Mu'tazilites. However, it is Muhammad Iqbal (1875-1938) who "dominates Islamic religious and political thought in the twentieth century."[63] Nevertheless, Gibb is able to remark that Iqbal's call for a 'reconstruction' of Islamic thought has "not yet had any deep effect upon Muslim thought as a whole."[64] Guillaume adds that "it may be doubted whether what he called a reconstruction will ever be regarded as such,"[65] in part because his most systematic work, *The Reconstruction of Religious Thought in Islam,* is so unsystematic and vague in specifics that "it is anything but easy to see what would be the practical outcome of his theories." In spite of these cautious assessments of Iqbal's work, it seems useful in an account of the concept of God in Islam, to turn to his writings as examples of attempts at modernization by one who has had as much influence upon Islam as anyone in this century.

(a) How God May Be Known

According to Iqbal there is a realm of experience beyond pure sense experience, and such an experience is mystical. One may experience the Ultimate Reality as directly as one experiences a tree, but not through the organs of sense. Intuition is an additional means of perception, is objective in its results, and grasps the Divine all at once.[66] Intellectual knowledge is an aid in the

63 *Ibid.,* p. 141.
64 Gibb, *Modern Trends,* p. 81.
65 Alfred Guillaume, *Islam* (Penguin Books Ltd., 1969), p. 160.
66 Iqbal, *Reconstruction,* pp. 2-3.

apprehension of Reality, particularly modern knowledge,[67] but the final vision is gained through Intuition, the way of love.[68] Intuition, or the 'heart' is not "a mysterious special faculty; it is rather a mode of dealing with Reality in which sensation, in the physiological sense of the word, does not play any part."[69] Iqbal lists five characteristics of Intuitional experience: (1) immediacy, (2) unanalysable wholeness (3) an association with a "unique other Self, transcending, encompassing, and momentarily suppressing the private personality of the subject of experience," (4) incommunicable ("more like feeling than thought"), and (5) contains a sense of the unreality of time without completely destroying all links with serial time.[70]

Iqbal never claimed to have had an Intuitional perception of God, and therefore is not himself a true mystic. At best, he may be considered sympathetic to the mystics and greatly influenced by Sufism. He does claim to have had a lesser form of mystical experience, viz. the direct apprehension of his own self.

(b) Knowledge of Self and Knowledge of God

If the self is spiritualized to a high enough degree, it will become immortal, enduring forever as a self and independent of God. Utilizing the dynamic philosophy of Henri Bergson, Iqbal affirms that both the human spiritualized self and the Divine Self may continually work toward an unending perfection. Iqbal conceives of two objective realities of which Intuition may become aware: the first is one's own self, the direct intuition of a potentially unlimited being whose essence is creativity, which is known only during moments of extreme emotional excitement.[71] Matter itself is but "a colony of egos of a low order out of which emerges the ego of a higher order, when their association and

---

67 *Ibid.*, p. 97.
68 Iqbal, *The Secrets of the Self*, pp. 76-77.
69 Iqbal, *Reconstruction*, p. 15.
70 *Ibid.*, pp. 18-23.
71 Enver, *op. cit.*, p. 5.

interaction reach a degree of co-ordination."[72] Taking this emphasis on ego to its extreme position, Iqbal writes that individuality is judged not by distance from the Ultimate Ego, but by closeness to God. The final absorption is not the absorption of self in God: "On the contrary he absorbs God into himself."[73]

The direct experience of God, the Ultimate Ego, was never Iqbal's. He conceives of the Ultimate Ego as being infinite in inner possibility of creative activity "of which the universe...is only a partial expression."[74] Iqbal also reaffirmed the "other important elements in the Quranic conception of God...Creativeness, Knowledge, Omnipotence, and Eternity."[75] The emphasis which Iqbal places on Western scientific knowledge, the Sufi tradition, and the mystical experiences of self and Ultimate Ego clearly mark him as a reformer of Islam in spirit, if not yet in effect. At all events, it is more than apparent that H.A.R. Gibb's comment on Sufism, that "...the mystics plunged down the rapids that ended in the whirlpool of pantheism,"[76] is not readily applicable to the emergent individualism of Iqbal.

Conclusion

Nothing has been said of the principle of the consensus of the community (ijmā). Public opinion over a period of time may reach a consensus concerning some matter falling outside the specific statements of the Quran, or the interpretations and dictates of the tradition as a whole. In such cases, the consensus may rule, and a precedent is set. Gibb speaks of three infallible sources of religious truth, *Vox Dei, Vox Prophetae,* and *Vox populi,* the latter being consensus of the community.[77] He also observes that the stricter theologians ("from the third century of

72 Iqbal, *Reconstruction*, p. 106.
73 Iqbal, *The Secrets of the Self*, p. 2.
74 Iqbal, *Reconstruction*, p. 64.
75 *Ibid.*, pp. 64-65.
76 Gibb, *Modern Trends*, p. 20.
77 *Ibid.*, p. 10.

Islam to the Wahhabis of today") reject the notion of the continuing power of this consensus, limiting it to the first generation of Muslims. At the same time he notes that "the modernists of all ages have relied upon it to provide their eventual justication."[78] For the purposes of this chapter, it is perhaps enough to recognize the possibility of a consensus as being a source of knowledge about God, and, as though to confirm Gibb's thesis that the modernists of all ages have turned to consensus for hoped for eventual support of their own position, to conclude that, in the eyes of one writer, "Iqbal's special contribution to the development of Muslim legal thought in Muslim India and Pakistan has been the re-establishment of the principle he advocated, i.e. the enlargement of the scope and authority of ijmā."[79] Whether modernism will become further enriched so as to provide a systematic and acceptable Islamic re-interpretation, or whether the consensus of orthodoxy will prove too great, if only because it is the fruit of countless generations of Muslims, cannot at this time be known.

A SELECT BIBLIOGRAPHY

Ahmad, Aziz, *Islamic Modernism in India and Pakistan, 1857-1964.* London: Oxford University Press, 1967.

Arberry, Arthur J., *An Introduction to the History of Sufism.* New York: Longmans, Green and Co., 1942.

————, *Revelation and Reason in Islam.* London: George Allen and Unwin, 1957.

————, *Sufism.* London: George Allen and Unwin, 1950.

Bilgrami, H., *Glimpses of Iqbal's Mind and Thought.* Lahore: Prientalla, 1954.

De Boer, T.J., *The History of Philosophy in Islam.* Translated by Edward R. Jones. New York: Dover Publications, Inc., 1967.

78 *Ibid.,* p. 11.
79 Ahmad, *op. cit.,* p. 155.

Burckhardt, Titus, *An Introduction to Sufi Doctrine.* Translated by D.M. Matheson. Lahore: Sh. Muhammad Ashraf, 1959.

Cragg, Kenneth, *The Call of the Minaret.* New York: Oxford University Press, 1956.

Dar, B.A., "Intellect and Intuition," in *Iqbal,* IV (1956), pp. 60-105.

Davis, F. Hadland, *The Persian Mystics: Rumi.* London: John Murray, 1912.

The Encyclopedia of Islam. New Edition. Leiden: E.J. Brill, 1960.

Fyzee, Asaf A.A., *A Modern Approach to Islam.* Bombay: Asia Publishing House, 1963.

Gibb, H.A.R., *Modern Trends in Islam.* Chicago: University of Chicago Press, 1947.

————, *Mohammedanism: An Historical Survey.* 2nd edition. London: Oxford University Press, 1953.

————, *Studies on the Civilization of Islam.* Edited by S.J. Shaw and W.R. Polk. London: Routledge and Kegan Paul, 1962.

Guillaume, Alfred, *Islam.* London: Penquin Books, 1969.

Hakim, Abdul, *The Metaphysics of Rumi.* Lahore: Ripon Printing Press, 1933.

Iqbal, Muhammad, *Poems from Iqbal.* Translated by V.G. Kiernan. London: John Murray, 1955.

————, *The Reconstruction of Religious Thought in Islam.* 2nd edition. London: Oxford University Press, 1934.

————, *The Mysteries of Selflessness.* Translated with an Introduction by Arthur J. Arberry. London: John Murray, 1953.

————, *The Secrets of the Self.* Translated with Notes by Reynolds A. Nicholson. London: MacMillan and Co., 1920.

Irving, T.B., "God's Oneness," *Studies in Islam,* I (1964), pp. 61-70.

Jadaane, F., "Revelation et Inspiration en Islam," *Studia Islamica,* XXVI, pp. 23-47.

MacDonald, Duncan Black, *Development of Muslim Theology, Jurisprudence and Constitutional Theory.* New York: Russell and Russell, 1965.

————, *The Religious Attitude and Life in Islam.* Beruit: Khayats, 1965.

Malik, Hafeez, "Iqbal's Conception of Ego," *The Muslim World,* LX (1970), pp. 160-169.

————, (ed.), *Iqbal: Poet-Philosopher of Pakistan.* New York: Columbia University Press, 1971.

Morgan, Kenneth W. (ed.), *Islam - The Straight Path.* New York: Ronald Press Co., 1958.

Nasr, Seyyed Hossein, *An Introduction to Islamic Cosmological Doctrines.* Cambridge, Mass.: Harvard University Press, 1964.

————, *Three Muslim Sages: Avicenna - Suhrauardi - Ibn Arabi.* Cambridge, Mass.: Harvard University Press, 1964.

Nicholson, R.A., *The Mystics of Islam.* London: G.G. Bell and Sons, 1914.

————, *Rumi, Poet and Mystic.* New York: the MacMillan Co., 1950.

————, *Studies in Islamic Mysticism.* Cambridge, England: Cambridge University Press, 1921.

Rahman, Fazlur, "The Qur'anic Concept of God," *Islamic Studies,* VI (1967), pp. 1-19.

Schuon, Frithjof, *Dimensions of Islam.* Translated by P.N. Townsend. London: George Allen and Unwin, 1970.

————, *The Transcendent Unity of Religions.* Translated by P.N. Townsend. London: Faber and Faber, 1954.

————, *Understanding Islam.* Translated by D.M. Matheson. London: George Allen and Unwin, 1963.

Shehadi, Fadlou, *Ghazali's Unique Unknowable God.* Leiden: E.J. Brill, 1964.

Smith, Margaret, *Readings from the Mystics of Islam.* London: Luzac and Co., 1950.

————, *The Sufi Path of Love.* London: Luzac and Co., 1944.

————, *The Persian Mystics: 'Attar.* London: John Murray, 1932.

Stace, W.T., *Mysticism and Philosophy.* London: MacMillan and Co., 1960.

Tritton, A.S., *Islam: Belief and Practices.* London: Hutchinson University Library, 1966.

————, *Muslim Theology.* London: Luzac and Co., 1947.

Underhill, Evelyn. *Mysticism.* New York: Meridian Books, 1955.

Upper, Claudia Reid, "Al-Ghazali's Thought on the Nature of Man and Union with God," *The Muslim World,* XLII (1952), pp. 23-32.

Vahid, Syed Abdul, *Iqbal: His Art and Thought.* London: John Murray, 1959.

Watt, W. Montgomery, *Islamic Philosophy and Theology.* Islamic Surveys, Vol. I. Edinburgh: Edinburgh University Press, 1962.

Wensinck, A.J., *The Muslim Creed: Its Genesis and Historical Development.* London: Frank Cass and Co., 1932.

Zaehner, R.C., *Hindu and Muslim Mysticism.* New York: Shocken Books, 1969.

Zwemer, Samuel M., *The Muslim Doctrine of God.* New York: American Tract Society, 1905.

China

CHAPTER III

THE CONCEPT OF THE TAO

Aloysius Chang*

In the history of Chinese philosophy, thinkers of the pre-Ch'in era were the most outstanding and influential. It was their thought which laid the solid foundation for later intellectual development in China. During that golden age numerous philosophical schools sprang up and academic centers were established. This historical period is also known as the era of *pai chia cheng ming* or a hundred schools contending in thought and learning. It was an era, then unprecedented and since unrivaled, of open competition and uninhibited discussion among a great number of schools contending for preeminence in ideological content and philosophical depth, in rhetorical presentation or logical argumentation, and in achieving the application of their principles to government and statecraft.

Since the Han Dynasty, Chinese historians have traced these schools as well as their writings and have classified their teachings into *shih chia* or ten principal schools. Aside from Confucianism and Taoism, the schools of the Naturalists, the Dialecticians, the Mohists and the Legalists also had a lasting impact in the years that followed.

Next to Confucianism, the most important and influential stream in Chinese thought has undoubtedly been that of the Taoist school. This school is often referred to as the "Teachings of Huang (the Yellow Emperor) and Lao (Lao Tzu)" or the "Teachings of Lao Tzu and Chuang Tzu." Although it was not a

---

*Professor of Foreign Languages and Literature at Washington State University, Pullman, Washington, U.S.A.

unified and homogenous school of thought, yet no other school of ancient times, especially in the late Chou period, has so strongly and effectively challenged Confucianism and firmly kept its vigor and attractiveness to the Chinese mind. It is quite possible that because of the analogical statements and frequent use of similar terms, many believed that the doctrines of Confucianism and Taoism complement each other, but the fact is that Taoism was in large part a "philosophy of protest."[1]

The Taoist school opposes the growing despotism of the ruling class and the rigidity of the Confucian moralists, and holds out a vision of the transcendental worlds of the spirit. Thus mysticism and poetic contemplations dominated its teaching what is clearly visible throughout the early writings of this school, notably those of Lao Tzu and Chuang Tzu. Taoism also focuses on the individual and his value, fosters the independence of the individual and strongly insists that the sole concern of an individual has to be how he should become eventually intoxicated by the beauties of nature and how he becomes fitted into the great pattern of the nature of the world or of the spirit of the man-made artificial society.

Wing-tsit Chan, the well known author and philosopher of our time, beautifully points out:

> On a higher plane, of course, the philosophy of Lao Tzu had much more to offer. Its vast concept of the oneness of Heaven, Earth and all things, its radically new idea of non-being not as something negative, but as the source of being, its strange synthesis of naive naturalism and profound mysticism, its doctrine of returning to the root, its fascinating emphasis on weakness as the way to a good life, and other equally significant concepts made its *Tao* (Way) unique, so that while practically all ancient Chinese philosophical schools had their

---

1 Edwin O. Reischauer and John K. Fairbank, *East Asia: The Great Tradition* (Boston: Houghton Mifflin Company, 1969), p. 72.

own *tao,* this system alone came to be identified with the name.[2]

It is important to note here and make a clear distinction between *Tao chia* (the Taoist school) and *Tao chiao* (the Taoist religion), as both are known in the West as Taoism. This is something unfortunate and the confusion is still present. It is difficult to determine when the Taoist religion began to utilize the Taoist philosophy as the basis of their teaching. But the fact is that Lao Tzu's philosophy was naturalistic and essentially atheistic, while the Taoist religion turned it into supernatural and polytheistic with a deity for almost anything thinkable.

The word "tao," literally the "road" or "way," is rich in meaning and was used by different philosophical schools and religious institutions. For Confucius and the Confucian scholars, Tao is the highest norm and the central principle that governs human behavior. For the Buddhists, Tao is the Way of enlightenment that leads man to nirvana. For the Chinese Christians, Tao is the Word, as read in the first chapter of St. John:

> In the beginning was the Tao,
> and the Tao was with God,
> and the Tao was God.

Thus, through more than two thousand years, Tao has been the central concept of Chinese thinking and worship.

The word "tao" has a special meaning for the Taoists as they give it a metaphysical as well as an ontological interpretation. Generally speaking, the Taoists seem to have meant something akin to what the Western philosophers call the Absolute, the Supreme, the One and the Ultimate Principle.

Meanwhile, the knowledge of the Tao is not to be attained by reason or study, but by the mystics' way of contemplation and

---

2 Wing-tsit Chan, *et al., The Great Asian Religions* (New York: The MacMillan Company, 1969), pp. 150-151.

inward illumination.[3] True knowledge therefore is of the transcendental kind, the mystical knowledge known only to the adept in trance. In trance, one sees the universe as a Unity, and indeed becomes identified with the One.[4]

There are numerous problems related to this study, such as the historicity of Lao Tzu and the authenticity of *Tao te ching,* which are clearly controversial in nature and require detailed and comparative examination. Our discussion will be centered on the Taoist concept of the Tao of the Taoist school. To present a synthetical view of the Tao, based on *Tao te ching* and *Chuang Tzu* is our main purpose.

1. The Tao of Lao Tzu

(a) Definition

The word "tao" is the most important term and central concept in the teachings of Lao Tzu. But the author of the *Lao Tzu* cautiously warns that a clear-cut definition of the Tao is something beyond one's comprehension. As we read from the *Lao Tzu* or *Tao te ching:*

> The Tao (Way) that can be told of
>   is not the eternal Tao;
> The name that can be named is not
>   the eternal name.
> The Nameless is the origin of
>   Heaven and Earth;
> The Name is the mother of
>   all things.[5]

---

3 Kenneth S. Latourette, *The Chinese: Their History and Culture* (New York: The MacMillan Company, 1968), p. 57.

4 W.A.C.H. Dobson, "The Religions of China" in *A Reader's Guide to the Great Religions,* ed. by Charles J. Adams (New York: The Free Press, 1966), p. 39.

5 *Tao te ching,* C. 1.

The essence of the Tao is thus extremely mysterious and rather difficult for the ordinary man to grasp; common terminology is by no means adequate to express the real nature of the Tao. "Tao" is the only possible word which can be used to describe the Tao somewhat. Besides the name "Tao," the name "Great" is also used to represent the unparalleled nature of the Tao.

> I do not know its name;
>   I call it Tao.
> If forced to give it a name,
>   I shall call it Great.
> Now being great means
>   functioning everywhere.
> Functioning everywhere means
>   far-reaching.
> Being far-reaching means
>   returning to the original point.
> Therefore Tao is great.[6]

The Tao of Lao Tzu and of the *Tao te ching* has a metaphysical and ontological meaning. It is the all-embracing first principle and the origin of the entire universe. Everything that exists has its own *principium vitale,* but the all-embracing first principle from which all the other things are produced is the Tao. The following is the most important passage of the *Tao te ching:*

> There was something undifferentiated
>   and yet complete,
> Which existed before heaven
>   and earth.
> Soundless and formless, it depends on
>   nothing and does not change.

6 *Ibid.,* C. 25.

> It operates everywhere and
>   is free from danger.
> It may be considered the mother
>   of the universe.[7]

The same profound idea is discussed in a different chapter:

> The Great Tao flows everywhere.
> It may go left or right.
> All things depend on it for life,
>   it does not turn away from them.
> It accomplishes its task, but does not
>   claim credit for it.
> It clothes and feeds all things but
>   does not claim to be master over them.
> Always without desires, it may be
>   called The Small.
> All things come to it and it does not
>   master them; it may be called The Great.
> Therefore (the sage) never strives
>   himself for the great, and thereby
>   the great is achieved.[8]

The behavior of the Tao is not performed reflexively or intentionally but rather instinctively as well as spontaneously:

> Man models himself after Earth.
> Earth models itself after Heaven.
> Heaven models itself after Tao.
> And Tao models itself after Nature.[9]

---

7 *Ibid.*
8 *Ibid.*, C. 34.
9 *Ibid.*, C. 25.

(b) Signification

As the text quoted above deals with the Tao as such, a brief signification is in order.

    1. "There was something" - This is the fundamental question of essence and existence. Tao is a being, as the Western ontologists call "ens." It is either an actuality or merely potentiality, and clearly its opposite is nonbeing.

    2. "Undifferentiated and yet complete" - It has the meaning that the Tao in itself is undifferentiated or formless, yet in relation with all other things it is complete and categorical. Using the scholastic terminology, this passage says that "ens est aliquid simplicissimum, in quo omnia conveniunt."

    3. "Which existed before heaven and earth" - The eternity of the Tao and its existence above time and space is expressively indicated. We should note the point of departure in the *Tao te ching*:

> Reversion is the action of Tao.
> Weakness is the function of Tao.
> All things in the world come from being.
> And being comes from nonbeing.[10]

The following passage will complete and present an integral view of the preceding statement:

> Tao produced the One.
> The One produced the two.
> The two produced the three.
> And the three produced the ten thousand things.[11]

It is clear that the being is exactly the same as the One that Tao produced. This being is not from the nonbeing which we

---

10 *Ibid.*, C. 40.
11 *Ibid.*, C. 42.

discussed above. It is our common knowledge that "ex nihilo nihil est." And Lao Tzu added:

> Therefore let there always be nonbeing
>   so we may see their subtlety.
> And let there always be being
>   so we may see their outcome.[12]

4. "Soundless and formless" - This passage presents another look at the Tao and indicates that the Tao is also nonbeing. Even if you look at it, you do not see; you listen to it and you do hear.

> The two (being and nonbeing) are the same,
> But after they are produced, they have different names.
> They both may be called deep and profound.
> Deeper and more profound,
> The door of all subtleties.[13]

5. "It depends on nothing and does not change" - Tao is subsistent and eternal, it is not dependent upon another being, it has no beginning nor end; it is what Lao Tzu calls the "eternal Tao." We may easily express the same notion in scholastic terminology: "Est ens subsistens, independens et immutabilis."

6. "It operates everywhere and is free from danger" - The Tao, being subsistent and unchangeable, eternal and independent, reaches and fills the entire universe. It is consequently immense, indestructible and imperishable.

7. "It may be considered the mother of the universe" - This is but a simple, logical and natural conclusion. It states that the Tao, being formless, eternal, subsistent, independent, immense and indestructible, is the real and sole lord and master of the universe. Like a mother, Tao gives birth, nourishes and protects the universe. Lao Tzu continues:

12 *Ibid.*, C. 1.
13 *Ibid.*

From the time of old until now,
    its name (manifestations) ever remains,
By which we may see the beginning
    of all things.
How do I know that the beginnings
    of all things are so?
Through this (Tao).[14]

An additional remark on the significance of nonbeing given by Fung Yu-lan will clarify this discussion, as perhaps some will judge the classical text contradictory. Fung Yu-lan writes:

I have said that Tao is nonbeing.
Nevertheless, this only means "nonbeing"
as opposed to "Being" of material objects,
and so it is not a mere zero or nothingness.
For how could Tao be nothingness when at
the same time it is the first all-embracing
principle whereby all things are produced?[15]

Lao Tzu concludes:

The all-embracing quality of the
    great virtue (te) follows alone
    from the Tao.
The thing that is called Tao is
    eluding and vague.
    Vague and eluding, there is in it
        the form.
    Eluding and vague, in it are things.
Deep and obscure, in it is the essence.

---

[14] *Ibid.,* C. 21.
[15] Fung Yu-lan, *A History of Chinese Philosophy,* tr. by Derk Bodde (Princeton: Princeton University Press, 1967), Vol. I, p. 179.

The essence is very real; in it
are evidences.[16]

2. The Tao of Chuang Tzu

(a) Quotations

Chuang Tzu, the second great figure of the Taoist school, shares with Lao Tzu and the *Tao te ching* the central concept of the Tao as the ultimate and supreme principle governing the universe. It is the origin of all things, master of life and the unity in which all the contradictions are ultimately resolved.

The principal texts are:

> Tung Kuo Tzu asked Chuang Tzu:
> "Where is the so called Tao?"
> Chuang Tzu said:
> "There is nowhere where it is not."
> Tung Kuo Tzu said:
> "Specify an instance of it."
> Chuang Tzu said:
> "It is in the ant."
> "How can it be so low?"
> "It is in the panic grass."
> "How can it be still lower?"
> "It is in the earthenware tile."
> "How can it be even lower?"
> "It is in excrement."
> To this Tung Kuo Tzu made no reply.
> Chuang Tzu said:
> "Your question does not touch
> the fundamentals of Tao. When Huo,
> inspector of markets, asked the

16 *Tao te ching,* C. 21.

managing director about the fatness
of pigs, the test was always made
in parts least likely to be fat.
You should not specify any
particular thing.
There is not a single thing without
Tao. There are three terms:
Completeness, All-embracingness and
the Whole. These three names differ
but denote the same reality; all
refer to the one thing.[17]

Tao is the "mother of all things." When there are things, there
must be Tao. What about Tao in itself?

Tao has reality and evidence, but no action and form. It
may be transmitted, but cannot be received. It may be
attained to, but can not be seen. It exists by and through
itself. It existed prior to Heaven and Earth, and indeed
for all eternity. It causes the gods to be divine, and the
world to be produced. It is above the zenith, but it is not
high. It is beneath the nadir, but it is not low. It is prior
to Heaven and Earth, but it is not ancient. It is older than
the most ancient, but it is not old.[18]

Tao is thus eternal, immense and subsistent. It constantly gives
birth to the universe.

Human skill is bound up with human affairs; human
affairs are bound up with what is right; what is right is
bound up with the Te; Te is bound up with Tao; and Tao
is bound up with Nature.[19]

17 *Chuang Tzu*, C. 22.
18 *Ibid.*, C. 6.
19 *Ibid.*, C. 12.

The conversation between Kuang-ch'eng Tzu and Yellow Emperor also illustrates the nature of Tao.

> Kuang-ch'eng Tzu said: "come and I shall tell you. The Tao is limitless and yet all men think it has an end. It is immeasurable and yet all men think it is finite.[20]

Tao is manifested in all things, thus these are born and grow, consequently all are transformed of themselves. But Tao, the origin of all these things, always remains and operates.

(b) Interpretation

The writings of Chuang Tzu clearly indicate and explain the concept of Tao, and set the solid foundation for the Taoist metaphysics. Let us briefly examine some of the basic aspects of Tao.

Tao is the all-embracing first principle:
> There is not a single thing without Tao. There are three terms: Completeness, All-embracingness and the Whole.[21]

Tao is the all-embracing first principle, through which all the other things come into being. The action of Tao is spontaneous:

> Tao has reality and evidence.[22]
> Tao is bound up with Nature.[23]

Tao is formless: Tao is formless, impalpable and incommensurable, or using the words of Lao Tzu it is "vague and eluding, deep and obscure."

---

20 *Ibid.*, C. 11.
21 *Ibid.*, C. 22.
22 *Ibid.*, C. 6.
23 *Ibid.*, C. 12.

Tao has reality and evidence, but no action and form.
It may be transmitted, but cannot be received.
It may be attained to, but cannot be seen.[24]

Tao is subsistent: Tao exists prior to Heaven and Earth. It
exists by and through itself. It is eternal, as it has no beginning
nor end. It is prior to Heaven and Earth, but it is ancient. Perhaps
we can quote God's word in the Old Testament: "Sum qui sum."

Tao controls gods and governs the world:

It causes the gods to be divine,
and the world to be produced.[25]

Chuang Tzu said in a different passage:
It is the Tao that overspreads and sustains all things.
How great it is in its overflowing influence.[26]

Tao is immense: Tao is immense, the greatest and the highest.

It is above the zenith,
    but it is not high.
It is beneath the nadir,
    but it is not low.[27]

Tao is eternal: Tao existed without beginning nor end; without
time nor space. It is eternal and eternally indestructible. As "It
existed prior to Heaven and Earth, and indeed for all eternity."[28]

Tao is ubiquitous: Tao brings the principles of all things into a
single agreement. It is thus both one thing and another, it is not in
one thing only. When Tung Kuo Tzu asked Chuang Tzu about

24 *Ibid.,* C. 6.
25 *Ibid.,* C. 6.
26 *Ibid.,* C. 12.
27 *Ibid.,* C. 6.
28 *Ibid.*

Tao and where Tao is, Chuang Tzu replied: "There is nowhere where it is not."[29]

Tao is the goal of great men: Each one has his goal which makes his living meaningful. For those born to do greater things, Chuang Tzu left the following:

> He who knows the part which the Heavenly in him plays, and also knows that which the human in him ought to play, has reached the perfection of knowledge . . . Being such they should ascend the loftiest heights without fear; they could pass through water without being made wet by it; they could go into fire without being burnt; so it was that by their knowledge they ascended to and reached Tao.[30]

Tao is God: The word "God" here means spirit. Since Tao controls the spirit and causes them to be divine, the very nature of the Tao should be of the similar nature. It is not only God, but the Supreme One.

Conclusion

The concept of the Tao has a great and lasting influence in the cultural and philosophical life of the Chinese. The philosophers of the Taoist school made many contributions and gave us excellent explanations. Scholars of later centuries have tried to search out and comment upon this fundamental idea and make the classical texts easy to understand even for common people.

It is my sincere hope that future Christian scholars will also become familiar with these texts and use them to explain the existence and the attributes of the Triune God.

29 *Ibid.*, C. 22.
30 *Ibid.*, C. 6.

A SELECT BIBLIOGRAPHY

Adams, Charles J. (ed.), *A Reader's Guide to the Great Religions.* New York: The Free Press, 1966.

Bahm, Archie J., *Tao Teh King by Lao Tzu Interpreted as Nature and Intelligence.* New York: Frederick Ungar, 1958.

Baumann, Carol, "Reflections Prompted by Laotze: A Psychological Approach" in *Bulletin de la société suisse des amis de l'Extrême-Orient,* 1946.

Blakney, R.B., (tr.), *The Way of Life: Lao Tzu.* New York: Mentor Books, 1955.

Bodde, Derk, "Myths of Ancient China" in *Mythologies of the Ancient World,* edited by Samuel N. Kramer. New York: Anchor Books, 1961.

Carus, Paul (tr.), *The Canon of Reason and Virtue.* Chicago: Open Court, 1945.

Chan, Wing-tsit, *A Source Book in Chinese Philosophy.* Princeton: Princeton University Press, 1963.

————, *Chinese Philosophy, 1949-1963: An Annotated Bibliography of Mainland China Publications.* Honolulu: East-West Center Press, 1967.

————, *Religious Trends in Modern China.* New York: Columbia University Press, 1953.

Chan, Wing-tsit, *et al., The Great Asian Religions.* New York: MacMillan, 1969.

————, (tr.), *The Way of Lao Tzu.* Indianapolis: Bobbs-Merrill Company, 1963.

Chang Chun-fang, *Yun Chi Ch'i Ch'ien* (Taoism). Taipei: The Commercial Press, Ltd., 1967.

Chang Chung-yuan, *Creativity and Taoism.* New York: Julian Press, 1963.

————, "The Concept of Tao in Chinese Culture" in *The Review of Religion,* March, 1953.

Chang, Constant C.C., "Wisdom of Taoism" in *Bulletin of National Taiwan Normal University,* Vol. XV, (June, 1970), pp. 241-386.

Ch'u Ta-kao (tr.), *Tao Te Ching.* London: Allen and Unwin, 1959.

Creel, H.G., *The Birth of China.* New York: John Day, 1937.

————, "What is Taoism" in *Journal of the American Oriental Society,* Vol. LXXVI (1956), pp. 139-152.

De Bary, Wm. Theodore, *et al.* (comp.), *Sources of Chinese Tradition.* New York: Columbia University Press, 1969.

Duyvendak, J.J.L. (tr.), *Tao Te Ching: The Book of the Way and Its Virtue.* London: John Murray, 1954.

Erkes, Eduard (tr.), *Ho-Shang-Kung's Commentary on Lao Tse.* Ascona: Artibus Asiae, 1958.

Eichhorn, Werner, "Taoism" in *Concise Encyclopedia of Living Faiths,* edited by R.C. Zaehner. New York: Hawthorne Books, 1959.

Ferguson, J.C., "Chinese Mythology" in *The Mythology of All Races,* edited by J.A. MacCulloch. Boston: Marshall Jones Company, 1930.

Fu Ch'in-chia, *Chung Kuo Tao Chiao Shih* (History of Chinese Taoism). Taipei: The Commercial Press, Ltd., 1967.

Fung Yu-lan, *A History of Chinese Philosophy,* tr. by Derk Bodde, 2 vols. Princeton: Princeton University Press, 1952.

———, (tr.), *Chuang Tzu.* Shanghai: The Commercial Press, Ltd., 1933.

Giles, Herbert A. (tr.), *Chuang Tzu: Mystic, Moralist and Social Reformer.* London: B. Quaritch, 1926.

Giles, Lionel (ed.), *Musings of a Chinese Mystic.* London: John Murray, 1906.

———, (tr.), *Taoist Teachings from the Book of Lieh Tzu.* London: John Murray, 1947.

———, (tr.), *The Sayings of Lao Tzu.* London: John Murray, 1905.

Granet, Marcel, *La Pensée Chinois.* Paris: Renaissance du livre, 1934.

Hail, William J., "Taoism" in *Living Schools of Religion* edited by V. Ferm. Ames, Iowa: New Students Outline Series, 1958.

Herbert, Edward (pseud. of E.H. Kenney), *A Taoist Notebook.* London: John Murray, 1955.

Hughes, Ernest R., *Chinese Philosophy in Classical Times.* New York: Everyman's Library, 1941.

———, and K. Hughes, *Religion in China.* New York: Hutchinson's University Library, 1950.

Kaltenmark, Max, *Lao Tzu and Taoism,* tr. by Roger Greaves. Stanford: Stanford University Press, 1969.

Kitagawa, Joseph M., *Modern Trends in World's Religions.* Chicago: Open Court, 1959.

Legge, James (tr.), *The Sacred Books of China: The Texts of Taoism.* New York: Dover Publications, 1962.

Li Hsien-chang (ed.), "Taoism" in *Sinological Researches,* Vol. V (1968), pp. 201-397.

Lin Tung-chi, "The Chinese Mind: Its Taoist Substratum" in *Journal of the History of Ideas,* Vol. VIII (1947), pp. 259-272.

Lin Yutang, *The Wisdom of China and India.* New York: Modern Library, 1942.

———, (tr.), *The Wisdom of Laotse.* New York: Modern Library, 1948.

Maspero, Henri, "Les procédés de nourir le principe vital dans la religion taoiste ancienne" in *Journal Asiatique,* Vol. 229 (1937).

————, "Le Taoisme" in *Les Religions Chinoises.* Paris: Musée Guimet, 1950.

— ————, "Le Taoisme" in *Melanges posthumes sur les religions et l'histoire de la Chine.* Paris: Civilisations du Sud, 1950.

Moore, Charles A., *The Chinese Mind.* Honolulu: East-West Center Press, 1967.

Morgan, Evan (tr.), *Tao the Great Luminant.* London: Kegan Paul, 1935.

Mote, Frederick W., "Confucian Eremitism in the Yuan Period" in *The Confucian Persuasion,* ed. by A.F. Wright. Stanford: Stanford University Press, 1960.

Nan Huai-chin, *Ch'an Yu Tao Kai Lun.* (Introduction to Tao and Zen). Taipei: Chen Shan Mei Press, 1968.

Tao Tsang. Taipei: Yiwen Publishing Company, 1963.

Waley, Arthur (tr.), *The Way and Its Power: A Study of the Tao Te Ching and Its Place in Chinese Thought.* New York: MacMillan, 1934.

————, *Three Ways of Thought in Ancient China.* New York: MacMillan, 1939.

Wang Gung-hsing, *The Chinese Mind.* New York: John Day, 1946.

Watson, Benton (tr.), *The Complete Works of Chuang Tzu.* New York: Columbia University Press, 1968.

Weber, Max, *The Religion of China,* tr. by Hans H. Gerth. New York: The Free Press, 1968.

Wei, Francis C.M., *The Spirit of Chinese Culture.* New York: Scribner's, 1947.

Wei, Shou, *Treatise on Buddhism and Taoism,* tr. by Leon Hurvitz. Kyoto: Kyoto University Press, 1956.

Welch, Holmes, *The Parting of the Way: Lao Tzu and The Taoist Movement.* Boston: Beacon Press, 1957.

Wieger, Leon, *A History of the Religious Beliefs and Philosophical Opinions in China from the Beginning to the Present Time,* tr. by Edward C. Werner. New York: Paragon Book Reprint Corp., 1969.

Wu, John C.H. (tr.), *Tao Te Ching.* Shanghai: Tien Hsia, 1940.

Yang, C.K., *Religion in Chinese Society.* Berkeley: University of California Press, 1961.

Yang, Y.C., *China's Religious Heritage.* Nashville: Abingdon-Cokesbury, 1943.

Yen Ling-feng, *Tao Chia Sse Tzu Hsin Pien* (Four Taoist Philosophers). Taipei: The Commercial Press, Ltd., 1968.

CHAPTER IV

THE CONCEPT OF GOD IN CONFUCIAN THOUGHT
Paul K.T. Sih* and Te-Sheng Meng**

Confucius' family name was K'ung, his private name Ch'iu, and his courtesy name Chung-ni (551-479 B.C.). He was honored as the "Great Master K'ung" or K'ung Fu-tzu, which the Jesuits westernized as Confucius. A self-educated man, he became a magistrate at fifty and minister of justice perhaps in the same year. He traveled for almost thirteen years trying to influence the rulers of various states to improve conditions but he did not succeed. This unsuccessful scholar-statesman turned to teaching and, according to tradition, had three thousand pupils during this phase of his career. It was the most successful period of his life.

Concerning his thought, there has been a grave misunderstanding in the West that Confucius was interested only in man and not in religion, because he "seldom talked about profit, destiny, and humanity."[1] He "never discussed strange phenomena, physical exploits, disorder, or shen (spiritual beings)."[2] He had kept silent on the way of T'ien (Principle of the Universe):

Tzu Kung said, "We can hear our Master's (views) on culture

*Professor of History and Director of the Center for Asian Studies at St. John's University, New York, U.S.A.

**Assistant at the Center for Asian Studies at St. John's University, New York, U.S.A.

1 James Legge (translator), *Four Books: Confucian Analects* (Hong Kong: The International Publication Society, n.d.), 9:1.
2 *Ibid.*, 7:20.

and its manifestation, but we cannot hear his views on human nature and the way of T'ien."[3]

He also had turned aside questions on serving spiritual beings and death:

> Tzu-lu asked about serving the spiritual beings. Confucius said, "If we are not yet able to serve man, how can we serve spiritual beings?" "I venture to ask about death." Confucius said, "If we do not yet know about life, how can we know about death?"[4]

Concerning spiritual beings the following words are ascribed to him:

> Fan Ch'ih asked about wisdom. Confucius said, "Devote yourself earnestly to the duties due to men, and respect spiritual beings but keep them at a distance. This may be called wisdom."[5]

Many such seemingly agnostic statements by Confucius have been repeatedly employed by Western as well as Chinese scholars to establish the agnostic nature of Confucius' thought and to divest it of any supernatural concepts.

In a study made by Professor Creel forty years ago to determine whether or not Confucius was an agnostic, he pointed out that none of the pre-Sung Chinese commentaries on the above-quoted and similar passages of the Analects considered Confucius to be agnostic and that, among the Sung and later Chinese commentaries, only four passages even suggested it. The agnostic impression of Confucius, according to Professor Creel, was mainly the result of the trend towards rationalism within the Confucian school, which reinterpreted Confucius' T'ien as "an

3 *Ibid.*, 5:12.
4 *Ibid.*, 11:11.
5 *Ibid.*, 6:20.

immanent . . . impersonal directive principle of the universe."[6] This "rationalization" of Confucius is particularly apparent in the case of modern Chinese scholars who have been heavily influenced by Western rationalism and the general social trend towards secularization in a period of revolution.

Whatever the interpretation of those statements by Confucius, it should be noted that, while they grant priority to knowledge about man in this world, they do not attempt to disprove the existence of supernatural forces. Instead, Confucius carefully kept the supernatural in the background but alive in his admonition to "respect the spiritual beings," in his emphasis on sacrificial ceremonies, and in his attitude towards T'ien and destiny.

Supernatural conceptions loomed large in people's minds during Confucius' time, in spite of some tendency towards secularization. Confucius himself could hardly have escaped entirely this concern for the supernatural, nor could he have ignored the importance of human affairs in his time.

In the *Analects*, the terms Shang-ti and Ti are not used, but the term T'ien occurs twenty times. A study of these instances shows that T'ien is the term used by Confucius in the following denotations.[7]

1. An Abstract Metaphysical Principle

An abstract metaphysical principle, not expressible in ordinary concrete terms:

Confucius said, "Great indeed was Yao as a sovereign! How majestic was he! T'ien alone is great, and Yao alone followed

6 H.G. Creel, "Was Confucius Agnostic?" *T'oung pao*, XXIX (1932), pp. 55-99, as cited in C.K. Yang's "The Functional Relationship between Confucian Thought and Chinese Religion," *Chinese Thought and Institutions*, edited by John K. Fairbank (Chicago: The University of Chicago Press, 1957), p. 271.

7 Vincent Yu-chung Shih, "A Study of the Concepts of Ti, T'ien, and Tao in Ancient Chinese Philosophy in the Light of Western Religious and Philosophical Thought" (unpublished Ph.D. dissertation, University of Southern California, 1939), pp. 69-78.

T'ien's way. How vast and immense! The people could not name it." *(Analects,* 8:19.)

It carries with it the idea of inexpressibility. Of course, in the passage it is Yao who is the subject described; but he was merely following the law of T'ien. Now, if the way of T'ien is inexpressible, we no longer wonder why Confucius' disciples did not have a chance to hear it.

2. A Moral Principle

Confucius said, "At fifteen my mind was set on learning. At thirty my character had been formed. At forty I had no more perplexities. At fifty I knew the decree of T'ien. At sixty I was at ease with whatever I heard. At seventy I could follow my heart's desire wtihout transgressing moral principles."[8]

What Confucius meant by the decree of T'ien seems to be the moral principle of life in religious terms, equivalent to "the will of God." The word decree in Chinese is ming 命 , which has the connotation of destiny.

However, it is not a kind of fatalism. We receive from T'ien our life with all it may become. This is the decree of T'ien. But it is our effort that is needed to realize its capabilities and possibilities. Therefore, in knowing the decree of T'ien we know in fact the aim of life. This knowledge gives one the principle or ideal of life from which one will not deviate for all the world. This knowledge also outlines the field of activity for us. We know what we have to accept with an attitude of acquiescence and fortitude that we can bring to a better and fuller state. This philosophy gives one, in the practical realm, a sense of poise and tranquility, without the effect of inactivity which so often accompanies determinism. It is "heroic" but not "fatalistic." All

8 *Ibid.,* 2:4.

this is based on a concept of T'ien as a moral principle, that bestows upon us certain conditions over which we have no control, and allows us to remake them in our effort to work out our own destiny. There are many passages containing the term ming or destiny, which refers to what is beyond our control in our life. The following are some of them:

Po-niu was ill. Confucius went to see him. He took hold of his hand through the window[9] and said, "It is killing him. It is the ming of T'ien. Alas! That such a man should have such a sickness. That such a man should have such a sickness."[10]

Ssu ma Niu,[11] worrying, said, "All people have brothers but I have none."[12] Tzu-hsia said, "I have heard (from Confucius) this saying: 'Life and death are the decree of T'ien; wealth and honor depend on T'ien. If a superior man is reverential (or serious) without fail, and is respectful in dealing with others and follows the rules of propriety, then all within the four seas are brothers.' What does the superior man have to worry about having no brothers?"[13]

In the second quotation, it was expressed very well just what is within the reach of human power and what is not. A superior man should develop what is within his power to its full, and should not be bothered with that over which he has no control. This is why Confucius said: "He who does not know ming (destiny) falls short of a superior man."[14] There is another passage where, though the term ming does not occur, the idea of destiny is unmistakable:

9 Po-niu probably had leprosy and therefore Confucius did not enter the house.
10 *Analects,* 6:8.
11 Confucius' pupil, whose family name was Hsiung.
12 Meaning that his brother Huan T'ui was not worthy to be a brother. (See *Analects,* 7:22.)
13 *Analects,* 12:5.
14 *Ibid.,* 20:3.

Confucius said, "If riches are to be sought, though I should become a groom with whip in hand to get them, I would do it. If they are not to be sought, I would rather follow what I love."[15]

When he said, "Alas! No one knows me!" Tzu-kung asked, "Why is there no one that knows you?" The Master said,

"I do not complain against T'ien. I do not blame men. I study things on the lower level but my understanding penetrates the higher level.[16] It is T'ien that knows me."[17]

In other words, we should not be concerned with circumstances that are brought about without our having anything to do with them. We should be concerned only with what is within our reach; and this is the development of ourselves to our best possibilities. All this sounds ethical rather than metaphysical. But it is an ethic built upon a metaphysical foundation which Confucius did not put into explicit statements.

3. Personalistic Concept

The following quotations admit of more than one interpretation, but the dominant note is personalistic.

(a) Wang-sun Chia[18] asked, "What is meant by the common saying, 'It is better to be on good terms with the God of the Kitchen than with the spirits of the shrine (ancestor) at the

---

15 *Ibid.*, 7:11.

16 The "higher level" refers to matters of T'ien such as T'ien's decree and the principle of T'ien, and the "lower level" refers to mundane matters.

17 *Analects*, 3:13.

18 Great officer in the state of Wei.

southwest corner of the house'?" Confucius said, "It is not true. He who commits a sin against T'ien has no god to pray to."[19]

(b) The border-warden at I requested to be introduced to the Master, saying, "When men of superior virtue have come to this, I have never been denied the privilege of seeing them." The followers introduced him, and when he came out from the interview, he said, "My friends, why are you distressed by your Master's loss of office? The empire has long been without the principles of truth and right; T'ien is going to use your Master as a bell with its wooden tongue."[20] and [21]

(c) The Master said, "T'ien produced the virtue that is in me. What can Huan[22] do to me?"[23]

(d) A high official asked Tzu-kung, "Is the Master a sage? How versatile is he?" Tzu-kung said, "Certainly T'ien has endowed him without limit the virtue of a great sage, and also made him versatile."[24]

(e) Confucius was very ill. Tzu-lu[25] told his pupils to be ministers to him (as if Confucius was an official). During a remission of his illness, he said, "Long has the conduct of Yu

19 *Analects*, 3:13.

20 *Ibid.*, 3:24.

21 The bell with a wooden tongue was used in ancient China to call the attention of the people to the enactment of new decree in civil matters. Hence the implication that T'ien, through the Master, would give new decree to the world, which commentators took to mean the moral laws of which Confucius has been thought of as the promulgator.

22 Huan T'ui was a military officer in the state of Sung who attempted to kill Confucius by felling a tree. Confucius was then 59 years of age.

23 *Analects*, 7:22.

24 *Analects*, 9:6.

25 Name of Confucius' pupil, whose family name was Chung and private name Yu (542-480). He was only nine years younger than Confucius and was noted for courage.

been deceitful. By pretending to have ministers when I don't
have any, whom do I cheat? Should I cheat T'ien?"[26]

(f) When Confucius was in personal danger in K'uang,[27] he
said, "Since the death of King Wen,[28] is not the course of
culture (wen) in my keeping? If it had been the will of T'ien
to destroy this culture, it would not have been given to a
mortal (like me). But if it is the will of T'ien that this culture
should not perish, what can the people of K'uang do to
me?"[29]

(g) When Yin Yüan died, Confucius said, "Alas, T'ien is destroying me! T'ien is destroying me!"[30]

These passages admit of different interpretations, but the personalistic element in them is the dominant note. A closer study
will reveal that the idea of destiny is also present in some of
them.

There is no doubt some allegorical meaning lies behind passage
(a). Whatever that is, the concept of T'ien as a spiritual being or
person to whom prayer is offered and against whom one may sin
is plainly given.

The personalistic concept in passage (b) is no less clear. T'ien
is conceived here as a ruler who uses man to declare his decrees.

In passage (c), T'ien is responsible for the virtue in man, which
idea already appears in the "Documents of Chou" in the *Book of
History*, where it is said that T'ien decrees three things: intelligence, happiness, misery, and the length of life. The same idea is
expressed in passage (d).

---

26 *Analects,* 9:11.
27 The people of K'uang, mistaking Confucius for Yang Hu, their enemy whom
Confucius resembled in appearance, surrounded him. This happened when Confucius
was 56.
28 Founder of the Chou dynasty (r. 1171-1122).
29 *Analects,* 9:5.
30 *Ibid.,* 11:8.

In passage (e), T'ien can be conceived either as a person, or as something which is impossible of being deceived. Passage (f) depicts T'ien as the governor of a moral order. This also finds expression in passages (c) and (d).

In passage (g) and in the *Analects,* 14:37 as previously quoted, T'ien may either be conceived as a person or as a sort of vague power. As a person, it destroys and is able to know. But these expressions may be like the common English sayings "God knows." If so, it is an emotional response to a situation over which we have no control. There is another possible interpretation, however. We may say that deep in the consciousness of the one who makes the utterance there is a tendency to appeal to the supernatural; and this native tendency is the evidence that the belief in a personal God is in the very nature of man.

With the exception of (b), which remark was made by the border-warden at I, and (d) which was the opinion of Tzu-kung, the rest represent Confucius' idea of T'ien. It may be interpreted as a spiritual being possessing personality, as the ruler of a moral order, or as a metaphorical expression used to indicate emotional tension.

4. The Naturalistic T'ien

In Book 17 of the *Analects* there is a passage in which the term T'ien appears to represent both the natural course of events and a metaphysical principle. The passage reads:

Confucius said, "I do not wish to say anything." Tzu-kung said, "If you do not say anything, what can we little disciples ever learn to pass on to others?" Confucius said, "Does T'ien (Heaven) say anything? The four seasons run their course and all things are produced. Does T'ien say anything?"[31]

---

31 *Ibid.,* 17:19.

Of course, we do not without intention say either a table or a stone speaks. But under certain circumstances we may with perfect legitimacy describe things which are incapable of speech as not speaking. We say "dumb animal" in contrast to man who is not dumb. Do we, in attributing dumbness to lower animals, commit ourselves to the belief that animals are capable of speech? If it is meaningless to speak of T'ien as "not speaking" without attributing to it the faculty of speech and hence personality, then all metaphorical allusions and allegorical statements will either have to be taken literally or relegated to the realm of meaninglessness. It seems sound to say that this passage would suggest a kind of naturalistic concept.

In short, for Confucius, T'ien was an abstract principle, a moral principle, a personal and spiritual being, a governor of a moral order, and on one occasion, the spontaneous principle of nature.

Having examined the meaning of the term T'ien as it occurred in the *Analects,* let us further discuss it as the basis of Confucius' philosophy.

(a) Heavenly Origin of Human Nature

Confucius seems to have entertained the idea that human nature is heavenly in its origin. And, indeed, it would seem that his concept of human nature can be explained only on this hypothesis. For, we may ask, how is it possible to maintain that one can understand others on the analogy of one's own experience? It can be maintained by postulating that there is a common source from which human nature springs and on account of which all manifestations of human nature will act according to certain general patterns. For since the general pattern or plan is the same for all individuals who are said to be human, it is no longer a mystery that one can appreciate and understand the experience of others under certain circumstances familiar to him. We have reason to believe that if Confucius were to give a name to this common source he would have named it T'ien, since it is T'ien to which he appealed in times of need for consolation, and it is T'ien which he conceived to have produced the virtue that was in him.

(b) T'ien, a Transcendent Moral Order

Confucius' T'ien can be said to be a moral order in some transcendent or Platonic sense, which is the origin of the moral order that we find in this world of concrete facts. This fundamental moral order also underlies Confucius' doctrine of rectification of names. For him, a name not only designates something real, it also signifies a certain attribute which is essential to the thing it designates. In other words, besides its logical signification, it also has an ethical significance. This significance or attribute is the virtue of the thing.

A virtue, when considered in relation to others, expresses the proper relationship among people. It defines for each member of society his status in it, and the conduct proper to him. Thus, the system of names Confucius had in mind represents an ideal society, in which every member holds his proper status and acts as he should act, as indicated by names.

(c) Confucius' Concept of Chun tzu

From Confucius' life and sayings, we find that he had a kind of moral fervor and earnestness which amounts to religious enthusiasm. In few other men do we find the sense of duty so strong as in Confucius. He knew very well that in his age his Way (Tao, Principle) could hardly prevail; but he kept right on wandering through all the states, hoping that some prince would use him for the good of the people. And the apparent breach in moral causality is reconciled by a philosophy of self-cultivation and satisfaction in its attainment. His idea of chün tzu (君子) meaning a superior man or the princely, which is Confucius' concept of a perfect personality, is an interesting topic in this connection. A few citations will serve to give us some idea as to how

Confucius proposed to deal with thwarted aspirations and defeated ideals in the realm of practical life.

> Confucius said, "The superior man is distressed by his want of ability. He is not distressed by men's not knowing him."[32]

> Confucius said, "The superior man seeks what is in himself. The mean man seeks what is in others."[33]

If we know that we have developed our nature to its fullest capability, we are not responsible if we are not advantageously employed. The attainment of our inner self is an endless source of happiness. Our happiness is permanent when it depends on ourselves; but it is as unsteady as the ship before the wind on an open sea if it is linked to external causes. One has to try as hard as one can to be of service to others; but if the external circumstances do not permit, one may rest satisfied in one's own attainment. This is why we have described Confucius' philosophy as "heroic" but not "fatalistic."

A SELECT BIBLIOGRAPHY

1. Sources in English

Barzun, Jacques and Graff, Henry F., *The Modern Researcher*. Revised edition. New York: Harcourt, Brace & World, 1970.

Bradley, David G., *A Guide to the World's Religions*. Englewood Cliffs, New Jersey: Prentice-Hall, 1963.

Cantor, Norman F. and Schneider, Richard I, *How to Study History?* New York: Thomas Y. Crowell Company, 1967.

Chan, Wing-tsit (compiler), *The Great Asian Religions*. London: The MacMillan Company, 1969.

---

32 *Ibid.*, 15:19.
33 *Ibid.*, 15:20.

———— (translator and compiler), *A Source Book in Chinese Philosophy.* Princeton, New Jersey: Princeton University Press, 1963.

Chang, Carsun, *The Development of Neo-Confucian Thought.* New York: Bookman Associates, 1957.

Chen Li-fu, *Eastern and Western Cultures: Confrontation or Conciliation.* New York: St. John's University Press, 1972.

Cornaby, W.A., "Chinese God," *Encyclopaedia of Religion and Ethics.* 6 vols. New York: Charles Scribner's Sons, 1914.

Creel, Herrlee Glessner, *The Birth of China: A Study of the Formative Period of Chinese Civilization.* New York: Frederick Ungar Publishing Co., 1937.

de Bary, Wm. Theodore; Chan, Wing-tsit; and Watson, Burton (compliers), *Sources of Chinese Studies.* Vol. I. New York: Columbia University Press, 1964.

Estlin, J., "Oriental Philosophy: China," *Dictionary of Philosophy and Psychology.* Oxford: Manchester College, 1901. Reprinted by P. Smith, Gloucester, Massachusetts, 1960.

Fung Yu-lan, *A History of Chinese Philosophy.* Translated by Derk Bodde. 2 vols. Princeton, New Jersey: Princeton University Press, 1952-1953.

————, *A Short History of Chinese Philosophy.* Edited by Derk Bodde. New York: Free Press, 1966.

————, *The Spirit of Chinese Philosophy.* Translated by E.R. Hughes. Boston: Beacon Press, 1962.

Gottschalk, Louis, *Understanding History: A Primer of Historical Method.* 2nd ed. New York: Alfred A. Knopf, 1969.

Latourette, Kenneth Scott, *The Chinese: Their History and Culture.* 3rd ed. New York: The MacMillan Company, 1948.

Legge, James (translator and commentator), *The Chinese Classics.* Vol. IV, Pt. I: *The She King.* Oxford, England: The Clarendon Press, 1895.

————, (translator), *The Four Books (Ssu Shu): The Great Learning; The Doctrine of the Mean; Confucian Analects; The Works of Mencius.* Chinese-English version. Hong Kong: The International Publication Society, n.d.

————, *The Sacred Books of the East.* 3 vols. 2nd ed. Oxford: The Clarendon Press, 1899.

McGuire, M.R.P., "Chinese Religion," *New Catholic Encyclopedia.* Vol. III. New York: McGraw-Hill Book Company, 1967.

Makra, Mary Lelia (translator), *The Hsiao Ching.* Edited by Paul K.T. Sih. New York: St. John's University Press, 1961.

Owen, H.P., "Concepts of God," *The Encyclopedia of Philosophy.* 8 vols. New York: The MacMillan Company, 1967.

Pelican, J. Jan, "Religion," *Encyclopaedia Britannica.* Vol. XIX. Chicago: Encyclopaedia Britannica Inc., 1970.

Shu Ching (Book of History), A modernized edition of the translations of James Legge by Clae Waltham. Chicago: Henry Regnery Company, 1971.

Sih, Paul K.T., *Chinese Culture and Christianity.* Taipei: China Culture Publishing Foundation, 1957.

Verwilghen, Albert Felix, *Mencius: The Man and His Ideas.* New York: St. John's University Press, 1967.

Waley, Arthur (translator and annotator), *The Analects of Confucius.* New York: Vintage Books, a division of Random House, Inc., 1938.

———, (translator), *The Book of Songs.* New York: Grove Press, Inc., 1937.

Walsh, W.H., *An Introduction to the Philosophy of History.* London: Hutchinson and Co., 1958.

Watson, Burton (translator), *Hsun Tzu: Basic Writings.* New York: Columbia University Press, 1963.

Weber, Max, *The Religion of China: Confucianism and Taoism.* Translated and edited by Hans H. Gerth. New York: The Free Press, 1951.

Yang, C.K., "The Functional Relationship between Confucian Thought and Chinese Religion." *Chinese Thought and Institutions.* Edited by John K. Fairbank, Chicago: The University of Chicago Press, 1957.

2. Sources in Chinese

Chü Wan-li 屈萬里 (translator and commentator), *Shang Shu Ching-chu Ching-yi* 尚書今註今譯 (The Book of History: Modern Translation and Commentary). Taipei: Commercial Press, 1971.

Huang, Te-shih 黃得時 (translator and annotator), *Hsiao Ching: Ching-yi Ching-chu* 孝經今譯今註 (Classic of Filial Piety: Modern Translation and Commentary). Taipei: Commercial Press, 1972.

Hsiung, Shih-li 熊十力, *Hsin Wei-shih Lun* 新唯識論 (New Doctrine of Consciousness-Only). Shanghai: Kwang-wen Book Company, 1947.

Hsu Shen 許慎, *Shuo Wen Chieh Tzu* 說文解字. Annotated by Tuan Yü-ts'ai 段玉裁, Taipei: Yi-wen Printing House, 1966.

Wang, Ching-chih 王靜芝, *Shih Ching T'ung Shih* 詩經通釋 (General Commentary on the Book of Odes). Taipei: Fu-jen Catholic University, 1968.

Wang, Meng-ou 王夢鷗, *Li Chi Ching-chu Ching-yi* 禮記今註今譯 (Book of Rites: Modern Commentary and Translation). 2 vols. Taipei: Commercial Press, 1970.

Wang, Yang-ming 王陽明, *Ch'uan-hsi Lu* 傳習錄 (Instructions for Practical Living). Taipei: Cheng Chung Book Company, 1954.

3. Unpublished Source

Shih, Vincent Yu-chung, "A Study of the Concepts of Ti, T'ien, and Tao in Ancient Chinese Philosophy in the Light of Western Religious and Philosophical Thought". Unpublished Ph.D. dissertation, University of Southern California, 1939.

CHAPTER V

NEO-CONFUCIONISM: ETHICS OF FUNG YU-LAN

Michel E. Masson*

This study focuses on the moral philosophy expounded by Fung Yu-lan in the two books he published around 1940, "China's Road to Freedom" and "A New Treatise on the Way of Life."[1]

In this investigation, the theme of *'continuity and discontinuity'* has been adopted as a *fil conducteur.* Those two terms are not definite concepts which would be used in order to categorize Fung's thought definitively, but neither are they merely rhetorical expressions.[2] The way the problem of change is approached *within a philosophical system* may provide us with a more

*East Asiatic Studies, Harvard University, Cambridge, Massachusetts, U.S.A.

1 *Hsin Shih-lun,* 1940. In his *Source Book on Chinese Philosophy* Wing-tsit Chan gives 1939, which is the date Fung completed his manuscript.

"China's Road to Freedom" is the subtitle of the book as indicated by Fung in his foreword.

Hsin Shih-hsün, 1943. The date given by Wing-tsit Chan, 1940, is the date of completion of the manuscript too.

"A New Treatise on the Way of Life" is the translation given by Wing-tsit Chan. "New self" as found in Boorman's *Biographical Dictionary of Republican China,* vol. 2, 34, might be a misprint; there are many of them in the article on Fung.

2 The problem of continuity and discontinuity is extensively dealt with in *Hsin Shih-lun,* c. 10. The title of this chapter *chi-k'ai* 繼 開 seems to be best translated as "continuity and discontinuity."

The preface to *Hsin Shih-hsün* too focuses, as we will explain later, on the "newness" in Fung's treatment of the way of life.

thorough understanding of the issues at stake. Last, but not least, the problem of continuity has been a recurrent theme in writings by Fung, or about him, since 1949 in Mainland China.[3]

The exposé has been divided into four 'sections.' *Section 1* contains some *introductary notations* on the two books and a few basic categories of thought which Fung has introduced and analyzed in his previous work, "The New Neo-Confucionism."[4] *Section 2* deals with *discontinuity in ethical values,* and refers mainly to "China's Road to Freedom." *Section 3* examines the continuity principle underlying "A New Treatise on the Way of Life." In *Section 4* we attempt to draw some conclusions: e.g. how Fung's treatment of the moral issues may modify our understanding of 'continuity and discontinuity' in the intellectual history of contemporary China.

1. Introductory Notations

Before undertaking a more detailed analysis, it is necessary to give a brief description of *Hsin Shih-lun* and *Hsin Shih-hsün,* and to introduce Fung's *basic conceptualization* in what we may call his moral philosophy.

---

3 An important list of those writings can be found in Wing-tsit Chan, *Chinese Philosophy, 1949-1963 - an annotated bibliography of Mainland China publications.* Some of those writings belong to the "confession literature," but other deal simply with the philosophical question of national tradition.

In the first category, continuity means reaction: "My concern was to preserve the superstructure of the feudal society...I said the major part of ethics cannot change, the mutable is only a small part. Accordingly to this theory, the major part of the feudal superstructure has to, and may, be preserved." (in *Che-hsüeh Yan-chiou,* 1959, 1: "Hsin Li-hsüeh ti yüan-hsing," p. 42.) Similarly, Fung was criticized for having "utilized economical determinism to counterfeit Marxism" and to fill the old bottles of feudalism with the new wine of imperialism" (in *Pei-chin ta-hsüeh hsüeh-pao,* 1955-1956: "P'i-p'ing Feng Yu-lan hsien-sheng kuo-ch'ü te szu-hsiang," p. 155).

4 *Hsin Li-hsüeh,* 1939. Wing-tsit Chan's translation, "The new rational philosophy," is too interpretative, and somehow misleading. "New neo-confucianism," given in Boorman, seems more exact.

Hsin Shih-lun is a "new discussion of the problems at hand" as well as "a road to freedom." In many aspects, too, it constitutes an interpretation of the history of ideas in China since the times of Tseng Kuo-fan and Chang Chih-tung. In the "augmented edition" of his *Fifty Years of Chinese Intellectual History,* Kuo Chan-po gives a somewhat detailed summary of the book, with this appreciation:

> During the eight years of the recent Japan war, the most important contribution in the field of thought - in terms of quality as well as of quantity - is Fung Yu-lan's.

> ...As to intellectual evolution in wartime China, *Hsin Shih-lun* has to be considered as the most important and most influential of his works.[5]

According to Kuo, the book is an attempt to give a new elucidation of the issues in wartime China "from the point of view of the Chinese people and of the nation."[6]

In Fung's own words, *Hsin Shih-lun* is conceived as a counterpart and complement of *Hsin Li-hsüeh:* as a theoretical work, *Hsin Li-hsüeh* does not deal immediately with actual concrete problems, although the latter are not alien to the content of it. *Hsin-Shih-lun* is the direct treatment of those problems, in the light of the general systematization elaborated in the previous work. And, as to the question of continuity and discontinuity, Fung states clearly in his foreword that *Hsin Shih-lun* is a *new* discussion of factual problems, and not a discussion of *new* problems; it is *new* in the same sense as *Hsin Li-hsüeh* is a new philosophy of immutable *Li.* We shall examine later in what sense he conceives the newness of his system.

In order to give a brief *aperçu* of *the content,* the twelve

---

5 Kuo Chan-po, *Chin we-shih nien chung-kuo szu-hsiang shih pu-pien* (Fifty years of Chinese intellectual history - augmented edition), pp. 195 and 198.

6 Kuo Chan-po, 209.

chapters may be arranged in three groups: in the first four chapters, Fung deals with the general question of change in contemporary China and explains the international, economic and social nature and implications of the problems. This theory is applied to cultural issues like filial piety, status of women, education and arts, in the next four chapters. Finally, Fung investigates some antithetic notions, like the permanent or transitory nature of national characteristics (c.9), continuity and discontinuity (c.10), resistance and construction (c.11), and he ends up with "Praising China" (c.12).

The *moral issues* here are mainly dealt with in terms of *ethical values:* filial piety, the ideal of womanhood, and education. But those problems are treated as part of the more general problem of China's destiny: one has first to appreciate correctly the whole process, in order to be able to analyze the question of ethics. The many references of Fung to Ch'ing statesmen or to iconoclasts of the Republican period are significant. Both generations have somehow identified every problem as an ethical issue; one of Fung's purposes is to show that this issue is only one among others. This approach to the question of ethics from the point of view of the global, national crisis is a distinctive feature of *Hsin Shih-lun,* quite different from the logical and deductive analysis of ethical categories in *Hsin Li-hsüeh.*

In *Hsin Shih-hsün,* moral issues are examined in terms of 'a way of living.' In the ten chapters of this work, Fung expounds what may be called 'virtues and practical wisdom', the fundamental attitudes man as a social being is invited to exert not only in order to be at peace with his fellowmen, but equally to be at peace with himself.

The essential point here is to understand correctly the different status given by Fung to 'ethical values' and these 'moral attitudes' developed in *Hsin Shih-Hsün.* The safest course is to refer to the terminology introduced in *Hsin Li-hsüeh.*

The first important distinction is: *moral/immoral/amoral.* Fung states that societies, as entities made of human beings, cannot survive unless the individuals act in accordance with the nature of that society. What is called 'moral' is the behavior which helps 'directly or indirectly to preserve the existence of that society' and, on the contrary, a behavior which directly or indirectly hampers the existence of the society is 'immoral'. There is a third term: the 'amoral' behavior which neither preserves nor hampers.[7]

The notion of 'amoral behavior' is essential because man is very often outside the sphere of morality/immorality:

> The 'amoral' is neither moral nor immoral: in other terms it does not belong to the sphere of ethical judgments. Man's behavior does not belong in its totality to that sphere, and cannot be in its totality labeled as moral or immoral. There are many forms of behavior originating in human nature which are simply amoral. For instance, eating and drinking, relations between men and women, all originate in human nature; in its own sphere, eating is not a moral behavior, nor an immoral one. There is no doubt about that, and it is the same with relations between men and women. In consequence, we must say that in a given sphere of activity, behavior becomes immoral only when it transgresses the limits of that sphere, with the result that it is no longer in accord with the basic norms (of the society).[8]

I do not think this conception could be qualified as "sociologism" (a western notion, and a very vague one indeed...). "Sociologism" implies the idea that transcendental values are being rationalized and levelled down. The preoccupation of Fung is quite alien to that problem. What he believes is that a society needs the cooperation of its members in order to survive at all: the *chün-tzu* is a "positive," a "constructive" element, whereas the *hsiao jen* is a negative and destructive one.

In the light of this distinction between moral/immoral/amoral, we may identify two kinds of questions. The problem of ethical

7 *Hsin Li-hsuen,* 165-166.
8 *Ibid.,* 167.

values in *Hsin Shih-lun* is to determine which behavior is moral or immoral. The scope of the way of living described in *Hsin Shih-hsun* is "indirectly moral" (my wording; not Fung's) or amoral: *jen* 仁 , sincerity, *wu-wei* 無為 or humility are indirectly moral in the measure that they contribute to the proper functioning of society; in other aspects they are only private virtues which do not affect society.

The second distinction is between *ethical values and virtues.* Fung says that societies cannot survive unless the individual behavior corresponds to the nature of those societies. The 'nature' of a society is not a simple element: it is both the nature of this society *as being a society,* a nature shared in with any other society, - and the nature of a *given type* of social organization.

Ethical values relate to a given type of social organization, they are part of a social system. In a given type of society, what is moral, immoral and amoral is clearly defined; for instance, the 'Five bonds' in traditional China draw the border line between moral and immoral, and at the same time indirectly define the limits of the amoral sphere.

"Virtues" are related to the nature of society as such. The traditional formulation of the basic virtues in China is the "Five constants." But, as in any philosophical system, the analysis of the notion of virtue here is complex. 1. Virtues are *"activities,"* through which any society achieves better unity. Traditional philosophy classifies those "activities" into 5 categories, each category having his own *li* 理 , for instance *jen* 仁 . 2. But virtues are not identified with the common good, in a mohist way; they are too *"spiritual conditions."* For instance, one could say that *jen* is not only the principle of altruistic actions, it is too 'the unity of Heaven and Earth'.[9] This ambivalence can be summed up as: although those activities are society-oriented,

9   *Ibid.,* 183.

their *li*, as virtues, is not part of the *li* of society; it is 'contained within the *li* of man'.[10]

In *Hsin Shih-lun*, Fung focuses on the problem of ethical values: what is the fate of traditional ethics in modern China? This question cannot be answered unless one examines what changes are taking place in this type of society. In *Hsin Shih-hsun*, he expounds several basic types of *virtuous activities*, as society-oriented, and describes the *spiritual condition* or attitude connected with each virtue. We have mentioned that the scope of 'a way of life' is partly moral, partly amoral; this is coherent with the definition of virtue.

Those complex notions cannot be satisfactorily summarized in a few paragraphs. Their significance will appear more clearly in the following pages. Moreover, the final interpretation of those notions has to be found in another work of Fung, *Hsin Yüan-jen*.[11]

2. *Discontinuity in Ethical Values (Hsin Shih-lun)*

Bearing in mind Max Weber's famous distinction, we may say that in *Hsin Shih-lun*, Fung Yu-lan advocates an *'ethics of responsibility'* (i) ideals cannot solve China's problems.[12] To be responsible means, first of all, to acknowledge the rule of *dual morality* (ii), especially in the field of international relations. No value can rescue China. Only effective strength can do what implies mechanization, and *mechanization means socialization* (iii), a complete transformation of the socio-economic organization. Because of the nature of that mutation in China, ethical values will be automatically *discontinuous* (iv). - That is a brief

10 *Ibid.*, 195- with this formulation, Fung avoids saying that the "Five constants" *constitute* man's nature.

11 *Hsin Yüan-jen* (A New Treatise on the Nature of Man), 1942.

12 But the dramatic contradiction between ethics of responsibility and ethics of conviction, which constitutes one of the main themes in Weber's thought, seems to be quite alien to Fung.

outline of how Fung introduces the question of ethical discontinuity, on the *significance* of which we shall add some final comments (v).

(a) Ethics of Responsibility vs. Ethics of Conviction

The fate of modern China is to discover its own particularity as a culture. Historically speaking, it is more exact to say that Chinese are rediscovering what they have forgotten since the times of the Han dynasty: for 2000 years of monoculturalism, culture could not be a problem. The fact that there has been different cultures - Shang, Chou, Chu - in the past was completely ignored as well as science-oriented theories dealing with cultural evolution and differentiation, such as the "three reigns," "small peace," "great peace."

This lack in premodern Chinese thinking has been well attested in the inability of the nation to solve the problems resulting from the *de facto* discovery of another culture in the mid-1800's. At the same time the new vogue for the "three reigns" or "great peace" theories among reformers was the sign that a scientific tool has to be found in order to cope with the problem of a universal Chinese culture, no longer existing.

In fact, states Fung, if this problem has to be solved at all, it has to be examined with a scientific method, that is one which analyzes a given cultural entity in terms of *types of culture,* instead of focusing only on the historical individuality of Chinese culture. The merit of the "three reigns" idea, and despite the somehow extravagant reinterpretations by K'ang Yu-wei, is to attempt to classify types of cultures. In the light of Fung's general principles as expressed in *Hsin Li-hsüeh,* each concrete individual culture may belong to several types and share in different *hsings* (nature). To detail all, or part of, the *hsings* in a particular individual is *history,* to study how an individual culture belong to one type and have the corresponding *hsing* is *science.* In Fung's words:

We may speak about culture either from the point of view of

particularity, or from the point of view of types. We call them "Western culture," "Chinese culture," according to their individuality: we mean a particular culture. We call them "capitalist culture," "socialist culture," according to types: we mean a type of culture. History is the study of cultures as individuals; science is the study of them as types of culture.[13]

Because this golden rule has been ignored or misunderstood, Fung gives some comments:

(a) This type-approach has been somehow followed at the end of the Ch'ing dynasty;[14] it was rejected by the following generation during the first decade of the Republic: this new generation got rid of the typology elaborated by its predecessors, but was unable to perceive what exactly was wrong in it. As a result they confine themselves to the particularity-approach: "West vs. China." Considering western culture as an *individuality* to be studied and imitated as a *whole,* they found themselves unable to distinguish within western culture the essential from the accidental, and they did not perceive the *contradictions* inherent to western culture, like Christianity vs. science. On the other side, the advocates of Chinese culture made the same error in their analysis of their own heritage.

(b) A step forward was made when the "westerner-Chinese" duality became "modernization vs. backwardness." The problem was no longer to imitate, but to adopt a type of culture. Nevertheless, modernization was still conceived as an individual entity, in which essential and accidental characteristics could not be distinguished.

(c) The scientific approach advocated by Fung is different:

13 *Hsin Shih-lun,* 3.

14 For instance, with the dichotomy: *wen* (spiritual and artistic aspects of a culture) and *chih* (practical, nature-bound aspects). This traditional distinction, which we find already in the *Lun-yü* (6,16) was used by late Ch'ing thinkers as a "sociological" concept: The West has discovered only plain practical know-how, whereas Chinese achievements are spiritual.

If we look at western culture in terms of types, then we are able to know why the so-called western culture is superior: not because of its being western, but because of its being a certain kind of culture. In consequence what we have to consider is not western culture as a particular culture, but the pattern of one kind of culture. Looking at western culture from the pattern-point of view, we can discern among the huge variety of its characteristics, which are important and which are accidental in regard to this type.[15]

And the same type of analysis must be carried out on Chinese culture.

In this perspective, says Fung, we may envision the cultural change as a *total transformation*, from one type of culture to another, or as a *partial transformation*, because it does not affect Chinese culture as an individuality: "it is not a matter of transforming our culture as a particular one into another particular one."[16] To adopt a new type of culture is not to lose one's own national identity; the question of a "fundamental Chinese culture" has not to be asked.

The scientific method so outlined in the first chapter of *Hsin Shih-lun* may appear as an awkward attempt to superimpose the logical concepts of *Hsin Li-hsüeh* over the maze of Chinese realities. In fact, what Fung is driving home is the impossibility of finding an overall solution. His main insistence is that there is no Chinese or western "culture" one can study or imitate *as a whole;* as long as the Chinese will try to deal with the whole of either culture, they will be unavoidably mistaken. Fung does not advocate a new way of dealing with the whole; its logical conceptualization is used as a tool to denounce the illusion of the whole-approach.

On the other hand, Fung emphasizes the fact that his scientific approach *is well rooted in Chinese tradition.* Doing so, is he an

[15] *Hsin Shih-lun*, 15.
[16] *Ibid.*, 16.

"orientalist," a "conservative" using a seemingly scientific language to buy the progressist votes? However, meaningless this question may be, it is difficult to skip over it; writing in 1940, advocating a scientific attitude, Fung refers at length to the bizarre theories of the *Kung Yang* school. The question is part parcel of the intellectual history of modern China; it is inherent to the complexity of the issues at hand, this complexity being more or less distorted by our own categories. For instance, in the present case, because we are easily inclined to identify "modernity"/"westernization"/"science," it is tempting to see an inner contradiction between the advocacy of a scientific method and the reference to the *Kung Yang* theories as prescientific. In fact, Fung recognizes that modern science is defined by many other features that are not found in the *Kung Yang* school; he simply stresses that both deal with types. In consequence he does not say that the *"three reigns"* theories may be a solution for the new problem of Chinese culture facing the West; he simply mentions that their cultural evolutionism, however China-centered and monoculturalist it may be, was already a deep understanding of cultural process.[17]

This being the case, there is no contradiction in his referring to *Kung Yang*: the development of anthropology or history in the West during the XIX and XX centuries shows that "science" did evolve out of monoculturalist evolutionisms. For instance, Wellhausen is a radical innovator in the field of biblical sciences, inspired by, and somehow fettered in, evolutionist patterns inherited from Hegel and Vatke.

At this juncture, the main question about Fung's endeavor is not so much whether he is traditionalistic or modernist, evolutionist or scientific, although those questions may be asked as ways of understanding where the issues are. The main question may be what Levenson calls "contemporaneity;" what are the multiple elements which constitute the *Geist* of 1940's China?

17 On this point, see *Hsin Li-hsüeh*, 167-168, where the *Kung-Yang* school and Tung Chung-hsu are mentioned in a similar context.

The safest course is to assume that Fung is coherent in his dealing with a situation which appears contradictory as long as we do not understand it. The fact that he has been widely read, that his books have been reprinted, may suggest that his answers ·are coherent in pre-1949 China. At this "coherence" or "contemporaneity" we have to aim.

(b) The Rule of Dual Morality

The problem of evaluating Western culture vs. Chinese culture has very often been more based on sentimental than realistic considerations. The fact is that ethical values were at stake. Many found refuge in advocating Chinese values against western materialism; in reaction, a new generation exalted the western spiritual values: individual liberty, courage, faithfulness, and rejected confucian cannibalism. At the same time, Darwinism gained many disciples, eager to negate any ethical standard and to preach the natural law of the struggle for life. Finally, the Marxist interpretation of human relations in terms of class struggle came in. Those different conceptions constitute the background of chapter 2, where Fung analyzes the dual relation between ethical values and a given society.

The shortcomings of the above mentioned theories, says Fung, are to express as universally true judgments which are only *relatively* so. Any ethical value is always relative to a given society. First of all, no behavior is completely immoral. The heroes of *Shui-Hu-chuan* follow the *tao* of their own group, in contradiction to the *tao* of the society at large, and in this sense their behavior is moral. Moreover, in fact, the heroes of *Shui-Hu-chuan* follow a *dual morality,* because they belong to two different societies at the same time: as "outlaws" they have their inner ethics, but they act sometimes as members of the society at large. For instance, if they want to buy or sell goods at the market-town, they follow the rules generally accepted (outer ethics).[18]

---

18 Similar reasoning in *Hsin Li-hsëh,* 172-173.

This pattern of dual ethics provides Fung with a general theory ethical systems. Firstly, ethical behavior and values cannot be dismissed at a single stroke on the basis of "Darwinist" interpretations: *no individual is taoless,* because nobody can do without a society to live in, and this implies that the individual complies with the laws and patterns of behavior of that society, as ethical values are the means by which individuals and society preserve their own existence. This principle of the *necessity* and *relativity* of ethical norms is the *fil conducteur* in Fung's analysis of China's new ethics.

On the other hand, *every national society is built on a dual system:* the different values reinforced within a given nation do not govern the behavior of the latter in regards to other states. Whereas individuals conform themselves to ethical values, nations relate to one another in terms of an unethical "struggle for life." International relations have not been civilized yet, since the times when Mo-ti wrote his famous "Against aggression" chapter, despite the first efforts towards an international society in the wake of World War I. Here again, Fung emphasizes the differences between two generations: the late Ch'ing statesman had advocated, quite rightly, self-strengthening, "navy and gun," but, among the following generation, many thought that treaties, international laws and world opinion were sufficient to preserve China's integrity; they did not perceive that the rules of the international game are unethical; they were praising western "spiritual values" at a time of colonial oppression.

The case of Marxism cannot be ignored in this discussion of ethics and violence. How does class struggle relate to this double set of behavior? Fung gives a quite precise answer: 1. Marxist class struggle has to be distinguished from struggle between individuals as well as struggle between nations. It is a specific type of struggle taking place within a given society on the grounds of a different conception of the rules to be followed within this society. The stake is an *ethical choice,* whereas it is not true in the cases of struggle between individuals or nations. In this sense, class struggle belongs to the realm of ethics, or is ethically oriented.[19] 2. But class struggle *cannot solve the problem of international barbarianism*. In Fung's view, a socialist world where reason would prevail between nations is but a dream in 1940. What we can only foresee is the formation of socialist nations which, as nations, will have to comply with the rules of the international game. "In the present situation, the expression 'red imperialism' is not a contradiction in terms."[20] In brief, socialist states will be "socialist within" and "states without."

In consequence of this unavoidable duality of ethical behavior, *the problem of cultural change is a question of Realpolitik*. The opposition is no longer: "barbarians vs. civilized China," or "western technology vs. Chinese spirit," or "western spirit vs. confucian anthropophagy" but between a type of culture which enables some nations to be powerful barbarians and a type of culture which condemns China to be a defeated barbarian.

By the same token, here the scientific approach to the problem of cultural change advocated by Fung finds its criterium. China needs only to turn to an economic type of society which enables her to survive on the international battlefield. Saying that, Fung is not going back to the old "wealth and power" motto: he does advocate self-strengthening, *but without mental reservation*. It is no longer strengthening China in order to preserve ethical, or Chinese values, it is only a matter of self-strengthening *per se*.

(c) Mechanization is Socialization

Cultural encounter as described in (i) was considered as a process to be analyzed in scientific terms. In (ii) we have discovered its political and antagonistic nature: the China/West relation is not only one between two different agglomerations of cultural

---

19 *Hsin Shih-lun*, 34 sqq. - See too *Hsin Shih-hsün*, 104: class struggle is not immoral.

20 *Hsin* Shih-lun, 36.

types, but also one between the stronger and the weaker, between exploiter and exploited. The problem of what type of culture China has to turn to is the problem of *the nature of that exploitation.*

The exploitation is *economic,* answers Fung. It originates from the industrial revolution in the West; since then, the general pattern has been exploitation of rural areas by industrialized cities, of oriental rural societies by the industrialized West. The peasant can no longer be self-sufficient - grow his own cotton and have his wife weave it for their own use; he has to buy clothing manufactured in the cities, and in the same way Chinese have to buy British cottoncloth. No ethical protest, no spiritual movement like Gandhi's or boycotts of Japanese goods, can break this pattern of economic oppression. The only solution is to replace the rural type of Chinese economy by an industrial one.

This primacy of economics was not acknowledged by the statesmen of the Ch'ing dynasty, because they could not understand properly the relation between industrialization and cultural values, but at least they advocated "western learning for practice." The next generation, criticizing the *t'i-yung* dichotomy, promoted "western learning for essence, industrialization for practice," understanding that China has to acquire firstly the *essence* - western philosophy, pure science, ethical values - in order to master the *practice.* They did not perceive that the necessary cultural mutation will follow, once the industrial basis has been set up: they were scholars, not social engineers. As to the Marxist emphasis on the oppression of urban proletariat by the bourgeoisie, Fung thinks that the major evil in China is not the oppression of the proletariat, but the oppression of China, as a rural entity, by urban industrial nations. The true nature of the Sino-Japanese conflict is the best expression of this situation: what Japanese call the "China affair" and Chinese "resist Japan" is not a war between the two nations, but a marketing operation, a "colonial war."[21]

21 *Ibid.,* 200 sqq.

If the unique task is industrialization, we can envision the necessary evolution of China in terms of cultural patterns. This evolution is not based on the abstract principles of wholesale westernization or partial westernization, neither can it be the result of a free selection of the best values at home and abroad; it is simply a direct, unavoidable *consequence of industrialization.* This process is considered by Fung essentially as a shift from a family - based and oriented type of society to a society-based and oriented one:

> In chapter 3, "Cities and Countryside," we have mentioned the revolution in the activities of production. We said that in this revolution, man gets rid of family-based methods of production, rejects a family-based system of production. Once this revolution is accomplished, man follows society-based methods of production and system of production. Cultures being centered around family-based systems of production and social systems are in our terms: *family-production based cultures,* those being centered around society-based systems of production and social systems are *society-production based cultures.*[22]

The criterion is socio-economic, but Fung makes it very clear that the determinant factor lies in the *methods* of production: are they mechanized or not? The changes in the social system are necessarily carried out as a consequence of mechanization. In a not yet mechanized society, the unit of production is the family, and in consequence the family becomes the basic social unity, essential to the survival of that society. With this strictly technical criterion, Fung avoids getting involved in the many discussions on modes of production, Chinese society, or Chinese economy, which have flourished in the 30's. As he put it, the basic factor is the identification of production activities and household, in a non-mechanized society.

22 *Ibid.,* 56-57.

As a commentary of this general principle, Fung draws a comparative tableau of the two types of culture: how as a result of mechanization, all aspects of life are modified, as well as the way the individual perceives himself. We may summarize his analysis of the socialization process as follows:

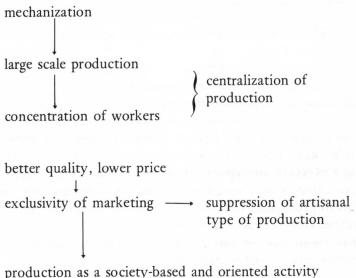

mechanization

large scale production

centralization of production

concentration of workers

better quality, lower price

exclusivity of marketing ⟶ suppression of artisanal type of production

production as a society-based and oriented activity

As for the *relation between the individual, his family* and the society at large, the shift can be outlined this way:

		family-based type	society-based type
work:	location	home	factory
	authority	familial bond	foreman
	professional ability	generalist personalized integral hereditary	specialized depersonalized abstract not hereditary

source of consumption goods and services	familial pro-duction & organization	society (money)
key unit for indiv. for society	family family	society society
model type	elder	younger genera-tion (ability to cope with changes

(d) Discontinuity in Ethical Values

The consequence of this shift in cultural patterns is mainly a *shift in ethical values,* accompanied by a morality crisis. The latter is a transient phenomenon; in a period where two sets of value coexist it is very tempting for the *hsiao jen* to turn this situation to profit, and to have his will in the void of a definite *Sittlichkeit.* One can observe too an identity crisis among many individuals who have to live in a dual universe: modern schools for girls, and traditional mothers-in-law.[23]

The basic change in ethical values originate in the disappearance of the family as a basic unit of social and individual existence. The "six bonds" which constitute the essence of traditional ethics are all family-oriented, including the relation between minister and prince. *Chung* and *hsiao* 忠孝 , explains Fung, can be considered as the two poles of the old ethical pattern. And in his analysis of those two notions, he elucidates their mutual connection through examining traditional terminology or *casus conscientiae.* He concludes that even when there is an apparent conflict between filial piety and loyalty to the prince, filial piety remains the fundamental obligation; *chung* is always conceived along the pattern, and for the sake of, *hsiao.* The priority of *hsiao* in the old culture is not the invention of a few

23 On those crisis, ib. 72-73, and *Hsin Shih-hsün,* 53-54.

illustrious sages of the past: it is the necessary product of, and
the sine-qua-non condition in, a family-based society. In Fung's
view, the attacks of the iconoclasts against "Confucius' shop"
and confucian "cannibalism" were completely irrelevant: they
did not perceive that Confucian values were not created by
Confucius, but imposed by the type of culture China has belonged to for centuries.

What is in consequence the fate of *hsiao* and *chung* in a
society-based culture? As far as *hsiao* is concerned, Fung writes:

> In a society-based culture, with society-based methods of pro-
> duction, the ramparts of the family are shaken. In that type of
> society, there are still families, but family is no longer the unit
> of economy, its social significance is completely different from
> the one in a family-based society. In the latter, man blends
> with society, economically and in all aspects of life. In such a
> society, as family is no longer the basis of social organization,
> man does not consider the consolidation of the family organ-
> ization as his first duty (...) In such a society, man does not
> consider *hsiao* as the priority. This does not mean that he may
> 'strike his father and slander his mother', but that *hsiao* is a
> virtue, and only one, no longer the center and root of all
> virtues.[24]

By the same token, traditional *chung* disappears too. It would
be erroneous to assume that *chung* could be transferred to the
society at large, and become the new ethical priority. In fact, in a
society-based type of culture, man does not serve the society the
same way as the minister "served" his prince. Now the individual
serves himself. Here the reasoning of Fung is not always crystal
clear, but his main emphasis is on the necessary discontinuity;
the difference between the two societies is not a quantitative one
(as if the society was a larger family), but a change in nature. It is
not possible to maintain traditional *chung* because it was defined

24 *Hsin Shih-lun*, 85.

as a supererogatory manifestation of filial piety. For the sake of his own family, the minister could commit himself to the service of an individual, his prince. But in the new type of society, it is no longer possible to envision this selfless, but family-oriented, commitment. The only thing one can do is to serve oneself. Using another terminology, we can say that Fung explicits the radical difference between a *Gemeinschaftlich* type of existence and a new one where the individual cannot be any longer identified with his family.

At this juncture, Fung discusses the case of *patriotism*. There is no continuity between "serving his prince" and "serving his country". The difference is that in a society-based culture, if the society is defined by the country, then the individuals are organically linked with "the country." The love of the country is ego-oriented, whereas in the old society the service of the prince was alter-oriented.[25] This does not mean that patriotism is selfishness: the point Fung is bringing home is that patriotism is not an empty ideal, an "ism" artificially imported. Patriotism originates in the deep feeling that to work for the country is to work for myself; any romantic or occidentalist idealization of patriotism misses that point.

We have said that *hsiao* and *chung* constitute the two major poles of the traditional ethics. A secondary bipolarity, filial piety and "virtue" *(chieh, 節)* has to be examined too. The "virtuous woman" is expected to be a filial daughter-in-law, a good spouse and a "worthy mother" in the family of her husband; her vocation is to serve her new family, in the same way as the vocation of the loyal minister was to serve his prince: "the loyal minister does not serve two princes; the virtuous woman does not serve two husbands."[26]

Both *hsiao/chung* and *hsiao/chieh* reflect the structure of a family-based economy. The difference is that the whole life of a woman is spent within the family circle, and that her social

25 *Ibid.*, 87 - see too 70-71.
26 *Ibid.*, 95.

position is inferior to man's. Without being very explicit, Fung relates this inferiority to the needs of a home economy: the principal function of a daughter-in-law is to add to familial manpower; this conception of marriage is simply the natural consequence in a society where individuals are totally dependent upon the family organization. On the contrary, the shift to a society-based culture means 'emancipation of women', 'free choice of a partner.' Within a socialized system of production man and woman become economically equal; the only aim of marriage is then "cohabitation and sexual life" between two partners who are effectively equal.[27]

However, this emancipation of women out of the old bonds is not completed as long as she is still expected to be a "worthy mother." If she has to stay home and look after her children, then she is not effectively on a foot of equality with man, she is "less equal" economically, and her professional aspirations have to be sacrificed for the sake of motherhood. The question is: does "motherhood" constitute an *exception to the rule of discontinuity?* Is there some "natural law" which would remain unchaged in the new society?

Fung's answer is *negative:* even in the case of motherhood there can be no continuity between the two systems. In the old one, women were required to devote themselves to the upbringing of children, but this self-denial was rewarded; doing so, women "fulfilled their vocation," and members of the family as well as the society at large would praise them as "worthy mother." In the new type of society, the conditions are different: motherhood is *no longer a socially rewarded achievement;* as long as the emancipation of women is not total, one could say that their social status is lower than in the old system. So, the problem is not a limit-case or an exception: it is too a matter of socio-economic organization. In Fung's view, the solution cannot be provided but in a completely socialized economic system, providing nurseries and day-care facilities; otherwise the equality

27 *Ibid.,* 102.

between sexes remains juridical and abstract. In that answer, we can see that Fung does not identify the new society with the capitalist system of the West; his preference for a socialist type of economy was already explicitly stated in *Jen-sheng che-hsüeh,* or "philosophy of life," published in 1923:

> For example, at present we all consider a socialist social system superior to a capitalist social system. Why? It is just because many of the human desires that can be satisfied by a socialist social system cannot be satisfied by a capitalist social system, while many of those human desires that can be satisfied by a capitalist social system can be satisfied by a socialist social system. The relative superiority of the socialist social system is due precisely to its ability to obtain a greater measure of 'harmony.'[28]

Another, and last, instance of total discontinuity is found in the *conception of education.* In the new society, education is a production process, conceived as an "industrialized," organizational type of activity. The old ideal of the quasi-filial relation between teacher and disciples, the generalist type of education focusing on the moral qualities of the gentleman, do not meet the requirements of the new society. The teacher has to be a professional in an educational "factory": he can be no longer a *guru.* This depersonalization of teaching does not mean, however, that in a society-based culture no close relationship is any longer possible between individuals:

> In the society-based culture, relationships between father and son, between brothers, and even between spouses, are less close than in the family-based culture. But we do not mean that in the society-based culture there is no extremely close relationships between individuals, but those close relationships are not necessarily limited to father and sons, or brothers.[29]

28 Translation given in H.L. Boorman, *Bibliographical Dictionary....* Vol. 2, p. 33.
29 *Hsin Shih-lun,* 124.

Nevertheless, the change in the educational process does cut very deep. The main aim of traditional education was to provide moral training, in addition to patterns of behavior inculcated within the family. In the new society where schooling has to be industrialized, no such training is offered in schools; at the same time the traditional family, as being the basic cell of life and education, has gone. In those conditions, no wonder that many ask who is going to teach moral behavior and advocate that moral values and way of life be taught at school.

The answer of Fung is somehow radical: moral behavior is not taught in the new schools, *because it cannot be taught at all*, and never it was, even at the times of Confucius. Distinguishing *chiao* (教) and *hua* (化) , Fung explains that individual morality has always depended on external *influence* (化) , on the *Zeitgeist* of a given society at a given time, not on teaching (教) . In the old culture, this influence was received from the family and the teacher who did stand for the society; now, the individual finds himself directly under the influence of the messages brought in by the *global society,* which functions as a massive propaganda machinery, dispatching ideals and idols indiscriminately. The problem cannot be underestimated, but its solution cannot be found in schools and textbooks.

(e) The Significance of Discontinuity

If we attempt now to define the *main characteristics* of Fung's approach to the problem of *ethical discontinuity*, we may say:

(aa) This ethical discontinuity is not conceived as the object of a decision that man may take or not; *discontinuity is a fact,* yet still in the making, and this fact is a necessary consequence of the change in social organization. In other words, the affirmation of discontinuity does not depend on an ideological stand. The only choice is to accept the fact of discontinuity as an unavoidable consequence of the new type of society. The moral issue is not whether one may or not get rid of the traditional virtues, but whether one is willing or not to come to terms with the new type of society. What Fung is advocating is not "discontinuity of values," but mechanization.

(bb) The necessity of discontinuity *cannot be called in* question. It is consequent with: 1) the way Fung conceives of the socio-economical changes brought along with mechanization and industrialization, 2) with his definition of ethical values as explicited in *Hsin Li-hsüeh;* ethical values are not dictated by a "natural law"[30] or any "categorical imperative," they are the norms of behavior within a given society, which enable that society to preserve its existence and cohesion:

> According to our conception, morality is not a unique behavior in accord with a definite law, but the behavior of the members of one society, as being in accord with the laws edicted by the *Li* of that society.[31]

Discontinuity is *total* because Fung thinks that the two types of organization (family-/ society-based) are basically contradictory.

(cc) This discontinuity in ethical values should not raise emotional reactions, because this discontinuity does not suppress the *continuity of China* as historical social unit. There is discontinuity from one system of values to another in China, but there is no discontinuity from *China* to another entity which *would not be China.* This discontinuity itself is neither Chinese nor non-Chinese: it belongs to any society, and as such the phenomenon of discontinuity is not alien to Chinese society.

(dd) On the contrary, *total discontinuity* allows us to *preserve totally the value of traditional ethics* and *morality.* The same principle which requires us to conclude that old values have to be discontinued now, allows us to recognize the moral achievements

---

30 Fung gives the example of the "natural right" to private ownership. In Soviet Union, even if private ownership is not completely abolished, it is clear that the "mentality" toward this natural right is already different from ours, because Soviet society provides for the emergency needs of the individual. Private ownership is a moral issue only in a given type of society (*Hsin Shih-lun,* 161 sqq.).

31 *Hsin Li-hsüeh,* 170.

of our predecessors in the old society. Chinese culture has never devoured her own children, there has been no cannibalism; 'filial sons' and 'virtuous women' were not the victims of a slave ideology; on the contrary, given the type of society they lived in, their values were the *best expression* of righteousness and human achievement. They were, and *they are* still so; although they are not *our* values, they have been *their* own ones, and as such they are still values:

> In a given society, the behavior which is in accord with the basic norms edicted by the *li* of this society is virtuous, in regard to this society. But this type of behavior is not necessarily in accord with the basic norms edicted by the *li* of another type of society; it may even be contrary to it. In consequence, from the point of view of another type of society, this behavior seems to be immoral, or at least amoral. But it only "seems to be so," because the behavior of the members of a society can be criticized only by the standard of the basic norms edicted by the *li* of this society. What is in accord with this standard is virtuous. If it is virtuous, it will remain so for ever.[32]

This is not Levenson's "museification," nor a traditionalistic approach: the traditionalistic concern is to preserve those values *as ours;* whereas Fung simply states: their values will preserve themselves as values of yesterday.

(ee) Discontinuity in ethical values *does not mean total discontinuity in the spiritual realm.* Very often, says Fung, traditionalists have advocated the preservation of "Chinese spirit," without distinguishing ethical values and aesthetics; in a similar way, many innovators have linked together the problem of the new ethics with the question of modern literature or arts. Both groups did not perceive that, whereas ethical values are determined by a type of socio-economic system, literature and arts

32 *Ibid.,* 171-172.

are essentially the creative *continuation* of a national tradition. 'English science' means 'science in England,' and 'English literature' points to the literary tradition which has evolved within the *emotional and historical heritage* of English language. Aesthetics is continuity: the only problem is to have genuine and creative artists, and not only imitators. The so-called discontinuity in arts is nonsense.[33]

(ff) There is no romantic worship of 'discontinuity' *for the sake of discontinuity* in Fung. His global approach to the problem of change is rather continuity-oriented. This 'continuity' does not mean conservatism or traditionalism; it is not incompatible with the idea of revolution, even a communist one. But revolutionary or not, change is always interpreted both as continuity and discontinuity, and envisioned more as a *natural process of development* than as a promethean sacrilege. Despite his logical apparatus, Fung is not a philosopher of immobilism, but he has no propensity toward revolutionary pathos either.

3. Continuity in the Way of Living (Hsin Shih-hsün)

(a) Continuity and Innovation

The purpose of Fung in *Hsin Shih-hsün* is to give "a new exposition of a method of living." 'Living' here does not include all aspects of human life: "When we say 'living' or 'human life' we mean the spiritual and social aspects of human life." Those aspects of life, like others, have their fundamental norms, that man has to follow in some degree at least, and those norms are universal:

For instance, 'veracity' is a norm of social life that man has to observe in a certain degree. Without distinction of epochs or nationalities, there are not many people indeed who are able

---

33 See *Hsin Shih-lun*, c. 8: "On Arts and Literature," and Fung's conception of national characteristics, ib., 165.

to fulfill perfectly this norm, but nobody can do without it.[34]

This notion of a way of life is not new; it is the *tao* of the ancient philosophers, it is too the *'method of learning'* in neo-confucianism:

> During antiquity, there has been already many expositions of a method of living; there has been still more of them among the neoconfucianists of the Sung-Ming period. We used to say that the latter are philosophers, but strictly speaking the major part of their work is not philosophical. Their most important topic is the 'method of learning.' In many respects 'method of learning' is a method of living.[35]

Although Fung is mainly *continuing* this illustrious tradition, his treatment of the subject is *new* in several respects; he enumerates five of them we are going to review.

(1) The first innovation brought in by Fung is the direct application of his conceptions of ethics as introduced in *Hsin Li-hsüeh* and developed at length in *Hsin Shih-lun;* some values are derived from the particular type a given society belongs to. However, some others are derived from the nature of society as such:

> For instance, the "five permanent virtues" are virtues derived from the existence of society: we have explained this point clearly in *Hsin Li-hsüeh.* As to *chung* and *hsiao,* according to their original significance, they are derived from the existence of a family-based society, as we have explained it in *Hsin Shih-lun.* Because of this distinction among ethical norms, the method of living in a given type of society may partially change accordingly to the changes in the ethical norms. The method of living in a given type of society may too not be

---

34 *Hsin Shih-hsün,* 2.
35 *Ibid.,* 4.

completely similar to the one in another type of society.[36]

This distinction, comments Fung, has not been perceived by the ancient philosophers; talking about "man," they were talking in fact about "man in a given type of society." On the contrary, the man Fung considers here is *man in any type of society*, as well as in any condition, young or old, Chinese or foreigner, modern or premodern.[37]

This innovation *does not mean discontinuity:* it is innovation within a philosophical tradition. To make his case clear, Fung gives the example of logic: however provincial Aristotle's logic may be, being conditioned by the particular characteristics of Greek language, the modern 'pure logic' is still a heritage and continuation of Aristotle's endeavor. We have already touched upon this matter of intellectual or artistic continuity, and it will remain one major concern for Fung after 1949.

(2) The method of learning in the Sung-Ming period was mainly expressed in terms of morality and virtue. According to those philosophers, every action or thought *had to be virtuous or immoral,* a moralistic conception which is well illustrated by their emphasis on 'merits' and their affection for detailed examination of conscience.[38] Fung's approach is broader: he will discuss many attitudes which can be considered as a-moral:

We assume that man's activities and thoughts may not be necessarily divided into 'virtue' and 'immorality'. In consequence the method of living we expose is in many respects a-moral.[39]

36 *Ibid.*, 5.
37 *Ibid.*, 12.
38 "merits": *kung-fu.* 功夫
    The importance of the examination of conscience is well illustrated in the *kung-kuo ko* 功過格 ("investigation of merits and defects"), quite similar to the "particular examination of conscience" in the Jesuit school of spirituality.
39 *Hsin Shih-hsün,* 7.

(3) Moreover, in the Neo-Confucian tradition, many problems used to be discussed which are *irrelevant to-day,* or may have been already worn out, bookish topics, for many generations.

(4) Altough theoretically, in Neo-Confucianism, everybody is invited to follow the way, nevertheless, one can say that ethical pursuit became the apanage of *'technicians'* or *'professionals'* bent over their codex and examining their conscience. Fung will address himself to the 'man of the street,' as ethical life is for everybody, and not reserved to an elite of specialists.

(5) The last point mentioned by Fung is the relation between "the method of living" and life itself. In Neo-Confucianism, man is striving for an ideal of morality; as long as the individual has not yet reached his summit, all his activities are considered as 'study,' as 'devices' or *means toward that end.* All in all Neo-Confucians had an ascetic conception of life, not so different from the Ch'an quest for enlightenment. Fung wants to go back to a more balanced conception; my life to-day is life, and can be virtuous; it is not only study and preparation for a state of perfection not yet achieved. As in (4) Fung tries to avoid any 'technical' or 'professional' conception of moral progress.

The above-mentioned points elucidate the way Fung envisioned philosophical continuity and discontinuity. Altogether one gets the impression that continuity is still the more important element; whatever innovations may be introduced, they are *innovations within the traditional framework.* For instance, Fung acknowledges the differences between types of society, but his conclusion is that *a fortiori* a general way of living is needed and can be described. He gives the example of warfare: bows and arrows have been replaced by guns, but the same universal professional qualities are still required in the warriors, 'quick eyes, quick hands.'

The 'way of living' is universal not only in regards to types of societies, but even in regards to the different *conceptions of life,* philosophical or religious:

The 'spiritual method' may be different according to dissimilar conceptions of life. But the method of living we expound here does not consider those differences. Our 'method of living' is a method of 'living': every living human being needs to follow it. Although conceptions of life are different, they are conceptions of 'life', not of 'death.' Whatever conception of life a man clings to, yet, until he dies, he has to live. Even if for buddhists life is suffering, even if they long to be delivered from it, as long as they are not yet delivered, they still have to live.[40]

So, the Buddhist monk who spends part of his life in the meditation hall, the citizen of Soviet Union or the revolutionary, cannot escape the fact that they are social beings; to describe the universal rules of social existence is the object of Fung's study. One could say that in his view *no society is totalitarian*: whatever the rules of the game may be, each individual has still to play his own part. The idea that a Marxist regime is evil, that is, totalitarian and contradictory to the spiritual essence of man, seems to be meaningless for Fung; a Marxist society is a *society;* the rules may be Marxist, and strictly imposed, they are only rules. From another point of view, no metaphysical system or spiritual doctrine can be conceived as an overall answer to the problem of life, Sutras, Vinaya, monastic rules, and "a way of living."[41]

(b) The Implications of Continuity

Without attempting to review the interpretation of individual virtues as found in *Hsin Shih-hsün,* we may analyze the main significance of continuity in that sphere. The question may be approached in two ways: on one hand, there is continuity of *content* - the virtues do not change -, on the other hand, that statement is expressed within a *philosophical discourse* which is conceived as a continuation of traditional thinking.

40 *Ibid.,* 16.

41 See *Hsin Li-hsüeh,* 308-309: Buddhist monks or taoist hermits do not "leave" society: they *ch'u chia* 出家 that is to say: "they leave only a type of organization within the society."

(aa) Content: The Virtues Are the Same

In *Hsin Shih-lun,* there is no 'human nature' or 'natural law' which may attenuate the total discontinuation of ethical values; 'human nature' means essentially that man is determined by the type of society he lives in. We may say that 'human nature' functions on the principle of discontinuity in ethical values and on the principle of continuity in the sphere of virtues. According to Fung, 'human nature' is what the holy men have fulfilled; moral cultivation is nothing else but 'becoming' fully human, that is, becoming fully adequate to the status of man as a rational animal. The 'rationality' of the human animal is understood by Fung as a self-conscious sociability, which is not yet completed and has to be consciously developed.[42] This conception, says Fung, is similar to Aristotle's *political animal,* and in fact a comparison between *Hsin Shih-hsün* and the *Nicomachean Ethics* would be very suggestive; in both cases, we would find a similar attempt to come to terms with the fact that moral philosophy is not a deduction of virtues from top down, but an investigation on the significance of culture.

However, this may be interpreted in various ways. In *Hsin Shih-hsün* moral continuity functions as an exorcism against the eventuality of any *tragic contradiction:* there can be no conflict between the pursuit of virtue and society-determined ethical values,[43] and the most striking feature of the book is probably that elimination of any 'Antigone' type of dilemma between the city and 'unwritten laws," or the absence of the Weberian opposition: responsibility/conviction. Fung states very explicitly that the general can fulfill his duties without hatred.[44] Similarly the Marxist class struggle should-and could- be carried out without hatred, - a statement which constitutes one of the few explicit criticism of communism in *Hsin Shih-lun* and *Hsin Shih-hsün.* Fung disapproves the communist propaganda aiming at arousing

42 *Hsin Shih-hsün,* 24-25.
43 *Ibid.,* 27.
44 *Ibid.,* 132-133.

peasant anger against landlords; the comparison he gives is very instructive on his non-conflictual conception of human condition: the child (symbol of the not yet morally accomplished ones) who stumbles over a stone, gets angry with the stone, but the adult simply removes the stone. Class struggle is simply removing stones on the road, there is no reason of hating whomsoever.[45]

In the same way, there is no cornelian debate about whether to join or oppose a revolution still in the making. The pattern here is the change of dynasty in traditional China: the loyal minister may follow the *rule of names (ming* 知 : 'let the minister be a minister, let the prince be a prince') and continue to serve his prince, he may too follow the *rule of realities (shih* 實 as found in Mencius stating that it is not a case of *shih* 弑 , but of *sha* 殺).

This absence of tragic conflict does not mean indifference, or absence of heroism, but moral life implies, first of all, continuity, effort, perseverance. Fung rejects the romantic idea that one may sacrifice one's life easily, in an impulsive gesture, thanks to euphoric circumstances; heroism has to be built up day after day, a lesson well illustrated in Chinese history, and in the western version of Socrates' death.[46] This morality is not synonymous with conformism, nor with lofty indifference in a taoist style; *the principle of no tragic dilemma and the possibility of heroism coexist,* coexistence which may be the core of Fung's moral philosophy. I do not mean that such a coexistence is not found elsewhere, in the West or in China, as a key-point in moral philosophy; I simply want to stress that this seems to be a cornerstone in Fung's philosophical construction. This leads us to the question of continuity of the philosophical discourse.

(bb) The Continuation of Traditional Thinking

The continuity of the way of life cannot be divorced from the

---

45 *Ibid.,* 129-130.
46 *Ibid.,* 29-30.

continuity of philosophical discourse itself. We have already mentioned how Fung introduces himself as a *innovator within tradition,* in the introduction of *Hsin Shih-hsün.* The general principle
of philosophical continuity have been expressed in *Hsin Li-
hsueh:* "from antiquity on, there has been no completely new
philosophy,"[47] "the philosophy of antiquity, the most philosophical part of it (metaphysics) is still philosophy to-day, and
not philosophy of an antecedent age. ...We may have only new
philosophers, and relatively new philosophies."[48]

We may say that philosophical continuity is first a continuity
of *language: jen,i,hsin,...* but it is, too, a *tradition of morality,*
well-rooted throughout Chinese history; even if Sung-Ming philosophy tends to a professionalized conception of moral endeavor,
history shows that virtue was not the apanage of a few scholars.
On the contrary, there has been a typical emphasis on morality
in China; for instance, a distinctive feature of art criticism in
China has been to consider the 'virtues' of the artist as a decisive
criterion. Here, Fung does not go back to some 'Chinese essence':
morality is not the exclusivity of China, but nevertheless there
has been a tradition of, and an emphasis on, morality proper to
China. This tradition survives the disappearance of traditional
ethics; *jen* cannot be erased.

We have indicated that virtues are related to the definition of
man as a rational and political being. But the different virtues
introduced in *Hsin Shih-hsün* are not deduced from the definition of man. They need not be deduced at all; they are already
there, in Chinese tradition. The philosopher may rationalize
them, and deduce them *a-posteriori,* but the main principle is still
continuity.

Those virtues are said to be identically true for Chinese and
foreigners, but they are not words in an *esperanto* of morality;

47 *Hsin Li-hsüeh,* 20.
48 *Ibid.,* 23. In a *Short History of Chinese Philosophy,* pp. 332 sqq., Fung gives
some comments on the difference between the historian of philosophy and the philosopher who is a creator, developing the old into the new.

this way of life is *universally valid* and *100% Chinese,* and this is the significance of philosophical continuity. More precisely, it is not universally true *because* it is fully Chinese, but it is fully Chinese because Chinese tradition has *already* uttered an universally true conception of man; it is not true because the Chinese have said it is so, they said it because it is true. The corollary is, the others have said it, too. In this context, continuity means that the best way for a Chinese philosopher to enunciate an universally true way of life is to use his own linguistic and philosophical tradition. Such a conception of continuity excludes (1) cosmopolitarianism -each tradition having a part of truth- (2) traditionalism -Chinese tradition having the whole truth alone, or the whole truth for Chinese- and (3) occidentalism -China having no truth at all.

(2) and (3) do not require comments. The problem of (1), *cosmopolitarianism,* is more intricate. Levenson has mentioned that even for a philosopher like Fung Yu-lan, the cosmopolitarian way was attractive, and it is true that Fung may envision from time to time a world philosophy, and have uttered statements in this sense. But, that can be said of many philosophers, Chinese or not, and may not obliterate the massive fact that Fung's philosophy is *not* cosmopolitarian. Referring again to Levenson's terminology, we have to say that in Fung the encounter with the West did enrich his language, but did not change it; he may refer to Aristotle or Hegel, but the result is not a westernized Chinese tradition. As to the enrichment of language, an equivocal expression as far as it seems to imply that the original language lacks certain important terms, it would be more exact to say Fung has learned another language, and so can control the use of his own native language in reference to another. The 'newness' is to know better than Chu Hsi how the Chinese tradition was and is universal.

But continuity within the tradition *does not mean imitation.* Fung is a 'new philosopher' and his way of living a 'relatively new philosophy' within Chinese tradition. He is a creator, in such a way that his work is at the same time a reinterpretation of tradition. The way of life expressed in *Hsin Shih-hsün* is not only the way of modern man, it is, too, the way of those in the past. Continuity is not pure repetition, it is *transmission within re-interpretation*. Interior to the notion of continuity is the assumption that our predecessors have not yet exhausted, to the utmost, the fullness of tradition. The challenge is not Kant or Hegel, but Chinese tradition itself which functions as an universe the center of which has still to be discovered. Continuity means somehow that tradition has become our future in a world which is no longer monoculturalist.

The implications of continuity in the philosophy of life may be summarized by a sentence of Fung in his introduction to *Hsin Yüan-jen* or "A New Treatise on the Nature of Man," *"The quotations from ancient philosophers are only a corroboration of my present views: 'The Six Classics are my commentators, I am not the commentators of the Six Classics'."*[49] This is an introductory remark, to apologize for publishing a book without references; it is too a clear allusion to a text in Lu Hsiang-shan: *"If in our study we know the fundamentals, then all the Six Classics are my footnotes"*—a text which is quoted in a post-1949 article on "The Legacy of Chinese Philosophy: the question of continuity."[50] In this text Lu Hsiang-shan is coming to terms with the fact that in the *Lun-yü* many sayings are desperately uninterpretable; in consequence the task of the philosopher is not to add another interpretative footnote, which interprets nothing, but to focus on the fundamentals, on passages which are self-explanatory. We have seen that Fung in his introduction to *Hsin Shih-hsün* adopts a similar attitude towards the

49 *Hsin Yüan-jen*, 1.

50 Lu Hsiang-shan, *Hsiang-shan ch'üan-chi* (The Complete Work of Hsiang-shan), 34, 1. - Translation given by Wing Tsit-chan, *A Source Book...*, 580.

The text is quotated in Fung's article: "Chung-kuo che-hsüeh i-ch'an ti chi-ch'eng wen-t'i" in: *Kuang-ming Jih-pao*, Jan 8, 1957, p. 4. - Article reprinted in: Feng Yu-lan, *Chung-kuo che-hsüeh shih lun-wen ch'u-chi* (A first Collection of Articles on the History of Chinese Philosophy), new ed. 1962. 98-105.

excessive, and sometimes fruitless, Neo-Confucian investigation of written things.

In this context, we may say: *'I am not a commentator of the Six Classics, the Six Classics are my commentators'* means that, as an historian of Chinese philosophy, Fung elucidates *what* the ancient philosophers *did say*, the essential, and that, as a new philosopher, he elucidates what their sayings *mean*. He can do it, because he knows better how the universal truths they have uttered were and are universal; they elaborated their thinking, identifying China and the universe, a given type of society with society as such; knowing now that China is only a part of the universe and Chinese traditional society only one type of social organization, Fung is able to read the authentic significance of the universally true Chinese way of life.

The reference to *Lu Hsiang-shan* indicates too that Fung's system is not necessary *only* a "reconstruction of rationalistic Neo-Confucianism";[51] the idealistic tendency of the School of Mind is not absent. Lu Hsiang-shan was turning away from the Ch'eng-Chu investigation of principles in things and devoted most of his time to moral principles and the interiority of mind. Although Fung develops a realist conception of *li*, nevertheless, finding himself in a world where science is taking over the task of investigating things, he did turn to the inner realm of morality. As a continuator, he recieves the 'realist' label - and *Hsin Shih-lun* is an investigation of things indeed -, but as a philosopher in the XX century, could he avoid focusing on the essential principles of the inner realm? Someone else could have turned to political philosophy, but Fung was not that man.

Final Remarks

We have said that the safest principle of interpretation was to assume that Fung's thought was coherent, or that "his significance at this time lies precisely in the representative nature of his

51 Wing Tsit-chan, *A Source Book...*, 751.

views."[52] We have already answered this question of *contemporaneity* in many aspects; the issues debated in *Hsin Shih-lun* and *Hsin Shih-hsün* are indubitably the problems of contemporary China culminating in the Sino-Japanese conflict. The representativeness of Fung's answers cannot be so easily appreciated; it is not enough to say that he has been widely read.

To my mind, this contemporaneity cannot be elucidated only by drawing up a comparative tableau of similar theses in Fung's system and other elaborated answers. The problem is rather to investigate how this *coexistence of seemingly contradictory answers may function,* how mutually exclusive theses may dissimulate at a given moment in history identical long range concerns or options. For instance, the contemporaneity of Fung with the Chinese communists is not a *minimal common denominator,* but rather the fact that he may envision the possibility of living in a communist Chinese society without denying himself. In one of his earlier 'confessions' in 1950, he describes his attitude during the decisive years 1947-49 in the following terms:

> If the proletarian society was to come, I could subsequently participate, and I would still be myself.[53]

When he writes this confession, Fung qualifies this attitude as 'capitalist,' 'idealist' and 'supraclass,' and we may be suspicious of his sincerity in doing so, but is there any reason to doubt that his attitude in 1947-49 is adequately described? In the light of the writings we have analyzed, I would be inclined to answer, there is no reason, this is quite coherent with the views expressed around 1940. Let us examine this coherence.

In his study of Fung in post-1949 China, Douglas Paal proposes an interpretation of Fung's decision not to leave China:

52 Douglas Paal, "Fung Yu-lan: tradition and scholarship in Communist China" (unpublished seminar paper, Harvard, 1971), 11.

53 Fung Yu-lan, *Wo ts'an-chia le ko-ming* (I have joined the revolution), 1950 (reprint, source unknown). Translation of the quotation given in Paal, 16.

Fung returned to Tsing Hua university in 1949, and chose to
stay in Peking rather than to flee to Taiwan, as the Chinese
Communists swept through China. To my knowledge, he has
never written his reasons for staying, but it is not difficult to
imagine that his concern for the long range history of China
and the ivory tower quality of his life's work, initially left him
relatively indifferent to the change in government. He sat
through the 'change of the dynasty and the replacement of the
emperor'.[54]

According to Paal's further comments, this *'ivory tower'* is not
only the unconcern of the scholar for political games, it is, too,
the fact that Fung may have considered himself already as an
essential piece on the Chinese chessboard; after all, he stood for
the history of Chinese philosophy... For all its subjectiveness, this
interpretation may be true, but Chinese philosophy may have
been transferred to Taipei, together with the T'ang paintings of
the National Museum. To identify oneself with China does not
suppress the necessity of a crucial choise between the two camps
who both claimed to be China. We have to search for a more
satisfactory understanding of the ivory tower attitude.

Wing Tsit-chan has approached the problem in a different way,
looking for what I have called a "common denominator." He
writes:

Fung's attraction of Marxism is by no means an unlikely
possibility. After all, as early as 1939, he wrote his *Hsin Shih-
lun* from the point of view of a materialistic interpretation of
history.[55]

This type of statement seems to me quite vague. I do not find a
"materialistic interpretation of history" in Fung. His thesis that a

54 Paal, 12.
55 Wing Tsit-chan, *A Source Book...*, 754.

shift to a mechanized type of society determines a new social and value system can be termed "economic determinism," but not a "materialistic interpretation of history," an expression which conveys the idea that all cultural and spiritual manifestations are levelled down. Moreover, even if one assumes only that Fung's view of the transformation of societies *may tend* to a "materialistic interpretation," this tendency is not an attraction to Marxism, or at least to the kind of Marxism advocated by the Chinese communists. The "materialistic" tendency in Fung could be one towards a sort of *mechanist evolutionism* of societies, whereas the communist outlook was articulated in terms of creating a new society. This difference is very explicitly stated in a notation about the theory of *tu-hua* 獨化 (self-transformation of things) in the *"Hsiang-Kuo* Commentary on the Chuang-tzu":

Everything that exists in the universe needs the universe as a whole as a necessary condition for its existence, yet its existence is not produced by any other particular thing. When certain conditions or circumstances are present, certain things are necessarily produced. But this does not mean that they are produced by any single Creator or by any individual. In other words, things are produced by conditions in general, and not by any other specific thing in particular. Socialism for instance is a product of certain general economic conditions, and was not manufactured by Marx or Engels, still less by the former's *Communist Manifesto*. In this sense we can say that everything produces itself and is not produced by others.[56]

This statement indicates the distance between Fung's economic interpretation of history and Marxist conception of revolution. We have already mentioned two other criticisms of communism by Fung: the one about communist propaganda aiming at arousing peasant anger and hatred against landlords, the other about the Marxist claim of an 'international socialist

56 Fung Yu-lan, *A Short History...*, 222.

world' where there will be harmony between nations. Both criticisms manifest the above mentioned 'evolutionist' conception of social change. In Fung's view, class struggle is not the agent of history, but only the historical epiphenomenon of a natural process of evolution; as such it is not immoral, but it is inessential and cannot define the fundamentals of a new morality.[57] In the same way, the rules of the international game cannot be modified by the virtues of proletarian dictatorship; only a supranatural instance may bring ethics into the sphere of international relations; whether nations are proletarian or not is inessential.

In this context, we may understand Fung's willingness to 'participate' in an already established 'proletarian society:' 1. this proletarian society would be socialist, that is, it would belong to the type of social organization Fung considers the most *appropriate* for a mechanized and industrialized society. 2. all the Marxist-Leninist elements which identify this socialist society as a proletarian one, and make all the difference from the Marxists' point of view, are inessential and make no difference in Fung's view. For him, the final victory of communism in China *would not demonstrate* the 'scientific value' of Marxist Scriptures; it would simply prove that objective conditions were there for the establishment of any type of socialist system in China. In other terms, Fung's conceptions would enable him to praise and explain the establishment of Chinese communist society for reasons which are quite heretical for a communist. 3. the proletarian society is only a socialist system, and *not a promethean process* through which a new type of man comes into existence; the basic vocation of man remains unchanged: to help the society function through the nourishment of the moral self, or 'kingness without, sageliness within.' The participation of Fung would not be a com-

57 However, one may keep in mind that class-struggle in *Das Kapital* is a function of the "mode of production," and that "economic determinism" is the basic principle of interpretation in Marx. In this sense Fung could stand closer to Marx himself than to many disciples of the latter.

promise with his own principles; when he wrote that he would still remain himself, he meant exactly what he was saying. This is not only an adroit way of avoiding any conflict between the inner and the outer realm, but once again a consequence of the same principle: the proletarian society cannot be preserved only by its own excellence or by the sacramental power of the dictatorship of the proletariat; as any society, it requires the moral achievements of each individual, a commitment which grows roots in the inner realm of morality. In this sense, Fung's participation would not be pure 'interventionism' nor face-about, but neither would it be the orthodox commitment to a moral ideal defined by the supernatural essence of the proletarian society. It would be a commitment, through society, to the inner realm.

It would be tempting to dismiss this whole analysis on the basis that this subtle adjustment has been blown up in Fung's subsequent history under the communist regime; his 'confessions,' his references to the orthodox jargon would demonstrate the irrealism of his conceptions - or, at least, an unstable compromise had to be made between his own tenacity and the desire of those in power to use his prestige to their own ends. The only question, however is to know whether 'compromise' is the only interpretation. Communist Chinese's ideology has been in flux; over a period of fifty years, we have been told that 'objective conditions' could not yet allow the dictatorship of the proletariat to display its virtues, that class affiliation was not necessarily the ultimate criterion, that proletarian societies could become imperialist, and finally that communist societies could not be preserved without the moral cultivation of individuals.

I do not mean that Fung may become a best-seller in communist China, but only that he deals with problems which will be with Chinese leaders for a long time.

Fung's philosophy is a systematic attempt to draw the lines of watershed between continuity and discontinuity, social and value system and the inner realm of morality, objective necessity of social change and the interior achievements of the individual. It is essential to Chinese communism to provide its own answer and draw up its own map. The solution cannot be found only in the scriptures of Marxism-Leninism, and they have been searching for a Chinese answer. Their fluctuations and uncertainties in doing so may suggest that Fung's own system is not yet irrelevant to the realities of proletarian society in China.

A SELECT BIBLIOGRAPHY

Boorman, Howard L., and Howard, Richard C., *Bibliographical Dictionary of Republican China*. New York: Columbia University Press, 1967-1971.

Chan, Wing-tsit, *A Source Book in Chinese Philosophy*. Princeton, New Jersey: Princeton University Press, 1963.

———, *Chinese Philosophy, 1949-1963 - An Annotated Bibliography of Mainland China Publications*. Honolulu: East-West Center Press, 1967.

Chu, Tzu-sung 主 于 崇 , "P'i-p'ing Feng Yu-lan hsien-sheng Kuo-ch'ü ti che-hsüeh szu-hsiang," 批 評 馮 友 三 先 生 過 去 的 哲 學 思 想 (Criticism of Mr. Fung Yu-lan's Philosophical Thinking in the Past), *Pei-ching ta-hsüeh hsüeh-pao (Journal of Peking University)*, 1955-1956, pp. 139-156.

Fung Yu-lan 馮 友 三 , *Chung-kuo che-hsüeh shih*, 中 國 哲 學 史 (History of Chinese Philosophy). 2 vols. Kow-loon, Hong Kong: Pai-ling Publishers, 1931-1934.

———, *History of Chinese Philosophy*. Tr. by Derk Bodde. Princeton, New Jersey: Princeton University Press, 1952-1953.

———, "Hsin Li-hsüeh ti yüan-hsing," 新 理 學 的 原 形 (The True Condition of Neo-Confucianism), *Che-hsüeh Yan-chiou 哲學研究 (Philosophical Research)*, I (1959), pp. 37-49.

Levenson, Joseph R., *Confucian China and Its Modern Fate*. 3 vols. Berkeley: University of California Press, 1958-1965.

CHAPTER VI

BUDDHIST APPROACH TO THE PROBLEM OF GOD
Charles Wei-hsun Fu *

Of all the major religions in the world Buddhism has perhaps suffered most from various kinds of misunderstanding or misinterpretation. This is particularly true when Buddhism *as a whole* is presented in connection with the notion of God or (in a more philosophical sense) the Absolute. As Professor Kenneth Inada rightly observes, "In the history of Buddhism as a religious force it has run the whole gamut of religious labels from monotheism, polytheism, and pantheism to agnoticism and atheism."[1] Not only are non-Buddhists often confused by different religious interpretations of Buddhism apparently contradictory to one another, but Buddhists themselves have never come to a universal agreement on where exactly their own tradition stands on the problem of God, the Absolute, the Ultimate Reality, whatever terminology one employs to describe this source. In this paper I shall discuss first the pragmatic and philosophical nature of the Buddhist religion as the teaching of the Middle Way *(madhyamā-pratipad)*, which makes no *ontic* commitment to anything whatsoever. I shall then introduce some religious interpretations given by Rahula, von Glasenapp, Getty, and Reichelt, and point out the reasons why Rahula's atheistic interpretation of Buddhism is not in accord with the principle of the Middle Way, as well as the reasons why all "theological" talks in Mahāyāna Buddhism are to

*Professor of Ethics and Eastern Philosophy at Temple University, Philadelphia, Pennsylvania, U.S.A.

1   Kenneth Inada, "Some Basic Misconceptions of Buddhism," *International Philosophical Quarterly*, Vol. IX, No. 1 (March, 1969), p. 111.

be considered pedagogical and symbolic. In this connection, Mahāyāna doctrines of (twofold) truth as skillful, which means *Trikāya*, Buddha-nature, as well as the philosophy of emptiness, will be philosophically clarified in the light of the principle of the Middle Way. Throughout the paper the central line of reasoning is based upon a philosophical understanding of the real meaning of the Middle Way, which must steer between theism ("God exists") and atheism ("God does not exist") from the highest standpoint of (Mahāyāna) Buddhism.

Buddhism can be characterized as essentially a pragmatic system of philosophical religion. As the historical Buddha's own religious experiences testify, Buddhism's starting point is a deep and sympathetic understanding of human suffering *(duḥkha)* from old age, sickness, death, etc., and Buddhism seeks very seriously for practical wisdom as a religious remedy for the total emancipation *(nirvāṇa)* from the ocean of existential imperfection *(saṁsāra)*. Since Buddhism is uniquely pragmatic, it does not engage itself in any futile or useless word-play *(hsi-lun)*, so to speak, with respect to purely metaphysical questions which are unanswerable *(sthāpaniya)*, inexplicable *(avyākṛta)*, and/or irrelevant to man's ultimate concern for the cessation *(nirodha)* of suffering. Speculative solutions of these questions are without sufficient evidence, and lead men only to different partial views likened to the conflicting one-sided accounts of an elephant given by a group of blind persons touching its different parts.[2] From the Buddhist viewpoint, the only urgent religious problem is how to stop suffering. As the Buddha declares:

I have explained *dukkha,* the arising of *dukkha,* the cessation of *dukkha,* and the way leading to the cessation of *dukkha.* Why...have I explained them? Because it is useful, is funda-

2 See Rhys Davids, *Dialogues of Buddha* (Pali Text Society), I, pp. 187-188; *Udana,* VI, 4. See also Christmas Humphreys, ed., *The Wisdom of Buddhism* (New York: Harper & Row, 1970), pp. 81-83.

mentally connected with the spiritual holy life, is conductive to aversion, detachment, cessation, tranquility, deep penetration, full realization, Nirvāṇa.[3]

It is important to add, however, that Buddhist religion is not only pragmatic, but is also philosophical in the sense that it fabricates no unexamined presuppositions which go beyond everyday human experience.[4] The Four Noble Truths as the historical Buddha announced above is established as the philosophical consequence of his phenomenological analysis of man's existential encounter with the external world, other men, and himself in particular, in the holistic context of relational origination *(pratitya-samutpāda).* Relying upon the principle of seeing things-as-they-are *(yathābhūta-darsana)* as the sole philosophical searchlight, the historical Buddha discovers that man's existential predicaments are in the final analysis conditioned by their own desire or "thirst" *(tṛṣṇā),* which has its roots in dark ignorance *(avidyā)* about the as-is-ness (non-permanence and non-substantiality) of the world and man. Philosophically speaking, to see things-as-they-are in Buddhism is to steer serenely and wisely to the middle path between all pairs of perverted views *(viparyāsa).* For example, the middle path in Buddhist practices, with reference to *Nirvāṇa,* is taken between extreme hedonism and extreme asceticism; the middle path in man's *karma* formation and *samsaric* state is between extreme determinism ("No one is responsible for his own action") and extreme indeterminism ("Every person is totally responsible for his own action"); the middle path in the mind-body relationship steers between extreme materialism ("Mind and body are identical") and extreme dualism ("Mind is different from body"); the middle path con-

---

3 Walpola Rahula, *What the Buddha Taught* (New York: Grove Press, 1962), p. 15. See also Henry Warren, *Buddhism in Translations* (New York: Atheneum, 1962), p. 122.

4 This point will become clearer in our subsequent discussion of the Mahāyāna conception of twofold truth.

cerning the ontological nature of all things lies in the acceptance of neither extreme realism ("Everything exists") nor extreme nihilism ("Nothing exists"); and the middle path concerning the reality of self or ego *(atman)* is expressed as the *anātmavāda* (theory of non-substantiality) standing between eternalist theory ("There is a self") and annihilationist theory ("There is no self").[5]

If the Buddhist principle of the Middle Way is strictly applied to the problem of God or the Absolute, the only possible conclusion one can draw is that Buddhism must naturally lie midway between theism and atheism. If the Buddhists themselves truly abide by the principle of the Middle Way, they must consistently avoid any propositional assertion about the existence or non-existence of God or the Absolute. According to *Cūla-Mālunkya-sutta* and other early Buddhist texts, the Buddha is said to keep *aryan* silence to the fourfold question regarding the ontic status of the *Tathagata* ("Thus-Come")--one of the Buddha's honorific titles--after his death.[6] This is one typical case of the application of the Buddhist logic of fourfold negation indicating the Buddha's non-committal attitude towards any *ontic* assertion about anything whatsoever. From the Buddhist point of view, especially Mahāyāna, it is philosophically unjustifiable to hypostatize a particular thing *t*--whatever it may be--in total isolation from the holistic context of the relational origination of all things in the world metaphorically expressed as Indra's Net, and then assert *t* to be existent or non-existent. The problem of (the existence of) God or the Absolute is simply a part of the whole ontic problem of all things. That is to say, according to Buddhist Middle Way, the problem of the existence of God or the Absolute is "null and void." It is in this sense that we cannot but agree with Professor Inada's following observation:

5 See K.N. Jayatilleke, *Early Buddhist Theory of Knowledge* (London: Allen & Unwin, 1963), pp. 359-360.
6 See Henry Warren, *op. cit.*, p. 117.

It should be remembered that the denial of atheism does not bring forth theism just as the denial of theism does not bring forth atheism. These are not mutually identifiable or mutually refutable concepts; and thanks to this, Buddhism is neither of the two....it has been argued that Buddhism is not monotheistic, atheistic, polytheistic, pantheistic, or agnostic. Then, what is it? To add another "ism" to the list will not do. We have no alternative but to keep the challenge open and to continue to call it Buddhism.[7]

In spite of the above clarification of the Buddhist approach to the problem of God, we cannot deny the fact that Theravāda (Hinayāna) Buddhists tend to regard their own tradition as an atheistic religion, whereas "theological" talks in terms of monotheism, polytheism, or pantheism have been prevalent among common, if not philosophical, Mahāyāna Buddhists. For example, Professor Walpola Rahula, who represents the best philosophical position of Theravāda Buddhism, strongly upholds the atheistic thesis that Buddhism from the beginning has never granted any notion of God. He even gives in a critical manner a psychological explanation about the origin of the notion of God, within or without, and the origin of the notion of an immortal soul, i.e., that man has created God out of self-protection and conceived the idea of an immortal Soul (Atman) out of self-preservation. Man clings to these notions deeply and fanatically, because he needs in his ignorance, weakness, and desire these two notions to console himself. And he concludes, "According to Buddhism, our ideas of God and Soul are false and empty."[8] To some extent Rahula's atheistic interpretation of Buddhism seems to be more justifiable than the theistic one, since it is very true that Buddhism never assumes the existence of a creator-deity or a ruler of the world, the world which is simply accepted as it is without any ultimate meaning. And it is also true that a (Hina-

---

7 K. Inada, *op. cit.*, p. 115.
8 W. Rahula, *op. cit.*, p. 52.

yāna) Buddhist phenomenological analysis of the existential factors of the world and man in terms of 5 aggregates (skandha), 12 bases (āyatana), or 18 realms (dhātu), etc., does not show any sign of positing an ultimate reality in the supernatural sense. Nonetheless, the atheistic position held by Theravāda Buddhists, as Rahula presented above, is not in perfect accord with the genuine spirit of the Middle Way, which must consistently dissolve the duality of theism and atheism. For, as we have clarified, the principle of the Middle Way leaves no room for any Buddhist speculation on or commitment to the existence or non-existence of God or Atman. That Buddhism does not assume the existence of God or the Absolute is logically very different from a flat *denial* of any divine existence. The latter violates the principle of the Middle Way, while the former only puts aside the notion of God as irrelevant to the Buddhist solution of *samsaric* problems.

The atheistic position of Theravāda Buddhism as Rahula has presented is somewhat softened in Mahāyāna Buddhism, especially in the Tantric tradition, Pure Land Buddhism, as well as in some popular sects mixed up with local animistic beliefs. In a book entitled *Buddhism: A Non-theistic Religion,* Professor Helmuth von Glasenapp notes--despite his careful analysis that Buddhism assumes neither a god (as creator-deity or world-ruler) nor a personal, immortal soul--that there are a number of Buddhist texts which "confirm unmistakably and authoritatively that since the oldest times Buddhists believed in the existence of gods *(deva),*" and that "both ancient authors and modern travellers almost always describe Buddha as a god."[9] If this account is accepted as true, then Buddhism, at least Mahāyāna Buddhism, must be considered "theistic" in some sense. By giving such a "theistic" report, however, von Glasenapp's treatment of the whole subject leaves the readers with more puzzlement or confusion, for no reasonable and satisfactory explanation is given as to

9 H. von Glasenapp, *Buddhism: A Non-theistic Religion,* trans. by I. Schloegl (New York: George Braziller, 1966), p. 1 and p. 64.

why and how there is no contradiction involved in both non-theistic and theistic versions of (Mahāyāna) Buddhism.

We find a stronger emphasis on the theistic aspect of Mahāyāna (Northern) Buddhism in Alice Getty's work *The Gods of Northern Buddhism,* in which she tells of some religious innovations the Mahāyāna adds to the old faith of primitive and Hinayāna Buddhism, such as the recognition of a supreme God (Adi-Buddha), the worship of the divinities, the heavenly Bodhisattvas, the Mānushi Buddhas who are said to be "inhabitants of earth and incarnations in flesh and bone of the *Dhyāni-Buddhas* or Buddhas of contemplation who dwell in heaven."[10] She then describes very extensively and specifically the nature and role of every divinity in the huge, dazzling pantheon of Mahāyāna Buddhism. Here again, no philosophical clarification is made concerning the symbolic meaning of Mahāyāna divinities, as well as philosophical clarification of why and how "theological" talk is justifiable within the Mahāyāna context.

There is one more interesting account of the polytheistic character of popular Mahāyānism in Karl Ludvig Reichelt's *Truth and Tradition in Chinese Buddhism,* in which the Scandinavian missionary gives a personal (Christian) criticism of the animistic belief and practice of Mahāyāna Buddhists in China, thus causing another kind of misimpression that Mahāyāna Buddhism is rather a perplexing mixture of religious belief and animistic superstition. He says:

It is only with the rise of Mahāyāna that there grew up the idea of representing the Buddhas in sculpture or painting, and it was also in Mahāyāna that the present large and motley collection of gods was developed. This characteristic has always been Mahāyāna's weakness, since it is polytheism which has in various ways drawn this doctrinal system, other-

---

10 A. Getty, *The Gods of Northern Buddhism* (Tokyo: Charles E. Tuttle, 1962), *Introduction,* xxviii-xxix.

wise on so high a plane, into the sombre shadows of animism.[11]

In the following sections we shall give a philosophical clairfication of the one-sidedness of Theravāda atheistic position, as well as of the pragmatic nature of Mahāyāna "theological" talks by way of a careful examination of Mahāyāna doctrines of emptiness, twofold truth, *Buddhakāya* (Body of the Buddha), Buddha-nature, and other notions related to the problem of God or the Absolute. Any possible misunderstanding about either "theistic" or "atheistic" versions of Buddhism as shown in the above examples can hopefully be removed through our clarification of the subject matter in the light of the Middle Way.

The atheistic thesis maintained by Theravāda Buddhists is in a deeper sense a corollary of their theory of the Absolute Truth (paramārtha-satya) that "there is nothing absolute in the world, that everything is relative, conditioned and impermanent, and that there is no unchanging, everlasting, absolute substance."[12] And the realization of this Absolute Truth in terms of seeing things-as-they-are without any illusion or ignorance is nothing but *Nirvāṇa*. The Pāli canon defines *"Nirvāṇa"* as the complete and utter dissolution of the three unwholesome roots of greed, hate, and delusion. *Nirvāṇa* is also expressed as the extinction of craving "thirst," the cessation of suffering, emancipation, the cessation of becoming, emptiness and deathlessness, etc.[13] Undeniably, the Hinayāna "negative" conception of *Nirvāṇa* is such that it is posited in contra-distinction to *saṁsāra* (the cycle of life-and-death). Based on their understanding of the duality of *Nirvāṇa* and *saṁsāra* as well as on the Buddhist conception of the

11 K.L. Reichelt, *Truth and Tradition in Chinese Buddhism* (New York: Paragon, 1968), p. 171.

12 W. Rahula, *op. cit.*, p. 39.

13 For a detailed discussion of various "attributes or names" of Nirvāṇa see Edward Conze, *Buddhist Thought in India* (London: Allen & Unwin, 1962), pp. 69-79.

non-substantiality of personal entity *(pudgalanairātmya)*, the scholastic *Abhidharma* philosophers classify all *dharmas* experimental (factors of existence) under two primary categories, *saṁskṛta* (compounded or conditioned states) and *asaṁskṛta* uncompounded or unconditioned states). The three *dharmas* of space, extinction due to lack of a productive cause, and *Nirvāṇa* (extinction through intellectual power) are placed in the category of *asaṁskṛta-dharma,* while the remaining *dharmas*, 72 in number, are placed in *saṁskṛta-dharma.*[14] Since *Nirvāṇa* is no more than the realization of the Absolute Truth about the "ultimate realities" of the world and man in terms of *saṁskṛta-dharma*, it cannot be talked about further.

In making such a dualistic distinction between *Nirvāṇa* and *saṁsāra* (or between *asaṁskṛta* and *saṁskṛta)*, the *Abhidharma* philosophers do not seem to realize that they are creating a Hinayāna ontic dilemma which is extremely difficult to resolve. Since *saṁskṛta-dharmas* that are held (or at least experienced) to be the "ultimate constituents" of the *saṁsaric* world-systems are defined as "actual existing realities," *Nirvāṇa* can only be described negatively as something non-existent, that is, the total cessation of *saṁsaric* provess or the total extinction of the phenomenal. In other words, *Nirvāṇa* and *saṁsāra* cannot be said to co-exist ontically: if *Nirvāṇa* is, then *saṁsāra* is-not, and vice-versa. But the *Abhidharma* philosophers have already dichotomized Reality into *asaṁskṛta* (which includes *Nirvāṇa*) and *saṁskṛta* (which ultimately constitutes *saṁsāra)*, and this dichotomization makes *Nirvāṇa* and *saṁsāra* ontologically interdependent. That is to say, if *saṁsāra* is ontic-ontologically extinguished, *Nirvāṇa* will have to be forsaken altogether. But what is so puzzling or confusing to us is that *Hinayāna* philosophers continue to assert (in Rahula's words again) that *"Nirvāṇa"* is not the result of anything....*Nirvāṇa* is neither cause nor effect. It is

14 For a complete chart of 75 *dharmas* see Junjiro Takakusu, *The Essentials of Buddhist Philosophy,* 3rd ed. (Honolulu: Office Appliance Co., 1956), p. 72a.

beyond cause and effect. Truth is not a result nor an effect. *Truth Is. Nirvana Is.*[15] Rahula goes on to say that *"Nirvāṇa* is the Ultimate Truth,"[16] and this makes both *Nirvāṇa* and Truth identical in reference ("is") and meaning. In making such a dilemmatic assertion about the "is" of *Nirvāṇa/Truth,* Rahula and almost all Hinayāna philosophers somehow deviate in their position from the original Middle Way, based on which the logic of fourfold negation must be employed to call into question all kinds of ontic commitment as a result of dualistic conceptualization.

Rahula also says, as we have already learned, that *Nirvāṇa* is the *realization* of the Absolute Truth. Does this help at all to resolve the Hinayāna ontic dilemma? Unlikely. The real difficulty here is that Hinayāna philosophers in general fail to understand the real meaning of the parable of the raft which exemplifies the pragmatic nature of Buddhist *Dharma* (Truth).[17] To illustrate this point we may ask a hypothetical question: Suppose that *Nirvāṇa* has been universally attained by all of us, or in Rahula's words, that we have realized the Absolute Truth (that "everything is relative, conditioned and impermanent," etc.), then it would still make sense to assert the "is" of this very Absolute Truth or *Nirvāṇa?* Wouldn't it be paradoxically true that if all sentient beings were from the beginning perfectly enlightened the problem of the Absolute Truth or *Nirvāṇa* (as understood by Hinayāna philosophers) could not arise at all? *Hinayāna* philosophers traditionally accept the Four Noble Truths announced by the historical Buddha as the Absolute Truth in the literal sense, but the First Noble Truth, for example, that "Life is suffering (or existentially imperfect)" can no longer be the Absolute Truth *if Nirvāṇa* is realized. By the same token, if and when *Nirvāṇa* is realized the Third Noble Truth about *Nirvāṇa*

15 W. Rahula, *op. cit.,* p. 40.
16 *Ibid.*
17 For this parable see *Ibid.,* pp. 11-12. See also Bhikshu Sangharakshita, *A Survey of Buddhism* (Bangalore: The Indian Institute of World Culture, 1957), pp. 210-211.

itself or *nirodha* (cessation of suffering) will turn out to be neither truth nor no-truth. In short, the realization of the Absolute Truth paradoxically cancels the legitimacy of the very question about the "is" of the Absolute Truth.

Thus, *Nirvāṇa* in the ontic sense *("Nirvāṇa is")* involves an unresolvable Hinayāna ontic dilemma, while *Nirvāṇa* in the sense of (personal, subjective) realization of Truth leads to a paradoxical cancellation of *Nirvāṇa* and Truth altogether. But the latter at least suggests to us a possibility of taking a new point of departure: If *Nirvāṇa* is not the realization of the so-called Absolute Truth (as understood by Hinayāna philosophers), it has to be the realization of the ontological non-differentiatability of *Nirvāṇa* itself and *samsāra* or of absolute truth and conventional truth. This is exactly where Hinayāna dualism ends and the Mahāyāna philosophy of emptiness *(sūnyavāta)* begins.[18]

18 In his insightful re-interpretation of the meaning of *dharma* (as factors of experience) in the *Abhidharma* philosophy, Professor K. Inada contends that the Traditional rendering of *dharma* as "elements of being" (Warren) or "elements of existence" (Warren, Th. Stcherbatsky) is based on the misleading interpretation of the *dharma* theory as a kind of pluralistic atomism. Then he says: "The *dharmas* do not have any a prior status. Rather, it is to indicate the existential nature of so-called 'elements' *(dharmas)* in the matrix of relatedness...the *dharmas* give a pluralistically factored nature or conception to experience and never the other way round, i.e., that they, the *dharmas,* underline experience in terms of an interplay or an aggregated construction out of them." See Inada, *Nāgārjuna* (Tokyo: Hokuseido Press, 1970), p. 9. Inada's re-interpretation (or re-discovery) of the original meaning of *dharma* in the existentio-experiental sense seems to be more justifiable than (e.g.) Stcherbatsky's, for it does among other reasons help to clarify the ideological continuity from the *Abhidharma* philosophy to the philosophy of eight-consciousnesses (Yogācāra-vijñānavāda). While I take side with Inada's thesis, I should add that my criticism of Hinayāna dualism in terms of the ontic dilema can still stand, regardless of whether *dharmas* are "actual existent realities" (Stcherbatsky, Sangharakshita, *et al.*) or "factors of experience" (Inada). The real point here is that there is a dualistic conceptualization of *Nirvāṇa/samsāra* or *asamskṛta/samskṛta* in the *Abhidharma* philosophy. My re-rendering of of *dharma* as "experiential factors of existence" is in a sense a synthesis of the above two interpretations by putting more emphasis on Inada's. In this connection, the word "ontic" used in this paper can be understood in either the sense of (1) really "ontic" or (2) conceptually "ontic."

According to the philosophy of emptiness, which is the central philosophy of Mahāyāna Buddhism, the Hinayāna teaching of the non-substantiality of all things in terms of *dharma*-analysis cannot be the final answer to the question of the Absolute Reality or Truth. Mahāyāna philosophers of emptiness first point out, by following the original spirit of the Middle Way, that all kinds of *dharma* Hinayāna philosophers have constructed under the two major categories of *saṁskṛta* and *asaṁskṛta,* such as 5 aggregates, 12 bases, 18 realms--all with their sub-divisions--are nonetheless unreal from the higher point of view, for all these *dharmas* are ultimately devoid *(sūnya)* of their self-nature or "own-being" *(svabhāva).* Thus, *Nirvāṇa* and *saṁsāra, asaṁskṛta* and *saṁskṛta,* absolute truth and conventional truth, or any such dualistic pairs are now logic-ontologically exposed as universally empty and non-differentiatable. But universal emptiness or sameness of all *dharmas* (sarvadharmasamatā) does not therefore establish the conclusion that emptiness (sūnyatā) itself constitutes a special kind of *dharma* as against all other *dharmas* devoid of self-nature, for the positing of emptiness as a *dharma* would be tantamount to committing a new ontic dilemma. In other words, emptiness is itself ultimately empty or devoid of its "own-being" and should never be conceived as a transcendental reality, i.e., "Nothingness" hypostatized, ontic-ontologically separated from all *dharmas.* Emptiness is, as Nāgārjuna says, "a provisional name for the mutuality (of being), and, indeed, is the middle path."[19]

What then would be the Absolute? The real key to the answer lies in the Mahāyāna conception of truth as a skillful means or pedagogical device *(upāya-kausalya).* We have already seen that Theravāda Buddhists literally accept the Four Noble Truths as the Absolute Truth; these are now to be considered Mahayanistically no more than a higher kind of conventional truth. This would seem to make (the philosophy of) emptiness or suchness *(tathatā)* the Absolute Truth of Mahāyāna Buddhism. Emptiness or suchness, however, cannot function as the Absolute because

19 K. Inada, *Ibid.,* p. 148.

it is devoid of self-nature. Emptiness, which is merely a provisional name (prajnāpti), is invoked only when all *dharmas*--whatever they may be--are mistaken for ultimate reality. Once this ignorance is removed, the so-called "emptiness" disappears altogether. There is thus a Mahāyāna middle path steering between emptiness and all *dharmas,* or between the so-called "Absolute Truth" and all kinds of conventional truth. It is for the sake of exposing the conventional nature of (e.g.) the Four Noble Truths that the Mahāyāna philosophy of emptiness is skillfully constructed to function as the "Absolute Truth/Reality" only in the provisional and pedagogical sense. As the greatest Chinese Mādhyamika monk Chi-tsang says, "The refutation of false views is itself the correct view."[20] By the same token, it is only because the non-enlightened worldlings are said to be ignorant about the true nature (suchness) of all things that (Mahāyāna) transcendental wisdom (prajnā) is called for; if the worldlings' ignorance (avidyā) is destroyed, the so-called "transcendental wisdom" will have to be denied of its "own-being". Here again, the dualistic distinction between ignorance and wisdom must break down in accordance with the principle of the Middle Way.

Thus, the dichotomy of *Nirvāṇa/saṁsāra, prajnā/avidyā, asaṁskṛta/saṁskṛta, paramārtha-satya/saṁvṛti-satya,* or the like, can be said, in the light of the Mahāyāna re-discovery or re-orientation of the Middle Way, to be a matter of mental construction by the non-enlightened. The so-called Absolute in Mahāyāna philosophy is then "nothing acquirable" (apraptavya-sūnyatā); it is the emptiness of emptiness (sūnyatā-sūnyatā) or absolute emptiness. If we still want to use philosophical speech to "define" it, it can be at best expressed as what is ontologically non-differentiable, though epistemologically differentiated by the non-enlightened. It is ontologically non-differentiable in the sense that, to apply the logic of fourfold negation, it cannot be said to (1) exist, (2) non-exist, (3) both exist and not-exist,

(4) neither exist nor not-exist. The Absolute (emptiness) is so-called provisionally and skillfully for the sake of refuting any particular theory which makes an attempt at dualistic concept-ualization of anything whatsoever to be real or non-real. Indeed, the Absolute in Mahāyāna Buddhism is none other than the Middle Way, as is typically expressed in the Arya-kāsyapa-parivarta-nāma-mahayanasutra:

> To see things-as-they-are is to see color as neither permanent nor non-permanent, and feeling, perception, mental formation, consciousness as neither permanent nor non-permanent....This is called the Middle Way of Seeing things-as-they-really-are.... Why? Because both "permanent" and "non-permanent" are onesided....Both "self" and "non-self" are one-sided....Both "being" and "non-being" are one-sided....Wisdom (non-ignor-ance) and ignorance are one-sided....Wisdom (non-ignorance) and ignorance are non-dual and non-differentiated, the realiza-tion of which is called the Middle Way of seeing all *dharmas* as they really are. Also, *karma*-formation and no-*karma*-formation....desire and extinction of desire, clinging and ex-tinction of clinging, becoming and extinction of becoming, rebirth and extinction of rebirth, old age and sickness and extinction of both old age and sickness: these are all non-dual and non-differentiated, the realization of which is called the Middle Way of seeing all *dharmas* as they really are.[21]

We may now ask: Since the Absolute (emptiness) is what is ontologically non-differentiatable and epistemologically non-conceptualizable, on what ground and for what purpose is the dualistic distinction between absolute truth and conventional truth, etc., still preserved in the Mahāyāna tradition? And in general, why and how is the Buddhist Dharma as such considered no more than a skillful, pedagogical device?

First, it should be noted that Mahāyāna conception of truth as

21 *Taishō Shinshū Daizōkyō*, Vol. 11, 633-634. (My translation).

a skillful means is not totally new, but is rather a re-discovery of the original meaning of the historical Buddha's parable of the raft and the parable of the arrow. Mahāyāna philosophers try to make explicit what is implied in these two famous parables: the Buddhist *Dharma* must be pedagogical and provisional in the sense that it is, like the raft, used for crossing over to the "other-shore" *(nirvāṇa)* and should be left behind after the task is accomplished; it is also pragmatic in the sense that it is, like a medicine used to heal a man wounded by a poisoned arrow, a religious remedy for the non-enlightened but is not to be grasped or got hold of as a purely objective truth set up in a conceptuo-propositional framework. The Mahayanistic distinction between absolute truth and conventional truth, etc., can only be provisional, pedagogical, and pragmatic; it can be neither real nor non-real.

Second, the essential point here with respect to the Buddhist *Dharma* as skillful means and to the dualistic distinction between absolute truth and conventional truth, etc., is that, from a Mahāyāna point of view, there is always an inseparable relation between (1) states of mind, (2) levels of truth, and (3) degrees of reality. All degrees of reality described by Buddhists presuppose the respective points of view taken in accordance with the respective higher or lower states of mind.[22] Of course, the dualistic distinction in question cannot be said to exist in any sense *sub specie aeternitatis,* for, if and when universal and perfect enlightenment is attained by all of us, there will be no dual mind engaged in the conceptual dichotomization of *Nirvāṇa/saṁsāra,* etc. It is however a matter of worldly fact that most of us who are non-enlightened do look at the world and man *sub specie temporis* from different, particular points of view in accordance with different dispositions or mental states. Hence men's construction of different levels of conventional truth. Fully recognizing this worldly fact, Mahāyāna philosophers have to treat all

---

22 See my article "Morality or Beyond: The Neo-Confucian Confrontation with Mahāyāna Buddhism," in *Philosophy East and West* (January, 1973), Section III.

kinds of Buddhist truth as pedagogically useful in satisfying all
the spiritual needs of different people yet to be enlightened.
Until universal emancipation is attained by all of us, the very
distinction between absolute truth and conventional truth, etc.,
will function properly as a skillful device. According to the
Dasabhūmikasūtra, all Bodhisattvas who aspire to attain Buddhahood by means of saving compassionately all *karma*-stricken
worldlings are required to practice assiduously, among others,
upāyakausalya-pāramitā (perfect virtue of skillful means) in order
to carry out the supreme task of universal emancipation. But
they must keep in mind, during the course of their practicing
upāyakausalya-pāramitā, that all different kinds and levels of
Buddhist *Dharma* they have mastered and skillfully used to
enlighten the worldlings should be completely forsaken once
their supreme task is accomplished. There is thus a famous paradoxical expression in the *Diamond Sūtra:*

> ...Someone who has set out in the Bodhisattva-vehicle should
> produce a thought in this manner: 'all beings I must lead to
> Nirvana, into that Realm of Nirvana which leaves nothing
> behind, and yet, after beings have thus been led to Nirvana,
> no being at all has been led to Nirvana.[23]

It should be now clear from the above discussion of the
Mahāyāna conception of twofold truth that if there is any possibility of "theological talks" in Mahāyāna "theological talks" are
constructed pedagogically and conventionally for the sake of
those who lack keen insight into what is ontologically non-
differentiable and epistemologically non-conceptualizable in the
light of the principle of the Middle Way. The pedagogical and
symbolic function of Mahayana divinity (or divinities) cannot be
too much emphasized, one of the most conspicuous examples
being the "theological" presentation of *maṇḍala* (sacred circle)

23 Edward Conze, *Buddhist Wisdom Books* (London: Allen & Unwin, 1968), p. 57.

in the Tantric tradition.[24] Professor Herbert V. Guenther, a worthy scholar on Tibetan Buddhism, notes the fact that there is a considerable amount of anthropomorphism and mythical thinking involved in Tibetan tantrism, but he quickly adds that "the gods are functions and their formulations in concrete forms are symbols for the inner experiences that attend man's spiritual growth."[25] He also rightly says that "unless we are constantly aware of the metaphorical character of the language and are prepared to recognize its psychological significance and to accept it as symbolic, almost all that the Tantras say is easily misunderstood, misrepresented, and highly vulnerable."[26]

In the main, Mahāyāna "theological" talks contain two important and inter-related doctrines: the doctrine of *Buddhakāya* or *Trikāya* (threefold body of the Buddha) and that of *Buddhatā* (Buddha-nature) inherent in all sentient (and non-sentient) beings. The former is often misleadingly compared to the Christian doctrine of the Trinity, while the latter is the main source of pantheistic misunderstanding. Let us now clarify these two "theological" teachings of Mahāyāna Buddhism.

With regard to the doctrine of *Buddhakāya,* there has been a long history of Buddhological speculations in both Hinayāna and Mahāyāna. Shortly after the historical Buddha's death *(parinirvāṇa),* or even during his life, speculations--super-humanization or mythologization--began as to the real nature of his body. Significant properties of a superhuman being are ascribed to him. He is said to have possessed 32 major physical marks and 80 minor physical characteristics, such as thousand-spoke wheel-sign on feet, hand reaching below the knees, well-retracted male organ, golden-hued body, forty teeth, etc. Ten supernormal powers are also ascribed to him: he has complete knowledge of what is the

24 The *maṇḍala* is a magic circle geometrically subdivided into circles or squares, in which are painted Buddhist symbols and divinities.

25 H.V. Guenther, *Treasures on the Tibetan* Middle Way (Berkeley: Shambala Publications, 1969), p. 32.

26 H.V. Guenther, *Buddhist Philosophy in Theory and Practice* (Baltimore: Penguin Books, 1972), p. 155.

karma of every being, past, present, and future, of what is right or wrong in every condition, of all causes of mortality and of good and evil in their reality, of the end of all beings and *Nirvāṇa,* etc. Although there is no significant development of the doctrine of the threefold body of the Buddha in Hinayāna schools, at least some heated debate arose among them concerning (e.g.) the physical body *(rūpakāya)* of the Buddha. The *Mahāsanghikas,* for example, argue that the Buddha's body has no limits, that he knows no fatigue, and that his personality is transcendental and free from the defilements that might be derived from his material existence. Against this deifying tendency, the *Sthaviras* contend that the corporeal body of the historical Buddha is the natural result of his full accumulation of good *karma* and should not be conceived as superhuman and beyond all limitations. Myths and legends about the previous lives and the birth and death of the historical Buddha have also piled up. According to an orthodox legend, for instance, the historical Buddha is predicted at the time of his birth to become in the future either a great wheel-king *(cakravarti)* or a great religious savior.

But there is very little "theological" talk in Hinayāna Buddhism, for the historical Buddha is considered in most cases no more than a great personality transcending our human (spiritual) limitations as the result of his unexcelled, perfect enlightenment at the age of 35. It is rather with the rise of Mahāyāna Buddhism, in which is found an interesting combination of philosophical intellectualism and religious emotionalism, that a new attempt is made at systematization of Buddhological speculations into the doctrine of *Trikāya,* which presents the status of the Buddha in the form of threefold body: (1) the *Dharmakāya* (Body of Reality or Truth), also identified with *Bhutatathata* (Suchness), *Dharmatā* (Dharma-nature), or *Tathāgata-garbha* (Matrix of Thus-Come), is regarded as the absolute reality, unconditioned, eternal, and infinite, constituting the "cosmic body" of the Buddha; (2) the *Sambhogakāya* (Body of Splendor or Bliss) is the celestial personification of the *Dharmakāya* enjoying the fruits of the meritorious deeds a Buddha attained as a Bodhisattva; and

(3) the *Nirmāṇakāya* (Body of Transformation) is the terrestial body of the Buddha appearing in various miraculous forms, such as a ghost, a dragon, or a human Buddha like *Śakyamuni* (the founder of Buddhism), in accordance with different spiritual needs of different sentient beings. The Buddhological relation between the *Dharmakāya,* the Absolute, and the other two bodies is such that the *Sambhogakāya* is the *Dharmakāya* as perceived and worshiped in the heavenly realms by the Bodhisattvas coursing in any one of the ten Bodhisattva *bhūmis* (stages), while the *Nirmāṇakāya* is the same reality as perceived on earth by *Śrāvakas* ("hearers" or "disciples"), *pratyekabuddhas* ("solitary enlightened beings"), and ordinary men, as well as those by Bodhisattvas who have not yet reached the first *bhūmi.* This Mahāyāna Buddhology is the main source of various religious misinterpretations. It is because of the *Dharmakāya* that Buddhism is often misidentified with monotheism; it is because of the *Sambhogakāya,* which is said to manifest itself in various divine forms such as *Vairocana* ("The Illuminator"), *Amitābha* ("Infinite Light"), *Ratnasambhava* ("The Jewel-Born"), etc., that a polytheistic label is often put on Buddhism; it is because of the *Nirmaṇakāya* that Buddhism is often mistaken to be a mixture of genuine religion and animistic superstition. More interestingly, the Buddhist idea of *Trikāya* is sometimes mispresented in such a way that it is said to correspond to Christian idea of Trinity. Reichelt, for example, sees the one-one correspondence between (1) the *Dharmakāya* and God, (2) the *Sambhogakāya* and the Son of God, (3) the *Nirmaṇakāya* and the Holy Spirit.[27] Even the late Dr. D. T. Suzuki, a Zen authority, once compared *Trikāya* to the Trinity as follows:

> If we draw a parellelism between the Buddhist and the Christian trinity, the Body of Transformation may be considered to correspond to Christ in flesh, the Body of Bliss either to Christ in glory or to Holy Ghost, and Dharmakāya to Godhead.[28]

27 K.L. Reichelt, *op. cit.,* p. 201.
28 D.T. Suzuki, *Outlines of Mahāyāna Buddhism* (London: Luzac, 1907), p. 256.

The truth is that the Mahāyāna doctrine of *Trikāya* defies any literal acceptance, for it functions symbolically for those Bodhisattvas who aspire to attain Buddhahood by means of practicing 6 or 10 *pāramitās,* especially *prajñā-pāramitā* ("perfection of wisdom"). It also functions pedagogically for the sake of the *Karma*-stricken worldlings who are unable to see (by self-power) into emptiness or suchness of all *dharmas.* Any comparison of *Trikāya* to the Trinity would be therefore misleading without a proper philosophical clarification.

It is quite understandable that in all the above Buddhological speculations the Buddha's disciples and later Buddhists intend to express their deep respect and profound admiration for the supernormal personality of the founder of Buddhism. Philosophically speaking, however, it is rather fruitless and meaningless to investigate whether or not there is some factual basis for these speculations. For what is fundamental or pivotal in Buddhism is the historical Buddha's attainment of insuperable *(anuttara)* and perfect enlightenment *(samyak-sambodhi)* as well as his teachings *(Dharma)* about the attainability of perfect enlightenment. It should be recalled that the Buddha himself, shortly before his *parinirvāna,* forewarned his disciples of any deification process thus:

...Be ye a lamp unto yourselves. Be ye a refuge to yourselves. Betake yourselves to no external refuge. Hold fast to the truth as a lamp. Hold fast as a refuge to the truth. Look not for refuge to any one beside yourselves.[29]

These last words of the historical Buddha clearly express his own wish that his disciples, indeed all Buddhists, may take refuge primarily in the *Dharma* itself, not in the Buddha. If his last instruction here is applied to the doctrine of *Trikāya,* it can be

---

29 See *The Mahâparinibbâna Suttanta,* trans. by T.W. Rhys Davids, reprinted in *Buddhist Suttas* (New York: Dover Publications, 1969), p. 38.

said that only the *Dharmakāya,* which is the "cosmic body" of the Buddha as Truth, remains as real, but not the other two bodies, celestial or terrestial. And even the *Dharmakāya* itself, which is identical with emptiness, suchness, or the true nature of all *dharmas,* is a pedagogical symbol pointing to what is ontologically non-differentiatable and epistemologically non-conceptualizable. In short, no ontic commitment should be made here to the *Dharmakāya* as the "Absolute" in *Mahāyāna* Buddhism. There is thus no inconsistency involved between the philosophy of emptiness and the doctrine of *Trikāya,* as is exemplified in the *Mahaparinirvana-sutra:*

> The *Tathāgata* is neither heavenly god nor no-god, neither man nor no-man, neither *asūra* (titanic demon) nor no-*asūra,* neither denizen of hell or no-denizen....neither sentient being nor non-sentient being, neither *dharma* nor no-*dharma,* neither form nor no-form, neither long nor non-long, neither short nor non-short, neither mark nor no-mark, neither mind nor no-mind, neither defiled nor undefiled, neither conditioned nor unconditioned, neither permanent nor impermanent, neither illusory nor non-illusory, neither name nor no-name, neither *samādhi* (concentration) nor no-*samādhi,* neither being nor non-being, neither speech nor non-speech, neither *Tathāgata* nor no-*Tathāgata.*[30]

This no-nonsensical and paradoxical expression about the *Tathāgata* or the Buddha warns us against any ontic commitment to the *Trikāya,* the doctrine of which must be considered a conventional truth at the highest level, but never the absolute truth. As long as there is a practical need of using a skillful means to help the non-enlightened climb up the spiritual ladder of (Mahāyāna) Buddhism, the doctrine serves as a good religious remedy; once all the non-enlightened reach the highest stage, i.e. Buddhahood, it must be spontaneously left behind.

---

30 *Taisho Shinshu Daizokyo,* Vol. 12, *chüan* 20. (My translation).

The second "theological" talk in Mahāyāna Buddhism concerns the conception of Buddha-nature inherent in all sentient (and non-sentient) beings. In Hinayāna Buddhism the problem of Buddha-nature or the attainability of Buddhahood cannot arise, for the reason that there is one and only one Buddha, the originator of Buddhism, and all of us can only be expected to attain arhatship. The notion of Buddha-nature is therefore another unique feature of Mahāyāna Buddhism.

Buddha-nature means the original nature of the Buddha; it also means the potentiality or "seed" inherent in all sentient beings for the attainment of Buddhahood. It is often identified with *Tathāgata-garbha,* which is the *Dharmakāya* in the midst of the defiled state of all sentient beings. The doctrine of Buddha-nature that "All sentient beings (are born to) possess Buddha-nature" is perhaps most explicitly presented in the Mahāparinirvāṇa-sūtra:

> I (the Buddha) always announce that all sentient beings do possess Buddha-nature, even the *icchantika* possess it. The *icchantika* has cut off his roots of good, but the very goodness of Buddha-nature is there because he can recover it in the future. All *icchantikas* possess Buddha-nature. Why? Because they will definitely be able to attain *anuttara-samyak-sam-bodhi* (unexcelled, perfect enlightenment).[31]

In the same *Sūtra* the Buddha also says that "if a man sees the dependent origination (of all things in the world), he sees in reality the *Dharma* (Truth), and to see the *Dharma* is to see the Buddha; and the Buddha is none other than Buddha-nature. Why? Because all Buddhas have it as their (true) nature."[32] This clearly means that there is a non-differentiatable relation between the Buddha, the *Dharma* (or the *Dharmakāya),* the dependent origination, the Buddha-nature itself. In truth, they

31 *Ibid., chüan* 25. (My translation).
32 *Ibid.* (My translation).

must be regarded as one and the same reality, though differently named. In most *Mahāyāna* texts dealing with the conception of Buddha-nature, including the *Mahāparinirvāna-sūtra,* only the Buddha-nature of *sentient* beings is emphasized and discussed, probably because only sentient beings can be said *in fact* to (have the mind to) realize the Buddha-nature if and when perfectly enlightened, although all beings, sentient or not, do *in principle* partake of universal Buddha-nature, which is also the true nature of all things *(Dharmatā)* in the world. But in the later development of Mahāyāna Buddhism, especially in Esoteric Buddhism (Mi Tsung) and the T'ien-t'ai school, a new emphasis is placed on the omnipresence of Buddha-nature, as is exemplified in the "pantheistic" expression "Every grass or every tree, every country or every land, all attains Buddhahood." Chan-jan, one of the *T'ien-t'ai* patriarchs, illustrates this new teaching in the light of the famous *T'ien-t'ai* jargon, "Everything, a color or a fragrance, is none other than (the manifestation of) the Middle Way,"[33] that since everything participates in the Middle Way, non-sentient beings must also possess Buddha-nature. From the highest perspective of Mahāyāna Buddhism, therefore, the true nature of all things in the world is called Buddha-nature in terms of potential *bodhi* (enlightened mind). Suchness in terms of things-as-they-are, *Dharmakāya* in terms of the cosmic (all-prevading) manifestation of the Buddha's wisdom, and Absolute Emptiness in terms of the non-acquirability of the ontologically non-differentiated. All of these provisional names are in the final analysis different ways of expressing the Middle Way, the best illustration of which can be found again in the *Mahāparinirvāna-sūtra:*

The dependent origination is called Buddha-nature; Buddha-nature is Emptiness in the absolute sense; Emptiness in the absolute sense is called the Middle Way; the Middle Way is called Buddha; and Buddha is called *Nirvāna.*

---

33 Chan-jan, *Chih-kuan fu-hsing ch'uan-hung-chüeh,* in *Taishō Shinshū Daizōkyō,* Vol. 46, 151.

Buddha-nature is called Emptiness in the absolute sense; this is called Transcendental Wisdom *(prajñā)*; what is spoken of as Emptiness (in the absolute sense) is neither empty nor non-empty. The wise sees both emptiness and non-emptiness, permanence and impermanence, suffering and happiness, self and no-self. The so-called emptiness is none other than all (cycles of) life-and-death *(saṁsāra)*; non-emptiness is none other than *parinirvāṇa*....To see emptiness of all things without seeing non-emptiness is not called the Middle Way; and to see non-substantially (non-self) of all things without seeing substantially (self) is not called the Middle Way. The Middle Way is called Buddha.[34]

Our philosophical clarification of Mahāyāna conception of Buddha-nature as well as of *Trikāya* brings us back to the original position of Buddhism as a philosophical religion of the Middle Way through and through, which is the real Absolute (Truth) of (Mahāyāna) Buddhism having no specific form and content of its own but functioning as the central guiding principle of Buddhism steering perpetually between all dualistic pairs conceptually posited. In conclusion, we can say that all religious misinterpretations of (Mahāyāna) Buddhism stem from the failure to comprehend the Middle Way which lies at a deep level beneath "theological" talks.

A SELECT BIBLIOGRAPHY

Aung, Shwe Zan, trans. *Compendium of Philosophy.* London: Luzac, 1910 and 1956.
Bharati, A., *The Tantric Tradition.* London: Rider & Co., 1965.
Bloom, A., *Shinran's Gospel of Pure Grace.* Tucson: University of Arizona Press, 1965.
Chang, Chung-yuan, trans., *Original Teachings of Ch'an Buddhism.* New York: Pantheon Books, 1969.

---

34 *Taishō Shinshū Daizōkyō,* Vol. 12, chüan 25. (My translation).

Chang, Garma C.C., *The Buddhist Teaching of Totality*. University Park: Pennsylvania State University Press, 1971.

Ch'en, Kenneth, *Buddhism in China*. Princeton: Princeton University Press, 1964.

Conze, E., *Buddhist Thought in India*. London: Allen & Unwin, 1962.

————, *Thirty Years of Buddhist Studies*, Columbia: University of South Carolina Press, 1968.

————, *Buddhist Wisdom Books*. London: Allen & Unwin, 1968.

————, *Buddhist Scriptures*. Baltimore: Penguin Books, 1959.

————, *The Large Sutra of Perfect Wisdom*. London: Luzac, 1961-4.

Cowell, E.B., ed., *Buddhist Mahayana Texts*. New York: Dover Publications, 1969.

Davids, T.W.R., trans., *The Buddhist Suttas*. New York: Dover Publications, 1969.

Dayal, Har, *The Bodhisattva Doctrine in Buddhist Sanskrit Literature*. London: Kegan Paul, 1932.

Dutt, Nalinaksha, *Aspects of Mahayana Buddhism and its Relations to Hinayana*. London: Luzac, 1930.

Evans-Wentz, W., ed., *Tibetan Yoga and Secret Doctrines*, London: Oxford University Press, 1928.

————, ed., *The Tibetan Book of the Dead*. London: Oxford University Press, 1927.

————, ed., *Tibet's Great Yogi Milarepa*. London: Oxford University Press, 1928.

Getty, A., *The Gods of Northern Buddhism*. Tokyo: Charles E. Tuttle, 1962.

Glasenapp, H.V., *Buddhism: A Non-theistic Religion*. New York: George Braziller, 1966.

Govinda, Lama Anagarika, *The Psychological Attitude of Early Buddhist Philosophy*. London: Rider & Co., 1961.

————, *Foundations of Tibetan Buddhism*. London: Rider & Co., 1959.

Graham, D.A., *Conversations: Christian and Buddhist*. New York: Harcourt Brace Jovanovich, 1968.

Guenther, H.V., *Treatures on the Tibetan Middle Way*. Berkeley: Shambala Publications, 1969.

————, *Buddhist Philosophy in Theory and Practice*. Baltimore: Penguin Books, 1972.

————, *Philosophy and Psychology in the Abhidharma*. Lucknow: Buddha Vihara, 1955.

————, tr., *The Jewel Ornament of Liberation*. London: Rider & Co., 1959.

————, tr., *The Life and Teaching of Naropa*. Oxford: Clarendon Press, 1963.

———, "The Concept of Mind in Buddhist Tantrism," *Journal of Oriental Studies,* Hong Kong, July 1956.

———, "Levels of Understanding in Buddhism," *Journal of the American Oriental Society,* 78/1, 1960.

Hakeda, Y.S., trans., *The Awakening of Faith.* New York: Columbia University Press, 1967.

Humphreys, C., ed., *The Wisdom of Buddhism.* New York: Harper & Row, 1970.

Inada, Kenneth, *Nagarjuna.* Tokyo: The Hokuseido Press, 1970.

———, "Some Basic Misconceptions of Buddhism," *International Philosophical Quarterly,* Vol. IX, No. 1. 1969.

———, "The Ultimate Ground of Buddhist Purification," *Philosophy East and West,* Vol. XVIII, No. 1 and 2, 1968.

———, "Buddhist Naturalism and the Myth of Rebirth," *International Journal for Philosophy of Religion,* Vo. 1, No. 1, 1970.

Jayatilleke, K.N., *Early Buddhist Theory of Knowledge.* London: George Allen & Unwin, 1963.

Keith, A.B., *Buddhist Philosophy in India and Ceylon.* London: Oxford University Press, 1923.

Kern, H., trans., *Saddharma-Pundarika or the Lotus of the True Law.* New York: Dover Publications, 1963.

Liebenthal, W., trans., *Chao Lun.* Hong Kong: Hong Kong University Press, 1968.

Luk, Charles, *Ch'an and Zen Teaching.* London: Rider, Series I, 1960; Series II, 1961; Series III, 1962.

Merton, T., *Zen and the Birds of Appetite.* New York: New Directions Book, 1978.

Morgan, K.W., ed., *The Path of the Buddha.* New York: The Ronald Press Co., 1956.

Murti, T.R.V., *The Central Philosophy of Buddhism.* London: Allen & Urwin, 1955.

Narada, Thera, *The Buddha and His Teachings.* Colombo, Ceylon: Vajira-rama, 1964.

Nyananonika Thera, *Abhidhamma Studies.* Kandy, Ceylon: Buddhist Publication Society, 1965.

Poussin, L., *The Way to Nirvana.* Cambridge, 1917.

Ramanan, K.V., *Nagarjuna's Philosophy as Presented in the Maha-Prajna-paramita-Sastra.* Tokyo: Charles E. Tuttle, 1966.

Reichelt, K.L., *Truth and Tradition in Chinese Buddhism.* New York: Paragon Reprint, 1968.

Sangharakshita, *A Survey of Buddhism.* Bangalore, India: The Indian Institute of World Culture, 1957.

———, *The Three Jewels.* London: Rider & Co., 1967.

Stcherbatsky, Th., *The Central Conception of Buddhism*. London: Royal Asiatic Society, 1923.

——, *The Conception of Buddhist Nirvana*. Leningrad: Publishing Office of the Academy of Sciences of the USSR, 1927.

Streng, F., *Emptiness*. New York: Abingdon Press, 1967.

Stryk, L., ed., *World of the Buddha: A Reader*. New York: Doubleday, 1969.

Suzuki, B., *Mahayana Buddhism*. 3rd ed., New York: MacMillan, 1959.

Suzuki, D.T., Essays in Zen Buddhism. London: Rider, Series I, 1950: Series II, 1953; Series III, 1953.

——, *Mysticism: Christian and Buddhist*. New York: Harper 1957.

——, *Outlines of Mahayana Buddhism*. London: Luzac, 1907.

——, *Studies in Zen*. New York: Philosophical Library, 1955.

——, tr., *The Lankavatara Sutra*. London: Routledge and Son, 1933.

Zürcher, E., *The Buddhist Conquest of China*. Leiden: E.J. Brill, 1959.

India

CHAPTER VII

THE HINDU CONCEPT OF GOD

Francis V. Vineeth *

It is not easy to define the Hindu concept of God just as it is not easy to state what Hinduism is. Hinduism is not a dogmatic religion with precise formulas to be believed in and prescriptions to be followed. It is rather a way of life with different religious beliefs and philosophical explanations. The marvellous character of Hinduism, capable of absorbing into itself any new thought, keeps it ever growing, widens the range of its beliefs and practices and thereby renders it all the more difficult to be defined by any standard of philosophical rigour.

This complexity of the nature of the Hindu religion certainly and most profoundly affects the concept of God, because religion in the last analysis is the encounter of the finite with the Infinite, man with God. Both man and God are explained and understood in a religion in accordance with the basic assumptions it has. Every religion, therefore, presents its own interpretations of man and God. To a certain extent varieties of interpretations do exist in all other religions, because a religion that curtails the freedom of thinking and nips off the philosophical growth of the world is no religion at all. But Hinduism with its great stress on the universal over against the particular has always cherished an overwhelming sense of tolerance thanks to which it could always keep its gates open to any religious thought blossoming in the country and call it 'Hindu'. Thus we find in the great Hindu body of beliefs schools and systems of contrary positions, and that too on such cardinal issues as the nature of Brahman, the existence of

*Professor, Lancaster University, Lancaster, England.

the world and so on. This is not because Hinduism is less philosophical, but because in its approach to and evaluation of the
ultimate reality it has a different norm. In expressing the ineffable nobody can ever claim to have expressed everything. To
express it differently, simultaneously as well as successively, is
the fate of any finite intelligence. And this is what man is. His
feeble knowledge about God is shrouded in mystery and even in
misunderstandings. Hinduism takes into account this fact as it
really is.

This does not, however, mean that nothing could be said about
the Hindu concept of God. We have only to bear in mind that the
Hindu concept of God is not a rigid one, but a very loose one, to
be fit into different systems of thought all of which have given
their own interpretations about God, world, man and their interrelationship.

This article is divided into five parts. In the first part we try to
trace the sources from which the Hindu concept of God has
drawn its main inspirations. The second part treats the Hindu
epistemology, according to *Nyāya, Yoga* and *Vedānta* with special reference to the knowledge of God. In this part, in connection with *Nyāya* epistemology we will also see Udayana's arguments for the existence of God. The third part is a brief exposition of the main philosophical systems dealing with the concept
of God. We have chosen three main systems of *Vedānta:* the
Non-dualism of Śankara, the Qualified Non-dualism of Rāmānuja
and the Dualism of Mādhva. Since all the post-Śankara vedāntic
systems are avowedly theistic and stand for a personal God, in
the fourth part we try to trace back the tendencies and developments of the personal concept of God in Hinduism. In this part
we deal with the theology of the *Bhagavad-Gītā,* the *Bhakti* movement, and the theistic philosophy of Śaiva Siddhānta. In the fifth
and the last part we hope to round up all the converging points
of different schools and systems so as to present the essential
elements of a Hindu concept of God.

1. The Sources of the Hindu Concept of God

As in many other religions in Hinduism too the concept of God was subject to evolution. It has grown from the infantile gropings of mankind to the fullfledged philosophical systems. Up to the recent times our knowledge about the pre-Aryan sources of the Hindu concept of God was almost exclusively confined to the Vedic literature. As regards the pre-Aryan sources, Vedas gave only very scanty references and that too in a tone of contempt as to be naturally expected from a people talking about the religion of the vanquished. Therefore, the reason for the striking difference of the Indian branch of the Indo-Iranian and Indo-European people in the development of their religious worship was a matter of guesswork for scholars. The remnants of the pre-Aryan civilization unearthed in Harappā and Mohenjo-Dāro have thrown much light on this guesswork. The discoveries of the Indus civilization show us that the Aryans came to a land of high civilization and met a people who had their own gods and had even developed their own script.[1] They had a mother-goddess which reminds us of the later resurgence of the female Hindu goddesses like Kāli, Durga etc. and a *yogin* who, though ithyphallic, is lost in meditation and is seated with his legs drawn to the body and the heels touching, a posture very similar to that of *padmāsana* (lotus posture) which is even today the favoured posture of meditation all through India. Later on a God called Śiva will come to prominence in the Indian scene whose favoured posture of meditation is *padmāsana* or a posture similar to it and his accepted emblem in worship is *linga* which, though despised in the Rig Veda, emerges once again as the symbol of the creative power of God. So also the term *paśupati* (Lord of beasts), an epithet of

1 For a detailed account of the archeological finds of the Indus civilization, cf. John Marshall, (ed.), *Mohonjo-Dāro and Indus Civilization* (London: Arthur Probisthian, 1931), 3 vols. Sir R.E.M. Wheeler, *The Indus Civilization* (Cambridge, 1953); for a brief account of the same, cf. Madho Sarup Vats, "The Indus Valley Civilization" in the *Cultural Heritage of India* (Culcutta: Ramakrishna Mission, 1958), Vol. I, pp. 110-128.

Śiva which assumes highly developed spiritual meaning in later *Śaiva Śiddhanta,* may have had drawn it original inspiration from the Harappā culture. Among other archeological finds of this ancient city we see also a seal representing a two-horned *yogin* surrounded by animals. All this shows, as R.C. Zaehner concludes, 'that the religion of the conquered people had once again emerged into the light of day and, as so frequently happens, transformed the religion of the conqueror into something that was not recognizably his at all'.[2]

But apart from a few stone-inscriptions, which are not yet deciphered, the Indus civilization has left behind no literature. The most ancient piece of literature we have is still the Rig Veda, an explicitly Aryan composition, which, according to R.C. Zaehner, a distinguished scholar both in Indian and Iranian religions, 'still looks back to its Indo-Iranian past'[3] without even mentioning some of the key-concepts of the classical Hinduism such as *Brahman, mokṣa samsāra* and *karma.* This suggests that in developing these key-concepts of the classical Hinduism India was certainly influenced also by the religion of the non-Aryans and hints at the same time the receptive nature of Hinduism from its very start.

Hindus divide their religious literature into two main classes called *śruti* and *smṛti.* *Śruti* means 'what is heared' and is considered to contain the eternal truth 'heard' and experienced by the sages of immemmorial aniquity, while *smṛti* meaning 'what is remembered' indicates the secondary sources for understanding the truth expressed in *śruti.* The four Vedas[4] with their four

---

2 R.C. Zaehner, *Hinduism* (London: Oxford University Press, 1966), p. 15.

3 *Ibid.,* p. 35.

4 The word 'Veda' is derived from the root *vid,* to know, and is related to the latin *vid-ere,* to see and Greek *oida,* to know. The four Vedas are: *The Rig-Veda,* the *Yajur-Veda,* the *Sāma-Veda* and the *Atharva-Veda.*

parts[5] *Mantras, Brāhmaṇas, Araṇyakas* and *Upaniṣads* constitute the *Śruti* literature whereas the *Dharma-Śāstras* (Law books), *Itihāsas* (Epics), *Purāṇas* (long mythological works), *Sūtras* (philosophical aphorisms) and *Agamas* (sacred books of the Saivites) etc. belong to *Smṛti*.

The Rig-Veda consists of 1017 hymns and speaks of several gods. As a rule the gods of Rig-Veda are the personifications of the natural forces at work in the universe. Even the great gods like Indra, Varuṇa, Mitra, Viṣṇu, Rudra etc. whose names are no longer so transparent were originally related to natural phenomena.[6] Though the Rig-Veda admitted the plurality of God one was free to adore the god he liked and to consider him as supreme. Max Müller called it Henotheism by which he understood the belief in individual gods alternatively regarded as the highest.[7] In fact this was a practical solution to the problem of the plurality of gods. But the search for a unifying principle went further on and some versicles of the Rig-Veda clearly show a tendency for unity.[8] The hymn of creation is a typical example for this:

Whence this emanation hath arisen,
Whether (God) disposed it, or whether he did not.[9]

5 According to S. Radhakrishnan these four parts correspond to the four stages of life. 'While the student *(brahmacārin)* reads the hymns, the householder *(gṛhastha)* attends to the Brāhmaṇas which speak of the daily duties and sacrificial ceremonies, the hermit, the man of the forest *(vānaprastha)*, discusses the Araṇyakas, the monk who has renounced wordly attachment *(samnyāsin)*, studies the Upaniṣads, which specialize in philosophical speculations'. S. Radhakrishnan, (ed.), *The Principal Upaniṣads* (London: George Allen & Unwin Ltd., 1969), p. 48.

6 S. Radhakrishnan and C.A. Moore, (ed.), *A Sourcebook in Indian Philosophy* (Princeton University Press, 1970), p. 4.

7 Max Müller, *The Six Systems of Indian Philosophy* (London: Longmans Green, 1899), p. 53.

8 I.164.46; X.121.1; X.129.1-7.

9 Rig-Veda, X.129.7. Eng. Trans., R.C. Zaehner, (ed.), *Hindu Scriptures* (London: Dent, 1968).

The hymn of the 'Golden Embryo' *(Hiraṇyagarbha)* gave a practical answer:

> In the beginning the Golden Embryo
> (Stirred and) evolved:
> Once born he was the one Lord of (every) being.[10]

But the question still remained:

> What God shall we revere with the oblation?[11]

The groping for the ultimate reality was yet to find its answer in the subsequent thinking of the Upaniṣads.

Leaving behind the *Brāhmaṇas* which are the elaborations of the sacrificial rituals outlined in the Vedas, and the *Araṇyakas* which are the interpretations of the sacrificial ceremonies we come to Upaniṣads.[12] According to S. Dasgupta 'the passage of the Indian mind from the Brāhmaṇic to Upaniṣad thought is probably the most remarkable event in the history of philosophical thought'.[13] The Upaniṣads are also called Vedānta, because they were the 'end' *(anta)* of Vedas, though later the term *Vedānta* meant the philosophical school which developed the doctrines contained in the Upaniṣads.

The Upaniṣads developed the quest for reality already found in the Rig-Veda, in the tenth book of the Cosmic hymns of the Atharva Veda and in some portions of the Brāhmaṇas and set the

10 Rig-Veda, X.21.1.

11 *Ibid.*, X.21.2.

12 The word 'Upaniṣad' is derived from *upa*, near, *ni*, down and *sad*, to sit. Upaniṣads speak of the high wisdom that ancient Gurus (Teachers) imparted to their pupils who sat near them. There are over 200 Upaniṣads, although the traditional number is 108. Sankara wrote commentaries on eleven of them and they, being the oldest, are generally considered to be the principal Upaniṣads. They are: *Isa, Kena, Katha, Prasna, Mundaka, Mandukya, Taittiriya, Aitareya, Chāndogya, Bṛhadāraṇyaka* and *Svetāsvatara.* The *Kausitaki* and *Mahānārāyaṇa* Upaniṣads both of which had been referred to by Sankara and the *Maitri* are also considered to be of great importance.

13 S. Dasgupta, *A History of Indian Philosophy* (Cambridge: University Press, 1922), Vol. I, p. 31.

path of the future philosophical thinking of India. The ultimate reality was called *Brahman,* a word which in all probability originally meant something like 'the spell', the word uttered in sacrificial formula.[14] It is also called *Atman* and is said to abide in the innermost recess of every being. According to Śankara, the great commentator on the Upaniṣads, the following four texts are the great utterances (Mahāvākyāni) of all the Upaniṣads: 'Thou art that';[15] 'I am Brahman';[16] 'This self is Brahman';[17] 'Brahman is consciousness'.[18] The great philosophers of the *Vedānta* school were very keen to base their teachings on some Upaniṣadic texts.

Along with the monistic doctrine which is stressed in many Upaniṣads we find also a theistic tendency taking shape of which the *Śvetāśvatara,* one of the later Upaniṣads, is the best example.

> Than whom there is naught else higher, than whom there is naught smaller, naught greater, (the) one stands like a tree established in heaven, by Him, the Person, is the whole universe filled.[19]

This is a prayer addressed to the Vedic god Rudra who was later called Śiva, the 'auspicious'. This theistic tendency found in the *Śvetāśvatara* finds its further development in the *Bhagavad-Gītā*[20], the Song of the Divine and later in the *Bhakti* movement of the Vaiṣṇavites and Śaivites.

---

14 R.C. Zaehner, *Hinduism,* p. 37.

15 *'Tattvam asi'. Chāndogya Up.* VI, 9.4. All references to the Upaniṣads in this article are according to *The Principal Upaniṣads* edited with introduction, Texts, Translation, and notes by S. Radhakrishnan (London: George Allen & Unwin, 1969, first published in 1953).

16 *'Aham brahmāsmi'. Bṛhadāraṇyaka Up.* I, 4.10.

17 *'Ayam ātmā Brahma'. Maṇḍukya Up.* 2.

18 *'Prajñānam brahma'. Aitarey Up.* III, 1.3.

19 *'...Tene'dam pūrṇam puruṣeṇa sarvam'. Śvetāśvatara Up.* III.9.

20 *Bhagavad-Gītā,* which has become a classic in religious literature and the most influential of the Hindu Scriptures, is an aphoristic dialogue between Sri Kṛṣṇa, the avatār of Viṣṇu, and Arjuna, the hero of the Pāṇḍavas at the point of waging war against Kauravas, their kinsmen. As to its date it is definitely post-Buddhistic and at least with regard to its essence pre-christian.

The various doctrines of the Upaniṣads were summarized in a
philosophical poem of 555 *sūtras*[21] attributed to Bādarāyaṇa.
This aphoristic work was known as *Brahma-sūtra*[22] and became
the basic text for the *Vedānta* school of philosophy. All the great
teachers of *Vedānta* develop their distinctive views commenting
upon this fundamental work. The *Brahma-sūtra*, the Upaniṣads
and the *Bhagavad-Gītā* are considered to be the three basic authorities of *Vedānta* and *Vaiṣṇavism*, the two great movement
that swept across the whole of India.

2. Hindu Epistemology and the Possibility of the Knowledge
of God

The logical school of *Nyāya*[23], one of the six Darśanas[24] of
the Indian Philosophy, has contributed most to the Indian epistemology. In developing an epistemology of their own the influence
of *Nyāya* on other schools is of paramount importance. As Dr.
Radhakrishnan points out 'its methodology is accepted by other
systems, though with slight modifications due to their metaphysical conceptions.'[25] *Nyāya* presents four valid means (*pra-*

21 'A *sūtra* is so called because it suggests wide meaning. It should be concise,
indicative of its purport, (composed) of few letters and words, in every way meaningful. Such are what the wise one called *sūtras* and aphorisms.' S. Radhakrishnan, *The
Brahma Sūtra* (London: George Allen & Unwin, 1960), p. 23.

22 *Brahma-sūtra* because 'it deals with the doctrine of Brahman'. It is also known
as *Śārīrika-sūtra* 'since it deals with the embodiment of the unconditioned self' and
Vedānta-sūtra 'since it deals with Vedanta or the final aim of the Veda' and is
supposedly composed between 500 and 200 B.C. Cf. S. Radhakrishnan and C.A.
Moore, *op. cit.*, p. 506.

23 The word *Nyāya* is derived from *ni*, into, *āya* (from *i*), to go, and literally means
that by which the mind 'goes into' the meaning of things and thereby led to conclusions. *Nīyate anena iti nyāya.* As a philosophical system it deals with the four factors of
right knowledge such as the means of right knowledge *(pramāṇa)*, the object *(prameya)*,
the state of cognition *(pramiti)* and the subject of right knowledge *(pramātṛ)*.

24 Indian Philosophy acknowledges six orthodox systems. They are called *darśanas*.
The word darśana means 'vision' or 'view' and roughly corresponds to the German
word *Weltanschauung*. The six systems are: *Nyāya, Vaiśeṣika, Saṁkhya, Yoga, Mīmāmsa*
and *Vedānta*.

25 S. Radhakrishnan, *Indian Philosophy* (London: George Allen & Unwin, 1962,
first published, 1923), Vol. II, p. 173.

maṇa) of right knowledge. They are: 1. Perception *(pratyakṣa),* 2. Inference *(anumāna),* 3. Comparison *(upamāna)* and 4. Verbal Testimony *(sabda).* Gautama, the founder of the school, in his *Nyāya Sūtra,* the basic work of the school, defines all these four means of right knowledge.

Perception is the immediate apprehension of an object with or without sense-contact.[26] It must be determinate and non-erratic. Commenting upon the erroneous character of perception Vātyāyana develops the classical notion of truth in the traditional western philosophy as agreement of the intellect with the thing.[27] 'That cognition is erroneous, says Vatsyāyana, in which the thing is apprehended as what it is not; while when a thing is perceived as what it is, the perception is not erroneous'.[28] Every other type of knowledge is based on perception and Gautama's insistence on sense-contact in perception reminds us of what Aquinas later said that 'the proper object of human intellect, which is united to a body, is a quiddity or nature existing in corporal matter.'[29]

Perception is followed by inference *(anumāna)*[30] which is the Indian syllogism. It is very closely parallel to the western syllogism except that the Indian syllogism has five parts. They are: 1. *pratijna* or the proposition to be established (the hill is on fire); 2. *hetu* or the reason (because it smokes); 3. *udāharaṇa* or the example (whatever has smoke has fire); 4. *upanaya* or the application (so does this hill); and 5. *nigamana* or the statement of the conclusion (therefore the hill is on fire). Inference thus develops method of argumentation and traces out the causal

---

26 *Nyāya-sūtra,* I.1.4. *Pratykṣa* originally meant sense-perception. But it soon came to include all immediate apprehension with or without sense-contact. Cf. Radhakrishnan, *Indian Philosophy,* p. 48.

27 Cf. *Summa Theologica,* 1.16.1c & 2c.

28 Vatsyāyana on *Nyāyasūtra* 1.1.4. Eng. Trans. Ganganatha Jha, (ed.), *Gautama's Nyāyasūtra with Vatyāyana's Bhāṣya* (Poona: Oriental Book Agency, 1939).

29 *Summa Theologica,* 1.84.7c.

30 *Nyāya-sūtra,* 1.1.5. Regarding the Indian method of induction and inference cf. Ninian Smart, *Doctrine and Argument in Indian Philosophy* (London: George Allen & Unwin, 1969), pp. 195-208.

connections. Later Udayana extended the Nyāya reasoning to arguments to prove the existence of God.

Comparison is the knowledge of a thing through its similarity to another thing previously well known.[31] In spite of its striking similarity to the western notion of analogy it did not gain momentum in the Indian way of knowing God. This was because of the Indian insistence on the direct experience of God rather than any mediate knowledge about God.

That is why *śabda* or the verbal testimony, the fourth of the valid means of right knowledge, became most important in the Indian way of knowing God. For the verbal testimony is, as Gautama defines it, 'the instructive assertion of a reliable person'.[32] That person is reliable to communicate the knowledge of God who has the direct experience of God. The philosophers of Vedānta school base their thinking on the Vedas, because the Vedas possess the verbal testimonies of those sages who had the direct experience of God.

Though *Nyāya* presented all the four means of knowledge it was beyond the intention of Gautama to make use of them for the knowledge of God. Supreme felicity was proposed as the ultimate goal to be obtained through the right knowledge of the categories.[33] But among the 12 objects proposed as the objects of the right knowledge[34] God does not come in. It was Udayana who presented God as the supreme object *(prameya)* of knowledge. In his *Nyāyakusumāñjali* he presents God as the supreme *prameya* and proposes several arguments for the existence of God.[35] M. Hiriyana in his *Outlines of Indian Philosophy* sum-

---

31 *Nyāya-sūtra*, 1.1.6.
32 *Nyāya-sūtra*, 1.1.7.
33 *Nyāya-sūtra*, 1.1.1.
34 *Nyāya-sūtra*, 1.1.9.
35 *Sāpekṣatvād anāditvād vaicitryād visvavṛttitaḥ Pratyātmaniyamād bhukter asti hetur alaukikaḥ* (1.4) From dependence, from eternity, from diversity, from universal practice, and from the apportionment to each individual self mundane enjoyment implies a supernatural cause. Eng. Trans. E.B. Cowell, *The Kusumāñjali or Hindu Proof of the Existence of a Supreme Being* (Calcutta: Baptist Mission Press, 1864). Cf. also V.I.

marizes Udayana's arguments for the existence of God as follows:

1. The world is an effect and like all other effects points, among other causes, to an efficient cause or agent who is by knowledge as well as power equal to the task of creating it.

2. There is observed in the created world physical order which indicates a controller or a law-giver; and

3. the moral government of the world implies a governor who dispenses justice in accordance with desert (*adrsta* or the merit and demerit of our actions).[36]

Udayana who lived about three centuries before Aquinas in some way anticipated his 'five ways'. Contingency of the created being and the order of the universe were the basic arguments also in Thomas Aquinas.

According to the Yoga school, it is through the practice of Yoga 'the light of wisdom reaches up to discriminative knowledge'[37] which alone removes the bondage of the individual self (*purusa*) and thereby brings about release (*moksa*). Yoga, as Patanjali, the founder of the school sees it, is concentration (*samādhi*)[38] by which one discriminates the subject from the object, *purusa* from *prakṛti*, and attains his true and eternal self.[39] Among the objects of concentration Patanjali presents also God[40] who is a 'distinct *purusa* untouched by the vehicles of affliction'.[41] By means of physical exercises (*āsanas*, breath-

---

36 M. Hiriyana, *Outlines of Indian Philosophy* (London: George Allen & Unwin, 1970, first published 1932), p. 243. For a brief survey of the Arguments for and against the existence of God in Indian Philosophy cf. Ninian Smart, *op. cit.*, pp. 149-158.

37 *Yoga Sùtra*, 2.28; Cfr also 2,25-27; Engl. translation by Rama Prasada, *Sacred Books of the Hindus*, IV (Allahabad: The Paṇini Office, 3rd ed. 1924).

38 *Yoga Sùtra*, 1, 1.

39 *Yoga Sùtra*, 2, 25-26; 4.34.

40 *Yoga Sùtra*, 1.23.

41 *Yoga Sùtra*, 1.24.

control), spiritual restraints *(yama)*, and observances *(niyama)*, Yoga prepares the aspirant for discriminative knowledge. However, in presenting God and his omnipresence as an object of concentration Yoga does not aim at a theistic form of religious worship. The goal of concentration is not union with God, but the liberation of *puruṣa* from *prakṛti*, self from nature.[42] In holding this Yoga follows *Saṁkhya* metaphysics, according to which the involution of *puruṣa* (the Self, the great male principle) into *prakṛti* (nature, the great female principle) caused the evolution of the universe. Yoga aims at the reversal of this process. But later on *Bhagavad-Gītā* takes up the same line of thought and presents union with God as the supreme goal of yogic *samādhi*.[43]

The Vedāntins accept the *pramāṇas* especially *pratyakṣa anumāna* and *sabda* but denounce all empirical knowledge as inadequate to know the real. Śankara holds that all empirical knowledge involves one in distinctions and therefore is incapable of reaching Brahman which is beyond all distinctions. The real never becomes the object of our perception.[44] But the real is sought after in every act of knowing. Because of this impossibility of attaining the real as the object our knowledge we feel a sense of the beyond in all our knowledge. What we can say about the real is that it is 'not so' 'not so'.[45] We can also say that the real is real. To say anything more about the real will be an error or superimposition *(adhyasa)*,[46] because it is attributing to one what it is not. Therefore the only way to know Brahman (God) is *anubhava* (integral experience) by which one realizes the supreme as oneself.[47] Because it is a process of realization *(sākṣātkāra)* rather than objectivization it transcends all subject-object distinc-

---

[42] *Yoga Sūtra*, 4.34.

[43] *Bhagavad-Gītā*, 18. 54-55.

[44] *Śankara-Bhāṣya* on *Vedānta-sūtra*, II.i.6. Eng. Trans. George Thibaut, *The Vedanta Sūtras with the Commentary by Sankarācārya*, Sacred Books of the East, Vol. XXXIV and XXXVIII (Oxford: Clarendon Press, 1890, 1896).

[45] *Śankara-Bhāṣya*, III.ii.22; *Brhadāraṇyaka Up.* 4.5.15.

[46] *Śankara-Bhāṣya*, Introduction.

[47] *Śankara-Bhāṣya*, I.i.2; II.i.4; III.iv.15. Cf. also Radhakrishnan, *Indian Philosophy*, Vol. II., pp. 510-520.

tions proper to all other forms of knowledge. This realization takes place when the misapprehension of reality *(avidyā)* is destroyed. *Avidyā* is the false identification of the self with something that it is not.[48] *Avidyā* and *adhyāsa* are thus very closely related. *Sākṣātkāra* is not the consciousness of this or that object but is realizing in oneself the truth of all, the ground of all. This is the way to know Brahman, the ultimate reality. If we have not yet experienced it we have to depend on the teachings of those who had the fortune of experiencing it. It is here we find the importance of *śruti*.[49] *Śruti* becomes the most important source of right knowledge about God, because it contains the eternal wisdom transmitted to humanity through the sages who had experienced God in themselves. Vedas are testimonies of divine experience on earth. However Vedas are to be interpreted. Thus the certitude of the intuitional experience supplemented by conceptual clarity. Argumentation or inference plays an important role in this interpretation.[50] But interpretation is only to understand the experience of the sages. Ultimately the knowledge of God is gained only through experience or intuitional consciousness.

Other systems of *Vedānta* school, though they do not accept Śankara's theory that reality is beyond all distinctions,[51] hold that reality is to be known by way of integral experience. While Śankara stresses the *jñānamārga,* the path of knowledge, by which the individual self tries to regain its lost identity with Brahman, the post-Sankara schools lay greater emphasis on the *Bhaktimārga,* the path of devotion, by which the individual self strives after its union with Brahman. The Indian religious literature proposes also *karmamārga,* the path of action, where action is under-

---

48 *Śankara-Bhāṣya,* I.iii.19.
49 *Śankara-Bhāṣya,* II.i.11.
50 *Śankara-Bhāṣya,* II.i.6.
51 For example cf. *Srī-Bhāṣya,* Rāmānuja's Commentary on Vedānta-sūtra, I.i.1. Eng. Trans. George Thibaut, *The Vedānta Sūtras with the Commentary of Rāmānuja,* Sacred Books of the East, Vol. XLVIII (Oxford: Clarendon Press, 1904).

stood as detached activity,[52] as a means of attaining Brahman. Whatever be the path one chooses, God is known only by way of intuitional experience which transforms the self of man.

3. The Philosophical Evolution of the Concept of God

As we have already seen the Hindu philosophy is not the development of one single thought. There had been different thought currents and complexities. Afterwards some of the predominant thoughts developed into particular systems. Six of them are generally known as darśanas.

The Brāhmaṇic period was predominantly ritualistic. When this ritualism came to its zenith naturally there arose reactions. The morality of killing the animals and the security of salvation through sacrifice were questioned. The three major 'schisms' such as Buddhism, Jainism and Cārvāka were the result. Because they all questioned the authority of Vedas, which was considered to be the orthodox way to religious realization, they came to be known as non-vedic or heterodox systems. The speedy growth of these systems, especially that of Buddhism, was a menace to Hinduism which seemed to be threatened by these new trends of thought. In the end, however, all these movements helped only the revival of Hinduism. The Hindu thinkers questioned the validity of Buddha's teachings and went back to the Upaniṣads that preserved the quintessence of the religious experiences of so many sages and saints. But the return to Vedas had to be at a different level. Buddhism had already developed a high level of thinking and its emergence had a lasting impact on the intelligentsia of India.[53] Hence it was a necessity that the orthodox Indian thought be presented in a strictly philosophical framework. Consequently there evolved six schools of thought generally known as six systems. These are the logical realism of the Nyāya,

---

52 Bhagavad-Gītā, 12, 10; 18, 23, 49.

53 The influence of the Mahāyāna school of Buddhism is especially manifest in the Non-dualism (advaita) of Śankara.

the atomistic pluralism of the Vaiseṣika, the metaphysics of the
Saṁkhya, the asceticism of the *Yoga,* the ritualism of the *Mīmāmsa* and the theology *(Brahmajijñāsa)* of the *Vedānta.* We have
already referred to some of these in our discussion on the Hindu
epistemology and the possibility of the knowledge of God. Of all
these systems, *Vedānta* has contributed very considerably to the
evolution of the Hindu concept of God. Hence here we treat
three main systems of *Vedānta.*

(a) God in the Non-dualism of Śankara: Advaita

The non-dualism of Śankara is definitely one of the most important schools of *Vedānta* which has gained wide acceptance all
over India. It draws its inspiration from the monistic trend of the
Upanisads and, as we have already seen, Śankara summarizes the
whole of his philosophy in the four great utterances of the
Upaniṣads.

Advaita unconditionally asserts the oneness of reality. Reality
is one and undivided.[54] It is beyond all possible distinctions. It is
existence in its purity and by its very nature absolutely transcendent. This reality is Brahman. By its very nature it is omnipresent, yet not confined to any particular space. Its true nature,
however, is beyond grasp and surpasses all attempts of human
understanding.[55] We can not attribute to it qualities of beings we
see here, because all of them involve one in distinction. The
reality, on the other hand, is the 'wholly other' and therefore is to
be designated as 'not this'. Hence it is called *'nirguna',* without
attributes or beyond all qualities.[56] This negative designation,
however, does not mean that Brahman is a mere blank devoid of
all perfections. In fact what is denied is the negations involved in
all finite perfections. Brahman is the supreme being and all perfections belonging to pure being belong to it, though we cannot

54 *Śankara-Bhāṣya,* I.iv.22.
55 *Śankara-Bhāṣya,* III.ii.23.
56 *Śankara-Bhāṣya,* I.i.11.

attribute anything to it, because our notions are derived from
things that are different from Brahman. As the supreme Being
(*sat*) it is the most real (*pāramārthikasatya*), by nature self-
luminous (*svayamprakāsatvam*) and therefore subsisting consciousness (*cit*) and bliss (*ananda*).[57] It is beyond all change[58]
and its nature is eternal and uniform (*ekarasa*).[59] But this Absolute is beyond all human grasp. The moment we think about
it, it becomes a part of the world of our experience.

The Absolute thus understood by man is called Īśvara. It is
Brahman itself, but Brahman as manifested in the universe.[60]
Īśvara is, then, not a product of mere imagination. He is the real,
the Absolute, not as in itself, but as understood by man. Īśvara
is the determinate Brahman (*saguṇa Brahman*), Brahman understood as the creator and the preserver of the universe. Īśvara is
the God of religion and the object of worship. In so far as Īśvara
does not have an existence of its own apart from that of the real
Brahman Īśvara could be considered as a postulate.[61] But it is a
true and reliable postulate and is supported by *śruti*, because
śruti presents Brahman as the cause of the origin and the dissolution of the universe.[62]

Though Brahman is absolutely transcendent it is also profoundly immanent in the heart of every being.[63] In fact it is the
Atman, the ultimate Self, of every being[64] and the individual
soul (*jīva*), in whom the eternal consciousness of Brahman reflects in a special way, is bound to discover it by way of intro-

57 *Śankara-Bhāṣya*, I.i.4.
58 *Śankara-Bhāṣya*, II. i.27.
59 *Śankara-Bhāṣya*, I.iii.1.
60 *Śankara-Bhāṣya*, II.i.14.
61 Radhakrishnan, *Indian Philosophy*, Vol. II, p. 545.
62 *Śankara-Bhāṣya*, I.i.2.
63 *Śankara-Bhāṣya*, I.ii.8.
64 *Śankara-Bhāṣya*, I.iii.19.

spective meditation.[65] But *jīva* on account of the physical adjuncts with which it is united thinks itself to be something different from the Self. This is *avidyā* or ignorance. This false sense of the identity of the self must be removed by true knowledge. Then the individual self will experience itself to be the Self, the Brahman. Thus the Upaniṣadic saying 'I am Brahman' will turn out meaningful. So also the saying 'That thou art' (*tat tvam asi*): thou thyself art that Brahman, the ultimate Self of everything.[66]

To answer the question how does Brahman manifests himself in the universe, Sankara brings in the idea of *Māyā*. The Brahman understood as Īśvara or Saguṇa Brahman is a Brahman with an infinite power of self-manifestation. This manifestative power of Īśvara is what he calls *Māyā*.[67] *Māyā* is, therefore, both the power of Īśvara and the manifestation of Brahman as the universe. As every revelation of God is at the same time revealing and concealing, so also *Māyā*, though it reveals Brahman, works also as veil (*āvaraṇa*) of the real Brahman. Since reality is Brahman, which is one and non-dual, the universe is only an appearance effected by the *Māyā* of Īśvara. Hence the reality of this universe cannot be said to be real (*sat*) because Brahman alone is ultimately real. Nor can it be said unreal (*asat*), because it does exist. It is both real and unreal (*sat-asat*) and therefore something indefinable (*anirvacanīya*). Though it is not real as Brahman is real, for all practical purposes it could be taken as real.

Brahman, world and the individual self are the three cardinal points in the non-dualism of Sankara. Of these three Brahman is

---

65 The way recommended is that of *śravaṇa*, *manana* and *nididhyāsana*. *Śravaṇa* is 'the study and discussion of the Upaniṣads with the assistance of a *guru* that has realized the truth they teach'; *manana* is 'arguing within oneself, after knowing definitely what the Upaniṣads teach, how and why that teaching alone is true' and *nididhyāsana* is 'meditation upon the identity between the individual self and Brahman'. M. Hiriyana, *Outlines of Hinduism*, pp. 379-380.

66 *Sankara-Bhāṣya*, I.iii.19; *Sankara-Bhāṣya* on *Chāndogya Up.* VI.9.4, on *Bṛhadāraṇyaka Up.* I.4.10.

67 *Sankara-Bhāṣya*, I.iv.3.

real, the world is illusion or *Māyā* and the individual self is not different from Brahman once release is obtained.

The *advaita* of Śankara is certainly one of the most dominating systems about the Indian concept of God. Its influence is great. The Indian mind still feels a great yearning for the philosophical acumen of Śankara in spite of its intricate subtleties.

(b) God in the Qualified Non-dualism of Rāmānuja (Viśiṣṭādvaita)

Rāmānuja, the great philosopher of the *Vaiṣṇavite* movement, attacks Śankara's absolute monism and in his commentary on *Vedānta-sūtras* Rāmānuja presents Śankara's view as that of the adversary against whom he has to defend his thesis. The thesis defended, however, is non-dualism itself, but a different sort of non-dualism. Reality is one for Rāmānuja too; but this one reality is not without distinctions. It is a complex reality. Reality includes God, souls *(jīva)* and matter *(acit)*. They are, however, inseperably united to form one Absolute which is Brahman. Souls and matter, though part of the reality, entirely depend on God for their existence. They are the attributes or qualifications *(viśeṣaṇa)* of God and God is the qualifiable *(viśeṣya)*. Reality is the complex whole which is, therefore, qualified *(viśiṣṭa)*. Hence the name qualified non-dualism *(Viśiṣṭādvaita)*.

The God of Rāmānuja is a personal God and possesses all good qualities to a supreme degree.[68] He is not very keen on the nirguṇa and saguṇa Brahman. Īśvara, the Lord of the universe is himself the ultimate reality[69] whose modes are the souls and the world. The relation between the universe and Īśvara is compared

---

68 Rāmānuja on *Bhagavad-Gītā*, 6.47. Cf. also R.C. Zaehner, *Hinduism*, pp. 98-99.

69 This ultimate reality is identified with Viṣṇu whose avatār (incarnation) is Lord Krishṇa. Rāmānuja conceives him as 'an ocean of boundless compassion, moral excellence, tenderness, generosity, and sovereignty, the refuge of the whole world without distinction of persons'. *(Gītā-Bhāṣya*, 6.47). R.C. Zaehner gives the following comment: 'Rāmānuja's Krishṇa is not the Krishṇa of Mahābhārata nor even of the Bhagavad-Gītā: He is the Krishṇa of the Bhagavada Purāṇa - the handsome cowherd boy who ravishes the hearts of all who hear the sweet sound of his flute'. R.C. Zaehner, *Concordant Discord* (Oxford: Clarendon Press, 1970), p. 158.

to that of a human body to its soul.[70] The world together with the innumerable souls constitute the 'body' of Brahman. 'The sensient and non-sensient beings in all their states constitute the body of the Lord while he constitutes their self'.[71] By body Rāmānuja means that which a soul controls, supports and utilizes for its own end.[72] Therefore, God controls the universe and every thing in it, including the human individuals, according to his plans and purposes.

The Lord of the universe is all perfect. He is 'the divine supreme person, all whose wishes are eternally fulfilled, who is all knowing and the ruler of all, whose every purpose is immediately realized'.[73] Though souls and matter are his attributes or modes of his being, he himself undergoes no change. He is the eternal changeless *viśeṣya* whereas all around him is in change due to his attribute that is matter. Īśvara is thus the unchanging center of the changing universe, the inspiring principle of every thing that is. As the support and substratum of every being he is the indweller *(antaryāmin)* and inner self *(antarātman)* of every thing, whether spirit or matter.

Rāmānuja distinguishes between Brahman in causal stage and Brahman in effected state. When Brahman is in his causal state the sensient and the non-sensient beings abide in Brahman 'in so subtle a condition as to be incapable of receiving designations different from that of Brahman itself'.[74] When, on the other hand, Brahman is in its effected condition 'its body is constituted by all those beings in their gross state'[75] and assumes distinct names and forms. This is how Rāmānuja explains the origin and the dissolution of the universe. The universe is not illusion *(mithya)* as in the philosophy of Śankara but real, and *māyā* is

70 *Śrībhāṣya*, I.ii.12.
71 *Śrībhāṣya*, II.iii.18.
72 *Śrībhāṣya*, II.i.9.
73 *Śrībhāṣya*, II.ii.3.
74 *Śrībhāṣya*, II.iii.18.
75 *Ibid.*

'God's mode of operation in it'.[76] It is the abode of *Jīva*, the soul, and God, the *Īśvara*.

Jīva, though essentially finite and dependent on God, is spiritual and of the same nature of God, a particle of pure consciousness. Only in release *(mokṣa)* it understands its true nature which is 'unlimited knowledge'[77] whereas in *samsāra* (the circle of birth and rebirth) 'it is obscured by ignorance, i.e. the influence of the beginningless chain of works'.[78] This ignorance is to be removed by true devotion *(Bhakti)* to the Lord who is kind and loving and mercifully guides and governs his devotees and punishes and rewards them according to their actions.[79] When at last the ignorance is removed, the soul enjoys the intuition of the Supreme Self 'which is the natural state of the individual selves'.[80] Consequently the upanisadic saying *'tat tvam asi'* receives an interpretation different from that of Śankara. By no means does it stand for an absolute identity of the individual with the Absolute. It means only that God who is the cause of the universe is also 'having the individual selves for its body' and thus becomes the Self of every finite self *(jīva)*.[81]

The influence of Rāmānuja's philosophy was remarkably felt in the *Bhakti* movements that followed him. Rāmānuja's philosophy was the justification of the *Bhakti* movement which promoted theistic devotion and worship and found numerous followers all over India, especially from among the common people.

(c) God in the Dualism of Madhva (Dvaita)

An extreme reaction to the *advaita* philosophy of Śankara we find in the philosophy of Mādhva. Mādhva's concept of reality is similar to that of Rāmānuja, but differs from it very considerably

76 R.C. Zaehner, *Hinduism*, p. 98.
77 *Śrībhāṣya*, I.ii.12.
78 *Ibid*.
79 *Śrībhāṣya*, II.ii.3.
80 *Śrībhāṣya*, I.ii.12.
81 *Śrībhāṣya*, I.i.1.

in some respects. With Rāmānuja Mādhva takes into account God, souls and the world. But as in Rāmānuja they do not constitute one reality. Reality is essentially dualistic. God is the only independent reality (svatantra). Every thing else is dependent on God (paratantra). Reality is thus svatantra and paratantra, two eternal principles, though the latter depends on the former. Hence the name dualism (dvaita). Of the dependent reality we have conscious and unconscious beings. The conscious beings are souls and the unconscious being is the universe and every thing that is in it.

Dualism is not a new theory in the history of India. The Samkhya school had already proposed it presenting puruṣa and prakṛti, Self and matter, as two independent but mutually co-operating sources of cosmic evolution. Mādhva's system is a Vaiṣṇavite version of the Saṁkhya dualism.

The independent reality which is Brahman is the creator of the universe and is identified with Viṣṇu.[82] Brahman is not the material cause of the universe, because the universe is different from him and is formed out of prakṛti[83] by Lakṣmi, the personification of God's creative energy.[84]

The curious thing about Mādhva's concept of God is his introduction of Vayu as the son of Viṣṇu who 'is the mediator'[85] between God and man. Man is saved only through the grace of Viṣṇu and Viṣṇu is free to elect souls for salvation or damnation as he likes. However, the divine decision is not merely arbitrary. It is also proportionate to the intensity of one's devotion. Devotion enriched by meditation[86] is the way to obtain release

---

82 Mādva-bhāṣya, on Vedānta Sūtras, I.iii.13. Eng. Trans. S. Subba Rao, Vedānta-sūtras with the Commentary of Srī Mādhwacharya (Tirupati: Sri Vyasa Press, 2nd. ed. rev., 1936).

83 Mādhva-bhāṣya, I.iv.27.

84 S. Rādhakrishnan, Indian Philosophy, Vol. II., p. 742.

85 Ibid., p. 747.

86 Mādhva-bhāṣya, IV.i.3.

(mokṣa) and release consists in the restoration of one's pure spiritual existence which is fellowship with God and not identification with him. The upaniṣadic dictum *'tat tvam asi'* (That thou art) is, therefore, to be understood only as expressing the similar qualities of both God and soul.[87]

Mādhva's school is also known as *Sad-vaiṣṇavism* (true Vaiṣṇavism) in contradistiction to the *Śrī-vaiṣṇavism* of Rāmānuja. The dualistic system of Mādhva, however, did not appeal to the Indian mind as that of Śankara and Rāmānuja and consequently did not succeed in gaining followers except a few devotees of Viṣṇu.

4. The Quest for a Personal God in Hinduism

The tendency to search for a personal God could be traced back to the beginnings of Indian Philosophy. Perhaps the human mind was never satisfied with the impersonal Brahman of the Upaniṣads. That is why already in the Upaniṣads along with the monistic trends we find a growing tendency for theism.[88] As we have already seen this tendency which had its pronounced appearance in the *Śvetāśvatara* Upaniṣad evolved further and found its high expression in the Bhagavad-Gītā, a professedly theistic poem, which though not a part of the *Śruti* literature, has secured a very high position in the religious literature of India. Composed in the form of dialogical verses and placed against the background of an imminent war representing the eternal struggle between good and evil and presenting the most enrapturing doctrines of love, grace and devotion, *Gītā* captured the heart of India in a very special way and transformed her religion profoundly.

God of *Gītā* is the Lord Krishṇa, Incarnation *(avatār)* of Viṣṇu who offers himself as the charioteer of Arjuna in the great Epic of *Mahābhārata* of which *Gītā* is a part. Viṣṇu, who was a minor

---

87 *Mādhva-bhāṣya,* I.i.17; II.iii.27, 28.
88 For a comparative study of theism and monism in Hinduism and in other religions, cf. R.C. Zaehner, *Mysticism Sacred and Profane* (Oxford: University Press, 1967, first published, 1957), Chs. VIII & IX, pp. 153-197.

god in Vedic times, has by now turned out to be a supreme deity. The Vaiṣṇavites, as the name signifies, have always considered Viṣṇu as their supreme God. This Viṣṇu is supposed to incarnate himself in the world 'whenever *Dharma* (righteousness) fails and *adharma* prevails'.[89] Ten of such incarnations or divine descents are commonly accepted[90] among whom Sri Rāma of Rāmāyana, another epic contemporary to *Mahābhārata* and Sri Krishna of *Mahābhārata* are most important. Krishna became all the more because of the doctrines of the *Gītā* of which he is the author.

In the *Gītā* Krishna reveals himself to Arjuna as the supreme God whose different forms are all other gods.[91] He is also the Lord of the universe and every thing in it, moving or unmoving, is unified in his body[92] or forms his lower nature. But his higher and real nature by which this world is upheld is different.[93] He is the Infinite Being, the Lord of gods, the refuge of the universe, the exalted one who is greater than Brahman.[94] As R.C. Zaehner rightly points out, Brahman here means 'the timeless state of Being which characterizes *Mokṣa* and the source and origin of all that has its being in space and time'.[95] Thus the God of the *Gītā* transcends both time and timeless eternity and is supremely personal. He superintends the universe[96] and guides His devotees to final release.[97] Man cannot see Him by his human eyes[98] nor approach Him by his own power.[99] But the Lord will give him

---

89 *Bhagavad-Gītā*, 4.7.

90 They are: a fish, a tortoise, a boar, a man-lion, a dwarf; Parasu-Rāma, who exterminated the Ksatriyas, Rāma, the hero of the *Rāmāyana*, Krishna, one of the heroes of *Mahābhārata*, the Buddha and the Kalkin who is yet to come.

91 *Bhagavad-Gītā*, 11.5-6.

92 *Bhagavad-Gītā*, 11.7.

93 *Bhagavad-Gītā*, 7.4-5.

94 *Bhagavad-Gītā*, 11.37; 14,27.

95 R.C. Zaehner, *Hinduism*, p. 93; Cf. also his *Bhagavad-Gītā with a Commentary based on Original Sources* (Oxford: Clarendon Press, 1969), pp. 313-325.

96 *Bhagavad-Gītā*, 9.10.

97 *Bhagavad-Gītā*, 18.66.

98 *Bhagavad-Gītā*, 11.8.

99 *Bhagavad-Gītā*, 11.48.

His grace provided he worships Him in true and loving devotion.[100]

This highly developed theism of the *Bhagavad-Gītā* was later
revived by two groups of Tamil saints who spearheaded the
Bhakti movement in India from the seventh to the ninth centuries. They were Aḷvārs and Aḍiyārs devoted to Viṣṇu and Śiva
respectively. Already Buddhism and Jainism had spread all over
India and there was little room left for theistic cult in these highly philosophical religions. The Tamil reaction to it, which is
supposedly of Dravidian origin, once again marks the resurgence
of the non-Aryan element in shaping the religious destiny of
India. The Aḷvārs and Aḍiyārs cherished a concept of God that is
supremely personal. The hymns they sang, the devotion they
preached were so influential that they found their way all over
India and changed the face of Hinduism very considerably.

Of the twelve Aḷvārs canonically recognized by the Tamil
Vaiṣṇavites, Nām Aḷvār was the most important. The famous
Nālāyira-prabandham (four thousand verses) collected by Nāth-
amuni is attributed to him. The movement had its greatest philosopher in Rāmānuja whose philosophical contributions we have
already seen.

Among the Saivite saints[101] Māṇikya Vāśakar, who composed
the loveliest hymns of the love of God, is considered to be the
greatest. The theology of the movement found in the Saivite
sacred books called *Āgamas* was later systematized by Maykaṇḍar
Karulturai in the thirteenth century in his work *Śivanānapōtam*
(Śivajnānabodham). The system came to be known as *Saiva*
Siddhānta.

The *Saiva Siddhānta*[102] considers Siva as the supreme God.

---

100 *Bhagavad-Gita,* 11.54-55.

101 For a critical study of the mystical and theological writings of the Saivite saints
cf. M. Dhavamony, *Love of God according to Saiva Siddhānta* (Oxford: Clarendon
Press, 1971).

102 Contemporary to *Saiva Siddhānta* there appeared in Kashmir, the extreme north
of India a Saivite movement which came to be known as Kashmir Saivism. Though
both accepted Siva as the supreme God, in its philosophical explanations Kashmir
Saivism tends to the Non-dualsim *(Advaita)* of Śankara.

He is a personal God who loves and cares for his people. He is the *pati*, the Lord, who lovingly takes care of his cattle *(pasu)* who are bound with fetters *(pāśa)*. Pati, pasu and pāśa are the three words that summarize the doctrines of *Śaiva Siddhānta*.[103] The word *Pasupati* reminds us of the pre-Aryan Yogin surrounded by animals found on the Harappa seal. Śiva, the Lord *(pati)* is wholly transcendent. His cattle *(pasu)*, the souls are bound by three kinds of fetters *(pāśa)*. They are: 1. *āṇava*, the principle of individuation which separates them from the lord, 2. *karma*, the individual action and 3. *māyā*, the world in which they act.[104] But the Lord will give his grace to his devotee and lead him to final release. The devotee, on the other hand, will consider the love of God as his supreme virtue and obedience to the divine command his highest *Dharma* (duty).

The creative power of the Lord is *Sakti,* the eternal consort of Śiva. As Śiva and Sakti, though separated, are eternally united, so will the soul, once released, be united with God for ever. In this blissful state of divine union he can say *soham*[105] (I am He), which, though reminds us of the upaniṣadic *Tat tvam asi* (Thou art that), does not in any way mean the absolute identity of the soul with God. However, the soul keeping its identity enters into the fulness of God and thanks to the divine transformation that takes place in it, becomes all in all.

The *Bhakti* movement of the Tamil saints with its stress on vernacular literature swept across the whole of India. From the fourteenth century onwards several saints appeared in the North, all singing devotion to a personal God in their respective languages.[106] Thus the religion that was more ritualistic and philosophical assumed a new devotional flavour all over India and

---

103 S. Dhavamony, *op. cit.,* p. 347.
104 R.C. Zaehner, *Hinduism,* p. 88.
105 *Ibid.,* p. 90, Cfr. also R.C. Zaehner, *Concordant Discord,* pp. 92-94.
106 The following are some big names who led the movement in the respective languages. Hindi: Rāmānda, Kābir, Nanak and Tulsī Das; Marāṭi: Jnānesvar, Nāmdev, Ekanāth and Tukārām; Bengali: Caitanya, Rāmprāsad Sen.

appealed much more profoundly to the heart of the common people.

But deep in the Indian mind the conviction still remains that the question of the personal God such as Viṣṇu or Siva is only a matter of choice which really does not exclude the possibility of having other forms of God for other people, because the Hindu believes that his religion, whatever it be, is but one of the mani-fold forms of religious expressions. This may be the reason the *advaita* of Sankara still appeals to the Indian mind even after the great wave of the *Bhakti* movement and its nation-wide influence.

5. The Essential Elements in the Hindu Concept of God

Having seen the different systems and movements centering around the Hindu concept of God in the preceding parts now we are trying to trace the converging points of all these systems, as far as they could be brought together. It is impossible to give a uniform concept of God as the typical Hindu concept of God. Even in tracing the common elements we have to make some distictions. There are two main trends in Hinduism: monistic and theistic. But since both of them stem from the same sources and to a large extent share the same backgrounds, they really have much in common. These common elements are to be pooled together along with the characteristic note of each trend. This may give a fair picture of the Hindu concept of God. But even this should not be taken in a rigid sense, because it contradicts the very nature of the Hindu concept of God, which is highly adaptive and very extensive.

Though with differences in details, the following may be said the main trends running through the different systems of the Hindu concept of God. God is the Absolute, independent, ulti-mate reality which is called Brahman, when impersonally con-ceived, and Iśvara, Viṣṇu or Siva, when personally conceived. At any rate essentially this reality is being, pure consciousness and bliss. The world is dependent on a God who sustains, controls and guides it. Whether the world is only appearance or reality is a matter of dispute among the schools. But except the *advaita* school of Sankara, all stand for the reality of the world. Even Śankara, according to some modern interpreters,[107] did not really deny the reality of the world, but denied only its equality with Brahman, which alone is really real.

Being the centre and substratum of the whole universe God is intimately present in every being. This is all the more true with regard to the human souls, who, created or uncreated, being pure consciousness are of the same nature as God, and could be explained as identical with or similar to God, the one ultimate reality.

Under the present conditions, however, the soul is in a strange existential predicament where it is united with matter. In this condition it is under the spell of ignorance *(avidyā)* and fails to know its real nature and falsely thinks that it is something else. This ignorance is to be removed and the true nature of the soul is to be realized either by way of knowledge *(jnānamarga)* or by way of devotion *(bhaktimārga)* or by both. Thus the intuitive meditations *(dhyāna, upāsana)* and integral experience *(anubhāva)* are the recommended means to attain this goal.

The removal of *avidyā* is itself the release *(mokṣa)* which is attaining the ultimate reality, the goal of one's life. It is always understood as the emancipation of spirit from matter. But as the understanding of the nature of the ultimate reality differs, the release could be understood either as a merging of the individual into the Absolute, where the individual realizes its identity with Brahman, or an intimate union with God, where the individual, keeping its self-identity, enters into the fulness of God and becomes all in all in the all pervading splendour of the divine love.

---

107 S. Radhakrishnan, *Indian Philosophy,* Vol. II., pp. 561-574. Cf. also S. Radhakrishnan and C.A. Moore, *A Sourcebook in Indian Philosophy,* pp.610, 611. "According to Radhakrishnan, *māyā* has not meant to Indian Philosophers, even to Śankara, that the world is illusion". *Ibid.,* p. 610.

A SELECT BIBLIOGRAPHY

1. The Principal Hindu Books in English Translation

The Vedas

Griffith, R.T.H., *The Hymns of the Rigveda.* 3rd ed. 2 vols. Benarea: E.J. Lazarus & Co., 1920-1926.
Macdonell, A.A., *Hymns from the Rigveda.* London: Oxford University Press, 1922.
Müller, Max, F., *Vedic Hymns,* Part I, The Sacred Books of the East. Oxford: Clarendon Press, 1889.
Oldenberg, Herman, *Vedic Hymns,* Part II. Oxford: Clarendon Press, 1897.
Whitney, W.D. and Lanmann, C.R., *Atharva-veda Samhita.* 2 vols. Harvard Oriental Series. Harvard: University Press, 1905.

The Upaniṣads

Hume, R.E., *The Thirteen Principal Upaniṣads.* London: Oxford University Press, 1921.
Radhakrishnan, S., *The Principal Upaniṣads.* New York: Humanities Press, 1953.

The Bhagavad-Gitā

Edgerton, F., *The Bhagavad-Gītā Translated and Interpreted.* 2 vols. Harvard: University Press, 1944.
Hill, W.D.P., *The Bhagavad-Gītā.* London: Oxford University Press, 1928.
Telang, K.T., *The Bhagavad-Gītā, with the Sanasugātiya, and the Anugitā.* Oxford: Clarendon Press, 1908.
Zaehner, R.C., *Bhagavad-Gītā with a Commentary based on Original Sources.* Oxford: Clarendon Press, 1969.

The Darśanas
Nyāya

Jha, Ganganatha, *Gautama's Nyāyasūtras.* Poona: Oriental Book Agency, 1939.
Vidyabhuṣaṇa, S.C., *The Nyāyasūtras of Gotama.* The Sacred Books of the Hindus. Allahabad: The Panini Office, 1930.

Vaiśeṣika

Sinha, Nandalal, *The Vaiśeṣika Sūtras of Kaṇada.* 2nd ed. Allahabad: The Panini Office, 1923.

Saṁkhya

Sastri, S.S. Suryanarayana, *The Saṅkhyakārika of Īśvara Kriṣṇa.* Madras: University of Madras, 1935.
Sinha, Nandalal, *The Saṁhkya Philosophy* (The Saṁkhya-pravacanasūtra of Kapila). Allahabad: The Panini Office, 1915.

Yoga

Prasada, Rama, *The Yogasūtras of Patanjali.* 3rd ed. Allahabad: The Panini Office, 1924.
Woods, J.H., *The Yoga System of Patanjali, or the Ancient Hindu Doctrine of Concentration of Mind.* Harvard: University Press, 1927.

Mīmāmsā

Jha, Ganganatha, *Śabara-bhāṣya* (The Mīmāmsā-sūtras of Jaimini with the commentary of Śabara). Baroda: Oriental Institute, 1933, 1934, 1935.
Sandal, P.M.L., *The Mīmāmsā Sūtras of Jaimini.* 2 vols. Allahabad: The Panini Office, 1923, 1925.

Vedānta

Thibaut, George, *The Vedānta-sūtras with the Commentary of Śankaracarya.* 2 vols. Oxford: The Clarendon Press, 1890, 1896.
———, *The Vedānta-sūtras with the Commentary of Rāmānuja.* Oxford: The Clarendon Press, 1904.
Rao, S. Subha, *Vedānta-sūtras with the Commentary of Sri Madhwacārya.* Tirupati: Sri Vyasa Press, 1936.

2. Selections from Different Books

Radhakrishnan, S. and C.A. Moore (eds.), *A Sourcebook in Indian Philosophy.* Princeton: University Press, 1957. Contains a useful introduction to each entry and an extensive bibliography.
Zaehner, R.C. (ed.), *Hindu Scriptures.* London: Dent, 1968. Contains a general introduction.

3. Works on Hindu Philosophy and Religion

Bergaigne, Abel, *La Religion védique.* 4 vols. Paris: Libraire Honoré Champion, 1963.

Chethimattam, John B., *Patterns of Indian Thought.* A student's introduction. London: Chapman, 1971.

Dasgupta, S.N., *A History of Indian Philosophy.* 5 vols. Cambridge: University Press, 1951-1955.

——, *Hindu Mysticism.* Chicago: The Open Court Publishing Co., 1927.

——, *Yoga as Philosophy and Religion.* New York: E.P. Dutton & Co., London: Kegan Paul, 1924.

Eliade, M., Yoga: *Essai sur les origines de la mystique indienne.* Paris: P. Geuthner, 1936.

Geldner, K.F., *Der Rigveda.* 3 vols. Harvard: University Press, 1951. The complete German translation of the *Rigveda* with notes.

Gonda, J., *Notes on Brahman.* Utrecht: J.L. Beyers, 1950.

Guénon, René, *Introduction général à l'étude des doctrines hindoues.* Paris: M. Riviére, 1921.

Hauer, J.W., *Yoga als Heilweg.* Stuttgart: W. Hohlhammer, 1932.

Hiriyanna, M., *The Essentials of Indian Philosophy.* New York: The MacMillan Co., 1949; London: George Allen & Unwin, 1932.

Jacobi, Herman, *Die Entwicklung der Gottesidee bei den Indern.* Bonn: K. Schroeder, 1923.

Lacombe, Olivier, *L'Absolu selon le Vedānta.* Paris: Libraire Orientaliste Paul Geuthner, 1966.

Lamotte Etienne, *Notes sur la Bhagavad Gītā.* Paris: Paul Geuthner, 1929.

Macnicol, N., *Indian Theism.* London: Oxford University Press, 1915.

Oldenberg, Hermann, *Die Indische Philosophie.* Leipzig: B.G. Teubner, 1913.

Otto, Rudolf, *West-östliche Mystik.* Gotha: L. Klotz, 1926.

——, *Mysticism East and West.* New York: The MacMillan Co., 1932.

Prasad, Jwala, *Indian Epistemology.* Lahore: The Panjab Sanskrit Book Depot, 1939.

Radhakrishnan, S., *Indian Philosophy.* 2 vols. London: George Allen & Unwin, 1923, 1927; rev. ed., 1929, 1931.

Smart, Ninian, *Doctrine and Argument in Indian Philosophy.* London: George Allen & Unwin; New York: Humanities Press, 1964. 2nd impression, 1969.

——, *The Yogi and the Devotee.* London: George Allen & Unwin, 1968.

Tucci, Giuseppe, *Storia della filosofia indiana.* Bari, 1957.

Zaehner, R.C., *Hindusim.* London: Oxford University Press, 1962.

CHAPTER VIII

GOD IN CONTEMPORARY INDIAN PHILOSOPHY
*Jitendra N. Mohanty**

This paper will be primarily epistemological in its orientation. Its chief concern shall be to explicate the manner in which God is supposedly known in contemporary Indian thought. Two preliminary sections, one dealing in broad outline with the concept of God in classical Indian thought, and another with the ways of knowing (pramānas) shall lead us to the central theme.

There are two distinct traditions in the history of Indian thought, in so far as speculations on the concept of God are concerned. One of these is mono-theistic; the other, simply monistic. Monotheism is latent in the hymns of the *Rg Veda,* forming an invisible underpinning of what would seem in a superficial examination to be a naturalistic polytheism. Often, however, monotheism is explicitly formulated even in the hymns, as for example in the conception of *Varuna.* Monotheistic thought comes to the forefront in the later Upanisads and in the rise of the *Krsna-Vāsudeva, Bhāgavata,* and *Pāsupata* cults, and then bifurcating into the *Vaisnava* and Saiva schools, reappears, in the classical period, in the theistic systems of *Vedānta* as well as in southern *Saiva-siddhānta.* The monistic tradition, according to which there is not only one God but one reality, the all-prevading universal spirit *Ātman,* is equally old and original in its sources and even possibly exercises a much stronger hold on Indian philosophical thought. It reaches back to such justly famous hymns of the *Rg Veda* as the *Purusa sûkta,* but finds its

*Professor of Philosophy at the New School of Social Research in New York, U.S.A.

chief support in the great early Upanisads and later on flowers into the magnificent systems of *Vedānta* and Kashmir *Saivism.*

Hindu thinking concerning the nature of God derives its immense complexity from the long and vital interplay of these two traditions. Their conflicts are as interesting and fruitful as are attempts at their harmony and reconciliation. The *Bhagavadgītā* embodies one such well-known attempt at reconciliation.

Without going into a detailed exposition of the systems and scriptures, let us look at some broad features which stand out prominently:

1. The most-often used Sanskrit synonyms for 'God' in the monotheistic tradition are: *'deva', 'devatā', 'Iswara'* and *'Bhagavān';* in the monistic tradition, the most frequently used words are: *'Brahman', 'Ātman'* and *'Paramātman'.* Often, both sets of words are used in both traditions with appropriate re-interpretations of meaning. However, etymologically, the former set of words connote 'he who gives (knowledge, illumination, prosperity)', 'the highest Lord' and 'One who possesses highest excellence'; the latter set means 'the greatest than which there is nothing greater', 'the source and ground of all that is', 'that which breathes, consumes or constantly accompanies, i.e., the inner self' and 'the highest self'.

2. Early in the mono-theistic tradition, in the hymns of the *Rg Veda,* the names for many deities ('Indra', 'Vayu', 'Yama', etc.) are recognized as being only different names of one Godhead. The conception of one cosmic order, also identified as a moral law *(Rta),* helped monotheism to emerge, but it also, in most of the later systems, served to limit the function of God. Creation, maintenance of the created world and its destruction are taken to be in accordance with this eternal law--later transformed, through an admixture of various other elements, into the law of *Karma* or *adrsta.* Otherwise regarded as omnipotent, God functions in accordance with the Law: the conflict is often sought to be resolved by regarding the Law as a part of God's being.

3. Not all of the orthodox classical systems--meaning by 'orthodox' those that accept the authority of the Vedas and/or

admit an eternal self in man--are theistic. The classical *Sāmkhya* is admittedly atheistic--the many theistic Sāmkhyas notwithstanding. The world and empirical individuals are not created by an efficient cause, but are regarded as evolutes of a primal matrix, *Prakrti* or Nature, in association with a plurality of eternal pure spirits *(Purusa)*--the process of evolution, being guided only by a final cause, the two-fold goals of enjoyment of the spirits and their ultimate liberation. The concept of God has no place in this scheme. The *Yoga* system of Pantanjali agrees in most significant points with *Sāmkhya* and does not make use of the concept of God to alter this scheme--but only introduces the idea of God as a person 'who is untouched by pain, sorrow and evil, eternally pure and free', only as a *regulative* notion for the aid of the practitioner or *Yoga* and aspirant after liberation. The *Mimāmsā*--a classical school of philosophy which sets down as its primary task a hermeneutic of Vedic injunctions--has no need of a God, but recognizes gods as posits for the purpose of performing Vedic rites and duties. No ontological status is assigned to them however. Of the orthodox Hindu systems of philosophy only the *Vedānta* and the *Nyāya-Vaiseṣika* are theistic, but even in regard to these several points need to be noted.

4. In the realistic pluralism of the *Nyaya-Vaiseṣika*, God is the efficient cause of the world, the moral ruler and dispenser of ethical justice, the destroyer and over-all maintainer of the universe, the author of the scriptures: a faultless, omniscient, perfectly pure and eternally free incorporeal self. This system has among its expositors some of the most ardent defenders of theism, however, God does not create the atoms, the individual souls, and the universals, all of which are eternal. God is responsible for the primal conjoining of the atoms and for seeing that individual souls are born in forms appropriate to their accumulated merits and demerits. Such a concept of God falls short of what is known as 'theism' in the fully developed sense.

5. Turning now to the *Vedānta,* we find it split into two main camps: the absolutistic and the theistic.

(a) In the absolutistic *Vedānta* of Śamkara, the world and finite individuals are false appearances, projected by a beginningless Ignorance *(avidyā)*, on the one, eternal, unchanging, in-determinate, difference-less spirit *(Brahman)*. The religious concept of God as the creator, maintainer and destroyer of the world implies the reality of the created world and finite individuals; it also implies the reality of the distinction between man and God, the worshipper and the worshipped. The concept of God, therefore, in Śamkara's system cannot have transcendental validity. God is what *Brahman,* the non-dual absolute spirit, appears to the ignorant man. God is, like the world and finite individuals of which he is the creator, a false appearance of *Brahman. Brahman* is neither creator nor destroyer, not an agent, not a person—but the eternally unblemished substratum of the world phenomenon: also the same as the universal spirit within, of which each individual self is an unreal fragmentation (as much as the many spaces are of the one space) or a reflection (as the one moon is reflected in various media).

(b) It is in the theistic schools of *Vedānta* that *Brahman,* the Absolute of Philosophy, is also regarded as the God of religion. But theistic *Vedānta* itself is diversified, ranging from Rāmānuja at one end to Madhva at the other. While Rāmānuja is still an absolutist, regarding *Brahman* or God as the totality of all beings, spirit *(cit)* and matter *(acit)* as well as their indwelling spirit, Madhva regards differences *(bheda)* between God and man, God and world, and man and world as being metaphysically ultimate and irreducible. Theistic Vedānta sought to understand the relation between God and the world by one central category which for Rāmānuja is identity-in-difference, for Madhva is difference, for some others unthinkable and supra-rational. Theistic *Vedānta* is personalistic (i.e., regards God as the supreme person), and realistic (i.e., glorifies the way of loving devotion to God as against the Absolutist's emphasis on metaphysical knowledge).

They all reject Śamkara's illusionism. For all of them finite individuality is real and survives in the state of salvation, though what is false, and therefore annulled, is the ignorant individual's sense of independence, autonomy and exclusiveness.

Indian philosophy has had a long and unbroken concern with 'ways of knowing' *(pramānas)*. The tradition of classical philosophy required that every system of thought had, first, to lay down and defend the 'ways of knowing' recognized by it, and then to elaborate its ontology or theory of being *(prameya)*. Throughout this long, uninterrupted tradition, several broad strands stand out with pre-eminence, so far as discussion of the 'ways of knowing' are concerned. We may first investigate them, and then consider their relevance to the specific problem of knowing God.

All the classical schools of philosophy *(darsana)* chose one or more from the following list of 'ways of knowing': perception *(pratyaksa)*, inference *(anumäna)*, verbal testimony *(sabda)*, comparison *(upamāna)*, postulation *(arthāpatti)*, non-perception *(anupalabdhi)*, historic tradition *(aitihya)* and possibility *(sambhava)*. The last two were, generally speaking, either disregarded or included within either inference or verbal testimony, and so were not accorded by the major systems, the dignity of being independent ways of knowing.

The naturalists and the materialists counted sense-perception as the only admissible way of knowing, questioned the validity of inference, doubted all verbal testimony as unreliable, and founded on the resulting sensualistic epistemology a materialistic, atheistic metaphysics on the one hand and an egoistic-hedonistic ethics on the other. The Buddhists recognized only two ways of knowing: perception and inference, and by an interesting doctrine of correlation *(pramana-vyavastha)* between ways of knowing and types of being, held the view that the true object of perception (or, rather the object of perception in the strict sense) is the momentary, bare particular, and the object of inference is the universal which for the Buddhists (who, in their ontology were nominalists) is but a construction of the mind. It is not the case that one and the same object can both be perceived and on some other occasion, if needed, be inferred. What counts ordinarily as perception, i.e., perception of enduring physical objects, is really inferential-founded though on perception in the strict sense. It is the latter alone which has epistemic priority and 'gives' the real, i.e., the momentary point-instant. Perception in this sense however is ineffable, non-linguistic, non-judgmental. Only the state of *nirvāṇa* restores this perception to its purity freed from all conceptual distortions. The logical atomists and pluralists, *Nyāya* and *Vaiseṣika* philosophers, recognized four ways of knowing: perception, inference, verbal testimony and comparison. They rescued the concept of perception from the narrow scope of 'bare sensation' to which the Buddhists had restricted it, extended it to include both pre-judgmental acquaintance and linguistic judgment, and made both physical things and their attributes and universals inherent in them possible objects of perception. Inference as a way of knowing is made dependent upon perception; of the two, perception and inference, the former is stronger in the sense that an inference which contradicts perception has to be *a forteriori* rejected. Upon perceiving a sensible mark (e.g. smoke) in a locus (e.g. yonder hill), we infer the presence in the same locus of another thing (e.g. fire) with which that mark (e.g. smoke) is previously known to be constantly conjoined. This general rule of constant conjunction is gathered from previous observation of cases of co-presence, non-observation of instances to the contrary, and indirect reasoning appealing to counterfactual conditionals. Both the mark and the inferred then must be things or properties that are known to exist, if not in this locus, certainly somewhere else. An entirely unknown property cannot then be validly inferred. Besides, the rules of disputation require that there should be an agreed instance of co-presence of the mark with the inferred--an instance about which no party to the dispute should have doubts and differences. These two rules make it particularly difficult to prove the existence of God by inference; for, the atheist simply rejects the concept of God as meaningless and God is unknown to him, while the theist cannot produce an agreed instance in which the divine properties coexist with whatever is to serve as a mark of God's existence. The *Nyāya* logicians accordingly had to exercise considerable ingenuity to formulate their inferential proofs of God's existence. One such causal argument is given by *Nyāyakusumānjali,* as follows:

The world is caused by an agent, for it is an effect, as for example is a pot. Here what is inferred is the property of "being caused by an agent" - a familiar and well-known property. This property is said to belong to all things of the world. The mark is 'being an effect' - also a well-known property. The rule "Whatever is an effect is caused by an agent" is exemplified in agreed instances like this pot. The atheist cannot produce a counter-example to this rule, for all other cases are under dispute (i.e. included within the extension of 'the world') and so cannot be used by either party to the dispute to his own advantage.

The most important way of knowing, however, is verbal testimony *(sabdapramāṇa)*, for this includes knowledge or belief derived from understanding the meanings of the sentences of reliable and authoritative texts, i.e. the scriptures. In matters that are supersensible, e.g. about what ought and ought not to be done, this is the ultimate court of appeal - for perception is of no avail in these matters, and where perception fails inference cannot be of any use either. Most orthodox Hindu philosophers accepted this 'way of knowing', and by way of explicating it and defending its status discussed such hermeneutical and semantical questions as: "What is the source of the authority of the scriptures?" "What are the principles of interpretation of scriptural texts?" "What is the meaning of words (ordinary and scriptural), and how does one construe the meaning of sentences (ordinary and scriptural)?"

Postulation is the name of a way of knowing by which - in a manner closely resembling a sort of transcendental argument - we proceed from a given fact A to the acceptance of another fact B, such that only under the assumption of B, A could have been possible. The more interesting use of postulation is in interpreting some texts of the scriptures and in deciphering the unstated implications of what is stated. For example, the scriptures state: 'One who knows the self overcomes all sorrow', but they *imply* thereby that sorrow is a product of ignorance for only ignorance (and its products) can be removed by knowledge. The way of knowing called 'non-perception' is not recognized by all; those who do recognize it do so in order to account for our direct experience of the absence of a thing. Its interest for us lies in the fact that non-perception of any X is a way of knowing that X is absent. It is rather the case that only if X be such that were it present would it have been perceived, would its non-perception count as a proof of its absence. This rider makes the atheist's naive argument 'There is no God, for we do not perceive such a being' baseless, for a supersensible being, even if it did exist, would not be perceived, so that non-perception in this case is no proof of absence.

Thus though inference and verbal testimony provides, for most classical Hindu philosophers, means of knowing *that* God exists (God either as the creator of the world and the Law giver, or as the indwelling universal spirit), yet such knowledge does not amount to knowing God in the sense of direct acquaintance with Him and His nature. The latter can only be an intuitive realization to which two major 'ways' are recommended (and several variations of each or even combinations of them):

(a) The path of knowledge *(jnāna):* According to those like Śamkara for whom God is the inner self, the *Ātman* and not the creator, knowledge alone is the path to his realization. Such knowledge amounts to a knowledge of one's essential identity with *Brahman* - the sort of identity that is taught in the Upaniṣads by the text *'Tat tvam asi'* ('Thou art That') and expressed in the recognitive pseudo-judgment *'So'ham'* ('I am He'). The means to such knowledge is constituted by the three steps of *'sravaṇa'* ('hearing' = study of the scriptures with a qualified teacher who has achieved wisdom), *'manana'* ('reflection' = intellectual reasoning carried on with a view to convince oneself that the thesis of identity of the self with *Brahman* is not impossible, to refute the arguments advanced by the opponents of the thesis, and to reach absolutely unwavering intellectual conviction) and *'nididhyāsana'* ('meditation' on the truth which has been intellectually fixed). The last is to lead to an intuitive realization of the identity - an intuitive knowledge *(aparoksa-jnāna)* resulting from meditation on words *(sabdajanya),* as happens when someone's utterance leads a person to discover his own identity.

(b) The path of devotion *(bhakti):* The theistic *Vedānta* distrusts the efficacy of knowledge and emphasizes the path of loving devotion to God, the supreme Person *(puruṣottama).* There were however different accounts of the nature of *bhakti* depending upon different emphases on the various shades of emotional and cognitive components of it. Rāmānuja, for example, emphasizes *dhyāna* or meditation; others emphasize *prapatti* or *saraṇāgati,* the attitude of absolute dependence on God and a sense of utter helplessness and self-surrender as a means of winning God's grace. Does God's grace depend upon man's merit, or is it unmerited result of God's free choice? Is it *nirhetuka* (without a cause) or *sahetuka* (with a cause)? Is God to be regarded, in *bhakti,* as the beloved or as the trusted friend, as Master or as Father? Human emotion directed towards an Other may take many and varied forms and there are as many complex forms of *bhakti* in whose description the theistic literatures of the Hindus abound.

(c) For the purposes of this paper, it may be in order to conclude this reference to classical Indian philosophy by referring to the teachings of Śri Kṛṣṇa in the *Bhagavadgītā.* The *Gītā,* as the work is briefly and lovingly called, seeks to synthesize not only diverse metaphysical trends present in Hindu thought, but also the many different 'ways' which were being recommended for reaching God or realizing the Divine. In brief, these were the 'ways' of knowledge *(jñāna)* taught by *Sāmkhya* and *Vedānta, bhakti* taught by the theistic *Bhāgavata* and *Kṛṣṇa-Vāsudeva* cults and the path of *karma* or performance of scriptural duties recommended by the Vedic tradition. As a result of this synthesis, or rather as a condition of its possibility, each of these concepts undergoes profound change: *karma* (action) is no longer performance of scriptural duties alone for attainment of heaven but disinterested performance of duties without attachment to likely consequences for oneself; *jñāna* (knowledge) of the distinction between the self *(ātman)* and non-self *(anātman)* now leads not to inaction but to life or action without attachment and with inner freedom and tranquillity; *bhakti* (loving devotion) is not mere emotional exuberance but is based on right knowledge of

God as the supreme Being whose aspects are Nature and finite individuals, and involves complete surrender of one's aspirations and the 'fruits' of one's actions to Him. Seen in this light, the three 'ways' complement and enrich each other.

Running through all these, there is to be discerned the peculiarly Indian conception of *Yoga* in various forms - the conception of a psycho-physical moral and spiritual discipline through which the individual gradually transforms himself into a fit medium for the manifestation of higher self-knowledge and/or love. The *Gītā* by giving this word a most welcome extension speaks of '*jnānayoga*' (the *yoga* of knowledge), *karmayoga* (the *yoga* of action) and *bhaktiyoga* (the *yoga* of devotion). A *yogin* is one who has achieved perfection through practice of *yoga*. Only the *yogin* knows God and *not* merely *that* there is God. Thus in the long run faith was subordinated to direct intuitive knowledge.

Contemporary Indian philosophy is rooted in the tradition we have outlined. In general, it shares that age-old spiritual concern. It still hovers between the conception of a universal, formless spirit or *Ātman* and the conception of a personal creator God, between 'ways' of *jnāna, karma* and *bhakti,* and still looks to the *Gītā* for the solution of its dilemma by way of a satisfying synthesis. The new motivations have been partly, contact with western science and philosophical thinking, and partly, the demands of modern life with its characteristic concern - social, political and economic - for the other at a purely secular level. We shall examine some typical and most influential figures to see in what form the concept of God appears in their thoughts and what they think about the ways of knowing God. We shall begin with the great Hindu saint Śrī Rāmakrisna who cast a profound influence on all shades of Hindu life and thought in the closing years of the 19th century; then we turn in that order to the Bengali poet Rabindranath Tagore, the political leader Mahatma Gandhi, the *yogi* Sri Aurobindo, the philosopher-statesman S. Radhakrishnan, and modern India's academic philosopher *par excellence* Krishna Chandra Bhattacharyya.

1. Through the tradition of Hindu thought, as we have seen,

the choice between the way of knowledge and the way of *bhakti* was closely connected with the choice between the conception of an impersonal *Brahman* and the conception of a personal God. The impersonal spirit had to be known or realized, the personal God had to be loved, adored, praised and worshipped. To the question, if God is with or without form, Sri Rāmakriṣna says: He is both. "God with form is just as true as God without form."[1] Is the phenomenal world real or illusory? Sri Rāmakriṣna believed that finite individuality, the 'I' and the 'Mine' are illusory;[2] yet again the universe is God's glory.[3] Darkness "reveals all the more the glory of light."[4] God is beyond 'knowledge' and 'ignorance'[5] - beyond the knowledge of abstract unity and belief in phenomenal plurality. Though Sri Rāmakriṣna did hold the view that knowledge (or experience) of *Brahman* is indescribable ("Once a salt doll went to measure the depth of the ocean. It wanted to tell others how deep the water was. But this it could never do, for no sooner did it get into water than it melted."[6]) and that perfect knowledge leads to silence,[7] yet he also emphasized that so long as the feeling of 'I' persists in us the path of love is easier to follow. This is how he contrasts the *jnāni* (one who knows) and the *bhakta* (one who loves): the former believes that the *Brahman* alone is real, the world being an illusory phenomenon, while the latter believes that the universe is a real manifestation of God's glory.[8] Of the two, the path of *bhakti* is easier to follow. The devotes does not renounce all sense of 'I'. Sri Rāmakriṣna distinguishes between the " unripe 'I' " (I am the leader) and the " ripe 'I' " (I am the servant of God). The *bhakta* throws away the former but retains the latter.

---

1 *Gospel of Sri Ramakrisna*, English trans. by Swami Nikhilananda (New York: Harper, 1952), pp. 80, 148.
2 *Ibid.*, p. 105.
3 *Ibid.*, p. 96.
4 *Ibid.*, p. 97.
5 *Ibid.*, p. 101.
6 *Ibid.*, p. 103.
7 *Ibid.*, p. 148.
8 *Ibid.*, p. 133.

However, the most distinguishing feature of Srī Rāmakriṣṇa's teachings is his recognition of the many different paths to God-realization ('*yata mat tata path*' = 'As many paths as there are views') leading to the same goal. In his own life he practised--and for his disciples he recommended--the precept: 'One should follow various paths. One should practice each creed for a time.'[9]

2. The poet Rabindranath Tagore emphasized the path of love as the best means of God-realization, and consciously continued the tradition of the great medieval poet saints Kabir and Vidyāpati and the contemporary Bengali sect of wandering mystics known as the Bauls. In his Hibbert lectures of 1929 published under the title *Religion of Man* Tagore develops the idea of the humanity of God whose correlate, for him, is the idea of the divinity of Man, the Eternal.[10] The former is contrasted with all concepts of God as cosmic force,[11] which hold no appeal to him. In the spirit of the medieval *Vaiṣṇaua* saints, he looks upon God as the supreme Person, and identifies Him with 'Man the Eternal' --without making it sufficiently clear what he means by the last concept. (Is it the eternal essence of man, of Humanity understood as the Human Race, or the most perfect Man, the supreme Person?) The world, even the realm of truth--the scientific truths not excluded—are human. The goal of human life is to make this inner divinity, the universality of the spirit within, explicit. The goal of the evolution of man is "the evolution of a consciousness that tries to be liberated from the bounds of individual separateness and to comprehend in its relationship a wholeness which may be named Man."[12] God is this unity of Mankind:

"Whatever character our theology may ascribe to him, in reality he is the infinite ideal of Man towards whom men move

9 *Ibid.*, p. 128.
10 Rabindranath Tagore, *Religion of Man*, 5th ed. (London: George Allen & Unwin, 1958), p. 17.
11 *Ibid.*, p. 19.
12 *Ibid.*, p. 47.

in their collective growth, with whom they seek their union of love as individuals..."[13]

To know this unity—to know not merely that there is such a unity, but to know the unity itself—requires renunciation, freeing oneself of the clutches of exclusive individuality: "religion is the liberation of our individual personality in the universal Person who is human all the same."[14] "From individual body to community, from community to universe, from universe to Infinity—this is the soul's normal progress."[15] Love is the intense feeling of union with that greater whole. Tagore concedes that other forms of experience of God are possible—the experience, for example, of the merging of the finite self in the infinite in the state of *samādhi,* but adds:

"While accepting their testimony as true, let us at the same time have faith in the testimony of others who have felt a profound love, which is the intense feeling of union, for a Being who comprehends in himself all things that are human in knowledge, will and action."[16]

God-realization is not an escape from an illusory world. In his *Gītānjali (Offering of Songs),* Tagore writes:[17]

"Deliverance?
Where is this deliverance to be found?"

God is not to be found in a solitude beyond:

13 *Ibid.,* p. 165.
14 *Ibid.,* p. 193.
15 *Ibid.,* p. 199.
16 *Ibid.,* p. 206.
17 Rabindranath Tagore, *Collected Poems and Plays,* (New York: MacMillan, 1951), p. 6.

"He is there where the tiller is tilling the hard ground and where the pathmaker is breaking stones."[18]

God is, for Tagore, both personal and impersonal. He writes:

"In love, at one of its poles you find the personal, at the other the impersonal. At one you have the positive assertion--Here I am; at the other the equally strong denial--I am not. Without this ego what is love? And again, with only this ego how can love be possible?"[19]

In his contribution to *Contemporary Indian Philosophy*, edited by Radhakrishnan and Muirhead, he writes:

Personality is "where infinite becomes finite without losing its infinity." "God is personal where he creates."[20]

3. If Tagore emphasizes the path of love, Mahatma Gandhi emphasizes the *Bhagavadgītā's* concept of 'action with detachment'. Neither Tagore nor Gandhi were academic philosophers. Both derived their wisdom from their experiences. The former's experience was that of a poet, the latter's of a man of action, social and political.

Gandhi oscillated all his life between the conception of God as a person and the conception of God as impersonal. In his *Autobiography*, he speaks of the 'grace' of God and of the need for "an unreserved surrender" to His grace. In 1925, he wrote:

"God is that indefinable something which we all feel but which we do not know...He transcends speech and reason...He

---

18 *Ibid.*, p. 6.
19 Rabindranath Tagore, *Sadhana*, (London: MacMillan), pp. 114-15.
20 J.H. Muirhead and S. Radhakrishnan, *Contemporary Indian Philosophy* (2nd ed. London: George Allen & Unwin, 1952), p. 37.

is a personal God to those who need His personal presence. He is embodied to those who need His touch. He is the purest essence. He simply *is* to those who have faith."[21]

In 1926 he asserts that though he was a non-dualist (advaitist) yet he could also support dualism *(dvaitavāda)*.[22] In 1928 he expresses his preference for 'God is truth' to 'God is love' on the ground that 'love' has many meanings while 'truth' does not have many meanings.[23] In his 1936 contribution to *Contemporary Indian Philosophy* he makes a notable advance in his thought:

> "I often describe my religion as Religion of Truth. Of late, instead of saying God is Truth, I have been saying Truth is God, in order more fully to define my Religion."[24]

And he justifies this change on the ground that God, as he now defines Him, is undeniable. "Denial of God we have known. Denial of Truth we have not known."[25] Since utter scepticism about truth is self-defeating, one's God is precisely what one accepts as the truth. He did allow that none of us has knowledge of that complete truth which is God:

> "We are all sparks of Truth. The sum-total of these sparks is indescribable, as-yet-Unknown Truth which is God. I am being daily led nearer to It by constant prayer."[26]

To sum up, it seems to have been Gandhi's maturer view that God as the Truth is the as-yet-Unknown supra-rational Change-less Being who is the source of all things. But how such a God appears to one would depend upon one's own need and perspec-

21 M.K. Gandhi, in *Young India,* March 3, 1925.
22 M.K. Gandhi, in *Young India,* January 21, 1926.
23 M.K. Gandhi, in *Young India,* November 11, 1928.
24 *Contemporary Indian Philosophy,* p. 21.
25 *Ibid.,* p. 21.
26 *Ibid.,* p. 21.

tive. "He is a personal God to those who need His personal presence."

How does one know God? Gandhi believed that the body, the senses and the ego were obstacles for knowing God. Consequently for him the indispensable condition for such knowledge is self-purification *(atma-suddhi)* through control of the senses, humility or self-effacement, service of suffering humanity, self-surrender and prayer. While self-purification was regarded in the classical non-dualism of Samkara as a necessary requisite for the *pursuit* of knowledge *(jijñāsā)*, Gandhi raises it to the status of a condition necessary for *jnāna* itself and replaces the emphasis on contemplation by that on self-less service of the other. God for him is beyond speech and reason.[27] His existence cannot be proved rationally[28] (although he found the argument from order more persuasive). Hence his great emphasis on faith which "does not contradict reason, but transcends it."[29] But he was in fact ascribing to faith a sort of cognitive value when he asserts:

"Faith is a kind of sixth sense which works in cases which are without the purview of reason."[30]

In the end of course Gandhi concludes that complete realization of God is impossible in bodily existence. One can only approximate towards it.

4. Sri Aurobindo combines the insights of personal spiritual experience with the construction of a grand metaphysical system. The intellectual and spiritual conflict which we have noted between the two opposed conceptions of God are sought to be harmonized by Sri Aurobindo in what he calls his Integral Non-dualism which recognizes three dimensions of the being of the

27 M.K. Gandhi, in *Young India,* March 3, 1925.

28 M.K. Gandhi, in *Young India,* November 11, 1928.

29 quoted in *All Men are Brothers. Life and Thoughts of Mahatma Gandhi As Told in His Own Words.* Complied and Edited by Krishna Kripalini. UNESCO (New York: Columbia University Press, 1958), p. 64.

30 *Ibid.,* p. 64.

Divine: the transcendent, the universal and the individual. Man is an individual expression of the divine being, and in Sri Aurobindo's view, the individual is necessary for the work of the Transcendent in the universe. Continuation of the illumined individual in the action of the world is an imperative need of the world-play, for which it is necessary that the individual must be an indissoluble center which no knowledge of the universal or of the transcendent should annul. Correlative to the conception of the integral *Brahman*, Sri Aurobindo develops the conception of integral knowledge which includes knowledge of all the terms of being,[31] the highest and the lowest with all intermediate links. Four grades of knowledge are distinguished: knowledge by identity (e.g. our direct awareness of our own essential existence), knowledge by intimate contact (e.g. our experience of our own subjective movements), knowledge by separative direct contact (e.g. introspection into subjective movements) and separative knowledge (e.g. knowledge of the external world). In all this, of course, for Sri Aurobindo, a knowledge by identity constitutes and continues to be the basis: consciousness is one in the subject and the object.[32] But this identity is concealed by differentiation, which is the function of Ignorance *(avidyā)*. But Ignorance, in Sri Aurobindo's system, is not the opposite of knowledge, not what is totally negated by knowledge—for, differentiation is also real—but a real movement of the spirit, to be perceived, in integral knowledge, in its real origin and function. Thus integral knowledge should combine knowledge of the one with knowledge of the many, which requires transcending the limitations of ordinary mental consciousness which works by setting up irreconcilable oppositions (e.g. the law contradiction), and growing into the level of supra-mental consciousness which balances unity with difference, and for which all differences are grounded in and sustained by unity. The growth of mankind into such supramental consciousness is, for Sri Aurobindo, a destiny immanent

---

31 Sri Aurobindo, *Life Divine.* (New York: Ambassador, 1951), p. 566.
32 *Ibid.,* p. 374.

in the process of cosmic evolution; while, at the same time, to accentuate this process, it is incumbent upon self-conscious individuals to make an effort to realize this higher form of consciousness in their own bodily and social existence—the means to which is provided by a supposedly new technic of *yoga,* as developed and practiced through the tradition—had two basic goals: the ascent of the individual to a higher form of consciousness, and freedom of the individual, to be achieved by the individual for himself. Sri Aurobindo considerably modifies these two conceptions: to the idea of ascent, he adds that of descent. It is as necessary for the individual to ascend to a higher mode of consciousness as to make the higher descend into the lower. These notions of ascent and descent correspond to the actual process of evolution in which there is a movement of ascent from the lower to the higher form (e.g. from matter to organic life), but also a descent of the higher into the lower and consequent transformation of the lower. The goal of spiritual life, according to Sri Aurobindo then, is not merely to rise up to a higher form of consciousness, but also to transform the lower forms (the body not excluding) so as to make them fit receptacles for the descent of the higher. The other respect in which Sri Aurobindo's conception of *yoga* differs from the traditional, consists in that for him the aim of integral *yoga* should be, not individual freedom, but the transformation of mankind into a higher form of consciousness.

It is important to note that in this philosophy, integral knowledge of the Divine depends as much upon the individual as upon the grace of the Divine being itself. This is implicit in the emphasis upon the concept of 'descent'. The individual's ascent is to be geared to the goal of making the descent of the divine possible.

5. Beginning as an *Advaita* Vedantist, K. C. Bhattacharyya moved towards a novel theory of alternate absolutes. Even in his early writings, he accords to the concept of God a more positive status than is to be found in the classical *Advaita* writings. Thus he writes in the early *Studies in Vedantism*:

"*Brahman* and *Īsvara* have sometimes been called the higher

god and the lower god. The distinction is, to say the least, misleading, and probably the over-definite language of some of
the systematizing scholiasts is responsible for this. No doubt
there is a distinction between the conceptions. Yet Isvara is
not in reality different from *Brahman.* "[33]

Bhattacharyya tries to make the distinction clear with the help
of an image:

"An image will make it clear—a light-sphere in circumambient
darkness. From the centre of it, the fullness of light radiates all
around, without a thought of darkness: it is the indeterminate
infinite *Brahman.* At the circumference, however, it reaches its
limit (not a resistance) and retires into itself, the limiting darkness falling outside of it; the sphere, as viewed from the circumference inwards, is the determinate Infinite or the closed-
in Absolute, *Īsvara.* "[34]

The *Īsvara* is then said to be revealed in an 'absolute consciousness' which is reached

"when there is a perfect chastening of the spirit, when it is
made the still mirror of truth, not simply by a discipline of
the intellect but by an ethical discipline of the will, when all
the desires of the individual self have been completely eliminated and the spirit is broadened out so as to comprehend the
truest interests of all beings."[35]

The experience of *Brahman* is not intellectual knowledge, but an
"enjoying intuition"[36] of the self's freedom from empirical

---

33 Krishna Chandra Bhattacharyya, *Studies in Philosophy*, (Calcutta: Progressive
Publishers, 1956), Vol. I, p. 49.
34 *Ibid.,* p. 49.
35 *Ibid.,* p. 52.
36 *Ibid.,* p. 106.

individuality. How such a freedom is to be reached is said to be a question of "meta-psychological" discipline.[37] The *jñāna* or knowledge which *Advaita Vedanta* emphasizes is not mere philosophical thought, but "a specific enjoyment of the thought as sacred,"[38] "an intuition which amounts to ecstasy."[39] Thus K. C. Bhattacharyya could say that *Advaita Vedanta* is not opposed to the religion of *bhakti*, for the higher stages of *bhakti* involve "the enjoyment of truth in one's being:"[40]

> "Although *bhakti* implies individuality, it represents the individual's joy in surrendering his individuality. The *bhakta* may feel his individuality restored through the Lord, but that is a mystery of the divine life with which the *Advaitin* would not dally."

However, soon, Bhattacharyya comes to develop his own distinctive theory of the alternate forms of Absolute. These alternate forms correspond to the three modes of consciousness: knowing, feeling and willing. The absolute of knowing is Truth, the absolute of feeling is Value, and the absolute of willing is Freedom.

> "In the reflective stage these absolutes or formulations of the absolute will be found to be un-unifiable and to be in a sort of alternation. Whether a mystical identity of the absolutes can be reached in the supra-reflective consciousness does not concern us. Our problem is to show how reflection demands a specific absolute in each case."[41]

Further:

> "It is meaningless therefore to cognitively assert that there are

37 *Ibid.*, p. 106.
38 *Ibid.*, p. 123.
39 *Ibid.*, p. 124.
40 *Ibid.*, p. 124.
41 Krishna Chandra Bhattacharyya, *op. cit.*, Vol. II, p. 128.

three absolutes or one absolute. The absolute has, however, to be formulated in this triple way. Each is absolute but what are here understood as *three* are only their verbal symbols, they themselves being understood together but not *as together.*"[42]

In fact, the Absolute may be regarded in this sense as an *alternation* of truth, value and reality.[43]

What Bhattacharyya seems to have in mind is the ultimacy of each of the traditional paths in the Hindu tradition: the paths of knowledge *(jnāna),* love *(bhakti)* and *yoga* understood as discipline of the will. Each path leads to its own absolute, its own God-realization (or, self-realization): the former to knowledge of the self-revealing, universal spirit as the only Truth, the second to the personal Godhead as the embodiment of all values (i.e. as Love), and the last to the realization of absolute will as freedom from all empirical objectivity. The will to achieve the highest stage of *samādhi,* in *yoga,* is "at once the culminating phase of willing and a contemplative surrender of the willing attitude."[44]

Now in the Hindu tradition, there were no doubt attempts to synthesize these paths. Bhattacharyya wishes to retain each in its purity and to grant each its own uniqueness and dignity. The alternation—the either-or—seemed to him an ultimate category of man's spiritual life; and the goal of this spiritual life, the Absolute, was also conceived in terms of this alternation.

6. Sarvepalli Radhakrishnan emphasizes that the essence of religion is a personal experience, unique and autonomous, which is also the reaction of the whole man to the whole reality. The distinctive characteristic of Hindu religion is its "insistence on the inward life of spirit."[45]

42 *Ibid.,* pp. 141-42.

43 *Ibid.,* p. 143.

44 Krishna Chandra Bhattacharyya, *op. cit.,* Vol. I, p. 227.

45 S. Radhakrishnan and C. Moore (ed.), *A Source Book in Indian Philosophy* (Princeton, N.J.: Princeton University Press, 1957), p. 615.

"To know, possess and be the spirit in this physical frame, to convert an obscure plodding mentality into clear spiritual illumination, to build peace and self-existent freedom in the stress of emotional satisfactions and sufferings, to discover and realize the life divine in a body subject to sickness and death has been the constant aim of the Hindu religious endeavour."[46]

Radhakrishnan describes religious experience as a sort of experience which is not split into subject and object, which is an integral and undivided consciousness "in which feelings are fused, ideas melt into one another, boundaries broken and ordinary distinctions transcended."[47] It is an intuitive experience, which claims to be self-sufficient, complete, self-validating, ecstatic and ineffable. Its expression has to be symbolic and metaphorical, and often negative.

Radhakrishnan sees no incompatibility between the notion of the all-embracing Absolute spirit and the concept of a personal God. The difference between the two is one of standpoint, not of essence.[48]

"We call it the "absolute" to show our sense of the inadequacy of all terms and definitions. We call it "God" to show that it is the basis of all that exists and the goal of all."[49]

The unity of the Absolute and God may be disputed by philosophers, but religious consciousness has felt that the two are one.[50]

Realization of God is also self-realization. It is not a matter of pleasing or placating God, it is a matter of transforming our being.[51] What is needed is a strict ethical discipline, absolute

46 *Ibid.*, p. 615.
47 *Ibid.*, p. 617.
48 *Ibid.*, p. 629.
49 *Ibid.*, p. 629.
50 *Ibid.*, p. 630.
51 *Ibid.*, p. 633.

inward purity through self mastery and self-renunciation, and meditation.

"It is the gathering up of all dispersed energies, the intellectual powers, the heart's emotions, the vital desires, nay the very physical being itself, and concentrating them all on the supreme goal."[52]

Several significant points may be noticed, as a consequence of the preceding survey:

The importance of *sabdapramāṇa*, or of the scriptural *words* as a source of valid knowledge, has been underplayed, although no one has explicitly rejected it. The Vedāntic tradition, as we have seen, rests upon it as much as on independent reasoning and reflection. None of the modern thinkers we have examined makes much use of it, none, however, questions it. Here is an area where contemporary Indian philosophers have to exercise constructive thinking in their relation to the traditional epistemological theories. The question is: are the scriptures to be regarded as independent and valid sources of *knowledge* of the supersensible (God, soul, *karma* and possibility of *mokṣa*)? The relevant concepts of 'independence', 'validity' and 'knowledge' require re-examination. Perhaps a distinction needs to be drawn between *'understanding* the meaning of a sentence p' and 'knowing that p'.

None of the modern Indian thinkers has sought to re-state, re-examine or rehabilitate the classical proofs for the existence of God. No attempt has been made to improve, for example, upon Udayana; or, possibly even to refute Udayana's famed arguments. The causal (from the world to its maker) and the moral (from the law to the lawgiver) arguments persist in the unreflective Hindu religious consciousness, and so are in need of re-examination with the help of modern logical and analytical techniques.

---

52 *Ibid.*, p. 633.

With Gandhi alone faith occupies a supreme place. All the other thinkers whom we have examined seek to move from an initial intellectual conviction to a living spiritual experience merging upon the mystical.

In its conception of the Divine, contemporary Indian thought is predominantly Vedāntic, though Śamkara's illusionism has been pretty well laid aside. The classical philosophies' sense of opposition between the conception of a formless spirit and the conception of a personal God has been sought to be overcome by Śri Rāmakriṣna (in the conception of varieties of religious *experience*), Sri Aurobindo (in his conception of Integral Brahman) and K. C. Bhattacharyya (in his rather strangely suggestive metaphor of a "light-sphere in circumambient darkness").

Attempts to synthesize, or at least reconcile, the different 'paths' to God-realization (or, better, Self-realization) abound and constitute a thematic link with the tradition deriving from the *Bhagavadgitā*. On the one hand, there is Śri Rāmakriṣna's bold declaration--almost a motto of modern Hindu liberalism--*'yata mat tata path'* ('As many paths as there are views'). On the other there is the poet Tagore's personal preference for the path of love and Gandhi's preference for the path of *karma* or non-attached action. A most striking construction is K. C. Bhattacharyya's recognition of the irreducibility of the category of 'either-or' in spiritual life and the resulting philosophy of the alternate forms of the Absolute.

A SELECT BIBLIOGRAPHY

Aurobindo, Sri, *Life Divine*. New York: Ambassador Publishing Co., 1951.

Bhattacharyya, Krishna Chandra, *Studies in Philosophy*. Calcutta: Progressive Publishers, (Vol. 1), 1956; (Vol. II), 1958.

Gandhi, Mohandas Karamchand (ed.), *Young India* (a newspaper published between 1919-1933). Ahmedabad, India: Mahadev Desai Publishing Co., March 3, 1925; January 21, 1926; November 11, 1928.

Kripalini, Krishna (ed.), *All Men are Brothers: Life and Thought of Mahatma Gandhi As Told by His Own Words*. UNESCO. New York: Columbia University Press, 1958.

Muirhead, J.H. and S. Radhakrishnan, *Contemporary Indian Philosophy.* London: George Allen & Unwin, 1952.

Radhakrishnan, S. and C. Moore (eds.), *A Source Book in Indian Philosophy.* Princeton, New Jersey: Princeton University Press, 1957.

Ramakrisna, Srí, *Gospel of.* English translation by Swami Nikhilananda. New York: Harper Publishing Company, 1952.

Tagore, Rabindranath, *Collected Poems and Plays.* New York: MacMillan, 1951.

———, *Religion of Man.* London: George Allen & Unwin, 1958.

———, *Sadhana.* London: MacMillan, 9140.

CHAPTER IX

NEO-HINDUISM of G. R. MALKANI

George B. Burch *

On February 25, 1971, on my way to Bengal, I stopped at Bombay to see my old friend and teacher Professor G. R. Malkani. We had a long talk about Vedanta philosophy, and he gave me a manuscript entitled *A Philosophy of Life.* Having finished writing this, he had no further interest in it, and said that I might keep it or throw it away as I pleased.

Malkani, born in 1892 at Hyderabad Sind and educated at Karachi, spent most of his life at Amalner, a small town two hundred miles northeast of Bombay. The economy of Amalner was transformed in 1908 when Pratap Seth, an agarwal business man, came there to build a cotton mill, which expanded to have 1000 looms and 2400 employees. With the profits of the mill he established and endowed a liberal arts college, a temple dedicated to Shankaracharya, a modern hospital and an ayurvedic pharmacy. In 1916, to encourage the study of Vedanta philosophy, to which he was passionately devoted, he established a research institution, the Indian Institute of Philosophy. Malkani was one of six young men chosen to be fellows the first year, was then sent to England for two years to get his M.Litt. at Cambridge, and soon after became the Institute's permanent director. It was a small institution with one academic building, a library of a few hundred volumes, and a block of living apartments, but it had considerable influence. Several of the leading philosophers of India were there for longer or shorter periods, and profited from the opportunity for study, meditation, and speculation in this

*Emeritus Fletcher Professor at Tufts University, Medford, Massachusetts, U.S.A.

secluded intellectual oasis. Malkani was the soul of the Institute, and informed it with his forceful personality.

From its beginning the Institute published a journal of articles by its members. In 1925 this was named the *Philosophical Quarterly,* and contributions were invited from all Indian philosophers. A year later the newly formed Indian Philosophical Congress adopted it as its official organ and Malkani was appointed editor. Under his vigorous and liberal direction it was the leading philosophical journal of India until its suppression in 1966.

The years 1933-1935 were the Golden Age of the Institute. K. C. Bhattacharyya, already "retired," was there, and Malkani ceded the title of Director to this distinguished philosopher while he was present. T. R. V. Murti, later professor at Banaras, and Rasvihary Das, later at Calcutta, were there. Bhattacharyya dominated the seminars. His oral presentation, unlike his writing, was clear, fluent, and persuasive, and Malkani told me he was never able to refute his subtle dialectic. In his address at the opening of the academic year in 1934 Bhattacharyya said, "We mean by philosophical research more a finding of our own place in thought than a contribution to the world of thought" (PQ, X, 2, iii). This also describes Malkani's attitude. He feels certain of the truth of his philosophy, but does not feel any mission to convert others.

When I resolved to spend my sabbatical year 1953-54 studying contemporary Indian philosophy, I knew nothing about it, but did know Malkani's name from seeing the *Philosophical Quarterly.* I wrote asking whether I might have some talks with him, and he replied that he was willing but advised against it because "the place is dusty; the available accomodations not suitable; European type of food not possible to arrange; no suitable places of entertainment." When my family and I arrived, Pratap Seth gave us an apartment in the mill, where we set up housekeeping and lived very comfortably. The Institute consisted of the director, one other professor, a shastri, and four fellows, two of whom had been there many years. Every day I talked with Malkani from eleven to twelve (exactly) and after tea joined him on his evening walk (by which the townsfolk might have set their clocks). "His erect bearing," I wrote in a report, "reveals an inner integrity of character, but his brusque manner conceals an inner warmth of devotion." Our friendship was both intellectual and personal, and my four months as the only Westerner to study at Amalner were a happy period of my life.

After Pratap Seth's death in 1965 the mill fell into bankruptcy. On September 30, 1966, Malkani was abruptly informed, by a letter from Pratap Seth's heir, that his services would terminate after one month and that the *Quarterly* was to be discontinued immediately. So ended the fifty-year career of this man, this journal, and this institute which did so much to make Vedanta a living philosophy in this century. He declined an offer of assistance; Malkani is neither a brahmin accepting gifts nor a guru supported by disciples. He and his wife now live with two of their sons at Bombay.

Malkani is a philosopher, not a scholar. He said it was his practice to read an author, then forget what was written, and then think out the same problem for himself. At Amalner he thought and wrote about philosophical problems every day. Almost every number of the *Philosophical Quarterly* included an article by him. Of his books, all published by the Institute, the most important are *Philosophy of the Self* (1939, American reprint 1966, in my opinion his best book), *Vedantic Epistemology* (1953, including a criticism of K. C. Bhattacharyya's philosophy), and *Metaphysics of Advaita Vedanta* (1961, the most comprehensive exposition of his philosophical position). The succession of writings does not involve any charge or development in the substance of his philosophical thought but only a persistent endeavor to formulate it with greater precision and clarity. His purpose is not to seek the truth, which he has already found, but to express it.

Each school of Vedanta philosophy claims to be the correct interpretation of the infallible but ambiguous Veda. The advaita or nondualist school, in which the oldest extant text is by the fifth-century philosopher Guadapada, teaches that the world is illusion, the self is reality, and freedom is attained by knowledge.

Malkani's philosophy is this ancient doctrine, not at all original, yet significant for its way of expression. Malkani frees nondualism from dependence on the Sanskrit language with which it has been associated by restating it in English, not merely translating Sanskrit terms into English equivalents but rethinking the whole doctrine in Western concepts. This might be impossible for Nyaya philosophy, in which the logical concepts are intimately related to the Sanskrit words. But Vedanta is universal. If true anywhere, it is true everywhere, and can be expressed equally well in any language. Malkani's English style is of extraordinary clarity, and this makes his works especially suitable as an introduction of Vedanta. "I am one of those who believe that philosophy should be freed from unnecessary technicalities, and made intelligible to all those intelligent lay persons who have not made philosophy their profession," he said in his Presidential Address to the Indian Philosophical Congress in 1949.

The traditional way of presenting Vedanta has been by commentaries on the classics -- especially the Vedanta Sutra, itself a commentary on the Upanishads -- and commentaries on the commentaries. For a modern reader this involves devious, repetitious unwinding of the doctrine and tedious anachronistic refutation of ancient arguments. By presenting the doctrine systematically Malkani frees it from dependence on the literary tradition. He makes few if any references to the classics or commentaries. He presents Vedanta rationally, on its merits, not on authority. His works constitute an independent body of nondualist philosophy intelligible without any acquaintance with the history of Indian philosophy. As a rationalist he has neither guru nor disciples; the true guru, he says, in the guru within us, which can never deceive us, always ready at hand, speaking to us -- only we do not listen (PQ XXXVIII, 2, 121).

His philosophy is significant, however, not only for its form of expression but also for its metaphysical substance. He carries out the analysis of experience with ruthless rationality. The commentators, beginning with the celebrated Shankaracharya, watered down Guadapada's nondualist system by compromises with common sense. Malkani makes no compromises with com-

mon sense, current opinions, or tradition, but pushes the arguments to their logical conclusions. He holds all those extreme
positions -- *drishtisrichtivada, ekajivavada, ajativada* -- which the
popular Vedanta teachers, traditional and contemporary, shy
away from. *Drishtisrishtivada,* "seeing-being-ism," is the doctrine
that the world exists only because it is seen; Malkani described
the more popular view, that the world, although illusory, is still
objective and so to be seen, as "advaita for the dull." *Ekajivavada,* "one-person-ism," is the doctrine that the person who has
the illusion is one, not many, since plurality of individuals is
itself part of the illusion. *Ajativada,* "non-origination-ism," is the
doctrine that the world has no origin -- because there isn't any
world; really there is no creation, no illusion, no world, no
individual, no bondage, no release, and no freedom, but only self.
Ajativada is not a theory of the world but denial that there is a
world to have a theory about. *Ekajivavada,* Malkani told me, is
the "most satisfactory philosophical theory," while *ajativada* is
the "last kick of philosophy" before it lapses into silence.

A theory of ignorance is essential to a philosophy which
teaches that experience is false. A central problem is the question
which is prior, ignorance or error. In our Bombay conversation
Malkani insisted that, although both are beginningless and ignorance does not explain error, ignorance is prior, because ignorance
makes error possible and the overcoming of ignorance by knowledge dispels error. This means, I take it, that error is a sufficient
condition but not a sufficient cause of ignorance, which has no
cause, but is itself the first cause of the world-appearance.

Malkani and K. C. Bhattacharyya, in my opinion the two most
important Vedanta philosophers of this century, are quite different in their style -- the primer-like simplicity of one and the
difficult precision of the other -- and in their philosophy. Malkani
clarifies and purses the perennial nondualism by his rigorous
logic. Bhattacharyya opens up new dimensions in it by his dialectical analysis. In *Reality and Value* Malkani acknowledges his
debt to Bhattacharyya's lectures: "but for him, my conclusions
would have been substantially the same, but the arguments
would have taken a less satisfactory turn." In *Vedantic Epistemo-*

logy he says: "Nothing shall be more gratifying to me than that I should be a correct interpreter or commentator of that great Indian thinker. But his thinking was of a short-hand and compressed type. It was too logical and precise. I can only get at his meaning with great effort, and sometimes not at all." He remarks that Bhattacharyya gives no clear indication of what he means by the knowledge of truth, and adds, "I have no misgivings on that point myself."

The philosophical issue is reduced to its simplest terms in the work here presented. The author discusses the three ways of spiritual progress recognized in Indian philosophy -- action, love, knowledge. For Bhattacharyya these are alternative ways leading ultimately to alternative forms of the Absolute. For Malkani the Absolute is nondual, one without a second. Perfect freedom of action, perfect love of God still leave something to be sought. Ultimately there is no distinction between the theoretical philosophy of knowing the truth and the practical philosophy of life; knowledge is the way, and knowledge is the goal.

1. The Secular Ideal

Life can be lived at many different levels. Most people live it at the unreflective level. They are not conscious of the ideals which govern their life. They do not ask themselves the questions: What is the meaning of life? Where are we going? Is there a worth-while goal which we can and should realize in life?

These questions are asked only by philosophers and religious-minded people. The rest live their lives blindly, guided by the needs of the body and certain secular ideals which have for their end the well-being of the individual here and now, and the well-being of the society of which the individual forms an integral part. *It all depends upon the concept of Man.* Is man a higher animal only? If so, he must live a life akin to that of animals with certain refinements which are peculiar to his nature. This nature differs from that of other animals inasmuch as he has a capacity for abstract thinking or reasoning, a capacity for aesthetic enjoyment, and a capacity for enduring family and social relations.

The communist ideology and the goals it sets for social and political action are based upon this concept of man.

It is possible to argue that communism has a philosophy of life, and that it has arrived at it not in any dogmatic way, as theologians and like-minded philosophers may be supposed to have done. The communist philosopher has reflected upon man and his situation and come to the conclusion that economic well-being is the basis of all other human values. No moral values are sacrosanct. There is no God or law of God. The so-called Christian values of forgiveness, humility, non-violence, etc. are only capitalistic virtues in disguise. Their purpose is to exploit the working class under the guise of future rewards in heaven. The fact is that violence and revolutionary wars and all else that these activities may imply are the normal methods for man to improve his economic well-being and to get permanently free from all forms of organized exploitation by well-to-do classes. If there is a heaven, it must be a heaven on earth, where all people are equal and where all their needs are well taken care of by the society. This is the only worth-while goal for all rational human beings, who use their reason for the improvement of the condition of man; and it is therefore the only true religion, if there is one. Religions based upon the dogmas of "an unknown and non-existent God," a future heaven or hell after death, sin, divine judgement, etc. are all myths, invented by an extremely clever class of capitalists to keep the working classes permanently in bondage, both politically and economically. They are all false religions. The working class should beware of them and not fall into the trap set for them. There is no sin and no redeeming grace of God. The workers should rely on their own inherent power and resources, if they want to improve their lot here and now, and not wait till eternity for imaginary rewards in the hereafter which will never materialize.

This is naturally a philosophy of life which will appeal to the *secular* man or the man interested in this life alone. For this philosophy, there can be no such thing as moral retribution or a system of rewards and punishments for good and bad deeds done in this life. There can be no law of *karma* which conserves our moral past and opens up an indefinite future of moral progress and achievement. Life on the physical and the animal plane is itself the end and the goal.

We certainly cannot disprove this communist thesis on the communist premise of a sense-ridden intelligence that can know nothing about a super-sensible order of things. The moral order is certainly a super-sensible order. Our only comment is that a satisfied communist can only live a type of life in which there is no room for the finest things in human life, -- the divine discontent and the joys of the spirit. Religion, with its high morality, an emotional life centered on the holy and the pure, and an emancipating knowledge which changes all the values of life and makes them look topsy-turvy, is alien to communist thinking. It is this loss which is to be deplored.

We are often enamoured of a life that is fully in consonance with science as we know it, and which is free from sentiment. But is that sufficient? We may have all our economic needs satisfied and more. We may have certain fringes of aesthetic, social and intellectual values added to those physical satisfactions to make them more satisfying. But will man ever be satisfied with a purely secular cup filled to the brim? If he is, we can have no argument with him. He lives in a world of his own which fully satisfies him. Only we have a doubt. The secular man needs God in some form or other in order to complete himself and to fulfill his destiny. There is such a thing as Life Eternal or life in God.

The reality of non-secular values cannot be denied. There are persons who have had some spiritual experience and an inkling of a joy that is not of this world. They naturally cannot be satisfied with the best that this world can give. They have tasted it and found it wanting, and even bitter. They need the consolations of religion. But religion does not come to man through any *natural* channel. It comes to him either through inspired individuals or through the recorded *word* of inspired individuals. It comes to him from above. It is the word of revelation *(sruti)*. It is accepted on faith alone.

Faith must be unquestioning and whole-hearted. But is not blind. A blind faith is no faith. We must go beyond the verbal formula to the inner experience which it suggests. Genuine faith is something "living." It is an invitation to a new form of experience, not available through any other method devised by man. This experience is not purely cognitive. It is an inchoate form of cognition, mixed with feeling and volition. What we seem to know, at the same time gives joy and spurs to noble activity. It elevates our understanding and purifies both feeling and will. Thus it has a direct connection with our whole life and reforms that life. It makes life different from within. It gives a many-sided satisfaction which is more convincing than any abstract argument. This faith, genuine faith, cannot be divorced from *truth*. It is truth in the *concrete,* not abstract and speculative truth.

It is obvious that there cannot be one universal form of faith acceptable to all mankind, just like the world of science based on sense-perception. The inspired teachings of different seers and sages reach only a limited segment of mankind. Here tradition plays an important part. Every community, big or small, has its own inspired teachers and its own scripture. This makes for different religious faiths. But can they all be *equally* true? That does not appear to be possible. Also there is no method by which we can decide the comparative truth or otherwise of different faiths. The only test is a *subjective* one. Does it satisfy me? Does it infuse a new meaning in life and make for integrated living for me? Do we see our goal clearly and the possibility of the consummation of our best aspirations? Does it make for Absolution or complete freedom from pain and bondage of every kind? Does it promise the crowning reward of life or the summum bonum?

Every man of faith must answer these questions to his own satisfaction. Naturally, there are men of religion who think that they have answered them to their own entire satisfaction, and that therefore their faith is a truly universal faith. It needs to be propagated both among unbelievers and believers in other and less satisfying faiths. They argue: "All religions may be true more or less. But the truth in them is mixed with falsehood and superstition. Their own religion, on the other hand, gives truth, pure and simple, direct and ultimate." That is what most people of different religious persuasions think.

That creates a problem for all thinking men. If all these claims are taken at their face value, they cancel each other out. Since there is no clear-cut and *objective* way of deciding truth from falsehood, there is no truth here at all, -- that is what most people think. It is all a matter of myth and fancy, or at best a subjective feeling which takes us nowhere. Men have invented a God and "salvation through God," in order to beguile themselves and to delude their fellow men. They play upon the feelings of the latter, and exploit them by preaching, "Give up the goods of this world, so that you inherit the heavenly world."

Is then all religion *non-sense?* That will be too sweeping a statement. It will be more in accordance with facts if we say that all religions are true. There are certain elements which are common to all advanced religions, and they are the most important elements in them. (1) Generally speaking, all religions preach some kind of morality or code of conduct. This means disciplining the will and making it subject to a higher law. The origin of this law may be differently understood and differently defined. But it is a *super-sensible* law. (2) All moral codes of different religions deprecate unrestricted indulgence in the pleasures of the flesh. They restrict them to the minimum possible in the tradition of a society. In general, they discourage and even prohibit subjection to animal impulses and all those propensities which create discord and disharmony among individuals of a society. (3) All important religions teach non-attachment to the fleeting things of the world and attachment to the permanent, everlasting and eternal things of the spirit. This spirit is invariably conceived in terms of the human spirit, with certain transcendent attributes added to it, -- attributes not found in man but which constitute the perfectibility of man.

(4) All religions take the present life on earth as a *prelude* to a greater, and possibly a better, life in the hereafter. What we sow, so shall we reap. There is a law of moral justice which determines a system of rewards and punishments in the hereafter. (5) There is some conception of "ultimate value" or the highest goal of life. What is common to this conception is the annulment of all forms

of pain and sorrow. It is therefore a state of peace. But in addition to this peace, there may be a positive element too, answering to the requirements of persons with different levels of inner refinement. (6) A body to the soul in the hereafter is not wholly denied. But it may be a very different sort of body from the present gross body. It will be a subtler or ethereal body, better suited to the new environment earned by the soul through his merit or demerit.

(7) All religions accept human intermediaries, who are personifications of the great Ideal at the human level. They shed light on the path for the common man. For they have already reached the goal themselves. This humanization of the Divine, this concept of guruship, is a great merit of all religions. It brings them down from heaven to earth, from abstract theory to actual reality. Is not this measure of agreement of all great and important religions sufficient to prove that they are all true and lead to the realization of a more or less common human goal?

However that be, we take it for granted that some sort of religion, with its belief in the reality of the super-sensible or the metaphysical, is necessary for meaningful living. No man can be satisfied with the good things of this life alone. We need a great and transcendent goal to give a new direction to life and infuse a new meaning in it. All men of religion have this direction and this meaning; but they have it in a more or less unreflective way and on the basis of the scriptural teaching of their own particular religion. What we are interested in here is to reflect on all those religious ideals which are unreflectively accepted, and try to construct a philosophy of life which will satisfy all thoughtful persons.

2. Freedom Through Action

Any worthy ideal of life should answer three most important questions: (1) What should I do? (2) What should I love? (3) What should I know? These questions can be answered most simply. I should do what is *good.* I love *beauty,* so I should love the most lovable thing of beauty. I should know all that there is to be known, or more simply *truth* in the most literal sense of the term. We shall tackle these questions one by one.

We should do the good. But what is *good?* We cannot define goodness. It is *sui generis.* But we directly *recognize* what is good. Pleasure is *the one thing* that all recognize as good. We therefore naturally do things which lead to pleasure. We can say that pleasure is a good *in itself,* while the things we do for its sake are good in a secondary or instrumental sense. Here criticism starts.

Pleasure is generally understood to be senuous pleasure. It is a type of good which many will regard as having only a low value. Sensuous pleasure we share with animals and uncultured human beings. We rise in the human scale with intellectual activity, aesthetic enjoyment and moral and religious behaviour. These things are good *in themselves* and *also* for the *goals* which we realize through them.

The question arises: Is there not something that is *common* to all the things that are good? We think there is. It is *emotional satisfaction* in the widest sense. This satisfaction may be direct and immediate or "deferred." But a doubt might arise here. Moral values at least appear to be in a class by themselves. They have no connection with emotional satisfaction. Many philosophers think that an act is morally good *only if* it is done without regard for its beneficial effects, either here or in the hereafter, upon the life of the doer. The moral is what *ought* to be done in a spirit of perfect dispassion. If there is any element of self-interest in it, it becomes immoral and so lacking in true moral value. The moral ought to be done for its own sake, *and because it is moral,* not because it will lead to our future happiness or any kind of emotional satisfaction.

We do not quite agree with this view. We know that there are theories, such as Hedonism and Utilitarianism, which reduce the moral to the pleasurable in some form or other. They may be discredited theories. But what is the alternative? Let us suppose that we somehow recognize the *ought* or morality or the moral law as such. But why should I act up to it? What is the *sanction* behind it? If it is the *sanction of reason*, we can counter it by saying that reason is only an instrument for our well-being or happiness. Reason has no other claim on us. We give up reason where we feel that our true end is not served. We then take shelter behind a higher reason which *serves that end*.

Let us now suppose that we directly intuit what is right, and the right is what we ought to do. *Truth-speaking* is right and moral. But there are situations in life where the moral becomes immoral. To save an innocent life, untruth may have to be spoken in quite good conscience. To save one's country, grievous injury has got to be inflicted upon the enemy and all those persons who inhabit the enemy's territory. Such examples can be multiplied. The theory that the moral should be done for the sake of the moral falls through. The moral is only done for the sake of a greater satisfaction beyond the act.

Society gets its law of morality from the scripture or the word of God. The natural man knows nothing about it. The natural man has no genuine morality or what is called *dharma,* the sacred law. *Dharma* is the super-natural law of morality, and its scope extends beyond our present life to the life in the hereafter. Our only source of information in this field is the revealed word of God. If we accept this view of the matter, the moral or the *dharmic* is that which is enjoined by the scripture, and the immoral is that which is prohibited. To the question, why should I do what is moral? the answer is simple: because it is so enjoined! To the further question, why should I do what is enjoined by the scripture? the answer again is equally simple: because what is enjoined is in my *best interest* both here and in the hereafter, and it will not lead to a balance of unhappiness in any conceivable circumstances! *This is a faith.* God or the scripture alone knows what is best for me. They do not, and cannot, deceive. The vision of the natural man is circumscribed by his natural environment. He can only extend his vision to the law of super-natural life through the sacred word of God.

It is clear then that some kind of *emotional satisfaction* or happiness is the only reason why I should do what I regard as morally right. This happiness is both this-worldly and other-worldly. But since the fruits of our actions which we enjoy in this life itself are uncertain, delayed and inadequate, belief in the hereafter is a *necessary element* of the moral consciousness. No hereafter, no genuine morality. Indeed, the hereafter as conceived by certain religions may only be an exaggerated copy of life on this earth. Heaven and hell may be very crude conceptions. But they are quite relevant to the emotional requirements of the common men of the world. There are however very refined conceptions of the hereafter also, such as company of like-minded persons and saints, nearness and intimacy with God, unlimited extension of love, etc. There is a hereafter to suit the taste of everybody, but still full of mystery.

To the question, what should I do? there are various answers. (1) Do what is beneficial to society in a purely secular way. (2) Do what is enjoined by the scripture, for that is in your best interest (3) Do what is enjoined, *simply because it is enjoined as a duty.* This is duty for duty's sake. Seek no regard or personal satisfaction for doing your duty. In other words, *dispassionateness* is itself the very highest reward for true moral behaviour.

This then is the highest ideal of morality -- doing duty for duty's sake and without regard to or desire for enjoying any fruits thereof. It is this *desire* for fruit that detracts from the purity of the moral ideal. It is also the same desire in all its various forms that makes for the pain of life. We, ordinary mortals, may not be interested in the absolute purity of the moral ideal. It is a hard ideal for the man of easy life. But everybody without exception is naturally interested in getting rid of the pain of life. Pain is what we reject. Pain originates in the restlessness of the spirit. In fact, restlessness is pain, and vice-versa.

This restlessness is the direct result of desire. If we can eliminate desire in all its subtle and incipient forms, we shall have no cause for worry, restlessness, sorrow, anxiety and the continuing pain of life. Life will be transformed. There will be an unbroken peace in it which nothing can break. This is a worthy ideal to be striven after.

Desire expresses itself in various acts of the will in life. We

want so many things. But the basic form of it is the "will to be."
We are all attached to life and to the Present existence in the
body. This desire is the cause of all the pain in life. It is our
biggest bondage. To be free from this bondage, we must negate
the will. But how is this possible? If we negate the will, the
negation will remain. We have then to negate this negation. Here
then is the great discipline of the will. We must train the will to
negate itself completely. When the will ceases to be will, a state
of placidity, peace and dispassion descends. It is the great Extinction (of desire) or the great Silence called *nirvāna*. It is the
goal and the ideal of all moral activity. We cease to will not only
what is bad, but also the good; and in the end we cease to will at
all. As we progressively realize this Ideal, we get rid of subtler
forms of desire. The end is only reached in a state of desireless-
ness, where the will has become passive and so ceased to be will,
and what life there is has become a life of unbroken and absolute
peace. It is the Dispassion of Buddha.

Life can now become fully meaningful. I should so act that
every form of desire is gradually eliminated and liquidated. In
the end, will itself will have to be negated, pacified and laid to
rest. It is what is significantly called *freedom beyond being.* This
ideal of the will is immanent in the will, and must therefore be
capable of complete realization. It is the last word in the philosophy of the will. Paradoxically enough, the question "what
should I do?" is best answered by saying, "do nothing" if you
have the right enlightenment. Or if that is very hard, do what
loosens your bondage to desire. When we resign our will to the
will of God in everything, we take a step in the right direction.
We are trying to get free from the bondage of the will.

3. The Love That Fulfils

We now come to the second question, what should we love?
We use this word "love" in common speech very vaguely to cover
all kinds of like-able things. We love sports, we love intellectual
activities, we love hearing stories, etc. We are however using the
term here in a specific sense. It is the sense in which the very

nature of the object is such that it evokes a certain feeling in us. We call this feeling "love," To *see* the thing is to *love* it. Every kind of beautiful thing, whether it belongs to nature or to human art, has this kind of effect on the human mind. A thing may be beautiful in itself, but it may have no charm for us; for we have not the capacity to see it for what it is, i.e., as beautiful. It leaves us cold. On the other hand, a thing may not be beautiful by common standards; but it may be quite beautiful in the estimate of a particular person. These differences are there. Sometimes we have not the capacity to appreciate *specialized beauty*, at other times we have an over-developed capacity which sees beauty where others do not. Some persons can see beauty in almost everything. In all these differences, one thing is clear. No-one can contemplate beauty dispassionately. To see beauty is to be attracted towards it, to love it. We cannot with-hold our love from a thing of beauty. We are not free in the matter. To see is to fall in love.

It is evident now that, in any appreciation of beauty, two factors are necessary. There is a contribution by the object and also a contribution by the subject. The contribution of the object is quite evident. One object does not evoke the same feeling as another. It is not equally beautiful. So there must be something *in the thing* to make it appear beautiful. In other words, the thing *itself* must be beautiful. But it is equally true that the thing does not mechanically determine the subjective feeling. The subject must be in a position to *appreciate* the beauty; and different subjects do it in varying degrees. While the beauty may be quite lost on some people, others go into raptures over it. This is a clear indication of the subjective factor in the appreciation and love of beauty. A beauty that does not evoke love in the person contemplating it is no beauty at all.

We know natural beauty and also human beauty. Unfortunately, human beauty is complicated with sensuous enjoyment. We seem to think that human females alone are beautiful; and so we have beauty contests among them. It is evident that this kind of beauty is loaded with sensuous elements, and our love of it therefore is not pure. It is not love of beauty for beauty's sake. Natural beauty cannot be so mixed up with purely personal feelings and personal desires. One therefore naturally remains more detached in its contemplation. There are however higher and more spiritual forms of beauty as well. True beauty not only pleases, but it also *elevates.* There is no suggestion in it of sensuous enjoyment or self-interest or even utility. It subserves no end beyond itself. It is lovable in itself. It invites us to contemplation. It does not invite us to make any *use* of it for a private end. Naturally, greater the beauty or purer the beauty, greater is our adoration and our absorption in it. It excites no crude passion. It is the purest kind of joy.

We hear of stories of love where the individual becomes oblivious of herself or himself. A gopi sees the child Sri Krishna and so far forgets herself that she does not notice that the flame in her hand has caught up the hand and is burning the hand. This is the real depth and purity of love, complete self-forgetfulness. It leads to a form of union in love which consumes all lower desires and separatist tendencies. It is only sentimental love, not real love, if the individual is always reverting to his own joys or sorrows in the love-business. It is love that is both selfish and egoistic. In real love, the individual is so simply and fully dedicated to the object of love that he completely forgets himself. He loves the object because it is *in itself beautiful* and lovable.

All secular beauty evokes aesthetic feeling in us. But it does not carry us far. We cannot become fully absorbed in the object. It is not big enough, nor important enough, nor true enough. The element of truth in beauty is particularly important. That beauty is found to be more pleasing and more lovable, which is at the same time found to be more lasting and more revealing of a higher spiritual truth. We are not only pleased, we are also lifted up.

We enjoy things of beauty in various different fields of experience. But in religion we enter a new field altogether. The beauty here is invariably sacred and elevating. Of all objects of religion which evoke our love, the religious man as such or the saint evokes our greater love. Of all such saints, our religious guide or *guru* takes precedence. And beyond the guru, and almost identical with him, is the great God with every possible perfection in Him.

Love is primarily the love of one person for another. There is reciprocity in it. Of the various different relations between persons, the relation of the mother to the child is in a class by itself. It is true, pure and disinterested. God is therefore often compared to the mother who loves the child; and the seeker of God is compared to the child, who has complete reliance on, and devotion to, the mother. The relation of love and beloved too has its own heights of blissful vision incomparable in its sweetness with any other human love. God is therefore pictured as the Great Lover, and man as the beloved who pines after her lover and who is one-pointedly and whole-heartedly devoted to him. The love of gopis for Krishna is a typical example. But beyond all these secular human relations is the relation of the *guru* and the *disciple*. For the disciple, if there is a supreme object of love on earth, it is the *guru*. The love for the *guru* is the purest, the most complete, and without limits or conditions of any kind. The disciple verily *sees God* in his *guru*. There is not a shade of pure thought or pure feeling in his own life which he will give to God but withhold from the *guru*. [*Guru* is verily God on earth. The biblical saying is literally true of the *guru* -- "those who have seen the Son have seen the Father in Heaven."] A devoted disciple is thus never in two minds about the existence of God. Does he not see God daily in human form in real life? Naturally, his love and his sense of dedication for his *guru* knows no bounds. It is the acme of love in all human relationships. There is not a thing in his life which the disciple will not give away for the sake of his *guru* without question.

The institution of the *guru* is in disrepute with the modern man of reason. But it is the most important contribution of Hinduism to religious life. Without the *guru*, religious life is both dull and difficult. One may read scriptures or listen to any number of religious discourses. One may go on thinking, practicing, and contemplating endlessly about religious matters. But he will still remain in the wilderness. What will throw light on his path and make his step easy is the guidance and the personal example of the *guru*. It is through the continuity of this *guru-disciple* relationship in an almost unbroken series that the Hindu religion tries to keep up the torch of spirituality in the lives of ordinary human beings. *The guru is as necessary to a birth in spiritual life as the father is to the physical life of the child born of him.*

Love-behaviour can take many different forms, sometimes almost contradictory to each other. The lover is sometimes filled with joy, at other times with despair. He may dance in rapture, he may also shed tears and weep. All these moods in the love-game are natural. There is no real contradiction. There is only richness of forms. What is common to all these forms is an inner yearning for one-ness. It can only be fully satisfied in a purely spiritual relationship, or the relationship of one spirit with another spirit. It takes us straight from the *guru-disciple* relationship of the individual soul with the divine spirit. Here there are bound to be levels and stages leading to the highest consummation in the union of the human with the Divine. What this union is like we cannot exactly know or define. But it is not unlikely that the I-thou relationship gradually gives place to a *distinctionless unity of the two entities,* in which the entities in question are no longer distinguishable as two or knowable as one. Those who reach this height of love do not return to tell their tale; and the tale can never to be told in human phraseology.

We said that beauty evokes love. From our present point of view, God is *beauty par excellence.* To *see God* is to be drawn towards Him or to *love Him.* At the same time, He is also the most real and the only enduring reality that we know. He is Eternity itself. Here is a link-up of *beauty* with what is *real, ever-lasting* and *true.* It is sometimes said, "beauty is truth, and truth beauty." We cannot go so far. For beauty is the object of love, and naturally evokes love. Truth, on the other hand, is the object of thought, not of feeling. The instruments of knowledge or truth are different from those of love. The instruments of love are a purified life and a highly developed and sensitive feeling. The instruments of knowledge include these, but they also include something else, which is all-important for knowledge, such as *pramāna* (evidence) and reason. Although therefore we cannot *equate* beauty with truth, this much is certain that beauty is more beautiful and therefore more absorbing when it is allied with truth. There are all the levels between purely sensuous beauty and the beauty of spiritual truths. A beautiful figure in the form of religious art or a beautiful literary composition in the form of spiritual truths is much more pleasing and satisfying than secular beauty in all its mundane forms. In other words, secular beauty of dance and song is one thing, sacred beauty in all its various different forms is another. There are songs and songs and there are dances and dances. The song and dance of religious rapture has a value which is not comparable to the song or dance which appeal only to sex or to our aesthetic sense at the purely sensuous level. In short, beauty becomes more beautiful as it is allied to spiritual truth. To the question, what should we love? our answer is quite simple: We should love not only what pleases aesthetically, but what also elevates and gives us a glimpse of the beauties and the realities of the realm of the spirit.

4. The Knowledge That Breaks All Bondage

We come now to the third question, what should I know? Evidently, we should try to know the truth. We should try to know what really is or the real state of things, whatever it may be. Ordinarily, we know this through our sense-organs. But science tells us that our sense-organs invariably deceive us. For example, the earth moves round the sun; but our senses give us the impression that the contrary is the case. Again, a solid thing like a chair is a dance of electrons, it is more hollow than solid, etc.; and yet our senses give us a different and misleading picture. Colour is nothing but certain electro-magnetic wave-lengths reflected from objects to our optical sense-organ. Similarly, certain wave-lengths projected into the air assume different forms of sound for our acoustic sense, and so on.

But then is science true? It is evident that it depends for all its *facts* and all its *problems* upon sense-given data or sense-data. The whole symbolism of science is supplied by the senses. All its descriptive formulas are given in sense-language. But apart from its dependence upon the senses which it has already condemned, science propounds only provisional truths. It propounds certain hypotheses which claim truth no doubt, but which are progressively replaced by new hypotheses of greater comprehensiveness and coherence; and so the theoretic consciousness in science proceeds almost endlessly to an imaginary goal of truth which is never in fact reached, and cannot be reached. The very method and procedure of science is such that no theory can hold the ground *for all time* or give truth which is final and absolute. Science uses imagination to formulate its theories; and imagination is not the right instrument of knowledge. It gives hypothetical knowledge only.

To imagine is not to know. To know is to see directly and at first hand. Sensible seeing is also a species of seeing. But it is *mediated* by our sense-organs and our thought. It is not truly direct or first-hand. All mediated knowledge is knowledge infected by doubt and error. And so our perceptions, however clear and definite, are still vitiated by doubt. "Is it this or something different?" "Is it really what it appears to be?" "May we not be deceived after all?" and so on. This fact of doubt and the possibility or error creates a new problem for us. Is there a higher and a better way of seeing? Is there a theoretic consciousness above sensible experience and above science? Can it give us *the truth*? If it can, what are the instruments which it utilizes for the purpose?

The theoretic consciousness above science is what we call philosophical consciousness. Philosophy is critical of science as a method of knowledge. Science can never give us a peep into the *thing-in-itself*, but only into its phenomenal appearances. But philosophy is not mere criticism. It is not purely negative, it is also constructive. It replaces the method of science by a new method. This method has three elements: (1) direct intuition; (2) authority of the revealed word; (3) rational criticism. Mere direct intuition will be too personal and unreliable. There will be a question about its genuineness and about its full implications. We cannot even discuss what is purely private. But we can discuss a public source of knowledge such as scriptural statements. We can here ask, what exactly do they signify? Do they signify something which we can directly know to be true? It is thus evident to us that we must go beyond intuition to the revealed word. It is the only public source of knowledge for super-sensible or metaphysical reality.

But the scripture alone is not sufficient. Reason has an important function to perform. (1) The statements of the scripture (sruti) have got to be interpreted. Do they have one universally acceptable meaning which is beyond all doubt? Reason alone can evolve a coherent meaning in diverse and apparently conflicting statements. When we have achieved this meaning, another problem confronts us. (2) Does our experience give any ground for the truth of the interpretation formally arrived at? If reason can be satisfied that the truth of the scripture is also the truth of experience on a proper analysis of the latter, then there should be no rational hindrance to the final acceptance of this truth. (3) If any hindrance continues, that can only be due to the dead weight of habit and false opinion. These are natural to a mind which is unreflective and uncritical. The remedy against this inertia of the mind is mental alertness and the counter-action of the mind to keep thought on the right lines and in full awareness of the enlightenment achieved.

This multi-form method ought to commend itself to all genuine seekers of truth. So far as direct intuition goes, nobody can possibly object to it. Only we must be able to point unerringly to a region available to everyone and part of the common experience of all mankind. So far as the function of reason is concerned, it is acceptable both to the believer as well as to the unbeliever. The only question here will be, what are the problems set to reason? Can reason answer any ultimate questions? There will be difference of opinion on this subject. But we agree with those who think that speculative reason or reason in its constructive aspect cannot solve any ultimate question. The activity of reason must be confined within definite limits already suggested by us. That brings us to the third and the most controversial element in the composite method of philosophy. This is our initial acceptance of the scripture *(śruti)* as evidence of a higher metaphysical truth.

We have no doubt on this score too. Man unaided by any revelation from above can know nature. He can build up science. He can also build world-views based on his knowledge of nature. But all such world-views (and they can be many) will convince only those who conceive them. It is not the business of philosophy to give us such uncertain knowledge. The knowledge it seeks must be absolutely certain and self-evidently true. This is not possible with *purely human* instruments of knowledge. We must take the aid of the word of God, which has played its part in the life of humanity through an unbroken series of sages and seers who have testified to its truth. This means an initial faith or a commitment. We must pay the proper price. We must seek divine aid in the fact of human helplessness. There is nothing derogatory in faith, if faith is the one and only method of raising human consciousness from things material to things spiritual. All we have a right to claim is full value for our initial faith. The faith must be transformed into knowledge which is certain and true. Those accordingly who have no use for faith have no use for the higher redeeming knowledge either. They are content with their ignorance and their boasted rationality, and it is useless to argue with them.

We now come to the three separate strands of the method of knowledge which we are adopting here. *(a) Direct Intuition.* The two most significant and universally acknowledged intuitions of reality refer to matter and spirit. The intuition of matter takes the form of "thisness" *(id-aitva)*. Nobody can deny this intuition in respect of objects of nature and our own physical body insofar as it is an object of perception. What about mental states and acts? Are they not supposed to be spiritual in some sense? They may be. And yet we want to draw a line. Whatever is presentable as *object* of some sort is inert and non-spiritual. It is material, in the sense in which we are using the term. In general we might say, anything that is *presentable* in any region or sphere of our experience is material *(jada)*. Mind as a *series of mental states*, which we can know introspectively, is certainly so presentable. But then is anything left for the reality of the spirit?

We now contend that, as against the intuition of physicality *(jadatva)*, there is another intuition which is clearly and wholly opposed to it. This is the intuition of "I." This intuition is common and universal. Nobody can deny it. Nobody can meaningfully say, "I am not." Everybody says, "I am." But what I am is a question. Different answers can be given to it. (1) Some say, I am a *spiritual substance* having the quality of *I-ness*. If that is so, the spiritual substance is a *qualified substance;* and a qualified substance, in principle, cannot be unobjective. We can only know it in the objective attitude -- it is *that,* it is *such and such*. The adjective to the substance can only be detected on an objective inspection. By our definition, a qualified substance can only be material *(jada)* in character.

(2) Others say, there is no substance, *unique and enduring,* called *I.* "I" is a momentary mental form, part of more complex mental states, such as "I know," "I imagine," "I desire," etc. Once again, *this momentary mental form is presentable to us,* and knowable only in the objective attitude. Even if it is known enjoyingly or subjectively, it is not unobjective. These philosophers, who substitute the notion of "event" for that of "substance" everywhere, find no evidence of spiritual substance anywhere. The unitary character of "I" for them is an *illusion* created by the quick succession of a series of I-s which are quite disparate and independent in time.

(3) Still others argue that we do know the self called "I," as *something empirical*, with its character, behaviour - peculiarities and its historical growth. *It is possible that this empirical self has a transcendental aspect also which we do not know.* But this empirical self cannot be wholly divorced from the transcendental self. There must be an inner unity between the two, so that when we know the empirical self we can claim to know the self as it

really is. There is no mystery about our knowledge of the self.

This argument suffers from a certain confusion. If we do not know the transcendental aspect of the self, why should we suppose that there is any such aspect at all? Perhaps the acceptance of it satisfies our theological conscience. Again, how can the empirical and the transcendental be one and the same thing? If they are not the same thing, why should we not try to know the transcendental for what *it* is? We are just suggesting a method for doing this, when we say that the real self is *beyond* the empirical self and the very *negation of it,* but it is not unknown. It is self-revealing for what it is. It is pure subjectivity or pure intelligence.

All these different views of the self, mentioned above, misinterpret our genuine intuition of it. We contend that this intuition refers to that which cannot be objectified, and which in fact is only reached through the *negation* of every objective association with it. Our ordinary intuition of the self is a mixed one. With the real self are simultaneously given elements of the not-self intimately associated with it. These elements range from the gross body to the subtler mental body, inclusive of the egoistic *I.* They constitute our superficial or empirical self which is "this" to us, and which can therefore be rejected as something non-spiritual. The real self, the spiritual "I," remains in the background. It is *absolutely opposed* to all forms of "thisness" *(id-amtva).* When we begin to analyze the intuition of "I," the non-spiritual reality meets our gaze. The spiritual core remains evasive, unobjectified and therefore unidentified, but nevertheless real to a perceptive mind. It reveals itself as what is absolutely immediate and innermost *(aparokṣa).*

There is a demand for the purification of our intuition of "I." As we come nearer and nearer to the true object of our intuition through a process of negation and rejection, we become aware of a new realm of the spirit altogether. It is something truly unique. There is only *one thing of the kind* -- never two or more. The moment we circumscribe the self and interpret it as something *within the body,* or as *numerically different* from some other self, it is degraded to some kind of *object.* Only objects can be different and so numerous. The real self is non-different and

without a second *(ekam-eva-adutiyam).* It may run in innumerable bodies, both human and divine, but it is unaffected by them.
It is always pure, whole, and blissful. The great Vedantic statement "that thou art" *(tattvasmasi)* is to be interpreted in this
sense of absolute identity of the human spirit and the divine or
jiva-Brahma-aikya. We may go further and say that the great
biblical statement "I and the Father are one" should also be so
interpreted, if it is really to be meaningful to us. There is *real
identity* of the spirit of man with the Divine Spirit. *To know
God, we must know this identity.*

(b) *The revealed word.* We may recognize the reality of the
spirit in us which is transcendental in character. But that is
perhaps all that we can know through an analysis of our intuition. The real significance of this spirit of man however will
still escape us. We shall also know nothing about God, the
Creator, and the great qualities we associate with Him. The scripture alone gives us an awareness of the Great Spirit called God
and poses the problem of our relationship with Him. It thus
opens the way to a new enlightenment.

When we think of greatness, we naturally think of the world
around us or space or time. These certainly are great. But the
scripture tells us that God is infinitely greater -- and greater than
Him there is nothing else. Everything in the world is born and
dies. The world is nothing apart from the things in it. So the
world too is born and it dies. What is born must have an efficient
cause; and the only efficiency we know anywhere is the efficiency of the will. All other efficiency is apparent only. Matter
can have no efficiency; it is essentially passive, and driven by
a power behind it. What then is the efficient cause of the birth
of the world as a whole? It cannot be any finite will, such as
man's will. It can only be the will of a world-spirit or God. Only
a God who is omnipotent and omniscient has the requisite
capability. And that is what the world's great scriptures declare.

God is the efficient cause like the potter who makes his pots.
The potter has power and also a purpose. But the potter has his
material given to him ready-made by nature. He does not create

the material, but only the form. Does God do likewise? But then where is the material to come from before the creation of the world? So He must be supposed to created the material out of nothing as the Christians hold, or alternatively out of Himself as the Hindus suppose. The Upanishads declare that God is both the efficient cause as well as the material cause of the world. God is the only uncaused cause of all that there is.

Being uncreated, he is the beginning and the end, the *alpha* and the *omega*. He puts forth the world and also takes it back into Himself. The whole thing is put in a nut-shell in the Brahmasūtra -- "From Him the birth, etc." *(janmādiyataka)*. Birth is invariably followed by a span of life, and the span of life by death. Thus the world has being in God alone. It comes from Him, stays in Him, and goes back to Him. God is infinitely greater than the world, and contains the world in all its three moments. This is the *first* step in the knowledge of the spiritual reality behind the world -- God is the *Creator*.

But the creativity of God is not fundamental to Him. It does not constitute his *essential nature*. It is a mere *accident* of His Being. God may create or He may not. He certainly *need not* create; and when He does not create, He does not cease to be God. He still has a nature of His own which is His abiding or permanent nature. What is this nature? The scripture says, it is "being, intelligence and bliss" *(sat-cit-ānanda)*; timeless, immortal *(anatam-amrtam)*; *sudha-budha-mukta-svarupam*; free from all kinds of limitations, infinite; without change, and without differences of any kind, internal or external; one without a second *(ekam-eva-adutiyam)*, etc. Such is the real nature of the Great Divine Spirit, also called Brahman.

But then how is it that Brahman who has this nature creates a world at all -- a world that appears to be external to Him and a limitation of Him? The answer is that He *does not really create*. Really He is non-active *(akriya)*. He only appears to create, when through the error of the onlooker He is conjoined to māyā. Māyā has no self-existence; as to existence *in Him*, it is the existence of a false or illusory adjunct. So we cannot *deduce* the world from Brahman or *trace it* to Him. It hangs midway between reality and unreality—an illusory appearance only. Brahman does not *need* to create a world, and He does not *really create.* He only appears to do so, and the appearance is *mayic. This means the world is real for us only.* It is the necessary stepping-stone towards God. God for us is present in the world, but He is no part of the world. He transcends the world. To know Him, we must negate the world—"as what the world is not." He is pure spirit opposed in nature to everything that is material *(jada).*

We have seen that God is the Creator. We have further seen that He has a nature of His own which goes beyond all creativity. He has a *svarūpa.* But all this knowledge of God is still inadequate, indirect and distant. We do not know Him face to face as He is. We are more or less groping in the dark with the help of vague conceptions and theories. We are still ignorant. We need a more direct and complete vision. We view a nut on our palm and we are satisfied that we know it from all sides and from top to bottom. There is no comparative knowledge of God to give us any such satisfaction. God in his essential nature as Brahman has both positive and negative attributes. The positive attributes may be supposed to be fully informative and helpful. But even these, in the case of Brahman, have to be interpreted negatively. We do not know pure being, pure intelligence, pure bliss anywhere. The being that we know is empirical, relative and illusory. We have to suppose that Brahman is the *negation* of all such being. But what He is in Himself cannot be directly known in a meaningful way. In the same way, we cannot directly know what is pure intelligence. We can only understand it as the *negation* of all those mental acts and states which we confuse with pure intelligence, and which are essentially objective to us and therefore non-intelligent. Such negative characterization cannot possibly take us to the inmost being or sanctuary, that is God.

This brings us to the *third level* of discernment recommended by *śruti.* It takes us direct to the *positive, unmistakable* and the *whole* being of God. If we do not still perceive the Absolute Truth, the fault is ours, not that of the scripture. The great statements *(mahāvākyās)* all point to something that is most *immediate* to us. They are: "Thou art that" *(tattvasmasi);* "I am Brah-

man" (aham-Brahmāsmi); "this Self is verily Brahman" (ayam-
atmā-Brahma-eva); "intelligence is Brahman." In other words,
Brahman is most truly, directly and conclusively known in identity with the Self of the individual.

Our knowledge of the Self is not mediated in any way. The
Self is not known as object of any kind. The Self does not even
know Itself in any form of self-awareness. The Self cannot be
both subject and object simultaneously, since these are diametrically opposed to each other. The truth is that the Self is never
known. For, who can know the knower (vijñātāram-are-kena-
vijaniyāt)? But although the Self is not known, it is always
spoken as immediate; and this speaking is quite meaningful to us.
We have no question about the immediacy of the Self -- is it there
or is it not there? is it such and such or different? All these
questions would be relevant, if the Self were some kind of object
open to our inspection. It is nothing of the kind, and yet assuredly it is. Other things become immediate to us when they are
related to our intelligence through the senses. They are not
immediate by their own nature. The Self is the one thing that is
immediate by its very nature, and not because it is related to our
intelligence through any outside agency (sākṣāt-aparokṣāt-Brah-
ma).

The Great Reality called God or Brahman is no other than our
own true and inmost Self, that is self-revealing and self-evidencing. Why seek the true God outside or in heaven, when He is
within and nearest to us? His greatness does not disappear thereby. It attains a new depth and immediacy. Pure intelligence has
no limits of any kind. It goes beyond all limits, which it naturally
knows objectively. The greatness of God only gains certainty of
truth by its identification with the Self. Both terms of the identity, the Self and Brahman, gain a new significance without losing
their own essential character. The Self gains greatness, infinitude,
freedom from pain and bondage, etc. God gains something most
invaluable to Him, namely intelligent being and immediacy. Thus
the scripture fulfils what we inadequately know in our own
direct intuition.

(c) We now come to the third factor in our methodology,

namely *reason.* It is evident that all knowledge is a matter of the intellect or *buddhi.* It is not a matter for *feeling* or of some kind of *mystic intuition.* If we are *enlightened* by knowledge, it is because our intellect comes into contact with reality, either through the *senses* or more directly through the *self-revelation* of reality itself to us. In the latter case, the intellect can be said to be *intuitive,* and we have what is called an *intellectual intuition.* Thus thought has two different levels, mediate and immediate. The *propositional form* is fundamental to all knowledge. There must be a subject and a predicate. In mediate knowledge, the predicate gives some additional information about the subject. But in immediate knowledge, the predicate gives no such information. It merely removes a certain misconception, and points to the essential identity of substance of the two terms in question. *It is the only form of unitive knowledge, where differences are introduced only to be negated.* We begin with two terms in a proposition, and end with the knowledge of their fundamental and undifferentiated unity.

The most conspicuous case of immediate knowledge is the knowledge which we get from the proposition, "I am Brahman." If "I" and "Brahman" are taken in their literal verbal sense, as representing the finite, and the infinite, the proposition is clearly false. Nothing can make two diametrically opposed things identical. But there is a sense in which the proposition is not only true, but absolutely true. This will require some interpretation of the terms. Part of their meaning has to be retained and part rejected. The "I" in its true inwardness is purely intelligent and spiritual, absolutely immediate, and free from all kinds of objective limitations of time, space and quality. Its finitude, its limitations of knowledge, power, etc., its transmigratory existence, pain of life, etc. -- all those belong to its envelopes, both physical and non-physical. We reject the envelopes and retain the essential nature. The same procedure of interpretation is to be adopted with regard to the other term. The greatness, the infinitude, the freedom from bondage, the fullness, the changelessness, etc. constitute the essential nature of Brahman. Its *distance from us* and its *objectivity to us* are not only incompatible with this nature, but they directly contradict it. Objectivity, for instance, clearly contradicts greatness, infinitude, etc. Thus Brahman can only fulfil its nature when it is diverted of incompatible characteristics and identified with the real Self or "I." This knowledge of identity is a new form of knowledge. It is propositional *in form,* but not *in substance.* In substance, the proposition with its two different terms is transcended; for the two terms coalesce in one undifferenced meaning. Thought here starts with divisions and differences, and then rejects them. It thus achieves knowledge of identity.

Reason is fundamental to all knowledge, including metaphysical knowledge. But metaphysical knowledge has its own problems. These relate to certain hindrances in the way of thought. (1) There is first the question of a proper interpretation of our two diametrically opposed intuitions of matter and spirit, symbolized by the terms "this" and "I." This involves the evaluation of sensible experience as such and the edifice of scientific knowledge raised on the same. It also involves a fuller elucidation of our intuition of "I" and its importance to the knowledge of the spirit. This is philosophy proper, without any encumbrances from theology. The end-result of all this thinking will be that there is no truth in sensible intuitions and their elaboration in science. Truth is more obviously available in our intuition of "I," which is not mediated either by sense or by thought, and which pertains to an entity that is both self-revealing and self-evidencing. But no amount of mere thinking can bring out the fuller significance of this intuition. For that, we must have recourse to the scripture that speaks of the Supreme Spirit or God, the Creator of the world, etc.

(2) The next set of questions to be solved by rational thinking is the interpretation of the scripture through recognized criteria. This will remove all doubts about the meaning of the scripture, which ought to be unitary and self-consistent. This is theological interpretation. We know what the scripture purports to say, contradictory statements notwithstanding.

(3) We have satisfactorily interpreted our intuitions of reality and satisfactorily interpreted the scripture. But do the two agree?

We cannot give up the scripture, because it is our only reliable and commonly accepted source of knowledge of the meta-physical and the super-sensible. We cannot give up our intuitions of reality, which alone can reveal the truth to us in our own personal life and experience. We have therefore to interpret and reinterpret the two sources of knowledge till they completely agree. What the scripture says must be seen to be the very truth in our own experience. All doubts concerning their conformity must thus be removed. In the end we are satisfied that we have known *the truth*. All this involves theoretical thinking of a very wide scope. We must examine all kinds of philosophical theories which claim to conform to our experience, but not to the scripture. We must see them to be infected with error. The scripture must hold the ground. Once again, this is philosophy proper.

(4) When all these hindrances have been removed, there re-mains the possibility that while the truth is *theoretically recog-nized*, it has not percolated into life and transformed it. All truth has a pragmatic aspect, whether it is scientific or metaphysical. Scientific truth changes society first, and the individual through the society. Metaphysical truth changes the individual first, and the society through the individual. This is because the mere perception of scientific truth changes nothing. It must be trans-lated into a technology, in order to be effective. This is not so with metaphysical truth. Its mere perception, direct and un-clouded, is effective in the life of the individual. This is a task to be achieved by the individual through a new thinking effort.

Old habits, erroneous views and common fallacies die hard. They are part of the natural man. They continue to sway the mind of the truth-seeker even after he has achieved some percep-tion of the truth on the theoretical level. He is quite sure that the truth is just as he has known it. But it does not quite click in his life. This demands more than mere theoretic thinking, which has its full innings. What is needed is a new spiritual effort to *discip-line* the mind. The mind must be made to stay in the truth and to function in life in full awareness of it. The inertness of the mind, its forgetfulness and its lapses must be resolutely corrected. Life must be transformed from its inmost depths. The Great Truth must be reflected in everything that we do. Philosophy at the purely theoretical level will not help here. Its value for life is small and remote. It may no doubt be called a philosophy of life. But it is still a philosophy which has yet to be *made good in life*. *Yoga*, the discipline of the mind par excellence, alone can do that.

Conclusion

The *way of knowledge* is hard and difficult. But it is a sure way and incomparable with all other methods of approach to the Ultimate Truth put together. Disinterested activity takes us to a stage. It purifies the mind, brings peace to it, and opens the path to the Truth. But there is no stopping here. There is still a stage to go. Any kind of activity, howsoever disinterested, has no tendency to annul itself. This is particularly so, when the intellectual hunger for truth is not fully satisfied. Man is whole, he is not merely will. As long as he is ignorant, his will will find itself at a dead end. The question must be answered, what is the Truth?

The starved human mind looks for love. The highest object of love is naturally God, for he is perfection personified. There is no object of love more resplendent and more beautiful than God. We can love Him more devotedly and more whole-heartedly than anything else. This love easily fills the cup of life. It makes life a perpetual joy, the joy of companionship with God or a spiritual union with Him. But we cannot stop here either. There is still a stage to go. Love is great. The joys of love have no limits. The individual is lost in the ocean of bliss. He can indeed wind up and rest here, it appears. But there is no rest yet. The upsurge of spirituality is bound to carry us forward and upward. The limit is God Himself or Divinity. Have we realized Him fully? Certainly not, so long as we know God to be external to us and somehow related to us. We are still ignorant of God as He is in Himself. We can dispel this ignorance. We dispel it when we realize God as no other than our own true Self; i.e., when we have the knowledge of *identity*. When that knowledge has taken full possession of the soul and the mind of man, that is the End and the Goal. There is nowhere to go beyond Divinity. Knowledge of Divinity thus crowns all other approaches to Reality and fulfils them. When we know, we are released for ever. There is no bondage any more. There is no coming back, no return, and no staying in any heavenly or other abode. We are lost to the world and to empirical living as such at all its earthly and unearthly levels. We have reached the Goal and become the Goal.

This philosophy of life, in our opinion, does justice to every aspect of human experience and human existence, and lifts that existence to the highest possible level of life in the Truth. Aspirants and seekers move by devious paths; and unconsciously, they all suppose that they are moving to the very highest goal of life. They are all *right;* for in fact they are moving to the highest goal. There is nowhere else to go. Only they do not *know* this goal. They imagine the goal in different ways, without realizing that that goal may be only a stepping-stone to something still higher and beyond their present conception. But the King among them, the person who knows, is not deceived. He supports all, sympathizes with all, but at the same time knows the limitations of all. Our salutation to the King among philosophers -- for he alone *knows.*

A SELECT BIBLIOGRAPHY

The Problem of Nothing. Amalner, India: Indian Institute of Philosophy, 1918.
"The Last Word in Philosophy," *Journal of the Indian Institute of Philosophy,* Vol. I (January, 1918), pp. 19-24.
"Advaitism and Nihilism," *Journal of the Indian Institute of Philosophy,* Vol. II (April, 1918), pp. 113-118; Vol. III (July, 1918), pp. 175-180.
"Mysticism," *Journal of the Indian Institute of Philosophy,* Vol. I, 3 (July, 1918), pp. 161-168; 4 (October, 1918), pp. 206-223; Vol. II, 4 (October, 1919), pp. 1-14.

"The Individual and the Absolute," *Journal of the Indian Institute of Philosophy*, Vol. II, 1 (January, 1919), pp. 1-15; 2 (April, 1919), pp. 30-43; 3 (July, 1919), pp. 1-15.

"Being," *Philosophical Quarterly*, Vol. I, 1 (April 1925), pp. 68-77.

"Existence," *Philosophical Quarterly*, Vol. I, 2 (July, 1925), pp. 32-40.

"Intuition," *Philosophical Quarterly*, Vol. I, 3 (October, 1925), pp. 179-189.

"The Problem of Proof," *Philosophical Quarterly*, Vol. II, 1 (April, 1926), pp. 33-41.

"Relations," *Proceedings of the Second Indian Philosophical Congress* (Benares, India, 1926), pp. 1-9.

"Negation," *Philosophical Quarterly*, Vol. III, 4 (January, 1928), pp. 273-284.

"Reason and Dogma," *Philosophical Quarterly*, Vol. IV, 1 (April, 1928), pp. 18-25.

"The Central Problem of Metaphysics," *Philosophical Quarterly*, Vol. IV, 2 (July, 1928), pp. 113-121.

"Intuition of Self," *Philosophical Quarterly*, Vol. IV, 3 (October, 1928), pp. 160-168.

"The Substantial Ground of Mental Life or The Self as Substance," *Philosophical Quarterly*, Vol. IV, 4 (January, 1929), pp. 244-252.

"Universal," *Philosophical Quarterly*, Vol. V, 1 (April, 1929), pp. 33-41.

"Intellect and Intuition," *Philosophical Quarterly*, Vol. V, 4 (January, 1930), pp. 262-269.

"The Duality of Subject and Object," *Philosophical Quarterly*, Vol. VI, 2 (July, 1930), pp. 83-93; 3 (October, 1930), pp. 149-161.

"Vedantic Mysticism," *Philosophical Quarterly*, Vol. VI, 4 (January, 1931), pp. 221-231.

"Are There Many Souls," *Philosophical Quarterly*, Vol, VII, 2 (July, 1931), pp. 125-131.

"The One and the Many," *Philosophical Quarterly*, Vol. IX, 2 (July, 1933), pp. 111-120.

"Reality and Value," *Philosophical Quarterly*, Vol. IX, 4 (January, 1934), pp. 19-24; X, 1 (April, 1934), pp. 28-53; 2 (July, 1934), pp. 105-126.

"The Absolute (a criticism of K.C. Bhattacharyya's 'Concept of the Absolute and its Alternative Form')," *Philosophical Quarterly*, Vol. X, 1 (April, 1934); 3 (October, 1934), pp. 199-224; 4 (January, 1935), pp. 351-364; XI, 1 (April, 1935), pp. 97-104; 2 (July, 1935), pp. 107-117.

"Some Reflections on the Nature of Philosophic Truth," *Philosophical Quarterly*, Vol. XI, 1 (April, 1935), pp. 58-65.

"Review of Bharata Kumaruppa's *The Hindoo Conception of Deity*," *Philo-*

sophical Quarterly, Vol. XI, 2 (July, 1935), pp. 208-209.

"The Universal and the Particular," *Philosophical Quarterly,* Vol. XI, 3 (October, 1935), pp. 220-243.

"Universal Religion," *Philosophical Quarterly,* Vol. XII, 1 (April, 1936), pp. 1-11.

"Significance of the theory of Evolution for Religion and Philosophy," *Philosophical Quarterly,* Vol. XIII, 2 (July, 1936), pp. 79-97.

"The Nature of Philosophical Reflection," *Philosophical Quarterly,* Vol. XII, 3 (October, 1936), pp. 213-222.

"Review of H.H. Henson's *Christian Morality - Natural, Developing, Final,*" *Philosophical Quarterly,* Vol. XII, 4 (January, 1937), pp. 330-335.

"Existence," *Philosophical Quarterly,* Vol. XIII, 3 (October, 1937), pp. 163-178; 4 (January, 1938), pp. 231-255.

"Mysticism," *Philosophical Quarterly,* Vol. XIV, 1 (April, 1938), pp. 1-13.

"Philosophical Knowledge," *Philosophical Quarterly,* Vol. XIV, 3 (October, 1938), pp. 239-247.

"Philosophy of the Self or A System of Idealism Based upon Advait Vedanta,*" Journal of the Indian Instiute of Philosophy* (1949), pp. 218ff.

"Rationalism in Philosophy," *Philosophical Quarterly,* Vol. XIV, 4 (January, 1939), pp. 281-290.

"Being and Negation," *Philosophical Quarterly,* Vol. XV, 3 (October, 1939), pp. 208-216.

"Review of S. Radhakrishnan's *Eastern Religious and Western Thought,*" *Philosophical Quarterly,* Vol. XV, 4 (January, 1940), pp. 342-349.

"The Principle of Inexplicability in Philosophy," *Philosophical Quarterly,* Vol. XVI, 1 (April, 1940), pp. 49-60.

"Reality of Time," *Philosophical Quarterly,* Vol. XVI, 3 (October, 1940), pp. 208-217.

"Are We Philosophically Progressive?" *Proceedings of the 16th Indian Philosophical Congress.* Madras, 1940, Part II, pp. 37-42. Reprinted, *Philosophical Quarterly,* Vol. XVII, 1 (April, 1941), pp. 37-42.

"Kant and Vedanta," *Philosophical Quarterly,* Vol. XVIII, 1 (April, 1942), pp. 1-8.

"Reason and Reality in the Philosophy of Kant," *Philosophical Quarterly,* Vol. XVIII, 3 (October, 1942), pp. 152-159.

"A Justification of Maya-vada (a criticism of Aurobindo's criticism of maya-vada in *The Life Divine),*" *Philosophical Quarterly,* Vol. XVIII, 4 (January, 1943), pp. 221-249.

"Sri Aurobindo's Theory of Creation," *Philosophical Quarterly,* Vol. XVIII, 4 (January, 1943), pp. 250-267. Reprinted together with the preceding, *Journal of the Indian Institute of Philosophy,* 1943.

"Sri Aurobindo's Synthesis of the Vedantic Schools of Thought," *Philosophical Quarterly*, Vol. XIX, 2 (July, 1943), pp. 67-79.

"Is Metaphysical Knowledge Possible?" *Philosophical Quarterly*, Vol. XIX, 2 (July, 1943), pp. 100-116.

"Is Time Real?" *Proceedings of the 20th Indian Philosophical Congress,* Trivandrum, 1945, pp. 46-55.

"The Problem of the One and the Many," *Philosophical Quarterly*, Vol. XX, 3 (October, 1946, next issue after XX, 2, July, 1944), pp. 198-208; 4 (January, 1947), pp. 254-266; XXI, 1 (April, 1947), pp. 38-49. Reprinted as separate pamphlet.

"Philosophical Significance of Negation," *Proceedings of the 23rd Indian Philosophical Congress,* Bombay, 1948, Part I, pp. 1-12.

"Comparative Study of Consciousness," *Radharkrishnan: Comparative Studies in Philosophy Presented in Honour of His Sixtieth* (1948). New York: Harper, n.d. pp. 231-257.

"Philosophical Truth," *Proceedings of the 28th Indian Philosophical Congress,* Patna, 1949. Reprinted, *Philosophical Quarterly*, Vol. XXII, 4 (January, 1950), pp. 197-227.

"Some Points on K.C. Bhattacharyya's 'Concept of Philosophy'," *Philosophical Quarterly*, XXIII, 2 (July, 1950), pp. 41-60.

"Maya-Vada: Sri Sankara and Sri Aurobindo," *Proceedings of the Indian Philosophical Congress, Silver Jubilee Session,* Calcutta, 1950, Part I, pp. 1-18. Reprinted, *Philosophical Quarterly*, XXIII, 3 and 4 (October, 1950 and January, 1951), pp. 87-104.

"A Note on Freedom," *Philosophical Quarterly*, Vol. XXIV, 2 (July, 1951), pp. 125-136.

"Examination of the Main Realist Argument," *Proceedings of the 26th Indian Philosophical Congress,* 1951, 179-185. Reprinted, *Philosophical Quarterly*, Vol. XXIV, 4 (January, 1952), pp. 253-259.

"Types of Metaphysical Thinking," *Philosophical Quarterly*, Vol. XXV, 2 (July, 1952), pp. 123-134.

"Unity and Difference," *Proceedings of the 27th Indian Philosophical Congress,* 1952, pp. 135-142. Reprinted, *Philosophical Quarterly,* Vol. XXV, 4 (January, 1953), pp. 195-202.

"Vedantic Epistemology," *Journal of the Indian Institute of Philosophy,* 1953, pp. 146 ff.

"The Spirit of Vedantic Philosophy," *Philosophical Quarterly*, Vol. XXVI, 1 (April, 1953), pp. 25-33.

"Our Knowledge of Nature (a criticism of B. Russell's *Human Knowledge, its Scope and Limits),"* *Philosophical Quarterly*, Vol. XXVI, 2 (July, 1953), pp. 111-123.

"The Conception of Reality as Dynamic," *Proceedings of the 28th Indian Philosophical Congress,* Baroda, 1953, pp. 179-186. Reprinted,

Philosophical Quarterly, Vol. XXVI, 4 (January, 1954), pp. 239-246.

"A Comparative Study of the Advaita Vedanta and the Madhyamika System of Buddhism," *Srimant Pratapsheth Amrita Jubilee Volume, Journal of the Indian Institute of Philosophy*, 1954, III, pp. 1-13.

"Methods of Knowledge or *Pramana*," *Journal of the Philosophical Association*, I, 3 and 4 (January-April, 1954), pp. 1-10.

"Being and Value," *Philosophical Quarterly*, Vol. XXVII, 1 (April, 1954), pp. 1-14.

"Moral Values," *Philosophical Quarterly*, Vol. XXVII, 3 (October, 1954), pp. 113-131.

"Rational Intuition," *Philosophical Quarterly*, Vol. XXVIII, 2 (July, 1955), pp. 107-121.

"On Philosophy," *Philosophical Quarterly*, Vol. XXIX, 2 (July, 1956), pp. 51-67.

"Immortality," *Philosophical Quarterly*, Vol. XXIX, 3 (October, 1956), pp. 155-156.

"Does Indian Philosophy Need Reorientation? (symposium)," *Proceedings of the 31st Indian Philosophical Congress*, 1956, pp. 71-78.

"Dialectical Consciousness," *Philosophical Quarterly*, Vol. XXX, 2 (July, 1957), pp. 77-85.

"Time and the Absolute," Presidential Address, 6th Session of the Philosophical Association, Amalner, 1957). *Journal of the Philosophical Association*, Vol. V, 17 (January, 1958), pp. 1-7.

"The Real, the Actual and the Possible," *K.C. Bhattacharyya Memorial Volume, Journal of the Indian Institute of Philosophy*, 1958, pp. 79-103.

"Matter for Science, Common-sense and Philosophy," *Philosophical Quarterly*, Vol. XXX, 4 (January, 1958), pp. 273-280.

"Review of C.A. Campbell's *On Selfhood and Godhood*," *Philosophical Quarterly*, Vol. XXXI, 1 (April, 1958), pp. 57-65.

"Ultimate Reality," *Philosophical Quarterly*, Vol. XXXII, 1 (April, 1959), pp. 21-29.

"The Logical and the Mystical in Advaita Vedanta," *Philosophical Quarterly*, Vol. XXXII, 4 (January, 1960), pp. 261-266.

"A Defense of Idealism," *Philosophical Quarterly*, Vol. XXXIII, 1 (April, 1960), pp. 23-29.

"Metaphysics of Advaita Vedanta," *Journal of the Indian Institute of Philosophy*, 1961, pp. 299 ff.

"Rational Method in Philosophy," *Philosophical Quarterly*, Vol. XXXIII, 4 (January, 1961), pp. 237-242.

"The Authority of Sruti or Revelation," *Philosophical Quarterly*, Vol.

XXXIV, 1 (April, 1961), pp. 35-38.

"The Concept of Evolution," *Philosophical Quarterly,* Vol. XXXIV, 2 (July, 1961), pp. 104-110.

"God and the Absolute," *Philosophical Quarterly,* Vol. XXXIV, 3 (October, 1961), pp. 179-182.

"Science and Advaita Vedanta," *Essays in Philosophy Presented to T.M.P. Mahadevan,* Madras, Ganesh, 1962, pp. 5-9.

"Concept of Spirit," *Philosophical Quarterly,* Vol. XXXIV, 4 (January, 1962), pp. 253-259.

"Has Indian Idealism Failed Us?" *Philosophical Quarterly,* Vol. XXXV, 1 (April, 1962), pp. 1-8.

"Philosophical Synthesis," *Philosophical Quarterly,* Vol. XXXV, 2 (July, 1962), pp. 79-87.

"The Problem of Evil," *Philosophical Quarterly,* Vol. XXXV, 3 (October, 1962), pp. 167-178.

"Relation of Ethics to Religion," *Philosophical Quarterly,* Vol. XXXVI, 1 (April, 1963), pp. 1-8.

"Ontological Reflections (Being and Necessary Being)," *Philosophical Quarterly,* Vol. XXXVII, 2 (July, 1963), pp. 85-91.

"Ontological Reflections (From Appearances to Reality)," *Philosophical Quarterly,* Vol. XXXVI, 3 (October, 1963), pp. 171-177.

"Gandhiji's Attempt at Modernizing Hindu Philosophy," *Organizer,* Divali, 1963, pp. 53-54.

"Ontological Reflections (from Non-Being to Being)," *Philosophical Quarterly,* Vol. XXXVI, 4 (January, 1964), pp. 235-244.

"Ontological Reflections (Absolute Reality or God)," *Philosophical Quarterly,* Vol. XXXVII, 1 (April, 1964), pp. 21-34.

"Spirituality Eastern and Western (a criticism of C.A. Moore's *Spirituality in the West),"* *Philosophical Quarterly,* Vol. XXXVII, 2 (July, 1964), pp. 103-110.

"The Relation of False Identity," *Philosophical Quarterly,* Vol. XXXVII, (October, 1964), pp. 141-149.

"The Rationale óf the Law of Karma," *Philosophical Quarterly,* Vol. XXXVII, 4 (January, 1965), pp. 257-266. Reprinted in Malkani Steinkraus, "A Discussion of the Law of Karma," *Journal of the Indian Institute of Philosophy,* 1966, pp. 11-26.

"Philosophy of Life," *Philosophical Quarterly,* Vol. XXXVIII, 1 (April, 1965), pp. 29-36.

"Concept of Philosophy (a sister-article to the one written for the seminar on the same subject held at Barnaras Hindu University on 23rd and 24th March, 1965)," *Philosophical Quarterly,* Vol. XXXVIII, 2 (July, 1965), pp. 75-82.

"Introduction to Malkani and Steinkraus, A Discussion of the Law of
        Karma," *Journal of the Indian Institute of Philosophy*, 1966, pp.
        1-10.
"The Absolute and the Individual," *Philosophical Quarterly*, Vol. XXXIX,
        1 (April, 1966), pp. 47-54.
"Identity versus Love," *Philosophical Quarterly*, Vol. XXXII, 2 (July, 1966,
        the last issue), pp. 97-108.
"Philosophy of the Will," *World Perspectives in Philosophy, Religion and
        Culture, Essays Presented to D.M. Datta*, Bihar Darshan Parishad,
        1968, pp. 1-10.

Japan

CHAPTER X

THE CONCEPT OF GOD IN SHINTO

*Virginia T. Johnson**

One of the hardest religions for Westerners to understand is the native religion of Japan — Shinto. It is barely understood even by the Japanese themselves. Shinto is not an ethical or doctrinaire religion. It had no founder, no images, no sacred scriptures, no commandments, no doctrines, no priests, no authentic interpreters, no metaphysics of any kind. It required no sacrifice as a penance or involving a renunciation and saw evil as something outside man's nature. It did not develop an inner spiritual life nor inspire intimate dialogue between man and his God. It offers no uniformity of answer to the question whether Shinto is truly a religion or merely an ethic or possibly a Japanese way of life. Some modern Japanese say it is more a state of mind than a religion. Yet for over 2,000 years it has shaped the lives of the Japanese people.

Primitive Shinto was a cult of nature in the form of animism. The fundamental belief of this Shinto was that everything which in the world of nature possessed power, beauty, or charm, everything which was gracious and sweet, everything which provoked awe, amazement, or mystery participated in divinity, sheltered it, revealed it.[1] These things included the sun, moon, sea, rocks, trees, waterfalls, rivers, mountains, caverns by the sea.

Unlike other people of that period the Japanese experienced no feeling of fear in the presence of nature. They felt there was

*Associate Professor of Asian Studies at St. John's University, New York, U.S.A.

1 R.P. Dunoyer, "The Religions of Japan," *Introduction to The Great Religions* by Jean Danielou, *et al.* (Notre Dame, Indiana: Fides Publishers, 1967), p. 96.

no conflict between man and nature for man was considered as a creature who has his place in creation and who is linked to it by an ontological bond.[2] Rather than feeling fear the Japanese felt great joy in living with the universe and the gods, for Nature was good and faithful.

So, the religious sentiment in early Japan consisted in a poetic intimacy with Nature and the gods in feelings of gratitude and joy over so much beauty. Man wanted their help, their approval. He gave them evidences of affection and hoped for theirs in return. This made early Shinto more than a religious faith. "It is an amalgam of attitudes, ideas, and ways of doing things that through two milleniums and more, have become an integral part of the way of Japanese people. Thus Shinto is both a personal faith in the kami and a communal way of life according to the mind of the kami."[3]

Who or what are these kami? The basic concept of a god or divine being in Shinto is the concept of kami and kami are the objects of worship. (In the Japanese sense worship means simply an act of reverence). "There was little differentiation between worship of an object as a deity, worship of its spirit, and worship of its attributes."[4] The literal meaning of the word kami is "above" or "superior." The term was applied to anything in the physical and cosmological world that possessed supernatural powers, extraordinary force or unusual features. Kami referred to deities of Heaven and Earth and to spirits, both good and evil, noble and mean, right and wrong. Each province, each village, and each clan had its own kami. In time, the term kami was applied even to the spirits of human beings, — ancestors, eminent emperors and national heroes. The word kami is poorly translated as gods or spirits in the Occidental sense but that is the nearest we can come to it. The term is obscure and vague

   2 *Ibid.*

   3 Sokyo Ono, *Shinto: The Kami Way* (Rutland, Vermont and Tokyo, Japan: Charles E. Tuttle Company, 1962), p. 3.

   4 William K. Bunce, *Religions in Japan* (Rutland, Vermont and Tokyo, Japan: Charles E. Tuttle Company, 1955), p. 100.

even to the Japanese themselves. They have a conscious awareness of kami rather than a conceptual or theological idea of it.
Motoori Norinaga (1730-1801), the greatest teacher of Shintoism and a leader in the Shinto Revival Movement in eighteenth
century Japan, wrote: "I do not yet understand the meaning of
the term kami."[5] He then went on to say that "human beings,
birds, beasts, trees, plants, seas, mountains, thunder, the echo,
dragons, foxes, tigers, wolves, peaches, a necklace, rocks, stumps
of trees, leaves of plants were all kami."[6] No kami in ancient
Shinto had a perceptible form. From this we can conclude that
"Shinto, at root, is a religion not of sermons but of awe. Not a
grasp of the conception of spirit, but a sense of its ubiquity, is
the proper end of Shinto."[7]

In ancient Shinto a structure was not a necessity to house a
kami. Kami-rites were performed wherever a manifestation of a
kami was first experienced. It might be before an unusual rock
formation or before an impressive waterfall or in a beautiful
grove. Gradually structures were erected. They were extremely
simple, being small single-structure, unpainted wooden buildings
(usually of cypress) with a thatched bark roof supported by
whole tree-trunks for beams. These shrines were built off the
ground and were usually located in a place of great natural
beauty. Since there were no images in primitive Shinto the Shrine
contained only a symbolic representation of a deity. However,
the main purpose of the shrine was to house one or several kami
and to provide a setting for the worship of the kami. The entrance to the shrine was marked by a torii, a wooden gateway to
indicate the separation of the sacred from the secular. If there
was no flowing water nearby then some sort of water container
was placed before the shrine so that the worshippers could

5   D.C. Holton, *The National Faith of Japan* (New York: Paragon Book Reprint
Corp., 1965), p. 23.
6   *Ibid.*, pp. 23-24.
7   Joseph Campbell, *The Masks of God: Oriental Mythology* (New York: The
Viking Press, 1962), p. 476.

cleanse their mouth and hands. From its earliest period Shinto exacted scrupulous cleanliness, for it equated physical uncleanness with moral impurity and considered it something revolting and intolerable to the gods. This exterior purification was to denote an interior one, which later increasingly became an act of spiritual significance. The holy place was marked out by a row of stones or a fence. A rope of twisted straw with small white paper cuttings tied to it usually dangled at the entrance.

Shinto worship consisted of prayers and practices. The prayers (norito) were very beautiful and simple, being usually prayers of thanksgiving or prayers of supplication for material favors such as the birth of a son, a good harvest, freedom from sickness or misfortunes, protection from dangers, success in undertakings and the like. There were no communal services. Practices included purification (misogi), making of offerings, sacred dances (kagura), music (gagaku), processions and celebration of festivals (matsuri).

Early Shinto was polytheistic, the number of gods being popularly reckoned as "eight hundred myriads." There was no idea of One Supreme Being, or Creator, or an Infinite personal being. There were the heavenly kami, — those who were born in Heaven, and the terrestrial kami, — those who came down to earth and had descendants here. The kami were regarded in anthropomorphic terms since they were begotten, born, lived, worked, played, and died as humans did. They had no individual names; they were related to specific regions. They were gifted with extraordinary and preeminent powers, some kami were benevolent, others malevolent. Each kami had its own work and function. There was the kami of agriculture, of rice, of the fishing season, of grains, of everything connected with food production. There were the nature deities and the kami connected with fertility and phallicism. There were the kami of the sea. There were the kami of the wind, storms, rain, fire, thunder, earthquakes. There were the kami of magical objects and ordinary utensils. There were the kami of particular families and clans, and of definite districts and communities. There were the kami of the crafts and every process of work. There were the kami of the household and ancestors.

To the primitive Japanese, all these natural phenomena were living beings, acting exactly as they themselves did. In the Shinto pantheon there were clear differentiations between the sexes and clearly defined hierarchical orders and family relationships. However, there were no kami personifying abstract qualities such as Love, Patience, Hope, Youth. Some of the higher kami were supposed to have a soul or spirit (mitama), which invisibly inhabited a shrine while the kami itself remained in the heavens. This mitama was represented in a shrine by an object (shintai), "in which part of the essence of a kami has lodged."[8] The shintai might be a stone, a mirror, or any little object meant to be the visible means of contact between the kami and its devotees.

Thus it can be seen to what extent polytheistic animism developed in early Japan. It was not organized or systematized; it was non-speculative. It did not even have a name. The main characteristic of early Shinto was its cosmic orientation."[9]

In the Japanese cosmogony three deities were supposed to have emerged from primordial chaos. The triad disappeared without leaving any posterity. A long succession of celestial deities appeared and vanished in the same manner until finally, in the seventh generation, Izanagi (The Male-who-invites) and Izanami (The Female-who-is-invited) appeared and were commanded by the other celestial deities to produce the terrestrial world.

They descended a floating bridge that connected heaven and earth and, after a courtship, Izanagi and Izanami procreated the islands (of the Japanese archipelago), and all the objects and forces of nature on them, such as the Mountains, Fields, Trees, Rocks, Clouds, and Fire. It was while giving birth to this last deity, Fire, that Izanami died and went to the nether world. The grieving Izanagi killed the Fire deity with his sword, then went

8 L. Aletrino, *Six World Religions* (New York: Morehouse-Barlow Co., 1968), p. 90.

9 Joseph M. Kitagawa, *Religion in Japanese History* (New York and London: Columbia University Press, 1966), p. 12.

to Hades, the underworld, to try to bring back his wife. Izanami agreed to accompany him provided he did not look at her. But he did look at her and he saw her decaying body. This angered Izanami and she sent other infernal deities to drive her husband out of the nether world where she remained to be the great goddess of Hades.[10] He returned to earth and immediately purified himself of the stains incurred during his visit to Hades. From this purification were born three very important deities in Shinto cosmology: Amaterasu, the Sun-goddess; Tsuki-yomi, the moon-god; and Susa-no-o, the Storm-god. This is one version of the myth concerning the creation of Japan.

Another tradition holds that Izanagi and Izanami jointly procreated Amaterasu, Tsuki-yomi and Susa-no-o. No matter which version is believed, the fact remains that Amaterasu was produced to be "lord of the universe." She was most beautiful and was her father's favorite. She gave light and life to all and was the protectress of the rice crops. She was also the guardian of peace and order. Because she was so beautiful her parents decided they should "send her at once to Heaven, and entrust to her the affairs of Heaven."[11] Tsuki-yomi was also radiant and beautiful so they put him in Heaven also to be the helpmate of his sister.

Susa-no-o was just the opposite of the other two. He was wild, impetuous, rebellious, and the perpetrator of cruelties and atrocities against his sister, the Sun-goddess, and others. Because of these acts he was expelled from Heaven and settled on earth in the Izumo region.

Eventually Amaterasu had her own family, and because of some misdoings of the sons of the Storm-god, she decided to send her grandson Ninigi, to pacify the Japanese islands. As tokens of his mission the Sun-goddess gave Ninigi three treasures,

10 John A. Hardon, *Religions of the World* (Garden City, New York: Doubleday & Company, 1968), Vol. I, p. 221.

11 From the *Nihongi* as quoted in *Sources of Japanese Tradition*, compiled by Ryusaku Tsunoda, Wm. Theodore de Bary, and Donald Keene (New York: Columbia University Press, 1958), p. 16.

— a mirror, a sword, and a jewel, with the command to rule Japan and the assurance that his dynasty would endure forever. The divine grandson descended from Heaven and landed with his entourage on the island of Kyushu. It was his grandson Jimmu Tenno who conquered the province of Yamato in Central Japan, in 667 B.C., and who established his capital there on February 11, 660 B.C. Jimmu is reckoned as the first human emperor of Japan and founder of the Imperial Dynasty. These mythological origins and genealogies of the gods were eventually recorded in the *Kojiki* and the *Nihongi* or *Nihon Shoki*. These works, which are the primary sources for primitive Shinto, will be enlarged upon later in this paper.

Though the credibility of these mythical traditions might put a strain on our credulity, at least they serve to denote certain features of Japan's primitive religion. These include the multitude of the gods, their ubiquity, their separation into superior and inferior divinities, their anthropomorphic characteristics, their qualities of good or evil. The people believed that both the visible and the invisible world were peopled with tremendous forces and influences and that every natural object, both animate and inanimate, harbored a spirit. Other important features were the stress on purity and purification, and the feeling of an intimate communion between gods and men.

For many, many centuries these religious traditions of Japan were loosely interwoven among the numerous clans but without any central organization, being determined mostly by local and tribal cults. All the clans claimed descendence from the deities. There were frequent struggles among the clans for supremacy but gradually the Imperial or Yamato clan overcame its rivals and assumed hegemony over all when it united both sacred and secular functions in its tenno or emperor.[12] When this clan gained the ascendancy so did its clan gods and that made the Sun-goddess the foremost and most important deity of all. These

12 Joseph J. Spae, *Shinto Man* (Tokyo, Japan: Oriens Institute for Religious Research, 1972), p. 20.

traditions were handed down orally because the Japanese had no
script at this time.

Then towards the end of the fourth century, A.D. came the
impact of Chinese civilization, especially Confucianist and Taoist
influences, both of which stimulated new developments within
Shinto. Taoism contributed "a sophisticated system of philosophical, astrological, and magical themes and practices."[13] Confucianism rationalized the cult of ancestor worship and structured an ethical system centered around the emperor. The Japanese let themselves be dominated by the intellectual and cultural
influences of China. They adopted the Chinese religions to their
own beliefs and practices and to the native religion which
emerged from this the Chinese gave the name Shen-tao, "The
Way of the Gods," (Shen meaning spirit; tao meaning way), but
which in Japanese is Kami-no-Michi.

Then in 552 A.D., Buddhism in its Mahayana form, came to
Japan from Korea and it tempered Japan's primitive Shinto. Its
acceptance by some clans provoked violent and bloody opposition from Shintoist clans but that was ended when the emperor
accepted the new faith. Within a few years Buddhism was elevated to a state religion but whereas it was accepted by the
aristocrats and courtiers the mass of Japanese peasants kept to
their Shinto beliefs and practices. It was now that Japan's religion was given the name Shinto, "The Way of the Gods" to
differentiate it from Buppo, "The Way of the Buddha." Thus,
although Buddhism exercised tremendous influences, especially
in new concepts of morality, prayer, and services for the dead,
it never was able to supplant Shintoism. This was due, not only
to the hold of Shinto on the Japanese mind, but also to the
tolerance and adaptability of Buddhism.

Soon there evolved a fusion, an amalgamation of Shinto and
Buddhism into a synthesis called Ryobu or Dual Shinto which
was maintained for the next thousand years. In this system the
Shinto gods were claimed to be manifestations of the Buddhist

13 *Ibid.,* p. 21.

gods and Buddhist ritual was blended with Shinto ceremonials. Many Shinto shrines were managed by Buddhist monks. Only the Ise Shrine, dedicated to Amaterasu, remained free from any Buddhist contamination. Seemingly, Buddhism had absorbed Shinto but, in reality, it never did. In fact, Shinto gained much through its association with Buddhism. While Buddhism was concerned with the hereafter Shinto was a religion of the present. It was also concerned with events in individual lives — like birth, children at various ages, youth festivals, and marriages. It was also the religion that was involved in every single matter pertaining to rice production. It was an inescapable facet of the daily living of the Japanese.

The basic myths which detailed for the early Japanese their origin, their social structure, and their pattern for daily life and worship can be found in the *Kojiki* (Records of Ancient Matters), dated 712 A.D. and the *Nihongi* or *Nihon Shoki* (Chronicles of Japan), and dated 720 A.D., which serve as sacred books. These gave the history of Japan from the creation of the world to the eighth century. It was in these works, influenced by Chinese and Buddhist ideas, that the Japanese became politically orientated and endowed their emperor with a sovereignty that had a divine origin from the earliest times and which was grounded and buttressed by a divine mandate to rule and last forever. Their purpose was to prove that the emperor was a direct descendant of the Sun-goddess and to strengthen the domination of the dynasty. By divinizing the emperor and their political institutions, they developed the cult of the emperor. The determined use of this and the other myths about the divine creation of the country itself and its people and customs developed into an aggressive nationalism from the eighteenth century onward which became the tool of a world-conquering ambition.

During medieval Japan codes were promulgated, some of which concerned Shinto. They fixed the number and dates of religious festivals, indicated what ceremonials were to be observed, and collected the oldest Shinto prayers, thus saving them from oblivion. Beginning with the eighteenth century, there was a Shinto revival vocalized and popularized by a number of philologists who wrote many commentaries on the *Kojiki* and *Nihongi*. Motoori Norinaga went even further and shifted emphasis in Japanese thought from the rational and moral to the emotional side of human nature. He cited Japan's greatest novel, *The Tale of Genji*, "as a masterpiece of human sensitivity,"[14] and felt that it provided "the key to all that is truest and best in the Japanese national life."[15]

After the Meiji Restoration of 1868 the unity of state and religion was stressed and Shinto came under the aegis of the national government. A movement purified Shinto of all foreign influences and attempted to restore it to its pristine purity. But the movement for the revival of Pure Shinto was more or less a failure. It was at this time, too, that by government decree Shinto was divided into State Shinto and Sect Shinto. From then on State Shinto was manipulated by the militarists as a tool for their imperialist and nationalist schemes.

State Shinto was disestablished on December 15, 1945 by General Douglas MacArthur. As a result rigid government control over all religions ended and no one religion in Japan was to have a privileged position in the State but all religions were to have equal position and protection before the Law. Moreover, there was to be freedom of religion for all.

On January 1, 1946 Emperor Hirohito, in a radio address to the entire nation, disassociated himself from the concept of his divinity and the nation from its illusionary and chauvinistic attitudes of racial superiority and supposed destiny to rule the world. He appealed to the mutual trust and affection that he said had always characterized the relationship between him and his people. This repudiation of his own divinity by the emperor not only had bewildering effects upon many of his subjects but also paved the way for many new religions and pseudo-religious cults to appear.[16]

14 *Sources of Japanese Tradition, op. cit.,* p. 509.
15 *Ibid.,* p. 532.
16 Joseph M. Kitagawa, *op. cit.,* p. 282.

People were shattered by the emperor's announcement and confused by the whole postwar religious situation. So many of their shrines had been destroyed or damaged. So many of their religious leaders had been killed or wounded. All at once the cult of the emperor was terminated. And at the same time Japanese society and culture were suffering from apathy, lack of leadership and resources, disillusionment. Not only were new religions increasing but Communism was also.

Although the Occupation officials ended State Shinto in 1945 they did not end Shinto. Many of its traditional cultic elements remain fairly much the same as they always were. There are still the daily ablutions, the family altar *(kami-dama)*, the homage at family shrines, village shrines, tutelary shrines. There are the celebrations of seasonal festivals and the Shinto wedding ceremonies. There is the wearing or carrying of paper amulets or badges to ensure the kami's protection. There is still the insistence on physical and moral cleanliness. The concept of sin is nebulous, the notion of immortality is vague, and the idea of an eschatological goal is negative.

The experience of Shinto salvation is still in the eternal present of the world; it is not an anticipation experience. "Shinto accepts this world; it does not want to change it."[17] Shinto still refuses to distinguish between the sacred and the secular, between the religious and the profane, between religion and government. Shinto is still polytheistic, never admitting the existence of a single Supreme Being. It is not that it denies the existence of any such Being but that it never seriously considers the question.

The younger Shinto scholars feel the need for reform. They are looking for a new view of man, of ethics, of society, of attitude towards the world. Already the shift from an agrarian to an industrial economy and from farm to city life has meant a loss for Shinto. A noted professor is quoted as saying, with

17 Spae, *op. cit.,* p. 65.

reference to the kami, "We are raising a nation of atheists in Japan."[18]

Perhaps, Shintoism without veneration of the emperor, is adapting to Christian models. There are profound changes going on in the world, and consequently also in Japanese religion. The family has always been the carrier of traditional Japanese religion. But present changes in family structure have resulted in a breakdown of the traditional relationship to the local Shinto Shrine and even in a fading interest towards ancestor worship. Community patterns have basically changed. This forces Shinto to transform itself from a community faith to a personal faith. For Shinto, this is a major problem.

At this point Shinto is not an organized religion as are Buddhism and Christianity. But it is "a noble expression of what is beautiful, and good, and true in the soul of Japan. It could possibly enrich the lives of people everywhere."[19]

A SELECT BIBLIOGRAPHY

1. Books on Shinto

Aston, W.G., *Shinto, The Ancient Religion of Japan.* London: Longmans, Green and Co., 1921.

Ballow, Robert O., *Shinto, The Unconquered Enemy.* New York: Viking Press, 1945.

Holton, D.C., *Modern Japan and Shinto Nationalism.* New York: Paragon Book Reprint Corp., 1963.

———, *The National Faith of Japan.* New York: Paragon Book Reprint Corp., 1965.

Ono, Sokyo, *Shinto: The Kami Way.* Rutland, Vermont and Tokyo, Japan: Charles E. Tuttle Company, 1962.

Spae, Joseph J., *Shinto Man.* Tokyo, Japan: Oriens Institute for Religious Research, 1972.

Underwood, Alfred C., *Shintoism: The Indigenous Religion of Japan.* London: The Epworth Press, 1934.

18 *Ibid.,* p. 45.
19 Joseph J. Spae, "The Shinto View of Man," *The Japan Missionary Bulletin,* XXV/8 (September, 1971), p. 490.

2. Books with Sections on Shinto

Aletrino, L., *Six World Religions*. New York: Morehouse-Barlow Co., 1968.

Anesaki, Masaharu, *History of Japanese Religion*. Rutland, Vermont and Tokyo, Japan: Charles E. Tuttle Company, 1963.

Bownas, G., "Shinto," *The Concise Encyclopedia of Living Faiths*. Edited by R.C. Zaehner. Boston, Massachusetts: Beacon Press, 1959.

Bradley, David G., *A Guide to the World's Religions*. Englewood Cliffs, New Jersey: Printece-Hall, Inc., 1963.

Bunce, William K., *Religions in Japan*. Tokyo, Japan: Charles E. Tuttle Company, 1955.

Campbell, Joseph, *The Masks of God: Oriental Mythology*. New York: The Viking Press, Inc., 1962.

Chamberlain, Basil Hall, *Japanese Things*. Tokyo, Japan: Charles E. Tuttle Company, 1971.

Chan, Wing-tsit; Al Faruqui, Ismail Ragi; Kitagawa, Joseph; Raju, P.T., *The Great Asian Religions*. New York: The MacMillan Company, 1969.

Dunoyer, R.P., "The Religions of Japan," *Introduction to the Great Religions*. Edited by Jean Danielou. Notre Dame, Indiana: Fides Publishers, Inc., 1964.

Earhart, H. Byron, *Japanese Religion: Unity and Diversity*. Belmont, California: Dickenson Publishing Company, Inc., 1969.

Frazier, Allie M. (ed.), *Chinese and Japanese Religions*. Philadelphia, Pennsylvania: The Westminster Press, 1969.

Fujisawa, Chikao, *Zen and Shinto*. New York: Philosophical Library, Inc., 1959.

Gaer, Joseph, *How the Great Religions Began*. Revised edition. New York: The New American Library, Inc., 1956.

————, *What the Great Religions Believe*. New York: The New American Library, Inc., 1963.

Hall, John W. and Beardsley, Richard K., *Twelve Doors to Japan*. New York: McGraw-Hill Book Company, 1965.

Hardon, John A., *Religions of the World*. Vol. I. Garden City, New York: Doubleday & Company, Inc., 1968.

Kitagawa, Joseph M., *Religion in Japanese History*. New York and London: Columbia University Press, 1966.

————, *Religions of the East*. Enlarged Edition. Philadelphia, Pennsylvania: The Westminster Press, 1968.

————, "Shinto," *Encyclopedia Britannica*, 1962 ed. Vol. XX. 517-21.

Noss, John B., *Man's Religions*. Fourth Edition. New York: The MacMillan Company, 1969.

Ross, Floyd H. and Hills, Tynette, *The Great Religions by Which Men Live*. Ninth Printing. New York: Fawcett World Library, 1969.

Schoeps, Han-Joachim, *The Religions of Mankind*. Garden City, New York: Doubleday & Company, Inc., 1968.
Spae, Joseph J., *Japanese Religiosity*. Tokyo, Japan: Oriens Institute for Religious Research, 1971.
Warner, Langdon, *The Enduring Art of Japan*. New York: Grove Press, Inc., 1952.

3. Books on Mythology

Aston, William G. (trans.), *Nihongi: Chronicles of Japan from The Earliest Times to A.D. 697*. London: Allen and Unwin, 1956.
Bruhl, Odette, "Japanese Mythology," *Larousse Encyclopedia of Mythology*. Edited by Felix Guirand, translated by Richard Aldington and Delano Ames. New York: Prometheus Press, 1959, pp. 412-426.
Chamberlain, Basil Hall (trans.), *Kojiki or Records of Ancient Matters*. 2nd ed. Kobe, Japan: J.L. Thompson and London: Routledge & Kegan Paul, 1932.
Saunders, E. Dale, "Japanese Mythologies," *Mythologies of the Ancient World*. Edited by Samuel N. Kramer. Garden City, New York: Doubleday & Company, Inc., 1961. Pp. 409-442.
Wheeler, Post (ed. and trans.), *The Sacred Scriptures of the Japanese*. New York: Schuman, 1952.

4. General Works

Anesaki, Masaharu, *Religious Life of the Japanese People*. Revised by Hideo Kishimoto. Tokyo, Japan: Kokusai Bunka Shinkokai, 1961.
Bellah, Robert N., *Tokugawa Religion*. Boston: Beacon Press, 1957.
Benedict, Ruth, *The Chrysanthemum and The Sword*. Meridian Books. Cleveland and New York: The World Publishing Company, 1946.
Branley, Brendan R., *Christianity and the Japanese*. Maryknoll, New York: Maryknoll Publications, 1966.
Hasegawa, Nyozekan, *The Japanese Character: A Cultural Profile*. Translated by John Bester. Tokyo, Japan and Palo Alto, California: Kodansha International, 1965.
Kidder, Edward J., *Japan Before Buddhism*. New York: Praeger, 1959.
Moore, Charles A. (ed.), *The Japanese Mind*. Honolulu, Hawaii: East-West Center Press and University of Hawaii Press, 1967.
Nakamura, Hajime, *Ways of Thinking of Eastern Peoples: India, China, Tibet, Japan*. Honolulu, Hawaii: East-West Center Press, 1964.
Reischauer, Edwin O., *Japan: The Story of A Nation*. New York: Alfred A. Knopf, Inc., 1970.

————, *The United States and Japan.* New York: Viking Press, 1965.
Sansom, G.B., *Japan: A Short Cultural History.* Revised edition. New York: Appleton-Centruy-Crofts, Inc., 1962.
Tsunoda, Ryusaku; De Bary, Wm. Theodore and Keene, Donald, *Sources of Japanese Tradition.* New York: Columbia University Press, 1958.

Judaism

CHAPTER XI

GOD IN THE BIBLICAL-RABBINIC TRADITION
Simon Greenberg*

This essay will be limited to an inquiry into the concept of God which emerges from a selective choice of passages primarily from the Hebrew Bible, the Tannaitic Midrashim, and the Babylonian Talmud. The choice of passages must of necessity be selective not only because of the vast amount of material available, but also because the theological content of this vast literature is not logically or psychologically ordered.[1] Statements reflecting a conception of the nature of God are usually introduced on the basis of association of ideas with legal or historic matters under discussion and are often contradictory.

This did not happen unwittingly. The rabbis restricted what we would designate as theological discussions to very small groups of the most learned and pious.[2] There is ample ground to assume that they discussed these questions in far greater detail than the extant literature suggests, but if these discussions were ever recorded, those records were not preserved.[3] Nevertheless, all who have taken the trouble to study this literature agree that

---

*Vice-Chancellor, The Jewish Theological Seminary of America, New York, U.S.A.

1 On the futile attempts to write a systematic theology of the Hebrew Bible see Gerhard Von Rad, *Old Testament Theology,* Vol. II, Postscript regarding efforts to do the same with Rabbinic Literature, see Kadushin's *The Rabbinic Mind,* p. VII, and S. Schechter, *Some Aspects of Rabbinic Theology,* p. 16.

2 Hagigah 11b.

3 The Talmud records that the schools of Shammai and Hillel debated the question of whether it would have been better for man not to have been born at all, for two and a half years, but we have no report of the arguments used on either side of the question (Eruvin 13b).

there emerges from it a concept of God which, in George Foote Moore's term may be designated as 'normative'[4] to Judaism for at least some twenty-five hundred years. Our understanding of the character of this normative concept will guide us in the selection of the materials and ideas to be included in this essay. That does not mean that what will be excluded is considered to be unimportant, schismatic, or in any way heretical.[5] Whatever is found in this literature is by the very fact of its inclusion a legitimate component of the Jewish heritage. But not every legitimate component is equally pervasive of the whole tradition.

There will be no attempt to follow a chronological order. The date of the 'birth' of an idea is at best of secondary importance. We are not here concerned with claiming priorities. Neither shall we be too fiercely constrained by the demands of a syllogistic logic. We shall be concerned with exploring the inter-relationships of the various ideas that in their totality constitute the 'normative' concept of God in this Biblical-Rabbinic tradition. Hence a theme dealt with primarily in one section of the essay will not always be completely treated in that section. Its further elucidation, if necessary, will be found in another preceding or following section.

Finally, we shall not be concerned with defending one or another theory of how the founders of Judaism arrived at their concept, whether it was by revelation, intuition or reason. We do not think that anyone can answer this question with any degree of scientific surety. Each one of us has his own intuitive predilection in this matter. My favoring the term 'intuition' in this essay should not be taken to imply my own theological position.[6] I use it here because it carries overtones of both revelation and reason.

---

4 G.F. Moore, *Judaism,* Vol. I, p. vii.

5 Thus, for example, very little attention will be given to the mystic trend in Judaism during this period, although Gershom Scholem has, in his *Major Trends* and other numerous works, demonstrated that it played an important role in Jewish religious life.

6 For that see S. Greenberg, *Foundations of a Faith,* pp. 45-69 and Chapter 3.

1. There is Only One Omnipotent God

Nowhere in the Bible is an attempt made to *prove* that there are gods or that there is only one God. The existence of gods or superhuman powers was universally assumed by all who had intellect enough to distinguish between themselves and their environment and who had sufficient curiosity to wonder how and what they beheld in the heavens or on the earth came to be. Everyone knew that neither he nor his fellowmen created themselves or the hosts of the heavens. However, there was nothing in the sensibly accessible environment which suggested to the observer that all were created by one God. On the contrary, it seemed eminently reasonable to assume that the same creator did not create phenomena that tended to cancel one another out, such as fire and water, or that had essentially different characteristics such as wetness and dryness, or air and earth. Above all it seemed to be inconceivable that tribes, families or nations that saw themselves as mortal enemies had the same creator or patron spirit.

Hence, in the mind of primitive man the world was populated with an infinite number of super-human spirits. Some were friendly, others hostile; each one was of limited potency. Some were restricted geographically. Some exercised control of some aspect of what we today identify as the natural order.[7] Some were more powerful than others. When pantheons were conceived they were organized under a chief god. But none of these gods was omnipotent. They all limited one another's powers and all of them together were subject to some primordial force, sometimes referred to as the Fates, whom even the gods sought to control by magic.[8] Greek philosophers later arrived at the idea of a first cause, an 'unmoved mover'. However, long before, and

---

7 See R.W. Smith, *The Religion of the Semites*, Chapters 3, 4, 5.
8 *Ibid.*, pp. 39-40.

completely unrelated to Greek philosophical thought, the people
of Israel were admonished:

"Here O Israel, the Lord our God, the Lord is One."

Those who maintain that the religion of the Israelites was for
centuries henotheistic interpret this affirmation as implying that
there are other gods and that other nations had many gods but
that Israel has but one God. They usually delay the rise of universal monotheism in Israel to the eighth century and the prophet
Amos.

If a reasonable difference of opinion about the implications of
this statement is conceivable, there can be no possible misunderstanding of the implications of such statements as:

> See, then, that I, I am He:
> There is no god beside Me.
> I deal death and give life:
> I wounded and I will heal:
> None can deliver from My hand.
>
> (Deuteronomy 32:39)

> Or: I am the Lord, and there is none else
> Beside Me there is no god:
> I form the light, and create darkness:
> I make peace, and create evil;
> I am the Lord, that doeth all these things.
>
> (Isaiah 45:5)

These go beyond the affirmation of the oneness of God. He is
declared to be "supreme" over all. There is no realm above or
beside Him to limit His absolute sovereignty. He is utterly distinct from, and other than, the world; He is subject to no laws,
no compulsions, or powers that transcend Him... This is the
essence of Israelite religion, and that which sets it apart from all
forms of paganism. This idea was not a product of intellectual
speculation, or of mystical meditation, in the Greek or Indian
manner. It first appeared as an insight, an *original intuition...*

The new religious idea never received an abstract, systematic formulation in Israel... Taking on popular forms, the new idea pervaded every aspect of Israelite creativity.[9]

Nothing in the Bible indicates that the Israelites arrived at the concept of one God by a process of logical reasoning. There are only polemics against idolatry. The idols are declared to be "not gods." The most telling argument was that the idols were made by man. The assumption that man makes his gods seemed on the face of it too absurd to deserve serious consideration. Isaiah's satire on idol making is devastating. "They that fashion a graven image are all of them vanity. And their delectable things shall not profit" (Isaiah 44:9). The prophet then goes on to describe how the smith and the carpenter cooperate in fashioning the idol. They take the wood of a tree, part of which they use for fuel to warm themselves, to bake bread, and to roast meat. "And the residue thereof he maketh a god, even a graven image: He falleth down unto it and worshipeth and prayeth unto it. And saith: Deliver me, for thou art my god . . . They know not . . . neither is their knowledge nor understanding to say: I have burned the half of it in the fire. Yea also I have baked bread upon the coals thereof. I have roasted flesh and eaten it; and shall I make the residue thereof an abomination? Shall I fall down to the stock of a tree?" (Isaiah 44:12-19). Moreover the idols were visible, and "the affirmation that God cannot be seen is written so deep in the Jewish heritage that it is not too venturesome to assert that the tradition may go back to Moses himself."[10]

Whether the average Israelite or even the prophets did or did not know that at least the sophisticated among the isolaters, distinguished between the idol and divinity that it represented or that was assumed to dwell in it, is an open question. Y. Kaufman argues with considerable cogency that the Israelites knew nothing or next to nothing about pagan mythologies, and that they assumed that the visible idol was worshipped as the

9 Y. Kaufman, *The Religion of Israel*, p. 60.
10 J. Muilenberg, *Isaiah*, Chapters 40-66; *Interpreter's Bible*, Vol. 5, p. 511.

actual god.[11] Whether Kaufman is right or not, the fact remains
that it obviously made more 'sense' to the idolaters, both Israelite as well as non-Israelite, to "fall down to the stock of a tree"
and pray than 'to fall down' before an invisible God, or else the
prophets would not have had to denounce the idolatry of their
own people with such vehemence and persistence for so many
centuries. Israel, the Rabbis say, was not weaned from the sin of
idolatry until after the Babylonian exile.[12]

2. Anthropomorphism in the Biblical-Rabbinic Tradition

Logically, there is nothing that of necessity follows from the
statement that there is only one omnipotent God, except that
there is not more than one. Thus, the question of whether the
one invisible God may be spoken of or thought of in anthropomorphic terms which occupied so central a place in the minds
of Jewish medieval philosophers, and particularly in the thought
of Maimonides, obviously did not seem to trouble either the
average Jew of the Biblical and Talmudic period or their prophets
and sages. Isaiah does not hesitate to tell us that he "saw the
Lord sitting on a throne, high and lifted up; and his train filled
the temple" (Isaiah 6:1). The Bible is replete with anthropomorphisms, as is Rabbinic literature.[13] The question did not seem to
trouble any of the Rabbis till about the tenth century when the
Aristotelian non-corporeal unmoved mover had become the
fashion in Arabic philosophical-theological circles and affected
the contemporary Jewish intelligentsia. They found their answer
in the second commandment forbidding the making of a visible
representation of God (Exodus 20:4) and in the admonition to
remember that "You saw no form on the day that the Lord

11 "...The biblical polemic against 'idolatry' - consistently misrepresenting the
religion of the pagans as fetishism," Y. Kaufman, *op. cit.*, pp. 3, 142, 236-237.
12 Yoma 9b.
13 "Nay, it would seem that the Rabbis felt an actual delight in heaping human
qualities upon God whenever opportunity is offered by Scriptures." S. Schechter, *op.
cit.*, pp. 37-38.

spoke unto you in Horeb out of the midst of the fire" (Deuteronomy 4:15). These served them as warrant enough to justify the
most casuistic interpretations of all anthropomorphic references
to God in the Bible as being mere metaphors.[14] Maimonides
pronounced anyone who conceived of God in anthropomorphic
terms as a *Min* - an idolater. Rabbi Abraham ibn Daud resented
it declaring that "many greater and better than he thought of
God in this way, because of what they read in the Scriptures, and
even more because of what they saw in the (Rabbinic) Aggadot
which tend to confuse man's opinions."[15]

This controversy between two of the giants of the tradition is
germane to our inquiry only in so far as it indicates that while
the question of whether speaking or even thinking of God in
corporeal terms was to be unequivocally proscribed, was argued
by the authoritative expounders of the tradition, *no one* ever
suggested that Judaism could tolerate the thought that there
was more than one God. The Rabbis of the Tannaitic Midrashim
and the Babylonian Talmud do not generally bother to interpret
Biblical anthropomorphisms as metaphors. They do insist, however, in maintaining that Biblical plural forms which refer to God
and might therefore be interpreted as indicating a belief in the
existence of more than one God are, in reality, only collective
forms and refer to only one God.[16]

The Biblical-Rabbinic tradition is fully aware of the ethical
dilemma presented by the belief in one omnipotent God. It
declares Him to be responsible for both the suffering of the
righteous and the prosperity of the wicked. Attempts are made
both in the Bible and in Rabbinic literature to grapple with this
problem directly, to meet it as it were head on. The variety of
plausible answers which were offered are not immediately ger-

14 M. Maimonides, *The Guide,* Part I, Chapters 1-49 - discusses every expression
found in Scripture that refers to God anthropomorphically, and proves that each one
can be interpreted and should be understood as a metaphor.

15 M. Maimonides, Mishna Torah, Hilchot Teshuva of the *Sefer Hamada,* Chapter 2,
par. 7, and ibn Daud's Comment *ad locum.*

16 Bereshit Rabba VIII: 9; Sanhedrin 38b.

mane to our theme; none of them is either logically or emotionally fully satisfying. Why then did the tradition remain so tenaciously loyal to a concept that for centuries not only brought
upon it the enmity of all with whom it came into contact but
also posed an insoluble ethical problem? The answer to this
question, I believe, is to be found in the fact that while there is
nothing which is logically of necessity deducible from the statement that God is one and omnipotent except that there are not
two such gods, there are other 'original intuitions' *which are
indispensable to human civilized existence which were made
possible or even stimulated by it and which being rationally
more congenial to it than to any other concept are nourished
by it.* Chief among these other 'original intuitions' is the concept
of the unity of mankind.

3. "Have We Not One Father?"

The most explicit association between the concept of one
omnipotent God and the concept of one mankind was made by
the prophet, Malachi. "Have we not one father? Hath not one
God created us? Why do we deal treacherously every man against
his brother, profaning the covenant of our fathers?" (Malachi
2:10).

There are those who argue that "the context seems to show
that Malachi is thinking more of God as the creator of the Jewish
nation than of individual men... Yet, the prophet gave utterance
to words which are capable of conveying a greater measure of
truth than he dreamed of. The ideal of common brotherhood
under a common fatherhood, which Malachi sets forth as the
true pattern of life for the Jewish community, is capable, under
the presuppositions of the prophetic faith itself of being extended to the whole of mankind."[17]

The prophet's statement, "is capable...of being extended to
the whole mankind," not merely "under the presuppositions of

---

17 R. Denton, *ad locum* in *Interpreter's Bible.*

the prophetic faith itself," but also because of the manner in which he formulated it. If the prophet had only the Jewish people in mind then he did not have to refer to God as the ground for their brotherhood. He could have reminded them that they were all descendants of Abraham, Isaac and Jacob, and while it is generally true that a primary characteristic of a genuine prophetic statement is that it is "capable of conveying a greater measure of truth than he dreamed of," the fact that Malachi does not refer to the patriarchs but to God would indicate that not only on the subconscious but even on the conscious level, he was 'dreaming' of a truth larger in scope than some of his commentators attribute to him.

This "greater measure of truth" is spelled out in the Rabbinic interpretation of the Biblical account of the creation of Adam. In contradistinction to his colleague, Rabbi Akiba, Ben Azzai designates the statement, "This is the book of the generations of Adam" (Genesis 5:1) rather than the commandment, "You shall love your neighbor as yourself" (Leviticus 19:18), as the spiritual zenith or culmination of the Torah.[18] The Rabbis would seem to agree with Ben Azzai for in one of their many extraordinarily profound interpretations of the Biblical narrative of the creation of Adam they say, "God created only one man so that no man should be able to say, 'My ancestor was superior to yours'." They thus explicitly posit actual consanguinity for the whole human race. The one omnipotent God created one physical ancestor for all of us.[19]

There is nothing in the historic experience of mankind to validate the concept that all men are brothers. Differences in color, in racial characteristics and in language, and the ongoing hostility among tribes and nations do not suggest it. The modern concept of evolution not only does not imply it, but tends to support the contrary view. Evolution does not posit one ancestor for the whole human race. It tends to assume rather that manlike

18 Yerushalmi, *Nedarim,* Chapter 9, Halacha 4.

19 Sanhedrin, 37a - for a more detailed discussion of this subject see S. Greenberg, *Foundations,* Chapter 4. A.E. Speiser, *Oriental and Biblical Studies,* p. 316.

creatures appeared at different periods in different areas of the earth. It surely does not posit the same rate of development for all of them. The idea of intellectually more endowed and less endowed races is more than merely congenial to the theory of evolution. It is well-nigh integral to it, for evolution presupposes haphazard forward and backward movement as well as inconceivably long periods of stabilization in which adjustment to environment is so perfect as to make movement in either direction highly unlikely.

Nor does the brotherhood of man logically and of necessity follow from the belief that one God created us. He also is said to have created the animals and the fish. The concept of one mankind is therefore another of the 'original intuitions' which are integral to the Jewish heritage, and which is rationally congenial to the concept of one omnipotent God.

4. The One Omnipotent God is a Just Ruler

One of the ongoing unresolved and unresolvable questions involves the relationship between the realities man experiences upon this earth and his beliefs about what goes on in heaven. There are those who insist that man's vision of the heavenly order is but a reflection of what he experiences on earth, and there are those who believe that it is the self-revelation to man of the heavenly order which sets men's goals for the human order. Both of these views we think contain significant elements of truth, and world views differ basically to the extent that they assign priority to either the one or the other of these attitudes. The first attitude is dominant in paganism. Pagan mythology pictures the heavenly order as being in essence a reflection of the human order. Gods are born and die. They copulate, they love, hate, are jealous and greedy. They require physical substance. Above all, the only restraint upon their activities is their limited power. Gods "do what they can do," and while the concept of justice is certainly known to the pagan world, it played little if any role in paganism's vision of the heavenly order. This view is articulated with utmost clarity in the address attributed by Thucydides to the Athenian delegates who came to Melos to demand that it join Athens in its war against Sparta or else be utterly annihilated. The Melians plead for justice and then express their hope that their cause being just, the gods will help them. To this the Athenians reply:

> When you speak of the favour of the gods, we may as fairly hope for that as yourselves; neither our pretensions nor our conduct being in any way contrary to what men believe of the gods, or practice among themselves. Of the gods we believe, and of men we know, that by a necessary law of their nature they rule wherever they can. And it is not as if we were the first to make this law, or to act upon it when made: we found it existing before us, and shall leave it to exist forever after us; all we do is to make use of it, knowing that you and everybody else, having the same power as we have, would do the same as we do. Thus, as far as the gods are concerned, we have no fear and no reason to fear that we shall be at a disadvantage...[20]

There was nothing in mankind's remembered experience twenty-five hundred years ago, nor is there today, that would suggest that things can and will be different. There are even those who question whether they should, in essence, be different. Concepts like "the struggle for existence" and "the survival of the fittest" which were and are integral to the evolutionary theory, have been interpreted in the most elementary terms of physical power and seen as offering the most satisfactory explanation for the appearance of the higher forms of life upon this planet.[21] The only concept which men have thus far con-

[20] Thucydides, *The Complete Works,* Chapter 17, p. 334.
[21] "To advance natural selection as the means of evolution meant that purely physical forces, brute struggle among brutes, could account for the present forms of powers of living beings. Matter and Force taken in any and every sense explained our whole past history and presumably would shape our future." J. Barzun, *Darwin*, p. 41. See also Index there under "Struggle for Existence" and "The Survival of the Fittest."

ceived which can supersede might as the arbiter in international, as well as in personal relations, is that of justice. But that concept must itself be conceived not as the defense mechanism of the lamb when confronted by the lion, but as inhering in the order to which they both belong.[22] Such a concept is not rationally congenial to a world order populated by warring gods, nor to a god who is not omnipotent, for impotent justice has nothing to offer to man. Nor does the concept of oneness and omnipotence logically and of necessity imply justice. The one omnipotent creator of the universe may be conceived as being a whimsical, morally indifferent tyrant and there is no objectively irrefutable evidence to disprove it. The concept that the one omnipotent God is just is therefore a discrete 'original intuition' which is rationally eminently congenial to the concept of omnipotent oneness. Abraham could rationally demand that God should act justly because he could address Him as "The ruler of the universe" (Genesis 18:25).

Rabbi Pinchas taught in the name of Rabbi Reuben: Five times in the first book of the Psalms, David calls upon God to "rise up" to help him. To which God responded, "Though you call upon me a thousand times, I will not arise. I will arise only when I see the poor plundered and hear the groans of the needy as it is written, 'Because of the groans of the plundered poor and needy, I will not act, says the Lord' " (Psalm 12:6).[23] Because God was omnipotent and just, the most highly 'nationalistic' of Jewish medieval philosophers, Yahuda Halevi could read the last verse of the 82nd psalm to mean that God is the *nachala*, the 'possession', and hence the defender, of "all who cry out against the injustices done to them among all the nations."[24]

Only when the concept of a multiplicity of deities, each one doing all that he or she *can* do, so that sheer power was the arbiter among them, was replaced by the concept of the one

22 See S. Greenberg, *Ethics*, Section IV, p. 109 and also Section VIII, p. 89.
23 Bereshit Rabba, Chapter 75, par. 1 - Comment on Genesis 32:4.
24 Quoted by Abraham ibn Ezra in his commentary on Psalm 82:8.

omnipotent and just God, did it become rationally possible for a prophet to envision the day when "the mountain"...of the Lord's house shall be established as the top of the mountain,

> And He shall judge between the nations,
> And shall decide for many peoples,
> And they shall beat their swords into plowshares,
> And their spears into pruning hooks;
> Nation shall not lift up sword against nation,
> Neither shall they learn war any more.
>
> (Isaiah 2:4)

5. Divine Forbearance and Forgiveness

In the narrative regarding the destruction of Sodom and Gemorrah, Scripture explains that God revealed His intention to Abraham because He had chosen him "that he may charge his children and his household after him to keep the way of the Lord by doing righteousness and justice" (Genesis 19:19). God, as it were, was not only to give Abraham an object lesson in the administration of justice but was, at the same time, testing him whether he would be sensitive to the demands of justice. Abraham lives up to God's expectations. But in pleading in behalf of the Sodomites Abraham does not ask God to give them an opportunity to repent, nor does he present extenuating circumstances which would call for forgiveness. He asks only that the innocent should not perish together with the wicked.[25] The concepts of forbearance and forgiveness appear for the first time in Scripture in the narrative regarding the golden calf which the Israelites had made and worshipped only forty days after the Sinaitic Theopany (Exodus 32-34).

The Israelites are not immediately punished for this egregious transgression. God, however, repudiates the Israelites and speaks

---

25 This problem is taken up by Ezekiel, Chapter 18.

of them as being Moses' rather than His people (*Ibid.* 7).[26] He says to Moses "Let Me be, that My anger may blaze forth against them that I may destroy them and make of you a great nation" (Exodus 32:10). The Rabbis sense in the words "Let Me be" that God was testing Moses even as He had tested Abraham earlier. He wanted to see how deep was Moses' concern for his people. Hence He hints to him that he can do something about it. Moses, like Abraham, rises to the occasion. He does not let God be! He pleads with God in behalf of Israel, but not on the basis of extenuating circumstances. He appeals to God's concern for His own reputation. "Let not the Egyptians say, 'It was with evil intent that He delivered them' " (*Ibid.* v. 12). And he asks God to remain faithful to the promises He made to the Patriarchs. Whereupon the Bible states somewhat elliptically, "The Lord repented of the evil which He thought to do to His people" (*Ibid.* v. 13).

Moses then comes down from Mt. Sinai, breaks the Tablets, grinds the golden calf into dust, punishes some of the people and returns to God to plead that if He still intends to destroy the people, then he too wishes to be "blotted out" from God's book. God responds that He will "blot out" those only who have sinned against Him, but it will not be done at once. Only a minor pestilence was visited upon them, but further punishment to be inflicted at some later time is foretold (Exodus 32:33-35).

Moses is then ordered to lead the people forward, but is at the same time told that only "My angel shall go before you" (*Ibid.* 32:34), "I will not go up among you, lest I consume you in the way, for you are a stiff-necked people" (Exodus 33:3). Moses is not ready to forego God's presence among them even though it involves the danger of being 'consumed' by His Holiness if they in any way profane it through their stiff-neckedness. He persists in pleading that God go with them. "For how shall it be known that I have found favor in Thy sight, I and Thy people? Is it not in Thy going with us, so that we are distinct, I and thy people

---

26 See also Exodus 3:7, 11; 5:1 ff.

from all other people that are upon the face of the earth?" (Exodus 33:16). Moses then makes his ultimate plea to be permitted to behold the "manifestations of God's character in its fullness."[27] He asks of God, "Let me know Your ways" (*Ibid.* 33:13), "Let me behold Your presence" (*Ibid.* v. 18). In response God says, "You will see my back; but my face shall not be seen" (Exodus 33:23). He then reveals Himself to Moses as "The Lord! The Lord! A God compassionate and gracious, slow to anger, rich in steadfast kindness, extending kindness to the thousandth generation, forgiving iniquity, transgression, and sin; yet He does not remit all punishment, but visits the iniquity of fathers upon children and children's children upon the third and fourth generation" (*Ibid.* 34:6-7).

In this passage the Rabbis identify thirteen *Middot,* thirteen different Divine Manifestations[28] in the world. *Adonay*—the Lord—denotes His manifestation as the Merciful one. "Yet He does not remit all punishment," denotes His manifestation as the Just One.

These two manifestations of God in the affairs of men are the most frequently referred to in Rabbinic thought. But there is another *Middah* - Divine Manifestation - listed among these thirteen to which far too little attention has been paid. It is the *Middah* of 'slow to anger', of Divine Forbearance. It too is a discrete concept and constitutes an 'original intuition'. It is usually overshadowed by or even absorbed into the concept of Forgiveness. But from the point of view of its implications for the religious and moral life of man, it is at least as important as

---

27 J.C. Rylaarsdam, Exodus 33:18, *Interpreter's Bible,* Vol. 1, p. 1074.

28 The Hebrew term, *Middah,* is usually translated as 'attribute.' I prefer to translate it is Divine Manifestation. The term, 'attribute' raises the theologicophilosophical question of the relationship of the 'attributes' to God which I think is avoided by the term 'Divine Manifestation.' For the Rabbinic interpretation of these verses, see J.H. Hertz, *Penteteuch,* on Exodus 34; 6-7; see also Torah Temima *ad locum.* On the question of the variety of God's manifestations and of hypostatical attributes - see S. Schechter, *op. cit.,* pp. 43, 44, 322n.2 also G.F. Moore, *Judaism,* Vol. I, pp. 392-93.

the concepts of Divine Justice and Mercy.[28a] God's forbearance is the opportunity given to man to repent. The concepts of For-bearance and Repentence are the indispensible religiously fructi-fying links between Sin and Forgiveness.

The Scriptural proviso that God will be gracious to whom He will be gracious (Exodus 33:19) ensured that the concept of Repentence would never have any traffic with magic. There was nothing that man could do that could force the hand of God and compel Him to forgive. But neither was the sinner left without any hope. No matter how grievously he may have sinned, he need not feel that punishment is inexorable. God's forbearance offers him an opportunity to do something about it. "For God does not desire the death of the wicked but that he abandon his ways and live" (Ezekiel 18:23, 33:11). How great is God's for-bearance? "Until the day of his death You wait for him. When-ever he returns You welcome him at once" (Mahzor p. 242). But lest one be inclined to postpone repentance until the very day of his death Rabbi Eliezer, the son of Hyrcanus (2d cent.) admon-ished his students to repent one day before death. Since no one knows the day of his death he should repent every day.[29]

Human sin and Divine Forbearance, human Repentance and Divine Forgiveness are discrete concepts and as such they are original intuitions rationally congenial to one another and to the Biblical-Rabbinic concept of one omnipotent God who makes Himself manifest to man through acts of justice and mercy.

6. The Inescapable Dilemma

It requires no superabundance of critical insight to discover that these two Middot are rationally irreconcilable. Justice implies punishment in proportion to the sin. Mercy implies either

---

28a "Israel is made aware from the beginning that Yahveh is never the hard *'creditor,'* relentlessly exacting the conditions of the covenant, but that his claim to honour rests on the fact that he owns the title *'erek appayim'* (slow to anger) (ex. 34.6) with as much right as he bears the name of *'el qana'* - the jealous god."

29 Avot, Chapter 2:15, and Shabbat 152b.

no punishment at all or one which is obviously less severe than the gravity of the sin would indicate. No theologian, philosopher, moralist or saint has ever been able to delineate the scope of the application of each of these *Middot*, so that we might know when justice violates mercy and when mercy infringes upon justice. Indeed God seems to have sensed what moved Moses to ask to be shown "His ways." Moses was at a loss to comprehend what saved the Israelites from suffering the full consequences of their transgression. He had received no verbal response to his plea after the incident of the golden calf. He therefore asked to behold God's "Presence" (Exodus 34:18). To which God replied, "I will make all My goodness pass before you as I proclaim the name Lord before you." Then Scripture continues with a statement that seems to have no reference to what preceded. God adds, "I will be gracious to whom I will be gracious, and show compassion to whom I will show compassion" (*Ibid.* 19). God forewarns Moses, that though He will show him all His goodness, he will not fully comprehend what he sees, "for man may not see Me and live" (*Ibid.* 20).

Many there are who refuse to accept this limitation upon man's ability "to see God." They cannot intellectually and emotionally tolerate the notion that such two contradictory manifestations reflect the will or the action of the same God. The simplest solution accepted by many was to replace the One Omnipotent God by at least two primordial powers or substances, the one manifesting itself in the good, the other in the evil. Attempts without number have, however, been made to reconcile the contradiction within the limits of a thoroughgoing monotheism. All resources of a desperate casuistry have been brought to bear upon this most disturbing of all theological problems confronting the sophisticated as well as the naive devotees of monotheism.[30] But the complete solution to this dilemma remains forever among "the secret things that belong to the Lord our God" (Deuronomy 29:28). There are, however,

---

30 See C.E.M. Joad, *God and Evil.*

things "that belong to us" because they "have been revealed to us" (*Ibid.*). Among them is the overwhelmingly attested fact that since man is sinful, human society simply could not exist if all transgression were completely unpunished. To live by love alone means to condone the holocaust and to treat its perpetrators with love. Neither could mankind exist if all transgressions were punished in proportion to the gravity of the sin, either by human or by divine agency. To act in accordance with the strict demands of justice alone is to inflict punishment equal to the sin of the holocaust, a prospect at which the heart recoils and the mind staggers.[31]

While the Rabbinic tradition never wavers in its insistence upon seeing in Justice one of the prime, all pervading manifestations of God, there is evident in a countless number of Rabbinic reflections an 'emphatic trend'[32] to accentuate the Divine manifestations of Mercy. Rabbinic Aggada has God conferring with the Torah before creating man. "The Holy One, blessed be He, said to the Torah, 'Let us create man.' The Torah replied, 'Master of the Universe, this man will be of few years and full of trouble' (Job 14:1) and will sin and if You are not patient with him, he will be as if he had not been born,' (i.e., he would be condemned very early to death). To which the Lord replied: 'Is it then for naught that I am called "slow to anger and rich in steadfast kindness'."[33]

In calling upon man to strive to be God-like, the Rabbis always ask man to imitate God's acts of mercy and loving kindness.[34]

31 "God said, 'If I create the world only with Love, sinners will multiply; only with Justice, how can it endure? I will therefore create it with Love and Justice'," Bereshit Rabba 12:15.

32 Kadushin, *The Rabbinic Mind*, p. 297. The Rabbis note that the statement that God is "rich in steadfast kindness" is meant to convey the idea that God always inclines to kindness rather than justice. Rosh Hashana, 17a.

33 L. Ginzberg, *Legends*, Vol. 1, p. 55, Pirke d'Rabbi Eliezer, Chapter 11.

34 Sotah 14a, Shabbat 133b. "Indeed, it is distinctly taught that man should not imitate God in the following four things which He alone can use as instruments. They are jealously (Deut. 6:5), revenge (Ps. 94:1), exaltation (Exod. 15:21, Ps. 93:1) and reacting in devious ways." S. Schechter, *op. cit.*, p. 204.

They never say "As He is just you be just" for only God can know when the punishment is equal to the sin and not greater than it. To bestow more mercy upon an individual than he deserves is hardly a sin, but to mete out more punishment than the occasion warrants certainly is.

The Rabbis see a manifestation of God's mercy in the very passage which deals with His punishment of sin. In commenting on the statement that God "visits the iniquity of the fathers upon children and children's children, upon the third and fourth generation" (Exodus 34:7) they say that God metes out rewards with a measure which is five hundred times greater than that with which he metes out punishment, for punishment is meted out only unto the third and fourth generation. His rewards extend unto (literally) two thousand generations.[35]

7. All of Creation is a Manifestation of God's Love

In Semitic and Greek mythologies the gods were themselves the progeny of variously conceived primeval forces. Man was conceived as being either the progeny of the gods or their special creation.[36] In addition, the gods, like men, were in need of physical sustenance. This mythological framework answered not only the question of how man came to be but the equally persistent question regarding his particular role. Whether as physical progeny or as a special creation man's role was to relieve the gods of the exhausting and menial labor of finding and preparing food. Man's joy and woes were dependent upon his proper fulfillment of this basic responsibility. The offerings placed upon the altars were therefore edibles.[37] But the one omnipotent God of Juda-

35 Tosefta Sotah, Chapter 4.

36 G.F. Moore, *History*, pp. 209-211, 432-33. "The relation between the gods of antiquity and their worshippers was expressed in the language of human relationships, and this language was not taken in a figurative sense but with strict *literality*. If God was spoken of as a father and his worshippers as his offspring the meaning was that the two make up one natural family with reciprocal duties to one another" R. Smith, *The Religion of the Semites*, p. 29-30.

37 *Ibid.*, p. 220; R. Smith, *op. cit.*, p. 224.

ism had no physical progeny. Nor did He have need for physical sustenance. And even if He were to have need of it, He was not dependent upon man for its acquisition.

> Hear, O My people, and I will speak;
> O Israel, and I will testify against thee:
> God, thy God, am I.
> I will not reprove thee for thy sacrifices;
> And thy burnt-offerings are continually before Me.
> I will take no bullock out of thy house.
> Nor he goats out of thy folds.
> For every beast of the forest is Mine,
> And the cattle upon a thousand hills.
> I know all the fowls of the mountains;
> And the wild beasts of the field are Mine.
> If I were hungry, I would not tell thee;
> For the world is Mine, and the fulness thereof.
> (Psalm 50:7-13)

A discussion of the role of the sacrificial cult in Israelite religion would take us far beyond the limits of this essay and is not immediately relevant to its basic theme. We shall therefore merely note that the rejection of the notion that God needed the offerings of edibles for His own sustenance required that a new answer be given to the question of man's role in relation to God. What was it then that moved God to create man? Judaism's answer to this question constitutes another 'original intuition' which the Biblical conception of one omnipotent God made possible. The creation of the universe is a manifestation of God's love. This concept underlies and pervades the Biblical-Rabbinic tradition.

The Psalmist calls upon us to "give thanks for His goodness and for His steadfast, everlasting love" (Psalm 136:1) which is manifest from time immemorial in that it was He who "made the heavens...spread out the earth upon the waters...made the great lights...the sun to rule the day...and the moon and the stars to rule over the night" (*Ibid.* 5-9). "In Thy goodness Thou renewest the creation every day continually...giving light to the whole world and to its inhabitants whom Thou didst create *bemiddat berachmim* as a manifestation of Thy mercy."[38]

The creation of man in God's image is the very acme of the manifestation of God's love. "Rabbi Akiba used to say: 'Man is beloved as is evidenced by his having been created in God's image.' God's surpassing love of man is evidenced in that man was told that he was created in God's image, as it is said, 'In the image of God, He created man" (Genesis 9:6).[39]

God's love embraces all of mankind. "When the Egyptians were drowning in the sea the angels wanted to sing God's praises. Whereupon He rebuked them saying: 'My creations are drowning in the sea and you want to sing'."[40]

God's love is steadfast and eternal. "And the Lord smelled the sweet savour; and the Lord said in His heart: 'I will not again curse the ground any more for man's sake; for the imagination of man's heart is evil from his youth; neither will I again smite any more everything living as I have done.' While the earth remaineth, seedtime and harvest, and cold and heat, and summer and winter, and day and night shall not cease" (Genesis 8:21-22). Even the afflictions visited upon man, are subsumed by the Rabbis under the category of manifestations of God's love.[41] Moses, after recalling the many positive manifestations of God's love, adds: "Know then in your heart that as a man disciplines his son, the Lord Your God disciplines you" (Deuteronomy 8:15).

The concept of creation as a manifestation of God's love constitutes the setting for the Biblical-Rabbinic concept of man's role in the world. For love, even Divine Love has need of, and delights in, reciprocity. Nothing is quite as distressing as unre-

---

38 Hertz, *The Authorized Daily Prayer Book*, p. 426. The translation in Hertz is "by the attribute of Mercy." I took the liberty of inverting the order of the two sentences quoted.

39 *Avot*, 3:18.

40 Sanhedrin 39b; Megillah 10b.

41 Berachot 5a.

quited love. And because love is not love unless it is freely given, and because God wants man's love and not his blind servile obeisance, He endowed man with freedom to choose to love or not to love Him. For though "loving God...means life and length of days" (Deuteronomy 30:19-20) man can refuse to do so. Hence, prophet, Rabbi and sage find it ever necessary to admonish man to "choose life" (*Ibid.* 19). Nowhere is the divine Pathos of which Abraham Heschel spoke so eloquently[42] more movingly reflected than in the repeated injunctions in Scripture to love God. Although it is the Jewish people which is addressed, the implications of the admonition are of a universal import. "You must love the Lord your God with all your heart and with all your soul and with all your might" (Deuteronomy 6:5). "And now, O Israel, what is it that the Lord, your God, demands of you? It is to revere the Lord your God, to walk only in His paths, to love Him, and to serve your God with all your heart and soul" (*Ibid.* 10:12).

To conceive of the creation of the universe as a manifestation of God's love is to take hold of a double-edged sword that has no handle. Exalted as the concept may be, it is also dangerously related to the blasphemous, for in its own way, it implies a certain dependence of God upon His creatures.[42a] A God who manifests Himself in love requires an object other than Himself through whom and to whom that love is manifested. The God of the philosopher, is eternally contemplating Himself. Aristotle's unmoved mover is so completely self-centered that man and his doings are altogether outside the realm of his concern. In Spinozistic pantheism man has no will of his own and cannot choose either to love or not to love God, for he is but an insignificant manifestation of the totality which is God. Thought contemplating itself may make some kind of sense to a philosopher, but love, loving itself is abhorrent to any normal human being and

---

42 Heschel, A., *The Prophets*, Chapters 12-14.

42a For this point of view see Eliezer Berkovits, *Dr. A.J. Heschel's Theology of Pathos*, Volume 6, Number 2, Spring-Summer 1964.

because Man is the only creature known to us who can freely
requite God's love, God is ever in search of man:[43]

> Wherefore when I came was there no man?
> When I called was there none to answer?
> Is my hand shortened that it cannot redeem?
> Or have I no power to deliver?
>
> (Isaiah 50:2)

> I was ready to be sought by those who did not ask for me:
> I was ready to be found by those who did not seek me.
> I said, 'Here am I, here am I'
> To a nation that did not call on my name.
> I spread out my hand all the day to a rebellious people
> Who walk in a way that is not good, following their own
> devices.
>
> (Deuteronomy 65:1-2)

In God's unrequited love, Judaism sees the root, and the substance of human tragedy and of cosmic travail.

8. God Establishes Covenants and is Faithful to Them

Next to the concept of the one Omnipotent God, nothing is
more distinctive of the Biblical-Rabbinic tradition than the concept of the covenant.[44] No known non-biblically rooted past or
present religious tradition contains anything even faintly resem-

---

43 A.J. Heschel, *God in Search of Man*. The whole volume in one form or another
is devoted to the theme "that it is precisely God's care for man that constitutes the
the greatness of man. *To be* is to *stand for,* and what man stands for is the great mystery of being His partner. *God is in need of man"* (emphasis in the original), p. 413.

44 For W. Eichrodt, *Theology:* "the covenant is the central concept by which to
illuminate the structural unity and the unchanging basic tendency of the message of
the Old Testament," (p. 13) even as the concept of the one omnipotent God is for Y.
Kaufman.

bling the notion that a god's relationship to a people is conditioned by a covenant between them. The bond between a people and its god was usually viewed as dependent upon "a kind of blood relationship or a link between the god and the country, which created an indissoluble association between himself and its inhabitants."[45] But these notions were rationally incompatible with the concept of One Omnipotent God. The concept of the covenant is therefore an 'original intuition' without which the one Omnipotent God would have become as totally removed from His creation as is Aristotle's unmoved mover. The covenant concept preserves the religiously indispensable personal, or - if you will - the anthropomorphic characteristics of the one God which involves Him in the affairs of man and makes Him accessible to man.

God established a covenant not only with Israel. After the flood he established a covenant with Noah and his descendants and with every living creature, the birds, the cattle and every beast of the earth that was with Noah in the ark (Genesis 9:9-10). The sign of that covenant was to be the bow in the clouds. "When the bow is in the clouds, I will look upon it and remember the everlasting covenant between God and every living creature of all flesh that is upon the earth" (*Ibid.* v. 17), "and the waters shall never again become a flood to destroy all flesh" (*Ibid.* v. 15), The 'bow in the clouds' is not so much a reminder to God but an assurance to man and to all creatures that there shall never again be a total devastation of creation.[46] This covenant is offered to man and beast as an "everlasting covenant," not as a reward for any particular virtue which inhered in Noah and the beasts that were with him, but rather as a manifest-

---

45 Eichrodt, *op. cit.*, p. 43. According to Eichrodt "these ideas were overcome by the concept of the covenant." I think rather that these ideas were overcome by the concept of the one omnipotent God with which the notion of blood relationship or geographic limitation are rationally inconceivable.

46 To the believer this assurance offers some comfort at a time when man somewhat boastfully proclaims that he now has the power to do what God promised never to do. What God will not do man cannot do. We can cause unprecedented destruction but the future of God's creation is not altogether at the mercy of man's evil inclination.

ation of God's grace and of His love for His creatures. God takes cognizance of man's evil inclination (*Ibid.* 8:21). It is as if God acknowledges that He, as man's creator, shares responsibility for man's backslidings so that though the sin be ever so grievous, the punishment will not equal its enormity.

The laws which govern the motions of the hosts of heaven and the relationships of the physical phenomena underneath the heavens which we designate as the laws of nature the Bible sees as the provisions of the covenant which God freely established between Himself and them. "Thus saith the Lord: If you can break My covenant with the day and my covenant with the night so that day and night may not come at their appointed time, then also my covenant with David my servant may be broken" (Jeremiah 33:19-20). The laws of nature are not autonomous. They are the creations of God.

> Thou hast established the earth and it stands fast.
> By thy appointments they stand this day
> For all things are thy servants.
> (Psalm 119:90-91)

The fact that they stand this day is testimony to God's "faithfulness which endures to all generations." The concept of the covenant and God's faithfulness to it excludes "the fear that constantly haunts the pagan world, the fear of the arbitrariness and caprice in the godhead...With this God men know exactly where they stand; an atmosphere of trust and security is created."[47]

It is within the framework of the concept of the covenant that the Prophets and Rabbis over the centuries elaborated and refined Judaism's unique philosophy of history and its understanding of the role that the Jewish people is called upon and is destined to play in bringing that history to a triumphant culmination. The covenant concept has been central to all Jewish and

---

47 Eichrodt, *op.·cit.*, p. 38.

Christian theology and its study has, in more recent years, become one of the chief preoccupations of scholars concerned with the theology of the Hebrew Bible. We cannot, within the limits of this essay, hope to treat it with any degree of adequacy. All we shall attempt to do is to indicate some of the questions raised by it and some of the answers suggested.

Both Biblical and Rabbinic sources waver in their answer to the question of why God chose to make a covenant with Israel. The dominant opinion would seem to be that it was due to the virtue of the patriarchs, particularly of Abraham. God promises to be with Isaac and to bless him because "I will fulfill the oath which I swore to Abraham, your father...because Abraham obeyed My voice and kept My charge, My commandments, My statutes and My laws" (Genesis 26:3-5). God is moved to redeem the Israelites from Egyptian slavery because their cry which reached heaven reminded Him of the covenant which He had made with Abraham, Isaac and Jacob. (Exodus 2:23-24). Nowhere in Biblical-Rabbinic tradition is it stated that God chose or made a covenant with Israel because it was the most virtuous of nations. He made a covenant with them because He loved them, and because He was faithful to the promise He made to the patriarchs. "It is not because you were more in number than any other people that the Lord set His love upon you and chose you for you were the fewest[48] of all the people, but it is because the Lord loves you, and is keeping the oath which He swore to your fathers...know therefore that the Lord your God is God, the faithful God who keeps covenant and steadfast love with those who love Him and keep His commandments, to a thousand generations..." (Deuteronomy 7:7-9).

The question whether the covenant with Israel was conditional and would be annulled has, of course been one of the chief 'bones of contention' between the Church and the Synagogue.

---

48 The term 'fewest' seems to be a circumlocution for 'stiff-necked', the usual Biblical description of Israel, or for some such idea as "for you were not the most virtuous of all people."

Many a scriptural passage has been quoted in support of either side. For the Biblical-Rabbinic tradition two things have been determinative. In the first place the promise made to Abraham was unconditional. "I will maintain My covenant between Me and you, and your offspring to come, as an everlasting covenant throughout the ages" (Genesis 17:7). It is a promise that is repeated in various prophetic pronouncements, "For the mountains may depart and the hills be removed, but My kindness shall not depart from thee. Neither shall My covenant of peace be removed, saith the Lord that hath compassion on thee" (Isaiah 54:10).

But God's love does not tolerate evil in the beloved. God's justice shows no favoritism. "For the Lord your God is the God of gods, the Lord of lords...who shows no favor and takes no bribe" (Deuteronomy 10:17). Moreover, His reproof is most severe against those whom He loves best. Others may, on occasion be excused for their shortcomings, but not Israel.

> You only have I known of all the families of the earth
> Therefore I will punish all your iniquities.
>
> (Amos 3:2)

However, though Israel may be severely reproved and sorely punished, it will never be rejected. Nay more. Even if Israel were to try to reject God, He would not permit them to carry out their designs. He, Himself, has too much at stake. He must vindicate His love for and choice of Israel.

> ...And that which cometh into your mind shall not be at all; in that ye say: We will be as the nations, as the families of the countries, to serve wood and stone.

> As I live, saith the Lord God, surely with a mighty hand, and with an outstretched arm, and with fury poured out, will I be king over you;

> and I will bring you out from the peoples, and will gather you

out of the countries wherein ye are scattered, with a mighty hand, and with an outstretched arm, and with fury poured out;

and I will bring you into the wilderness of the peoples, and there will I plead with you face to face.

Like as I pleaded with your fathers in the wilderness of the land of Egypt, so will I plead with you saith the Lord God.

And I will cause you to pass under the rod, and I will bring you into the bond of the covenant...

(Ezekiel 20:32-37)

But in addition to the promises specifically recorded in Scripture, Israel has even in exile and dispersion tangible evidence of God's everlasting love and of His faithfulness to the covenant. It has the Torah. Rabbi Akiba taught: "Beloved are Israel for a most precious gift was given unto them. It was an act of especial love to tell them that, that whereby the world was created (the Torah) was given as a gift to them," as it is said 'For I give you good doctrine, forsake you not my teaching' (Proverbs 4:2).[49] "With everlasting love hast Thou loved the House of Israel, Thy people. A Torah and commandments, statutes and judgments hast Thou taught us."[50] The Torah is the ever present manifestation of God's love for Israel. It nourishes the 'everlasting life' which He has bestowed upon Israel. It is the very embodiment of the covenant which He established with Israel at Sinai as an everlasting covenant and His faithfulness to it is made manifest by the fact that through it Israel lives.

---

49 *Avot*, Ch. 3:18.
50 J.H. Hertz, *Daily Prayer Book*, p. 367.

9. God Communicates with Man

There is nothing uniquely Israelitish in the notion that "man in the bush with God can meet." The pagan world was full of gods of whose presence men were aware and whom they encountered wherever they turned.

The distinctive uniquely Israelitish aspect of man's encounter with God is not that man was overawed by the awareness of His presence, but that there were those among men with whom God *communicated*. God did not merely reveal Himself to them. He conversed with them. They could react to what He said, and He responded. The tradition designates one with whom God has thus communicated, as a *Navi* - a prophet. "Surely, the Lord, God, does nothing without revealing his secret to the prophets. The lion has roared, who will not fear." The Lord, God has spoken *"mi lo yinavay"* - who can but prophesy (Amos 3:7-8). Abraham Heschel has analyzed with extraordinary profundity and detail the authentically unique characteristics of Biblical prophecy which distinguish it from all manner of communication between man and the supernatural depicted in all other religious traditions.[51] We shall not distort his brilliant presentation by attempting to summarize it. We shall merely call attention to those basic distinguishing characteristics which are specifically referred to in the Bible.

In rebuking Miriam and Aaron for their evil talk against Moses, the Lord says: "If there is a prophet among you, I the Lord make myself known to him in a vision. I speak with him in a dream. Not so with my servant Moses...with him I speak mouth to mouth, clearly, and not in dark speech" (Numbers 12:6-8). Moses, whom the tradition reveres as the greatest of all the prophets (Deuteronomy 34:10), had, as it were, free access to God. No one before him or after him was granted a more or even an equally significant and comprehensive communication from Him. But all the other prophets of Israel whose messages are

---

51 A.J. Heschel, *The Prophets,* Chapters 19-28.

recorded in the Bible shared with Moses two precious privileges!
To them also, God did not speak "in dark speech." The communication they received was clear and could be understood without commentary by any normal human being. And while God
may not have spoken to them "mouth to mouth," they are never
pictured as losing an awareness of themselves while receiving
the divine communication. There was no merging of personality
with the divine. They were keenly aware that they were being
spoken to and could respond even if, as in the case of the patriarchs, the communication is said to have occurred in a dream
(Genesis 16:1, 12-16. 28:12-16).

But the privilege of being spoken to 'mouth to mouth' which
was not granted to any other individual prophet was granted for
a brief moment to the whole people at Sinai. Even though they
had been prepared for the encounter when the unprecedented
moment arrived, the people were afraid and trembled and stood
afar and said to Moses, "You speak to us and we will hear, but
let not God speak to us lest we die...and the people stood afar
off..." And the Lord said to Moses, "Thus you shall say to the
people of Israel, You have seen for yourselves that I have talked
with you from heaven" (Exodus 20:18-22). The prophetic encounter did take place.[52] Scripture takes pains to stress that the
whole people who gathered at the foot of Mt. Sinai were fully
aware that they were spoken to by God.

The tradition is not unanimous on exactly how much was
directly communicated to the people and how much was later
communicated to them through Moses. About that and about its
relationship to the covenant concept we shall have somewhat
more to say in the next section. Here we want merely to note the
effect that the presence among the people of the divine communication associated by them with the Sinaitic theophany had
upon their attitude to future communications that claimed to be
of divine origin. It became the litmus test of their authenticity.
No man's claim to have been spoken to by God could be ac-

52 See Footnote 6.

cepted as authentic, no matter how many great miracles he may perform, if the message he brought in the name of God called for a violation of the communication that had been granted to the whole people at Sinai, or for adding to, or subtracting from it (Deuteronomy 13:1-7).

The prophet never spoke in his own name; his words were invariably associated with the formula, "Thus saith the Lord" or by some variation of it. Only the first of the divine communications which the prophet was granted was intended for him personally. It consisted of a charge committing him to be *God's messenger* to Israel and to other peoples.[53] The message itself was almost invariably related in one form or another to the Sinaitic communication. The prophet either denounced the violations of the ethical and ritual laws and statutes that were enjoined in it, or he would warn of the dire consequences that would inevitably follow such violations, or when the foretold catastrophe struck, he sustained the spirit of the disconsolate by references to events that preceded and occurred at Sinai and to the divine promises recorded in the covenant which was there sealed between Israel and God.

Malachi was the last of the line of apostolic prophets whom the tradition acknowledges.[54] Henceforth anyone who prefaced his message by the words, "Thus saith the Lord," or by any other words that implied that he had been directly commissioned by God to bring His message to another individual or nation, or mankind, was not only suspect, he was rejected. Is one therefore to infer that since Malachi, God withdrew and no longer communicates with man? Not at all. But He no longer appoints prophets to bring His message to us. He communicates with us as individuals in one or more of an infinite number of ways and those of us who have 'ears' to hear receive His message and may in our own way even converse with Him. We may come out of such an experience with a firm conviction committing us to actions in-

---

53 Amos 7:14-15, Isaiah 6:8, Jeremiah Ch. 1.
54 Baba Bathra 12a.

volving great effort and sacrifice.[55] But a divine communication commits only the one who receives it and no one else. Even the authentic prophet was, according to the tradition, commissioned only to exhort the people to obey the communication which the whole people had received and to which they had all voluntarily been pledged, at Sinai. The Scribes, and the Rabbis carried on from where the prophets left off, but instead of merely exhorting their listeners to observe the Torah, the Rabbis took on the task of teaching the Torah, thus bringing their students into direct contact with the divine light that inheres in the Torah. That is perhaps why the Rabbis could make bold to say that the *Talmud chacham*, the student and teacher of the Torah, stands above or is to be preferred to the *navi*,[56] the prophet; for he who studies Torah is as if he were standing at Sinai and receiving it anew from God.

10. God as Lawgiver

The term, *law*, has two basic categories:
a) Natural Law,
b) Humanly-oriented Law.

A Natural Law is a statement whose substantive content describes the immutable relationship assumed to exist between phenomena which, to the best of our knowledge, are not endowed with a will of their own. A Humanly-oriented Law is a statement whose substantive content constitutes a directive for human action, violation of which is assumed to have unpleasant and even dire consequences and obedience to which will presumably bring happy consequences.

Regarding a natural law we ask two questions: 1) Who is its author? Who formulated the statement? 2) How did the regulari-

55 See "with firmness in the right as God gives us to see the right," A. Lincoln's *Second Inaugural Address.*
56 Baba Bathra 12a.

ties reflected in the law come into being? Thus, the statement that water when not interfered with by any external impediment or when not seeking its own level, or when not being propelled by an external force will always flow from a higher to a lower level, is a natural law. We know that, that statement was formulated by a human being who observed the phenomenon and recorded his observation. The second question we ask is, How did the relationship between water and an inclined plane originate? The first of these two questions we ask also in regard to a humanly-oriented law. Who formulated the statement that one shall not bear false witness, or that he shall rest on the Sabbath day. The second question we ask about humanly-oriented law is regarding the guarantor of the dire or happy consequences which violation of, or obedience to its directive may involve.

Man cannot suspend even for a brief moment the functioning of a natural law. The fact that he can build a dam which impedes the water's down-hill flow does not constitute a suspension of the law. Only water flowing uphill to a point higher than its original source would constitute a suspension of this natural law. Nor can he violate a natural law without at once experiencing the consequences. He can, however, act contrary to the directives of a humanly-oriented law. He can bear false witness, without at once experiencing any untoward consequences.

Biblical-Rabbinic literature is practically devoid of natural law, but it does not equivocate on the question of the origin of the regularities reflected in it. They are not self-created. They are not eternal. They are not sustained by any autonomous force that inheres within them. It is God who "established the ordinances of heaven and earth" (Jeremiah 33:25), and it is He who by His love sustains them and renews them daily. If He so desires He can suspend those regularities, and have the phenomena in question behave in a manner contrary to that indicated in the humanly formulated natural law.

It is "He alone who can do great wonders" (Psalm 119:4). The Biblical-Rabbinic tradition therefore provides for the possibility of miracles. He can create events whose occurrences requires a temporary suspension of the divinely established "ordinances of heaven and earth." The tradition does not limit its concept of 'miracle' to events of such nature. But for obvious reasons we shall not here pursue any further the role of 'miracle' in the tradition.

In regard to a natural law then, it is God who created the phenomena that man observes and on the basis of which he formulates the law. But the phenomena never became subject to the law. They are always subject to their Creator who is obviously not subject to a humanly formulated law.

The situation is radically different in regard to a humanly-oriented law. It is not a statement descriptive of observed regularities in the behavior of human beings. It is rather a directive related to a concept of what human behavior *ought* to be. There are two fundamental differences between the humanly-oriented law of the Biblical-Rabbinic tradition and that of the tradition associated with the ancient Mesopotamian civilization to which Israelite religion was related, but from which it radically departed. In Mesopotamian civilization, the *"ought"* of human behavior was autonomous. It was the creation of neither God nor of man. In addition, the individual laws whereby that *ought* was to be implemented were recognized as being humanly formulated...

"In Mesopotamia the law was conceived of as an embodiment of cosmic truths (Kinatum, sing. Kittum). Not the originator, but the divine custodian of justice was Shamash, the magistrate of gods and men, whose lot is justice and to whom truths have been granted for dispensation." The Mesopotamian king was called by the gods to establish justice in his realm; to enable him to do so Shamash inspired him with "truths." In theory, then, the final source of the law, the ideal with which the law had to conform was above the gods as well as man. "The Mesopotamian King...was not the source of the law but only its agent." However, the actual authorship of the laws, the embodying of the cosmic ideal in statutes of the realm, is claimed by the king. Hammurabi repeatedly refers to his laws as "my words which I have inscribed on my monument." They are his 'precious' or 'choice' words. "The judgment...that I have judged (and) the decisions...which I have decided."[57]

In the Biblical-Rabbinic tradition God is the author of both the *ought* and the specific directive whereby it is to be implemented. The central event that occurred at Sinai when God entered into a covenant with Israel was the communication to them of divinely ordained humanly-oriented law. Some of those laws were communicated orally directly to the people. Others were later communicated by God to Moses. All of them were then recorded in a book which was known as the *"Sefer Habrit"*, the Book of the Covenant. "And Moses wrote all the words of the Lord...then he took the book of the covenant and read it in the hearing of the people, and they said, "All that the Lord has spoken we will do and we will be obedient" (Exodus 24:4-7).

The tradition has identified the Five Books of Moses of the Hebrew Bible, as the Book of the Covenant, and has designated it as the Written Law to differentiate from the Oral Law. The Oral Law was for many centuries actually transmitted orally and its recording in writing strictly forbidden. In its earliest form in the legal *Tannaitic Midrashim* each law was attached to a specific passage of the written law. The Oral Law was not structurally severed from the Written Law until the second half of the second century, C.E., when Rabbi Judah, the Prince, edited what was immediately accepted as *The* Mishna. Whether the Mishna was written down by its editor or by others in his day or whether it continued for a while to be studied only orally is a question that need not concern us. It did however immediately become *the*

---

57 M. Greenberg, in Kaufman Jubilee Volume, p. 9. The article by E.A. Speiser referred to in the notes there and quotations of which are here included may now be found in E.A. Speiser, *Oriental and Biblical Studies*, pp. 313-323. In Note 7, on p. 9, Greenberg quotes the following from a communication he received from Professor J.J. Finkelstein: "What the god 'gives' the king is not 'laws' but the gift of the perception of *Kittum*, by virtue of which the king, in distinction from any other individual, becomes capable of promulgating laws that are in accord or harmony with the principle of *Kittum*. Greenberg here adds in the following note. "This Mesopotamian conception of cosmic truth is a noteworthy illustration of Professor Kaufman's thesis that paganism conceives of morality not as an expression of the supreme free will of the deity, but as one of the forces of the transcendent, primordial realm which governs the deity as well."

text studied in all the Rabbinic schools. The discussions that took place in the schools of Babylonia when edited at the end of the fifth century together with the Mishna became known as the Babylonian Talmud. Those that took place in the schools of the Holy Land and were edited about one hundred years earlier together with the Mishna became known as the Jerusalem Talmud.

Was God in any significant way related to the Oral Law? That there was a relationship was obvious from the fact that the Written Law served as the source of the Oral Law. Theoretically, nothing in the Oral Law could contradict or supersede or annul any provision of the Written Law. All it could do was to explicate the Written Law.[58] But there were those who conceived of God's relationship to the Oral Law in much more explicit terms. The Rabbinic tradition tended emphatically towards the belief that the Oral Law was also communicated to Moses at Sinai, that he transmitted it orally to Joshua, Joshua to the elders, etc.,[59] but that much of it had been forgotten. But that which had been forgotten is from time to time recovered by the insight of the learned as reflected in their explications of the Written Law, so that "all future explications of a *Talmud Vatik* of a recognized scholar are viewed as having originally been communicated by God to Moses."[60]

But the Rabbis were well aware that there existed among them significant differences of opinion regarding the legal implications of any specific Pentateuchal Verse. How was one to decide which was the right one? One of the most dramatic and imaginative passages in the Babylonian Talmud records the following incident. Rabbi Eliezer (end of the first and beginning of the second century C.E.) disagreed with his colleagues on a matter of comparatively little moment. It involved the laws of purity as they affected a stove built in a given fashion. Rabbi Eliezer presented

---

58 For the relationship of the Oral to the Written Law, see S. Greenberg, *Foundations,* Chapter 6.

59 *Avot,* 1:1.

60 Yerushalmi, *Peah,* Chapter 2 - Halacha 6; Shmot Rabbah 28:6; Tmurah 16a.

all his arguments, but his colleagues did not find them convincing. Where upon he said: "If I am right, then let this carob tree testify to it." We are told that the carob tree was uprooted and carried away some hundred yards. But his opponents were not convinced. They said: "One does not appeal to a carob tree in an argument."

"If I am right," said Rabbi Eliezer, "then let this stream of water testify to it." The stream reversed its course, but his opponents said, "The action of a stream of water is not a convincing argument." Rabbi Eliezer then called upon the walls of the house of study to testify. The walls were about to fall, when Rabbi Joshua rebuked them with the words, "What affair is it of yours if scholars dispute a matter of law?" We are told that out of respect for Rabbi Joshua the walls did not fall, but out of respect for Rabbi Eliezer they did not right themselves completely and remained in their inclined position.

Finally Rabbi Eliezer called upon a Voice from Heaven to testify in his behalf. The Voice responded that he was right. Whereupon Rabbi Joshua arose and quoted the Scriptural verse. " 'It (the Torah) is not in heaven' (Deuteronomy 30:12). We pay no heed to heavenly voices."

The Talmud then goes on to relate how some time thereafter Rabbi Nathan, when visited by the prophet Elijah, asked him, "What did the Lord do at the time when the Rabbis refused to accept the testimony of the heavenly voice?" Elijah answered, "The Lord smiled and said, 'My children have prevailed over me. My children have prevailed over me'."[61]

All Rabbinic laws derive their authority from the fact that they are presumed to be implied in the divinely communicated text of the Pentateuch and that the explication of a Pentateuchal text which represents a Rabbinic consensus, is as divinely inspired as is the text itself.

The Biblical-Rabbinic notion that God was the author of the moral law as well as of the ritual law presented a difficult prob-

---

61 Baba Metzia, 59b.

lem to both Jewish and non-Jewish theologians from whom the
Sinaitic theophany constitutes a central pillar of religious faith.
Why did God have to descend from heaven to command the
Israelites not to kill or steal or bear false witness? Could they not
have arrived at these precepts by applying their reasoning powers,
even as the Gentile philosophers had done? Within the limits of
this essay we can do no more than raise the question. We discussed it at some length elsewhere.[62]

God who is the author of the humanly-oriented laws of Judaism is also the guarantor that their observance will bring blessing
and their violation penalties. But neither blessing nor penalty
follow automatically. The laws of Judaism are not magical formulas which produce results independent of God's will. The
ultimate source of blessing and sorrow is the will of God and of
Him it was said that "He is gracious to whom He wills to be
gracious and shows mercy to him He wills to show mercy"
(Exodus 33:19).

Judaism has ever been wary of any notion bordering on the
magical. To maintain that observance of the law guarantees
divinely bestowed blessings - mundane, tangible blessings - and
its violation divinely ordained mundane, tangible punishment is
to attribute to them magical powers. For the essence of magic is
the assumption that man by his acts can, as it were, bypass or
constrain God and produce anticipated results. In Judaism God
cannot be bypassed or commandeered. He can only be thanked,
implored and revered.

11. God, the Holy One

The concept, Kadosh, 'holy', is ethically and religiously the
most inclusive of all the concepts related to God. The term,
Hakadosh baruch Hu (The Holy One, blessed be He) is probably
the most frequently used in Rabbinic literature to designate God.
When Isaiah beholds God in the Temple, he at the same time

---

62 S. Greenberg, *Ethics, Religion*, Section VII, p. 78-82.

hears the Seraphim proclaiming Him as "Holy, holy, holy is the Lord of hosts, the whole earth is full of His glory" (Isaiah 6:3). He is "the Holy One of Israel" (II Kings 19:22) and enjoins Israel to "Be Holy, because I, the Lord your God, am holy" (Leviticus 19:1).

The root meaning of *Kadosh,* holy, refers to that which was set apart from the rest of the community whether it be a place, an object, or a person. It belonged to the realm of tabu. Whoever approached the Holy without adequate and proper preparation was exposed to dire consequences which were usually inexorable and immediate, for there resided in the Holy an "intrinsic power to vindicate itself against encroachment."[63]

This conception of the holy is reflected in the account of the "fire that came forth from the presence of the Lord...and devoured the two sons of Aaron who had offered strange fire before the Lord, such as He has not commanded them" (Leviticus 10:1-2); and in the death of Uzzah whom "God smote because he put forth his hand to the ark" to keep it from falling when the oxen who were drawing the cart on which it stood, had stumbled (II Samuel 6:6-7), and in other similar passages.[64]

The conception of the holy which attributes to it an immediate and inexorable dire reaction to inappropriate 'encroachment' upon it is finally discernable in Abraham's plea in behalf of the people of Sodom and Gomorrah. We noted previously that Abraham does not plead for forgiveness or even for forbearance. He asks only that the innocent be not consumed together with the wicked. The implication seems to be that not only does the wickedness of the Sodomites merit their being consumed, but also that the punishment would be swift and inexorable. There was no alternative, and no escaping it. The same is true of Isaiah's spontaneous outcry when he realizes that he was in the presence of the Lord. "Woe is me! For I am lost; for I am a man of un-

---

63 R. Smith, *op. cit.,* p. 162. On the relationship between holiness and tabu, see *ibid.,* p. 450.

64 Eichrodt, *op. cit.,* pp. 272-273.

clean lips, and I dwell in the midst of a people of unclean lips, for my eyes have seen the King, the Lord of hosts." He is saved by the quick action of one of the Seraphim who touched his lips with a burning coal taken from the altar and said, "Behold, this has touched your lips; your guilt is taken away, and your sin forgiven" (Isaiah 6:5-6).

But these faint shadows of the root idea that underlies the concept of the holy which are discernable in some Biblical narratives are heavily overlaid by revolutionary connotations which came to be associated in Judaism with the concept of the holy. In the case of Sodom, the "encroachment" upon God against which He was about to vindicate Himself, did not consist in the failure of the inhabitants to offer proper and adequate sacrifices. God was not roused because He was not properly worshipped. Scripture is very specific regarding what it was about Sodom's people that God could not tolerate. Though "the Jordan valley (in which Sodom was located) was well watered everywhere like the garden of the Lord..., the men of Sodom were wicked, great sinners against the Lord" (Genesis 13:10,13). They were sexual perverts, inhospitable to strangers (*Ibid.* 19:5) and, in accordance with Rabbinic legend, cruel and unjust to the defenseless in their own midst. Thus also Isaiah fears that he is "lost," not because of any ritual oversight on his part nor because of any act of violence which he may have committed, but because he is of unclean lips.

Though Isaiah does not specify what he had in mind when he spoke of unclean lips, we can with considerable confidence surmise. Hosea, his contemporary, speaks of "the Lord's controversy with the inhabitants of the land" because there is "swearing and lying, killing, stealing and committing adultery" (Hosea 4:1-2). Micah, another contemporary, complains that "the godly man has perished from the earth, and there is none upright among men. ...Put no trust in a neighbor, have no confidence in a friend, guard the doors of your mouth from her who lies in your bosom; for son treats the father with contempt, the daughter rises up against her mother...a man's enemies are the men of his own home" (Micah 7:2, 5-6). The psalmist repeatedly refers to those who "utter lies to their neighbors..., speak with flattering lips and a double heart," and warns that "the Lord will cut off all flattering lips, and the tongue that makes great boast" (Psalm 12:2-3).

That injustice, sexual perversity, inhospitality to strangers and unclean lips should be viewed as encroachments upon the holy, that was another one of Judaism's "original intuitions" whose implications were explicated by the prophets and the Rabbis, and which eventually revolutionized the course of man's religious development. The One Omnipotent God who was the Holy One, and whose glory filled the whole earth thus became the God with whom evil, whether in the form of man's inhumanity to man, or in the form of perversion of the divine image bestowed upon him, "cannot abide" (Psalm 5:5). The concepts of divine forbearance and forgiveness, which we previously discussed, eliminated from the concept of the holy the connotations of immediate, inexorable, automatic and hence, 'thoughtless' reaction on the part of the Holy to that which encroached upon it. Thus, "the element of moral perfection was incorporated into the concept of holiness" and "the whole system of tabu is pressed into the service of a loftier idea of God."[65] The concept which, in early Semitic civilization, was completely devoid of any moral or spiritual connotations was thus transformed into a concept more richly endowed with moral and spiritual connotations than any other known to man.

Those connotations are more fully and specifically spelled out in the Holiness Code (Leviticus 17-26), which enjoins upon Israel to be holy, because "I the Lord your God am Holy." The original root idea of the concept does not completely disappear. God's Sabbaths are to be kept, idols are not to be worshipped or made (*Ibid.* 19:34). Sacrifices are still to be offered. God is still to be worshipped in an acceptable manner (*Ibid.* 19:5-8). He cannot be approached without proper mental and physical preparation and one's behavior must reflect an awareness that he stands in God's presence. But preceding and following these

---

65 *Ibid.*, pp. 277, 274.

injunctions are the commandments to revere one's father and mother (*Ibid.* 3); not to reap the field to its very border, nor gather the gleanings...nor strip the vineyard bare but to leave these for the poor and the sojourner (*Ibid.* 9-10); not to curse the deaf or put a stumbling before the blind (*Ibid.* 14); to judge in righteousness (*Ibid.* 15); nor to hate your brother in your heart (*Ibid.* 17). The holiness code reaches its climax in the commandments of "love your neighbor as yourself" (*Ibid.* 18) and to love "the stranger who sojourns with you as yourself" (*Ibid.* 34). The only reason given for the observance of these commandments is the statement "I am the Lord," which is repeated fifteen times in the thirty-seven verses of the chapter.

Man has a two-fold relationship to the holiness of God. On the one hand he must be ever aware that he is always in God's presence (Psalm 16:8), for God's glory fills the whole earth, and He cannot abide evil. Man must, therefore, act accordingly either out of fear or out of reverence and love. He dare not mistake God's forbearance either for forgiveness or as indicative of God's indifference. "The heart of the sons of man is set to do evil" either "because sentence against an evil deed is not executed speedily" (Ecclesiastes 8:11) or because he "says in his heart 'God has forgotten. He has hidden His face, He will never see it...(He) will not call to account' " (Psalm 9:11-13).

On the other hand, man should ever be mindful of the fact that the reason why he can be commanded to observe these laws is because he was endowed with the capacity to do so. He was not made in the physical image of his Creator, for Judaism has no physical image of God. Man was made in the spiritual image of God, which makes it possible for him to stand in the presence of the holy without being consumed because he has the capacity to achieve a measure of holiness himself. But this capacity is tenuous and fragile. It can all too easily be submerged, suppressed or dissipated. It is nurtured and fortified by the observance of the divinely ordained Sabbaths, festivals and home and personal rituals. Hence, before performing a ritual act, Judaism asks its adherents to recite a benediction in which God is thanked for giving us these commandments whereby we are 'sanctified.'

The holiness thus nurtured by the ritual commandments could then all the more readily be embodied in deeds of love, of justice, of truth and of charity.

12. God Is Eternally Other

Gershom Scholem divides the historical development of religion into three stages. In the first stage the world was "full of gods whom man encounters at every step and whose presence can be experienced without recourse to ecstatic meditation." This coincides with "man's mythical age...when the universe was truly monistic," the age of "the immediate consciousness of the interrelation and interdependence of things, of their essential unity." In the second stage, "Religion's supreme function is to destroy the dream-harmony of Man, Universe and God...and the creation of a vast abyss conceived as absolute, between God, the infinite and transcendental Being, and Man, the finite creature." Mysticism arises after "the abyss between Man and God has become a part of the inner consciousness... It does not deny or overlook the abyss...but proceeds to a quest for the secret that will close it in, the hidden path that will span it."[66]

For most non-Jewish mystics, the 'spanning' of the abyss means recapturing, if for only a fleeting moment, the sense of the essential unity of things, of obliterating from consciousness the distinction between the self, the universe and God and of experiencing the 'truly monistic universe of Man's mythical age.'

Biblical-Rabbinic Judaism has no room either for the monism of man's mythical age nor for any ancient or modern philosophic version of it. Just as the universe is forever different from its Creator and its Creator can never be identified with it, so God is eternally other than man, and man can never in any ontological sense be one with God. But nothing is more characteristic of the founders and adherents of Biblical-Rabbinic Judaism than the

[66] G. Scholem, *Major Trends*, pp. 7-8.

awareness of being ever in the presence of God. For primitive man the world is full of gods. For Biblical-Rabbinic man God's glory, His presence, "fills the world."

> Whither shall I go from Thy spirit?
> Or whither shall I flee from Thy presence?
> If I ascend up into heaven, Thou art there;
> If I make my bed in the netherworld,
>   behold, Thou art there.
> If I take the wings of the morning,
> And dwell in the uttermost parts
>   of the sea;
> Even there would Thy hand lead me,
> And Thy right hand would hold me.
> And if I say: 'Surely the darkness
>   shall envelop me,
> And the light about me shall be night';
> Even the darkness is not too dark for Thee,
> But the night shineth as the day;
> The darkness is even as the light.
>   (Psalm 139:7-12)

We noted previously that in the Biblical-Rabbinic Tradition men are aware of being spoken to by God. Isaiah does not hesitate to say that he *saw* God sitting on His throne (Isaiah 6:1). Ezekiel describes in considerable detail the vision of the 'divine chariot' above which he saw "the likeness of a throne...above which was seated "a likeness as it were of a human being." After describing the "likeness of the human being" he concludes "Such was the appearance of the likeness of the glory of the Lord" (Ezekiel, Chapt. 1). The psalmist declares being "near to God" to be his 'good' or his 'bliss'[67] (Psalm 73:27). But nowhere in Biblical-Rabbinic literature is there a report of any one experi-

---

67 Thus translated by James Moffatt.

encing the kind of *unio mystica,* of a mystical *union* with God accompanied by a loss of consciousness of self and ineffable ecstasy and illumination which are reported by non-Jewish mystics. As far as our records go, the most that Jewish mystics of the Talmudic period sought to achieve was to behold "His majesty, and the aura of sublimity and solemnity which surrounds Him... the mystic who, in his ecstasy has passed through all the gates, braved all the dangers, now stands before the throne; he sees and hears--but that is all... Ecstasy there was...but we find no trace of a nuptial union between the soul and God. Throughout there remained an almost exaggerated consciousness of God's *otherness,* nor does the identity and individuality of the mystic become blurred even at the height of ecstatic passion."[68]

But no matter what the ultimate goal of the mystic was, the path leading to the achievement of the goal was always strewn with well-nigh insurmountable impediments. Only the rare chosen could muster the spiritual and physical resources required to traverse it. It demanded indefinitely long periods of fasting, prayer, self-flagellation, renunciation of all physical pleasure and ecstatic meditation. The term, mystic, thus came to designate an individual engaged in abnormal activities and the mystic experience itself, an abnormal experience not necessarily in a pejorative sense, as being aberrant or unnatural, but rather as being extraordinarily exceptional or unusual. If Rufus Jones is correct in designating such a mystic experience as "religion in its most acute, intense and living stage,"[69] achievable only via abnormal preparatory exercises, then by definition we deny the average person the hope for ever experiencing the 'living stage' of religion.

The Biblical-Rabbinic tradition does not identify the "most acute, intense and living stage of religion" with this kind of abnormal experience. On the contrary, it is very wary of it, and while it does not condemn the quest of Jewish mystics of the

---

68 Scholem, *op. cit.,* pp. 54-55.
69 Quoted by Scholem, p. 4.

Hellenistic-Rabbinic period to "pass through all the gates in order to stand before .the throne," it does not encourage anyone to undertake the quest. It rather warns in most solemn pronouncements of the dangers such a quest involves, and sets stringent limitations upon the manner in which such a quest may be undertaken.[70]

Judaism wants its followers to feel that they are ever in the presence of God and to act accordingly. To achieve that sense of God's all encompassing presence one need not engage in any abnormal activities. The psalmist whom we have quoted refers to no special exercises that enable him to experience God's presence as an "acute, intense and living" experience. Anyone who recites that psalm with a normal degree of spiritual and intellectual concentration can identify with its sentiments. We shall be forever indebted to Dr. Max Kadushin for creating the concept whereby to identify this experience. He designated it as *normal mysticism,* explicated its connotations and identified the manner of its concretization in the observance of the commandments, in prayer and in the study of Torah.[71]

At the risk of inviting obvious misunderstanding, and of raising more questions than we can hope to answer, we shall suggest that the Torah and its ritual and ethical commandments are the bridge which the Biblical-Rabbinic tradition has built across the abyss between God and man. That bridge is accessible to all. Man never crosses over to God's side of the bridge nor does God ever pass over to man's side. At any one of the infinite points along that bridge man and God may meet. In that meeting He is glorified. His creation of the universe is vindicated, and Man is privileged to experience the "acute, intense and living stage" of his religious faith.

70 Mishna-Hagiga, Chapter 2, par. 1.

71 See Kadushin, *The Rabbinic Mind,* and *Worship and Ethics,* index under "Normal Mysticism."

A SELECT BIBLIOGRAPHY

Barzun, Jacques, *Darwin, Marx, Wagner*. Boston: Little, Brown & Co., 1941.

Eichrodt, Walter, *Theology of the Old Testament*. Vol. 1, trans. by J.A. Baker. Philadelphia: The Westminster Press, 1961.

Frazer, Sir James, *The Golden Bough*. Abridged edition. New York: The MacMillan Co., 1923.

Ginzberg, Louis, *Legends of the Jews*. Philadelphia: Jewish Publication Society, 1913.

Greenberg, Moshe, *Some Postulates of Biblical Criminal Law*, in Yehezkel Kaufman Jubilee Volume, edited by Menahem Haran. Jerusalem: The Magnes Press, Hebrew University, 1960.

Greenberg, Simon, *Ethics, Religion and Judaism*, Sections I-IV, in "Conservative Judaism," Volume 26, No. 4, Sections VII-XI, in "Conservative Judaism," Volume 27, No. 1, pp. 75-129. New York: Burning Bush Press, 1972.

———, *Foundations of a Faith*. New York: Burning Bush Press, 1967.

Hertz, J.H., *The Authorized Daily Prayer Book*. London: National Council for Jewish Religious Education, 1943.

———, *The Penteteuch and Haftorahs*, London: Oxford University Press, 1930.

Heschel, Abraham J., *God in Search of Man*. Philadelphia: The Jewish Publication Society, 1956.

———, *The Prophets*. New York: Burning Bush Press, 1962.

Joad, C.E.M., *God and Evil*. New York: Harper and Brothers, 1943.

Kadushin, Max, *The Rabbinic Mind*. 2nd ed. New York: Blaisdell Publishing Co., 1965.

Kaufman, Yehezkel and Greenberg, Moshe, *The Religion of Israel*. Chicago: The University of Chicago Press, 1960.

Kohler, K., *Jewish Theology*. New York: The MacMillan Co., 1918.

Mahzor - for Rosh Hashanah and Yom Kippur. New York: The Rabbinical Assembly, 1972.

Maimonides, Moses, *Guide to the Perplexed*. Translated with an Introduction and Notes by Shlomo Pines. Chicago: The University of Chicago Press, 1963.

Moffatt, James, *The Holy Bible*. New York: Harper Brothers, 1922.

Moore, G.F., *History of Religions*. New York: Charles Scribner's Sons, 1925.

———, *Judaism-In the First Centuries of the Christian Era-The Age of the Tannaim*. Cambridge, Massachusetts: Harvard University Press, 1927.

Schechter, Solomon, *Some Aspects of Rabbinic Theology*. New York: The Macmillan Co., 1910.

Scholem, Gershom, *Major Trends in Jewish Mysticism.* Jerusalem: Schocken
        Publishing House, 1941.
Smith, Robertson, *The Religion of the Semites.* London: Adam and Charles
        Black, 1914.
Speiser, A.E., *Oriental and Biblical Studies.* Collected writings edited by J.J.
        Finkelstein and Moshe Greenberg. Philadelphia: University of
        Pennyslvania, 1967.
Thucydides, *The Complete Works.* New York: The Modern Library, 1934.
Von Rad, Gerhard, *Old Testament Theology.* Translated by M.G. Stalker. 2
        vols. New York: Harper and Row, 1965.

CHAPTER XII

GOD IN THE WITNESS OF ISRAEL'S ELECTION
Carroll Stuhlmueller, C.P. *

The Old Testament witnesses the response of Israel to God's presence in her midst. The task of Old Testament theology, then, is not to penetrate the mystery of God *in se* but to explain that mystery as operative *in Israel*. Biblical study, moreover, does not endeavor to abstract God's ideals for Israel in their purity and grandeur, but to determine realistically how this ideal was

*Professor of the Old Testament at The Catholic Theological Union, Chicago, Illinois, U.S.A.

ABBREVIATIONS

ATANT	*Abhandlungen zür Theologie des Alten und Neuen Testaments.* Zürich.
BZAW	*Beihefte zür Zeitschrift für die Alttestamentlich Wissenschaft.* Berlin.
CBQ	*Catholic Biblical Quarterly.* Washington.
EvT	*Evangelische Theologie,* N.S. München.
HTR	*Harvard Theological Review.* Cambridge, Mass.
KAT	*Kommentar zum Alten Testament.* Gütersloh.
KHCAT	*Kurzer Hand-Commentar zum Alten Testament.* Tübingen.
NRT	*Nouvelle Revue Théologique* (Louvain)
OTS	*Oudtestamentische Studien.* Leiden.
RB	*Revue Biblique.* Paris.
SBT	*Studies in Biblical Theology.* Chicago. Naperville, Ill.
SchwTUm	*Schweizer Theologische Umschau.* Bern.
TB	*Theologische Bücherei.* München.
TZBas	*Theologische Zeitschrift.* Basel.
ZAW	*Zeitschrift für die Alttestamentliche Wissenschaft.* Berlin.
ZBK	*Zürcher Bibelkommentare.* Zürich.

expressed in the words of her leaders and in the morality of her daily life.[1]

This article investigates one aspect of Israel's response to God—her sense of special election or choice.[2] Election, according to G. Ernest Wright, "is the chief clue for the understanding of the meaning and significance of Israel."[3] Through election we ought to be able to appreciate the special significance of God for Israel. Election manifests God's love as free, unmerited and personal.

"Election-faith," wrote Paul Volz, "is as old as Israel."[4] While the *fact* of being Yahweh's specially chosen people goes back to the very beginning, the *realization* of what this fact meant for herself and revealed about God developed slowly within Israel. Only as Israel came into contact with more and more peoples and was forced to ponder the meaning of her own existence in relation to these people did she understand her role as Yahweh's specially chosen nation.[5]

---

1   The extent to which Old Testament theology can be abstracted from the sequence of Israel's evolving history has been debated by W. Eichrodt, "The Problem of Old Testament Theology," *Theology of the Old Testament* (Philadelphia: 1961), Vol. 1, pp. 512-520, whose charge was answered by G. von Rad, "Postscript," *Old Testament Theology* (New York: 1965), Vol. II, pp. 410-429.

2   A select bibliography on the question of election-faith includes: P. Altmann, *Erwählungstheologie und Universalismus im Alten Testament (BZAW,* 92; Berlin: 1964); F.M.T. De Liagre Böhl, "Missions und Erwähltheitsgedanke in Alt-Israel," *Festschrift, A. Bertholet* (Tübing: 1950), pp. 77-96; K. Galling, *Die Erwählungstraditionen Israels (BZAW,* 48; Giessen: 1928); F. Holmgren, *The Concept of Yahweh as Go'el in Second Isaiah* (Ann Arbor, Mich.: University Microfilms, 1963), ch 5, pp. 115-120; K. Koch, "Zur Geschichte der Erwählungsvorstellung in Israel," *ZAW* 67 (1955), pp. 205-266; R. Martin-Achard, "La Signification theologique de l'election d'Israel," *TZBas* 16 (1960), pp. 333-341; *ibid., Israel et les nations: La perspective missionaire de l'Ancien Testament* (Paris, 1959); G.E. Mendenhall, "Election," *Interpreter's Dictionary of the Bible* (Nashville, 1962), Vol. II, pp. 76-82; G. Quell, "Eklegomai," *Theological Dictionary of the New Testament* (Grand Rapids, Mich., 1967), Vol. IV, pp. 144-192; G. von Rad, *Das Gottesvolk im Deuteronomium* (Stuttgart, 1929); *ibid., Studies in Deuteronomy (SBT,* 9 London, 1953); H.H. Rowley, *The Biblical Doctrine of Election* (London, 1950); Th. C. Vriezen, *Die Erwählung Israels nach dem Alten Testament (ATANT,* 24; Zürich, 1953); H. Wildberger, *Jahwes Eigentumsvolk (ATANT,* 37; Zürich, 1960); *ibid.,* "Die Neuinterpretation des Erwahlungsglaubens Israels in der Krise der Exilszeit," *Wort-Gebot-Glaube (ATANT,* 59; Zürich, 1970), pp. 307-324.

3   G. Ernest Wright, *The Old Testament Against Its Environment (SBT,* 2; London, 1950), p. 47.

4   P. Volz, *Jesaja II Übersetz und erklärt (KAT;* Leipzig, 1932), p. 17.

5   G. von Rad, *op. cit.,* (in fn 1), Vol. 1, pp. 69-70.

Election, we can see, raises the problem of the "non-elect."[6] The choice of Israel eventually precipitated the serious question— what about the non-elect gentiles? Here we come up against the agonizing mystery, still with us today, the salvation of those outside the pale of God's chosen people.[7]

These problems about the nations as well as the glorious conviction of being Yahweh's chosen people reached a peak of development in Deutero-Isaiah, the brilliant poet-theologian within the Babylonian exile (587-539 B.C.), who composed the poems on chapters forty to fifty-five in the book of Isaiah.[8] Within the writings of this "Great Unknown" there occurred, perhaps for the first time in any conspicuous way, the transition from Israel's election to universal salvation. The latter doctrine comes to the fore in the Songs of the Suffering Servant.[9]

Universalism of salvation—a mirroring of God's unity within his love and redemptive designs—lies beyond the scope of this piece of research. Here we confine ourselves to Israel's election, a foil to God's free, personal love. At the close of this article, we will simply indicate some reasons for this extraordinary leap in Deutero-Isaiah's thinking from Israel's election to universal salvation.

This investigation will center particularly upon the meaning and the use of the Hebrew word *bāḥar* "to choose." As we will see,

---

6   Cf., Samuel Sandmel, *The Several Israels* (New York, 1971).

7   Vatican II, "Dogmatic Constitution on the Church," n. 14, *The Documents of Vatican II,* ed. by Walter M. Abbott (New York, 1966), p. 32 ff.

8   Cf., R.F. Melugin, Jr., *The Strucrue of Deutero-Isaiah* (Yale University Ph.D., 1968; Ann Arbor, Mich.: University Microfilms) has established, at least for this writer, that the poems in Is. 40-55 are "a collection of originally separate units which can be isolated by form . . . [and] which only occasionally display continuity in message with the surrounding context." There is a logical unity, in that the poems are grouped together according to three large themes (the Jacob-Israel block in 40:12-48:21, the Zion-Jerusalem section in 49:14-52:12, and the covenant theme in ch 54-55), but there is "not a continuous progression in message." (p. i—abstract).

9   Cf., P.E. Dion, "L'universalisme religieux dans les différentes couches redactionnelles d'Isaie 40-55," *Biblica* 51 (1970), pp. 161-182.

bāḥar, as well as its Greek equivalent *eklegesthai* (or *eklektos*),[10] became a technical term for "election-faith." But the idea, or shall we say, the divine mystery, communicated by the term *bāḥar,* transcends any human word. Although *bāḥar* is practically without synonym in the Hebrew Bible,[11] nonetheless, many similar expressions occur, especially in the earlier traditions of the Bible and once again in the brilliant richness of Deutero-Isaiah. These phrases will also receive some attention. But first we clear the way for deeper probing by attending to some surface details about the word *bāḥar.*

I. Statistics on bāḥar

Details on the occurrence of *bāḥar* are supplied by G. Quell:

The verb *bḥr* "to elect" occurs 164 times in the Heb. Bible, predominantly as qal, only 7 times as niph'al and once (Qoh. 9:4 in doubtful ketib) as pu'al. Its theological significance may be seen from the fact that in 92 instances the subject is God, and in 13 instances of the pass. *bāḥir* the election is by God. When used of God's electing the verb is always act . . . Among the instances in which *bḥr* denotes a human decision a particular place is occupied in which the object of choice is God, His Law, or similar normative definitions of the divine will. These are few in number . . . [12]

Quell proceeds to group the uses of *bāḥar* in three types: (1)

---

10 *Eklegesthai* (middle) translates *bḥr* 108 x; *eklektos,* 44 x. If in 6 out of 146 uses of *eklegein-eklegesthai* in LXX, it translates a different Hebrew word than *bḥr,* a stylistic (Joel 2:16) or a doctrinal reason (Deut 1:33) is involved.

11 *Cf.,* Quell, *op. cit.,* p. 149; Mendenhall, *op. cit.,* p. 76. Mendenhall also remarks: "In the NT similarly, the verb *eklegomai,* 'choose,' and derived forms *eklektos,* 'chosen,' and *ekloge,* 'election,' are without true synonyms. . . . In both languages [Hebrew and Greek] the terminology of 'choice' with 'God' as subject has become technical usage with a specific meaning not communicated by any other word." Quell, *op. cit.,* p. 150, speaks of "ein schon fest umrissener dogmatischer Terminus."

12 Quell, *op. cit.,* p. 146.

without any specifically theological meaning: i.e., the sensuous
way in which men chose wives for themselves in Gen. 6:2; (2) in
the sacral area, God and his norms are chosen by men; (3) God
makes the choice. The third function of *bāḥar* with God as
subject, occurs the grand total of 92 to 105 times, out of 164
appearances of the word. Not only, therefore, is God or Yahweh
the subject in the larger number of instances, but the verb is found
almost always in the active gal form, thereby stressing the divine
initiative.

We add a few more pertinent facts, relative to the books where
the verb *bāḥar* occurs. *Bāḥar*, for the most part, is concentrated in
books of Deuteronomic influence: 31 x in Deut itself;[13] 37 x in
Josh-Jdg-Sam-Kgs;[14] 19 x in the Book of Isaiah, including 8 x in
the Book of Consolation; 13 x in Psalms;[15] and 21 x in 1-2 Chron.

II. The Significance of Israel's Election

In Israel the general idea of "election" included two essential
components: separation from other nations because of the
particular love of Yahweh for Israel; and secondly, readiness for
Yahweh's special task or commission.[16] Not till the time of
Deutero-Isaiah, will we see that both of these elements come

---

13 Except in Deut 23:17, the Subject is always Yahweh or Elohim.

14 18 x, the subject is Yahweh or Elohim; always so in 1-2 Kgs.

15 A penetrating study of *bahar* in the psalms is given by K. Koch; his article, in
many ways, is a response to Vriezen. K. places the election tradition before Deut by
tracing Pss 33; 47; 65; 78; 105; 135–either in themselves or in their earlier stages–to a
pre-Deuteronomic composition. He then concludes, too quickly perhaps, that Deutero-
Isaiah depended upon the psalms, rather than upon Deut, for his own election-theology.

16 Vriezen, *Die Erwählung*, p. 41, writes: "Der Kern des Wortes Erwählen im
Allgemeinen hat die Bedeutung: etwas bestimmen, über etwas verfügen. . . . In der
religiösen Sprache liegt der Nachdruck auf der Liebe oder noch besser auf der Gnade als
Motiv der Erwählung–der Mensch, in diesem Fall das Volk Israel, hat im A.T. Gott
gegenüber keinen eigenen Wert, un dessentwillen Gott es erwählt hätte. Eine zweite
Nebenbedeutung, die dem Wort inhärent ist, ist die *des Beauftragens.* Erwählen heisst
einen bestellen, bestimmen zu einer Aufgabe; der Erwählte wird erwählt zu einem
bestimmten Zweck." On pg 48 Vriezen stresses the idea of *separation* from others in the
understanding of election. On p. 53 he thus explains the notion of election in *bāḥar:*
"Dies alles ist der Inhalt des Wortes *bachar:* Israel ist von Gott herausgenommen aus den
Volkern und hat einen Auftrag in der Welt; nur mit Jahwe als Auftraggeber hat er zu tun;
er ist von Gott dazu berufen, seinen Namen zu verherrlichen."

consciously and fully to the surface. Election-theology took a long time to develop and emerge, and one of the major factors in this evolution is to be located in the Deuteronomist tradition.[16a]

1. In Deuteronomy

Deuteronomy is clearly a crisis-book, urgently demanding a decision "this day" (Deut 5:1-5), to turn away from apostasy and to cultivate from this moment onward, "one God" (Deut 6:4; 13:7), "one sanctuary" (Deut 12), and "one law" (Deut 4; 17:18-20; 31:9-13). Thus will a people who have been destroying one another and their entire nation by centuries of apostasy[17] be reunited among themselves and with Yahweh. One final chance, to salvage what was left and hopefully to regain what was lost, is granted Israel. The people are back again at Horeb, without law or sanctuary and even without Yahweh, their God. But what God did once at Horeb, he is ready to do now. One would conclude, from looking at the people, that the situation was hopeless; but by directing one's eyes to Yahweh, one knows that his goodness will accomplish now what it did formerly in the desert.

Israel, therefore, does not so much choose Yahweh, as it is Yahweh who chooses Israel. Israel's response is the immediate and spontaneous one of faith. Interiorly, she knows, by a mystic awareness, the reality of Yahweh's loving choice (11:1-2).[18] Deuteronomy is the fruit of long and vigorous thought over a choice by which Israel felt herself set apart by Yahweh from all other nations. Deuteronomy is the *first* instance in biblical tradition of *frequent* references to Israel's worldwide relationships.

16a It is difficult to determine exactly the historical age of various portions in the Deuteronomic corpus. We treat the entire tradition at once, because of its homogeneous development. We admit the great moments of crystallization in the reform of Josiah and during the exile.

17 Cf., G. von Rad, *Studies in Deuteronomy*, p. 70.

18 Cf., Quell, *op. cit.*, p. 163, "The strength, theological value, and didactic fruitfulness of the concept derive from the unique blending of rational and demonstrable thought with the supra-rational certainty of faith, from the taking up of concrete history into the sphere of experience of God. It is hereby shown to be of universal and not just national and restricted validity."

Yahweh "has made" all other nations (26:19), and "created mankind upon the earth" (4:32), and therefore "the Lord is God in the heavens above and on earth below, and there is no other [god]" (4:39).[19] Deuteronomy has come to grips with crucial problems: the role of Israel in relation to all other nations; the relation of the nations to Yahweh. The answers are inadequate, but they are sufficient to warrant our speaking of an "election theology" in Deuteronomy.

The key text on election-theology in Deuteronomy is 7:6-9,[20] where we meet a modulation between the 2nd person singular and 2nd person plural. The latter, referring to Israel in the plural, is usually considered to be a later, more homiletic addition by the Deuteronomic redactor of Josh-Judg-Sam-Kgs.[21] The plural sections reflect, therefore, the continuing contemplation of the election theme by Israel's leaders.

6. (in 2 sg) For you are a people sacred to the Lord, your God; he has chosen you from all the nations on the face of the earth to be a people peculiarly his own.

7. (in 2 pl) It was not because you are the largest of all nations that the Lord set his heart on you and chose you, for you are really the smallest of all nations.

8. (8a, in 2 pl) It was because the Lord loved you and because of his fidelity to the oath he had sworn to your fathers, that he brought you out with his strong hand from the place of slavery (8b, in 2 sg) and ransomed you from the hand of Pharaoh, king of Egypt.

9. (in 2 sg) Understand, then, that the Lord, your God, is God,

---

19 Cf., G. von Rad, *Das Gottesvolk im Deuteronomium,* p. 23.

20 H. Wilberger, *Jahwes Eigentumsvolk,* p. 8, claims that the fundamental text is Ex 19:3b-8, which is not Deuteronomic, according to him, but "mit einen alten, festgeformten Überlieferungsstoff zu tun haben." It is "jünger als J and E" and is associated with "ein Fest der Erwählung Israels," which W. identifies with "Mazzenfest" (p. 12). On pp. 46-50 he summarizes his reasons.

21 Cf., E.W. Nicholson, *Deuteronomy and Tradition* (Philadelphia, 1967), pp. 26-32, relying on G. Minette de Tillesse, "Sections 'tu' et sections 'vous' dans le Deuteronome," *VT* 12 (1962), pp. 28-87.

indeed, the faithful God who keeps his merciful covenant down to the thousandth generation towards those who love him and keep his commandments.

Deut 7:6-9 ought to be studied in close connection with other election texts like: 4:37; 10:15; 14:1-2; 26:18-19. From these passages, we draw the following conclusions:[22]

(a) Deuteronomy makes it clear enough that Israel is Yahweh's special property, chosen from all other nations as his own people. "Legitimacy" or blood descent from the patriarchs seems to be demanded, for that is how Deuteronomy apparently distinguishes Israel from the other nations. "Legitimacy"[23] is certainly required, and Deuteronomy adamantly condemned all mixed marriages. But were the Deuteronomic preachers so naive, we might ask, as to accept unhesitatingly the theory of a pure blood stream within Israel?[24] Very much closer to the times than ourselves, the Deuteronomists must have realized what a mixture was Israel, particularly in her early historical origins (cf., Ez 16:3; Josh 24:2). God's love and human faith, not carnal descent, formed the family-bond of Israel; faith distinguished the true from the false Israelite, or, we might say, faith separated the Israelite from the non-Israliete. Yahweh's love, therefore, possessed a certain "creative" power to form the true worshipper and the genuine Israelite. This love, nonetheless, also possessed a destructive force—during the exile and the previous age of Josiah—because Deut. 7 announces the holy war of *ḥerem* destruction against the non-elect gentile nations.

(b) Deuteronomy immediately associates laws and commandments with divine election. Laws, however, are a consequence, not

---

22 Cf., Vriezen, *op. cit.,* p. 61.

23 Cf., Mendenhall, *op. cit.,* p. 80, "The evidence is thus rather impressive for concluding that Yahweh's choice is clearly bound up with legitimacy." Wilberger, "Die Neuinterpretation des Erwahlungsglaubens Israels," 318, differs with this position, and sees the major question with Israel's acceptance of Yahweh as the öne and only God.

24 Cf., R. de Vaux, "Israel," *Supplement au Dictionnaire de la Bible* (Paris, 1949), IV, pp. 733-735.

the cause of election.[25] Laws externalized in a fitting way the presence of Yahweh within Israel. Yahweh bestowed life upon Israel, and this life expressed itself in a well-ordered, peaceful, kindly way of action. The "law" of life would also be prosperous and fruitful. Deuteronomy accredits the fertility of man, his live stock and his land, not to Israel's action and obedience, but to Yahweh's power and goodness.[26] The ancient creed in Deut. 26 attributes the first fruits of the soil to Yahweh's ever continuous renewal of his redemptive acts in Israel's midst. Obedience to laws expressed the way in which Yahweh's life and power moved through Israel.

Some later additions to Deut, particularly to the curses in ch. 28-29, tended to direct attention away from God's election and to emphasize Israel's activity. We can establish, however, that the main thrust of Deut's thought lay in an opposite direction, not only from the sequence of election-life-law-obedience, discussed in the preceding paragraph, but also from two other facts: (1) Deut remains within the prophetic tradition which combatted all superstitious trust that man can be perfected from external observance of the law; (2) Deut envisages Israel again in the desert, being covenanted with Yahweh, and *in view of this covenant or election* newly receiving the law. In all cases election precedes obedience and requires only faith.[27]

(c) Yahweh's love, as stated above in # a, not only "elected" and thereby brought Israel into existence, but it also formed a happy, prosperous Israel. Deut extends the results of Yahweh's election to "everything that furthers life . . . even to the kneading-trough of the individual household" (*cf.*, Deut 28:8-14).[28]

---

25 Cf., Dieter Baltzer, *Ezechiel und Deuterojesaja (BZAW,* 121; Berlin, 1971), pp. 73-82, especially the treatment of Ez 11:20 & 36:27 wherein creation of a new heart and a new spirit within Israel precedes Israel's keeping of the commandments and is a *conditio sine qua non* for the latter.

26 Cf., G. von Rad, *Studies in Deuteronomy*, p. 72.

27 Cf., G. von Rad, *Old Testament Theology*, I, pp. 228-231.

28 *Ibid.*, p. 229. When the blessings and curses are read against the larger theological patterns of Deut, then Israel's obedience is a condition for fertility and prosperity, but not the cause of them. They are due to Yahweh's living presence among his people. This "conditional" note extends throughout Deut: *i.e.*, 6:18; 11:8 ff; 16:20; 19:8.

Yahweh's redemptive activity possesses a cosmic scope; Deut is not too far removed from Deutero-Isaiah's idea of "creation."

The plural passages stress all the more that God's election of Israel is motivated by his love and fidelity.

How far back before Deut, we now seek to know, can election-theology be found in biblical tradition? Some authors, like K. Koch and S. Mowinckel,[29] lay stress upon the royal tradition of Jerusalem. Others, like K. Galling[30] and G. von Rad[31] include the patriarchal narratives of the Yahwist (or "L" according to Eissfeldt). We will touch down upon both of these traditions.

2. In the Royal Tradition of Jerusalem

Bāḥar occurs in the royal traditions of Jerusalem. These early accounts have been preserved for us by the Deuteronomist[32] and also by the Psalmists.[33] Saul, David, Absalom, Solomon and Zerubbabel are all said to be the object of a divine election. It is worth noting that no royal person after Solomon, with the sole exception of the messianic figure, Zerubbabel, is said to be "chosen" *(bāḥar)* by Yahweh.[34] In these cases, *bāḥar* presumed a *divine* choice, externally manifested, usually by the anointing by a *nābî*.[35]

The pre-Deuteronomic use of *bāḥar* contains *in germine* the two essential ingredients mentioned earlier in this chapter: divine choice of one from among many; commission for a special office. The king is taken, by Yahweh's free choice, from the multitude of Israel; Yahweh lays upon the king the special office of fulfilling the divine promises among the people. The king, therefore, *is* the

29 Cf., fn 2.
30 Cf., fn 2.
31 Cf., G. von Rad, *Das Gottesvolk im Deuteronomium,* p. 65.
32 Cf., Quell, *op. cit.,* p. 156, fn 54, summarizing the royal choices of Yahweh.
33 Cf., below, fn 37.
34 Cf., Mendenhall, *op. cit.,* p. 78.
35 Quell, *op. cit.,* pp. 156-159 recognizes the important role of the *nabi* in election-theology of the royal tradition.

people in the fulness of their life and calling from Yahweh. The idea of kingship is not at all unique with Israel but was taken over from other nations in a specially modified and adapted form.[36] When royalty within Israel degenerated to its condition outside Israel and lost its particularly Israelite character, then the quality of the king's being Yahweh's "chosen" or "elect" one is returned to all the people—partially in Deut; completely in Deutero-Isaiah (Is 55:3).

Bāḥar is also found in some of the royal psalms, both those psalms in honor of the Davidic king of Jerusalem as well as those in honor of Yahweh-King.[37] Koch emphasizes the importance of these psalms in the election-tradition as it reaches Deutero-Isaiah.[38] The actual dependence of Deutero-Isaiah upon the psalms in a most difficult and accordingly a very controverted question. It seems that the problem will remain unsettled for still some time.[39] Restricting himself to the psalms where *bāḥar* occurs, H.J. Kraus will see a pre-exilic date only in three instances (Pss 65; 89; 105), and even here for Pss 65 and 105 he admits that the date is only probable.[40] For the rest (Pss 37; 47; 78; 106; 135) he prefers a postexilic date of composition. Koch, for his part, places either the psalms themselves or at least the oral, liturgical form of the psalms before the exile. He argues, for instance, that Ps 78 still speaks of Jacob in a favorable way (v 5), even though the rest of the psalm is a polemic against the northern kingdom; hence Ps 78 manifests vestiges of its early origin.[41]

---

36 The extent to which Israel accepted and absorbed the royal ritual of other nations and in particular the ancient Jebusite ritual is a major discussion in contemporary biblical research. Cf., J. de Fraine, *L'Aspect Religieux de la Royauté Israelite* (Rome, 1954); E. Lipinski, *La Royauté de Yahwé* (Brussel, 1965); R. de Vaux, *RB* 73 (1966), pp. 481-509; R.E. Clements *God and Temple* (Oxford, 1965).

37 Koch, *op. cit.,* pp. 212-213, thus summarizes the presence of *bahar* in the Psalms: (a) in the hymns, similar to the ancient credo's, where the object of election is *Jacob:* Pss 105:6 ff; 135:4 ff; 106:5 ff; 47:5; 33:12; (b) psalms in reference to Yahweh's creation-acts, in which the *king* is the chosen one: Pss 78:68; 89:2 ff; and (c) where the object of election is the *Priest:* Pss 65:5 105:26; (106:23).

38 Koch, *op. cit.,* p. 221.

39 Lipinski, *op. cit.* (in fn 36), attempts to reach a solution but it is thoroughly unacceptable to R. Tournay, *RB* 63 (1966), pp. 420-425.

40 Kraus, *Die Psalmen* (Neukirchen, 1960), 1:450.

41 *Art. cit.* (in fn 2), p. 209.

If we should grant for the moment that the above mentioned psalms precede Deutero-Isaiah and the exile, we might still ask if the tradition of election, which they reflect, says anything more than the same tradition within the royal-Davidic passages in the Deuteronomic books of Sam-Kgs. The idea of choosing the king (or priest or Jacob) and in him the nation of Israel from all other nations, is only vaguely implied in the psalms just discussed.

3. In the Patriarchal Traditions

A better case, at least for an indirect influence on Deutero-Isaiah, can be made for the patriarchal narratives of the Yahwist tradition. K. Galling deserves the credit for first drawing attention to *die Erzvätererzählungen* in the discussion of election-theology.[42] The idea of election, but not the word *bāhar*, occurs in such passages as: Gen 12:2f; 18:18; 22:17f; 26:4; 27:14; Ex 32:13. All of these texts are concerned with the privileged place which God granted Abraham in relation to other nations.[43]

The patriarchal traditions were recalled by Israel at important moments of her existence, as when the invading tribes formed alliances with some of the more indigenous inhabitants to Palestine or when the united tribes celebrated the renewal of these alliances at Shechem. Israel could worship Yahweh, the God of the Exodus and the Sinaitic covenant, with greater union among the tribes and with a deeper appreciation of her God, if she recalled the way in which the patriarchs worshipped God, for instance, as ʾel šadday and the God of the Fathers, titles more familiar than the name Yahweh to the tribes with longer roots in Palestine. The patriarchal traditions, and their appreciation of Yahweh's election

---

42 *Ibid.* (in fn 2). In his attempt to disentangle and abstract the patriarchal religion from the biblical account, M. Haran arrives at the conclusion that "at the beginning of the Patriarchal period, the religious consciousness of the Hebrew tribes (or part of them) was profoundly altered. The Bible sees this change as concentrated mainly in the figure of Abraham, and pictures him as an initiator of a new era," "The Religion of the Patriarchs, An Attempt at a Synthesis," *Annual of the Swedish Theological Institute,* 4 (1965), p. 43.

43 Galling, *op. cit.,* p. 63.

of Israel's forefathers, were integrated into the Mosaic Religion already established on the basis of the exodus and/or the Sinaitic covenant.[44]

Among the reasons why the germs of election-theology within the patriarchal traditions never developed too prominently during the pre-exilic preaching of the prophets,[45] we can cite: (1) the patriarchal traditions stressed the unconditional and eternal aspects of election-theology;[46] (2) they also tended to favor a "pride of race."[47] These qualities threatened Israelite religion in the time of the prophets. These men insisted that Yahweh was not the God of the Israelites in the same way in which, for instance, Yah (or whatever his name may have been) was their god of the Kenites. Rowley comments: "To the Kenites Yahweh was their God because He always had been; to Israel He was their God because He had chosen them, and His character as revealed in the deliverance, which Moses both promised and interpreted, was understood as the Kenites did not understand it."[48] The prophets very well realized that Yahweh had been baalized or deformed

---

44 M. Haran, *art. cit.* (in fn 42), pp. 45-46, " . . . at the beginning of the Patriarchal period, when the Hebrew tribes moved from the Euphrates Valley westward, they experienced a certain spiritual transformation which cast them into a new religious framework. . . . The distinct conceptional traits which appear from Abraham onward can provide us with a certain historical foothold. Accordingly, it may be said that those Hebrew tribes were attracted to various *'Elim—'El Shaddai* being the most prominent— and to the specific religious concept of the 'father's god,' and they adopted the practice of circumcision. It is also probable that the religion of the ancient Hebrews contained something which made it close to Yahwism—something which helped to make the acceptance of the latter by the tribes of Israel so swift and easy. Haran provides rather full, critical, bibliographical details. We call special attention to the articles of A. Alt, "The God of the Fathers," *Essays on Old Testament History and Religion* (Oxford: 1966), pp. 1-77; F.M. Cross, Jr., "Yahweh and the God of the Patriarchs," *HTR* 55 (1962), pp. 225-259; V. Maag, "Jahwas Heerscharen," *SchwTUm* 20 (1950), pp. 75-100; C. Westermann, "Arten der Erzahlung in der Genesis," *Forschung am Alten Testament (TB*, 24; München: 1964), pp. 9-91.

45 Mendenhall, *op. cit.,* p. 80, "Jer. 33:23-26 . . . [is] the only prophetic usage [of *bahar*] before Ezekiel and Second Isaiah."

46 Cf., Rowley, *op. cit.* p. 33, fn 1.

47 As though no matter what happened, Israel is still Yahweh's people: see Mi 3:11; Jer 5:12; 7:4, 10; 6:14.

48 Rowley, *op. cit.,* p. 43, calls attention to his other book, *Rediscovery of the Old Testament* (London, 1945), pp. 65-66.

into the kind of deity worshipped by neighboring peoples (cf., Hos 2:18). We shall soon see that Deutero-Isaiah could revive the patriarchal aspects of election-theology because he also insisted repeatedly that Yahweh was different from all other gods. Yahweh was the *one* God, not just in the modern idea of monotheism, but in the singular and unparalleled character of his goodness towards the people he freely chose.

Election, accordingly, is as old as Israel; Israel started to exist only when God began to exercise redemptive acts which singled out this *one* people from all others. But the full meaning of such an election dawned slowly. The first, adequate expression appears only in the Deuteronomic tradition. The Deuteronomist shows that he is conscious not only that Israel has been singled out from all other nations by the loving kindness of Yahweh, but also (though to a much less degree) that Israel has a role to perform towards other nations. Both of these essential components of election-theology, however, come clearly to the surface only in the poems of Deutero-Isaiah. This same prophet, as we shall now observe, also incorporated in one way or another the two other aspects of election-theology: the choice of the Davidic king; the call of the patriarchs.

How Israel responded to Yahweh's choice of her revealed Yahweh's presence; how she articulated her understanding of this divine election contributed to the biblical concept of God.

III. Election-Faith in Deutero-Isaiah

Authors generally recognize the importance of election-theology in the poems of Deutero-Isaiah and the importance of this prophet for the full development of election-theology. Professor Mendenhall wrote: "In Deutero-Isaiah . . . the concept of election reaches a culmination."[49] Vriezen, for his part, has this to say: "Noch tiefer als im Deuteronomium sind hier Liebe

---

[49] G. Mendenhall, *op. cit.*, p. 80.

und Erwählung verbunden."[50] According to Martin-Achard, "les oracles d'Es. 40-55 expriment mieux que les ecrits deutéronomistes qu'être élu par Iahvé signifie le servir . . . . Bref la théologie de l'élection chez le Deutéroésaïe reprend et prolonge, en les précisant, les indications du Deutéronome sur la peuple de Iahvé;"[51]

The *idea* of election extends throughout the Book of Consolation and comes repeatedly to the surface of the prophet's words. Volz lists these expressions of Deutero-Isaiah, frequently met in the prophet's book, for emphasizing Yahweh's special choice of Israel:

Yahweh is the God of Israel; your (sg) God, your (pl) God, our God; the Holy One of Israel; your (pl) Holy One; the King of Israel; your (pl) King, your (sg) Redeemer; your (pl) Redeemer, the Holy One of Israel, your (sg) Redeemer, the Stong One of Jacob; our Redeemer, Yahweh Sebaot, the Holy One of Israel; your (pl) merciful One; . . . the Creator and Former of Israel . . . ; my people . . . ; my sons and daughters . . . ; offspring of my friend Abraham . . . [52]

In order to keep our study of Deutero-Isaiah's election-theology within proper limits, we restrict ourselves to those texts where *bāḥar* occurs.[53] A study of Deutero-Isaiah's uses of *bāḥar* seems justifiable, not only because the word maintained a technical sense of Israelite religion (i.e., that Israel was apart from all others and commissioned for a special service), but also because the word began to include some idea of Israel's relation to the cosmos and its fertility.

---

50 Th. C. Vriezen, *op. cit.,* pp. 70-71.

51 E. Martin-Achard, *La signification théologique de l'élection d'Israel,"* *TZBas* 16 (1960), p. 338. H.H. Rowley, 63, writes similarly: "It is to be observed that for Deutero-Isaiah universalism did not spell the rejection of the thought of Israel." Cf., Begrich, *Studien zu Deuterojesaja,* reprinted in *Gesammelte Studien zum Alten Testament (TB,* 20; München; 1963), 107 ff.

52 Volz, *op. cit.* (in fn 4), p. 18. The full text of Volz is twice as long as that quoted here.

53 *I.e.,* 41:8-9; 43:10, 20; 44:1-2; 45:4; 49:7. We omit 42:1, which belongs to the first Servant Song.

41:8-10
8   But you, Israel, my servant,
          You, Jacob, whom I have chosen,
          Offspring of Abraham, my friend.
9   You I take hold of from the ends of the earth,
          from its remote places[54] I call you.
      I am saying to you: you are my servant.
      I have chosen you and I have not cast you off.
10   Do not fear! I am with you.
          Do not be dismayed,[55] for I am your God.
      I strengthen you, indeed I help you.
      Yes, by my victorious right hand I uphold you.

These lines, part of a slightly longer poem (41:8-13), are composed in the style of an Oracle of Salvation *(Heilsorakel)*.[56] Yahweh's words are intended as an answer to a sorrowing plaint or *Volksklagelied*. We learn from v 11-12 that the people are being persecuted. Yahweh assures them that their oppressors will be totally destroyed. Israel's victory shall be complete and unconditional.

Yahweh's announcement of salvation is acceptable only to the person of faith, only to the Israelite who believes that Yahweh has chosen his people and continuously abides by that choice. The word *bāḥar* occurs twice in the poem, but the idea of election is presented in a number of other ways. One of those ways, most impressive in the Hebrew text, is the I-Thou relationship, the *I, Yahweh* and *Thou, Israel*. The Hebrew verb in its *qatal* form puts

---

54 *Ūmé-sîlèhā.* The hapax *āsîl* is from sl[2] (Num 11:17, 25; Gen 27:36), to set aside or take away. G. Fohrer, *Das Buch Jesaja.* 3. Band *(ZBK;* Zürich, 1964), p. 36, translates it: "aus ihren fernstern Winkeln."

55 The Massoretes understood *tista* as the Hithpael of *s'h,* to gaze (anxiously), because of the qamets (also in 41:23). Because of the Ugaritic *tt'* and because of the parallel word *yare',* the word is better considered the Qal of *st',* "to fear." Cf., C.H. Gordon, *Ugaritic Textbook* (Rome, 1965), p. 507, Glossary, 2763.

56 Cf., Begrich, *op. cit.* (in fn 51), pp. 13-15; Fohrer, *op. cit.* (in fn 54), p. 37. H. Wildberger, "Die Neuinterpretation," p. 319, cites Is 41:8-10 and its oracle style as a reason for Deutero-Isaiah's dependency upon a Jerusalem tradition. This reasoning is difficult to follow.

I-Thou into the last two syllables of the word: b^eḥartîka . . .
heḥ^{e}zaqtîkā . . .   q^{e}ra\`tîkā . . . b$^e$ḥartîka . . .      m$^e$\`astîkā . . .
immaṣtîkā . . ^{a}zartîkā . . . t^{e}maktîkā: •   i.e.,   choose-I-you . . .
grasp-I-you . . . call-I-you . . . etc. The first singular and the second
singular pronoun suffix occur in still other ways quite frequently
in these lines, and thus still more trenchantly enforce the personal
bond by which Yahweh joins his people to himself.

Yahweh evidently takes the initiative. He is the subject of all
the verbs. Israel is scattered to the most remote corners of the
earth, helpless and dismayed. Yahweh calls Israel, grasps her,
strengthens her, upholds her by his victorious right hand. At the
same time Israel must react on her own part. A personal relation
demands a personal response. Israel's first and absolutely necessary
response must be *faith:* that deep realization, and the confidence
thus inspired, that Yahweh is her God and she is his people. But in
this Oracle of Salvation of Deutero-Isaiah, Yahweh seems to
expect more than faith; he wants the response of a servant. Twice
the prophet parallels "I have chosen you" with "my servant."
'ebed (servant), as Volz has remarked, is "ein feines Bild für den
Erwählungsglauben."[57]

It is in conjunction with election-faith that Deutero-Isaiah uses
'ebed for the first of many times. "Servant" brings out clearly one
of the essential components of "election," i.e., a special commission for a particular work. "Servant" also implies, what is
explicit in the word "to choose," loyalty and attachment; work is
undertaken by the servant for the master's sake. *bāḥar,* moreover,
lifts the work from the basis of master-servant to a more personal
relationship. We might recall that, as the word *'ebed* was used in
the ancient Near East, the "servant" was frequently a high
functionary at court, one at the immediate beck and call of the
monarch, one who constantly had the king's ear.[58] The *'ebed*

<hr>

57 Volz, *op. cit.* (in fn 4), p. 18. With those words Volz begins his discussion of
"servant." Wildberger, "Die Neuinterpretation," pp. 319-320, recognizes also the
important contribution of the *'ebed* theme to that of election in Deutero-Isaiah.

58 Cf., especially C. Lindhagen, *The Servant Motif in the Old Testament* (Uppsala,
1950), pp. 6-39, for many examples drawn from ancient Near Eastern literature; also
Gordon, *op. cit.* (in fn 55), pp. 452-453, Glossary, 1901.

responded immediately and whole-heartedly to whatever the king wanted.

Just what work was given to the servant Israel by Yahweh is not stated in this Oracle of Salvation. Other *bāḥar* passages, like the one to follow (43:8-13) will be more explicit on this point.

In order to manifest the special love of election and in order to inspire faith in her privileged place of Yahweh's chosen one, Deutero-Isaiah introduces two motives: very explicitly, the call of Abraham; more implicitly, the exodus. We first discuss the Abraham-reference. Pre-exilic prophets do not mention him. This fact by itself manifests the traditionalism of Deutero-Isaiah—to reach as far back as Abraham—as well as his radical innovative-ness—to strike out differently from the prophetic tradition.[59] By his grammatical style Deutero-Isaiah brings the past tradition about Abraham into the present moment. The participle, *'ōhⁱbî,* presents a nuance of present, contemporaneous action; secondly, the suffix is a subjective genitive.[60] *'Ōhⁱbî,* consequently, can be translated: whom I am loving." The exiles *are* "Abraham, whom I am loving," and by that love, redeeming. Because the love is total, the redemptive action of Yahweh will completely transform Israel's esistence into unmitigated joy.

Just as Abraham's situation had once been hopeless—he did not even know Yahweh (Jos 24:2)—yet, God's election made him the father of offspring as numerous as the stars in the sky or the sand along the seashore; likewise, the same love of Yahweh is now calling out to a hopeless and tragic people, scattered to the remotest corners of the earth.

In this passage then Yahweh appears, through the response of faith evoked in his prophet and through the prophet in Israel, as continuously faithful to Israel by a loving promise which reaches

---

59 Cl. Westermann, *Isaiah 40-66* (Philadelphia, 1969), p. 70.

60 It has already been pointed out that the subject of the verbs in this passage is consistently "I, Yahweh." K. Marti, *Das Buch Jesaja erklart (KHCAT;* Tubingen, 1900), 280, comments that if the meaning lay in Israel's loving me (i.e., Yahweh), then the Hebrew form would be *'ohⁱbeni.* LXX re-enforces the interpretation of God's activity: *'on agapesa.*

back as far as Abraham; by an intimate I-Thou bond with Israel
the Lord is gathering his people from the ends of the earth and
re-constituting them as his servants for some special work.

43:8-13

8   Lead out[61] the people, blind, though they have eyes,
        and deaf, though they still have ears.

9   Let all the nations gather together.
        Let the peoples assemble.
    Who among them is accustomed to announce this,
        that the court may hear and say, "It is true!"

10   You are my witnesses—the oracle of Yahweh—
        my servant,[62] whom I have chosen,
    that you may know and trust in me,
        and understand that I am [God].
    Before me no god was formed,
        and after me there shall be none.

11   I [alone], I am Yahweh,
        and besides me no one saves.

    . . .

12   You are my witnesses—the oracle of Yahweh—
        I am God. (13) From eternity I am the same.

In this judgment speech (*Gerichtsrede*) against the gods,
Deutero-Isaiah argues that by what Yahweh accomplishes within
and for Israel, he reduces all other deities to nothing. Something
divine takes place *within* the people—a work which only a God
could achieve—enabling Israel to know, trust and understand that
Yahweh alone is God. This divine achievement, though centered
within Israel, radiates a divine activity before the eyes of the
nations. In fact, the light is so blinding as to surround all their
gods with darkness. They no longer can claim existence.

---

61 TM *hosi*, "he led forth," Hiph perf 3 sg masc; read with IQIs[a] hosi'u, Hiph imper
pl.

62 We follow the TM, *wᵉ'abdi* (sg suff), which, as North explains, "is supported by
all versions except P[eschitta]," *The Second Isaiah* (Oxford, 1964), p. 121.

Deutero-Isaiah's main argument against the gods is based on what Yahweh has announced and fulfilled.[63] Another argument, however, almost as cogent in the eyes of the prophet, is the *wondrous transformation,* announced and fulfilled within Israel. A people, once blind and deaf, march back, free and victorious, to their homeland. Deutero-Isaiah is describing poetically or symbolically how Yahweh redeems Israel from her hopeless and helpless situation. Redemption is *like* a new creation which gives eyes that see and ears that hear. Israel, thus re-created, "witnesses" to the nations; Israel reveals the overwhelmingly divine, redemptive force surging through her and making her a new creation.

Yet, Israel is not new in the sense of being completely different from the past. What Yahweh is doing within Israel, he has always been doing. "From eternity I am the same." The past which has relevancy for the prophet is the one which always teemed with Yahweh's redemptive activity in Israel and which now converges with finality and completion in the moment just ahead.

What this poem adds to our understanding of Deutero-Isaiah's election-theology is the role of Israel, chosen by Yahweh, to witness to the nations by what is happening primarily within her but radiated outside her. The interior source of the re-creation is stated in v 10, "my witnesses . . . my servant, whom I have chosen, that you may know and trust in me, and understand that I am [God]."[64] Clearly, something decisive happens within Israel. Yet, the results of her election are seen outside for the evidence of her redemption is produced in court, to obtain a favorable verdict for Yahweh against all other deities.

43:19-21

19   Look! I am doing something new!
       Now it springs forth, do you not perceive it?

63 Cf., C. Stuhlmueller, " 'First and Last' and 'Yahweh-Creator' in Deutero-Isaiah," *CBQ* 29 (1967), pp. 495-205.

64 Westermann, *op. cit.* (in fn 59), pp. 122-123 insists upon the interior results achieved by Yahweh and Yahweh alone.

> In the wilderness I am placing a way,
>> rivers in desolate wastes.
>
> 20 . . .
>
> For I put water in the wilderness,
>> rivers in desolate wastes,
>> to provide drink for my chosen people
>>> (*l^{e}hašqôt 'ammî b^{e}ḥîrî*)
>
> 21 The people whom I form for myself,
>> let them recount my praises.

These lines belong to an Announcement of Salvation, beginning at 43:16. Within the larger context of the poem, wherein the first exodus and the new exodus are deftly interwoven, Deutero-Isaiah speaks of a cosmic transformation.[65] Wherever Israel goes to live, even momentarily, on her journey back to the Promised Land, the area is re-created into a paradise. Similar to the garden of Gen 2:4b-14, everything—plants, trees, animals and the whole earthly terrain—is put at the service of Israel for her joy.

Deutero-Isaiah uses the word, *bāḥar,* in the strictly technical sense. He includes what we have come to recognize as the two component parts of election: separation from others; commission for a special work. The separation appears clearly enough in the violent way in which Israel's enemies (the nations) are utterly destroyed (v 17). The commission is related immediately afterwards: "Let them [my chosen people—*'ammî b^{e}ḥîrî*] recount my praises." While the preceding poem (43:8-13) cast the "service" of Israel in the form of a witness against the pagan gods, this poem describes her service as one of *praise.*

Finally, Deutero-Isaiah parallels "my chosen people" with "people whom I *form* for myself." He employs creation-vocabulary (*yaṣar,* "form") for the act of election. Deutero-Isaiah sees that election contains within itself the power to re-create. What Yahweh has been doing from the beginning for his people, he now does so much more wondrously that they are no longer to think about the events of the past (v 18).

---

65 C. Stuhlmueller, *Creative Redemption in Deutero-Isaiah* (Rome, 1970), pp. 67-70.

Election-theology enables the prophet to realize the intimacy of God's love and the Lord's transforming power, so that a liturgy of praise breaks forth across the cosmos. The same theology has the unfortunate by-product of rejecting the nations, so that another aspect of Yahweh's plans remain hidden.

44:1-5[66]

1   But now! Listen, Jacob, my servant,
        and Israel, whom I have chosen.
2   Thus says Yahweh, your maker,
        who forms you within the womb, your helper.
     Do not fear, my servant, Jacob,
        Yeshurun, whom I have chosen.
3   For I will pour out water upon the thirsty ground,
        and streams upon the dry land.
     I will pour out my spirit upon your offspring
        and my blessing upon your descendants.
4   They shall spring up like the verdant poplar,
        like willows beside the flowing waters.
5   This one shall say, "I am the Lord's!"
        and another shall call himself by the name Jacob.
     Yet another shall inscribe on his hand, "The Lord!"
        and ennoble himself by the name Israel.

Again, as in 41:8-10, the election term *bāḥar* not only occurs twice but also each time in the perfect tense: *bāḥartî*. It is helpful to note that all the other verbs in this Oracle of Salvation (except the introductory: *kōh-'āmar yahweh*) are in a tense other than the perfect. Consequently, Yahweh's election of Israel is considered a completed fact, fully in existence, before any of the other actions are undertaken. This priority, however, need not be chronological; it might be more in the nature of what upholds something else.

In this Oracle of Salvation Deutero-Isaiah attributes the formation of Israel and the prosperity of her existence to her

66 For the textual criticism and commentary on this poem, see *ibid,* pp. 125-131.

election by Yahweh. In the first part of the poem the initial
bāḥartî is followed by creation-vocabulary in the participial form,
'ōśekā wᵉyōṣerkā. Furthermore, these latter words point explicitly
to the creation of a new Israel, therefore to the "new creation."
The second occurrence of *bāḥartî* governs the announcement that
Yahweh will pour water[67] and spirit[68] upon his people and thus
not only relieve them of the desert conditions of their life but also
surround their life with abundant joys.[69] Because he has chosen
them, the redemptive acts of the past will continue still more
effectively, with repercussions throughout the earth, in what
Yahweh is about to perform for his people. Election-theology,
consequently, unfolds and extends into a creation-theology.

Deutero-Isaiah certainly foresees a redemptive renewal of life
within Israel, but it is not clear, and therefore is disputed, whether
or not this passage describes redemption under the image of a new
exodus.[70] If Deutero-Isaiah is using exodus-phraseology, then he
is clearly enough placing the moment of election before the
exodus.[71] Because of the election, the (new) exodus takes place.
Yet, the prophet does not go back as far as first creation, only to

67 Water is one of Deutero-Isaiah's favorite symbols for Yahweh's power to bring life
abundantly: 41:17-20; 43:19; 45:8; 48:18, 21; 49:10; 51:3; 55:1, 10-11.

68 Beginning with the exilic literature, *ruah* takes on an important place in Israel's
traditions: in the prophetical line: Is 28:6; 61:1; 63:10; Hab 2:5; Joel, ch 3; Zech 12:10;
in the psalms, Pss 33:6; 51:12-14; 143:10; in the wisdom books, Job 26:13; 33:4; Dan
5:12; Sir 48:12 (LXX); Wis 1:5-7; 9:17.

69 E. Hessler, "Die Structur der Bilder bei Deuterojesaja," *EvT* 25 (1965), p. 364,
writes regarding 44:1-5, "Jahwes segenspendendes handeln soll als ein schöpferischer Akt
aufgefasst werden durch den Jahwe seinem glaubenslosen Volk neuen Glaubensmut
verleiht, so dass es sich zu ihm bekennt."

70 In favor of the exodus theme, we cite these reasons: a) similarity of ideas with
43:19-20 and 41:17-20; b) *ruah,* which holds a prominent place in the Mosaic exodus
traditions: the strong wind to divide the waters (Ex 10:13, 19; 14:21; 15:8, 10) and to
bring the quail (Num 11:31); the spirit granted to the artisan by God (Ex 28:3; 31:3,
31); the spirit of Moses (Num 11:17, 25bis), given to Joshua (Num 27:18) and to
Balaam (Num 24:2); the spirit of Caleb (Num 14:24); the spirit of wisdom (Deut 34:9);
or the spirit of God (Num 11:29; 16:22; 27:16); c) and the LXX paraphrase in v 3, "I
will give water to the thirsty, walking in a dry terrain."

71 J. Muilenburg, "The Book of Isaiah, Chapters 40-66," *Interpreter's Bible*
(Nashville, 1956), p. 501 recognizes the need, felt by Deutero-Isaiah, "to ground Israel's
unique character in something more ultimate than the Exodus." Muilenburg adds:
"Observe that election precedes creation. It is reality and significance of the election that
evokes the reflection upon creation."

the patriarchal stage. For Deutero-Isaiah the thought of creation here is confined to the new re-creation of Israel.

"Election," we have already seen, includes the notion of a special commission or a work to be performed. This aspect of Israel's election is explicitly present in 44:1-5, only if one interprets v 5 as a reference to the conversion of the gentiles. Here is another, seriously controversial question.[72] Does the Book of Consolation, independently of the Servant Songs, explicitly refer to the conversion of the gentiles and their incorporation within the people of Israel? The question is a very involved one, and it can be laid out here only in broad outline. It does concern us, because we are interested in knowing whether Deutero-Isaiah's creation-theology is limited to Israel or has a universality, extending to all the nations who come into contact with Israel. How the Bible reacts towards the nations indicates what it is saying about God's universal love and practical monotheism.

Taken just by itself, 44:5 *might* indicate the conversion of *individual* gentiles to the community of Yahweh's chosen people. The larger context, however, of the Book of Consolation raises doubts about anything more extensive than scattered proselytes. Deutero-Isaiah arrived at a more generous outlook only in the Servant Songs.[73] Ordinarily in the Book of Consolation the prophet presents the gentiles as: foolish worshippers of helpless gods (40:15-20; 43:8-13; 44:9-20), people who are to be completely defeated (43:17), disgraced (41:11), and given away in exchange for Israel (43:3b). Many of Deutero-Isaiah's expressions

---

72 Many commentators maintain that some kind of gentile conversion is announced here: Duhm, 303; Marti, 301; Volz, 48-49; Kissane, 11:60; Fischer, 11:69; North, 134; Muilenburg, 504; Westermann, 136-7. However, Fohrer, 72, rejects v 5 as a later addition to the original text; its universalism evidently jars too much in his opinion with Deutero-Isaiah's position in the Book of Consolation.

73 This paragraph and its footnotes depend largely upon E. Vogt, *Isaias 40-55* (Rome, 1966), pp. 11-17. P.A.H. de Boer, *Second-Isaiah's Message* (OTS, 11; Leiden, 1956), pp. 80-101, devotes an entire chapter entitled, "The Limits of Second-Isaiah's Message," not only providing bibliographical material on the question of Deutero-Isaiah's universalism, but also arguing firmly that "Second-Isaiah's only purpose [even in the Suffering Servant Songs] is to proclaim deliverance [exclusively] for the Judean people."

about the nations' recognizing Yahweh (40:5; 42:12; 52:10) are to be accounted merely stylistic and exaggerated ways of presenting the wondrous work of Yahweh within Israel (cf., Pss 117; 126:2). Excluding 44:5, therefore, "the solicitude of God for the salvation of the gentiles is clearly enuntiated in only two places [45:22-25 and 51:3-8]."[74] We can eliminate from ch 51 these following verses: 4b, 5b, 6b," and arrive not only at a smoother flowing poem but also at one in which the salvation of Israel is the sole concern. The excision of verses from ch 51, then, leaves us only one verse in the entire Book of Consolation (45:22), with reference to the conversion of many or all gentiles! Because of the otherwise overwhelming number and even violent form of expressions against the gentiles, the force of 45:22 pales in significance.

If an *incipient universalism* is present in 44:5, then we can conclude that Deutero-Isaiah is thinking of a kingdom within Israel, less nationalistic than it had been under the pre-exilic monarchy (cf., 55:3-5), less enclosed within itself against foreigners than had been the community formed by Moses in the desert. In this poem, in fact, Deutero-Isaiah addresses himself to "Jacob" and "Israel" and therefore constructs the framework of thought from the patriarchal days, before Israel existed as a distinct national or ethnic unit. Deutero-Isaiah's community is thus much more "spiritual" or, shall we say, "supra-national." 44:5 would thus be one of those exceptional statements in the Book of Consolation, a germ of thought which will develop more fully when the prophet or his disciple composes the Servant Songs.

Conclusion

In the course of this essay, our attention has been focused upon two major biblical traditions—the Deuteronomic books and Deutero-Isaiah—because of their thorough appreciation of Israel as the Lord's elect people. Election reflected the great attributes of

---

74 Vogt, *op. cit.* (in fn 73), p. 14.

God's goodness, mercy and provident care. For a long time election-theology not only announced the Lord's free and personal love (*cf.*, Deut 7:6-9), but it also restricted that love to Israel. Unfortunately, the election of a chosen people implied the rejection of the non-elect. Only one side of God's goodness was visible, and the full meaning of God's personal interaction with man was not seen.

If, however, God's choice of Israel reached back before the days of the exodus and covenant, as we saw to be the case with Deuteronomy and Deutero-Isaiah, then at the basis of election lay a factor which would eventually include the gentile nations within the ambit of God's redemptive love. If it was not Israel's goodness or greatness but solely God's merciful love and fidelity that motivated the choice of Israel, then nothing could prevent the Lord from choosing the gentiles and making them one with his originally chosen people.

It seemed that the whole development of election-theology was leading against such a solution. Not only did Deuteronomy take a fierce stand against gentile nations, but Deutero-Isaiah insisted upon the separation of Israel from all other nations. The "Great Unknown" employed *bāḥar* in the context of such a distinction: 41:9, Israel is called from the ends of the earth; 43:10, Israel witnesses against the gods of the nations; 43:17, other nations are snuffed out and destroyed.

Besides being separated from all other nations, Israel's election also laid a special commission upon her—the second component in the technical idea of election. As the chosen people, she is Yahweh's servant (45:4). What Yahweh accomplishes within Israel (the conscious acceptance in faith of being his specially beloved one—43:10) radiates outside of Israel, transforming her entire earthly existence wherever she might be, and as such witnessing before all the nations that Yahweh alone is God-Savior (43:9-11). In another poem Israel is chosen in order to recount Yahweh's praise. Finally, there is a possibility that Deutero-Isaiah sees Yahweh as giving his chosen people a mission to attract at least individual converts from the gentiles (44:5).

As Deutero-Isaiah began to associate election with (re-)creation, the extent of election began to widen. Creation was viewed as the earthly repercussion of Yahweh's choice of Israel. Yahweh will make his chosen people completely joyful and prosperous. In 44:1-5, where *bāḥar* is in the perfect tense and all the other verbs (including *'āśâ* and *yāṣar*) are in another tense or form, we see clearly enough that all other blessings follow, because Yahweh's choice is perfect and complete and everlasting. Election expands into (a new) creation. We also saw in 43:19-21 that election *is* the act of (re-)creation. Earlier in that same chapter of Deutero-Isaiah (43:8-13), election is expressed through the image of providing sight to the blind and hearing to the deaf. The symbol expresses creation rather well, for such an action can be performed only by Yahweh, replacing vital organs which no longer existed in the earthly substance of Israel's life.

Towards the end of his career, Deutero-Isaiah—or was it his disciple?—made the extraordinary leap from Israel's redemption achieved across the panorama of the ends of the earth, to the redemption of all the earth.[75] The Suffering Servant Songs reflect such a universalistic view (42:1-4; 49:1-4,5c; 50:4-9a; 52:13-53:12). Was such an unusual transition, dormant for a long time within election theology, made a living reality by suffering and rejection? Does such a poem as 45:9-13 in the Book of Consolation, speak of the prophet's rejection by his own fellow-countrymen?[76]

We end this article with a question. Are suffering and rejection always necessary to appreciate the full potential of what God's election can achieve? Election blossoms when confronted with what seems to be its opposite, rejection! Seemingly in darkness the full appreciation of God is experienced, but such a mystic perception leaps beyond the careful, controlled bonds of theology.

---

[75] G. von Rad, *Old Testament Theology* (New York, 1962), 1:404 writes about Pss 16 and 73:23 ff, "Here too we are dealing with one of those ancient sacral phrases which were handed on through many generations and all of a sudden released quite unexpected contents."

[76] C. Stuhlmueller, *op. cit.* (in fn 65), 200-207.

Addenda

The mighty leap towards universal salvation, executed in the Suffering Servant Songs, influenced only a few postexilic writers of religious leaders. The voice of Deutero-Isaiah resonates in some of the psalms (Pss 47; 93; 96-99),[77] and again in Deutero-Zechariah (Zech 9-14) with the poignant tone of the Servant Songs.[78] The spirit of the "Great Unknown" lives in such a book as Jonah and Malachi. For the most part, however, chapters 40-55 of the Book of Isaiah remain in view like a grand monument erected over a dead hero! The Targums, in fact, translate and paraphrase the Servant Songs so that the martyr in Deutero-Isaiah's book becomes the enemy of God and God's people.[79]

When the sights of postexilic Israel turned in upon itself, Israel's appreciation of God also shrunk in size and in glory.

The next great leap is made by St. Paul, who sees himself as the Suffering Servant,[80] and at the cost of much pain and rejection he preaches the salvation of the gentiles. He too like Deutero-Isaiah reached back to the patriarch Abraham for inspiration. The "image of God" in St. Paul expands and opens into an apostolate which extends to the end of the earth and to the last moment of time.

The biblical "Question of God" then is intertwined with the "Question of a Chosen People" and with their willingness to open their arms towards their non-elect neighbors.

The Bible seldom takes up the further question: Can the

---

77 Cf., A. Feuillet, "Les psaumes eschatologiques du règne de Yahweh," NRT 73 (1951), pp. 244-260, 352-363.

78 Cf., M. Delcor, "Les sources du Deutéro-Zacharie et ses procedes d'emprunt," RB 59 (1952), 384-411.

79 See the English Translation in The Fifty-Third Chapter of Isaiah According to the Jewish Interpreters. Vol. II, translations by S.R. Drivers and Ad. Neubauer (New York, Ktav, 1969, reprint of 1877 edition), pp. 5-6; and commentary in S. Mowinckel, He That Cometh (Nashville: Abingdon, 1954), pp. 330-333.

80 A. M. Denis, "L'election et la vocation de Paul, faveurs célestes," Revue Thomiste, 57 (1957), pp. 405-428.

81 S. Lyonnet, Les Etapes de l'histoire du salut selon l'épitre aux Romains (Paris: Les Editions du Cerf, 1969); L. Ligier, Péché d'Adam et péché du Monde, II (Montaigne: Aubier, 1960), pp. 169-186.

gentiles be saved, separate from Israel? Eventually all men must belong to Israel, one way or another—the Book of Revelation uses the image of the twelve tribes (Rev 7) and Romans that of the olive tree (Rom 11), to describe the final assembly of the redeemed saints at the end of time. Our discussion, therefore, swings around one hundred and ninety degrees to our starting point—the election of a chosen people. While Wisdom 13:1-9 and later Romans 1:18-21 state that all men *can* know God "from the greatness and the beauty of created things . . . by analogy" (Wis 13:5), *neither* passage explicitly declares that the gentiles *actually did come* to a saving knowledge of God. A great gulf separates what man *can* do and what man *actually does*. St. Paul implies that all men, gentiles and Jews, are called by the same God to the same goal.[81] Once again, only in the union of all men in God—when all are equally members of God's chosen people—is the mystery of God complete and the vision of God revealed.

A SELECT BIBLIOGRAPHY

Clements, R.E., *God and Temple: The Idea of the Divine Presence in Ancient Israel.* Oxford: Blackwell, 1965.

Dentan, R.C., *The Knowledge of God in Ancient Israel.* New York: Seabury, 1968.

Eichrodt, W., *Theology of the Old Testament.* 2 vols. Philadelphia: Westminister Press, 1961-1967.

Giblet, J., *The God of Israel, The God of Christians.* New York: Paulist Press, 1961.

Imschoot, P. van, *Theologie de l'Ancien Testament.* 2 vols. Tournai: Desclée, 1954-1956. English Translation of Vol. One, 1965.

Jacob, E., *Theology of the Old Testament.* New York: Harper & Row, 1958.

Knight, G.A.F., *A Christian Theology of the Old Testament.* Richmond Va.: John Knox Press, 1959.

Kohler, L., *Theologie des Alten Testament.* 4th ed. Tübingen: Mohr, 1966.

Laurin, R.B., *Contemporary Old Testament Theologians.* Valley Forge, Pa.: Judson Press, 1970.

Rad, G. von, *Old Testament Tehology.* 2 vols. New York: Harper & Bros, 1962-1965.

Renckens, Henry, *The Religion of Israel.* New York: Sheed & Ward, 1966.

Ringgren, H., *Israelite Religion.* Philadelphia: Fortress Press, 1966.

Vaux, R. de, "Is it Possible to Write a 'Theology of the Old Testament'?" *The Bible and the Ancient Near East* (Garden City, N.Y.: Doubleday, 1971), pp. 49-62. Reprint from *Melanges Chenu* (Paris: Bibliothéque Thomiste, 1967), pp. 439-449.

Vriezen, Th. C., *The Religion of Ancient Israel.* Philadelphia: Westminster Press, 1967.

Wright, G.E., *The Old Testament and Theology.* New York: Harper & Row, 1969.

We call special attention to *Biblical Theology Bulletin,* whose first volume appeared in February 1971 from the Biblical Institute Press, Rome 00186. Two articles in particular deserve note: J. Harvey, "The New Diachronic Biblical Theology of the Old Testament," 1 (Feb. 1971), pp. 5-29; and G.F. Hasel, "Methodology as a Major Problem in the Current Crisis of Old Testament Theology," 2 (June 1972), pp. 177-198.

Part Two
God in the Christian Tradition

PRELIMINARY REMARKS

The following discussions of the notion of God in the Christian tradition are divided according to the main branches of Christianity, namely Roman Catholicism, Protestantism, and the Orthodox Churches.

This Part is introduced by the essays on Plato's and Aristotle's thinking, the basis of the philosophical concept of God in Christianity.

Christianity is a religion which, generally speaking, is followed by one-third of the population of the world. In 1970 about 1,000,000,000 people were identified as Christians; half of them are in Europe and most of the other half in North and South America. Principally Christianity may be called a Western religion which spread through the whole world and influenced other religions.[1]

---

[1] "Christianity," *Encyclopedia Britannica*, 1970.

Pre-Christian God

CHAPTER XIII

PLATONIC AND CHRISTIAN THEISM

John P. Rowan *

Considering the similarities that undoubtedly exist between the descriptions of the divine found in the dialogues and those provided by the Scriptures, it is not surprising that so many of Plato's interpreters, from the early Christian period to the present, have asked whether his conception of god is not in a last analysis very close to if not identical with the one recognized by Christianity.[1] And neither is it surprising, when one takes account of the exposition of his theological views, that there has been no general agreement among his interpreters as to the way in which this question ought to be answered: some affirming and others denying that the two conceptions are the same, and still others arguing that any comparison is impossible because Plato has no god in any distinctively singular sense of the term; for what he has to say about the divine and the way in which this is presented, unlike the Biblical account, often appears to leave his exact position a matter of conjecture.

His thoughts on the subject, like those on others of which he treats, are not set forth in any systematic way such as one meets in treatises by later authors, but are scattered throughout different

---

*Professor of Philosophy at St. John's University, New York, U.S.A.

[1] Philo's interest in the possibility of reconciling some of Plato's ontological and theological views with those found in the Old Testament antedates that of early Christian writers, and often influenced their approach to the problem. He drew heavily, for example, upon the *Timaeus* in explaining the Mosaic account of the world's creation, and was the first to make Plato's Ideas the thoughts of God *(De Opificio Mundi,* V, 20). For an analysis of the use Philo makes of Plato consult H.A. Wolfson, *Philo,* 2 vols. (Cambridge, 1947); on the use made of the *Timaeus,* see I, ch. V; and on the Ideas as the thoughts of God, see I, pp. 280 ff. A brief description of the themes developed by Philo is presented by J.K. Feibleman, *Religious Platonism* (London, 1959), pp. 103-119.

dialogues from the *Euthyphro* to the *Epinomis,* and from these, as his commentators readily concede, a coherent body of doctrine that is clear and comprehensive cannot easily be formulated. Comparing what he has to tell us about the divine in earlier dialogues up to the *Republic* with the statements made in later ones, his opinions on the subject would appear to have undergone some kind of evolution, although what transpired during the process—which it would be most. helpful to know—can only be surmised in a vague and general way.

During the earlier stages of his speculations he does not seem to have been interested in any special way in theological issues, his concern being chiefly centered on the Ideas.[2] When the divine is mentioned, as it often is, it is generally referred to in a purely casual way, and usually in conventional terms that are simply indicative of Greek piety. Occasionally there are remarks which appear to be philosophically significant, but these, being unduly brief and standing in need of development, do little more than suggest possible lines of inquiry.[3] In later dialogues, where the divine emerges as an essential part of his world-view, his treatment of it also proves to be anything but satisfactory. Some statements are found to be obscure or ambiguous, and sometimes even difficult if not impossible to reconcile with one another, so that one is often at a loss to say what their real meaning is. Even passages of a positive kind can prove to be disappointing, since they are rarely as informative as the matter under discussion would seem to warrant, and such restraint together with his silence where explanations are desperately needed, add to the difficulty

---

2   The discussions in the dialogues would indicate, as is often noted, that Plato at first was primarily interested in the theory of Ideas and its application to moral and practical matters, and that the divine, as the highest kind of soul, began to become significant only after the need to include a dynamic principle in the realm of the "really real" to account for motion was recognized, a conclusion which was reached by the time of the writing of the *Sophist:* "And, oh heavens, can we ever be made to believe that motion and life and soul and mind are not present with perfect being?" (*Soph.,* 249A).

3   Some remarks appear to anticipate later doctrines. The conception of self-motion referred to in the *Charmides* (168E-169A), for example, is later taken up in the *Phaedrus* (245C ff.), and the creation myths of the *Symposium* (189E ff.) and *Protagorss* (320C) are forerunners of the one in the *Timaeus* (29D ff.).

of establishing his views in any precise and definite fashion.[4]

Different reasons have been offered to explain the abstruseness and restraint that is characteristic of much that he has to say. Some have argued, for example, that he did not wish to express himself more clearly, either because he was afraid of being charged with impiety,[5] or because he preferred to reserve his teaching on such a sublime subject for the members of the Academy.[6] Others have maintained that since for him the end of wisdom was political action and not metaphysical speculation, he never experienced the need to formulate any precise and comprehensive doctrine about god. And still others have claimed that he was unable to give his theological thought a coherent and determinate form because of the novelty of the enterprise.[7]

While the cogency of some of these explanations may be questioned for want of corroborative evidence, the last can hardly be challenged on this score. History clearly indicates that theology in the traditionally accepted philosophical sense of the term originates in large measure with Plato, and from anyone attempting to explore a subject for the first time a clear and comprehensive understanding and exposition of it cannot reasonably be expected, especially when the subject by its very nature is the one least amenable to human investigation, as the divine is reputed to be according what Plato has to tell us. His remarks to this effect in fact often create the impression that nothing at all, or almost nothing, can be known with certainty about the gods or god. In the *Cratylus,* for example, Socrates frankly admits that "Of the gods we know nothing, neither of their natures or the names they give themselves," and "we do not

---

4   Interpreters seldom fail to comment on the difficulties in one form or another that stand in the way of establishing his theological views. See, for example, R. Demos, *The Philosophy of Plato* (New York, 1966), pp. vii-x, 99-103; A. Diès, *Autour de Platon* (Paris, 1927), pp. 571 ff.; and J.K. Feibleman, *op. cit.,* pp. 21-24.

5   See L. Robin, *Platon* (Paris, 1938), p. 246.

6   Passages in several dialogues seem to suggest that Plato had certain doctrines which he did not care to reveal, and his reference in *Epistle* II to secret doctrines which are not to be committed to writing tends to lend support to this belief.

7   For a summary of the various opinions on this issue see O. Reverdin, *La Religion de la Cité Platonicienne* (Paris, 1945), p. 41.

presume that we are able to do so."[8] Man's ignorance of the gods
is also readily acknowledged in the *Critias*,[9] and in an often cited
passage of the *Timaeus* the principal speaker cautions his audience
that "The father and maker of the universe it is a hard task to
find, and having found him it would be impossible to declare him
to all mankind."[10]

Little wonder, then, that Plato's whole approach to the problem
of god should turn out to be tentative and suggestive, obscure and
hesitant, rather than definitive and conclusive in its results, and
thus open to any number of interpretations, for whatever stand
one takes with regard to Plato's views, there are always grounds, as
Feibleman points out, to support a different one.[11] Thus, if his
interpreters are not denying that he had a highest deity, they are
crediting him with one, though disagreeing as to whom this deity
is: some claiming that he is the Demiurge, Father, or Maker of the
universe, described in the *Timaeus,* and probably referred to in
certain other dialogues, or, if not this divine artisan, then the
Good of the *Republic.* And when the Good is considered in this
capacity, it is believed either to be the highest of the Ideas (or
even the Ideal world *in toto),* or to be a principle that transcends
the Ideal world, which is then conceived either as a unique Being,
or as a purely self-subsistent mind (not unlike the one proposed by
Anaxagoras), or as the deity of whom the Demiurge is either the
equivalent or merely the symbol.[12] And having visualized Plato's
god along one or the other of these lines, some interpreters have
not hesitated to credit him with a view of the divine that is for all
intents and purposes indistinguishable from the one commonly
recognized by Christian theologians and philosophers. Are they
justified, however, in making such a claim on the basis of

---

8 *Crat.,* 400D, 401A. Unless otherwise noted the dialogues are quoted according to
B. Jowett's translation, *The Dialogues of Plato,* 2 vols. (New York: Random House,
1937).

9 *Crit.,* 107A: "We know how ignorant we are concerning the gods."

10 *Tim.,* 28C; F.M. Cornford, trans. from *Plato's Cosmology* (London, 1956), p. 22.

11 *Op. cit.,* p. 22.

12 The list is not intended to be exhaustive. The positions mentioned, however,
appear to be the ones most commonly taken.

everything that Plato has to say, or is this not simply a case of textual misinterpretation, of reading into Plato conceptions which are in fact alien to his thought?[13] Is it even certain to begin with that he has a unique god with whom the Christian God can be compared?

Several reasons have been advanced in support of the claim that the existence of such a god is doubtful, if not to be discounted altogether, and while these may not prove in the long run to be necessarily conclusive, they do serve to point up some of the obstacles in the way of too readily accepting those statements in which Plato is supposed to acknowledge a highest divinity in one or the other of the ways indicated above.

Some have questioned the existence of such a deity for Plato because of the indefinite way in which the terms god *(theos)* the the gods *(hoi theoi)* are frequently used throughout the dialogues from beginning to end. [14] It is very unlikely, they argue, that the apparent references to a unique and highest deity, either by the term god or by some special title, are intended to be taken literally. For, with the exception of those instances in which the term denotes some particular divinity of whom mention has already been made, it is commonly employed as an equivalent for

13 Those who identify Plato's god, whatever form he is thought to have, with the Christian God, are frequently accused of reading Christian conceptions into Plato. On this point see the remarks of E. Gilson, *The Spirit of Medieval Philosophy* (New York, 1940), p. 432; G. M. Grube, *Plato's Thought* (London, 1935), p. 177; and F.M. Cornford, *op. cit.,* pp. 35-36.

14 On the confusion created by the use of these two terms, and the term divine *(theios),* see the comments of I.M. Crombie, *An Examination of Plato's Doctrines* (New York, 1962), p. 371; G.M. Grube, *op. cit.,* pp. 150-151; P.E. More, *The Religion of Plato* (Oxford, 1921), pp. 139-140, 203; L. Robin, *op. cit.,* p. 246; U. Von Willamowitz-Moellendorf, *Platon*, 2 vols. (Berlin, 1920), I, p. 248.

For special studies devoted to the problem see G. François, *Le polythéisme et l'emploi de mots Theos et Daemon* (Paris, 1957), ch. X, pp. 294-304, and R. Mugnier, *Le sens du mot theios* (Paris, 1930), pp. 116-142.

the gods,[15] as their alternate use on so many occasions clearly indicates.[16]

According to this line of reasoning any mention of a world artisan, father, maker, or pilot of the universe, would have, in all probability, to be understood in a purely collective sense as signifying the gods as a whole or divine reason as such operative in the cosmos.[17] This conclusion, which has been stoutly defended by Cornford, Grube, and others, is also demanded they believe by reason of certain of Plato's cosmological commitments, since the perpetuity of the universe, to which he, in keeping with the whole tradition of Greek thought, appears to definitely subscribe, precludes the need for a highest god such as the one described in the *Timaeus* at least. For, granted that Plato's world is eternal in duration, it requires no highest cause either to bring it into being or to initiate becoming within it. The description of its supposed beginning as found in the *Timaeus* having been adopted merely for the purpose of exposition and not to be understood literally, Plato's divine craftsman must therefore be judged to be a purely mythical figure symbolizing the intelligence of the gods at work in

---

15 For examples of the alternate use of these terms see *Republic* II, 379 AB: Having first rejected the poets' descriptions of the gods, Socrates then proceeds to give the genuine attributes not of the gods, as might be expected, but of god. In the *Phaedo*, 62B-D, the gods are said to be the guardians of men, and men their possessions, but a little later it is said that "a man should not take his life until god summons him." And in the *Laws* X, 902E-903D, the terms god, the gods, and "the ruler of the universe," are all employed interchangeably.

16 On this and related points see the conclusions of G. François, *op. cit.,* p. 295, n.1. In the authentic dialogues alone, according to his investigations, the term god *(theos)* is used 155 times and the term the gods *(hoi theoi)* 543 times to designate divine power, and in many of these instances they are employed interchangeably. In those cases in which THEOS designates some particular god (159 times), the definite article accompanies the term, but in others its presence or absence appears to be of no significance.

The difficulty, in fact, in often ascertaining Plato's meaning, is created by the absence of the definite article when *theos* is used, since without it the term becomes ambiguous. The lack of an indefinite article in the Greek language has much the same effect. It is often difficult, as G.C. Field notes, "to decide if one should translate *theos*, without any article, by *god* (with or without a capital letter) or by *a god.*" See *Plato and His Contemporaries* (London, 1949), p. 149.

17 Statements of the kind found in the *Laws* cited above (p. 6, n.2) would seem to confirm this opinion.

the world.[18] This interpretation, they believe, is confirmed by the fact that the formative functions first assigned to the Demiurge are later attributed to a host of lesser deities.[19]

Whether one can appeal to the authority of Aristotle in support of this interpretation on the basis of the criticisms, offered in the *Metaphysics* and in other works, of the Demiurge as a primary source of motion, is perhaps questionable; for he does not dismiss him specifically as a symbolic or mythical figure, although the way in which he treats him might be thought to imply something of this kind.[20] He simply rejects him as being in any way capable of causing motion in the world, and therefore often speaks as though he did not exist;[21] for example, in criticizing the supposed beginning of the universe described in the *Timaeus,* he avoids making any reference to this god of Plato,[22] and in another passage he says that no one has said anything about the (motive) cause of becoming,[23] adding that "those who believe in the

18 See F. M. Cornford, *op. cit.,* pp. 37-38, and G.M. Grube, *op. cit.,* pp. 169, 177. For the same opinion see F. Copleston, *A History of Philosophy* (Westminster, 1948), vol. I, p. 249; Cl. Piat, *Platon* (Paris, 1906), pp. 156-157; U. von Willamowitz, *op. cit.,* vol. I, pp. 598 ff. Other interpreters, however, deny that the Demiurge is mythical. See, J.B. Skemp, *The Theory of Motion in Plato's Later Dialogues* (Amsterdam, 1967), p. xv, and A.E. Taylor *Plato, The Man and His Work* (Edinburgh, 1926), p. 442.

19 See F. M. Cornford, *op. cit.,* pp. 38, 280: H. Cherniss, *Aristotle's Criticism of Plato and the Academy* (Baltimore, 1944), vol. I, p. 608; G.M. Grube, *op. cit.,* p. 169; U. von Willamowitz, *op. cit.,* p. 260. Such an interpretation is dismissed by other interpreters. See, for example, P.E. More, *op. cit.,* p. 201.

20 See Cherniss' account, *op. cit.,* pp. 609 ff.

21 In one passage of the *Metaphysics* (XII, 1071b 37 − 1072a 2) he takes Plato to task for failing to provide a cause that would account for motion in the world, noting that what Plato considers to be the cause–"That which moves itself"–which is clearly a reference to the divine as soul in the *Phaedrus,* 245C-E, and in the *Laws* X, 892A, 896A-D, must not even be mentioned. The rejection of the Demiurge as a genuine motive cause is also implied in Aristotle's remark that Plato recognized only two of the causes, the formal and material, to the neglect of the motive cause (*Metaph.* I, 988a7-11). The main reason for his dismissing the motive cause proposed by Plato is that a self-moved mover entails a contradiction, since it requires that one and the same thing be both mover and moved at the same time. (See *Physics,* VIII, 257b2 -13, and *De Anima,* I, 404a20-25). But this line of criticism does not, as Cherniss points out (*op. cit.,* p. 411), touch Plato's self-moving soul, for it is not a self-mover but a self-moving motion.

22 See *Physics,* IV, 218a33-35; VIII, 251b14-16, and *De Coelo,* I, 279b17-283b22.

23 Speaking of Plato and Leucippus: "for they say there is always movement. But why and what this movement is they do not say, nor . . . do they tell us the cause of its doing so" (*Metaph.* XII, 1071b31-35: Ross trans.).

Forms" do not explain why things participate in them.[24] The same thought is expressed where, after noting that the Forms are patterns, he asks "what is it that works looking to the Forms?"[25] Yet if the discourse of Timaeus is taken seriously, it is the Demiurge who performs this function.

The existence of a supreme god for Plato can also be questioned on the grounds that when he undertakes to establish the existence of the divine, as he does in the *Phaedrus*[26] and in the *Laws*,[27] it is always the existence of a plurality of gods that is demonstrated.[28] The reasoning in the *Phaedrus* does not aim primarily to prove that there are gods but that souls are immortal. Yet in so doing it makes clear that souls are the ultimate and ungenerated source of movement in the universe, because "it is only the self-moving which, being constant in its own nature, never ceases to be in motion, and which, moreover, is the fount and origin of everything else that moves." And some of these souls are obviously gods, since "It is the soul in all its forms," that is, both human and divine, of which Socrates treats,[29] and it could only be through the destruction of the divine in Plato's opinion, as the argument concludes, that "the whole heaven and all coming-into-being within it must collapse and come to a standstill."[30] And any doubts that the gods are souls are laid to rest in the light of what is said in later dialogues. In the *Timaeus,* for example, the Demiurge and lesser gods clearly possess intelligence,[31] and this, as is frequently noted, can only exist in soul.[32] The same

24 *Metaph.* XII, 1075b17-20; see also VIII, 1045b8-9.

25 *Ibid.* I, 991a22-23; XIII, 1079b26-27.

26 *Phdr.,* 245C ff.

27 *Laws* X, 893B ff.

28 Remarks to this effect are made at the beginning of the demonstration in the *Laws* (893B): "Come, then, and if we are ever to call upon the Gods, let us call upon them now . . . to come to the demonstration of their own existence." See also Cleinas earlier question: "But is there any difficulty in proving the existence of the gods?" (885E)

29 *Phdr.,* 245C.

30 *Phdr.,* 245E.

31 The Demiurge is described as "taking thought" (30B), and what he produces as "the works of intelligence" (47E).

32 See *Tim.,* 46D; *Phil.,* 30C, and *Soph.,* 249A.

conclusion is inescapable in the light of the discussion in the *Laws* where the argument from motion is given more comprehensive treatment.[34] Here "error of the true meaning of the gods" is identified with ignorance of "the nature and power of soul," and the souls under discussion there are unequivocally said to be gods.[35]

As persuasive as these arguments may appear to be, they have not dissuaded those for whom Plato's recognition of a supreme deity, envisioned at least as a divine artisan—and this is the more popular view—is or seems to be beyond a reasonable doubt.[36] Plato speaks on several occasions of such a god, it is pointed out, and in such a way that he cannot be merely written off as a symbol of the gods as a whole.[37] In the *Timaeus* he is clearly distinguished from the other gods, since he is by nature ungenerated whereas their existence and perpetuity are contingent upon his will.[38] He is referred to again in the *Politicus*. Here it is claimed that "there are not two gods that make the world go round, but only one," and this external divine power—the Maker,

---

[34] *Laws* X, 893B-899D. The argument from motion is complemented by appeal to universal consent, and to the order found in the universe.

[35] *Ibid.*, 891E-892A; see also 899C.

[36] The Demiurge is Plato's god according to the following: E. Brehier, *A History of Philosophy: The Hellenic Age* (Chicago, 1963), p. 124; V. Brochard, *Études de philosophie ancienne et de philosophie moderne* (Paris, 1926), p. 97; R.S. Brumbaugh, *The Philosophy of Plato for Modern Times* (New York, 1966), ch. 2; J. Burnet, *Greek Philosophy, Thales to Plato* (London, 1920), pp. 189 ff.; 273 ff.; R.G. Collingwood, *An Essay in Metaphysics* (Oxford, 1962), p. 36; I. M. Crombie, *op. cit.*, pp. 274-376; R. Demos, *op. cit.*, p. 118; J. K. Feibleman, *op. cit.*, ch. V; G. François, *op. cit.*, pp. 295 ff.; P. Friedländer, *Plato* (New York, 1954), pp. 198-201; E. Gilson, *God and Philosophy* (Hartford, 1941), ch.1; W.K.C. Guthrie, *The Greeks and Their Gods* (Boston, 1954), pp. 305-351; P.E. More, *op. cit.*, ch.V; J. Owens, *A History of Ancient Western Philosopy* (New York, 1959), pp. 235-237; 247-248; W.D. Ross, *Plato's Theory of Ideas* (Oxford, 1951), p. 238; P. Shorey, *What Plato Said* (Chicago, 1933), p. 349; J.B. Skemp, *op. cit.*, pp. 65 ff.; A.E. Taylor, *op. cit.*, pp. 441-442; W. Windelband, *History of Philosophy* (London, 1901), p. 130.

[37] See, for example, the comments of G. François, *op. cit.*, p. 301; P.E. More, *op. cit.*, p. 201; J. Owens, *op. cit.*, p. 248; W.D. Ross, *op. cit.*, p. 238; J.B. Skemp, *op. cit.*, p. xii.

[38] *Tim.*, 41A: "When all the gods had come to birth . . . the author of the universe addressed them in these words: Gods, of gods whereof I am the maker and of works the father, those which are my own handiwork are indissoluble except with my consent."

Father of the world, Orderer of all, and the Pilot of the universe, as he is variously called—is the one from whom the world received life and immortality, and all that was good in it,[39] as it does in the *Timaeus*. Allusions to this divine craftsman are also made, it is believed, in the *Republic*, where Socrates speaks of "the artificer of the senses,"[40] and of "the maker of the heavens and the stars."[41] The *Sophist* contains a similar reference to a world-forming god, who is thought to be he.[42] And the "cause" singled out in the *Philebus* as the ultimate source of things, which is described as "a marvellous intelligence and wisdom," is called maker and demiurgos.[43]

Whether these statements provide adequate evidence to settle the issue definitively may well be a matter of dispute, although it is difficult to see how some of them could be understood to refer to anything else than a singular and supreme deity. However, the fact that this god is mentioned on so few occasions, with such marked reserve, and appears, with the exception of the *Philebus*, in the context of myth, which Plato frankly admits is fiction mixed with some degree of truth,[44] makes it difficult to draw any hard and fast conclusions. And the fact, too, that he omits giving any formal argument, along the lines proposed by later writers, to show that an absolutely primary source of becoming, a first mover, which the Demiurge appears to be, is necessary, only adds to the difficulty, although something of this kind might be

39 *Polit.*, 273AD. The inferior deities are also contrasted here with the supreme power: "All the inferior deities who share the rule of the supreme power . . . let go the parts of the world under their control" (272E).

40 *Rep.*, VI, 507C.

41 *Ibid.*, VII, 530A.

42 *Soph.*, 265C.

43 *Phil.*, 26E; 28D; 30C.

44 Attention is drawn to this in several dialogues. See, for example, *Republic*, II, 337A; *Phaedo*, 114D; *Meno*, 86B. On this point note especially the passage in the *Timaeus*, 29D: "If, then, Socrates, among the many opinions about the gods and the generation of the universe we are not able to give notions which are altogether and in every respect exact and consistent with one another, do not be surprised. Enough if we can adduce probabilities as likely as any other."—See P. Friedländer's comments on the role of myths in Plato, *op. cit.*, pp. 179-209.

thought to be implied in the discussion in the *Laws.*[45]

There seems, however, to be no reason why Plato should not have recognized a unique and highest deity in some form even from the beginning of his career,[46] or at least have contemplated the possibility of his existence, since the idea of such a deity was not by his time totally foreign to Greek thought. For want of sufficient evidence it would be idle to try to make a case for the influence that some of his predecessors had or may have had on the formation of his theological views, but it is worth noting that some of them were already exponents of the very theses about the divine which are often found in the dialogues. Xenophanes, for example, openly objected to the popular anthropomorphic representation of the gods, and to the attributing to them of activities which are infamous and shameful.[47] He also combatted pure polytheism and supported the conception of a unique, supreme, eternal, and immutable god, who is exempt from every imperfection.[48] A similar position was maintained by Socrates, according to Xenophon, who credits him with a conception of the divine which he appears to consider original, for he tells us that while others commonly spoke of god or of the divine in a collective sense, Socrates posited a supreme deity, who is concerned with the general direction of the universe and allots tasks of a secondary nature to subordinate divinities.[49] Inasmuch as these doctrines were known to Plato and so strongly resemble

45 In *Laws,* X, 987C, Plato speaks of "the best soul," which "takes care of the world and guides it along the good path." And in Book VII, the Athenian says: "Men say that we ought not to enquire into the supreme God and the nature of the universe, nor busy ourselves in searching out the causes of things, and that such enquiries are impious: whereas the very opposite is the truth" (821A).

46 E. Zeller is of this opinion with regard to the Good: "The Idea of the Good was identified by Plato both in its earlier and later forms with God." See *Outlines of the History of Greek Philosophy* (New York, 1955), p. 152.

47 See the fragments of his writings in K. Freeman, *Ancilla to the Pre-Socratic Philosophers* (Oxford, 1948): *Frags.* 11, 12, 14, 15, 18, 27, 34, 38, pp. 95-99. See also R. Mugnier, *op. cit.,* pp. 8-11.

48 *Frag.* 23.

49 *Memorabilia* (London, 1965; Loeb, edt.), I, 4, 14; 17; 18; IV, 3, 12; 16. See also the comments of G. François, *op. cit.,* p. 234, and of E. Zeller, *Die Philosophie der Griechen* (Leipzig, 1875), pp. 176 ff.

his own, it is difficult to imagine that they had nothing to do with the shaping of his thought. Plato could at least have had a conception of an absolute deity from the very start, although the grounds on which his existence could be established and the cosmological or ontological role that he might play would still remain to be determined. And these would be the problems which he eventually undertook to resolve along the lines that begin to appear in the later dialogues, as those who see some kind of development in his thought are accustomed to maintain.[50]

It is not impossible, then, that the Demiurge is Plato's god. Indeed, the possibility at least of conceiving him as a supreme god in the role that is literally assigned to him is one to which all parties would have to agree, whatever differences of opinion they might otherwise have; for the idea of a primary cause that is responsible for the order and motion observable in the world is not self-contradictory. Assuming, then, for the sake of argument, that the Demiurge is to be understood in this way, is he or is he not one and the same as the God recognized by Christian writers?

The answer to this question on the part of those who adhere strictly to the account given of the Demiurge in the *Timaeus*, and refuse to confuse him with the Good of the *Republic*, is generally in the negative. That there are many respects in which this divine artisan appears to be indistinguishable from the Christian God is readily admitted.[51] For like the latter he is described not only as a personal and provident god on whose mind and will the visible universe as an ordered system of things in motion ultimately depends, but as one who supposedly brings it into being at some

50 Scholars are not always in agreement, however, on the course and outcome of such development. See P. Bovet, *op. cit.,* pp. 177-179; G. Grote, *Plato and Other Companions of Socrates* (London, 1975), pp. 249-251; G. M. Grube, *op. cit.,* p. 158; W.D. Ross, *op. cit.,* pp. 225-245; J.B. Skemp, *op. cit.,* ch. 1; F. Ueberweg, *History of Philosophy* (Berlin, 1926; trans. Morris), I, p. 116; E. Zeller, *op. cit.,* p. 148.

51 The similarities are such that some early Christian writers thought it possible that Plato had become acquainted with the Scriptures on his visit to Egypt. See St. Augustine, *De Civitate Dei* (New York, 1948; Dods trans.), VIII, 11, p. 332, and St. Justin, I, *Apology,* lix, in *The Anti-Nicene Fathers* (New York, 1925-1965), I, p. 182. (This edition will be referred to hereafter simply as AN.)

remote moment in the past.[52] He is also said to be supremely good and perfect, and it is because he is such, and thus the best of causes, that the world was formed by him.[53]

Such similarities, however, are usually judged to be merely superficial. What is distinctive about the Christian God is that He is one, Being itself, and the sole cause of everything else, which He calls into existence from nothingness, and nothing of this kind, it is claimed, can be attributed to the Father of Plato's world. He is not, for one thing, a single god, notwithstanding his uniqueness and supremacy, but one god among many, and thus quite different from the Christian God, to whom the title divine by right exclusively belongs.[54] Neither can he be said to be creative in the strict sense in which that term has come to be used, unless one wants to ignore some of the points that Timaeus is concerned to make, or to interpret them in a way that runs counter to their obvious meaning. Conceived along lines analogous to those of a human craftsman, as he usually is in the *Timaeus* and in other dialogues in which he reputedly appears, he is primarily a mover or generator. For just as the human artisan produces his effects by informing a preexistent matter in likeness to an intelligible model or pattern, so also does the Demiurge, looking to the Ideas, the eternal model, fashion a world by taking over and giving order to something that is "in discordant and unordered motion."[55] But to produce something out of something already given is not an *ex*

---

52 For the description of the Demiurge, see *Tim.*, 28B-30B.

53 See *Tim.*, 29A: "For the world is the best of things that have come to be, and he is the best of causes." It is also the best because of the model after which it is patterned: "For the god, wishing to make this world most nearly like that intelligible thing (i.e., the "Living Creature") which is best and in every way complete, fashioned it as a visible living thing" (*Ibid.*, 30CD). The emphasis placed here, and in other passages, on the goodness of the Demiurge and his model (the Ideal world) have led some to identify him with the Good and to make the Ideas his personal thoughts.

54 Some writers have tried to make Plato a monotheist. B. Russell, for example, claims that there is only one God in Plato—the Good. See his *History of Western Philosophy* (New York, 1964), p. 5. So also does G. Murray: *Five Stages of Greek Religion* (New York, 1925), p. 92. And A.E. Taylor often speaks in this way. See the comments on Taylor by E. Gilson, *The Spirit of Medieval Philosophy* (New York, 1925), p. 430, and those of F.M. Cornford, *op. cit.*, pp. 34-35.

55 *Tim.*, 30A.

nihilo activity.[56] And neither therefore is he omnipotent, as the creative God is understood to be, since he is described as making things in such a way as to be "as good as possible,"[57] implying that his causal power is restricted by something other than himself, that is, by Necessity, the intractableness of the precosmic stuff out of which the body of the universe is made. "For the generation of this universe was a mixed result of the combination of Necessity and Reason," with Reason persuading Necessity but never fully subordinating it.[58]

It might be objected that this commonly accepted account fails to consider Timaeus' remark at the start of his discourse on the world's origin, where, in answer to the question whether the world "has always been without any source of becoming, or has come to be starting from a beginning," he says that "It has come to be,"[59] which seems tantamount to admitting that it initially received existence and thus was created in the strict sense. But this interpretation, as Cornford, More, and others have so aptly noted, misses the real point at issue, since it is not a question here of any absolute beginning of the world, but of the need of a "source of becoming," that is, of a cause or principle of the continuous coming into being and passing away of mutable things, as the text itself clearly indicates.[60] And this process would have to be

56 Most scholars who consider the Demiurge to be Plato's god deny that he is creative. On this point see the remarks of R. S. Brumbaugh, *op. cit.,* pp. 118, 128; J. Burnet, *op. cit.,* pp. 273-274; F. M. Cornford, *op. cit.,* pp. 35-36; R. Demos, *op. cit.,* p. 106; G. Grube, *op. cit.,* p. 164; W. Guthrie, *op. cit.,* p. 128; P.E. More, *op. cit.,* pp. 139-140, 203; J. Owens, *op. cit.,* p. 235.

57 *Tim.,* 30B; 46C.

58 *Tim.,* 48A. The same point is also made in the *Laws,* VII, 818B: "not even God himself can fight against necessity."

59 *Tim.,* 28BC. A passage in the *Sophist* (265C), in the English translation, would also seem to indicate that for Plato the divine can be credited with a genuinely creative activity. Speaking of the various things found in the world the Stranger asks, "shall we say that they come into existence—not having existed previously—by the creation of God, or shall we agree with the vulgar opinion about them?" See B. Jowett's translation, *op. cit.,* Vol. II, p. 276.

60 On the ambiguity of the word to become *(gignomai)*, see the observations of F.M. Cornford, *op. cit.,* pp. 24-26; P.E. More, *op. cit.,* p. 167, n.1; and J. B. Skemp, *op. cit.,* pp. iii-iv, 65.

perpetual, notwithstanding the fact that the various orders of things composing the world are described as coming to be in temporal succession, following an initial act on the part of their producer.

Timaeus' story, in short, is not to be received as a historical account, even though some modern interpreters and some of the ancients believe that it should be taken in this way. Aristotle, for example, takes the story literally to mean that the universe and time came into being at some moment, and he rejects this as an error on Plato's part, since in his opinion motion and time are eternal.[61] However, if the opinion generally subscribed to by later Platonists means anything, Aristotle misunderstands Plato's position. From what they have to tell us, Plato's universe is of infinite duration, and the description of it as having a beginning was employed by him merely for the purpose of exposition, without his ever supposing that it came into existence.[62] This explanation, first proposed by Xenocrates,[63] was commonly accepted by the Neoplatonists. Proclus, citing Porphyry and Iamblichus, states the case for Plato in this way: "They say that Plato desiring to exhibit the Maker's providence descending into the universe, the government of reason and the presence of the soul, and all the great benefits these confer on the cosmos, first contemplates the whole bodily frame by itself in its disharmony and disorder, so that you may see also by itself the order due to soul and to the dispositions of the creator, and distinguish the nature of the bodily in itself from the nature of the created order. The cosmos itself exists everlastingly; but the discourse

61 What Aristotle has to say on the subject, however, is confusing. In the *De Coelo* (280a 28-32) he maintains that Plato considered the universe to be generated, and he cites the *Timaeus* to that effect. And again in the *Physics* (251b 14-16) he says that Plato generates time for he makes it simultaneous with the universe, which he describes as having come to be. In the *Metaphysics* (1071b 32), on the other hand, he claims that Plato said that motion always existed. For a criticism of Aristotle's interpretation of Plato see H. Cherniss, *op. cit.,* pp. 414-431.

62 Aristotle recognizes this explanation, although he attributes it to the Platonists and not to Plato. See *De Coelo,* 279b 33.

63 For an account of Xenocrates position see Plutarch, *De Animae Procreatione in Timeo,* 1013b ab – 1014e.

distinguishes that which becomes from its maker and introduces in temporal order things which co-exist simultaneously, because whatever is generated is composite.[64] This interpretation is certainly in line with Plato's general thought and also with the whole Greek philosophical tradition with which he remains in substantial agreement.

The acknowledgement of such differences as those just noted between the two conceptions of deity, and the refusal on the part of some of Plato's modern interpreters to identify them, re-echoes the stand commonly taken by Christian writers beginning with the Fathers, notwithstanding the claim sometimes made that their theological views are largely derived from and thus no different than those of Plato himself.[65] Nowhere when Plato's theological views are considered do they mistake Plato's god for their own, although Plato's language is often used to describe Him. St. Justin, for example, can speak of God as the Demiurge, Father, and Maker of the universe,[66] and even refer to Him as the "being beyond essence,"[67] as Plato does of the Good in the *Republic*, but the Maker of the universe, the supreme reality, whom he recognizes, is by no means the same. Plato may well be Moses speaking Greek, as Justin and others were fond of saying,[68] but the meaning behind their words was profoundly different.

For all of these writers the absolute unicity of the God revealed in the Bible stands in marked contrast to the polytheism of Plato and of Greek thinkers as a whole. And while some of these, as Athenagoras notes, have sometimes vaguely spoken in monotheistic terms, their thoughts on the subject were largely a

64 *In Platonis Timaeum Commentaria* (Amsterdam, 1965: ed. E. Diehl), i, 382. Quoted in Cornford, *op. cit.*, p. 37-38, n. 1.

65 A better case can be made for their "anti-Platonism." See E. Gilson, *History of Christian Philosophy in the Middle Ages* (New York, 1954), p. 601, n. 73.

66 He speaks of God in these terms throughout both Apologies. See *I Apology*, lix; AN., I, 186, and *II Apology*, x; AN., I, 191. See also Clement of Alexandria, *Stromata*, V, 12; AN., III, 462, and Theophilus of Antioch, *To Autolycus*, I, 4; AN., *III*, P. 191.

67 *Dialogue with Trypho*, xi; AN., I, 199.

68 *Intercession for the Christians*, vii; AN., II, 382. On this point see also St. Justin Martyr, *I Apology*, lxiii; AN., I, 184; Clement of Alexandria, *Miscellanies*, v, 12; AN., I, 76-79; and Tatian, *Address to the Greeks*, v, 4; AN., II, 66.

matter of conjecture, and cannot compare with those of the Christians, which are clear-cut and definitive. The lack of creative power in the strict sense on the part of Plato's divine craftsman is also frequently acknowledged when the account of the world's formation in the *Timaeus* is compared with the one given in the Scriptures. Only the Christian God, as Theophilus points out, is capable of producing something from nothing, Plato's demiurge, being merely a mover or generator, can only modify something already existing.[69] And if the Christian God is the sole source of things, it is because being in an absolute sense can be predicated of Him alone.[70] He is, as the anonymous author of the *Hortatory Address to the Greeks* observes, "He who is," whereas Plato's god is "that which is."[71]

Medieval Christian writers are no less explicit in rejecting any identity between the creator whom they recognize and the one projected by Plato, and their reasons for doing so are the same as those of their predecessors. St. Bonaventure and St. Thomas are two cases in point. According to both of these men, Plato's Demiurge may well be the ultimate source of things coming to be, but he does not in any sense give them existence. His abilities are limited to informing something already existing. Plato's god, as St. Bonaventure points out, is not the God of Peter, nor capable of doing the same things, since he is not the plenitude of being in virtue of which alone things can be made to be.[72] The same view is expressed by St. Thomas when he calls attention to the priority of being to motion or becoming, and the necessity of a cause of being prior to a cause of motion.[73]

69 Theophilus of Antioch, *To Autolycus,* ii, 4; AN., III, 67; ii, 9; AN. III, 74. On this same point see also Irenaeus, *Contra Haereses,* I, 2, 1; AN., I, 347; Origen, *De Principiis,* I, 1-7 (in Eusebius, *Preparatio Evangelica,* vii, 2; AN., III, 334-335).

70 See St. Augustine, *De Trinitate,* V, 2, 3: Pl. 42, 912.

71 To bring out the difference, the author presents several versions of God's description of Himself given in the Mosaic account: "I am the being." "I am He who is." "I am the really existing." *Op. cit.,* xx-xxvi; AN., I, 281-283.

72 *In Hexhaemeron,* IX, 24.

73 *Sum. Cont. Gent.,* II, 16.

In the light of all of the foregoing observations it is difficult to understand how some, in comparing the two conceptions of god, can come to the conclusions that they do; how Decharme, for example, can claim that the Demiurge is almost analogous to the Christian God,[74] and how Ritter can insinuate that they are one and the same,[75] and how Taylor, in answering the question, "whether God in the *Timaeus* is quite all we mean by a creator," can maintain that the *Timaeus* gives no indication of any kind of limitation placed upon God's will by anything other than Himself. The Demiurge's supreme goodness, being the sole source of the existence of the physical world, provides sufficient justification for maintaining that Plato considered the Demiurge to be a creator properly speaking.[76] In making such claims are not these writers and others of a similar opinion simply attributing the doctrines of a later theological age to Plato? Their critics believe they are, and the evidence seems to be clearly on their side.

Attempts to visualize the Good as Plato's god,[77] and to treat

[74] P. Decharme, *La critique des traditions religieuses chez les Grecs* (Paris, 1904), p. 217.

[75] C. Ritter, *The Essence of Plato's Philosophy* (London, 1933), pp. 371-374, and *Platon,* 2 vols. (Munich, 1910-1923), II, pp. 776 ff.

[76] *Op. cit.,* pp. 442-444. The same interpretation is found in his *A Commentary on Plato's Timaeus* (Oxford, 1928), p. 70: "The physical world, then, has a maker . . . This means exactly as the dogma of creation does in Christian Theology, that the physical world does not exist in its own right, but depends on a really self-existing being, the "best *psyche*," God, for its existence."

[77] The following understand the Good in one form or another to be Plato's god: J. Adam, *The Religious Teachers of Greece* (Edinburgh, 1908) pp. 442 ff.; E. Caird, *The Evolution of Theology in the Greek Philosophers* (Glasgow, 1904), pp. 171-172; J. Chevalier, *Histoire de la Pensée: La Pensée Grecque* (Paris, 1953), p. 215; C. De Vogel, "On the Neoplatonic Character of Platonism," *Mind,* LXII, pp. 43-64; A. Diès, *Autour de Platon* (Paris, 1927), II, pp. 506 ff.; J. E. Erdmann, *A History of Philosophy* (Hull, 1869), pp. 109-119; A. J. Festugière, *L'Ideal religieux des Grecs et l'Evangile* (Paris, 1932), pp. 20-32; A. Fouillée, *La Philosophie de Platon* (Paris, 1890), II, Ch. IV; E. Gonzalez, *Histoire de la Philosophie* (Paris, 1890), II, pp. 248 ff.; M. J. Lagrange, "Platon Théologien," *Revue Thomiste,* 1926, pp. 189-218; W. Lutoslawski, *The Origin and Growth of Plato's Logic* (London, 1897), p. 525; R. Mugnier, *op. cit.,* pp. 118-142; C. Ritter, *op. cit.,* Ch. VI; L. Robin, *op. cit.,* pp. 248-252; W. T. Stace, *A Critical History of Greek Philosophy* (London, 1928), pp. 202-203; J. Souilhé, *Histoire de la Philosophie: Platon* (Paris, 1927), IV, iv, pp. 203-241; F. Ueberweg, *History of Philosophy* (New York, 1889), II, p. 116; U. von Willamowitz-Moellendorf, *Platon* (Berlin, 1920), pp. 408-409; 583; E. Zeller, *Die Philosophie der Griechen* (Leipzig, 1889), II, p. 712.

this supreme principle in such a way that it sometimes becomes indistinguishable from the Christian God, if not actually considered to be identical with Him, also run into difficulties. The principal point at issue here is whether the Good can be considered to be a god at all in characteristically Platonic terms, and this it seems necessary to deny.

In so far as it is taken to be an Idea or pure essence, following Plato's description of it in the *Republic,* there appears to be no genuine grounds on which its divinity in any proper sense can be based. In no dialogue, it is argued, does Plato explicitly state or even intimate that any Idea, including the Good, is a god,[78] nor could he have done so, considering everything that he has to say about each of them.[79] Alike inasmuch as both are eternal, immutable, and self-subsistent, they differ in their essential constitution and in the kind of causality that each exercises—an Idea being an impersonal nature or essence, whose causal role is exemplary, and a god, a person, a soul endowed with intelligence, and a motive cause responsible for cosmic order and becoming. This is not to say that Plato does not describe the Idea of the Good in terms characteristic of such a cause, since he speaks of it as "the parent of light and the lord of light in this world and the immediate source of reason and truth in the intellectual,"[80] and as being "not only the author of knowledge to all things known but of their being and essence."[81] But it would appear that these statements are not to be understood literally, unless Plato is thinking of the Good by the time of the writing of the *Republic* as a principle to which both types of causality can be attributed, as

---

78 Whenever the Ideas and gods appear together they are spoken of as distinctly different kinds of entities. See, for example, *Euthyphro,* 10A ff., *Phaedrus,* 247A-249D, and especially the *Sophist,* 248A-251A, where the gods (as souls) are assigned to the sphere of true being along with the Ideas without being equated with them.

79 According to More, the language use of God and the gods in the *Republic* "is such as to make their identification with impersonal Ideas almost a wilful perversion of Plato's plain meaning" (*op. cit.,* pp. 211-212). Against the identification of the Good or any Idea with a god, see also R. Demos, *op. cit.,* pp. 119, 123-124; E. Gilson, *op. cit.,* p. 431; G.M. Grube, *op. cit.,* pp. 152-153, 168; W. D. Ross, *op. cit.,* pp. 43-44, 78-79; P. Shorey, *op. cit.,* p. 65; J. B. Skemp, *op. cit.,* p. 115, n. 1.

80 *Rep.,* VII, 517C.

81 *Rep.,* VI, 509C.

some believe.[82] Yet if he is, there is no later confirmation of this in the *Republic* or in any subsequent dialogue, nor for that matter in any earlier one.[83]

Any claims, then, of the kind made by Stace, that "The Idea of the Good is the one supreme creator, controller, and ruler of the world," and "the final explanation of all other Ideas and of the entire universe,"[84] and by Gonzalez, who says that "For Plato, God is the absolute being, the supreme Good, creative of things,"[85] can only be accounted for on the grounds that they have been inadvertently misled by the ambiguity of some of Plato's remarks into believing that the kind of causality exercised by the Good is efficient rather than exemplary, or that it is capable of both at the same time. These two writers do not, however, maintain that the Idea of the Good is one and the same as the Christian God, although what they have to say about it could easily pass for a description of the latter. And neither do others who take the Good to be an Idea usually identify the two. The Ideal nature of the Good being recognized for what it is—the highest intelligible essence—it is not to be confused with the self-subsisting existence whom the Christian God is acknowledged to be.

The objection that the Ideal status assigned to the Good makes any claims to its divinity impossible, would seem to have little if any force, however, against the many writers who consider it to be Plato's supreme god, since it is on just the opposite assumption that they base their case. For, if the Good is not an Idea, it must be the "author," "source," and "parent" of the world in the sense of its motive or efficient cause, and this kind of causality is clearly a prerogative of the divine. The evidence on which the Good is

82 According to A. Fouillée (*op. cit.*, p. 129), the Good is both an exemplary and efficient cause (although he comes to this conclusion by identifying the Good with the Demiurge). V. Brochard (*op. cit.*, p. 130) understands the Good to be both a final and efficient cause.

83 In the *Phaedo*, 99C, Socrates rejects efficient causality (Anaxagoras' mind) in favor of the causality proper to the Ideas.

84 *Op. cit.*, pp. 202-203.

85 *Op. cit.*, II, p. 248.

thought to be other than an Idea is supposedly found in a much disputed passage in the allegory of the sun. Having described the Good as "that which imparts truth to the known and the power of knowledge to the knower," and having likened it to the sun, Socrates goes on to say that "just as the sun is not only the author of visibility and visible things, but of generation and nourishment and growth, though he himself is not generation," so too "the Good may be said to be not only the author of knowledge to all things known but of their being and essence, and yet the Good is not essence, but far exceeds essense in dignity and power."[86]

Concluding that the last words of this statement are a clear denial by Plato of the Ideal status of the Good, it has not been too difficult for some commentators to visualize it as his highest divinity in one or the other of the ways noted earlier, and, if not to conclude that it is one and the same as the Christian God, to at least treat it in such a way that any difference between the two is not always easy to discern.

This proves to be the case especially when the Good, as a principle transcending the Ideal world, is conceived as a unique Being, for in being "beyond essence" it would appear to be definable only in existential terms, that is to say, as something that simply is, and thus in being its own existence, and the source of the existence of everything else, as the *Republic* suggests, its identity with the Christian God seems to be incontestable. A.E. Taylor, among others, understands the Good in this way, for according to him "the distinction, valid everywhere else, between *essentia* and *esse, So-sein* and *Sein,*" falls away in the case of the Good, "the supreme value" on which all other existence depends,[87] and this being the case the Idea or "Form of the Good is exactly what is meant in Christian philosophy by the *ens realissimum.*"[88] He makes it clear, however, that in so identifying the Good with the God of Christianity, it is not to be understood as Plato's highest god (nor did Plato so consider it), but simply as

86 *Rep.,* VI, 509C.
87 *Op. cit.,* pp. 288-289.
88 *Ibid.*

that supreme principle of the metaphysical sphere which fully accords with what Christian thinkers mean by God when they use the term.[89]

The emphasis placed upon the Good as a purely self-subsistent mind, can also lead to its confusion with the Christian God inasmuch as He is reputed to be His own intelligence. Festugière is of this opinion respecting the Good, and though he does not equate it with the Christian God in so many words, he does remark on how closely they resemble one another in definition.[90] According to him, the Good, which is "the most divine of all that which is divine," "the first Being,"[91] and "the true God of Plato,"[92] must be "a perfect intelligence."[93] And it is obviously a self-subsistent one, since in being "beyond essence . . . it is pure existence, . . . the being whose essence is indistinguishable from its existence," and who brings things into being from non-being.[94] The line of reasoning employed by Festugière, Robin, Zeller, and others,[95] in coming to the conclusion that the Good should be interpreted as a self-existing mind, would seem to be as follows: if the Good is not an Idea, yet belongs to the intelligible order, it can only be a mind which knows the Ideas (whether as independent

---

89 Grube makes a similar observation, *op. cit.*, pp. 151-152.

90 A. J. Festugière, *L'Ideal religieux des Grecs et l'Evangile* (Paris, 1932), p. 191.

91 *Ibid.*, p. 44.

92 *Contemplation et Vie contemplative selon Platon* (Paris, 1936), pp. 264-265.

93 *Ibid.*, p. 207.

94 *Ibid.*, 263.

95 According to Robin, the Good, as a supreme being, a supreme mind (*Platon*, p. 262), is a higher kind of Demiurge than the one described in the *Timaeus (La Pensée Grecque*, p. 234). Along with the passages commonly cited in support of the present interpretation, he employs the one in the *Republic* (597B-E) where God is described as creating the Ideal bed, and presumably the Ideas as a whole; but this passage has been generally dismissed as mere humor of Plato's part. See W. D. Ross's comments, *op. cit.*, p. 235.–For others who understand the Good to be a pure self-conscious, self-subsistent mind, see E. Caird, *op. cit.*, p. 171. In his opinion the Idea of the Good is only a step from the idea of a supreme intelligence, the *nous thetos* of the *Philebus* 22C; 28D); J. Adam, *op. cit.*, pp. 442 ff.; C. de Vogel, *art. cit.*, pp. 52-53. R. Hackforth, "Plato's Theism," *Class. Quart.*, XXX, pp. 4-9) also argues that Plato's god is a pure mind, though he does not take up the question of its possible identity with the Good.–There are also some who would make the Good a purely impersonal mind. On this point see E. Zeller, *Die Phil. Griech.*, pp. 710-715, and U. von Willamowitz, *op. cit.*, p. 598: in his opinion a personal god in Plato is a fiction.

objects, or as its personal thoughts)[96] and fashions things in likeness to them. And since it is described as a cause of universal power and scope, it must be to it that Plato is referring when he speaks of a divine mind or reason that organizes and rules the world. Passages in several dialogues provide the grounds on which this reasoning is based. An allusion to the Good as an independently existing mind is supposedly found in the *Phaedrus* where the divine intelligence is described as contemplating the Ideas,[97] and again in the *Laws* where reference is made to "the dominion of mind which ordered the universe."[98] And the statement in the *Republic* in which the Good is said to be the author of the intelligible world is often adduced as evidence for this interpretation.[99] It is on certain remarks in the *Philebus,* however, that these writers principally rely in support of their position, and the one that is most commonly cited occurs in discussing the question whether pleasure or mind is the principal cause of that happy life which is the *summum bonum.* Philebus has been arguing on behalf of pleasure, and Socrates on behalf of mind, and having dismissed pleasure, which Philebus recognizes as a god, Socrates answers Philebus' gibe: "And neither is your 'mind' the good, Socrates," by saying that "it may be far otherwise with the divine mind."[100] And any doubts as to Plato's meaning in making this remark are supposedly dispelled by a later one in which "a marvellous intelligence and wisdom" rather than "unreason and chance medley" is admitted to be the "cause of no

---

96 Some interpreters understand the Ideas to be personal thoughts of Plato's god, whatever form he may be thought to take, but any attempt to assign them this role has to be rejected because of what is said in the *Parmenides* (132C) where Socrates' suggestion that perhaps they might be so considered is unequivocally rejected. On the Ideas as thoughts of god see P. Bovet, *op. cit.,* p. 160; A. Diès, *op cit.,* II, pp. 550 ff.; W. Lutoslawski, *op. cit.,* p. 525; R. Mugnier, *op. cit.,* p. 134; E. Ritter, *op. cit.,* II, 280 ff.; L. Robin, *La physique de Platon* (Paris, 1919), p. 73; A. Fouillée, *op. cit.,* p. 132; M.J. Lagrange, *art. cit.,* p. 196.

97 *Phdr.,* 247C-E.

98 *Laws,* XII, 966E. See also *Ibid.,* IX, 875CD, where genuine *nous* is said to be the ruler of everything.

99 *Rep.,* VI, 508E; 509A-C.

100 *Phil.,* 22C.

mean power which orders the months, seasons, and years."[101]

The more popular approach taken by those who would bestow divinity upon Plato's highest Idea, is to equate it with the Demiurge,[102] and this undoubtedly results in the conception of a supreme deity which can readily pass for that of the Christian God, since it combines certain ontological and cosmological features which are understood to be proper to Him alone. The identity of these two Platonic principles is thought to be clearly implied in passages of several dialogues on the understanding that, if Plato speaks of a divine artisan, or of a world-forming god who is believed to be he, as supremely good and perfect, it is only because he considers him to be the Good itself.

The passages in the *Republic* containing the account of the Good, and those in the *Timaeus* describing the Demiurge as fully good and the best of causes, provide the primary evidence on which this conclusion is based.[103] Ritter, for example, believes that what is said there leaves no question that Plato considered them to be one and the same. The highest Idea, he says, can be nothing else than God. For, since the *Timaeus* tells us that God, as supremely good, wanted everything to resemble Himself as closely as possible, He was clearly the model after which the universe was formed, and in contemplating Himself He drew from the fullness of his own being everything that He bestowed upon the world.[104]

101 *Ibid.*, 28D; 30C-E.

102 The following authors are of the same opinion on this point as those cited in the body of the article: Ch. Bernard, *Platon, sa philosophie* (Paris, 1892), pp. 285-299; A. Fouillée, *op. cit.*, p. 176; E. Hofmann, Supplement to Zeller, *Die phil. griech.*, II, 1, pp. 1098-1105; W. Lutoslawski, *op. cit.*, p. 525; P.M. Schuhl, *L'oeuvre de Platon* (Paris, 1933), p. 161. R.D. Archer-Hind goes even further by identifying the Good with the Demiurge and with the world-soul, and thus achieves, as Cornford puts it, "an absolute spirit evolving everything out of itself by a timeless process of thought." See Archer-Hind, *The Timaeus of Plato* (London, 1888), p. 167. For Cornford's comments, see *Plato's Cosmology*, p. 163.

103 For the role assigned to the Good in the *Republic* whereby its identification with the Demiurge is thought to be implied, see Bk., VI, where it is said to be the "author" of the intelligibility of things and "of their being and essence;" and Bk., VII, 517B, where it is "inferred to be the universal author of all things beautiful and right, the parent of light and of the lord of light in this visible world, and the immediate source of truth in the intellectual."

104 C. Ritter, *The Essence of Plato's Philosophy*, p. 372.

Diès views Plato's God in the same way, since he believes that the reference to the Demiurge as the best of the intelligibles is a clear indication of his identification with his model, the Ideal world as a whole.[105] And Ueberweg says much the same thing in noting that when Plato speaks of his world-forming deity, he intends the Good.[106] The same conclusion is presumably implied in the *Politicus* where reference is made to "an external divine power" which causes motion in the world and gives it life;[107] and also in the *Sophist* where things are said to "come into existence—not having existed previously—" by the power of God rather than by chance.[108] And the frequently cited remark in the *Philebus,* noted above, to the effect that the absolute good is a universal mind (interpreted now as the mind of the Demiurge) is made to serve the same purpose.[109]

That some of those who credit Plato with this conception of a highest divinity should speak as though it were the equivalent or near equivalent of that of the Christian God is perhaps to be expected, since their investigations would show that what has been traditionally considered to be distinctive of the latter is in fact distinctive of the former. A number of Ritter's statements indicate that he sees a profound similarity between the two conceptions (and he has been accused of confusing the two). "This demiurge appears before us," he says, "much like the transcendent Creator of the Old Testament;"[110] and later in speaking of Plato's remarks regarding divine destiny, he notes that "this is an expression of a belief in providence which resembles the Christian so much that

---

105 A. Diès, *op. cit.,* p. 554, n. 1. The reference is to *Tim.,* 36E-37A.

106 F. Ueberweg, *op. cit.,* p. 116.

107 *Polit.,* 270A.

108 *Soph.,* 265CD.

109 Other statements commonly referred to are found in *Republic* II, where god is said to be truly good "and if good, . . . not the author of all things, but of good only" (380C), and that "god and the things of god are in every way perfect" (381A); and in the *Laws,* where the perfectly good soul (if this is the way in which the Demiurge happens to be interpreted) is proclaimed to be the "lord of heaven and earth" (X, 896E), and is presumably "the supreme god . . . who has ordered all things with a view to the excellence and preservation of the whole" (X, 903B).

110 *Op. cit.,* above, p. 371.

we can scarcely be wrong if we take these two words in the sense of having the world-ruling power take a personal interest in the fate of a people, nay of an individual."[111] Lagrange, too, would appear to identify the two in one important respect at least, since he claims that Plato's Demiurge is capable of bringing things into existence from non-being.[112]

None of these interpretations of the Good, however, if their critics are correct, are acceptable, and for several reasons. For one thing, the claim that Plato denies Ideal status to the Good on the grounds that it is said to "surpass essence"—the premise on which all of these attempts to make the Good a god are initially based—is contradicted by several statements in which just the opposite state of affairs seems to be affirmed; for the Good is first of all described in the allegory of the sun as an Idea or pure essence,[113] and on two latter occasions in the allegory of the cave, following the remark regarding its supposed transcendence, it is again spoken of as an Idea: "My opinion," Socrates says to Glaucon, "is that in the world of knowledge the Idea of the Good appears last of all,"[114] and in speaking of the soul's ascent into the intelligible world, he says that it must "learn by degrees to endure the sight of being *(ousia)*, and of the brightest and best of being, or, in other words, of the Good."[115] However, if the Good is a pure essence, as Plato's final words on the subject would indicate, one may ask how the remark that it "surpasses," "exceeds," or is "beyond essence," is to be interpreted without involving Plato in a contradiction. It is admittedly not always easy to speak for Plato, but the answer to such a query seems obvious enough when the last statement cited above is taken literally, for according to what is said there, Plato simply means that the Good differs from the Other Ideas or Forms, not in kind, but in priority, perfection, and self-sufficiency, for the others depend upon it, whereas it depends

---

111 *Ibid.,* p. 374. For other examples see his *Platon,* II, pp. 771 ff.; G. Grube *(op. cit.,* p. 177) accuses him of confusing the two.

112 *Art. cit.,* p. 199.

113 *Rep.,* VI 508E.

114 *Ibid.,* VII, 517B.

115 *Ibid.,* VII, 518E.

upon nothing. Any contradiction, then, is apparent and not real. And such being the case, any attempts to conceive the Good along the lines proposed by Taylor, or those proposed by other interpreters, and to bring it into line in one way or another with the Christian God, can only be dismissed for want of genuine evidence.

There are, moreover, formidable difficulties of a specific kind, as is often noted, in the way of making the Good a divine mind, or of identifying it with Plato's world-craftsman. To interpret the *Philebus'* statements in the way mentioned above, fails, as Cherniss points out, to take account of a subsequent passage in which any identity of the "absolute good" with mind is unequivocally denied.[116] And in the *Republic* passage the Good is not in fact said to be a mind but the cause of mind.[117] The principal obstacle, however, to treating the Good in this way, is that mind, whatever form it takes, belongs to soul, and lays no claim to independent existence.[118] On this score, then, any visualization of Plato's god such as that proposed by Festugière and others of the same opinion, and any resemblance, weak or strong, that might thereby appear to exist between him and the Christian God, have to be dismissed as purely illusory.

The view that the Good is one and the same as the Demiurge appears to be no less inadmissable than any of the others which commit Plato to acknowledging its divinity, because it is not, properly speaking, an Ideal entity at all. This premise, as its critics seem to have clearly shown in the light of Plato's text, must be taken to be a pure assumption for which there is no corroborative evidence, or none that has been discovered to date. So long as the Good is understood to be an Idea or Form, and the Demiurge a god, and this he can hardly be denied to be, there is no way in which they can be reconciled as two sides of the same being, or

116 *Op. cit.,* p. 605. The reference is to *Phil.,* 672A: "The claims both of pleasure and mind to be the absolute good have been entirely disproved in this argument, because they are both wanting in self-sufficiency and also in adequacy and perfection."

117 *Rep.,* VII, 517E.

118 See *Phil.,* 30C; *Tim.,* 30B; 46D; *Soph.,* 249A.

one made the symbol of the other, as has sometimes been suggested. Both belong to the sphere of "true being," but this does not entail their being equated, nor does the argument, commonly employed, that their identity is implied in Plato's describing the Demiurge as good and perfect in the highest degree succeed in proving this to be the case, since this turns out to be nothing more than a covert attempt to make him an Idea. Plato speaks on many occasions of the goodness and perfection of the gods,[119] and of that of his divine artisan, when he makes an appearance, but this is not to say that any god is goodness *per se.* When goodness is attributed to the gods, it is adjectival rather than substantive, for according to the theory of Ideas, which Plato does not appear to have abandoned, what any god possesses, be it truth, wisdom, or goodness, he *has,* like everything else, by participation in the appropriate Form, which is something other than, and perhaps even superior to, him.[120] The Good, then cannot be the Demiurge, nor can either of them be identified with the Christian God. For He is not an Idea any more than a Platonic god is, and He cannot be equated with the Demiurge, since the latter, if the theory of participation holds true, can only be admitted to *have* being and goodness, whereas He is Being and Goodness *per se,* eternal and underived.

A SELECT BIBLIOGRAPHY

Cherniss, H., *Aristotle's Criticism of Plato and the Academy.* Baltimore, Maryland: The Johns Hopkins Press, 1944.
Feibleman, J.K., *Religious Platonism.* London: Allen and Unwin, 1954.
Festugière, A.J., *Contemplation et Vie contemplative selon Platon.* Paris: J. Vrin, 1936.
Foster, M.B., "Christian Theology and the Modern Science of Nature," *Mind,* XLIV, pp. 439 ff.

119 For references to the goodness of the gods see the *Phaedo,* 63C, and the *Republic,* II, 379A-381C.
120 On this point see *Phdr.,* 249CD: the realm of "true being" is pictured here as that wherein "God abides, and beholding which He is what He is."

Gilson, E., *God and Philosophy*. New Haven, Connecticut: Yale University Press, 1941.

Grube, G.M., *Plato's Thought*. Boston, Massachusetts: Beacon Press, 1958.

Hartshorne, C., *Philosophers Speak of God*. Chicago, Illinois: University of Chicago Press, 1953.

Lagrange, M.J., "Platon Théologien," *Revue Thomiste*, IX (1926), pp. 285-297.

More, P.E., *The Religion of Plato*. Princeton, New Jersey: Princeton University Press, 1921.

Mugnier, R., *Le sens du mot THEIOS*. Paris: J. Vrin, 1930.

Ritter, C., *The Essence of Plato's Philosophy*. Trans. by A. Alles. New York: Russell and Russell, 1968.

Roberts, A. – Donaldson, J. (eds.), *The Anti-Nicene Fathers*. New York: Charles Scribner's Sons, 1925-1965.

Skemp, J.B., *The Theory of Motion in Plato's Later Dialogues*. Amsterdam, Holland: A.M. Hakkert, 1967.

Taylor, A.E., *Plato, The Man and His Work*. London: Methuen, 1960.

CHAPTER XIV

ARISTOTLE ON GOD

Joseph Owens, C.Ss.R. *

The puzzling nature of Aristotle's reasoning about God has received considerable attention throughout the past century. The initial difficulty is quite general. For the ancient Greeks the notion of God was predicative.[1] The pagan and polytheistic mentality of the classical Hellenic world could not be expected to locate the notion of God in a unique being, and in that way forestall its use as a predicate for any other subject. God has to be approached in their writings as an object common to many instances, quite as the notion of man is common to an indefinite number of individuals. The notion of God, one must stress, is not to be restricted to a single instance alone when it is found in an ancient Greek writer.

Even this type of caution, however, turns out to be insufficient in the case of Aristotle. Not only is the predicate "God" applied by him to different subjects, but the notion itself as predicative is found to take on different meanings as it is used in turn for

*Professor of Philosophy at the Pontifical Institute of Mediaeval Studies, Toronto, Canada.

1 On this topic, see Werner W. Jaeger, *The Theology of the Early Greek Philosophers* (Oxford: Clarendon Press, 1947), p. 173. The question of capitalizing the word "God" when used in the Greek sense, and especially when it occurs in the plural, is a delicate one. At present the common usage still seems to capitalize the term in the singular, but to employ lower case for the plural. This insinuates the difference between Judeo-Christian monotheism and pagan polytheism, and makes a philosophical discussion of the Greek notion of God difficult. In the Greek setting no sharp difference of nature should be implied between the meanings of the term in the singular and in the plural. Accordingly, in the present paper the term will be capitalized in both singular and plural, as less offensive to prevailing usage and mentality than lower case in the singular. But the capitalization in the singular does not imply that in Aristotelian texts the nature of the Judeo-Christian God is meant.

provident divinities, for the stars, for separate or entirely immaterial and supersensible substances, and, from particular viewpoints, for men. Accordingly "God" in Aristotle has been regarded as a notion having various levels,[2] a notion with a primary instance set apart from other instances,[3] or as a notion that exhibits inconsistency. In a word, the notion "God" in the Stagirite's writings would appear to bear the usual marks of an Aristotelian equivocal. Like "being" or "good," the notion "God" seems to have in this way markedly different meanings, even though the meanings may be related to one another or to a common primary instance.[4]

There need not be anything surprising in this apparently polyvalent bearing of the notion "God" in Aristotle. The situation is quite general with key metaphysical notions in the Stagirite's works. Accordingly, it is to be expected in the present context, if God is with him a genuine philosophical object having metaphysical implications. Should this turn out to be the case, the notion "God" has to be approached in his writings with all the caution required in dealing with multivalent objects. What holds of the notion when predicated in one sense need not be true when it is used in its other meanings, any more than the aspect of inherence as found in accidents need be present in the notion of being as applied to substance. This would mean that one cannot infer without further ado the presence, in a particular sense, of characteristics present in other senses. From texts asserting that God does things, or knows things other than himself, one cannot

---

2 See synopsis in Walter Potscher, *Strukturprobleme der aristotelischen und theophrastischen Gottesvorstellung* (Leiden: E.J. Brill, 1970), pp. 65-68. The conceptual *Schichten* (p. 66.13-14,20) have to be distinguished from proposed chronological *Entwicklungsstufen.*

3 I.e., separate substance is "der Gott schlechtin und damit als erster Gott auftritt"–Hans Joachim Krämer, *Der Ursprung der Geistmetaphysik* (Amsterdam: P. Schippers, 1964), p. 131. On Krämer's conception of the other separate substances as *Momente* of the first, see *ibid.,* pp. 170-171.

4 A discussion of the alleged phenomenon of inconsistency, hesitation, vacillation, ambiguity and contradiction in Aristotle's basic philosophical concepts may be found in my study *The Doctrine of Being in the Aristotelian Metaphysics,* 2nd ed. (Toronto: Pontifical Institute of Mediaeval Studies, 1963), pp. 107-135.

straightway conclude that separate substance is an efficient cause or has knowledge of what goes on in the sensible universe. Rather, one would have to show first that the notion "God" was being used in the same sense in both cases. If in each case the sense of the notion is partially different, the reasoning cannot be cogent until it is shown to follow strictly from an aspect in which both senses agree in some proportional or relational manner.

Even with these preliminary cautions about God as subject and predicate admitted, however, the approach to the topic in Aristotle today is still complicated by centuries of Judeo-Christian tradition. A glance at the discussions from the German controversy in the last quarter of the nineteenth century to the recent (6th) Aristotelian symposium at Cerisy-la-Salle in France,[5] will show readily enough that the participants are governed to a large extent by the traditional Western notion of God. In back of their problems lies the concept of the deity found in the Bible or the Christian creeds. The maker of heaven and earth, the supreme being who knows and cares about what goes on in the world, the ultimate arbiter before whom one is in conscience responsible for one's actions, the recipient of a deeply religious cult and devotion—all this seems involved in the notion of God that interests the modern commentators as they approach the Aristotelian text. They seem bent on asking whether or to what extent this notion is found in the Aristotelian reasoning and conclusions. They disagree sharply in their answers, but they leave little doubt about their concern with the issue from this particular angle.

Correspondingly the centuries of Scholastic interest in Aristotle's philosophy about God have manifested a frankly

---

5 To be published under the title "Recherches sur la metaphysique d'Aristote." On the nineteenth century German discussions, see Anton Bullinger, *Aristoteles und Professor Zeller in Berlin* (Munich: Ackermann, 1880), pp. 39-58; Franz Brentano, "Über den Creationismus des Aristoteles," *Wien. Sitzungsberichte,* Phil.-hist. Classe, 101.X (1882), pp. 95-126; Eugen Rolfes, *Die aristotelische Auffassung vom Verhaltnisse Gottes zur Welt und zum Menschen* (Berlin: Mayer & Müller, 1892), pp. 1-9; Konrad Elser, *Die Lehre des Aristoteles über das Wirken Gottes* (Münster: Aschendorff, 1893), pp. 19-31, 85-117, 153-167.

apologetic motif. The Stagirite's reasoning was assessed in terms of its ability to provide a philosophical demonstration for the existence and nature of the God accepted on faith by Jews, Christians, and Moslems. For Aquinas, demonstrations presented as taken from Aristotle lead directly to the primary movent, first cause, and supreme being that all call God.[6] With John Duns Scotus there are reservations about the ability of the Aristotelian reasoning to attain the notion of a God whose omnipotence extends immediately to all things.[7] Suarez, noting the thorough-going dependence upon the eternity of the world in the Aristotelian argument, maintains that it cannot reach even an immaterial movent, not to speak of an uncreated substance.[8] The Neoscholastics tended quite generally to look upon the pure actuality reached by Aristotle as identical with the infinite God of Christian revelation.[9] The interest throughout focuses upon the extent to which Aristotle's reasoning can be used to. establish philosophically the existence and nature of the Judeo-Christian God.

From these observations there emerges the conclusion that today one may not expect to find the problem of God in Aristotle approached with the same detachment that would prevail, for instance, in a scrutiny of his tenets on the parts of animals. One

---

6 See Aquinas, *Contra Gentiles,* I, 13. Here the procedures by way of motion, efficient causes, and grades of being are attributed to Aristotle. Two ways by means of motion, and the way by efficient causality, are directly ascribed to the Stagirite. On the grades of being, Aquinas (*CG,* I 13, Potest etiam) is more cautious. He states merely that the argument can be gathered from the words of Aristotle in the *Metaphysics* on the degrees of truth and being. In a lost work of Aristotle, however, the argument from the degrees of goodness led expressly to the divine; see *Fragments,* Ross[2], *On Philosophy,* 15,1476b13-39, especially b15,18-19-24, and 28-29 (Ross, *The Works of Aristotle,* XII, pp. 87-88). Simplicius, in quoting the passage, placed its background in Plato's *Republic.* The argument is developed in Augustine (*De Lib. Arbit.,* II, pp. 3-17) against the general Platonic background. In Aquinas, however, it receives its cogency from the role of existence as a distinct and participated actuality.

7 "Concedo ergo, quod Aristoteles secundum sua principia negaret Deum multa posse immediate causare . . . " *Quodl.,* VII, p. 26; ed. Vivès, XXV, p. 304. Cf. VII, 12, pp. 293-294.

8 *Disputationes Metaph.,* XXIX, pp. 1, 7; ed. Vives, XXVI, p. 23a.

9 E.g., Josef Gredt, *Elementa Philosophiae Aristotelico-Thomisticae* (7th ed. Freiburg i. Breisgau: Herder, 1937), II, pp. 203-204, 211-212.

might like to approach the problem in just that way, but in the actual situation it is not done. In any attempt to do so one would not be meeting the questions that would keep arising in one's audience or readers, and one would be continually leaving oneself open to misunderstanding. Complete abstraction from the circumstances in which one is writing is accordingly not desirable even though it were achievable. The writing in this case is directed towards readers who have learned to think against a background in which the notion "God" is generally taken to be that of Judeo-Christian tradition. They have been saturated with this notion in the "death of God" controversy and in the philosophical discussions of recent years on the ontological and cosmological arguments. The use of the notion outside this context is strange and, one might say, unconvincing. The extraneous use, moreover, tends to be taken without much seriousness. To treat of a star or a planet as a God, for instance, requires mental effort. Men, after all, have walked on the moon and brought pieces of its surface back for our museums. To regard noted figures, even presidents of the United States, as becoming Gods would seem rather ludicrous when one recalls what was said by opponents in election campaigns. To see the notion of God in an intelligence completely wrapped in self-contemplation and utterly unaware of what is going on outside itself may be asking too much of a modern mind. Yet if the texts show that these notions seriously come under Aristotle's conception of God, the effort has to be made. The notions and needs of today are to be kept in mind, but the basic task should be genuine concentration on the original meaning of the Aristotelian texts themselves. This will be the aim of the present paper.

* * *

The dominant philosophical interest in God for the contemporary era has been in the moral rather than in the cosmological order. Modern cosmologies are as a rule developed without recognition of any need of God for their completion. But Kantian stress on the role of God in the practical sphere, and

existentialist and personalist concern with human destiny, have
located the present philosophical approach to God in man's moral
life. For Aristotle the origin of moral action is choice.[10] His
ethical procedure is focused on the guidance of human choice
through intellectual and moral virtue. But towards the end of the
Eudemian Ethics there is considerable acknowledgement of divine
influence. Human choice is able to make use of the superior
causality of God:

> The answer is clear: as in the universe, so in the soul, God
> moves everything. For in a sense the divine element in us moves
> everything. The starting point of reasoning is not reasoning, but
> something greater. What, then, could be greater even than
> knowledge and intellect but God? . . . those are called fortunate
> who . . . attain the attribute of the prudent and wise—that their
> divination is speedy . . . both experience and habituation use
> God . . . and so the lucky seem to succeed owing to God . . . [11]

10 "The origin of action—its efficient, not its final cause—is choice"—*E N*, VI
2,1139a31-32; Oxford tr.). Cf. *Metaph.*, E 1,1025b22-24. Book VI of the *Nicomachean
Ethics* belonged to the *Eudemian Ethics* as Book V, and accordingly is presupposed by
the texts about to be cited.

11 *E E*, VII 14,1248a25-b4; Oxford tr. In this passage, "reasoning" *(logos)* quite
apparently refers to human reason. When the passage suggests that God may be greater
than knowledge, the meaning required by the context is that God is greater than human
knowledge. A possibly corresponding assertion in Aristotle's lost work *On Prayer*
maintained that "God is either mind *(nous)* or something beyond *(epekeina)* the
mind"—*Fragments*, Ross[2], 46,1483a27-28. Here the language is Platonic. Its notion of
God was interpreted in a strongly Neoplatonic sense in later traditions—see Anton-
Hermann Chroust, "Comments on Aristotle's 'On Prayer'," *The New Scholasticism*,
XLVI (1972), p. 311. The context in the *Eudemian Ethics*, however, does not allow this
interpretation to be transferred to its own statement, in any sense that would make the
statement imply something superior to intelligence in general instead of something
superior to human prudence. Yet the opposite conclusion is suggested at the end of a
comprehensive discussion by Jean Pépin, *Idées grecques sur l'homme et sur Dieu* (Paris:
Les Belles Lettres, 1971), pp. 249-294.

On the Platonic background for this type of divine inspiration, see *Meno*, 99BD,
and *Ion*, 534CD. Cf. Clement, *Strom.*, V, 13,88; ed. Stählin, *op. cit.*, p. 384.3-5. See also
comments of Jean Pépin, *op. cit.*, pp. 220-222. Immediate divine influence as a cause of
human happiness is proposed aporematically at *E E*, I 1,1214a23-24 and *E N*, I 9,
1099b9-18. Cf. *Ph.*, II 4,196b5-7. Against the notion of "using" the higher part of the
soul or of "ruling" the Gods, see *E N*, VI 13,1145a6-11. The verb means "are provided
with" at Ross[2] *Fr.* 188,1511b16 (Ross, 3; p. 137).

The way God imparts motion within the soul's activities is accordingly paralleled with his causality upon the universe as a whole. But neither the nature of the causality nor the nature of the divinity is specified. Final causality would suffice for this text. Earlier the *Eudemian Ethics* (VII 3, 1238b27-28) mentioned the love or friendship received by men from God, and stated (10,1242a33) that this friendship is the same as of father to son. But likewise in these passages no explanation of the way God can love men had been given, nor any indication of what was meant by "God." How human choice can "use God" remains undetermined. Would not the divine aspect of things, intuited as in the wisdom of Heraclitus (*Frs.* 32,67,114), suffice?

Some help for interpreting this text of the *Eudemian Ethics* may be had from the *De Anima*. There the "immortal and eternal" (III 5,430a23) mind, dealt with under the heading of a "part of the soul" (4,429a10), is described as the active principle *in* the soul "which is what it is by virtue of making all things: this is a sort of positive state like light; for in a sense light makes potential colours into actual colours" (5,430a15-17; Oxford tr.). The terminology, with the use of the verb "make" or "produce" (*poiein*—430a12; 15; 16; 19), suggests efficient causality more definitely than do the phrases of the *Eudemian Ethics*. But is the notion really expressed with decisive clarity? Why is the comparison made with "a state *(hexis)* like light"? Why is the "making" in the comparison qualified by the phrase "in a sense" *(tropon gar tina)*? Efficient causality is verbally asserted, and in express contrast with undergoing or passivity. But the strong sense of the notion seems dissipated. No explanation is offered about the way the separate and impassive principle can make contact with the perishable mind or perform any activity upon it. Though the separate principle is not called "God" in this passage, the epithets of divinity, namely "immortal" and "eternal," are used to describe it. It seems just as divine as the separate substances of the *Metaphysics,* which are explicitly called "God." What is said about it should accordingly be open to approach for an answer to questions about the manner in which "in a sense *(pos)* the divine element in us moves everything" (*E E,* VII 14,1248a26-27), or for an explanation how God could have love or friendship for men.

Yet no satisfactory account is found. One has to remain content with the assertions of the *Eudemian Ethics* that in human conduct God is a moving force owing to which a lucky person is successful, and that God in an unequal way has friendship to man. The causality on the part of God is still unspecified. "The divine element in us" could move everything merely by way of final causality, as far as this text from the *Ethics* requires. In fact, the *Eudemian Ethics* ends by regarding God as ruling only by way of final causality, as health governs medical science. God is to be contemplated and served.[12] Though "in us," the divine element just as in the *De Anima* is given self-sufficient status: "the perfection of God is ... in being superior to thinking of aught beside himself ... the deity is his own well-being" (*E E,* VII 12,1245b16-19; Oxford tr.) All goes as though final causality alone is being emphasized for God's influence on human affairs, and as though the good imparted in this way suffices for friendship between God and man even though God has no knowledge of those men who benefit by this friendship. The use of the term "friendship" where there is no return of love seems allowed by the *Eudemian Ethics* (3,1238b26; 29).

The *Nicomachean Ethics,* on the other hand, seems to exclude any friendship on the part of God for men.[13] But it emphasizes the service and honor due to God.[14] Intellect is regarded as the

---

12 " ... For God is not an imperative ruler, but is the end with a view to which prudence issues its commands ... What choice, then ... will most produce the contemplation of God, that choice or possession is best; this is the noblest standard, but any that through deficiency or excess hinders one from the contemplation and service of God is bad; this man possesses in his soul"—*E E,* VII 15,1249b13-21; Oxford tr. See comments by W.J. Verdenius, "Human Reason and God in the Eudemian Ethics," in *Untersuchungen zur Eudemischen Ethik,* ed. Paul Moraux & Dieter Harlfinger (Berlin: Walter de Gruyter, 1971), pp. 285-297. Verdenius argues (pp. 290-291, 294) that "God" is not identified here with the human mind, even though the human mind is regarded as "divine." However, the reason seems to lie in Greek usage rather than in Aristotelian doctrine. See *Oxford Classical Dictionary,* 2nd ed. (Oxford: Clarendon Press, 1970), s.v. "Ruler-Cult."

13 *E N,* VIII 7,1158b35-1159a5. Cf. 14,1163b15-18; IX 1,1164b5-6; and *M M,* II 11,1208b27-34.

14 *E N,* VIII 14,1163b16-18. Cf. IX 2,1165a24.

divine element in man.[15] In accord with its activity men lead a divine life.[16] In pure thinking they are most akin to God.[17] The life of God or the Gods is described as most happy and pleasant, without change and without action on anything external.[18] Nevertheless the possibility that human happiness is a gift of the Gods is proposed (*E N,* I 9,1099b11-18), and seems to be answered in the affirmative: "Nature's part evidently does not depend on us, but as a result of some divine causes is present in those who are truly fortunate" (x 9,1179b21-23; Oxford tr.). This is in full accord with the view of the *Eudemian Ethics* on the influence of the divine factor in human fortune (above, n. 11). But here the identity of the Gods in question is indicated somewhat more clearly:

Now he who exercises his reason and cultivates it seems to be both in the best state of mind and most dear to the gods. For if the gods have any care for human affairs, as they are thought to have, it would be reasonable both that they should delight in that which was best and most akin to them (i.e. reason) and that they should reward those who love and honour this most, as caring for the things that are dear to them and acting both rightly and nobly. And that all these attributes belong most of all to the philosopher is manifest. He, therefore, is the dearest to the gods (x 8,1179a22-30; Oxford tr.).

---

15 *E N,* X 7,1177a15-16. For texts from other Aristotelian works, see Pépin, *op. cit.,* pp. 223-226, with the Platonic background given on p. 225.

16 *E N,* X 7,1177b30-34. Cf. I 12,1101b24-25.

17 *E N,* X 8,1178b21-23. At VII 1,1145a23-24, a saying was quoted that "men become gods through excess of virtue." The saying is used aporematically, and in a context of epic virtue rather than of contemplation. Nevertheless Aristotle registers no marked opposition at the idea of men becoming Gods. He is also quoted (*Fr.,* Ross, 2,48,1483b15-17) by Cicero as calling man "a sort of mortal god" (tr. Ross, p. 42), and in a fragment from Iamblichus there occurs the statement "man seems a god in comparison with all other creatures" (tr. Ross, *ibid.*). But in both these statements the designation "God" is sharply qualified.

18 *E N,* VII 14, 1154b26-28; X 8,1178b8-22. For a discussion, see Pépin, *op. cit.,* pp. 229-233. Cf. *Pol.,* VII 1,1323b21-26.

The Gods that love men and exercise providence towards them seem identified in this passage with the Gods publicly recognized in Greek culture, those "thought to have" care for human affairs. They do not seem to be other than the Gods referred to (I 12,1101b18-35) as honored in the standard encomia. What is strongly emphasized, however, is their intellectual nature. Aristotle speaks as though in his own view intelligence is the outstanding characteristic of deity. For cultivating (*therapeuein*—cf. *E E,* I 12, VII 15,1249b20) and honoring (*timan*—cf. *E N,* I 12, 1101b11-1102al) intelligence he uses the same terms as for serving and revering the Gods. He groups together "the gods and the most godlike of men" as being called "blessed and happy" (*E N,* I 12,1101b23-25; Oxford tr.). In these passages he is quite obviously thinking against the background of traditional Greek cult. He is rationalizing those Gods as intelligent beings that are concerned with and provide for human affairs. He makes no attempt, however, to identify them individually with the names given them in Greek mythology. This overall picture of the encounter of men with God in their moral life is supported by occasional references in other Aristotelian works.[19] Nothing definite emerges about the nature of the Gods who exercise providence, though the texts have furnished a springboard for plunges into speculation that would make Aristotle basically a religious thinker and even a mystic. What the texts do center around, though, is intellection. Life according to this divine element in man is divine in comparison with human life, and in that way we "must, so far as we can, make ourselves immortal" (*E N,* X 7,1177b31-33; Oxford tr.).

That is the extent, then, to which one may legitimately press in Aristotle's own thought the application of the saying quoted by him in the epic context: " . . . men become Gods" (*E N,* VII 1,1145a23; see above, n. 17). There is a quite noticeable Platonic background for the Stagirite's use of terminology in stressing the

---

19 See texts cited in Pépin, *op. cit.,* pp. 218-231, and for Aristotle's attitude towards mythology and its Gods, see Pépin's comments, pp. 207-209.

kinship of man to God.[20] Yet for Aristotle himself intellection was the mark of divinity. It assured the immaterial nature that grounded philosophically the eternal and immortal character of divine beings.[21] No doubt need arise that Aristotle meant literally and in the context of his own philosophy the application of the term "divine" to the highest part of the human intellect, and likewise literally, though in a secondary sense, its application to a human life lived on the intellectual plane. But he does refrain from an unqualified use of the term "God" in reference to men. Men were sharply distinguished from Gods throughout early Greek literature. Before Alexander the Great apotheosis was not the fashion. Aristotle could accordingly give literal meaning in his own philosophical context to divinization of men through intellection without thereby being required to look upon them as becoming Gods in any current Greek sense.

One final text may be noted from the *Topics:* " . . . for even God and the good man are capable of doing bad things, . . . Moreover, a capacity is always a desirable thing: for even the capacities for doing bad things are desirable, and therefore it is we say that even God and the good man possess them; for they are capable (we say) of doing evil" (IV 5,126a34-39; Oxford tr.). The context shows that physical capacities for actions like stealing and slandering are meant. The reference seems clearly enough to bear on the epic Gods. They are paralleled with men in regard to moral conduct.

To sum up, Aristotle quite apparently recognized the civic Gods of Greece. He could, it would seem, pay them the customary public respect, acknowledge their tutelary functions, and acquiesce in prayer to them. In all this there would be less occasion for conflict with philosophical views than there was a generation or so later with Epicurus, who urged belief in the Gods

---

20 Pépin, *op. cit.,* pp. 228-229.

21 Separation from matter, the principle of change, is the characteristic of the eternal things with which primary philosophy deals (*Metaph.,* E 1,1026a10-30 E 1,1026a10-18), and also the characteristic of intellection (*De An.,* III 4, 429a24-b5).

while denying them any influence on human conduct.[22] Rather, Aristotle was able to rationalize them as intelligent beings in the context of his own philosophy. But opportunity for strictly philosophical development of the mythologically received notions was not thereby offered. So one can hardly look for further expansion of them in later Peripatetic tradition. Christian tradition drew rather upon Neoplatonic sources for philosophical development of doctrines of grace, assimilation to God, and divine friendship.[23] The occasional assertions of Aristotle about the role of deity in moral life were in fact without notable philosophical influence on subsequent Western thought.

*   *   *

Leaving the sphere of personal action for that of cosmology, one finds Aristotelian passages in which the stars are called Gods, and the visible world as a whole is regarded as in some way divine. In the *De Caelo* the observed circular movement of the heavens is shown to be a simple motion requiring location in a simple body, which accordingly is immune from generation, destruction and alteration (I 2-3,268b17-270b25). On account of this eternal nature the substance in which the everlasting motion is located is termed divine and identified with the immortal deity located in the topmost place by the traditions of both barbarians and Greeks

22 See Epicurus, *Letter to Menoeceus,* 123-124. Cf. A.J. Festugière, *Epicurus and his Gods,* tr. C.W. Chilton (Cambridge, Mass.: Harvard University Press, 1956), pp. 51-65. On Aristotle's reverence for traditional religious practice, see Ross, 2, *Frs.* 44-45,1483a15-22 (Ross, *Frs.* 14-15; p. 87); cf. Ross, 2, *Fr.* 14,1476a35-b10 (Ross, *Fr.* 13; pp. 85-86).

23 On the tradition in regard to friendship, see doctoral dissertation of Yvon Migneault, "Aelred de Rievaulx, théologien de l'amitié au XIIe siècle" (Université de Montréal, 1971), pp. 82-84; 135-136. For Aristotle, man "man partakes of the divine" (*P A,* II 10,656a7-8), and along with all animals possesses "by nature something divine" (*E N,* VII 13,1153b32).

(3,270b5-19). The heavens are looked upon as besouled.[24] The celestial activity is effortless, because perfect (II 1,284a18), in accord with the inspired mythological conceptions (b2-5). The more perfect heavenly bodies attain their end with fewer activities, the less perfect require more (II 12,292a22-b25). The first heaven moves all the other divine bodies, while each of these has also its own particular movement (292b25-293a10).

This general conception in the *De Caelo* is supported by the more developed and cogent reasoning of the *Physics*. Perceptible movement, as the starting point of the reasoning, is explained in terms of actuality and potentiality (*Ph.* III 1,201a10-11). Anything that is being moved is being moved by something. This is shown by the essential dependence of movement on its parts (VII 1,241a24-242b34), and by induction (VIII 3-4,253a22-256a3). The requirement of a previous movement to initiate any particular movement establishes cosmic motion as eternal (VIII 1,251a8-252b6). On the other hand the actuality that initiates the movement is not possessed by the moved thing, unless it be a self-movent; and even in this case the above principle requires that the movement of the self-movent be caused by an unmoved part (5,256a4-258b9). The eternal cosmic movement accordingly requires one or more eternal unmoved movents: "Since there must always be motion without intermission, there must necessarily be something, one thing or it may be a plurality, that first imparts motion, and this first movent must be unmoved. . . . Motion, then, being eternal, the first movent, if there is but one, will be eternal also: if there are more than one, there will be a plurality of such eternal movents" (6,258b10-259a8; Oxford tr.). Since the only continuous eternal movement is rotatory locomotion, this will be

---

24 *Cael.*, I 7,275b26; II 2,285a29-30; 12,292a18-21; b1-2. In spite of these explicit assertions, the tenet that for Aristotle the heavens were animate, is sometimes found denied on the ground that it is asserted only in *De Caelo* and there in a mythological setting, and that it is a product of systematization in supplying the link between the heavens as efficient movents and the separate substances as final causes. On the history of the division of opinion in Aristotelian tradition, see Harry A. Wolfson, "The Problem of the Souls of the Spheres from the Byzantine Commentaries on Aristotle through the Arabs and St. Thomas to Kepler," *Dumbarton Oaks Papers,* no. 16 (Washington: Center for Byzantine Studies, 1962), pp. 65-93.

the one motion of the primary movent, which will be located at the circumference of the universe and will be without parts or magnitude (7-10,260a20 ff.). The continued efficient causality of the heavenly bodies in every sublunar change is asserted at *De Generatione et Corruptione,* II 10,336a31-b9 and *Metaphysics,* A 5,1071a13-17.

What is the overall picture of cosmic motion given in this natural philosophy of Aristotle? The starting point is clearly observable movement, shown to be caused by a self-movent. The background is evidently enough the reasoning of Plato (*Phdr.,* 245CE; *Lg.,* X,894B-897C) that movement originates in a self-movent, which is soul. Aristotle reasons further that since the self-movent as a whole is something moved, it must be moved by one its own parts, a part that remains unmoved in imparting the motion. There are countless such principles that come into being and perish (*Ph.,* VIII 6,258b16-259a2), all unmoved movents. The reference can hardly be to anything but souls of plants and animals (cf. 9,265b32-34). The doctrine is not easy to grasp, since at first sight it would seem to regard plant and animal souls as agents in themselves, instead of taking each as the formal principle of the agent. Nevertheless, the form of an inanimate thing is not a formal principle of self-motion, while a soul is. The soul can accordingly be regarded as the unmoved origin of self-motion, even though it is not an agent in itself as with Plato. In this way Aristotle could accommodate his reasoning to the Platonic background, while at the same time having no special motive for explicitly identifying the unmoved part as soul. A self-movent has to have motion from one its parts that remains unmoved in imparting the motion. That suffices without having to explain how the soul functions as a principle of a body's self-motion.

These unmoved principles of self-movents, however, may be moved *per accidens* with the movement of the whole body, as in the case of perishable self-movents (i.e., plants and animals). The same holds for the unmoved principles of heavenly bodies whose movements are complex (*Ph.* VIII 6,259b28-31). These would be the planets. Heavenly bodies are accordingly regarded as self-movents. A primary movent, even though because of the eternally simple motion it imparts, cannot be moved even *per accidens* (b23-24); it does not seem to escape this status of part of a self-movent. All goes as though the heavens are regarded in the *Physics* as besouled, just as they were in the *De Caelo.* The unmoved movents to which the *Physics* leads are souls then, and the primary unmoved movents that are the principles of eternal motion are the souls of the heavenly bodies. These souls are consequently the source of cosmic motion by way of efficient causality.[25]

Further, in human generation the Gods along with the parents are recognized (*E N,* VIII 12,1162a4-7; cf. IX 2,1165a21-24) as "causes of being," obviously in the sense of efficient causes. This seems but an instance of the celestial efficient causality in all sub-lunar generation (*G C,* II 10,336a31-32; cf. *Metaph.,* A 5,1071a13-17). The same may be said for Aristotle's under-standing of the dictum "God and nature do nothing in vain" (*Cael.,* I 4,271a33). However, Socrates' alternative that the *daimones* may be "children of Gods" (*Rh.,* III 18,1419a11-12) is to be located rather in the background of traditional belief.

What value may be accorded the Aristotelian reasoning in this area? Its analysis of motion in terms of actuality and potentiality is correct from the viewpoint of natural philosophy, and has had enduring significance in Western philosophical tradition. It continues to be acceptable. The conclusion that motion so analyzed must be eternal, is valid, however, only where movement has to be caused by way of another movement. It was un-acceptable in the middle ages, when movement was regarded as caused originally in creation; and it does not accord with modern cosmologies. Likewise, the conclusion that the primary causes of cosmic motion are celestial souls could not be accepted by the medievals, nor is it consonant with modern knowledge of the planets and stars. But what of the more general reasoning that

---

[25] The contrast with final cause is explicit at *Ph.* VII 2,243a3-4. A discussion of the overall problem may be found in Jean Paulus, "La théorie du premier moteur chez Aristote," *Revue de Philosophie,* XXXIII (1933), pp. 259-294, 394-424. Types of soul proposed by Aristotle at the beginning of *De Anima* are those of "horse, dog, man, god" (I,1,402b7; Oxford tr.).

movement must ultimately have an unmoved movent as its primary efficient cause? In its generality this principle was retained by Aquinas and used to locate the primary efficient movent of the universe in the Christian God. By others it has been rejected as insufficient for this purpose.[26] When it is kept in its generality, however, the efforts to show flaws in Aristotle's reasoning have not proved decisive. Once movement is accepted as involving potentiality, the thing being moved cannot possess the actuality towards which it tends. This has to come from an outside source, and ultimately from something that has the actuality solely through itself. There are difficulties that have to be met, for instance how a new actuality can be brought into the universe, and how it can be imparted by one thing to another. These are real difficulties, which have to be carefully dealt with. But they leave the basic cogency of the Aristotelian principle unimpaired. The principle that whatever is being moved is being moved by something, and ultimately by an unmoved movent, remains a valued heritage in Western philosophical thought. But the unmoved movent must be located elsewhere than in a multiplicity of celestial souls, if the principle is to have permanent validity.

* * *

Finally, there is the remarkable conception of God presented in the Aristotelian *Metaphysics*. Basing itself on the eternity of cosmic motion as established in the *Physics*, the reasoning concludes that the ultimate cause of eternal movement must be something whose very substance is actuality. Potentiality present in its substance would allow for change, and would not permit it to be the ultimate ground of the eternally unchanging circular motion of the heavens. But matter is potentiality, and cannot be present in something whose substance is actuality. The ultimate causes of world motion are consequently without matter or

26 E.g., Suarez; see above, n. 8. Cf.: "Bref, la *prima via* est plutôt un acheminement vers la preuve authentique, qui commence là où la *prima via* finit"—F. Van Steenberghen, "Le problème philosophique de l'existence de Dieu," *Revue Philosophique de Louvain*, XLV (1947), p. 164.

potentiality (*Metaph.*, A 6,1071b5-22).

Aristotle's reasoning has in this way reached immaterial substance or substances. As with the unmoved movent of the *Physics,* the singular and plural seem used more or less indifferently.[27] But the celestial souls are forms of material things, the heavens. The substance they actuate is material in nature. They do not meet the conception of substance without matter, any more than any sublunar form would meet it. The immaterial causes of motion now reached are different beings, different substances, from the movents reached in the *Physics.*[28]

How they cause motion is investigated in the next chapter of Book Lambda. The eternal substance and actuality that moves the first heaven imparts motion as does the object of thought and desire, namely by way of final causality. On a principle of this kind the heavens and nature depend (7,1072a21-b14). No other kind of causality is mentioned for the immaterial movents. Nor should any of the other three types of causality be expected. Formal and material causality would be excluded by the absence of matter, while an efficient cause for Aristotle has its actuality in the *passim*[29] and accordingly presents a notion incompatible with an entirely actual substance.

The *Metaphysics* then rises to lyric tones in describing the life of this immaterial substance. The starting point for the reasoning is the life of thought that is experienced by men. It is the best life men can enjoy, even though it be only for short intervals. In the thinking so experienced, thought and the object of thought are identical. With God, the situation is still better—God is the actuality of thought, and this actuality is life (7,1072b14-28). The reasoning presupposes the notions of cognition developed in the *De Anima.* In actual cognition, whether sentient or intellectual,

---

27 *Metaph.,* A 6,1071b20-22; 8,1073a14-1074a31. Cf. *Ph.,* VIII 6,258b11; 259a7-9; 20-31; and *G C* II 10,337a17-22. Efforts to explain the use of the respective use of the singular and the plural as indicating different chronological stages in Aristotle's development have not proven very convincing.

28 See above, n. 25; also Augustinus Nolte, *Het Godsbegrip bij Aristoteles* (Nijmegen-Utrecht: Dekker & Van De Vegt, 1940), pp. 126, 172-175.

29 *De An.,* III 2,426a4-6; *Metaph.,* O 8,1050a30-31; K 9,1066a26-34 (=*Ph.,* III 3,202a13-b22).

agent and object are identical *(De An.,* III 2,425b25-426a17; 4,429a22-430a7). The "better" situation in regard to divine cognition emerges clearly enough from the entirely immaterial condition just demonstrated in the *Metaphysics* for the supreme final cause. In human cognition the forms of the things perceived and known have first to be received immaterially, and then serve as instruments for the union of the sentient or intellective subject with the object, a union in being that takes place in the actuality of cognition.[30] Effort and mental toil are involved in this type of cognition, experience testifies, and the duration is limited to comparatively short intervals. The divine substance, on the other hand, is of its very nature a form without matter. It is accordingly cognitive without presupposing any other prior activity or toil, and in consequence continues forever without the least effort or interruption.

Book Lambda of the *Metaphysics* then applies the argument from the *Physics* (VIII 10,267b17-26) to prove that separate substance has neither parts nor magnitude. The conclusion would appear sufficiently established by the already demonstrated immaterial character of separate substance. Why should a different ground be now introduced as a basis for the proof? This presents a real difficulty for readers of Aristotle today. The procedure to be expected would be that the entirely immaterial nature of separate substance precludes extension through material parts and therefore does not allow any magnitude. But would Aristotle's different procedure appear at all strange to his hearers? He has been presuming a live knowledge of the *Physics* in them all along, and has been drawing upon it without attempt at explanation or justification. Aristotle has been reasoning as though his hearers accept the tenets of the *Physics* without any hesitation. He has been basing his thought as far as possible upon what the *Physics* had already established. At the end of this chapter of Book Lambda he rapidly summarizes (7,1073a3-13) that he has made clear the existence of separate substance and that also absence of parts and magnitude has been proven for this substance. The first

30 See *De An.,* III 8,431b26-432a3. For soul as an instrument, cf. I 4,408b14-15.

conclusion had been drawn in the *Metaphysics,* but the latter had been proved in the *Physics* and is referred to as though it were well-known to the hearers. They are presumed well enough acquainted with it to see at once that it applies equally to separate substance. In a Peripatetic school *logos* this procedure is understandable, and could be considered more satisfactory and more in solidarity with the physical basis of the reasoning than an argument grounded on the new knowledge of immaterial being, something more remote from sensible cognition and presumably grasped as yet very tenuously by the hearers. There is at least no clearcut case here for seeing strict identity between the unmoved movent of the *Physics* and the separate substance of the *Metaphysics.*

The eighth chapter of Book Lambda asks about the number of the separate substances, and concludes that the number corresponds exactly to the number of original eternal movements observable in the heavens (8,1073a14-1074a17). It sees these movements arranged hierarchically under one supreme movent, making all into a single universe (1074a17-38), and it justifies the basic truth in the mythological traditions that the first substances are Gods (1074a38-b14). There can be no doubt that Aristotle is asserting multiplicity in separate substance. It is a nature that is at least able to be found in a plurality of individual beings. It is consequently something finite, for an infinite being would exclude any other infinite being and would be unique. The Aristotelian separate substance called God in the *Metaphysics* is beyond doubt a finite being.[31]

The following chapter returns to the topic of the divine intellection. Lacking any potentiality, separate substance cannot change from thinking on itself: "Clearly, then, He is thinking of that which is most divine and most honorable, and He is not changing; for change would be for the worse, and this change would then be a motion. . . . Moreover, it is clear that something

31 A discussion of this point may be found in my article "The Reality of the Aristotelian Separate Movers," *The Review of Metaphysics,* III (1950), pp. 319-337.

else would be more honorable than The Intellect, namely, the object of thought. . . . It is of Himself, then, that The Intellect is thinking, if He is the most excellent of things, and so Thinking is the thinking of Thinking. . . . It is in this manner that Thinking is the thinking of Himself through all eternity" (9,1074b25-1075a10; Apostle tr.). The conclusion in this passage is stated very definitely, but it proves to be a scandal for modern readers.[32] The notion of God who spends all eternity thinking only on himself as object, turns out to be incomprehensible to people trained in a morality that gives highest value to thought about others. Yet the Aristotelian reasoning is cogent, given the background of the *De Anima.* There (II 12,424a17-24; III 2,425b23-24; 4,429a15-430a9) human cognition, the type with which men have immediate experience, was explained through reception of forms without matter. This requires passivity, that is, potentiality for change, on the part of the knowing agent. The Aristotelian form is the cause of being, and when it is received in physical matter it makes the physical matter to be the material thing in question. When it is received in the cognitive agent, it makes the soul to be actually, and no longer just potentially, the perceptible object.[33] But in the case of separate substance this cognition of other things is impossible. Separate substance has absolutely no potentiality to receive their forms. Existing as form without matter it is cognitional according to the notion of cognition given in the *De Anima.* But the only object it can make known is itself.

The notion of God developed in the *Metaphysics* is accordingly that of a plurality of immaterial beings that, while perfect, can exercise no efficient causality on anything else and cannot even know anything other than the individual substance in which each consists. None of them can be infinite, none of them can be a creator, none can have any concern or love or providence towards men. They can be loved and desired, but cannot return the love. It

---

32 E.g., "a sort of heavenly Narcissus"—R. Norman, "Aristotle's Philosopher-God," *Phronesis,* XIV (1969), p. 63.

33 On the form as cause of being, see *Metaph.,* Z 17,1041a6-b28.

would be hard to find a highly philosophical conception of God more different from the creator of heaven and earth, who exercises loving and universal providence towards all his creatures. Small wonder that some writers have been prone to regard the Aristotelian thought as a baneful and restrictive influence on Judeo-Christian religious belief![34]

Paradoxically, however, this Aristotelian metaphysical conception of God turned out to be the greatest of all philosophical contributions to the development of Christian thinking about the divine nature. The notion of actuality without potentiality became labeled "pure actuality" in the middle ages and was regarded as identical with the "infinite ocean of being" signalized in patristic thought.[35] This was possible because actuality meant perfection, and in the Christian God all perfection without the least imperfection was found. This God could be understood philosophically as pure actuality, with only slight modification of the Aristotelian terminology. With Aquinas the basic actuality of anything whatsoever was existence. So approached, the reasoning from actuality and potentiality as found in perceptible movement led to subsistent existence as the one and only pure actuality. It was existence itself, containing within itself the existence of everything else. This "pure actuality" was accordingly infinite and unique, infinite truth and infinite goodness. Knowing itself, it knew everything contained within itself, and that meant every creature down to the smallest detail. Infinitely good, it was motivated to exercise the most loving and most finely focused providence towards all. As first cause in this order of existence, it was able to be understood philosophically as the creator of all things out of nothing, as the conserving agent that sustained all things in being, and as the being most intimately present to all things in continually imparting to them their deepest actuality,

34 E.g., "to impose on Gothic evangelical inspiration the deforming tyranny of Aristotelianism"—José Ortega y Gasset, *Man and Crisis*, tr. Mildred Adams (New York, 1958), p. 118.

35 Gregory Naz., *Oratio XXXVIII*, 9; *PG*, XXXVI, 317B. John Damascene, *De Fid. Orth.*, I, 9; *PG*, XCIV, 835B. Cf. Aquinas, *In I Sent.*, d. 2, q. 1, a. 1, ad 3m (ed. Mandonnet, I, 61); d. 8, q. 1, a. 1 (I, 194-197); *Summa Theologiae*, I, 4, 2.

their existence. From the thirteenth century on, through the influence of Scholastic thought, Aristotle's metaphysical reasoning became in this way the most penetrating philosophical tool for the Christian *fides quaerens intellectum,* for faith seeking understanding in regard to God.

* * *

Aristotle's notion of God turns out, then, like so many of his other philosophical notions, to have a number of different though commonly focused meanings. The focal point in this case seems obviously enough, and fully in accord with Greek religious and mythological tradition, to be that of eternally living and thinking substance. For Aristotle that notion finds its highest instance in separate substance, the only thing that can ultimately account for the eternity of cosmic process. In separate substance the notion of thought predominates. In this highest instance, God for Aristotle is a plurality of separate substances, each finite in character and each a thinking that contemplates itself only. None can think of anything outside itself or produce anything at all. But as final causes they give the ultimate guarantee of eternal continuity in the cosmic processes.

The stars and planets seem to be the next highest instance of deity for the Stagirite. They are regarded as besouled, as intelligent beings that eternally love and desire the perfection of the separate substances, and come as closely as they can to it by their uninterrupted circular motion. They are efficient causes eternally at work in all that goes on in the sublunar world. In this sense Aristotle may speak of the visible universe or of celestial substance as divine.

Still further down the scale there are unspecified divinities that exercise providence and show concern and love for men. They have only occasional mention in the Aristotelian texts, and do not seem to play any functional role in the Stagirite's philosophy. Men may live a divine life through the cultivation of intelligence, the divine element in them, and presumably from this angle a man may be regarded as "a sort of mortal god" (above, n. 17).

As may be readily seen, these various instances are too different in nature to allow tenets asserted for one instance to be applied without further scrutiny to the others. Because the heavens exercise efficient causality it does not follow that the separate substances do. Because the unspecified divinities are provident towards men it does not follow that the higher instances of divinity are. The common characteristics throughout the various instances seem to be intelligence and eternal duration, and through these characteristics the others have their relation to the highest instance, the separate substances. But in their special characteristics the instances differ too sharply from one another to allow conclusions based on them to be transferred from one instance to another.

Finally, great care has to be used in applying the Aristotelian reasoning to the God of Judeo-Christian revelation. The divinization of men through cultivation of intelligence offers possibilities of tranformation through the theological doctrine of grace, and the sharing of everything in the divine might be exploited in sacred theology for understanding the elevation of all things to a supernatural end. But so far the Aristotelian teaching has not been called upon for this function. Where it has been drawn upon copiously is in the metaphysical area, and in the tenet of the celestial efficient causality at work in every terrestrial and human event. But here one is not justified in reading back the Christian implications into the pagan Greek notions. The inestimable worth of the Aristotelian notions for the philosophical understanding of the Christian tenets is amply safeguarded without giving in to that confusion. It is true that Aristotle did not reach even the Christian philosophical notion of God. But that is a far cry from saying that philosophy itself cannot reason to the existence and the nature of the God known to Abraham, Isaac and Jacob. Aristotle and philosophy are not convertible terms. Christian philosophy has in point of fact made genuinely philosophical advances over Greek thought in regard to God. It can claim to demonstrate the existence of a creator God, and to use Aristotelian principles for doing so, without thereby implying that Aristotle himself had reached or even intended to reach that goal.

In a word, Aristotle either acknowledges or reaches philosophically many of the characteristics of the Judeo-Christian God, viz. providential care, object of cult, intelligence, efficient causality at work in every sub-lunar happening, and final cause of all movement in the celestial as well as sub-lunar world. But he does not unite all these characteristics in any one single being. Nor do his principles, as applied in his own context, reach the concept of creation. On the contrary, his thinking remains within the traditional Greek philosophic tenet that nothing can come into being out of nothing. Neither does his ethics revolve around responsibility to a personal God for every human action. The inestimable service he rendered in advance to Christian thought lies rather in the development of profound metaphysical principles that when applied to the existence of sensible things lead in fullest cogency to the God who is subsistent existence, the *I am who am* of *Exodus*.[36] Aristotle's thinking remains close to reality, and thereby achieves an openness that permits its use on a level to which he himself did not attain. His texts on God, though they form an imposing collection when gathered, are in fact scattered through his works and are often merely occasional. They are comparatively few in the context of his total writing. They do not present a final, systematic doctrine on God. But their worth for metaphysical and theological reasoning remains unsurpassed.

---

36 On the traditional understanding of the *Exodus* (III, 14) text, and its use in patristic thought, see Cornelia J. De Vogel, " 'Ego sum qui sum' et sa signification pour une philosophie chrétienne," *Revue des Sciences Religieuses,* XXXV (1961), pp. 346-354. A discussion on this meaning of the Scriptural text may be found in M.M. Bourke, "Yahweh, The Divine Name," *The Bridge,* III (1958), pp. 274-278.

A SELECT BIBLIOGRAPHY

1. Primary Sources

(a) Text

Aristotelis Opera. 5 vols., ed. Prussian Academy. Berlin: Reimer, 1831-1870.

(b) Translation

The Works of Aristotle Translated into English. 12 vols., ed. W.D. Ross. Oxford: Clarendon Press and Oxford University Press, 1908-1952.

2. Commentaries

(a) Greek

Commentary on *Metaphysics* lambda by Pseudo-Alexander in *In Aristotelis Metaphysica Commentaria,* ed. Michael Hayduck. Berlin: Reimer, 1891. In *Commentaria in Aristotelem Graeca,* ed. Prussian Academy, I, 2.

Paraphrase of *Metaphysics* lambda by Themistius, *In Aristotelis Metaphysicorum Librum A Paraphrasis,* ed. Samuel Landauer. Berlin: Reimer, 1903. In *Commentaria in Arist. Graeca,* V, 5.

(b) Medieval

St. Thomas Aquinas, *Commentary on the Metaphysics of Aristotle.* 2 vols., tr. John P. Rowan. Chicago: Henry Regnery, 1961.

(c) Modern

Apostle, Hippocrates G., *Aristotle's Metaphysics.* Bloomington and London: Indiana University Press, 1966.

————, *Aristotle's Physics.* Bloomington and London: Indiana University Press, 1969.

Ross, William David, *Aristotle's Metaphysics.* 2 vols. Oxford: Clarendon Press, 1924.

————, *Aristotle's Physics.* Oxford: Clarendon Press, 1936.

Reale, Giovanni, *Aristotele, La Metafisica.* 2 vols. Naples: Luigi Loffredo, 1968.

3. Studies on God in Aristotle

(a) General

Boehm, Alfred, *Die Gottesidee bei Aristotales auf ihren religiosen Character untersucht.* Strassburg: Goller, 1914.

Nolte, Augustinus H.J.A., *Het Godsbegrip bij Aristoteles.* Nijmegen-Utrecht: Dekker & Van De Vegt N.V., 1940.

Pauler, Akos von, "Über den Theismus des Aristoteles," *Archiv für Geschichte der Philosophie*, XXXVII (1926), pp. 202-210.

Pépin, Jean, *Idees grecques sur l'homme et sur Dieu* (Paris: Les Belles Lettres, 1971), pp. 207-263.

(b) Particular

Bousset, M., "Sur la théologie d'Aristote: monothéisme ou polythéisme?" *Revue thomiste*, XLIV (1938), pp. 798-805.

Brentano, Franz, "Uber den Creatianismus des Aristoteles," *Sitzungsberichte der Akademie der Wissenschaften in Wien, philosophisch-historische Klasse*, 101, X (1882), pp. 95-126.

Busnelli, G., "Il Dio d'Aristotele e il Dio di Tommaso d'Aquino secondo il prof. A. Carlini," *La Civilta Cattolica*, LXXXIV, 4 (1933), pp. 142-150.

Capelle, W., "Zur antiken Theodicee," *Archiv für Geschichte der Philosophie*, XX (1907), pp. 173-195.

Cauchy, V., "La causalité divine chez Aristote," *Mélanges á la memoire de Charles De Koninck* (Quebec: Les presses de l'université·Laval, 1968), pp. 103-114.

Christensen, Johnny, "Actus Purus," *Classica et Mediaevalia*, XIX (1958), pp. 7-40.

Chroust, A.H., "The Concept of God in Aristotle's Lost Dialogue on Philosophy (Cicero, *De Natura Deorum I 13, 33),*" *Emerita*, XXXIII (1965), pp. 205-228.

_____, "A Cosmological Proof for the Existence of God in Aristotle's Lost Dialogue *On Philosophy,*" "*The New Scholasticism*, XL (1966), pp. 447-463.

_____, "Comments on Aristotle's 'On Prayer,' " *The New Scholasticism*, XLVI (1972), pp. 308-330.

De Corte, Marcel, "Le pluralisme dans la théologie aristotelicienne," *Revue belge de philologie et d'histoire*, IX (1930), pp. 869-877.

_____, "La ćausalite du premier moteur dans la philosophie aristotelicienne," *Revue d'histoire de la philosophie*, V (1931), pp. 105-146.

Dockx, J. "De theorie van den onbewogen beweger bij Aristoteles," *Tijdschrift voor philosophie*, I (1939), pp. 747-800.

Elser, Konrad, *Die Lehre des Aristoteles uber das Wirken Gottes.* Münster: Aschendorff, 1893.

Festugière, A.M.J., "Les premiers moteurs d'Aristote," *Revue philosophique de la France et de l'étranger*, CXXXIX (1949), pp. 66-71.

Forsyth, T.M., "Aristotle's Concept of God as Final Cause," *Philosophy*, XXII (1947), pp. 112-123.

Fuller, B.A.G., "The Theory of God in Book A of Aristotle's *Metaphysics*," *The Philosophical Review*, XVI (1907), pp. 170-183.

Guthrie, W.K.C., "The Development of Aristotle's Theology," *Classical Quarterly*, XXVII (1933), pp. 162-171; XXVIII (1934), pp. 90-98.

Jackson, Henry, "On Some Passages in Aristotle's *Metaphysics* A," *Journal of Philology*, XXIX (1904), pp. 139-144.

Jolivet, Regis, "Aristote et la notion de création," *Revue des sciences philosophiques et théologiques*, XIX (1930), pp. 5-50, 209-235. Reprinted with Appendix, in Jolivet, *Essai sur les rapports entre la pensée grecque et la pensée chrétienne* (Paris: Vrin, 1931), pp. 3-84.

Kramer, Hans-Joachim, *Der Ursprung der Geistmetaphysik* (Amsterdam: P. Schippers, 1964), pp. 164-171.

Lagrange, M.J., "Comment s'est transformee la pensée religieuse d'Aristote d'aprés un livre recent," *Revue thomiste*, XXXI (1926), pp. 285-329.

Leveque, Charles, *Le premier moteur et la nature dans le systéme d'Aristote.* Paris: Firmin Didot, 1852.

Lindbeck, G.A., "A Note on Aristotle's Discussion of God and the World," *The Review of Metaphysics*, I (1948), pp. 99-106.

Mansion, A., "L'action du Dieu moteur d'Aristote sur le monde," *Library of the Xth International Congress of Philosophy* (Amsterdam: North-Holland Publishing Co., 1949), I, pp. 1091-1093.

————, "Le Dieu d'Aristote et le Dieu des chrétiens," in *La philosophie et ses problémes* (Offert a R. Jolivet, Lyons-Paris: Vitte, 1960), pp. 21-44.

Merlan, P., "Aristotle's Unmoved Movers," *Traditio*, IV (1946), pp. 1-30.

————, "Two Theological Problems in Aristotle's *Met. Lambda* 6-9 and *De Caelo* A.9," *Apeiron*, I (1966), pp. 3-13.

Mugnier, Rene, *La théorie du premier moteur et l'evolution de la pensée aristotelicienne.* Paris: Vrin, 1930.

Norman, R., "Aristotle's philosopher-God," *Phronesis*, XIV (1969), pp. 63-74.

Oehler, K., "Der Beweis fur den unbewegten Beweger bei Aristoteles," *Philologus*, XCIX (1955), pp. 70-92.

Owens, J., "The Reality of the Aristotelian Separate Movers," *The Review of Metaphysics*, III (1950), pp. 319-337.

————, "The Relation of God to World in the *Metaphysics*," to be published in *Recherches sur la métaphysique d'Aristote*, ed. Pierre Aubenque (Sixième Symposium Aristotelicum).

Patzig, G., "Theologie und Ontologie in der 'Metaphysik' des Aristoteles," *Kant-Studien*, LII (1961), pp. 185-205.

Paulus, J. "La théorie du premier moteur chez Aristote," *Revue de philosophie*, XXXIII (1933), pp. 259-294, 394-424.

Rolfes, Eugen, *Die aristotelische Auffassung vom Verhältnisse Gottes zur Welt.* Berlin: Mayer & Muller, 1892.

————, "Die angebliche Mangelhaftigkeit der aristotelischen Gotteslehre," *Jahrbuch für Philosophie und Spekulative Theologie*, XI (1897), pp. 129-139.

Ross, W.D., "Review" of F. Brentano's "Aristoteles' Lehre vom Ursprung des menschlichen Geistes," in *Mind*, N.S. XXIII (1914), pp. 289-291.

Siwek, P., "Le Dieu d'Aristote dans les dialogues," *Aquinas*, XII (1969), pp. 11-46.

Verbeke, G., "La structure logique de la preuve du premier moteur chez Aristote," *Revue philosophique de Louvain*, XLVI (1948), pp. 137-160.

Verdenius, W.J., "Traditional and Personal Elements in Aristotle's *Religion*," *Phronesis*, V (1960), pp. 56-70.

Vuillemin, Jules, *De la logique á la théologie.* 5 ed., La théologie d'Aristote (Paris: Flammarion, 1967), pp. 164-224.

Wolfson, H.A., "The Knowability and Describability of God in Plato and Aristotle," *Harvard Studies in Classical Philology*, LVI-LVII (1947), pp. 233-249.

————, "The Plurality of Immovable Movers in Aristotle and Averroes," *Harvard Studies in Classical Philology*, LXIII (1958), pp. 233-253.

————, "The Problem of the Souls of the Spheres from the Byzantine Commentaries on Aristotle through the Arabs and St. Thomas to Kepler," *Dumbarton Oaks Papers*, no. 16 (Washington, 1962), pp. 65-93.

God in Christian Teaching

CHAPTER XV

GOD IN THE CATHOLIC TRADITION
Gerard A. McCool, S.J.

The name "Catholic tradition" will be used in this chapter as a descriptive label for a stream of thought which has occupied a central place in Roman Catholic theology for many centuries. It is not intended to be a normative or essential definition. Distinguished Catholic preachers, philosophers and theologians have worked outside of it in the past. Doubtless many will continue to do so in the future. Nevertheless the term has been a useful designation for a way of thinking which has had a discernible historical existence and which still stands today in clear and conscious opposition to the faith-reason, Law-Gospel dialectic of Reformation theology. For practical purposes therefore it will be used to designate the intellectual tradition in Roman Catholic religious thought associated with the phrase, *fides quaerens intellectum.* This is the intellectual tradition through which Patristic thought reached the Latin West primarily, though by no means exclusively, in its Augustinian interpretation. Augustinian theology is a synthesis in which religious encounter with the Word of God is united to the philosophical heritage of the ancient world. Consequently the representatives of the tradition, sometimes in heated disagreement with each other, have repeatedly addressed themselves to the question whether knowledge of God acquired through religious experience and prayerful meditation on the Scriptures can be reconciled with knowledge of God obtained through rigorous philosophical reflection and mystical encounter. Different though they are from each other, Boethius, Anselm,

*Professor of Philosophy at Fordham University, New York, U.S.A.

Bernard, Abelard and the Victorines helped to shape this Western Catholic tradition of the manifold ascent of the soul to God. Bonaventure and Thomas can be safely listed among its great representatives in the High Middle Ages. Baroque Scholasticism, less happily united than were Bonaventure and Thomas to the Church's mystical tradition, endeavored to carry it forward into the modern period and the Catholic thinkers of the Scholastic Revival tried to renew its vigor in the nineteenth and early twentieth centuries.

1. God in the Western Catholic Tradition

From Augustine on, God, as He is understood in the Western Catholic tradition, is the Triune God of classical Roman Catholic theology. Coming after a long evolution of Patristic thought and violent Trinitarian and Christological controversies, Augustine's *De Trinitate* was a work of mature theological development. Likewise, his *City of God*, originally intended as a defense of Christianity against the charge of causing Rome's misfortunes, turned into a prolonged reflection on the relations between the provident God and His historical creation. In his *Confessions* Augustine had written movingly of the call of the indwelling Triune God to the human soul. After his controversy with the Pelagians, however, he was more explicitly aware that without the grace of God the fallen soul has not the freedom to turn away from its sinful love of finite beings and return to the God of whom it is the disfigured image.

Augustine's works established the theology of the Triune God which, despite the influence of Pseudo-Dionysius, became the common property of the Western Middle Ages. According to His nature, God is One, Infinite, Eternal, Immense, Immutable. He is the Wisdom or Measure in the imitation of whose Divine Ideas all things are made. He is the Free Creator from whose nature (common to all three Persons) all finite beings flow as the effects of His creative causality. He is the end toward whom all creatures move. All-knowing and provident, God sees in his timeless gaze all past, present and future events in the changeless present of His own being. All good, He guides creatures to their destiny, willing nothing but their benefit. Sin, the non-being of moral evil, is not the effect of God's activity. Rather it proceeds from the free will of man which can fall away from God because of the essential mutability of human nature.

God, however, is not simply the Supreme Nature. He is the Supreme Community of the Trinity. We can call Him Creator, Conserver, Provident because of the relation of His nature to His creatures. More fundamental than this relation, however, are the essential relations intrinsic to God Himself which constitute the Trinity. We can call the whole Trinity Creator and Provident because all predicates are affirmed by identity of the divine nature except where there is opposition of relation. There is such opposition, however, between the Father and the Son who proceeds from Him by way of generation. Likewise there is opposition of relation between the Holy Spirit and the Father and Son, who together constitute the principle from which the Holy Spirit proceeds. God is all three Persons and all three Persons are God, distinct yet inseparable in their being and activity. Since there is no opposition between the three divine Persons and God's essential being, Father, Son and Holy Spirit are identified with the divine nature. Man and the world proceed by creation from that unique principle of God's external action.[1]

One Person alone of the Blessed Trinity, however, became man. The Son, the Word of God, united to His person the human reality which, as a finite being, proceeded from God's nature by way of creation. Christ, the subsistent personal union of God and man, is the redeemer because of whose salutary theandric activity sinful creatures can return to God, healed and elevated by the power of

---

1 This theology is by no means confined to the works of Saint Augustine. It can also be found in both the theological tractates and the *Consolation of Philosophy* of Boethius. In the twelfth century St. Anselm's *Monologion* and *Proslogion* cast it in the highly unified and systematic form which was taken up and developed more profoundly by the great Scholastic theologians of the thirteenth century. For St. Thomas' development, see his *Summa Theologiae,* I, qq. 2-43.

faith and grace.[2]

The infinite divine nature and the different sets of relations, within God in the Trinity, between the Son and His human nature in the Incarnation, between God and His creatures in creation and redemption, are the fundamental elements which remain constant in the classical Catholic doctrine of God. There are variations in their interpretation and expression, however, which, without changing the essentials of the classical doctrine, permit important differences in the theology of God and the world. One such difference, for example, is the diverse interpretation of the relation between the Divine Ideas and the Person of the Word in Augustine and Pseudo-Dionysius.[3] Another difference is the diverse understanding of the relation between the Incarnation of the Son and His place within the Trinity. Augustine believed that any one of the Divine Persons could have become man. The earlier Patristic teaching on the other hand insisted that, because of His peculiar place in the Trinity, the Son alone could do so. The importance of these differences will appear later in the chapter.

2. The Three-fold Knowledge of God in the Catholic Tradition

Knowledge of God in the Augustinian tradition is three-fold. Sacred Scripture, through which the Christian revelation reaches

---

2 The saving mission of the Word Incarnate is the theme of Book IV of St. Augustine's *De Trinitate*. A classical example of medieval soteriology can be found in St. Anselm's *Cur Deus Homo*. For St. Thomas' theology of Christ the Savior, see *Summa Theologiae*, III, qq. 1-59.

3 The Dionysian tradition has presented a more dynamic conception of the procession of the divine ideas through the Word from the One Divine Originating Principle, associated with the Father. The procession of the divine ideas is even more strongly emphasized in Scotus Eriugena's *Division of Nature* than it was in Pseudo-Dionysius' *Divine Names*. Eriugena believes that, although the divine ideas are in the Son, they are *less eternal* than the Son. In St. Thomas the Augustinian tradition takes the form in which it became familiar to succeeding generations of Catholic theologians. The divine ideas are the *divine essence,* seen by the divine mind as imitable *ad extra.* Thus the Dionysian tradition unites the procession of creatures from God much more closely to the procession of the Son from the Father than the Augustinian tradition in its Thomistic form. The ideas proceed from the Father through the Son and through them, as creative causes, finite realities proceed from God. Under the influence of Hegel, Catholic theologians are returning to the Dionysian tradition.

the individual soul, is the primary source of man's encounter with the divinity. God is reached through faith in God's Word, communicated by His Scriptures and preached in His Church. Nevertheless, under the guidance of grace, the Christian believer can reach a deeper understanding of the revelation to which he assents in faith. He will do so by "despoiling the Egyptians," that is, by employing the resources of the liberal disciplines and philosophy to discover the literal and symbolic meaning of the Sacred Scriptures. The soul which unites this intellectual discipline with a life of prayer and moral purification may hope to pass, with the help of grace, through this deeper understanding of the Sacred Scriptures—the form of "intellectus" which Augustine calls "scientia" or science—to the higher form of mystical encounter with God's own changeless reality which Augustine calls "sapientia" or wisdom.[4] This ascent from simple faith to mystical wisdom structures the entire second half of Augustine's *De Trinitate.* It also underpins the educational system, proposed in his *De Doctrina Christiana,* in which the liberal arts are employed to reach the understanding of the literal and symbolic meaning of the Scriptures, whose source and goal is supernatural charity. The educational theory of *De Doctrina Christiana* profoundly influenced religious life in the Middle Ages. We find its echoes in the *lectio divina* practiced in the Benedictine monasteries, in the mystical theology of Bernard, and in the *Itinerarium Mentis in Deum* and the *Reductio Artium ad Theologiam* of Bonaventure.

Man's three-fold knowledge of God is the result of his concrete relation to the Trinity. Man is the image of the Trinity. His intellect and will make man a spirit whose restless drive to know and love will be appeased by nothing less than God Himself. The mind's metaphysical constitution as an image of the Trinity provides grounds and experience of transcendence through man's innate longing for perfect truth and goodness. Because of the

---

4 St. Augustine, *De Trinitate,* Books XII and XIII. See Etienne Gilson, *The Christian Philosophy of St. Augustine* (New York: Random House, 1960), pp. 115-126. The title which St. Anselm originally chose for his *Proslogion* was *Fides quaerens intellectum.*

mind's metaphysical relationship to God, once man has been enlightened by faith and healed by grace, he can enter into himself and acquire the religious experience through which the illuminated and purified soul grasps the inner meaning of God's word and His creation. Faith must lead the way, since it is the mind's awareness that it is the image of the *Triune* God which enables it to acquire an adequate knowledge of its own reality as an image of the Trinity. Likewise it is the mind's awareness that all creation bears the traces of the Triune God which enables it to discover the hidden symbolism, the religious and moral meaning, which lies beneath the sensible exterior of material creation. Man's knowledge of God in faith leads him to a deeper religious understanding of the world and of himself. Then this knowledge of the world and his own mind doubles back in turn on Scripture to deepen the religious man's ever growing understanding of God's written word.

The ascending spiral of man's knowledge of God, despite the primacy accorded to faith, rests on the metaphysics of God's being. God is the infinite end toward which man's spiritual dynamism is directed. He is the supreme exemplar whose reality created beings imitate according to their measure. He is the provident creator whose personal activity in the human intellect and will explains man's movement toward the good. He is the omnipresent, omnipotent knower, whose loving direction makes each human life a personal vocation. The intelligibility of the world and of the metaphysical and moral norms through which we pass judgment on it are manifestations of His immutable divine intelligibility. Thus there is a continuity between man's intellectual and moral response to created being and value in the philosophical order and his response in faith and love to the God of revelation. Unless man first submits himself in faith to God, human pride and sinfulness will keep man's reason from reaching true knowledge of the universe and its Creator. Nevertheless, the metaphysics of the soul and God explain why, in the converted man, the evolution of faith and philosophy merge harmoniously into a single, unified movement. It also explains why the immanent dynamism of this movement, in order to reach its full development, must pass beyond a conceptual grasp of God through the contingent, historical words of Scripture and ascend to mystical encounter.[5] For the God of grace and revelation is also the Supreme Good. The Triune God is the necessary One, to whom the purified soul, when it has mounted above all conceptual diversity, unites itself in the cloud of unknowing.

3. Interrelation of Elements in the Three-fold Knowledge

The faith-reason controversies of the twelfth century revealed, however, that, within the Western Catholic tradition, the conflicting claims of faith, reason and mystical encounter as normative sources of knowledge of God were not easily reconciled. The rise of dialectic introduced a tendency to restrict intellectual knowledge of God to an exercise of discursive reasoning. Beneficial though the rise of dialectic was, through its contribution to the establishment of the Scholastic method, there was within it an unmistakable tendency toward rationalism of the *Verstand.* An unusually well rounded thinker like Anselm could resist this tendency and do justice in his writings to dialectic, speculative theology and mystical encounter. Abelard, however, could not, and his incautious application of discursive reason to the mysteries of faith provoked the violent reaction of Bernard, the eloquent defender of the mystical tradition of the monastic *lectio divina.* Unfair as Bernard was to Abelard at times, he saw more clearly than the latter that the intellectual approach to God in the Western Catholic tradition is not an exercise in abstract discursive thought. The mind reaches God through an ascent which is nourished by the Scriptures and through a conversion, by the healing power of grace, which repairs God's distorted image in the soul and purifies its love.

The clarification of the relation among the elements of the

---

5 For both Augustine and Pseudo-Dionysius the wisdom of the soul which has made the ascent from the world to God involves mystical encounter with the Divinity. Thus St. Bonaventure could say that the ascent to God described in his *Itinerarium Mentis in Deum* leads to the same goal as the mystical ascent of St. Francis on Mount Alverna.

three-fold knowledge of God in the twelfth century enabled the Scholastics of the thirteenth, despite very significant differences among themselves, to reach agreement concerning its broad lines. God is reached through faith by the help of grace. The science which gives us adequate knowledge of Him therefore is theology. Nevertheless, although the infidel, who cuts himself off from God by his lack of faith, will not reach the truth, man's intellect can arrive at true and certain knowledge of God by metaphysical reflection. Consequently Bonaventure, Thomas and Scotus, for example, propose philosophical arguments for God's existence, although they are not in agreement about their grounding and validity. Similarly all three draw upon the heritage of Plato and Aristotle to work out their classical theology of the divine attributes and explain, as far as this is possible, the relations and processions of the Trinity. One of Thomas' great achievements in fact was his explicit grounding of the status of theology as a *scientia* on the model of the *Posterior Analytics* and his justification of the place of philosophical reflection as an integral part of his Aristotelian science of God. Despite their increased philosophical sophistication and their acceptance of the corpus of Aristotle, however, the thirteenth century Scholastics still looked on their conceptual reflection on God in scientific theology as a stage in an integral spiritual ascent whose term was mystical encounter. This is clear in Bonaventure's *Itinerarium Mentis in Deum*. It is also evident in Thomas' echoing of the Augustinian dictum that action has contemplation as its goal. For in saying so he is simply incorporating into his own synthesis the passage from action to contemplation which accompanies the ascent from science to wisdom in Augustine's *De Trinitate*.

Thus, despite the almost complete occupation of the place of the liberal arts by heavily Aristotelian philosophy in their interpretation of the Scriptures, the thirteenth century *Commentaria, Quaestiones* and *Summae* remained faithful to the three-fold knowledge of God of the *fides quaerens intellectum* tradition. They did so because in their authors' metaphysics of God and man God remained the infinite immutable Creator who made man and the world in His image. Since God remained the eternal creative Beauty, man could find in himself, the world and Scripture the timeless intelligible patterns through which creation speaks of God to the purified conceptual intellect. But, since God was still the supreme Good, the end of creation's striving, human love, purified and elevated by grace, could not reach its satiating goal until the soul passed beyond all intelligible patterns, which are only symbols of God, and touched His perfect Unity in the wordless silence of mystical encounter.

4. The Western Catholic Tradition after Vatican I

Two great events influenced Catholic theology in the last quarter of the nineteenth century, the First Vatican Council and the Scholastic Revival. Both had their roots in the Church's dialogue with nineteenth century thought. In many respects the dialogue was a defensive one. Empiricist and Idealistic philosophy and the growing influence of positive science joined with the political liberalism of the age to create a climate of thought, especially in educational circles, which was often actively hostile to the Catholic Faith. In self-defense the Church felt obliged to reaffirm clearly, in the teeth of her philosophical opponents, her firm conviction that human reason can reach true and certain knowledge about God's existence and nature. She also felt obliged, in the face of rationalistic anti-clericalism, to reassert the possibility of divine revelation and its necessity for salvation.[6]

The God whose existence was discussed at Vatican I was the Triune God of traditional Catholic theology. Evolutionary pantheism was clearly irreconcilable with the Catholic conception of God as transcendent creator. The more recent question about a limited applicability of process categories to the divine attributes in orthodox Catholic theology did not occur to the Bishops at

6 The Council's defense of the ability of natural reason to come to certain knowledge of God is contained in the Dogmatic Constitution, *Dei Filius*. For an excellent discussion of the content and background of *Dei Filius*, see Bernard J.F. Lonergan, "Natural Knowledge of God," in *Proceedings of the Catholic Theological Society of America*, 23 (1968), pp. 54-69.

Vatican I. Their concern was rather with the ability of the traditional God to reveal Himself and with the capacity of the human mind to know Him. The human mind, Vatican I declared, is capable of knowing God through its natural power by reflecting on the visible creation. Furthermore, although, as a matter of fact, revelation is morally necessary for men in their concrete situation to reach accurate knowledge of God by the exercise of their reason, that natural knowledge of God, based as it is on rational evidence, must be clearly distinguished from the salutary act of faith, a supernatural assent whose motive is the revealing word of God.

Thus Vatican I clearly distinguished between natural knowledge of God and salutary faith and firmly defended the power of the natural reason to arrive at certain knowledge of God. Divine revelation, it declared, is absolutely necessary for the supernatural act of faith of which it is the motive. Revelation is also morally necessary for historical man's effective use of his natural reason. Adequate knowledge of God requires an historical revelation which is mediated to man through the authority and infallibility of the teaching Church. Reason must operate within the context of the faith, without which it is impossible to please God, and its reflections must be clarified and supported by ecclesial teaching.

The relation between faith and reason affirmed by Vatican I excludes both fideism, which denies the ability of the human mind to reach true and certain knowledge of God by natural reason, and rationalism, which, by rejecting divine revelation, confines man's knowledge of God to the deliverances of natural reason. It also excludes the Reformation position, reaffirmed in Barthian Neo-Orthodoxy, which denies the possibility of natural knowledge of God in man's present fallen state. Also excluded is Liberal Protestantism in the Schleiermacher tradition, in which man's knowledge of God is restricted to the *a priori* content of universal religious experience. In this type of Protestant theology God no longer manifests Himself as the ontologically transcendent, infinite cause, who freely created the world, providentially rules it, and discloses His hidden personal depths in historical revelation. Against every type of religious immanentism, Vatican I defends the existence of a positive, historical revelation with a clearly distinguishable cognitional content. Furthermore, in the case of strict mysteries, this content transcends the grasp of unaided human reason.[7]

If the theology of God affirmed by Vatican I took issue with certain types of Protestant theology, it left considerable freedom to Catholic theology. No definite proof of God's existence was defended. No definite system of philosophy was prescribed. Beyond its rejection of fideism and rationalism and its clear distinction between faith and natural knowledge of God, the Council did not develop its understanding of the relation between philosophy and theology in any great detail. The focus of its preoccupation did not include a discussion of the relation between scientific theology and religious experience or mystical encounter. The living presence of monastic and religious institutes in the Catholic Church, the Catholic understanding of the relation between faith and natural reason, and the Catholic teaching on the intrinsic nature of grace and the theological virtues had already undercut the thesis of many Reformed theologians that there is an unbridgeable opposition between mysticism and genuine Christian faith. For the Catholic, contact with God does not take place through faith alone. God does not stand over against human reason as the Wholly Other. Man's nature is intrinsically affected by grace and the theological virtues. Thus he can grow in his intrinsic capacity to know and love God. Law and Gospel are not in opposition to each other. Moral growth can and does lead to deeper supernatural insight. Thus mystical encounter with God, far from standing in opposition to Christian contact with the Word of God in faith, is its legitimate development.

In the years following Vatican I the adherents of the Scholastic Revival worked out a philosophy and theology which supported the affirmations of the Council. Basing themselves on Saint Thomas, they presented a series of proofs for the existence of God

---

7 For a discussion of the teaching of *Dei Filius* concerning divine revelation and its relation to nineteenth century Protestant Theology, see Avery Dulles, S.J., *Revelation Theology* (New York: Herder and Herder, 1969), pp. 62-82, esp. pp. 75-77.

which expanded, and sometimes reinterpreted, the celebrated five ways of the Angelic Doctor.[8] A theory of analogy, which the stricter Thomists (but not the Suarezians) built on Thomas' distinction between essence and existence, justified the human knower's right to affirm the traditional attributes of the Infinite God, whose essence or nature was identified with His existence. Thus a Scholastic natural theology was established to prove the existence of an infinite personal God who could manifest Himself to man through His historical revelation. This natural theology laid the groundwork for an apologetic of signs, miracles and prophecies, which in turn established the reasonableness of the act of faith. Then theology, reflecting on the data of revelation, proceeded to work out a Scholastic theology of the Trinity and Incarnation in which the metaphysics of person and relation played a major role.

Nevertheless, Scholastic philosophy and theology were never identified with Catholic doctrine. Other systems of philosophy and theology had flourished in the nineteenth century before the Scholastic Revival and, even in the heyday of its restoration, there were Catholic thinkers who had difficulties with the Scholastic proofs for God's existence. Few, if any Catholic philosophers, however, showed any hesitation about accepting the traditional attributes of God and, after the Modernist crisis, a combination of official encouragement and scholarly activity insured the dominance of scholastic theology in the Church's seminaries and universities. Two of the masterpieces which classical Neo-Scholastic theology produced in the period of its intellectual dominance were Billot's *De Deo Uno et Trino* and Garrigou-Lagrange's *Dieu*.[9]

---

8 For a reworking of St. Thomas' proofs from a Marechalian point of view, see Joseph Defever, S.J., *La Preuve Réelle de Dieu* (Paris: Desclée de Brouwer, 1953) and Joseph Donceel, S.J., *Natural Theology* (New York: Sheed and Ward, 1962).

9 Louis Billot, S.J., *De Deo uno et trino* (Rome: Gregorian University Press, 1895). Reginald Garrigou-Lagrange, O.P., *Dieu, Existence et sa Nature* (Paris: Beauchesne, 1915).

5. The Western Catholic Tradition after Vatican II

In the last quarter century, however, the Catholic tradition has undergone a remarkable evolution. The philosophical challenge to Scholasticism, which reached significant proportions in the years following the Second World War, the increasing difficulty of reconciling traditional Scholastic epistemology and metaphysics with the procedures and discoveries of the physical and behavioral sciences, and the inability of classical Scholastic theology to cope with the problems of Biblical exegesis and hermeneutics created an uneasy feeling among Catholic scholars that all was not well with the Scholastic Revival. Furthermore, the abstract and, to some, historically conditioned character of Scholastic reasoning created a gap between the Church's scientific theology and the religious experience of the faithful. These growing tensions within the Catholic tradition prepared the way for the violent reaction against Scholasticism which followed Vatican II.

This reaction, like most reactions, was not always reasonable. Accusations of extremism and over-kill could well be levelled against some of the anit-Scholastic polemicists, and, when philosophical pluralism became respectable again in Catholic intellectual circles, naive proposals to restructure Catholic theology in terms of Hegelianism, phenomenology and various types of process philosophy soon appeared, often in rather popular form. Unfortunately, a number of these popular proposals were distinguished more for their revolutionary enthusiasm than for their theological profundity, and, after a brief *succes de scandale,* ceased to attract much attention. Nevertheless, the reaction has proved to be healthy in the long run. Modern and contemporary philosophy have entered fully into the main stream of Catholic thought and are being employed consistently and carefully by competent theologians. Within the Scholastic community, the historically oriented Thomism of Gilson and Maritain, with its comparatively negative attitude toward modern philosophy has yielded its dominant place to Marechalian Transcendental Thomism, which has always felt an affinity to post-Kantian thought. Rahner and Lonergan, who today are profoundly influential conservative theologians, are Transcendental Thomists.[10] Their reflections on the knowledge and nature of God, although hostile to the more extreme forms of historicism or process theology, show the influence of post-Kantian and contemporary philosophy. Both have moved far beyond the Thomism of Billot, Garrigou-Lagrange, Gilson and Maritain.

Since Vatican II there has been a growing consensus among Catholic theologians that the natural theology, apologetics, dogmatic theology sequence of post-Vatican I Scholasticism did not do justice to the *fides quaerens intellectum* tradition. The proofs for the existence of God were presented in an abstract and general manner which paid too little attention to the concrete experience of their recipient and the actual working of grace in the human soul. The apologetics were rationalistic and exterior in form and increasingly subject to criticism in the light of contemporary hermeneutics. Revelation appeared to be an extrinsic, secondary source of knowledge about God, confined to a limited portion of the human race and unconnected with the religious experience of non-Christians, which Vatican II acknowledged could be a genuine, salutary contact with God. These criticisms of Neo-Scholastic natural theology and apologetics had been advanced years before Vatican II by Maurice Blondel.[11] If

---

10 The major work of Joseph Maréchal, S.J. is his famous five-volume *Le Point de départ de la métaphysique* (Paris: Desclée de Brouwer, 1944). An English translation of selected texts, with a highly illuminating commentary, can be found in *A Maréchal Reader,* ed. by Joseph Donceel, S.J. (New York: Herder and Herder, 1970). Karl Rahner's major works are *Spirit in the World* (New York: Herder and Herder, 1968), *Hearers of the Word* (New York: Herder and Herder, 1969) and *Theological Investigations* (Baltimore: Helicon, 1961 ff), of which nine volumes have appeared in English. Bernard Lonergan's major works are *De Deo Trino,* 2 vols. (Rome: Gregorian University Press, 1964), *Insight* (New York: Philosophical Library, 1957), *Verbum* (Notre Dame, Indiana: University of Notre Dame Press, 1967), *Method in Theology* (New York: Herder and Herder, 1972) and *Grace and Freedom* (New York: Herder and Herder, 1972).

11 Blondel's major work is *L'Action* (Paris: Alcan, 1893). Blondel's criticism of post-Vatican I apologetics is found in his famous "Lettre sur les Exigences de la Pensée contemporaine en matière d'Apologetique et sur la Methode de la Philosophie dans l'Etude du Problème Religieux" in *Les Premiers Ecrits de Maurice Blondel* (Paris: Presses Universitaires de France, 1956). For a clear and thorough exposition of Blondel's thought, see James M. Somerville, *Total Commitment: Blondel's L'Action* (Washington: Corpus Books, 1968).

divine revelation is addressed, not to a restricted group of people, but to *all* men, in all ages and places, Blondel insisted, revelation must correspond to the deepest exigencies of the human spirit. If men reflect on the fundamental dynamism of the human spirit, they will see that the intellectual and volitional action through which man wills every finite object will be satisfied with nothing less than personal contact with God Himself. Thus an adequate philosophy of human experience must inevitably raise the question of a possible revelation without which that personal contact is impossible. Blondel's philosophy had already influenced Transcendental Thomism profoundly. Marechalian Thomists, including Rahner and Lonergan, traditionally prove the existence of God through the movement of the mind to its Infinite End. De Lubac's *Surnaturel* provoked a famous controversy by its claim that God could not create a being with an intellectual drive toward intuitive knowledge of God without also destining that being to the Beatific Vision.[12] To preserve the gratuituous, supernatural character of the Beatific Vision, Rahner refined Lubac's position by the addition of his supernatural existential.[13] The positive decree of God through which historical man is destined to the supernatural end of the Beatific Vision, Rahner claims, produces an intrinsic ontological effect in man's intellect and will. This effect, the positive offer of the Indwelling Presence of the Trinity through Uncreated Grace, is the supernatural existential. Whether man accepts the offer of grace or not, the very offer itself, the supernatural existential, has already elevated his intellect and will to the supernatural order. The end of historical man's intellectual dynamism is now the Triune God of the Beatific Vision. His experience of the world and its Infinite Horizon is already supernatural and religious. If man responds rightly to God, the Horizon of his world, by responding rightly to the beings in it, his love of the world and its Horizon is already charity, and the

12 Henri de Lubac, S.J., *Surnaturel* (Paris: Aubier, 1946).
13 "Concerning the Relationship between Nature and Grace," in *Theological Investigations*, I, pp. 297-317.

knowledge of God that comes with it, vague thought it be, is
already implicit faith.

6. Religious Experience and Process Philosophy

Through this development the *fides quaerens intellectum*
tradition returns clearly to its starting point in faith. All men are
challenged by the supernatural character of their intellectual
dynamism to an act of at least implicit supernatural faith and love.
Many respond to the challenge and, through their act of implicit
faith, become anonymous Christians. Only the explicitely
believing Christian, however, who has been instructed by revelation understands the true nature of man's spirit and so can
explicitate accurately the significance of man's universal religious
experience. When the believing Christian speaks to the unbeliever,
he is not speaking to a man who has had no contact whatsoever
with God's revealing action. He is speaking to a man in whom he
may reasonably assume that implicit faith and love are already at
work. He is bringing the message of revelation to men prepared to
receive it by what is best in contemporary culture and philosophy.
And, since culture and philosophy are explicitations and
thematizations of man's supernatural drive toward God, they are
already implicitly Christian. Christian and non-Christian will
engage in a dialogue in which, under the influence of grace,
implicit and explicit faith will move toward understanding through
their intellectual wedding with what is best in human culture and
philosophy.

Thus the God of faith, as always in the *fides quaerens
intellectum* tradition, is the key to man's self-understanding. But
the God of faith in this tradition is also the God of philosophy
whose attributes can be derived from rational reflection on man's
experience of himself and exterior reality. Once we admit that
what is best in contemporary philosophy is implicitly Christian,
why should we not consider its objections against the Platonic-
Aristotelian metaphysics which has dominated Catholic theology
since the time of Augustine? For contemporary philosophers claim
that the Aristotelian philosophy of substance, act and potency is

inadequate not only to their experience of themselves and the world but to their experience of God.

For this reason Protestant theology in the United States has been strongly attracted to the process philosophy of Alfred North Whitehead. Abandoning substance in favor of his actual entities, or basic, structured units of process, Whitehead proposes an evolutionary universe in which every actual entity, including God, is always open to novelty. Changelessness is found only in abstractions. The basic character of every concrete reality is to be in process. Continuity in the evolving universe is due to the universal influence of the omnipresent, all-knowing, provident God. Yet God too changes. Although His primordial nature, which contains the eternal objects (the Platonic patterns prehended by the evolving actual entities) is eternal, God's consequent nature, on the other hand, evolves and develops through His ceaseless interaction with the other actual entities of the universe.

Whitehead arrived at his concept of an evolving God through his reflection on man's scientific, cultural and religious experience. Charles Hartshorne, in a series of books and articles, has defended the position that Whitehead's conception of God, the actual entity who surpasses Himself, although He cannot be surpassed by others, represents the only coherent notion of the infinitely perfect being.[14] Whitehead's God corresponds to Anselm's idea of the being than which no greater can be conceived. And it is to Whitehead's God that Anselm's argument (the only valid proof for God's existence in Hartshorne's eyes) really concludes. Other Whiteheadians argue that Whitehead's changing God is more suited to the God of Biblical revelation and religious experience than the Aristotelian Pure Act. The Biblical God repents, changes His plans, rejoices at man's actions. The God of religious experience is involved in our lives, grieved at our sins, moved by our prayers.

14 For a clear and sympathetic exposition of Hartshorne's neo-classical theism, see Eugene H. Peters, *Hartshorne and Neo-Classical Metaphysics* (Lincoln: University of Nebraska Press, 1970). For an equally sympathetic exposition of Whitehead's philosophy and its applicability to Christian theology, see Norman Pittenger, *Alfred North Whitehead* (Richmond, Virginia: John Knox Press, 1969).

The infinite Pure Act cannot change. Consequently his relation to the world is only a relation of reason. He remains the same no matter what we do. Nothing we do, whether it be good or bad, makes any difference to Him.

In recent years the religious challenge of process philosophy has been taken very seriously by philosophers and theologians in the Western Catholic tradition. If God is the key to a universal human experience which is fundamentally religious, He must be religiously available. He cannot be an utterly impassive divinity to whom our prayers and religious acts mean nothing. From the Catholic point of view, however, there are serious theological difficulties with Whitehead's God. He is not the creator of the world, for example, and whether an orthodox Christology or Trinitarian theology can be worked out in terms of Whitehead's metaphysics is problematic. Furthermore, the Transcendental Thomist God, the infinite Good of the human intellect, has the characteristics of Pure Act, and in Lonergan's *Insight,* the traditional attributes are assigned to God in virtue of his being the pure act of insight. Nevertheless, cautiously, and with considerable reservations, conservative Thomists have begun to modify their teaching on the traditional attributes of God in an effort to show that God is really involved with the world and really responds to our religious approach to Him. A number of years ago, in an article which drew considerable attention, the late Walter Stokes, S.J., endeavored to establish that, even though God is the infinite Pure Act, His relation to the world as its intelligent creator is a real one.[15] More recently, W. Norris Clarke, S.J. has argued that the Pure Act is mutable, although only in the intentional order.[16] Joseph Donceel, S.J. has taken a more radical approach. The Pure Act is really mutable, although only in respect to some of His attributes. Father Donceel, one of the foremost interpreters of

---

15 Walter Stokes, S.J., "Is God Really Related to the World?" in *Proceedings of the American Catholic Philosophical Association* (Washington: Catholic University Press, 1965), pp. 145-151.

16 "A New Look at the Immutability of God," in *God Knowable and Unknowable* (New York: Fordham University Press, 1972), pp. 43-72.

Transcendental Thomism in the United States, does not hesitate to call his position "panentheism" and claims to be carrying further some hints which he has discovered in Karl Rahner's theology.[17]

7. Karl Rahner and Process Philosophy

The hint concerning the mutability of God to which Father Donceel referred is found in Rahner's Christology. Contrary to the classical tradition of Catholic theology, Rahner claims that, although God is infinite Pure Act, the Divine Logos *as divina* (and not just *per communicationem idiomatum*) is really changed through the Incarnation. He is changed, however, Rahner continues, *in His other,* the human nature of Christ, the real symbol, through which the Logos expresses Himself.[18] As Donceel rightly observes, Rahner's metaphysics of the symbol, which he applies to the Logos in his theology of the Incarnation, is an effort to incorporate into a Thomistic synthesis a major thesis of Hegelian philosophy that the immutable Absolute can really change in its other. Rahner's use of Hegel is significant as an indication of the growing tendency of European Catholic theologians to make use of Hegelian metaphysics.[19] Far more significant, however, is the absolutely central role which this Hegelian-Thomistic metaphysics plays in Rahner's theology of God. A real symbol is the other through which a being comes to fulness by expressing itself. In St. Thomas' metaphysics of man, for example, the soul reaches its fulness by expressing itself in its real symbol, the faculties which it unites to itself as its proper accidents. All reality, even the divine reality, Rahner claims, is symbolic, for the Son is the real symbol through whom the Father expresses Himself and whom He unites to Himself in the unity of His divine being. Because the Son is the real symbol through whom the Father expresses Himself, the Son

---

17 "Second Thoughts on the Nature of God," *Thought,* 46 (1971), pp. 346-370.

18 "On the Theology of the Incarnation," *Theological Investigations,* IV, pp. 105-120.

19 One of the most significant among the recent efforts in this direction is Hans Küng's *Menschwerdung Gottes* (Freiburg: Herder, 1970).

is the Word. Because He is the Word, God's word *ad extra* in creation proceeds from Him, and, contrary to Augustine's teaching, He alone of the Persons of the Trinity can become man. Through the real symbol of His body, the Word unites Himself to the natural and religious history of the world, *changing as Logos* in the course of its development. United to the world by the Incarnation, God makes the offer of His grace to every man, thus raising all men to the supernatural order.[20]

Rahner's metaphysics of the symbol, which owes so much to Hegel, links the three mysteries of the Trinity, the Incarnation and grace to form the unified structure around which he has built his whole theology. Rahner believes that God as Triune, not the God of natural theology or even of the theological *tractatus de Deo Uno,* is and must be the key to the understanding of man and the world. The mystery of the Trinity, he insists, must be restored to the central place which it has lost in theology and popular devotion.[21]

So Rahner unites again the relations of the Trinity, Incarnation, creation and redemptive elevation which are central to the classical Catholic theology of God. Like Augustine, he makes the Trinity the key to the understanding of man and the universe. Unlike Augustine, and like Pseudo-Dionysius and especially Scotus Eriugena, he links the procession of the Logos to the dynamic operation of creation in a way that the Augustinian metaphysics of creation as an operation of the divine nature would not allow. Yet Rahner's theology of the mutability of the Word through His identification with an evolutionary creation has parted company with the static Greek metaphysics of both Augustine and Eriugena. His divergence from them is due to Hegel, whose reflections on the Trinity and Incarnation, have had a significant effect on Rahner. Thus, through this distinguished German Transcendental Thomist, German process philosophy has had a

---

20 "The Theology of the Symbol," *Theological Investigations,* IV, pp. 221-252.
21 "The Concept of Myster in Catholic Theology," *Theological Investigations,* IV, pp. 36-76.

profound influence on the contemporary Catholic understanding
of God and His relation to the world.

8. Historicity and Catholic Theology

Well before Vatican II phenomenology and Heideggerian
philosophy had begun to influence Catholic theology. Karl
Rahner's first two major works are dialogues with Heidegger and,
in the past decade and a half Schillebeeckx, Lonergan and many
other major theologians have engaged in a fruitful give and take
with phenomenology. For a theist who restricts himself purely to
the phenomenological approach, however, God can appear only as
the Horizon of the human subject's world. He is the being who
manifests Himself in and through the historical subject pole of
human consciousness and the finite subjects and objects toward
which the subject pole's intentionality is directed. Since the
human subject is intrinsically finite and temporal, the world of
subjects and objects toward which his conscious intentionality is
directed is essentially finite and temporal also. Yet, if the knower
is confined to what appears in the world of consciousness and is
consequently forbidden to use metaphysical causality as an
approach to a transcendent God, he has no other grasp of being.
Therefore he knows being only in its finite, historical
manifestations. Neither metaphysical argument, analogous conceptual knowledge, nor direct intuitive contact with the Supreme
Being are available to him as ways of knowing the transcendent
Absolute in His own reality.

Therefore the risks for Catholic philosophers and theologians
who confine themselves to a purely phenomenological approach
are rather obvious. The result is bound to be historicism, since
God is known exclusively through His finite and temporal
manifestation in human consciousness. No objective statements
with abiding cognitional content can be made concerning God. It
was inevitable therefore that when Leslie Dewart abandoned the
metaphysical being reached in the Scholastic judgment in favor of
the presence which manifests itself through the differentiation of
consciousness into its subject and object pole, his reconstruction

of Catholic theology would be characterized by radical historicism. We are not surprised therefore to learn in *The Future of Belief* that all our statements about God and His relation to the world are intrinsically mutable.[22] If they are to remain true to the historical manifestation of Being as Presence, they must change, sometimes radically, with the temporal development of human consciousness. Nor are we surprised that Henry Duméry, once he united his Plotinianism to an existentialist projection of objective meaning by individual consciousness, no longer permits us to make abiding objective statements about God.[23]

Nevertheless the historicity of human consciousness, on which phenomenology has focussed the attention of philosophers, presents a challenge to the abiding objectivity of statements about God which contemporary theologians cannot ignore. Both in Europe and in America, Catholic theologians have met the challenge and have modified their teaching on the abiding nature of Catholic tradition as a consequence. They are much more conscious than they were in the past of the historical and contextual nature of human truth, of the culturally conditioned character of objective statements, and of the place of a philosophical hermeneutics in any theological reflection upon Catholic tradition. The more conservative theologians, however, have combined a phenomenological starting point with a meta-physics which can make objective statements about the divine reality as it is in itself. In his popularly written *Man Becoming,* Gregory Baum has endeavored to apply Blondelian metaphysics to a contemporary philosophy of human consciousness.[24] By doing so, he endeavors to do justice to the immanence of God in human history and to the mutability of culturally conditioned statements about Him without destroying the divine transcendence. More carefully, and more successfully, Transcendental Thomists,

---

22 *The Future of Belief* (New York: Herder and Herder, 1966).
23 For a fine selection of Duméry's major texts, see *Faith and Reflection*, ed. by Louis Dupré (New York: Herder and Herder, 1968).
24 *Man Becoming* (New York: Herder and Herder, 1970).

especially Rahner, and more recently Lonergan, have united a phenomenology of the human mind to their metaphysics of its dynamic finality. In this manner they justify their ascent from human experience to valid, though analogous statements, about God Himself. They also lay the philosophical groundwork for the incorporation of historical studies and scientific hermeneutics into the essential structure of a theology of God's revelation of Himself.

Indeed the impact of this heightened consciousness of the historical character of human concepts is most strongly felt in the theology of revelation. The influence of Heidegger can be clearly seen in the conception of revelation as an event through which God manifests Himself in historically conditioned human concepts. Catholic theologians now distinguish much more carefully than they did in the past between the abiding manifestation of God to His Church and the historical, and to some degree at least, mutable, contextually modified statements through which the ecclesial community objectifies that revelation.

Consequently a highly developed hermeneutics has become an important part of systematic theology. Rahner has devoted many articles to the theology of revelation and to the development of doctrine and theology. He has placed in the very center of his system the distinction between God, as the Absolute Mystery, and the objective statements in which we formulate our knowledge of Him conceptually. Some, though by no means all of the latter, Rahner concedes, are historically and culturally conditioned and therefore mutable. Nevertheless, in his famous controversy with Hans Küng, Rahner insisted vehemently that immutable dogmatic statements, with abiding conceptual content, may and must be made about the content of divine revelation. Nevertheless, he must admit, the number of such abiding dogmatic statements may be much more limited than we thought in the past.[25] A similar concern with the historicity of human knowledge and with the

---

25 For an English translation of the whole Rahner-Küng controversy, see the *Homiletic and Pastoral Review* for May, June, July and September, 1971.

hermeneutic problem which it presents appears in the major works of Bernard Lonergan. In his *Insight* and, more recently *Method in Theology,* Lonergan has developed his four-fold theological method as the central element of a new theology, whose model is contemporary science rather than the Aristotelian science of the *Posterior Analytics.* He has done so in the belief that a theology based on Aristotle is no longer serviceable in an intellectual community which has become explicitly conscious of the historical diversities of human cultures and the different complexes of meaning which determine the sense of objective statements made in diverse human communities. Schillebeeckx too has made a major contribution to the growing awareness of the historicity of consciousness in the Catholic theology of revelation in his *Revelation and Theology.*[26]

9. Fides Quaerens Intellectum

Process philosophy and phenomenology have worked major changes in the Catholic *fides quaerens intellectum* tradition. The immutable Pure Act and the changeless intelligibilities of the created world have been called into question. It is safe to assume that this questioning will continue. Nevertheless, the fundamental doctrines of the Trinity, creation and the Incarnation retain their essential character and their central position in the Catholic theological synthesis. Theologians in the Catholic tradition still demand that the ascent to God begin with faith. Once the ascent has begun, however, the Christian will find in the metaphysics of man the road to the understanding which will both manifest the connection of revelation with man's deepest exigencies and enable him to grasp more clearly the coherent connection of the mysteries among themselves. True theological understanding, however, is never simply the work of discursive reasoning. Rahner, Lonergan and Schillebeeckx all insist that personal conversion is

---

26 Edward Schillebeeckx, O.P., *Revelation and Theology,* 2 vols. (New York: Sheed and Ward, 1968).

an intrinsic element of the process. Only through personal conversion, by means of charity, can man become a genuine theologian and authentically participate in the tradition of the converted community which is the bearer of God's word. The aim of the theologian's understanding is to bring himself and others to personal union with the Absolute Mystery who, in His infinite intelligibility, transcends all conceptual expression.

In its contemporary expression the *fides quaerens intellectum* is much more complex than it was either in the Middle Ages or in its post-Vatican I form. The education which it requires of the theologian is more flexible and sophisticated than the theory of education which underpinned Augustine's *De Doctrina Christiana.* Catholic theology is moving away from Greek philosophy and has already discarded the classical conception of culture. Yet the God it proposes remains essentially the same and the road of the soul to God remains fundamentally unaltered. Like all living things, the *fides quaerens intellectum* tradition retains its identity through growth and change.

A SELECT BIBLIOGRAPHY

Bouilliard, Henri, *The Knowledge of God.* New York: Herder and Herder, 1968.

Collins, James D., *God in Modern Philosophy.* Chicago: Regnery, 1959.

Daniélou, Jean, *God and the Ways of Knowing.* New York: Meridian Books, 1959.

Defever, Joseph, *La Preuve Réelle de Dieu.* Paris: Desclée de Brouwer, 1953.

Donceel, Joseph F., *Natural Theology.* New York: Sheed and Ward, 1962.

Garrigou-Lagrange, Reginald, *God: His Existence and Nature.* St. Louis: Herder, 1934.

Gilson, Etienne H., *The Christian Philosophy of St. Thomas Aquinas.* New York: Random House, 1956.

———, *Elements of Christian Philosophy.* Garden City, New York: Doubleday, 1960.

———, *God and Philosophy.* New Haven, Connecticut: Yale University Press, 1941.

Hawkins, Denis John Bernard, *The Essentials of Theism.* New York: Sheed and Ward, 1950.

Lonergan, Bernard J.F., *Collection.* New York: Herder and Herder, 1967.
———, *A Second Collection.* Philadelphia, Pennsylvania: Westminister Press, 1975.
———, *Insight.* New York: Philosophical Library, 1957.
———, *Philosophy of God and Theology.* Philadelphia, Pennsylvania: Westminister Press, 1973.
Lubac de, Henri, *The Discovery of God.* New York: Kennedy, 1960.
Mascall, Eric Lionel, *He Who Is.* New York: Longmans Green, 1948.
———, *The Openness of Being,* London: Darton, Longman and Todd, 1971.
———, *Words and Images.* New York: Ronald, 1957.
Maritain, Jacques, *Approaches to God.* New York: Harper, 1954.
———, *God and the Permission of Evil.* Milwaukee, Michigan: Bruce, 1966.
———, *Man's Approach to God.* Latrobe: The Archabbey Press, 1960.
Matczak, Sebastian A., *Karl Barth on God: Our Knowledge of the Divine Existence.* New York: St. Paul Publications, 1962.
———, *Le Problème de Dieu dans la pensée de Karl Barth.* Louvain: Nauwelaerts, 1968.
Mitros, Joseph F., *Religions: A Select Classified Bibliography.* Louvain: Nauwelaerts, 1973.
Rahner, Karl, *A Rahner Reader.* New York: Seabury Press, 1975.
Trethowan, Illtyd, *The Basis of Belief.* New York: Hawthorn Books, 1961.
———, *Absolute Value: A Study in Christian Theism.* New York: Humanities Press, 1970.

CHAPTER XVI

THE CONCEPT OF GOD
IN THE REFORMATION TRADITION
Geddes MacGregor*

Since my assignment was the concept of God in Protestantism, I begin with an historical note to exhibit a difficulty the term "Protestant" presents. For several technical reasons I would avoid it.

The term relates to a casual historical incident. By the time of the Diet of Speier in 1526, Germany was divided between those who followed Luther's way and those who preferred allegiance to Rome. That year the Diet of Speier devised an arrangement whereby each prince should order affairs within his own territory according to his own conscience. This was an early expression of the principle later known as *cujus regio, ejus religio,* which indeed was a convenient and sensible one in those days in which pluralistic societies were still unknown and would have been no doubt unworkable. In 1529, however, when the Diet met again at Speier, there happened to be a strong papalist majority, causing legislation to be passed that would have put an end to all toleration of Lutherans in the territories earmarked for the Pope while at the same time enjoining toleration for papalist sympathizers who were in the Lutheran territories. That was unfair legislation, to say the least, and it was the occasion of a formal *protestatio* that was made by six princes in fourteen cities to the Archduke Ferdinand on April 19, 1529. It was what would be called today a "minority rights" protest. Those who supported it were dubbed "Protestants," and the name happened to stick as a sort of nickname for all who supported the Reformation of the

*Distinguished Professor of Philosophy, University of Southern California, Los Angeles, California, U.S.A.

Church. It is on that account alone objectionable as are all nicknames. Scholars should object to it for the still better reason that it refers far too exclusively to an incidental occurrence in the story of what we call the Reformation, which is really a series of movements extending from the fourteenth to the seventeenth centuries in Western Europe. To call the heirs to these movements Protestants is somewhat like calling Latin Catholics *filioquists,* in reference to the *filioque* clause that the Eastern Orthodox repudiate in the Creed and that was nominally the occasion for the schism between East and West in 1054.

No scholar could care much for the term. Educated Roman Catholics today could not like it much, for it suggests that there was no protest within their own heritage, and that of course is absurd. Lutherans certainly do not like the term, and Calvinists were, at least at first, very resistant to it, contending that they did not seek to protest against the Catholic Church but to achieve the Catholic Church Reformed. Most Anglicans, claiming the apostolic succession through bishops and having today special relations to Eastern Orthodoxy as well as historical roots both in Celtic and in medieval Latin Christendom, find themselves far too much identifiable with the Catholic heritage and ethos not to find the term objectionable, though they would be ready also to acknowledge themselves heirs to the Reformation. Those Anglicans who think of themselves simply as Catholics would find the "Protestant" designation simply odious. Moreover, there are many manifestations of religion that are widely listed as products, however remote, of the Reformation (for example, the Aimee Semple MacPherson cult) that can properly be called part of the Reformation heritage only if we allow the Bogomils to be accounted Orthodox and the Albigenses Catholic.

* * *

In the light of that preliminary note we may see at least a little more clearly what we are to consider. The legitimate heirs of the Reformation, Anglican, Lutheran or Calvinist, inherit a concept of

God that is fundamentally the same as the traditional one in Orthodoxy and in Rome. That is, if we were distinguishing it from the concept of the Tao in Chinese thought or Brahman in Vedanta or even Yahweh or Allah, we might well overlook any distinction at all in the mode of conceptualizing God among the heirs of the Reformation on the one hand and those who, on the other, renounce that heritage or have been unaffected by it. When we look, however, at the rich and multifaceted character of the Christian way, (in many respects as much a clearing-house of ideas as has been India), we do find that the question is proper and useful: has the Reformation heritage produced any distinctive contribution to the concept of God within the spectrum of Christian thought?

First we may do well to rehearse what is really distinctive in the Christian concept of God in general. To the Greeks the term *theos* originally meant any wonder, whether a permanent wonder like Venus (symbolizing human sexual love) or a more temporary one, a "nine-day wonder," which might be a hurricane such as nowadays we might call Bertha or Hilda. When Christians used the Greek term, however, they gave it the special biblical monotheistic connotation. *Theos,* with or without the definite article, is used to designate the God of Israel, Yahweh; but the character of God is exhibited in a new way: God reveals himself in and through Jesus the Christ. The Spirit of God dwells in the Church, the Body *(soma)* of Christ. God and Christ are sometimes identified ("I and the Father are one");[1] but the title *ho theos* is used specifically to designate the Father.

The early Christian Fathers, in their discussion and development of the Christian concept of God, took three factors into consideration: (1) the biblical data, (2) the discussions with pagans, heretics and others, and (3) the intellectual climate of their age, which was very deeply influenced by Platonist thought. Very important in any concept of deity in the thinking of the early Fathers was the notion of God as the ground of all things.

---

1 John 10:30.

God is metaphysically "required," so to speak, as the ground of all that is non-God. God may act; but he cannot be acted upon. To suffer is to be acted upon; therefore God cannot suffer. Here can be seen very easily the germ of the development of the doctrine of the Trinity that has become a norm of Christian orthodoxy, as it certainly was for all the Reformation Fathers.

The doctrine of the Trinity is developed in answer to many questions, but notably to questions such as: if God is by definition impassible (incapable of suffering), how could Jesus Christ be God, as Christian faith insists, since he suffered? To put the matter more crudely: who was holding the universe together while God was (as Christians proclaimed) in Christ? Again, when Jesus was a baby in Mary's arms was he omniscient, omnipotent, and otherwise in possession of all the attributes of deity? These were puzzles that even the plain man, to say nothing of the philosopher, could not leave unexamined. The doctrine of the Trinity is, though much else besides, an answer to them, in terms of the best thought of the day. It served well, though the Latin mind, literalistic and unphilosophical as it was, never understood the subtleties of Greek modes of conceptualizing. One modern writer puts the case well in reference to the Council of Chalcedon (A.D. 451): "the clumsy Occident intervened as teacher in a matter which it had not properly learned and did not really understand."[2]

To the Fathers of the Reformation, more than a millenium later, it could still be seen as the hallmark of orthodoxy. Those who, like Servetus (1511-1533), abandoned the doctrine of the Trinity were accounted the most abominable of heretics in the eyes of Calvin as well as in Rome's. That such a doctrine, couched in the terms of such a specifically Greek philosophical outlook should have remained as inviolable to the followers of Luther and Calvin as to the adherents of the Pope is remarkable only to those unaccustomed to the history of religious ideas. In the East, where the Orthodox feel themselves cheek-by-jowl with an exceedingly

2   G.L. Prestige, *God in Patristic Thought* (London: S.P.C.K., 1952), p. 279.

hostile Islam, the Trinity becomes a watchword for Christian orthodoxy. Among Greeks to this day, the frequent use of the sign of the cross is taken to be the surest guarantee of authentic Christian allegiance in a part of the world that feels itself "up against" its Jewish and Muslim neighbors in a way the West has never known even in the days of the Crusades.

Even before the official formulation of trinitarian doctrine, however, the Christian concept of God underwent considerable development in many ways. For example the great Alexandrian theologians, including Athanasius, Didymus and Cyril, while recognizing the incomprehensibility of God (a vehement traditional insistence in Christian as in Jewish thought), taught that man could know God through the human soul, since that soul is made in the divine image. The consequences of developments of this kind are far-reaching, and we shall see that they attain special importance among heirs of the Reformation. From patristic times, the whole Christian tradition of thought about God has been extremely agnostic: God's essence is unknowable. That view is rooted in biblical Hebrew teaching: Moses, in his attempts to speak face to face with God, learned that no man could see God and live. Yet there are also other strands in Christian teaching that appear within that same Alexandrian school: St. Gregory of Nazianzus, for instance, taught that to God, though he is most properly called Being, may also be attributed certain names such as wisdom and justice. Many such Greek patristic proposals about God were distilled into the thinking of the West by Augustine, to whom both the Roman and the Reformed traditions have looked as the most authoritative of the Latin Fathers.

By the time of Luther the medieval scholastic method, which in its Thomistic form was to become quasi-official within the Roman Church, had already been subjected to penetrating criticism. Nicholas of Cusa in the fifteenth century had maintained that God is necessarily unknowable and that he is also immanent in the world. This unity of God and the world can be seen even more explicitly much later in the thought of the sixteenth-century Italian philosopher Giordano Bruno, who after many years of confinement at Rome, was burnt at the stake in 1600 on the

Campo dei Fiori. He had taught an extreme form of what a later age would have called pantheistic immanentism. Bruno's is an extreme case; but we should remember that already by Luther's time Italian and even the more restrained German types of medieval humanism had already produced some fruits that the theologically orthodox would have considered very wayward indeed. The thought of the Reformers cannot be well interpreted simply in terms of a revolt against medieval scholastic methods, though that was of course an obvious part of the reformation movement.

Also very important, however, is the ambivalent attitude of the Reformers to the humanism that had already so radically affected the late medieval outlook. True, they accepted and used much of the work of the humanists and were imbued with their zest for going to the original sources. How else could they have accomplished the biblical renaissance that was so central to their purpose? Yet at the same time the Reformers were even more suspicious of the tendencies of "secular" humanism, especially in the forms it was sometimes already assuming by even the beginning of the sixteenth century, than they were of the theological traditions of the Latin Church. What Luther saw, at first fumblingly but seemingly with increasing clarity, was that whatever the contemporary theologians said and whatever they upheld, their understanding of the divine nature had been vitiated. What had vitiated it was certainly not any excess of conservative adherence to ancient theological models but, on the contrary, a gradual erosion of the authentic teaching of Augustine. The exaggerated place of Mary in the late medieval Church was only a symptom of the error into which, according to Luther, the medieval Latin Church he knew had fallen.

The cause, Luther saw, was a departure from the teaching of the early councils. Though the Church had been officially Chalcedonian, recognizing therefore that Christ is, in the language of piety, "True God and True Man," it was, in effect, crypto-Monophysite, playing up his divine and soft-pedalling his human character. So, since Christ had become too de-humanized, too divinized, to function as Mediator, popular feeling demanded instead a Mediatrix, who was conveniently found in Mary.

Similarly, though in respect to the controversy between Augustine and Pelagius in the fifth century the teachings of Augustine on original sin, grace and predestination had officially triumphed, the majority of the faithful did not really understand, let alone accept, their implications. They were crypto-Pelagian. The Pelagian attitudes of the masses accounted for the development of those emphases that Luther especially deplored, such as reliance on fasting, barefoot pilgrimages and other penitential practices which, in the monastic tradition that had become the official exemplar of the Catholic ideal, included the use of hair shirts and other instruments for the discipline of the spirit through the mortification of the flesh. Whatever the Church taught *de deo* in the theological schools, the widespread understanding was of a deity who was to be placated through such "good" works. The spiritual effect of them was calculable in the sense that if one performed too many one need not fear the "extras" would be redundant, for these "supererogatory" works would overflow and become available to others who had performed too few. Against such mechanistic and radically non-Christian concepts of the workings of God Luther lodged his protest in many forms, all of which appealed to patristic teaching against these medieval innovations. The innovations had indeed become traditional attitudes; but against these traditions Luther put the more venerable traditions of antiquity: the early Fathers, particularly Augustine.

Calvin, leader of what is sometimes called the Second Reformation, shared much of Luther's outlook; but his principal attack was on whatever in medieval thought and practice derogated from or undermined the sovereignty of God. This, too, is very much a return to a primitive Christian emphasis. Whatever else may be said in enunciating a doctrine of God, the divine sovereignty is to be jealously guarded above all else. Calvin's is a revival of the primitive Christian horror of idolatry, a horror that went back to the days of persecution under Nero and Diocletian. In those times of persecution the Roman officials had been often if not generally very reasonable in their demands for acquiescence in the requirements of State worship; yet Christians felt bound in conscience to refuse to offer even the formal pinch of incense or libation of wine before a statue of the deified Emperor that would have satisfied the authorities but would have constituted in the eyes of the Christian community, an idolatrous act. Calvin was by no means alone in his dissatisfaction with the concept of God that had developed in the late medieval Church he knew; but no one else saw it so simply and unequivocally as widespread idolatry destroying the concept of God presented in the Bible and expounded by the early Fathers of the Church. Calvin also had immense respect for these. Not only does he see God as sovereign over all, including, of course, Nature; he sees mankind in very Augustinian terms as *massa peccati,* a mass of sin, tainted and diseased by a morally corrupt inheritance that makes right attitudes impossible without divine aid.

Calvin's teaching *de deo* is eloquently expressed in the opening prayer of confession in the French Calvinist liturgy for regular Sunday worship: "Seigneur Dieu, Père éternel et tout-puissant, nous reconnaissons et nous confessons, devant ta sainte majesté, que nous sommes de pauvres pécheurs, nés dans la corruption, enclins au mal, incapables par nous-mêmes de faire le bien, et qui transgressons tons les jours et en plusieurs manières tes saints commandements, ce qui fait que nous attirons sur nous, par ton juste jugement, la condamnation et la mort." Whatever derogates from the divine sovereignty is nothing less than idolatry.

With the name of Calvin is associated a strongly predestinarian doctrine, and indeed Calvin did spell out a particular doctrine, sometimes called double predestination. His teaching on this subject did not radically differ, however, from what had already been familiar to theologians in Thomistic teaching. The doctrine of Thomas on predestination could have been seen to be just as horrific and just as consoling as was Calvin's; but it was much less prominently displayed. The reason is that while Thomas included it as a metaphysical consequence of his general teaching *de deo,* Calvin, in the later editions of the *Institutes,* dealt with it as a soteriological theme. That made it more likely to become a topic of preaching, and that of course is what in fact happened.

Nevertheless, it remains true that Calvin did take a more dismal view of the human plight and of our total depravity apart from the miracle of divine grace. Calvin, in his zeal to purify Christian thought of every *soupçon* of idolatry, desiccated the concept of God. Formally, he was saying about God little that was fundamentally different from what was predicated of divine Being by the medieval schoolmen; but what he said did indubitably convey the impression of a deity coldly aloof from human affairs, human longings and human needs, though graciously condescending to come to our aid, our hopeless depravity notwithstanding. As correctives of late medieval aberrations, Calvin's emphases were of incalculable value; but in themselves they could result in, and in later Calvinism often did result in, an unfortunate distortion of the concept of God as developed by the early Fathers. Some might go so far as to suggest that Calvin's God is more like an orthodox Muslim concept of deity than of any Christian one; but that would be an exaggeration. Nevertheless, he does show how easily the traditional Christian concept of God could be attenuated and perverted, when peremptorily cut adrift from its metaphysical moorings.

The deistic concept of God, contradistinguished both from the pantheistic concepts of thinkers like Bruno and Spinoza and from the traditional theistic concepts of Christian orthodoxy, emerged chiefly as a result of the influence of the *Aufklärung* on the attitudes of many people within the general Reformation tradition. Because of the exaltation in the eighteenth century of the highly ambiguous notion of Reason, which was literally deified in the apse of the Cathedral of Notre Dame de Paris for several years after the French Revolution, there was a considerable demand, in those countries that had come within the Reformation heritage, for a "natural" theology, that is, a theology that would proceed philosophically according to "rational" principles and free from what were accounted the superstitious accretions of traditional Christian thought. From many a pulpit, Lutheran, Anglican, Presbyterian and Congregationalist, were preached sermons that implied, patently or latently, a concept of God that made the trinitarian doctrine seem otiose *not because* it had expressed the

truth about God in a form that had become outmoded but
because the preacher no longer believed what the doctrine had
been originally designed to express.

Since what such preachers did believe about God tended to be
for obvious reasons more or less deliberately veiled, one can never
be sure of what it was. The general tendency, however, was toward
a concept of God as the disinterested architect of the universe,
which the Newtonian physics of the day encouraged them to
regard as mechanistic. God is too far removed from the affairs of
this world to be expected to care about falling sparrows and the
rescue of wayward men and women. Nevertheless, there is a God
who transcends the universe, and that God ought to be
worshipped, chiefly through virtue as conceived rationalistically
after the manner of the Nichomachaean Ethics, and that somehow
or other virtue will be in the last resort rewarded and vice
punished. These notions had already been adumbrated in the
seventeenth century, for the English-speaking world, by Lord
Herbert of Cherbury,[3] who greatly influenced Locke and, through
him, the Founding Fathers of the United States who were
predominantly deistic in their concept of God.

Alongside of such developments was a very different one:
Pietism in Germany and Methodism in England propagated a type
of religious devotion that expressed an extremely personalistic
concept of God. The outlook of such people may have owed
something, though very indirectly, to the Quattrocento humanists,
such as Pico della Mirandola, whom Savonarola clothed on his
deathbed in the habit of a Dominican friar. It was at any rate
impatient of and even consciously antipathetic to traditional
theology. Because of the personalistic warmth in its attitude
toward God it has often been likened, *mutatis mutandis,* to Indian
bhakti. Certainly it had some affinities with at least some of the
medieval mystical traditions. Hence there is a tendency to care
little for metaphysical expositions of God's nature and to lay

---

3 W.R. Sorley, "The Philosophy of Herbert of Cherbury," *Mind,* N.S. iii (1894), pp.
491-508.

emphasis, rather, on religious experience. To this point we shall presently return.

A crucial blow was dealt to the enterprise of "natural" theology by Kant; hence his great importance in the later formulation of thought about God among the heirs of the Reformation. His importance in these quarters has not escaped the notice of Neo-Thomists. Through his attack on speculative metaphysics in all its forms, Kant strove to show the impossibility of any rational proof of the existence of God, even the teleological, which he seems to have considered somewhat more plausible than the others. Kant's intention was, of course, anything other than destructive of belief in God. Moreover, when we ask what kind of God, he provides at least a clue in his plea for the only argument he considers valid: the argument from moral experience. "I had to remove knowledge *(Wissen),*" he wrote, "in order to make room for faith *(Glauben)*." From the way in which moral obligation is interiorly known, we can go on to affirm the existence of a wise and holy and almighty God. Kant's conviction that all men enjoy such an interior experience of moral obligation suggests an underlying belief in the presence in our inner life of a spiritual "cell" such as is seen in the medieval mystical tradition that saw in *synteresis* the "ground of the soul." This notion is not as fanciful as it might seem: the term first appears in Jerome's Commentary on Ezekiel, apparently as a scribal error for *syneidesis,* which is the standard Greek word for "conscience." *Synteresis,* latinized, runs through a medieval mystical tradition exemplified by Eckhart; but it is used also as a technical term in Thomist ethics,[4] where it signifies our knowledge of the first principles of moral action. At any rate, to modern ways of thinking, Kant seems to many to have shared an older presupposition about the inner life that may not be as universal as he accounted it. We all know of people whose inner life seems either to be extinct or not yet to have come about.

Be that as it may, Kant's undermining of speculative meta-

---

4   E.g., Thomas Aquinas, *De veritate,* 17, 2.

physics had also another and very different consequence for the development of the concept of God among the heirs of the Reformation. The pietistic development already noticed had in some measure prepared the way for it. If we cannot have any certainty about the meaning of the term "God" in the sense of the ontological reality that is acclaimed in traditional Christian thought as beyond all experience, and therefore cannot usefully talk about such a Being, we can nevertheless recognize in our inner life a sense of dependence on a something-beyond-ourselves. The criterion of the authenticity of religious experience can lie only in feeling *(Gefühl)* and intuition *(Anschauung)*. Schleiermacher expressed that mood of the rising nineteenth-century Romanticism, in its religious aspect. His influence on the thought of the Reformation tradition has been immense. To him, for example, Rudolf Otto, whose much criticized but important book *Das Heilige,* was partly indebted. Schleiermacher's intellectual progeny have not always been so creditable, however. From him the transition was easy to a view that became not uncommon among those heirs of the Reformation in whom the connection with Luther and Calvin was growing dim, namely, that the mode of conceptualizing God is unimportant: what matters is the experience attending religious conviction. That experience, on this view, is sufficient to provide a calculus of religious value. The susceptibility of such a view to the ravages of modern psychologism is too obvious to need exposition.

Schleiermacher's expression of the Romantic spirit was not without parallels in the Roman Church. In France, Francois René, Vicomte de Chateaubriand, published his *Génie du christianisme* in 1802, just after the Concordat between Pius VII and Napoleon. After the deaths of his mother and sister, he experienced a deep personal crisis that resulted in his conviction of the value of the Christian faith. But what was that value and what was the nature of his belief? "Ma conviction est sortie du coeur; j'ai pleuré et j'ai cru." Whether the traditional Christian concept of God that the rationalists of the Enlightenment seemed to have undermined was tenable or not, Chateaubriand noted that the treasures of European art and the splendor of European civilization had as their mainspring the Christian religion, and he thought that this reflection should be enough to rehabilitate Christian faith. Once again the quality of the experience had become the calculus of religious value.

One might well suppose that by this time, post-Reformation thought had undergone almost every influence that could have affected it without totally destroying its original stance. No sooner, however, was the old rationalism decently buried than a new and still more influential rationalism was to appear in the monumental speculative edifice erected by Hegel, whose effects on nineteenth-century thought, not least among the heirs of the Reformation, were immense. Anyone who was exposed to the Hegelian influence seems to have been unable, despite himself, to shed it. Hegel enabled those post-Hegelians who wanted to arraign themselves with the Christian cause to re-interpret the Christian concept of God in terms the secular thought of the day could understand. Nor was it implausible to argue, as they did, that if it had been proper to couch the faith in the intellectual terms of the fourth century, as the patristic exponents of trinitarian doctrine had done, why was it improper to engage in a similar enterprise in terms of nineteenth-century thought? The Christian doctrine of God as the Creator who transcends his creation seemed to be lost in face of bows of respect to a Spinozistic immanentism. Origen, the greatest scholar of the early Church, had been generally accounted heretical for his opinion *inter alia* that creation is an eternal activity of God (contrary to the commonly received interpretation of the first chapter of Genesis) since without a universe God would be at some point inactive and not almighty. Origenism, however, no longer seemed to scholarly heirs of the Reformation so terrible a heresy as once it had been accounted. Then was Hegel to be deprecated as a destroyer of the Christian faith or was he not, rather, to be acclaimed a nineteenth-century Thomas Aquinas for the Reformation tradition?

The story of the collapse of such hopes is well known. The twentieth-century flight from rationalism took many forms, and Hegelianism lost favor in every one of them, though there are signs of his possible rehabilitation in some quarters. Hegel's influence, though felt in France and Italy, was most pervasive in those lands that had entered into the Reformation heritage. Nor need we seek far for the reason. Hegel, as is well known, had theological interests before developing his immense philosophical system, and despite his denigration of religion as a sort of "baby philosophy" he remained always a religious philosopher. Indeed, were we to forget that, he would become, as for many he has become, unintelligible. He is, however, a neo-Gnostic. That was what made him so intolerable to Kierkegaard. Christian faith from its infancy has always held Gnosticism suspect and, while it has been tolerant of it up to a point, if not hospitable, it always has ended by resisting it. What happened in the second century in the Mediterranean world and in the twelfth in Provence, where the Albigenses had almost succeeded in destroying the Church, was re-enacted in yet another form in the twentieth, when the long-unheard voice of Kierkegaard began, soon after World War I, to bring about a revolution in the thinking of every theologian within the Reformation heritage.

Yet throughout the nineteenth century Hegel's influence among theologians in Germany, England, Scotland and the Scandinavian countries was astounding. F.C. Bauer, D.F. Strauss, and the rest of the Tubingen school that revolutionized the study of ecclesiastical history, as well as the great German scholars who developed modern literary methods of biblical exegis and criticism within the Reformation heritage, were deeply affected by Hegel. That England and Scotland, whose philosophical traditions are empiricist, both came heavily under his spell is noteworthy. The nature of his influence on the concept of God in the Reformation heritage within the English-speaking world may be seen from books such as A.S. Pringle-Pattison's Gifford Lectures.[5] Of course men such as Bradley, Bosanquet and Pringle-Pattison were far too explicitly Hegelian to receive the *imprimatur* of any Church within the Reformation tradition; nevertheless they exerted incalculable

---

5   A. Seth Pringle-Pattison, *The Idea of God.* New York: Oxford University Press, 1917.

influence on the more reticent and conservative churchmen who enjoyed that ecclesiastical approval, especially those among them who hoped to achieve the marriage of theology to the science of the day, which Hegel's evolutionary view of the universe seemed to promise. That Hegelianism could go into reverse, so to speak, in the thought of Feuerbach and Marx is no more remarkable than that the existentialism of Kierkegaard should re-appear a century later in the nihilism of Sartre.

Towards the end of the nineteenth and at the beginning of the twentieth century, there was a considerable movement among scholars and theologians in the Reformation tradition to develop a thoroughgoing evolutionary approach to religion that would have given the traditional concept of God a new dimension. Henry Drummond and John Fiske are examples of leaders of that movement, about which I have written elsewhere.[6] It was in many respects a forerunner of the kind of process-thought we find in Teilhard de Chardin, and indubitably provided a foundation for understanding the Christian faith in a way that made the old Platonic formulations seem inadequate. Not only could God now be seen as more directly involved in the evolutionary process; the biological evolutionism of Darwin and Huxley could be seen as only part of a spiritual evolution.

Unfortunately, that movement was halted. The catastrophic effects of World War I arrested such developments in thought, and in their place came a wave of anti-intellectualism, which in its various forms has considerably affected the concept of God among the heirs of the Reformation, without, however, proportionally clarifying it. Among the masses it has done nothing to mitigate the insensitive literalism of so-called "fundamentalist" groups, and among the educated professional classes it has brought about much bewilderment. For the ordinary churchgoer is naturally perplexed by the seemingly great intellectual contradictions with which he is confronted when he tries to grapple with the

---

6 See the sections "The Superman in Early Christian Thought" and "The Superman in Late Nineteenth-century Thought" in my *Philosophical Issues in Religious Thought* (Boston: Houghton Mifflin, 1972), pp. 194 ff.

theological ideas of those who expound the Christian faith in terms of the Reformation tradition. Nor is his perplexity remarkable. For in the amalgam of numerous kinds of humanism, pragmatism and revelationism he can find no sure, helpful guide in interpreting his own experience in a situation in which the intelligent reading of the Bible had become very difficult for the layman. The only common element he is able to find in almost all his teachers is a repudiation of metaphysical inquiry, about which the only disagreement he finds among them seems to him to be whether it is untrustworthy, incredible or meaningless.

That the *succès fou* of Bishop Robinson's *Honest to God* should have shown that thousands of well-bred, well-educated and technologically skilled professional people can still suppose that they are expected to conceive of God as being seated on a throne in the "middle" of the sky sufficiently establishes the failure of the leaders of the Reformation tradition to provide ordinary men and women with an intelligible concept of God by which they might be enabled to interpret the experience of the God-dimension in their own lives. Linguistic analysis, however useful an instrument for the philosopher, is certainly not enough to accomplish what is needed to help contemporary people to conceptualize God in such a way as to exhibit the value of their Reformation heritage instead of traducing it. Whatever methods are used for that end, they will have to include ontological and metaphysical procedures, and that is to say they will have to be philosophical in the sense intended by Gilson when he remarked that "philosophy always buries its undertakers."[7]

A SELECT BIBLIOGRAPHY

Note: The bibliography of works on the concept of God in the Reformation Tradition is, of course, enormous. The following short list, confined to works in English, is offered by way of introduction to the distinctive theological emphases.

[7] E. Gilson, *The Unity of Philosophical Experience* (London: Sheed and Ward, 1938), p. 312.

Baillie, John, *Our Knowledge of God.* New York: Charles Scribner's Sons, 1959.

Barth, Karl, *Credo,* tr. J.S. McNab. London: Hodder and Stoughton, 1936.

———, *The Humanity of God,* tr. J.N. Thomas and T. Wieser. Richmond, Virginia: John Knox Press, 1960.

———, *The Word of God and the Word of Man.* New York: Harper Torchbooks, 1957.

Calvin, John, *Institutes of the Christian Religion,* ed. John T. McNeill. 2 vols. Philadelphia: Westminster Press, 1960.

> Especially to be noted are the passages as follows.
>> Divine attributes: 1, 10,2; 1,16,2; 3,20,40 f.
>> Majesty of God: 3,12,1-3.
>> Omnipotence: 1,14,3.
>> Unity: 1,10,3.
>> Triune God: 1,13,2; 1,13,20.
>> God as creator: 1,6; 1,10,1.
>> God as sustainer: 1,16.
>> God as ruler: 1,17,2.
>> Justice of God: 2,11,13f.; 3,23,3-7.
>> Mercy of God: 2,8,21; 3.,12,4-8.
>> Love of God: 2.16, 1-4.
>> Grace of God: 2,3,3; 3,13,5; 4,1,24-26.

De Senarclens, Jacques, *Heirs of the Reformation,* tr. G.W. Bromiley, with foreword by T.F. Torrance. Philadelphia: Westminster Press, 1958.

Dowey, E.A., *The Knowledge of God in Calvin's Theology.* New York: Columbia University Press, 1952.

Farmer, H.H., *The World and God.* London: Nisbet, 1935.

Gerrish, B., *Grace and Reason: A Study in the Theology of Luther.* New York: Oxford Univeristy Press, 1962.

Heppe, H., *Reformed Dogmatics.* London: George Allen and Unwin, 1950.

Leith, John H. (ed.), *Creeds of the Churches.* New York: Doubleday, 1963.

McGiffert, A.C., *Protestant Thought Before Kant.* New York: Charles Scribner's Sons, 1911.

Mackintosh, Hugh Ross, *Types of Modern Theology: Schleiermacher to Barth.* London: Nisbet, 1937.

Matczak, Sebastian A., *Karl Barth on God: Our Knowledge of the Divine Existence.* New York: Alba House, 1962.

Ogden, Schubert M., *The Reality of God.* New York: Harper and Row, 1963.

Parker, T.H.L., *The Doctrine of the Knowledge of God.* Edinburgh: Oliver and Boyd, 1952.

Paterson, W.P., *The Rule of Faith,* 4th enlarged edition. London: Hodder and Stoughton, 1932.

Schlink, E., *Theology of the Lutheran Confessions,* tr. P.F. Koenneke and H.S.A. Bouman. Philadelphia: The Board of Publication of the Lutheran Church of America, 1961.

Tillich, Paul, *Systematic Theology.* 3 vols. Chicago: University of Chicago Press, 1951-1963.

Walker, W., *The Creeds and Platforms of Congregationalism.* New York: Charles Scribner's Sons, 1893.

CHAPTER XVII

GOD IN THE ORIENTAL
ORTHODOX BELIEF

*Gabriel Abdelsayed**

The Oriental Orthodox Churches are the Coptic, Ethiopian, Syrian, Armenian, and Malabarite, so-called non-Chalcedonian Churches that separated themselves from the communion of both the Roman Catholic and Eastern Orthodox Churches,[1] in the year A.D. 451,[2] because of a misunderstanding of the latter group that committed them to Monophysitism. To designate these churches as Monophysite and to address them as such, as some historians and theologians still do today, is a polemically motivated misunderstanding. In reality there are no substantial dogmatic differences between them and the Eastern Orthodox Churches. Rather, the basis of their separation is the fact that in the formulation of certain fundamental truths of faith in the ancient Christian period, terms were used which did not correspond to the meaning presupposed by subsequent precise definitions. This separation is based on misunderstandings, national and social conflicts, intolerance, and jurisdictional arrogance.[3]

However, the seeds of Christianity were first sown by the Apostles of Christ in the countries where these churches belong. But, before that time, some other Jews from various Oriental countries who happened to be present at Jerusalem on the day of

---

*Assistant Professor of the African Studies at St. John's University, New York, U.S.A.

1   The Byzantine Orthodox Churches.

2   At the Council of Chalcedon in 451.

3   Elias Tsonievsky, "The Union of The Two Natures In Christ According To The Non-Chalcedonian Churches and Orthodoxy," *The Greek Orthodox Theological Review,* XIII, 2 (Fall, 1968), p. 170.

Pentecost, returned to their dwelling countries where they established Christian congregations.[4]

St. Mark, the writer of the second Gospel and a Jewish native of
Cyrene,[5] who was early instructed in the Christian faith and
appointed one of the seventy disciples chosen by Christ, came to
Egypt to establish the Coptic Church in the year 42.[6] Moreover,
the story of the Flight of the Holy Family from Palestine into
Egypt strongly tied the latter to the history of Oriental Orthodox
Christianity.[7] At a very early time Christianity was also introduced informally into Ethiopia. An eunuch of Queen Candace had
gone on a pilgrimage visit to Jerusalem and on his way back was
baptized.[8] But the church was formally organized and the
sacraments administered only from the later years of the reign of
kings Abreha and Atsbaha, the two brothers who inherited the
throne from 290. It was Frumentius, from Tyre, early in the
fourth century who undertook this great work, supported by the
royal brothers, until 332 when Christianity became the state
religion in Ethiopia. Since then, the Coptic Church has been
undertaking the responsibility to send a metropolitan to
administer the Ethiopian Church affairs. In 1967, the church
moved to a rather decentralized system when an Ethiopian Bishop
was ordained to replace the Coptic Metropolitan. However, in
1959 his position was raised to Patriarch Catholicos of Ethiopia
and subsequently was vested the right of ordaining diocesan
bishops to his own church.[9]

The Syrian Orthodox Church of Antioch believes itself to be

4 A.J. Arberry (ed.), *Religion in the Middle East,* 2 vols. (London: Cambridge
University Press, 1969), I, p. 423. Cf. *Acts,* 12:25.

5 In Libya, an outlying province of Egypt since the days of Ptolemy I.

6 According to Eusebius, this took place during the second year of the Roman
Emperor Claudius. See *Ecclesiastical History,* 2 vols. Tr. from Greek by Kirsopp Lake
and E.L. Oulton (London: Heineman, 1926-1932), I, pp. 11-24.

7 M. Jullien, *Traditions et legendes Coptes sur le voyage de la Sainte Famille en
Egypte* (Paris: Missions Catholiques, Vol. XIX, 1886), pp. 3-12. D. Meinardus, *In the
Steps of The Holy Family* (Cairo: Dar Al-Maaref, 1963), pp. 10-12.

8 *Acts,* 8:26-40.

9 *The Oriental Orthodox Churches, Addis Ababa Conference,* ed. by the Interim
Secretariat Oriental Orthodox Conference (Addis Ababa: Artistic Printers, 1965), p. 47.

directly related to the earthly life of our Lord Jesus Christ in that it has Syriac, the mother tongue of Christ, His blessed Mother, the Apostles and the Apostolic community in Jerusalem, as its liturgical language. It was early in Antioch where the disciples of Christ were first called Christians. St. Peter spent a time there preaching the word and is said to have founded the Syrian Church. The Supreme Head of this Church is the Patriarch of Antioch who has the right to appoint the Catholicos of the Syrian Orthodox Church of India or the Malabarite Church.[10]

The origin of the Armenian Orthodox Church dates back from the Apostolic age too. According to the ancient tradition which is well supported by historical evidence, the two Apostles of Christ, St. Thaddeus and St. Bartholomeus, laid the foundation of the Armenian Church.[11] The greatest saint whose missionary life and work were given as a living sacrifice in efforts to spread Christianity, was St. Gregory the Illuminator, who has been recognized and venerated as the Patron Saint of the Armenian Church.[12]

1. How Do Oriental Orthodox Churches Know God?

The Oriental Orthodox Churches basically derive their belief in God from five main sources: the structure of the universe, the conscience, the human instinctual accord, inspiration and history.

A famous contemporary Coptic theologian, Father Michael Mena, explains the impact of the elements of the universe on the Oriental mind: "If you look up to the sky or down to the earth, right or left, you find the universe abundant of concrete proofs that obviously proclaim the existence of the Supreme Being that must be eternal, self-conscious, wise, rational, existent in every place and can never be limited."[13] He also adds that God granted

---

10 *Ibid.,* p. 27.

11 Cf. *John,* 14:22-24 and *John,* 1:43-50.

12 *Op. cit.,* p. 35.

13 Fr. Michael Mena, *Ilm Al-Lahut* (Theology according to the Coptic Orthodox Faith), in Arabic, 2 vols. (Cairo: Al-Mahaba Publications, 1948), I, p. 107.

man a free will towards his own belief. The various elements of the beings that were and are still efficiently functioning introduce to man the natural reason for his existence. Facts about the organs of the body, such as the minute functioning of the eyes and the heart and the various elements of the air that spontaneously match together in order to develop life on earth, are all adequate natural reasons that a wise Supreme Being created them, controls them, and continues to keep them functioning.[14]

Perhaps Egypt, as one of the Oriental countries, gives us the simplest case of the development of man's experience in the natural reason about God's existence.

The physical reasons and social background of the Egyptian stand as important elements that massively contributed to his discovery of a Supreme Being. Egypt is cut off relatively, from the direct contact of the Western World by the Mediterranean on the north, and by a vast barren desert rising in the east. In the west stretching over more than a thousand miles of Sahara wasteland and fenced off too on the south by wild equatorial mountains, Egypt lay for centuries quiet under the sun, with her river of life in that rainless land. Since ancient history the Egyptian realized that his material needs were assured by the annual overflow of the great stream of the Nile. During the neolithic period the first permanent residents of the Nile Valley were mainly attracted by its national privileges. Later on, after being housed in wood, bricks and then stone, they organized themselves into communities that appeared in the predynastic period in the city-state system. Depending mainly on the Nile for its agriculture, each city-state learned from its neighbors how to regulate and control its overflow. Yet, influenced by local environment, they had separate customs and gods. Then, as cultures grew more attractive and inter-communication increased, there came amalgamation, usually by way of conquest of one city-state by another. For centuries this process went on until two kingdoms were established; one in Upper Egypt in the Nile Valley and the other of lower Egypt in

14 *Ibid.*, pp. 108-111.

the Delta. Finally, these two kingdoms were united into one by Nermer Mena the founder of the First Dynasty, about 2900 B.C.[15]

Since the very beginning of ancient history, the Egyptian has made up his mind to know God. But he knew Him through various aspects of animism and natural phenomena too. Apparently his beasts and birds were not worshipped for their animal qualities but for their super-human powers and characteristics that challenged the Egyptian's mentality. However, in evident recognition of the belief that the divine as such could manifest itself in either man or beast and so showed itself in both, they acquired human bodies under their animal heads, and vice-versa. For the gods seemed pictured best as composite beings. The God, Khnummu, for instance, had a man's body with a ram's head, while Anubis, the guardian of the cemetery and guide of the dead, possessed a jackal's head. Most curious was the greyhound form of Set, with an upright tail suggestive of the wart hog, though his legs were human. His great adversary, Horus, had a hawk's head to signify that he was the sun.[16]

The movement of the sun appeared to them as a cycle, rising in the early morning, then, moving on its way in the sky from east to west until it sets or, as he believed, dies for the night then rises again to resume its constant uninterrupted activity on the following day, shimmering so gloriously in the cloudless Egyptian sky. This inspired the Egyptians with the belief of a supernatural power that gives life to man and to all existing beings and in the meantime, taught them about death and resurrection. This Supreme Being to be approached or rather contained in their minds could only be embodied in the greatest power in the cosmos, the sun. This notion was symbolized by setting the sun's disk in the middle of the serpents with their heads reared and two wings of a falcon. In this form the Sun-god, or Re (or Amen Re) as it became known to the masses, was believed to be a falcon flying

15 John B. Noss, *Man's Religions* (New York: The MacMillan Co., 1963), pp. 52-53.
16 *Ibid.,* p. 54.

across the sky, dominating not only Egypt but also the whole world. Other nations of the Near East adopted this Egyptian symbol.[17]

When Upper and Lower Egypt were united under the First Dynasty Horus, the chief god of the Delta and Set dominant in Upper Egypt continued their bitter struggle; for since Horus was now conceived to be the Sun God, Set became the power of darkness. Even after their enmity was caught up and made a minor theme in the dramatic myth of Isis and Osiris, they went on with their feud, Horus as the son-avenger (he was now the son of Isis by Osiris) and Set, the brother of Osiris, as the fratricidal uncle, his heart full of murderous jealousy. But, triads and enniads (or groups of nine) were formed also for other and quite natural reasons.

However, during the higher life of the ancient empire, Egyptians were advancing in their knowledge of God until they reached a monotheistic structure. In 1375 B.C. when Amenhotep IV became King, he was convinced that the Sun God was the god of the whole world and also that he was the only god. There was an old Egyptian word "atun" which meant "sun" and Amenhotep IV took this word as the name for his new God. Amenhotep believed that one God created not only all the lower creatures but also all races of men, both Egyptians and foreigners. Moreover, the King saw in his God a kindly Father, who maintained all his creatures by his goodness so that even the birds in the marshes were aware of his kindness and uplifted their wings like arms to praise him, as a beautiful line in one of the hymns tells us. In all the progress of men, no one had ever before caught such a vision of the great Father of all.[18] Therefore, Amenhotep commanded that all the people of the Empire should worship only the sun, as the source of all life and power in the universe and forget all the old gods. In order that they might do this, he closed all the temples, especially those of the god of Amen, and cast out their priests. All over his

17 J.H. Breasted, *Ancient Times: A History of The Early World* (New York: Ginn and Co., 1935), pp. 69-70.
18 *Ibid.*, p. 117.

country he had the names of the gods erased and cut out. Consequently, he began to use new symbols to identify his one God, Atun. His dedication to his monotheistic religion also motivated him to change his royal name, Amen-Hotep (meaning "Amen is satisfied") to Ikhnatun, which means "Profitable to Atun."[19]

However, a new faith like this, though nourished by symbols and hymns, could not easily spread among common people in such an early age of the world. It came to its end right after the King's death due to the discontent of the Amen priests who managed to recover the worship of their god and his temples. But this had showed, after all, that, there was a readiness among the people of the country to believe in one God, Creator, above all, Father of all, and a life-giving God. In the meantime, during the Greco-Roman period the newly introduced religions were consequently unable to deeply infiltrate in the life of both the Egyptians and the Syrians. These oriental beliefs in Incarnation, Resurrection, and the readiness to accept a monotheistic religion, undoubtedly paved the way for Christianity to spread easily among the masses rather than any other area in the world.

Also, at the time of the Apostles, the same reasons were introduced. St. Paul, in his epistle to the Romans, says: "Ever since the creation of the world, His invisible nature, namely, His eternal power and deity, has been clearly perceived in the things that have been made. So, they are without excuse; for, although they knew God they did not honor Him as God or give thanks to Him but they became futile in their thinking and their senseless minds were darkened."[20]

Father Michael Mena of the Coptic Church quotes St. John Chrysostom: "If God had only informed us about His existence through the Scriptures, His knowledge should have been only confined to the literate or the rich who are able to acquire such books. Therefore, God made Himself manifest in elements of

19 *Ibid.*, p. 116.
20 *Romans* 1:20-21.

nature and the way they technically function."[21] King David had
had such a perception and had been inspired to say: "The heavens
are telling the glory of God; and the firmament proclaims His
handiwork."[22]

St. Athanasius (325-373), who is the founder of the Coptic and
Oriental theology, explains this issue: "We dare to say that all
things in the universe should be either created or not created. In
case it is created it should be changing; and so far it is changing, it
continues to be characterized with this phenomenon of change.
This change either makes it perishable or translational . . . And,
since all things in the universe are changing, they must be created
and consequently, must have a Creator. This Creator must not be
created or even changing. Therefore, He should be the God who
regulates and controls the various elements of the universe,
whether fire, water, air or earth. He should be omnipotent, and
also keeps them without annihilation or rather perishing one
another . . . Who established the heavens, the earth, fire and water,
and everything therein, and planned for the functions of each
without exceeding its limits?"[23] St. Athanasius then raises a
question: "In case these elements are self-formed, could the sun be
able to continue giving light to all the universe at a time?" He also
discusses the circulation of the earth, the moon and the other
planets and how, according to the Creator's plan, they efficiently
function. "If we believe in God the Creator, we could realize that
He, unlike creatures, has no limits and can never be described."[24]

The conscience, in turn, is another source of the knowledge of
God. Although the atheist may deny the existence of God, yet, in
his subconscious still something urges him not to do what is
ethically prohibited, as it is also the cause of any inner conflict in
man that arises between his evil and good tendencies. The Oriental
Orthodox Churches quote St. Augustine in this concept where he

21 Fr. M. Mena, *op. cit.*, p. 112.

22 *Psalms* 19:1.

23 St. Athanasius, *Kamal Al-Burhan Ala Haqiqat Al-Eman* (Complete Proof on the
Authenticity of the Faith), in Arabic (Cairo: Al-Mahaba Publications, 1947), pp. 7-8.

24 *Ibid.*, p. 8.

says: "The Almighty God set up in man's heart a court where the mind acts as a judge, the conscience as a prosecutor and the thought as a witness. He wrote on the heart, the token of His existence, His oneness, eternity, creation and care of the world."[25]

St. Paul in reference to this point says: "Their conscience also bears witness and their conflicting thoughts accuse, or perhaps excuse them."[26] The thoughts of men are either accusing or approving man's actions before a Being to whom they feel accountable.

But, because conscience does not alone reveal the true God, the third source from which these Oriental Churches derive their belief in God is the human instinctual accord. It is an innate feeling that makes men always have the inclination to believe in the existence of God. An instinctual tendency as such was also taken by St. Paul as an incontestable principle when he addressed the Athenean philosophers: "For as I passed along and observed the objects of your worship, I found also an alter with this inscription: 'To an unknown god'. What, therefore, you worship as unknown God who made the world and everything in it, being Lord of heaven and earth, does not live in shrines made by man nor is he served by human hands as though He needed anything since He Himself gives to all men life and breath and everything."[27]

However, these three previous elements or resources of knowledge of God cannot stand alone as dependable. The true God has more fully revealed Himself in the Scriptures, inspired by The Holy Spirit. Inspiration and history stand as the important evidences for the existence of God. All the incidents of the scriptures are inspired and have their coincidence with the mainstream of history. As an instance, the demolition of Babylon and Ninwah, mentioned in Isaiah and of Jerusalem as had been preached by Jesus Christ, are some of the historical tangible evidences for the prophecies on issues as such.[28]

25 *Ibid.*, p. 114.
26 *Romans,* 2:15.
27 *Acts,* 17:23-25.
28 Father Michael Mena, *op. cit.,* pp. 119-120.

The belief of natural man may lead his conscience to think of the Supreme Being in one of various ways. Some people believe in one God (monotheism), others in many gods (polytheism), and still others say that all is God (pantheism). Therefore, the natural knowledge of God is insufficient in the Oriental Orthodox Churches to arrive at the right knowledge of God, as the Scriptures plainly teach. While natural man knows something about God, he is, nevertheless, by nature spiritually dead, and therefore he cannot by his own reason or strength know the true God. Rational thinking only leads to certain rational conclusions on the basis of his limited knowledge of God, and these conclusions prompt him to individual—misapplied—worship.

Thus, we should say that the Oriental Orthodox Churches, founded by the Apostles, recognized the Holy Scriptures as potential means for man's knowledge of God and for his salvation too. "The Holy Scriptures . . . are able to make thee wise unto salvation through Faith which is in Christ Jesus. All Scripture is given by inspiration of God and is profitable for doctrine, for reproof, for correction, for instruction in righteousness, that the man of God may be perfect, thoroughly furnished unto all good works."[29]

The Scriptures are recognized as the Word of God because they were inspired by Him.[30] The word inspiration means a "breathing in." "Divinely inspired" means "God breathed." When we speak of the inspiration of the Bible by God, we mean that God gave the writers the impulse or driving force to write; that they wrote as God wanted them to write, and that they used the very forms of words God wanted to express His divine thoughts. This is called "verbal inspiration." God moved the writers when they were to write, what they were to write, and how they were to write. Just how God inspired these writers, we are not told. While under the Spirit's direction, each writer was an individual who employed his individual talents, and used expressions, general knowledge, and

29 *2 Timothy*, 3:15-17.
30 *2 Peter*, 1:20-21.

style peculiar to him.[31] There is a concrete evidence in history about the authenticity of the scriptures.

History itself is not in contradiction with the historical books of the Scriptures. Both are used by the Oriental Orthodox Churches as potential elements for their faith in God. Each church includes in her liturgical prayers a portion of the historical events related to certain ecclesiastical incidents added as proofs for the existence of God, His omnipotence, and providence.

2. Who Is God In The Oriental Orthodox Churches?

The Oriental Orthodox Churches know God as One, undivided and indivisible Essence, in which there are three distinct Prosopons (Persons), that are the Father, the Son, and the Holy Spirit. They believe in the "Triune" or "Trinity" meaning "Three in One." The Scriptures teach a strict monotheism, that there is but One God, however, in the Gospel according to St. Matthew 28:19 we read: "Go ye, therefore, and teach all nations, baptizing them in the name of the Father and of the Son and of the Holy Spirit." Each of the Three Prosopons of the Trinity is to be acknowledged as God; but the Three constitute One God only.[32] The Father is true God. "But to us there is but one God, the Father of whom are all things and we in Him."[33] Jesus Christ, the Son, is true God. "Truly, truly, I say to you, before Abraham was, I am."[34] "In His Son, Jesus Christ, this is the true God and eternal life."[35] According to the flesh is the Christ God Who is over all, be blessed forever.[36] The Holy Spirit is true God. In Acts 5:3,4 the Holy Spirit is called God and in 1 Corinthians 3:16 the Christians are called "the temple of God" because the Holy Spirit dwells in them.

---

31 Bishop Gregorius, *Mohadarat Fi Lahut Al-Massih* (Lectures on Christology), in Arabic (Cairo: Coptic Seminary Publications, 1968), p. 129.

32 St. Athanasius, *op. cit.,* pp. 31-33.

33 *1 Corinthians,* 8:6.

34 *John,* 8:58.

35 *1 John,* 5:20.

36 *Romans,* 9:5.

St. Athanasius, on whose theological writings the Oriental Churches still rely, adds that man's perception of the Essence of God is unattainable since He, unlike material beings, is not limited to any space or place.[37] "The angels even created by God, unlike earthly creatures, can see God, due to their tenuity. They are, nevertheless, of another essence from God. However, men like Abraham, Daniel or Job, of the Old Testament could see Him only when He became manifest in a semi-material state of being."[38] "God can only be known as the Creator of the whole Cosmos, of the Heavens and Angels, the earth and everything therein; man and animals. Man knows God as life-giver, Merciful, Righteous, Omnipotent but after all He is Intangible and Invisible. He is All-knowing or Omniscient since He is present in everything and every place."[39]

"He is not a part of His creation and nothing may happen to Him as it does to His creation. He is eternal without any beginning or end, above quantity or quality."[40]

"Many human characteristics and names have been attributed to God in the Scriptures; however, they fail to designate His essence."[41] For instance, God, Who is not composite, is unlike man who has two eyes, with a limited eyesight, and hearing, nor can His eyesight be limited to two eyes and his hearing limited to two ears. It should not be said that God speaks with a mouth, a tongue, teeth and lips that give out a structure and harmony as such, a voice reaching through the air . . . God's word is generated from Him to the hearer without the need of a tongue or mouth while never disunited from Him.[42] God gave himself these characteristics because He knew that man would be unable to perceive His essence.

When God wanted to manifest His existence to men, the Incarnation of His Word took place. Thus, in our Lord Jesus

---

37 St. Athanasius, *op. cit.*, p. 10.
38 *Ibid.*, p. 12.
39 *Ibid.*, pp. 13-14.
40 *Ibid.*, p. 16.
41 *Ibid.*, p. 14 (as speaking of the eyes, ears, hands, lips or feet of God).
42 *Ibid.*, pp. 15-16.

Christ, the God Word Incarnate, the Divine nature united with the human nature into one hypostasis or physis.[43]

St. Athanasius, in the meantime, obviously explained the Oneness of God by referring many times to the Scriptures, for instance Ex., 2:8; Deut., 6:4; Isaiah 23 & 10; John 17:4 and others. He denounced, with clear logic and dogmatic proofs, the sanctimony that believed in two gods—one of the light and good and the other is of darkness and evil.[44] He said that the One God is the source of good, and all that He created is good. However, if the human being does not behave in the straight path of goodness, he consequently sins and falls into evil. Hence, good is relatively natural of his nature, while evil is casual and results from his disobedience.[45]

The Oriental Orthodox Churches always use the Nicene Creed that embodies their belief in God, and it is used in most of their liturgical prayers. The Creed itself was an outcome of the anti-rational thinking and literal misinterpretation of the Scriptures. It was Arius, a Libyan Priest in the Church of Alexandria, Egypt, who introduced this misinterpretation in the year A.D. 318.

The dogmas he invented contrary to the Scriptures, are these: That God was not always the Father, but that there was a period when he was not the Father; that the Word of God was not from eternity, but was made out of nothing; for that the ever-existing God ('the I AM'—the eternal One) made him, Who did not previously exist, out of nothing; wherefore there was a time when He did not exist, inasmuch as the Son is a creature and a work. That he is neither like the Father as it regards his essence, nor is by nature either the Father's true word, or true Wisdom, but indeed one of His works and creatures, being erroneously called Word and Wisdom, since He was himself made by God's own Word and the Wisdom which is in God, whereby God both made all things and Him also. Wherefore, he is as to his nature mutable and susceptible

43 *Ibid.*, p. 16.
44 *Ibid.*, pp. 17-18.
45 *Ibid.*, p. 18.

of change, as all other rational creatures are: hence the Word is alien to and other than the essence of God; and the Father is inexplicable by the Son, and indivisible to him, for neither does the Word perfectly and accurately know the Father, neither can he distinctly see Him. The Son knows not the nature of his own essence: for He was made on our account, in order that God might create us by Him, as by an instrument nor would He ever have existed unless God had wished to create us.[46]

Arius quoted some texts of the Gospel according to St. John, literally misusing them in support of his heresy that Jesus Christ, the Logos Incarnate, was inferior to God the Father. He added that God adopted Him as a Son, forseeing His merits, for the Logos is free, subject to change and determined to good by His own will. From this adoptive Sonship there does not result any real share in the Divine Nature, any true likeness to it.[47]

Arianism was therefore an oriental rationalization of Christianity. Faith was dried out by its logical analysis and distorted into an abstract construction. Arianism was in tune with the times in its strict monotheism and desire to prune out everything irrational and incomprehensible. It was more accessible to the average mind seeking a rational faith than were the biblical images and expressions of Church tradition.[48]

Arianism spread from Alexandria throughout all Egypt, Libya and at length diffused itself over the rest of the provences and cities. Many others adopted the opinion of Arius. When Alexander, the Patriarch of the Coptic Church that displayed the right theological teachings in the Near East, became conscious of these things, he convened his Synod in A.D. 320 that discussed the issue, then excommunicated Arius and the abettors of his heresy.[49]

[46] Socrates, *Ecclesiastical History from the Accession of Constantine A.D. 305 to the 38th Year of Theodosius II,* tr. from the Greek with some account of the author and notes selected from Valesius (London: Henry G. Bohn, 1853), fasc. II, pp. 4-10.

[47] P. Hughes, *A History of the Church: An Introductory Study.* 3 vols. (New York: Sheed and Ward, 1934-1947), I. pp. 232-233.

[48] Alexander Schmemann, *The Historical Road of Eastern Orthodoxy* (Eng. tr. by Lydia W. Kesich. Chicago: Henry Regnery, 1966), p. 75.

[49] Socrates, *op. cit.,* fasc. II, p. 3.

This resolution of the Alexandrian Synod was followed by a cyclical epistle sent by Alexander to the other patriarchs and bishops. In it he explained the problems and laid the dogma which the Coptic and other Oriental Orthodox Churches had to believe and still teach: Who ever heard such blasphemies? Or what man of any piety is there now hearing them that is not horror-struck, and stops his ears, lest the filth of these expressions should pollute his sense of hearing? Who that hears John saying, 'In the beginning was the Word,'[50] does not condemn those that say, 'There was a period when the Word was not?' or who, hearing in the Gospel of 'the only-begotten Son,' and that 'all things were made by Him,' will not abhor those that pronounce the Son to be one of the things made? How can He be one of the things which were made by Himself? Or how can He be the Only-Begotten, if He is reckoned among created things? And how could He have had His existence from nonentities, since the Father has said, 'My heart has indited a good matter;'[51] and 'I begat thee out of my bosom before the dawn?'[52] Or, how is He unlike the Father's essence, Who is 'His perfect image,'[53] and the brightness of his glory'[54] and says: 'He that hath seen me, hath seen the Father?' Again, how if the Son is the Word and Wisdom of God, was there a period when He did not exist? For that is equivalent to their saying that God was once destitute both of Word and Wisdom. How can He be mutable and susceptible of change, who says of Himself, 'I am in the Father, and the Father in Me;'[55] and 'I and the Father are one;'[56] and again by the Prophet, 'Behold me because I am, and have not changed.'[57] But if any one may also apply the expression to the Father Himself, yet would it now be even more fitly said of the Word; because He was not changed by having become man, but as the Apostle says, 'Jesus Christ, the same yesterday, today

[50] *John*, 1:1-3.
[51] *Psalms*, 45:1.
[52] *Psalms*, 109:3.
[53] *Colossians*, 1:5.
[54] *Hebrews*, 1:3.
[55] *John*, 10:30.
[56] *John*, 10:30.
[57] *Malachi*, 3:6.

and forever.'[58] But what could persuade them to say that He was made on our account, when Paul has expressly declared that 'all things are for Him, and by Him?' One need not wonder indeed at their blasphemous assertion that the Son does not perfectly know the Father; for having once determined to fight against Christ, they reject even the words of the Lord Himself, when He says,[59] 'As the Father knows me, even so I know the Father.' If therefore the Father but partially knows the Son, it is manifest that the Son also knows the Father but in part. But if it would be improper to affirm this, and it be admitted that the Father perfectly knows the Son, it is evident that as the Father knows His own Word, so also does the Word know his own Father, whose Word He is. And we, by stating these things, and unfolding the Divine Scriptures, have often confuted them; but again as chameleons they were changed, striving to apply to themselves that which is written, 'When the ungodly has reached the depths of iniquity, he becomes contemptuous.'[60] Many heresies have arisen before these, which exceeding all bounds in daring, have lapsed into complete infatuation; but these persons, by attempting in all their discourses to subvert the Divinity of The Word, as having made a nearer approach to the Antichrist, have comparatively lessened the odium of former ones. Wherefore they have been publicly repudiated by the Church, and anathematized. We are indeed grieved on account of the perdition of these persons, and especially so because, after having been previously instructed in the doctrines of the Church, they have now apostized from them. Nevertheless we are not greatly surprised at this, for Hymenaeus and Philetus[61] fell in like manner, and before them Judas, who had been a follower of the Saviour, but afterwards deserted him and became his betrayer. Nor were we without forewarning respecting these very persons: for the Lord himself said: "Take heed that no man deceive you: for many shall come in My Name, saying, I am Christ, and shall

---

58 *Hebrews*, 13:8.
59 *John*, 10:15.
60 *Proverbs*, 18:3.
61 *2 Timothy*, 2:17-18.

deceive many;[62] and the time is at hand; Go ye not therefore after them."[63] And Paul, having learned these things from the Saviour, wrote, 'That in the latter times some should apostatize from the faith, giving heed to deceiving spirits, and doctrines of devils,'[64] who pervert the truth. "Seeing then that our Lord and Saviour Jesus Christ has himself enjoined this, and has also by the Apostle given us intimation respecting such men, we having ourselves heard their impiety, have in consequence anathematized them, as we before said, and declared them to be alienated from the Catholic Church and faith."[65] However, when the disputes on the essence of the Faith threatened the peace of the empire, Emperor Constantine I ordered an ecumenical Council to be convened under his auspices in June of 325 at Nicaea. In the sessions disputes among the delegates were very heated until they reached an agreement on the structure of the Christian belief in God, to which Athanasius, at that time, a preeminent Archdeacon of the Coptic Church, contributed a great deal. The agreement of the Faith, assented to with loud acclamation at the great council of Nicaea is this:

We believe in one God, the Father Almighty, Maker of all things visible and invisible; and in One Lord Jesus Christ, the Son of God, the only-begotten of the Father, that is of the substance of the Father; God of God and Light of Light; true God of True God; begotten, not made, consubstantial[66] with the Father: by whom all things are made, both which are in heaven and on earth; who for the sake of us men, and on account of our salvation, descended, became incarnate, and was made man; suffered, arose again on the third day, and ascended into the heavens, and will come again to judge the living and the dead. (We) also (believe) in the Holy Spirit. But the holy

---

62 *Matthew,* 24:4.
63 *Luke,* 21:8.
64 *1 Timothy,* 4:1 and *Titus,* 1:14.
65 Socrates, *op. cit.,* fasc. II, pp. 4-10.
66 Of the same essence.

Catholic and Apostolic church anathematizes those who say "There was a time when He was not," and "He was not before He was begotten," and "He was made from that which did not exist," and those who assert that He is of other substance or essence than the Father, or that He was created, or is susceptible of change.[67]

This creed was recognized and acquiesced in by three hundred and eighteen (bishops), and being, as Eusebius says, unanimous in expression and sentiment, they subscribed it. Five only would not receive it, objecting to the term *homoousius*, 'of the same essence,' or consubstantial. "For" said they, "since that is consubstantial which is from another, either by partition, derivation or germination; by germination, as a shoot from the roots; by derivation, as children from their parents; by division, as two or three vessels of God from a mass, and the Son is from the Father by none of these modes." Therefore they declared themselves unable to assent to this creed. Thus having scoffed at the word consubstantial, they would not subscribe to the deposition of Arius. Upon this the Synod anathematized Arius, and all who adhered to his opinions. Some more phrases were added in the second ecumenical Council convened at Constantinople in A.D. 381 and still constitute a part of the Creed in these churches. First to the clause, 'maker of all things visible and invisible' was added: 'of heaven and earth,' against the Marcionites and Manicheans, who asserted the doctrine of two Principles. Secondly, was inserted 'born before all ages,' to combat the teaching of Photinus that the Word was not eternal but temporal, having an origin in the womb of Mary, and in the man Christ. Thirdly, the heresy of Apollinarius caused the introduction of 'by the Holy Ghost, of the Virgin Mary took flesh.' Fourthly, where the Nicene Creed reads only 'suffered,' the clause 'was crucified for us under Pontius Pilate and was buried,' was added. It was also added: "He sat at the right hand of the Father, and He is to come again in glory." And, as Apollinarius

---

67 Also included in the Acts of the Council of Chalcedon of 451.

taught the doctrine of the millenial reign of Christ, and to Marcellus of Ancyra was imputed the assertion that Christ would one day surrender His Kingdom to the Father and then be reduced to the order of the just, the council wrote, 'Of whose Kingdom there shall be no end.' To serve as a definition against the Pneumatomachoi who denied the Divinity of the Holy Spirit and defended the Macedonian heresy, to the ending, 'and in the Holy Spirit,' was added: "Lord and Giver of life, Who proceeds from the Father,[68] is adored and glorified with the Father and the Son, Who spoke through the prophets and in one Holy Catholic Church, Amen."[69]

These churches, along with the Eastern and Roman Catholic, also express in their liturgical prayers their rejection to the Nestorian heresy. It said that the Virgin Mary could not be called Theotokos 'the Mother of God,' that the Man formed in the womb of Mary was other than the word 'Logos' of God; that the Incarnation was simply a dwelling of the Word in man as a temple so that Jesus Christ was not born, and did not suffer and die; that Christ therefore was not God but only the temple of God. Nestorius then proceeded to establish his doctrine on the two natures of Christ. The Oriental Orthodox Churches insisted on calling the Virgin Mary 'Theotokos,' anathematized Nestorius and introduced dogmatic interpretation to their knowledge of God which they embodied in their liturgical services in order to easily demonstrate the knowledge of God to every common worshipper. However, the contemporary Oriental Orthodox churches have the same belief in God and identify Him as their predecessors did during the era of the first three councils. They believe that Our Lord is perfect in His Godhead and perfect in His Manhood. They dare not say that He is God and Man together, for this expression

---

[68] As to the assertion made by some that the Pope Damasus added the celebrated phrase "Filioque," (and From the Son) to the Constantinopolitan Creed, there is no foundation whatever for it. In the Roman Catholic Church, this addition was probably made in the time of Pope Nicholas I A.D. 858 as we gather from the encyclical sent by the Constantinopolitan Patriarch Photius to the Orientals on this issue.

[69] J.D. Mansi, *Sacrorum Conciliorum nova et amplissima collectio,* 31 vols. (Florentiae: Expensis Antonii Zatta Veneti, 1759-98), III, col. 557-565.

implies separation. He is rather God Incarnate. The Godhead and the Manhood are united in Him in a complete union, i.e. in essence, hypostasis and nature, without any separation or division between both.[70] The two-natures formula affirms Christ's unity and confesses that He is 'from two natures.' The 'one incarnate nature of God the Word' is composed of two natures, which continue in Him, each in its own absolute integrity and perfection in a condition of union, without being mixed or confused one with the other. The natures are so indissolubly united that neither of them can be viewed in separation from the other. Thus, Jesus Christ is at once consubstantial with God the Father as to Godhead and consubstantial with us as to manhood. Taking these affirmations seriously, one is entitled to say that, though Christ does not exist 'in two natures,' the two natures exist in Him, each in its own perfection and reality. That is why it is better to call these churches Meaphysite.[71]

This belief is expressed in various parts of the Divine Liturgies of these Churches. The Creed also constitutes an important part. We hereby select some instances from three of these Oriental Orthodox Churches:

3. God In The Liturgical Prayers Of The Coptic Church

In her prayers of Raising of Incense, particularly in the Prayer of Thanksgiving, the term 'The Only Beggotten Son, Our Lord and God,' is repeated. The same prayer ends with: "With goodness, mercy, and the love to mankind which are for the Only Beggotten Son, our Lord, our God and Saviour Jesus Christ."[72]

The priest raises the incense burner three times and addressing the Holy Virgin, says:

---

70 Bishop Gregorius, *The Christological Teaching of The Non-Chalcedonian Churches* (Cairo: Coptic Seminary Publications, 1965), p. 6.

71 V.C. Samuel, "The Manhood of Jesus Christ in the Tradition of The Syrian Church," *The Greek Orthodox Theological Review*, XIII, 2 (Fall 1968), p. 152.

72 *Alkholagi Al-Mokkadas* (The Book of the Divine Liturgy), in Coptic and Arabic (Cairo. Coptic Patriarchate, 1957), p. 29.

"Rejoice, O Mary, the beautiful dove that begat for us God the Word, we greet thee."

"Hail to Thee, Virgin, the real and true Queen, greetings to the pride of our race. She begat for us Emmanuel."

"We ask Thee, our honest intercessor, to remember us before our Lord Jesus Christ in order that He may forgive us our sins."[73]

In the morning prayers of the Raising of the Incense, the priest says inaudibly: "Jesus Christ is He Himself in the past, today and forever. In one hypostasis we bow to Him and glorify Him."[74]

Before the reading of St. Paul's epistle in a Coptic mass, the choir chants this hymn: "The golden incense-burner is the Virgin and its scent is our Saviour. She begat Him and He saved us and forgave us our sins."[75]

In the Coptic Synxarium of which a part is read as a reminder to the faithful of the history of Church martyrs, the Union of the two natures in Christ is expressed as the union of the soul with the body as as the union of fire with iron, which, although they are of different natures, yet by their union they become one. It is added, "Likewise, the Lord Christ is one Christ, One Lord, One Nature, and One Will."[76]

The Prayer of Reconciliation with which the priest begins the Divine Liturgy of St. Basil reads, "O Great and Eternal God, He who made man without corruption, and through the life-giving revelation of Thy Only Son, our Lord and God, our Saviour Jesus Christ, Thou hast destroyed death that entered the world through Satan's temptation."[77]

In the Prayer of Blessing that comes after a hymn for the Virgin Mary, the priest expresses the Christian belief in these words: " . . . Holy, Holy, Holy, O True God, Our Lord, He who created us, sustained us, and put us in Paradise. Once we were tricked by

73 *Ibid.*, p. 47.

74 *Ibid.*, p. 48.

75 *Ibid.*, p. 233—see also *John* 1:1-3 and *Matthew* 1:18-25.

76 R. Basset, *Le Synxaire Arabe Jacobite,* in Patrologia Orientalis, in Arabic and French (Paris: Firmin-Didout, 1935), 1, fasc. 3, p. 23.

77 *Ibid.*, pp. 300-302.

the serpent and broke Thy commandment, we were lost from eternal life and cast out of Paradise. Yet, Thou didst not leave us to perish, but sent us Thy Prophets, and at the end of the days through Thy only Begotten Son, Our Lord God and Saviour, Jesus Christ, Thou appeared to us, we who were in darkness and in the shadow of death. For He who was conceived of the Holy Spirit and the Virgin Mary, became Man and taught us the way of salvation."[78]

However, at the end of the Divine Liturgy the priest says the Confession audibly: "Amen, Amen, Amen, I believe, I believe, I believe and confess to the last breath that this is the life-giving Flesh of the Only Begotten Son, Our Lord, God and Saviour, Jesus Christ. He took it from Our Lady and Queen, the Mother of God, the Pure and Holy St. Mary, and made it One with His Godhead without mingling, confusion, or change. The good confession He did make before Pontius Pilate, and by His own will He gave Himself up on the cross to redeem us. Truly, I believe that His divinity was never separated from His Humanity for one moment nor for a wink of an eye. This is to be given for our redemption, forgiveness, and eternal life for those who partake from it. I believe, I believe, I believe this is true, Amen."[80]

Some of the characteristics of God the Son are also expressed in the Prayer of Reconciliation according to the St. Gregory's Divine Liturgy which the Coptic Church also uses:

"Thou Eternal, Who existeth forever, Thou the Homoousion, Creator, seated beside Himself and Partner with the Father. He Who for goodness and out of nothing created man and entered him in Paradise, and when he fell through the temptation of the enemy, and disobedience of Thy Holy commandment, Thou wast willing to renew him and to return him to his position. To save us, Thou didst not trust an Angel or Archangel or Prophet, but descended unto us and took the shape of man to be like us except in sin, being our Mediator with the Father. Thus, breaking the wall

78 *Ibid.*, pp. 319-320; see also *Genesis* 3:7-17.
80 *Ibid.*, pp. 400-402.

of partition, and destroying the old enmity, Thou hast bound those of the earth with those in the heaven, and made the two into one, and when Thy Body ascended into heaven, Thou didst fill us all with Thy Divinity . . . "[81]

More characteristics are contained in another liturgical prayer used on Christmas Eve:

"Our Father and Our Lord, Our God the Creator, the Invisible, the Uncontained, the Non-alterable, the Incomprehensible, He Who sent His true and only light, Jesus Christ, the Word, existing in the Bosom of His Father at all times, He Who came to the Pure Virgin's womb. She bore Him in complete virginity, while the Angels praise Him saying: Glory, glory, glory to the Lord of the Sabaoth."[82]

The Theotokia hymns chanted daily for the intercession of the Virgin Mary include other explanations of the knowledge of God. We hereby select some of the Theotokia.

Theotokion of Monday:

"He who has been is He who will be; He who came comes again, Jesus Christ the Word was made flesh without change of substance and was a perfect man. He does not destroy or disturb or divide in any way as concerns the Unity. . . . But is the same nature, is the same substance, the same person, that is God the Word."[83]

Theotokion of Tuesday:

"She bore to us God the Word Who became man for our salvation. After He became man, He was still God, therefore, she who born Him remained Virgin."[84]

"And again thus He took flesh in Her without change in substance, a reasonable body consubstantial with us, perfectly complete, at one with His mother, a soul superna."[85]

---

81 *Ibid.*, pp. 449-450.
82 *Ibid.*, pp. 668-669.
83 O'Leary De Lacy, *The Daily Office and Theotokia of the Coptic Church* (London: Luzac and Co., 1923), p. 153.
84 *Ibid.*, p. 158.
85 *Ibid.*, p. 159.

4. God in the Teachings and Liturgical Prayers of the Syrian Church

Severus of Antioch (6th century) who is an outstanding character of the Syrian Orthodox Church, contained his interpretations of Cyril of Alexandria in his prolific writings that represent the Syrian understanding of God as follows.

(a) God is One and a simple spirit and can never be visible to human eyes, however, was revealed to man though the Incarnation of the Womb.

(b) God the Son who is eternally born of God the Father, took upon Himself a second birth from the Virgin for the salvation of the human race.

(c) Christ's Manhood was an individuated Manhood, fully like and continuous with our manhood, with the only exception that He was absolutely sinless.

(d) The Manhood of Christ was individuated only in a hypostatic union with God the Son, and the Manhood continued in perfection and reality in its union with God the Son.

(e) The union did not lead the Manhood to a state of confusion or mixture with the Godhead. Therefore, Godhead and Manhood were there in Christ with their respective properties. When it is said that the natures were inseparably united, the point made was that Christ was a unity. In concrete terms this meant that the words and deeds of Jesus Christ as they are recorded in the Gospels, were expressions of the One Christ, Who is God the Son, the Word Incarnate.

(f) The Manhood of Christ was real, perfect and dynamic in the Union. Severus opposed Julian of Halicarnassus who taught that the Manhood of Christ was the Manhood of Adam before the fall and insisted that it was our manhood.[86] Thus, even though Christ was sinless, which is a point of difference from our manhood, He was essentially related to men in the world of time and space.[87]

In the Christmas service of the Syrian Church the Incarnation of Jesus Christ is expressed in most of the hymns and prayers of that day. It is stated that Mary the Virgin, really conceived Him in Her womb. She received Him at the time of the annunciation of Archangel Gabriel through Her ears, and He formed for Himself a body from Her very body. Like any human child, He remained in the womb for a period of nine months and was brought forth at the completion of the days of Her conception. When He was born, He cried like any human child, and His mother gave Him food from Her breast. He was borne and carried around by Mary in her bosom; He was fondled and carefully looked after by His mother. He crawled like a babe and grew like a child. As God the Son who became Incarnate, He passed through all these different stages of human life in order to redeem us from the fall which has come upon us in consequence of the trespass of our first parents. These stages however, were necessary for our salvation.

In the services of the Holy Week, it is affirmed that Our Lord suffered mental and physical agony. While being spit at, scourged and ridiculed, He endured physical and mental pain in a genuine sense. He was then crucified at Golgotha after enduring many sufferings. All these sufferings were necessary for our salvation. The union of Godhead and Manhood also was so real that even when Our Lord died and was buried, His body remained indivisibly united with the Godhead.

In St. John Chrysostom's Syrian Liturgy we read:

"Thou art a true God, thou hast taken a body for the sake of

---

86 Michel le Syrien, *Chroniques de Michel le Syrien,* ed. and tr. from Syriac by J.B. Chabot, 4 vols. (Paris: L'Academie des Inscriptiones et Belles Lettres, 1899-1910), III, p. 461.

87 V.C. Samuel, *op. cit.,* pp. 159-160.

our salvation without changing from being God; Thou art the Word that is with God from the beginning. . . . Thou art the ray of the Father's glory; Thou hast taken from our race . . . a body without defilement or sin. Although Thou wast veiled with a pure bodily veil, I invoke Thy Lorship and acknowledge thy divinity."[88]

The Kokay, a hymnal prayer says:

"God has ascended on the cross and tasted death, then descended into the abyss of the dead, smashed its high fences and broke the doors and the brass locks, and raised Adam, His image that had been corrupted."[89]

In a supplication of Mar Ephrem:

"God has entered the tomb and lain as a human being and has shown in the bones of the righteous the power of His Divinity, and they knew Him to have come to raise their bodies from the dust, and they hailed glory to His blessing because He condescended to serve them."[90]

Since there is a union of both natures, the Syrian Church believes that all the words and deeds of Christ were expressions of a Union of the volitional and energistic faculties of Godhead and Manhood.

Mar James of Seroug in one of his "Maimars" (religious essays) explains that:

"We know the One with His Divinity and humanity and He has proved it to us by His crucifixion as He was exercising both the high and the only matters together. . . . He ascended the cross and the creatures were terrified by their inherent nature, as it is utterly difficult for a human being to do likewise. Then He made audible his moanful sufferings which He was bearing in fulfillment of His human nature that He had taken from David's daughter. O redeemed Church, bow down to Christ and worship Him with one accord; how truly to the Son of God who has saved thee with His

---

88 Cf. *Greek Orthodox Theological Review* (Fall, 1968), XIII, p. 313.
89 *Ibid.*, p. 314.
90 *Ibid.*, p. 315.

blood. . . . Let the Church come and reveal the truth to the liars, and acknowledge openly His Divinity and Humanity."[91]

Emmanuel also should be understood. "He who acts is one, and that is God the Word Incarnate. The operating power is also one. But the things done are different; they are accomplished by the one operation. To walk bodily on earth, for instance, and to move from one place to another is human. To raise the maimed and command them to run is most certainly God-befitting. However, the Word Incarnate is One, and His operation is also One, for He did them both. Because of the fact that the things done are different, we do not say that the two natures did them; for as we have said, it is God the Word Incarnate that did them both."[92]

5. God as Expressed in the Liturgical Services of the Armenian Church

In the Armenian Orthodox Church the "Profession of the Orthodox Faith" is expressed as follows:

"We believe in God the Logos, uncreated, begotten and originated from the Father before the eternal times; neither after nor younger, but just as the Father is the Father, so with Him, the Son is Son."[93]

The Armenian tradition compares this wonderful birth from the Father with that of a beam from the light. "O Light, rising from the Light, righteous Sun, unspeakable birth of the Father, Son, Thy name is praised before the sun."[94]

Christ, although born from the Father, nevertheless, 'was not after or junior,' but equal in glory and power. He also shared the creation together with the Father and the Holy Ghost.[95]

---

91 *Ibid.,* p. 315.

92 Severi Antiocheni, *Orationes ad Nephalium.* Ed. and tr. from Syriac by Iosephus Lebon (Louvain: E Typographeo Linguarum Orientalium, 1969), fasc. 64-65, pp. 82-83.

93 *"Zamagirq Hayastaneayc Ekclecwoy* (Prayers of the Hours of the Armenian Church)," in Armenian (Jerusalem: The Armenian Brotherhood of St. James Press, 1955), p. 6.

94 *Ibid.,* p. 368.

95 Mesrob Krikorian, "Christology in the Liturgical Tradition of the Armenian Church," *Greek Orthodox Theological Review* (Fall 1968), pp. 213-214.

"God the Word who is with the Father equal in creation and power in the third day separated the waters, brought forth the herbs and the plants. The Creator of heaven and earth, being God and Man, appeared in the stream of the river Jordan, His body united with the Divinity, and washed the world from sins, glorify Him forever."[96]

In the Armenian hymns we read that God is without beginning and became Incarnate: "O Word without beginning, consubstantial with the Father, who wast before all eternity, and came from the deliverance of thy creatures, we bless thee God of our Fathers."[97]

Jesus Christ, the only begotten Son of God the Father, in order to redeem man, took upon Himself the form of man and was born of the Virgin Mary.

"The Word without beginning was unoriginate as from the Father, and He took His beginning from the Virgin by being clothed with flesh. He was contained in the womb and at the same time He was with the Father and being bounded by time, He was born as God and Man."[98]

Dr. Krikorian, speaking of the birth of Jesus as a great and wonderful mystery, quotes from the Armenian Hymnal:

"O unspeakable unity, Thou wast born of the Virgin; but being indivisible, never didst Thou depart from the bosom of the Father. We bless Thee God of our Fathers."[99]

"The Child of the Father outside time, of the Virgin without sperm; the Creator of Heaven and earth today He was cherished in the arms of His Mother."[100]

"O Theotokos and Holy, who bore God the Word in thy womb by conception without sperm, we glorify thee with unceasing song."[101]

---

96 *Zaynqal Sarkan,* (Hymnal Book of the Armenian Church), in Armenian (Jerusalem: The Armenian Brotherhood of St. James Press, 1914), p. 51.

97 *Ibid.,* p. 28.

98 Nersoyan, Archbishop T., *Divine Liturgy of the Armenian Apostolic Church* (New York: Armenian Archdiocese, 1950), pp. 45-46.

99 *Zaynqal Sarkan,* p. 28.

100 *Ibid.,* p. 26.

101 *Ibid.,* p. 27.

God the Logos, when taking flesh and blood, in accordance with natural laws, took everything from the Virgin, except sin, and thus "the perfect God became the perfect Man." In other words, the birth or body of Jesus was incorrupt and incorruptible.[102] As His Godhead has no beginning, likewise there is no end for His humanity, for as Jesus Christ was yesterday and is today, so He will be the same forever.[103]

M. Ormanean states that: "The Armenian Church's doctrine is similar to that of Julian, in not saying that the body of Christ was subjected to corruption necessarily and from the beginning, which would be to dishonour the unity with the Godhead, but she does not thus become Julianist and phenomenalist. Moreover, adding the word 'who wast crucified' in the Trisagion for the person of Christ in view of the unspeakable unity, does not imply that she approves of theopaschism."[104]

The death of Jesus Christ on the Cross is the triumph over death for all men who believed and would believe in Him, and who are granted through His Resurrection, new and eternal life:

"Thou (Christ), unchangeable as Thou art, didst become man and wast crucified and didst trample down death by death."[105]

"Christ is risen from the dead. He trampled down death by death, and by His Resurrection He granted life unto us, glory unto Him for all ages, Amen."[106]

After His Resurrection, Christ, as stated in all Oriental Orthodox Churches, ascended into heaven and sent us the Holy Spirit of consolation and grace. Christ will come again with the same body and with the glory of the Father to judge the quick and the dead, and that will be the resurrection of all men.

---

102 Mesrob Krikorian, *op. cit.*, p. 216.

103 *Zamagirq Hayastaneayc Ekelecwoy*, p. 6.

104 M. Ormanean, *Azgapatoum* (History of the Armenian Nation), in Armenian. 3 vols. (Beirout: Cevan Publishing House, 1961), I, p. 841.

105 *Divine Liturgy of the Armenian Apostolic Church*, p. 35.

106 *Ibid.*, p. 137. This hymn is also included in the liturgies of both the Oriental and Eastern Orthodox Churches.

A SELECT BIBLIOGRAPHY

Al-Kholagi Al-Mokkadas (The Book of the Divine Liturgy), in Arabic and Coptic. Cairo: Coptic Patriarchate, 1957.

Arberry, A.J. (ed.), *Religion in the Middle East.* 2 vols. London: Cambridge University Press, 1969.

Athanasius, St., *Kamal Al-Burhan Ala Haqiqat Al-Eman* (Complete Proof on the Authenticity of the Faith), in Arabic. Cairo: Al-Mahaba Publications, 1947.

Basset, R., *Le Synaxaire Arabe Jacobite,* in Patrologia Orientalis Series, in Arabic and French. Paris: Firmin-Didout et Cie, 1907.

Breasted, J.H., *A History of the Early World.* New York: Ginn and Company, 1935.

Eusebius, *Ecclesiastical History.* 2 vols. Tr. from Greek by Kirsopp Lake and E.L. Oulton. London: Heineman, 1926-1932.

Gregorius, Bishop, *Mohadarat Fi Lahut Al-Massih* (Lectures on Christology), in Arabic. Cairo: Coptic Seminary Publications, 1968.

———, *The Christological Teaching of the Non-Chalcedonian Churches.* Cairo: Coptic Seminary Publications, 1965.

Hardy, E.G., *Christian Egypt: Church and People.* New York: Oxford University Press, 1952.

Holy Bible. King James version. Revised ed. New York: Nelson and Son, 1952. First published the New Testament in New York: Nelson and Son, 1946.

Hughes, P., *A History of the Church: An Introductory Study.* 3 vols. New York: Sheed and Ward Inc., 1934-1947.

Jullian, M., *Traditions et legendes Coptes sur le voyage de la Sainte Famille en Egypte.* Paris: Missions Catholiques, 1886.

Krikorian, M., "Christology in the Liturgical Tradition of the Armenian Church," *Greek Orthodox Theological Review* (Brookline, Massachusetts) Vol. XIII, No. 2, Fall 1968.

Mansi, J.D., *Sacrorum Conciliorum nova et amplissima collectio.* 31 vols. Florentiae: Expensis Antonii Zatta Veneti, 1759-1798.

Meinardus, O., *In the Steps of the Holy Family From Bethlehem to Upper Egypt.* Cairo: Dar Al-Maaref, 1963.

Mena, Michael, *Ilm Al-Lahut* (Theology according to the Coptic Orthodox Faith), in Arabic. 2 vols. Cairo: Al Mahaba Publications, 1968.

Michel le Syrien, *Chronique de Michel le Syrien Patriarche Jacobite d'Antioche 1166-1199.* Ed. and tr. from Syriac by J.B. Chabot. 4 vols. Paris: L'Academie des Inscriptiones et Belles Lettres, 1899-1910.

Nersoyan, Archbishop Tiran, (ed.), *Divine Liturgey of the Armenian Apostolic Orthodox Church.* New York: Armenian Archdiocese, 1950.

Noss, John B., *Man's Religions.* New York: Macmillan, 1963.

O'Leary, De Lacy., *The Daily Office and Theotokia of the Coptic Church.* London: Luzac and Company, 1923.

The Oriental Orthodox Churches, Addis Ababa Conference. Ed. by the Interim Secretariat, Oriental Orthodox Conference. Addis Ababa: Artistic Printers, 1965.

Ormanean, M., *Azagapatoum* (History of the Armenian Nation), in Armanian. 3 vols. Beirut: Cevan Publishing House, 1961.

Samuel, V.C., "The Manhood of Jesus Christ in the Tradition of the Syrian Orthodox Church," *Greek Orthodox Theological Review* (Brookline, Massachusetts), Vol. XIII, No. 2, Fall 1968.

Severi Antiocheni, *Orationes ad Nephalium.* Ed. by Iosephus Lebon, also in Syriac. F. 64-65 of Corpus Scriptorum Christianouim Orientalium Scriptores Syri. Lovanii: E Typographio Linguarum Orientalium, 1969.

Schmemann, Alexander, *The Historical Road of Eastern Orthodoxy.* Tr. from Russian by Lydia Kesich. Chicago: Henry Regmery, 1966.

Socrates, *Ecclesiastical History From the Accession of Constantine A.D. 305 to the 38th Year of Theodosius II.* Tr. from the Greek with some account of the author and notes selected from Valesius. London: Henry G. Bohn, 1853.

Tsonievsky, E., "The Union of the Two Natures in Christ According to the Non-Chalcedonian Churches and Orthodoxy," *Greek Orthodox Theological Review,* (Brookline, Massachusetts), Vol. XIII, No. 2, Fall 1968.

Zamagirq Hayastaneayc Eklecwoy (Prayers of the Hours of the Armenian Church), in Armenian. Jerusalem: The Armenian Brotherhood of St. James Press, 1955.

Zayanqal Sarakan (Hymnal Book of the Armenian Church), in Armenian. Jerusalem: The Armenian Brotherhood of St. James Press, 1914.

CHAPTER XVIII

GOD IN GREEK ORTHODOX THOUGHT

Constantine N. Tsirpanlis*

This paper proposes to deal with two basic questions: 1) Who is God; 2) How do we know that this is a God. It will try to give an answer to these questions from the point of view of Greek Orthodox Spirituality and Theology.

The revelation of God—the Holy Trinity—is the basis of all Christian theology; it is, indeed, theology itself, in the sense in which that word was understood by the Greek Fathers, for whom *theology (theologia)* most commonly stood for the mystery of the Trinity revealed to the Church. Moreover, it is not only the foundation, but also the supreme object of theology; for, according to the teaching of Evagrius Ponticus (developed by St. Maximus), to know the mystery of the Trinity in its fullness is to enter into perfect union *(henosis)* with God and to attain to the divinization *(theosis)* of the human creature: in other words, to enter into the divine life, the very life of the Holy Trinity, and to become, in St. Peter's words, "partakers of the divine nature"— *theias koinonoi physeos.*[1]

Theology, in the traditional Orthodox thought, means something more and deeper than mere intellectual or speculative exercises. It means the soul's experience *(pneumatic* or *esoteric vioma)* of divine grace and bliss which derives from a complete union with God.[2]

---

*Associate Professor of Church History and Greek Studies at the Unification Theological Seminary, Barrytown, New York, U.S.A.

[1] II Peter 1:4.

[2] Cf. St. Athanasius, *Ad Adelphium* 4; *De Incarnatione* 54. St. Irenaeus, *Adv. Haeres.* V, *Praefatio.*

Trinitarian theology, therefore, is a theology of union, a mystical theology which appeals to experience (*vioma* or *peira*), and which presupposes a continuous and progressive series of changes in created nature, a more and more intimate communion of the human person with the Holy Trinity.[3]

God, in Greek Patristic Thought, is beyond reason, but not against reason, incomprehensible, ineffable, invisible, inaccessible, undescribable. Even the christological terminology of the Greek Church Fathers, as well as the Definition of the Council of Chalcedon (451) are negative, because the Orthodox Theology is *Apophatic,* that is to say that it is impossible to know God positively or rationally.

Yet the questions remain: How can this divinization of man be compatible with the Divine Transcendance? What is the nature of this *henosis* with God? If man is able to be united to the very essence of God, he should be God by nature. God would then no longer be Trinity, but "myriypostatos," "of myriads of hypostases." The paradox was especially sharp in the Eastern theology, which has been always committed to the belief that God was absolutely "incomprehensible"—*akataleptos*—and unknowable in His nature or essence.[4] The Eastern Church was therefore compelled to recognize in God an ineffable distinction, other than that between His essence and His persons, according to which He is, under different aspects, both totally inaccessible and at the same time accessible. This distinction is that between the essence of God, or His nature, properly co-called, which is inaccessible, unknowable and incommunicable, and the energies or divine operations, forces proper to and inseparable from God's essence,

---

3 See. St. Symeon, the New Theologian, *Centuries* 2, ch. 16; 3 ch. 22. Ed. of *Sources Chretienne* (Cheventogne, Belgium). The pseudo-Dionysius introduced in the Church the notion of "Mystical theology;" he understands by that name a supernatural and unspeakable intuition, as distinct from "apodeictic" or demonstrative theology. He develops a complete theory of the union with God *(theia henosis).*

4 See especially St. John Chrysostom's magnificent discourses *Peri Akataleptou;* St. Athanasius, *De Decretis* II; St. Basil, *Adv. Eunomium* 1:14; Epist. 234, *ad Amphilochium.*

in which He goes forth from Himself, manifests, communicates, and gives Himself.

The principal and most comprehensive exponent of this distinction is St. Gregory Palamas. Palamas was not, however, the originator of this doctrine; the same distinction is found, though with less doctrinal precision, in most of the Greek Fathers—even amongst those of the first centuries of the Church. It is in fact an integral part of the tradition of the Eastern Church, and is closely bound up with the dogma of the Trinity.

St. Gregory Palamas begins with the distinction between "grace" and "essence:" "The divine and divinizing illumination and grace is not the essence but the energy of God,"[5] a "divine power and energy common to the nature in three."[6] Thus, according to Palamas, "to say that the divine nature is communicable not in itself but through its energy, is to remain within the bound of right devotion" (eusebia).[7] It should be noted that this basic distinction was formally accepted and elaborated at the Great Councils in Constantinople, 1341 and 1351. Those who would deny this distinction were anathematized and excommunicated. The anathematisms of the council of 1351 were included in the rite, for the Sunday of Orthodoxy, in the Triodion. Orthodox theologians are bound by this decision.

The energies might be described as that mode of existence of the Trinity which is outside of its inaccessible essence. God thus exists both in His essence and outside of His essence. Palamas says, referring to St. Cyril of Alexandria, that "Creation is the task of energy; it is for nature to beget."[8] If we deny the real distinction between essence and energy, we cannot fix any very clear borderline between the procession of the divine persons and the creation of the world; both the one and the other will be equally

---

5 St. Gregory Palamas, *Capita physica, theologica, moralia et practica*, 68-9. *P.G.*, CL, 1169C.

6 'Theophanes,' *ibid.*, 941C.

7 *Ibid.*, 937D.

8 *Ibid.*, 143. *P.G.*, CL, 1220D. Cf. St. Cyril of Alex., *De Sancta Trinitate*, dial, VI, *P.G.* 75, 1056A.

acts of the divine nature.[9] This distinction, however, does not
imply or effect division or separation. Nor is it just an
"accident"—*symvevikos*.[10] Energies "proceed" from God and
manifest His own Being. The term "proceed"—*proienae* simply
suggests distinction—*diakrisis*, but not a division: "the grace of the
Spirit is different from the Substance, and yet not separated from
it."[11] Undoubtedly, the formulation of this doctrine is an
antinomy: the energies express by their procession and ineffable
distinction—they are not God in His essence—and yet, at the same
time, being inseparable from His essence, they bear witness to the
unity and the simplicity of the being of God. The opponents of St.
Gregory Palamas—eastern theologians who had been strongly
influenced by Aristotelianism (in particular the Calabrian monk
Barlaam who had received his theological training in Italy, and
Akindynus, who quotes the Greek translation of the *Summa
theologica*)—saw in the real distinction between the essence and
the energies a derogation of the simplicity of God, and accused
Palamas of ditheism and polytheism. Their philosophy of God,
that is, was a philosophy of pure act which cannot admit anything
to be God that is not the very essence of God. Thus God is, in this
philosophy, limited by His essence; that which is not essence does
not belong to the divine being, is not God. Consequently, in the
mind of Barlaam and Akindynus, the energies are either the
essence itself, understood as pure act, or are produced by the
outward acts of the essence, that is to say, the created effects
which have the essence for their cause—creature, that is. In other
words, the adversaries of St. Gregory Palamas recognized the
divine essence and also its created effects; but they did not
recognize the divine operations or energies. Obviously, they failed
to understand that like every doctrinal statement about God, this
divine simplicity can only be expressed in terms of an antinomy: it
does not exclude distinction, but can admit neither separation nor
division on the divine being. One may say that the energies are

9 *Ibid.*, 96, 1189B.
10 *Ibid.*, 127.

attributes of God, which, however, have nothing in common with the concept—attitudes with which God is credited in the abstract and sterile theology of the manuals. The energies manifest the innumberable names of God, according to the teaching of the Areopagite: Wisdom, Life, Power, Justice, Love, Being, God. Like the energies, the divine names are innumberable, so likewise the nature which they reveal remains nameless and unknowable—darkness hidden by the abundance of light.

The speculative and intellectual stream has penetrated modern Orthodoxy. Greek theologians are on the whole traditionalist, strictly patristic, and even to a certain extent scholastic. But, from the time of Skovoroda (18th century) Russian theologians such as Soloviev, Frank and Lossky have returned to the Alexandrian tradition and not without contact and sometimes collusion with German idealism, have carried on what V. Ern called the "fight for the Logos:" Berdyaev occupies a special place, as he has been deeply influenced by Eckhart and the gnosis of Boehme. Paul Florensky and Bulgakov,[12] who have developed into a systematic *Sophiology* certain elements present in Soloviev's books, must also be set apart. Their doctrines concerning Holy Wisdom constitute much controverted *theologumena* (i.e. theological opinions only) and do not belong to the common teaching of the Church. Their error lies in their effort to identify the attributes or energies of God with His essence. In fact, God is not determined by any of His attributes; all determinations are inferior to Him, logically posterior to His being in itself, in its essence. When we say that God is Wisdom, Life, Truth, Love—we understand the energies which are subsequent to the essence and are its natural manifestations, but are external to the very being of the Trinity. That is why, in contrast to western theology, the tradition of the Eastern Church never designates the relationship between the Persons of the Trinity by the name of attributes. We never say, for

---

11 'Theophanes,' 940.

12 Especially Bulgakov made the fundamental error to try to see in the energy of Wisdom—*Sophia*, which he identified with the essence, the very principle of the Godhead.

example, that the Son proceeds by the mode of the intelligence and the Holy Spirit by the mode of the will, The Spirit can never be assimilated to the mutual love of the Father and the Son. The "trinitarian psychologism" of St. Augustine is viewed rather as an analogical image than as a positive theology expressing the relationship between the Persons. St. Maximus refused to admit in the Trinity qualifications of a psychological order in connection with the notion of the will; he saw in such qualifications that which is posterior to the nature of God, in other words, His exterior determinations, His manifestations.[13] That is why, according to Maximus, our divinization is worked out by the identification of our human will with the divine will. Here we have a striking instance of the application of Christological dogma to the inner life: our Saviour and within Himself, constantly brought His human will under the subjection of His divine will; we ought, *mutatis mutandis,* to do the same. Maximus, who in his fight against monothelitism had much to suffer for the sake of the dogma of the two wills of Christ, took his Christology over into concrete life.

It should be emphasized, here, that the starting point of the Eastern Theology, and especially of the theology of St. Maximus and of St. Gregory Palamas was *the history of salvation* and the clear distinction between "nature" and "will" of God: on the larger scale, the Biblical story, which consisted of Divine acts, culminating in the Incarnation of the Word and His glorification through the Cross and Resurrection; on the smaller scale, the story of the Christian man, striving after perfection, and ascending step by step, till he encounters God in the vision of His glory. It is usual to describe the theology of St. Irenaeus as a "theology of facts." With no lesser justification we may describe also the theology of St. Gregory Palamas as a "theology of facts." The Christological definitions of the Ecumenical Councils, completing what St. Irenaeus had written long before on the "recapitulation" of all men in Christ, have illuminated not only the beliefs but also

---

13 St. Maximus, *De ambiguis, P.G.,* XCI, 1261-1264.

the inner life of Christians. These conciliar formulae may seem dry and remote from personal experience; in reality the Chalcedonian Christology, in defining the relation between the divine and human natures in the Person of Christ, draws the main lines of the spiritual life of the man in whom Christ operates and who takes Christ as a pattern. What is the second anathematism of Cyril against Nestorius if it is not a source from which the Orthodox spirit and doctrine on Christian's divinization spring out?[14]

We should keep in mind, furthermore, that Clement and Origen wanted to oppose to heretical gnosticism a Christian gnosis. The "true gnosis" described by Clement of Alexandria is very near the idea of the Gospel. Clement writes: "Our own gnosis . . . is our Saviour Himself."[15]

The great theologians of Alexandria were not merely intellectualists. They were also heroic ascetics. J. Quasten has shown the close links which Christian Hellenism established between the Logos theology and the symbol of the Good Shepherd.[16]

Clement of Alexandria, in the hymn which closes the *Pedagogue,* prays thus: "Be the guide, and Shepherd, of the *logical* sheep." The *Logical* sheep—the reasonable sheep—the sheep of the Logos. It is difficult to realize the central place occupied by the Logos in Christian Greek thought and piety. As has been rightly said, what "reason" was for the eighteenth century, "science" for the nineteenth, and "life" for the beginning of the twentieth century, the *Logos*—at the same time intellect, divine Word and first cosmic principle—was for the Hellenistic world, both heathen and Christian. Identified with Christ, the Logos is the medium between the Father and man, the light of the soul, the master of the inner life. Christian life consists in the perfect subjection to the Logos, a subjection not only of the mind but of the flesh as

---

14 See my study: "Christological Aspects of the Thought of St. Cyril of Alexandria," (Athens, 1973), pp. 11-12.

15 Clement of Alexandria, *Stromateis,* VI, I.

16 J. Quasten, *Der Gute Hirte in hellenisticher und frühchristlicher Logostheologie in Heilige Ueberlieferung,* Maria Laach (Münster, 1938).

well. For, through the Incarnation "the flesh has become logified"—*sarkos logotheises*.[17]

The Eastern Church is rooted in a specific inter-relation between the World and God. Orthodoxy has produced a definite system of thought and world-view. It stresses, in fact, the cosmological aspects more strongly than the West, which places unquestioned emphasis upon anthropology. This is of course the Hellenistic legacy to Eastern theology, clearly discernible from Origen to John of Damascus. A symbolic expression of this can be seen in the representation of the *cosmos* on the Icons of the Pentecost which are found in the Orthodox Churches. Around the Blessed Virgin, the twelve Apostles are depicted receiving the fiery tongues of the Holy Spirit; but beneath their seats, a half-figure of a bearded man with a crown on his head is seen coming from under the earth. This is the "King Cosmos," participating in the outpouring gifts of the third Person of the Holy Trinity.

In concluding this brief study a few basic points must be emphasized. Orthodoxy seeks to understand and interpret the common principle uniting God and man. Orthodoxy means not only correct thinking or teaching (*orthe doxa*), but also and primarily the right way of life—divinization. In Eastern theology it is God and not a fate, not an impersonal abstract determining power, not a law, not a something which is above everything that is and happens, but "He, the Creator Spirit, the Creator Person." God is personal, is active and dynamic, who posits everything and is not posited. He is the *actus purus*, Trinity, and absolute free will, free in such a way that the world, His creation, is at every moment conditioned by His will, through His *creatio continua* above the abyss of nothingness. God exists, and then He also acts. There is a certain "necessity" in the Divine Being, indeed not a necessity of compulsion, and no *fatum*, but a necessity of being itself. God simply is what He is. But God's will is eminently free. He in no sense is necessitated to do what He does. Thus generation—*yennesis* is always according to essence—*kata physin*, but creation

---

17 St. Athanasius, *Orat. contra Arianos*, III, 33.

is an energy of the will—*vouleseos ergon.*[18] These two dimensions, that of being and that of acting, are different, and must be clearly distinguished. Of course, this distinction in no way compromises the "Divine simplicity." Yet, it is a real distinction, and not just a logical device. St. Gregory Palamas was fully aware of the crucial importance of this distinction. At this also point he was a true successor of the great Athanasius and of the Cappadocian hierarchs. If one does not accept this basic distinction between "nature" and "will" of God, Gregory argued, then it would be impossible to discern clearly between the "generation" of the Son and "creation" of the world, both being the acts of essence, and this would lead to utter confusion of the Trinitarian doctrine.[19] Actually, Greogry echoes also Cyril who quite clearly shows the difference between God's essence and energy stating that to generate belongs to the Divine nature, whereas to create belongs to His Divine energy or operation.

Finally, the distinction between the essence and the energies makes it possible to preserve the real meaning of St. Peter's words "partakers of the divine nature." The union to which we are called is neither hypostatic—as in the case of the human nature of Christ—nor substantial, as in that of the three divine Persons: It is union with God in His energies, or union by grace making us participate in the divine nature, without our essence becoming thereby the essence of God. In divinization we are by grace (that is to say, in the divine energies), all that God is by nature, save only identity of nature *(horis tes kat' ousian tautotetos),* according to St. Maximus.[20] We remain creatures while becoming God by grace, as Christ remained God in becoming man by the Incarnation.

---

18 *Ibid.,* 64-66.
19 St. Gregory Palamas, *Capita* . . . , 96 and 97.
20 St. Maximus, *De ambiguis, P.G.,* XCI, 1308B.

A SELECT BIBLIOGRAPHY

Campenhausen, H.V., *The Fathers of the Greek Church*. New York: Pantheon Books, 1959.

Fedotov, G.P., *The Russian Religious Mind*. New York: Harper and Brothers, 1960.

Florovsky, G., *Bible, Church, Tradition: An Eastern Orthodox View*. Belmont, Massachusetts: Nordland Publishing Company, 1972.

Grillmeier, A., *Christ in Christian Tradition*. New York: Sheed and Ward, 1965.

Lossky, V., *In the Image and Likeness of God*. Crestwood, New York: St. Vladimir's Seminary Press, 1974.

Lossky, V., *The Vision of God*. Crestwood, New York: St. Vladimir's Seminary Press, 1974.

Meyendorff, J., *Byzantine Theology*. Bronx, New York: Fordham University Press, 1974.

Meyendorff, J., *St. Gregory Palamas and Orthodox Spirituality*. Crestwood, New York: St. Vladimir's Seminary Press, 1974.

Meyendorff, J. *Christ in Eastern Christian Thought*. Washington and Cleveland: Corpus Books, 1969.

Prestige, G.L., *God in Patristic Thought*. London: S.P.C.K., 1959.

Wolfson, H., *The Philosophy of the Church Fathers*. Cambridge, Massachusetts: Harvard University Press, 1956.

Part Three
Selected Thinkers On God

PRELIMINARY REMARKS

This Part presents some significant trends in modern philosophical thinking. The coverage is not exhaustive and could not hope to be. In addition to some important individual figures—Whitehead, Tillich, Heidegger, Marcel and Sartre—this section approaches five characteristic schools of thought: process theology, analytic philosophy, death-of-God theology, the Unification movement and Marxist atheism. We also include essays on God by representatives of literature, psychology and art. We introduce this Part with: general characteristics of the period, John of the Cross' mysticism and David Hume's agnosticism. All of them present influencing themes in the search for knowledge of God throughout contemporary thought.

Philosophy

CHAPTER XIX

MODERN RELIGIOUS THOUGHT

*Peter Fuss**

If one generalization about contemporary religious thought is fairly safe, it is that, even more than usual, confusion abounds. There is conceptual confusion as to what is meant by fundamental terms: God, transcendence, spirit, person. There is historical confusion regarding which traditions in Western and even non-Western culture are potential wellsprings of renewal or reconstruction amidst the current perplexities, and which of these have helped cause or perpetuate them. There is existential confusion as to what it is to be religious ("ultimately concerned"), and what being religious has to do with being moral, being politically engaged, and in general being responsive (including sexually) to the presence of another.

In this essay, I shall make no attempt to address myself directly to these puzzling matters. As a historian of philosophy familiar with confusion, and not wholly unsympathetic with the tribulations of a theology in crisis, I should like instead to comment briefly on what I regard as several of the conceptual "high moments" in our more recent cultural history, from the point of view of their actual and possible effect on the current state of religious thought. My intentions are quite likely as ambivalent as the subject matter I shall deal with. On the one hand, I think that present-day theologians deserve some encouragement: the difficulties they face, by no means least the conceptual ones, are well founded and by no means easy to overcome. Just what it was that Descartes established and Kant refuted, what Hegel reconceived

*Professor of Philosophy at the University of Missouri, St. Louis, Missouri, U.S.A.

and Nietzsche once again helped undermine,—these matters are
not at all clear, textbook accounts to the contrary notwithstanding. I want to suggest that contemporary theology may be
freer of its philosophical past than it realizes, just because very
little in that confused and ambiguity-ridden past is definitive or
decisive. On the other hand, the tradition I wish to examine is at
the same time, indeed partly for the same reasons, more
thoughtful, more alive and alert to *experienced* dilemmas than is
usually recognized. I want to urge that there are some specific
lessons for contemporary religious thought to learn from its past,
that these lessons reinforce the seriousness of the present
quandary, and that they stand as powerful warnings against simple
solutions.

* * *

Descartes is the acknowledged "father of modern philosophy,"
and with good reason. Generations of readers have been fascinated
by the lucid, selfconscious, yet almost relentlessly paradoxical
(one is tempted to say perverse) character of his thought. His
Meditations, still a best seller among philosophy's "perennials,"
focuses, familiarly enough on the topics self, God, and world. But
by the time Descartes is finished reshaping their traditional
identities, all three have become exceedingly strange. What has
occurred amounts to a new kind of thinking, whose implications
have to this day been only imperfectly understood.

The "I" of Descartes' *cogito* (the rock-bottom certainty that
withstands methodic doubt) is shockingly impersonal. It is in
essence a being-that-thinks, its existence validated by a logical
feature of utterance (I cannot deny *"cogito, ergo sum"* without
contradicting myself), its abstract identity as *res cogitans* hastily
affirmed by appeal to an abstruse and backward-looking piece of
metaphysics (where there are mental "predicates" there must be a
subject of predication, namely a mental substance). But Descartes'
attention is already elsewhere. What for him makes this being
unique is not the vague generalization that he is rational, but, of

all things, a single thought which may or may not occur to him, whose content he can never fully comprehend, and for the thinking of which he is in no way himself responsible. This remarkable thought is the idea of an infinitely perfect being, to a demonstration of whose existence Descartes quickly turns.

The elaborate proof in Meditation Three bears superficial resemblance to Aquinas' Five Ways. But Descartes' God is ushered in on the wings of a thought in a thinker's mind—I have a very clear and distinct idea of an all-perfect being; whence could it have come?—not on the basis of the reflection that a cosmos (dismantled in the *Meditations* by the very *dubito* that could not dislodge the *cogito*) is surely in need of a divinely powerful and intelligent Creator. Indeed, most of Aquinas' proofs had been in one form or another "cosmological;" and cosmological arguments (*vide* Hume and Kant), if left unbolstered by tacit appeal to the ontological argument, could only succeed in establishing at most a more perfect, not an all-perfect being. Not so with the Cartesian proof in Meditation Three. Against the common view that although we are able to imagine God in various ways, we are not able to conceive of him clearly, Descartes insisted that the truth is exactly the reverse: although in a muddled hour I can *imagine* that God does not exist, once I entertain the *concept* of an all-perfect being and clearly understand its logical implications, I cannot conceive how that idea could fail to refer to something real. And that something cannot be less than an all-perfect being. For what I conceive, once purified of what I imagine, is nothing less than an absolutely infinite, all-perfect being—an idea whose adequate cause, just because neither I nor any other less-than-perfect being, in isolation or in combination, could concoct it,[1] can be nothing

---

1 This idea is itself paradoxical. For although Descartes insists that it is a "supremely clear and distinct" idea, and its content more than sufficient to carry us inexorably to a demonstrative certitude that such a God really exists, he also concedes that insofar as the very notion of absolute infinity boggles a finite mind, which can neither fully comprehend it nor fully analyze it, the idea of God, taken from the point of view of its own content rather than its radical difference from all other ideas, is in one respect not really "distinct" at all. See *Five Philosophers,* Descartes' "Meditations," (New York: Odyssey, 1963), p. 64.

but an absolutely infinite all-perfect being. The entire argument would be pointless, instead of merely weak, were a less-than-all-perfect being its avowed or unintended conclusion.

In Meditation Five, Descartes gives us his version of the old ontological argument. This time the resemblance is with Anselm. But although the content of their arguments is strikingly similar, the contexts are *toto caelo* different. The classical objection to the ontological proof is of course that it is itself guilty of an ontological fallacy: it confuses the order of mere thought with the order of real existence. Aquinas had long ago suggested that this was the trouble with Anselm's argument. Hume did the same for Descartes, and Kant attacked with such epistemological force and sweep that his refutation of this and other types of rational demonstration of God's existence (Kant tried to show that their seeming force is in every instance due to the disguised presence of the ontological maneuver) has been generally accepted as definitive.

But the matter isn't that simple. Anselm's argument, as recently renewed controversy indicates, is ambiguous. It seems to succeed in showing what type of existence must logically be predicated of God's nature, even if it should fail to prove that God exists. But Descartes' argument allows less latitude for interpretation. After all, Descartes clearly anticipates the major Kantian objections—and quite offhandedly dismisses them.[2] Moreover, as we have already seen and shall presently have occasion to see again, Descartes is in principle indifferent to, even contemptuous of the finite, dependent aspects of being.[3] Rationalist that he was, he would never accept the governing assumption of Kant's entire refutation, namely that real existence is a surd, a radically contingent event, beyond the powers of mind to establish *a priori.* Yet without some

2 *Op. cit.,* pp. 79-80.
3 And why not? If *res cogitans* is superior to *res extensa* largely because the mathematically infinite character of the latter is but a pallid reflection on the conceptually infinite powers of the former, then perhaps only *res cogitans* exists necessarily and really and fully—the rest contingently and as it were negatively, as privation. Descartes is the father of modern idealism too. See two paragraphs below.

such premise, it is not at all clear what force the vaunted distinction between the conceptual and the existential order is supposed to have.[4] Descartes, for what he regards as good and sufficient reasons, simply rejects it.

In between these two demonstrations of God's existence, in a manner that must seem downright perverse to anyone taught to regard him as the embodiment of the fanatical rationalist, Descartes, in Meditation Four, refuses to indulge in the rationalist theologian's favorite pastime: theodicy. Asking himself the inevitable question, why the benevolent Lord who created him should allow him to err and sin, our arch-intellectual makes do with the reply, "it would be presumptuous of me to investigate the impenetrable purposes of God."[5] But this unexpected intellectual humility is probably once more deceptive.

Descartes' new turn of thought is at its most original, and paradoxical, when it confronts the physical world. In the wake of what Copernicus' astronomy and Galileo's nefarious glass had done to the old world order and its trust in the cognitive reliability of the unaided senses, it was Descartes the mathematician, in dialogue with Descartes the philosopher who perceived a way out of the skeptical morass. Suppose that the constitution of matter is in its very essence mathematical. In that case, it is not implausible to suggest that the reality of the physical world is itself epiphenomenally conceptual. And if that is so, then mind and matter are not so alien to one another after all. This, I believe, is what the famous analysis of that piece of wax in Meditation Two is really trying to get at, whether the unregenerate dualist Descartes was fully aware of the implications or not.[6] Everything

---

4 I believe that it has the fragile force of simply being true, beyond the reach of argument and counter-argument. Kant, I think, believed likewise. His brave display of supporting argumentation *(Critique of Pure Reason,* A598-601=B626-629) is rather obviously question-begging, since it presupposes the validity of his own epistemological doctrine.

5 *Five Philosophers,* p. 71. Quite likely an offense more grievous than methodological inconsistency preys on Descartes' mind here, and prudence resolves the tension. Recall the Horatian words inscribed, apparently at his own request, on Descartes' tombstone: "Bene vixit qui bene latuit."

6 We cannot forget the pineal gland. But then—the pineal gland indeed!

about that piece of wax seems to change, radically at that. Yet we keep calling it by the same name. With what justification? Well, there is one property that remains constant throughout its many metamorphoses: extension—or better extendedness, since no *particular* dimension of its extendedness remains unchanged either. In the end, the reality of that very concrete lump of wax turns out to be that it incidentally exemplifies a most abstract, conceptual property: mathematical extendedness as such. For Descartes, matter = extendedness; it's almost as simple as that. By implication, the whole of nature, now bereft of teleological structure as well as inherently significant qualitative distinctions, has been reduced to neutral stuff.

A mind that thinks abstract and infinite thoughts now confronts an abstract, infinite universe: the Archimedean Point has been won. Descartes has achieved a pan-mathematical monism that undercuts the awkward dualism which permeates his official teaching. Spinoza will be swift to discern that there's now little reason any longer to continue the two-substance tradition. A young and vigorous bourgeois society will be far slower, but no less surer, to recognize in a "nature" of mathematically calculable but indifferent stuff an unbounded terrain for a less and less scrupled technological imperative.

A mind everywhere master and nowhere at home, an ego whose self-objectification is won at the price of its self-estrangement: this is the long-range "cultural" upshot of the Cartesian *cogito.* But it is not so different with the Cartesian God. If he did geometrize when he created—the in retrospect remarkably pious hope of the mathematician-scientists of the Renaissance—then the Creation is safe in its structural foundations, and we, who have inherited the power to think infinitely, can, indeed must, take over. Enlightenment Deism is a conceptual offspring of the Cartesian *Meditations* too.[7] But so are the peculiarly modern forms of pantheism,

---

7 I'm well aware that Descartes insists upon a continuing Providence to sustain the world in being at any moment. But his reasoning is unconvincing—the implicit force of the argument is once again that there cannot be thought-predicates (a creation) without a mind thinking them (the Creator)—and the Providence in question is in any case of such an abstractly logical character that the resulting evisceration is just one more telltale sign of how thoroughly the Age of Belief has collapsed.

culminating in Hegel. For if our growing mastery of the world is taken to provide fresh evidence that our minds are God-like, and if secular history becomes increasingly the focus of all human attention and concern, then, in spite of all the use and abuse to which the modern age will subject God's name, it is really a moot question, indeed a matter of indifference, whether he is conceived as remotely transcendent to secular history (the Deists), or as the very source, inner meaning, and literal unfolding of the world-historical process (Hegel). On either view, mundane activity is all that matters. On the Deist view, God, a mere First Cause and lingering shade, cannot make more of secular history than it already is. On the Hegelian view, God, reconceived as world-historical Absolute, cannot possibly be other than what secular history itself becomes. Abstracted away from history or reduced to it: either way such a God represents the demise, not the continuation let alone strengthening, of a transcendental dimension to which we might find ourselves meaningfully related. Modern monotheism conceptualizes a world become more and more emphatically mono-dimensional, less and less believably theistic.

It is not my intention to lay responsibility for recent Western history at Descartes' door. What I am concerned with is the inner logic of a philosophy of transcendence of a certain kind, namely one that seeks, in the fashion of Descartes, an Archimedean Point from which to reconceive, and eventually to redesign, the universe. The moral of the Cartesian story seems to be something like this: One must be profoundly dissatisfied with one's world merely to start dreaming of an Archimedean Point. But actually to begin travelling in the direction of such a Point is already to change the place where one began. Descartes' functionalization and de-concretization of self, God, and world *is* his voyage toward the Point. By the time he has arrived at it, therefore, he will find himself exerting leverage on a world already altered. The Archimedean dream, once realized, seems to be inherently self-defeating: what is at last in one's power to move is no longer what one set out to move. The result is that eerie and airy experience—a hallmark of modern sensibility—that nothing one says or does ever comes up hard against anything, that one is thinking and acting in a void, that all echoes and reverberations are somehow hollow, as though they too were self-impelled and self-confined. The theoretical expression of this experience is of course solipsism[8] —a position no major modern philosopher holds, none entirely avoids.

* * *

There is no doubt that Immanuel Kant made it one of the major objectives of his "Critical Philosophy" to help stem the Cartesian rationalist-apriorist tide. Actually, the Critical Philosophy is the imperiled attempt of a masterful navigator to sail between the Scylla of an unbridled rationalism and the Charybdis of a skeptical empiricism—imperiled, perhaps even doomed from the outset, because our navigator, for all his skill, seems mesmerized by those two rocks, hence unable to chart an alternative route.

What may well be the one controversial point upon which the Cartesian and the Humean agree—namely that our sense experience of the world is far too atomistic, chaotic, sub-rational to provide any sort of adequate foundation for science, for a systematic conceptualization of what's "out there"—is also the underlying assumption of the *Critique of Pure Reason.*

When Galileo caused balls, the weights of which he had himself previously determined, to roll down an inclined plane; when Torricelli made the air carry a weight which he had calculated beforehand to be equal to that of a definite column of water . . . a light broke upon all students of nature. They learned that reason has insight only into that which it produces after a plan of its own, and that it must not allow itself to be kept, as it were, in nature's leading-strings, but must itself show

---

8   The familiar textbook definition, I alone am real, is quite misleading. When there is nothing over against the self, its reality dissolves very quickly,—into the boundless auto-problematics Dostoevsky illuminated so brilliantly in his *Notes from Underground.*

the way with principles of judgment based upon fixed laws, constraining nature to give answer to questions of reason's own determining.[9]

Kant is quick to see the implication for metaphysics, the much abused queen of the sciences, prey of boundless speculative affronts and center of never-ending methodological strife.

Hitherto it has been assumed that all our knowledge must conform to objects. But all our attempts to extend our knowledge of objects by establishing something in regard to them *a priori*, by means of concepts, have, on this assumption, ended in failure. We must therefore make trial whether we may not have more success in the tasks of metaphysics, if we suppose that objects must conform to our knowledge. . . . We should then be proceeding precisely on the lines of Copernicus' primary hypothesis. Failing of satisfactory progress in explaining the movements of the heavenly bodies on the supposition that they all revolved around the spectator, he tried whether he might not have better success if he made the spectator to revolve and the stars to remain at rest. A similar experiment can be tried in metaphysics, as regards the intuition of objects. If intuition must conform to the constitution of the objects, I do not see how we could know anything of the latter *a priori;* but if the object (as object of the senses) must conform to our faculty of intuition, I have no difficulty in conceiving such a possibility.[10]

It is for passages like these that Kant justly deserves his great reputation. Perceiving the epistemological quandary of the modern age more clearly than anyone before him, he proposes a radically new thought-experiment, his own "Copernican Revolution" in

---

9 Preface to the Second Edition, Bxiii-Bxiv, translated by Norman Kemp Smith, (London: Macmillan, 1950), p. 20. See the parallel passage about the conceptual revolution in geometry at Bxii (*op. cit.,* p. 19).

10 *Ibid.,* Bxvi-Bxvii (*op. cit.,* p. 22).

philosophy. If, and only if, our basic perceptual forms (space and time) and conceptual categories (causality, substance, etc.) have their source in ourselves rather than in the inner constitution of things "out there" can we know something of the nature of objects *a priori.* In this way alone can we have genuinely universal and necessary knowledge. But only on one condition, namely, if we restrict the play of our perceptual and conceptual forms to things as they appear, not as they are in themselves. And they cannot help but appear in conformity with our mental forms. Hence about the basic nature of and laws governing the appearances we can be certain; the realities beyond or behind them remain forever inaccessible to us.

Thus Kant completes the Cartesian "subjective turn" by carefully circumscribing it. Euclidean geometry and the foundational principles of Newtonian physics are systematic conceptual articulations of the basic ways in which human sensibility and human understanding structure the experiences we have. These sciences are, at least at their core, universally and necessarily valid—of the world as it appears to us, and in fact of the world in which we ourselves appear. The beyond is no man's land: there our forms of sensibility, our conceptual categories, our sciences determine nothing. It is logically possible, therefore, that God exists *beyond* the strictly Euclonian[11] realm of appearances, and that we too exist there in "noumenal" form as free, morally responsible beings with immortal souls. What's more, since it is impossible to disprove such possibilities, and since the non-Euclonian aspects of our own beings implicate such possibilities (how could we be morally responsible agents unless we indeed are free?), our beliefs in such things are reasonable. It is this that inspires Kant's most famous prefatory remark: "I have therefore found it necessary to restrict *knowledge,* in order to make room

---

11 My coinage, so far as I know. I don't want to keep saying "Euclidean . . . and Newtonian . . . "

for *faith*."[12] And unquestionably Kant's lucid discussion of Reason's inevitable shipwreck when embarked on trans-phenomenal expeditions does cut with equal critical force against what the skeptical empiricists and positivists have attempted to preclude as it does against what the rationalists have sought to demonstrate.

Still, a closer cost-accounting of Kant's "Copernican" bargain disposes one to have second thoughts. There is, to be sure, a profound wisdom in Kant's ambivalent but stubborn clinging to the noumenal self, the intelligible world, and the things-in-themselves, realities and principles we seem unable by our very nature either to grasp or to let go. There is something compellingly true, not just strange and paradoxical, about the notion that we must in some sense have crossed a limit in order to be clearly aware of it. But to admire Kant's instincts is not yet to accept his philosophy, whose internal incoherencies are more than reason, conceive it as you will, can bear.

Kant has his *cogito* too. Perhaps more than any philosopher before him, he was cognizant of the inevitably self-referential character of human experience—on its cognitive side the ultimate unity of the "I think," which he termed the "transcendental unity of apperception." The more Kant found himself compelled, in the absence of an actively contributing object, to multiply trans-cendental functions and levels of subjective synthesis[13] in order to account for the complexity of human knowing, the more desperately he clung to the "t.u. of a" as their single and ultimate, however mysterious, source. But the paradoxical result is a progressively impoverished notion of self. As Kant adamantly pursues his attempt in the very teeth of his own skepticism to provide adequate epistemological and metaphysical grounds for

12 Preface to the Second Edition, Bxxx (Kemp Smith, *op. cit.*, p. 29)–but I have emended his translation, which has the more ambiguous word "deny" in place of "restrict."

13 Note in particular how belatedly the transcendental imagination enters upon the scene in the *Critique,* and how quickly it has heaped upon it an almost swarm of synthetic functions.

what he takes to be a rigidly Euclonian transcendental structure of apprehension, he reduces the self more and more to a set of meta-Euclonian functions. Originally postulated as a spontaneous experientially conditioning subject, the Kantian self little by little becomes the very archetype of a blindly conditioned object.

This is equally true of Kant's "practical" self. The Kantian moral philosophy is almost bizarrely abstract and perplexity-ridden. Its touchstones are (1) a Categorical Imperative which is unable to command anything more specific than rational consistency; (2) a Kingdom of Ends which compounds rather than compensates for the irrelevance of individuality on the phenomenal plane by dissolving the irreducible plurality of noumenal persons into the uniformity of "rational self-legislation;" and (3) a Rational Moral Will without a viable sphere of action, because the only realm in which it could act, one in which there is a closeable but never fully closed gap between is and ought, namely our experiential realm, has been reconstrued as a strictly determined Euclonian "force field" in which action to close the gap is in principle impossible, indeed in which the gap itself can have no logically consistent meaning.

Into this tissue of paradoxes Kant, in double despair of thinking out either a Euclonian or a trans-phenomenal world in which moral striving might make sense, inserts what even Descartes foreswore: a theodicy. As if blocked by the depth of his own spiritual convictions from turning the critical power of his teaching in the Antinomies against himself, Kant postulates, as objects of a reasonable faith and hope for paraphenomenal beings, a noumenal immortality and a God who rectifies phenomenal wrongs. Both however are, by Kant's own demonstration in the Transcendental Dialectic, repudiated "Metaphysical Ideas" whose content is ineluctably sense-bound and whose extension into the noumenal domain is therefore inherently confused. Freedom, Immortality, and God, Kant's Metaphysical Ideas, confronting themselves as "theoretically" proscribed yet "practically" indispensable, tempt one to suspect that something is fundamentally wrong with the Kantian account of both theory and practice. Whereas it is merely doubtful that the "empirical reality" of space and time presupposes or in some other way entails their "transcendental ideality," it is almost certain that Kant is unable to give an intelligible account of how the moral and religious life can be either transcendentally real or experientially ideal. The cost of Kant's Copernican turn is high. It appears that he found it necessary, in spite of himself, to trivialize faith and hope if he was to entrench a narrowly Euclonian knowledge.

The upshot of Kant's teaching is that we are doubly barred: On the one side, from an open-ended and multidimensionally rich immanence by a self-imposed Euclonian straightjacket which condemns to irrelevance what is not scientifically determinable. On the other side, from a full-fledged openness to transcendence by the very monoform transcendental determination which, although, on Kant's own analysis illegitimate just insofar as it is transcendentally determined, pins us down to a pre-fixed Euclonian immanence. In the final analysis, the greatest antinomy Kant unearths is his own system. Starting from the commonplace but uncritical assumption of post-Cartesian philosophy that mind and world, subject and object, rather than interpenetrating and reciprocally conditioning one another, stand on opposite sides of a chasm of epistemological uncertainty, Kant seeks to fill this chasm with a Euclonian world of appearances. Alleged to be the joint product of the constituting activity of subject and object (qua thing-in-itself), this world of appearance, instead of filling that gulf, seems rather to engulf both subject and object, usurping the unpredictable outcome of a spontaneous and natural interaction between them. As Theodor Adorno has argued, Kant's greatest failure is to ground the very thing he set out to ground: experience. A living experience, with its no-holds-barred dynamic, cannot be grounded in the barren invariability of Forms and Categories. The more open and alive experience is, the more its very forms must be susceptible to change. "An incapacity for this is tantamount to an incapacity for experience itself."[14]

14 *Negative Dialektik,* (Frankfurt a.M.: Suhrkamp Verlag, 1966), p. 378. This is a good place to acknowledge the extent of my indebtedness to this outstanding late

But does Kant "save" even the scientific phenomena? When he maintained that "we can know *a priori* of things only what we ourselves put into them,"[15] Kant enunciated something that was truly revolutionary in his own day, although it has become a virtual truism in some quarters of twentieth century science. Of course modern science, even before the advent of the pragmatists, the instrumentalists, and the operationalists, had come to perceive the usefulness of so-called "mental constructs"—especially in science's more practical, manipulative roles, those in which its aim is to control nature in accord with rational human decisions. But it is by and large only in the twentieth century that the theoretical distinction between "pure" and "applied" science has been brought into question by some of the leading scientists themselves. First it dawned on them that nature seems always to answer our questions in accordance with how we ask them. Next it was suggested[16] that Nature's very promiscuity, her tendency to lie willy-nilly with most any conceptualizer provided only that he is energetic and persistent enough (and "internally consistent," of course), makes it questionable that she confirms *any* of our conceptual schemes, just because she so readily accommodates to them *all*. And finally, the obvious circularity involved in much of current "experimental method" suggested to some of our contemporaries that science is a self-enclosed conceptual system, hermetically sealed off from any such dubious entity as a really existing external physical world.[17] After all, on good Kantian premises, the very same mind which is seeking "objective validation" designs the instruments used in the experiment, whose defining conditions are almost exclusively the mind's in the first place. Scientific hypotheses often are designed in such a way as to

German philosopher. Although almost all of the Descartes section, and most of the Kant, was conceived independently, it was a recent study of Adorno that led me to see the need for a fresh critical look at the modern philosophical tradition. An earlier impulse had come from Hannah Arendt's excellent and unjustly ignored work, *The Human Condition.*

15 *Critique of Pure Reason, op. cit.,* Bxviii.

16 I believe it was by Bertrand Russell.

17 A jaunty union of Rationalism and Idealism that must make their respective philosophical founders turn over in their graves.

"program" experimental conditions—which experimental conditions are thereupon used to verify the hypotheses. From beginning to end we never leave the charmed circle of hypothesis. No matter how much one multiplies on how often one repeats such an experience, it is and remains solipsistic.

If one were to read Kant backwards, in the light of recent developments, the implications of the account just given would seem to be three-fold: (1) Science is at bottom nothing but the organized autobiography of the conceptual structures existing in our minds. (2) Its so-called "confirmatory experiments" confirm not that what we think corresponds to what is out there, but rather that we are indeed consistently thinking what we think. (3) This inveterate circularity, this endless spinning of the human mind around its own conceptual axis, is not in the least objectionable, for it is the inescapable first premise of all strict, i.e. universal and necessary, knowledge. Kant himself did not, of course, draw these implications. Had they been called to his attention, he would in all probability have been appalled. They may nevertheless be the further consequences of his own Copernican-Euclonian logic.

Even then our cost-accounting is not complete. There are socio-political implications as well. The formalism and purism of Kant's philosophy, its much-vaunted freedom from the sensual and the concrete, is to some extent illusory, to some extent responsible for a lack of critical distance from the reigning status quo. Adorno observes that the Kantian cognitive machine grinds out Euclonian phenomena all too much like the machines of bourgeois society grind out commodities. Kant's phenomenal matter, like the Cartesian matter-as-extension, is as sheerly denumerable, neutral, and indifferent as is a bourgeois economy's raw material, the former as completely subject to the mind's rules of conceptual appropriation as the latter is to the exigencies of profit. It is difficult to overlook the striking parallel between exchange values as end-products and Kant's subjectively fashioned yet objectively accepted "empirical objects."[18]

18 Adorno, *op. cit.,* pp. 373-377.

But more than mere analogies are at stake here. Kant's radical separation of sensibility and understanding, his conceptual underpinning for the strict limits he imposes on the world of experience, is itself socially conditioned and conditioning. For, as Adorno argues, it parallels and, more importantly, rationalizes a social psychology of self-denial (the "Protestant ethic") at the very moment when the historically familiar basis for self-denial, natural scarcity, had for the first time shown some promise of being overcome. To a remarkable degree, the uniquely Kantian synthesis of Protestant sensibility with Euclonian conceptual rigor has become "modern philosophy," explains its descriptive moment of truth alongside its normative and critical poverty, and helps account for the high esteem in which Kant is held.[19] Implicit in Adorno's criticism, I believe, is the suggestion that the universally accepted rationale for anything and everything we do, however outrageous—"After all, I've got to make a living!"—is so false in the face of an economy of abundance powered by a sophisticated technology, that only an ideology with very deep religiophilosophic roots could sustain it. To this ideology Kant, whatever his intentions, made no small contribution.

*   *   *

For the limited purposes of this essay, it might be said that Hegel's philosophy rests on two principles, at once presupposed and to be justified by the development of his system. The first, that "substance" is in essence "subject," involves a radical reworking of the Cartesian claim that matter is at bottom conceptual. The second, that human consciousness is self-corrective and ultimately all-inclusive, involves an equally radical reconstruction of the Kantian "transcendental unity of apperception." Both principles rest on the prior assumption that there is a whole called Reality, and that it has an intelligible structure. Before Hegel, this ideal of universal intelligibility was of course a

19 *Ibid.*, p. 380.

commonplace of Western philosophy. It seemed as natural and
inevitable that this should be the foundational assumption of
philosophy as it has always seemed for the principle of cosmic
determinism to be the ubiquitous methodological ideal of Western
science. Ironically, it was the great conceptual power with which
Hegel clarified the implications of the philosophers' ideal, alongside the failure of his "System" to embody it as fully and
convincingly as its own methodology demanded, that he has led
many of those coming after Hegel to suspect that if The Great
Tradition really does culminate in Hegel's system, then that
tradition is now, and perhaps implicitly always has been, bank-
rupt.

What kind of "substance" (external reality, matter) is it that
can be fully intelligible in principle? Sounding very much like a
classical realist instead of the idealist he is supposed to be, Hegel
answers that it must be a substance capable of exemplifying in its
very particularity and diversity a universal meaning or pattern of
order to a consciousness. Clearly it cannot do this if it is in essence
an irremediably lifeless, impenetrable, "brute" externality—even if
one tacks on, as did the men of the Enlightenment, the notion
that it is so to speak written in mathematical equations. For Hegel,
ordinary mathematical conceptualization is as much on the level
of mere "abstract understanding" as are the syllogisms of the old
formal logic. Mathematical knowledge is limited both in regard to
the "poverty of its purpose" and the "defectiveness of its
material."[20] Its purpose or principle is quantity; its material is
space and numerical units. It fails, therefore, to penetrate to the
heart of what is concretely actual, for this is driven by principles
which are qualitative and immanent. A reality we can truly
comprehend, Hegel insists, must be an organic whole whose parts
are internally related, whose movement is from within because it is
driven by an inherent "principle of negativity" ceaselessly forcing

<hr />

20 *The Phenomenology of Mind,* translated by J.B. Baillie, revised second edition
(New York: Macmillan, 1949), pp. 101-102. Hereafter referred to as Baillie. The German
edition (consulted throughout) is *Phänomenologie des Geistes,* sechste Auflage
(Hamburg: Felix Meiner, 1952), p. 37.

it to seek to transcend its given limitations. The real substance, the stuff of the Hegelian world is not matter in space but spirit in time, spirit in its dialectically attenuated rather than spatially externalized manifestation. It is, in a word, *history*.

Of this universal history, man is at once the prime agent, the main subject-matter, the interpreter, and the culmination.[21] This history charts man's subsequent efforts to achieve the vantage-point of absolute knowledge, and appears, on one level at least, to come to an end when he has attained the freedom afforded him by having reached that vantage-point. In Hegel's world a person is a focal unifying center in a very special sense: his is a "self-referring and self-relating identity and simplicity."[22] Strikingly like Schelling's[23] processive God, Hegel's human self has at its very core a principle of dialectical self-differentiation. This principle makes it the most "metastable" of all organic realities; "precisely this unrest," as Hegal puts it, *"is* the self."[24]

All this is possible and even plausible, Hegel believes, because of the implications of his other cardinal principle, the self-sufficiency of human consciousness. Well aware that Kant's dualism amounted to a confession of failure to bridge the Cartesian epistemological gulf between subject and object, Hegel makes a fresh approach to the nature of our consciousness through reinterpreting some familiar facts about it. Merely to be aware of something, I must be sufficiently at a distance from it to be able to contrast it with what it is not. But to call experience "mine," I must be able in addition to disengage universal characteristics and general patterns of order from the sea of particulars I confront. I hereby possess

21 It is noteworthy that in the *Phenomenology*—for many in the nineteenth century the philosophical Bible of the modern age—history properly speaking begins only in chapter four, with the dawning of man's *self*-consciousness in the struggle for mutual recognition.

22 Baillie, *op. cit.,* p. 84; Meiner, *op. cit.,* p. 22.

23 This highly influential doctrine was adumbrated in *The System of Transcendental Idealism* and developed into a more coherent doctrine in *Philosophical Inquiries into the Nature of Human Freedom* (1809). It is fascinating to observe what the omnivorous Herman Melville did with this bit of radical theology in *Moby Dick*; see in particular chapter 119, "The Candles."

24 Baillie, *op. cit.,* p. 83, italics added; Meiner, *op. cit.,* p. 22.

principles of intelligibility with which I can enter, noetically speaking, into any set of empirical determinations without losing my identity as transcending consciousness. All experience is potentially mine just because my consciousness is not bound down to anything in particular but is free to range over all there is. In this sense, I *am* the unity and universality of all my conscious experience—in content as well as in form. But the ability to know that all the preceding is so involves still another level of disengagement or, to use Hegel's word, "negation." I realize at last that the universality I have struggled so hard to extract from objects of experience was mine all along.[25] What makes all reality intelligible need now be no longer sought outside self: it is "in and for" self. Substance, the underlying principle of unity and intelligibility in the "objective" world, is in actuality subject.

Upon its distinctively metastable, processive character Hegel bases the claim that human consciousness in principle encompasses the knowledge of its object and the object of its knowledge. It is able to know when the subject-term and the object-term correspond because it is essentially knowledge of its own knowledge.[26] When it compares these two terms, it is actually comparing itself with itself. The Cartesian epistemological gulf has been closed. For the criterion for determining whether and when consciousness is adequate to its object, knower and known are face to face, falls within consciousness itself.

But not only is human consciousness inherently self-corrective, its ultimate goal is inescapably all-inclusive. That goal

is fixed for knowledge as necessarily as the succession in the process. The terminus is at that point where knowledge is no longer compelled to go beyond itself, where it finds its own self,

25 To this extent, Kant had of course been on the right track. He had simply, in Hegel's estimation, not gone far enough.

26 Baillie, *op. cit.*, p. 80; cf. p. 140; Meiner, *op. cit.*, pp. 19-20; p. 71. Only on this hypothesis, Hegel is convinced, can we account for our ability to recognize error.

and the concept corresponds to the object and the object to the concept.[27]

Hegel's name for this ultimate goal is of course "the concrete universal"—the fully articulated totality of the real in which the moments of thought and being, consciousness and object, are dialectically interfused. Once attained, the concrete universal, as final achievement of "the tremendous power of the negative" at work in human consciousness, will justify both of Hegel's foundational principles in one stroke.

It may well be that the power, the perplexities, and in the end the perniciousness of this sort of dialectical monism all have the same source: a refusal to allow extra-mental reality to have an essential structure of its own that differs significantly from that of mind itself. Nature can be fully intelligible if at its core there is the same dynamic negating-and-reconciling, self-differentiating and self-relating principle as there is in human consciousness, in the person. Once that is assumed, Hegel is free to admit,[28] in a way Descartes and Kant were not, that persons are a part of nature too. The natural world, in itself *Geist* or *Geist*-like, imbued with Reason, need no longer be posited as problematic "other," left unmediated as "matter" or "thing-in-itself," its inexplicable effects at best externally related to minds who quantify it into orderly "appearance." It was precisely their impoverished, bifurcated notion of experience that trapped the modern philosophers from Descartes through the British Empiricists to Kant in a self-contradictory subjectivism in which an abstractly formal consciousness, the sole ascertainable reality, was in constant need of an alien impact for its concrete, empirical content.[29]

At the same time, there is no longer any justification for Kant's transcendental bars. For Kant, transcendental dialectic had been a

27 *Ibid.*, pp. 137-138; Meiner, *op. cit.*, p. 69. I have changed the notoriously misleading term "notion" in Baillie's translation to "concept" *(Begriff)*.

28 Indeed insist.

29 Baillie, *op. cit.*, p. 279; Meiner, *op. cit.*, pp. 180-181.

mere "logic of illusion."[30] We are led by our very natures to conceive an "intelligible sphere;" but so soon as we attempt to think it through, our own finitude compels us to deform it, to reduce it to an appearance in the worst sense. Hegel turns all this around. Since by virtue of the very nature of our consciousness we are infinite beings, all experience that is limited is deformed, not yet fully real, merely apparent. The logic of our own condition and the inner nature of what stands over against us conspire together to compel us to reach the Really Real. With a show of exasperating innocence, Hegel is now in a position to echo what realists from Aristotle to the latest blear-phenomenologist"[31] demand: humility before the fact; avoidance of conjectural apriorism, mists of notions, chains of uncontexualized reasonings; a willingness to take on the burden of comprehension.[32] Hegel can even afford to reintroduce into his philosophy the wealth of detail and descriptive richness that Kant was so concerned to excise from his. After all, the principles of dialectical synthesis animating the effort of description must in the end be identical with those animating its objects. To guarantee we're on the right track, we need only to keep going. The apparent solipsism here is deceptive: the "I" is big enough to be all-embracing. Its phenomenology is nothing less than the story of the life of the Absolute.

Descartes, to lay hold of a reality from which he felt cut off, reconstructed it in terms of pure thought. The paradoxical result was a greater alienation than before. Kant, to "save the appearances," found it necessary to detach them from a reality to which he promptly barred access. The prohibitive cost of this experiment led Hegel to try the Cartesian approach once more, but in a far bolder and more comprehensive way. For just these reasons, the costs of the Hegelian transaction are more difficult to assess. No rationalistic, "speculative" philosophy had ever been so

30 *Critique of Pure Reason,* A 293 = B 350 ff.

31 A term coined, I believe, by Prof. (emeritus) Donald Williams of Harvard for the descriptivist whose eyes water from the strain of gazing at what's actually there.

32 Cf. Baillie, *op. cit.,* p. 116; Meiner, *op. cit.,* p. 48.

earthy, so historically oriented, so dense-textured, no descriptive account of man's history so single-mindedly dedicated to the revelation of rational structure. The father[33] of contemporary phenomenology may well have had the most ambitious conception of its methodological ideal. The *concrete universal:* to be fully illuminated in its concreteness, the object of a phenomenological description must be exhibited in a context that is systematically comprehensive.

In pursuit of this ideal, Hegel ontologizes history and historicizes ontology. He ontologizes history because it is in history, and in history alone, that the structures of being become concretely transparent. He historicizes ontology because without a temporal, historical biography being is an empty abstraction. The concrete historical forms of being are the actual content of being's very essence[34] —whether the being in question is human or divine. History is truly the proving-ground of ontology. But then of course nothing is allowed to "go wrong" in history, there must not be any historical accidents. History must be through and through coherent, "logical," determined by an inner rational necessity. And so, for Hegel, it is. The notorious "cunning of Reason"[35] is the control mechanism of the historical *Weltgeist* whereby it transforms the follies and vagaries of its human agents into its own necessary means to its own immanent end. By now one cannot help but ask whether Hegel is justified in predicating such an ontology of history, then looking to history to establish the validity of his ontology. Hegel may be right that in the end philosophy, queen of the sciences, can and must justify itself only by itself,[36] i.e. circularly. But when philosophy appeals to history, to empirical actuality to bear witness to a cunning Reason which it

33 Or grandfather; we don't wish to raise the hackles of the Husserlians needlessly.

34 Baillie, *op. cit.,* pp. 80-81; Meiner, *op. cit.,* pp. 20-21.

35 *The Philosophy of History,* translated by J. Sibree (New York: Dover, 1956), pp. 27, 30, 33.

36 Baillie, *op. cit.,* pp. 70-71: "The inner necessity that knowledge should be science lies in its very nature; and the adequate and sufficient explanation of this lies simply and solely in the systematic exposition of philosophy itself." See Meiner, *op. cit.,* p. 12.

takes a Hegelian doctrinal eye to see in the first place, the circle would seem to have become vicious.

Naturally, the obverse question must also be asked: Can ontology justify history? If ever an entire system can be said to have been a theodicy, it is Hegel's. It is a mightly effort to "take in" transcendence. The world itself is the Absolute. The Absolute becomes history. History is its sacrificial altar, on which number-less individuals are required to shed their blood[37] so that Freedom and Reason may ultimately be secured. "The history of the world is not the theatre of happiness."[38] Pain and suffering are justified because they are necessary to the tortuous process of the Absolute's self-unfolding. The reality of the Concrete Universal implies that individuals are after all *not* ultimately real. The universal moving and driving force in which they are caught up is their reality. Before the exigencies of the Absolute, individual and collective moral decision and action can be little more than "local color:" they may, at best, incidentally coincide with or express a fleeting, dialectical episode in the Absolute's story.

Theodicy is supposed to justify the ways of God to man. But Hegel's God, the Absolute, is a clever narcissist[39] who generates out of his cold innards a realm of existence and history in which beings suffer and die for what is presumably his transcendental pleasure. Human individuals, on the other hand, are supposed to be very real indeed—so much so that it is in and through their moral and spiritual exertions, their fleeting days of glory and long black nights of despair, that the Concrete Universal is gradually to realize itself. A bit of a dilemma here. If Hegel's Absolute is real, he is a monster who, in sanctioning everything, justifies nothing; if Hegel's human individual is real, then Hegel's Absolute seems not to have been conceived correctly.

For better than a century now, the Hegelians have been pilloried for equating logical categories with those of philosophy

---

37 Or blow their minds, as the ambivalent but vivid current jargon has it.

38 *Philosophy of History, op. cit.,* p. 27.

39 Notice to what extent Hegel himself concedes this narcissism: Baillie, *op. cit.,* pp. 80-81; Meiner, *op. cit.,* p. 20.

of history or of social process. This, we are told over and over again, is the *hubris* of a speculative idealism which must inevitably flounder in face of the unreconstructability of the empirical. But, as Adorno argues, that reconstruction is all too real. The panlogism which the Hegelians seek in vain to interpret into the historicosocietal process is already there, albeit in self-contradictory form. "What tolerates nothing particular gives itself away as being the ruling particular."[40] Nothing is more irrational than a *ruling* Reason—necessarily a polarized, narrow, hypostatized one. Indeed, "the principle of absolute identity is in itself contradictory. It perpetuates nonidentity in repressed and impaired form."[41] Adorno concludes:

> What was once named by the mythological term Destiny is no less mythical when given the demythologized name of secular "logic of things." . . . It is this that provided the objective impulse for Hegel's construction of the World Spirit. The latter on the one hand accounts for the emancipation of the Subject: he must first have stepped back from the Universal in order to recognize it *per se* and for himself. On the other hand, the nexus of society's individual transactions must be yoked to a seamless predetermining totality with a lack of loophole unheard of in the feudal era.[42]

Eventually, our seamless web constricts its own weaver. Hegel radically transformed the nature of the philosophical enterprise. It is itself historicized, temporalized: "the study of the history of philosophy is the study of philosophy itself."[43] There are no timeless philosophical problems which are answered (or for that matter left unanswered) in the same way by one philosophical

---

[40] *Negative Dialektik, op. cit.,* p. 309.
[41] *Ibid.,* p. 310.
[42] *Ibid.,* p. 311.
[43] From the 1820 preface to Hegel's lectures on the history of philosophy; reproduced in Walter Kaufmann, *Hegel: Reinterpretation, Texts, and Commentary* (New York: Doubleday, 1965), p. 285. Kaufmann is, I believe, quite mistaken in claiming that this contention of Hegel's is no longer controversial.

generation as by another. Philosophy keeps pace with the historical unfolding of man's self-consciousness on the one hand, and that of the concrete universal on the other. Philosophy is in fact nothing more or less than their systematic com-prehension. That is why Hegel characteristically incorporates rather than refutes previous philosophical positions. As he says, "the ceaseless activity of their own inherent nature makes them at the same time moments of an organic unity, where they not merely do not contradict one another, but where one is as necessary as the other; and it is just this equal necessity of all moments which constitutes the life of the whole."[44] Ironically, by interpreting philosophy in this way, Hegel tolls its death-knell. The task of philosophy is to achieve an all-embracing conceptual synthesis adequate to the concrete universal in its Absolute form. The two, concept *(Begriff)* and Absolute, must arrive on the historical scene simultaneously. But once they do arrive—and Hegel seems to insist that they have, in his own era—philosophy no longer has a task to perform. It has accomplished its distinctive mission and is henceforth obsolete. If anything remains to be done it is to see that the *Begriff* realized by thought is put uniformly into practice—a task for social scientists and social engineers.[45] That such a development has actually tended to take place, and to that extent supports the descriptive side of Hegelian philosophy, is small consolation. Hegel's radical reconstruction of the Cartesian Turn is no less self-defeating than the original. To relocate the Archimedean Point within the immanent is to forsake once and for all the critical and imaginative leverage needed to power an escape from the immanent's toils.[46]

It would appear that the unequaled descriptive richness and comprehensiveness and the ultimate abdication of critical force in Hegel's philosophy have a common root. At the same time, all claims to the contrary notwithstanding, the phenomenological and

---

44 Baillie, *op. cit.,* p. 68 (translation slightly emended); Meiner, *op. cit.,* p. 10.

45 Compare, and contrast, Herbert Marcuse's interpretation of this matter in *Reason and Revolution.*

46 Consider, for instance, how surprisingly little was changed, from a conceptual and critical point of view, by the Marxists' celebrated "turning of Hegel on his head."

the philosophical-critical dimensions of Hegel's thought do not and cannot coimplicate one another. As matters stand, it is more likely that they contradict. The presupposition of pan-noetic identity (substance = subject) and the assumption of the self-sufficiency and all-inclusiveness of consciousness, Hegel's foundational principles, may well be, for all of their implicit solipsism, the unavoidable methodological ideals of a systematic phenomenological description. But if the system were in fact to achieve what Hegel wanted it to, if its results actually were to render these methodological working principles real or true, they would condemn the system to being closed, uncritical, and, worst of all, uncriticizable. The explosive dynamism never absent from the events Hegel describes rests on the ever-renewed empirical, historical falsification of these two principles. Just in so far as the *Phenomenology* is, as Hegel claims, the story of the emergence of freedom in history, its true purpose must be, exactly contrary to Hegel's, to prove those two principles to be in reality wrong, not right.

If Kant's own system falls prey to the lesson of the Antinomies which is its greatest critical achievement, no less is true of Hegel's.[47] On closer look, Hegel's Absolute Idealism is by no means simply the antithesis of Kant's doctrine of an absolute limit. If Kant's transcendental bar is procured at the price of overstructuring the immanent, all the more is this true of Hegel's historicization and phenomenalization of the Absolute. By containing the transcendent within the immanent, Hegel surreptitiously reconstitutes an even more formidable version of the very Kantian bar he tried so hard to remove. There is irony in the fate of Hegelianism: unable to keep its rationalization within bounds, its historical effects have been more positivist than idealist.

---

[47] For a brilliant account, in a somewhat different context, of the Hegelian antinomy see Ulrich Sonnemann's *Negative Anthropologie* (Rowohlt, 1969), especially the section entitled "Exkurs zu Cusanus," pp. 141-163.

* * *

There is a remarkable passage in the *Phenomenology*[48] where Hegel, for a moment free of the spell of his theological optimism, suggests that cultural development is inherently—I would venture to say "systematically"—ambivalent. Viewing Western history as a series of oscillations between eras of faith and periods of enlightenment, Hegel (who delights in such things) construes their interrelation in terms of a double ironic reversal. On the one hand, an age of faith is the anguished expression of a divided consciousness, bifurcating itself into two estranged worlds, one all too actual, the other all too remote, hence neither nor both together *real* for us. However, the pure consciousness into which spirit at such times retreats or to which it rises is not merely a realm of faith; the pathos of distance which stirs the religious imagination is also the wellspring of man's conceptual power: the animating force of secular rationalization. On the other hand, the worldliness characterizing epochs of enlightenment takes the form of a two-fold process. The inevitable depopulation of heaven coincides with, and appears to be internally related to, a de-essentialization of earth, i.e. a pervasive skepticism, relativism, and subjectivism, a freedom and license to invent, remake, reduce everything to instrument and means: the upshot a world-alienation if anything still deeper than that experienced by the religious consciousness. From dialectics such as these one might plausibly conclude (1) that a secular humanist religion, one which attempts to sanctify concern with the world on the world's behalf, is an unlikely, perhaps an impossible spiritual achievement; and (2) that a fulfilled culture, a culture at equilibrium, one whose culmination is *not* its own undoing, is a Utopian notion.[49] Through aberrant

48 Chapter VI, opening pages of section B, entitled "Spirit in Self-Estrangement." Baillie, *op. cit.,* pp. 512-513; Meiner, *op. cit.,* p. 350.

49 This is not the only time Hegel, the bourgeois-Christian apologist, flew into the nest of perplexities associated with the tradition of "pagan" civic humanism (Aristotle, Machiavelli, Harrington, etc.), Hegel, I believe, must be interpreted from the perspectives of both traditions, in large measure because he was reluctant to give up either. But the matter cannot be pursued here.

Hegelian eyes like these, modern philosophy's Archimedean Point begins to look like a singularly inappropriate metaphor: far better even now is the classical Wheel of Fortune, on which, the more historically self-conscious we become, the more painfully we are stretched. But to the official Hegel, he of the great reconciliation, such a perspective and its consequences are of course inimical, hence sooner or later suppressed or subordinated to a progressivist ideology.

It is otherwise with Nietzsche. This extraordinary critical thinker planted himself squarely in the middle of the Western tradition's unresolved perplexities and refused to budge—the only "fixed position" he ever held. For Nietzsche the dialectical, systematically ambivalent character of any significant cultural phenomenon is axiomatic. There is no better illustration of this than the "death of God," a long-developing phenomenon of the modern age which Nietzsche dissected so brilliantly that he himself has become an inseparable part of it. His parable of the madman, by now a *locus classicus* in "death of God" literature, is anything but what is so often associated with Nietzsche: philosophizing with a hammer.

> "Where did God go?" he cried out. "I'll tell you. *We killed him*—you and I. We are all his murderers. But how did we do it? How did we manage to drink up the ocean? Who gave us the sponge to erase the whole horizon? What did we do when we unhinged this earth from its sun? Where is it going now? Where are we going? Away from all suns? Aren't we in an endless fall—backwards, sideways, forwards, every which way? Is there still an above and a below? . . . Hasn't it become colder? . . . The holiest and mightiest the world has ever possessed has fallen to our knife—who'll wipe the blood from us? Where is the water that could wash us clean? What ceremonies of atonement, what sacred games shall we be forced to invent? Isn't the magnitude of this deed too great for us?

Don't we have to become Gods ourselves, just to appear worthy of it?"[50]

What *did* we do when we unhinged this earth from its sun? Having won the Archimedean Point, did we, who are still human-all-too-human, hence bizarre caricatures at such remote places, perhaps . . . lose everything? Nietzsche spent a brief and anguished lifetime projecting thought-experiments (*der Übermensch,* the Eternal Recurrence) in a desparate effort to avoid an affirmative answer. He kept wanting to believe that Western man, once emancipated from a repressive, other-worldy moral ontology, once rid of a self-crippling guilt and the destructive forms of the will to power to which such guilt gives rise (*resentiment:* seedbed of much of our tyrannizing over our fellow men), might somehow recapture his spontaneity, his joy in creating (yes, even new gods), his love of life,—in the end, perhaps even the "innocence of becoming."[51] But try as he might, Nietzsche couldn't quite convince himself. He suspected, and subsequent events seem to bear him out, that we mortals can no more survive a naked immanence than effectuate a demystified transcendence.

In this he was not alone. Of the four men who sensed most sharply and pondered most imaginatively the spiritual crisis that followed in the wake of Hegel's pantheosecular optimism— Kierkegaard, Melville, Dostoevsky, and Nietzsche[52]—the fact that two were devout Christians and two pagan humanists is far less decisive than that all four were truculently "reactionary," and deeply pessimistic about man's future. While Kierkegaard and

50 *Die Fröhliche Wissenschaft (The Gay Science),* §125, in all editions. First published in 1882. The translation of the text in Karl Schlechta, *Friedrich Nietzsche: Werke in drei Bänden* (München: Carl Hanser, 1966), Volume II, pp. 126-127, is my own. Philosophizing with a hammer, by the way, is Nietzsche's own expression; it is part of the title of *Twilight of the Idols* (1888).

51 This is of course the Nietzsche who is forerunner of the "human lib" movement: Freud and D.H. Lawrence, Shaw and Reich, Marcuse and Norman O. Brown. But this Nietzsche is only one of many; one need only recall how he celebrated the "pathos of distance."

Dostoevsky came to have an undoubted other-worldy center to their thought, all four detested religious rationalism, which each independently discerned as being but a short dialectical step away from solipsism and nihilism. Since of the four Melville is perhaps least known and almost never read in such a context, it may be fruitful to let his demonic Captain Ahab round off our tale.

*   *   *

"Vengeance on a dumb brute!" cried Starbuck, "that simply smote thee from blindest instinct! Madness! To be enraged with a dumb thing, Captain Ahab, seems blasphemous."

"Hark ye yet again—the little lower layer. All visible objects, man, are but as pasteboard masks. But in each event—in the living act, the undoubted deed—there, some unknown but still reasoning thing puts forth the mouldings of its features from behind the unreasoning mask. If man will strike, strike through the mask! How can the prisoner reach outside except by thrusting through the wall? To me, the white whale is that wall, shoved near to me. Sometimes I think there's naught beyond. But 'tis enough. He tasks me; he heaps me; I see in him outrageous strength, with an inscrutable malice sinewing it. That inscrutable thing is chiefly what I hate; and be the white whale agent, or be the white whale principal, I will wreak that hate upon him. Talk not to me of blasphemy, man; I'd strike the sun if it insulted me. For could the sun do that, then could I do the other; since there is ever a sort of fair play herein, jealousy presiding over all creations. But not my master, man, is

---

52 One cannot help wondering how much more they might have enriched our culture had they known one another. Nietzsche stumbled on some of Dostoevsky's work, and read it with enthusiasm, in 1887, less than two years before he went mad; he was unaware of the existence of Kierkegaard, whom he never had a chance to read, until early in 1888. See *Nietzsche: A Self-Portrait from His Letters,* translated and edited by Peter Fuss and Henry Shapiro (Harvard University Press, 1971), pp. 97f, 107f, 127, 132. There appears to have been no other contact among the four.

even that fair play. Who's over me? Truth hath no confines . . . "[53]

Melville's Ahab remains one of the most lucidly conceived shatterers of the delicate here-yonder balances. His refusal to let be, his pathological determination to flush the gods out of their hiding places, is much less the apogee of the very human desire for truth, than it is the absolutization of the will to power, to undisputed mastery over all there is. In the process of giving forced object-lessons to a crew (the *Pequod* is Melville's microcosm) that shies away from greatness, our demigod destroys its objective pole: the silent, unseizable Other, out of relation to which there can be no human greatness. Obsessed by what has affronted him,[54] Ahab, in his rage against the deceptiveness of the apparent, seeks to wash white the very coloration which not only sustains life but hints at realities beyond life. To violate appearance, to politicize the heart, to absolutize the relative[55] and to pinpoint the absolute—all are the same crime, the crime against being. The consequence is always the same, a destruction not only of that which one was seeking to remake, but that in the name of which one embarked on this misadventure in the first place: transcendence. Ahab's reverberations from Beyond are hollow, are in the end the mere echoes of his own strident voice. The harpooneer of the Absolute draws no blood, not so much because none is there, but because the would-be impaler is the only one impaled: it is always only the image of his own progressive etiolation that is reflected back to him.

Sometimes, our Captain seems little more than a swaggering *naif,* daring the gods to put him back in his place lest he take theirs:

53 *Moby Dick,* Chapter 36, "The Quarter-Deck" in all editions—the first of Melville's great "black mass" chapters, in which Ahab bends the crew's will to his purpose.

54 Cf. Chapter 42, "The Whiteness of the Whale," for an elaborate (but hyperselfconscious and obscure, to the point of self-mockery) theoretical explanation.

55 Hannah Arendt is persuaded that precisely this is the underlying issue of Melville's later drama *Billy Budd.* Cf. *On Revolution* (New York: Viking, 1965), pp. 78-83. I believe she's right.

I will not say as schoolboys do to bullies,—Take some one of your own size; don't pommel *me!* No, ye've knocked me down, and I am up again; but *ye* have run and hidden. Come forth from behind your cotton bags! I have no long gun to reach ye. Come, Ahab's compliments to ye; come and see if ye can swerve me. Swerve me? Ye cannot swerve me, else ye swerve yourselves! Man has ye there.[56]

But his sporting words belie their own ultimate consequences. A century after the likes of him, the gods still remain hidden, and we could today count ourselves lucky if a mere succession of Ahabs had stepped forth to impersonate them. If one were to judge by recent events, there may be no limit to the crimes man must commit before the gods can no longer stay their wrath.

In February of 1887, Nietzsche experienced an earthquake in Nice. Unable just then to take the incident very seriously, he wrote:

Quite a bit has caved in, so total panic reigns. I found all my friends strewn pitifully under green trees, all wrapped up because of the bitter cold, and responding to every little tremor with gloomy thoughts of death. . . . Apart from an old, very pious woman who is convinced that her God is not *permitted* to do her any harm, I was the only cheerful person amidst the ghostly faces and heavy hearts.[57]

At first blush, what can that pious old woman inspire but pity for her old-fashioned superstition? If one should happen to read Marx—in context, for a change—one might be led to more sober reflections:

Religious distress is at the same time the *expression* of real

---

56 Chapter 37, "Sunset."
57 Fuss-Shapiro (eds.), *Nietzsche: A Self-Portrait from His Letters, op. cit.,* p. 97.

distress and the *protest* against real distress. Religion is the sigh of the oppressed creature, the heart of a heartless world, just as it is the spirit of a spiritless situation. It is the opium of the people.[58]

But after Dachau, even this seems slightly out of focus. That old lady's faith would be as obscene now as it must be irresistably tempting. When opiates are many and cheap, religion is no longer *the* opium, nor, for that matter, the opium of *the people.* Often the final copout of the damned, it is sometimes their most human sound.

* * *

In my view, the religious emancipation toward which we seem currently to be groping has two aspects to it, each corresponding to a very real human need. Its immanent face seeks to liberate the man of action and hope from the fetters of institutional conformism—what to believe and how to behave: long the "dirty work" of the Church in its self-destructive alliances with secular power. Its transcendental face seeks to liberate man's metaphysical urgency, his need to dream himself beyond his entanglement, be it wretched or rewarding, in secular affairs; liberate it not so much any longer from magic and superstition (these have by now emigrated to the domain of the sciences), but from the hard-dying conceptual fetishism of the theological metaphysics which once claimed to have replaced them.

But in its recoil, long overdue, against its own history and tradition lies contemporary theology's greatest danger too: a certain spiritual cowardice, an all too eager willingness to replace an escapist devotion to the Four Last Things with a fuzzy notion of "relevance." In an age convinced that all problems and all solutions are "social," a theology that embraces rather than resists

58 Karl Marx and Friedrich Engels, *On Religion* (New York, Schocken Books, 1957), p. 42.

an ideology of pan-socialization betrays what is best in itself. The very sensible insistence on first things first is self-defeating if it is allowed to lead, however slowly and subtly, to Last Things never. Any theology worthy of its name today must be a theology of refusal: not a refusal to be concerned with elemental social needs, but a refusal to be part of *any* self-contained whole, *any* status quo. Adorno, no optimist in such matters, is convinced that bourgeois society, locked into a psychology of desperation, is prepared to perish *en masse* rather than risk the results of questioning itself radically, down to its very foundations. But without such questioning, essentially nothing will ever change. "Only when what is is opened to change will it cease to be all there is."[59]

In the wake of a cost-accounting like Nietzsche's, it is possible that we shall come to recognize in any major cultural phenomenon a systematic ambivalence. But if the conceptualization of such a phenomenon (before, during, or after is immaterial) often seems somehow purer than the event it reflects, that is because appearances are, after all, deceiving. To the ambivalences of motive and intention, action and happening correspond the antinomies of thought. For theological thinking, the antinomy it confronts is nothing new: an ever-elusive transcendence can only be held fast by being reified—that is, compromised, betrayed to the point where the spirit dies; yet giving up the slimmest hope of incarnating the transcendent in the immanent reduces spirit to an illusion and leads inescapably to the deification of the here and now—by far the worst of all possible mystifications.[60]

The most abrasive demythologizing agent in the religious history of the modern age has been, of course, the positivist tradition. It is this positivism which inspired, long before it began to impoverish, secular culture. It is this positivism whose relentless struggle with all forms of obfuscation flattened obstacle after obstacle in the path of an aggressive bourgeoisie—until finally, no

59 Adorno, *op. cit.,* p. 389.
60 Cf. Adorno, *op. cit.,* p. 390.

longer in touch with its first and purest impulse, it itself was transformed into that bourgeoisie's most stubborn and pervasive myth: the vaunted and flaunted exigencies of something we call Modern Society. Both the religious and the secular humanist traditions have long regarded positivism as the enemy, and have recently come more and more to make common cause against him. But they have never given him his due. In pruning both of them of their arrogance and their tendency toward mystification, he has empowered them for the struggle. As Nietzsche advised, one should be grateful to one's enemy.

A SELECT BIBLIOGRAPHY

Adorno, Theodor, *Negative Dialektik*. Frankfurt a.M.: Suhrkamp Verlag, 1966.

Arendt, Hannah, *The Human Condition*. Chicago: University of Chicago Press, 1950.

———, *On Revolution*. New York: Viking Press, 1965.

Descartes, Rene, "Meditations," in *Five Philosophers*. Translated and edited by Philip Wheelright and Peter Fuss. New York: Odyssey Press, 1963.

Dostoevsky, Fyodor, *Notes from Underground* (1864). New York: Dell, 1960.

Hegel, G.W.F., *The Phenomenology of Mind* (1807). New York: Macmillan, 1949.

———, *The Philosophy of History* (1830-1831). Translated by J. Sibree. New York: Dover, 1956.

Kant, Immanuel, *Critique of Pure Reason* (1781, 1787). Translated by Norman Kemp Smith. London: Macmillan, 1950.

———, *Foundations of the Metaphysics of Morals* (1785). Indianapolis, Indiana: Bobbs-Merrill, 1959.

Kierkegaard, Soren, *A Kierkegaard Anthology*. Edited by Robert Bretall. New York: Modern Library, 1946.

Marcuse, Herbert, *Reason and Revolution: Hegel and the Rise of Social Theory*. New York: Humanities Press, 1954.

Marx, Karl, *Karl Marx: Early Writings* (1844). Translated and edited by T.B. Bottomore. New York: McGraw-Hill, 1964.

Marx, Karl and Engels, Friedrich, *On Religion*. New York: Schocken Books, 1957.

Melville, Herman, *Moby-Dick* (1851). Indianapolis, Indiana: Bobbs-Merrill, 1964.

Nietzsche, Friedrich, *Werke in drei Banden.* Edited by Karl Schlechta. Munich, W. Germany: Carl Hanser, 1966.

————, *Nietzsche: A Self-Portrait from His Letters.* Translated and edited by Peter Fuss and Henry Shapiro. Cambridge, Massachusetts: Harvard University Press, 1971.

Schelling, F.W.J., *Of Human Freedom* (1809). Translated and edited by James Gutmann. Chicago: Open Court, 1936.

Sonnemann, Ulrich, *Negative Anthropologie.* Hamburg, W. Germany: Rowohlt, 1969.

CHAPTER XX

MYSTICISM: ST. JOHN OF THE CROSS

*Robert A. Herrera**

William James once noted that *mysticism* is an ambiguous term, often used as a reproach for opinions considered vague, vast, and sentimental.[1] The ambiguity of the term has lately served to include a veritable host of *esoterica*, from the pathological and downright weird, to nature's *historia praetergeneratione*. Philosophy, from Xenophanes to Lord Russell, has tended to regard mysticism, however this ambiguous term may have been interpreted, as antithetical to thought. Many studies on the subject originating in religious sources, such as Gorre's *Mystik* (two volumes of 'divine' mysticism parallelled by two volumes of 'diabolical' mysticism), tend to confirm this opinion. Although Watkin, Otto, and others,[2] have helped restore a certain seriousness to the study of mysticism, philosophy, perhaps remembering its ancient, unsatisfactory flirtation with the hermetic tradition and its adjuncts, has never really welcomed it into the fold. An opinion such as Otto's that mystical conceptions lie behind the higher speculation of more modern times, behind the thought of Descartes, the occasionalists, Malebranche, Spinoza, Shaftesbury, Leibniz, and Kant,[3] may well be somewhat fanciful but still cannot be rejected without seriously exploring its possibilities.

What is mysticism? Even if we were to banish from the field all 'mysticisms' except those that have endured the test of time,

---

*Professor of Philosophy at Seton Hall University, South Orange, New Jersey, U.S.A.

1 *The Varieties of Religious Experience* (New York: Modern Library, 1922), XVI, pp. 370-371.

2 See bibliography.

3 *Mysticism East and West* (New York: Meridian, 1960), Appendix II, p. 233.

piety, and criticism—a procedure not really adequate to the task involved—would it be possible to include, under one heading, the Persian verse of Rumi, the Teutonic Gothic of Meister Eckhardt, the mystagogical treatises of Ibn' Arabi, the poetry of St. John of the Cross, and the speculations of Isaac Luria? We are here, limiting ourselves to 'the people of the book.' Perhaps the best approach, among many poor ones, is to outline some of the fundamental themes of mysticism as found in Christianity and center our attention on one mystical writer, St. John of the Cross, as he developed his insights. The Christian mystical tradition, if we are to distinguish it from the predominantly ascetical bent of mind of the primitive Church, has its inception with Macarius and Nilus, continues in the *Scala Paradisi* of John Climacus and the *Mystica Theologiae* of the Pseudo-Denis, is brought to the West in seminal form by Cassian and is developed by Augustine, Gregory the Great, the Victorines, Bernard and Bonaventure among others. It extends to Meister Eckhardt, the Rheinland mystics, and to sixteenth century Spain with Teresa of Avila and John of the Cross. After the sixteenth century, with few exceptions, the literature of mysticism becomes either parochial, fantastic, or professorial, in spite of instructive controversies such as the Bossuet—Fenelon exchange. Contemporary man senses rightly that something is wrong, that the 'sense' of the sacred has been lost, or at least misplaced, and seeks confusedly a new opening to the divine.

Mysticism distinguished itself from the usual *theology* in that it claimed to teach a deeper 'mystery' and reveal profundities otherwise unknown. There is, then, a *mystical* sense and a *mystical* interpretation of the scriptures, unveiling a hidden meaning of the text. At an early period, a 'tasting' of unencompassed truth, a 'penetration' of the invisible and incomprehensible, was included as a further aspect of this new and deeper scriptural sense. This 'knowing,' far from being limited to pure cognition, includes an 'experience,' a fortaste of ultimate union with God. The use of tactile analogy is current at a very early date: 'seeing,' 'hearing,' 'touching,' 'tasting' and so forth. Paradoxically, this 'experience' is ineffable, something that can be compared to our normal, everyday experience only by analogy.

Spiritual life is viewed as a journey, even after the original 'leap of faith' and acceptance of Christ, has been made. In the early Middle Ages those monasteries in which the vow of stability (permanence) was enforced, the physical pilgrimage to the holy places was replaced by their archetype: the spiritual pilgrimage to God, a *peregrinatio in stabilitate.* The mystical life has the same goal as any variation of the Christian life: the ascent to God and ultimate deification by participation. However, it differs from other variations in that the working of God in the soul is, in some way, perceived. This life is 'experienced' *as is God* in an ineffable manner.

There is a road to traverse, a journey to be made, knowledge to be acquired, an 'experiencing' transcending experience, before arriving at union with God. The human condition is mysticism's point of departure, spiritual and moral ascesis its method, and the end in view is ultimate union with God. Mysticism, then, embraces a unique dialectic between the existential ground of a supra-rational faith and the practical life of spiritual ascesis which organizes the lower tendencies of sensibility. The contact with this ground, God, is *experiential;* at its most intense, it is called ecstacy. Ecstacy has both positive and negative aspects; negatively, it brings about a cessation of conceptual thought and imagination; positively, it is an intensification of intellectual activity on a totally new level or dimension.[4]

Philosophical inquiry is certainly not a propaedeutic to mysticism: a mention of Teresa of Avila and other 'unlettered' mystics is enough to rid us of this academic illusion. But the mystical experience, whatever it is, does not itself provide the mystic with a vocabulary adequate to this intensification of spirit. The mystic is forced to express himself in language, if he is to express himself at all, and consequently is wedded to its categories. It is only when he can, in some way, escape from these

---

4 Refer to Joseph Marechal, "Features of Christian Mysticism" in *Studies in the Psychology of the Mystics* (Albany: Magi Books, 1964).

categories, by impregnating them with an additional dimension
that he is most adequate. Language, as such, is an insufficient
vehicle to express the ineffable mystical experience. Nevertheless,
it may point to this experience by stammering out whatever it can,
thus indicating the poverty of language and intimating another
dimension.

St. John of the Cross is particularly interesting because of his
use of language and poetry to attempt an articulation of mystical
experience. The Scriptures provided him with the instrument
necessary to supercede discursive reasoning: in his terminology,
"natural knowledge." It is the metaphor. Through it he attempts
to outline that hidden domain which "natural knowledge" based
on cause and effect is structurally incapable of penetrating.
Because of this the poem always 'says more' than any commentary. It is impossible to exhaust "the abundance of the Holy
spirit" by words.[5] We are not dealing with rational explication but
rather with experiences which "overflow" into figures and similes
(*figuras, comparaciones y semejanzas*): "it would be foolish to
think that expressions of love arising from mystical understanding . . . are fully explainable."[6] Metaphor perhaps may overcome those barriers which prevent conceptual discourse from
probing into mystery.

The role of the metaphor in the interpretation of reality is as
old as mantic poetry. Within a Christian context it is established
by Boccaccio in his commentary on the *Divine Comedy:* "poetry
is theology."[7] Dante himself, in his letter to Can Grande della
Scala, notes that there are many things for which we do not
possess an adequate word and must then recur to the metaphor
"as Plato did."[8] Aquinas, in the *Expositio in Psalmos*, indicates
that when words are lacking, man breaks into song: "the leap of

5 *Sudiba,* Prol., 1.
6 *Ibid.*
7 Cited by Jacques Maritain, *The Frontiers of Poetry* (New York: Scribners, 1962),
p. 224, note 179.
8 *Obras Completas* (Madrid: B.A.C., 1960), p. 1063.

the mind in the eternal breaking into sound."[9] Authentic use of the metaphor in poetry is not a mere *contrafactum,* the substitution of a profane by a sacred meaning. It is a real though partial penetration into mystery, the paradigm of all mysteries, which is God. Poetry may well permit a 'knowing' which transcends the limits of discursive reason and penetrates the incomprehensible cloud of unknowing.

A discussion of some of the principle metaphors used by John of the Cross might even be considered a *philosophical* endeavour, especially if philosophy is understood as a continuing quest for those metaphors adequate to express reality. The metaphor, by the way, is also a clue to thematic presuppositions of the author. Through a brief exegesis of the metaphor we hope to accompany the soul as a somewhat myopic observer in a journey from its earthly prison to the heights of divine union. As 'observers,' we cannot hope to experience God vicariously. There are no mystics at second remove. We can, nevertheless, attempt to partially comprehend, the language of the mystic. Much may seem bizarre, even repugnant. A familiarity with these strange cadences, an attunement of the inner self towards this alien domain, is the most we can expect.

Mystic and poet, John of the Cross lived in an unique age that witnessed the twilight of the Medieval Schools and the dawning of the new world of the mathematization of nature. Chronological poles set by the death of Erasmus and the birth of Descartes, it is the age of Justus Lipsius, Giordano Bruno, Galileo, Campanella, and Francis Bacon. It is a time, as Dilthey has pointed out, characterized by the affirmation of the world and nature, 'the gospel of infinite nature.'[10] John is antithetical to this vision. In a Promethean world he is an anti-Prometheus, leaving to one side man and nature in the wake of his quest for an alien God. Even from a contemporary perspective he appears to be overly

---

9 *Prol.*
10 *Hombre y mundo en los siglos XVI y XVII* (México: Fondo de Cultura Económica, 1947), p. 458.

engrossed in God, a rather uncomfortable God who resists domestication and imprisonment in conceptual schema, referred to in strange metaphorical allusions.

I would like to center attention on three metaphors employed by John of the Cross in which his thought is concentrated, illustrating the ascent from the human condition such as it is, to union with God. These metaphors are those of the *imprisoned soul*, the *sculpting of a statue*, and a metaphor uniquely his, that of *night (noche)*. Together, in progression, they illustrate an ascent which greatly resembles those other spiritual journeys depicted in the literature of mysticism. The ascent to God, the 'Absolute,' the 'One,' remains, at least at its spiritual apex, beyond the province of language. The further we ascend the greater is the distance between our statements and the reality signified. An awareness of this disproportion will prevent us from constructing a straw God or a parody of mystical contemplation, a temptation to which, as history indicates, man is all too prone.

The state of the human soul resembles that of a prisoner in a "dark dungeon," a "noble lord" in the "prison of the body."[11] This metaphor, most probably of Orphic ancestry, is adopted by Plato and expands into the metaphors of *burial* and *entombment*, so dear to Plotinus. They illustrate his theory of the "fall" grounded in the *Phaedo* and the *Phaedrus*. The point of departure for a christian 'ascent' is the notion of original sin, somewhat different from the Plotinian 'fall,' in which the soul descends from the intelligible real to the domain of matter because of its lusting for embodiment. In the Platonic tradition philosophy possesses therapeutic powers: it effects the purification of the soul and its liberation from the body, suppressing the 'desires and evils' of the body.[12]

This notion of the therapeutic role of philosophy is alien to St. John of the Cross. The only 'fall' he comprehends is original sin, the fall of mankind from its primitive rectitude. This 'fall' is

---

11 *Cántico*, 18, 1.; *Subida*, I, 3, 3.
12 *Phaedo*, 81 c ff.; *Cratilus*, 404 ff.

reflected in the human race through its debilitating effects. Originally, reason ordered the "sensory part" of the soul.[13] In overthrowing this hierarchical government, original sin throws the soul into captivity: "the soul, through original sin, is a captive in the mortal body, subject to passion and natural appetite."[14] The ordered harmony which prevailed *ab initio* is destroyed.

None the less, St. John does agree with the Platonic tradition, at least in two particulars. First of all, he identifies the individual man with his highest aspect, the soul. The term soul *(alma)*, used in a wide sense signifies the whole man, body and soul, although primarily, it refers only to the spiritual and life-giving power, and only secondarily does it apply to the body.[15] In fact, it is the soul which, properly speaking, possesses a body, "the soul does not live in the body, but rather gives life to the body."[16] John, in the spirit of the Platonic tradition, does not believe that the present state of man is his original state. The human condition does not faithfully mirror human nature; man is neither what he once was nor what he should be. Because of some catastrophe hidden in the darkness of prehistory, man has been severed from his true self. As we have noted, the Platonic remedy to this unfortunate state of affairs is *philosophy,* a noble spiritual exercise which puts purification within our grasp, opening the way to a participation in divinity. St. John is situated at quite a distance from any such optimistic humanism. Philosophy is, after all, a human endeavour open to all who enjoy sufficient leisure. For St. John of the Cross, in the last instance, God acts alone, doing everything *in* man, always *with* man.

In describing the ascent to God, he stresses the Pauline distinction between the 'old man' and the 'new man.' He speaks of the 'animal man' who lives by "natural appetite" and suffers from "embotamiento de la mente," blunting of the mind.[17] The 'old

---

13 *Subida,* III, 26, 5.
14 *Ibid.,* I, 15, 1.
15 *Cántico,* XXV, 6 *(Primera Redacción).*
16 *Ibid.,* VIII, 3.
17 *Subida,* III 19, 3.

man' must die if the soul is ever to 'taste' God.[18] This required metamorphosis is called a *'desnudar'* (stripping), a *'vaciar'* (an emptying or voiding).[19] The soul must be emptied so that God will clothe it with a new and blessed life.[20] The 'nights' of sense and spirit, involving as they do ascetical and moral purification grounded on prayer and humility under the aegis of God, will constitute the new man. The metaphor of *sculpting a statue* is used to illustrate the process by which this 'stripping' or 'voiding' of the 'old man' takes place. The soul, at its point of departure—St. John speaks of a *principiante* or novice—is compared to the 'first draft of a painting' which 'calls out to the one who drew the sketch to finish the painting.'[21] In a small ascetical treatise called the *Cautelas,* directed to these novices, he advises them to think of all the members of the religious community as artisans destined to mould them: "in all you must be submissive as is the statue to the craftsman who moulds it, to the artist who paints it, and to the guilder who embellishes it."[22] The final touches on the statue, "the ultimate perfection of delicate painting" is assigned to God *alone,* so as to emphasize His preeminence.

This metaphor comparing spiritual purification to the production of a work of art also enjoys an illustrious ancestry having been used among others, by Plotinus, the Pseudo-Denis, and St. Gregory of Nyssa. Plotinus invites the 'initiate' to polish the statue of his true being, to proceed as the creator of a statue that is to be made beautiful, "he cuts away here, he smooths here, he makes this line brighter, this other purer, until a lovely face has grown upon his work."[23] In this way, cutting away what is excessive and straightening the crooked, the soul will arrive at the godlike

---

18 *Noche,* II, 16, 4.
19 *Ibid.,* II, 3, 3.
20 *Ibid.,* II, 13, 11.
21 *Cántico,* XII, 1.
22 *Cautelas,* 15.
23 *Enneads,* 1, 6, 9.

splendour of virtue.[24] Pseudo-Denis, in the *De Mystica Theologiae,* advises Timothy to emulate those sculptors who "carving a statue out of marble, remove all the impediments that hinder the clear perception of the latent image and . . . display the hidden statue in its hidden beauty."[25]

The soul, in Plotinus' conception, can select, at any given moment, the spiritual level on which it will dwell. Its hierarchy is dictated by its own efforts, the strivings of an autonomous being. For St. John of the Cross, the individual can be said to take the initiative (always *in* and *with* God) but this initiative is ultimately a situating of himself in potency to divine action. Only God can initiate the vertical ascent of the soul. There is no 'ladder' among created things to bring man to union with God. We must, St. John insists, rely on the 'ladder' which God has given us: namely, *faith.* In advancing by faith we ascend by *unknowing* rather than by *knowing,* "by (the soul) blinding itself and remaining in darkness rather than opening its eyes."[26] The propositions of faith in this life implicitly contain and prepare us for the 'seeing' and 'enjoying' of their 'substance' in the next.[27] God's love alone, however, not theoretical knowledge, draws us to Him.

The metaphor which is the key to the thought (and poetry) of St. John of the Cross is that of night *(noche),* and its fulfillment in flame *(llame).* It is a truly unique combination of lyric and dialectical genius. Not only have the very best Sanjuanist scholars stressed its importance but a few have attempted their own interpretation of the metaphor at times in rather audacious terms. Jean Baruzi essayed a Leibnizian interpretation of the *nights,* while Jacques Chevalier has returned to Descartes in an attempt to interpret the *nights* in the light of Cartesian doubt.[28] But these

---

24 *Ibid.*
25 De Mystica Theol., 2.
26 *Subida,* II, 8, 5.
27 *Cántico,* XII, 4.
28 Jean Baruzi, *Saint Jean de la Croix et le problème de l'expérience mystique* (Paris: Alcan, 1924), p. 574 ff.
    Jacques Chevalier, 'Le réalisme spiritual des mystiques espagnols,' *Stromata,* V, a, 1940, pp. 315-316.

interpretations appear to contradict both St. John's use of the metaphor and whatever we know of *night* as a cosmic symbol. In primitive belief it signifies death, the entrance into another level of existence. In the cosmic night all the basic structural principles of the universe lose their form (limits) and descend into chaos. Fire signifies a new genesis, generating a new universe out of chaos. It is interesting to note that this correlation between night and fire seems also to hold in John of the Cross. A Spanish exegete, Fray Crisogóno indicates that night does not terminate in darkness; "it is a night whose darkness is born of light, feeds on light, and is ultimately reduced to light."[29] It is, in fact, · the slow metamorphosis of *night* into *flame* that illustrates man's spiritual odyssey. In brief, the soul enters darkness, empties itself through the mediation of the 'nights' of sense and spirit, and then encounters God; flame is recognized as the obverse of night, and night as an adumbration of flame.

God is both mover and end of this spiritual pilrimage. "The very loving light and wisdom into which the soul will be transformed is that which in the beginning purges and prepares it, just as fire transforms the wood into itself and first prepares it for this transformation.[30] The life of flame pulsating within the night is the index of spiritual vitality. This occult life expands until night is transformed into the unlimited dynamism of flame. *Mystical contemplation* is "an infused knowledge that both illumines and enamours the soul, elevating it step by step to God, its Creator."[31]

The sketches of the mystical Mount Carmel drawn by the saint himself present one salient detail: a path going directly to the summit of the mount, the "path of Mount Carmel, the spirit of perfection." On it is inscribed, "nothing, nothing, nothing, nothing, nothing, and even on the Mount, nothing." Though at first reading this may seem an exercise in nihilism, it decidedly is

29 *San Juan de la Cruz: su obra científica y su obra literaria* (Madrid: Mensajero de Santa Teresa, 1929), II, p. 269.
30 *Noche,* II, 10, 3.
31 *Ibid.,* II, 18, 5.

not. On the contrary, it represents the necessary limitations which the soul in its 'powers' of intellect will, and memory, must respect so as to arrive at union with God. The *Nadas* are not ends in themselves but rather the means of purification necessary to ascend to the *Todo,* the means of penetrating through the night to God Who is flame.

Although St. John of the Cross in his commentaries[32] catalogues wide range of phenomena from 'spiritual touches' to 'ecstacks' he is far from recommending a spectacular mysticism, centering around physco-physical or spiritual *esoterica.* Still less, would he be in sympathy with a 'mysticism' which sought to generate these experiences. This he characterizes as spiritual gluttony. Natural Reason, Divine Law, and the Gospel are sufficient from human guidance. God has fixed "natural and rational limits" by which man is to be ruled, and any desire to transcend these limits is illegitimate.[33] Even if God were to vouchsafe a genuine supernatural experience, man should not shift his loving attention from the imperceptible God to the all too perceptible experience. This would be tantamount to idolatry, as no experience, no matter how sublime, legitimate, or ineffable, may be equated with God.[34]

St. John of the Cross has an important lesson for the contemporary world. Man is not the absolute value. The Promethean posture must be rejected. It is near insanity to advocate either *homo homini lupus* or *homo homini Deus.* Man is created so that he can "rise from the crumbs of creatures to the uncreated Spirit of their Father."[35] All creatures "whet the appetite," that is, serve as a stimulus to man in his ascent to God. Once this function of creatures is perverted or distorted, man himself becomes perverted and distorted. The soul must either

32 The *Subida del Monte Carmelo* and the *Noche Oscura* should be regarded as one Treatise: the *Noche* was originally the fourth book of the *Subida.* The other commentaries are the *Cántico Espiritual* and the *Llama de Amor Viva.*

33 *Subida,* II, 21, 1.

34 Refer to this remarkable letter "To a religious," dated Segovia, April 14, 1589; *Vida y Obras de San Juan de La Cruz* (Madrid: B.A.C., 1960), pp. 1147-1149.

35 *Subida,* I, 6, 3.

ascend to God or fall to the level of the creature it desires. God, though he may be *dark night* to us, is very much alive. Our being is rooted in Him. To fail to ascend to God is to lose both God and self.

A SELECT BIBLIOGRAPHY

1. Works

Vida y Obras Completas. Madrid: B.A.C., 1960. *Concordancias de las Obras y Escritos del Doctor de la Iglesia San Juan de la Cruz,* ed. Luis de San José, O.C.D. Burgos: El Monte Carmelo, 1948.

Translations

Allison Peers, E., *Complete Works of St. John of the Cross,* 3 vols. London: Burns, Oats, 1934-1935.
Kavanaugh, K. & Rodriguez, O., *Collected Works of St. John of the Cross.* New York: Doubleday, 1964.

2. Studies

Biographies

Bruno de Jesus-Marie, O.C.D., *St. John of the Cross.* New York: Sheed and Ward, 1932.
Crisógono de Jesús Sacramentado, O.C.D., *Vida de San Juan de la Cruz.* Madrid: B.A.C., 1960.
Allison Peers, E., *A Handbook to the Life and Times of St. Teresa and St. John of the Cross.* London: Burns, Oats, 1954.

Doctrinal Studies

Baruzi, Jean, *Saint Jean de la Croix et le problème de l'expérience mystique.* Paris: Alcan, 1924.
Crisogóno de Jesús Sacramentado, O.C.D., *San Juan de la Cruz su Obra Científica y su Obra Literaria.* 2 vols. Madrid: Editorial Mensajero de Sta. Teresa 1929.
McCann, Leonard A., *The Doctrine of the Void.* Toronto: Basilean Press, 1955.

McNabb, Vicent, *The Mysticism of St. John of the Cross.* Aylesford: St. Alberts Press, 1955.

Sanson, Henri, *L'Esprit Humain selon saint Jean de la Croix.* Paris: P.U.F., 1953.

———, *Jean de la Croix entre Bossuet et Fénelon: Contribution à l'étude de la querelle du pur amour.* Paris: P.U.F., 1954.

Stein, Edith, *The Science of the Cross.* Chicago: Henry Regnery, 1960.

Literary Studies

Alonso, Dámaso, *La Poesía de San Juan de la Cruz.* Madrid: Aguiar, 1958.

D'Ors, Eugenio, *Estilos del Pensar.* Madrid: Editorial y Publicaciones Españolas, 1945.

Groult, P., *Les Mystiques de Pays-Bas et la Litterature Espagnol du XVIe Siècle.* Louvain: Louvain University Press, 1927.

Hatzfeld, Helmut, *Estudios Literarios sobre mística Española.* Madrid: Gredos, 1955.

Icaza, Sra. Rosa María, *The Stylistic Relationship between Poetry and Prose in the Cántico Espiritual of St. John of the Cross.* Washington: Catholic University Press, 1957.

CHAPTER XXI

DAVID HUME ON GOD

Sebastian A. Matczak *

One of the philosophers whose writings have been constantly examined and have had a particular influence on our century is David Hume (1711-1776). His views on God are of special importance; this was a question that preoccupied him during his whole life. The results of this preoccupation are presented in his *Dialogues Concerning Natural Religion,* posthumously published in 1779. The *Dialogues* provide abundant material for the study and examination of the arguments concerning the existence of God. For this reason we shall concentrate on them, particularly on their method of reasoning, their arguments and their value.

1. Importance of the "Dialogues"

According to Norman Kemp Smith, David Hume in his *Dialogues* was the first thinker in English literature to subject the proofs for the existence of God to "a careful and dispassionate critique."[1] Smith goes so far as to affirm that Hume's critique is complete and definitive.[2] Alfred North Whitehead[3] and Leslie Stephen[4] expressed similar opinions. Looking further back, we

---

*Professor of Philosophy at St. John's University, New York, U.S.A.

[1] Smith (ed.), *Hume's Dialogues Concerning Natural Religion* (New York: Social Sciences Publishers, 1948), p. 30.
[2] *Ibid.*
[3] Whitehead, *Adventures of Ideas* (New York: Mentor Books, 1953), p. 173.
[4] Leslie Stephen, *English Thought in the Eighteenth Century,* 3rd edition (London, 1902), Vol. I, p. 311; cf. Smith, *op. cit.,* p. 30.

find Immanuel Kant (1724-1804), who was not only awakened from his "dogmatic slumbers" by the philosophical writings of Hume, but who was particularly impressed by the *Dialogues*. We can see the effect of Hume's influence in Kant's criticism of the theological argument both in the second edition of the *Critique of Pure Reason* (1787)[5] and in his *Critique of Judgement* (1790).[6]

We should not be surprised by this influence. Hume's reasoning in the *Dialogues* is very subtle and embraces a large number of problems essential to the search for the knowledge of God and for our knowledge in general.

Hume himself attributed very specific importance to the *Dialogues*. As a matter of fact, he tried persistently to have them published and was willing to allow the destruction of all his other works if only the *Dialogues* be preserved.[7] He apparently foresaw that they would be like a wind which, as La Rochefoucauld observed, "extinguishes a candle, but stirs up a blaze."[8]

Continuing interest in the *Dialogues* convincingly proves their importance. Many of the ideas and arguments found in them recur in various trends of contemporary philosophical thought. A careful study of the varieties of naturalism vividly points up their close relation to the *Dialogues*. Logical empiricism finds strong support in them, particularly in its tasks of clarifying concepts by examining language and verifying ideas in order to rediscover the very meaning of terms. Hume himself seems to emphasize these tasks by the voice of Philo in his discussion between the theist and the atheist, the skeptic and the dogmatic.[9] The analytical method,

---

[5] Kant, *Kritik der Reinen Vernunft*, English translation by Max Müller, *Critique of Pure Reason* (New York: Doubleday, 1961), pp. 360 ff. The first edition of this work was published at Riga in 1781; the second edition appeared in 1787. See W. Windelband, *A History of Philosophy*, translated by J.M. Tufts (New York: The Macmillan Co., 1954), p. 536.

[6] Kant, *Kritik der Urtheilskraft*, English translation by J.H. Bernard, *Critique of Judgement* (New York: Hafner, 1961), pp. 312 ff.

[7] J.H. Burton, *Life and Correspondence of David Hume*. 2 vols. (Edinburgh: William Tait, 1846), Vol. II, p. 1490;–*Letters of David Hume*, ed. by J.Y.T. Greig, 2 vols. (Oxford, 1932), Vol. II, p. 317. See the *Dialogues*, p. 89; also Ch. W. Hendel, *Studies in the Philosophy of David Hume* (New York: Bobbs-Merrill, 1963), p. 310.

[8] *Letters*, II, p. 316; see the *Dialogues*, p. 89, also Hendel, *op. cit.*, p. 361.

[9] *Dialogues*, Part IX, pp. 189-190; Part XII, pp. 217-219.

widely applied by G.E. Moore (1873-1958) was also inspired by Hume.[10]

With regard to contemporary probabilism and its tendency toward either skepticism or a sort of vague certainty, it was Hume, among others, who advanced that kind of thinking.[11] Dialectical materialism, although not anticipated by the *Dialogues* in the sense of the same concept of dialectical development, has been suggested by the idea of matter in motion more or less spontaneously producing the variety of things and the constant order in the universe.[12] There is even a suggestion of an idea of existentialism, with its phenomenological method, the idea of the mystery of being (G. Marcel) and the being conceived as a factual, although not gnoseological solution of all problems.[13] To be sure, however, existentialism is not really found in the *Dialogues*.

Pragmatism's notions of the workableness of ideas and their consequences also have their precedence in the *Dialogues*.[14] The same can be said of the conception of a rational instinct as a means to our knowledge of the cause of the universe, a concept which was advanced by Charles Sanders Peirce (1839-1914).[15] Even a kind of deism, or better, limited theism, finds support in the *Dialogues*.[16]

Besides these particular ideas, we also find in the *Dialogues* the great questions which various philosophical systems have debated all along evaluated in a new light. Among them are the eternity of the world, its external and internal unknown causes and its

---

[10] *Ibid.*, p. 219. See also Moore, *Some Main Problems of Philosophy* (New York: Collier, 1962), pp. 104-143, 157-160, 168-171, 257, 296, 327, 340; *Philosophical Studies* (Paterson, New Jersey: Littlefield, 1959), pp. 147-167.

[11] *Ibid.*, Parts IV, pp. 163; Part V, pp. 165, 167; Part VIII, p. 182.

[12] *Ibid.*, Parts IV, pp. 163; Part VII, p. 179; Part VIII, p. 185.

[13] *Ibid.*, Part VIII, p. 183, cf. p. 162, see also Richard H. Popkin, "Hume and Kierkegaard," *The Journal of Religion*, Vol. XXXI (1951), pp. 276-281.

[14] *Dialogues*, Part IX, p. 188. See also G.B. Marthur, "Hume and Kant in Their Relation to the Pragmatic Movement," *Journal of the History of Ideas*, Vol. XVI (1955), pp. 198-208.

[15] Peirce, "A Neglected Argument for the Reality of God," *Values in a Universe of Change*, ed. by Ph. P. Weiner (New York: Doubleday, 1958), pp. 366, 369, 371-373. *Dialogues*, Part XII, p. 218.

[16] *Dialogues*, p. 36; Part IV, p. 160.

evolution; the problem of suffering and the origin and usefulness of religion.

All these questions are organized in a conversational manner around the ultimate questions of the nature and existence of God. Thus, the *Dialogues* constitute the most complete work of Hume on God.

2. Other Writings by Hume on God

Hume also discusses various aspects of God in other works. In his *Treatise of Human Nature* (1739),[17] Hume elaborates on the problem of the conceivability of God and, consequently, the origin of the idea of God. He treats the proof of God's existence through order and movement;[18] they are explained by force and energy identical with the entity of every creature and being.[19] However, Hume is particularly interested in our ideas; all of them being derived from particular impressions, "none of which contains any efficacy, nor seems to have any connection with any other existence."[20] Thus, they cannot lead us to the "knowledge of cause or productive principle, nor even the deity himself."[21]

Another writing, the *Enquiry Concerning Human Understanding* of 1748,[22] adds an important study on miracles, providence, and the future life of man.[23] Hume had previously pursued these researches for the *Treatise,* but had published them

---

[17] Hume, *A Treatise of Human Nature,* reprinted from the original edition of three volumes and edited by L.A. Selby-Bigge (Oxford: The Clarendon Press, 1958), pp. 159-160, 248, 249, 633.

[18] *Ibid.,* pp. 159-160, 248-249, 633. *Dialogues,* Part XII, pp. 214-220; Hume's opening to this issue has been shown by James Orr, *David Hume and His Influence on Philosophy and Theology,* Edinburg, 1903; H.N. Price, "The Permanent Significance of Hume's Philosophy," *Philosophy,* Vol. XV (1940), pp. 7-37.

[19] Hume, *Treatise,* p. 633.

[20] *Ibid.,* p. 248; see also pp. 162-163, 249.

[21] *Ibid.,* p. 248.

[22] Hume, *Enquires concerning the Human Understanding and concerning the Principles of Morals,* reprinted from the posthumous edition 1777 and edited by L.A. Selby-Bigge (2nd ed. Oxford: The Clarendon Press, 1957), VIII.

[23] *Ibid.,* Sections X-XI, pp. 108-148; see also pp. 90-99.

later in the *Enquiry*.[24] He also wrote *The Natural History of Religion* (1757), a study of the origin and historical value of religion, questions that the *Dialogues* treat.[25] We must add a special essay *On the Immortality of the Soul* (1777), which rejects immortality on the basis of the lack of a sensory evidence.[26] Some relevance is also found in *An Enquiry Concerning the Principles of Morals* (1751),[27] where Hume sees determination in man's interpretation of the problems called free will, and reduces man's responsibility and destiny to earthly satisfaction.

Since, as we can see, several topics presented in the *Dialogues* find their elaboration in other writings of Hume, we may conclude that he studied the question of God on various occasions and under numerous aspects. In addition, the basis of Hume's reasoning, especially his theory of knowledge which reduces our concepts to sensory nature, plays an important role in our understanding of his position on our knowledge of God.

3. Personalities of the "Dialogues"

In order to throw a better light on the particular problems regarding the existence of God, Hume adopts the form of a debate between three persons. One of them, Demea, is a theist who accepts religion on the basis of faith. His knowledge of the philosophical foundation of religion leaves a lot to be desired. Another interlocutor is Cleanthes; although a theist, he is more critical than Demea and an advocate of experience as the foundation for our knowledge of God. The third is Philo, the hero of the *Dialogues*,[28] who advances a penetrating and careful

---

24 *Dialogues*, p. 45.

25 Hume, *The Natural History of Religion,* ed. by H.E. Root. Standford, California: Standford University Press, 1957. See also Hume, "My Own Life," in the *Dialogues,* pp. 237 ff.

26 Hume, "On the Immortality of the Soul," *Essays, Moral, Political and Literary,* ed. T.W. Green and T.H. Grose (London, 1975), Vol. II, p. 399, *Treatise,* pp. 114-115, 240-242, 276; also the *Dialogues,* pp. 42, 199.

27 *Ibid.,* also *Treatise,* pp. 403 ff.

28 See below, #5.

critique of belief in God. The conclusion, at the end of the
Dialogues, is presented by Pamphilus, the listener, who sums up
the arguments and modifies the atheistic suggestions found in the
work.[29]

4. Subject of the "Dialogues"

The main theme of Hume's *Dialogues* is an analysis and critical
evaluation of the proof for the existence of God from order in the
world. That proof was of supreme importance during Hume's life.
Indeed, it was considered to be the conclusive demonstration of
the existence of God, particularly in the works of Samuel Clarke
(1675-1729).[30] By undermining that proof, Hume could destroy
the primary basis of a rational belief in God. In the course of his
study, Hume was nevertheless logically obliged to discuss other
arguments that serve as foundations to the proofs generally
proposed for the existence of God. Thus, Hume examines, through
some of its stages, the principle of causality essential to Thomist
philosophy and to the classic *a posteriori* proofs for the existence
of God.[31] Hume treats mainly the second and third ways as
advanced by St. Thomas, namely that from secondary causes to
the prime cause and that from contingent being to necessary
being. He also mentions the first way, from movement to the
prime mover,[32] and the fourth way, that from degrees of
perfection.[33] In addition, Hume discusses *a priori* proofs; rejecting
them as a whole and accepting experience as the only means of an
eventual demonstration of God's existence.[34] In the final analysis,

---

29 See below, #8.

30 *Dialogues,* p. 44. Hume thought especially of S. Clarke's *A Discourse concerning
the Being and Attributes of God, the Obligations of Natural Religion, and the Truth and
Certainty of the Christian Revelation.* 4th edition. London: James Knapton, 1716. First
published in 1775 under the title, *A Demonstration of the Being and Attributes of God.*
London: James Knapton, 1705. See also Hendel, *op. cit.,* p. 61.

31 *Dialogues,* Parts II, especially pp. 143, 145-146, 151; cf. Part IX, p. 188.

32 *Ibid.,* Part IV, p. 159; Part VII, pp. 178-179; Part VIII, pp. 182-184; see also pp.
161, 172.

33 *Ibid.,* Part X, p. 202.

34 *Ibid.,* Part IX-XI, pp. 188, 191-193, 200, 205.

however, he completely excludes any knowledge of God's existence through reason and suggests that faith alone is the basis of such knowledge.[35] Thus, religion is grounded solely in a popular feeling, without a truly rational base.[36]

A final attack against the most general principles of religion and the existence of God is presented in the exposition of Philo. Given the disorder that exists in the world, he concludes that no natural or revealed religion can justify the existence of suffering on earth.[37] Because of this situation, no reason exists why anyone should be obliged to believe.[38]

5. Hume's Order of Proceeding

Despite the fact that Hume discusses various proofs for the existence of God, he invariably returns to the proof through order in the universe. He does this because this argument, as we noted above, was frequently used in his time as a conclusive proof for God's existence.

We should remember that Hume was conscious of another fact, a widespread religious feeling throughout his country; we well know that he encountered such great difficulties in publishing his *Dialogues* that they were published posthumously.[39] In fact, it was because of this religious atmosphere that Hume, throughout the *Dialogues,* proceeded in a systematic and prudent manner, handling the presentation of the arguments in the form of calm debates. The debate format ensures a deeper insight into the content of the arguments; and it also provokes in the reader a strong desire to evalute the momentum of their reasoning. In proceeding this way the *Dialogues* accomplish their ultimate goal, a genuine skepticism about the proofs usually advanced for the existence of God.

---

35 *Ibid.,* Part X, pp. 200-202.
36 *Ibid.,* Part X, p. 202; Part XI, pp. 205, pp. 205-213; Part XII, pp. 226-228.
37 *Ibid.,* Parts VIII-XII, especially, p. 200.
38 *Ibid.,* Parts I-II, see also pp. 71-75, 97-101, 186-187.
39 *Ibid.,* pp. 88-96; see above, Introduction to this essay.

Of the interlocutors Demea, Cleanthes, and Philo, there is no doubt that Philo represents the position of Hume. This is evidenced by Philo's penetrating critique, a confirmation found in Hume's letters, and also in the agreement of Philo's reasons with the rest of Hume's philosophical writing.[40] However, the reasoning displayed by the other persons who occasionally express Hume's views and their arguments serve to sharpen the attention of the reader. Thus, Cleanthes asserts that experience constitutes the only sure basis for proving the existence of God,[41] that our conclusions concerning the cause of the universe are simply hypotheses,[42] and that the principle of causality does not lead to God's existence.[43]

The essence of these subtle and systematic discussions throughout the *Dialogues* can be summed up in this way: choosing experience as the criterion of certitude, Hume begins with a defense of the skeptical attitude in general (Part I) in order to apply it later to our knowledge of God. Hume assures this result by proceeding along this line: he prudently opens the discussion on the nature of God and attempts to prove through various arguments that God is inconceivable; we cannot make conjectures on His nature, unless completely arbitrary, since we do not know Him.[44]

By defining the limits to our knowledge of the nature of God, Hume prepares the ground for denying His existence. Thus, he shows that if we conceive God in one manner or another, we must understand Him as a fininte God (Part V). Consequently, He can be thought of as the soul of the world, and the world can be eternal (Part VI). If God is the soul of such a world, then He could

---

[40] *Letters,* Vol. 1, p. 154, see also the *Dialogues,* p. 88, cf. pp. 36, 41, 68-69. The opinion of G. Elliot, according to which Cleanthes is "the hero of the *Dialogues*" is questionable for the reason that we have given above. Other reasons are to found in Copleston, *A History of Philosophy,* 8 vols. (Westminister, Maryland: the Neuman Press, 1959), Vol. V, pp. 308-309. See also below, #8.

[41] *Dialogues,* Part II, p. 146, and *passim.*

[42] *Ibid.,* Part II, p. 145; Part IV, p. 163; see pp. 169-170, 183.

[43] *Ibid.,* Part II, pp. 144-145; Part VII, pp. 178-179; IX, p. 190; see also pp. 144, 167.

[44] *Dialogues,* Part II, pp. 143-145.

be the ground of all beings, living beings included (Part VII), and the order of the universe could be conceived as both the spontaneous development of matter and the natural adjustments of the component parts of the universe (Part VIII). Hume's reasoning to this point paved the way for him to discuss and reject the basic principle of the classical proofs for the existence of God, namely causality (Part IX). Belief in God and in His existence have become progressively deprived of their rational base, and soon only faith is left. Moreover, any rational basis for religion is discredited by the existence of disorder and suffering in the world, which is incompatible with an idea of God (Parts X and XII). Hume goes even further, submitting that existing religions are ill conceived, perverted, and even absurd (Part XII). He thus expresses in the *Dialogues* the idea that there is total lack of justification for the existence of God, and the idea of the uselessness of religion.

This conclusion is modified by Pamphilus in summing up and concluding the discussion, who remarks that belief in God is more plausible than disbelief.

6. Classification of the Problems

The order of Hume's reasoning in the *Dialogues* allows us to group his arguments according to the subjects on which they focus. Three principal problems are discussed, around which the other questions are organized: the nature of God, the existence of God, and the value of existing religions. Also discussed is the method of Hume's philosophical research: our experience which serves as a means of verification. We may summarize the problems of the *Dialogues* and the solutions suggested as follows.

a) God is known from religions, but His existence cannot be justified by rational, philosophical arguments.[45]

b) Experience is the only means of philosophical verification. By experience Hume means sensible evidence rather than intuitive

---

45 *Ibid.*, Part I, pp. 130, 138-139; see also Parts X-XII.

or discursive conclusions. Such experience should be at the beginning and also at the end of the reasoning.[46]

c) God is invisible and incomprehensible; therefore, our conjectures about His nature must remain uncertain. Generally it is accepted that He is infinte and omnipotent. But since the world is full of imperfection, disorder, evil and suffering, we should conclude that He is finite rather than infinite. If He were infinite, He would not permit the lamentable conditions that exist in the world,[47] since they would be incompatible with His goodness.

d) The Existence of God, inculcated by religion, cannot be proved. Traditionally *a priori* and *a posteriori* arguments are advanced to prove it. However, we cannot prove a fact of existence by *a priori* proof since what is conceived existent can be non-existent as well.[48] *A posteriori* proofs are also not conclusive for various reasons, particularly for the need of perfect similarity (analogy) between causes and effects,[49] because of the impossibility of examining innumerable causes of each effect, and because of the lack of equality between the parts and their whole since the whole may exceed its parts.[50]

e) Hume returns to the question of religions and sees the lack of their rational justification also in their origin, since they are reducible to imagination and superstition, and in their degeneration, to inconsistency and even absurdity.[51]

Hume concludes by suggesting a course of religious skepticism and the need for more revelation.[52]

46 *Ibid.*, Part II, pp. 142-143, 145-146; Part VII-VIII, pp. 177-186; Parts X-XIII; see above note 41.

47 *Dialogues*, Part II, pp. 142-145; Part V, p. 166; Part X, pp. 201-202; Part XI, pp. 203-211.

48 *Ibid.*, Part IX, pp. 188-191; see also pp. 114-116.

49 *Ibid.*, Parts II, V.

50 *Ibid.*, Parts II, pp. 144, 147; Part III, p. 152; Part V, p. 165; Part VIII, pp. 182-183.

51 *Ibid.*, Parts X-XII.

52 *Ibid.*, Parts X, XII.

7. Foundation of Hume's Reasoning

Throughout the *Dialogues* there are some fundamental ideas on which Hume's argumentation is grounded. One of them is that all of our perceptions are of a sensory nature. Hence, not only our sensory impression, but also even the universal ideas of our mind are, in the final analysis, of a sensory nature; they are essentially linked with their origin, that is to say, with some particular ideas and then with sensory impressions. Due to this fact our general concepts are governed by the psychological laws of association, which are equally sensory. Hume discusses these questions in his *Treatise* and in the *Enquiry*. He admits, however, as N.K. Smith correctly noted, that knowledge of "the ultimate cause of our mental acts is impossible;" this cause is therefore mysterious and secret.[53] Hume tries to prove the sensory character of our ideas by reducing them to copies or images or impressions;[54] he denies the existence of spirits and of spiritual souls.

In the same writings, Hume examines another basic idea—the principle of causality. Our knowledge of the causal relation is governed by psychological laws and expresses a feeling of necessity produced by habit in the mind of the observer, and not by a direct influence of the observed events.[55]

It is evident that Hume does not suppose a purely phenomenological existence of the whole world, as he tried to prove it in his *Treatise*. The reason might be that Hume himself feels the lack of precision and coherence of the proofs of his new epistemological theory.[56] Yet it seems more probable that Hume tried, as much as possible, to come closer to theistic doctrines, and to evaluate them by placing himself in their point of view. Hume

---

53 *Treatise*, I, I Section 7, p. 22; see also pp. 14, 78-82, 110, 149, 168-170, 207, 248-249, 461, 636. *Dialogues*, p. 27; Copleston, *op. cit.*, Vol. V, p. 273.

54 *Treatise*, I, I, Section 7, pp. 17 ff. See also Copleston, *op. cit.*, Vol. V, pp. 272-273, 280.

55 *Treatise*, I, III, Section 14, pp. 155, 170, see also Copleston, *op. cit.*, Vol. V p. 283-284; Smith, *The Philosophy of David Hume* (London, 1949), pp. 92-93.

56 Some aspects of this lack of coherence have been well found by H.H. Price, *Hume's Theory of the External World*, Oxford, 1940. See also Leroy, *David Hume* (Paris, 1953), p. 339.

could do it so much easier since his strictly epistemological study was secondary in relation to the validity of the arguments themselves concerning God's existence.

8. Modifications

Hume, as we noted above, tried to temper the skeptical impression of the *Dialogues* with the final remarks of the listener Pamphilus, who accords to the theistic position of Cleanthes a greater probability than to the skeptic position of Philo.[57] The modifications of this impression are serious but obvious. Philo insists on his belief in God, understood as a kind of deist's conception of the Supreme Being, after he has discredited the ordinarily accepted proofs.[58] Likewise, Cleanthes becomes more theistic, in the traditional sense of the term, when the inter-locutors tackle the problem of the value of religion.[59] One can ask why Hume introduces these modifications,[60] since they change nothing in the fundamental conclusion of the *Dialogues*. We can agree with N.K. Smith that these modifications were dictated by the conformist tendency of Hume that grew out of the atmosphere of his time and place. But the modifications in question do not express Hume's true convictions at the final stage of his intellectual development, when he was more inclined toward an atheistic view.[61] His conformist inclination, however, led him to retain the words "God" and "Religion" in his *Dialogues*.[62]

We can equally admit that Hume, at the time of the first writing of the *Dialogues* around 1751, doubted the existence of God rather than denied it.[63] These doubts find their expression in the modifications of which we spoke above. They are in close agreement with the fact that in the *Dialogues* Hume sought to

---

57 *Dialogues,* Part XII, p. 228. Hendel, *op. cit.,* pp. 275, 357.
58 *Dialogues,* Part XII, pp. 202, 214-219, 287.
59 *Ibid.,* Part XII, p. 216.
60 *Ibid.,* pp. 25-44.
61 *Ibid.,* pp. 25, 37-38, 40-41, 44.
62 *Ibid.,* pp. 75, 40-41.
63 *Ibid.,* pp. 88, 92, 96.

show that the proofs for God's existence are not so convincing as was commonly believed in his time.[64] Smith thinks that at that time the *Dialogues* show that Hume's position must be qualified as non-atheistic. We will later see how Smith characterizes the final religious attitude of Hume.[65] Hendel, however, insists that Hume was represented by Cleanthes.[66] In spite of his arguments Hendel's opinion seems questionable mainly for the reasons mentioned above, that Philo's position agrees with other writings of Hume.[67]

9. Influences

In order to estimate with greater precision the internal force of the arguments presented by the *Dialogues* and the coherence of the conclusions which are drawn from them, it is useful to keep in mind the main features of the religious evolution of Hume.

He was born into a Calvinist family of Edinburgh. His father died when David was three. The child received a strictly Calvinist religious education.[68] According to N.K. Smith, his orientation began to change at the age of sixteen when he finished his university studies and began his personal works.[69] Hume himself wrote to James Bonweld that he did not believe in any religion at the time he began to read John Locke and Samuel Clarke.[70] The theistic arguments of Samuel Clarke appeared too naive to Hume, especially since he was probably already convinced of the importance of the experimental method in philosophy. This idea could have been imprinted on his mind by the Newtonian teacher whose courses he took at the university.[71] In addition, Hume was attacked by serious and persistent doubts in matters of religion[72]

64 *Ibid.*, pp. 37-38.
65 Below, #10.
66 Hendel, *op. cit.*, pp. 267, 309; see above, #5, below, #10.
67 Hendel, *op. cit.*, pp. 367 ff., also above, #2, 10.
68 *Dialogues*, pp. 4-5.
69 *Ibid.*, p. 7.
70 Leroy, *op. cit.*, p. 5; see above, #4.
71 *Letters*, ed. by Creig, I. p. 154; see *Dialogues*, p. 71.
72 *Ibid.*, pp. 37-38, and Leroy, *op. cit.*, pp. 10-11.

so that he became unbeliever, or close to it. The skeptical attitude which he reached regarding God and religion is clearly evident in the letter of his friend Adam Smith, where Smith presents the state of Hume's mind during his last days. According to Smith, Hume showed at that time a total absence of belief in God and in the future life. He had been moved more than before toward disbelief by his last stay in Paris, which took place from 1763 to 1766.[73] There he met D'Alembert, Diderot, Helvetius and Holbach, whose atheistic attitudes could not have failed to seriously influence Hume.

These influences are perceptible in the *Dialogues*. When Hume began to compose them (about 1751), he presented them with a noticeable atheism, but still filled with doubt and ambiguities. In subsequent corrections (the last one most probably in 1776), his inclination towards religious skepticism, or better towards agnosticism, becomes more evident, and even quite clear.[74]

10. Final Characterization of Hume's Position

In light of the explanations given above, how shall we characterize the position of Hume? Is his theory, finally, atheistic, theistic, or something else altogether? The historians who have studied this problem do not give the same answer.

James Collins calls Hume's theory on God "the minimum skepticism of empirical theism."[75] According to Copleston, Hume "reduced the religious hypothesis to such thin content that it is difficult to know what to call it." The substance of this remainder, continues Copleston, is so poor that it can be accepted by nondogmatic atheists, but its content is ambiguous.[76] Hendel considers Hume "no atheist, nor a complete skeptic," but rather a representative of a "philosophic skepticism," which is an attitude

---

73 *Dialogues*, p. 38.
74 See particularly the end of the *Dialogues*, Part XII, pp. 226-227, cf. pp. 37 ff. See also Leroy, *op. cit.*, p. 10.
75 Collins, *God in Modern Philosophy*, p. 114.
76 Copleston, *op. cit.*, Vol. V, p. 311.

adopted when the difficulties faced by reason appear insuperable.[77] N.K. Smith concedes equally that Humes is not an
atheist, but that he is also not a theist. He is therefore
non-atheistic; for the atheist expresses a more positive view of
reality than that which Hume maintained at the moment of the
last composition of the *Dialogues*. The final revisions of the
Dialogues (1776), as well as the private life of the author,
nevertheless show a more negative attitude concerning theism.
Concerning this final period, Smith says of Hume's "theism" that
it is no more than a recognition of the mysterious character of the
final causes of existence and "a refusal to admit as possible or
necessary any affirmation of a more positive nature."[78]

It seems, however, that the most proper conclusion would be to
qualify the position of Hume as religious skepticism, or still better
as agnosticism, a designation already suggested by Copleston[79]
and quite well justified by the conclusion of Philo, who says that
we need more light from above to dispel our ignorance.[80]

It is not necessary to add that the value of Hume's *Dialogues*
lies, in the end, in the force of conviction of their arguments. The
acceptability of the opinion of N.K. Smith concerning the
arguments also depends on this force. According to him, Hume
presented a definitive and complete critique of the proof of the
existence of God through order in the universe. It seems,
nevertheless, that both the argumentation of Hume and his
method of reasoning are highly debatable.

11. Value of Hume's Position

The significance of Hume's position concerning God, and
consequently the value of his *Dialogues,* lies not so much in his
own view, dictated by the historical circumstances in which he
advanced his ideas, or in the positions of any particular person of

---

77 Hendel, *op. cit.*, pp. 369-370, see also pp. 367, 376.
78 *Dialogues,* p. 38.
79 Copleston, *op. cit.,* Vol. V, p. 310.
80 *Dialogues,* Part XII, p. 227. See also above, #8.

the *Dialogues*, but rather in the arguments which are suggested. These suggested arguments decide the perennial importance of Hume's reasoning. In this light we should look now at his arguments and their value.

We can touch here only on some of the most important reasonings. They concern Hume's treatment of religions, particularly their fruits, their origin and the justification of suffering; the reason for his rejection of the *a priori* and *a posteriori* proofs for God's existence; his insistence on experience; the indefinite number of causes to each effect; the possibility of a spontanous generation of the world and the world's eternity. Of special interest is the value of his argumentation against infinity of God based on suffering. We should also mention the degree of acceptability of some specific tenets which may be brought out in support of Hume's position, such as the nature of universals, causality, permanency of ego and man's freedom.

(a) Religions

We should agree with Hume that the idea of God has been supported and spread by religions. For this reason Hume rightly asks these questions: Why do religions exist? Have they any rational ground? In supporting his negative answer, Hume connects the origin of religions with fear, hope, distress, superstition and imagination.[81] He also finds the justification of this position in the arguments which he advances against the proofs for God's existence.

Before we examine the value of those arguments, we would like to mention that the persistance of religions among all sorts of people, highly educated and uneducated, may suggest a different cause from that indicated by Hume, namely a sort of rational, intuitive and reflective grasping of God's existence. This grasping was correctly described by Charles S. Peirce (1839-1914) as

---

81 *Dialogues*, Parts I, XI-XII; *Natural History of Religion*, pp. 11-14. For different opinions from Hume on this matter, see above Introduction, note.

rational instinct.[82] Henri Bergson (1859-1941) sees it in mysticism, particularly Christian mysticism.[83] These writers, among many others,[84] are of the opinion that religions have their origin in reason, and not necessarily in sensuous perception alone as Hume suggests. Consequently, Hume's account of the origin of religions and their basis, i.e. our knowledge of God's existence remains controversial, to say the least.

In Hume's study of religions we also find other points of disagreement and of oversimplification. He did not see much good coming from religions.[85] He elaborated at length their un-reasonable results; we do not learn much, however, as H.E. Root correctly observed, about the charity, kindness, trust and dedication caused by religious beliefs.[86] Moreover, Hume seems to reduce all the religious facts to the same pattern; such a homogeneity obviously becomes suspicious.[87] We can also ask the question whether religions, Christianity included, explain suffering and evil without rational satisfaction. Hume's negative attitude in this matter seems far from being justified, especially since he did not discuss in detail reasons offered by religions. These obvious oversimplifications are all the more disappointing, since Hume was also a historian. Thus, we may doubt that Hume proved that religions are not supported by man's reason. This may be clearer when we examine Hume's argumentation against proofs of God's existence.

We also may find a rational support of religions in man's need of such a belief. For man finds the meaning of life and its goal in

82 Peirce, "A Neglected Argument," *Values in the Universe of Chance,* pp. 264 ff. "The Concept of God," in the *Philosophical Writings of Peirce,* ed. by Justus Buchler (New York: Dover Publications, 1955), pp. 365-368. See also "The criterion of Validity in Reasoning," *ibid.,* pp. 12-128; "Religion," in *Collected Papers of Charles Sanders Peirce,* ed. by Charles Hartshorne and Paul Weiss, 8 vols. (Cambridge, Massachussetts: Harvard University Press, 1931-1960), II, pp. 281 ff.

83 Bergson, *The Two Sources of Morality and Religion,* tr. by R. Ashley Audra and Claudesley Brereton (New York: Doubleday, 1956), especially pp. 241 ff.

84 See below, Chapter XXV.

85 Hume, *History of Natural Religion,* p. 17; see also pp. 13-14.

86 *Ibid.,* p. 17.

87 *Ibid.*

God's existence; without such a goal life with all its difficulties seems to lead to complete frustration, despair and in the last result to the extermination of mankind. For man would ask himself what is the purpose of continuing such a worthless life? Would it not be better to end it for one-self and for everyone else also? Who would be hurt if this existence is terminated? No one; just the opposite, it would be beneficial for everybody since suffering would be completely eliminated once and for all. Yet man spontaneously resents such an extermination; he intuitively feels that it is against human nature. Hume, however, does not seem to grasp this logical consequences in spite of his quite detailed and penetrating description of disorder, suffering and evil in the world. He rather tends to see the absence of reason in those disorderly events. Neither does he comprehend the reason for mankind's resentment toward extermination. It seems nonetheless, that this resentment could be dictated by man's rational intuitive knowledge of the goal of his existence and that this is related to his intuitive knowledge of some superior Being and a future life. Hume, however, also rejects a future life on the basis of the lack of sensory evidence.[88] This kind of evidence is for Hume the only criterion of truth. Such a criterion, however, remains highly debatable, as we shall see below.[89]

(b) "A priori" Proofs

Although we may agree with Hume that we cannot prove the existence of any object, God included, by *a priori* reasoning alone, we may question whether or not *a priori* proofs for God's existence are completely deprived of any value, or whether they are deprived even of an experimental basis.

It seems that they have some experiential support at their starting point, but not necessarily in their further development and final conclusion. Moreover, the force of those arguments

88 See above, note 26.
89 See below, b.

seems to be quite stringent, and dismissing it requires argumentation stronger than just Hume's insistence on the need of experience.

Thus, we touch upon Hume's more basic argumentation, namely that all the proofs must be based on experience from their inception to their result. This contention does not seem to be certain even in scientific procedure, for even hypotheses and theories leading to successful results are not based on experience alone. "Two Dogmas of Empiricism," an essay of W.V.O. Quine, quite clearly presents evidence to this effect: need of such a criterion is not empirically proved, neither is it always applicable.[90] Moreover, the persistence of *a priori* proofs, particularly the formulations of Leibniz based on the notion of the possibility of necessary Being,[91] requires that their existence must be contended with; Kant's posulates of practical reason, Whitehead's need for a divine primordial nature,[92] and Hartshorne's insistance on creative actuality[93] require much deeper reasoning then Hume advances and suggests in order to dismiss all of them.

(c) "A posteriori" Proofs

As to the *a posteriori* proofs concerning God's existence we must agree with Hume in a number of instances. One of them is that each effect has indeed an indefinite number of causes; thus, an analysis of all the causes of a given effect presents an insurmountable task for the human mind. However, since every effect

90 W.V.O. Quine, "Two Dogmas of Empiricism," in *Classics of Analytic Philosophy,* ed. by R.R. Ammerman (New York: McGraw-Hill, 1965), pp. 196-213. See also A. J. Ayer, *Logical Positivism* (Glencoe, Illinois: The Free Press, 1959) particular pp. 108-126. A.G. Ewing, "Meaningfulness," in P. Edwards and A. Pap (ed.), *A Modern Introduction to Philosophy* (Glencoe, Illinois: The Free Press, 1957), pp. 577, 604, 609.

91 G.W. Liebniz, *New Essays Concerning Human Understanding,* tr. by A.G. Langley (Lasalle, Illinois: Open Court, 1949), pp. 503-505. See also Copleston, *op. cit.* Vol. IV, P. 3211.

92 See below, Chapter XXV, 1.

93 Charles Hartshorne, *The Logic of Perfection* (Lasalle, Illinois: Open Court, 1962), pp. 28-117, particularly pp. 116-117; see below, Chapter XXV, 2.

has the same essential feature, namely *dependency*, all of them ultimately require an independent cause. Dependent causes do not become independent either by their indeterminable (or infinite) number or by the fact that the whole results in something different from its parts. For dependency is an essential feature of each part, and thus of the whole; whereas other features of each part differ from each other; consequently they must produce a whole different from the individual parts.

Hume supports his position by suggesting that the world could emerge from other worlds or beings according to the pattern of vegetation and generation of living beings. In this supposition, however, Hume seems to overlook the basic problem, namely, from where is the ultimate element? Moreover, if we have to be based on experience, as Hume contends, we can only imagine or purely suppose, without any proof, such a non-living being, or nothing, out of which other beings emerge. Hume resorts to the world-soul in further supporting his position. Such a soul raises the same question, however, as the existence of any other being: where is it from? If eternal, its eternity should be proved.

Beyond that, Hume points out the possibility of an eternal world;[94] thus, the first cause of the world becomes a needless postulate. It does not seem, however, that the eternal world excludes the cause of its existence. We can refer to Aquinas' position defending such a need[95] and to the discussion that has arisen on this subject, particularly in the Middle Ages.[96]

(d) Suffering

Hume insists forcibly and reasonably on the existence of evil and suffering in the world. From these facts he draws the

---

94 *Dialogues,* Parts, VII-VIII.

95 S. Thomas Aquinas, "De aeternitate mundi contra murmurantes," in P. Mandonnet's *S. Thomae Aquinatis Opuscula Omnia* (Paris, 1927), IV. See also *De Potentia,* q. 3, a. 13-17; *Contra Gentiles,* II, 31-38; *Summa Theologiae,* I, 2. 46, a.1.

96 M. Gierens (ed.), *Controversia de aeternitate mundi.* Rome: Pontifica Universitas Gregoriana, 1933.

conclusion that if God exists He must be a finite God. This conclusion, however, raises questions. If God creates man and creates him as a free being, then He must live up to His decision and respect man's freedom. Consequently, it is up to man to choose his destiny. In such a choice man must be exposed to some sort of suffering even if it is only in obedience to God's will. If this choice is removed, freedom is removed and suffering with it. As a result, the world would consist of inanimate and irrational creatures alone, since these creatures would be deprived of their freedom.

Hume further supports his position by insisting that animals suffer. The suffering of animals, however, has a different character than that of man, due to animals' limited foreknowledge and consequently limited worry about the future. In addition, animals are subordinated to man and serve him, so they become a reminder to man, even in their sufferings, of the need of right choice since the consequences of choice may result in suffering. This factor seems to be quite important and even indispensable for an understanding of suffering and its role in the world.

Hume's reasoning prompts further questions, namely could God eliminate suffering? It seems that He could not if He wanted to create a free being, and if we understand by suffering a choice with its consequences. If we understand by suffering a physical, senuous pain, its removal would lead to a creation of spirit only. In this respect God can be considered finite; but his finitude is the result of His own decision to produce free creatures whose freedom He must honor, and not, as Hume suggests, from the genuinely limited power of God.

We may add, since Hume treats the reasonableness of religions, that the Bible speaks of the creation of man without physical pain as a special gift of God to man. Physical pain was introduced by man's disobedience to God. However, obedience is a sort of suffering, although of different kind than physical pain, as mentioned. Hence, God can eliminate physical pain if he wants to, but, once He decided to create a free, rational being, He could not eliminate suffering resulting from the use of man's free will.

Thus, religions provide some support to human reasoning and

they are not completely deprived of a rational foundation, contrary to what Hume tries to suggest. Moreover, religions quite often advance solutions to man's problems which cannot be solved by reason alone. The cause of that limitation of reason lies in the fact that God is much superior in intelligence to man; He is infinite, whereas man is finite. Hence, man's questioning of God and of our relation to Him cannot be answered by limited human reasoning only, unsupported by divine intervention. The fact of this intervention and its reasonableness as presented by some religions seems to have rational support, contrary to Hume's contention. Hume, however, did not discuss in detail the answers which religions, mainly Christianity, offer to problems concerning God and the reasons for man's suffering; his discussions are quite fragmentary and consequently create doubts as to their validity.

(e) Specific Tenets

We should add that Hume's philosophical reasoning concerning the problems brought out in the *Dialogues* is marked by his specific tenets which are themselves not without serious questions. These questions mainly relate to the nature of our universal concepts, particularly the concepts of causality and causation, the permanency of our empirical ego, and the problem of freedom—to mention only a few. They require separate treatment; here we may treat them only briefly.

In regard to universals, we may mention that although our universal concepts are accompanied by imaginative pictures, as Hume correctly argues, we distinguish their imaginative character from their meaning and concept; we are well aware that the meaning of prudence is distinct from any picture of prudence which we may bear in our mind.[97]

We equally distinguish succession from causation. We also are aware that the association of ideas is caused by a "certain gentle

---

97 Hume, *Treatise*, pp. 18 ff.

force" as Hume says;[98] and that this force is not reducible to repetition of events, but causes the connection of ideas. Hume, when stressing gentle force, does not seem to grasp its meaning and role in relation to causation and to the principle of causality. As a matter of fact he tries to reduce causation to repetition and association and thus to disprove the validity of the principle of causality. Still, he stresses that there is a *mysterious force.* Is not this mysterious force causation? Furthermore, can it be substituted by repetition as Hume tries to do? Thus, Hume's explanation of causation in terms of repetition becomes highly questionable. This reminds us of his application of the criterion of experience to the validity of our knowledge concerning the permanency of our *ego.*

This permanence of our ego is our deepest *reflective* conviction, based on our internal and external experiences. It is not just the persuasion of popular common sense as Hume contends. If we deny this conviction resulting from reflection on our perceptions and our actions, we deny the essence of Hume's principle of his own phenomenological method, namely the need to be based on experience in our conclusions; and thus we deny the correctness of his reasoning. We might reconcile his position only by contending that Hume's denial of the permanency of ego is based on unilateral experience which does not include our deepest, *reflective* conviction. But in such a case our reasoning becomes deprived of any basis, i.e. not only of popular common sense but of philosophical reflective conviction as well.

Finally, we may add that Hume is right in his denial of absolute freedom of man and in his insistence that man's actions are always prompted by the satisfaction of ego. However, Hume's restriction of man's motives to pain and pleasure alone seems to be a misinterpretation of our deepest and most reflective convictions and experiences, since man is also acting in contrast to his sensuous satisfaction when he acts to fulfill his duty, charity, etc. Thus, Hume's conclusions seem to be against his own criterion of

---

98 *Ibid.,* p. 10.

truth residing in experience, since his interpretation of experience has not taken into account all its aspects.

Conclusion

Thus, the *Dialogues* and Hume's reasoning in general concerning God's existence are very deep indeed and contribute greatly to the discussions of the problems directly or indirectly involved. Still, they are far from being the last word concerning even the traditional proofs for God's existence, as shown, we hope, from this essay. We attempted to draw attention in this essay at least to some reasonings of Hume and their weaknesses without entering into much detail due to the limits and purpose of this study.

A SELECT BIBLIOGRAPHY

1. Bibliographies

Jessop, T.E., *A Bibliography of David Hume and of Scottish Philosophy from Francis Hutcheson to Lord Balfour,* London: A Brown and Sons, 1938.

Metz, Rudolf, "Bibliographie der Hume–Literatur," *Literarische Berichte aus dem Gebiete der Philosophie* (Erfurt), Hft. 15-16 (1928), pp. 39-50.

J.L., "Notes bibliographiques," *Revue Internationale de Philosophie* (Bruxelles), Vol. VI (1952), pp. 250-253.

Matczak, Sebastian A., "A Select Classified Bibliography of David Hume," *The Modern Schoolman* (St. Louis University), 1964, pp. 70-81.

————, *Philosophy: Its Nature, Methods and Basic Sources.* Louvain: Nauwelaerts, 1975.

2. Works of David Hume

(a) Monographs

A Treatise of Human Nature. Ed. by A. Selby-Bigge. Oxford: The Clarendon Press, 1958. First edition of the Vols. I-II, London, J. Noon, 1739; Vol. III, London, Thomas Longman, 1740.

A Treatise on Human Nature and An Inquiry concerning Human Understanding. Together with 2 biographical documents edited with an introduction by Antony Flew. New York: Collier Books, 1962.

Enquiries concerning the Human Understanding and concerning the Principles of Morals. Ed. by A. Selby-Bigge, 2nd edition. Oxford: The Clarendon Press, 1957.

An Enquiry concerning Human Understanding. First published as *Philosophical Essays concerning Human Understanding.* London: A. Millar, 1748. Later editions contain essays on miracles, providence and the immortality of the soul.

Essays, Moral and Political. Edinburgh: R. Fleming, 1741; 2nd edition, Edinburgh, A. Kincaid, 1742; 3rd edition, Ibid., 1748.

An Enquiry concerning the Principles of Morals. Ed. by Charles V. Hendel, New York: Bobbs-Merrill, 1955.

Two Essays on Suicide and the Immortality of the Soul. London, 1777.

The Life of David Hume, Esq., Written by Himself. London: W. Strahan, 1777. Reprinted in Smith's edition of the *Dialogues,* 1948. See below.

Hume's Dialogues Concerning Natural Religion, ed. by Norman Kemp Smith. Oxford: The Clarendon Press, 1935. First published by nephew of Hume (London: Robinson), 1779. 2nd edition in London; Thomas Hughes, 1779. Recently published by Morris Philipson in *Foundations of Western Thought: Six Major Philosophers* (New York: Alfred A. Knopf, 1962), pp. 629-704.

"Two Unpublished Essays on Mathematics in the Hume Papers," edited by Lionel Grossman in *Journal of the History of Ideas* (New York), Vol. XXI (1960), pp. 442-449.

Abstract of a Treatise. London: S. Borbet, 1940.

Essays, Moral, Political and Literary, with an essay of T.H. Green et T.H. Grose. London: Longmans Green and Co., 1875. First published in 1752.

Political Discourses. Edinburgh: R. Fleming, 1752.

Writings on Economics. Ed. by Eugene Rotwein. Edinburgh: Nelson, 1955.

Four Dissertations: I, The Natural History of Religion; II, Of the Passions; III, Of Tragedy; IV, of the Standard of Taste. London: A. Millar, 1757.

The Natural History of Religion. Ed. by H.E. Root, Stanford, California: Stanford University Press, 1957. First published in 1757; see *Four Dissertations.*

The History of England from the Invasion of Julius Caesar to the Revolution of 1688, 6 vols. London: A. Millar, 1759-1762.

Letters of David Hume. Ed. by J.Y.T. Greig. 2 vols. Oxford: The Clarendon Press, 1932.

Letters of Eminent Persons, Addressed to David Hume. Ed. by John H. Burton. Edinburgh: W. Blackwood and Sons, 1849.

Letters of Hume and Extracts from Letters referring to Him. Ed. by T. Murray. Edinburgh: A. and C. Black, 1841.

New Letters of David Hume. Ed. by Raymond Klibansky and Ernest L. Mossner. Oxford: The Clarendon Press, 1954.

"Some Unpublished Letters of David Hume," *Nineteenth Century and After* (New York), Vol. XCVIII (1925), pp. 293-306.

(b) Collective Editions

The Philosophical Works of David Hume. 4 vols. Edinburgh: Adam Black and William Tait, 1826.

The Philosophical Works of David Hume. 4 vols. Boston, Massachusetts: Little, Brown and Company, 1854.

The Philosophical Works of David Hume. Edited by T.H. Green and T.H. Grose. 4 vols. London: Longmans, Green and Company, 1898.

Hume Selections. Ed. by Charles W. Hendel. New York: Scribner, 1971.

3. Studies

(a) On Hume

See Bibliographies, above I.

Anderson, Robert F., *Hume's First Principles.* Lincoln, Nebraska: University of Nebraska Press, 1966.

Farbes, D., *Hume's Philosophical Politics.* Cambridge, Massachusetts: Cambridge University Press, 1975.

Flew, Antony G., *Philosophy of Belief.* New York: Humanities Press, 1961.

Hendel, Charles W., *Studies in the Philosophy of David Hume.* New York: Bobbs-Merrill, 1963. First published in 1925.

Laird, John, *Hume's Philosophy of Human Nature.* Hamden, Connecticut: Shoe String Press, 1967. Reprint of 1932 edition.

Leroy, A.L., *David Hume.* Paris: Presses Universitaires de France, 1953.

Maud, Constance, *Hume's Theory of Knowledge: A Critical Examination.* New York: Russell, 1972. Reprint of 1937 edition.

Smith, Norman Kemp *et al.* (eds.), *The Credibility of Divine Existence.* New York: St. Martin's Press, 1967. Pp. 456.

Todd, William B. (ed.) *Hume and the Enlightenment: Essays Presented to Ernest Campbell Mossner.* Austin, Texas: University of Texas Press, 1975.

Whitehead, Alfred N., *Adventures of Ideas.* New York: Macmillan Co., 1933.

———, *Process and Reality.* New York: Macmillan Co., 1929.

Zabeeh, Farhang, *Hume Precursor of Modern Empiricism.* Revised edition. Paramus, New Jersey: Humanities Press, 1973.

(b) Related Studies

Cousins, Ewert H. (ed.), *Process Theology*. Paramus, New Jersey: Paulist Press, 1971.

De Lubac, Henri, S.J., *Le Drame de L'humanisme athée*. 6th ed. Paris, France: Editions Spes, 1959.

Dhanamony, Mariasusai, S.J. *et al., Phenomenology of Religion*. Chicago, Illinois: Loyola University Press, 1972.

_____, *Revelation in Christianity and Other Religions*. Rome, Italy: Gregorian University Press, 1971.

Ducasse, C.J., *A Critical Examination of the Belief in a Life After Death*. Springfield, Illinois: Charles C. Thomas, 1961.

Eister, Allan W., *Changing Perspectives in the Scientific Study of Religion*. New York: Wiley-Interscience, 1974.

Fabro, Cornelio, *God in Exile: Modern Atheism*. Translated by Arthur Gibson. Paramus, New Jersey: Paulist-Newman, 1968.

Hick, John, *Evil and the God of Love*. New York: Harper and Row, 1966.

Johnson, A. William, *The Search for Transcendence: A Theological Analysis of Nontheological Attempts to Define Transcendence*. New York: Harper & Row, 1974.

Miceli, Vincent P., S.J., *The God of Atheism*. New Rochelle, New York: Arlington House, 1972.

Mitros, Joseph F., *Religions: A Select, Classified Bibliography*. Louvain: Nauwelaerts, 1973.

Plantinga, Alvin, *God, Freedom and Evil*. New York: Harper & Row, 1974.

Staudinger, Joseph, S.J., *L'home moderne devant le problème de l'au-delá*. Translated by Rene Guillaume. Paris: Casterman, 1950.

Whitson, Robley E., *The Coming Convergence of World Religions*. Paramus, New Jersey: Paulist Press, 1971.

CHAPTER XXII

ON THE WHITEHEADIAN GOD

R.M. Martin *

It should not be forgotten that Whitehead (1861-1947) was a professional mathematician for most of his academic life and that he spent ten years or so collaborating with Bertrand Russell on *Principia Mathematica.* Logico-mathematical methods and procedures must have become thoroughly ingrained as habits of thought by the time he wrote the later metaphysical works. The suggestion that Whitehead may have forgotten these methods or no longer trusted them must surely be in error. For him, it would seem, to think at all was to think mathematically. Even in *Process and Reality*[1] it is interesting to discern mathematical or quasi-mathematical notions, definitions, and statements creeping in almost unawares on every page. The great categoreal scheme of this book, in fact, it will be contended, may be viewed as a kind of logico-mathematical system in disguise. In a previous paper a few first, tentative steps towards substantiating such a claim were put forward.[2]

It might be objected that Whitehead himself, in the opening chapter, writes (p. 12) that "philosophy has been misled by the example of mathematics; and even in mathematics the statement of the ultimate logical principles is beset with difficulties, as yet insuperable." Also, (pp. 11-12) "philosophy has been haunted by the unfortunate notion that its method is dogmatically to indicate

*Professor of Philosophy, Northwestern University, Evanston, Illinois, U.S.A. The material of this paper is adapted from the author's *Whitehead's Categoreal Scheme and Other Papers* (The Hague: Martinus Nijhoff, 1974), and is used here with the kind permission of the publisher.

1   New York: The Macmillan Co., 1929.
2   "An Approximative Logical Structure for Whitehead's Categoreal Scheme," in *Whitehead's Categoreal Scheme Etc.*

premises which are severally clear, distinct, and certain; and to erect upon those premises a deductive system of thought." On the other hand, Whitehead also emphasizes that the categoreal scheme must be "coherent" and "logical," and that (p. 5) "the term 'logical' has its ordinary meaning, including 'logical' consistency, or lack of contradiction, the definition of constructs in logical terms, the exemplification of general logical notions in specific instances, and the principles of inference." Also (p. 13) "the use of the categoreal scheme . . . is to argue from it boldly and with rigid logic. The scheme should therefore be stated with the utmost precision and definiteness, to allow of such argumentation." "Speculative boldness (p. 25) must be balanced by complete humility before logic, and before fact."

There is no conflict between these two types of statements if it is recognized (p. 12) that "the accurate expression of the final generalities is the goal of discussion and not its origin" and that "metaphysical categories . . . are tentative formulations of the ultimate generalities." Thus even tentative statements are to be expressed "with the utmost precision and definiteness" and with "complete humility before logic." If "the logician's alternative, true or false" is applied to the scheme of philosophic categories regarded "as one complex assertion . . . the answer must be that the scheme is false. The same answer must be given to a like question respecting the existing formulated principles of any science." The categoreal scheme is put forward rather in a provisory way and to be improved upon by further reflection, better formulation, discovery of further facts, scientific laws, and so on. Thus it is not "dogmatically" contended that the items of the categoreal scheme are "severally clear, distinct, and certain." Such a contention would indeed be unfortunate, and has been abandoned for the most part even in mathematics. Not only the "difficulties, as yet insuperable" that infect *Principia Mathematica* (as Whitehead noted, p. 12, footnote 3), but also the presence now of various kinds of set-theoretic alternatives, Gödel's incompleteness theorem, the Löwenheim-Skolem theorem, various intuitionistic and constructivistic systems—all of these militate against any dogmatically certain rendition of the fundamental notions of mathematics. Whitehead's strictures against mathematics, written before 1929, are based upon an inadequate conception of its foundations and are no longer applicable.

Some readers may question the importance of exhibiting the logical format of a metaphysical or cosmological theory in such detail. Some readers may question whether such a format can be given at all. They are convinced in advance that something fundamental will be left out that can never be accommodated in a logical system. They say in effect: *Mathematica sunt, non leguntur.* On the other hand, there are philosophers and logicians whose attitude is rather: *Metaphysica sunt, non leguntur* (Frege, it will be recalled, berated both attitudes). What is needed is an exact account of how the two are interrelated. "The solution I am asking for," Whitehead commented of another context, "is not a phrase, however brilliant, but a solid branch of science, constructed with slow patience, showing in detail how the correspondence is effected."

The logistical account of Whitehead's categoreal scheme and of his theory of God, to be given, is thought to be of interest on several grounds. In the first place, Whitehead himself would have welcomed it. On one occasion, in fact, in conversation with the present author, he commented to this effect, adding that he would have attempted such an account himself had he had the time, but that it was essential to make the intuitive sketch first in the few remaining years allotted him for philosophical writing.

Secondly, many readers are puzzled as to the exact character of the categoreal scheme. What are "categories" for Whitehead anyhow? Which statements are supposed to be definitions? Which are supposed to lay down fundamental principles axiomatically? Which are supposed to be logical consequences of which? Which are in effect semantical rules or mere informal explanations? What is the logical structure of the language Whitehead uses? What are its primitives? How are the eternal objects related to sets? What precisely are prehensions? How are they related to relations? What precisely is a concrescence? How are they related to actual occasions? And so on. Whitehead's manner of writing invites these questions and sensitive readers ask them. However, one must work very hard indeed to get even inadequate answers. In fact they cannot be answered, it would seem, except on the basis of the detailed exhibition of a full logical format.

Especially important here is the treatment of prehensions. It has usually been supposed that prehensions are a kind of event, but no one seems to have explored how they may be handled on the basis of an exact logic.

Another merit of the logical reconstruction to be given it would seem, is that it makes Whitehead easier to understand. Whitehead's opaque style is a stumbling block to many and is often difficult if not impossible to follow. Logical systems, on the other hand, are easy to "read," provided of course one is familiar with modern logic and the methods of system building and logical analysis.

It is often lamented that Whitehead's system is so general as to lack content or relevance for specific philosophical problems. Whitehead's thought is thus sometimes regarded as a *cul-de-sac* and without interest for contemporary analytic philosophy. To be sure, most of Whitehead's statements are couched in terms of universal quantifiers and only a few of them contain specific constants. As soon as a constant is introduced, however, there remains the task of characterizing it explicitly. To do so is not the function of metaphysics, it might be thought, but of the specific discipline to which the term belongs. Consider, for example, 'Val' for valuations, 'Dcsn' for decisions, or the like. To help characterize the latter, the theory of decision would be useful. To help characterize 'Val,' much analytic philosophy concerned with 'valuable,' 'good,' and so on, is needed. Whitehead does not seek to provide specific analyses of these constants—that is the task of more special disciplines. He seeks only to characterize notions of vast generality, which can then be exemplified in specific instances. In the light of this, Whitehead's work is seen to be of direct interest for contemporary analytic philosophy, in particular, if we replace his quantifiers and variables by suitable constants and then seek to determine their behavior.

* * *

It is significant that Whitehead makes no explicit reference to God in the preliminary delineation (pp. 27-45) of the categoreal scheme in *Process and Reality*. This is no accident, for Whitehead's God emerges only as a construct in terms of the metaphysically basic entities, namely, actual occasions, eternal objects, and prehensions, prehensions in turn being themselves a kind of actual occasion. Immediately, however, amends are made in the following chapter, "Some Derivative Notions." We are straightaway told that the "primordial created fact is the unconditional conceptual valuation of the entire multiplicity of eternal objects. This is the 'primordial nature' of God . . . God is the primordial creature; but the description of his nature is not exhausted by this conceptual side of it. His 'consequent nature' results from his physical prehensions of the derivative actual entities . . . "

In the previous paper, Whitehead's categoreal scheme was discussed in the light of the author's event logic. It was shown there how, at least approximatively, that logic seems to provide the necessary structural underpinning. The notion of God, however, the most important of the "derivative" notions, was left out. It will be of interest in the present paper, which is self-contained, to see how this notion in its full complexity may be accommodated within that approximative logical reconstruction.

That the notion of God is handled as derivative does not mean of course that it is in any way less fundamental or less important than the non-derivative ones. For Whitehead, "God (p. 521) is not to be treated as an exception to all metaphysical principles, invoked to save their collapse," as in some of the great historical systems. "He is," rather, "their chief exemplification." The entire system, in fact, may be viewed as providing "a certain rendering of the facts" concerning God's nature. "There is nothing . . . in the nature of proof" in the sense of any of the traditional proofs for God's existence, and the system is supposed to stand or fall pretty much as a whole. In adding another speaker to Hume's *Dialogues Concerning Natural Religion,* as he says he does (p. 521), Whitehead is inviting us to dwell "upon the tender elements of the world, which slowly and in quietness operate by love." He wishes to elucidate "somewhat exceptional elements in our conscious experience—those elements which may roughly be classed together as religious and moral intuitions." The extraordinary appeal of Whitehead's approach is that it seeks to accommodate these exceptional elements in the same categoreal framework that it seeks to accommodate logic, mathematics, and empirical science, and not just superficially in a telling phrase or two, but with a reasonably full and careful delineation of basic notions, definitions, fundamental principles, and so on.

Here as in the previous paper, there is no question of merely keeping to the letter of what Whitehead has written. It is the spirit that guides us, even if the result should seem somewhat remote from the text. Thus it is perhaps not literally Whitehead's view that is discussed here, but merely an approximation to it.

*   *   *

In the previous paper, it will be recalled, an expression for the relation of *prehending,* 'Prhd,' was taken as primitive, so that

$$\text{'}\underline{e}_1 \text{ Prhd } \underline{e}_2\text{'}$$

expresses that actual occasion $\underline{e}_1$ *physically* prehends actual occasion $\underline{e}_2$, and

$$\text{'}\underline{e} \text{ Prhd } \propto,\underline{e}_1\text{'},$$
$$\text{'}\underline{e} \text{ Prhd } \propto, \underline{e}_1, \underline{e}_2\text{'},$$

and so on, respectively express that actual occasion [AO] *conceptually* prehends the monadic eternal object [EO^1] $\propto$ with respect to the AO $\underline{e}_1$, that AO $\underline{e}$ conceptually prehends the dyadic eternal object [EO^2] $\propto$ with respect to AO's $\underline{e}_1$ and $\underline{e}_2$, and so on.

In event logic, the so-called *event-descriptive predicates* are introduced as applicable to events, enabling us to describe events of such and such a kind.[3] Thus, where 'j' is short for 'John,' 'K' for 'kisses' and 'm' for 'Mary,' the predicate

'$<j,K,m>$'

concatenated with an event variable '$\underline{e}$' gives us a sentential function

'$<j,K,m>\underline{e}$',

expressing that $\underline{e}$ is an event of John's kissing Mary, one of perhaps many such events. Thus here

'$<\underline{e}_1,\text{Prhd},\underline{e}_2>\underline{e}$'

enables us to express that $\underline{e}$ is a (or the) *prehension* of the "datum" $\underline{e}_2$ by the "subject" $\underline{e}_1$.

Because for Whitehead actual entities prehend different data to different degrees of "intensity," a numerical measure may be introduced, so that forms such as

'$\underline{e}_1 \text{ Prhd}^{\underline{i}} \underline{e}_2$'
'$\underline{e}_1 \text{ Prhd}^{\underline{i}} \propto, \underline{e}_2$'

and so on, for $0 \leqslant \underline{i} \leqslant 1$, are in practice more useful than the non-numerical ones.

The "subjective forms" of prehensions may be handled as certain classes of prehensions. Thus, Val may be the class of *valuations,* Purps$_e$ the class of $\underline{e}$'s *purposes,* Desn$_e$ the class of $\underline{e}$'s free *decisional acts,* and so on. To say

'$\underline{e} \; \epsilon \; \text{Val}$'

---

3 See the author's *Belief, Existence and Meaning* (New York: New York University Press, 1969), Chapter IX; *Logic, Language, and Metaphysics* (New York: New York University Press, 1971), Chapters VII and VIII.

is thus to say that $\underline{e}$ is a valuation, and so on.

The calculus of individuals is presupposed with a part-whole and allied relations available therein. Thus given any two AO's $\underline{e}_1$ and $\underline{e}_2$, their "sum" ($\underline{e}_1$ U $\underline{e}_2$) is also an entity. Where $\underline{e}_1$ and $\underline{e}_2$ are both prehensions with the same "subject" the sum ($\underline{e}_1$ U $\underline{e}_2$) is an "intergrated" prehension. It is also the *fusion* of the class $\{\underline{e}_1, \underline{e}_2\}$, i.e., the class whose only members are $\underline{e}_1$ and $\underline{e}_2$. In general, if μ is a class of prehensions with a common "subject," Fu'μ is the "integrated" prehension consisting of them all.

Let 'α', 'β', and 'γ' be variables as above for eternal objects. Each eternal object has a fixed degree depending upon whether it is monadic, dyadic, and so on. Let '$\alpha \in EO^1$', '$\alpha \in EO^2$' and so on, express respectively that α is a *monadic* EO, a *dyadic* EO, and so on. Further, for specificity, let $\underline{k}$ be the degree of the eternal-object constant *of highest degree admitted as primitive*. Other eternal-object constants may be defined in terms of these, but some at least are presumably picked out as primitive.

Further items in the vocabulary needed are as follows. '$\underline{e}_1 = \underline{e}_2$' expresses that $\underline{e}_1$ and $\underline{e}_2$ are identical, and '$\underline{e}_1$ P $\underline{e}_2$' that $\underline{e}_1$ is a *part* of $\underline{e}_2$. The forms

'$\underline{e} \in$ CncptlPrhn' and '$\underline{e} \in$ PhysPrhn'

are defined to express respectively that $\underline{e}$ is a *conceptual* prehension, and that $\underline{e}$ is a *physical* prehension. Then

'$\underline{e} \in$ Prhn' abbreviates '($\underline{e} \in$ CncptlPrhn v $\underline{e} \in$ PhysPrhn)'.

'Cnsc' is to stand for the class of *conscious* AO's and 'SA$_{\underline{e}}$' for the class of $\underline{e}$'s *subjective aims*.

'α Ing $\underline{e}_1, ..., \underline{e}_n$'

expresses that the $\underline{n}$-adic eternal object α *ingresses* into the AO's $\underline{e}_1, ..., \underline{e}_n$ (in that order).

Perhaps 'Ing' is definable in terms of 'Prhd$^{\underline{i}}$' as follows.

'$\propto$ Ing $\underline{e}$' abbreviates '$\underline{e}$ Prhd^1 $\propto,\underline{e}$',

'$\propto$ Ing $\underline{e}_1,\underline{e}_2$' abbreviates '($\underline{e}_1$ Prhd^1 $\propto,\underline{e}_1,\underline{e}_2$ v $\underline{e}_2$ Prhd^1 $\propto,\underline{e}_1,\underline{e}_2$)',

and so on. AO $\underline{e}_1$ prehends AO $\underline{e}_2$ *positively if the degree is* >0; otherwise *negatively.* And similarly for conceptual prehensions. Further notational matters will be explained in the appropriate contexts.

* * *

Nothing was said of God in the preceding section, and nothing was said of him in the previous paper. However, definitions of separate expressions for the consequent nature and for the primordial nature were given in another previous paper devoted to Hartshorne's recent *Creative Synthesis and Philosophic Method.*[4] Let us suggest an improvement upon those definitions now as a basis for further discussion.

The consequent nature, cng, was introduced as the fusion of the class of all AO's, so that

'cng' abbreviates 'Fu'$\hat{\underline{e}}\underline{e} = \underline{e}$'.

The cng thus comprises, in its total cosmic fullness, all occasions, all sums of them [nexūs], all prehensions both physical and conceptual, and thus all valuations, adversions, aversions, hopes, fears, loves, hates, and so on.

The primordial nature, on the other hand, was regarded as the fusion of the class of the conceptual valuations of the cng with respect to all EO's relative of course to all AO's. Thus 'png' was taken to abbreviate 'Fu'$\hat{\underline{e}}$(E$\propto$)(E$\underline{e}_1$)...(E$\underline{e}_k$)((<cng,Prhd,$\propto,\underline{e}_1$> $\underline{e}$v...v<cng,Prhd,$\propto\underline{e}_1$,..., $\underline{e}_k$>$\underline{e}$) • $\underline{e}$ ϵ Val)'. The png is, according to this definition, the fusion of *all* of the cng's conceptual

---

4 "On Hartshorne's *Creative Synthesis and Philosophic Method,*" in *Whitehead's Categoreal Scheme Etc.*

prehensions that are valuations and with respect to all EO's.

This definition is not quite adequate, however, for it does not take into account the numerical degrees of the valuations. The valuation is complete of course, in the sense that every EO is valuated with respect to all AO's. "By reason of this complete valuation," Whitehead writes (p. 46), "the objectification of God in each derivate actual entity, results in a graduation of the relevance of eternal objects to the concrescent phases of that derivate occasion." The "graduation" here, it seems, can best be provided by a numerical measure. Thus, in place of the preceding definition, the following is suggested.

'$\underline{png}$' may abbreviate 'Fu'$\underline{\hat{e}}$ $(E\underline{i})(E\alpha)(E\underline{e}_1)...(E\underline{e}_k)$ $((<cng,Prhd^{\underline{i}},\alpha,\underline{e}_1> \underline{e}$ v ... v$<cng,Prhd^{\underline{i}},\alpha,\underline{e}_1,...,\underline{e}_k>\underline{e}) \cdot \underline{e} \, \epsilon \, Val \cdot 0 \leqslant \underline{i} \leqslant 1)$'.

Here each EO is valuated to just such and such a degree with respect to its "relevance" to each AO.

In the definientia of these two definitions of '$\underline{png}$', it should be noted, it is the $\underline{cng}$ as a whole whose valuations determine the "relevance" or order of all eternal objects. However, Whitehead nowhere stipulates this nor does he anywhere say just *whose* primordial valuations constitute the primordial nature. This seems an important omission. The valuations cannot be those of any AO, for all such valuations would be "conditioned" by the world antecedent to that AO. There thus seems to be in Whitehead's cosmos nothing to perform the primordial valuations other than $\underline{cng}$ as a whole. These valuations would then seem to be "conditioned," however, for $\underline{cng}$ is merely the cosmos as a whole. The $\underline{cng}$'s conditioned valuations should be distinguished from his unconditioned ones. Also it might be thought that $\underline{cng}$'s valuations are given only *after* all creation, not *with* it, as Whitehead insists (p. 521). Their "relevance" could thus never be operative in actuality. A way out of these difficulties suggests itself as follows.

Consider again a form of a kind

'$<\underline{e}_1,Prhd,\underline{e}_2>\underline{e}$'.

Ordinarily where an instance of such a form holds, e is one of the prehensions constituting e_1's "real internal constitution," in which case e bears P to e_1. Ordinarily a prehension e must have a "subject" e_1 *distinct* from itself and distinct from its "object." or "datum" e_2. Clearly the subject e_1 must always be distinct from the datum e_2 and the prehension e must also always be distinct from the datum. The question arises, however, as to whether a prehension could ever be *its own subject*. In orther words, could

$$\text{'} \langle e_1, \text{Prhd}, e_2 \rangle e_1 \text{'},$$

ever hold? The e_1 here would be the merest "puff of experience." Such a puff itself would undergo only *minimal* concrescence, but it could be ingredient in other concrescences. Their concrescences would be minimal in the sense that the various "phases" would be degenerate. (A prehension that is its own subject is presumably the fusion of a unit class, i.e., of a class whose only member is itself, a phase in general being a suitable fusion.)

Similarly forms such as

$$\text{'} \langle e, \text{Prhd}, \alpha, e_1 \rangle e \text{'},$$

and so on, could be admitted, for conceptual prehensions that are their own subjects. And similarly with 'Prhd^1' in place of 'Prhd'. The admisssion of both physical and conceptual prehensions that are their own subjects seems not incompatible with Whitehead's actual text.

If such prehensions are admitted, then the png could be regarded as consisting of such only. It is then not cng's conceptual valuations that give the primordial nature, but only those valuations that have themselves as their own subjects. Thus,

'png' could now abbreviate 'Fu'$\hat{e}(Ei)(E\alpha)(Ee_1)...(Ee_k)((\langle e, \text{Prhd}^1, \alpha, e_1 \rangle \; e \; v \; ... \; v \langle e, \text{Prhd}^1, \alpha, e_1, ..., e_k \rangle e) \cdot e \; \epsilon \; \text{Val} \cdot 0 \leqslant i \leqslant 1)$'.

Prehensions that are their own subjects are genuinely "unconditioned" in the sense of undergoing only minimal or degenerate concrescence, in no way depending upon other prehensions or AO's. But they enter into other concrescences, of course, because the subjects of those concrescences prehend God's primordial valuations.

Perhaps this third definition of 'png' is the most satisfactory, and it will be presupposed in what follows.

It should be noted that, in view of the foregoing definitions, the png is a *part* of the cng, and hence of course God would be identified with the cng alone. It might be thought better to restrict the definition of 'cng' in such a way that this would not hold and so that cng and png would be mutually exclusive. This could be done by letting

'cng' abbreviate 'Fu'$\hat{\underline{e}}{\sim}(E\mu)(\underline{png} = Fu'\mu \bullet \underline{e} \in \mu)$',

where 'μ' is some class variable. The cng in this way contains none of png's valuations, although of course many of the valuations that it does contain may accord with them. This second definition also has the advantage of making the cng contain only "conditioned" prehensions, no "unconditioned" ones, and thus being more closely tied with the creative advance. Again, this second definition will be presupposed in what follows.

What now is God in his total fullness as comprising both his primordial and consequent natures? The logical sum of the two in the sense of the calculus of individuals. Thus,

'*God*' may now abbreviate '(png U cng)'.

In other words, *God* is cng, the fusion of the class of all actual entities, together with the fusion of all conceptual prehensions that are unconditioned and whose subjective forms are valuations. *God* is thus for Whitehead a highly complex entity with a very involved internal structure—an understatement indeed.

Is *God* an AO? Yes, he is a fusion of various prehensions, all such prehensions being AO's. In this way, *God* is not "treated as an exception to all metaphysical principles, invoked to save their collapse. He is their chief exemplification." He is an AO undergoing concrescence in the creative advance; one among many, but somewhat exceptional all the same owing to his unconditioned valuations.

Whenever God is mentioned hereafter, it should always be borne in mind precisely what is being referred to, whether just png, or rather cng, or *God* himself in his total fullness. Some of Whitehead's statements may seem puzzling if these three are not clearly distinguished. Some statements seem to refer primarily to one, others to another.

* * *

Let us comment now upon Chapter III, Section I, where God is first introduced in *Process and Reality,* in the light of the foregoing.

The "relevance" of an EO for a given AO is given or fixed in the primordial valuation. "There will be additional ground of relevance (p. 46) for select eternal objects by reason of their ingression into derivate actual entities belonging to the actual world of the concrescent occasion in question. But whether or not this be the case, there is always the definite relevance derived from God." A given AO may conceptually prehend EO's (relative to the AO's in its actual world) in modes other than just those of the png's valuations of those EO's relative to those AO's. But no matter; each EO relative to all AO's is conceptually valuated to some degree in png. "Apart from God, eternal objects unrealized in the actual world would be relatively non-existent for the concrescence in question," or for that matter for any concrescence. If an EO is null in the sense of never, never ingressing into any AO, in other words, "relatively non-existent," it at least fully "exists" in the sense of being a datum in one of the valuations of the png. "For effective relevance requires agency of comparison, and agency belongs exclusively to actual occasions." The "agent" is the "subject" in concrescence, and "effective relevance" is always that of an agent. The "ordering" of the valuations in the png is effective in the process of actuality and "has a real relevance to the creative advance."

"This divine ordering is itself matter of fact, thereby conditioning creativity." The valuations of the png in fact takes place *in* and *with* the creative advance itself (p. $\overline{521}$). As metaphysical facts or principles we have seen that

$$(\propto)(\underline{e}_1)(\propto \ \epsilon \ EO^1 \ \supset \ (E\underline{e}) \ (E\underline{i})(<\underline{e},Prhd^{\underline{i}},\propto,\underline{e}_1> \ \underline{e} \bullet \underline{e} \ \epsilon \ Val \bullet$$
$$0\leqslant\underline{i}\leqslant1)), \ (\propto)(\underline{e}_1)(\underline{e}_2)(\propto \ \epsilon \ EO^2 \ \supset \ (E\underline{e})(E\underline{i})(<\underline{e},Prhd^{\underline{i}},\propto,\underline{e}_1,\underline{e}_2> \ \underline{e}$$
$$\bullet \underline{e} \ \epsilon \ Val \bullet 0\leqslant\underline{i}\leqslant1)),$$

and so on. These are *Principles of Existence* for png. In addition, *Principles of Uniqueness* are needed to assure that for each EO relative to given AO's there is *at most one* valuation of the desired kind of that EO relative to those AO's. More particularly,

$$(\propto)(\underline{e})(\underline{i})(\underline{e}_1)(\underline{e}_2)((\propto \ \epsilon \ EO^1 \ \bullet \ <\underline{e},Prhd^{\underline{i}},\propto,\underline{e}_1> \ \underline{e} \ \bullet \underline{e} \ \epsilon \ Val \bullet$$
$$<\underline{e}_2,Prhd^{\underline{i}},\propto,\underline{e}_1>\underline{e}_2 \bullet \underline{e}_2 \ \epsilon \ Val \bullet 0\leqslant\underline{i}\leqslant1) \supset \underline{e} = \underline{e}_2),$$

$$(\propto)(\underline{e})(\underline{i})(\underline{e}_1)(\underline{e}_2)(\underline{e}_3)((\propto \ \epsilon \ EO^2 \ \bullet \ <\underline{e},Prhd^{\underline{i}},\propto,\underline{e}_1,\underline{e}_2> \ \underline{e} \bullet \underline{e} \ \epsilon \ Val \bullet$$
$$<\underline{e}_3,Prhd^{\underline{i}},\propto,\underline{e}_1,\underline{e}_2> \ \underline{e}_3 \bullet \underline{e}_3 \ \epsilon \ Val \bullet 0\leqslant\underline{i}\leqslant1) \supset \underline{e} = \underline{e}_3),$$

and so on, as well as

$$(\propto)(\underline{e})(\underline{e}_1)(\underline{i})(\underline{j})((\propto \ \epsilon \ EO^1 \ \bullet <\underline{e},Prhd^{\underline{i}},\propto,\underline{e}_1> \ \underline{e} \bullet <\underline{e},Prhd^{\underline{j}},\propto,\underline{e}_1> \ \underline{e},$$
$$\underline{e} \ \epsilon \ Val \bullet 0\leqslant\underline{i}\leqslant1 \bullet 0\leqslant\underline{j}\leqslant1) \supset \underline{i} = \underline{j}),$$

$$(\propto)(\underline{e})(\underline{e}_1)(\underline{e}_2)(\underline{i})(\underline{j})((\propto \ \epsilon \ EO^2 \ \bullet <\underline{e},Prhd^{\underline{i}},\propto,\underline{e}_1,\underline{e}_2> \ \underline{e} \bullet <\underline{e},Prhd^{\underline{j}},$$
$$\propto,\underline{e}_1,\underline{e}_2> \ \underline{e} \bullet \underline{e} \ \epsilon \ \overline{Val} \bullet 0\leqslant\underline{i}\leqslant1 \bullet 0\leqslant\underline{j}\leqslant1) \supset \underline{i} = \underline{j}),$$

and so on. These principles of existence and uniqueness together assure us that the png *as a matter of metaphysical fact* contains uniquely the primordial valuations.

"Creativity" or the creative advance is always found under conditions, and described as conditioned. The non-temporal act of all-inclusive unfettered valuation is at once a creature of creativity and a condition for creativity. It shares this double character with all creatures. The png is both a creature, being a fusion of prehensions, and a "condition for creativity," being the primordial "lure for feeling." Each AO is a creature and also a condition for creativity in the sense of being in the "actual world" of every subsequent concrescence. The png is a "non-temporal act" in the sense of being an "integrated" prehension so complex that to attempt to locate it spatiotemporally would be hopelessly difficult if not impossible. "By reason of its *(God's)* character as a creature, always in concrescence and never wholly in the past, it receives a reaction from the world; this reaction is its consequent nature." The png is operative in each concrescence and each concrescence is a "reaction" to it. The cng is never wholly in the past, but is always being augmented with each new concrescence.

The cng is appropriately a part of *God*, and so-called, "because the contemplation of our natures, as enjoying real feelings derived from the timeless source [valuation] of all order, acquires that 'subjective form' of refreshment and companionship at which religions aim." This "refreshment and companionship" is for Whitehead a matter of fact, not of conjecture. Perhaps not everyone feels them, but some at least do, as a matter of fact. Let 'Refr and 'Cmpn' stand respectively for the subjective forms of the kind of consciously-felt refreshment and companionship "at which religions aim." Then

$$(E\underline{e})(E\underline{e}')(E\underline{e}'')(E\propto)(E\underline{e}_1)...(E\underline{e}_k)(E\underline{i})((<\underline{e}',Prhd\overset{i}{\underset{}{-}},\propto,\underline{e}_1> \underline{e}' \text{ v } ... \text{ v }$$
$$<\underline{e}',Prhd\overset{i}{\underset{}{-}},\propto,\underline{e}_1,...,\underline{e}_k>\underline{e}') \bullet \underline{e}' \in \text{Val} \bullet 0\leqslant\underline{i}\leqslant1 \bullet <\underline{e},Prhd\overset{i}{\underset{}{-}},\underline{e}'> \underline{e}'' \bullet$$
$$(\underline{e}'' \in \text{Refr v } \underline{e}'' \in \text{Cmpn})).$$

That this and allied principles concerning religious experience hold for Whitehead is eloquent testimony that God is needed in his system in a most fundamental way. To excise it, as some have attempted to do, is to alter the system unrecognizably and to allow no place for principles that are integral to the system and not mere appendages.

A word more concerning the "non-temporal" character of png. It was suggested a moment back that to attempt to locate png in the temporal flow would be hopelessly difficult if not impossible. The reason is that the valuations constituting png are "unconditioned." More needs to be said about this, but only after time and space have been introduced into the system. In any case, the png is presumably the only non-temporal creature, and the doctrine of spatiotemporal order must be so arranged that this circumstance is in no way exceptional but rather a "chief exemplification" of it.

"This function of creatures, that they constitute the shifting character of creativity, is here termed the 'objective immortality' of actual entities. Thus God has objective immortality in respect to [both] his primordial nature and his consequent nature." The objective immortality of an AO may be regarded as, put loosely, just the fusion of the class of all the prehensions (physical or conceptual) that are borne e by something or other, as in the previous paper. The objective immortality of png is then just png itself, for all its constituent valuations are prehended to some degree by all AO's. The objective immortality of the cng likewise may be regarded as just cng itself, for all its constituent AO's other than itself are prehended by some e or other to at least some degree.

* * *

Let us comment now on the most significant passages in the last chapter, "God and the World" (*Process and Reality,* pp. 519-533), especially Sections II ff., in the light of the foregoing.

"Viewed as primordial," Whitehead notes again (p. 521), God "is the unlimited conceptual realization of the absolute wealth of potentiality." The use of 'conceptual valuation' would perhaps be better here then 'conceptual realization.' Potentialities become realized only with actualization. The png, however, involves no actualization, only valuations. "In this aspect, he is not *before* all creation, but *with* all creation." Clearly png is not before all creation, for at any time some prehensions in png may not yet have come into existence. In what sense now is the png *with* all creation? Just in the sense that "there is an order in the relevance of eternal objects to the process of creation," as already noted. The png's "unity of conceptual operations is a free creative act,

untrammelled by reference to any particular course of things."
Thus we have the Principle of Freedom, that

$$(\underline{e})((\underline{e} \in CncptlPrhn \bullet \underline{e} \ P \ \underline{png}) \supset \underline{e} \in Dcsn_{\underline{e}}).$$

Every conceptual prehension that is a part of the png is a free
decision by some entity, namely itself. These valuations are
"deflected neither by love, nor by hatred, nor what in fact comes
to pass." If they were, they would be conditioned by the physical
world, whereas it is the *ideality* of the png that is relevant here.

"The *particularities* of the actual world presuppose *it* (the png);
while *it* merely presupposes the general character of creative
advance, of which it is the primordial exemplification." The AO's
presuppose the realm of order—no EO's, no concrescences. On the
other hand, the png involves the unconditioned valuations of the
EO's, and it is the EO's that determine "the general character of
creative advance." Finally, the png is the "primordial exemplification" of this general character in the sense that it consists after all
of the "unfettered" valuations of all EO's and not of anything less.

The png is of course "deficiently actual" in comprising no
physical feelings, and also in lacking consciousness. A prehension
is conscious, it will be recalled, when and when it is "integrated"
with a physical prehension. Thus

$$\sim (E\underline{e})(\underline{e} \in PhysPrhn \bullet \underline{e} \ P \ \underline{png})$$

and

$$\sim \underline{png} \in Cnsc,$$

whereas

$$\underline{cng} \in Cnsc.$$

The png, although devoid of actuality, is of course replete with
ideality. The png is, strictly, God's vision of the ideal eternal order
of the cosmos. The valuations comprising png "exemplify in their

subjective forms their mutual sensitivity and their subjective unity of subjective aim." The "unity of subjective aim" is provided by the principle that the cosmos as a whole always has as its subjective aim the "realization" of the valuations of the png. Thus, we have principles of cosmic aim—to the effect that

$$(\underline{e}_1)...(\underline{e}_n)(\propto)(\underline{i})((E\underline{e}')(\underline{e}' \ \epsilon \ Val \bullet 0 {\leq} \underline{i} {\leq} 1 \bullet <\underline{e}',Prhd^{\underline{i}},\propto,\underline{e}_1,...,\underline{e}_n> \\ \underline{e}') \supset (E\overline{\underline{e}}')(\underline{e}'' \ \epsilon \ SA_{cng} \bullet <cng,Prhd^{\underline{i}},\propto,\underline{e}_1,...,\underline{e}_n> \underline{e}'')),$$

and so on, for each $\underline{n}$ ($1 {\leq} \underline{n} {\leq} \underline{k}$). The valuations are mutually harmonious with the one unified subjective aim no doubt of achieving maximal realization of truth, beauty, and goodness, and all derivative excellences. In any case, these valuations determine, in the sense of providing "the lure for feeling, the eternal urge [better perhaps, object] of desire," the "relative relevance [or degree of relevance or value] for each occasion of actuality." Each occasion in actuality prehends each eternal object as it will, but in ideality always values each eternal object to just the degree that it is valued unconditionally. However, there is always failure of actual achievement in this regard, as recorded by the following principles, for each $\underline{n}$ ($1 {\leq} \underline{n} {\leq} \underline{k}$).

$$(E\underline{e}')(E\propto)(E\underline{e}_1)...(E\underline{e}_n)(E\underline{i})(\underline{e}' \ \epsilon \ Val \bullet (\underline{i} > 0 \bullet <\underline{e}',Prhd^{\underline{i}},\propto,\underline{e}_1, \\ ...,\underline{e}_n> \underline{e}' \bullet \sim \propto Ing \ \underline{e}_1,...,\underline{e}_n) \ v \ (\underline{i} = 0 \bullet <\underline{e}',\overline{P}rhd^{\underline{i}},\propto,\underline{e}_1,...,\underline{e}_n> \underline{e}' \bullet \propto \\ Ing \ \overline{\underline{e}}_1,...,\underline{e}_n)).$$

These existence laws are at the root of the presence of evil in the cosmos.

The png is thus relevant "to each creative act [i.e., decisional conceptual prehension] as it arises from its own conditioned standpoint in the world" and constitutes "the initial 'object of desire' establishing the initial phase of each subjective aim." In other words, each AO, no matter what its standpoint in the world, values initially each EO precisely as it is valued unconditionally.

Thus

$$(\underline{e})(\underline{e}_1)...(\underline{e}_n)(\propto)(\underline{i})((E\underline{e}')(\underline{e}' \in \text{Val} \bullet 0 \leqslant \underline{i} \leqslant 1 \bullet <\underline{e}', \text{Prhd}^{\overset{\cdot}{\underline{i}}}\propto, \underline{e}_1,...,$$
$$\underline{e}_n > \underline{e}') \supset (\overline{E\underline{e}}')(\underline{e}' \in \text{Val} \bullet <\underline{e}, \text{Prhd}^{\underline{i}}, \propto, \underline{e}_1,...,\underline{e}_n > \underline{e}')),$$

for each $\underline{n}$ ($1 \leqslant \underline{n} \leqslant \underline{k}$). Further, it has as its subjective aims the purpose to realize that valuation in its own concrescence. Thus also

$$(\underline{e})(\underline{e}_1)...(\underline{e}_n)(\propto)(\underline{i})((E\underline{e}')(\underline{e}' \in \text{Val} \bullet 0 \leqslant \underline{i} \leqslant 1 \bullet <\underline{e}', \text{Prhd}^{\underline{i}}, \propto, \underline{e}_1,...,$$
$$\underline{e}_n > \underline{e}') \supset (\overline{E\underline{e}}')(\underline{e}' \in \text{SA}_{\underline{e}} \bullet <\underline{e}, \text{Prhd}^{\underline{i}}, \propto, \underline{e}_1,...,\underline{e}_n > \underline{e}')).$$

Of course it may not actually succeed in realizing this subjective aim, and it is free not to choose even to try to do so if it so wishes. Again, self-seeking evil prevails, and as a result of one of $\underline{e}$'s decisions. Thus

$$(E\underline{e})(E\underline{e}')(E\propto)(E\underline{e}_1)...(E\underline{e}_n)(E\underline{i})(\underline{e}' \in \text{Val} \bullet 0 \leqslant \underline{i} \leqslant 1 \bullet <\underline{e}', \text{Prhd}^{\underline{i}}, \propto,$$
$$\underline{e}_1,...,\underline{e}_n > \underline{e}' \bullet \sim (E\underline{e}'')(\underline{e}'' \in \text{Dcsn}_{\underline{e}} \bullet <\underline{e}, \text{Prhd}^{\underline{i}}, \propto, \underline{e}_1,...,\underline{e}_n > \underline{e}'')).$$

Each EO is lured by the valuations in the png but is free to do and decide as it will, and some reject that lure. Self-seeking is the root of all evil, and comes into play by the agent's rejection of the primordial valuations in favor of those of his own making.

* * *

The png acts on the world as "the principle of concretion—the principle whereby there is initiated a definite outcome from a situation otherwise riddled with ambiguity." The "situation . . . riddled with ambiguity" is perhaps the entire multiplicity of eternal objects with no unconditioned valuations thereon. For any given AO, the "definite outcome," i.e., its conceptual valuation of a given EO, may or may not accord with the unconditioned valuations with respect to that EO. But in any case, there is present the "lure for feeling," the object of desire, guiding with gentle persuasiveness and love the actual valuation to accord with the ideal one. Without such guidance, the concrescence is "riddled with ambiguity" and confusion, not knowing what valuations to make nor why.

The cng, unlike the png, "is the beginning and the end" and the middle as well. "He is not the beginning in the sense of being in the past of all members." He is the beginning in the sense that given any $\underline{e}$, the $\text{cng}^{\underline{e}}$ (the whole cosmos anterior to $\underline{e}$) is an initial part of the cng itself. And similarly he is the end in the sense that given any $\underline{e}$, the

$$\text{Fu}^{\prime}\hat{e}_1(\sim \underline{e}_1 \text{ P } \underline{\text{cng}}^{\underline{e}} \bullet \sim (\text{E}\mu)(\underline{\text{png}} = \text{Fu}^{\prime}\mu \bullet \underline{e}_1 \in \mu))$$

is a part of the cng itself.

"He is the presupposed actuality of conceptual operation, in unison of becoming with every other creative act. Thus by reason of the relativity of all things, there is a reaction of the world on God." The cng "becomes" in the sense that every concrescence is a part of it, and the whole "becomes" with the becoming of each and every one of its parts. And cng is "the presupposed actuality of conceptual operation" of any AO in the sense that all antecedent AO's with their completed conceptual prehensions are themselves parts of it. Each EO "presupposes" all such conceptual prehensions. There is "a reaction of the world on God" in the sense that the entire cosmos *up to* any $\underline{e}$ is also a part of the cng. Each $\underline{e}$ is of course objectively immortal in the cng, and the "completion of God's nature into a fullness of physical feeling," the cng itself, "is derived from the objectification [objective immortality] of the world [up to any $\underline{e}$] in God." Also he "shares with every new creation its actual world; and the concrescent creature is objectified in God as a novel element in God's objectification of that actual world." Clearly the actual world of any new $\underline{e}$ is a part of the cng, as is $\underline{e}$ itself. "This prehension into [inclusion in] God of each creature[5] is directed with the subjective aim, and clothed with the subjective form, wholly derivative from his all-inclusive primordial valuation." The use of 'prehension into

5   On p. 16.

God' here is merely informal. Each concrescence has the primordial valuations available as a lure for feeling, even if it heeds them not. The all-inclusive "conceptual nature [png] is unchanged by reason of its final completeness. But his derivative nature [cng] is consequent upon the creative advance of the world." Clearly the png is fixed once and for all. Of course the cng is also in the sense of including all e whatsoever. On the other hand, the cng contains within its "real internal constitution" each concrescence and in this sense depends upon them.

The sum God, (png U cng), is genuinely dipolar, just as each AO is. Each AO is dipolar in the sense of being a concrescence of both physical and conceptual feelings. "The consequent nature of God is conscious; and it is the realization of the actual world in the unity of his nature, and through the transformation of his wisdom." The consciousness of the cng is dependent upon the consciousness of its parts and arises only with the integration of physical with conceptual feelings. Thus only the cng can be said to be conscious, not the png, devoid as it is of physical feelings. This has been noted above. "The primordial nature is conceptual, the consequent nature is the weaving of God's physical feelings upon his primordial concepts," where 'weaving' is taken to express the integation of physical and conceptual prehensions.

The png is "infinite, devoid of all negative prehensions." It is infinite in the sense that it is "limited by no actuality which it presupposes." It is "free, complete, primordial, eternal, actually deficient, and unconscious." It is free in the sense of consisting of the all unconditioned valuations. It is complete in the sense that the valuation of every eternal object is a part of it. It is eternal in the sense of being fixed once and for all. It is actually deficient, as already noted, in involving no complex feelings integrated with physical ones. The cng, on the other hand, is "determined, incomplete, consequent, 'everlasting,' fully actual, and con-scious"—determined in the sense of consisting of AO's, the finite determined actualities, incomplete in the sense of not containing at any given time all AO's but of increasing continually with the creative advance of the cosmos, "everlasting" in the sense that given any AO there is always an AO that prehends it and one that it prehends (everlasting in the future as well as in the past), *fully* actual in the sense of comprising all actualities, and conscious of course in the sense of containing integrated conceptual and physical prehensions from which consciousness can arise. "His necessary goodness expresses the determination of his consequent nature," the subjective aim, i.e., of each AO to make its primary valuations in accord with those of the png.

"Conceptual experience can be infinite" in the sense of not being limited by actuality, "but it belongs to the nature of physical experience that it is finite" in the sense of being thus limited. "An actual entity in the temporal world is to be conceived as originated by physical experience with its process of completion motivated by consequent, conceptual experience initially derived from God." A concrescence consists of both physical and conceptual prehensions, the latter being always available as the primordial lure for feeling. On the other hand, "God is to be conceived as originated by conceptual experience with his process of completion motivated by consequent, physical experience, initially derived from the temporal world." God seems fundamentally the png but fully or completed only with adding as a logical summand the cng. No special significance should be attached in these two sentences to Whitehead's use of 'originated by,' 'consequent,' or 'initially derived.' They could be deleted without loss of content.

* * *

A "perfect" valuation is one in accord with those of the png. Thus

$\text{'}\underline{e} \ \epsilon \ \text{PerfVal'}$ may abbreviate $\text{'}(\underline{e} \ \epsilon \ \text{Val} \bullet (E\underline{e}\text{'})(E\alpha)(E\underline{e}_1)...$
$(E\underline{e}_{\underline{k}})(Ei)(\underline{e}\text{'} \ \epsilon \ \text{Val} \bullet 0 \leqslant \underline{i} \leqslant 1 \bullet ((<\underline{e}\text{'},\text{Prhd}^{\underline{i}},\alpha,\underline{e}_1>\underline{e}\text{'} \bullet (E\underline{e}\text{''})<\underline{e}\text{''},$
$\text{Prhd}^{\underline{i}},\alpha,\underline{e}_1>\underline{e}) \ \text{v} \ ... \ \text{v} \ (<\underline{e},\text{Prhd}^{\underline{i}},\alpha,\underline{e}_1,...,\underline{e}_{\underline{k}}>\underline{e}\text{'} \bullet (E\underline{e}\text{''}) <\underline{e}\text{''},\text{Prhd}^{\underline{i}},$
$\alpha,\underline{e}_1,...,\underline{e}_{\underline{k}}>\underline{e}))))\text{'}.$

Similarly, a "perfect" subjective aim is one in accord with those of the png. Thus

$$\text{'}\underline{e}\text{' } \epsilon \text{ Perf } SA_{\underline{e}}\text{' abbreviates '}(\underline{e}\text{' } \epsilon \text{ } SA_{\underline{e}} \bullet (E\underline{e}\text{''})(E\propto)(E\underline{e}_1)...$$
$$(E\underline{e}_k)(E\underline{i})(\underline{e}\text{'' } \epsilon \text{ Val} \bullet 0 \leqslant \underline{i} \leqslant 1 \bullet ((<\underline{e}\text{''},\text{Prhd}^{\underline{i}},\propto,\underline{e}_1> \underline{e}\text{'' } \bullet <\underline{e},\text{Prhd}^{\underline{i}},$$
$$\propto,\underline{e}_1>\underline{e}\text{'}) \text{ v } ... \text{ v } (<\underline{e}\text{''},\text{Prhd}^{\underline{i}},\propto,\underline{e}_1,...,\underline{e}_k> \underline{e}\text{'' } \bullet <\underline{e},\text{Prhd}^{\underline{i}},\propto,\underline{e}_1,...,$$
$$\underline{e}_k>\underline{e}\text{'}))))\text{'}.$$

"The wisdom of [the primordial] subjective aim [p. 525] prehends every actuality for what it can be [even this wisdom being limited by the physical factors] in such a perfected system—its sufferings, its sorrows, its failures, its triumphs, its immediacies of joy—woven by rightness of feeling into the harmony of the universal feeling, which is always immediate, always many, always one, always with novel advance, moving onward and never perishing." This famous sentence is not to be interpreted as saying that the "wisdom" of the png sees no evil, but only that the evil is absorbed by and harmonized into the ever emerging universal feeling. "The revolts of destructive evil, purely self-regarding, are dismissed into their triviality of merely individual facts; and yet the good they did achieve in individual joy, in individual sorrow, in the introduction of needed contrast, is yet saved by its relation to the completed whole." Every concrescence becomes absorbed in the cng, as do all valuations (other than the primordial ones), all rejoicings, all sorrowings, and so on. Each is thereafter ever present to be valuated in accord with the valuations of the png. Such valuations "save" the temporal world and future valuations may yet accord with those of the png, even if past ones have not.

"The consequent nature of God is his judgment on the world. He saves the world as it passes into the immediacy of his own life. It is the judgment of a tenderness which loses nothing that can be saved. It is also the judgment of a wisdom which uses what in the temporal world is mere wreckage." The cng receives each item of the passing world into its real internal constitution. This reception is the "judgment," the saving "tenderness" that preserves each AO in its status of having been just what it was, even if mere "wreckage." All AO's are "covered" by the cng as creatures in his internal nature.

Whitehead speaks of the "infinite patience" of the cng. What he says of it indicates that he means to refer rather to the infinite patience of *God.* "The universe includes a threefold creative act" composed of (i) the png, (ii) all purely physical prehensions, the *World,* and (iii) the cng. "If we conceive the first term and the last term in their unity over against the intermediate multiple freedom of physical realizations in the temporal world, we conceive of the patience of God, tenderly saving the turmoil of the intermediate world by the completion of his own nature . . . [God] does not create the world, he saves 't" by receiving it into his own real internal constitution; "or, more accurately, he is the poet of the world, with tender patience leading it by his vision of truth, beauty, and goodness" incorporated in the primordial valuations.

*   *   *

The final summary as to the interrelations between flux (or "fluency") and permanence, the one and the many, immanence and transcendence, and creation is given by Whitehead in the six "antitheses" (p. 528) concerning God and the World.

"It is as true that God is permanent and the World fluent, as that the World is permanent and God is fluent." The use of 'is as true that' here is insignificant, for all that is asserted is presumably intended to be true. For God to be permanent is for him to contain all and only the primordial valuations, and for the World to be permanent is for it to contain *all* physical prehensions. On the other hand, both the World and *God* are fluent in the sense of containing at least one (fluent) concrescence. Let

'$\underline{e} \ \epsilon$ PrimVal' abbreviate '$(\underline{e} \ \epsilon \ $Val $\bullet \ (E\propto)(E\underline{e}_1)...(E\underline{e}_k)(E\underline{i})$ $(0 \leq \underline{i} \leq 1 \bullet (<\underline{e},$Prhd$^{\underline{i}},\propto,\underline{e}_1> \underline{e}$ v ... v$<\underline{e},$Prhd$^{\underline{i}},\propto,\underline{e}_1,...,\underline{e}_k>\underline{e}))\check{)}$'.

Then

$(\underline{e})(\underline{e} \ \epsilon \ \text{PrimVal} \supset \underline{e} \ P \ \underline{png}) \bullet (E\underline{e})(\underline{e} \ \epsilon \ AO \bullet \underline{e} \ P \ \underline{God}) \bullet (\underline{e})(\underline{e} \ \epsilon$ PhysPrhn $\supset \underline{e} \ P \ \underline{World}) \bullet (E\underline{e})(\underline{e} \ \epsilon \ \text{PhysPrhn} \bullet \underline{e} \ P \ \underline{World})$,

where

'$\underline{World}$' abbreviates 'Fu'PhysPrhn'.

"It is as true to say that God is one and the World many, as that the World is one and God many." God is one in the sense that both the $\underline{cng}$ and the $\underline{png}$ are unique fusions and hence that $(\underline{cng} \ U$ $\underline{png})$ is, and the World is one in the sense that the fusion of the class of physical prehensions is also unique. On the other hand, both the World and God are many in the sense of containing at least two concrescences.

$\underline{World} = \text{Fu'PhysPrhn} \bullet \underline{God} = (\underline{cng} \ U \ \underline{png}) \bullet (E\underline{e}_1)(E\underline{e}_2)(\underline{e}_1 \ P$ $\underline{World} \bullet \underline{e}_2 \ P \ \underline{World} \bullet \sim \underline{e}_1 = \underline{e}_2) \bullet (E\underline{e}_1)(E\underline{e}_2)(\underline{e}_1 \ P \ \underline{God} \bullet \underline{e}_2 \ P$ $\underline{God} \bullet \sim \underline{e}_1 = \underline{e}_2).$

"It is as true to say that, in comparison with the World, God is actual eminently, as that, in comparison with God, the World is actual eminently." God is "actual eminently" in the sense of containing all concrescences, but the World is not, in the sense of not being conscious. On the other hand, the World is eminently actual in the sense of containing all physical prehensions, whereas the $\underline{png}$ lacks eminent actuality because it contains none such.

$(\underline{e})\underline{e} \ \text{Pt} \ \underline{God} \bullet \sim \underline{World} \ \epsilon \ \text{Cnsc} \bullet (\underline{e})(\underline{e} \ \epsilon \ \text{PhysPrhn} \supset \underline{e} \ P \ \underline{World}) \bullet$ $\sim (E\underline{e})(\underline{e} \ \epsilon \ \text{PhysPrhn} \bullet \underline{e} \ P \ \underline{png}).$

"It is as true to say that the World is immanent in God, as that God is immanent in the World." The World is "immanent" in God in the sense of bearing P to it. And God is "immanent" in the World in the sense of supplying the initial SA's for all concrescences. Thus

$\underline{\text{World}}$ P $\underline{\text{God}}$ • $(\underline{e})(E\underline{e}_1)(\underline{e}_1 \in SA_{\underline{e}} • \underline{e}_1$ P $\underline{\text{png}})$.

"It is as true to say that God transcends the World as that the World transcends God." Clearly God contains prehensions not included in the World, and the World contains prehensions not included in the png.

$(E\underline{e})(\underline{e} \in \text{Prhn} • \underline{e}$ P $\underline{\text{God}} • \sim \underline{e}$ P $\underline{\text{World}}) • (E\underline{e})(\underline{e} \in \text{Prhn} • \underline{e}$ P $\underline{\text{World}} • \sim \underline{e}$ P $\underline{\text{png}})$.

"It is as true to say that God creates the world as to say the World creates God." God "creates" the World in the sense of providing items in it with the initial valuations or subjective aims, but the World creates God in the sense of providing the physical data for these valuations. Thus

$(\underline{e})(\underline{e} \in \text{PrimVal} \supset (\underline{e} \in \text{Val} • (E\underline{e}')(\underline{e} \in SA\underline{\overset{\cdot}{e}}')) • (\underline{e})(\underline{e}$ P $\underline{\text{World}} \supset (E\underline{e}')(E\propto)(E\underline{e}_1)...(E\underline{e}_k)(Ei)(\underline{e}' \in \text{Val} • 0 \leq \underline{i} \leq 1 • (<\underline{e}', \text{Prhd}^{\underline{1}}, \propto, \underline{e}_1,...,\underline{e}_k> \underline{e}'$ v ... v$<\underline{e}', \text{Prhd}^{\underline{1}}, \propto, \underline{e}_1,...,\underline{e}_k> \underline{e}') • (\underline{e} = \underline{e}_1$ v ... v $\underline{e} = \underline{e}_k)))$.

The renditions given of these six "antitheses" are by no means the only ones, the antitheses themselves being highly ambiguous.

It might seem "philistine to lay the rude hands of logic"—C.I. Lewis's phrase—upon a subject so lofty as the "real internal constitution" of God. It should not be forgotten however, as suggested earlier, that Whitehead for most of his adult life was a professional mathematician, and it is interesting to note that even when he writes about God the movement of his thought is that of a mathematician, first giving definitions and then in effect theorems based on them. Especially important are the definitions. From the strict point of view of just developing a logical system, the definitions are regarded merely as notational conventions of abbreviation. However, as Whitehead himself pointed out in an early writing,[6] " . . . if we abandon the strictly logical point of view, the definitions . . . are at once seen to be the most important part of the subject. The act . . . (of giving a definition) . . . is in fact the act of choosing the various complex ideas which are to be the special object of study. The whole subject depends upon such a choice." Once the definitions have been chosen, the derivation of theorems should come out easily enough in terms of previously proved theorems, the axioms, and of course the principles of the underlying logic.

It is interesting to note that in the foregoing the definitions have been crucial. Alternatives have been suggested and it is not always clear which ones are preferable for the intended purposes. Also various metaphysical principles have been suggested, in addition to those required (in the previous paper) for the categoreal scheme. Some of these, or similar ones, might be suitable to take as axioms. Strictly the axioms and definitions go hand in hand and should be given together. To suggest a suitable set of axioms for the whole of the Whiteheadian cosmology, however, would be a formidable task indeed. Meanwhile, the tentative definitions and comments above may be useful as a first step in helping to clarify the logical structure of Whitehead's theory of God. The exhibition of such structure is not only an aid to understanding, it would seem; it is so important that without it we cannot be said to know what that theory really is.

A SELECT BIBLIOGRAPHY*

Works

Whitehead, Alfred North, *Adventures of Ideas.* New York: Macmillan, 1933.
_____, *Process and Reality.* New York: Macmillan, 1929.
_____, *Religion in the Making.* New York: Macmillan, 1926.
_____, *Science and the Modern World.* New York: Macmillan, 1925.

*Compiled by Robert Hall at St. John's University, New York, U.S.A.

6 *The Axioms of Projective Geometry* (Cambridge: Cambridge University Press, 1906), p. 2.

Studies

Bennett, John, "Nature—God's Body: A Whiteheadian Persepective," *Philosophy Today,* Vol. XVIII (Fall, 1974), pp. 248-254.

Cobb, John, *Christian Natural Theology: Based on the Thought of Alfred North Whitehead.* Philadelphia: Westminster, 1965.

Ely, S.L., *The Religious Availability of Whitehead's God.* Madison, Wisconsin: University of Wisconsin Press, 1942.

Ford, Lewis, "The Non-temporality of Whitehead's God," *International Philosophical Quarterly,* Vol. XIII (1973), pp. 347-376.

Hamilton, Peter, *Living God and the Modern World: Christian Theology Based on the Thought of Alfred North Whitehead.* Philadelphia: United Church, 1967.

Lundeen, Lyman, *Risk and Rhetoric in Religion: Whitehead's Theory of Language and the Discourse of Faith.* Philadelphia: Fortress, 1972.

Overman, Richard, *Evolution and the Christian Doctrine of Creation.* Philadelphia: Westminster, 1967.

Platt, David, "Does Whitehead's God Possess a Moral Will?" *Process Studies,* Vol. V (Summer, 1975), pp. 114-122.

Reese, William, and Freeman, Eugene (eds.), *Process and Divinity: The Hartshorne Festschrift.* La Salle, Illinois: Open Court, 1964.

Schilpp, Paul (ed.), *The Philosophy of Afred North Whitehead,* 2nd ed. New York: Tudor Publishing Co., 1951. Contains complete bibliography of Whitehead's works.

CHAPTER XXIII

PAUL J. TILLICH ON NATURAL THEOLOGY

*Joseph Fitzer**

Paul J. Tillich's (1886-1965) views on natural theology are to be found chiefly in the first volume of his *Systematic Theology,* especially Section II-D. Further insight into his position can be gained from the last section of *The Courage to Be* and in the essays "The Two Types of Philosophy of Religion" and "The Nature of Religious Language" in the volume *Theology of Culture.*[1] With respect to secondary literature, unfortunately, the picture is rather bleak: most theologians have been much more concerned to show where Tillich has gone wrong than simply to show where he has gone. Apart from the critiques of John Herman Randall, Charles Hartshorne, Gustave Weigel, and Carl Armbruster, there is painfully little of what Jacques Maritain has called "the consideration of the *place* which each system could, according to its own frame of reference, grant the other system as the legitimate place the other is cut out to occupy in the universe of thought."[2] Any any rate, the present essay will not presume to

---

*Associate Professor of Theology at St. John's University, Jamaica, New York, U.S.A.

[1] *Systematic Theology,* Vol. I (Chicago, 1951); *The Courage to Be* (New Haven, 1952), pp. 178-190; *Theology of Culture* (New York, 1964), pp. 10-29, 53-67. *Systematic Theology,* Vol. I: abbreviated *ST.*

[2] *The Range of Reason* (New York, 1952), p. 40. Cf. J.H. Randall, "The Ontology of Paul Tillich," and C. Hartshorne, "Tillich's Doctrine of God," in *The Theology of Paul Tillich,* ed. C.W. Kegley and R.W. Bretall (New York, 1964), pp. 132-161, 164-195; G. Weigel, "Contemporaneous Protestantism and Paul Tillich," and "Recent Protestant Theology," *Theological Studies* XI (1950), pp. 177-202, and XIV (1953), pp. 568-594; *ibid.,* "The Theological Significance of Paul Tillich," and "Myth, Symbol, and Analogy," in *Paul Tillich in Catholic Thought,* ed. T. O'Meara and C. Weisser (Dubuque, 1964), pp. 3-24, 184-196; C.J. Armbruster, *The Vision of Paul Tillich* (New York, 1967).

stand in judgment over Tillich, but will concern itself only with showing, in terms of Maritain's twentieth-century Thomism, what place Tillich's thought might legitimately occupy.

*   *   *

To move on, then, to a summary of Tillich's position, "The basic theological question is the question of God. God is the answer to the question implied in being."[3] The task of the theologian, therefore, is to become for a time a philosopher, to ask the "ontological question." And the ontological question is "What is being itself? What is that which is not a special being or group of beings, not something concrete or something abstract, but rather something which is always thought implicitly, and sometimes explicitly, if something is said to *be*?" The task of philosophy, in other words, is "to investigate the character of everything that is in so far as it is," and philosophy does this, sometimes on its own initiative and sometimes, as here, as part of the theological concern. What others would call philosophy, in other words, becomes theological for Tillich by reason of its motivation.

The ontological question arises from "the shock of non-being," the sense of being able imaginatively to remove all that is; and thus it is not really so much a question as a state of experience, a kind of perspective taken on the phenomena of human life. If one enquires how this question can be answered, in as much as the question seems to imply the removal of all that inspired the question, the answer is that when one asks "What is being itself?" he is not expecting the reply "Being is being: *to be* is to be given in phenomenal experience." The simple *fact* that beings of some sort emerge from the shadows is taken for granted, masked, so to speak, behind the ontological question in the form in which it is here asked. He is rather expecting to be told, in an exploratory, descriptive way, *what it is like* to be. In what manner, how characterized, do these beings emerge? For Tillich, the ontological

---

[3] *ST*, p. 163.

question seems to be, not *an sit,* but *quid sit.* "Ontology is possible because there are concepts which are less universal than being but more universal than . . . any concept designating a realm of beings."[4]

It is extremely important, I think, to understand what is being said here. Without such an insight the rest of what Tillich will say will seem highly confusing, if not absurd. The crucial point is this: for Tillich, *being-itself* is an ambiguous term. As the above quotations indicate, *being* is something you can think: it is the most universal concept. *Being,* therefore, means the mental mirroring of *essence,* not of phenomenal givenness, or existence. When the term *being* is used to designate *existence*—and this is the case with any philosopher—there is in it no thinkable content beyond the recognition of a certain state of things, a certain givenness—as Kant's example of the real and the possible hundred dollars brings out quite clearly. The additional note of objective factuality seems to add nothing when existence is included in, assumed by, or masked behind the discussion of essence.

To continue, the expression *being-itself* can mean simply *to be present in experience, to be real, to be a "being."* It is in this sense that being is the most universal of concepts. For Tillich, however, this is the loose, conversational sense of the expression. On the other hand, *being-itself* can also be the entire and unrelated content of a concept—not phenomenal givenness any more, not being as qualified in any fashion by internal differentiation, not being as threatened and limited by non-being—no, just being-itself. *Being-itself* in this sense is quite as univocal as "a being," *this one*—and this sense is the primary one with Tillich. As the only proper name of God it is the keystone of his whole system. The great paradox of the system is, then, that its highest concept is arrived at through the subtraction of all qualification such as would characterize "a special group of beings." The result is that, for the human mind that conceives it, the notion *being-itself* is quite without proper content. All that it designates is a certain

---

[4] *ST,* p. 164.

state of affairs, namely, that the beings of experience can elicit the ontological question as stated above. A further result, of course, is that they cannot supply its answer; because the system takes the *esse* of phenomena for granted and turns resolutely to the study of essences, and because, consequently, its highest essence is simply what remains after the lower ones have been distilled of differences—because of this it becomes impossible for the philosophical side of the system to go beyond the limits set by phenomena. So the philosopher's task is to discover and relate the categories that structure experience.

What are these categories? Says Tillich, "It is possible to distinguish four levels of ontological concepts."[5] The first of them is "the basic ontological structure that is the implicit condition of the ontological question." This structure, as will be the case with the other categories or concepts as well, is a polarity of principles, not a genus.[6] The two principles at the first level are "an asking subject and an object about which the question is asked;" the question "presupposes the subject—object structure of being, which in turn presupposes the self-world structure as the basic articulation of being."[7] Tillich's intent here is not, as his subsequent exposition indicates, to posit some Absolute Self from which a world emanates; or at least it is not his intent to posit it as falling within the experience of man. It seems, rather, that he is saying that the first thing every being notices about itself (or would notice, were it conscious) is that there are other beings around it, a world. The second level of ontological concepts is derived immediately from this presupposition; it deals with "the elements which *constitute* the basic structure of being."[8] Here we find three polarities; identity and universality, dynamics and form, and freedom and destiny.

It would appear that Tillich is here simply restating in more up-to-date language the traditional philosophical problems of the

---

[5] *ST,* pp. 164-165.
[6] *ST,* p. 164.
[7] *Ibid.*
[8] *Ibid.*

one and the many, or participation, of change, and of necessity. An explanation is sought for the relation of the self to the whole in which it finds itself; then of the changeability of the self-whole relation; and then of what makes such a changing relation possible, freedom in man, and in other beings at least their contingency: the entire given might have been otherwise.

The third level of ontological concepts flows immediately from the consideration of freedom, or contingency. It is that of "the conditions of existence."[9] "Finite freedom is the turning point from the idea of being to existence,"[10] because "whatever exists, that is, 'stands out' of mere potentiality, is more than it is in the state of mere potentiality and less than it could be in the power of its essential nature."[11] The third level of ontological concepts, then, is the place where existence, having been tossed out of the system at the beginning, climbs back in. It should be noted, just in passing, that the discussion is about, not temporally successive moments, but levels of simultaneously given experience. In any case, it is the experience of freedom that leads one to notice the discrepancy between ideas and things. No thing embodies in itself all the perfection that the idea of it implies. Thus it is that what was spoken of before simply as freedom must now be qualified as *finite* freedom. "All the categories of thought and reality express this situation. To be something is to be finite."[12] Finally, the fourth level of ontological concepts is that of "the categories of being and knowing."[13] There are many of them, but the chief ones are time, space, substance, and causality. They are the fields within which the self-world relation is seen to change. Since the finite is finally encountered only through these categories, and not in any other way, "systematic theology must deal with them, of course not in terms of a developed system of categories, but in a way which shows their significance for the question of God, the

9 *Ibid.*
10 *ST*, p. 165.
11 *ST*, p. 203.
12 *ST*, p. 190.
13 *ST*, p. 164.

question to which the entire ontological analysis leads."[14]

Still, "in order to experience his finitude, man must look at himself from the point of view of a potential infinity . . . He is able to do so, although not in concrete terms, but only as an abstract possibility."[15] Thus, "infinity is a directing concept, not a constituting concept. It directs the mind to exprerience its own unlimited potentialities, but does not establish the *existence* of an infinite being."[16] One can therefore summarize the moves made thus far in the following manner: 1. Phenomena are given. 2. A postulate is given, namely, that philosophy is the study of essences. 3. Turning to phenomena, one abstracts the essence *being,* or *being-itself,* or *being-unlimited.* Because of its limitlessness, however, this concept is philosophically useless. 4. One therefore begins again, this time by abstracting the polar principles of the phenomenal free subject. Because of the polar principle of freedom the subject is seen to stand in contradistinction to its own essence, and therefore to that essence above all which resulted from the purification of its own essence, namely, *being-itself.* 5. Philosophy thus arrives at the perception of a super-polarity between the free subject and being-itself, or between the phenomenal finite, encountered in the categories of time, space, substance, and causality, and the ideal infinite.

* * *

Before going any further into Tillich's system, however, one really ought to stop and reconsider a problem occurring in what has already been said of it. It is this: what does Tillich understand of participation in being? If the idea or essence of being-itself is, in effect, univocal, how can he speak, for example, of the participation of the self in the world? What does he mean by participation, further, if *being,* as used to speak of the beings of

---

[14] *ST,* p. 192.
[15] *ST,* p. 190.
[16] *Ibid.*

experience, simply means *givenness,* the givenness of phenomena, each of whose existence is seen only in comparison with its own—totally enclosed—essence? The answer to these questions, it would seem, is to be found in the *examples* that Tillich uses in his treatment of participation.

> An individual leaf participates in the natural structures and forces which act upon it and which are acted upon by it. ... Man participates in the universe through the rational structure of the mind and reality. Considered environmentally, he participates in a very small section of reality; he is surpassed in some respects by migrating animals. Considered cosmically, he participates in the universe because the universal structures, forms, and laws are open to him. ... The universals make man universal; language proves that he is *microcosmos.* Through the universals man participates in the remotest stars and the remotest past. ... Man participates in all levels of life, but he participates fully only in that level of life which he is himself—he has communion only with persons. ... In the resistance of the other person the person is born.[17]

From these examples I can draw but one conclusion: for Tillich, participation takes place on the level of *operation.* And this is quite consistent with his essentialism, for essence, or nature, is ordinarily understood to be the principle, not of existence, but of operation. Still, where there is no participation at the level of pure existence, must one not conclude to philosophical nominalism? Tillich answers:

> According to nominalism, only the individual has ontological reality; universals are verbal signs which point to similarities between individual things. Knowledge, therefore, is not participation; it is an external act of grasping and controlling things. ... Even the empiricist must acknowledge that every- thing approachable by knowledge must have the structure of

17 *ST,* pp. 176 f.

"being knowable." And this structure includes by definition a mutual participation of the knower and the known. Radical nominalism is unable to make the process of knowing understandable.[18]

Granted that Tillich is not a *radical* nominalist, he yet seems to be very much of a *moderate* one. The answer he presents here appears to beg the question: to be knowable by another is entirely compatible with being rather like him, with mutually participating in the same similitude—*but only on the operational level*. One would still like to know what, for Tillich, *founds* the possibility of this known likeness. In *The Courage to Be* Tillich describes participation as "a partial identity and a partial non-identity."[19] The question is whether this gap can ever be closed with selfhood remaining intact. There would be no point in speaking of participation at all if there were complete identity at all levels; but, on the other hand, is it logical to speak of (unqualified) partial non-identity? The root problem seems to be that Tillich thinks nominalism is merely a logical problem, not an ontological one. Logically, or operationally, it is true, he is not a nominalist; ontologically, he seems to remain one.

* * *

But to continue with our summary of Tillich's outlook, his disavowal of the traditional proofs for the existence of God, which at first blush strikes the traditionally-minded theologian as so alarming, is only the entirely consistent result of the philosophical stance he has taken. Tillich considers in turn the ontological and the cosmological arguments. The ontological argument, he says, shows that the question of God is possible. "The ontological argument in its various forms gives a description of the way in which potential infinity is present in actual finitude."[20] That is to

18 *ST*, p. 177.
19 *The Courage to Be* p. 100.
20 *ST*, p. 206

say, "the arguments for the existence of God neither are arguments nor are the proof of the existence of God. They are expressions of the *question* of God which is implied in human finitude."[21] To begin with, the expression *existence of God* embodies a contradiction *in adiecto:* given the meaning of *existence* in Tillich's philosophy, God cannot possibly *exist.* Tillich remarks: "The scholastics were right when they asserted that in God there is no difference between essence and existence. But . . . actually they did not mean existence. They meant the reality, the validity, the truth of the idea of God, an idea which cannot carry the connotation of some*thing* or some*one* who might or might not exist."[22] And it is precisely the reality or validity of the idea of God that makes the construction of a proof about God impossible: God is already present in the situation into which he was argumentatively to be brought. The ontological argument is inescapably circular. "The question of God is possible because an awareness of God is present in the question of God. This awareness precedes the question. It is not the result of the argument but its presupposition. . . . An awareness of the infinite is included in man's awareness of finitude."[23] In other words, when man compares his existence with his essence, or with any more general essence, he must necessarily, in effect, compare his own existential finitude with the ideas of absolute being, truth, and goodness. There is no proof here at all, but only the complementary awareness of real finitude and ideal (not yet necessarily real) infinity. Could you not conceive, let us say, truth itself, you would not know you are finite when you make true judgments.

The cosmological argument, on the other hand, shows that the question of God is necessary.[24] It is the result of the frustrations of the Tillichian ontology. If, after all, you have taken this ontology seriously, you have thereby reduced yourself to meaning-

---

21 *ST,* p. 205.
22 *Ibid.*
23 *ST,* p. 206.
24 *ST,* pp. 208 ff.

lessness. Because time, space, substance, and causality, and also teleity, are simply the field of action of finite being, you really do not know where you have come from or where you are going—or, to continue the metaphor, where the whole field is. Nor can the cosmological argument tell you; because its ingredients are simply the (essential) categories of Tillichian existence, they cannot meaningfully be employed beyond the confines of it. They are but the schematization of your anxiety. Tillich summarizes: "These arguments being the ontological analysis to a conclusion by disclosing that the question of God is implied in the finite structure of being. In performing this function, they partially accept and partially reject the traditional natural theology, and they drive reason to the quest for revelation."[25]

* * *

There is, then, a way out. "Revelation," for Tillich, "is first of all the experience in which an ultimate concern grasps the human mind and creates a community in which this concern expresses itself in symbols of action, imagination, and thought."[26] Faith is correlative to revelation; it is "the state of being ultimately concerned,"[27] That is to say, of accepting revelation, of allowing oneself to be grasped. It is important to note, apropos of Tillich's use of the terms *revelation* and *faith*, that he does not, by these terms, mean to suggest any kind of supernatural solution to the problem of God. Because of Tillich's view of the fundamental subject-object structure of being it is in principle impossible for him to make any meaningful distinction between natural and supernatural. *Revelation* and *faith*, then, simply refer to a kind of gnostic experience in which man attains to "the courage to be," or discovers that life under conditions of "existential estrangement" from his essence can yet have meaning and value.[28] Now if faith is

25 *ST*, p. 210.
26 *Dynamics of Faith* (New York, 1958), p. 78.
27 *Ibid.*, p. 1.
28 Cf. *ST*, pp. 111-115; *ST*, II, pp. 173-176; *ST*, III, pp. 111-114.

this consoling discovery of or admission of ultimate concern,

> God . . . is the name for what concerns man ultimately. This does not mean that first there is a being called God and then the demand that man should be ultimately concerned about him. It means that whatever concerns a man ultimately becomes god for him, and conversely, that a man can be concerned only about that which is god for him.[29]

It is evident that in terms of traditional theology *faith* and *ultimate concern* can, as used here, be explained entirely in terms of the "natural," even if the "supernatural" is not in principle excluded. Some critics have wished to go further, however, and have seen in the "god" that this "faith" discovers a mere symbol of the ideals of atheistic humanism. Such a conclusion seems excessive, however, and really quite at variance with Tillich's intentions. In the light of Maritain's essay, "The Immanent Dialectic of the First Act of Freedom," it seems more reasonable to suggest that Tillich has in mind something very close to Aquinas' view of ethical responsibility in the unsophisticated mind. For Aquinas and Maritain, man is thoroughly capable of opting for or against the ultimate Good even though that Good is far from adequately conceptualized:

> When man begins to have the use of reason, he is not entirely excused from the guilt of venial or mortal sin. Now the first thing that occurs to a man to think about then is to deliberate about himself. And if he then direct himself to the due end, he will, by means of grace, receive the remission of original sin: whereas if he does not then direct himself to the due end, *as far as he is capable of discretion at that particular age,* he will sin mortally, through not doing that which is in his power to do.[30]

---

29 *ST,* p. 211.
30 *Summa theologiae,* tr. English Dominicans (New York, 1948), I-II, 89, 6. Italics added. Cf. Maritain, *loc. cit.,* pp. 66-85.

These lines of Aquinas suggest that there is a place in traditional theology for Tillich's ultimate concern, for, in effect, creative and loyal receptivity vis-a-vis an unknown God. All Tillich seems to be saying is that, in any case, the real God is perforce the "god" of man's conceptualization.

Still, *ultimate concern* is a troublesome expression; it "points to a tension in human experience."[31] A concern has to have an object: God, as what concerns man, or man's "concern," must therefore be concrete. At the same time, an ultimate concern must be truly ultimate: it must transcend all the concrete but finite concerns in man's life—but such transcendence is a hard thing to maintain. Thus, says Tillich, "The conflict between the concreteness and the ultimacy of the religious concern . . . is the key to understanding the dynamics of the history of religion, and it is the basic problem of every doctrine of God."[32]

Moving through a typological analysis of the history of religion, Tillich comes, on the side of ultimacy, to the expression *being-itself*. This expression, or its variants *ground-of-being* and *power-of-being,* is the *proper* name of God, of man's ultimate concern. Man, imprisoned within finite existence, is dissatisfied with his lot. He wants to get beyond finite existence, but the god who is the highest *existent* remains finite. Man wants to get beyond finite essence, even, but the god who is the highest knowable *essence* is the pantheist god, and he, too, is finite.[33] The only solution is to move backward from the four levels of ontological concepts, back, that is, to the idea of being-itself. Only at this point a serious problem arises.

When the notion being-itself first appeared it was characterized as being quite empty of content. It was unlimited by particularities; in a word, it was in-finite—but with a negative, vacuous infinity. When being-itself appears this time it is meant to designate an inconceivable fullness—a positive infinity, so to speak. How did this happen? As nearly as I can determine, no

[31] *ST,* p. 211.
[32] *Ibid.*
[33] *ST,* p. 236.

explanation is offered. Tillich appears to argue *ab esse ad posse.* In other words, one is invited to make the experiment, or more exactly, offer oneself for the experiment. The man who is grasped by ultimate concern *knows* that *being-itself* is no longer an empty abstraction but the proper name of ultimate reality.[34]

Be that as it may, a philosophically more satisfying explanation is suggested by these Augustinian-sounding lines from *The Courage to Be:* "The vitality that can stand the abyss of meaninglessness is aware of a hidden meaning within the destruction of meaning. . . . Even in the state of despair one has enough being to make despair possible."[35] The argument here is rather like Augustine's refutation of total scepticism. Meaninglessness and despair are given, as indisputable facts of experience, but precisely because they are given, God, too, is posited. The *fact* of anxious ultimate concern truly appears to be a sort of intellectual bridge from negative to positive infinity. From the reality of ultimate concern as a subjective disposition, then, one can argue to the reality of ultimate concern in the objective, concrete sense, that is, as being-itself, or God. Once again, one might add, existence has found a way to climb back into the system.

So God is being-itself. And also the "ground," or "power," of being—which two expressions some have found rather disturbing. Still, there does not seem to be any reason for not reading these expressions in a quite traditional manner. In speaking of providence, for example, Aquinas writes:

Now every creature may be compared to God as the air is to the sun which enlightens it. For as the sun possesses light by its nature, and as the air is enlightened by sharing the sun's nature, so God alone is being by virtue of his own essence, since his essence is his existence; whereas every creature has being by participation, so that its essence is not its existence. Therefore, as Augustine says, "if the ruling power of God were withdrawn

34 *ST,* pp. 211-215.
35 *The Courage to Be* (New Haven, 1952), p. 177.

from his creatures, their nature would at once cease, and all nature would collapse."[36]

Whether one moves from the sun downward or the ground upward, the relationship does seem to be the same. It might even be said that Tillich's ground and power metaphors tend to correct the ontological poverty of his notion of participation. Nevertheless, they do not correct it enough to allow Tillich actually to frame a proof for the reality of God. Such would-be proofs merely raise the question of God, or what comes to the same, precipitate man into despair. A little ironically, perhaps, it is not the formulation of the question of God, but the fact that someone formulates this question that demonstrates the reality of God. But then, one wonders, was not this just what the rejected formulation fundamentally set out to do? After all, Aquinas' first way *does* begin with the words, "Certum est enim, et sensu constat, aliqua moveri in hoc mundo." If, therefore, Tillich's grasp of the niceties of medieval thought seems a bit shaky now and then, it is precisely in these suspicious-sounding ground and power metaphors that his fundamentally sound intent reaffirms itself.

Even if the best name for God is being-itself, however, most of mankind have preferred other names for him. They have spoken of him in symbols, terms that are "affirmed and negated at the same time."[37] Symbolic language is possible "because that which is infinite is being-itself and because everything participates in being-itself. . . . The *analogia entis* gives us our only justification for speaking at all about God. It is based on the fact that God must be understood as being-itself."[38] Curiously, this passage could be read meaningfully in either a Tillichian or a Thomist context. To the writer, though, it seems that here the *analogia entis* is nevertheless located in the realm of understanding, not that of existence. This interpretation at least coheres with Tillich's

---

36 *Summa theologiae*, I, 104, 1.
37 *ST*, p. 239.
38 *ST*, pp. 239 f.

statement that "the doctrine of creation is the *basic* description of the relation between God and the world."[39] The primary reality of the creature seems here to be, not its own act of being, simply, but its act, so to speak, of being-a-creature. The dominant essentialism of Tillich's thought seems to preclude his speaking of creator and creature purely in terms of being. Nonetheless, in the course of history, in the interval between creatures' "falling out of" God and their eschatological "essentialization" in him, it is perfectly permissible to employ their existentially wounded essences as fragmentary analogates, or symbols, of their primal ground.[40]

The symbols that men use for God correspond to the first, second, and fourth levels of ontological concepts.[41] In terms of the first level, God is holy, omnipotent, eternal, omnipresent, omniscient, just, and loving. In terms of the second level, God is the Living God, and as living in such a way as to be fulfilled in himself, he is Spirit.[42] In terms of the fourth level, he is creator. The final synthesis of Tillich's picture of God revolves around two words, Lord and Father.

> The symbols "life," "spirit," "power," "love," "grace," etc., as applied to God in devotional life are elements of the two main symbols of a person-to-person relationship with God, namely, God as Lord and God as Father. . . . While Lord is basically the expression of man's relation to the God who is holy power, Father is basically the expression of man's relation to the God who is holy love. The concept "Lord" expresses the distance; the concept "father," the unity.[43]

The fact remains, nevertheless, that the guarantee of religious picture-thinking is a carefully worked-out philosophical theology.

---

[39] *ST,* p. 252. Italics added.
[40] Cf. *ST,* pp. 252-261; *ST,* III, 396-401.
[41] *ST,* pp. 241-289.
[42] Regarding Tillich's theology of the Trinity, cf. *ST,* III, pp. 283-294.
[43] *ST,* p. 287.

In other words, the language of prayer and the language of philosophy have nothing to fear from one another. While "the ego-thou relation . . . always is implicit," prayer moves freely: "Often a prayer which starts with addressing itself to God as Lord and Father moves over into a contemplation of the mystery of the divine ground. Conversely, a meditation about the divine ground may end in a prayer to God as Lord or Father."[44]

*   *   *

The purpose of the foregoing comparative exposition was not—appearances notwithstanding—to show that Tillich is a bashful Thomist! It is perfectly plain that he is not. It was to point out, rather, that there is a "legitimate place" for his system in the universe of tradition-conscious theological thought. Just where, then, does he fit in? Three possible, complementary, categorizations will be suggested here.

In the first place, despite all the show of system, Tillich is basically an intuitionist. As noted above, the mainspring of Tillich's way to God is the gnostic moment of being grasped by ultimate concern, what Tillich himself calls a "mystical a priori."[45] What "reasoning" fails to do, a moment of lived insight, or intuition, accomplishes. Along this line, Jacques Maritain himself has written some surprisingly Tillichian-sounding lines. In his essay "A New Approach to God" he states:

Three intellective leaps—to actual existence as asserting itself independently from me; from this sheer objective existence to my own threatened existence; and from my existence spoiled with nothingness to absolute existence—are achieved within that same and unique intuition, which philosophers would explain as the intuitive perception of the essentially analogical content of the first concept, the concept of Being.

[44] *ST*, p. 289.
[45] *ST*, p. 9.

In "a wordless process of reasoning," Maritain continues,

> I see that the universal whole, whose part I am, is Being-with-nothingness, from the very fact that I am part of it; so that finally, since the universal whole does not exist by itself, there is another Whole, a separate one, another Being, transcendent and self-sufficient and unknown in itself and activating all beings, which is Being-without-nothingness, that is, self-subsisting Being, Being existing through itself.[46]

Furthermore, when a man does not despair over "being-with-nothingness," but instead

> directs his life, toward the good for the sake of the good, then he directs his life, even without knowing it, toward the absolute Good, and in this way knows God vitally, though unawares, by virtue of the inner dynamism of his choice of good—even if he does not know God in any conscious fashion and by means of any conceptual knowledge.[47]

The point here is simply that there is considerable similarity between Maritain's intuitive natural reason and Tillich's courage-through-faith. At least in Maritain's universe, there is a legitimate place for an intuitive, non-conceptual way to God. And, because of the crucial importance of the "mystical a priori" in Tillich's "system," what Tillich actually does seems very like what Maritain has described in the lines just quoted. Still—and Maritain would surely agree—all the intuition in the world does not of itself make one a metaphysician, or metaphysical theologian.

In the second place, therefore, some interpretation must be made of Tillich's extensive preoccupation with philosophy. It is clear that he is not a metaphysician in the grand style, such as Aquinas or Hegel, or their latter-day interpreters. Despite his

---

[46] *Op. cit.*, pp. 88 f.
[47] *Ibid.*, p. 91.

penchant for metaphysical *language,* a good case might be made for considering him a kind of phenomenologist, if that designation be understood very broadly. What Tillich's celebrated "method of correlation" seeks to do is to show how the traditional Christian symbols answer the questions that arise out of man's existential situation.[48] The method of correlation thus demands a dual venture into phenomenal analysis: both man's present situation and the symbols that come to his rescue must be subjected to scrutiny. It is important to bear in mind, however, that the symbols are vehicles of salvation precisely as symbols, not as metaphysical statements, even if metaphysical language should happen to be the literary *genre* to which they belong. At no point in Tillich's system is the basically phenomenological character of his thinking more evident than in the question of God. Here, it will be recalled, the metaphysical language of the traditional proofs is to be valued, not for what it actually says, but solely as a symptom of a human problem. The link between existential problem and Christian symbol, or between being as negative vacuousness to being as positive fullness, is precisely the phenomenologically described moment of being-grasped by ultimate concern. In a word, Tillich's treatment of the area of natural theology is a kind of natural history of the question of God and the answers made to it.

For a self-proclaimed Christian theologian, at any rate, such an approach is not without its problems. One of Tillich's most perceptive critics, the late Gustave Weigel, put the matter thus:

> Tillich rejects natural theology on principle, but his whole theology is not only a natural theology, but more ominously, a naturalistic theology. . . . The question a Catholic asks is this: Does the theology of Tillich add anything to his phenomenology, or is it only the phenomenology written theologically? One reluctantly feels that the theology does nothing to correct the phenomenology.[49]

[48] *ST,* pp. 59-68.
[49] *Paul Tillich in Catholic Thought,* p. 17.

As has already been pointed out, Tillich's moment of gnostic insight is capable of either a naturalist or a supernaturalist interpretation. Entirely correctly, according to his principles, Tillich attempts neither. Still, one would like to know, who or what produces this moment? Is "ultimate concern," like the Buddhist nirvana, something one can do for himself, or can it be brought about solely by some supernatural agency? For reasons of economy in argument, the naturalistic explanation seems preferable. But then does not this essentially descriptive theology appear to sacrifice what might be termed the prophetic element in the Christian proclamation of God? Even at the purely natural, philosophical level, moreover, Tillich's God, strictly speaking, remains unnamed. There is no organic link of philosophical understanding between the experience of the nature of being and language about being. Unlike Maritain, Tillich is not in a position to have the philosopher *explain,* as opposed to merely *record,* what happens in the intuitive life of the ordinary man. Whether Tillich's philosophical theology is thereby better or worse off is surely open to further debate, but no debate is likely to go very far if the radically non-metaphysical character of Tillich's thinking is not fully appreciated.

The question of the philosophical *genre* of Tillich's God-talk leads to a third, and final, consideration. As a philosophical theologian Tillich is a system-builder, not a historian. As a friend who once studied the history of Christian thought under Tillich observed to the writer, "All the great thinkers of the past are grist for his mill." The remark is a trifle unkind, perhaps, but it does point to something that the reader of Tillich may find disconcerting. On one page Augustine is cited, on another Kierkegaard, and on another Jakob Boehme—the resulting impression being one of slap-dash eclecticism. Even if the charge of quotation out of context often has a certain plausibility, however, it must be borne in mind, in fairness to Tillich, that he had no pretension to be a historian of doctrine. Rather, it would seem, he was simply citing illustrations from the past of elements of an adequate contemporary theology—in a fashion not althogether unlike Aquinas' marvellously tendentious reading of the Church

Fathers! Still, what is the unifying scheme for this apparent eclecticism?

The Ariadne's thread for Tillich's passage through metaphysical language, existentialism, and phenomenology to Christian symbolism would seem to be the mature philosphy of Schelling. This philosophy was the subject of Tillich's dissertations for both the doctorate in philosophy and the licentiate in theology.[50] It could even seriously be argued that Tillich is to Schelling what Maritain is to Aquinas: in both cases throught from the past is put to use in answering twentieth-century questions. To a surprising extent the Christian symbols that rescue Tillich's modern man from despair are Christian symbols as interpreted by Schelling. In particular, it would seem that it is Schelling's conception of the fall that causes Tillich's way to God to take such a circuitous path. As K.B. Osborne notes,

> In essence there is no split or estrangement (between man and God), but in Schelling's view a transcendent Fall has occurred, for Schelling's "leap" occurs on the level of *Sein* and not on that of the ego. . . .

> For Schelling, then, sin, particularly in reference to the transcendent fall, is irrational. It is the actualizing of something particular, *der Partikularwille,* over against the actualizing of the universal, *der Universalwille.* Tillich sees in this the irrational transition from essence to existence.[51]

If it be granted that existence is irrational, then, as Tillich quite consistently argues, natural theology is impossible. Schelling's and Tillich's *Urgrund* can be discerned and discussed only in terms of the "powers of reality which grasp the unconscious, or which come out of the unconscious and grasp the consciousness of men

---

50 Cf. below, *A Select Bibliography,* 4.
51 K.B. Osborne, *New Being* (The Hague, 1969), pp. 74 f.

and produce the symbolism in the history of religion."[52]

Tillich's way to God, then, would seem to be an intuitive, phenomenological representation of the mature philosophy of Schelling. To compare this way with the traditional, classical ways of Augustine and Aquinas is by no means to stand in judgement over Tillich, but simply to make clear the real nature of Tillich's achievement. We do not happen to live in a metaphysical age, and thus, despite its lack of metaphysical elegance, Tillich's way to God answers a real need. Its basic value lies, perhaps, in its delineation of the question of God, a delineation shot through with the awareness that this question can, ultimately, be answered.

A SELECT BIBLIOGRAPHY

Autobiographical Statements by Tillich. See "Autobiographical Reflections," *The Theology of Paul Tillich,* ed. C.W. Kegley and R.W. Bretall (New York, 1964), pp. 3-21; *On the Boundary* (London, 1967).

Tillich's Works. A complete bibliography of Tillich's works from 1910 to 1945 is to be found in James Luther Adams, *Paul Tillich's Philosophy of Culture, Science, and Religion* (New York, 1965), pp. 281-294. A complete bibliography of Tillich's works up to 1959 is contained in Tillich's *Gesammelte Werke,* ed. Renate Adler (Stuttgart, 1959), Vol. I, pp. 389-427. Extensive bibliographies are also to be found in C.J. Armbruster, *The Vision of Paul Tillich* (New York, 1967), pp. 311-315; K.B. Osborne, *New Being* (The Hague, 1969), pp. 216-222.

It is important to point out that Tillich's *Systematic Theology* (University of Chicago Press, 3 vols., 1951-1963) stands in relation to the rest of Tillich's *oeuvre* somewhat the way Calvin's *Institutes* stands to the rest of Calvin's equally extensive literary output: the finished, mature, quintessential Tillich can be encountered only in the *Systematic Theology.* Other works must be read either as studies for or abstracts of this work. As Tillich himself remarks, in Vol. III, p. 7, "I consider my lectures on "Systematic Theology" in Marburg, Germany, in 1924 as the beginning of my work on this system." The German edition of *Gesammelte Werke* mentioned above will eventually run to 14 vols.

---

[52] Tillich, *A History of Christian Thought,* ed. C.E. Braaten (New York, 1968), Part II, p. 152.

Secondary Works. See the bibliographies in Adams, pp. 295-303; Armbruster, pp. 314-318; Osborne, pp. 222-225. Of particular interest are the two collections, *The Theology of Paul Tillich,* ed. Kegley and Bretall, mentioned above, and *Paul Tillich in Catholic Thought,* ed. T. O'Meara and C. Weisser (Dubuque, 1964). Armbruster's work is perhaps the best overall study of Tillich's thought. Also of great value is Wilhelm and Marion Pauck, *Paul Tillich: His Life and . Thought,* Vol. I, *Life* (New York, 1976).

Tillich and Schelling. See Tillich, *Die religionsgeschichtliche Konstruktion in Schellings positiver Philosophie, ihre Voraussetzungen und Prinzipien* (Breslau, 1910), and *Mystik und Schuldbewusstsein in Schellings philosophischer Entwicklung* (Gutersloh, 1912, repr. *Gesammelte Werke,* Vol. I, pp. 11-108); D.J. O'Hanlon, *The Influence of Schelling on the Thought of Paul Tillich* (Rome: Gregorian University, dissertation, 1957); G.F. Sommer, *The Significance of the Late Philosophy of Schelling for the Formation and Interpretation of the Thought of Paul Tillich* (Durham, N.C.: Duke University, dissertation, 1960); J.W. Rathbun and F. Berwick, "Paul Tillich and the Philosophy of Schelling," *International Philosophical Quarterly* (1961), pp. 373-393.

CHAPTER XXIV

GABRIEL MARCEL ON GOD

Clyde Pax *

To understand and appreciate Gabriel Marcel's reflection on
the question of God it is necessary to see the context in which
these reflections arose and grew. Marcel did not set out in his
philosophical work to write a philosophy of religion. He was
lead to inquire into the meaning of God in human experience
because his reflections on everyday events left him unsatisfied
until he had dug down to the ultimate, and for him the
religious, dimensions of these experiences. Unless one has an
appreciation of what Marcel means by philosophy and some
knowledge of the route he has followed, his philosophy of
religion will appear to lack rigor and in the end may appear
simply as the record of one individual's inability to cope with
life without God.

For Marcel philosophizing begins in dissatisfaction with the
situations in which we find ourselves. He likens the metaphysician to a sick person who is tossing and turning to find a
comfortable position. If there is no discomfort, that is, if there
are no antinomies in our experience, there is no need and, in
fact, no sense or possible meaning in trying to make the
antinomic intelligible by philosophical reflection.[1] This understanding of philosophy gives to all of Marcel's work a certain
pragmatic dimension; it is, however, a pragmatic dimension
which seeks the ultimate meaning of life, or more specifically,
the ultimate meaning of "my life." Because it is my life which

---

*Professor of Philosophy, College of the Holy Cross, Worcester, Massachusetts, U.S.A.

1 *The Mystery of Being*, I, Ch. 1; cf *Metaphysical Journal*, p. 290.

has to be understood and made meaningful in the total experience of the world and of other people, each one of us must do his philosophizing for himself even though others may lead us or prod us to further effort.

This personal and practical character of philosophy makes it impossible to separate the result, or the fruit of philosophy from the search itself. The goal of philosophical reflection is nothing else but the concrete resolving of the difficulties which originally gave rise to the search.[2] Nothing of philosophical worth is gained from the study of the history of philosophy unless one can first step into the questions which prompted the philosophers to reflection.

Although such a linking of the result to the origin of the search makes it necessary that philosophy be an affair of the individual, it is by no means Marcel's intention to make philosophy into a purely subjective experience. His meaning is rather to show that philosophy possesses a universality different from that of the objective sciences. Since philosophy is the attempt to bring light and meaning, by means of reflection, to on-going life it can never leave the individual who is experiencing out of account. Its fruit is not some "product" which is simply there for the would-be taker or spectator, and the universality possible in philosophy is not the objectively necessary judgment which is available without reference to the origin and route by which it was uncovered. If there is a universality in philosophy, and Marcel does not doubt its possibility, it must arise from a common effort to resolve difficulties and to bring understanding and reason to experiences which are present in my life and also present in the lives of others. This understanding of philosophy carries all the way through Marcel's work and in his philosophy of religion leads him eventually to an appeal to thou my Ultimate Recourse rather than to the affirmation of an objective First Cause or an *ens realissimum*.

---

2   *The Mystery of Being,* I, 6.

More than any other area of experience, the presence of conflict and lack of mutual understanding among persons has troubled Marcel all of his life. It is this area, therefore, which provided him with the data for his philosophical reflection as well as for his dramatic work and set him on the path which leads him ultimately to reflection on the question of religion. Who am I, what is my life, who are we who can both respect and betray one another? It is questions such as these which caused Marcel to philosophize and to bring his reflections to bear on the themes of hope, fidelity, betrayal, death, as well as on the necessity of questioning who am I who can pose such questions about the *total* meaning of my life.

The experiences indicated by such questioning make it clearly impossible to exclude the one who is experiencing from the content of the experience and still to have any content remain. My life has no content apart from my living it. Hope and betrayal are real as the hope and betrayal of those who are hoping and betraying. Consequently to ask about such actions within Marcel's concrete understanding of philosophy means to include the one acting in the "content" of the question. This encroachment of the content upon the one who is experiencing, and in philosophical reflection upon the one who is questioning, Marcel developed into the notion of mystery and distinguished it from the notion of problem.[3] Some issues which arise in life allow me to step back from the matter, to take an objective look and to propose an objective solution. I can, for example, take an objective look at a business operation and make an objective judgment that the volume of business makes it necessary to hire additional personnel. Or if I am planning to make a trip, I can make an objective determination of which route is most direct. The field of geometry might be taken as providing a paradigm for this kind of question, that is, a paradigm of the problematic question.

In contrast to this realm of the problematic, which allows us to set the matter clearly outside of ourselves and to view it from

---

3   "The Ontological Mystery," *The Philosophy of Existence,* pp. 1-31; *Being and Having,* p. 126.

every angle, the realm of persons and of personal actions does not allow us to step back from our involvement with the issue. There is no locus except from within freedom, for example, from which I might question the value and meaning of freedom; nor is it possible to speak about the personal worth of friendships or the pain of betrayal if I first step back from the experience. Similarly, it is only from within my life that I can ask who I am and from within our lives that we can ask who we are.

The distinction between problem and mystery is a fundamental epistemological distinction inasmuch as mystery indicates an order of experience and knowledge beyond the realm where the distinction of subject and object are strictly applicable. The indication of this order is not the rejection of the distinction of subject and object nor the rejection of objective knowledge but it is a pointing toward a kind of knowledge in which the categories of objective universality and necessity are not useful categories for understanding and explaining our experience. In Marcel's view this realm of mystery pervades all issues and experiences in which we are involved in a personal way. This means, therefore, that a concrete philosophy, one that does not leave the experiencer out of account, must be chiefly a probing of mystery and the worth of this probing cannot be measured totally by objective criteria.

In the light of his explanation it would be a serious mistake to think that Marcel's use of the word mystery indicates something akin to a supernatural order as, for example, the mysteries of a religion, or something shrouded in semi-darkness. He is using the term in a precise technical sense to underscore the fact that some kinds of experience cannot be objectified and studied in an objective fashion without denaturing the experiences as they present themselves. Stated in a more positive way, Marcel is contending that a concrete analysis of personal and inter-personal experiences will reveal the necessity of accepting a meaning of truth and of universality beyond and different from objective truth and universality.

The order of experience indicated by the word mystery can be approached in a somewhat different fashion by means of another distinction central to Marcel's work, namely, the distinction between primary and secondary reflection. A first level of reflection, by which we distance ourselves from on-going lived experience, separates us from the objects of experience and makes possible the recognition of objects as other than ourselves as well as the recognition of ourselves as subjects distinct from the objects of experience. This distancing makes possible a clear view of the matter thus set before us and gives a definite content to experience, which content can be properly studied in itself with no need to ask who the experiencer is. Together with the clarity which results from the setting of definite boundaries limiting and defining the content and separating it from the present knower there arises the basis and possibility of objective universality.

It is important to note, however, that the clarity thus achieved is not in the lived experiences but is the result of a mediation by consciousness in its moment of reflection; the clarity and objectivity are the result of a modification of lived experience. It is within this modification that the empirical sciences, common sense and objective universality have their locus. However, when we advert to the fact that the distinction between subject and object is a result of a modification of lived experience, it becomes meaningful to ask how this modification was possible. By asking this question consciousness opens to itself a further level of reflection. In reference to the uncovering of objectivity, this further reflection represents a meta-reflection or what Marcel calls secondary reflection. This secondary reflection takes the fact of primary reflection itself as its "object" and asks what were the conditions which allowed primary reflection to take place, that is, the conditions which allowed me to see objects in the world and I myself as a subject independent of these objects.[4]

The most significant result of this secondary reflection is that it reveals that the distinction and separation of the subject and object rests upon a more fundamental belonging together or *commercium* which was already in operation and provided the basis for the distinction between what is designated in primary reflection as subject and object. Only if knower and known have

4 *The Philosophy of Existence*, p. 14.

already been together in a kind of union more fundamental than their separation is experience understandable. Consequently, in revealing this fundamental belonging together of knower and known, secondary reflection, in one stroke gives the basis for primary reflection (and its resultant objective account of experience) and is "recuperative" of the divisive account of experience rendered by primary reflection. In the light of this understanding of primary and secondary reflection Marcel can argue, without falling into a simple begging of the question, that secondary reflection must be possible and the order of being which it reveals existent, or else primary reflection also would be impossible.

If we recall that to philosophize for Marcel means to bring reflection to bear on life it is clear that his philosophy must be principally a probing of the order of mystery. This probing is, however, a work of reflection; it is a reflection that does not denigrate objective knowledge but by being more fully reflection than primary reflection invites us to an understanding of truth beyond that truth which is objectively valid. Consistent with his understanding of the nature and goal of philosophy Marcel directs most of his work toward the consideration of our personal involvements: toward perception, toward my having a body which is in some way my *own* body, toward friendship, promise-making, betrayal, hope and death. A brief examination of the way Marcel's reflection unfolds in reference to several of these themes will lead us to his reflections about God. The act of perceiving will serve well as a place to begin.

True to his desire to be faithful to concrete experience Marcel's concern with perception is a concern to know who I am as perceiver. He describes his approach as phenomenological, meaning thereby that he wishes to understand perception without failing to take notice of the link between perceiver and what is perceived. When this link is respected it becomes clear that perception cannot be understood as the transmission of a message between a sender called the object or stimulus and a receiving subject. Such an explanation, which Marcel takes to be typical of empirical philosophy and common sense, leaves totally unexplained the *act* of perceiving. No more successful is the idealistic account which seeks to explain perception entirely in terms of the action of the knowing subject; this account fails to take seriously the character of the perceived as *presenting itself* to the perceiver. A concrete description of experience must take seriously both the act of the perceiver and the data given in perception. When both are taken seriously, reflection upon the conditions which make perception possible reveals, according to Marcel, the necessity of affirming an *immediate* openness of the perceiver to the world. What is given in perception is neither *I* nor the *world* but I-to-the-world. This conclusion is, of course, in harmony with the understanding of perception generally among the phenomeno-logical thinkers. The importance for our study is that it brings to light what might be called a first level of ecstasis. The perceiver is not real in himself but as standing out of himself into the world in a non-mediatized fashion. Similarly the reality of the world and its objects is a reality which is toward consciousness. Thus the dichotomy of perceiver and perceived rests upon an order of being which is a plurality-in-unity, that is, an order in which knower and known are mutually constitutive of one another.

This does not deny the existence or value of individuality but rather insists upon individual uniqueness and value as necessary for the constitution and thereby re-defines individuality as one moment or pole in a bi-polar plurality-in-unity. To deny the individuality of either subject or known would again be to fail to take either the act or the given data seriously. Since it is in perception that we first meet existence and since the conscious knower stands out to the world, our experience of existence does not allow us to speak of existence as applying exclusively to a particular existent. What we saw above as an epistemological realm, namely the realm of mystery which is prior and founda-tional to the distinction of subject and object, is now seen as an order of being. For the perceiving subject, to be means to be beyond oneself, to have the center or at least one necessary dimension of its reality in the other than self. This same immediate openness to the world constitutes the conclusion of Marcel's analysis of my having a body which is *my* body. If I reflect upon my body not as an object but as mine, it is clear that my body is not merely an object among other objects but is the way in which I am in the world.

We have in Marcel's discussion of perception and incarnation an exposition of a first ecstasis of the experiencing individual. For a full understanding of Marcel's work it is important to emphasize that this ecstasis is where we affirm our own existence and that of the world and its objects. What is given experientially as existent is not the self or the other than self, but an order of being in which subject and object are mutually constituted and defined.

In addition to this first level which we have just considered, there is another level of ecstasis, and hence of being and knowledge, of the person not as perceiver but as free and self-conscious. In the more mature philosophizing of Marcel a third ecstasis comes to the fore, namely the ecstasis of the intersubjectivity itself, that is, an ecstasis which defines the human condition itself. It is in the uncovering of this third level of ecstasis that Marcel's philosophy of religion finds its place.

The dependence upon the other than self which we have noticed in the act of perception becomes increasingly more profound and more significant as we move to a consideration of actions which involve our persons more fully and more intimately. Entry into a relation of friendship implies the willingness to trust the other to care for my self. The recognition that another person must be respected rather than merely used implies the recognition that the other has a lien against me, that he can place a demand on my person which I can disregard only at the risk of losing standing in my own eyes. Here again I find myself as person only in an ecstasis but now in an ecstasis into another freedom rather than into the world.

In Marcel's discussion of promise-making and in his discussion of the need to bear witness, the elucidation of this ecstasis is carried to still further lengths. When I make a promise to another person—and it is only to other persons that a promise can be made—I commit myself not only to the other person but also to a future myself, whom I know at present only in hope and in commitment. Considered in its full concrete presence this means that in promise-making I am real as person in an ecstasis directed both toward the other and toward a myself who will be real in the future. When we consider the act of bearing witness, further implications come into view. When one accepts the need to bear true witness he is placing himself under the necessity of not concealing the light of truth to which he (and perhaps he alone) has access.[5] At times the necessity of revealing this light of truth works for the individual standing under judgment, at times against him. At times the weight of testimony may jeopardize my own interests or support them, or what is more telling, may jeopardize the interests of those whom I love. What is this truth that can so bind me?

Unlike the act of perceiving, personal acts of encounter are available to us only in freedom and most generally only in the freedom of others as well. It is only by free choice that I can enter into friendship or promise-making or into the realm of experience where witnessing takes place. This dependence upon freedom means that I can also refuse to enter into a possibility of friendship and commitment, or having entered, I can betray that trust placed in me. The possibility of bearing witness is also the possibility of false witnessing.

If we keep in mind that this world of persons is brought into reality by the mutual openness and mutual constitution of one another it is clear why Marcel can call fidelity the "place of being."[6] Fidelity is not the place of being in the sense of the locus of being; it is the necessary condition for the existence and reality of the personal realm. Marcel's view of persons makes it necessary to see personhood not as mere givenness but as goal to be achieved by fidelity and trust. Intersubjectivity, or human society, is likewise not simply given but is real only if and to the extent that it is nurtured and held in being by the willingness, the courage and the fidelity of its members. It is in this context that truth becomes inseparable from fidelity, that it becomes "that for the sake of

5 *Ibid.*, pp. 68 ff.
6 *Being and Having*, p. 41.

which" something is done.[7] A true friendship is one which lasts through the various obstacles which call for its dissolution, and being is that which withstands all pressures and attempts to nihilate it.[8] This view of Marcel, in which the person is real only in a mutual constitution with others, does not deny the worth of the individual person but insists upon the fact that the worth of the individual is real and is needed for others. It does, however, define individual personal worth in terms of the ability to be freely responsible and freely available to others.

We have seen part of the answer which Marcel gives to the question 'Who am I?' The experience of perception and of my having a body reveal that as perceiver I am real only by standing in an immediate openness to the world. Thus the world is given as equiprimordial with myself and existence is first experienced as designating not a particular existent but the order of experience in which I and the world are given to each other. An analagous openness or lack of identity within my own boundaries is revealed in the analysis of acts of personal encounter. In this personal order, however, the mutual constitution is accomplished in freedom and thus the reality of this order of being is brought into existence and nurtured by creative fidelity—and lessened or destroyed by the refusal by persons to become or remain available to one another. We have spoken of these two orders of experience as two levels of standing-out-of-oneself, which define the perceiver and the person.

Marcel's reflections on religion can best be seen as a continuation of the questions 'Who am I?' and 'Who are we?' As his analyses of perception and of intersubjective relations are intended to show, a lack of simple identity becomes manifest as soon as we ask who we are. This lack of identity within myself leads me to ask where in fact the center of my reality lies. In acts of friendship my center cannot lie simply within me because as friend I must wait upon the acceptance of the other and the reality of our

7 *The Mystery of Being*, I, 79 ff.
8 *The Philosophy of Existence*, p. 5.

friendship is inseparable from the standing out of self in availability to the other. My promise is real to the extent that I accept the rightfulness of the claim of the other upon me. Similarly, an analysis of perception reveals the presence of what Marcel calls an intelligible background[9] which makes possible the truth of both perception and judgment.

To attempt to answer the question of where my center lies it is necessary to carry the analyses a bit further. A careful consideration of inter-personal relations reveals not only that the personal realm is constituted by mutual availability but also that these relations can be either absolute or non-absolute. The conditional character becomes evident in that they can and often do deteriorate and fail. There is, however, an absolute or unconditional dimension possible in personal relations inasmuch as once I have committed myself to another, no obstacle including even the rejection by the one to whom my commitment has been made, can break the bond of my care and concern unless I choose to be unfaithful. From the vantage point of objective thought it is, of course, always possible to say that there is no necessity, no unconditionality, involved in the commitment because future events may well show that the commitment is broken and forgotten. This way of arguing, however, fails to note that the claim to unconditionality is not made as an objective claim but from within freedom. Evidence for the truth of commitments is provided by the example of those who do sacrifice themselves for others either in a single act or an act that is spread over many years.

Marcel refers to the presence of unconditionality in human pledges as the true sign of God's presence.[10] His question is, 'What are the conditions which render intelligible unconditional pledges, testimony in the face of death and hope which refuses to be overcome?' It is insufficient to look for the reason for the success of the promise and the testimony which endures merely within the

---

9 *The Mystery of Being,* I, 93.
10 "Theism and Personal Relationships," *Cross Currents,* Vol. I, I (Fall 1950), p. 40.

act itself because the act can either be successful or not. It is because there is no objectively necessary bond between the act of commitment and its terminus that the objective order can break into the personal realm and when the bond does not last it is often possible to point to some obstacle which interposed itself within the free realm and against which the love was unable to triumph. It is those relationships which do not fail, the love and commitment which do not end even in death and in the face of death, which call for a different order of explanation. It is in such actions that Marcel claims we must either appeal to thou my Ultimate Recourse or leave the experiences ultimately unexplained. It is in every instance possible not to make the appeal, to refuse to invoke an order of fidelity beyond myself, but the price of such refusal is that I remain unable to answer the question of my, or our, identity. The appeal is not to an exterior hypothesis or exterior being but is from within my freedom which I experience as being unable of itself to account for its own presence and movements; the "necessity" of the appeal is the necessity of retaining my own worth and it is in the appeal that I am truly given to myself.[11] In order for my limited acts of fidelity to be meaningful they must find their place in an order of reality in which it is already *given* that fidelity is preferable to infidelity. It is this *givenness* of fidelity itself, in which my fidelity partakes, which is the unconditional basis for my finite fidelities and which is ultimately the "place of being." It is always possible to immerse myself in my conditional affairs and to forget or refuse to acknowledge this more ultimate order. This satisfaction with the limited is not unlike what Heidegger calls the forgetfulness of Being. Like the forgetfulness of Being which is characterized by an excessive engagement with beings, the refusal to invoke the transcendence of God can be covered by acts of humanistic endeavor. Such acts do not become meaningless when viewed and performed in this truncated fashion, but neither do they reveal who man is except by an arbitrary closure of the question within

---

11 *Creative Fidelity*, p. 145; cf. *Problematic Man*, p. 44.

the human condition. In Marcel we have an existentialism which is courageous enough to go all the way into an existential ontology not only of human acts of perception and intersubjectivity but of the human condition itself. To begin the analysis of the human situation in terms of intentionality of consciousness and to end it with the mere givenness and opacity of the facticity of man or of human freedom is to begin with an existential analysis and to revert to an essentialism. This amounts to a failure of nerve, an unwillingness to stand before the abyss opened by self-questioning. It is in this connection that Marcel can say that perhaps my soul would remain only the him or it of the psychologists if I could not converse about my soul with God.[12] The "necessity" of the appeal is seen also in testimony when this is made in the face of death and perhaps most clearly in the condemned man who insists upon his innocence. An appeal to his innocence loses all meaning unless it is an appeal to truth and fidelity beyond all possibility of betrayal. Testimony is always an appeal beyond the given evidence, that is, an appeal to trans-cendence, and when made in the face of death is an appeal to an order of truth and faithfulness beyond the whole human condition.

The necessity of the appeal may be seen not only in testimony but in our experience of truth generally. Why do we prefer truth to falsehood and ignorance, even in those ambiguous instances when we fight against the truth? How, in the last analysis, does consciousness get its tasks suggested to it? If such questioning is serious and ultimate it does no good to tell ourselves that truth arises in particular judgments or in perception because the questioning asks about the possibility of our making judgments and our having perceptions. Any answer to such questioning can be only an appeal and the effort to lead others can serve only to awaken in them the need to advance to a level of reflection where such questioning is possible. For the individuals or the people who have already *decided* that some limited experienced good, for

12 *Metaphysical Journal*, p. 200.

example, the limited freedom which we experience, is the
sovereign good, there is no need or possibility of asking radically
'Who am I?' In such a one the metaphysical unrest which is the
spring of philosophical reflection has been stifled or has not yet
arisen.

Hope also, when it is more than mere expectation, is a creative
appeal beyond all objective evidence. Hope becomes hope
precisely in discrediting in advance the very evidence which would
wish to challenge it.[13] When a mother continues to hope for a son
who has according to all available evidence repudiated her she is
not going against the empirical evidence but by her hope is
involved in a creative effort which shall destroy or make
inconclusive all the previous evidence. Here, as in the faith of the
religious believer, the appeal is not to an exterior force but is from
within the creativity of human action and freedom and rests upon
a denial of any clearly identifiable boundaries between the person
acting and the one to whom the appeal is directed. In this, the
stance of the believer is phenomenologically very different from
that of the non-believer. The believer is affirming thou who are the
internal foundation of my own self-presence, whereas the non-
believer is concerned with the denial of an external reality which
he supposes the believer is affirming without sufficient evidence.
The non-believer says he "does not believe or know that . . . " The
believer, on the other hand, is living in the order of "I believe
in . . . "[14] While the non-believer does not find any reason to
affirm the existence of God because the circumstances and
experiences of his life do not reveal the necessity or likelihood of
the hypothesis that God exists, the believer is affirming and
appealing to thou who are beyond all structures and thus not
challenged by any set of circumstances. In the sense that faith is
an appeal to the *ultimate* it is truly self-authenticating since the
ultimate is either gratuitously given or it is not ultimate. In that it
is an *appeal,* its authentication comes from thou who cannot fail

13 *Homo Viator,* p. 67.
14 *The Mystery of Being,* II, 76 ff.

me. For Marcel as well as for the religious believer the appeal is made in freedom and can always be refused or neglected; however, once a person (or a people) begins to ask the ultimate meaning of his life he is either condemned to a lack of ultimacy within the human condition or is on the way: he is either *homo absurdus* or *homo viator.*

The insistence by Marcel that the appeal to God rests in freedom and always entails the possibility of refusal is what sets his way of creative fidelity off most sharply from that tradition of natural theology which would wish to give a logical demonstration of the existence of God. His chief concern is to bring us to a recognition of the significance of God in our daily experience and thereby to assist in the creation of a viable bond among men. In the framework of Marcel's personal and existential metaphysics a logical proof for the existence of God—and in a number of passages Marcel accepts the logical validity of the traditional arguments—[15] would bring us only to an ultimate Him or It.[16] Such an ultimate Him would be of no concern to the believer and of no help to the unbeliever. In contrast, Marcel's concern is so to change a person's view of his own reality and of his relations to others that he can awaken to his divine filiation.[17] If the task of philosophy is to go from life and back again to life, Marcel's philosophy of religion is the attempt to infuse a new vision into our interpersonal relations and with this vision a creative fidelity strong enough to withstand the evil and the absurd which constantly invite us to abandon our hope for mankind.

A SELECT BIBLIOGRAPHY

1. Works of Gabriel Marcel

Being and Having. Translated by Katherine Farrer. Westminster: Dacre Press, 1949.

---

15 Cf. *Creative Fidelity,* p. 180.
16 *The Mystery of Being,* II, 147.
17 *Homo Viator,* p. 160.

"Contemporary Atheism and the Religious Mind," *Philosophy Today,* (Winter 1960), pp. 252-62.

Creative Fidelity. Translated by Robert Rosthal. New York: Noonday Press, 1964.

The Decline of Wisdom. Translated by Manya Harari. New York: Philosophical Library, 1955.

The Existential Background of Human Dignity. Cambridge, Massachusetts: Harvard University Press, 1963.

Homo Viator: Introduction to a Metaphysics of Hope. Translated by Emma Crauford. Chicago: Regnery, 1951.

Man Against Mass Society. Translated by G.S. Fraser. Chicago: Regnery, 1952.

Metaphysical Journal. Translated by Bernard Wall. Chicago: Regnery, 1952. Includes as an appendix the essay "Existence and Objectivity."

The Mystery of Being. 2 vols. Translated by G.S. Fraser and Rene Hague. Chicago: Regnery, 1960.

Philosophical Fragments 1909-1914 and *The Philosopher and Peace.* Translated by Lionel A. Blain. Notre Dame, Indiana: University of Notre Dame Press, 1965.

The Philosophy of Existence. Translated by Manya Harari. London: Harvill Press, 1948. Issued as *The Philosophy of Existentialism,* New York: Citadel Press, 1961.

Presence and Immortality. Translated by Michael A. Mackado. Pittsburgh, Pennsylvania: Duquesne University Press, 1967.

Problematic Man. Translated by Brian Thompson. New York: Herder and Herder, 1967.

Royce's Metaphysics. Translated by Virginia and Gordon Ringer. Chicago: Regnery, 1956.

Searchings. New York: Newman Press, 1967.

"Theism and Personal Relationships," *Cross Currents* (Fall, 1950), pp. 35-42.

For a complete bibliography of Marcel's writings see Roger Troisfontaines, *De l'existence a l'être.* 2 vols. Louvain: Nauwelaerts, 1953; 2nd ed. 1968.

2. Studies

Bagot, Jean-Pierre, *Connaissance et amour: Essai sur la philosophie de Gabriel Marcel.* Paris: Beauchesne, 1958.

Bernard, Michel, *La philosophie religieuse de Gabriel Marcel.* Paris: Les Cahiers du Nouvel Humanisme, 1952.

Bertman, Martin A., "Gabriel Marcel on Hope," *Philosophy Today* (Summer, 1960), pp. 101-105.

Blain, Lionel A., "Marcel's Logic of Freedom in Proving the Existence of God," *International Philosophical Quarterly* (June, 1969), pp. 177-204.

Cain, Seymour, *Gabriel Marcel's Theory of Religious Experience.* Chicago: Microfilm 4914B, 1956.

Davis, George W., *Existentialism and Theology.* New York: Philosophical Library, 1957.

Gallagher, Kenneth T., *The Philosophy of Gabriel Marcel.* New York: Fordham University Press, 1962.

Gerber, Rudolph J., "Gabriel Marcel and the Existence of God," *Laval Théologique et Philosophique* (1969), pp. 9-22.

Gilson, Etienne, *Existentialisme chrétien: Gabriel Marcel.* Paris: Librairie Plon, 1947.

Hocking, William E., "Marcel and the Ground Issues of Metaphysics," *Philosophy and Phénomènological Research* (1954), pp. 439-469.

Jarrett-Kerr, M., "Gabriel Marcel on Faith and Unbelief," *Hibbert Journal,* (July, 1947), 321-325.

Le Thank Tri, Joseph, *L'idée de la participation chez Gabriel Marcel: Superphénomènologie d'une intersubjectivité existentielle.* Saigon: Nguyen Dinh Vuong, 1961.

Luther, Arthur, "Marcel's Metaphysics of the 'we are'," *Philosophy Today* (1966), pp. 190-203.

McCarthy, Donald, "Marcel's Absolute Thou," *Philosophy Today* 10 (1966), pp. 175-181.

Ogiermann, Helmut, "Gottes Existenz im Denken Gabriel Marcel," *Scholastik* (1954), pp. 274-289.

O'Hara, Sister M. Kevin, "Person in the Philosophy of Gabriel Marcel," *Philosophy Today* (1964), pp. 147-154.

O'Malley, John B., *The Fellowship of Being: An Essay on the Concept of Person in the Philosophy of Gabriel Marcel.* The Hague: Martinus Nijhoff, 1966.

Pax, Clyde, *An Existential Approach to God: A Study of Gabriel Marcel.* The Hague: Martinus Nijhoff, 1972.

Prini, Pietro, *Gabriel Marcel et la méthodologie de l'invérifiable.* Paris: Desclée, 1953.

Shaldenbrand, Sister M. Aloysius, "Gabriel Marcel and Proof for the Existence of God," *Studies in Philosophy and the History of Philosophy* (1961), pp. 35-56.

Schilpp, Paul A. (ed.), *The Philosophy of Gabriel Marcel.* La Salle, Illinois: The Open Court Publishing Company, (forthcoming).

Sweeney, Leo, "G. Marcel's Position on God," *The New Scholasticism,* (Winter 1970), pp. 101-124.

Troisfontaines, Roger, *De l'existence a l'être.* 2 vols. Louvain: Nauwelaerts; Paris: Vrin, 1953; 2nd ed. 1968.

For a full bibliography of studies on Marcel see Lapointe, Francois H., "Bibliography on Gabriel Marcel," *Modern Schoolman* (1971-1972), pp. 23-49.

CHAPTER XXV

THE MYSTERY OF GOD IN PROCESS THEOLOGY
Owen Sharkey *

Process Theology is not a collection of vague and isolated affirmations about the mystery of God but a vision of reality as an organic whole marked by activity, movement, change, life. The terms and concepts are related to the philosophical perspectives of Alfred North Whitehead, Charles Hartshorne, and, to a certain extent, to those of Nicolas Berdyaev and Karl Rahner.

According to this viewpoint, God, or the Absolute, is not the universe or any created thing. God is a personal loving Subject; and the created universe is not God. Yet, at the same time, the whole of reality is a connected organic unity. God enters into a living, creative, relationship with the universe. Everything in the universe exists in a connected relationship.

The emphasis in such a metaphysics is placed on God as a dynamic Act. "Whitehead," Charles Hartshorne writes, "holds the definite and carefully considered opinion that the classical versions of theism are one and all unsound, collectively a 'scandalous failure.' "[1] Alfred Whitehead, on his part, had written: "Undoubtedly, the intuitions of Greek, Hebrew, and Christian thought have alike embodied the notions of a static God

---

*Professor of Theology, St. John's University, New York, U.S.A.

1 Charles Hartshorne, "Whitehead's Idea of God," *The Philosophy of Alfred North Whitehead* (The Library of Living Philosophers, Vol. III, Northwestern University, Evanston, Illinois, 1941), p. 515. "Process Theology" originated in American theology after 1925 but may be expressed in terms associated with pure Act, Idealism, Process, or Action. Cf. R.J. Blaikie, "Being, Process, and Action in Modern Philosophy and Theology," *Scottish Journal of Theology* (1972), pp. 129-154.

condescending to the world . . . "[2] As a consequence, it has been
said that Whitehead's idea of God is an intentional departure from
most of the philosophical past.

But such statements raise the problematic: Are they true? Has
not Whitehead, himself, fallen into the error of what he termed
the "fallacy of misplaced concreteness"? Has he not become so
specific in what he affirms that the statements are not true? In
Israel, at least by the time of Jeremiah, Yahweh was a *living God.*
"Yahweh is the true God: he is the living God and the everlasting
King" (Jer. 10.10). The God of the New Testament is the God of
Israel who enters into living relations with an historic community
of people. The God of Christianity is the God of Israel (Mt.
15.31), a Personal Mystery who enters into direct relation with
men in creative, revealing, and redeeming acts and makes it
possible for men to enter into direct communion with Him.
Certainly one cannot say, either, that this tradition was not known
to the community. Thomas Aquinas will speak of the same living
God: "in Deo maxime est vita" (*Summa Theologiae,* I, q. 18, art.
3); and he will add that God is always in act: "semper in actu."

There is, however, some real issue at stake. Whitehead affirms
that God can change yet remain himself. He will say that God's
nature is *dipolar.* "He has a primordial nature and a consequent
nature."[3] Similar thoughts are found in the viewpoint of Charles
Hartshorne, Nicolas Berdyaev, and Karl Rahner. The questions
become: Can God change yet remain himself? Can God actualize
himself in new ways?

In considering, then, the theme *Process Theology and the
Mystery of God* such questions are always placed. The problem is:
How should we answer?

In such a context, I shall describe the explanations of Alfred
Whitehead, Charles Hartshorne, Nicolas Berdyaev, and Karl
Rahner. In the final portion of this essay I shall offer my personal
observations, indicating, at the same time, certain possible
consequences included in these observations. A basic difficulty

2   Whitehead, *Process and Reality,* p. 526.
3   *Ibid.,* p. 524.

appears throughout in the use of words. Each of the authors whom I shall consider uses his own words and perceives his own particular meanings. The words point towards reality yet are symbols at the same time. The use of human language reflects the choice of one description rather than another.

1. The God of Alfred Whitehead

Alfred Whitehead relates man's manner of knowing to a coherent interpretation of the whole of reality. From his perspective, coherence is the great preservative of rational sanity. What philosophical scrutiny seeks for is an interconnected interpretation of the whole.

> Speculative Philosophy is the endeavour to frame a coherent, logical, necessary system of general ideas in terms of which every element of our experience can be interpreted. By this notion of "interpretation" I mean that everything of which we are conscious, as enjoyed, perceived, willed or thought, shall have the character of a particular instance of the general scheme. Thus the philosophical scheme should be coherent, logical, and in respect to interpretation, appliable and adequate.[4]

Whitehead, in his general manner of thinking and explaining, never seeks to dogmatize but seeks, rather, to carry out a critical examination of man's manner of knowing, which has an empirical side and a rational side.

From the empirical side man knows and interprets the world of phenomena. From the rational, or subjective, side man experiences the sense, or meaning, of the whole of reality. Impressions from the senses awaken the entire faculty of knowing which then produces a living *experience* confronting a particular content, engages in intuition, and represents the intelligibility through

4 *Ibid.,* p. 4.

concepts. Whitehead agrees with Kant in saying: Thoughts without content are empty; intuitions without concepts are blind. But whereas Kant would say experience is a process from subjectivity to apparent objectivity, Whitehead inverts the analysis maintaining that human knowledge is a process from objectivity to subjectivity.

According to the epistemology of Whitehead there is, then, a possibility of metaphysics based on man's intellectual functioning in the act of experience.

We confront in our lifetime, Whitehead observes, a universe in process with an interplay of opposites:

> Joy and sorrow, good and evil, disjunction and conjunction— that is to say, the many in one—flux and permanence, greatness and triviality, freedom and necessity, God and the World. In this list, the pairs of opposites are in experience with a certain ultimate directness of intuition, except in the case of the last pair. They embody the interpretation of the cosmological problem in terms of a fundamental metaphysical doctrine . . . [5]

From the perspective of Whitehead, man has a vision of this dynamic universe. He *conceptualizes* or pictures it out. At the same time, we observe that man has a living *experience* of reality from a situation in this world. Man experiences the interplay of opposites marked by signs or data, which we call activity, change, movement, life. The universe is perceived to be caught up in the movement, process, a creative advance, and, at the same time, there appears to be a complex interrelationship of one thing to another and to the whole.

When man conceptualizes or pictures out the universe, he tends to think and speak in terms of *things* and *everything*. In such a perspective, the universe is imaged out as a world of things. But in the larger context of living experience, Whitehead maintains, one perceives a wholeness in the actuality—or presentness—of activity,

5 *Ibid.,* p. 518.

change, movement and life. At the same time, there are things in which one finds a focusing of energies, and we are able to think of particular things as energy events. These things appear to be moving towards some goal or end. We are able to speak of everything in terms of a possibility of fulfillment.

For Whitehead everything has meaning and significance but within the framework of a whole or societal universe. The significance is disclosed in what is actually going on, or is happening, in the creative advance of the universe. There are no bare facts without some meaning and significance. Further, there is no moment without some meaning and significance, and that significance is related to the significance of every other moment and the total movement. The consequences are apparent in our own human experience. We perceive that every moment has some meaning and importance. We know also that every human decision selects some possibility and cuts off others. Free decisions are effective in bringing about set events, conditions, circumstances, and situations which could have been otherwise.

> The actual world, the world of experiencing, and of thinking, and of physical activity, is a community of many diverse entities; and these entities contribute to, or derogate from, the common value of the total community. At the same time, these actual entities are, for themselves, their own value, individual and separable. They add to the common stock and yet they suffer alone. The world is a scene of solitariness in community.[6]

The relevance of Whitehead's epistemology to the problem of God's existence is obvious. Human knowledge has an empirical and rational side. From the empirical side man confronts, senses, knows, and interprets the world of phenomena. From the rational, subjective, side man experiences the intelligibility or meaning of the whole of reality. Basically, human knowledge is a process from objectivity to subjectivity, but it can and does proceed from subjectivity to objectivity. Particular attention and emphasis must

---

6   Whitehead, *Religion in the Making,* p. 88.

be given to objective evidence and the coherence of reality.

For Whitehead a reasonable interpretation of objective data, which can be pragmatically verified, allows man to ascribe coherent meaning and purpose to the universe as a whole and to affirm God's existence as the creator of all things. But such a statement is but a small part of the actual historical situation. Obviously the modern world has lost God and is seeking him. Further, today there is one central dogma in debate: What do you mean by "God"? Whitehead also adds: today is like all of man's yesterdays.[7]

When we consider the problem of God's existence, both sides of man's modes of knowing come into play: man's *subjective religious experience* and *empirical evidence*.

Whitehead takes it for granted that mankind has a common religious experience. The religious experience is a fact. The basic issue, however, concerns the ultimate nature of such experience. Men have a felt sense of an encounter with a divine person, a sense of addressing and being addressed. But does man encounter God directly without some mediating factor?

Whitehead rejected Ontologism as the answer. If you make religious experience to be the direct intuition of a personal being substrate in the universe, there is no objective basis to appeal to. If you proceed entirely by way of internal religious experience, you are seeking to supersede reason. "Then you can prove anything, except to reasonable people. But reason is the safeguard of the objectivity of religion: it secures for it the general coherence denied to hysteria."[8]

Whitehead favored the classical Catholic opinion that man's personal encounter with God is mediated through the experience itself, through insight, and through an extended relation to the knowledge of external reality. Obviously faith has its foundation in intuition, but it remains a private psychological act without some reference to objective evidence.

7 *Ibid.*, pp. 62-80.
8 *Ibid.*, p. 64.

Christian theology has also, in the main, adopted the position that there is no direct intuition of such an ultimate personal substratum for the world. It maintains the doctrine of the existence of a personal God as a truth, but holds that our belief in it is based upon inference. Most theologians hold that this inference is sufficiently obvious to be made by all men upon the basis of their individual personal experience. But, be this as it may, it is an inference and not a direct intuition. This is the general doctrine of those traditionalist churches which more especially claim the title of Catholic; and contrary doctrines have, I believe, been officially condemned by the Roman Catholic Church; for example, the religious philosophy of Rosmini.[9]

Whitehead perceives the wisdom in the mainstream of Christian theology which refuses to countenance the notion of a direct vision of a personal God. At least for those persons who, for one reason or another, must rationalize their outlook, ideas need to be anchored in the rightness and coherence of things. "The rational satisfaction or dissatisfaction in respect to any particular happening depends upon an intuition which is capable of being universalized. This universalization of what is discerned in a particular instance is the appeal to a general character inherent in the nature of things."[10]

At the same time Whitehead observed that Christianity had a genius for keeping its metaphysics subordinate to the religious facts to which it appeals.[11] A Catholic theologian would say, perhaps, that God always acts first and is a God of grace. Yet to be reasonable and coherent, Whitehead maintains, rational religion must have recourse to metaphysics for a scrutiny of its terms. "It is impossible to fix the sense of fundamental terms except by

9 *Ibid.*, pp. 62-63, cf. Norman Pittenger, "Whitehead and 'Catholicism'," *Theological Studies* (1971), 32(4), 659-670. On process Theology as used in Catholic thought itself, cf. A.J. Kelly, "Trinity and Process," *Theological Studies* (1970), pp. 393-414.

10 *Ibid.*, p. 67.

11 *Ibid.*, p. 72.

reference to some definite metaphysical way of conceiving the most penetrating description of the universe."[12] In a Christian context, at least, Whitehead would say, religion and metaphysics manifest a mutual dependence.

It is at this juncture that we come to the image or model of the "God" of Alfred Whitehead.

In the first place, the God of Whitehead is the God of the Christians. He believed God to be a personal, transcendent, yet immanent Actuality. He believed the divine Logos had become incarnate and was immanent in Jesus. He believed there is a third divine Person in the Godhead. He believed God to be a loving Actuality. He knew this from reading the epistles of John. At the same time he was a philosopher. The question arises, of course: Was he a Christian first and a philosopher second; or was he a philosopher first and a Christian second? We notice that his Lowell Lectures, *Religion in the Making,* were given in 1926 and his Gifford Lectures, *Process and Reality,* were delivered in 1927-1928. Whitehead, most likely, would answer the question by saying that he was a Christian and a philosopher at one and the same time. The totality of human knowledge cohered in a universal unity. Religion, "while in the framing of dogmas it must admit modifications from the complete circles of our knowledge, still brings its own contribution of immediate experience,"[13] and "religion is the longing of the spirit that the facts of existence should find their justification in the nature of existence."[14] Whitehead stressed, obviously, the active immanence of God in creative things; but he remarked at the same time: "Immanence is a well-known modern doctrine. The points to be noticed are that it is implicit in various parts of the New Testament and was explicit in the first theological epoch of Christianity."[15]

One might say that Whitehead lived as a Christian but thought as an empirical philosopher. He recognized that religious

12 *Ibid.,* pp. 78-79.
13 *Ibid.,* pp. 79-80
14 *Ibid.,* p. 85.
15 *Ibid.,* p. 74.

experience had its own particular evidence and certainty. Yet he insisted at the same time that religion requires a metaphysical backing. In his viewpoint, the Christian faith was a live option only if it was connected with the rest of our interpretation of the universe.

Second, Whitehead, as an empirical philosopher, thought and spoke of God from within a total and coherent image of the universe. In this world we discern a *complexity of inter-relationships.* When man studies and describes the universe, he tends to simplify its nature through the simplicity of his dominant ideals. But, Whitehead adds, modern physics does not disclose a simple world.

In simplifying through thought the all-inclusive universe, what basic formative elements do we find?

Whitehead says we are able to discern through evidence three such elements:

(1) A creativity, or a creative process, whereby the actual world has its character of temporal passage to novelty.

(2) In the world of real entities, being manifests itself in fundamental determinations. There is a fundamental unity or coherence, truth, goodness, and beauty (the aesthetic factors). In the concrete world particular entities are qualified by these fundamental determinations, and conversely these ideal forms are qualified by each particular entity.

(3) The actual but non-temporal entity whereby the indetermination of mere creativity is transmuted into a determinate entity is what men call God.

When we look closely at the third factor of "God," we notice that Whitehead would speak of God as an *actual but non-temporal entity.* There are many problems associated with the use of such language. I make no attempt to remove the difficulties beyond the limited observations that first, Whitehead tended to speak as an empirical philosopher; second, the term *non-temporal* seems to point towards transcendence; and third, Whitehead's use of the term *entity* seems to mean that God is a *reality* and an *actuality* rather than one thing among all the other things. He can and will define God in this way by saying: "God is that non-temporal actuality which has to be taken account of in every creative phase."[16]

God, in the description of Whitehead, is not introduced as a transcendent Principle to complete a logical chain of causation, as in classical Metaphysics. Rather, God is the necessary, immanent, Grounding, creating Principle or Actuality which has to be taken account of to explain every creative phase of the evolving universe and the concretion of every particular entity. He is, then, in a living dynamic relationship to the creative process, the Principle of concretion, or "the principle whereby there is initiated a definite outcome from a situation otherwise riddled with ambiguity."[17]

According to Whitehead's image of God, there is an ongoing living relationship between God and the universe. This means that God realizes his Actuality in affecting everything and being affected by it. God experiences and uses the consequences of what happens for his loving purpose. Everything matters and has its consequences even in the intimate life of God. Everything is itself and does its own thing; and everything is on the move. This statement is true even for God as the societal whole is caught up in an intimacy of real reciprocity.

Whitehead, however, does not say that God evolves or changes. God is and remains Himself. He never experiences a loss of what He is. God is *above change.* "He is exempt from transition into something else. . . . This must mean that his nature remains self-consistent in relation to all change."[18] A personal subject always remains himself and keeps his identity, but in and through an on-going complex of living relationships.

Whitehead speaks of his organic view of the whole universe as "panentheism." By this term he wishes to reject any notion of a dualistic conception of God and the universe and any pantheistic conception. Rather, God is the immanent yet transcendent

16 *Ibid.,* p. 94.
17 Whitehead, *Process and Reality,* p. 523.
18 Whitehead, *Religion in the Making,* p. 99.

Ground of the universe and enters into intimate and reciprocal relationships with everything. The term "panentheism" indicates, however, that this particular manner of describing the relation between God and the universe has its origins in empirical philosophy rather than in religious experience or Theology.

Correlating known empirical evidence with man's internal human experience, Whitehead came to the following conclusions: First, God is not to be treated as an exception to all metaphysical principles; rather, he is their chief exemplification. Second, God, then, is to be conceived as the Creator-with-the-creatures. Third, God, as well as being primordial, is also consequent. He is the beginning and the end. "Each actuality in the temporal world has its reception into God's nature. The corresponding element in God's nature is not temporal actuality, but is the transmutation of that temporal actuality into a living, ever-present fact."[19]

Whitehead's concept of God is based on an analysis of "order" and the "coherence" of the whole of reality.

2. The God of Charles Hartshorne

No one has studied, analyzed, and developed Whitehead's conception of God more than Charles Hartshorne. He has, following the same general viewpoint and method, directed attention to the philosophical contributions of Whitehead and to a new alternate idea of God which Hartshorne speaks of as a "neo-classical" theism. Speaking of Whitehead, Hartshorne has written: "What he offers us is rather the most technically adequate version of a conception of God which a score of philosophers and theologians of great distinction, and hundreds with humbler attainments, have been working out since the fifteenth century, and especially during the last one hundred years."[20] Hartshorne thinks that Whitehead has thought out and set down in writing a

---

19 Whitehead, *Process and Reality,* p. 531.

20 Hartshorne, "Whitehead's Idea of God," *The Philosophy of Alfred North Whitehead,* p. 515.

new balanced synthesis of the more extreme tendencies found in recent theism.

From Hartshorne's perspective of understanding, when we consider the problem of God, three basic questions must be answered. First, what is a philosopher to mean by the term "God"? Second, what does the term *perfection* mean when applied to God? Third, what is one saying, as does Whitehead, when he declares that God's nature is *dipolar?*

(a) The Meaning of the Term "God"

When one asks the question, What does a philosopher mean by the term "God"? the answer according to Hartshorne is given by man through his total manner of knowing: a correlation of empirical data of the universe with his total human experience. God from this viewpoint is known not only by way of reasonable inferrence but also through the mediation of human experience itself. What one experiences is the living "Immanence" of God.

> Basic ideas derive somehow from direct experience or intuition, life as concretely lived. Moreover, it is demonstrable from almost any classical conception of God that he cannot be known in any merely indirect way, by inference only, but must somehow be present in all experience. No theist can without qualification deny the universal 'immanence' of God. Even Aquinas did not do this. And if God is in *all* things. He is in our experience and also in what we experience, and thus is in some fashion a universal datum of experience.[21]

Such a total manner of human knowing lifts to the level of explicit awareness the integrity of an individual responding to reality. One integrates his thoughts and purposes, all perceptions and conceptions, all valuations and meanings. In this context, the

21 Hartshorne, *A Natural Theology for our Time,* p. 2. Cf. Merold Westphal, "On Thinking of God as King," *Christian Scholar's Review* (1970), pp. 27-34.

conscious wholeness of the individual is correlative to an inclusive wholeness of the universe. God is the Ground of the wholeness of the universe and the Correlative to an inclusive wholeness in the world of which the individual is aware.

However, as Hartshorne observes, there are two possible theories explaining man's religious experience of wholeness: the theistic and the nontheistic.

According to the former, the conscious wholeness of the individual is correlative to an inclusive wholeness in the world of which the individual is aware, and this wholeness is deity. According to the nontheistic view, either there is no wholeness, or if there is one, it is not what religions have meant by deity. Perhaps it is just The Unknown, or Nature as a Great Mystery, not to be thought of as conscious, or as an individual in principle superior to all other. Perhaps it is even Humanity.[22]

What Hartshorne is saying is that a man's conscious experience of the wholeness of reality embraces the all-inclusive reality, or the Grounding Omnipresence, or the living God. Men come to affirm, as did Paul the Apostle, that we live, move, and have our being "in" God. The atheist and the agnostic feel the need and possibility of raising integrity, wholeness, coherence to a conscious level, but do not quite know how to do so. They are in the human condition of "lossness" or some degree of conflict with oneself.

Hartshorne, as one can see, trusts reason and man's intuitive religious experience of God's omnipresence. At the same time he agrees with Whitehead that Metaphysics must complement man's internal experience of wholeness.

I incline to think (with Freud, for example,) that the impossibility of any rational argument for belief, supposing it really obtained, would be a strong and quite rational argument

22 *Ibid.*, pp. 5-6.

against belief. I suspect that most unbelievers agree with me here. And so, officially, does the Roman Catholic Church.[23]

Hartshorne agrees with Whitehead in affirming that everything in the universe has some intelligibility, meaning, significance, value, some integrity of order. This situation is equally true of every moment and every event. It is true for plants, animals, man. What reason perceives is that particular things can have intelligibility and significance only if the whole has intelligibility. The ontological or metaphysical fact of coherent purpose or intelligibility in the universe complements the religious experience of man with God given as the adequate referent. It is only because the whole of reality has intelligibility that particular things and events have significance. If and only if life has meaning, Hartshorne writes, do particular forms of life have meaning.

> William James in his 'will to believe' failed to make the above distinction with sufficient clarity, and this was what spoiled his insight. Where contingent alternatives, particular instances of value, are concerned, truth 'facing reality' has priority. Here it is absurd to argue, 'This view is good, the belief in it yields value, hence we shall take it as true.' For until we know that it is factually true in some further sense than that of giving satisfaction by being believed we do not know what its value will prove to be.[24]

This is Hartshorne's global or religious argument for God's existence based on the coherent order found in the universe and man's total reasonable experience of wholeness. From this horizon of understanding there is, as Hartshorne says, something irrational in choosing not to believe in God: a form of illusion.

From the viewpoint of Hartshorne, the temporal world exhibits two sides: *Order,* or a coherence of intelligibility and purpose; and

---

23 *Ibid.,* pp. 31-32.
24 *Ibid.,* p. 47.

second, a *creativity* whereby the actual world has a character of passing to novelty. The order is both *local* and *universal*, or cosmic. Thus, if it is assumed or supposed that all interaction in the universe is only local material interaction, how can one explain the unified cosmic order? "Only universal interaction can secure universal order or impose and maintain laws of nature cosmic in scope and relevant to the past history of the universe."[25] If such reasoning is correct, the alternative to God's existence is not an existing chaos but nothingness. The *creativity,* from the perspective of Hartshorne, is a universal actuality.

> A theistic philosophy must take 'create' or 'creator' as a universal category, rather than as applicable to God alone. It must distinguish supreme creativity from lesser forms and attribute some degree of creativity to all actuality. It must make of creativity a 'transcendental,' the very essence of reality as self-surpassing process.[26]

When we ask the question, then, what does Hartshorne mean by the term "God," we must say that his God is the same God as that of the Jews, Christians, and Moslems. He is not a being but Pure Actuality, Self-individuated, a loving Subject, the immanent and transcendent Ground of all things, Omni-Present, yet experiencing the intimacy and reciprocity of the cosmic interaction. Where Hartshorne breaks with classical theism is in his affirmation that the creating and omnipresent God *interacts* with created things. God is Pure Actuality but always interacting and responding. "He remains entirely free, in his full reality, to be receptive, enriched by his creatures, perpetually transcending himself, a genuinely active and loving subject, sympathetic companion of all existence."[27]

What Hartshorne is saying is that if the universe is in some real way the manifestation of the wholeness of reality, if man is as a microcosm a manifestation of the wholeness of reality, then God

25 *Ibid.,* p. 53.
26 *Ibid.,* p. 26.
27 *Ibid.,* p. 44.

must be a creative Actuality and capable of reacting to all created things. Within such an horizon of reality he affirms: "The conception of an ideal power of response has much better basis in ordinary categories than that of 'greatest possible actuality.' "[28]

God is eternal and everlasting. He always remains himself and keeps his self-identity. He is the Unsurpassable; yet as a creating Actuality he can surpass himself in a living relationship to created things. As a genuinely acting and loving Subject, he is the sympathetic companion of all existence.

Natural and rational theology began to collapse in the eighteenth century and has come to such a situation today that some speak of doing a non-Metaphysical Theology.[29] Hartshorne reacts to this by saying that some philosophers and theologians have over-simplified the complexities of life and the universe. Hartshorne, then, is attempting to do not a "descriptive" metaphysics but a "revisionist" metaphysics. He is of the opinion that modern man has been too passive and unsuspecting in the face of these simplifications. First, Hartshorne says, man has come to deny as "unreal" some aspects of experience. He fails to perceive the significance behind man's religious experience and the meaning of worship. God, because he is ubiquitous, can be experienced. Second, Hartshorne maintains, man fails to perceive what the universe and human reason can tell him about God. Man's idea of God is too narrow. For over two thousand years he has been living with philosophically baseless suppositions of an "Unmoved Mover," and associated this with an abstract idea of "the greatest possible actuality." Whereas some today can only hope and trust in "The Mystery," the metaphysics of Hartshorne offers definable positive characteristic by which we can conceptually identify him in contrast to other things.

We come, as a consequence, to the second question: What does the term *perfection* mean when applied to God?

---

28 *Ibid.*, p. 42.
29 Claude Geffre, *Un Nouvel Age de la Theologie*, pp. 67-81.

(b) The Perfections or Characteristics of God

Men, as Hartshorne says, through an intuitive and rational experience of *wholeness*, both in themselves and in living relation to the universe, come to affirm an immanent yet transcendent, creating, Omni-Presence. They say: "God exists." But to merely say, "God exists," without giving some specifying content to the idea, is an empty statement. As Kant said: "Concepts without precepts are empty." The *perfection* of a reality is the definitive actuality possessed by it.

> So the empty conceptual knowledge that God exists does tell us that his individuality is actualized *somehow*. How it is actualized is for science, revelation, personal experience, some form of empirical knowledge, to tell us, so far as we can know it at all.[30]

One can speak of God's perfections in one of two ways. He can, first, make some *a priori* or Platonic idealist affirmation about God's nature; or second, one can point to the perceived universe and to particular individuals. In the first case one will speak either in a projected idealism or by way of negation. He will say that God is all Good, Perfect, Transcendent, Absolute, as was done in classical Greek metaphysics; or he will speak as Kant did of the "most real being." If he speaks negatively, he will say that God is non-finite, the uncaused Cause, the unmoved Mover; or, since he is Pure Act, that he *cannot* react or interact. If, however, one follows the second option and points to the perceived universe and the world of particular individuals, he must notice "the apparent impossibility of making sense out of an acting agent which cannot *interact*, or of an individual which cannot relate itself to other individuals."[31]

Hartshorne follows the path indicated by the perceived universe and particular individuals. Following " . . . the well-founded rule

30 Hartshorne, *A Natural Theology for Our Time*, p. 77.
31 *Ibid.*, pp. 68-69.

that to be an individual power is to interact, we have excellent ground for taking universal interaction to be the positive feature in the divine mode of action."[32] At the same time, although God's universal creative interaction is still affirming that God is Pure Actuality, "the concrete content of this absolute universality must be relative, varying with the actual world."[33] God always remains what he is, Pure Creative Actuality; yet, in relation to the world of creation, he interacts with whatever is. "This is the contingent, relative, or empirical aspect, yet it is integral to the concrete realization of the absolute aspect. One cannot interact except with existing individuals."[34]

Hartshorne is of the opinon, as one can observe, that modern empiricism and logic, related to man's total experience of wholeness, indicate that God is Pure Creative Actuality able to react and interact both within his Self and in relation to particular things and events in the external created universe. Further, he is convinced that the basic metaphysical issues were not clearly seen by Kant and Hume, or by Green and Bradley. These philosophers were thinking within the framework of a metaphysics of being. They failed to perceive from the evidence in the universe that the perfection of being included creativity.

> Traditional metaphysics was too enamored of the supposed idea of an absolute, immutable maximum to follow the inherent logic of the idea of unsurpassable individual (or unsurpassable subject of interaction—they are really the same). It was held that while ordinary individuals interact, God's superiority is that he acts only, and does not interact. Unfortunately, this destroys all analogy between God and creatures, and it contradicts the very meaning of worship and related religious ideas. Nor is there any justification for the notion that interaction, as compared to simple action, indicates a weakness.

32 *Ibid.*, p. 70
33 *Ibid.*, p. 70.
34 *Ibid.*, p. 70.

Man's sensitivity to influences is just as superior to that of the lesser creatures as is his power over them, and analysis shows that the two superiorities belong logically together. Similarly, the gulf between us and God is no less shown in the limitations of our responsiveness to, than in those of our power over, others. But metaphysicians for two millennia almost unanimously missed all this and dogmatized instead about the 'superiority of agent to patient,' or of cause to effect, immutable to mutable, self-sufficient or independent to dependent. This procedure was, I believe, equally bad as philosophy and as theology.[35]

Such a metaphysics, then, is a metaphysics of *creativity*. Being, even the Pure Act of God, presupposes creative interaction and advance. Such a creative Actuality in God brings with it, both within His nature and in relation to created things, free opportunities and responsibilities for creative becoming. It is based on the idea that reality coheres in a logical or intelligible wholeness. Creatures manifest the hidden nature of God. In this sense God and creatures are correlative. Mistakes in perceiving the inner nature of things tends to produce mistakes about the Actuality of God. On the other side, our understanding of God as creative, free Actuality enables us to understand the intelligibility of creation and human existence. "If Supreme Creativity inspires all lesser creative action and takes it up into its own imperishable actuality, then the opportunities of existence outweigh its risks, and life is essentially good."[36]

We perceive, then, that we are in a situation where we may define *divine perfection* in one of two ways: either classically or neoclassically.

God's perfection is his definitive *Actuality*. Classical metaphysics maintained that God's Actuality is pure act *(actus purus)*. All that God has power to be, he is. Neoclassical metaphysics maintains that God is *creative* Actuality and can take on new

35 *Ibid.*, p. 134.
36 Hartshorne, *The Logic of Perfection*, p. 14.

modes of existing and interacting. "God cannot conceivably be surpassed or equalled by an other individual, but He can surpass himself, and thus His actual state is not the greatest state. This implies that there is potentiality as well as actuality in the divine reality."[37]

What Hartshorne is saying is that God is and always remains God. He possesses his own necessary existence. Yet, he adds, God's potentiality for change is coextensive with the logically possible. At the same time, God in grounding and effecting lesser creative action takes it up into his own imperishable actuality. "The absolute infinity of the divine potentiality might also be called its *coincidence with possibility as such.*"[38]

God is thought of as actually knowing the existence of whatever does actually exist. His actuality, like His potentiality, is all inclusive. Item for item, everything actual is accounted for in His actual knowing, as everything possible in His potential knowing.[39]

The new changes in God are called the divine property of *modal coincidence.*

A being necessarily all-inclusive must be one whose potentiality for change is coextensive with the logically possible. I call this property 'modal coincidence.' All actual things must be actual in God, they must be constituents of his actuality, and all possible things must be potentially his constituents. He is the Whole in every categorical sense, all actuality in one individual actuality, and all possibility in one individual potentiality. This relatively simple idea was apparently too complex for most of our ancestors to hit upon. They did not reject it, they failed so much as to formulate it.[40]

37 *Ibid.*, p. 35.
38 *Ibid.*, p. 38.
39 *Ibid.*, p. 38.
40 Hartshorne, *A Natural Theology for Our Time*, p. 20-21.

God, then, from Hartshorne's point of view, possesses both necessary and contingent properties. We are back to Whitehead's conception of a *dipolar God.*

But what is one saying when he declares that God's nature is dipolar?[41]

Hartshorne answers this question by saying that if one looks at the universe as we know it, he may observe two facts: first, it is a creative process, which is objective evidence for saying that *creativity* is a fundamental principle applicable to all reality;[42] second, "unactualized possibilities increase, rather than decrease, with the rank of a being, and that, accordingly, perfection does not mean a zero, but a maximum of potentiality, of unactualized power to be, as well as to produce beings in others."[43] The universe appears to disclose that becoming is an aspect of being. It would follow then

> that if God is purely immutable, he is merely an abstraction from process. This is reason enough for avoiding the doctrine. God must not have any external "and" connecting him with the natural process; rather, he must literally and absolutely embrace his own togetherness with it.[44]

Hartshorne maintains, as one can perceive, that God possesses his own proper and necessary nature; yet, as he is present in all things and interacts with them, he also has *contingent* properties, and these may be known to man through his knowledge of the empirical universe.

> God must be necessary and contingent, and our knowledge of him must have an a priori and also an empirical aspect.

41 Hartshorne, "The Dipolar Conception of Deity." *The Review of Metaphysics* (Dec. 1967) Vol. 21, pp. 273-289. This essay is in reply to the article of Merold Westphal, "Temporality and Finitism in Hartshorne's Theism," *The Review of Metaphysics* (March 1966) Vol. 19, pp. 550-564.

42 Hartshorne, *Creative Synthesis and Philosophic Method*, p. 1.

43 Hartshorne, *The Logic of Perfection*, p. 37.

44 Hartshorne, *Creative Synthesis*, p. 17.

The empirical aspect of God, however, concerns not his existence or eternal character, but only the accidental or generated qualities constituting, with the eternal aspect, his full reality.[45]

It has been stated, in opposition to the viewpoint of Hartshorne, that if God is *eternally* Pure Actuality *(Actus Purus)*, then he must possess the perfection of divine life and existence at every moment of the duration of eternity and cannot acquire anything or change. In such a context, God is related to everything as its grounding cause and as omnipresent; yet, at the same time, each thing is constituted by the divine activity while God is not dependent on the thing.[46] The weakness in the position of Hartshorne, then, is that he has capitulated to the demands of positivism and created a God in the image of man.

In meeting the basic classical objection to his position, Hartshorne does two things. First, he indicates a possible weakness in the classical manner of speaking about God's *eternity* by saying that at each and every moment of his existence God possesses the perfection of divine life and, as a consequence, cannot acquire anything or change. Second, Hartshorne concedes that his metaphysics is based on empirical evidence. He thinks that it is the total concrete universe, time, and becoming which explain the meaning of *eternity* and *being* and not *vice versa.* Having this viewpoint, he maintains God is truly *dipolar.*

(aa) Hartshorne indicates that there could be a possible weakness in speaking of God as being eternally immutable, in the sense that he possesses the perfection of divine life at every moment of his existence and, as a consequence, cannot interact or change. Such an idea could be no more than an abstract conjecture based on Aristotle's notion "eternal" and "unconditionally necessary" are equivalent. Aristotle also apparently thought the heavenly bodies were immune from decay. But modern empirical

---

45 Hartshorne, *A Natural Theology for Our Time,* p. 52.
46 See M. Westphal, *op. cit.,* pp. 561-564.

evidence does not verify such a conjecture. On the other hand, when one looks at the concrete world, he notices that becoming is inherent in being. What appears to be objectively necessary is that the creative process must produce and continue to produce creatures, and thereby continue to be, as creative.[47]

If creative becoming is a property of concrete things, then it is logical to say that God's must always exist with his proper nature yet be open to new modes of actualizing himself. If creativity embraces the whole of reality, then, Hartshorne says, one may define God's eternity as referring to his necessary existence.

> If the epistemic meaning for 'eternal' is 'necessary,' then eternity should be defined as necessary existence. The eternal always exists because it cannot not exist . . . [48]

(bb) In replying to the observation that he "has unwittingly capitulated to positivism's demands and created God in man's image," Hartshorne concedes that his metaphysics is based on empirical evidence and the total human experience of being a man. From this viewpoint an empirical metaphysics is an absurdity; yet, on the other hand, metaphysics is the perception of the intelligibility of concreteness. How, he asks, if one starts from zero, can there be a path to the supreme case? Again, Hartshorne observes, one must admit some anthropomorphism in speaking of God or one will use words from which all meaning has departed. Further, Hartshorne affirms that the classical philosophical picture of God is not the Biblical God.

If one observes the universe as a whole, he should be able to affirm its dynamic or creative nature. *Creativity,* Hartshorne says, appears to be a fundamental principle applicable to all reality. This creating mode of acting is found in the world of atoms, molecules, and man. Atoms respond to stimuli and even appear to exhibit signs of spontaneous activity. Human personal experience has its

---

47 See Hartshorne, *Creative Synthesis,* pp. 28-29.
48 Hartshorne, *The Dipolar Conception of Deity,* p. 275.

final unity and meaning in a self-created actuality and if its deepest motives and character are simply received from the past, it must be a *creation* of the present. The whole of reality appears to be a "sharing" of creativity.

What is at stake, then, from the viewpoint of Hartshorne, is the *principle of self-creativity and shared creativity,* whose materials are prior acts of self-creation by some or other individuals. Within such a framework of reality, "the highest form of individual life or consciousness must be, not an unsurpassable possession of value, but a combination of actual possession with capacity for further possession, which combination is surpassable only by the being itself."[49]

Hartshorne is not saying that God is *finite* or *relative.* He is saying that God is *pure creative Actuality,* the transcendent yet immanent Ground of all things, yet possessing unlimited capacity for new modal actualizations. In this sense God possesses a dipolar nature. "I hold, with Whitehead, but also with Hocking, Brightman, Montague, Pfleiderer, and still others, some of whom helped me to reach this doctrine before I knew anything of Whitehead's view on the subject, that God is (and without any contradiction or irreducible dialectical difficulty) both finite and infinite, limited and unlimited, relative and absolute. There has been no intention of avoiding a 'straightforward' admission of finitude in God, provided it be accompanied by an equally literal affirmation of infinity in him."[50]

3. The Dynamic God of Nicolas Berdyaev

In general, Eastern Christian conceptions of God have been more dynamic than traditional Western ideas. In the Eastern Church God is a Dynamic Act, and the Word, or Logos, is a Dynamic Personal Mode of Existing in and from the Father. With

---

49 *Ibid.,* p. 280.
50 *Ibid.,* p. 282.

the ideas of substance *(substantia)* and person *(persona)* introduced into Western Latin Theology by Tertullian, theology tended
to emphasize the static and to affirm that becoming, as such,
belongs to creatures and finite things. Eastern theology, on the
other hand, tended to emphasize the dynamic and living aspect in
God together with modal actualizations. This particular viewpoint
was expressed by Origen, the Father of Eastern Theology.

> The Father himself and the God of the whole universe is
> "longsuffering, full of mercy and pity." Must he not then, in
> some sense, be exposed to suffering? So you must realize that in
> his dealing with man he suffers human passions. For the Lord
> your God bears your ways, just as the son of God bears our
> "passions." The Father himself is not impassible. If he sought to
> show pity and compassion, then he experiences, in some way,
> the passion of love, and is exposed to what he cannot be
> exposed to in respect to his greatness, and for us men he
> endures the passions of mankind.[51]

Eastern theology, though it knew and followed the path of
reason, lived on a tradition of mystical theology, in which one
affirmed that he possessed an experienced knowledge of God's
dynamic Presence, a living *gnosis.* But with such a form of
theology the question was always placed: How can God's
unknowable nature be reconciled with our living knowledge of
him? Gregory Palamas (c. 1296-1359) answered this question by
speaking of a *dipolar* God. The divine nature, he said, must be
incommunicable and communicable at the same time. We participate in a living knowledge of God through his expressed *energies,*
yet at the same time God remains inaccesible. We must affirm
both things at once yet preserve the antinomy. Russian theology
knew and followed the General Eastern tradition; so we find
Vladimir Solovyov (1853-1900) affirming: "The eternal God
forever realizes himself in realizing his content, i.e. in realizing

51 Origen, *Homily on Ezekiel,* 6, 6.

all." At the same time, we find Russian theologians following classical theism and stating that God is both immutable and impassive. In such a situation we are able to appreciate the importance of Nicolas Berdyaev (1874-1948), who, following insights he received from Boehme and Schelling, spoke in terms of an open dipolar theology. God has a divine becoming, a divine need, a divine suffering, a divine history.[52]

Here I merely indicate some of the many statements of Berdyaev on this subject matter. One should, however, observe the difficulties inherent in the theology of this religious philosopher. Berdyaev never treated or developed a specific theme logically within the framework of a discussed whole. He simply *affirmed* out of his position of self-understanding. He did think, nevertheless, within a specific metaphysics. He thought that Kant's philosophical investigations made possible a metaphysics based on the *personal subject;* hence he expressed a metaphysics of *freedom.* Personality becomes the meeting point of two orders of being: the universal-infinite and the individual particular. It is personality which allows for a correlation of the whole of reality, for a meeting and communion with God. "Two natures, God and man, exist side by side in the very depths of the spiritual life."[53] For Berdyaev, God is at the center of man's personality and consciousness; and man is in God, not over against him. "I believe only in a method which is existentially anthropocentric and spirituality religious."[54]

(a) The God of Berdyaev Has a Divine Becoming

Berdyaev defines God as Spirit. By this he means that God is not a thing, but a transcendent yet immanent Presence, Subject or Energy, penetrating human existence and giving man his inner

---

52 See Hartshorne and Reese, *Philosophers Speak of God,* pp. 285-294; Hartshorne, "Whitehead and Berdyaev: Is There Tragedy in God?," *The Journal of Religion,* 37 (1957), pp. 71-84; S.L. Frank, *A Solovyov Anthology* (SCM Press LTD, 1950); V. Lossky, *The Vision of God;* C.S. Calian, *Berdyaev's Philosophy of Hope.*

53 Berdyaev, *Freedom and the Spirit,* p. 38.

54 Berdyaev, *The Divine and the Human,* p. vi.

freedom and unity. "Spirit is, as it were, a Divine breath, penetrating human existence and endowing it with the highest dignity, with the highest quality of existence, with an inner independence and unity."[55] The Spirit, he says, affirms its reality through man who is a manifestation of spirit. The Spirit exercises a primacy over being.[56] It is identified with power and energy, a holy energy overflowing from another world into ours. Freedom is its chief attribute, together with creativity and love. The Spirit emanates from God but is not a divine creation like nature; rather, it is a divine infusion. The Spirit is not some ideal premise of the world; rather, it manifests itself in man's personal existence in a concrete manner. God is not man and man is not God. Yet man enters into the very life of God. Man is God's other self, and without man God could not come to personal, concrete self-expression.

For Berdyaev, man is truly an image of God. God, then, manifests his hidden nature in man and in human history. What he is indicating is that every existent is in process. He will say: "In true humanity not only is the nature of man revealed but God Himself is revealed also."[57] God, then, in Berdyaev's mind is a dynamic, free, creating personal Presence. "The divine is understood either in terms of social images—master, tsar, father—or in terms of dynamic images—power, life, light, spirit, truth, fire. Only the second interpretation is worthy of God and worthy of man."[58] "God is spirit. God is freedom and love. His final and definitive revelation of Himself is in a creative act of Spirit; in a creative act of Spirit God is realized. In a creative act of Spirit, in the creative act of knowing God and proving God, the birth of God takes place in vital fashion."[59] What Berdyaev is saying follows an Eastern Christian manner of thinking: God manifests his hidden mysterious nature in and through his creating, modal,

55 Berdyaev, *Spirit and Reality*, p. 6.
56 *Ibid.*, p. 15.
57 Berdyaev, *The Divine and The Human*, p. 4.
58 *Ibid.*, pp. 6-7.
59 *Ibid.*, p. 58.

concrete actualizations. The image is one of Power from Power, Light from Light, Energy from Energy. One tends to think of the Sun with its sparks of light and energy.

Berdyaev does not think he is saying anything radical or new. He is speaking as man knows and experiences himself in relationship with a grounding Spirit, with the same viewpoint as the Bible, and in full agreement with the Eastern Church Fathers. He knows that others, following Aristotle's Pure Act, associated potentiality with imperfection and created things. In his opinion such a system of thought is too narrow and restrictive. It cuts man off from a living and interacting relationship with God.

> Thus the intellectualist rationalistic doctrine of God as pure act, which has played such a part in Catholic scholasticism, is derived not from the Bible, nor from revelation but from Aristotle. That doctrine, professing to meet the needs of abstract reason, turns God, so to speak, into stone; it deprives Him of any interior life and of all dynamic force. But God is life; life, not being, if by this term the rational concept of being is understood. Being is secondary, not primary . . . [60]

(b) Berdyaev Spoke of the Divine Need

According to the viewpoint of Berdyaev, God is Spirit: a creative Act, Power, Life, Freedom, and Love. Within God, then, there is a tendency of freedom to create and to realize his Spirit in and through new actualizations. God at the same time as Creator brings intelligibility, meaning, order, purpose, value into being with new modes of freedom. In this context the universe and man are, truly, an enrichment of the divine life.

> God is spirit. God is freedom and love. His final and definitive revelation of Himself is in a creative act of Spirit; in a creative act of Spirit God is realized. In a creative act of Spirit, in the

---

60 *Ibid.*, p. 15. See also, *Freedom and Spirit*, p. 50.

creative act of knowing God and proving God, the birth of God takes place in vital fashion.

The old doctrine according to which God created man and the world, having in no respect any need of them and creating them for His own glory, ought to be abandoned as a servile doctrine which deprives the life of man and the world of meaning. God with man and the world is a greater thing than God without man and the world. Man and the world are an enrichment of the divine life.[61]

God is present in the universe and in man as the grounding creating energy granting to each thing a share in the creative process. God, however, as Berdyaev says, is not present in the universe as an object or thing, but as Spirit. One may say that God is in the universe *incognito.* The mystery of God, rather, discloses itself perfectly only in and through the spiritual life of the human person. In such a meeting or living communion, both God and man are active. It is at this juncture that one finds the meaning in divine revelation and religion.

The religious phenomenon has two sides: it is the disclosure of God in man and of man in God. The yearning of man for God comes to light in it and the yearning of God for man. Traditional rational theology denies this yearning of God for man from the fear of introducing affective passionate life into God. For the rational concept of perfection does not admit of yearning and need in the notion of completeness; it prefers the perfection of a stone. In that case the relations between God and man cease to be a drama of two which is capable of resolution in a third.[62]

The tragedy of man's life, if one looks at the universe from the

---

61 *Ibid.,* p. 7.
62 *Ibid.,* p. 15.

viewpoint of Berdyaev, is that God creates the universe and man in loving freedom. He allows everything to be itself. He does not create and rule over things and persons as a master or a wielder of power. "In opposition to this stands the tragic feeling for life. God is present in freedom and love, in truth and right and in beauty, and in the face of evil and wrong. He is present not as judge and avenger but as appraisal and as conscience."[63] In such a universe change, fate, necessity have their place. In this world of ours not only God acts; but fate, necessity, chance, also act. Fate continues to operate when the world abandons God or when God abandons the world. Moments and times of God-forsakenness are fateful in human life. Man and the world are subject to inevitable necessity as a result of falsely directed freedom. The deepest tragedy is this: man too often wants to be man without God; whereas, on the other hand, God does not want to be without man. Because of this living need, God became man in Jesus Christ.[64]

(c) Divine Suffering

From the viewpoint of Berdyaev, God both shares in and is enriched by the lives of other persons. Here the question arises: Can God suffer? Can God participate in the sufferings of others through a specific awareness, sympathy, love, and compassion? God, as far as Berdyaev is concerned, is no spectator God. God lives fully, experiences fully, and understands fully. Between God and man there is a shared experience and communion. "That which comes to pass in the depths of man comes to pass in the depths of God also."[65]

As a rule, Berdyaev says, theology tends to shy away from any thought that there could be any experience like genuine suffering in God's life. Theologians tend to remember those who were condemned for saying the Father suffered when Jesus suffered. Again, there could be no genuine sympathetic suffering in a

63 *Ibid.*, p. 8.
64 *Ibid.*, p. 21.
65 *Ibid.*, p. 46.

system of Pantheism or in a rigid dualism but only in some dipolar conception of God which would allow him to actualize his understanding in new ways. Yet, rather strange, Christianity has always affirmed the hard reality that the Son of God suffered in Jesus. In such a situation we notice a paradox in the Christian understanding.

> ...Theological doctrines have always been afraid to recognize suffering in God, and have condemned what is known as patripassianism. But here, too, as in every case which brings us into contact with mystery, everything is on a razor-edge, for the suffering of the Son of God, of the God-man, is acknowledged. Here everything turns upon the union of the suffering of the human with the suffering of the divine, for in that the disruption and alienation between the human and the divine is overcome.[66]

In the opinion of Berdyaev, God truly suffers with a sympathetic understanding as he confronts the universe and man. Why? Because of what God is and what creation is. God is a dynamic, free, creating Spirit or Power and creation is a free creative process. He allows things to be what they are. He does not merely create man but allows man to be free. Hence, Berdyaev says, there is a powerlessness of God himself as Creating Power. There is order and purpose in everything but also chance, fate, and tragedy. It would be degrading to God to assume in any sense that the sufferings of human beings and of other objects in the universe are pleasing and acceptable to him. Rather, if we judge from the nature of God and the creating process, we realize that "divine suffering exists and this divine suffering is evoked by a lack of congruity between God and the condition of the world and man."[67] We can even perceive, Berdyaev thinks, a living experience of tragedy in the divine life. "Divine life is tragedy. Even at the beginning, before the formation of the world, there

66 *Ibid.*, p. 68.
67 *Ibid.*, p. 73.

was the irrational void of freedom which had to be illuminated by the Logos."[68]

The terms "divine suffering" and "divine tragedy" are difficult expressions. What we know of suffering and tragedy belong to facts, events, conditions associated with man's world. From the perspective of process theology, we may say that God experiences in them the meaning of such misfortune and is sympathetic as he enters into living relationships with men. Yet, obviously, these terms do not mean in God what they do in the world of man. God is truly Other in some real way. Berdyaev, then, throws the meaning of suffering and tragedy into God's intimate life. God is *creative, free* Act. What these terms point to is expressed in God's Word, Light, or Meaning. What is expressed through the Word (the Logos) is the Spirit: creative Love, Need, Longing, Freedom. This Spirit is a Divine Infusion in God. The Spirit of God yearns for free love. Out of this Freedom, Berdyaev affirms, comes both suffering and tragedy.

(d) Divine Historicity

Berdyaev rejects the conception of an absolute immobility in God. He speaks only of a living God, possessing a concrete inner and dramatic existence. He thinks the idea of an impassible God to be no more than an abstract projection cut off from the intelligibility of the universe, from a religious understanding of man and his life, and from history. The mystery of the Trinity, he declares, hidden in the Godhead, is made manifest in man and in time. Man's deepest knowledge comes from the experience of life; in this connection, religious experience means that being reveals itself to the knower. Christian thinking, then, allows one to comprehend, in some limited way, the concrete life of God and the idea of God as a *coincidence of opposites.* Hence, he says:

68 Berdyaev, *Freedom and The Spirit,* p. 165.

We cannot regard absolute fulness and perfection from the static and abstract point of view, for they can only be thought of in terms of concrete dynamism, as life and not as substance.[69]

He adds to this observation:

The theological and metaphysical doctrine of the absolute immobility of the Divine Being, which is the one traditionally and officially recognized, is in striking contradiction to the essential mystery of Christianity. A really profound Christianity does not order the relations between God and man and between God and creation upon a basis of static categories.[70]

Berdyaev is of the opinion that the dynamic of God's life will always manifest itself in a concrete manner. He thinks this is true in God's own internal life and in the world of creation and time. God always remains God, the Spirit, yet actualizes his divine life in creation and in each man. In this perspective he will say: "The process of divine birth which transpires in heaven (in God) takes place in us, in the very depths of our being."[71] God is becoming God in his living relationship to creation. "The Creator is manifested at the same time as creation, God and man appear simultaneously."[72] As a consequence of this, Berdyaev will say that God's plan of creation, as an externalization of the dynamic life of God, can be realized only through man's cooperation and the participation of creation itself. "The Kingdom of God is that of God-humanity, in which God is finally in man and man in God, and this is realized in the Spirit."[73]

What is disclosed concretely in creation and in man is manifested uniquely and most perfectly in one man: Jesus, the

69 *Ibid.*, p. 191.
70 *Ibid.*, p. 192.
71 *Ibid.*, p. 193-4.
72 *Ibid.*, p. 194.
73 *Ibid.*, p. 197.

God-Man. The divine creating Power or Energy (the Spirit) grounds each and everything and is poured or infused into each concrete thing. Yet to man, judging by visible appearances, the universe appears to be no more than external nature. Its grounding energy or life remains beyond his comprehension. In such a situation he is solitary, alone, for the Ground of his life is not in and from himself. But through Christ, the divine Word, or Logos, the deepest meaning of creation and human life is manifest and responded to. This Person, the God-man, meets every other person, and there is a new fulness of life in community (*sobornost*). As Berdyaev phrases it, the meeting of one person with another person finds fulfillment in a third. "In Christ, the God-Man, the free activity not only of God but also of man is revealed."[74]

Nicolas Berdyaev is, obviously, a process theologian but one who follows a line of thinking developed by the Eastern Church Fathers. He strongly protested that he was not a Pantheist. He would say that his view was *Panentheism* rather than Pantheism. But even here he preferred to say that his perspective was one of *Pan-pneumatism:* the infusion of the Spirit (the divine, loving and creating Energy) into the cosmos. God is creating, free Power. He is somewhat like Light, Energy, Fire, the Sun. He manifests his Presence in two forms: at *rest* or in *motion.* Light in a lamp is at rest but it is also in process. Energy appears as a *quantum* but also as a *wave* in motion. Fire, too, appears as a quantum at rest; but it is also an active energy and can actualize itself in new ways in new concrete places. The Sun appears to be a quantum and at rest; but it is also alive with energy and can extend its energy to new places. We may speak of God in like manner. He possesses within himself a coincidence of opposites. He may manifest Himself at rest or in motion as alive. He can and does actualize his Spirit in new ways.

4. Process Theology in the Christology of Karl Rahner

In Catholic systematic theology today one rarely hears of

74 *Ibid.*, p. 207.

process theology as such. Instead one speaks of an evolutionary world view, following the path of Pierre Teilhard de Chardin; or one speaks in terms of an I-Thou metaphysics in which being is disclosed dialogically. God enters into living personal relationships with men.[75]

Christian belief, however, centers on Christology, and the deepest crisis in the Christian community is always a crisis of its belief in Jesus Christ. As a consequence, it is not at all surprising that Karl Rahner, the German theologian, has associated the problem of divine becoming with the Incarnation of the Logos in Jesus. Can God *become* anything?

> The Word of God has *become* man: this is the assertion which we are trying to understand better. We take the word "become." Can God "become" anything? This question has always been answered in the affirmative by pantheism and all other philosophies in which God exists "historically." But it leaves the Christian and all really theistic philosophers in a difficult situation. They proclaim God as the "Unchangeable," he who simply is—*actus purus*—who in blessed security, in the self-sufficiency of infinite reality, possesses from eternity to eternity the absolute, unwavering, glad fullness of what he is. He has not first to become, he has not first to acquire what he is.[76]

Yet the Christian community affirms: The Word *became* flesh. Traditional Catholic theology usually says that the change takes place in the created reality, in the human nature of Jesus, and not in the divine Word. In this perspective the Logos *takes* or *assumes* human nature somewhat like a person putting on an overcoat.

---

75 See Ewert H. Cousins (ed.), *Process Theology*, pp. 229-350; also Michael Schmaus, *God and Creation (Dogma 2)* (Sheed and Ward, N.Y. 1969), pp. 28-47.

76 Karl Rahner, *Theological Investigations*, Vol. IV, p. 112. Cf. Jurgen Moltmann, "Gesichtspunkte der Kreuzestheologie heute," *Evangelische Theologie (1973)*, 33(4), 346-365; also Walter Kasper, "Krise und Neuanfang der Christologie im Denken Schellings," *Evangelische Theologie* (1973), pp. 366-384.

But in the opinion of Rahner, this is not what the affirmation declares when it says: The Word *became* flesh. Further, if the Logos did *become* flesh, or man, then the changing history of this human reality is his history, human time becomes a shared time with the Son of God, and he truly shares in and experiences the meaning of human death. From the meaning of the declaration, as Rahner understands it, the Logos *became* incarnate so that what happened to Jesus on earth is precisely the history of the Word of God himself, and a process which He underwent.

> If we face squarely the fact of the Incarnation, which our faith testifies to be the fundamental dogma of Christianity, we must simply say: God can become something, he who is unchangeable in himself can *himself* become subject to change *in something else.* This brings us to an ontological ultimate, which a purely rational ontology might perhaps never suspect and find it difficult to take cognizance of and insert as a primordial truth into its most basic and seminal utterances: the Absolute, or more correctly, he who is the absolute, has, in the pure freedom of his infinite and abiding relatedness, the possibility of himself becoming that other thing, the finite; God, in and by the fact the he empties *himself* gives away himself, poses the other as his own reality.[77]

One may say, of course, that the created thing is the humanity of the Word itself. This affirmation is correct. But one should not conclude, says Rahner, that because this happened, it must be the change. If one places the change in the humanity of Jesus, he can say, as has been said, that the Logos *assumed* human nature, but he is not saying: The *Logos became* flesh. The becoming is in no way an event affecting the Logos. What the Incarnation means, from Rahner's understanding, is that the Logos *became* man—God became the finite—through a new actualization that was a *kenosis:*

---

[77] *Ibid.,* pp. 112-3.

a self-emptying. This self-emptying of God himself was a becoming to be man.

The difficulty found in accepting such a conception, Rahner thinks, lies in the traditional affirmation that God is *immutable* and *unchanging*. But there is a way out of this difficulty. We may define *immutability* in a *dialectical* manner. God, from the perspective of Rahner, is a personal Spirit of love, a dynamic Will to fill the void. God always remains what he is: this dynamic Spirit of love. In this sense God is immutable and unchanging. Yet, at the same time, because he is this dynamic Will to fill the void, God can utter himself as himself into the *void,* speak out through his immanent Word and become man. We are able to say: God can become something; he who is unchangeable in himself can himself become subject to change in something else.

> And this possibility is not a sign of deficiency, but the height of perfection, which would be less if in addition to being infinite, he could not become less than he (always) is. This we can and must affirm, without being Hegelians. And it would be a pity if Hegel had to teach Christians such things.[78]

The questions placed in process theology are these: Can God change yet remain himself? Can God actualize himself in new ways? In answering these questions Rahner would say: Yes, if we are able to define the *immutability* of God in a dialectical manner.

Concluding Observations

In evaluating the significance of Process Theology for contemporary Catholic philosophy and theology, we need but observe the specific difficulties. First, it is extremely difficult for a Catholic to understand how one can speak of God in terms of process, change, and becoming. This is the problem of language. Second, there is the difficulty of *Metaphysics.* On all sides we find theologians

---

78 *Ibid.,* p. 114, note.

proclaiming that the future of theology will be found in a non-metaphysical theology. Third, as Heidegger has pointed out, classical philosophy and theology tend to affirm in terms of being, objects, and things. We tend *to thing* God out. We tend to say God is the *Supreme Being* and the *primum Ens.* Berdyaev, as we have indicated, speaks of God as a *creative Act* or *Spirit.* He will say that God is not a thing or a being. The fourth and last difficulty has to do with thinking in terms of *a dipolar God.* Such an idea seems openly opposed to our received definition of God's *immutability.* Scripture (*Mal.* 3, 6) states, as Thomas Aquinas pointed out in the *Summa* (1a, 9, 1): "I, the Lord, do not change."

(a) The Problem of Human Language

Part of the crisis in contemporary philosophy and theology is a crisis over language. With the appearance of the *Death of God* theologians, problems over the term *God* have become more complex than they were in the past classical period. Today, to a large extent, philosophers and theologians use their own words and define them in their own particular way. When one uses such words, for example, as change, process, becoming, evolution, Catholic theology respects traditional usage and defines them according to a basic reference to matter and material energy. Process theology, on the other hand, sets aside all traditional definition of terms and goes back to ordinary language, as used in the ordinary way, to recover the meaning embodied in the language. In such a shift of understanding, ordinary modes of speaking are accepted as making sense, provided one keeps in mind that philosophical purposes may differ from ordinary ones. It will say, then, that the terms change, process, becoming, evolution may be used in speaking of God as a creative *Act* or *Spirit* and in a context of living relationships and interaction. It will insist, and I think rightly, that God is not a being nor the *primum Ens.* Hartshorne will even protest against Whitehead speaking of God as an "actual entity."

It cannot be true, as Whitehead observed, that contradictory notions can be applied to the same fact. Yet, at the same time, a reconcilement of contrary concepts can and should be sought in a more searching analysis of the meaning of the terms in which they are phrased.

(b) The Problem of Metaphysics

Associated with the problem of human language is that of metaphysics. One hears it affirmed on almost every side that Kant's *Critique of Pure Reason* has made all metaphysics an impossibility. Or, one hears it proclaimed that Hume and Kant have refuted all natural theology. Even in contemporary Catholic theology one hears it suggested that theology should and must free itself from metaphysics and rely completely on a theology of Revelation and Personal Encounter.

From the viewpoint of contemporary Process Theology, which presupposes a neo-classical metaphysics, Kant failed to deal with the living and true God, the God of religion; and constructed for himself some image or idol of some far off Supreme and Absolute *Being.* Kant was *thinging* God and creating his own abstract idea of God. He had little or no conception that God is a creative Act or Spirit: the creating *Ground* of everything.

In such a context, I think it is true to say that classical metaphysics was too narrow in its ideas, and I agree with Process Theology in affirming that metaphysics from Aristotle to Hegel was something less than a success. At the same time, its failures were no worse than the fate that overtakes most scientific views. Kant thought it was attempting the impossible, but perhaps as Process Theology thinks, it merely took on a weakness and bias: stressing *being* at the expense of *becoming, identity* at the expense of *diversity,* the *absolute* at the expense of the *relative,* the *non-physical* at the expense of the *physical, origins* or *causes* at the expense of *events, outcomes* or *effects.* Everywhere and at all times man's future is uncertain: death threatens everyone. No clear edge can be set to the limits of his uncertainty. The simplest remedy is to attack the idea of change itself and affirm that the first Being, the Supreme Being, is immutable and free of change. In such a context there is no utlimate danger or fear: change has been transcended in the First Principle.

The God of the Bible and of religious experience appears to respond as a Person to other persons and to interact with creatures and historical events. Perhaps, instead of trying to free oneself from metaphysics, one should examine more closely a metaphysics of *Creativity.*

(c) The Problem of God as the Supreme Being

If I were to say: "God is not the Supreme Being," someone could certainly object that I seem to be affirming that God is not a *Reality,* or that one cannot use the analogy of being in speaking of God. Obviously, if God exists, He must be a Reality, an Act of existing. Again, from the perspective of Process Theology, there must be an analogy of being or one could not say anything positive about God. When Whitehead says that God is an *actual entity,* he wishes to affirm that God, most truly, is a personal, individual reality.

Yet, there is a real problem in speaking of God as the Supreme Being. In such a perspective, the temptation is to picture God out as a thing, one thing among other things. We picture out an immutable being; but, God is not a thing or a static being. He is a creative, dynamic *Act,* Spirit. Metaphysics tends, in its moments of weakness, to picture out its intuitions and interpret them as if they were a being, either a being of the mind or a real being. After all, it is said that the aim of Ontology is to discover objective being. But, as Berdyaev says, Spirit is not only a reality of a different kind from that of objects, but it is an altogether different reality. God is Spirit because He is not an object but a creative, loving Subject. In such a context, following the insights of Eastern Christian theology and American Process Theology, I think it is true to say that God is, most truly, a creative, loving, dynamic Act or Spirit; he can, as a consequence, actualize himself in new ways. If God's creative Energy or Power means a potentiality for actualizing in a new modes what he already is, then God has an unlimited capacity for such actualization.

(d) Finally, We Come to the Problem of the Immutability of God

Here we are tempted to say, as others before us, that God cannot change because God says of himself, as witnessed to by a prophet: "I, the Lord, do not change." Furthermore, we answer questions without knowing what the words really mean. In this context, we realize today that the changelessness of God, as used in the Bible, refers to his fidelity and steadfast purpose. Far from implying a static immutability of nature in God, such trustworthiness indicates a committed creative love which acts freely in new ways: in creation, in history, in the decisions of men, even in the incarnation of the Logos.

Can there be a strictly immutable Act or dynamic Spirit? I think the answer is No, and here we must say that God is a living dynamic Spirit who can and does actualize himself in constant new ways.

Can God change and remain himself? Can God actualize himself in new ways? Yes! God can and does change yet remains what he is: a dynamic creating Spirit. God can and does actualize himself in new ways. We make such affimations because created reality, cohering with man's religious experience, indicates that God's *immutability* should be defined in a dialectical manner. God, who is unchangeable in himself, as He is always God, can actualize himself in new modes of existing and even become subject to change and response in something else.

A SELECT BIBLIOGRAPHY

Baltazar, Eulalio R., *God Within Process.* New York: Newman Press, 1970.
Berdyaev, Nicolas, *Freedom and The Spirit.* London: Geoffrey Bles, 1948.
_____, *Slavery and Freedom.* London: Geoffrey Bles, 1944.
_____, *Spirit and Reality.* London: Geoffrey Bles, 1939.
_____, *The Destiny of Man.* London: Geoffrey Bles, 1948.
_____, *The Divine and The Human.* London: Geoffrey Bles, 1949.

Brown, Delwin (ed.), *Process Philosophy and Christian Thought*. New York: Bobbs-Merril, 1971.

Clifford, Paul R., *Interpreting Human Experience*. London: Collins, 1972.

Cobb, John B., *A Christian Natural Theology*. Philadelphia: Westminister, 1969.

Cousins, Ewert H., *Process Theology*. New York: Newman Press, 1971.

Ely, Stephen L., *The Religious Availability of Whitehead's God*. Madison, Wisconsin: University of Wisconsin Press, 1942.

Emmet, Dorothy M., *Whitehead's Philosophy of Organism*. New York: Macmillan, 1966.

Geffre, Claude, *Un Nouvel Age de la Théologie*. Paris: du Cerf, 1972.

Hamilton, Peter, *The Living God and the Modern World*. London: Hodder and Stoughton, 1967.

Hartshorne, Charles, *Anselm's Discovery*. La Salle, Illinois: Open Court, 1965.

————, *A Natural Theology For Our Time*. La Salle, Illinois: Open Court, 1967.

————, *Creative Synthesis & Philosophic Method*. La Salle, Illinois: Open Court, 1970.

————, *Man's Vision of God*. Hamden Connecticut: Archon Books, 1964.

————, *The Divine Relativity*. New Haven, Connecticut: Yale Press, 1967.

————, *The Logic of Perfection*. La Salle, Illinois: Open Court, 1962.

————, "Whitehead and Berdyaev: 'Is There Tragedy in God?'," *The Journal of Religion* (1957) 37, pp. 71-84.

Hartshorne, Charles and Reese, William, *Philosophers Speak of God*. Chicago: University of Chicago Press, 1953.

James, Ralph E., *The Concrete God*. Indianapolis, Indiana: Bobbs-Merril, 1967.

Lossky V., *The Vision of God*. Clayton, Wisconsin: Faith Press, 1963.

Mays, W., *The Philosophy of Whitehead*. New York: Macmillan, 1959.

Ogden, Schubert, *The Reality of God*. New York: Harper and Row, 1966.

Overman, Richard H., *Evolution and the Christian Doctrine of Creation*. Philadelphia: Westminster, 1967.

Peters, Eugene H., *The Creative Advance*. St. Louis, Missouri: Bethany Press, 1966.

Pittenger, W. Norman, *Alfred North Whitehead*. Richmond, Virginia: John Knox Press, 1969.

Rahner, Karl, *Theological Investigations*. 4 vols. Baltimore, Maryland: Helicon Press, 1966.

Reese, William L. and Freeman, Eugene (eds.), *Process and Divinity*. La Salle, Illinois: Open Court, 1964.

Robinson, John A., *Exploration Into God*. Stanford, California: Stanford University Press, 1968.

Schlipp, Paul A., (ed.), *The Philosophy of Alfred North Whitehead.* Evanston, Illinois: Northwestern University Press, 1941.

Westphal, Merold, "Temporality and Finitism in Hartshorne's Theism," *The Review of Metaphysics,* Vol. 19, pp. 550-564.

Whitehead, Alfred N., *Adventures of Ideas.* New York: Macmillan, 1967.

_____, *Modes of Thought.* New York: Macmillan, 1968.

_____, *Process and Reality.* New York: Macmillan, 1930.

_____, *Religion in the Making.* New York: Meridian Books, 1971.

_____, *Science and the Modern World.* New York: Macmillan, 1925.

_____, *Symbolism: Its Meaning and Effect.* New York: Macmillan, 1927.

_____, *The Function of Reason.* Princeton, New Jersey: Princeton University Press, 1929.

CHAPTER XXVI

THE UNIFICATION VIEW OF GOD

Lee Sang Hun *

The Unification view of God was made public by Reverend Sun Myung Moon (1920-   ). It is summarized in *Divine Principle,* a synthesis of theology, history and Biblical exegesis which is used by the Unification Church in conjunction with the Bible. The Bible is accepted as the basic source and the Unification view of God is founded on these Scriptures; certain indications in the Bible, however, need clarification. In addition to the summary in *Divine Principle,* Reverend Moon has discussed many points related to the entity of God while teaching or answering questions. In this essay, I have presented a gist of these explanations together with the relevant material from the *Divine Principle.*

As does the traditional view, the Unification view regards God as the infinite and perfect Creator, first and ultimate cause, omnipresent, omniscient and omnipotent, absolute, the unique God of *Logos* and Trinity and the source of love and life. Since God considered thusly is inifinite and beyond space and time, whereas we are finite and our conceptions are marked by those dimensions, we speak of the image of the features of God.[1] He is One, unified in simplicity.[2]

The Unification understanding of God seeks to deepen the insights of traditional Christianity regarding the nature of God's fatherhood and love. For this reason, it also adds further notions

---

*Director of the Institute for Unification Thought, Seoul, Korea. His article written in Korean for this cumulative work, has been translated into English.

[1]   See below, II, 3; III.
[2]   See below, III.

and explanations of the features of God. It is these notions that are summarily dealt with in this essay.

The Unification view sets forth the image of God as having both internal or spiritual and external or energetic aspects. We call the spiritual or internal aspect of God "Sung Sang" and the energetic or external aspect "Hyung Sang;" we call them together "the duality of God." Besides the *Sung Sang* and *Hyung Sang* duality of the image of God there is another pair of complementary features, not dealt with in the traditional view, called "Positivity" and "Negativity." We also refer to them as "duality of God," but strictly speaking they are characteristics of the *Sung Sang* and the *Hyung Sang.*

Among the many features of God, Heart, which belongs to the *Sung Sang,* is essential and fundamental. Heart is the source of love and the motive for the creation of the universe.

Taken collectively, the features of God are called "The Original Image." The Original Image has both content and structure. Here, "content" means the classification and description of the essential features and "structure" means the mutual relationships appearing among them. The structure of the Original Image can also be considered from the view point of its formation (or activity), and this constitutes a dynamic aspect of God.

I. The Content of the Original Image (Static Aspect of God)

Among the features of God, there are some that are seen as the source of the essence and appearance of each creature, and there are others that are seen as the source of the activity (nature) and function of each creature. The former grouping of features is called "Divine Image" or General Image of God and the latter "Divine Character" or Specific Image of God.

1. Divine Image (General Image of God)

As stated above, the image of God appears as the union of the internal spirit and external energy: the internal spiritual aspect being called "Sung Sang" and the external energetic aspect being called "Hyung Sang;" also, each of these can be perceived in terms of relative characteristics, of "Positivity" and "Negativity." "Individual Images" of specific beings are also understood to be located in the image of God.

When beings are created, these features are manifested in the essence and activity of each. In other words, the entity of each being is derived from these features. In this sense, the *Sung Sang* and *Hyung Sang,* the Positivity and Negativity, and the Individual Images of creatures are the features of God which are manifested in all creatures.

(a) Sung Sang and Hyung Sang

First, *Sung Sang,* called also the mind of God, contains in one of its aspects functions corresponding to emotion, intellect and will, and in another aspect functions corresponding to ideas and laws. These two aspects of the *Sung Sang* are referred to as the *Inner Sung Sang* and the *Inner Hyung Sang.* God's *Sung Sang* is manifested in all creatures, in various ways, such as in the minds of men and animals, in the life of plants, and in the reactiveness of inorganic material. Understanding of *Sung Sang's* two aspects may be helped by looking at the example of man. We experience that the active mind always thinks of something. This is due to the fact that in thinking there are both the subjective aspect and the objective aspect.

Emotion, intellect and will belong to the *Inner Sung Sang.* Here, "intellect" refers to the composite of sensibility, understanding and reason; "emotion" refers to the function of feeling, such as joy, melancholy, anger, etc.; and "will" refers to the function of intention to realize a certain purpose. On the other hand, ideas (mental images), concepts, and laws, conceived by God "before" creation, belong to the *Inner Hyung Sang.* In the process of creation, the ideas and principles of each forthcoming creation would be found "first" in the mind of the Creator.

Thus, the mind of God *(Sung Sang)* consists of the *Inner Sung Sang* which is the subjective aspect, and the *Inner Hyung Sang* which is the objective aspect. The relationship between the former and the latter is that of a subject relative to an object. The subject is relatively active and governs the object; the object is relatively passive and cooperative with the subject.

Next, *Hyung Sang* is the aspect of God's image corresponding to the energy found in the created world. Thus the energy of the world has its origin in God in the same sense that the love and spiritual laws of the world have their origin in God.

The Unification view of God holds that this energetic aspect must exist in God as relative object to the *Sung Sang*. This aspect of God is seen as the origin of the energetic aspect of all created beings. All creatures—men, animals, plants and minerals—have definite material structures. If they all appear with such structures, there must exist in God that which is the source from which these structures are formed. There is no effect without a cause. Thus, although God is an invisible Being, we consider that His features must be manifested in the beings which He creates.

The *Sung Sang* and *Hyung Sang* compose the duality of "God's image." They occupy different positions. *Sung Sang* is in the subject position and *Hyung Sang* is in the object position.

(b) Positivity and Negativity

It is written in the Bible (Gensis 1:27) that God created man and woman after His own image. This means that God, as the source of man and woman alike, has both the natures of masculinity and femininity in His entity. In *Divine Principle* we call the former Positivity and the latter Negativity. Positivity and Negativity are not independent features separated from the *Sung Sang* and *Hyung Sang,* but are characteristics of them. In other words, both *Sung Sang* and *Hyung Sang* have aspects of positivity and negativity. Thus, when the *Sung Sang* and *Hyung Sang* of God are manifested in the phenomenal world of His creation, these manifestations have positive and negative aspects.[3]

---

[3] God, not being material, does not actually contain masculine and feminine, nor positive and negative parts, but rather this duality lies in His being virtually a cause of masculine and feminine or positive and negative phenomena of His creation.

For example, when the mind of God *(Sung Sang)* is manifested in the mind of man, it becomes either the mind of a man (masculinity) or the mind of a woman (femininity). And when the *Hyung Sang* aspect of God's image is manifested in the body of man it becomes the body of a man (masculinity) or the body of a woman (femininity). Positivity and Negativity are a duality of God and thus are manifested in every creation. The aspects of positivity and negativity determine not only the characteristics of the *Sung Sang* and *Hyung Sang* of man (resulting in men and women), but also those of animals, plants, and minerals, (resulting in male and female animals, the stamen and pistil of plants, the cation and anion of molecules, and the proton and electron of atoms, etc.). It is the aspects of positivity and negativity that also, through alteration, allow for change in the mind and body of each individual being.

As has been said above, positive and negative aspects appear in all things—animal, plant and mineral. This fact requires us to think that God, the Creator of all things, has Positivity and Negativity as relative features or complementary characteristics of His *Sung Sang* and *Hyung Sang.* The reciprocal relationship between the positive and the negative, where positivity is the relative subject and negativity is its object reminds us of a similar relationship between *Sung Sang* and *Hyung Sang.*

Sung Sang and *Hyung Sang,* Positivity and Negativity are also called the "Universal Image" because they are seen throughout the whole creation.

(c) Individual Images

Another feature of God the Creator consists of countless Individual Images, and in creation each created being takes after one of them.

What is the relationship between the Individual Images and the *Sung Sang* and *Hyung Sang?* The Individual Images are not independent or separated from *Sung Sang* and *Hyung Sang.* As the Individual Images are features of God individually given to a creature at creation, they could not have existed prior to the *Sung*

Sang of God. In other words, in creating the universe, God had the image of each creature in His mind, and each image in His mind was an Individual Image. So, the Individual Images are merely the ideas of creatures which appear in the mind of God. Thus the Divine Image consists of the Universal Image (*Sung Sang* and *Hyung Sang* and Positivity and Negativity) and the Individual Images.

2. *Divine Character* (Specific Image of God)

While the "Divine Image" refers to those features of God which cause each creature to have a definite essence and appearances, there are other features of God which are the cause of the specific activity (nature) and functions of all creatures. These features together may be called the "Divine Character." Thus, love, a practice of justice, piety, dignity, honesty, creativity, respect and indignation, all originate in the Divine Character. They are all features of God and they belong directly to the *Sung Sang.* The Divine Character also includes such features as omniscience, omnipotence, absolute goodness and eternal life. In the Unification view of God, *Heart, Logos,* and *Creativity* are considered the most important among them and they can be considered as Specific Image of God. Here I will explain these three characteristics.

(a) *Heart* (Shim-Jung)

Heart is the essential and fundamental feature of God. Because of this feature, God appears as a personal Being, the Father of man. The location of Heart is in the *Inner Sung Sang.* Heart lies deeper in the total mind than emotion, intellect or will; that is, it is the core of the mind, and controls its other functions. Heart moved the mind of God to create the universe. As Heart performed its role being the motive and cause, all the features of the Divine Image and the Divine Character interacted with each other . . . creation began.

Heart is the impulse that seeks joy through loving an object.

One cannot receive joy unless he has an object that resembles himself and he loves it. Therefore, the impulse of Heart necessarily requires an object; the purpose for the object and the thinking in creating it accord with this requirement.

When we analyze the spiritual aspect of man, we can understand that heart is the essential feature of God. Man wants to live happily, being peaceful and joyful throughout his whole life. Many Christians have experienced that true joy and true happiness can be realized when we love people and serve God and mankind. This is because God's motive for creation was the impulse of Heart that seeks joy. The purpose of creation is to love an object, thereby producing joy.

We cannot explain the personality of God or His creative activity without recognizing Heart, nor can we otherwise solve the problem of why a perfect and faultless God would create the universe. Joy cannot result from merely interior interactions. Even if God is omniscient and omnipotent, He feels joy only when He has created an object that resembles Him (especially man). In this sense, it is not too extreme to say that all other features, including omniscience and omnipotence, are means for accomplishing the purpose of Heart.[4]

Heart, being the source of love, is the central and essential dimension of God. The Heart of God being central, each human, resembling God, has a fundamental desire to seek joy by relating with other beings, especially other humans, and giving love to them. Because others, like oneself, have been created in the image of God, with both the same desire for joy and the aspects of spirit and matter, one can have confidence that harmonious reciprocal relationships are possible.

---

4 This is the Heart of God the Creator: the Heart of God the Father, God the Lover, God the Sovereign. But through man's fall, all mankind fell into ruin; man could neither fully resemble God and fully receive His love nor could he respond to God returning joy to Him. Because only man was created as God's partner in joy, the Heart of God has been manifested in history as His long-suffering Heart, the Heart in search of restoration.

(b) Logos

According to the Gospel of John, Chapter 1, verses 1-3, "In the beginning was the Word, and the Word was with God and the Word was God . . . all things were made through him. . . . " (Similar meanings can be found in Gensis 1-3 and Psalm 33). The Unification view of God understands the *Logos* not as God Himself but as God's standard, by which all things were created. It is comparable to the blueprint of an idea. When one wants to make an industrial product or a work of art, one first sets up in his mind the standard for it, including standards such as shape, structure, size, color, and efficiency, and then makes the blueprint on this basis. Only then does one begin to make the object according to one's thought or blueprint. God's creation of the universe was accomplished in the same way, and His blueprint is the *Logos* or the Word. This means that the *Logos* is formed in the mind of God. It is formed through the interaction between the *Inner Sung Sang* (emotion, intellect and will) and the *Inner Hyung Sang* (idea and principle).

Reason (a function of intellect) found in the *Inner Sung Sang,* and law, in the *Inner Hyung Sang,* play the most important roles in forming the *Logos.* When we view each creature, we see that it has both intellectual and mathematical reason, as well as law acting in it; therefore, we can assume that reason and law have played important roles in creation. This is why we think of the *Logos* as a synthesis of reason and law.

The fact that the universe was created by the *Logos* means not only that all existing beings have been created by the *Logos,* but also that all interactions between individuals have been carried out according to the norm established by the *Logos,* that is by "reason and law." Thus, the Word is God's conception of creation, and is one of the features in the Creator's Divine Character.

Because man, who is also created according to God's *Logos,* is modeled directly after the Divine Character, he should be governed by the *Logos.* Reason and law operate in man through the principle of give and take. This means that man is created to have harmonious give and take with others, centering on Heart and Love. As a subject or object he is connected with those around him in various positions. (Because of the fall of man, however, he has become unable to follow this "reason and law." Therefore, society has become filled with hatred, repulsion, plunder and struggle. Saints have appeared throughout history to try to restore man to a life in line with the *Logos.)*

Because the image of God is manifest in each man, each person can apprehend within himself the blueprint for his own becoming and relating,[5] and can recognize that every other creature has an innate God-given blueprint for its becoming and relating. These blueprints are designed for harmonious relationships of love and beauty.

(c) Creativity

What is Creativity? As mentioned before, the creation of the universe was caused by the desire of God's Heart. Creation was accomplished through the *Logos;* the *Logos* was formed by the interaction of the *Inner Sung Sang* and *Inner Hyung Sang.* This means that before the actual creation of each thing, the *Logos* has always been formed beforehand. This ability to form *Logos* is the Creativity of God. God's Creativity is the ability to form and develop ideas through the interaction of the functions of the mind (emotion, intellect, and will) with ideas and principles which are held in the mind.

Because man is given a corresponding creative ability, he wants to invent new things and develop new ideas: he is not content with repetition. When man invents new things, he first establishes the purpose or aim and then utilizing wisdom, knowledge and experience develops the specific idea. Man's ability to develop new ideas is the creativity given to him by God.

We must note, however, that because of the fall, man has lost

---

[5] For the notion of "relationship," see below, 3 (Remarks).

his ability to reveal the Heart and love of God and therefore creative and technological activity is not directed by a true view of value.

3. Remarks

God's purpose is to relate to an object with love. God's creativity formed the *Logos* for creation and relation. Creatures in His image, therefore, also have the nature to relate.

A relationship requires recognition, selection, communication, the readiness to relate, the design for relationship, and the flexibility to form relationships.

Creatures in whom the features of the Divine Image are manifested have the possibility of a relationship. Recognition is possible because of the commonality of the features of the Universal Image; selection is possible because of the manifestation in each being of an Individual Image; communication is possible because individualized *Sung Sang* and *Hyung Sang* appear in each created being and possess individualized characteristics of positivity and negativity. The possibility of relationship exists because the features of the Divine Image are manifested in each existing being.

Also, relationships can exist only because the features of the Divine Character are manifested in the created beings: sharing the manifestation of God's Heart, such beings have the tendency to relate; with the manifestation of *Logos*, they have the capacity for normal relationship; and with the manifestation of creativity, they have the necessary flexibility to form relationships.

It is existing beings with images manifesting the features of the Original Image that have capabilities for relationship. But the basis for actual relationship lies in the structure for relationship.

Since the capabilities for relationships between created beings originate in the features of the Original Being, the structure for relationship of these beings may be discovered in the structure for relationship of the features of the Original Image. Actual relationship is possible only with reference to the living Creator, in whom already exists the structure for relationship.

It is traditional to consider relationships between the different qualities attributed to God; for instance, the relationship between God's love and God's wrath, or between His power and love. The Unification View of God, perceiving features of the Original Image, explains the principles of relationship among these features. These principles are also the principles for the actualization of relationship in the created world.

II. The Structure of the Original Image: The Quadruple Base (Dynamic Aspect of God)

As mentioned before, the features of God consist of *Sung Sang* and *Hyung Sang*, Positivity and Negativity, Individual Images, Heart, Logos and Creativity. These features are not a disordered mix, but are closely connected and interacting with each other. They form a certain orderly structure; therefore, order and interaction appear certainly structured in creation. The apparent structure of the image of God and of any creation or unity of reality is a quadruple system, a structure with four positions (see below, Figures 1 and 2). We call this system the "Quadruple Base."[6]

1. The Quadruple Base Centering on Heart

The basic model for order and interaction in the Original Image has four positions which are occupied by the four factors of the origin, subject, object, and their synthesis. This is called the "Quadruple Base." The features of God are connected with each other, and each feature is found in one of the four positions of the quadruple base. Heart always occupies the central position, and

---

6 Of course it is technically impossible to explain the interactions of the many features of an invisible God with the concepts of "structure" and "quadruple base." Strictly speaking, it is not even appropriate to discuss the interactions of the features of God with the concept of a "structure" similar to that of a machine, (such as watches which are composed of many parts). For convenience of understanding I am figuratively explaining the relationship of the features of God as if they were distinct parts put together. I *metaphorically* am communicating something about the features of God.

the relative pairs, *Sung Sang* and *Hyung Sang* or Positivity and Negativity, occupy the positions of the subject and object. Centered on Heart, the paired subjects and objects, such as *Sung Sang* and *Hyung Sang* become harmonious and unified to occupy the position of synthesis.

The features of God form the quadruple base because the subject and object perform give and take action centering on Heart. Give and take is the action of giving and receiving between the subject and object. *Sung Sang* and *Hyung Sang* or Positivity and Negativity become harmonious and unified by their give and take action. Accordingly the four positions come about. This relationship is seen in Figures 1 and 2.

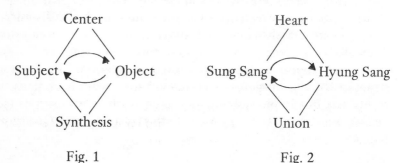

Fig. 1

Fig. 2

Basic Model of the Quadruple Base

Quadruple Base of *Sung Sang* and *Hyung Sang* (Outer Identity-Maintaining Quadruple Base)

The Unity of God's features is due to the centrality of Heart and the appropriateness of relationship of His features.

(a) The Quadruple Base Formed by Give and Take between "Sung Sang" and "Hyung Sang"

We call the features of God viewed as grouped into an interacting and unifying duality His "dual characteristics." As mentioned before, there are many features of God and all of them belong to either the *Sung Sang* or *Hyung Sang* of God's image. Therefore, *Sung Sang* (or internal aspect) and *Hyung Sang* (or external aspect) are the representative features of God.

How is give and take action between *Sung Sang* and *Hyung Sang* possible? Because *Sung Sang* is the mind, it can control *Hyung Sang* or the energetic-external aspect. However, the basic reason that they can have give and take action is that, although different in position, *Sung Sang* and *Hyung Sang* in God are not different in essence. If they were essentially different as are mind and matter in the created world, the *Sung Sang* of God could not dominate His *Hyung Sang.*

In the created world, mind alone cannot move matter (such as instruments or machines). To move matter, we need similar matter such as hands or tools. Similarly, in God, the dominating *Sung Sang* and the submitting *Hyung Sang* must be of the same quality. In God, *Sung Sang* is at the same time *Hyung Sang.* Mind *(Sung Sang)* is power *(Hung Sang)* and power is mind. This means that power is actually power with mind, and the mind is actually mind with power.

In the created world, the mental or internal and the energetic or external appear as completely different, but they are of basically the same quality in the image of God. The only difference between them is one of balance. The predominance of *Sung Sang* (internal-mind) results in a more active manifestation; the predominance of *Hyung Sang* (external-power) results in a more passive manifestation. Still, the action of give and take between them is possible because they are essentially of the same quality, including both natures. Through give and take action their complete unity is possible.

In the give and take action of *Sung Sang* and *Hyung Sang,* Heart must always be the center. There is no give and take action without a center. That give and take action appears centering on Heart can be easily understood due to the fact that Heart (or purpose which is established by Heart) induces the interactions of the features of God which lead to creation. Such give and take action realizes the harmony of His features.

There is no change in the quadruple base formed by such give and take action. It is unchanging; it maintains its identity forever, and we call it the "Identity-Maintaining Quadruple Base." The eternity and unchangeability of God show that His features form an Identity-Maintaining Base.

God's Heart is the center of all creation. We apprehend it through consideration of His unified internal or mental and external or energetic aspects. Heart is expressed in energy directed by mind or as will which is energized. All appearances of God express eternal, unchangeable Heart and love. Reflecting its Creator, every unit in reality presents itself as a union of *Sung Sang* and *Hyung Sang,* and of positivity and negativity.

(b) Inner Quadruple Base of the Sung Sang

As explained before, there are relative aspects of the *Sung Sang.* Just as the *Sung Sang* and *Hyung Sang* are seen as necessarily having give and take centering on Heart, so the relative aspects of the *Sung Sang* also appear having give and take action centering on Heart, and forming a quadruple base. The resultant synthesis is the *Sung Sang (Original Sung Sang)* itself. In other words, the mind of God *(Original Sung Sang)* appears as the union of the *Inner Sung Sang* (emotion, intellect and will) and the *Inner Hyung Sang* (idea and law). We call this the "Inner Quadruple Base."

Because of this unchanging, identity-maintaining quadruple base the mind of God is eternal and unchanging.

Whereas the quadruple base inside the *Sung Sang* is called the "Inner Quadruple Base," the quadruple base formed by the action of give and take between the over-all *Sung Sang* and *Hyung Sang* aspects is called the "Outer Quadruple Base," in order to avoid confusion.

In the Outer Quadruple Base, the *Sung Sang* is subject and the *Hyung Sang* is object, and in the Inner Quadruple Base, the *Inner Sung Sang* is subject and the *Inner Hyung Sang* is object. Therefore, the *Inner Sung Sang* dominates the *Inner Hyung Sang;* the *Inner Hyung Sang* is never in a dominating position. This fact is important because it is the standard for the perfection of human personality.

The quadruple base formed by the give and take action between a man's spiritual mind and physical mind is his Inner Quadruple Base. Here the subject should be the spiritual mind which is the location of our ongoing desire to seek after and to realize truth, goodness and beauty; the object to the spiritual mind should be the physical mind, which focuses on physical maintenance and development. Accordingly, we should be primarily concerned with our spiritual life—seeking the values of goodness, justice and love. Secondary to this should be our physical life of seeking food, clothing and shelter. Through this we can make our physical mind submit to our spiritual mind, with the desire to love governing the desire for physical maintenance. This will result in a unified mind, the mind of love. In such a mind, the physical desires can be very great providing only that they are in harmony with the spiritual desires for love and beauty. Then, as these unified desires are fulfilled through actually doing the will of God, God's creation of Heaven and Earth will be realized through individual spiritual growth and substantial cultural progress.

I have now explained the Inner and Outer Quadruple Bases centering on Heart. The basic character of these quadruple bases is that their subjects and objects centering on Heart harmonize completely with each other and form a synthesis, a union. Such relationships are seen in all things and in the universe as a whole. Together they form one great harmony. However, due to the Fall, man lost the inner harmony of his mind (the Inner Quadruple Base), and has also lost the harmony of his relationships with others (corresponding to the Outer Quadruple Base).

From their origin in the individual many difficult and complicated problems in the family, the nation and the world have arisen. However, by comprehending the structure of relationships in the image of God, we can understand the nature which is desirable for our own relationships.

(c) Clarification

Identifiable and enduring relationships in the Original Image and in the world of creation are those of subject and object uniting around a center to express God's Heart. For a person to enter such a relationship there should be a connection with God's Heart, identification of self and another being, and comprehension of how oneself and the other can fulfill positions of a quadruple base in order to express Heart.

What is identity? God's identity is not the omnipotent speaking God or the omniscient acting God, for essentially He is the heartistic God, the living Creator and Father. For this reason, Christians do not say that God is Intellect or that God is Power; nor do we describe Him as a dualistic God of mind and power. Rather, we identify God as a monistic Being; we have said that God is Love, the One source of existence and development.

Then what is man's identity? Just as with God, we cannot identify man as mind or body. The persons in a human quadruple base cannot relate simply as minds or bodies which only express centers of identity. (Within a human it is neither feeling nor other internal content that specifies the human spirit; rather it is the identifying center). Initial self-identity must be as a child of God, as a person with a spirit and body to express love. With this identity, we relate to another human as another child of God, and we relate to non-human creatures as also being of value to God. Then, united under God we may form the quadruple base centering on Him.

That the quadruple base is formed as an orderly system implies that in the created world, order must be formed and maintained in both nature and human society. A very stable system of order is found in nature, but in human society one finds very confused relationships.

2. The Quadruple Base Centering on Purpose

In the previous section I explained the structure of God's image "before" He began to create the universe. Here, I will clarify the structure as involved in the process of creation, that is, the quadruple base formed by give and take between the *Sung Sang* and *Hyung Sang* in the process of creation, and also explain the Inner Quadruple Base with the *Sung Sang* in this process.

(a) The Quadruple Base Formed by the Give and Take Action between "Sung Sang" and "Hyung Sang"

Give and take action is performed and the quadruple base formed "during" as well as "before" the process of creation. During creation, not Heart but the purpose of Heart appears in the center (origin) position for give and take action, and rather than a union of *Sung Sang* and *Hyung Sang* or a harmonized body as the result a multiplied body (a new individual) occupies the fourth position. In creation, the purpose of creation is established first, then the activity of creation begins centered on the purpose, and finally a new creation (multiplied body) is created. Accordingly, the four elements—purpose, *Sung Sang*, *Hyung Sang* and multiplied body—form the quadruple base. In this Quadruple also, *Sung Sang* is the subject and *Hyung Sang* is the object.

Heart and its purpose, which are the centers of these quadruple bases, are not different from each other because the purpose is established by Heart, seeking joy and desiring to love.

Purpose cannot exist isolated from Heart; on the contrary, it is established and maintained by Heart. Of course, countless new individuals have been created since the beginning of creation through the formation of quadruple bases centering on purpose. Accordingly, the details of the purpose, *Sung Sang, Hyung Sang* and multiplied body are continuously changing. For example, if God created the amphibians after fish, the purpose, *Sung Sang, Hyung Sung* and multiplied body of the amphibians would have been quite different from those of the fish. Thus, the details of the four elements of the quadruple base are not fixed throughout a period of continuous creation, but are always changing. We call such a quadruple base the "Developing Quadruple Base."

(b) Inner Quadruple Base of the "Sung Sang"

(aa) Of the four elements in the quadruple base, it is the *Sung Sang* in which the change is most remarkable; this is because an Inner Developing Quadruple Base is formed in the *Sung Sang* itself.

Once a purpose for creating something, for example a fish, is set up by Heart, the idea or image of a fish is formed in the *Inner Hyung Sang,* while the *Inner Sung Sang* (emotion, intellect and will) interacts with this idea. The requisite conception *(logos)* of the fish is formed through this give and take action between the *Inner Sung Sang* and the *Inner Hyung Sang,* and this "logos" or concept is the new entity in the Inner Quadruple Base. Then, in God, the *Sung Sang* in which the "logos" has been formed performs give and take action with the *Hyung Sang,* centered on the same purpose which formed the "logos." Consequently, a substantial fish in the created world results.

As the creation of different individuals progresses, the contents of the Inner Quadruple Base change each time. Thus, it is a developing quadruple base which is formed in the overall *Sung Sang.* Actually, this quadruple base is the Inner Identity-Maintaining Quadruple Base which has become dynamic and developmental. Therefore, we call it the "Inner Developing Quadruple Base." We call the Outer Quadruple Base formed by the give and take action of *Sung Sang* and *Hyung Sang* centering on purpose the "Outer Developing Quadruple Base."

(bb) The Inner Developing Quadruple Base and the Outer Developing Quadruple Base are understood to be formed consecutively during the creation process. As God creates something, the specification of *logos* or the Inner Developing Quadruple Base is first formed inside the *Sung Sang,* and the actual "multiplied body" (the created being) is made according to this *logos* through the give and take action of the *Sung Sang* and *Hyung Sang* in the Outer Developing Quadruple Base. We call the structure involving these two quadruple bases, which are formed during the creation process, "the two-staged structure of creation." The Word is with God in the first place; in the second place, the Word has power and is effective in the created world. This being the process of creation, the Word and the power are both centered on the purpose of creation.

(cc) To state that God has a purpose of creation raises the issue of just what that purpose is. It seems that traditional theologies have not answered this question adequately. *Divine Principle* maintains clearly that the purpose of creation is to realize the Kindgom of Heaven, a world of great harmony and eternal happiness in which people love each other centering on God's love. In such a world, God loves all men, men love each other and all things, all things give back beauty and joy to man and man gives back beauty and joy to God. This means that all things as well as man contribute to the creation of the Kingdom of Heaven. This is the world in which the *logos* of creation is fully realized.

Logos being a blueprint to be realized in the created world of time and space, and development being able to occur only through the establishment in this world of Outer Dynamic Bases (of Origin, Positivity, Negativity, and multiplied body), the *Logos* specifies the norms for harmonious interactions of positivity and negativity. *Logos* (word) is always expressive of purpose, and God's purpose is to realize relationships of love; therefore, every true norm expresses God's love.

When the *logos* of creation is fully realized in the Kingdom of Heaven, all things, including man, will exist, move, and develop in accordance with the norms of God's *Logos.* Man will not feel restrained or inconvenienced by these norms, because the foundation of the Kingdom of Heaven is the love of God. Because God-centered rulings were violated by the fall of man, these original rulings (norms) need to be restored.

(dd) In the process of creation, the conception of a new entity precedes its substantiation. But the new concept is an elaboration of an already given potential, for the Inner Developing Quadruple Base centering on purpose is logically preceded by the Inner Identity-Maintaining Quadruple Base of which it is a dynamic and developmental form. This Identity-Maintaining Base is centered ultimately on God's Heart which established purpose.

The Kingdom of Heaven is the fulfillment of the potential of the cosmos—it is the world of the complete realization of love—and any true *logos* or plan delineates a step toward it. Therefore, a true *logos* or plan can be developed only by centering on God's purpose of creation. Man is created as a child of God; his development is towards his potential of "attaining the stature of manhood of Christ[7] . . . to be as He is."[8]

A two-staged structure is also formed when man creates. That is, man first engages in a thinking process, forming an inner quadruple base, and next, according to the result of the thinking, mobilizes energy/matter to make an actual entity, forming an outer quadruple base. The application of this principle to philosophical fields such as epistomology, logic, etc. makes the establishment of many new theories possible.

The *Logos* includes norms for social units as well as for individuals. Ultimately, human society is to direct the cosmos. When the stable society of the original standard is restored, it always will develop according to the potential of *Logos*.

3. Origin-Division-Union Action

As already mentioned, the quadruple base is the structure of the Original Image. The structure has four positions, being formed of four factors. It can be explained by considering its factors and their relationships. Indeed, to understand fully the structure of the Original Image, it is necessary to explain the formation process of the structure as well as the interactions between factors of the structure. However, since God is outside of time, there is actually no formation process of the structure of God; this is merely a *metaphorical* expression to facilitate understanding. Such understanding of God will enable a clear view of the formation process of structure in the world of time and space.

Among the four factors of the quadruple base, which is established first? In the Identity-Maintaining Quadruple Base, Heart exists first, then the subject, the object, and finally the synthesis appears. In the Developing Quadruple Base, the purpose is set up first, then the subject and object, and finally the multiplied body.

The general principle is that the center is established first, then

7   Ephesians 4:13.
8   I John 3:2.

the realative factors of the subject and object (in this order), and finally the synthesis or multiplied body. Centering on Heart or purpose, the subject and object perform the harmonious action of give and take which results in a synthesis or in the formation of a multiplied body. We call this process the Origin-Division-Union action or, briefly, O-D-U action. Thus the O-D-U action is the formation process of the quadruple base. Therefore, in the sense that the subject and object perform give and take action and thereby form a synthesis or a new body centering on Heart or purpose, the quadruple base and the O-D-U action are quite the same. The O-D-U action deals with the quadruple structure in relation to time. As there are both Identity-Maintaining and Developing Quadruple Bases, there are also Identity-Maintaining and Developing O-D-U Actions. There are also both Inner and Outer O-D-U Actions.

The fact that both Developing and Identity-Maintaining O-D-U actions appear in the image of God indicates that God not only continues His creation of all things but also perpetually maintains His own eternity and immutability. As there are both immutability and developmentality of God's features, all creatures also necessarily have simultaneously the Identity-Maintaining and Developing aspects. We can easily see that during their lives, men, animals, plants, etc. have both a growing, changing aspect and an unchanging aspect which maintains their individual characters. This is the principle of "the union of changeability and un-changeability."

The principle of "the union of changeability and un-changeability" and the principle of "the harmony of the give and take action," should replace materialist dialectics. Materialist dialectics emphasizes only the changing and dynamic aspects of things and neglects or ignores the unchanging or static aspects. Besides, materialist dialectics insists that struggle is the essential cause of development, ignoring harmonious give and take. From the Unification viewpoint, these assertions of materialist dialectics are fundamentally objectionable.

Through continual O-D-U action, God participates in the life of His creation. Limitation of space prevents discusssion here of

God's continuous activity in human living. God provides the opportunities and gives loving impulses, standards and encouragement for attaining increasing unification. In the Kingdom of Heaven on Earth, God's feelings and thoughts are fully accessible to perfected man. His commandments have always been given to imperfect man and He accepts the efforts of fallen man desiring to return to him.

III. Unity of the Original Image

To conclude the explanation of the Original Image and our understanding of God through the concepts marked by space and time I would like to mention one important point, that being the unity of all the features of God. I have dealt with the features of God from various perspectives, specifically from the standpoint of content and structure, and from the standpoint of space and time. As I have explained frequently, however, there is not time nor space in the dimension of God, and concepts of structure and time pertaining to Him are of imagination. Actually, all of God's features must be comprehended as unified in simplicity. The four positions of the quadruple base are unified in one position. Movement and quiesence, development and identity-maintenance, the inside and outside, large and small are all one. The center and circumference are together; the past, present and future all exist in simultaneity. There is no difference between the infinite and infinitesimal, nor between eternity and moment. God exists as in one *locus* and immediately as in an infinite number of *loci.* The features of God are united as in one simplicity, and they ever spread out infinitely. There are an infinite number of features of God and equally there is only one. Therefore, the features of God form one complete unity. Hence, the theory of the Original Image is a unitive theory.

As these features of God are manifest and reflected in the world of time and space, they invariably show the previous mentioned structure and process. In this sense the use of the metaphorical expressions in this article to explain the Original Image seem to be justified.

A SELECT BIBLIOGRAPHY

1. Sources

Divine Principle. Washington, D.C.: The Holy Spirit Association for the Unification of World Christianity, 1973.

Unification Thought. New York: Unification Thought Institute, 1973.

Moon, Sun Myung, *The Role of United Science in the Moral Orientation of the World.* New York: The International Conference on the Unity of the Sciences, 1972.

————, "Modern Science and Man's View of Moral Values," *Modern Science and Moral Values, Proceedings of the Second International Conference on the Unity of the Sciences* (Tarrytown, New York: The International Cultural Foundation, Inc.), 1973, pp. 571-574.

————, Founder's Address, *The Centrality of Science and Absolute Values, Proceedings of the Fourth International Conference on the Unity of the Sciences* (Tarrytown, New York: The International Cultural Foundation, Inc.), 1975, pp. 7-9.

2. Studies

Kim, Young Oon, *Unification Theology and Christian Thought.* New York: Golden Gate Publishing Co., 1975.

Lee, Sang Hun, "Eradication of Poverty and the Realization of Well-Being of Society," *The Centrality of Science and Absolute Values, Proceedings of the Fourth International Conference on the Unity of the Sciences* (Tarrytown, New York: The International Cultural Foundation, Inc.), 1975, pp. 1097-1108.

The Divine Principle Study Guide. Washington, D.C.: The Holy Spirit Association for the Unification of World Christianity, 1973.

CHAPTER XXVII

GOD IN THE THOUGHT OF MARTIN HEIDEGGER

Hans Köchler *

In the thought of Martin Heidegger** two distinct "periods" can be discerned: the early *phenomenological* approach (*Sein und Zeit*, 1927) and the later approach *based on a philosophy of being* (*Zur Seinsfrage*, 1955; *Was heisst Denken?* 1954). In the earlier period Heidegger remains "neutral" as regards the God-question (phenomenological neutrality, abstention from any statement). In the later period the *transcendence of Being* (ontological difference) appears to him as being something truly "divine," in

Abbreviations

EH	*Erläuterungen zu Hölderlins Dichtung*	(1944)
EM	*Einführung in die Metaphysik*	(1953)
FD	*Die Frage nach dem Ding*	(1962)
Gel	*Gelassenheit*	(1959)
HB	*Brief über den "Humanismus"*	(1947)
HW	*Holzwege*	(1950)
ID	*Identität und Differenz*	(1957)
KM	*Kant und das Problem der Metaphysik*	(1929)
KT	*Kants These über das Sein*	(1962)
NI	*Nietzsche*, Vol. I/II	(1961)
PW	*Platons Lehre von der Wahrheit*	(1942)
SF	*Zur Seinsfrage*	(1955)
SG	*Der Satz vom Grund*	(1957)
SP	*Unterwegs zur Sprache*	(1959)
SZ	*Sein und* ...	(1927)
TK	*Die Technik und die Kehre*	(1962)
VA	*Vorträge ufsätze*, Vol. I/II/III	(1954)
WD	*Was heisst Denken?*	(1954)
WG	*Vom Wesen des Grundes*	(1929)
WM	*Was ist Metaphysik?*	(1929)
WW	*Vom Wesen der Wahrheit*	(1943)

*Assistant Professor at the University of Innsbruck, Austria.
**Born 1889, died 1976.

opposition to a merely objectivistic-anthropomorphous understanding of God. In our paper we unfold the God-problem in
Heidegger's works primarily under the aspects of his later mode of
thinking, as here an affinity to a theological, though not dogmatic,
approach is apparent. In the part concerned with "philosophy and
theology" we briefly refer to Heidegger's early position which we
want to present in its implications regarding his later thinking on
the philosophy of being.

1. The Systematic Presentation of the God-Question within the Framework of the Problem of Being

The God-problem, as it exists for Heidegger, can first be
adequately understood when viewed from the perspective of the
systematic, historical development of the problem of Being. The
God-question, as it historically appears, is held by him to be a
modification of the question of Being, a possible way of
experiencing Being as "Ground" (although this experience of the
Ground offers only one given form of the experience of Being!)[1] :
"The Ground, as the first existing reason for all essents (alles
Seienden), is called God."[2] Heidegger believes that the reason why
the first "Being" is experienced as "Ground" at all, and further,
that this "Ground" was conceived of as an existing God, lies in the
historical necessity of the experience of Being, a necessity which
itself is founded (and hidden) in one of the principle characteristics of Western man. Such a principle feature of the human
experience of the Real is the "possessive placing before oneself"
(das bemachtigende Vor-stellen),[3] through which man asserts his
position within the world. This placing before does not take
cognizance of the inaccessibility (Unverfügbarkeit) of Being and
therefore searches for a supreme grounding (oberste Begründung)
for the existing phenomena in the sense of a supreme existing
cause from which everything can be totally deduced on the basis

1   See especially SG; NI, I.
2   SG, p. 55.
3   See, for example, SG, p. 132; NI, I, p. 427; VA, II, p.15.

of necessity.[4] Thus the Being of "that which is" *(das Sein des Seienden)* "reveals" itself "as the Ground which both founds *(begrunden)* and discovers *(ergrunden)* itself."[5] It is conceived of as the highest essent *(oberstes Seiendes),* the *summum ens,* and is thus removed from the realm of actual ontological difference. It is no longer experienced as Being which withdraws itself from an objective fixation. "The original concern *(Sache)* of thought portrays itself as the primal concern *(Ur-sache),* as the causa prima which corresponds to the substantiating return to the *ultima ratio,* the final justification."[6] This *ultima ratio* is the God of the Western Greek metaphysics which exhibits its "theological" character in such a presentation of a supreme existing Ground. "The greatest justification for the universal order *(Berechenbarkeit),* for universal accountability, is *Deus,* God."[7] Metaphysics thus becomes an "onto-theo-logy" to the extent it views "that which is" *(das Seiende)* "in the founding unity *(begrundende Einheit)* of 'all that is' *(Allheit),* that is, of the highest *(essent)* over everything," [8] God,[9] and allows the ontological difference between Being and "that which is" to become a "theological" difference between *ens* and *summum ens.*[10] Metaphysics must therefore "think beyond to God in that the basis *(Sache)* of thought is Being which is Ground in many ways: as *logos,* as *hupokeimenon* as substance, as subject."[11] The thus objectified ontological difference (which also determines the very nature of "technical science") limits the appearance of the

4 Against which, for example, H. Krings firmly reacts *(Transzendentale Logik,* p. 179).

5 *ID,* p. 48.

6 *Ibid.,* p. 51. See also, "Die Metaphysik als Geschichte des Seins," VA, III, p. 399ff.

7 *SG,* p. 169 (formulated in connection with a Leibniz-interpretation).

8 *ID,* p. 49.

9 Heidegger also understands the Christian, Catholic teaching on Trinity from the "Logos" involved in such an "Onto-theo-logy." See *WD,* p. 170.

10 See M. Müller, *Existenzphilosophie im geistigen Leben der Gegenwart,* p. 66.

11 *IS,* p. 51.

"Divine" to but an objectified relationship.[12] The theological difference bars the appearance of the genuine experience of transcendence, as Heidegger demonstrated in his experience of Being, and the manner in which it must also be the base of a deepened God-experience.[13]

On the other hand, Heidegger stresses that the "Holy" first makes its "appearance" "when previously and through long preparation Being itself has made itself visible and has been experienced in its Truth."[14] For "it is only from the Truth of Being that the nature of the Holy can first be conceived."[15] Thus a "theology" built upon the metaphysical basis described as a "statement about God from conceptual (vorstellende) thought"[16] does not succeed in achieving the depths of Heidegger's question of Being, and thus neither can nor should see itself as a critical stage in relation to Heidegger's discussion of "Being" and "God." Heidegger attempts to understand this God-concept of metaphysics and theology in its historical development and thus, through such an "understanding," to "destroy" it in order to free the way to an experience of the "God who is divine."[17] The Christian concept of God as the "highest essent" (höchste Seiende) as "Ground in the sense of that which allows all that is to rise into Being,"[18] is actually an expression for the "transfer" (Verlegung) of Being into a highest existing cause,[19] that is, the restructuring of the ontological difference into a derived theological one. To permit this difference to appear in its very character of derivation, Heidegger completes the "step back-

12 Thus Heidegger in one place speaks about the "theological at work in all of metaphysics," SF, p. 24. See also PW, p. 141: "Thus since the explanation of Being, thinking about the Being of 'that which is' (Sein des Seienden) is metaphysical, and metaphysics theological."

13 On this, see esp. TK.

14 HB, p. 169.

15 Ibid., p. 181ff.

16 ID, p. 44.

17 Ibid., p. 65; also: HB, p. 179. He speaks here about a "minimizing of the nature" of God through certain metaphysical, theistic value judgements.

18 KT, p. 277.

19 PW, p. 141.

ward"[20] which leads out of "metaphysics" into its (hidden) nature which is the manner in which Being "sends itself forward" *(sich zuschickt)* from time to time through events *(vorgängig)* and leads to a given interpretation of the "whole of reality" as the Ground, the Divine in the sense of an *ens creator*, etc.[21] The knowledge of the "onto-theo-logical" character of Western metaphysics[22] which, according to Heidegger, centralizes everything upon conceptual "calculation" *(vorstellendes Berechnen)*, and thus has always objectified (verdinglicht) a clear experience of "Being" and "God" (which is expressed in its extreme in the nature of modern "technical science."),[23] does not permit it to renounce a discussion of the God-question on the basis of the existing ("metaphysical") categories (according to which also the understanding of God is determined).[24] The historically achieved level of the problem is insufficient for a discussion of the question. It is first necessary that the experience of Being again be shown

20 See *ID,* p. 40: "Before Being, thought steps back and thus brings that which was considered *(das Gedachte)* into an opposite in which we see the whole of this history, and this indeed in the light of that which constitutes the source of this whole area of thought in that it prepares the confines of its stay."

21 For metaphysics cannot itself consider the conditions of its possible existence *(Möglichkeitsbedingungen)* which lie in a hidden "nihilism," a having forgotten *(Vergessenheit)* about Being. Compare *SF,* p. 25: "How is this to be done when even the language of metaphysics and metaphysics itself, be it that of a living or a dead God, *as* metaphysics built that boundary which . . . prevents the overcoming of nihilism?" And according to Heidegger it is the theology of Being *(Ontotheologie)* which is the decisive expression of such a "nihilism." Compare *NI,* I, p. 348.

    Heidegger therefore decisively distances himself from a theological, metaphysical interpretation of the basic concepts of his philosophizing (since he wants to come to know the "metaphysical-theological" in its very nature and thus "overcome" it): In relation to the concept of "existence," he stresses that what is being dealt with here is not a "secularized transference unto man of a thought (expressed) about God in Christian theology," *HB,* p. 159.

22 This character exists above all in that, when the "Grounding" of "that which is" is asked about, the "that which is" appears as Ground in two ways: as "that which is" as such and as the "highest essent," see especially *ID,* p. 31; *KT,* p. 277. "The two forms of the question about Being are brought together in the title Onto-Theo-Logie." For a more precise meaning of "logos," see below.

23 See especially, *TK,* p. 26; *SG,* p. 99.

24 In addition (in connection with the relationship between the traditional understanding of God and the basic structures of "metaphysics") compare also, *Die Frage nach dem Ding,* p. 84; *WD,* p. 44; *KM,* p. 18.

from its origin.[25] "He who has experienced theology, both that of
the Christian faith as well as that of philosophy, from its
developed origin prefers today to remain silent in the area of
thought about God."[26] This does not have its basis "in an
indifferent attitude but rather comes from a respect for the
boundaries drawn up for thought as thought through . . . the truth
of Being."[27] When Heidegger considers Nietzsche's statement on
the "death of God,"[28] he sees in it the final conclusion of the
metaphysically depicted nature of God: the change of the already
established Ground of Being as the grounding subjectum to man as
"Ground."[29] The hidden cause of this change is the previous
establishment of Being as the "existing cause" (seiende Ursache),
the inattention to the ontological difference. For only in this
manner can "the position which, metaphysically speaking, belongs
to God" as "the place of the effectual 'bringing about'
(Bewirkung) and preserving of 'that which is' as something
created,"[30] be suddenly fixed in the human nature itself. The
metaphysical God, "against" whom such change was directed, was
not a God. The conception of him as the highest existing cause
was always a "killing" of God to the extent that un-objectifiable
(nicht-vergegenständlichbares). Being was thus forced into a
categorical schema of "that which is" (des Seienden). "For this
striking out (against God) does not come from the bystanders who
do not believe in God, but rather from the believers and their
theologians who speak about 'the most fully existing' (das
Seiendsten alles Seienden) of all that is without ever remembering

25 Compare with this esp. W. Schulz, Der Gott der neuzeitlichen Metaphysik, p. 43.

26 ID, p. 45.

27 HB, p. 182.

28 HW, p. 193. See also NI, p. 320.

29 Thus Heidegger can become acquainted through it with the "fate of Being in 2000
years of Western history" as the "fate of Being" of "metaphysics," HW, p. 196). See NI,
I, p. 275: "To the extent that metaphysics has received a specific character from
Christianity, the devaluation of the until now supreme values must also be expressed
theologically through the saying, 'God is dead'."

30 HW, p. 235.

to think about Being itself . . . "[31] Viewed in this way, Nietzsche's cry is the by nature necessary final result of the establishment of Being as the highest essent, that is, the "forgetting about Being" *(Seinsvergessenheit)* of Western philosophy. Heidegger sees the inner necessity of this event as already posited in the change of the nature of truth since the time of the Greeks, who determined the metaphysical way of conception *(das Vorstellen)* from that time on as *orthotes* (see *Platons Lehre von der Wahrheit*).

2. The Question of Being as an Ontological "Corrective" of the God-Question

(a) The "Neutrality" of the Ontological Formulation of the Question

When Heidegger sets aside the God of metaphysics through the arguments contained in his philosophy, this is not to be understood, viewed systematically, as "atheism," a belief which rather is to a greater extent possible only upon the *same* metaphysical basis. The denial of the existence of God as an *"essent" (eines seienden Gottes)* which is the *causa prima,* is in itself always a metaphysical consideration, as is demonstrated, for example, by J.P. Sartre.[32] A decision regarding atheism or theism does not yet contain within itself the question of Being but remains at the stage of an investigation[33] of "that which is" on the basis of Grounds and Causes (that is, according to the presence of lack of Grounds) within "that which is." An a-theism only has "meaning" upon the level of such an "onto-theological" understanding of world and Being; therefore, "one has already proceeded wrongly when he maintains that the explanation . . . (of

31 *Ibid.,* p. 240. Thus the "death of God" can never be understood (from the dogmatic standpoint of Christian religion) only theologically and apologetically; much more must it rather be placed within the whole of the history of "metaphysics" according to ontological relevance. *HW,* p. 202.

32 See Heidegger, *HB,* p. 159.

33 As it is carried out in the various individual sciences.

the nature of man) in relation to the Truth of Being is atheism."[34]
Thinking about Being can be no more theistic than atheistic.[35]
The dimension of the questioning is a different one. The
determination of the nature of man as an equivalent *(Ent-
sprechung)* to Being still says nothing about a possible or
impossible relationship to God: "Therefore, through the existential determination of the nature of man, nothing has yet been
determined about the *'Dasein* of God' or his 'not-existing,' nor
about the possibility or impossibility of the existence of gods."[36]
This phenomenological neutrality, in the way in which it already
directed the analyses in *Sein und Zeit*,[37] sometimes however
appears to withdraw before a "divinization" of Being, especially as
it presents itself in the personal categories which Heidegger uses to
discuss the relationship between man and Being. When he
interprets Nietzsche's statement on the "death of God" as an
expression for the "killing of the Being of 'that which is',"[38]
which has its roots in the forgetting about Being *(Seinsvergessenheit)* of metaphysics, there already exists at least a
justified cause for the identification of the still un-objectified
(vorgegenständlichen) "Ground of Being" sought by him with the
purely "Divine." This is also suggested by his joining of
"experience of Being" and experience of the "Holy" (which in
connection with Hölderlin he made a central theme of his thought
in his later works), the last of which is possible only in the
presence *(Gemeinschaft)* of the former: "The Holy . . . , which is
but the place for the nature of the Godhead, which again itself
only guarantees the dimension for the gods and for God, only
appears when previously and through long preparation Being itself
has made itself visible and has been experienced in its

---

34 *HB*, p. 181.
35 *Ibid.*, p. 182.
36 *Ibid.*, p. 181; Compare also *WG*, p. 55, footnote.
37 See esp. §6 ("Die Aufgabe einer Destruktion der Geschichte der Ontologie"), p.
19.
38 *HW*, p. 246.

Truth . . . "[39] Heidegger himself speaks of a "God of Being" who is only experienced in the Truth of Being. It is only from the "Truth of Being that the nature of the world and the earth is obtained for man and that man, through the conflict involved, experiences the answer of his nature to the God of Being."[40] In such a statement, the area of the "personal" *(des Personalen)* is not more clearly defined; what is meant remains undecided. The still un-objectified *(vor-gegenständliche)* "Being" (as "Nature") is designated as before with merely symbolic designations; it is never conceptually determined. This of course also causes the difficulty of the significance of the statements and a structural comparison with a theological, e.g. Christian, God-concept.

(b) Philosophy and Theology

As Heidegger already said in a conversation after the Second World War, philosophy "does not go beyond the idea of Being, in which is meant the Absolute (God), about which philosophy, independent of the experience of a communication by God, cannot assert that it is God."[41] The only possible consideration of Being for philosophy is, on the one hand, a critical "destruction" of the traditional metaphysical God-concept, as it is developed in philosophy qua ontology *(summum ens),* and a criticism of a premature objectification *(Vergegenständlichung)* of the Divine; and on the other hand, philosophy can, hypothetically, formally describe the concept of the nature of the Divine on the basis of its experience of Being and determine its ontological, systematic place within the framework of the problematic of the Real (an undertaking which Heidegger carried out in his later publications in a varied and not completely clear manner). A concrete, substantial experience of the Divine itself is not possible for philosophy; it is beyond its phenomenological concept of

---

39 *HB*, p. 169.
40 *NI*, I, p. 29.
41 R. Scherer, "Besuch bei Heidegger," *Wort und Wahrheit*, p. 781.

"givenness" (Gegebenheit).[42] "God is a given of religious experience, not of philosophy."[43] This leads Heidegger to a strict separation of theology and philosophy, as he already clearly formulated in a talk ("Phänomenologie und Theologie") given in 1927: "Theology is a positive science[44] and as such is thus completely different from philosophy."[45] In contrast to the ontologically, transcendentally orientated philosophy which always goes beyond the concrete, individual ways of experiencing the Real in the manner in which they underlie the "positive" sciences, "theology is the science which is motivated and justified by faith."[46] "It founds itself through faith and has no need of a "philosophical theory of God."[47] In one way there is indeed an inner relationship to the philosophical problematic: the basic theological concepts are themselves obtained through concrete, ontic experience of the world as it underlies philosophical, ontological reflection. This statement taken from Bultmann simply verifies that theological concepts possess an "ontically

42 For the whole of this problem as it presented itself to the early Heidegger and thus led to a confrontation with Catholic theology, cf. J. Möller, *Existentialphilosophie und katholische Theologie.* Baden-Baden, 1952.

43 Scherer, *op. cit.,* p. 781.

44 That is, "what is present *(das Vorliegende, Positum)* for theology is Christianity," *in his* "Théologie et Philosophie," *Archives de Philosophie* (1969), pp. 364-366.

45 *Ibid.,* p. 360. In connection with the whole of this problematic, compare the excellent critical study of K. Löwith, "Phänomenologische Ontologie und protestantische Theologie," in O. Pöggler, *Heidegger* (Köln, 1969), pp. 54-77. Löwith seeks here to limit the universality of the previous ontological statement, through which there also results a different determination of the relationship between philosophy and theology, in that he refers to its connection and independence from the momentary ontical factors (p. 64). On this separation, see also Scherer, *op. cit.,* p. 782.

46 "Théologie et Philosophie," *op. cit.,* p. 372. For what reflectively articulates itself in theology is the direct "being placed *(Gestelltwerden)* before God" as a "rearranging *(umgestelltwerden)* of existence in and through the mercy of God as understood by faith," *ibid.,* p. 366.

47 Thus theology must keep itself free from elements "alien to its purpose"; as a positive science, it has its own method of procedure. Therefore, in a letter to H. Ott, Heidegger criticizes its manifold dependence upon present "trends" of science: "Until the anthropological, sociological and the existential philosophical manner of conception *(Vorstellen)* are placed on the side, theology will never achieve the freedom of the area of consideration *(das Sagen)* assigned to it," H. Ott, "Was ist systematische Theologie?," J. Robinson (ed.), *Der späterer Heidegger* (Zürich, 1964), p. 132. See similarly Heidegger, *HW,* p. 19.

invalidated content, but for that very reason a pre-Christian one which ontologically determines them, and thus one understandable on a purely rational plane."[48]

Thus philosophy cannot be an inner constitutive moment of theology; it is however, which is related to the establishment of theological concepts in the "profane," pre-religious ways of experience related to "being in the world" *(In-der-Welt-sein-)*, "the formally proclaimed corrective of the ontic, and indeed of the pre-Christian content of theological concepts."[49] There does not exist, however, a "Christian philosophy" which can substantially incorporate theological premises (e.g. divine revelation) into its ontological reflections. Such a philosophy would be "no more

---

[48] "Theologie et Philosophie," *op. cit.,* p. 386. That is, "that in the existence of the believer there is also existentially, ontologically included the overcome pre-Christian *Dasein,*" *ibid.,* p. 386. For "all theological concepts of necessity have buried within themselves the understanding of Being which the human *Dasein,* as *Dasein,* possesses within itself to the extent that it exists at all," *ibid.* See in the same work p. 382: "Faith does not need philosophy, though science as positive science does need faith," to the extent that the ontical, ontological moments of common human "existing" express themselves in it.

Theology therefore always remains related to and bound up with philosophy "to the extent that it can explain its basic concepts as concepts of existence only on the basis of an understanding of the 'Being' of Dasein *(das Sein des Daseins)* and to the extent that it is dependent *(angewiesen)* upon philosophy for an analysis of the meaning of Being," R. Bultmann, "Die Geschichtlichkeit des Daseins und der Glaube," *Die Zeitschrift für Theologie und Kirche* (1940), p. 344.

[49] "Théologie et Philosophie," *op. cit.,* p. 390. That is, "if in faith the existence previous to the time of belief is *"existentiell,"* ontically overcome, this does not mean that the existential *(existential),* ontological conditions of existing are destroyed," Bultmann, *op. cit.,* p. 346. Heidegger also expresses this in *WG* where he refers to the phenomenological neutrality of his investigations concerning the God-problem and also to the ontological establishment of what the God-experience can actually "be": "Through the ontological interpretation of *Dasein* as 'being in the world' *(in-der-Welt-sein),* neither a positive nor a negative decision about a possible Being in relation to God has been made. To be sure, through a better understanding of transcendence there will first of all be gained a more satisfactory concept of Dasein, about which, in regard to its Being, there can be asked from now on how it is ontologically ordered to the relation to God of the *Dasein,"* *ibid.*, p. 55, footnote.

See also Bultmann, *op. cit.,* p. 340. Bultmann too makes clear the relationship of philosophy and theology in the ontical-ontological *(existentiell-existential)* difference (whereby the ontical concretion of a previous ontological structure, which philosophy works out, is investigated by theology); philosophy, therefore, "investigates existence with regard to existentiality, but does not concern itself with concrete existence," *(ibid.,* p. 342), something which is much more the duty of theology.

than a paradox."[50] Regardless of the way in which it is attempted to more precisely describe the relationship between philosophy and theology, the experience of the "Divine" can only be described for an ontologically orientated philosophy in its deficient character and in its formal, systematic meaning, but cannot be sufficiently "understood" in a substantial manner through the means of this philosophical, ontological systematic. An investigation related to the "history" of Being *(seinsgeschichtliche),* whose theme is the withdrawal of Being in history (as Heidegger, for example, gave in the second volume of his Nietzsche work), can never of its own ability already grasp and explain this withdrawal in a theological, Christian manner; it can only reach the conclusion of a possible "lack of God" in the sense of an absence of "salvation" *(Heil),* which is to be understood in a neutral rather than Christian manner, in order to thus more accurately describe the way and manner in which "Being" withdraws itself. Heidegger himself offers such an ontological, and to a certain extent "neutral," approach to the God-problem when he considers the necessity of the fate of Being in relation to the human experience of Being: The absence of the non-hiddenness *(Unverborgenheit)* of Being as such releases the disappearance of all that is salvific in "that which is" *(im Seienden).* This disappearance of the salvific takes along and obstructs the openness of the Holy. The incommunicativeness of the Holy darkens every glimmer of the Divine. This incommunicativeness strengthens and conceals the lack of God.

(c) The Problem of Determining the "Divine"

According to Heidegger, this "Divine" (so as to briefly present what has been achieved in a systematic manner) is, on the level of the classical, "onto-theological" metaphysics, the "purely Existing" *(das schlechthin Seiende)*[51] as the *summum ens,* that is,

---

50 "Théologie et Philosophie," *op. cit.,* p. 392. See also *EM,* p. 6: "A 'Christian philosophy' is a paradox, a misunderstanding."
51 *KT,* p. 277.

"that which exists most fully" *(das Seiendste)*.[52] However, it thus remains outside of the actual ontological difference and does not extend down into the origin of the problematic of the Real in the manner in which Heidegger attempts to reveal it through the discussion of the question of Being.

Heidegger determines "God" and the "Divine" as the symbols of a mythical, as yet unobjectified, experience of Being in a more essential regard in that he sees a possible new access to the Ground of things as to "the Hidden" *(das Geheimnis)*.[53] The essential meaning is expressed in that which Heidegger conceives of as the *Geviert*,[54] in which a non-object *(ungegenständliche)* relationship to the World Ground *(Weltgrund)* becomes visible in relation to it. Beside this on the whole rather vague designation of the "Divine" (the gods), which can also be considered a falling back into a mythical cosmology (which perhaps could correspond to a need of modern man for hiddenness), he is concerned with a new experience of the basic characteristics of the Divine as they already underlied the metaphysical God-concept but were given insufficient consideration. The Divine which is to be determined in this way is indeed, even when Heidegger himself makes no clear observations which support the interpretation, Being itself[55] in the *How* of its appearance-for-man.[56] "Being" is to an extent the leading theme of the investigation. "Reality," neutrally considered

---

52 *ID*, p. 62.

53 On "Geheimnis," cf. esp. *EH*, p. 23; *SG*, p. 186.

54 See *VA*, II, p. 51; *TK*, p. 47; *SP*, p. 22.

55 This interpretation is also held by H. Meyer, although—on the basis of his Catholic standpoint—he criticizes Heidegger's definition of Being: "The hypostatized Being is simply personified and surrounded with the divine nimbus," *Martin Heidegger und Thomas von Aquin* (Paderborn, 1964), p. 69.

56 Therefore, "God" is to that extent "dependent" upon Being, bound up with it. Cf. esp. Vom Wesen und Begriff der *physis*, p. 310. "Nature" as "Being" stands above the gods, formulated in the explanation of a Holderlin poem. See also *EH*, p. 59, 71. A twofold type of dependence remains to be more critically distinguished: namely, the dependence of the experience of God upon a (preceding or concomitant) experience of Being; and on the other hand, the dependence of God himself upon the "Ground of Being" which also encompasses him. Whether the last distinction is meaningful can only be decided when it is explained whether Heidegger conceives of "God" as existing in a "real, ontic" sense, which interpretation we believe can be rejected. See below.

(as the concept of the limit of knowledge), is according to Heidegger to be studied from the viewpoint of how it appears in my finite consciousness. For such an application, the reference leads to an experience of "Salvation" (which Heidegger himself frequently expresses), in which God can first reveal himself (whereby this "Salvation" can again only be determined in an original experience of Being).[57] The Divine would thus be the expression of how "Being" is to be experienced in a new "secureness" (Geborgenheit). It would be the symbolic formulation of the human relationship to Being in regard to the form of this relationship. It itself, however (in such an interpretation), would have no "substantial" anchorage in the sense of a fixation as an essent, but it is this very "existing" (seiende) God which Heidegger wants to overcome in his thought. The manner of being (Seinsweise) which could adequately describe this God remains in darkness, as does also what "God" actually means and can mean on the level of the problem of the experience of Being. Heidegger only makes suggestion from which no fast solutions can be drawn. Does the Divine lie in the How of the experience of Being, therefore, in an ontological occurrence which somehow unites subject and object, or in Being itself (which, of course, is not to be thought of as separate from man, but rather to a much greater extent as including him), or in both? Is it to be understood as pantheistic or personal? We do not know; nor does Heidegger himself "know" since he is only on his way to the Divine without being able to grasp it through a substantial (inhaltlich) experience.

3. The Abandoning of the "Transcendental" as an Indication of the God-Experience

A different possible way to the God-experience from the thinking of Heidegger remains to be briefly mentioned and systematically discussed in relation to its relevance for the God-question so that it will become clearer what Heidegger means by "God." In Sein und Zeit Heidegger considered Being in the

57 See NI, I, p. 394; EH, p. 61; HW, p. 294.

transcendental relationship to man.[58] He conceived of his systematic as being the fully worked out development of the transcendental concept and wanted to thus finally complete Kant, on the basis of the universal, "experiential" *(lebensweltlicher)* world, in that he sought to carry out the logical consequences of his thought.[59] On the basis of Husserl, he believed that a basic ontology could only be established through an existential analysis of the modes of the human, subject *(subjektiver)*, not subjective *(subjektivistisch)*, experience of the world; thus *Sein und Zeit* became for him a phenomenological description of the human *Dasein*, although always in relation to the therein appearing Being which first makes the human *Dasein* transcendentally possible. Such a description, of course, had to exclude every concealment of *Dasein* through traditional, metaphysical conceptions of man (anthropologies). The very concept of "God" too had to be excluded from the transcendental subject-object relationship in which Heidegger posited the *Dasein*.[60] The phenomenologically given objectum of the subjective, transcendental fulfillment presented itself to him, and could only present itself to him, as the encounterable *(vorfindliche)* "World," that is, as indeterminate *(unbestimmte)* Being, as the boundary-concept of a metaphysics. In all the pages of *Sein und Zeit*, there is no mention of God; he does not determine man's original experience of himself.

This phenomenological positiveness *(Positivität)* of the transcendental statement is later fundamentally questioned by Heidegger.[61] If in the beginning Being was only understood (transcendentally) from the point of view of *Dasein*, how could it ever itself appear in its pure inaccessibility *(Unverfügbarkeit)* and

---

58 See esp. *SZ*, p. 212.

59 See E. Coreth, "Heidegger und Kant," *Pullacher Philosophische Forschungen,* I. Pullach, 1955.

60 And this also precisely by phenomena which are customarily placed in the proximity of the religious, as for example, conscience. See esp. *SZ*, pp. 269, 275. The resistance of a "moral" explanation of conscience on the basis of traditional faith in a transcendent God.

61 See my work, *Hegel und die "Metaphysik" aus der Sicht des spateren Heidegger,* esp., p. 34.

difference *(Unterschiedenheit)* from the "that which is" *(das Seiende)* about which a transcendental analysis of Dasein is concerned? Does not *Dasein* itself close off genuine access to an experience of this Being in that, in the transcendental development *(Wendung),* to a certain extent it remains concerned with itself and thus can only consider itself and not Being as Being? Was it not in this very point that the metaphysical dominion in the mannor of conception *(Vorstellen)* was still intact?[62] And was it not here that there was expressed in an intensified (though only more hidden) form the modern Subjectivism which can only discover a meaning in everything through the establishment of a relationship to an (ontologically undertermined, non-reflecting) "Subject?" In that, in his much discussed *"Kehre,"* Heidegger experienced the insufficiency of the "horizontal, transcendental relationship,"[63] there was opened to him a new dimension of the experience of Being, and thus also of the Divine: The experience of Being is no longer determined only by man but essentially appears according to the manner in which Being itself "shows itself;" the "Truth" of Being is thus removed from the accessibility *(Verfügbarkeit)* of a transcendental Subject; it depends much more on an overcoming of the transcendental Subject-Object framework if Being is ever to be experienced as such in pure receptivity *(Gelassenheit)* as becoming an equivalent *(Entsprechung)* to the *Gegnet* which Heidegger views as the encompassing medium of Subjective and Objective in which the ontological occurrence of Truth *(Wahrheitsgeschehen)* brings itself to completion. "The nature of man is therefore only relinquished into the *Gegnet,* and accordingly used by the *Gegnet,* because man of himself has no power over Truth and it remains independent of him."[64] The thus experienced "inaccessibility" *(Unverfügbarkeit)* of Truth and Being leads to a genuine, meta-transcendental openness toward an encompassing *(umgreifenden)* Reality in

---

62 See W. Schulz, "Über den philosophiegeschichtlichen Ort Martin Heideggers," *Heidegger,* ed. by Pöggeler, pp. 95-139, esp. p. 106 (on the "metaphysical" character of Heidegger's own thought).

63 See *Gel,* p. 53.

64 *Ibid.,* p. 63.

which nothing can be forced to appear, nor can anything be placed in an isolated, transcendental relationship to a "Subject." The pure receptivity thus required "is actually the freeing of oneself from transcendental conception *(Vorstellen)*, and thus an ignoring of the wish for a horizon."[65] The pure receptivity indicated here cannot be conceived of as "the horizontal, transcendental relationship;"[66] it is much more the "relation to the *Gegnet*" as "waiting," "and waiting means a participation in the openness *(Offene)* of the *Gegnet.*"[67] Thus man no longer determines himself transcendentally from himself. What "experience" means is no longer determined exclusively by the person experiencing; transcendental thought is now finally brought to its full significance (and thus at the same time "overcome"). For as the highest "transcendental" condition of being man, as of Human experiencing and coming to know, "Being itself" determines itself in its pure transcendence qua ontological difference. Man thus first becomes open for an "other" which addresses him.[68] For "only to the extent that the nature of man does not experience its character from man, but rather from that which we designate as *Gegnet* and its *Vergegnis* (the appearing as an occurrence of the Truth *(Wahrheitsgeschehen)* of Being),"[69] can Being be spoken about in the medium of historical experience. And only thus does there also exist the openness toward its possible historical, concrete ways of appearing which are also ways of divulgence *(Entäusserung)* and also the critical reservation and distance toward the conceptual fixation of these forms of appearance. When at all, it is first in this receptiveness that the condition for a possible experience of God is realized, a condition which in principle can have no place in the transcendental Subject-Object relationship. What is meant is the openness toward the forms of the appearance of Being, which implies a potential openness for an

---

65 *Ibid.,* p. 57.
66 *Gel,* p. 53.
67 *Ibid.,* p. 48.
68 See also, *Der innere Bezug von Anthropologie und Ontologie,* p. 19.
69 *Gel,* p. 55.

appearance of the "Divine" as a manifestation of Being. Not given, however, is a substantial reference to a "Divine."[70] What is indicated in the *"Kehre"* of Heidegger's thought is actually "only" the possibility of an experience which was not present in this way in his earlier model as he expressed it in *Sein und Zeit.*[71]

What has thus been achieved in regard to the God-question is therefore more a habitus of experience than an experience itself.[72] It is thus the experience of the "inaccessible" *(Unverfügbaren)* as such. As the state of thought *(Erkenntnishaltung)* which places the transcendental approach in question and overcomes it, it creates only the methodological, transcendental pre-requisite for a discussion of the God-question; it also points out its fundamental possibility within a philosophy of Being, as we already attempted to present briefly above, which understands itself as an "openness" toward Being and does not reject from the start the appearance of "God" because it is not explainable and understandable from the transcendental Subject-Object relationship; for "it is not man who decides whether and how God and the gods . . . come into the clearing *(Lichtung)* of Being, are present, and absent."[73] Thus, there remains for him only the pure receptiveness *(Gelassenheit)* of "waiting"[74] which,

70 To a much greater extent, everything here remains undefined. See also *Der Feldweg*, p. 7, where this uncertainty in the experience of Being is expressed in a manner of mystical, timeless experiencing: "The suggestion of the *Feldweg* is now very clear. Does the soul speak? The world? God?"

71 Nevertheless, in regard to his thought, as the actual "building." See "Bauen-Wohnen-Denken," *VA*, II, p. 19; he says: "Such building can scarcely contrive the erection of a house for God and dwelling places for the mortals," *SF*, p. 41.

72 V. Vycinas expresses this (regarding the experience of God as an experience of transcendent "Being"—not meant in the "metaphysical" sense) very appropriately: "Heidegger, the ex-theological student, returns to a sort of piety: a man does not anymore 'transcend himself,' rather he 'waits' for the Transcendent," *Earth and Gods*, p. 91. See also *Gel*, p. 71.

73 *HB*, p. 162. See also *TK*, p. 46: "Whether lives or remains dead" is not left to human arbitrariness. See *NI*, p. 336 where he stresses that the *gods* "can never merely be taken over from tradition."

74 See *Gel*, p. 71.

however, is more than a mere "neutrality"[75] toward the Divine (as Heidegger clearly and decisively stated in a talk).[76]

4. The Divine as "the Hidden"

Thus it all depends upon whether we experience "Being" (as "Nature," *physis*) in its fundamental, understood in the sense of the ontological difference,[77] inaccessibility (*Unverfügbarkeit*) and withdrawnness (*Abgehobenheit*),[78] whether we, in the manner in which we encounter it, can still comprehend the "Holy" which first makes visible its true "Divineness," one radically different from all personal, ontic, subsistent character,[79] and whether we "still experience" this Holy "as the clue to the Divinity (*Göttlichkeit*) of the Divine."[80] A philosophy which frees itself from the traditional concepts of God so as to reach this goal, one which "destroys" them, is necessarily in this sense "godless"[81] since it renounces all claims to an object-ive (*gegenständliche*)

---

75 See Scherer, *op. cit.,* p. 782. See also *HB,* p. 181. Heidegger does not want his phenomenological, ontological concern to be understood as mere "indifference" about the God-question.

76 His speech on the "Fehl Gottes."

77 A very similar tendency, though in different terminology and from a somewhat different systematic background, is found in the important work of K. Jaspers, *Der philosophische Glaube angesichts der Offenbarung* (München, 1962). Unfortunately, the inner relationships of the conceptions of Heidegger and Jaspers cannot be more closely investigated here. See esp. *ibid.,* p. 527.

78 In this is shown the inner relation to the idea of dialectical theology; in fact, one can glimpse in the thought of Heidegger the ontological basis of dialectical theology!

79 Of a "metaphysical" God.

80 *HW,* p. 253. Just as perhaps many a poet succeeds in doing whose self-fulfillment *(erfülltes Selbstsein)* (as the true human state) consists in "standing in the presence of the gods and being affected by the nearness of the nature *(Wesensnähe)* of things," *EH,* p. 39.

However, already when we experience the "lack" of God we indirectly experience a "trace" of him in existential nearness. On such experience of "God" in withdrawal (in the "hiding of himself" *("Sichverbergen"),* see *VA,* II, p. 74.

81 See *ID,* p. 65. It is also "godless" in the dogmatic sense—from the standpoint of a "metaphysical" way of conception (since this way of conceiving always arrives at a fast definition of the nature of God as a clare et distincte understood essent *(Seienden)*). See esp. V. Vycinas, *Earth and Gods,* p. 320: "For one who does not transcend metaphysical thinking, such Heideggerian thought may appear a godless thought." (However: "Disrespecting of God as *causa sui* is no atheism," *ibid.*).

conception of the Divine as esse in se subsistens, experiences in it,[82] in fact, a too circumscribed basis for the Divine.[83] When such thought asks about the "Truth of Being," and makes an experience of the nature of the Divine dependent upon the former, it does this out of "respect for the boundaries of thought"[84] and not because of any atheistic tendency.[85] If it wanted to consider itself "atheistic," it would again succumb to the very tendency it is trying to "overcome;"[86] it would again take refuge (as is the case by Sartre) in the "metaphysical" way of conception and the created *(gemacht)*, all-too-human "gods." "It is therefore not only too hasty a conclusion, but already wrong in approach when it is insisted that the explanation of the nature of man from the relationship of this nature to the Truth of Being is atheism."[87] And thus it is possible that the very Christian, personal, theistic conception of God, and "Christendom itself, is a

82 Heidegger, esp. *NI*, I, pp. 131, 163, 414; *HB*, p. 179.

83 At the basis of this view there lies a deeply believing stance of Heidegger which clearly shows itself, for example, in his critism of a subjective atheism: "Man can never place himself in the position of God since the scope of man's nature never attains the nature of God," *HW*, p. 235.

However, such thought "is more open toward him (God) than the onto-theo-logic would like to admit," *ID*, p. 65.

84 *HB*, p. 182. But , says Heidegger in *TK*, in thinking in this way, in the counterpart *(Ent-sprechung)* to the "event" *(Ereignis)* "man as finite is capable of seeing the Divine in the visible element of World," p. 45.

85 See also *NI*, p. 471; *HB*, p. 177 where he separates himself very decisively from it. Heidegger also holds a mere accusation of "atheism" in regard to Nietzsche's more critical position for too superficial. See *HW*, p. 202, 196). The determination of the nature of man through "Being" as the "Other than itself" *(Anderes seiner selbst)*, and not through "God" or other metaphysical "constants" is in no way something "inhuman," something detrimental to humanitas, *ibid.*, p. 178.

See also *HB*, p. 177. "Since Nietzsche's statement on the 'death of God' is referred to, such an action is designated atheism." Whereby it must be pointed out that it is in such a "death of God" that Heidegger sees the basis for the possibility of an experience of the "true" God! At the most, one could talk about an "atheism" in the sense of a present "lack" of God which is experienced by Heidegger as such. See Scherer, *op. cit.,* p. 782: "Heidegger thus allows the designation of his philosophy as 'atheistic' only insofar as God is present or absent for philosophy, but not in the sense of a denial of God."

Bultmann already appropriately described the situation as follows (1930): "The 'atheism' of philosophy is not identical with the theological concept of lack of faith." Bultmann, *op. cit.,* p. 340.

86 See *SF*, esp. p. 35.

87 *HB*, p. 181.

result and development *(Ausformung)* of nihilism"[89] which, as the "forgetting about "Being" *(Vergessenheit des Seins),* determines Western "metaphysics" and obscures the truly "Divine" which appears in Being.[90] Thus, what Heidegger wrote in 1947 on the natural place of modern man retains and proves its validity: "We have come too late for the gods and too early for Being."[91]

Conclusion

With the discussion of Heidegger's concept of "Being" it was our aspiration to show, how in philosophical research, without the presupposition of "divine revelation," direct experience of the "Divine" for Heidegger is conceivable. Starting from a neutral viewpoint in the ontological question concerning the God-problem Heidegger experiences the essence of the truly "Divine" in the ontological difference, in the *transcendence* of Being, in its un-objectivity and withdrawness. Here he emphasizes that concrete experience is no longer possible as would be given in "revelation." At the same time, however, he insists, that "openness toward the Hidden" enables a much *profounder* experience of the Divine than was known in the entire traditional metaphysics which operated mainly with an objectified concept of God. In distinction from this tradition Heidegger tries, as has been shown in this paper, to experience the Divine in a new way based on the concept of transcendence, without relying exclusively on a defined religion or tradition.

89 *HW,* p. 204. Heidegger seeks to understand this 'nihilism" as the necessary fundamental characteristic of Western "metaphysics," *HW,* p. 201.

90 To that extent, Heidegger's systematic model, seen as a whole, is completely directed toward "God"; he does not exclude a "philosophical theory of God" (understood in the correct sense).

91 *Aus der Erfahrung des Denkens,* p. 7.

A SELECT BIBILIOGRAPHY

1. Works of Martin Heidegger

Sein und Zeit. 11th ed. Tübingen: Max Niemeyer Verlag, 1967. First published in 1927.

Vom Wesen des Grundes, see below, *Wegmarken.* First published in 1929.

Platons Lehre von der Wahrheit, see below, *Wegmarken.* First published in 1942.

Erläuterungen zu Hölderlins Dichtung. 3rd ed. Frankfurt a.M.: Klostermann, 1963. First published in 1944.

Brief über den "Humanismus," see *Wegmarken.* First published in 1947.

Der Feldweg. 4th ed. Frankfurt a.M.: Klostermann, 1969. First published in 1949.

Holzwege. 4th ed. Frankfurt a.M.: Klostermann, 1963. First published in 1950.

Einführung in die Metaphysik. 3rd ed. Tübingen: Max Niemeyer Verlag, 1966. First published in 1953.

Vorträge und Aufsätze. 3 vols. 3rd ed. Pfullingen: Günther, 1967. First published in 1954.

Was heisst Denken? 2nd ed. Tübingen: Max Niemeyer Verlag, 1961. First published in 1954.

Zur Seinsfrage. 3rd ed. Frankfurt a.M.: Klostermann, 1967. First published in 1955.

Der Satz vom Grund. 3rd ed. Pfullingen: Günther, 1965. First published in 1957.

Identität und Differenz. 4th ed. Pfullingen: Günther, n.d. First published in 1957.

Gelassenheit. 3rd ed. Pfullingen: Günther, n.d. First published in 1959.

Unterwegs zur Sprache. 3rd ed. Pfullingen: Günther, 1965. First published in 1959.

Nietzsche. Vols. I and II. Pfullingen: Günther, 1961.

Kants These über das Sein, see *Wegmarken.* First published in 1962.

Die Technik und die Kehre. 2nd ed. Pfullingen: Günther, N.Y. First published in 1962.

"Theologie et Philosophie," *Archives de Philosophie* (1969), pp. 355-415.

Wegmarken. Frankfurt a.M.: Klostermann, 1967.

2. Studies

Bultmann, Rudolf, "Die Geschichtlichkeit des Daseins und der Glaube: Antwort an Gerhardt Kuhlmann," *Zeitschrift für Theologie und Kirche* (1930), pp. 339-364.

Jaspers, Karl, *Der philosophische Glaube angesichts der Offenbarung.* München: Piper-Verlag, 1962.

Löwith, Karl, "Phänomenologische Ontologie und protestantische Theologie," *Heidegger* (1963), pp. 54-77. See below, Pöggeler.

Meyer, Hans, *Martin Heidegger und Thomas von Aquin.* Paderborn: Schöningh-Verlag, 1964.

Möller, J.P., *Existenzialphilosophie und katholische Theologie.* Baden-Baden: Verlag für Kunst und Wissenschaft. 1952.

Müller, Max, *Existenzphilosophie im geistigen Leben der Gegenwart.* 3rd ed. Heidelberg: Kerle-Verlag, 1964. First published in 1954.

Ott, Heinrich, "Was ist systematische Theologie?" *Der spätere Heidegger und die Theologie* (1964), pp. 95-133. See below, Robinson.

Pöggeler, Otto (ed.), *Heidegger: Perspektiven zur Deutung seines Werks.* Köln: Kiepenheuer & Witsch, 1969.

Richardson, William J., *Heidegger: Through Phenomenology to Thought.* The Hague: Martinus Nijhoff, 1963.

Robinson, James M., Cobb, John B. (eds.), *Der spätere Heidegger und die Theologie.* Zürich: Zwingli-Verlag, 1964.

Scherer, R., "Besuch bei Heidegger," *Wort und Wahrheit* (1947), pp. 780-782.

Schrey, Heinz-Horst, "Die Bedeutung der Philosophie Martin Heideggers für die Theologie," *Martin Heideggers Einfluss auf die Wissenschaften.* Ed. by C. Astrada *et al.* Bern: Francke-Verlag, 1949, pp. 9-21.

Schulz, Walter, "Über den philosophiegeschichtlichen Ort Martin Heideggers," *Heidegger,* see above, O. Pöggeler, pp. 95-139.

_____, *Der Gott der neuzeitlichen Metaphysik.* Pfullingen: Günther, 1957.

Vycinas, Vincent, *Earth and Gods: An Introduction to the Philosophy of Martin Heidegger.* The Hague: Martinus Nijhoff, 1961.

CHAPTER XXVIII

DEATH-OF-GOD THEOLOGY

Eric C. Meyer, C.P. *

Fundamentally, theology is that disciplined "talk about God" which expresses both the critical and self-critical reflection the believer does when he is trying to bring his faith to greater understanding and more effective activity in his current situation. Now, most Jewish and Christian theologians would not deny that there has long been a progressive fading away of faith in God (i.e., of course, in the God of Judeo-Christian tradition: the eternal, transcendent, all-holy, all-powerful, etc. Creator and Savior); nor would many deny that this development seems to be climaxing in the modern process of radical secularization; but relatively few are willing to affirm this situation in a radical way. Radical or death-of-God theologians are those relatively few who do "talk about God" in various ways that *more or less* radically affirm what has happened to faith in God in the extremely secular situation of modern man; and so it is that they speak positively about the disappearance or absence, eclipse or hiddenness, or even demise or death of God. What one must emphasize, however, is the *more or less;* for the differing extent of their various affirmations of this situation, besides revealing that radical or death-of-God theology describes something very inclusive, also supplies a kind of slide rule for distinguishing radical or death-of-God theologies from one another. Thus, if we move from those that are *less* to those that are *more* radically affirmative of what has happened to faith in God in the present situation, we will see that radical or death-of-God theologies are: theistic, panentheistic, pantheistic, agnostic and atheistic.

*Professor of Philosophy at the Catholic Theological Union, Chicago, Illinois, U.S.A.

Our descriptions of these various divisions of radical or death-of-God theology will necessarily be only very brief and generic, for the principal concern of this article is not to examine radical or death-of-God theology itself, certainly not in the particular systems elaborated by individual representatives of these major divisions,[1] but simply to equip the reader with a schematic summary of radical or death-of-God theology in its major divisions that is precise enough to give him an adequate introduction to what *is* our principal concern here: to examine the most important elements in Judaism, Christianity, Protestantism and radically secular humanism that have given rise to radical or death-of-God theology as a whole.

Theistic and panentheistic radical or death-of-God theologians are "soft," as opposed to "hard," radical or death-of-God theologians[2] because they speak of the death only of an idea of God (even if it be the very idea of God in traditional Jewish or Christian belief) rather than of the death of *all* ideas of God or of God *himself.* Thus, they continue to believe in a real God of one sort or another.

Theistic radical or death-of-God theologians, echoing the very negative theology of the early Barth, proclaim that the God who has died is the one Western man associated too closely with Judeo-Christian religion and culture which are now passing away due to the process of radical secularization and the rise of empirical and technological man. All religious and cultural gods must always be dying, for man's religions and cultures are always passing away. God himself, however, who is wholly other than men and their religions and cultures, remains alive and continues to reveal himself to man in every new future. Vahanian and Cox are the principal representatives of such theistic radical or death-of-God theology. Among Catholics, one might include here: Leslie Dewart and Raymond Nogar, but even more especially,

---

1 See the bibliography for works by and works on the more important of these individual radical or death-of-God theologians.

2 This is an adaptation of terminology already used by W. Hamilton, "The Shape of a Radical Theology," *The Christian Century,* Vol. LXXXII, No. 40, October 6, 1965, p. 1220, cols. 1-2.

Jacques Durandeaux. By placing these thinkers under this one heading, we do *not* mean to imply, of course, that their particular theologies are simply the same, but rather only very generically alike in this regard.[3]

Panentheistic radical or death-of-God theologians, on the other hand, striving to merge the best of theism with the best of pantheism into a third option, proclaim that it is the God who is wholly other, or a transcendent person or being, that has died. All things come from and live and move and have their being in God[4] who will finally be all in all;[5] hence, God is fully immanent in them and their entire process, even if he does transcend them in as much as he is their ground and antecedent and consequent nature. Some of the principal representatives of this very large and diverse school of thought about God are: Whitehead, Hartshorne, Pittenger, D.D. Williams, J.B. Cobb, Jr., Ogden, J.A.T. Robinson and Peter Hamilton. Among Catholics who parallel such thinking are, besides Teilhard and his many followers, E. Baltazar and G. Baum. Once again, these people hold positions that are really only very generically alike. How different they can be is well illustrated by the variety of stands taken on the question of whether man will enjoy afterlife in the consequent nature of God as a genuine subject. Teilhard believes that the answer is certainly yes;[6] Ogden believes that an affirmative answer is possible but not at all necessary;[7] Peter Hamilton leaves only the very remotest possibility of an affirmative answer but repeats again and again that the answer is almost surely no.[8] Further, the more radical panentheists come closer than the others to making God little more than a quality of the universe (in which case it would really be God who lives and moves and has his being in the universe

---

3 See below, footnote 21.

4 Acts 17:24, 28.

5 1 Cor. 15:28.

6 Teilhard de Chardin, *The Phenomenon of Man* (New York: Harper and Row, 1961), pp. 262, 308 and *The Future of Man* (London, 1964), pp. 308, 309.

7 S.M. Ogden, *The Reality of God* (New York: Harper and Row, 1966), pp. 229-230.

8 P. Hamilton, *The Living God and the Modern World* (Philadelphia: United Church Press, 1967), pp. 108-141, esp. pp. 125, 132, 137, 140-141.

rather than the universe in God); and, in so doing, they come closer to pantheism than to theism, closer, i.e., to "hard" radical or death-of-God theology.[9]

Pantheist, agnostic and atheist radical or death-of-God theologians are "hard" radical or death-of-God theologians because they speak either of the death of God *himself* or of the death of *all* ideas or experiences of a real God.

The most well known of the pantheist radical or death-of-God theologians is Altizer. He adopts the following view. All things and their process derive from an Original or Primordial Totality which undergoes a kenotic self-negation by which it empties itself out into sacred (God) and profane (the world and man) opposites which then themselves negate this negation by also undergoing kenotic self-negation so as to empty themselves out into one another and compose the Final or Eschatological Totality. Thus, according to this cosmo-historical dialectic, God *himself* dies and he does this especially in becoming incarnate in and dying in Jesus of Nazareth who rises only as a universally immanent or incarnate Spirit that becomes ever more universally immanent or incarnate "in every human hand and face" until men became especially conscious of this in the nineteenth century and until eventually both the world and man will also undergo kenotic self-negation and empty themselves out into God and one another, i.e. until all of the sacred and profane will have passed into one another to form the Final or Eschatological Totality.[10] There are, of course,

---

9 Perhaps Whitehead himself is more guilty of this charge than the many other panentheists he has inspired. It also seems to be true in large part of people like Albert Schweitzer and perhaps even of G. Todrank.

10 Eric C. Meyer, *A Critical Analysis of the Death-of-God: Theology of Thomas J.J. Altizer in its Origins and Development,* A Doctoral Dissertation, Münster University,

other versions of pantheistic radical or death-of-God theology which are very different, such as the evolutionary thought of W.F. Loomis in which God, God as Nature or Exterior, becomes God, God as Man or Within; but Altizer's very gnostical fusion of Hegel, Blake, Nietzsche, Tillich, Barfield, Teilhard and others has certainly stolen most attention, despite the fact that it remains very confused and does not seem to have won over any significant disciples.

Agnostic radical or death-of-God theologians would contend that God-talk cannot be shown to be of God as he is in himself but only as men think of him. Hence, they concede too that saying that "God is dead" refers to nothing more than to the *human* experience of having lost faith in a living God. Theologians who adopt this position (not only the agnosticism but also the human experience of loss of faith in a living God) do so for different reasons. Braun, a disciple of Bultmann, goes beyond his master in demythologizing even God. When man speaks of God, he is really speaking of himself. Hence, speaking of God objectively as existing in himself is naive; speaking of him symbolically to express authentic and unconditional engagement with one's fellow man is sophisticated. Further, Braun claims that this process of demythologizing God had already begun in the Johannine literature, even though both ideas of God are still to be found there side by side. Van Buren adopts an agnostic death-of-God position

---

1972, 633 pp. Altizer has confused as many people as he has, not only because of his disregard for language, logic and verification, but especially because he himself has moved from a traditional theism to the process-pantheism described above by first going through a very negative theistic phase and then a genuine atheistic phase. Indeed, his current process-pantheism itself has undergone several mutations (including reversals). In short, then, to be assessed properly, anything he says must be situated in its proper time and place and in relation to what precedes and follows it. While this may be true enough of any thinker, it is especially true of all radical or death-of-God theologians, even if less so in most cases than in the case of Altizer, for they are all *moving* away from theistic positions once held, and it is difficult to calculate exactly just how far away they were at this or that time or now are. Hence, though the major divisions of radical or death-of-God theology are quite clear, an assignment of this or that individual to this or that division might easily be contested.

because he claims that we cannot verify talk about a God who is real in himself. This kind of talk, when tested in the contexts in which it is used, cannot be shown to refer to any reality other than one's basic *blik* or view about how life should be lived. Thus, if love of God can be verified only by love of man, then it can mean only love of man. Beyond this, however, van Buren replaces God-talk with Jesus-talk which refers to a *blik* patterned on the example of Jesus and to the experience of actually being taken hold of by this contagious freedom of his to live for others. Rubenstein adopts an agnostic death-of-God position, largely at least, because of the problem of evil as concretized for him as a Jew in the overwhelming experience of "Auschwitz" which has made faith in an all-good and all-powerful God (indeed, in any other God except final nothingness) impossible for him.

Atheistic radical or death-of-God theologians do not believe that there is now nor ever was a real God, which contention should not be confused with the fact that atheistic radical or death-of-God theologians themselves did at one time believe in a real God. Indeed, William Hamilton and Dorothee Sölle still believed in some kind of a real God even after they had adopted their initial death-of-God stands; i.e., it was only some time before they became *genuine* atheistic death-of-God theologians.[11] Therefore, when they had become genuine atheistic death-of-God theologians, what they taught was, not that God *himself* has died (God *himself* never existed), but that there once was *a real experience* of God and that it is *this entire real experience* of God that has actually died and not just certain aspects of it. This real experience of God died for many reasons. It was not merely that the problem of evil became more acute than ever before and that the traditional "proofs" for God were effectively countered by

---

11 William Hamilton once still waited for a real God he did not need but might enjoy *(The New Essence of Christianity,* New York, Association, 1961, pp. 63-65) and then gave up waiting for the return of any God ("The Shape of a Radical Theology", *ut supra,* pp. 1220-1221 and "The Death of God," Playboy, Vol. XIII, No. 8, August, 1966, p. 84, col. 1). Dorothee Sölle once still seemed to believe in something of a real God whom Christ represented to us and us to *(Stellvertretung,* Freiburg im B., 1965), a God she later dispenses with *(Atheistisch an Gott Glauben,* Freiburg im B., 1968, pp. 77-96).

people like Hume and Kant. It was above all the gradual rise and triumph of empirical and technological man that finally led to the death of this real experience of God. Not only was belief in a real God not verifiable by empirical man, it contradicted his reason and truth. Not only was belief in a real God no longer necessary for technological man (who fills his own needs), it contradicted his dignity and freedom. These atheistic radical or death-of-God theologians, however, like van Buren, strive to cling to the example of the human Jesus or to see in him the powerful symbol of a way of living totally for others.

* * *

With this schematic summary of radical or death-of-God theology in hand, we can now turn our attention to the principal concern of this article and ask what is ultimately responsible for the various tendencies in radical or death-of-God theology to affirm the progressive fading away of faith in God within the Judeo-Christian tradition which is now climaxing in the modern process of radical secularization. 1. Was it something inherent to Judaic religion which also became a component of Christianity? 2. Was it something peculiar to Christianity in the way it transformed Judaic religion? 3. Was it something more or less particular to Protestantism as it distinguished itself from Catholicism? 4. Was it something unique to the radically secular humanism which has emancipated itself from the Judeo-Christian tradition? The answer to *all* of these questions is yes! Judaism, Christianity, Protestantism and radically secular humanism, each accounts in its own way—but only in progressive connection with the others—for radical or death-of-God theology.

1. Judaic Religion

The idea that secularization finds, in one sense or another its initiation and vindication in Judaic religion is a common conviction. It has been argued by, among others,[12] especially Harvey Cox[13] and Erich Fromm.[14]

For Cox, secularization (the liberation of man from religious and metaphysical tutelege and the turning of his attention from other worlds to this one) represents an authentic consequence of biblical faith because: Creation disenchants nature, the Exodus desacralizes politics and the Sinai Covenant deconsecrates values— especially in its prohibition of idols. Further, he distinguishes secularization from secularism (an ideology or closed world-view which functions like a new religion). Hence, he insists that those whose orientation to reality is shaped by biblical faith must not oppose but rather nourish the almost certainly irreversible process of secularization. They can and should do so by clarifying its biblical roots, guarding against movements which attempt to stop it and preventing it from hardening into secularism.[15]

Erich Fromm finds a still more radical initiation and vindication of secularization in Judaic religion. He divides the history of man's religious evolution into four stages: the totemistic (in which primitive man seeks to recover his original unity with nature by linking himself to and worshipping animals as gods), the idolatrous (in which man, now a craftsman less dependent on nature, projects his own skills into the idols he makes, unconsciously worshipping the former in this alienated fashion), the anthropomorphic (in which man comes to a greater awareness of himself as the highest of beings in as much as he projects the gods as glorified human beings) and the humanistic (in which modern man finally comes to realize that "God" is not a power outside of himself but a symbol for the ever fuller unfolding of his own human powers and the

12 G. Vahanian, *The Death of God* (New York: Braziller, 1961), pp. 60-78; M. Marty, "Whenever God Dies: Protestant Roots of the Problem of God," *Speaking of God,* edited by D. Dirschel (Milwaukee: Bruce, 1967), p. 78.

13 Harvey Cox, *The Secular City: Secularization and Urbanization in Theological Perspective* (New York: Macmillan, 1965), pp. 17-37.

14 Erich Fromm, *The Art of Loving: An Enquiry into the Nature of Love* (New York: Harper and Row, 1956), pp. 63-82 and *You Shall be as Gods: A Radical Interpretation of the Old Testament and its Tradition* (New York: Holt, Rinehart and Winston, 1966), pp. 17-62.

15 H. Cox, *op. cit.,* pp. 17-18, 20-21, 36.

totality of what he is striving to become).[16] The anthropomorphic stage is subdivided into earlier mother-centered religious (mother is the supreme being; her love is unconditional; hence, it cannot be acquired by obedience but envelopes all equally) and later father-centered religions (father is the supreme being; his love is conditioned on the observance of his laws; hence, it must be acquired by obedience, and the more obedient is more loved).[17] *Judaic religion,* the evolution of strict monotheism, is a progressive phase which links father-centered anthropomorphic religion to humanistic religion by moving the former *toward* the latter. This progressive phase also passes through four periods. In the first, God is a father in the sense of a despotic tribal chief who makes man in his image and treats him as his property. When man breaks God's laws, God drives him from paradise and later even kills all men except his favorite son, Noah. The second period begins when God makes a covenant with Noah, for God then binds himself to his own laws and is transformed thereby from a despotic tribal chief into a constitutional monarch. Indeed, at the end of this period, he has become a *loving* father bound to his own principles of justice, as can be seen from the way Abraham argues with him to spare Sodom. In the third period, God answers Moses' question about his name with "Eheyeh asher Eheyeh," which Fromm interprets as both "I am becoming that which I am becoming" and "my name is nameless." The prohibitions against making any image of God, of taking his name in vain and later of pronouncing his name at all are also part of this period. In the fourth period, this development of pure monotheism is carried into radically negative theology, such as that of Moses Maimonides, in which the more I know God, the more I know what he is *not.* Thus, the whole evolution of monotheism is *in the direction of* freeing man from the idea that God is a father or person and of realizing that he is a symbol of truth and justice and love and unity, that God is

16 E. Fromm, *The Art of Loving.* For stages one to three, cf. p. 64; for stage four, cf. pp. 70-71, 81. Fromm does not deny that these stages overlap; indeed, he grants that all of them are still in existence, see pp. 70-71, 82.

17 *Ibid.,* pp. 65-68.

I in as much as I am human and the totality of what is coming
from the longing and striving and ever fuller unfolding of human
powers.[18] Hence, while Fromm does not claim that the radically
negative theology of this fourth period is simply the equivalent of
the religious systems of non-theistic mysticism or atheistic
humanism,[19] he does claim that the logical consequence of the
mature monotheism of Judaic religion is the absurdity of theology
and its negation[20] and that, therefore, the next logical step would
be a religious system without "God," even though it is impossible
for a theistic religious system to take this step without losing its
own identity.[21]

One may justly criticize many of the details in the theories
which Cox and Fromm put forth to explain how modern
secularization is a process that finds its initiation and vindication
in the rise of the strict monotheism of Judaic religion—but even
more so the *extent* to which they argue that this is the case.
Nevertheless, it does seem that one must concur with them at least
to the following degree. Judaism's mature faith in God emerged in
large part from its opposition to the idolatrous beliefs of
surrounding religions, especially to their diverse tendencies to
understand the whole of nature or a part of nature or the forces of
nature or animals or men or the works of men as divine. Further,
it was only with the evolution of the strict monotheism of Judaic
religion that the divine was set over against the worldly and the
human as *radically other.* God alone is Creator; everything else,
regardless of how good it is, is not divine but only created. God is
so holy, i.e. so other, that he cannot even be imaged nor named.
Now, we can see in this development a kind of seminal beginning
of that later process of ever more radical secularization which
many have called "the death of God" in the sense that, if the
divine was liberated from the worldly and the human, *so too were*

18 *Ibid.,* pp. 68-70, 71, 72 and *You Shall be as Gods,* pp. 22-37. See also his shorter
summaries of this development: *The Art of Loving,* p. 81 and *You Shall be as Gods,* pp.
61-62, 225-226.

19 E. Fromm, *The Art of Loving,* pp. 71, 71-72.

20 *Ibid.,* pp. 70, 71 and *You Shall be as Gods,* pp. 37, 47.

21 E. Fromm, *You Shall be as Gods,* p. 53.

the worldly and the human liberated from the divine. In a much deeper sense, of course, Judaic religion liberated the worldly and the human from the divine only in a way that made the former all the more bound to the latter, for it replaced their confusion with a differentiation that involved a total dependence of the world and man on God for their own existence and goodness. However, it is still true that one of the consequences of the Judaic faith in God as the wholly other Creator was the belief that the world and man have a created existence proper to themselves, that this created existence proper to themselves is good and that it is proper to man to name and work the world as his own. All of these ideas entered into Christianity.

2. Christianity

The origins of radical or death-of-God theology, however, are still more closely connected with the way in which Christianity transformed Judaic monotheism. Christians came quickly to the belief that Jesus was not only the Messiah but that he was so as "Emmanuel" (God-with-us) who saved us from sin and death by *becoming man* and *dying on the cross.* Hence, in as much as (but only *in as much as*) Christians continued to believe that God is one but that Jesus is God and that, therefore, in Jesus God became man and died for us, to this extent at least, radical or death-of-God theology does have an even more definite rooting in what is peculiar to Christianity's faith in God than in what is peculiar to Judaism's faith in God or shared by both Judaism and Christianity. No genuinely orthodox Christian theologian should be unwilling to concede as much. Nevertheless, this does *not* mean that he must concede that radical or death-of-God theology is the logical and legitimate consequence of the evolution of Christian monotheism. Indeed, he cannot concede this because of the character of Christian monotheism: a. as Trinitarian and b. as Incarnational.

(a) As Trinitarian

Even in what appears to be the earliest known confession of faith in the pre-existence and kenotic incarnation of Jesus Christ,[22] it is not said simply that God became man by emptying himself out into the man Jesus who then died on the cross. Rather, it is said that Jesus Christ, subsisting in the form of God, did not think being equal to God a prize but emptied himself and took the form of a slave, that he, becoming like men and found in the fashion of a man, humbled himself and became obedient even to death on a cross.[23] Now, given this internal evidence, and also the external evidence of what Christian monotheism was to become, it is clear *enough* that this hymn should be understood as an incipient, albeit *a very incipient,* expression of emerging Trinitarian belief in God. It is true, of course, that the hymn concerns itself only with the relationship between Jesus Christ and God or God the Father. Furthermore, although it does not say so in any evident way, most exegetes can agree that Jesus Christ is God, nevertheless, at one and the same time, it: 1. does say that Jesus Christ was "in the form of God" and implies that this means "equal to God"[24] and 2. yet makes it clear also that Jesus Christ is not identical with God or God the Father.[25] It is especially this

22 Phil. 2:6-11. It is generally conceded that this is a prepauline, liturgical hymn; hence, it would probably have been in use even before 56 A.D. Cf. Joachim Gnilka, *Herders Theologischer Kommentar Zum Neuen Testament,* X:3, *Der Philipperbrief* (Freiburg: Herder, 1968), pp. 131-133, 145-146 and also p. 24.

23 Phil. 2:6-8.

24 Phil. 2:6. The most difficult words in this verse are: morpha and arpagmon. Cf. J. Gnilka, op. cit., pp. 112-117 for a competent treatment of how they have been and should be exegeted. With regard to our own claims here (the hymn does not provide any real basis for the idea that God simply became man and died on the cross; the hymn does show a very incipient Trinitarian faith), the following should be noted: 1. Those who argue that 6a (Jesus Christ was "subsisting in the form of God") means that he was a manifestation of God only in an extrinsic sense and not God in any intrinsic sense and that 6b means that he did not "snatch at being equal to God" only strengthen our first claim. 2. Nevertheless, their position, of course, undermines our second claim. We answer, not only that their exegesis is poor, but also that their lack of proportionate concern about 7b (verse 6 comes closer to saying that Jesus Christ was equal to God than 7b does to saying that he was equal to man—that is our point) indicates their one-sided and prejudicial approach to the problematic of this hymn.

25 Phil. 2:9, 11.

last element of the hymn that does not allow any real basis here
for the idea that God in any simple sense (i.e., God the Father or
the Father and Jesus Christ) emptied himself, became man and
died. Further, there is no basis for such an idea anywhere in the
New Testament, for, even though there are cases where the New
Testament seems to call Jesus God, it never confuses Jesus with
the Father.[26] Indeed, toward the end of New Testament times,
the author of the fourth gospel is still repeating basically the same
thought as that of the hymn Paul cites in Philippians 2.

The author of the fourth gospel teaches that before creation
Jesus Christ, as the Word of God and the only begotten Son of the
Father, was with God and was God;[27] and he adds that he who
sees Jesus has seen the Father[28] because Jesus and the Father are
one in as much as Jesus is in the Father and the Father is in
Jesus.[29] Nevertheless, the author of the fourth gospel also, even
though he is more insistent on the divinity of Jesus and his unity
with the Father than is the pre-pauline hymn of Philippians 2,
makes it clear again and again that the Father and he whom the
Father has sent (the Word of God, the Son of God, the only
begotten Son of the Father) are distinct.[30] Thus, it was not God
as Father or as Father and Son who became flesh and died on the
cross but the Word of God, the only begotten Son of the Father,
who became flesh in Jesus and died on the cross.[31] Furthermore,
though the one clear evidence of a Trinitarian faith in the New
Testament, the Matthean baptismal formula, was probably added
only later,[32] both Paul and especially the author of the fourth

26 See R.E. Brown, *Jesus God and Man* (Milwaukee, Wisconsin: Bruce, 1967), pp.
1-38.

27 Jn. 1:1-2, 14, 18; cf. also 3:16-18; 5:16-18; 8:54-59; 10:22-39; 17:5, 24.

28 Jn. 12:45; 14:7-9; 17:21-23.

29 Jn. 10:30, 38; 14:10a, 11; 17:11, 21-23.

30 This distinction is abundantly clear throughout the fourth gospel, above all in
chapters: 5, 6, 8, 12, 14, 15 and 17. Especially significant are verses such as 14:23-24,
28; 20:17 and 13:15 in the light of this gospel's constant emphasis from 3:17 to 20:21
on the Father's sending the Son.

31 Jn. 1:14 and 19:32-35.

32 Mt. 28:19. 1 Jn. 7b-8a, the Johannine comma, was certainly added later since it
first appears in Latin manuscripts.

gospel, in contrast to the more primitive pre-pauline hymn of Philippians 2, speak also of the Spirit of God or the Spirit of Christ and sometimes seem to speak of this Spirit as more than just the power of God or of Jesus Christ, as more than a mere personification of their saving and sanctifying power, for sometimes they speak of the Holy Spirit as a kind of divine subject who is distinct from the Father and the Son or Jesus Christ.[33] At any rate, underdeveloped as all of this admittedly very incipient Trinitarian monotheism is, it is clear enough to rule out the idea that God in any simple sense (the Father and the Holy Spirit, as well as the Son) became man in Jesus and died on the cross.

The very fact that modalistic monarchism was: 1. later than adoptionism and subordinationism,[34] 2. not as long lasting in the ancient Church as those heresies in their recurrent forms[35] and 3. everywhere quickly opposed[36] serves only to confirm our

[33] Romans 8:14-17, 26-27; 1 Cor. 12:4-6; 2 Cor. 13:13 and Jn. 14:15-17, 25-26; 15:26; 16:7-16.

[34] Noetus, the first known patripassianist, was condemned by a synod in Smyrna about 190 or 200. Praxeas brought patripassianism to Rome thereafter, where later Epigonus, a disciple of Noetus, built up the faction, among whose members were Cleomenes and Sabellius. Pope Zephyrin's (198-217) apparent toleration of this group may well have been due more to their opposition to Montanism and to the subordinationism and ditheism of their opponents than to any understanding and approval of modalistic monarchism.

[35] In Rome, Sabellius was excommunicated by Callistus (217-222); in Bostra, Beryll surrendered patripassianism at a synod in 244; and, in Alexandria, bishop Dionysius (247-264) condemned patripassianism. In the case of the latter's opposition to patripassianism, he so emphasized the difference between the Father and the Son that he was accused of saying the Son was created by the Father and came into being. Dionysius of Rome opposed Dionysius of Alexandria on this point as Callistus had the author of the tenth book of the *Refutatio Omnium Haeresium* who also revealed an Arian-kind-of subordinationism or ditheism in his opposition to modalistic monarchism. While Dionysius of Alexandria accepted the correction of Dionysius of Rome at this time, this kind of thinking was to surface again in Alexandria with Arius a half-century later. Here are yet further confirmations of the persistent importance of adoptionism and subordinationism as opposed to modalistic monarchism which had largely passed by 250 or 260, even though there was a partial rebirth of it in the fourth century in Marcellus of Ancyra and in the Priscillians and was still important enough to be included among the condemnations of First Constantinople in 381.

[36] Besides the opponents of modalistic monarchism mentioned in footnotes 23 and 24, reference should also be made to Origen, Tertullian, Hippolytus and Novatian. While Hippolytus' authorship of the *Syntagma* and *Contra Noetum* and *Refutatio* is disputed today, there is no doubt that Tertullian and the author or authors of the above works were the principal foes of modalistic monarchism during the time of popes Zephyrin, Callistus and Urban (198-230).

contention that the idea that God simply became man in Jesus and died on the cross has no real basis in the New Testament because of the Trinitarian character of Christian monotheism already emerging in the New Testament itself. This in turn, however, confirms the further claim that radical or death-of-God theology cannot be seen as the logical and legitimate consequence of the evolution of Christian monotheism, for, if that were true, then modalistic monarchism would have to have a real basis in the New Testament. This is not to deny, however, that patripassianism (Jesus is the Son who is God but not a person distinct from the Father for "he" is the Father himself become flesh to suffer and die as Jesus) and Sabellianism (there is one God in eternity who progressively manifests himself to us in time in three different prosopa (masks or roles): as Father in creation, for example, and as Son in incarnation and as Spirit in sanctification) have real importance. Confronting these heresies led to a much greater explicitation and clarification of Christianity's faith in the one God as Father, Son and Holy Spirit, especially through the work of Tertullian (one of the first to speak of unity in trinity and to describe God as one substance and three persons), even if he did himself retain a quasi-subordinationist monarchism in his own thought.[37] Furthermore, there has been an extensive resurgence of patripassianism or Sabellianism, though in vastly modified forms, in much modern reflection on God.[38] Nonetheless, neither ancient nor modern forms of modalistic monarchism have a genuine basis in what the New Testament says about the incarnation and death of Jesus Christ, for, as we have seen, even though the New Testament does speak of Jesus Christ as God, it

37 Tertullian, *Adversus Praxeam,* c. 213.

38 Unitarianism, Idealism (especially in its Hegelian form) and the theologies influenced by such thinking, the Anglo-American process theologies influenced by the process-panentheism of Whitehead and Hartshorne, all of these witness to the modern resurgence of elements of modalistic monarchism. Perhaps this is nowhere more the case, however, than in the patripassianistic-like process-pantheism adopted by Altizer to explain the fading away of faith in God in the consciousness of modern man: God finally died in the consciousness of modern man (God as other than man) precisely because God himself has been in the process of becoming ever more incarnate in or immanently one with man.

never confuses him with the Father nor says that the Father himself, nor the Father and the Son, nor the Father and the Son and the Holy Spirit, became flesh and died in Jesus Christ.

(b) As Incarnational

However, if the Father and the Son and the Holy Spirit are one God, and if the Son really emptied himself in becoming man and suffered and died, then why can we not say that, *in and through the Son,* the one God was emptied out, became man, suffered and died? Wouldn't this claim be confirmed, not merely by various traditional ways of speaking, such as the communicatio idiomatum, but also by such central doctrinal formulations of the Church as: the creedal definition of Nicea that the Son is "omoousion to Patri," i.e., consubstantial in the sense of the same one substance,[39] and the *later* Trinitarian definitions of Florence, those of perichoresis (each of the divine persons is wholly in the other two) and of the unity of the divine operations ad extra (all the acts of God ad extra are common to the three persons)?[40] If the Son really emptied himself in becoming man and suffered and died, then so did the Father and the Holy Spirit, because the Father and the Holy Spirit are wholly in the Son. If the Son's saving acts of incarnation, suffering and death are really divine operations ad extra, then they are also the acts of the Father and the Holy Spirit, because divine operations ad extra are common to all three persons of God.

This position seems formidable because of the subtle way it

---

39 This doctrine of Nicea was not extended to the Holy Spirit until First Constantinople in 381. Nevertheless, it was implicit in the early creeds in as much as they put the Holy Spirit on a par with the Father and the Son; and it was taught explicitly by Tertullian as early as the *Adversus Praxeam,* c. 213.

40 The Council of Florence, *Decretum pro Jacobitis,* 1442. Perichoresis was not applied to the relationship of the Father and the Son and the Holy Spirit until the early sixth century by Fulgentius in his *De Fide ad Petrum.* The doctrine on the unity of the divine operations ad extra has basis in Augustine's *De Trinitate,* c. 400-416, and was given synodal and conciliar expression at the Lateran in 649, Toledo in 675 and the Fourth Lateran in 1215.

combines an exclusive use of the kenosis-model of the incarnation, as well as a literal interpretation of it, with later Christological and Trinitarian formulations. But the combination is invalid. 1. This position uses exclusively the kenosis-model to interpret the incarnation; however, that puts an undue limitation on the idea of how the Son of God became man, for the kenosis-model (i.e., that the Son of God *emptied himself out* in becoming man) is rare, even in the New Testament,[41] whereas the assumption-model (i.e., that the Son of God *took on manhood* in becoming man) is more frequent in the New Testament and dominant thereafter.[42] 2. The position outlined above interprets the kenosis-model of the incarnation too literally. It has God, in and through the Son of God, becoming man in Jesus Christ by ceasing to be God through emptying out his divinity into that humanity. Yet Philippians 2:7 itself cannot be interpreted in such a literal sense, for: a. it does not say that Jesus Christ emptied out his divinity but *himself* (supposedly, what he emptied himself out from was his being in the form of God and equal to God); b. it does not say that he emptied himself (much less his divinity) into man but describes that eauton ekenosen as morphan doulou *labon* (taking) and c. the latter part of the verse lends itself more easily to a semidocetic interpretation than to any other: en *omoiomati* anthropon genomenos kai *schamati euretheis os* anthropos. 3. Moreover, even if one were to allow a literal interpretation of Philippians 2:7, one

41 The only explicit text is Phil. 2:6-11; however, 2 Cor. 8:9, Heb. 2:5-18, 5:5-10, 9:23-29 and Jn. 17:1-5 may be counted among those texts which imply incarnation by kenosis.

42 By "the assumption-model of the incarnation," we are referring, not to the assumptus-homo theologies of Sertillanges, de Basly, Galtier, etc., but to those expressions of the incarnation which conceive of it as consisting basically in the only begotten Son of God's becoming man by taking on manhood without ceasing to be God, regardless of how much the Godhood was hidden thereby. This concept of the incarnation does not exclude that of kenosis unless the latter be interpreted in an exclusive and literal sense. In actual fact, every expression of the incarnation in the New Testament seems to involve the assumption-model, not only the more obvious texts (Gal. 4:4-7; Col. 1:15-20; 2:3, 9; Heb. 1:1-12, 10:5-7 and Jn. 1:1-18), but also those texts which imply incarnation by kenosis (e.g., 2 Cor. 8:9, for how could Jesus Christ's becoming poor for our sake make us rich if it meant that he simply surrendered his being rich to become as poor as we are?) and, indeed, even Phil. 2:7 itself (for Jesus Christ's emptying himself is explained as: "taking the form of a servant").

would have to insist that this pre-pauline hymn indicates quite clearly that it is not God or God the Father who empties himself out but only he (Jesus Christ) who was in the form of God and equal to God. Hence, one could not claim to be faithful to the hymn when "himself" is interpreted with later Christological and Trinitarian formulations in such a way as to make the hymn involve what it quite clearly does *not* involve: the idea that God or God the Father emptied out his divinity or self into man in the incarnation.

Even the major Christological heresies of ancient times (adoptionism, subordinationism, docetism, Arianism, Nestorianism and Monophysitism) show by their virtually unanimous opposition to the radically kenotic position that it cannot be the logical and legitimate consequence of the evolution of Christian monotheism, for they all kept the Godhood from any simple identification with or transformation into the manhood of Jesus Christ. Indeed, even modalistic monarchism in its Sabellian form would also be evidence for our contention, for it too emphasized that God is one in eternity and that his manifestations in time as Creator, Savior and Sanctifier are but prosopa in the sense of masks or roles.

Finally, the radically kenotic position outlined above runs counter to the mainstream of orthodox incarnational theology as it evolved from its earliest expressions and in the New Testament writings, through the early apologetes and fathers and Christological councils, to the watershed of Chalcedon. That development increasingly clarified and defended: the reality and integrity of the humanity (against docetism, Arianism and Monophysitism) and of the divinity (against adoptionism, subordinationism and Arianism) of Jesus Christ but also the hypostatic unity of these, without any confusion or change, without any division or separation, in the one person of the Word or only begotten Son of God (against Nestorianism) who it is that became man, without ceasing to be God, in Jesus Christ.

Thus, radical or death-of-God theology cannot claim to be the logical and legitimate consequence of the evolution of Christian monotheism, not only because of the Trinitarian character of that monotheism (the Father and the Holy Spirit, even though they are one God as the same one substance with the Son, are persons distinct from the Son and do not become man in Jesus Christ) but also because of the Incarnational character of that monotheism (the Word or only begotten Son of God becomes man in Jesus Christ, not by emptying or transforming the divinity into his humanity but by taking his humanity into a personal union or oneness with the divinity in which neither is confused with, changed into, nor divided and separated from the other). Because *this* is the Christian idea of the Incarnation, and *not* that of kenosis understood in any exclusive or literal way, the addition of the later Trinitarian ideas of perichoresis and the unity of divine operations ad extra does not really strengthen the case of radical or death-of-God theology in its claim to be the logical and legitimate consequence of the evolution of Christian monotheism.[43]

3. Protestantism

One of the evident things about radical or death-of-God theology, especially "hard" radical or death-of-God theology, is its predominantly Protestant character; most of its principal pro-

---

43 The doctrine of perichoresis is actually only a kind of alternate way of emphasizing that the three divine persons are the same one divine substance to combat any tritheistic misunderstanding of Christian monotheism in as strong a language as possible. The statement that each of the divine persons is wholly in the other two must not be interpreted as denying that the Father and the Son and the Holy Spirit are really distinct or that it is the Son alone who becomes man in Jesus Christ, for, in the very same context in which perichoresis is made use of, these other doctrines are also explicitly re-affirmed and Sabellianism condemned once again (Cf. DS 1330-1332, 1337). With regard to how the doctrine of the unity of the divine operations ad extra applies to the incarnation, the Church later adopted what the synod of Toledo taught in 675: that actively the Father and the Son and the Holy Spirit effect the incarnation but that passively only the Son becomes man because the human nature is attached immediately to his person (to that proper to the Son as really distinct from the Father and the Holy Spirit) and not to the one divine substance as such (to that common to the Father and the Son and the Holy Spirit as one God) (cf. DS 535). Nevertheless, despite this qualification of this doctrine, we would agree with Rahner that this idea of the unity of the divine operations ad extra cannot do real justice to Christianity's belief in the incarnation and grace. In one sentence, "The 'economic' Trinity is the 'immanent' Trinity and the 'immanent' Trinity is the 'economic' Trinity." See *The Trinity*. New York: Herder and Herder, 1970.

ponents are Protestant[44] and most of its principal sources, positive and negative, are or were Protestant.[45] It is also true, of course, that most of the principal opponents of radical or death-of-God theology have been Protestant,[46] that there are Jewish "hard"[47] and Catholic "soft"[48] radical or death-of-God theologians, and that there are many thoroughly secularized sources for "hard" radical or death-of-God theology from Jewish and Catholic milieus.[49] These qualifications are important; they witness to the fact that radical or death-of-God theology is not a problem restricted to Protestantism but is acute for any believer in the modern world (for *all* within the Judeo-Christian tradition) and, further, that radical or death-of-God theology is not the logical and legitimate consequence of the way in which Protestantism modified Judeo-Christian monotheism. Nevertheless, despite these qualifications, it is still evident that radical or death-of-God theology is more Protestant than either Judaic or

44 Among the "hard" radical or death-of-God theologians, e.g., there are, besides Paul van Buren, William Hamilton and Thomas Altizer: Herbert Braun, Dorothee Sölle, Werner and Lotte Pelz, John Cooper, Ernest Harrison, William R. Miller, Mary J. Irion, William Mallard and Manfred Hoffmann.

45 The principal positive sources (authors whose thought "hard" radical or death-of-God theologians have largely repeated) would include especially: Hegel, Feuerbach (but almost never explicitly), Marx and Nietzsche; the principal negative sources (authors whose thought "hard" radical or death-of-God theologians have either a. directly opposed or b. wanted to go beyond) would include especially: in the case of a., Kierkegaard and Barth; in the case of b., Bultmann, Tillich and Bonhoeffer. Needless to say, they also wish to go beyond the thought of such "soft" radical or death-of-God theologians as: Vahanian and Cox or Robinson and Cobb.

46 Among so many others, there are especially: Eric Mascall, Kenneth Hamilton, R.M. Brown, Martin Marty, Langdon Gilkey, J.W. Montgomery, J.D. Bales, C. Van Til, G.D. Kaufman, J.V.L. Casserley, A.A. Vogel, T.W. Ogletree, G.J. Fackre, H.H. Barnette and S.P. Schilling. Furthermore, "soft" radical or death-of-God theologians, especially Vahanian and Cox, have been very critical of "hard" radical or death-of-God theologians.

47 There is at least Richard L. Rubenstein. One might include Erich Fromm here, however, for his position is somewhat closer to that of Rubenstein than it is to that of Freud. Further, it is difficult to see how the final stance of such Jewish thinkers as Ira Eisenstein, Richard Israel, David Lieber and Ezra Spicehandler is really much different from that of Rubenstein and/or Fromm. Cf. *The Condition of Jewish Belief* (New York: Macmillan, 1966), pp. 50-51, 102-103, 140-141 and 233-234.

48 There are, besides Teilhard and his followers, especially: Brian Wicker, Raymond Nogar, Jacques Durandeaux, Leslie Dewart and Gregory Baum.

49 Such Jewish sources would include: Kafka, Freud, Jung and Fromm; such Catholic sources would include: LaPlace, Comte, O'Neill, Joyce, Camus and Sartre.

Catholic; and, thus, the question arises: in what sense are the origins of radical or death-of-God theology more closely connected with the peculiar way Protestantism transformed Judeo-Christian monotheism?

Not long after the death-of-God movement surfaced in the public consciousness, Martin Marty published a schematic summary of the pseudo, minor and major reasons for the Protestant character of death-of-God language,[50] but without limiting it to the Protestant ambit alone.[51]

The two pseudo reasons Marty lists are: 1. being "born in a parsonage" causes earlier and more radical reaction against Christian belief in God; 2. the divided state of Protestantism and its lack of papal authority have led to the chaos, irresponsibility, experimentalism and radicalism from which has arisen "the death of God."[52]

The four minor reasons Marty notes are: 1. the initial, poetic exaggeration can be found in Johann Rist's Good Friday chorale: "Gott selbst ist tot"; 2. Hegel exploited this kind of language, coupled with his interpretation of "kenosis" as the self-emptying of God in Jesus and the Lutheran emphasis on God as hidden in history but revealed supremely in his self-giving and loving death

---

[50] Martin Marty, "Whenever God Dies: Protestant Roots of the Problem of God," *Speaking of God,* edited by D. Dirschel, Bruce, Milwaukee, 1967, pp. 74-93. Although he claims that language about "the death of God" is only metaphorical (it can be used phenomenologically to describe a human event in a cultural or personal experience but not metaphysically to describe a divine event in a transcendent realm of experience), Marty concedes that this language is more accurate for Western Christian tradition than that of classical atheism ("God is not and never was") in as much as what is being described is the historical process by which the language of faith, once appropriate, has become inappropriate, i.e. the God once alive for Western Christian man has been killed for him. Cf. pp. 74-75, 89.

[51] Marty affirms that it is possible to see god-killing tendencies in the Bible's opposition to all forms of idolatry, its desacralization of nature and secularization of politics and prophetic criticism of religion; but he denies that the Bible itself, by way of these iconoclastic tendencies, leads logically to a nature and history autonomous from God or to the death of God himself. Furthermore, there is a kind of partial preparation for death-of-God language in the *via negativa* language used by mystics. Finally, language about "the death of God" is not limited to Protestantism; it has occurred on Catholic terrain also, as is evident in the works of Sartre and the films of Fellini. Cf. pp. 75, 78, 89.

[52] *Ibid.,* pp. 75-76, 92.

in Jesus on the cross, in order to obscure any distinctions between the divine and human natures in Jesus so as to argue that man was now able to undergo spiritual crisis or the "Golgatha of absolute spirit" without resorting to false religious props (such as the Reformation's stress on the resurrection) or false philosophical props (such as the Enlightenment's Deism which sought to preserve God by making him a philosophical abstraction rather than a living presence); 3. Nietzsche later made more of the Hegelian experience; 4. Protestantism, from Luther to Barth and Tillich, has valued the honest atheist as an ally against pious righteousness, human religion and institutional or idolatrous religiosity.[53]

The six major reasons Marty gives are the following.

(1). Luther understood the effort of man to know the hidden God by speculative reason as: making claims on God, a spiritual pride blinding man to his need for Christ's sacrifice, the "Devil's damned whore" preventing man's acceptance of God's grace. Man must despair of himself completely to be fit for the grace of Christ; his whole old self must be annihilated by God before his new self can be brought forth. Not he who beholds what is invisible of God through what is made but what is visible of God in the sufferings and cross of Christ is a true theologian. Only "the theologian of the cross" says what a thing is; "the theologian of glory" calls the bad good and the good bad. This anti-philosophical epistemology has run into difficulty in modern times, for, when historical criticism has made the very narrative of God's revelation in the sufferings and cross of Jesus suspect, how can one jump from that narrative to any objective reality called "God?" Thus, Luther's epistemology lies at the heart of the death-of-God problem as peculiarly Protestant, for asserting revelation without or against speculative reason no longer has any advantage since revelation itself has been put in question. Further, death-of-God theologians have accepted Luther's theology of the cross but denied his theology of the resurrection as both outside

53 *Ibid.*, pp. 76-78, 92.

of the empirical and in anticlimactic opposition to the effectiveness of Christ's death.[54]

(2). Luther rejected man's speculative efforts to find the hidden God through nature and man. God remains hidden in Christendom itself and partly hidden even where he reveals himself most: in the sufferings and cross of Christ, in all the weak and powerless things of the world and in death. Hence, Lutheranism speaks of revelation in terms of "transcendent immanence" and goes so far, especially in Hegel, that there is danger of identifying God and man, making God's thought in us his being in us, allowing man to swallow up God. Though this extreme was avoided by Kierkegaard and Bonhoeffer, the tendency is still present in them. Calvin claims that God, radically other and inscrutable, is manifest and known in the spiritual life of the individual when he experiences his election by God. Hence, Calvinism speaks of revelation in terms of "immanent transcendence;" and Barth intensified this attitude, even if the later Barth tends to be more Lutheran. Both of these efforts to relate the transcendence and immanence of God lead to paradox or contradiction without enjoying, since both attempt to rely on revelation alone, the cushioning effect which philosophical theism can provide against death-of-God language.[55]

(3). Pietistic Protestantism tended toward a "Unitarianism of the Second Person." It confessed that Jesus is "the Lord of Hosts" and "there is no other God" (Luther's *Ein Feste Burg*), while neglecting witness to God the Father and God the Holy Spirit. Thus, even though it meant only that the Christian knows no other God than that revealed in Jesus and still condemned patripassianism and Sabellianism, pietistic Protestantism tended also toward modalism: "God himself is dead" (Rist's Good Friday chorale). Its Christological emphasis makes God empirically manifest in our history only in Jesus; hence, the fate of Jesus becomes the fate of God himself.[56]

(4). Protestantism has so accentuated the subject of faith, man,

---

[54] *Ibid.,* pp. 79-82.
[55] *Ibid.,* pp. 82-84.
[56] *Ibid.,* pp. 84-85.

that it has neglected the object of faith, God. Besides stressing personal salvation, it ruled out speculative philosophy and good works as avenues to God; it concentrated entirely on the faith of the believer where the revelation of God is near and manifest. For Luther, faith is the creator of divinity in man and man has as he believes; but faith was not yet separated from the agency of God as revealer and still had the content of the promises made by God in Jesus. Radicals in the Protestant tradition, however, such as Feuerbach, could stress how close such an approach to faith brought theology to anthropology and claim that talk about God is really only talk about man. Neither Barth (his connection of revelation with faith and emphasis on God as "wholly other" only continued to draw attention to the subject of faith) nor Tillich (whose separation of "faith" from "belief" maximized the existential, the subject or man, and minimized any content-relation to the object or God) nor the generation after them (when it is all the more difficult to talk about revelation and meta-physics) have been able to arrest this tendency.[57]

(5). Modern secular (industrial, scientific, technological, etc.) culture was encouraged more on Protestant terrain, and Protestants have been more willing to welcome this development as a fulfillment of Christian goals.[58] Bonhoeffer and others understood: (a) secular man's growing concern with and mastery of creation as the fulfillment of a Scriptural mandate[59]) and (b) his overcoming of any need for God in his understanding of nature and himself as a purgation of the God of the gaps and of the immanent God of our religiosity in accord with Scriptural injunctions against all idols.[60] When it is then objected, however,

---

57 *Ibid.,* pp. 85-87.

58 Protestants who did not welcome an autonomous secular order abetted its development, according to Marty, in as much as they were ill-prepared to interpret it, either because they reacted to it with a revivalism which appealed only to the heart or because they perceived its arrival late and then wavered in their appeal to constructive reason. Cf. p. 90.

59 Gen. 1:26-29.

60 Ex. 3:13-15, Dt. 5:6-10, the prohibitions of images, the practice of not using the name of God directly, etc.

that faith's talk about God adds nothing substantial to human discussion, these Protestants must fall back on the empirical Jesus of history. But conventional historical inquiry finds Jesus elusive; whereas unconventional historical inquiry issues in talk about Jesus as the Christ, which is equivalent to God-talk. Hence, the apologist must either reopen God-talk or become a Jesus-oriented humanist inside the Christian community; and the death-of-God thinkers, who do the latter, can accuse those who do the former of having failed to make any real progress in meeting the challenge of secularization despite their initial claim that it should be welcomed as a fulfillment of Christian goals.[61]

(6). Sacramental symbolism has broken down more among Protestants than Catholics and Orthodox. Ever since Zwingli reduced the Eucharist to an allegory representing what it itself is not, sacrament has increasingly become for Protestants *mere* symbol. It has been ever more isolated from nature, until the empirical no longer seems transparent to any transcendent "beyond." The transcendent has become ever more spiritual but less real, and the mundane ever less spiritual but more real, until any "object" beyond the mundane or worldly has "disappeared" and man experiences himself as "alone" in the universe.[62]

Now, for the most part, I wish to agree with these important reasons Marty has given for the Protestant character of death-of-God language, as well as his insistence that it is not the final logic of orthodox Protestantism itself but a distortion or restrictive selection of certain of its principles and tendencies which leads to death-of-God atheism,[63] and that is why I have repeated these reasons at such length. Nonetheless, there are two qualifications and two crucial additions which must be made.

Marty's dismissal of the divided state of Protestantism as any kind of a real reason at all for the frequency of death-of-God theology among Protestants should be qualified. While it is true

---

61 Martin Marty, *op. cit.*, pp. 87-90, esp. pp. 87-88.
62 *Ibid.*, pp. 90-91.
63 *Ibid.*, pp. 75, 77, 78, 93.

that this has not simply caused death-of-God theology, neverthe-less, Protestantism has been split *so* many ways that it is difficult today to know what the word really means unless one synthetically limits himself to some principal traditions still in living contact with their classical origins—as Marty himself does by attending exclusively to Lutheranism and Calvinism. This is, however, to overlook at least two things with regard to the relation of the fractured state of Protestantism to the frequency of death-of-God thinking among Protestant theologians. For one thing, some of the more secularized and minimally Christian forms of Protestantism have been close to later death-of-God theologies, such as Unitarianism, which, like death-of-God theology, can represent any variety of beliefs about God, including the denial of a transcendent and personal God. For a second thing, and much more important than offering proto-types of one or another death-of-God theology, the fractured state of Protestantism has made it almost natural for death-of-God theologians to feel that they can remain in the Christian community (at least as humanists with a special dedication to Jesus) even if they do reject belief in God.

A second qualification should also be made, for, while it would be true to say of Feuerbach and Marx that they were "later to make more of the Hegelian experience," it is not even fair to say this of Nietzsche. Not only is Nietzsche's thought very different from that of Hegel (e.g., Nietzsche sees history as eternally recurrent and stresses the individual, but Hegel sees history as an irreversible dialectical process and stresses the social), but also the few references he does make to Hegel are almost all as uniformly negative as his warning that whoever once gets sick on "Hegelei" will never be cured again.[64] Further, the thing that most disturbed Nietzsche about Hegel was what he took to be the religious nature of Hegel's philosophy which he considered a last-ditch pantheism that only delayed the triumph of "scientific atheism" in Germany until Schopenhauer, translating Divinity into a process of world

---

64 *Friedrich Nietzsche: Sämtliche Werke* (Stuttgart: Kroner, 1964), Vol. 71, p. 38.

history which makes God detectable as "Spirit" in the sense of "the self-disclosing and self-realizing Ideal" which is always revealing and actualizing something more of itself in "process" and "becoming," something to which we belong by our impulse toward the Ideal.[65]

This serious qualification brings us to our first addition because it brings us to the *real* Nietzsche whose protests against belief in God have something much more central and disturbing to reveal about the way in which Protestantism has transformed Judeo-Christian monotheism than the secondary role Marty has assigned to him. As Marty himself has pointed out, it was Luther who taught that man's own speculative and practical efforts to reach God are to be condemned, for, to be saved, man must "completely despair of himself" and "his whole old self" must be "annihilated" by God. Although Nietzsche attacks virtually every concept of God, in his own way duplicating the attacks of Feuerbach[66] and Marx,[67] as well as anticipating those of Freud[68] and even Bonhoeffer's assault on the God-of-the-gaps,[69] there can be little doubt that his favorite target is precisely the God who annihilates man. This is especially clear in passages where Nietzsche calls the Christian concept of God the lowest of all because it is the will to nothingness pronounced holy, the contradiction of life rather than its transformation[70] and, therefore, a "deification of nothingness" that must itself be killed by man so that he can become "superman," i.e. a man in a way beyond the way in which he is now a man, a unique creator and master rather than an ordinary creature and subject. Now, it is true that Nietzsche himself does not blame Luther alone for the idea of the God who annihilates

---

65 *Ibid.,* Vol. 74, pp. 262-263 and Vol. 78, pp. 182-183, 282.

66 *The Antichrist,* No. 16.

67 *Ibid.,* Nos. 25 and 26.

68 *The Geneology of Morals,* "Guilt, Bad Conscience, etc.," No. 19.

69 *Thus Spoke Zarathustra,* II, "Of the Priests."

70 That we have to do here with the Lutheran God, i.e. the God that saves man only by wholly negating him, is especially clear in: *The Antichrist,* Nos. 18, 19, 47 and *Thus Spoke Zarathustra,* IV, "Retired", esp. the latter part, and "The Ugliest Person." Cf. also: *The Will to Power,* No. 54 and *The Geneology of Morals,* "Guilt, Bad Conscience, etc.," Nos. 7, 19-23, esp. 22.

man. In fact, he usually blames, besides Paul, Judaism and Christianity in general. Furthermore, it is true enough that Augustine, Thomas, Calvin, Jansen and others are guilty of the same, each in their own way and to a different degree. In short, Catholicism itself has almost always been *too* anti-Pelagian and not Molinist *enough* about how it is that man is saved by God's grace alone. Nevertheless, Catholicism did not insist that man is totally degraded and incapable of meriting. It did accuse Lutheranism of doing this; so did Nietzsche, even if he did tend to do so by unconsciously yeasting all of Judeo-Christian monotheism with Lutheranism. No, there can be little doubt that the God Nietzsche rejects is above all Luther's God (and that of Paul or Judeo-Christianity especially as seen through Lutheran glasses), a God who saves man only by negating him. This is a way in which "Protestantism," i.e. *Lutheranism,* has peculiarly transformed Judeo-Christian monotheism; and it is a way that has done much more to precipitate death-of-God language than Luther's epistemology or the reasons Marty has catalogued. I would not expect a Lutheran to make nor even to grant this point; and a Catholic does neither without trepidation in this ecumenical age. But the point *must* be made. It is true. It is even fairly obvious. And it is my own firm conviction that Lutheranism shall never be able to confront death-of-God theology, except with a "false consciousness" or even bad conscience, by overlooking or avoiding this crucial self-confrontation. Of course, the same is also true for all other Christian traditions to the degree to which they share in this predicament, especially for Calvinism (which found a kind of lesser Nietzsche in Melville) with regard to the God its doctrine of predestination implies and for neo-Thomism.[71]

---

71 Neo-Thomists teach that God is *Pure Act.* Thus, he cannot even know anything except by himself determining it, otherwise he would be passive in this regard and so not really *Pure Act.* Hence, God actually determines *all* things, and, with reference to predestination, whether saved or damned, man is really destroyed as any kind of a genuinely free person. Election means that God freely chooses to give a man *efficacious* grace which infallibly premoves him to salvation. Reprobation means that God freely chooses *not* to give a man efficacious grace. Therefore, damnation is really due to one's not being elected by God rather than to any misuse of his own freedom in the face of God's saving presence and activity. Of course, neo-Thomists try to free themselves from

Another reason I would add for the predominantly Protestant character of death-of-God theology is that death-of-God theology has been nourished directly by the frustrating results of the quest for the historical Jesus. There is, of course, nothing *per se* Protestant about this quest; nevertheless, it has been de facto Protestant, indeed, largely Lutheran. Now, if one first limits all true knowledge of God to knowledge of Jesus, but it is shown after this commitment that there is really very little that can be known about Jesus, then most of what we thought we knew about God passes away. This is all the more true if the little we can know about the real or historical Jesus shows he was a fanatical, eschatological prophet who is so strange and enigmatic to us that we cannot keep him for our time but must let him go, let him return to his own time.[72] Despite the fact that, according to Schweitzer, the result of the critical study of the life of Jesus is supposed to do away with, not only the Jesus of traditional orthodox theology, but above all with the Jesus of nineteenth-century liberal Protestant theology, we see a Schweitzer himself trying to retain an interior something of Jesus (and that without God) by which to direct his life.[73] Indeed, Jackson L. Ice has argued very ably that Schweitzer is one of the first "prophets" of radical or death-of-God theology.[74] This seems to be born out by some very striking resemblances between Schweitzer and modern

the dire consequences of this position by saying things like: 1. all men receive *sufficient* grace for salvation (but one would like to know how grace can be sufficient for anything if it has de facto no effect unless it is efficacious); 2. efficacious grace—even though it premoves us infallibly—moves us only "sweetly in accord with our nature" (but one would like to know how what is by nature free can be premoved infallibly by another without ceasing to be free); 3. no one is lost without his own fault (but one would like to know how a man can be at fault for not being elected—especially since he cannot be *not* elected on the basis of God's seeing ahead of time that he would refuse God's grace since he would "refuse" it only if God did not give him efficacious grace, i.e. only if God did not elect him). No, when all is said and done, the truth of the matter is that the God who is *Pure Act,* just as the Lutheran and Calvinist God, annihilates man as any kind of a genuinely free person.

72 Albert Schweitzer, *The Quest of the Historical Jesus* (New York: Macmillan, 1961), pp. 398-399.

73 *Ibid.,* pp. 398-403.

74 Jackson L. Ice, *Schweitzer: Prophet of Radical Theology.* Westminster, Philadelphia, 1971. Cf. esp. p. 192 for a short summary of his position.

"hard" radical or death-of-God theologians, such as his pantheistic-sounding claim, akin to that of Altizer, that the spirit of Jesus has risen into and lives in the spirits of men today[75] and his emphasis, akin to that of van Buren and Hamilton, on a life of service for others as the only way to discover Jesus.[76] It might be objected that since the publication of *Von Reimarus zu Wrede* in 1906 there has been a whole "new quest" which has been more successful. However, this would only confirm the argument that radical or death-of-God theology draws some of its especial Protestant character from the "original quest" for the historical Jesus, because radical or death-of-God theology has been in large part a return to nineteenth-century thinkers, by way of revolting against more recent Protestant theologians as not positive enough toward their own forebears, in order to modify faith in accord with the radically secular findings of those forebears and make faith, thereby, more adequate to our even more radically secular world today.

These, then, are the important reasons why the way Protestantism (i.e., especially Lutheranism and Calvinism) has transformed Judeo-Christian monotheism has made it more responsible for the rise of radical or death-of-God theology than Judaism or Catholicism, even though it is still true: that all of

---

75 Schweitzer, *op. cit.*, pp. 399, 401.

"Jesus means something to our world because a mighty spiritual force streams forth from Him and flows through our time also. This fact can neither be shaken nor confirmed by any historical discovery. It is the solid foundation of Christianity."

"But the truth is, it is not Jesus as historically known, but Jesus as spiritually arisen within men, who is significant for our time and can help it. Not the historical Jesus, but the spirit which goes forth from Him and in the spirits of men strives for new influence and rule, is that which overcomes the world."

"The abiding and eternal in Jesus is absolutely independent of historical knowledge and can only be understood by contact with His spirit which is still at work in the world. In proportion as we have the Spirit of Jesus we have the true knowledge of Jesus."

76 *Ibid.*, p. 403. "He comes to us as One unknown without a name, as of old, by the lake-side, He came to those men who knew Him not. He speaks to us the same word: 'Follow thou me!' and sets us to the tasks which He has to fulfil for our time. He commands. And to those who obey Him, whether they be wise or simple, He will reveal Himself in the toils, the conflicts, the sufferings which they shall pass through in His fellowship, and, as an ineffable mystery, they shall learn in their own experience Who He is."

these have contributed something to the development of radical or death-of-God theology, that radical or death-of-God theology is not the logical and legitimate consequence of Protestantism either nor a problem limited to Protestantism alone.

4. *Radically Secular Humanism*

It may occur to the reader at this point to object that the leaders of "hard" radical or death-of-God theology itself are or were Episcopal (van Buren and Altizer) or Baptist (Hamilton) and, therefore, that the real reason for the Protestant character of radical or death-of-God theology must lie elsewhere. Nevertheless, these two forms of Protestantism are not as radical or death-of-God-prone as Lutheranism and Calvinism; rather, these three theologians, precisely as "hard" radical or death-of-God theologians, are or were actually more Lutheran or Calvinist than Episcopal or Baptist. Van Buren was a student of Barth, and his agnostic death-of-God theology is shaped by his effort to go beyond Barth toward a radically secular expression of Christian faith. Altizer's "Christian Atheism" (even though much more affected by Hegel and an Hegelianized Nietzsche and Blake) has been deeply affected by Tillich whose theology he goes beyond toward a more radical process-pantheism. Finally, the principal influence on Hamilton's atheistic brand of death-of-God theology has been the Bonhoeffer of the prison letters, whom he recognizes he is going beyond. Hence, not only are or were these theologians actually more Lutheran and Calvinist than Episcopal or Baptist, but they go beyond their already much secularized Lutheran and Calvinist sources in their willingness to adapt faith yet more radically to our modern, radically secular world. Thus, it is not true that *the real reason* for the *Protestant* character of radical or death-of-God theology lies elsewhere but rather that *the most immediate and important reason* for the rise of radical or death-of-God theology *at all* lies elsewhere; i.e. it is not something in Judaism nor Catholicism nor even Lutheran or Calvinist Protestantism as such (even though each of these has contributed to its development in progressive connection with one another) but our modern, radically secular world and the willingness of radical or death-of-God theologians to adapt faith to it in a radical way. Actually, this willingness of their's is itself, for the most part, but another aspect of our modern, radically secular world—an indication of how pervasive and thorough its influence has become.

Our modern, radically secular world has been a long time in coming. It is largely, not totally, the result of the advance of the empirical sciences; i.e., the continuously growing success of the empirical sciences has led to the general conviction that the only genuine reality man can know, even that the only genuine reality there actually is, is that which can be verified in accord with the criteria and methodology of the empirical sciences. This has led very directly to the continuous decrease of belief in God, soul, afterlife, miracles, etc. and to the continuous increase of "belief" in man, body, this life, technology, etc. Thus, Judeo-Christian religion, despite the fact that it inspired much of what went into science and secularization, finally became their victim and so opponent.

This gradual process of radical secularization began to reach a crucial turning point from the end of the eighteenth century on. Nietzsche later aptly described this turning point as "the death of God," i.e. as actually arriving at the realization that the Judeo-Christian faith has *become* unbelievable (essentially: that there *no longer* is a transcendent personal God who created all things and bestows everlasting life on the good and everlasting punishment on the evil) and, therefore, that man's horizon was now open as never before but also that the shock of this discovery left him plunging into a directionless void.[77] This death-of-God feeling, whether suspicion or conviction, eventually permeated virtually all of philosophy, art, literature and everyday life until even the faithful Jew or Christian senses that his religion is dangerously divided from the rest of his existence and fears that he may be trapped in the impossible position of one who is trying to *believe* what he

77 See esp. *The Gay Science,* not only No. 125 but also No. 343.

knows is not actually true. Kierkegaard's well-intentioned efforts: to oppose objective and subjective truth and opt for the latter as somehow more true or to defend genuine faith as necessarily a "leap in the dark" and base it on the claim "credo quia absurdum," not only reflect precisely this situation but also the futility of trying to solve it simply be brazenly emphasizing and affirming it.

At any rate, ever since the process of radical secularization has reached this crucial turning point, an increasing number of the leading spokesmen of modern Western thought have attempted consciously and explicitly to reduce Judeo-Christian religion to, or replace it with, other systems of human meaning and morality more in accord with what man can seemingly know as truly real. Even though all genuine *radically secular* humanisms do away with any real God and afterlife, there is, of course, no one radically secular humanism; and it is not my aim here to try to summarize or compare the efforts in this direction of a Hume, Hegel, Feuerbach, Marx, Comte, Schopenhauer, Nietzsche, Freud, Jung, Fromm, Russell, Camus, Sartre, Garaudy, Bloch or any of the other outstanding figures which come to mind. The only point I wish to make is that radical or death-of-God theologians are really *less* radically secular than these radically secular humanists.

Radical or death-of-God theologians are really less radically secular than these radically secular humanists because, though they wish to go beyond the Tillichs and Bultmanns and later Bonhoeffers in adapting faith to our radically secular world today, they are unwilling to go as far in doing so as radically secular humanists have gone; i.e., they are simply unwilling to go all the way.

"Soft" radical or death-of-God theologians, whether theist or panentheist, are really less radically secular than radically secular humanists because they retain belief in a kind of real God and afterlife. It is true, of course, that some of the more radical panentheists seem to reduce God to little more than a quality of the universe and afterlife to little more than continued existence as an "object" somehow "remembered" in the universe following upon subjects presently alive. Now, such a position would roughly approximate that of a radically secular humanism; indeed, the conscious clinging to religious language and images and feelings, despite complete demythologization, recalls Feuerbach. Nevertheless, even these more radical of the panentheist versions of "soft" radical or death-of-God theology have not become radically secular humanisms if only because their creators have refused to be as frank as a Feuerbach whom radical or death-of-God theologians in general ignore or disown.

"Hard" radical or death-of-God theologians, whether pantheist or agnostic or even atheist, are also really less radically secular than radically secular humanists, for, although these theologians do away with God and afterlife,[78] they cling: 1. to a kind of Jesus whom they find indispensible (be this Jesus what they think they can know of the historical Jesus or what they still like about the kerygmatic Christ or a Jesus Christ they claim to discover experientially in themselves or in others or among men or in the world) and, therefore, 2. to membership in the Christian community (be this membership no more than the fellowship that happens wherever men consciously or unconsciously live for one another on the pattern of Jesus Christ, regardless of whatever else they believe or do not believe). Because of this minimal christology and ecclesiology, these "hard" death-of-God theologians are not truly as radically secular as radically secular humanists. This is very likely the reason why they ignore or disown people like Feuerbach or Russell, for these radically secular humanists illustrate embarrassingly well both the true logic of "hard" death-of-God theology and also the few remaining steps "hard" death-of-God theologians have yet to take in "adapting" faith *radically* to the radically secular world of today.

---

[78] Except for Altizer, whose process-pantheism retains something of a "God" and an "afterlife" and, thus, may best be seen as a kind of bridge between the more radical panentheist versions of "soft" radical or death-of-God theology and "hard" radical or death-of-God theologies, i.e. the agnostic or atheist versions of Christianity taught by van Buren and Hamilton.

A SELECT BIBLIOGRAPHY

Because listing them would make this bibliography much too long, the works of panentheistic radical or death-of-God theologian are not included.

Altizer, Thomas J.J., *Oriental Mysticism and Biblical Eschatology*. Philadelphia: Westminster, 1961.

———, *Mircea Eliade and the Dialectic of the Sacred*. Philadelphia: Westminster, 1963.

———, *The Gospel of Christian Atheism*. Philadelphia: Westminster, 1966.

———, *Radical Theology and the Death of God*. Philadelphia: Westminster, 1966.

———, *The Altizer-Montgomery Dialogue*. Chicago: Inter-varsity, 1967.

———, *The New Apocalypse*. East Lansing, Michigan: Michigan University, 1967.

——— (ed.), *Toward a New Christianity*. New York: Harcourt, Brace, World, 1967.

———, *The Descent into Hell*. Philadelphia: Lippincott, 1970.

Bales, James D., *The God-Killer*. Tulsa, Oklahoma: Christian Crusade, 1967.

Barnette, H.H., *The New Theology and Morality*. Philadelphia: Westminster, 1967.

Baum, Gregory, *Man Becoming*. New York: Herder and Herder, 1971.

Beardslee, W.A. (ed.), *America and the Future of Theology*. Philadelphia: Westminster, 1967.

Bent, C.N., *Les théologiens de 'la mort de Dieu'*. Paris: Cerf, 1967.

Braden, William, *The Private Sea*. Chicago: Quadrangle, 1967.

Buri, F., *Wie können wir heute noch verantwortlich von Gott reden?* Tübingen: Mohr, 1967.

Burkle, H., *The Non-existence of God*. New York: Herder and Herder, 1969.

Carey, J.J. and J.L. Ice (eds.), *The Death of God Debate*. Philadelphia: Westminster, 1967.

Casserley, J.V.L., *The Death of Man*. New York: Morehouse-Barlow, 1967.

Christian, C.W. and G.R. Wittig, *Radical Theology: Phase Two*. Philadelphia: Lippincott, 1967.

Cobb, John B., *God and the World*. Philadelphia: Westminster, 1969.

———, (ed.), *The Theology of Altizer: Critique and Response*. Philadelphia: Westminster, 1970.

Cooper, John C., *The Roots of the Radical Theology*. Philadelphia: Westminster, 1967.

———, *Radical Christianity and Its Sources*. Philadelphia: Westminster, 1968.

———, *New Mentality*. Philadelphia: Westminster, 1969.

———, *A New Kind of Man*. Philadelphia: Westminster, 1972.

Cox, Harvey, *The Secular City.* New York: Macmillan, 1965.
———, *On Not Leaving it to the Snake.* New York: Macmillan, 1968.
———, *Feast of Fools.* Cambridge, Massachusetts: Harvard University Press, 1969.
Dewart, Leslie, *The Future of Belief.* New York: Herder and Herder, 1966.
———, *The Foundations of Belief.* New York: Herder and Herder, 1969.
Dirscherl, D. (ed.), *Speaking of God.* Milwaukee, Wisconsin: Bruce, 1967.
Durandeaux, Jacques, *Question vivante à un Dieu mort.* Paris: Desclée de Brouwer, 1967.
Fabro, Cornelio, *God in Exile.* New York: Newman, 1968.
Fackre, G.J., *Humiliation and Celebration.* New York: Sheed and Ward, 1969.
Fromm, Erich, *The Art of Loving.* New York: Harper and Row, 1956.
———, *You Shall be as Gods.* New York: Holt, Rinehart and Winston, 1966.
Gilkey, Langdon, *Naming the Whirlwind.* Indianapolis, Indiana: Bobbs-Merrill, 1969.
Glicksberg, C.I., *Modern Literature and the Death of God.* The Hague: Martinus Nijhoff, 1966.
Hamilton, Kenneth, *God is Dead: The Anatomy of a Slogan.* Grand Rapids, Michigan: Eerdmans, 1966.
Hamilton, William, *The New Essence of Christianity.* New York: Association, 1961.
———, "The Shape of a Radical Theology," *The Christian Century,* Vol. LXXXII, No. 40, October 6, 1965, pp. 1219-1222.
———, *Radical Theology and the Death of God,* Indianapolis, Indiana: Bobbs-Merrill, 1966.
———, "The Death of God," *Playboy,* Vol. XIII, No. 8, August, 1966, pp. 79, 84, 137-139.
Harrison, Ernest, *A Church Without God.* Philadelphia: Lippincott, 1967.
Hayes, J.H. and L.D. Kliever, *Radical Christianity.* Anderson, South Carolina: Droke, 1968.
Herzog, F., *Understanding God.* New York: Scribners, 1966.
Ice, Jackson L., *Schweitzer: Prophet of Radical Theology.* Philadelphia: Westminster, 1971.
Irion, Mary J., *From the Ashes of Christianity.* Philadelphia: Lippincott, 1968.
———, *Yes World.* New York: Baron, 1970.
Kaufman, Gordon, *God the Problem.* Cambridge, Massachusetts: Harvard University Press, 1972.
Kereszty, R.A., *God Seekers for a New Age.* Dayton, Ohio: Pflaum, 1970.
Killinger, J., *Hemingway and the Dead Gods.* New York: Citadel, 1965.
Lelyveld, A.J., *Atheism is Dead.* Cleveland, Ohio: World, 1968.

Loomis, W.F., *The God Within.* New York: October House, 1967.

Macquarrie, J., *God and Secularity.* Philadelphia: Westminster, 1967.

Marty, M.E., *Varieties of Unbelief.* New York: Holt, Rinehart and Winston, 1964.

Mascall, Eric L., *The Secularization of Christianity.* London: Libra, 1967.

Metz, J.B. (ed.), *Is God Dead?* New York: Paulist, 1966.

Miller, J.H., *The Disappearance of God.* Cambridge, Massachusetts: Belknap, 1963.

Miller, William (ed.), *The New Christianity.* New York: Delacorte, 1967.

————, *Goodbye, Jehovah.* New York: Discus-Avon, 1969.

———— (ed.), *Contemporary American Protestant Thought, 1900-1970.* Indianapolis, Indiana: Bobbs-Merrill, 1971.

Montgomery, John Warwick, *The 'Is God Dead?' Controversy.* Grand Rapids, Michigan: Zondervan, 1966.

————, *The Altizer-Montgomery Dialogue.* Chicago: Inter-varsity, 1967.

————, *The Suicide of Christian Theology.* Minneapolis, Minnesota: Bethany Fellowship, 1970.

Murchland, B., editor, *The Meaning of the Death of God.* New York: Vintage, 1967.

Murray, J.C., *The Problem of God.* New Haven, Connecticut: Yale University Press, 1964.

Nogar, R., *The Lord of the Absurd.* New York: Herder and Herder, 1966.

Ogletree, Thomas W., *The Death of God Controversy.* Nashville, Tennessee: Abingdon, 1966.

Pelz, Werner and Lotte, *God is No More.* London: Gollancz, 1963.

Richard, R.L., *Secularization Theology.* New York: Herder and Herder, 1967.

Richardson, A., *Religion in Contemporary Debate.* London: SCM, 1966.

Robinson, J.A.T., *Honest to God.* Philadelphia: Westminster, 1963.

————, *The New Reformation?* London: SCM, 1965.

————, *Exploration into God.* London: SCM, 1967.

————, *But that I can't Believe.* London: Fontana, 1967.

————, *In the End God.* London: Fontana, 1968.

————, *The Difference in Being a Christian Today.* Philadelphia: Westminster, 1972.

Rubenstein, Richard, *After Auschwitz.* Indianapolis, Indiana: Bobbs-Merrill, 1966.

————, *The Religious Imagination.* Indianapolis, Indiana: Bobbs-Merrill, 1968.

————, *Morality and Eros.* New York: McGraw Hill, 1970.

————, *My Brother Paul.* New York: Harper and Row, 1972.

Schilling, S.P., *God in an Age of Atheism.* Nashville, Tennessee: Abingdon, 1969.

Smith, R.G., *Secular Christianity*. New York: Harper and Row, 1966.

_____, *World Come of Age*. Philadelphia: Fortress, 1967.

_____, *The Whole Man*. Philadelphia: Westminster, 1969.

_____, *The Doctrine of God*. Philadelphia: Westminster, 1970.

Sölle, Dorothee, *Stellvertretung*. Freiburg im B.: Walter, 1965.

_____, *Die Wahrheit ist Konkret*. Freiburg im B.: Walter, 1967.

_____, *Atheistisch an Gott glauben*. Freiburg im B.: Walter, 1968.

Todrank, G.H., *The Secular Search for a New Christ*. Philadelphia: Westminster, 1969.

Vahanian, Gabriel, *The Death of God*. New York: Braziller, 1961.

_____, *Wait Without Idols*. New York: Braziller, 1964.

_____, *No Other God*. New York: Braziller, 1966.

Van Buren, Paul, *The Secular Meaning of the Gospel*. New York: Macmillan, 1963.

_____, *Theological Explorations*. New York: Macmillan, 1968.

Van Til, C., *Is God Dead?* Philadelphia: Presbyterian and Reformed, 1966.

Vincent, John J., *Secular Christ*. London: Lutterworth, 1968.

Vogel, A.A., *The Next Christian Epoch*. New York: Harper and Row, 1966.

Weiland, J.S., *New Ways in Theology*. New York: Newman, 1968.

Wicker, Brian, *Culture and Theology: Toward a Contemporary Christianity*. London: Sheed and Ward, 1966.

Wolff, Richard, *Is God Dead?* Wheaton, Illinois: Tyndale, 1967.

Zahrnt, Heinz, *Gott kann nicht Sterben*. München: Pieper, 1970.

CHAPTER XXIX

"GOD" IN ANALYTIC PHILOSOPHY
David Stagaman, S.J. *

Once upon a time two explorers came upon a clearing in the
jungle. In the clearing were growing many flowers and many
weeds. One explorer says, 'Some gardener must tend this plot.'
The other disagrees, 'There is no gardener.' So they pitch their
tents and set a watch. No gardener is ever seen. 'But perhaps he
is an invisible gardener.' So they set up a barbed-wire fence.
They electrify it. They patrol with bloodhounds. (For they
remember how H.G. Wells' *The Invisible Man* could be both
smelt and touched though he could not be seen.) But no shrieks
ever suggest that some intruder has received a shock. No
movements of the wire ever betray an invisible climber. The
bloodhounds never give cry. Yet still the Believer is not
convinced. 'But there is a gardener, invisible, intangible,
insensible to electric shocks, a gardener who has no scent and
makes no sound, a gardener who comes secretly to look after
the garden which he loves.' At last the Sceptic despairs, 'But
what remains of your original assertion? Just how does what
you call an invisible, intangible, eternally elusive gardener differ
from an imaginary gardener or even from no gardener at all.'[1]

This parable was used by Antony Flew to illustrate how the
God-hypothesis dies the death of a thousand qualifications. In its
present form, the parable is based upon, but differs from one

*Professor of Philosophy at The Jesuit School of Theology, Berkeley, California, U.S.A.

1   Antony   Flew   and   Alasdair   MacIntyre   (eds.),   *New   Essays   in   Philosophical
Theology* (London: SCM, 1955), p. 96.

written by John Wisdom. The point of Wisdom's parable had been that the willingness or unwillingness to make use of the word "God" turns on a difference in attitudes on the part of the believer and the non-believer and not on a divergence in the experimental data available to each. Flew has re-written Wisdom's parable so that it illustrates how evidence is lacking for the God-hypothesis.

Historically, the challenge to believers laid down in Flew's version of the parable is the origin of the falsification controversy. And this controversy has set the tone for much discussion concerning God within the framework of analytic philosophy on both sides of the Atlantic. It will undoubtedly be helpful to get a clear idea of what Flew means by falsification before exploring the controversy further. The term indicates a criterion for distinguishing between factual and non-factual assertions. A statement of fact claims that a state of affairs stands thus and thus, *and not otherwise.* As a consequence, in understanding any statement, we grasp not so much what is being asserted, but how the state of affairs described by that statement differs from one or more other states of affairs. In other words, comprehension of a factual assertion requires that we know how the assertion can be falsified. Any utterance which would be compatible with all states of affairs would have no empirical content. For example, if we are told, "San Francisco is on the west side of the Bay," we can readily grasp the meaning of that statement because we can stipulate what would be required for San Francisco not to be there. But if we are told, "The governor is the chief executive of the state," we would soon recognize that we have been given no factual information about the governor, but a definition of what the governor is. We could specify no instance of the governor not being the chief executive.

Flew contends that, if we attend carefully to how Christians speak, we will see that their assertions are compatible with all states of affairs. He challenges the Christian to explain how the assertion "God loves the world" is in any sense a statement of fact. An innocent child dies of an incurable disease or in a meaningless and unnecessary accident. Yet Christians continue to insist that God's love for the world extends to each and every person in it. What, then, asks Flew, counts against the divine love? Does the utterance "God loves the world" communicate any genuine information at all?

R.M. Hare conceded that Flew was completely victorious on his own ground. Hare contended, however, that Flew had missed the point of Christian assertions. They are in no sense factual. And he proposed a counter-parable to indicate how religious sentences have meaning:

A certain lunatic is convinced that all dons want to murder him. His friends introduce him to all the mildest and most respectable dons that they can find, and after each of them has retired, they say, 'you see, he doesn't really want to murder you; he spoke to you in a most cordial manner; surely you are convinced now?' But the lunatic replies 'yes, but that was only his diabolical cunning; he's really plotting against me the whole time, like the rest of them; I know it I tell you.' However many kindly dons are produced, the reaction is still the same.[2]

According to Hare, religious beliefs are *bliks.* They are fundamental attitudes towards the world which determine what does and what does not count for an explanation. They provide us with frameworks for explaining other things. They do not in themselves require explanation.

Flew found Hare's response unorthodox. Most religious believers, he contended, speak as if their statements communicate some information about God.[3] Furthermore, Hare was asked: how does the believer or anyone else distinguish correct from incorrect bliks, the folly of the cross from sheer madness? For the present, suffice it to say, that Hare illustrates one type of response to Flew's challenge. Religious language is not factual. It can be properly understood only in terms of its non-cognitive features.[4]

2 *Ibid.,* pp. 99-100.
3 *Ibid.,* p. 108.
4 D.R. Duff-Forbes, "Theology and Falsification Again," *Australasian Journal of Theology* (1961), pp. 145-146.

The other type of response is that of Basil Mitchell. He accepts
Flew's challenge that believers must indicate how religious
language has factual meaning. And he illustrated why this was so
in a parable of his own:

> In time of war in an occupied country, a member of the
> resistance meets one night a stranger who deeply impresses him.
> They spend that night together in conversation. The Stranger
> tells the partisan that he himself is on the side of the
> resistance—indeed that he is in command of it, and urges the
> partisan to have faith in him no matter what happens. The
> partisan is utterly convinced at that meeting of the Stranger's
> sincerity and constancy and undertakes to trust him.
>
> They never meet in conditions of intimacy again. But some-
> times the Stranger is seen helping members of the resistance,
> and the partisan is grateful and says to his friends, 'He is on our
> side.'
>
> Sometimes he is seen in the uniform of the police handing over
> patriots to the occupying power. On these occasions his friends
> murmur against him: but the partisan still says, 'He is on our
> side.' He still believes that, in spite of appearances, the Stranger
> did not deceive him. Sometimes he asks the Stranger for help
> and receives it. He is then thankful. Sometimes he asks and does
> not receive it. Then he says, 'The Stranger knows best.'
> Sometimes his friends, in exasperation, say 'Well, what *would*
> he have to do for you to admit that you were wrong and that he
> is not on our side?' But the partisan refuses to answer. He will
> not consent to put the Stranger to the test. And sometimes his
> friends complain, 'Well, if *that's* what you mean by his being on
> our side, the sooner he goes over to the other side the better.'[5]

Human suffering does count against the Christian's belief in
God, but not decisively. The believer, according to Mitchell, is not

5 *New Essays in Philosophical Theology*, pp. 103-104.

a detached observer, but one who trusts in God. Like the partisan in the parable, he finds the evidence for the love of God ambiguous, but he accepts this ambiguity as a trial of his faith.

Mitchell's parable of the partisan, however, has not satisfied many proponents of the falsification challenge. They feel that, in the final analysis, Mitchell's position differs little from that of Hare.[6] Human suffering only appears to count against belief in God for the Christians. But Christians never do finally permit anything to count against their belief in God. Mitchell may insist that religious sentences are falsifiable and therefore factual, but he fails to explain adequately how this is the case.

In analytic philosophy today, much discussion of the God question takes place against the background of Flew's challenge. But it would be misleading to proceed as if little progress has been made in clarifying the issues since Flew's original statement. In that statement, Flew assumed that the criteria for the valid use of language as delineated by the logical positivists are essentially correct. That assumption has been extensively criticized. In the remainder of this article, I propose to examine three such critiques with special attention how they clarify our use of the word "God." The three critiques have been made by Ian Ramsey, by John Austin and applied to the religious use of language by Donald Evans, and by Ludwig Wittgenstein and interpreted theologically by Dallas High.

According to Ian Ramsey,[7] religious language rests on a double foundation, the discernment of the "odd" in certain situations and the ensuing commitment of ourselves without reserve. We discern the "odd" whenever "the light dawns," "the ice breaks," "the penny drops," that is, in any situation in which we come alive to ourselves and the world around us. We discern the "odd" in those moments of memorable insight in which we pass from being

---

6 William Blackstone, *The Problem of Religious Knowledge* (Englewood Cliffs: Prentice Hall, 1963), pp. 73-74.

7 Throughout my treatment of Ian Ramsey, I am following the outline laid down in *Religious Language* (London: SCM, 1957). I am also using material from his other writings, but will indicate the book or article only when I am drawing extensively from another source.

spectators to being participants, from being detached observers of events to becoming involved in what transpires in and around us. An example which Ramsey gives is that of a judge noted for the impartiality of his court who looks down from his bench one day to see before him as the accused his own wife or a long lost friend. The situation has ceased to be impersonal.

We know commitment in loyalty to a school or a nation. Some commitments, like patriotism, have as their object something universal, but they often become quite abstract in the course of life. Other commitments remain very concrete, but usually have as their object a very particular person or thing, e.g., devotion to one's wife. Christian love combines features of both kinds of commitments: it is a concrete commitment to the whole universe, embracing and including all the other commitments we make. All religious commitments are total, i.e., objectively, they refer to something all-inclusive while, subjectively, they require an unconditioned giving of ourselves.

Religious languages reflect our breakthrough discernments by being logically odd, and reflect our total commitments by making assertions such as "God is love" where subject and predicate are synonomous. We need logically odd language to articulate experiences of heightened consciousness. So we take the object-language of ordinary experience and give it appropriately strange qualifications. In the assertion, "God is my refuge and my strength," we use two quite ordinary words, "refuge" and "strength," but their combination creates a situation of logical oddity: God is simultaneously him to whom I flee because I am weak and he who gives me courage not to take flight. The two apparently opposed terms are paradoxically related, and the seeming contradiction proves enlightening. So the sentence has meaning. Significant tautologies, such as "God is love," commend the word "God" as a key-word or ultimate of explanation. An analysis of the predicate reveals what we mean by "God." The statement also casts light on the depths of all personal language interpreted in terms of love. Theological statements, then, are affirmations about the ultimacy of personal relationships and instructions how these relationships are finally to be explained.

Braithwaite has inquired in what this odd logic of Christianity consists. Can it be taught to non-believers or is it a secret doctrine open only to an elect?[8] Keith Ward has asked whether religious language has any basis in non-religious discourse.[9] A response to Braithwaite is contained in Ramsey's discussion of models, qualifiers, and disclosures. Ward's difficulties will be cleared after an examination of Ramsey's views on duty and I-language.

Models are familiar situations which enable us to understand the unfamiliar.[10] They are constituted by objects or sets of objects whose properties are sufficiently known so that we can use these objects to investigate phenomena which presently elude our grasp. Models do not picture their objects, i.e., they do not reproduce selected features of the original so that an identity of representation is achieved. Rather they are isomorphic with their objects, i.e., they reproduce in a new medium the structure of relationships present in the original. In theology, models enable us to be articulate. By means of them, we interpret religious phenomena in terms of related discourse (e.g., the Christ-event in terms of *logos*-language) or make sense of otherwise perplexing discourse (e.g., exploring grace through the language of love). Religious models, therefore, ground theological language in human experience; but they thereby prevent religious discourse from reflecting adequately its infinite object.

Theological models are deemed reliable whenever they are isomorphic with situations of a cosmic character and whenever the discourse articulated on their basis "empirically fits" the phenomena. Cosmic isomorphism is a matter of seeing the relationship between the model and its situation; empirical fit is obtained whenever the model harmonizes a number of events and

---

8 R.B. Braithwaite, "Discussion," *Christian Ethics and Contemporary Philosophy,* Ian Ramsey, ed. (London: SCM, 1966), pp. 93-94.

9 Keith Ward, "Myth and Fact in Christianity," *Scottish Journal of Theology* (1967), p. 68.

10 The present discussion goes well beyond the treatment of models in *Religious Language.* Ian Ramsey has elaborated this concept in *Models and Mystery* (London: Oxford, 1964) and "Talking About God: Models, Ancient and Modern," *Myth and Symbol,* F.W. Dillistone, ed. (London: SPCK, 1966).

so demonstrates its stability over a wide range of religious phenomena. Empirical fit is a distinguishing factor not only of theology, but also of all personal sciences. In the personal sciences, personal models are both appropriate and necessary because both observation *and* participation are required. In the personal sciences, theology included, the word "I" is a logical peculiarity necessary for adequate understanding. The analysis of any human behavior requires the use of both scientific and social predicates (third- and first-person language). Among personal models, metaphors have a special place. They evoke further insights through the tangential meeting of two diverse contexts. In the assertion, "God is a mighty fortress," "God" and "mighty fortress" are related tangentially. God is wholly spiritual while mighty fortresses are thoroughly material; but both are reliable sources of protection against the vagaries and vicissitudes of life. Metaphors also possess an eccentricity which generates an un-limited number of articulation possibilities. As a consequence, they are highly suitable for the explication of mystery. Religious models are the means of achieving theological relevance. They permit us to compare religious language with other kinds of discourse, especially scientific language.

At the heart of theology lies a mystery. And all theological language must bear witness to this mystery. So theological models, which are taken from ordinary experience, must be strained to tell the proper tale, i.e., they stand in need of qualification. *Qualifiers* are operators which indicate how models should be developed so that a characteristically religious experience will be evoked. Qualifiers are logically second-order rules to guide and direct our talk about God. Their primary function is to bring about situations in which the use of the word "God" is inevitable.

Qualifiers can be negative or positive. Some divine attributes, such as immutability or impassibility, have a negative operator, the prefix *im*, which instructs us to develop our models of change and suffering until a discernment occurs in which we are aware of the perceptual *and the more*. For instance, one might meditate upon the whole of one's experience until one sees that interaction (the phenomenal) can never be the last word, and that no scientific account will ever exhaustively explicate one's experience. The need for a radically different kind of explanation becomes evident, and "God" occurs as an explanatory ultimate outside the domain of perceptual language. Or one might approach our use of "God" positively, beginning in the goodness we observe around us. We recognize first that this goodness is to be admired and imitated. We also become aware that some things are better than others. So we begin to imagine instances of greater and greater goodness until God occurs to us as someone so good that adoration and worship are the appropriate responses. We place the word "God" outside of all ordinary goodness-language by our use of the operator "infinite." "Infinite goodness" instructs us to refine all models of goodness within our experience in the direction to a goodness to be adored and worshipped.[11] Ramsey, by these examples, is not interested in proving the existence of God. He is attempting to describe how a religious experience (or, as he calls it, a cosmic disclosure) is evoked. God is not deduced from the existence of change- or goodness-models. The experience that all mutability- and ordinary goodness-language is finally unsatisfactory requires the word "God" for its adequate articulation.

The process of qualification terminates in a disclosure. Disclosures are intuitions or insights. Ramsey prefers the term *disclosure* because disclosure emphasizes the sense of objectivity given in each intuition and highlights the apprehension of mystery which lurks in the background of every insight. Not all disclosures reveal God; only those which are cosmic. They are so whenever they reveal a non-empirical feature of the situation in the context of personal interaction or love. Ramsey is attempting to call our attention to the fact that cosmic wonder or awareness of mystery is the very condition of insight. Any articulation is always inadequate as an expression of the originating insight; and this

---

11 Ramsey's characterization of "infinite" as a positive operator is unfortunate. "In-finite" obviously means not finite and is, therefore, a negative qualifier. A closer examination of Ramsey's examples, however, indicates what he intends when he asserts that some qualifiers are positive: certain situations, traditionally called transcendentals such as unity, truth, goodness, etc., are more appropriately used in speaking of God than others.

inadequacy is the condition for further insight. Ramsey is not saying that men experience this presence of mystery which conditions all knowledge and speech as such, but that a man can, in the course of his life, acknowledge that religious language is necessary to articulate what he is only vaguely aware of in his every act of understanding and speaking.

William Austin has made an enlightening suggestion as to what Ramsey means when he says that cosmic disclosures reveal God.[12] The basic principle involved is that mystery and specifiability are the two components of our intellectual experience: as articulation increases, the sense of mystery decreases; and *vice versa*. Yet mystery is ever present for no single articulation does full justice to the generative insight. Consequently, we can construct a continuum within our intellectual experience. We could begin with gestalts where mystery is minimal, then work through major scientific theories like gravitation and theological theories such as the intuition relating the crucifixion and Isaiah 53, and end in the crucifixion itself where mystery is paramount and articulation minimal. This continuum of insights would remind us of Berkeley's SIRIS, a comprehensive view of all reality from tar water to trinity. (And Ramsey is a great admirer of the eighteenth century bishop.)[13] What is important for Ramsey, however, is that mystery pervades the entire continuum of our rational consciousness, and man can sooner or later come to the realization that this all-pervasive mystery is articulated in the word "God."

The most important clue to the meaning of the word "God" is our use of the word "I." "I" refers to a distinctive awareness that we have of ourselves. "I" also indicates a particular kind of existence which we know to be ours. The "I" can never be completely described in observational terminology because the experiential basis for "I" is a disclosure in which we know ourselves to be more than our observable (i.e., perceivable)

---

12 William Austin, "Models, Mystery, and Paradox in Ian Ramsey," *Journal for the Scientific Study of Religion,* 1968.

13 Cf. Ian Ramsey, "Berkeley and the Possibility of an Empirical Metaphysics," *New Studies in Berkeley's Philosophy,* W.F. Sternkraus, ed. (London: Holt, 1966) and "Sermon Preached at Festival Service in Chapel of Trinity College," *Hermathena,* 1953.

behavior. Hence we are required to use a logically peculiar word. The self-awareness, which grounds our use of "I," can never be displayed in purely descriptive (i.e., strictly empirical) terminology. We can only tell stories which illustrate the inadequacy of descriptive terms taken as a whole. The word "I" is like the word "this." "I" is demonstrative and not descriptive. We survey a set of distinct perceptions and recognize them to be our own. Furthermore, self-awareness is always and also other-awareness. Human intellectual experience is never a wholly private or a wholly public affair. We only become aware of ourselves when we become aware of an environment which transcends the observable. Awareness of subjective transcendence is simultaneously awareness of objective transcendence. The word "I" commits us to a pluralism of persons.

Ramsey's favorite example of self-disclosure is the story of Nathan and David. King David, the spectator, listens to the prophet Nathan's account of a rich man who, in spite of the numerous sheep in his own flock, took the poor man's single ewe lamb in order to prepare a meal for a visitor. The impartial David pronounces an impersonal judgment, "the man who has done this deserves to die." But Nathan tells David, "You are the man," and the king comes to self-knowledge and changes into a participant. According to Ramsey, it is no accident that David's response to Nathan takes the form of religious language.[14]

The word "God" is modeled on the word "I." "I" is the presupposition of all the descriptive language which I use about myself. The statement, "I am blonde" would be utter nonsense if "I" did not exist. In a not altogether dissimilar fashion, the statement "the world exists" presumes the statement "God exists." "God" is the contextual presupposition of the universe. All finite descriptions presuppose the existence of God. Furthermore, "I exist" entails no verifiable deductions about myself (e.g., about my hair or eye color), but all verifiable statements about myself do presuppose "I exist." Likewise, "God exists" entails no

---

14 *Religious Language,* pp. 112-113.

verifiable deductions about the world, but all statements about the world presuppose the truth of "God exists." For Ramsey, the previous sentence is the logical equivalent of the traditional metaphysical assertion that the world depends upon God, but God does not depend upon the world. In the final analysis, a threefold analogy obtains between the words "God" and "I." Neither word can be reduced to statements in purely descriptive language. Both are integrator words for descriptive statements. Personal models are the most appropriate in any attempt to understand the use of either word.[15]

The story of Nathan and David indicated that we come to ourselves most characteristically in the face of a moral challenge. According to Ramsey, ethics, the discipline which analyzes these moral challenges, requires a theological interpretation for two reasons. First, descriptivity leads naturally to prescriptivity (all factual knowledge must ultimately be submitted to the bar of value-judgments). Secondly and in contradistinction to the first reason, prescriptivity requires descriptivity to attain universality (the public features of moral judgments indicate that they are not just private affairs). The precise function of the theological interpretation is to relate the value-claims of ethics to the non-moral features of the universe. The integrating word, then, on the believer's language map is "God" who, as creator, is related to the universe through I-propositions and, as Lord of the promise, to duty situations by means of moral language. "God" names the larger context which envelops both scientific and ethical language.[16]

Ramsey concedes that the theist hypothesis does not seem capable of being falsified. Human suffering, even of the innocent, does not apparently count for Christians against their just and good God. For Ramsey, the question, "What would be different if God did not exist?" must be transposed into another, "What

---

15 "On the Possibility and Purpose of a Metaphysical Theology," *Prospect for Metaphysics,* Ian Ramsey, ed. (London: Allen and Unwin, 1961) and "The Systematic Elusiveness of 'I'," *The Philosophical Quarterly,* 1955.

16 Ian Ramsey, *Religion and Science* (London: SPCK, 1964), esp. pp. 63-88.

would be different if we did not have 'God' as a metaphysical index, i.e., as an integrator of all our language?" If God did not exist, our whole language scheme would be utterly transformed. In the final analysis, religious language is now falsifiable. But its speaker can be converted to infidelity. Religious speech along with the religious commitment is abandoned only after a personal revolution.[17]

In many ways this truncated account of Ramsey's language philosophy does not do justice to his contribution. Suffice it to say that his individual intuitions are often brilliant, but that his overall theory leaves much to be desired. First, Ramsey fails to explain with precision why the word "God" is necessary for human speech. He adds example upon example until the reader wonders whether "God" is not just another name for "penny dropping" experiences. His explanations how the word "God" can be modeled on the word "I" and how ethical language can be integrated with scientific discourse are plausible, but they are not cogent. Only Austin's continuum of insights provides us with some idea of what Ramsey is trying to elucidate. Secondly, is the logic of religious language actually "odd"? Or is the logical oddness, at least as Ramsey explains it, merely the result of a philosophical prejudice? On Ramsey's analysis, not only religious language, but also all personal language would seem to be logically odd. But such an assertion is true only if scientific discourse is taken to be the primary analogue of all speech-activity. And there is no compelling reason why we should concede science such a primacy. Rather we should argue that intersubjective language is the more fundamental mode of human expression. The religious use of language might still prove to be odd (a preferable word would be paradoxical), but for reasons other than those given by Ramsey. Finally, the theory of models and qualifiers conflates important differences in our various and varied uses of language and thereby blinds us to the complexity of ordinary language. Ramsey assumes that we have immediate access to the nature of our speech activity. Both John

---

17 *Religious Language*, p. 36.

Austin and Ludwig Wittgenstein have disputed that assumption. They have argued that a grasp of what actually happens in human language comes only at the end of a long and arduous analysis. It is to their understanding of our speech activity that we must now turn.

The application of John Austin's ordinary language philosophy to the religious use of language can be best discussed in terms of the work of Donald Evans. Evans studied under Austin at Oxford until the latter's untimely death and then completed his doctoral studies under the direction of Ramsey. Evans' doctoral thesis was subsequently published as *The Logic of Self-Involvement.*[18] This book is, in my estimation, the best single volume available on the religious use of language. The subtitle is most enlightening: *A Philosophical Study of Everyday Language with Special Reference to the Christian Use of Language about God as Creator.* One might pithily summarize the point of Evans' book in the following manner: the assertion "God created the world" is more like the assertion "I dub thee a knight of the realm" than it is like the statement "Joe made a table." Language is self-involving whenever there exist logical connections between a man's utterances and his practical commitments, attitudes, and feelings. Self-involving language is opposed to neutral, impersonal statements of fact.

Some self-involving language is *performative.* I perform a speech-act whenever I say what I do. Performatives are propositions whose principal function is to accomplish an act, not to describe a fact or action. They are of five kinds and can be divided into (1) *constatives* which report, state, guess, warn, bet, estimate, etc.; (2) *exercitives* which order, decree, appoint, name, give, etc.; (3) *verdictives* which judge, rate, find, grade, value, etc.; (4) *commissives* which promise, pledge, threaten, covenant, undertake, etc.; and (5) *behabitives* which thank, praise, apologize, blame, confess, etc. Those performatives which are commissive or behabitive are the most important for the study of the religious use of language; most of our talk about God implies certain

---

18 Donald Evans, *The Logic of Self-Involvement* (London: SCM, 1963).

attitudes and/or commits us to certain kinds of behavior. Furthermore, performatives can be correlative; I can show in a reply that I have taken another's words or actions as having performative force.

It is important to note that performatives are not true or false. They may be null and void if I am morally incapable of doing what I purport to be doing, e.g., a judge who grants a decree of divorce, but lacks the necessary authority. Or they may be insincere if I lack the attitude or intention necessary for the procedure, e.g., I swear a false oath. Or they may go unfulfilled if I fail to carry out my commitment, e.g., I promise money and then send none.[19]

Evans believes that world-creation in the Old Testament exemplifies a performative use of language. World-creation included the creation of man with a subordinate status and in a certain role. It was also an action in which God rendered an evaluation and made a self-commitment. To believe in God as Creator was to acknowledge him as one's Lord and accept one's status as his obedient servant. Belief in a Creator God also meant that man embraced his role as God's steward, a role to which man had been divinely appointed in the very act of creation. God's creative word then had exercitive force: it created men in a subordinate status so that their very existence became an act of obedience, and it produced creatures with a very definite role—they were designated as the stewards of nature and God's articulate worshippers. Belief in the Creator God was likewise to concur in the divine evaluation that creation was good, even to the extent that the very value of Israel as a nation depended on the divine approval. Such belief entailed further a reliance upon the divine guarantee or commitment to maintain creatures in existence. Faith in the creator, then, is not an assent to a flat (non-performative) constative which narrates a supernaturally powerful act; it is the grateful response of a creature who

---

19 *Ibid.*, pp. 27-80 *passim.*

recognizes and acknowledges God's authoritative verdict that his creation is good.[20]

Language can be used not only performatively, but also expressively. Some language and behavior reveal our inner feelings. My face blanches when I am afraid; I grit my teeth when I feel pain; I smile when I am happy; I report "I am sad" when I feel that way. Of these four examples, the most important is smiling. It *expresses* my feeling rather than just being a symptom (the face turning white) or manifesting a feeling (gritting one's teeth) or reporting the feeling ("I am sad"). Evans finds that such expressions of feeling have three significant characteristics: (1) they are open to understanding or misunderstanding insofar as they have a rudimentary meaning which may or may not be understood; (2) they can be appreciated only to the extent that two requirements are fulfilled—viz., (a) our personal life experience and attitudes give us some affinity with the agent who is expressing the feeling, and (b) we have sufficient insight to appraise the adequacy of the "correspondence" between the expression and inner feeling; and (3) since expressions of feeling can have different meanings for different people, we can speak of *the* expressive meaning only if we make one man's understanding authoritative. The previous three points can be exemplified thus. Smiling, to be understood, must have some generally accepted meaning for us; it usually means that we are happy. A particular man's smiling, however, will be understood only insofar as we have some rapport with that person and can grasp how smiling is related to an internal feeling of happiness. Finally since smiles are ambiguous, i.e., they can express happiness, mocking superiority, idiocy, etc., depending on who is doing the smiling, we can talk of *the* meaning of smiling only if we are prepared to accept one person's definition of *smiling* as authoritative. The second characteristic of expressions of feeling with its two conditions makes evident that language or behavior which expresses feelings is rapportive: the agent's action is understood only to the extent

20 *Ibid.*, pp. 145-165 *passim.*

that one has rapport or affinity with that agent.[21]

On the basis of behavior which reveals feelings, Evans constructs a concept peculiarly his own which he calls *soul-revealing-behavior* (SRB). SRB represents a portion of what we mean when we talk of a quality of soul. For we refer in part to a certain kind of behavior. SRB resembles behavior which expresses feelings inasmuch as its understanding requires the existence of a widely shared interpretation of the behavior involved, an affinity of the observer with the possessor of the quality of soul in question, and a willingness to make one man's understanding authoritative in order that we might talk about *the* behavior and *the* quality of soul.[22]

In the Old Testament, the notion of a divine attribute involved three different aspects of the divine reality: God's hidden self, certain revelatory observables, and the response of men to those observables. The divine *glory*, for instance, had a threefold meaning. The term *divine glory* referred to God's internal glory (that quality, as it were, of the divine soul), then to his external, visible expression of that glory in events, things, and persons (the divine impressive behavior), and finally to the acknowledgement of and response to that glory on the part of men or personified nature (the human, correlative feeling-response). Israel's response could be explicit, in acts of worship, or implicit, by being what she was—the revelation of God's glory to the world. The recognition of God's glory in His creation was rapportive. Biblical knowledge was a sort of doing. Knowing God implied a set of attitudes and committed one to a way of life. Only insofar as one acquired the appropriate attitudes and lived a proper way of life, could one understand the glory of God.[23]

Jesus Christ was the perfect revelation of the divine glory. First of all, his own personal inner glory was identified with the internal glory of God. Secondly, he constituted the epitome of the

---

21 *Ibid.*, pp. 80-106 *passim.*

22 *Ibid.*, pp. 196-189. Jean Ladriere has suggested that SRB is the most important contribution of Evans. Cf. *L'articulation du Sens* (Paris: Cerf, 1970), p. 133.

23 *The Logic of Self-Involvement*, pp. 174-201 *passim.*

observable expressions of God's internal glory. Thirdly, he represented the man who rendered perfect acknowledgement of the divine glory. This revelation of God's glory in Jesus, however, can be understood only rapportively. Only inasmuch as we become like Jesus and through him like God, can we grasp his revelation.[24]

Evans next considers *onlooks:* I look on x as y, e.g., "I look on Jones as a father." Onlooks can be of several kinds. I can say "I look on Brown as the cause of the trouble" when I expect to be taken literally or "I look on students as vermin" when I don't. An important type of non-literal onlook Evans calls *parabolic:* x is such that the attitude appropriate to y is similar to an attitude appropriate to x, e.g., "I look on Henry as a brother." In the case of religious parabolic onlooks such as "I look on God as my father," it is not possible to specify the similarity between God and my father. I must trust in the testimony of Jesus that attitudes appropriate for a loving father are also appropriate responses to the love of God.[25]

Grasping the parabolic meaning of a creation story consists in adopting an attitude which enables us to lead a life in rapport with God and thereby relate the parable to our own personal situations. Thus, the language in creation-parables is both self-involving and rapportive. In the parable of the potter, we learn that God has formed man somewhat like a craftsman forms a clay vessel. The appropriate attitude is humility towards our creator. In the parable of the victor, we learn that God has banished chaos to the outskirts of human life and protects us against its return. So we have been rescued from a fundamentally meaningless existence. It behooves us, therefore, to accept the authoritative divine onlook that human actions have meaning, that man does have an ultimate status and role, and that human existence is intrinsically good.

There exists a core in all human casual acts which can be observed and reported neutrally. World-creation possesses no such

---

24 *Ibid.,* pp. 204-209 *passim.*
25 *Ibid.,* pp. 124-141 *passim.*

core. It is accessible exclusively in terms of onlook-attitudes. These commit us to a certain mode of living which affects both our thinking and our behavior. But we are never able to specify the similarity between the two terms of our comparison (e.g., the potter and God or the victor and God) except by means of a similarity in the attitudes which constitute an appropriate response. We trust the divine authority that these attitudes are fitting. But we do have corroborative evidence insofar as these attitudes are self-verifying: we conduct our lives in the light of these attitudes and thereby make them existentially true, and we believe that God's grace alone enables us to carry on in such a manner.[26]

In *The Logic of Self-Involvement*, Donald Evans simply assumed that religious language was a valid form of discourse. The task he set himself there was an explanation of how the religious language functions. Since the publication of that book, however, almost all his effort has been expended on an exploration of the foundations of religious discourse: what permits us to speak of God? One might describe Evans' progress as a movement from a malaise over Karl Barth's views of language[27] to a re-interpretation of Thomist analogy in the light of Preller's *Divine Science and the Science of God.*[28]

For Barth, God reveals himself as hidden, as beyond the scope of human language. In contrast to Thomas Aquinas who said that, while the order of being was from the creator to creature, the order of knowing was from creature to creator, Barth insists that the way of signifying with regard to God must correspond exactly to the reality signified. Knowledge about divine things, therefore, must start with the meanings words possess when they are applied by God to himself. Otherwise we know not God, but an idol. As a consequence, the descriptive applicability (the non-religious use) of a word has nothing to do with God's taking possession of that

26 *Ibid.,* pp. 220-257 *passim.*
27 "Barth on Talk About God," *Canadian Journal of Theology,* 1970.
28 Victor Preller, *Divine Science and the Science of God* (Princeton, N.J.: Princeton University Press, 1967).

word for purposes of divine revelation. God simply bestows his truth upon the words which appear in the Bible. When God selects a word such as "Lord," he applies it to himself as a proper name. When we make use of that same word to speak of God, we do so on the divine authority that we are permitted to use "Lord" in that very manner.

Evans objects that the authority of someone who performs an act of naming is not enough to justify another's use of that name for whatever has been so named. No amount of authority, as a matter of fact, can render a name applicable unless the person or thing named has the characteristics which the name connotes. For example, if we apply a nickname to someone, the moniker does not stick unless it is somehow appropriate. The case of the divine names does not seem to be altogether dissimilar. The titles which have perdured over the centuries do appear to be those which have conformed to man's experience of God.

According to Barth, God bestows his truth upon human words, supplying himself as the referent for religious language and thereby enabling the man of faith to speak religiously. In other words, the words men use of God have religious meaning only because God has revealed their use in the Bible. Here Evans counters that the application of the same word to both God and man makes sense only if there exists some continuity in the word's meaning when applied to men and when referred to God. The meaning of the word when used of God may be normative and thus set a standard according to which we should understand the word even when applied to men. But the paradigmatic meaning is available only after the word's meaning when used of men has provided some provisional understanding. "God is love" may dictate what the full meaning of "love" will be, but it is difficult to imagine what "God is love" could mean to a man who had never learned to use the word "love" to describe his relationships with other people.

Evans conjectures that Barth's error lies in a conviction that grace, like creation, must be *ex nihilo*. No pre-existing capacity in man or his language could provide any basis for divine revelation. One should certainly concede that talk about God is subject to and dependent upon the divine initiative in revelation, but, if God's word is to be somehow intelligible and its author somewhat comprehensible, a context is necessary even for divine revelation. In other words, a doctrine of analogy is unavoidable. One must speak of an analogy of being (i.e., between human and divine activity) in which the decisive clue seems to be the loving activity of Jesus Christ. One must also speak of an analogy of faith (based on the fact that human attitudes and commitments do constitute an appropriate response to divine revelation) with the faith-response of Jesus providing the decisive clue.[29]

At the beginning of an extended review of Preller's *Divine Science and the Science of God,*[30] Donald Evans notes that Preller represents two tendencies which have been prominent in recent Thomistic writings on analogy: towards a more agnostic understanding of analogy which stresses how little we know about God by means of analogy and towards an interpretation of analogy in the formal rather than the material mode (as a set of relations between words rather than beings). For Preller, God is absolutely unique and radically unknowable. We cannot, therefore, refer intelligibly to God, but we can talk intelligently about the word "God." We should not interpret the previous statement to imply that, when we use "God," we do so meaningfully; only that we can mention "God" in our language. But God can use the word in his language, and we can talk about what such a language might be. What Preller offers us, then, is a two-language-theory in which there is a formal analogy between some human language and a postulated divine language.

In Preller's system, the meaning of a word is its role within the language. And that role is determinable from what can and cannot be done with that word in the language. And what can and cannot be done may be observed from the function of the word in the formation and derivation of sentences. Preller also insists that an analogy is an isomorphism, and an isomorphism is defined as the

29 "Barth on Talk About God," pp. 175-192 *passim.*
30 Donald Evans, "Preller's Analogy of 'Being'," *The New Scholasticism,* 1971.

sameness or similarity of structures. We can, thus, distinguish three types of analogy: *linguistic* isomorphisms which obtain between two or more linguistic structures; *judgmental* isomorphisms between one or more linguistic and one or more real structures, and *real* isomorphisms which operate between two or more real structures. While linguistic structures dictate what can or cannot be said, real structures determine what can or cannot be the case. Real structures, however, cannot be understood apart from linguistic structures which have been shown to be judgmentally isomorphic with real structures. Consequently, we must abandon hope of comparing man with God, and confine ourselves to comparing talk about God with talk about man, where talk about God is understood as God's own discourse and not our human talk about God.

Whenever we make a judgment, we imply several things: that there is at least one entity in the world, something which exists extra-linguistically as an individual unit in rational connection with other entities, something to some extent intelligible to us, and we claim that our judgment is true. Existence, unity, rational connection, intelligibility, and truth constitute the transcendentals of our language. When we say that a word is a transcendental, we assert that every possible language, if it is to be a genuine language, must have words which fulfill roles the same as or similar to those which the transcendentals perform in our language. Hence a postulated divine language would have to have transcendentals.

For Preller, the only justifiable moves are between assertions in our language, that is, moves which conform to syntactical rules. But every time we pass judgment, we express *esse* and refer to something outside our language. No syntactical rule warrants such an extra-linguistic move. If the existence of the world is intelligible, it must be inferrable from a cause according to syntactical rules in some language other than our own. We perceive here two claims: that a world-cause exists, and that a divine language exists.

In the case of God, real structures in the world are identical with the divine linguistic structures. The world is entirely passive to the divine intellect. God alone knows things as they really are.

Yet our language is at least relatively adequate. We do apply our linguistic structures judgmentally. Our human language, however, is never completely adequate because we are not world-creators and because we are sinful.

Man as a language user, therefore, cannot render intelligible the existence of the world. This fact provides us with a clue of not only what God is not, but also with a basis for thinking in the direction of a perfect language-user. But the analogy between man and God as language-users is directly intelligible to us only in terms of a linguistic isomorphism. In other words, from the divine point of view, there is an analogy of being; from our point of view, there is only an analogy of "being." But this limitation characterizes not just our knowledge and talk about God, but all our linguistic activity.[31]

The overarching value in Evans' work is that he is rigorously linguistic and not dogmatically empiricist. He is eminently conscious of the varied religious uses of language and does not conflate differences the way Ramsey does. He has learned well from Austin that the essential structures of any language are less than obvious and come to light only after the most careful analysis. Yet Donald Evans is quite capable of appreciating work done outside the point of view of the British empiricist tradition. In his analysis of the language of creation, he shows a keen awareness of the values of biblical theology, and, in his subsequent writings, of the theology of Karl Barth and of the structuralism of Victor Preller.

The same objection, however, which Evans brought against Barth, viz., that an appeal to the authority of God to justify our application of certain words to God is unacceptable unless some continuity exists between those words when applied to God and to man, can be made against Evans' discussion of parabolic onlooks. There he said that we know that certain attitudes are appropriate responses to God's revelation only on the authority of certain religious teachers like Jesus. First, we might well ask, in the

---

[31] *Ibid.*, pp. 1-26 *passim*.

light of recent developments in christology, how Jesus knew that these attitudes were appropriate. But, more importantly, we must inquire why we should accept the word of Jesus. It does not seem that we do so reasonably unless the putting on of the attitudes recommended in the parables touches us at a level where we are most profoundly human. Furthermore, if the Christian tradition of speculation teaches us anything, it teaches us that God is a pure spirit, and that his self-communication to us is in accordance with what he is—a mind and a will. As a consequence, we should expect that the revelation of God to men would be a new set of attitudes and commitments. When Evans states that we know only that these attitudes are similar to the appropriate attitudes, he is affirming a merely banal truth: that God is totally other and reveals himself as who he is. There is an appeal to authority which is necessary here, but it is not located where Evans would have it—in the external religious teacher. We must appeal to authority because our first awareness of ourselves as religious users of language has been unmasked as false consciousness. Our language betrays us. God touches us most profoundly not in what we actually say about him, but in the realization that everything we say about him is hopelessly inadequate and impregnated with our sinfulness. God is first the one who renders us dumb and, in that experience of silence, instructs us that we are in need of redemption. Then, in the death and resurrection of Jesus Christ, he commissions us to utter our meagre words in the conviction that his Word is truly present within us, healing the brokenness of our own language and making it possible for us to say something worthwhile. Because the overcoming of our sinfulness and its linguistic expression in inauthentic language is never final given our present condition, we must appeal to the divine authority as our justification for speaking about God: that he has been and is visiting his people and making authentic speech possible in his son Jesus Christ.

Nor does Evans' uncritical acceptance of Preller's two-language-theory appear to be much help in the analysis of the religious use of language. Again, the tradition does talk about a Word, but hardly about a set of divine words. It would seem that this divine language is one of those beings which our medieval predecessor William of Occam told us were not to be multiplied without necessity. Preller appears to want his Barthian cake and to eat it too. God is radically unknowable, but the divine language can be talked about. If this divine language is what we ordinarily call God's creation, let us call it the world, deal with it in terms of our ordinary language about the world, and be done with talk about a divine language. If this divine language is not a creature, but God himself, then we're right back to the problem of God's unknowability. And if God has in no way taken the initiative in breaking down the barriers between himself and us in language we can use, there is no possibility of talk about God.

Evans would have done better to explicate further the conclusion of his article on Barth than to investigate Preller's notion of analogy. First, there exists an analogy of being—of the being unto death. We know this analogy initially in the finitude of all our language: it is radically incapable not so much of expressing who God is, but more so of articulating who we are. But we confront this being unto death not merely in our radical incapacity to verbalize who we are, but more acutely in the fact that we are wounded. We not only cannot say who we are, but we lie about who we think we are and want to be. We are born into a culture where human sinfulness operates as a surd element, poisoning the atmosphere we breathe as we begin to speak, and we acquiesce in that situation of alienation at almost the very first opportunity. So we discover that, as spokesmen for being, we are both tongue-tied and mendacious. The appropriate response to our condition as finite and sinful is, of course, silence. This silence, however, is the beginning of wisdom. For, in these moments of silence, the Word of God can and does enter into our minds and hearts and lives, and teaches us how to speak.

There is also an analogy of faith. Here the faith of Jesus constitutes the decisive clue. He was the one who went like a lamb to the slaughter. He is our dumb exemplar who teaches as that silent trust in the Father's will is the only way to authentic manhood. He shows how the being unto death is destined also for the resurrection. Resurrection is new being, the power to say truly who we are and what we are about. We partake of this new life in Christ Jesus whenever we experience this world as perfect (relishing a good meal, taking delight in a lilting melody, or standing in awe before a sunset) and utter a simple "It is good;" whenever we truly encounter our neighbor (being loved by him for what we are, coming to self-acceptance by recognizing those things in ourselves which make us lovable, and thereby being enabled to accept others for what they are and not for what we would have them be), and say quietly "I love you;" finally, whenever we undergo the seering experience of being called radically into question in the presence of a light which reveals the tragic darkness within us and then the saving experience of being invited to transcend the hopelessness of our human condition, and say worshipfully "Lord, I believe, help my unbelief." In the final moment, Christ Jesus comes into our lives as the one who first shatters the idols we construct of his Father and exposes what we had hitherto considered faith as infidelity and, then, as the gift of the Father who brings us the possibility of forgiveness and of answering the query "who we are" by saying "Sons of God." It should be noted that, here, we come face to face with the mystery of Jesus Christ: as he who ever eludes our ability to define and thereby take hold of who he is. We know him only as the presence who brings order out of the chaos that we are without him and frees us to encounter him once more at the frontiers of our linguistic activity by singing new songs about his universe and telling more stories about our encounters with his brothers, yet destined finally to be rendered dumb in his presence.

After this extended discussion of analogy, the reader may well wonder whether the present essay has come to an end. No discussion of "God" and analytic philosophy, however, would be complete without a consideration of Ludwig Wittgenstein. His posthumously published *Philosophical Investigations* has become, as it were, the gospel within of the canon of linguistic philosophy.[32] Dallas High has provided an enlightening commentary on

---

32 Ludwig Wittgenstein, *Philosophical Investigations*, G.E.M. Anscombe, tr. (Oxford: Basil Blackwell, 1958).

the three principal contributions of Wittgenstein to our understanding of religious use of language.[33] The present essay will
follow the outline of High's presentation.

Wittgenstein pictured language as an extension of the person
into the world. People, who ask whether certain language is
meaningful, are actually inquiring whether the persons who speak
that language are justified in being what they are. As a
consequence, an analysis of the meanings words have must be an
analysis of how those words are used. Meaning as use should be
seen at the outset as a rejection of four other theories of meaning.
First, words are sometimes thought to be labels for things other
than themselves, and sentences to be combinations of such labels.
On this view, every word has a meaning, and this meaning
corresponds to the word and enables it to refer to an object. This
theory has merit in that it calls our attention to the fact that by
means of words we refer to objects outside of as well as inside of
language. But it oversimplifies the situation considerably. To what
objects do "if," "because," and "and" refer? How do we explain
words such as "you," "he," "here," and "this" which systematically change their reference depending on the conditions of their
expression? Secondly, linguistic expressions are often viewed as
deriving their meaning from images, conceptions, ideas, or mental
pictures which the speaker is attempting to communicate. But to
what kind of idea do "or," "but," or "the" refer? Besides, images
and ideas are of themselves ambiguous. They require subsequent
interpretation or application in order to be grasped. Thirdly, the
meaning of a word is occasionally said to be its disposition to
provoke a certain behavioral response. Overt behavior, however,
resembles ideas and images. It can always be variously interpreted
and is never unambiguous. Finally, the meaning of a statement has

---

33 Dallas High, *Language, Persons, and Belief* (New York: Oxford, 1967). It should
be noted that High presents those elements of the *Philosophical Investigations* which are
applicable to the analysis of the religious use of language. Wittgenstein's lone foray into
the matter of religious discourse consisted of some lectures he gave at Cambridge in the
late thirties. Cf. Ludwig Wittgenstein, *Lectures and Conversations on Aesthetics,
Psychology and Religious Belief,* Cyril Barrett, ed. (Oxford: Basil Blackwell, 1970).

been said to be its method of verification. At the outset, one should note that the principle, "The meaning of a word is its verification empirically" is itself empirically unverifiable. But more significantly the principle constitutes a preconceived formula for stipulating how language must work rather than a methodology for clarifying how in fact it does work. The principle rests on two assumptions that the primary function of language is to inform, and that scientific explanation is the paradigm for all linguistic activity. Neither assumption is warranted.

Common to all four of these theories are three important presuppositions: that language exists as an object which can be investigated and criticized from a detached point of view; that meaning can be separated from the words uttered and from the understandings which speakers and hearers share as they interact linguistically (meaning is thought to reside in a self-intelligent universe of ideas, a quantifiable world of bodily responses, an external world of objects and informative facts, or conventional sets of logical, semantic, and taxonomical rules); that there exists a radical dualism about speakers and hearers, and language can be reduced to an affair of one side or the other.

Wittgenstein viewed as a temptation to be resisted, the conviction that our understanding of another person or act of meaning must be accompanied by a separate mental process. Understanding, in his opinion, was not a mental process, but a being able to go on, i.e., to continue the conversation in such a way that at least one other person could grasp and be satisfied with what the speaker had said. Understanding and meaning are public insofar as their circumstances are shared by a speaker and a hearer. In other words, speaking and understanding are more intimately connected than we ordinarily construe them to be. There exists no extra-logical order above the human order of spoken language. Understanding cannot be analyzed apart from what we do in and with our speech.

Meaning as use suggests at least two things. First, we must surrender our preconceived notions how language must function, especially the notions that words express ideas or that any particular form of speech, e.g., scientific language, has priority over all the other forms, and we must look at how language actually does work. Secondly, although there is order present in language, a complete knowledge of all possible grammatical, syntactical, and logical rules would not enable us to predict what a word will mean when used by human speakers. Men change the rules as they proceed. This latter suggestion needs and will receive further elaboration when language-games are discussed. Use, however, does not mean that we must consult the speaker to know the meaning of a word or a sentence, nor that describing the logical environment of a word amounts to knowing its meaning. Wittgenstein warned us against both these fallacies. Use suggests that meaning is better observed in the skills, confidence, and agreements which speakers and hearers share in common while they put language to work. Using words and sentences is best conceived as a linguistic activity in which words, sentences, and even paragraphs occur.[34]

Thiselton has observed that British empiricism took a decisive turn with Wittgenstein. Locke had assumed that we initially have rational ideas which we then communicate by means of language. Wittgenstein took his stand with von Humboldt and insisted that language emerges on a pre-rational level. Language determines the limits of what can and what cannot be thought.[35] Meaning as use is a major contribution of Wittgenstein. It explains why this essay has concerned itself with an analysis how the word "God" is used. God is not to be understood, as Flew would have it, as someone independent of our talk about him or as something verifiable within our sense-experience. God is to be understood in terms of the self-involving language, as Evans would have it, which we use about him. He is only accessible through our talk about him. The meaning of God is the meaning of "God."

Language-game is the most famous term used by Wittgenstein in the *Philosophical Investigations*. Unfortunately, it has been among

34 High, pp. 27-69 *passim.*
35 A.C. Thiselton, "The Parables as Language-Event: Some Comments on Fuchs' Hermeneutic in the Light of Linguistic Philosophy," *Scottish Journal of Theology* (1970), p. 448.

the least understood. The term was never meant to suggest that language consists of neatly separated compartments of discourse which are mutually exclusive of one another. It makes no sense, therefore, to speak of the religious language-game. Attention to the actual performance of language reveals that there are subtle and overlapping differences in great quantity. With the term language-games, Wittgenstein hoped to dispose of the conception that language was a fixed and ideal calculus and show that language nonetheless had some unity whereby we can recognize that words do have roughly the same meanings when they are employed in similar contexts. Language does have regularity and order. But this order should not be understood as a set of rules. Rather it is a set of regular uses, institutions, and customs. Logical rules do not determine what and how we speak; we learn such rules in an explicit, self-reflexive, after-the-fact act which pre-supposes a before-the-fact tacit reliance upon a more primitive sense of order, mean, and form.

Wittgenstein did not urge upon us the idea that language can be divided into autonomous games. He knew that we have a tendency so to divide it, but he declared such a crystalization of our speech activity the result of prejudice. Language games do not have strict boundaries, but are complicatedly and inextricably inter-connected and never hermetically sealed off from one another. The unity of language, then, is characterized by a certain plasticity. Actual use reveals a complicated, but unified network of uses which crisscross and overlap one another. The unity of a language is a reflection of its players who stand in and behind speech and move freely about within its manifold forms.

When we look at language and do not speculate in advance what is there, we notice a series of relationships where common features constantly come into and pass out of existence. This feature of language Wittgenstein called *family-resemblances.* With the term, he hoped to banish two prejudices: that the use of the same word in similar contexts presupposed some single feature in common; and that such use presupposed no features in common. The basic metaphor is obvious enough. When we say that members of a family resemble one another, we do not mean that they are identical in all respects. So, when we use the same word several times in similar contexts, it does not follow that we always mean exactly the same thing. Nor does it follow that the meaning of a word one day bears no likeness to its meaning the next. In traditional scholastic terminology, one would say that Wittgenstein has taught us that analogy characterizes our use of language generally. Univocity is a violence done to language— usually for scientific purposes. In everyday speech, univocity is about as frequent as equivocity.

The concept family-resemblances allows two seemingly opposed principles to operate simultaneously. Language functions creatively. Horizons of meaning expand without pre-determined limit. The use of language, therefore, is characterized by flexibility, suppleness, and adaptability. But meaning does not expand arbitrarily, i.e., in every and any direction. As a consequence, two closely related members in the same linguistic family have numerous features in common, although they may have next to nothing in common with less closely related members.[36] It would appear, then, that Wittgenstein's concept of family-resemblances rather than Preller's isomorphism between human and divine language is more promising as a perspective from which to re-interpret the medieval doctrine of analogy.

The central concept in the later philosophy of Wittgenstein was *form of life*. Words, symbols, and sentences reside upon a foundation of human life in all its social, cultural, and inter-personal forms. These forms of life are for Wittgenstein the logically primitive concept. They constitute the *conditio sine qua non* for all comprehension and meaning.

Logical rules are best viewed as being kept rather than as determining what is logically compulsory. All such rules are dependent upon certain *agreements,* implicit judgments which people make while doing language. These agreements display the trust and confidence shared by at least two persons in one another's ability, skill, and activity. Without such agreements,

36 High, pp. 70-98 *passim.*

communication would be impossible. These agreements found all our expressions from highly abstract mathematical and logical symbols to the very concrete words and sentences of everyday language. Unless our utterances are backed by common responses, they can have no meaning or use at all. All the meaningful modalities of human discourse have in common that they are fiduciary, i.e., they are grounded in the reciprocal trust of men as they communicate with one another.

Person and person-words are indispensable. Only persons can perform self-reflexive acts and interact with others as centers of particularized self-identity. Speech presupposes the notion of an "I" who stands back of his words in such a way that he can disclose himself to his hearer. It does not suffice to assert that an utterance has a meaning; one must also say that the utterance has a user who is known to use that utterance. All speech-acts are self-involving and may be self-revealing. Agreements and person-words constitute together the natural conditions for there being human language and knowledge.[37]

We may inquire at this point what Wittgenstein's analysis of ordinary language has done to the challenge of Flew. Flew said that the meaning of a word was its verification, or more accurately, its falsification. Such a theory of meaning has been shown to rest on two pillars: that the purpose of language is to communicate facts, and that scientific language is the paradigm of all speech-activity. And both those pillars came tumbling down when they were measured against the theory of meaning as use. Use indicates that the word "God" is employed quite intelligently by people, expecially when they are united in a church—as a community, not necessarily in every congregation. When these people use the word "God," they are hardly prepared to say anything whatsoever—which would be our expectation if Flew were right that all religious discourse is meaningless. For instance, Christians know that certain qualities of life here, e.g., material properties, cannot be attributed to the Godhead. And they also

---

37 *Ibid.*, pp. 99-103 *passim.*

know that some (usually personal) qualities are more properly attributed to God than others: "God is love" as opposed to "God is simple." Nor does the actual use of language indicate that scientific usage is paradigmatic. Rather does it indicate that the various language-games are related mutually by means of family-resemblances. In fact, if one were to speak of a kind of norm, person-words would seem to be more primitive than scientific terms. Finally, the ground of all linguistic activity seems to be not the communication of factual information, but the trust that speakers and hearers have in one another. Their tacit agreements indicate that man, if he would speak and listen, must have faith—at least in his fellow man. By this standard, the religious use of language appears far less logically odd than it did to Flew and Ramsey.

The task I set myself at the inception of this essay is now completed. The reader may object that the essay has been, in fact, as much influenced by Heidegger as by Austin or Wittgenstein. Suffice it to say the work of any one casts light on the thought of both the others. My personal conviction is that the work of both Husserl and Wittgenstein has its origin in similar mathematical problems, and that their philosophies are generalizations upon their discussions of the foundations of mathematics. As a result, ordinary language philosophy and phenomenology constitute complementary techniques for understanding the phenomenon of human speech.[38] Hopefully, as I have discussed "God" in analytic philosophy, the reader has heard not only what I have said, but also what I did not say, and even what I could not say. For there are certain things whereof we must be silent—if the Word of God is to be heard in our midst.

---

38 Cf. Granville Henry, "Mathematics, Phenomenology, and Language Analysis in Contemporary Theology," *Journal of the American Academy of Religion,* 1967.

A SELECT BIBLIOGRAPHY

1. The Falsification Challenge

(a) The Basic Documents

Crombie, Ian, "Arising from the *University* Discussion," *New Essays in Philosophical Theology.* Ed. A. Flew and A. MacIntyre. London: SCM Press, 1955.

_____,"The Possibility of Theological Statements," *Faith and Logic.* Ed. B. Mitchell. London: George Allen and Unwin, 1957.

Flew, Antony, *God and Philosophy.* London: Hutchinson, 1966.

Flew, A., Hare, R., Mitchell, B., "The *University* Discussion," *New Essays in Philosophical Theology.* Ed. A. Flew and A. MacIntyre. London: SCM Press, 1955.

Mitchell, Basil, "The Grace of God," *Faith and Logic.* London: George Allen and Unwin, 1957.

_____, "The Justification of Religious Belief," *New Essays On Religious Language.* New York: Oxford University Press, 1969.

(b) Critical Evaluation of the Challenge

Allison, Henry, "Faith and Falsifiability," *The Review of Metaphysics,* Vol. XXII (1968-69).

Clifford, Paul, "The Factual References of Theological Assertions," *Religious Studies,* Vol. III (1967).

High, Dallas, "Belief, Falsification and Wittgenstein," *International Journal for Philosophy of Religion,* Vol. III (1972).

McPherson, Thomas, "The Falsification Challenge: A Comment," *Religious Studies,* Vol. V (1969).

2. Ian Ramsey

(a) Books by Ian Ramsey

Christian Discourse. London: Oxford University Press, 1965.
Freedom and Immortality. London: SCM Press, 1960.
Models and Mystery. London: Oxford University Press, 1964.
On Being Sure in Religion. London: London University Press, 1963.
Religion and Science: Conflict and Synthesis. London: SPCK, 1964.
Religious Language. London: SCM Press, 1957.

(b) Articles by Ian Ramsey

"Berkeley and the Possibility of an Empirical Metaphysics," *New Studies in Berkeley's Philosophy.* London: Holt, 1966.

"Biology and Personality: Some Philosophical Reflections," *Biology and Personality.* Oxford: Basil Blackwell, 1965.

"The Challenge of Contemporary Philosophy to Christianity," *The Modern Churchman,* Vol. XLII (1952).

"The Challenge of the Philosophy of Language." *The London Quarterly and Holborn Review,* Vol. CLXXXVI (1961).

"The Concept of the Eternal," *The Christian Hope.* London: SCM Press, 1969.

"Contemporary Philosophy and Christian Faith," *Religious Studies,* Vol. I (1965).

"Discernment, Commitment and Cosmic Disclosure," *Religious Education,* Vol. LX (1965).

"Empiricism and Religion," *The Christian Scholar,* Vol. XXXIX (1956).

"Hell," *Talk of God.* London: Macmillan, 1969.

"History and Gospels: Some Philosophical Reflections," *Studia Evangelica,* III. Berlin: Akademie, 1964.

"The Intellectual Crisis of British Christianity," *Theology,* Vol. LXVIII (1965).

"The Logical Character of the Resurrection-Belief," *Theology,* Vol. LX (1957).

"A Logical Explanation of Some Theological Phrases," *The Chicago Theological Seminary Register,* Vol. LIII (1963).

"Miracles: an Exercise in Logical Mapwork," *Miracles and the Resurrection.* London: SPCK, 1964.

"Moral Judgements and God's Commands," *Christian Ethics and Contemporary Philosophy.* London: SCM Press, 1966.

"On the Possibility and Purpose of a Metaphysical Theology," *Prospect for Metaphysics.* London: Allen and Unwin, 1961.

"Paradox in Religion," *New Essays on Religious Language.* New York: Oxford University Press, 1969.

"A Personal God," *Prospect for Metaphysics.* Digwell Place, England: James Nesbitt, 1966.

"Persons and Funerals: What Do Person Words Mean?" *The Hibbert Journal of Theology,* Vol. LIV (1956).

"Polanyi and J.L. Austin," *Intellect and Hope.* Ed. T. Langford and W. Poteat. Durham, North Carolina: Duke University Press, 1968.

"Religion and Science: A Philosopher's Approach," *New Essays on Religious Language.* New York: Oxford University Press, 1969.

"Some Further Reflections on 'Freedom and Immortality'," *The Hibbert Journal of Theology,* Vol. LIX (1961).
"The Systematic Elusiveness of 'I'," *The Philosophical Quarterly,* Vol. V (1955).
"Talking about God: Model, Ancient and Modern," *Myth and Symbolism.* (Ed. E. Dillestone). London: SPCK, 1966.
"Toward the Relevant in Theological Language," *The Modern Churchman,* Vol. VIII (1964).

(c) Articles About Ian Ramsey

Austin, William, "Models, Mystery and Paradox in Ian Ramsey," *Journal for the Scientific Study of Religion,* Vol. VII (1968).
Cohen, Cynthia, "Some Aspects of Ian Ramsey's Empiricism," *International Quarterly for Philosophy of Religion,* Vol. III (1972).
Evans, Donald, "Ian Ramsey on Talk About God," *Religious Studies,* Vol. VII (1972).
Owen, H. "The Philosophical Theology of I.T. Ramsey," *Theology,* Vol. LXXIV (1971).
Robinson, Norman, "Mystery and Logic," Canadian Journal of *Theology,* Vol. XX (1967).

3. Analysis of Religious Language in the Austin Tradition

Austin, John, *How to Do Things with Words.* Ed. J. Urmson. New York: Oxford University Press, 1965.
Evans, Donald, "Barth on Talk About God," *Canadian Journal of Theology,* Vol. XVI (1970).
———, *The Logic of Self-Involvement: A Philosophical Study of Everyday Language with Special Reference to the Christian Use of Language.* London: SCM Press, 1963. Now available under the title *About God as Creator.* New York: Herder and Herder, 1969.
———, "Preller's Analogy of 'Being'," *New Scholasticism,* Vol. LIV (1971).
McClendon, James and Smith, James, "Religious Language After J.L. Austin," *Religious Studies,* Vol. VIII (1972).
———, "Saturday's Child: A New Approach to the Philosophy of Religion," *Theology Today,* Vol. XXVII (1970-71).
Searle, John, *Speech Acts: An Essay in the Philosophy of Language.* Cambridge: Cambridge University Press, 1970.

4. The Analysis of Religious Language in the Wittgenstein Tradition

(a) The Basic Writings

Wittgenstein, Ludwig, *Lectures and Conversations in Aesthetics, Psychology and Religious Belief.* Ed. C. Barrett. Oxford: Basil Blackwell, 1970.
―――, *Philosophical Investigations.* 2nd edition. Translated by G. Anscombe . Oxford: Basil Blackwell, 1958.
Malcolm, Norman, *Ludwig Wittgenstein:* A Memoir. London: Oxford University Press, 1958.

(b) Application of Wittgenstein's Philosophy to the Religious Use of Language

Bell, Richard, "Wittgenstein and Descriptive Theology," *Religious Studies,* Vol. V (1969).
Daly, C., "Polanyi and Wittgenstein," *Intellect and Hope.* Ed. T. Langford and W. Poteat. Durham, North Carolina: Duke University Press, 1968.
High, Dallas, *Language, Persons and Belief.* New York: Oxford University Press, 1967.
Hudson, W., *Ludwig Wittgenstein.* London: Lutterworth Press, 1968.
―――, "Some Remarks on Wittgenstein's Account of Religious Belief," *Talk of God.* London: Macmillan, 1969.
Kellenberger, James, "The Language-Game View of Religion and Religious Certainty," *Canadian Journal of Philosophy,* Vol. II (1972).
Phillips, Dewi, *The Concept of Prayer.* London: Routledge and Kegan Paul, 1965.
―――, *Faith and Philosophical Inquiry.* London: Routledge and Kegan Paul, 1970.
Van Buren, Paul, *The Edges of Language: An Essay in the Logic of Religion.* New York: Macmillan, 1972.
Wisdom, John, *Paradox and Discovery.* Oxford: Basil Blackwell, 1955.
―――, *Philosophy and Psychoanalysis.* Oxford: Basil Blackwell,

(c) Some Comparative Articles

Henry, Granville, "Mathematics, Phenomenology and Language Analysis in Contemporary Theology," *Journal of the American Academy of Religion,* Vol. XXXV (1967).
Mood, J., "Poetic Language and Primal Thinking: A Study of Barfield, Wittgenstein and Heidegger," *Encounter,* Vol. XXVI (1965).
Thiselton, A., "The Parables as Language-Event: Some Comments on Fuchs' Hermeneutic in the Light of Linguistic Philosophy," *The Scottish Journal of Theology,* Vol. XXII (1970).

CHAPTER XXX

ATHEISM OF JEAN-PAUL SARTRE

Thomas M. King, S.J. *

> *Atheism is a cruel and long-range*
> *affair: I think I've carried it through.*
> Jean-Paul Sartre[1]

In 1943 Jean-Paul Sartre (1905-   ) published *Being and Nothingness,* an abstract philosophical work occasionally illuminated by vivid dramatic phrases. In the same year he published *The Flies,* a vivid dramatic work set in the context of an abstract philosophy. Existentialism quickly became a popular fad and Sartre became an international celebrity. The Existentialism of Sartre offered a despair that was eloquent and absolute, and this despair was carefully based on the radical atheism that Sartre repeatedly professed. Sartre argued that the very concept of God is contradictory—by definition there cannot be a God—from this followed man's unfortunate condition.

Human reality therefore is by nature an unhappy consciousness with no possibility of surpassing its unhappy state.[2]

The rhetorical language of Sartre had a power of its own:

Thus the passion of man is the reverse of that of Christ, for man loses himself as man in order that God may be born, but the

---

*Associate Professor of Philosophy, Georgetown University, Washington, D.C., U.S.A.

1 *The Words* (New York, 1966), p. 158. For the list of the abbreviations, see *A Select Bibliography,* at the end of the article.

2 *BN.,* 110.

idea of God is contradictory and we lose ourselves in vain. Man is a useless passion.[3]

God is silent, that I am not able to deny—everything within me demands God, that I am not able to forget.[4]

The impossibility of God produces this total human frustration because God enters into the very definition of what is meant by man: "To be a man means to reach toward being God. Or if you prefer, man fundamentally is the desire to be God."[5] Thus man is frustrated by definition, but human society as a whole is also frustrated by definition: Sartre argues that the limiting-concept of humanity and "the limiting-concept of God imply one another and are correlative."[6] Thus in *Being and Nothingness* atheism is at the root of both the individual's despair and the failure of human society as a whole.

During the decades that have passed since 1943 Sartre has moderated his absolute despair and has even hinted at the eventual unity of mankind. His atheism has remained, but it too has undergone some changes. The point of this article will be to present the original atheism of Sartre and follow it through its subsequent mutations.

In *Being and Nothingness* Sartre develops at length the dualism that is announced in the title. Being is a substance in the most radical sense of the term, it is perfect self-identity, a total plenitude without the slightest duality, an infinite compression with an infinite density, it is fully itself and enters into no connection with what is not itself;[7] it contains no reason for its being for a reason would suggest a slight duality, to be perfectly one with itself it must be apart from the separation of time, thus it is without reason (*de trop*) for eternity. Other than Being there is only Nothingness: Nothingness is totally without substance, it is

3 *BN.*, 754.
4 *S.I.*, 4.
5 *BN.*, 694.
6 *Ibid.*, 6.
7 *BN.*, LXXIX.

the reverse of Being, it is not even itself, it escapes the principle of contradiction as that "which is not what it is and which is what it is not."[8] Being and Nothingness are thus two ultimate and opposed regions; they resemble the ultimate categories set up by Plato in *The Sophist,* and Sartre points out the parallel. In *The Sophist,* Plato had argued for the reality of both being and non-being and thus acknowledged two ultimate categories: the Same (Being) and the Other (non-being). Sartre argues for a similar duality, but Sartre identifies this Otherness (Nothingness) in a way that is unique: it is human consciousness. Consciousness is always other than what it is (if it were not it would not be Other but would be simply the Same). In itself consciousness is nothing, but apart from itself it can be all things (which it is not). The world (Being) is simply a given totality, but consciousness is a nihilating withdrawal from the given world; in its negation it makes Being stand forth (exist), it makes "the world irridescent, casting a shimmer over things."[9]

In *Being and Nothingness* God is identified with the synthesis of these radically opposing terms, God would be Being-Nothingness. But such a synthesis is impossible by the very meaning of the terms. The two regions of being are "absolutely separated" they are "Two regions without communication."[10] Sartre develops the opposition at length and concludes that for God to exist he would have to be what he is in full positivity, and at the same time not be what he is in order to be his own foundation,[11] God would have to be absolute transcendence in absolute immanence.[12] This is the basic contradiction that Sartre sees in God and the reason that he offers for his atheism.

Sartre has been criticized for his radical dualism. Certainly the oppositions that Sartre points out have been recognized by many theists and many mystics have spoken of God as the reconciliation

8   *Ibid.,* 37.
9   *Ibid.,* 28.
10 *Ibid.,* LXXVI.
11 *Ibid.,* 110.
12 *Ibid.,* 111.

of opposites. In *Being and Nothingness* Sartre bases his atheism on the non-reconciliation of oppositions; in his literary works he exacerbates the differences. In his first novel he presented what might be considered a mystical experience in reverse: the central character has an insight into reality that is described in the language of the mystics ("suddenly the veil is torn away, I have understood, I have *seen.*") But the content of the experience is reversed: instead of the ultimate unity of all things there is total alienation ("We were a heap of living creatures . . . (each) felt in the way in relation to all the others"). In later novels he would present the attempts of alienated loners to come together in love, but all of their attempts are futile for love itself involves the same basic contradiction found in the definition of God: "Love finds its failure within itself."[13]

It is in these terms that the atheism of Sartre is generally understood. But there are also many Sartrean texts which speak of a non-contradictory God: a God who is so wholly positive to the exclusion of any negative property, that is, God is sometimes presented as pure Being, the first of the two opposing terms. This was even suggested in *Being and Nothingness,*[14] but first developed at length in an essay on Descartes written in 1945; here God is identified with the totality of the Good and the True to the *exclusion* of the negative properties of evil, ignorance and error. In 1953 Sartre again spoke in these terms when considering the mentality of Jean Genet:

> . . . As a being I am encircled and hemmed in by being, God's eye sees me. But since God, the infinite Being, cannot conceive nothingness, in nothingness I escape him and derive only from myself.[15]

The same totally positive understanding of God is involved when Sartre considers the mentality of Jouhandeau:

13 *Ibid.*, 498.
14 *Ibid.*, 120-121.
15 *G.*, 159.

God who is all-positivity, an infinite being and infinitely being, is blinded by his omnipotence: He perceives the creature only insofar as it is a positivity. In order for the divine understanding to conceive the negative, it would, to a certain degree, have to be affected with negativity. Thus, the nothingness which is secreted by the creature is a veil that hides it from the sight of the Almighty, like the ink in which the cuttlefish envelops itself.[16]

In each of these texts Sartre speaks of a God that is not contradictory, one that is so positive that all nothingness is excluded, in short, the Being of *Being and Nothingness.*

The problem of Sartre's atheism becomes even more complex when Sartre presents still another way of speaking of God; one that is wholly negative. He explains a character found in the fiction of Genet that is called Divine: "Divine is a hole through which the world empties into nothingness, that is why she is called Divine: when she appears, she causes a hemorrhage of being." The same negative understanding of God occurs in one of Sartre's plays *(The Devil and the Good Lord)* when the hero comes to a moment of truth he explains:

You see this emptiness over our heads? That is God. You see this gap in the door? It is God. You see that hole in the ground? That is God again. Silence is God. Absence is God.[17]

This wholly negative way of speaking of God to the exclusion of anything positive runs through Sartre's study of Flaubert; he terms it negative theology or negative theodicy. For example Sartre considers the possibility of a hypothetical priest speaking to Flaubert:

God is nowhere: neither in time nor in space, nor in your heart,

16 *Ibid.,* 214.
17 *DGL.,* 141

and this infinite emptiness, everywhere, this cold, our eternal despair, what do you think it is if not Him?[18]

These passages make problems for anyone trying to understand Sartre: the basic difficulty is that when Sartre presents a wholly negative or a wholly positive God Sartre is not really trying to state his own mind (with the possible exception of the character cited from the play above); rather Sartre is developing by rhetorical elaboration the mentality of Descartes, Genet, Jouhandeau, Flaubert etc. But then one can ask if he was really able to do anything different in *Being and Nothingness* when he was denying the existence of God. That is, if one denies the existence of God, he cannot intend to be talking about a *something* which does not exist; all that he can really do is deny existence to what *other* people have meant by the term. This he did in *Being and Nothingness* by developing the oppositions presented above; which oppositions he presumably found in what theists had meant by God. When Sartre wrote his studies of different French literary figures, he presented the God with whom he judges them involved (many of them considered themselves atheist). This would turn out to be a God wholly positive to the exclusion of all negativity, or a God wholly negative to the exclusion of any positivity. Whatever difficulty there might be in these divinities they are at least not contradictory and therefore not subject to the logical objections to the existence of God made in *Being and Nothingness*. Rather the wholly positive God and the wholly negative God resemble nothing so much as the two regions that *Being and Nothingness* had set in radical opposition. There both of these regions of being were acknowledged to be real. Still this would not mean that Sartre would accept God, or at least what these authors meant by God, or accept two opposing Gods. Sartre has moved away from the radical opposition between Being and Nothingness that he had presented so forcefully in 1943. In 1953 he even suggested that eventually there will be an Hegelian

---

18 *IF.,* 532.

Aufhebung, "a concrete totality," in which Being and Nonbeing will achieve a synthesis.[19]

Certainly men have meant very different things by the term God; in denying the existence of God all Sartre can do is deny existence to what others have meant by the term. But in 1953 Sartre seems to be accepting that which he himself had once meant by God and denied: since 1953 this synthesis is suggested as the eventual outcome of history,[20] while the contradiction that had ruled out the existence of God in 1943 is presented in different terms: "The abstract separation of these two concepts expresses simply the alienation of man."[21] Here the separation is only an abstraction and the implication of the whole passage is that eventually this human alienation can be overcome and the synthesis achieved. Accordingly Raymond Aron points out that in the later works of Sartre the alienation of man is no longer an essential alienation (true by definition) but true only in the present historical situation.

But in the writings of Sartre God is not presented simply in essential or ontological terms; God is also basic to Sartre's understanding of intra-personal relations. Again God is of central importance, but again the texts of Sartre are difficult to reconcile. The problem is of central importance.

> The problem of God is a human problem which concerns the rapport between men. It is a total problem to which each man brings a solution by his entire life, and the solution one brings to it reflects the attitude one has chosen towards other men and towards oneself.[22]

In *Being and Nothingness* interpersonal relations are considered in a long section that is devoted to "the look" *(le regard);* by the look the one who is looked at loses his own subjectivity as he feels

---

19 *G.,* 186.
20 See also *CRD.,* 61, 377.
21 *G.,* 21.
22 *S.,* 22.

himself reduced to the status of an object under the gaze of another. The person looked at can regain his own subjectivity only by returning the look and thus reducing the other into an object in return. In this context God is spoken of as "the being-who-looks-at and who can never be looked-at."[23] Before God there is no possibility of gaining our own subjectivity. But in this context Sartre will explain that "God" is only the purely formal notion of an omnipresent, infinite subject which can never be looked at in return.[24] With this understanding Sartre interprets the God of Kafka ("only the concept of the Other pushed to the limit"), the God of Parrain ("that quintessence of the Other"), the God of Mauriac ("a concrete totality of the Others"). God is the condemning gaze of other men absolutized within me; it trans-forms me into a guilty thing. Many of the religious experiences of Genet are interpreted in this way, and a character in the fiction of Sartre has a religious conversion because he feels penetrated by an omnipresent gaze and is objectified in guilt.

> No one was there . . . But the look was there . . . I did not see it as one sees a passing profile, a forehead, or a pair of eyes; for its essential character is to be beyond perception . . . It's the night that looks at you, but it's a dazzling night . . . I am infinite and infinitely guilty.[25]

Sartre's phenomenology of the look and his interpretation of the look of God is not without its merits. But Sartre does not always understand the look of God this way (i.e. the look of human society absolutized): sometimes the look of God *reverses* the judgment of society. Genet is the thief and homosexual rejected by all men, even by his fellow criminals; then a sacred and loving regard appears above his interior life which supports him and *opposes* the condemnation of society.[26] Again in Sartre's

---

23 *BN.*, 517.
24 *Ibid.*, 345.
25 *R.*, 315.
26 *G.*, 143.

study of Gustave Flaubert there is this reverse interpretation of the look of God. Gustave was condemned by the stern judgment of his patriarchal father, but the look of God reverses the judgment. "The absolute Regard would substitute itself for the surgical regard" of Gustave's father (a surgeon who analyzed Gustave to the point of destroying him); the look of God would erase "the cross-hatchings of analysis to restore Gustave to his natal transcendence."[27] Not only does the regard of God reverse the human judgment, but in restoring Gustave to his "natal transcendence" it does the reverse of what any look is said to do: it restores transcendence (subjectivity) instead of making transcendence into an object.

There are also difficulties in understanding what Sartre means by God when one tries to reconcile texts concerning appearance and reality. At times God is associated with the surface appearance to the point that the ultimate reality escapes Him: "Everything happens as if the world, man, and man in the world succeeded in realizing only a missing God;"[28] it is only as "as if," a matter of appearing that way. A character in Sartre's fiction explains: those around me "let themselves be taken in: they see only the thin film which proves the existence of God. I see beneath it!"[29] There are other texts of Sartre where the situation is reversed: God is spoken of as if he were the ultimate reality from whom the appearances escape: "In the eyes of God, Who cuts through appearances and goes beyond them, there is no novel, no art, for art thrives on appearances."[30]

The basic difficulty in understanding the atheism of Sartre is that it has taken innumberable forms: God is the synthesis of Being and Nothingness, God is Being to the exclusion of Nothingness, or God is Nothingness to the exclusion of Being. God is the absolutizing of the look of the Other, or God reverses the look of the Other. God's look renders my subjectivity into an

27 *IF.*, 513, 2077.
28 *BN.*, 762.
29 *N.*, 124.
30 *LPE.*, 25; *G.*, 355; *S.*, 37.

absolute object, or God's look restores my subjectivity. God is found in and through appearances, but not in reality; God is reality to the exclusion of appearances.

Perhaps it would be better to understand his atheism more in the context of several references to his childhood found in his brief autobiography, *The Words*. There he reaffirms his atheism ("atheism is a cruel and long-range affair, I think I have carried it through"). But he does not trace his atheism to a radical opposition of opposites, he refers instead to a brief experience at the age of twelve.

> After a while not knowing what else to do to occupy my mind, I decided to think of the Almighty. Immediately he tumbled into the blue and disappeared without giving any explanation. He doesn't exist I said to myself with polite surprise . . . [31]

Sartre follows this passage (written in 1963) with a consideration of the despair that he had preached in 1943; he writes with playful amusement.

> I gaily demonstrated that man is impossible; I was impossible myself and different from the others only by the mandate to give expression to that impossibility. . . . I was a prisoner of that obvious contradiction, but I did not see it, I saw the world through it. Fake to the marrow of my bones and hoodwinked, I joyfully wrote about our unhappy state.[32]

The passage was surprising to those who took Sartre too seriously. The meaning of the passage can be better understood in the context of Sartre's autobiography. It is the study of how a child began to become an author. As a child Jean-Paul lived among books and adults: he liked to play only in the presence of adults, there he was only a fake child putting on a performance. He would repeat adult-sounding phrases, not because he knew what he was

---

31 *W.*, 157.
32 *Ibid.*, 158.

saying, but because he wanted to startle people by what he said; language was used to strike a stunning pose. Later he would develop at length this alternate use of language wherein a person speaks not to communicate what he sees, but to have a stunning effect on his listeners—and on *himself* (so he calls himself both "fake" and "hoodwinked"). In his autobiography he explains that he would measure the truth of a statement by the effect it would have on others and himself: "(I went) to the extent of measuring the obvious truth of an idea by the displeasure it caused me."[33] His autobiography also explains a rhetorical technique that he had learned as a boy: "I had read de Musset, I knew that 'the most despairing songs are the loveliest,' and I decided to capture Beauty by a decoy-despair."[34] The early works of Sartre are filled with despairing songs that often have a poignant beauty, but Sartre has suggested that the despair is only a decoy, a stunning pose; he adds that he is "waking up, cured of a bitter-sweet madness."

With the end of the bitter-sweet madness, one could ask what has become of the rhetorical skill by which Sartrean despair produced passages of stunning beauty. Perhaps the best way of answering this question is to consider Sartre's recent study of Flaubert (1971). Sartre is at his rhetorical and despairing best, but it is all set in the context of the mind of Flaubert. But through the eloquent conjectures about Flaubert, it is the plaintive voice of the author of *Being and Nothingness* speaking again of atheism and essential despair.

Flaubert is presented as desiring God with all of his heart; but Sartre explains that this is the *reason* he has no God: "he has *need* of God . . . *therefore* God is refused him."[35] Flaubert is said to have sought total frustration, for his essence "can be nothing but despair," the lack of God then becomes "frustration carried to the infinite."[36] Flaubert choses to live in this absolute stripping.

---

33 *Ibid.*
34 *Ibid.*, 116.
35 *IF.*, 546.
36 *Ibid.*, 560.

Empty of God for having understood too well that he cannot fill himself with Him, he will live the impossible Alienation, letting his finitude cry towards an inconceivable and necessary infinite.[37]

The Devil has expressly created a religious soul which aspires after the infinite, to the ravishings, to the elevations, to cast it into a universe without values and without God.[38]

Since God does not exist, we (Flaubert and other writers of the last century) witness by the non-being that is in us to our vain and inconsolable refusal of his non existence.[39]

These passages are supposed to explain the mind of Flaubert, but they sound more like the author of *Being and Nothingness*; the difference is that Sartre no longer claims the despairing texts as his own. Sartre's study of Flaubert is permeated with passages of atheistic-despair, but they are presented with a sense of gentle irony that is hard to convey out of their context. It is a decoy-despair that captures Beauty, but it no longer produces the displeasure that once was a measure of truth. In any case, it would seem that Sartre's atheism remains; it is still a long-range affair, but perhaps it is no longer quite so cruel.

A SELECT BIBLIOGRAPHY

1. Works of Jean P. Sartre

Being and Nothingness. Translated by Hazel Barnes. New York: Washington Square Press, 1966. Abbreviated *BN*.
Critique de la Raison Dialectique. Paris: Gallimard, 1960. Abbreviated *CRD*.

37 *Ibid.*, 586.
38 *Ibid.*, 470.
39 *IF.*, 1592.

The Devil and the Good Lord, and Two Other Plays. Translated by Kitty Black. New York: Random House (Vintage Books), 1965. Abbreviated *DGL*.

Saint Genet, Actor and Martyr. Translated by Bernard Frechtman. New York: The New American Library (Plume Books), 1971. Abbreviated *G*.

L'Idiot de la famille. 2 vols. Paris: Gallimard, 1971. Abbreviated *IF*.

Literary and Philosophical Essays. Translated by Annette Michelson. New York: Macmillan (Collier Books), 1962. Abbreviated *LPE*.

Nausea. Translated by Lloyd Alexander. New York: New Directions, 1969. Abbreviated *N*.

The Reprieve. Translated by Eric Sutton. New York: Bantom Modern Classics, 1968. Abbreviated *R*.

Situations, I. Paris: Gallimard, 1947. This is a collection of articles written by Sartre between 1938 and 1945. Abbreviated *S,I*.

Situations. Translated by Benita Eisler. New York: Fawcett World Library (Fawcett Crest Books), 1966. This is a collection of articles written by Sartre between 1950 and 1961. Abbreviated *S*.

The Words. Translated by Bernard Frechtman. New York: Fawcett World Library (Fawcett Crest), 1966. Abbreviated *W*.

2. Studies

Desan, Wilfrid, *The Tragic Finale.* Revised edition. New York: Harper and Row, 1960.

Jeanson, Francis, *Sartre: Les ecrivains devant Dieu.* Paris: Editions du Seuil. 1965.

Jolivet, Regis, *Sartre: The Theology of the Absurd.* Translated by Wesley Piersol. Westminster, Maryland: Newman, 1967.

Marill-Alberez, Rene, *Jean-Paul Sartre: Philosopher without Faith.* Translated by Wade Baskin. New York: Philosophical Library, 1960.

CHAPTER XXXI

THE CHALLENGE OF MARXIAN ATHEISM
Jan Milič Lochman *

For those of us who are concerned about social cooperation, and thus intellectual encounter between Marxists and Christians, Marxist atheism has always presented a special problem. Here one seemed to encounter from the beginning a built-in barrier, which for most Marxists and Christians made any ideological rapprochement very difficult. Here the mutual prejudices hardened: The Christians are believers, theists; the Marxists, on the other hand, are conscious unbelievers, atheists. What can these two groups—in view of such a basic difference—really have in common?

This type of entrance into encounter is unfavorable and unfortunate. The focusing on the problem of religion—which also caused tempers to run especially high—has threatened to cover up the multiplicity of possible encounters. How often have Christians refused "on principle" to cooperate with Marxists in concrete social areas! How often have Marxists considered Christians as backward or second class citizens, and discriminated against them upon coming to power! Under these circumstances it was and is necessary to "demythologize" and "de-dogmatize" the problem of the criticism of religion as we move along the path "from anathema to dialogue," a path to which I have felt myself committed for several decades as a theologian in the East and West. This does not mean an undervaluation of the problems: the question of Marxian atheism represents a serious matter for both

*Professor of Theology at the University of Basel, Switzerland.

This article, written for the present collection, was translated by Gareth Putnam. With the exception of the passage cited from *The German Ideology* which was translated from *Die Deutsche Ideologie,* Berlin, 1953, all quotations from Marx were translated from *Die Frühschriften,* ed. by S. Landshut, Stuttgart, 1953.

sides. It should not, however, be tackled in an abstract and isolated way, but in the open horizon of a more comprehensive encounter. For Christians this means asking about the context and the reasons for the Marxian criticism of religion, differentiating and taking into account its various elements and layers. This I would like to attempt in the following by outlining three dimensions of Marxian atheism: The philosophical, the socio-critical, and the anthropological—dogmatic.

1. The Philosophical Dimension of Marxian Atheism

"For Germany the criticism of religion is essentially complete, and the criticism of religion is the presupposition of all criticism." In this introductory sentence of his famous treatise, "Introduction to the Critique of Hegel's Philosophy of Law" (Karl Marx, *Die Fruhschriften,* ed. by S. Landshut, Stuttgart 1953, p. 207), the historical position of Karl Marx's criticism of religion is programmatically defined. Marx assumes the rich heritage of the German criticism of religion, acknowledges his debt to it and feels himself at the end of it. What heritage is meant?

The beginnings of Marxian thought are very closely connected with the controversy over the philosophical legacy of Hegel, which determined the intellectual scene in Germany in the 1840's. In *The German Ideology,* one of Marx's early writings which he composed with Engels, the situation is described: "In the general chaos powerful empires came into being and soon disappeared again, heroes momentarily appeared and were hurled back again into obscurity by bolder and more powerful rivals. It was a revolution which makes the French Revolution look like child's play, a world battle which makes the battles of the Diadochi appear trivial. . . . In the three years from 1842-45 more of the past has been cleared away in Germany than otherwise in three centuries" (*Die Deutsche Ideologie,* Berlin 1953, p. 13).

The controversy crystallized predominantly around two complexes of themes: The Hegelian philosophy of law and the Hegelian philosophy of religion. This is understandable, for here lay the social need of the times. On the one hand Germany experienced at this time an upsurge in economic and political power. On the other hand there developed in Prussia a quite authoritarian, bureaucratic-militaristic system with a lot of police, censorship and chicanery, against which many rebelled, especially of the young students. This system had two authoritative columns: throne and altar. "The Christian state" was, in the self-understanding of the Prussian monarchy, the political ideal. And a strange mixture of pietistic devoutness with Prussian "rigidity" characterized the public mentality of the country.

In this context Hegel's philosophy of the state and of religion became relevant. Is Hegel's heritage to be claimed for the established order? This was the opinion of most of the "orthodox" Hegelians. At his chair at the University of Berlin Hegel was after all the great ideologist of the system, the ingenious interpreter (and defender) of the system. But others of his followers asked whether the same Hegel did not also have a different side. The great systematizer was at the same time also the great dialectician. His philosophy was not only a philosophy of reconciliation with the previously given, but also a philosophy of the destruction of obsolete forms. It was precisely here that the explosive question presented itself: Where does the real legacy of this thinker lie? Which Hegel is the true and relevant one? The official political and clerical orthodoxy was clearly on the side of the "right Hegel." The other revolutionary group of "Young Hegelians" made themselves heard louder and louder with the proclamation: the left Hegel is the right one. In their circle—which included to a certain extent such important thinkers as Heinrich Heine, David Friedrich Strauss, Bruno Bauer, Ludwig Feuerbach and Max Stirner—that tradition of German criticism was developed which Marx followed also (although in no way uncritically).

It was characteristic of these thinkers that criticism meant above all (and at times almost exclusively) the criticism of religion. Let us try to briefly outline their position.

The philosophically most important figure in the criticism of religion is indeed *Ludwig Feuerbach*. Originally a theologian, he converted under the influence of Hegel to philosophy. He remained, however, faithful to religion throughout his life to be sure, only with completely reversed premises: in a concentrated, almost monothematic way he announced his implacable fight against religion. Religion is fundamentally the lie, the radical evil in the world of man. In it man becomes estranged from himself. He is the creator of religion, God is his idea, religious ideas and values his projections. This state of affairs, however, becomes obscured and reversed in religion: the religious man, the true creator, places himself at the disposal of his creation, the idea of God, and surrenders himself to it, losing his sovereignty. The self-estrangement of man is then carried through in all important areas of life. The religious man—since he sells himself to his idols—becomes estranged from his true origin, from nature, from other men and ultimately from himself. Thus religion proves to be plain misanthropy (which is especially visible in the ascetic tendencies of religion).

Man can only become liberated by a radical overcoming of religion. The estranging strategy of the religious mind needs to be seen through, the lie needs to be exposed by a criticism of religion. Then the truth will be apparent: theology is anthropology—God is the projection of man. Where this is understood the path of human emancipation and enlightenment begins.

Alongside of this great radical critic of religion there are the smaller ones, many who are, significantly enough, theologians by profession. One example is D. F. Strauss. In his book The Life of Jesus Strauss objected to the Hegelian reconciliation of philosophy and Christianity. In light of his historical examination of the New Testament it appeared to him that the Jesus portrayed there (whom Strauss first wanted to verify) never existed. Christ is a myth. God is not to be thought of as a person, and the revelation of God is not to be connected with the history of Christ or of Christians, but with world history. In this sense the Hegelian philosophy of history is to be carried further and decisively "de-Christianized."

More important for Marx was the no less radical religious-critical approach of the Bonn theologian Bruno Bauer. Bauer was originally a New Testament theologian, who at first—in the controversy over D. F. Strauss—stepped forward against Strauss.

Soon, however, he became a decisive critic of orthodox doctrine. His main thesis reads: the mystery of the New Testament message is the mystery of the self-consciousness of the early Christian community. The pious mind of the biblical authors is the true subject of the gospel. In the development of this point of view Bauer distinguished himself from Hegel (Christianity is in no way the highest manifestation of the religious spirit) as well as from Strauss (Christianity has in no way a relative-divine substance). Human self-consciousness is all in all. It is to this that Bauer then dedicates all his energies in the inexorable battle against the theological interpretation of religion. "Critical criticism" becomes a program for him. He thereby exercised a considerable influence also on the young Marx, who was one of his personal friends. They even published together a satirical-ironic essay entitled "The Trumpet of Doom against Hegel, Atheists and Anti-Christians." But Marx did not participate for long in this all too impractical and thus unfruitful campaign of "critical criticism." He separated himself from the "holy family" of Young Hegelians—and from his "Saint Bruno"—and pursued a path of his own—beginning, to be sure, from this starting point which remains: the criticism of religion is also for Marx essentially complete—and the criticism of religion is the presupposition of all criticism.

What results from these brief philosophical references for our understanding of Marxian atheism? Only a preliminary, but certainly not to be underestimated, piece of information: the religious critic Marx thinks in conscious continuity with the criticism of religion of his times. He finds a radically irreligious element present in the spiritual situation of his times and accepts it as almost self-evident. The emphatic conviction of his critical friends that religion fundamentally endangers the emancipation of man, and hence that the overcoming of religion is necessary for human liberation, also has for him an axiomatic validity.

One occasionally argues among Marxologists whether atheism belongs essentially or only accidentally to Marxism. In my opinion such considerations are not very fruitful: the abstract concepts can hardly do justice to the complexity of the question. It is certain, however, that the Marxian criticism of religion has its side which is determined by the situation, and in this sense is limited by the times and thus "accidental." This needs to be critically considered by dogmatically thinking Marxists who are inclined to perpetuate positions limited by the times; but also by dogmatic Christians, which implies that especially the connection between this criticism of religion and the social situation, i.e. the complicity of the Church in conditions which provoked the response of the radical criticism of religion, needs to be reflected on critically. We shall now proceed to the second part of our considerations.

2. The Socio-Critical Approach of Marxian Atheism

Karl Marx's atheism would be misunderstood if one would attempt to explain it simply in light of its philosophical presuppositions. It is in no way merely a reflection of the intellectual situation of the times. It shares the religious-critical axiom, but develops it independently, or better: it puts it into the socio-critical context of a radically new understanding of the world and man. This becomes clear in Marx's most important critical remarks on religion, especially as he formulated them in the initial stages of his thinking—e.g. in the essays, "Introduction to the Critique of Hegel's Philosophy of Law" and "On the Jewish Question" (both Paris 1844). The position of the Young Hegelians—especially the position of Feuerbach is presupposed: "The basis of irreligious criticism is: man makes religion, religion does not make man" (*Die Frühschriften, op. cit.,* p. 207). But this basis is then—in the framework of a fundamental and comprehensive criticism of Young Hegelian thinking as it is programmatically formulated, for example, in the important "Theses on Feuerbach"—interpreted quite differently and set in motion. The human essence is the "ensemble of social relations" (Thesis 6, *op. cit.* p. 340). "Man is the world of man, the state, society" (*op. cit.,* p. 208).

Important consequences follow from this for the understanding of human estrangement and for the role of religion in this context. The Hegelian and Feuerbachian concept of estrangement is taken over by the young Marx, but it is concretized and radicalized. Not only is the narrow area of intellectual life, including religion and speculative philosophy, the source and the stage of estrangement, but the world of man as a whole, especially in its *ens realissimum,* in the socio-economic sphere. The work of the working man, which under the rule of private property was deprived of its products and emptied of its creative joy is the root of the universal perversion. What Feuerbach saw rooted in the religious perversion, the suppression of man (who is the actual creator) by God (who is actually the human creature), Marx looks for in the socio-economic conditions. *Here* man becomes enslaved by his product and universally estranged.

It is only in this primary context that the religious form of estrangement then arises secondarily. The social and political conditions, the state and society "produce religion, a perverted world consciousness, because they are a perverted world" (*ibid.,* p. 208). Indeed it is in this concrete context that the most famous words of the Marxist criticism of religion are to be understood: "Religious distress is the expression of real distress and at the same time the protest against real distress. Religion is the sigh of the oppressed creation, the heart of a heartless world, just as it is the spirit in a spiritless situation. It is the opium of the people" (*ibid.,* p. 208). One should note the dialectic of the two motifs "expression" *and* "protest" in the Marxian statement: Marx differentiates, he does not think in negative generalities or in a stubborn, rectilinear way as was so often the case among "critical critics" before and after him (It is characteristic, for example, of the vulgarized criticism of religion of later Marxism that the expression "opium *of* the people" was changed to "opium *for* the people," which implies that religion is basically an instrument of malevolent manipulation).

In this approach Marx's criticism of religion differs considerably from the criticism of religion of his predecessors. For them religion often appeared to be the quintessence of all misanthropy. Their "critical" or "total" criticism was burdened by an anti-religious complex. Therefore they occupied themselves with religion almost monothematically. This attitude is foreign to Marx.

Religion is not the basic evil, the radical evil or the original sin of mankind. Religion is not the cause of the perverted world, but rather the perverted world is the source of religion. Therefore one should not make a "scapegoat" theory out of the criticism of religion. The criticism of religion is never to be pursued as the primary front and as an end in itself: "The fight against religion is indirectly the fight against that world whose spiritual aroma is religion" (ibid., p. 208). Only on the socio-critical horizon is the criticism of religion meaningful.

This approach has important consequences: Marx's relationship to religion is more concrete than the criticism of religion of his time. Religion is mainly attacked in its concrete forms. It is important, therefore, to establish which religious phenomena especially provoked the Marxian protest. In my opinion there are above all two phenomena: the misuse of Christianity for power political aims and the mammonism of the religion of the times.

The first point appears in connection with Marx's remarkable and even today relevant criticism of the "Christian state." We have pointed to the oppressive presence of this "ideal" in the official philosophy of the state and the social climate of the Prussian monarchy. Marx suffered in this climate and protested against the ideology of the "Christian state." The alliance of throne and altar seemed to him an evil misalliance. Of course he did not attack it because of its theological adversity. His reasons were socio-critical and political. Thus it is all the more remarkable that in the context of his political argumentation he also clearsightedly diagnosed and denounced the religious contradiction of the "Christian state." In clear reference to the biblical message, which should be taken absolutely seriously precisely by the "Christian state," he emphasized how "the infamy of its (the Christian state's) worldly aims, which are cloaked by religion, gets into an insoluble conflict with the integrity of its religious consciousness" ("Zur Judenfrage", op. cit., p. 187)—a statement which as a theologian one would have like to have seen written by the leading theologians of his time.

In Marx's writings the second main reason for his polemic of religion appears even more clearly and persistently: the religious mammonism of the times. Money, mammon, capital represents in his view the greatest power in the estranged world. It is also the greatest God of the religiously estranged. Marx tries to demonstrate that this is above all true for the Jewish religion: "Money is the zealous God of Israel before whom no other God may exist" (*op. cit.* p. 204). Bartering is the "worldly cult of the Jews." But not only of the Jews. The God of the Jews has become the God of the world. Very soon especially Christianity was in this respect contaminated by the Jewish leaven, indeed: in the Christian-bourgeois society "the Jewish spirit," mammonism, reached its apex. Marx points this out with respect to typical "pious Christians" of his time. Even the gospel became a commodity for many of them. Thus Christianity, which arose out of Judaism, dissolved again into Judaism. The exceptional pointedness of the Marxian criticism of religion is applicable to this form of Christianity.

It is in the socio-critical dimension of Marxian atheism that I see its continuing challenge to theology and the church. One should not overlook that it was the political power and mammonistic form of Christianity which provoked this protest. And one must acknowledge without hesitation that an assault on these phenomena was and is justified—and indeed also and expressly for theological reasons. Precisely in the biblical perspective the perversion of every church established in political power becomes evident: it fails to see the authentic initiative of Jesus, which urged a love expressed in service rather than the love of power; and it also ignores his unequivocal concern for the poor and oppressed. And mammonism is quite sharply and uncompromisingly rejected by the prophets and apostles—and by the extremely challenging saying of Jesus (Matt. 6. 241). Thus when the Marxian criticism points so energetically to these facts, it does not simply address Christians "from the outside," but also "from the inside" of their radical heritage. If one would attempt to dilute or pass over this critical voice in silence—possibly with the occasionally mentioned alibi that it is a resolute atheistic voice—then this would be a sign of an unconvincing impenitence. In avoiding Karl Marx the church with such an attitude would only all too easily avoid the biblical summons itself. Here there still remains a chronic need for Christians to catch up.

A theology which is self-critically conscious of this may and must ask also critical questions of Marxian atheism. Karl Marx himself, for example, must be asked whether his remarkably differentiated religious-critical attitude does not fall short at one point, namely at that point where his justified criticism of the actual conditions of the church disregarded the question of whether these conditions did not represent a "decay" of Christianity, and not exactly its "essence." Marx seemed to know that Christianity had other possibilities in its origin and also in its history; but in his theory of religion they were not taken into account.

Another analogous and far reaching question concerns later Marxism: it needs to be asked whether in its theory of religion Marx's concrete socio-critical approach was not weakened and pushed aside in favor of a general antireligious theory. Above all where Marxism became the official ideology of Marxist-socialist societies it tended to freeze its atheistic standpoint into a general world view which did not allow for the concrete form and changes of Christianity. This dogmatism hindered the openness and dynamism of socialist society and at the same time endangered the possibility of social cooperation between Christians and Marxists.

These two questions suggest the presence of another, more general and more abstract—in my view even more questionable— dimension of the Marxist criticism of religion. With that we come to the third part of our considerations.

3. The Anthropological–Dogmatic Dimension of Marxian Atheism

Already our historical orientation has underlined the anthropological motif in the background of the Marxian criticism of religion: the pseudo-mystery of religion is the mystery of the human self-consciousness. As our discussion of the socio-critical dimension has shown, this Young Hegelian thesis is filled with meaning and concretized in Marx's writings by his rejection of every unhistorical and abstract anthropology: man—that means the world of man. This important concretization, however, is not the last word of the Marxian view of man. It has—especially in the religious-critical context—also a polemic edge: Marx advocates the aseity of the world of man, and it is only in light of this thesis and in this context that he establishes atheism as an integral part of his philosophy.

In using the key-word "aseity" (*aseitas mundi hominis*) I am consciously employing a typically theological formula: classical theology spoke of the "aseity of God" in order to assert the sovereign independence of the Creator from creation. Is not the Marxian position theologically manipulated from the beginning by using such a formula? I don't think so. Marx himself develops a corresponding anthropological-cosmological thesis in a clearly theological horizon—and that precisely in the context of his discussion of the doctrine of creation.

I am thinking of one of the key passages in his "Paris Manuscripts." It deals with the central set of problems concerning humanism and emancipation: with the question of the true nature of man, as considered not only from a speculative, but also from a deeply practice-related, revolutionary perspective. This eminently anthropological concern has an immense religious-critical component. Marx argues: "A being becomes independent as soon as he stands on his own feet, and he stands on his own feet only when he owes his existence to himself. A man who lives by the grace of another views himself as a dependent being. But I live completely by the grace of another person when I owe him not only the continuance of my life, but when he has also created my life . . . when it is not my own creation" (*Die Frühschriften, op. cit.,* p. 246).

In referring to this being who puts man under his tutelage Marx has the biblical creator God in mind. It is imperative for human freedom that this God be abolished. In so far as I believe in him, I do not stand on my own feet, and thus am not truly emancipated, indeed—in order to resume the decisively positive concept: I am not yet "really" man. Hence this God needs to be abolished in the eminent interest of human emancipation and reality.

This is precisely what Marx attempts. Negatively, in a directly religious-critical way, by trying to mobilize—certainly not in a concentrated way, but rather with the "left hand"—a type of "negative proof of God" by borrowing from the attack of the naturalistic philosophy of his time against the belief in creation; but above all indirectly, positively, by outlining a kind of socialist-communist doctrine of creation: "Since . . . for socialist man the entire so-called world history is nothing other than the generation of man through human labor, and the development of nature for man, he therefore has clear and irresistible proof of his self-creation, of his own formation process" (*op. cit.,* p. 247 f). One should keep the implication of this argument in mind: the socialist-communist man—the community of freely associated socialist individuals, as Marx later expresses it—takes up the heritage of the biblical creator God. This man proves to be the true subject of the only real human history of creation and salvation. Through his "objective activity," through his work and revolution in history, a solution of all those problems arises which the biblical religion anticipates only eschatologically in the "kingdom of God"—a healing of all conditions in the world of man: the theological promise of an *apokatastasis ten panton* appears as a genuine restoration and real bringing home "of the human essence through and for mankind" in the realm of history, the "complete and conscious return of man to himself as a social, i.e. human being within the total wealth of previous development." And not only the history of mankind but also world history, indeed in a certain sense even nature attains its goal: "This communism . . . is the authentic resolution of the antagonism between man and nature and between man and man; it is the true resolution of the conflict between existence and essence, between objectification and self-affirmation, between freedom and necessity, between individual and species. It is the solution of the riddle of history and recognizes itself to be this solution" (*op. cit.,* p. 235).

In my opinion this dimension of the Marxian criticism of religion represents the other challenge and the real problem for

Christian theology, and indeed in the positive as well as in the burdening sense.

First of all I would like to point unmistakably to the *positive* side of this radical criticism of religion. In this connection I am not only thinking of the emphatically positive approach of this criticism. This should nevertheless also be appreciated: here no "atheism" of angry or despairing negation is offered, as is quite often the case in the history of atheism. This atheism is not concerned with destroying but with constructing, not with renouncing but with healing. The positiveness of this phenomenon, however, is in no way exhausted by its positive approach. Marxian atheism carries weight not only formally, but above all in its content. I will mention some aspects of this positiveness in key words. Marxian atheism thinks *comprehensively*: it is in no way "obsessed" with its set of problems, and in no way isolates them from broader connections in order to pounce in a sectarian and narrow-minded way on religion as the real hydra of the human race—as was quite often the case in bourgeois-freethinking atheism. Marxian atheism thinks in a *concentrated* way: it does not get stuck in arbitrary details, but pointedly asks about the essence and liberation of man. Thus it stands in the best tradition of European humanism—and indeed also in the best tradition of Christian humanism. The Marxian criticism of religion is also unique in not tackling the central humanistic question in an idealistic-abstract way, but in searching for the "essence" of man in the context of real human history, i.e. it attempts to set the concrete *social world of man* in motion toward hope and liberation. In all these accents the Marxian criticism of religion serves as a moving challenge to theology and the church.

In its openness for the central concern of the Marxian theory of religion, however, Christian theology must also certainly ask *critical* questions of Marxism, especially concerning the concrete form and execution of the humanistic concern of the Marxian criticism of religion. Concretely it must ask whether switches are thrown and positions established in this criticism which sooner or later endanger, both theoretically and in reality, precisely its humanistic concern. In my opinion Marxian atheism—however justified it may be in concrete contexts—constitutes at the same time a serious problem, and indeed precisely at that point where its strength lies in its concentration on the theme of the true essence and liberation of man. This holds true for its positive as well as for its basic critical accent. I would like to suggest primarily two basic questions for reflection:

(1) Is the anthropological thesis true which holds that man attains his "essence" when he "owes his existence to himself" and is not dependent on any grace? I cannot agree with this thesis. It advocates an abstract and negative concept of freedom: freedom means here "non-dependence." Of course the element of a legitimate independence and emancipation belongs inalienably to human freedom. Genuine freedom, however, is at the same time more. It is freedom for the other person, a neighborly freedom. With the ideal of "aseity" in the understanding of freedom a real concept of man (and also a true concept of God!) is not yet described. Also a feeling of indebtedness and undeserved love belongs to concrete and free humanness. This important element of freely being human, which is expressed in the original words of the Christian message, grace and love, gets cut short in the positive-anthropological approach of Marx.

(2) I do not want to overlook that this Marxian one-sidedness is corrected in other contexts: in his materialistic knowledge of the "neediness" of the individual, for example, or in his socialist emphasis on community. In my opinion, however, this correction also is obstructed by the atheistic element of his thinking. The religious-critical decision in favor of atheism implies that God as the life-giving and supporting vis-a-vis of man is eliminated in the interest of human emancipation and liberation. But does the emancipatory interest really lead forcibly to an elimination of God? In my opinion, certainly not. The pre-supposition that God is a rival of man was indeed suggested by some distortions of popular theology and piety; however, if one thinks of the concept of God in the Old and New Testaments, the thought of a "competition" between God and man appears to be a decidedly

unbiblical, or rather "pagan" idea. The biblical God is the God of covenant, of "partnership," the God who from the beginning is intent on the liberation of men and not on their enslavement and dependence. One thinks of the Old Testament Exodus, and of the history of Jesus Christ. To appeal to Jesus is suggestive of initiatives of freedom. Therefore the presupposition of atheistic argumentation is hardly valid. The deletion of God is no necessary postulate of human liberation, but rather a faith decision of unbelief, an ideological dogma.

This dogma can have burdensome effects. What does it mean to "delete God"? In my opinion this is no merely intellectual operation of ideological cosmetics. Rather it is a potential "revaluation of all values," and indeed for Marx in a concrete sense: the transfer of the absolute from the "world of God" to the "world of man." In the "elimination" of God, his predicates in no way automatically disappear with the renounced subject. They tend to be transferred into "worldly contexts." In religious-critical operations salvation-historical elements of the biblical heritage are indeed secularized; but this secularization proves to be an ambiguous matter; the worldly questions become "theologized," "mythologized," absolutized. The political ideology then inclines toward becoming an untouchable dogma; the political organization identifies itself with the avant-garde of an absolute future; the field of political action becomes the eschatological battle field. Legitimate attempts toward the realization of the Marxist theory are thus dangerously handicapped—as became brutally evident especially in the theory and practice of Stalinism.

In order not to be misunderstood, I do not assert that this development results "with logical necessity" from the Marxian approach and certainly not that it was "caused" by the atheistic component of Marxism. Also I consider the humanistic approach of Marxism in no way refuted, and the possibility of a self correction of Marxist thought is not excluded. On the contrary, it seems to me to be possible and due. Humanistically oriented Marxists deserve in this connection the sympathy and support of all democratically oriented men. It is my conviction in this connection also that a critical examination of the anthropological-dogmatic dimension of Marxian atheism could play a modest but meaningful role. It seems desirable—not in order to make life easier for Christians and theologians, but in order to make all of us freer for mutual encounter and social cooperation by reducing dogmatized prejudices.

A SELECT BIBLIOGRAPHY*

Adelmann, F., *From Dialogue to Epilogue*. The Hague: Nijhoff, 1968.
Aptheker, H. (ed.), *Marxism and Christianity*. New York: Humanities Press, 1968.
————, *The Urgency of Marxist-Christian Dialogue*. New York: Harper and Row, 1970.
Aron, R., *Marxism and the Existentialists*. New York: Harper and Row, 1969.
Ash, W., *Marxism and Moral Concepts*. New York: Monthly Review Press, 1964.
Bakunin, M., *God and the State*. Freeport, New York: Books for Libraries, 1971.
Bennett, J., *Christianity and Communism Today*. New York: Association Press, 1970.
Block, E., *Atheism in Christianity*. New York: Herder and Herder, 1972.
Brown, H., *Christianity and the Class Struggle*. New Rochelle, New York: Arlington Press, 1970.
Crossman, R. (ed.), *The God that Failed*. Freeport, New York: Books for Libraries, 1972.
De George, R., *Soviet Ethics and Morality*. Ann Arbor, Michigan: University of Michigan Press, 1969.
Desan, W., *The Marxism of Jean-Paul Sartre*. New York: Doubleday, 1965.
Flakser, D., *Marxism, Ideology and Myth*. New York: Philosophical Library Press, 1970.
Garaudy, R. and Lauer, J., *From Anathema to Dialogue*. New York: Vintage Press, 1968.
————, *A Christian Communist Dialogue*. New York: Doubleday Press, 1968.

*Compiled by Robert D. Hall, St. John's University, New York, U.S.A.

Girardi, G., *Marxism and Christianity*. New York: Macmillan Co., 1968.

Gollurtzer, H., *The Christian Faith and the Marxist Criticism of Religion*. New York: Charles Scribner's Sons, 1969.

Hecker, J., *Religion and Communism*. London: Hyperion Press, 1973.

Klugmann, J., (ed.), *Dialogue of Christianity and Marxism*. Los Angeles: Lawrence Publications, 1968.

Kim, D., *Victory Over Communism and the Role of Religion*. New York: Vantage Press, 1972.

Kolakowski, L., *Marxism and Beyond*. London: Pall Mall Press, 1969.

Korsch, K., *Marxism and Philosophy*. London: NLB, 1970.

Lacroix, J., *The Meaning of Modern Atheism*. New York: Macmillan, 1965.

Laski, H., *Faith, Reason and Civilization*. Freeport, New York: Books for Libraries, 1972.

Leeuwen, A. van, *Critique of Heaven*. New York: Charles Scribner's Sons, 1972.

Lewis, J. (ed.), *Christianity and the Social Revolution*. Freeport, New York: Books for Libraries, 1972.

Lochman, J., *The Church in a Marxist Society*. New York: Harper and Row Co., 1970.

MacIntyre, A., *Marxism and Christianity*. London: Duckworth, 1969.

MacIntyre, A., and Ricoeur, P., *The Religious Significance of Atheism*. New York: Columbia University Press, 1969.

Magno, J., and Lamotte, V., *Atheism and Christianity*. Dubuque, Iowa: Listening Press, 1972.

Masterson, P., *Atheism and Alienation*. South Bend, Indiana: Notre Dame University Press, 1973.

Miceli, V., *The Gods of Atheism*. New Rochelle, New York: Arlington Press, 1971.

North, G., *Marx's Religion of Revolution*. Nutley, New Jersey: Craig Press, 1968.

Odajnyk, W., *Marxism and Existentialism*. New York: Doubleday, 1965.

O'Dea, T., *Alienation, Atheism and the Religious Crisis*. New York: Sheed and Ward, 1969.

Oestreicher, P. (ed.), *The Christian Marxist Dialogue*. London: Macmillan Co., 1969.

Ogletree, T. (ed.), *Openings for Marxist-Christian Dialogue*. Nashville, Tennessee: Abingdon Press, 1968.

Petulla, J., *Christian Political Theology*. Maryknoll, New York: Orbis Books, 1972.

Schilling, S., *God in an Age of Atheism*. New York: Abingdon Press, 1969.

Singh, S., *Communism, Christianity, Democracy*. Richmond, Virginia: John Knox Press, 1965.

Suda, J., *Manu, Marx and Gandhi*. Meerut, India: Jan Prakash Nath and Co., 1967.

Tucker, R., *Philosophy and Myth in Karl Marx*. Cambridge, England: Cambridge University Press, 1972.

Ward, H., *God and Marx Today*. Philadelphia: Fortress Press, 1968.

West, C., *Communism and the Theologians*. New York: Macmillan, 1963.

Literature

CHAPTER XXXII

GOD IN MODERN LITERATURE

*Barry Ulanov**

The terms remain the same; the themes, the signs and symbols, everything in the language of modern man proclaims his Christian inheritance. He is more preoccupied than ever with finding some purpose for his suffering, some explanation, however obscure or illogical, to match the ingenuity with which new forms of pain seem to be invented in the twentieth century. He is more deeply thrust into his own interiority, more anguished in his sense of isolation in an unfriendly universe with each of the developments of psychology, anthropology, and the physical sciences. All of this his literature reflects and more than reflects, insists upon. How easy it is, then, to construct an elaborate Christian apologetics upon such a foundation, with such evidence, and how often it has been done, and with what meager results!

To the argument from design and the unmoved mover and all the other classical demonstrations of the existence of God have now been added the arguments from James Joyce, D.H. Lawrence, William Faulkner, Samuel Beckett, Jean Genet, and Albert Camus. Nothing so clearly proclaims the divine presence as a loud and firm *non serviam*. Look for the rhetoric of antithesis, especially if its negations are directed against religious belief, and there you will find the grounds of faith. Clarity in ambiguity, light in darkness, ultimate reality in the denial of any reality beyond the hourglass— these are the canons of an anti-metaphysical metaphysics for which modern literature has too often provided the fables and the exemplary tales. They reveal little about modern literature and

*Professor of English and Religion at Barnard College, Columbia University, New York, U.S.A.

modern man, I suspect, and too much about the yearnings of the
critics and philosophers and theologians who can find their
theodicy only in the forced conversion of the literary atheist and
agnostic.[1]

To the convinced Christian the presence that lurks everywhere
is, of course, divine. A stab at the arras will discover not only
Polonius hiding beneath an embroidered apothegm but a type of
the crucifixion. The inverted ritual of Genet will turn a whore-
house into a church and, inevitably, every sexual or political
gesture into a liturgical movement. Whoever Beckett's tramps
thought they were waiting for, it was clearly the God in Godot
that they were expecting. Stephen Dedalus's pilgrimage was, in
fact, the old Adam's and Finnegan's wake was the resurrection
that produced the new Adam, bloody wine, fleshy bread, and all.
There is no mistaking the meaning of Faulkner's Joe Christmas,
however reduced in stature the Godman may seem to have
become, and even Mellors, the fun- and gameskeeper of Lady
Chatterley, can be seen to have some of the lineaments of a sacred
figure, for every coupling adumbrates the Creation and
tumescence and detumescence are ancient configurations of the
resurrection to set beside the daily rise and fall of the sun as
tellings and retellings of the great mystery.[2]

But having said this, what has one said? At best, one has
perpetrated a commonplace, and at worst a vulgarization that
serves neither literature nor religion. To find God everywhere is a
splendid spiritual exercise; it is not useful literary criticism or
acceptable theology if in order to do so one must turn the
self-proclaimed non-server into a religious zealot and make over his
works into a library of Christian apologetics. The point surely is

---

1 This is not to say that the measured criticism of such writers as Nathan A. Scott,
Jr., Amos Wilder, Martin Jarrett-Kerr, Martin Turnell, Wallace Fowlie, Charles Moeller,
and others of their quality has not been useful in exposing Christian elements in modern
literature. It is simply to suggest that any less balanced approach to literature from a
religious viewpoint is an exercise in futility, whether regarded as criticism or apologetics.

2 The references are to Hamlet, Genet's The Balcony, and Beckett's Waiting for
Godot; Joyce's Portrait of the Artist as a Young Man, Ulysses, and Finnegan's Wake;
Faulkner's Light in August, and Lawrence's Lady Chatterley's Lover.

that suffering, compassion, redemption, hope, despair, evil, and transformation have no more compelling associations or drama- tizations than the gospel stories and that there is no longer or more impressive witness to this fact than the literature of the West of the past two millennia. And so the poems and plays and novels of the moderns are filled with Christian allusion and constructed out of people and places and events that can be traced back to both Testaments, just as the literature of the Middle Ages and the Renaissance was, even if in our time this is accomplished with a good deal less understanding and a comparatively impoverished idea of the possible refractions of sign or resonances of thing.

There is undoubtedly some small value in tracking down the points of Judaeo-Christian reference in modern poetry or dis- covering the Christ-figure or John the Baptist who stands behind the dead American gangster in Faulkner or the unfrocked French lawyer in Camus,[3] whether or not the poet or novelist recognized his holy sources. It is not much more than a kind of literary busy work, however, and it hardly reveals a serious contemplation of the problem of God in the literature of our time. It is all too much like the bemused Freudian adventuring among the bookstacks who lets out a strangled cry of delight everytime he finds a chimney or a crater, a sword or a pot, and can demonstrate once again that the world is full of symbols of masculine or feminine sexuality which a hopelessly repressed humanity has been unwilling or unable to acknowledge.

In modern literature, as in all the modern arts, as in philosophy or psychology or theology, the concern for God and the interaction of the human and the divine that makes most sense is the conscious one. The depths in this subject-matter are those that have been sounded by artists and craftsmen who have known exactly what they have been doing, whether or not they have been doing it in the service of faith or anti-faith or any clearly identifiable set of religious convictions. What has been important is the writer's conscious pursuit of understanding in what we call

---

3 See Faulkner's *Light in August* and *Sanctuary,* and Camus's *The Fall.*

the religious situation, not his demonstration of understanding, not his manipulation of character or plot to prove anything, whether sympathetic or antipathetic to religious doctrine, and certainly not his own assertion of religious or anti-religious feeling. Understanding comes hard in these precincts. It almost always involves some more than superficial examination of religious tradition, of the writings of those who have lived and worked within religious tradition, and the associated theology, philosophy, psychology, and, most important, literary theory. Thus it was that Thomas Mann immersed himself in the *Urfaust* and the medieval style and human experience that stand behind and move so profoundly into the living textures of his great religious novel, *Dr. Faustus*. Similarly, T.S. Eliot sought out analogies for the interior journey he narrated in his *Four Quartets*, sometimes appropriating, sometimes glossing, sometimes merely turning over the words and experiences of Dante's encounter with his teacher Brunetto Latini in the *Inferno*, of John of the Cross's theological rationalization of his dark night of the senses, of Julian of Norwich's "shewings" of the case for Christian confidence, of the resolution of the paradox of action in inaction and inaction in action in the explications of Krishna to Arjuna in the *Bhagavadgita*.[4]

There is a special probity that pursuers of this understanding of the divine display, often after having failed to do so in an earlier work. So, it seems to me, Mann is reduced to ironies, sometimes at the edge of a duelling sarcasm, in his attempts to deal with even the vocabulary of religion in *The Magic Mountain*. Then, with the Joseph books, he moves, with a grasp of the psychology of belief that has an almost Augustinian majesty, into a plotting of character that make it possible to find, accept, reject, fence with, destroy, and be destroyed by the devil dressed in his artist's habit in *Dr. Faustus*. Eliot could legitimately, I think, ask for Ezra Pound's editing for *The Waste Land*, a work which deals with religion, searches for the liberation of religious affect, and flirts

---

4   See *Little Gidding*, II; *East Coker*, III; *Little Gidding*, III, and *The Dry Salvages*, III, in Eliot's *Four Quartets* (New York, 1943).

now comfortably, now nervously, but never altogether openly and honestly with religious experience. Equally, he could declare himself in *Ash Wednesday,* as he had in the preface to *For Lancelot Andrewes,* making a public profession of faith rather like his assertion of the royalist and classicist persuasions in politics and literature. It was all rather tidy, elegant even, but never much more penetrating as a presentation of belief than the signature of a distinguished figure in an advertisement in support of a political candidate: T.S. Eliot endorses God, the King, and John Dryden; not necessarily in that order. The same distance from the ostensibly sought-for presence, from the faith so publicly proclaimed, continues in the Canterbury Festival performance that yielded the choruses from *The Rock* preserved in the *Collected Poems.* Then came the change with the detailed treatment Eliot gave the figure of Thomas a Becket in *Murder in the Cathedral,* tortured by his hopes for a bloody martyrdom and horrified by the temptation to pride that the hopes represented. This was no longer copybook Christianity, though it was as public as ever, written like *The Rock* for a Canterbury Festival and very satisfying to that sort of listening and viewing audience as it continued to prove in college and commercial theater performances and even as a film. But now the public Eliot was a writer with a habitual mode for whom the mode was no more significant, really, than the choice of a cadence or a fixed number of syllables to give shape to a verse line. Eliot, the Christian on open pilgrimage, had found the same grace of understanding as Mann, the philosophical novelist, whose professed faith never went beyond the literary essay, the friendly introduction to selections from the works of Schopenhauer, the expression of horror at the development of McCarthyism and other political lapses in his temporarily adopted American homeland.

After the complexities of Thomas a Becket's temptations, Eliot had found his Christian voice. It never deserted him. It made possible an elegant fable for the stage, *The Cocktail Party,* in which psychoanalytical jargon and drawing-room repartee were turned into the language of pure spirit and three characters out of Oscar Wilde were made to play the role of guardian angels.

However much he may have faltered technically in his other dramatic adventures—*Family Reunion, The Confidential Clerk,* and *The Elder Statesman*—his literary world was a world on pilgrimage, mixing the memory of Aeschylean, Sophoclean, and Euripidean antiquity with the desire for the *lumen gloriae*,[5] relieving personal sentimentalities with impersonal ironies, saying now over and over again that he did not want to turn again, but never in so many words; he had learned the lesson of Christian modesty, which, properly enough, made it harder and harder to call his works Christian, at least on the surface. It was something he had in common with Boethius and Rabelais, not a bad pair of associations for a modern man.

In an introduction that Eliot wrote for a 1961 edition of David Jones' long 1937 prose poem, *In Parenthesis,* he pointed out an "affinity" in the work of Jones "with that of James Joyce (both men seem to me to have the Celtic ear for the music of words) and with the later work of Ezra Pound, and with my own." But he insisted that whatever the influences, they were "slight and of no importance."[6] It is probable that Jones will not find his audience until the connections of his work with *The Waste Land* and *Finnegan's Wake* and Pound's *Cantos* are established, even if in so doing a small nexus is inflated into a central influence. For then the willingness of the reader of Eliot and Joyce and Pound to work through deliberate obscurities, polyglot plays on words, and a whole encyclopedia of citations and paraphrases and densely figurative fables will have been summoned forth and Jones the Welsh bard, the re-maker of Arthurian legend, the troubadour of the Mass, will be seen for the master of sacramentality that he is. Divine substance has rarely in recent centuries been given such beguiling human shadows as in *The Anathemata* ("the devoted things"), the great 1951 offertory poem of David Jones. Where the

---

5 As, for example, in the mixing of Christian theme and the figures of the Eumenides from Aeschylus's *Oresteia* in *Family Reunion* or the central characters in Euripides' *Alcestis* with the contemporary London world and Eliot's own Christian concerns in *The Cocktail Party*.

6 See T.S. Eliot, "A Note of Introduction," in David Jones, *In Parenthesis* (New York, 1961), pp. vii-viii.

earlier work gathers the experience of the 1914-1918 War into eternity, the later one somehow makes sacred things accessible to us, no matter how remote the language, or how far from us the Welsh world of this water colorist and engraver turned poet. The work begins—

> We already and first of all discern him making this thing other. His groping syntax, if we attend, already shapes: *Adscriptam, ratam, rationabilem* . . . and by preapplication and for *them,* under modes and patterns altogether theirs, the holy and venerable hands lift up an efficacious sign.[7]

—And thus with the Latin of the Mass lifts us into a modality that, no matter what the liturgical fashion or decree, must make sense to those who worship the Lord of the two Testaments. The concluding words have an eloquence of their own, but larger, much larger, for the medieval pageant and rite, gest and hymn and legend which have preceded them:

> He does what is done in many places
> what he does other
>   he does after the mode
> of what has always been done.
> What did he do other
>   recumbent at the garnished supper?
> What did he do yet other
>   riding the Axile Tree?[8]

The Lord lives as priest and king and prophet in *The Anathemata,* sits comfortably beside and within Merlin and Mary, a part of the ancient world, the medieval, and the modern. He demands—or rather, Jones does for him—a rigorous attention and responds with an understanding of divine persons and human

---

7 See David Jones, *The Anathemata* (New York, n.d.), p. 49.
8 *Ibid.,* p. 243.

nature at least as far-reaching as that offered by the multiple masks of Humphrey Chimpden Earwicker and Anna Livia Plurabelle, Shem and Shaun and their sister Isabel in the *Wake* or Ezra Pound's mixture of social and economic jeremiads and literary autobiography in the *Cantos.* There is, it must be said, a gusto in Joyce's application of Giambattista Vico to Irish myth, English literature, and depth psychology that Jones cannot match. And Pound, for all the determined eccentricity of his social doctrine and the dubious scholarship of his reading of the Italian renaissance and Confucian thought, is an incomparably witty and entertaining glosser of European literature, whose very off-center approach to history and contempt for scholarly procedure permit him insights and lovely, singing lines that will keep large parts of the *Cantos* alive long after their detractors have been forgotten and their articles and books buried in the dust. But Jones offers a presence and an encounter that neither Joyce nor Pound can touch or, one suspects, begin to understand. He has to make his obeisances to Joyce and Pound, no doubt, and to Eliot, too, for some of his manner, but not for his matter. When he speaks in Part IV of *In Parenthesis,* for example, of war and death, he speaks as well of all sacrifice and of *the* sacrifice, and manages to do so without cliche or the rhetoric of preaching or the reduction in any way of truth to platitude—

> But I held the tunics of these—
> I watched them work the terrible embroidery that He put on.
> I heard there, sighing for the Feet so shod.
> I saw cock-robin gain
> his rosy breast.
> I heard Him cry:
> *Apples ben ripe in my gardayne*
> I saw Him die.[9]

---

9 *In Parenthesis,* p. 83. For a deepening of one's understanding of Jones's thought and procedures, his book of critical essays and theoretical speculations, *Epoch and Artist* (London, 1959), is very much worth consulting.

This is the authentic meeting of the divine and the human, close to Dante and Boccaccio and Chaucer in spirit and texture and trust in the strength of ancient patterns of figurative language to penetrate some of the layers of the central mysteries. It is the quality one finds in the French writers Peguy and Claudel, each so much of his time, now strongly Englished and directed toward a harsher world, a less sympathetic audience, a less certain faith than the French poets faced. This is the world, the audience, the organized doubt that modern literary men, believers or not, must face. It offers from within the worst kind of assurance—the words are Edwin Muir's—

> Packed in my skin from head to toe
> Is one I know and do not know.
> He never speaks to me yet is at home
> More snug than embryo in the womb.
> ....
> .... He is safe, he has no doubt,
> He sits secure and will not out.
>
> His name's Indifference.
> Nothing offending he is all offence;
> Can stare at beauty's bosom coldly
> And at Christ's crucifixion boldly...[10]

For without, it presents the emptiness that looks and feels like fullness, a world apparently so complete and so completing that salvation is an irrelevance in it. W.H. Auden's bitter comment at the end of the time of Compline in his *Horae Canonicae* is not without hope; the question he asks is not rhetorical—

> Can poets (can men in television)
>   Be saved? It is not easy

10 See "Variations on a Time Theme," in Edwin Muir, *Collected Poems* 1921-1951 (London, 1952), p. 31.

To believe in unknowable justice
 Or pray in the name of a love
Whose name one's forgotten: *libera*
 Me, libera C (dear C)
  And all poor s-o-b's who never
   Do anything properly, spare
  Us in the youngest day when all are
   Shaken awake, facts are facts,
  (And I shall know exactly what happened
   Today between noon and three)
  That we, too, may come to the picnic
   With nothing to hide, join the dance
  As it moves in perichoresis,
   Turns about the abiding tree.[11]

Poets like Muir and Auden are enough of this world, have lived enough in this world, seen enough of others' suffering, suffered others' suffering enough to write at various times, in their journeys from indifference and an environment unconcerned with salvation, with the tones of bitterness or disillusion or different shades of detachment. But they do not scold, nor do they make easy disjunctions between the saved and the lost as sometimes the sterner moralizers of modern literature have seemed to do, speaking for God or Anti-Christ or whatever summary judgment has made them its oracle in their plays and novels. The Jansenist nightmares of Francois Mauriac's novels, to take the most scrupulously crafted example, offer their victims to the justice of a God who seems to present more of the stern face of a papal commission to our view than a loving heart. The people are honestly described; their sins are not exaggerated; the atmosphere of evil in which they move is no more to be doubted than the world of Balzac's characters—it is in fact that same world a century later. But the worst that Balzac's men and women can do, really, is to accuse themselves. Mauriac's not only accuse them-

---

11 See "Compline," in W.H. Auden, *Selected Poetry* (New York, 1959), p. 172.

selves and each other but stand accused, delated, one by one, to that terrible Holy Office into which his version of the Trinity seems to have dissolved.[12]

Graham Greene's sympathies are more openly with his stumbling adulterers and crumbling confessors of the faith. But the net effect of his multi-volume *Pilgrims' Regress* is the same as that of Mauriac's moral theology or Evelyn Waugh's sentimental parody of it in *Brideshead Revisited.* Chastity is the impossible burden. Love is something that occurs in spite of it sometimes, more often in deliberate, delicious transgression. Then human relations of some quality may develop, but they are always doomed: if a wronged husband or wife cannot make legal trouble, he or she can turn whatever remains of pleasure and goodness in the relationship into fantasies at the very least of bad faith and at the worst of eternal damnation. Joy is invariably a fugitive, like the stoic narrator of *Brideshead* or Greene's whiskey priest, from the Holy Office-God.[13] How much more satisfying—and satisfied —are the agonists and protagonists of Waugh's ironic allegories, *A Handful of Dust* or *Scott-King's Modern Europe* or *The Loved One,* or the superb *Sword of Honour* trilogy![14] They disport themselves, these variously happily miserable figures, it is true, in a landscape designed by Hieronymous Bosch or Brueghel or Cranach, where pitchforks are always about to descend. But they are very little pitchforks and wielded by minor devils and everybody of importance in the allegories knows about the devils and accepts them as inevitable features of a fallen world which is also a redeemed one. It is, though with much more humor, rather like the complex mixture of goodness and misery, beatitude and cancer and senseless killing, in the best of the novels of Georges

---

12 The Mauriac novels I have in mind are *The Desert of Love, Vipers' Tangle, Therese Desqueyroux,* and *The Woman of the Pharisees,* but almost any of his novels will support my point, I believe.

13 The Graham Greene novel about the whiskey priest is, of course, *The Power and the Glory.*

14 In the United States, the novels which make up the trilogy are better known by their individual titles, *Men at Arms, Officers and Gentlemen,* and *Unconditional Surrender* (first published in the U.S. as *The End of the Battle*), than by their group title.

Bernanos, *The Diary of a Country Priest* and *Joy.*[15] There is something like a perfectly made chronicle of a mystic's dark journey toward union in the Bernanos tales and also, I think, in Waugh's, though the English ironist must make all his best points by inversion and indirection and leave his saintly victims just beginning to be instructed in the ancient science of extracting heroic virtue from homely victimhood rather than fully delivered as holy martyrs in the great continental manner so handsomely affected by Bernanos. What is most important, we can take either the French hagiography or the English bestiaries seriously and recognize in their people and the situations in which they find themselves and the dreams which they dream and the language they speak either ourselves or our friends or our enemies, neighbors at the communion rail or companions on the confessional line.

It is an extraordinary accomplishment to turn the central characters in a hagiological drama or an ironic allegory into recognizable types. It is also an essential one if they are to be exemplary and not merely acceptable. There seems little question that Waugh and Bernanos—and no doubt Mauriac and Greene as well—were trying their hand at the art of the exemplary, whether to provide cautionary tales or some variations on the *De Imitatione Christi* or some less lofty or more cutting morality. The mere making of a plot on the part of a tale-teller assures a moral tone, according to the Italian novelist Cesare Pavese:

> The motive force in every plot is simply this: To discover how such and such a character extricates himself from a given situation. Which means that every plot is invariably an exercise in optimism, in so far as it is a research into how a character responds. It goes without saying that even if he fails, that is still

15 See also, by Bernanos, the novel which preceded *Joy* by three years, the 1926 *Sous le soleil de Satan*, the related *Nouvelle histoire de Mouchette* (1937), and the comparatively early *Monsieur Ouine*, which was not published until 1946. In all of these the hagiological tone is present, though in more muted fashion than in the *Diary* and *Joy*, and as always with Bernanos, his sense of the complexity of the human condition, even when it is firmly directed by a Christian faith.

a reaction. If the failure is the author's fault, if, that is, he did not manage to get out of the difficulty, the unspoken question arises as to what he should have done to bring matters to a successful conclusion. Here is the message in every plot: this is how one ought, or ought not, to act. It follows that if immoral works exist, they are works in which there is no plot.

Plotless modern works, Pavese goes on to explain, offer "artless" narratives of the ordinary, with a single character, *"the average man,* who can be any one of us and, indeed, is, under the old clumsy psychological classifications." At its best, this sort of performance presents us with someone beyond the ordinary, but seen "in his normal state, his 'averageness.' " Thus the writer transcends convention with "an abnormal, pathological hero (that being the common conception of 'extraordinary'), and follows his activities with a sort of uncritical homeliness (Faulkner? O'Neill? Proust?)."[16]

Pavese's categories may not exhaust the typologies of tale-telling, but they do make an important distinction for the writer who comes, by whatever kind of religious or moral or psychological or philosophical or even anthropological conviction, to a story in which absolute value figures. Sooner or later the absolute will take on the literary trappings, at the very least, of Judaeo-Christian rhetoric and some configuration of deity will make its appearance. That assures the development of plot as an exercise in optimism, to use Pavese's term, a confrontation with the absolute, viewed honorifically or pejoratively: a character either should or should not act in such and such a way to achieve his peace with the Almighty (Jewish version, Christian version, Hindu version, Moslem version—it makes no difference) or to find Nirvana (Buddhist version, Virginia Woolf version—or whatever) or to face the simple truth that there is no absolute except that there is no absolute (John Dewey version, Peter De Vries version, or anybody

16 See Cesare Pavese, *The Burning Brand: Diaries 1935-1950,* translated by A.E. Murch and Jeanne Molli (New York, 1961), pp. 114-115.

else's). Those whose interest in the absolute is the most obsessive seem to me to combine this exercise with the second of Pavese's performing categories: they throw into moral combat, against all the familiar *oughts* and some new ones as well, an extraordinary creature somehow reduced for the occasion of combat to the level of his averageness. He is the saint at home, suffering with constipation or migraine; she is the earthly Venus, just about to go to work and frustrated with a run in her pantyhose or a broken strap in her brassiere. Even in the monumental exchanges of the Russian Revolution, there is time for a Yuri Zhivago to be acutely aware of changes of temperature, to sweat and to know that he is sweating, to look out at peaceful or violent scenes and to note all the homely details that remind him and us that war and revolution occur in ordinary places to ordinary people. When Pasternak's giant of a man discovers that his consciousness of personhood is impossibly affronted by the doctrines and practises of Communism, it is in a setting of commonplace elements. Everything that marks the world as divine also proclaims its small-scale human associations:

It was Holy Week, the end of Lent, and winter was almost over. The snow on the roads was turning black, betraying the beginning thaw, but on the roofs it was still white, and covered them as with tall hats.

The "ancient post road" which leads to the town in which we are granted this incidental meditation, "the oldest highway in Siberia," cuts through "towns like a knife, slicing them like a loaf of bread along the line of their main streets." When Dr. Zhivago dies, on a trolley-car, fittingly enough, or more precisely trying to get off the trolley and falling dead of a heart attack as he reaches the pavement, he has time to gather a few thoughts, and once again somehow to bring together the divine and human orders and to leave them inextricably and mysteriously associated. Confusion and clarity mix. School-arithmetic problems, in which different train speeds must be sorted out to produce a schedule of arrivals, come to mind, reasonably enough, in a public conveyance. Zhivago cannot remember any general rule, but one set of associations leads to another—

> He tried to imagine several people whose lives run parallel and close together but move at different speeds, and he wondered in what circumstances some of them would overtake and survive others. Something like a theory of relativity governing the hippodrome of life occurred to him, but he became confused and gave up his analogies.

> There was a flash of lightning and a roll of thunder. The ill-starred trolley was stuck for the nth time . . . [17]

It is a homely death for a heroic figure. It is also a remarkable reduction in scale of the events of the Pasternak novel, bringing the heroic down to more approachable proportions. This is the way literature achieves its moral force and out-sized beings fall into place in average lives. In this sense, every such figure is a demonstration of the *analogia entis* and the God of the philosophers and of the theologians is inseparable from the God of the modern novelist and poet and playwright. Not many twentieth-century writers have worked with such a directed consciousness toward the contemplation of being as Pasternak or the novelist who must be bracketed with him, Alexander Solzhenitsyn. Not many have been provided such a richness of material for this particular contemplative exercise as these writers working in Lenin's and Stalin's and Khruschev's and Brezhnev's Russia. But one does not need to experience the events of 1917 or to endure a slave-labor camp or a cancer hospital in a totalitarian society to discover the tragic textures of human existence or the

---

17 See Boris Pasternak, *Doctor Zhivago,* translated by Max Hayward and Manya Harari (New York, 1958), pp. 307, 306, 490. For the Zhivago poems, I strongly recommend the Donald Davie translation and commentary, *The Poems of Doctor Zhivago* (Manchester, England, and New York, 1965), in which see particularly the notes to "Magdalene I," leading up to the conclusion, "what makes Zhivago identical with Christ is above all his capacity as an artist."

transfiguring elements which so often grow out of them.[18] One can lead a life that is almost a caricature of tragedy and makes transfiguration little more than a lighting effect in an expressionist drama, as August Strindberg did, and still find the materials for a stunning meeting with the divine,—literally stunning, for no one has made more of the blinding, baffling, generally immobilizing effect of conversion than Strindberg did in his trilogy *To Damascus.*

In the *Damacus* plays, Strindberg has brought together almost all the oblique angles of human contradiction. His agonist-protagonist, the Stranger, turns up in a number of unmistakable disguises and is reflected as well in one way or another in all the many male roles, even the most inconspicuous and passing ones. To the Stranger's playing of Saul and Paul, an equally multifaceted Lady gives ample room to Strindberg's passionate love and hatred of woman and through her to the darkest, least predictable, most frequently unconscious sides of human behavior. The triple drama, which moves in each of its sections from conversion to de-conversion (and, with the beginning of each new part, to re-conversion), is as successful, as confounding, as touching, and as unresolved as the other Strindberg adventures in the theater of the metaphysical macabre, *The Ghost Sonata, A Dream Play,* and *The Great Highway.*[19] It is possible to translate the adventures in psychoanalytical, philosophical, or sociological terms or simply to assign them their large part in the development of German expressionist drama and the modern theater of the absurd and of cruelty, and all of this has been done, with ample credit to

---

18 The references are to Solzhenitsyn's *One Day in the Life of Ivan Denisovich, The First Circle,* and *Cancer Ward.* For a direct insight into Solzhenitsyn's sensibility as an artist and a Christian, see his *Stories and Prose Poems,* translated by Michael Glenny (New York, 1971), especially the prose poems, in which a form associated in Russian literature with the work of Turgeniev assumes the stature of a religious meditation. Another vital Solzhenitsyn document is, of course, the undelivered *Nobel Lecture,* excellently translated by Thomas Whitney (New York, 1972).

19 There are a variety of translations of Strindberg's plays now available, some of them very good indeed. In my own work, I have preferred to use those of Arvid Paulson, Elizabeth Sprigge, and Evert Sprinchorn. I also have found useful and reliable those of Michael Meyer.

Nietzsche and all the other figures and currents of thought that helped produce the disciplines peculiar to our time. But though it is fair enough it does not go far enough. It neglects, I think, the true wildness within Strindberg, which defines even if it does not altogether explain his astonishing achievement. He was surely an *anima naturaliter Christiana,* never a gentle one, except in moving up or down his fearful pursuits to an always more strenuous struggle with his demons, which he himself, occasionally, recognized as angels. He chose the role of Paul, but it may be that Jacob was closer to his gifts.

Our deepest investigations of human interiority continue to require the support of ancient mythologies and their appointed diviners. We have no better material with which to take apart and put together again our research into the nature of the human, whether it is clinical, literary, theatrical, on canvas or musical manuscript, as the work of Freud, Jung, Eliot, Mann, Yeats, Joyce, Strindberg, Picasso, Stravinsky, and Schönberg shows so clearly. The quality and profundity of the material is indicated by the depth of the investigators' projections into the myths and onto their ancient explicators. Thus we have Strindberg openly playing Paul and more covertly Jacob, Freud somewhere in the coils of the Oedipal cords, Yeats now this, now that ancient Celt, Picasso got up as the Minotaur, and Schönberg caught up in the characters of both Moses and Aaron, not to speak of the possible embroilments of Mann with the Devil, Joyce with Ulysses, Penelope, Adam, and Eve, and Eliot with Thomas a Becket, Orestes, and Alcestis. One can quickly object with the cry of "the biographical fallacy!" and all its surrounding arguments. But the power of this sort of investigation remains the power of participation and thus of projection, even after one has made all the honorable exceptions and freed the artist of precise identification with his creation. The exact distance of Proust from the Marcel of *A la recherche du temps perdu* does not matter, nor does the separation of fact from fantasy in the association of Joyce with Stephen Dedalus or Mann with either Adrian Leverkuhn or Serenus Zeitblom or any of the other persons or personifications of his version of Faust. The participation in every case, when we are dealing with artists of this quality, is like nothing else on earth; it is a case of that splendid paradox in which man becomes so profoundly concerned with man that he is all but transformed into pure spirit.

The most remarkable example of this transmutation is, I believe, what is demonstrated by Hermann Broch in *The Death of Virgil*.[20] Though the book is written in the third person, Broch, or the narrator, or the spirit entrusted with the tale, or whatever one wants to call the extraordinary being in charge of events, is very much the figure around whom the work takes its shape. He is Virgil; he is not Virgil. He is the voice of history, of the chronology of the ancient poet's last days. He is the nature of consciousness, of whatever can be spoken or written. He is just as much the medium through which what cannot ordinarily be verbalized is somehow brought to earth and given narrative structure and poetic clarity. Here, at the last boundary of life, everything is more completely alive than it has been before. For Virgil, the impossible aim of experiencing death while still alive is achieved, or at least seems to be. For us, aware as no century has been before of the complexity of human events and the opacity of our own nature, a dialectic of the states of consciousness is attained in which inner and outer worlds mingle freely and at their most obscure meetings become, of all things, clear, for pages at a time, in sentences of unbelievable length and tortuousness and syntactical precision and beauty.

Broch's Virgil is the Virgil of the messianic eclogue, of *pietas,* of all the human foibles, but also of a sometimes incomparable rectitude. He is a poet of astonishing graces of comprehension. He is a fallible human, a sinful one, a loving one, a compassionate and merciful man to whom wisdom was given and who in Broch's book at least as much as in his own writings gives us wisdom. In a way which no summation of the book can adequately reveal, this allegory of modern man confronts the human with the divine, questions authority, supports authority, gives man unlimited

---

20 See Hermann Broch, *Der Tod des Vergil* (Frankfurt, 1958), handsomely translated by Jean Starr Untermeyer (New York, 1945), with great sympathy for the German text and unmistakable understanding as well.

freedom and then takes it all away from him as death must take it all away unless it promises something more to come. In a mixture of styles as handsomely brought together as the themes of transcendence and immanence, which are what *The Death of Virgil* really contemplates, Broch presents the twentieth century with itself. Here are the possibilities of hell, purgatory, and something even more mysterious than the paradise of Scripture or Dante because it is never reduced to systematic description. Here is description, never reconcilable to an exact system, but still purposeful; a book wonderfully alive to the surface world of Virgil and at the same time extraordinarily rich in the techniques of interior monologue.

The Death of Virgil is very much a book of our time and very much a book of earlier times. It offers us that sort of self-contemplation that can come only from seeing ourselves under the rubrics of both earth and eternity. Like Eliot's *Four Quartets*, it is divided into four parts, following the ancient division of the elements—water, fire, earth, and air—and is liberally provided with fateful epigraphs, including the *fato profugus* of the opening lines of the *Aeneid* which invokes the force of fate. The remaining two quotations bring us the meeting of Aeneas and the ghost of his father in the sixth book of Virgil's epic—"O father, allow me to join my right hand with yours, and do not withdraw yourself from my embrace . . . "—and the last seven lines of Dante's *Inferno*, in which Dante and Virgil enter on "that hidden road" which leads from hell to the bright land of earth, a journey which permits Dante a glimpse of "some of the lovely things that heaven bears" as they come forth to see the stars again.[21] In the passage from the *Aeneid*, Aeneas reaches to embrace his father three times and three times the shadow of his father slips away. One can hardly avoid reading Broch's book in these terms, or any of the other works of high seriousness that I have tried to deal with in this essay. One is offered, with the full consciousness of the writer and all the equipment of his own time which he has been able to

---

21 The exact passages are *Aeneid,* VI, 697-702; *Divine Comedy, Inferno,* XXXIV, 133-39.

appropriate, a glimpse of heavenly beauty, but it is always on the road from hell or toward purgatory. One looks on, perhaps even participates, in all sorts of movement toward the shadow, the image, the ghost of the Father, but, to complete the quotation from Virgil, one reaches it only to find that it has escaped one's hands, "like light winds or even more like a fleeting dream."

A SELECT BIBLIOGRAPHY

Auden, W.H., *The Dyer's Hand and Other Essays.* New York: Random House, 1962.

Berdyaev, Nicholas, *The Meaning of the Creative Act.* Translated by D.A. Lowrie. New Collier, 1962.

Camus, Albert, *L'Homme revolté.* Paris: Gallimard, 1951.

Claudel, Paul, *Un Poete regarde la croix.* Paris: Gallimard, 1938.

Eliot, T.S., *For Lancelot Andrews.* London: Faber, 1928.

_____, *Notes Towards the Definition of Culture.* London: Faber, 1948.

_____, *Selected Essays.* New York: Harcourt, Brace, 1950.

Fletcher, Angus, *Allegory: The Theory of a Symbolic Mode.* Ithaca, New York: Cornell University Press, 1964.

Friedman, M.J. (ed.), *The Vision Obscured: Perceptions of Some Twentieth-Century Catholic Novelists.* New York: Fordham University Press, 1970.

Gilson, Etienne, *The Arts of the Beautiful.* New York: Scribner's, 1965.

Heller, Erich, *The Artist's Journey to the Interior.* New York: Random House, 1965.

Jennings, Elizabeth, *Christianity and Poetry.* London: Burns & Oates, 1965.

_____, *Every Changing Shape.* London: Andre Deutsch, 1959.

Jones, David, *Epoch and Artist.* London: Faber, 1959.

Mann, Thomas, *Essays of Three Decades.* Translated by H.T. Lowe-Porter. New York: Knopf, 1947.

_____, *Last Essays.* Translated by Richard Winston and others. New York: Knopf, 1959.

_____, *The Story of a Novel.* Translated by Richard and Clara Winston. New York: Knopf, 1961.

Maritain, Jacques, *Creative Intuition in Art and Poetry.* Princeton, New Jersey: Princeton University Press, 1953.

Moeller, Charles, *Litterature du XXe siècle et Christianisme.* 3 vols. Tournai: Desclee de Brouwer, 1953.

Neumann, Erich, *Der Schöpferische Mensch.* Zürich: Rhein-Verlag, 1959.

Pavese, Cesare, *The Burning Brand: Diaries 1935-50.* New York: Walker, 1961.

Scott, Nathan, *Modern Literature and the Religious Frontier.* New York: Harper, 1958.

———, *Negative Capability.* New Haven, Connecticut: Yale University Press, 1969.

———, *The Wild Prayer of Longing.* New Haven, Connecticut: Yale University Press, 1971.

——— (ed.), *The New Orpheus.* New York: Sheed & Ward, 1964.

Ulanov, Barry, *The Two Worlds of American Art: The Private and the Popular.* New York: Macmillan, 1965.

——— and James Hall (eds.), *Modern Culture and the Arts.* 2nd edition. New York: McGraw-Hill, 1972.

CHAPTER XXXIII

THE TWO DOMINANT VIEWS OF GOD IN MODERN POETRY
*Francis L. Kunkel**

Gerard Manley Hopkins (1844-1889), priest and poet, shows the greatest preoccupation with God of any poet in the past one hundred years. Thomas Hardy (1840-1928), novelist and poet, displays an almost comparably intense, if very different, preoccupation with God. The major poems of Hopkins and Hardy are concerned with man's relationship to God. Man's relationship to his fellow man is only a subsidiary theme. We might call both of them "theologians in mufti": in mufti since neither was a systematic thinker, but of course poets rarely are and when they are it is usually to their detriment as poets. On account of the relative brevity of this chapter, it will be necessary for me to limit my analysis of God in modern poetry to Hopkins and Hardy almost entirely. But since this particular pairing of modern poets on God will yield insight into the two general ways most modern poets who address themselves to the problem resolve it, the limitation is not unfortunate. In other words, Hopkins and Hardy exemplify the two dominant views of God in modern poetry.[1]

Their creative work shows God-concerned impulses which emanate in either theistic humanism or secular humanism.[2]

*Professor of English at St. John's University, Jamaica, New York, U.S.A.

1 Lest an objection be raised as to how two poets born prior to the mid-nineteenth century can be construed as moderns, let me point out briefly why the chronology is misleading. Hardy was less Victorian than modern in spirit, since most of his poetry was composed in this century and it anticipates the direct speech of this epoch. Hopkins likewise deserves to be considered a modern poet. During his lifetime his work was regarded as much too innovative and idiosyncratic for publication, which did not take place until 1918.

2 Hopkins' theistic humanism usually took the form of celebrating God; Hardy's secular humanism usually took the form of mocking God.

Probably the similar point of departure is to be accounted for by the common spiritual crisis they underwent as young men. The 1860's was the great decade of the Victorian age, intellectually speaking. Christianity came under attack from two quarters at once. First the publication of *The Origin of Species* (1859) and then around the same time publications devoted to "higher criticism" of the Scriptures greatly disturbed the religious outlook of the late Victorians. Hopkins' response was to move to the right. He forsook Anglicanism for Roman Catholicism and ultimately ordination as a Jesuit. Hardy's response was to move to the left. He lapsed from Anglicanism and allowed himself to be engulfed by the rising wave of agnosticism. But though he became a disaffected religionist he never wavered in his search for the Unknown God, as Hopkins never rested in his search for the Known God. When Hopkins is ranged besides Hardy, the following antitheses are pitted against one another: conformist theology vs. rebellious theology, orthodox piety vs. unorthodox piety, supernaturalism vs. naturalism, and faith-science allegiance vs. science-faith allegiance.[3]

* * *

Serene acceptance of God and stormy acceptance of God are not exclusive chronological phases—one early; the other late—in the poetical development of G.M. Hopkins. Bewildered belief both precedes and follows a period of buoyant belief. The poet traversed a circular route beginning with troubled faith, illustrated by *"Nondum"* (1866), transcribing an arc through a period of less troubled faith, illustrated by "The Wreck of the *Deutschland"* (1876), reaching the apex in tranquil faith, illustrated by "God's Grandeur" (1877), and finally closing the circle with sorely

---

3   Hardy placed ultimate faith in science, so his poetry is structured by the scientific thought of his time. Because Hopkins is God-driven, however, it does not follow that he is anti-scientific. There are for example in his journals (See *The Journals and Papers of Gerard Manley Hopkins,* ed. Humphry House) entries on horticultural and astronomical lore that would reflect credit on a professional.

troubled faith again, illustrated by the sonnets of desolation (1885-1889).

"Nondum" (No. 23),[4] dated Lent, 1866, was composed just a few months before Hopkins' conversion to Catholicism. It carries an epigraph from Isaiah, "Verily Thou art a God that hidest Thyself," and shows clearly the character of this young poet's preoccupation with God. Thrice he complains of the "silence" of God:

> Our prayer seems lost in desert ways
> Our hymn in the vast silence dies.
> > (Stanza 1)

> And still the unbroken silence broods
> While ages and while aeons run . . .
> > (Stanza 4)

> And Thou art silent, whilst Thy world
> Contends about its many creeds . . .
> > (Stanza 6)

"Nondum" ends with a prayer for enlightenment and support however which must have been answered prior to "The Wreck of the *Deutschland"* where the emergence of God from hiding is plain.

W.H. Gardner describes well the modification of troubled faith which issues from "The Wreck of the *Deutschland"* (No. 28). "We perceive that there has been a mental struggle, in which the problem of evil and the Christian doctrine of Divine Love and Omnipotence have been with difficulty reconciled by reason and faith."[5] The reconciliation he writes of, Hopkins achieved by a coincidence of contraries which John E. Keating clarifies as

---

4 Throughout this study, the poems of Hopkins are identified by numbers in parentheses. These numbers correspond to the numbers in *The Poems of Gerard Manley Hopkins,* ed. W.H. Gardner, 4th ed.

5 *Gerard Manley Hopkins: a Study of Poetic Idiosyncrasy in Relation to Poetic Tradition,* I, 51.

follows: "It seems to me that Hopkins is first of all concerned, and honestly, tormentedly concerned, with what we may anthropomorphically call the character of God. The poet believes that God reveals himself in 'stars and storms,' in 'fall-gold mercies' and in 'dark descending[s],' in 'pied and peeled May' and in December tempests, in the Incarnation of the Word and in the threat of 'hell-fire.'[6] The problem, as Hopkins saw it then, is how is man to reconcile these seemingly contradictory divine revelations? And the resolution of the problem, again as Hopkins viewed it at that time, hinges on the acceptance of inevitable paradoxical difficulties associated with faith.

This accounts for the shifts in mood which, in the course of "The *Deutschland,*" range from abject terror to ecstatic joy. But before delving into theme and mood, let me explain briefly the genesis and structure of the poem. The incident which recalled Hopkins to the writing of poetry, after seven years of neglect attributable to scrupulosity, was the foundering of the North German Lloyd steamship *Deutschland.* He explained the circumstances in a letter to Canon R.W. Dixon. "When in the winter of '75 the Deutschland was wrecked in the mouth of the Thames and five Franciscan nuns, exiles from Germany by the Falck Laws, aboard of her were drowned I was affected by the account and happening to say so to my rector he said that he wished someone would write a poem on the subject. On this hint I set to work and, though my hand was out at first, produced one."[7]

"The *Deutschland,*" an elegiac ode, is divided into two parts. *Part The First,* comprising the first ten stanzas, treats the poet's private religious experience without explicit reference to the sea disaster. *Part The Second,* comprising the remaining twenty five stanzas, relates the shipwreck of the nuns to the poet's own mystical shipwreck. Stanzas 1-4 recount Hopkins' terrifying encounters with God's grace, stressing the mastery of the

    6 John E. Keating, *The Wreck of the Deutschland: an Essay and Commentary,* p. 17.
    7 *The Correspondence of Gerard Manley Hopkins and Richard Watson Dixon,* ed. Claude Abbott, p. 14.

Almighty. Stanzas 5-10 recount Hopkins' ecstatic encounters with God's grace, stressing the mercy of the Almighty. Stanzas 11-17, the narrative portion of the poem, describe the *Deutschland* in the storm. The tall nun is introduced at the end of stanza 17. Her heroic behavior, calling on Christ to "come quickly," is the prime concern of the poem through stanza 31. Touched by the finger of God, as the poet had been, she creates faith and hope in her fellow passengers. The concluding four stanzas contain reflections on the omnipotence and universal salvific will of God, and a plea to the drowned nun for intercessory prayers for the conversion of England.

In substance, "The *Deutschland*" presents a paradoxical God who is at once severe and compassionate:

> Thou art lightning and love, I found it, a winter and warm;
>   Father and fondler of heart thou hast wrung:
> Hast thy dark descending and most art merciful then.
>
> (Stanza 9)

"The *Deutschland*" thematically confirms the nature and ways of God by suggesting that "the mysteries of our inner and outer lives point back to a God who, to human intelligence, must remain endowed with a paradoxical combination of opposing attributes. But, in his glimpse of the divine inscape, the poet sees that these attributes are not really set against one another . . . God's justice is his mercy, his chastisements are his blessings."[8] God's terrible omnipotence is simultaneous with His infinite love. Hopkins here dramatizes two traditional Christian solutions: salvation through suffering—no crown without a cross; divine utilization of physical evil to effect good—man's extremity is God's opportunity.

The overcast faith of *"Nondum"* and the partly cloudy faith of "The *Deutschland*" are succeeded by the sunny faith of "God's Grandeur." Nowhere more so than in the sonnets that were composed in that highly productive year, 1877—which includes

---

8 Keating, *op. cit.*, p. 20.

besides "God's Grandeur" such well known sonnets as "The Windhover" and "Pied Beauty"—is there discernible that "hierarchic identification betwixt God and nature and Hopkins himself, of such a sort as that the natural images will convey the religious exaltation which he experiences mystically."[9] These sonnets all have a common theme: God manifests Himself through visible creation. The poet "inscapes" the Infinite through finite nature: that is, the supernatural inscape is "instressed" by natural objects.[10]

Since the common theme is most overt in "God's Grandeur" (No. 31)

> The world is charged with the grandeur of God.
>> It will flame out, like shining from shook foil;
>> It gathers to a greatness, like the ooze of oil
> Crushed. Why do men then now not reck his rod?
> Generations have trod, have trod, have trod;
>> And all is seared with trade; bleared, smeared with toil;
>> And wears man's smudge and shares man's smell: the soil
> Is bare now, nor can foot feel, being shod.
>
> And for all this, nature is never spent;
>> There lives the dearest freshness deep down things;
> And though the last lights off the black West went
>> Oh, morning, at the brown brink eastward, springs—
> Because the Holy Ghost over the bent
>> World broods with warm breast and with ah! bright wings.

9 Stanley Hopper, *Spiritual Problems in Contemporary Literature,* pp. 101-102.
10 "Inscape" and "instress" are technical terms used by Hopkins as both nouns and verbs:

> In his vivid descriptions of skies, cloud-formations, trees, waves breaking, flowers opening and withering, and other phenomena, Hopkins is mainly fascinated by those aspects of a thing, or group of things, which constitute its individual and 'especial' unity of being, its 'individually-distinctive beauty', or (if beauty is not involved) the very essence of its nature. For this unified pattern of essential attributes (often made up of various sense-data) he coined the word 'inscape'; and to that energy or stress of being which holds the 'inscape' together he gave the name 'instress'. This 'instress' is often referred to as the force which also, as an impulse from the 'inscape', carries it whole into the mind of the perceiver.

(Gardner, *op.cit.,* p. xx)

Let it bear the burden of explication. The lengthiest and most felicitous commentary on this poem is Father Boyle's.[11] However the curtal nature of this chapter permits nothing more than a *précis.* "In the first line . . . the electrical image carried in the verb 'charged' . . . is a preparation for the introduction of moving gold foil as a revelation of God's grandeur,"[12] and also a preparation for the next image. "The oil which oozes from the olive is intrinsic to the olive, hidden within, saturating without revealing its presence, as the grandeur of God saturates the world."[13] The question in line 4 expresses wonder why it is that men once having discerned God in nature now no longer do so. The remainder of the octave suggests the answer. "The world is now a big place, literally a stamping ground for generations of shod feet. And the flame from creatures which should reveal God is from greed abused so that it sears the earth, and the oil which should bear witness to God is smeared on the earth, and the smudge of smoke and the smell of sweat . . . wipe out the evidence of God's grandeur." In these lines Hopkins implies more than an indictment of industrial squalor; he implies that "the situation of man is a tragic one after the Fall."

This is borne out by the fact that the sestet, "the cosmic close of the poem . . . has no direct reference to the growth of factories."[14] The poet is expressing a Franciscan love of nature, albeit a "shod" one. And the sestet contains the formula for recovering an unshod Franciscan love of nature. The continuous resurgence of the Holy Ghost will overcome the wanton destruction of nature and renew "the dearest freshness deep down things." An earlier commentator, Brooks Wright, anticipated this view by showing how "God's Grandeur" "culminates in an unforgettable picture of the Holy Ghost, brooding over the earth, rousing it to life and infusing it with beauty and freshness."[15]

---

11 Robert Boyle, *Metaphor in Hopkins,* pp. 25-44.
12 *Ibid.,* p. 26.
13 *Ibid.,* p. 31.
14 *Ibid.,* p. 36.
15 *The Explicator Cyclopedia,* I, 159.

In the overall view, as Thomas McDonnell points out, "when Hopkins says, 'The world is charged with the grandeur of God,' he is not simply using, as some may think, an over-wrought figure of speech; he literally means it. He is declaring in poetry the doctrine of the *immanence of God* in the world."[16] That the immanence of God is the central doctrine poetized in the sonnets written between 1877 and 1885 can be illustrated by parading a series of quotations:

> Look at the stars! look, look up at the skies . . .
> These are indeed the barn; withindoors house
> The shocks. This piece-bright paling shuts the spouse
>   Christ home, Christ and his mother and all his hallows.
>   (No. 32, composed in 1877)

> All things counter, original, spare, strange;
>   Whatever is fickle, freckled (who knows how?)
>   With swift, slow; sweet, sour; adazzle, dim;
> He fathers-forth whose beauty is past change:
>   Praise him.
>   (No. 37, composed in 1877)

> I walk, I lift up, I lift up heart, eyes,
> Down all that glory in the heavens to glean our Saviour . . .
> And the azurous hung hills are his world-wielding shoulder[17]
> Majestic—as a stallion stalwart, very violet-sweet!—
> These things, these things were here and but the beholder
> Wanting; which two when they once meet,

---

16 "Hopkins as a Sacramental Poet," *Renascence*, XIV, 1 (Autumn, 1961), 28-29.

17 Taken out of context such lines as these might be construed as pantheistic. But to charge Hopkins with pantheism is to fail to contrast Hopkins' insight into the transcendent God in nature with other nineteenth century poets who were . . . inevitably turning to a 'god' in or of nature, who, if they got Him in, could not get Him above it. Wordsworth and Emerson are excellent examples of pantheistic views which locked God in nature and left Him there, perhaps because locked there He could serve as the ultimate dimension of nature without making Him the ultimate but transcendent end of man. (David Downes, *Gerard Manley Hopkins: A Study of His Ignatian Spirit*, pp. 76-77)

The heart rears wings bold and bolder
And hurls for him, O half hurls earth for him off under his
feet.

(No. 38, composed in 1877)

Man's spirit will be flesh-bound when found at best,
But uncumbered: meadow-down is not distressed
For a rainbow footing it nor he for his bones risen.

(No. 39, composed in 1877)

. . . . Christ plays in ten thousand places,
Lovely in limbs, and lovely in eyes not his
To the Father through the features of men's faces.

(No. 57, composed about 1882)

What do then? how meet beauty? Merely meet it; own,
Home at heart, heaven's sweet gift; then leave, let that alone.
Yea, wish that though, wish all, God's better beauty, grace.

(No. 62, composed in 1885)

In each of these quotations—and surely they are not all that could have been selected—what Alan Heuser calls Hopkins' "sacramental vision" is given poetic manifestation. Hopkins believed with Duns Scotus "in Christ's eucharistic or sacramental Presence working in created nature since the beginning of time."[18] "To what serves Mortal Beauty?" composed August 23, 1885, is perhaps the last of the sacramental sonnets. "Spelt from Sibyl's Leaves," composed from all evidence at about the same time, is a transitional poem between the sacramental sonnets and the desolate sonnets, variously called the dark sonnets and the "terrible sonnets."[19] The terminology requires clarification. When we pass in 1885 from the sacramental sonnets to the terrible

---

18 Alan Heuser, *The Shaping Vision of Gerard Manley Hopkins,* p. 38.

19 Hopkins himself called them the "terrible sonnets," meaning what his friend Canon Dixon before him had meant in saying that Hopkins' poems contained a quality of "terrible pathos . . . a right temper which goes to the point of the terrible; the terrible crystal." *(Correspondence to Dixon,* p. 80)

sonnets, "the sacramental intuition, whereby he had greeted Christ
in the naturalistic ideal of inscape, was darkened, then fled away:
this was the mystery of Christ's absence in the dark sonnets."[20]

The differences behind the terminology require clarification,
and the differences are a matter of inscape, mood, tone, faith, and
technique. In terms of the poet's concept of inscape, the transition
is marked by a passage from objectivity to subjectivity: from
inscaping God's earthly revelation Hopkins turns to inscaping
man's abandonment by God. So in the terrible sonnets, he gives up
his optimistic religious outlook and strikes a note of deep tragedy.
This effects the tone and the nature of the faith expressed. In the
earlier sonnets, ecstasy was pitched on an even keel; there was no
oscillation between degrees of despair and hope. And near
complacency suffused the expression of religious faith; there was
no hint of faith put to the test. But perhaps the most important
change was in the area of technique where a diminution of
sensuous imagery sets in. His earlier sonnets reveal a Crashaw-like
gift for lush sensuous imagery. The concluding images in "The
Windhover" (No. 36) are typical:

> . . . Sheer plod makes plough down sillion
> Shine, and blue-bleak embers, ah my dear,
> Fall, gall themselves, and gash gold-vermilion.

By contrast images are employed less frequently in the later
sonnets and when they do occur they differ in kind. The opening
line of the sestet in No. 67 is typical:

> I am gall, I am heartburn . . .

The language retains startling imaginative appeal, but it is now
concise, more controlled and less fanciful—attributable in part to
the absence of anything similar to the *quasi*-precious phrase of
direct address, "ah my dear." All too often however in the terrible

---

20 Heuser, *op. cit.*, pp. 72-73.

sonnets, Hopkins by-passes imagery in favor of direct statement. The result is that the sacramental view of nature is blighted. And this is unfortunate, because the purpose of the sacramental vision is to incarnate existence, not to abstract it. That is to say most of Hopkins' mature poetry exemplifies Incarnational tenets: the supernatural is evoked by the sensuous. But when he relies on direct statement to perform the unique task of an image, the poetry suffers and exemplifies Jansenistic tenets: the direct evocation of the supernatural.

To explain the reasons for the change and the attendant qualitative decline in the poetry, in detail, would be a luxurious digression into Hopkins' psychological makeup that I cannot afford. Suffice to say that his chronic melancholic outlook was darkest during his Dublin years, the years he was writing the terrible sonnets. David Downes suggests that this period of intense dejection which became a crucial test of the poet's spirit resulted, in part, from a substitution of spiritual mentors. Prior to 1885, the influence of Ignatius Loyola structured the feelings and thoughts which Hopkins converted into his mature verse. Downes sees as especially Ignatian a sacramentalization of the sensuous world: a movement by grace through nature to divinity—the very pattern of Hopkins' best poems. But then around 1885, the poet came under the spell of Thomas a Kempis, and so the astringent poems of his last years owe more to the *Imitation of Christ* than to the *Spiritual Exercises.* The last poems show their affinity to the *Imitation* by stridently underscoring an opposition between nature and grace.[21]

The trio of the joyful sonnets, nature-God-poet, is shrunk to a duo, God and poet, in the sorrowful sonnets. This is evident in the first of them, No. 64, where "Hopkins' immediate plan of operation is to set up a Despair vs. Self antipathy, later shifting the equation to Despair vs. Self vs. God and then to Self vs. Despair-who-is-God-in-disguise." The Despair vs. Self antipathy occurs in the octave:

---

21 Downes, *op. cit.,* Chapters IV-V.

. . . O thou terrible, why wouldst thou rude on me
Thy wring-world right foot rock? . . .

The equation is shifted to Self vs. Despair-who-is-God-in-disguise
in the sestet:

. . . The hero whose heaven-handling flung me, foot trod

And the reader gets the eerie impression that "no one exists in the
world except God and His antagonist, the soul,"[22] when the poem
ends:

That night, that year
Of now done darkness I wretch lay wrestling with (my God!)
my God.

In the self-regarding, self-enclosed world of the dark sonnets,
God is increasingly devalued. From "The *Deutschland*" epithets

World's strand, sway of the sea;
Lord of living and dead
(Stanza 1)

to the notion of God as despair turned hero is a long step down.
But there is a further step down in No. 65 where God appears to
have abdicated. At least His presence is nowhere felt by the
poet—no wrestling with Christ—just a sense of total abandonment:

No worst, there is none. Pitched past pitch of grief,
More pangs will, schooled at forepangs, wilder wring.
Comforter, where, where is your comforting?

And the poem closes with scant comfort:

22 Sister M. Joselyn, "Herbert and Hopkins," *Renascence*, X, 4 (Summer, 1958),
193.

> . . . Here! creep,
> Wretch, under a comfort serves in a whirlwind: all
> Life death does end and each day dies with sleep.

This is Hopkins' most intense expression of spiritual anguish. Man is seen out of context with hope and grace as absolutely barren spiritually. There is only despair in this sonnet.

The mystic sense of emptiness and drought is scarcely less in No. 67, a poignant poetic expression of the inveterate insomnia attendant upon the awful separation from God.

> I wake and feel the fell of dark, not day . . .
> With witness I speak this

cries Hopkins as he laments his life estranged from the "Comforter," so remote that he must send Him letters—"dead letters" at that, since they seem never to reach their divine destination. In the sestet

> I am gall, I am heartburn. God's most deep decree
> Bitter would have me taste: my taste was me;
> Bones built in me, flesh filled, blood brimmed the curse.
> Selfyeast of spirit a dull dough sours. I see
> The lost are like this, and their scourge to be
> As I am mine, their sweating selves; but worse

the poet, soured by self-ferment, concludes that hell is the inability to love God.

A measure of reconciliation with God comes in No. 69, however. After futilely casting about for comfort, Hopkins finally resigns himself and resolves to trust in the grace of God:

> . . . Let joy size
> At God knows when to God knows what; whose smile
> 's not wrung, see you; unforeseen times rather—as skies
> Betweenpie mountains—lights a lovely mile.

The result is that joy's smile, which cannot be forced, lights up a lovely mile of sky unexpectedly glimpsed between piebald mountains.

But the consolation is short-lived. For in the last of the terrible sonnets, No. 74, Hopkins feels himself a eunuch. He concludes his complaint to God, "my friend," with these images:

. . . Birds build—but not I build; no, but strain,
Time's eunuch, and not breed one work that wakes.
Mine, O thou lord of life, send my roots rain.

In a happier time, when nature was depicted as a vessel of grace bearing tidings from God to man, this contrast between the fecundity of nature and the sterility of the poet would have been inconceivable.

And so we have returned to the starting point, *"Nondum":*

And still th' abysses infinite
Surround the peak from which we gaze.
Deep calls to deep, and blackest night
Giddies the soul with blinding daze
That dares to cast its searching sight
On being's dread and vacant maze.
                    (Stanza 5)

We are back to the starting point, subject to this difference. "In the relatively feeble imagery of 'Nondum' . . . we heard the young Hopkins speak of the 'chastening wand' of patience and ask God to lead him through the darkness and to whisper to his frightened and watching heart one word, to make him smile in confidence of love and protection. The patience we have seen in these last poems is no chastening wand, but a rack and a torment. The journey through the darkness is one of sterility, of whirling blasts on the mountainous cliffs, of utter blackness through towering mountains. And the whisper his heart echoes in horror is, 'Our night whelms, whelms, and will end us.' The foretelling of the young Hopkins was in a general way correct, but almost incredibly pale beside the violent and vigorous colors of the reality."[23]

To summarize, we have seen in our consideration of the Divine Presence in Hopkins' poetry how in a pre-Jesuit poem ("*Nondum*") he "searched the 'glories of the earth' but found no host in the lighted but empty hall;" how in his first poem as a Jesuit ("The *Deutschland*") he proffers an act of adoration to a God whom he sees through a glass darkly; how in a host of later poems (sonnets prior to 1885) he "kisses his hand to the stars, because behind them and in them he sees the Host, the Word"[24] and how in a handful of last poems (sonnets between 1885-89) he takes the Gethsemane view: "Father . . . remove this chalice from me; but not what I will, but what thou wilt" (Mark 14, 36). In Boyle's judgment, the Catholic view of God "is presented in Hopkins' work with a depth, a fullness, and a sweep that English poetry has not known since the Reformation."[25]

* * *

Although Thomas Hardy devoted himself primarily to writing novels from 1871 to 1896, poetry was always his favorite means of expression. He began his literary career by writing poetry. "About forty poems are dated as being written in the 1860s, the majority in the middle of the decade; 1866 is by far the most frequent date."[26] Since he was able to get only four of them published at the time, however, he shelved poetry for fiction. But after the publication of *Jude the Obscure* (1896), he ceased writing novels and returned to poetry. In the remaining thirty two years of his life, he composed over eight hundred short poems.

Hardy's attitude towards God, at least as expressed in his poetry, does not show the ups and downs characteristic of Hopkins' stance. Hardy was not alternately optimistic and pessimistic; he was consistently the latter. God was always heavy

23 Boyle, *op. cit.*, p. 161.
24 *Ibid.*, p. 196.
25 *Ibid.*, p. 195.
26 Kenneth Marsden, *The Poems of Thomas Hardy: A Critical Introduction*, p. 182.

going for him. Some of this pessimism he attributed to the influence of Karl von Hartmann. For in the course of an interview William Archer had with Hardy, the poet raised the question: " 'Do you know Hartmann's philosophy of the Unconscious? it suggested to me what seems almost a workable theory of the great problem of the origin of evil—though this, of course, is not Hartmann's own theory—namely, that there may be a consciousness, infinitely far off, at the other end of the chain of phenomena, always striving to express itself, and always baffled and blundering just as the spirits seem to be.' "[27]

But the ultimate source of this overemphasis on evil—for Hardy himself points out that the problem antedated Hartmann—is Gnosticism, which Charles Williams defines as follows: "They [the Gnostics] removed from that supreme Godhead of theirs any tendency to creation, especially any tendency to the creation of matter, and most especially any tendency to the creation of anything capable of 'evil.' They regarded creation in a Deity not so much as impossible as indecent. But they allowed to It certain emanations or supernatural outputtings and to those yet others, and to those yet others again, until they had imagined 'a long chain of divine creatures, each weaker than its parent,' and came at last 'to one, who while powerful enough to create is silly enough not to see that creation is wrong.' This was the God of this world."[28] This is also the God of Hardy, a non-omnipotent God who erred in creating the world. His lack of omnipotence and omniscience are adequately revealed by an investigation of six or seven appropriate poems.

God is a party to an imaginary conversation in "New Year's Eve" (1906).[29] The poem opens with God accounting for "his" stewardship over the expiring year:

---

27 *Real Conversations*, pp. 45-46.
28 *The Descent of the Dove*, p. 23.
29 In parentheses, after each poem of Hardy's appears the date of composition. The poems themselves are to be found in *The Collected Poems of Thomas Hardy*.

"I have finished another year," said God,
  "In grey, green, white, and brown;
I have strewn the leaf upon the sod,
Sealed up the worm within the clod,
  And let the last sun down."

In the second stanza, the "I" of the poem, the persona, criticizes
God for having created the world at all in as much as "nine-and-
ninety" reasons can be cited against the creation. A chorus in the
third stanza—another mouthpiece for the poet—also takes God to
task for the creation of the world, an exercise in futility, since the
world provides so little joy.

In the next two stanzas, God confesses a certain impotence: to
"logicless" labors and to having endowed mankind with a
teleological insight surpassing his own. And in the last stanza

He sank to raptness as of yore,
  And opening New Year's Day
Wove it by rote as theretofore,
And went on working evermore
  In his unweeting way.

notice God's ways are "unweeting," unwitting, which implies that
what "he" achieves, he achieves inadvertently. Needless to say this
is at variance with the orthodox concept of an all-knowing God
whose every deed perfectly reflects the divine intention.

The fragility of joy is a recurrent theme in Hardy's poems about
God. In the sestet of the sonnet "Hap" (1866), the poet expresses
a familiar lament:

. . . How arrives it joy lies slain,
And why unblooms the best hope ever sown?
—Crass Casualty obstructs the sun and rain,
And dicing Time for gladness casts a moan . . . .
These purblind Doomsters had as readily strown
Blisses about my pilgrimage as pain.

To "Crass Casualty" and the "purblind Doomsters," not God, is attributed the overwhelming presence of sorrow and pain in this bleak world. The implication that God is subject to these unconscious and unintelligent impulses in cosmic affairs explains the creator's inability to direct his work to any rational end in "New Year's Eve."

The top link in Hardy's "long chain of divine creatures" is Chance and Predestination, the "twin halves of one august event." The line occurs in "The Convergence of the Twain" (1914) and in context refers to the historic collision of an iceberg with the *Titanic*. But I use it here as an appropriate description for the two components jointly responsible for any important event. Coincidence and design, incompatibles for many people, are conceived as partners by Hardy for whom "Chance, as an idea, is a chameleon in its behaviour. Place it upon one twig of circumstance, and it will suggest an impact of blind fate; upon another, and it seems a junction of two determinate life-lines."[30] "Crass Casualty" and "purblind Doomsters" ("Hap"); the "Immanent Will" and the "Spinner of the Years" ("The Convergence of the Twain") are various synonyms for Chance and Predestination.

Of these terms, the most impressive is the Immanent Will. In certain respects, this concept has a little in common with some concepts of modern theoretical physics and with what the Vedanta philosophers call "Vaishvanara." Hardy's concept, however, was not only considerably less sophisticated, but it was curiously twisted. Whereas Vaishvanara is Consciousness conditioned by that mode which is the aggregate of the physical universe known to science, the sum total of its collectivities, its billions of atoms and quanta, Hardy's Immanent Will was a kind of blind unconscious. This, having produced God as an accidental and fortuitous by-product, is itself, in the process of infinite change and of becoming aware of itself. This hypothesis shows clearly the influences of the century which formed Hardy and the texts which shaped his thinking: the mechanism, the confidence in progress

---

30 Arthur McDowall, *Thomas Hardy: A Critical Study,* p. 30.

and in time as a one-directional flow, and—above all—what he had imperfectly absorbed from Darwin. It is the idea, extended and transposed, of development through the fortuitous mutant.

The idea of a Guiding Providence called God, so close to Hopkins' orthodox heart, is clearly rejected in Hardy's universe. God, the product and agent of the Immanent Will, is the penultimate link and like the ultimate link, undergoes a process of infinite change and of becoming aware of himself. How different is this debased immanence from Hopkins' concept of a God who is at once transcendent in Paradise and gloriously immanent on earth: transcendent in the sense of totally other; immanent in the sense of having created man in His own image and likeness. And how different is Hopkins' response to God's transcendence in the form of adoration, if not his response to God's immanence in the form of fraternal charity.

The so-called "Subalterns" are the third link in Hardy's chain of nonhuman beings. The Subalterns, in a poem of the same name composed in 1901, are four in number: "the leaden sky," "the North wind," "Sickness," and "Death." They possess no initative of their own, for they are merely junior officers in the service of the Immanent Will—and perhaps to a lesser degree responsible to God. They reluctantly do what they do, working without care for human creatures, for they may not stray from their appointed rounds. The leaden sky must depress the wanderer; the North wind must chill the "shorn" soul. The physiological agents fare no better; they too must obey "laws in force on high." Sickness and death have no alternative but to own "their passiveness" and attack their designated innocent victims. Throughout the poem, especially in the last stanza, nature, in the form of the four Subalterns, expresses compassion for man but pleads helplessness. Nature has sympathy with man and undoubtedly would treat him benevolently if allowed.

John Crowe Ransom, discussing "The Subalterns," draws attention to the theological configuration of the poem. "If we wish to bring Hardy's views as much as possible under some variant or other of orthodox Christian doctrine, he might seem to us here a sort of eighteenth century Deist; but the term does not occur in Hardy's usage . . . Nature as the complex of natural forces must appear to Hardy, as to any other naturalist, as the effective agent of evil when the Subalterns come to execute the laws . . . In other poems of Hardy's, Nature is personified as the general Mother, doing the best she can to bring her creatures to birth and care for them; that is only the extension of the spirit of the Subalterns, and of course it is a theologism to which a great many poets are given in one form or another."[31]

In relation to man, this view of nature is somewhat ambivalent: nature is usually involuntarily injurious, if occasionally maternally benign. But Hardy's view of nature in relation to God is thoroughly gloomy. The poem that sets forth this relationship most clearly is "Nature's Questioning" (1898). Here a number of natural forces, dawns, pools, fields, flocks, and trees, speak— although clearly Hardy is the ventriloquist—[32] and reflect on the purpose of their creation:

> "Has some Vast Imbecility,
>> Mighty to build and blend,
>> But impotent to tend,
> Framed us in jest, and left us now to hazardry?
>
> "Or come we of an Automaton
>> Unconscious of our pains? . . .
>> Or are we live remains
> Of Godhead dying downwards, brain and eye now gone?
>
> "Or is it that some high Plan betides,
>> As yet not understood,
>> Of Evil stormed by Good,
> We the Forlorn Hope over which Achievement strides?"
>> (Stanzas 4-6)

---

31 John Crowe Ransom (ed.), *Selected Poems of Thomas Hardy,* pp. xv-xvi.
32 Marsden, *op. cit.,* p. 96.

Far from the Hopkinsesque notion that God sometimes interposes in the execution of natural laws, Hardy would not allow that God is free to interpose even if he chose—perhaps he is a "Vast Imbecility . . . impotent to tend." Or Hardy theorizes that God and nature may illustrate evolution in reverse: nature is the devolution of the Godhead. Or again he theorizes that evil may not be a spinoff from good, as commonly thought, but the other way around.

Earlier in assessing Hardy's indebtedness to von Hartmann and the Gnostic heresies, I implied that his was a temperament close to Manichaeism, a position which these stanzas abundantly support. Less apparent, and so in need of comment however, is the fact that these same stanzas reveal Hardy to be far less Victorian in this matter than Hopkins. Tennyson, the Victorian poets' Victorian poet, traditionally depicted nature as conveying news about the power and majesty of God. An untitled lyric of just six lines is typical:

Flower in the crannied wall,
I pluck you out of the crannies,
I hold you here, root and all, in my hand,
Little flower—but *if* I could understand
What you are, root and all, and all in all,
I should know what God and man is.[33]

Nature is the vesture of God: in beholding a humble flower the poet is contemplating God's terrestrial manifestation, not worshiping God swallowed up in nature. Even to the Tennysonian disavowal of pantheism (see "The Higher Pantheism"), this outlook is shared by Hopkins. For Hopkins, nature conveys the joyful news that the world is charged with the grandeur of God; for Hardy, nature conveys the abject news that the world is rotten with the remains of the dying Godhead.

Hardy was a precursor of the popular death of God pheno-

---

33 *The Complete Poetical Works of Tennyson*, p. 274.

menon which created so much consternation in orthodox theological circles a short time ago. This "should be considered by anyone who feels inclined to write off Hardy's views as Victorian relics. The problem of how Man is to behave in a Universe which seems to have no values other than those Man can create himself is hardly a dead issue . . . Man ought to devote himself to the doing of good deeds."[34] To the extent he allowed God is alive at all, Hardy asserts that God is immanent in man: God is to be found only in involvement with other people. The opposed notion championed by Hopkins that God can be found directly in Himself through prayer and contemplation was alien to the naturalistic Hardy, as was Hopkins' corollary: the immanence of God depends upon His transcendence.

In his zeal to show that nature is cut off from God, Hardy has multiple aspects of nature reflect in ventriloquistic fashion on the possibility that they came

> . . . Of an Automaton
> Unconscious of our pains . . .
> > ("Nature's Questioning," Stanza 5).

The charge is made again and again. The most overt statement occurs in "Hap" where God is said to be utterly indifferent to human suffering:

> If but some vengeful god would call to me
> From up the sky, and laugh: "Thou suffering thing,
> Know that thy sorrow is my ecstasy,
> That thy love's loss is my hate's profiting!"
>
> Then would I bear it, clench myself, and die,
> Steeled by the sense of ire unmerited;
> Half-eased in that a Powerfuller than I
> Had willed and meted me the tears I shed.

---

34 Marsden, *op. cit.*, p. 235.

But not so . . .

So galling is this alleged divine indifference that Hardy tells us he
would experience relief even if he were to discover what is
patently not so: heaven is guilty of sadism. His neo-Manichaean
side manifests itself again in the fascination-fear that some god
would will pain and mete it out.

Hardy misses two tenets essential to the Christian concept.
There is potential merit in human suffering. God permits it, but
He does not cause suffering. Hopkins embodies both tenets in his
poetry. For example in "The *Deutschland*," he shows at length
how the tall nun is ennobled by agony: how Christ manifests
Himself more intensely to her in the midst of "wind's burly and
beat of endragoned seas" (stanza 27) than if she were at rest from
the "wild-worst" (stanza 24) of nature. Her salvation is assured by
the heroic response she makes to the suffering she has undergone.
Christ "cure[s] the extremity" (stanza 28) into which He has
allowed her to be cast. In the divine plan, evil is tolerated that
good may be wrested from it.

Hardy comprehends this not at all. The pain produced by
ongoing evil in the world seems so useless, of profit to no one—a
charge he makes perfectly clear in the afore quoted octave of the
sonnet, "Hap." Closely related to this is his recurring obsession
with man's impotence to overcome evil and change things for the
better. The fantastic situation dramatized in "Channel Firing," a
parable-poem written two months before World War I, provides an
instance of this. The practice firing of battleships at night in the
English channel disturbs the sleep of the dead in a churchyard
cemetery near the coast. The dead, thinking it is "the Judgment-
day" sit upright in their coffins:

> . . . Till God called, "No;
> It's gunnery practice out at sea
> Just as before you went below;
> The world is as it used to be:
> "All nations striving strong to make
> Red war yet redder. Mad as hatters

They do no more for Christ's sake
Than you who are helpless in such matters.

"That this is not the judgment-hour
For some of them's a blessed thing,
For if it were they'd have to scour
Hell's floor for so much threatening . . .

"Ha, ha. It will be warmer when
I blow the trumpet (if indeed
I ever do; for you are men,
And rest eternal sorely need)."

(Stanzas 3-6)

Ransom's commentary on this fatalistic and somewhat ironical view of the persistence of evil is illuminating. "The deity here is particularly obliging in Hardy's free and easy version of the orthodox Christian God. He reassures them, and after some menacing asides against the bellicose sinners he suggests that he may even reconsider his scheme of a universal resurrection, which will be too painful for the good ghosts to bear. He may just let things go on as usual. His part in the poem reminds us of many Old Testament stories in which the Lord spoke to the faithful about his grand designs and complained of the incorrigible sinners who perverted them." In three closing stanzas, the ghosts react to God's words with resignation. "And the guns resume, with a roar which reaches even to the ancient shrines of the region. The poem ends, and the poet-theologian has not found his triumphant theology which will overthrow the powers of evil."[35] Here, may I add, is another instance of Hardy's anticipation of modernity. He is anti-war, but he is decidedly dubious of man's ability to abolish war.

Despite his repeated naturalistic theologizing, a residual orthodoxy reemerges in that tender but untypical lyric, "The

35 Ransom, *op. cit.,* p. xii.

Oxen," written to celebrate Christmas Eve, 1915. It is a deeply felt tribute to the power of the Christian legend:

Christmas Eve, and twelve of the clock.
    "Now they are all on their knees,"[36]
And elder said as we sat in a flock
    By the embers in hearthside ease.

We pictured the meek mild creatures where
    They dwelt in their strawy pen,
Nor did it occur to one of us there
    To doubt they were kneeling then.

So fair a fancy few would weave
    In these years! Yet, I feel,
If someone said on Christmas Eve,
    "Come; see the oxen kneel,

In the lonely barton by yonder coomb
    Our childhood used to know,"
I should go with him in the gloom,
    Hoping it might be so.

The desire for the legend to be true is explicit and pathetic. For as Babette Deutsch observes: "Here the simplicity of the language, even to the use of such old words as 'barton' for farmyard and 'coomb' for upland valley, the subdued tone, and the quiet verbal music help to create the endearing homeliness and half-shadowy radiance of some medieval Nativity."[37]

---

36 The elder is referring to a folk belief that as the ox fell on its knees in Bethlehem when Christ was born, so oxen ever since fall on their knees at midnight Christmas Eve. Hardy had ridiculed the belief in *Tess of the D'Urbervilles* (1891), chap. 17, with his story of William Dewy making the bull kneel by fiddling the Nativity hymn; yet he had Angel Clare remark, "It's a curious story. It carries us back to medieval times, when faith was a living thing."

37 *Poetry in Our Time,* p. 12.

"The Oxen," however, is more than a superstition viewed wistfully. It is a poem which regards "nostalgically the simple secure past, untroubled by thought and spiritual difficulties."[38] This implies a simplistic dichotomy in Hardy's theologizing: either you are a naive believing supernaturalist oversimplifying, through ignorance or intellectual dishonesty, the difficulties that beset modern belief; or you are a hardheaded skeptical naturalist who, having sincerely pondered God, accepts the grim truth of the situation. Needless to say, the example of Hopkins strenuously repudiates this dichotomy. Nurtured by the self-same Darwinian crisis, as we have seen, Hopkins hammered out his orthodoxy over the opposition of a thousand difficulties, a thousand difficulties that stopped short of a doubt. While there is no reason to suppose that his intellectual honesty was any less than Hardy's, there is every reason to suppose that his theological subtlety, Jesuit-crafted, was the greater. Still this was no barrier to the acquisition of an uncynical, mostly optimistic, yet profound, faith in God.

"In embracing Catholicism," as Keating points out, "Hopkins definitely rejected such images of God as are suggested by even a few random phrases from Victorian literature—'the stream of tendency by which all things fulfill the law of their being,' 'the President of the Immortals,' 'the grand Perhaps.' Still, within the framework of Catholic dogma, there was the possibility of speculation and questioning, even of trials of faith. And the faith which is victorious in the *Deutschland* is not of the sort that eradicates difficulties, but of the sort that lives in the face of them." Keating then rightly likens the faith of Hopkins to that of Cardinal Newman. After Hopkins' "acceptance of Catholicism, he apparently never experienced even the onset of a change in outlook such as that which led his fellow-converts Challis and Addis out of the Church. Yet as a young man, he had, like Newman, been exposed to and attracted by religious liberalism;

---

38 Marsden, *op. cit.*, p. 76.

and though he turned away from it, he remained conscious of the problems which it raises."[39]

* * *

In conclusion, I wish to declare a preference and indicate the influence these two overviews of God have had on poets who have been contemporaneous with or come after Hopkins and Hardy. The quality of the versification is foremost in passing a judgment with the theological content, if any, usually a minor criterion. But here where the craftsmanship is roughly even, the theological content—particularly because it bulks so big in both poets— becomes a major consideration. On that count, the nod must be awarded to Hopkins. I opt for him—not because I happen to be of the same religious persuasion—in keeping with T.S. Eliot's dictum that when ideas inform a poem it is not necessary for the reader to share the poet's ideas, it is merely necessary that the ideas be intellectually respectable. [40] Orthodox Catholicism is so accepted world-wide. Granted that this is now also the case with "Hardy's doubt as to the existence, identity and power of the Ruler of the Universe."[41] It is scarcely so when his "crude home-made mythologies"[42] prevail, as they so often do. I repeat the *Weltanschauung* is only important when the craftsmanship of one poet or the other is not clearly superior. For example, if the comparison were Yeats and Hopkins, instead of Hardy and Hopkins, then the inferior stature of the private eclectic religion Yeats infuses into his poetry would matter very little.

Be that as it may, Hardy's theological point of view has been widely embraced by other poets, like himself, lusting after strange gods. A.E. Housman, E.A. Robinson, Robinson Jeffers, and even Robert Frost have cultivated a similar skepticism, pessimism, and

---

39 Keating, *op. cit.*, p. 18.
40 *Selected Essays*, p. 230.
41 Marsden, *op. cit.*, p. 51.
42 *Ibid.*, p. 42.

mood of pagan melancholy. The Asiatic mystery-mongering of W.B. Yeats and Ezra Pound may owe something to Hardy. And Hardy's agnostic speculations on man's bewilderment and despair, the adequacy of the physical and material world could well have strengthened the comparable position of Wallace Stevens. If I seem to flinch from asserting any direct influence, it is only because I am aware of major differences—especially with the last three who, unlike Hardy, were delicate stylists much concerned with a sort of "absolute" poetry, dependent upon tone rather than passion. But estheticism aside, what all the foregoing share with Hardy is a purely naturalistic view of God.

The orthodox progeny of Hopkins is both less notable and less numerous. With the exception of T.S. Eliot, Hopkins' sacramental view of God has been bequeathed to minor poets. It has been left to Thomas Merton, Daniel Berrigan, and Brother Antoninus to court the familiar God of the New Testament.

A SELECT BIBLIOGRAPHY

1. Main Works

Collected Poems of Thomas Hardy. New York: The Macmillan Company, 1961.

Selected Poems of Thomas Hardy. Ed. by John Crowe Ransom. New York: The Macmillan Company, 1960.

The Poems of Gerard Manley Hopkins. Ed. by W.H. Gardner. Fourth edition. London: Oxford University Press, 1970.

The Correspondence of Gerard Manley Hopkins and Richard Watson Dixon. Ed. by Claude Colleer Abbott. London: Oxford University Press, 1935.

The Journals and Papers of Gerard Manley Hopkins. Ed. by Humphry House. London: Oxford University Press, 1959.

2. Secondary Works

Archer, William, *Real Conversations*. London: G. Allen & Unwin, 1904.

Boyle, Robert, *Metaphor in Hopkins*. Chapel Hill: University of North Carolina Press, 1960.

Deutsch, Babette, *Poetry in Our Time*. New York: Doubleday, 1963.

Downes, David, *Gerard Manley Hopkins: A Study of His Ignatian Spirit*. London: Vision Press, 1960.

Eliot, T.S., *Selected Essays*. New York: Harcourt, Brace & Company, 1932.

Gardner, W.H., *Gerard Manley Hopkins: A Study of Poetic Idiosyncrasy in Relation to Poetic Tradition*. 2 vols. New Haven: Yale University Press, 1948.

Heuser, Alan, *The Shaping Vision of Gerard Manley Hopkins*. London: Oxford University Press, 1958.

Hopper, Stanley, *Spiritual Problems in Contemporary Literature*. New York: Harper & Row, 1957.

Joselyn, Sister M., "Herbert and Hopkins," *Renascence*, X, 4 (Summer, 1958), 192-195.

Keating, John E., *The Wreck of the Deutschland: an Essay and Commentary*. Ohio: Kent State University Press, 1963.

Marsden, Kenneth, *The Poems of Thomas Hardy: A Critical Introduction*. New York: Oxford University Press, 1969.

McDonnell, Thomas, "Hopkins as a Sacramental Poet," *Renascence*, XIV, 1 (Autumn, 1961), 25-33.

McDowall, Arthur, *Thomas Hardy: A Critical Study*. New York: Books for Libraries Press, 1931.

Tennyson, Alfred, *The Complete Poetical Works of Tennyson*. Boston: Houghton Mifflin, 1898.

Williams, Charles, *The Descent of the Dove*. New York: Meridian Books, 1956.

Wright, Brooks, *The Explicator Cyclopedia*. 3 vols. Chicago: Quadrangle Books, 1966.

Psychology

CHAPTER XXXIV

GOD AND DEPTH PSYCHOLOGY

*Ann Belford Ulanov**

Depth psychology must in the future be considerably involved with the transcendent. I use the word "transcendent" to encompass both analysts and patients who specifically focus on God and the life of the Spirit, and those who reject the notion and experience of a personal god but see the necessity of dealing with values directly. Both groups have strong convictions about the need to find and define a transcendent meaning for themselves and its role in the recovery and maintenace of health. Hope is based on one's experience of the transcendent—hope which consoles and permits one to survive the kind of terrible rears and unseen pressures that attack the mentally ill. On a sense of the transcendent participating in one's own life is based the vision of getting "weller than well," as Menninger puts it, of shunning a mere adjustment to the *status quo ante* as too meager for the life of a whole person.[1] From such an experience of the transcendent grows a value system that gives one a reason for living, Pascal's reason of the heart, for the sake of which one will persevere when all else—good feeling, firm resolve, self-interest—has fallen away.

Every analysis, directly or indirectly, touches on transcendence. Indeed one can correlate the specific presenting symptomatology of a patient with basic life-attitudes and visions of reality, so much so that the attitudes and visions come to be necessary information for accurate diagnosis. The main difficulty is that anyone's secret vision of reality and its value associations is first of all hard to verbalize and second of all often the last confidence a patient will

*Professor of Psychiatry and Religion at Union Theological Seminary, New York, U.S.A.
1   Karl Menninger, *The Vital Balance* (New York, 1963), p. 406.

entrust to an analyst. We are dealing here with the ineffable, the unspeakable, with what lends itself to direct communication only with the utmost difficulty.

We are dealing here with the primitive sides of a person, with his primary experience of religion, not with what he may have been taught in school or church or synagogue, but with the unknown as it has somehow touched his life and his person. Thus the confession of this experience—and it can only be that, a declaration, an avowal of an extraordinary experience that he lived through—proves the basis of his deepest apperception of reality, both as it reveals itself to him and as it reveals him for what he is. There is no sophisticated talk to hide behind. There is no grand doctrine to adhere to. There is only mystery as he has known it and as it has known him. Most patients, most people, feel a keen sense of shame in such confessions. As Helen Lynd's excellent book *On Shame and the Search for Identity* makes clear, shame overcomes us today much as it did those eloquent figures in the Old Testament; we feel bared, exposed, completely seen by the other, and yet altogether unready for such self-revelation.[2] We feel so overtaken by awe in the face of some revelation from "the other side" that we cover our faces or fall to the ground. We are further confounded by an awareness that piercing as this primary religious experience may be to us, it is a great distance from the grand reaches of dogma handed down to us through tradition. We feel convinced of our smallness. How can we compare our raw experiences of god as a threatening spider, or god as a numinous pig, to take two examples from patients, to the large, majestic visions of God as vibrant love related to others and to himself in the mysteries of the Trinity?

The temptations of psychoanalysis, as Freud so ably demonstrates in his "interpretation of suspicion," to use Paul Ricoeur's phrase for it, is to trace these powerful visions to their source in

2   See Helen M. Lynd, *On Shame and the Search for Identity* (London, 1958).

undigested personal problems involving sex and aggression.[3] Freud's analysis of religion is masterful, exposing to the light of consciousness our fear of consciousness, our shrinking away from the need to give up infantile retreats and childish pleasures. We insist, Freud shows, on fatherly protection from the harshness of reality; we need to compensate for our suffering in this life through the promise of bliss in an after life; we need to be guarded against the rampant energies of unchecked sexual and aggressive drives in order to preserve human society, and thus we renounce our lust for vengeance and give it up to the Lord. Theodore Reik applies Freud's analysis to the Eucharist, pointing out that in that sacrament we preserve an ancient ritual of aggression through incorporation: we are what we eat. In eating the host in the Eucharist, we reenact both the primitive tribal crime of the sons' incorporation of the father's power, through murder and cannibalism, and act out our own present wish, however unconscious, to supplant those in authority over us. We usurp the power and privilege of all our "fathers"—parent, teacher, employer, government official, religious leader—by ingesting the symbol of the son and identifying with him, in effect against the father. The Father-centered religion of the patriarchs is replaced by the religion of the Son and all those who believe in Him. Thus the religion of peace, Reik argues, provides for secret release of murderous impulses against the father.[4]

But when we have said all this what have we said? Freud helps us scour away the dross of our religious experience; he purifies it of its self-interested hiding-places. But what does he put in place of it when he declares there is no future to this "illusion?" He offers instead his own illusion, of a future pulsating with faith in his science of psychoanalysis. That alone, he proclaims, leads to

---

3 Paul Ricoeur, *Freud and Philosophy: An Essay on Interpretation,* translated by Denis Savage (New Haven, 1970), p. 32.

For pertinent works of Freud on religion, see *The Future of an Illusion,* translated by W.D. Robson-Scott (London, 1949); *Totem and Taboo,* translated by James Strachey (New York, 1950); *Moses and Monotheism,* translated by Katerine Jones (New York, 1962); *Civilization and Its Discontents,* translated by Joan Riviere (London, 1955).

4 See Theodore Reik, *Myth and Guilt* (New York, 1957).

reality as it is; that alone rescues people from falsehood and illness, leaving them free "to love and to work." A later follower, Melaine Klein, even prophesied a coming utopia—a secular *eschaton*—based on an application of Freud's truths to primary education. She promises a new generation, untouched by the sicknesses and sins of the fathers.

We may ask if our religious experiences can ever be free from our childish wishes or should be. We may wonder if these wishes are not our connecting links to the life embedded in our bodies—to our instincts, needs, and desires—our true life in the flesh. For are not wishes the instinctive foundation of what becomes the consolation of hope? Wishes are fresh, insistent, energetic, exciting us to act. Hope is a dull, pedantic holding-on if it lacks the freshness of the driving wish. And the wish that fails to connect with the steady seriousness of hope falls and dies without igniting any lasting zeal. Wishes and hope feed each other, live upon each other.

Freud clarifies, even purifies, our understanding of the mixtures of wish and hope, health and neurosis, infantilism and maturity, but in the last analysis offers only a substitute faith of his own that, with unconscious humor, fulfills his own theory of the oedipal complex. His young science of psychoanalysis presumes to slay the father-centered religion of Moses and the patriarchs, exposing its illusory promises, focusing on its fundamental oedipal drama. Thus Freud, the son, fathers a new religion in psychoanalysis, and hands down new laws—the pleasure and reality principles, latent and manifest contents, resistance and transference, and the life-long struggle against each other of the instincts of eros and death. No, we must go back again to our primary religious experience where God has sought us and see how clearly it informs our health and our sickness.

Our religious orientation to transcendence, however young, undeveloped, barely beyond the sense of self, nonetheless patterns the flow of psychic energy and is intrinsically related even to symptoms of neurotic disorder. Images of life's religious meaning configure both the childish source of neurosis and the direction in which healing can be found.[5]

One such attempt to envision the nature of reality is R.D. Laing's notion of the void, which functions in his system much as a kind of transcendence. The void underlies all other existents; it dwells at the core of being and overarches all behavior and experience. For Laing, as for so many patients, "the dreadful has already happened":[6] we are all alienated from our true experience and thus cut off from genuine interiority. "Experience" for Laing parallels the notion of soul in religious thought; it is the center of the person, his means of connecting to the essence of life. Because we are cut off from our experience, Laing reasons, our behavior no longer reflects who we truly are, but rather divorces us from ourselves in a masquerade of "normal" and "related" human exchanges. Instead of connecting with each other, we invalidate all our experience through what Laing calls a process of mystification. We urge on each other adaptation to a sick world by falsifying each other's experience. For example, we maneuver others so that they will not remind us of what we want to forget:

5   I say this not only out of knowledge of the literature of depth psychology, but also out of that speculative knowledge that comes to any working psychoanalyst from his or her own patients. Some very brief examples may serve as illustrations. A young woman suffering from anorexa nervosa confided her vision of the essential coherence of reality, a coherence portrayed by the elemental connectedness of physical life. This vision compensated for the splitting of her own experience of her body and psyche. In her vision she saw herself lying in the sun on a beach, "held in an encircling completeness of sand touching water and the water touching the sky." Thus all the elements—fire (in the sun's rays), earth, water, and air—surrounded and encompassed her own small reality. She felt "a liberation from complication and burden, able to deal with my problems because I am connected in my own body, just as the sky, earth, and water are connected around me."

Another patient, a married woman in her forties, mother of three children, created a sand-box scene of her image of the nature of reality. In the middle of the sand-box she placed a large rock, next to it a smaller rock and a piece of driftwood. Around this grouping of rock and wood there was only sand; nothing else, no human figures, no animals, not even any insect life or creatures from the sea. In her own life this woman produced desolation by alienating her family and friends. Yet the sand-box scene also hinted at a way out of this wasteland: see it, look at it, accept that you feel this way and that you see loneliness afflicting every person. She did, in fact, break out of her self-imposed prison, moving toward people who felt equally alientated from human contact. With remarkable generosity of spirit, she brought the simple warmth of her presence to a dying friend, to a child afflicted by a terminal disease, to a neighbor whose son had died in a car accident. She perceived that these people also suffered from a sense of desolation, and that forged a link between them and herself.

6   R.D. Laing, *The Politics of Experience* (London, 1967), p. 12.

we challenge their recollection of a shared experience by insisting the event really did not happen the way they remember it—"that's just your imagination" (as if imagination were nothing but delusion). We invalidate the content of others' thought, labeling it "mere propaganda, political distortion." We invalidate their capacity to remember by calling them "prejudiced" and "subjective." We invalidate their intentions by attempting to instill guilt: "Good people don't do that."

For Laing, such mystification is a means of destroying experience. The only hope of salvation from this sickness, this exchange of violences under the name of loving concern, is a breakdown of the whole system. Laing reminds us that we live in a secular world; and to adapt to it (quoting Mallarme) "L'enfant abdique son extase." The presence of God is segregated from objective facts and we must blast through this separating wall, even at the risk of madness.[7]

Although Laing claims a break*down* may be a break*through* to some experience of the transcendent that will then grant us a sense of "ontological security," his vision of the transcendent itself remains a formless void.[8] We may discard our alienated state, shed our complicated subterfuge, and burst through "outer reality" to enter the world of inner space, but what do we find when we get there? What guidance does Laing offer? Very little, I am afraid, though he does put forth some excellent suggestions for the creation of communities of former patients to sustain those in therapy in their attempt to recover the connections between their inner experience and their outer behavior. Though Laing underscores the necessity in the quest for sanity of the experience of the transcendent, he tells us little of what we might find in that experience or how to integrate it in our day-to-day existence.

Laing overemphasizes, I believe, the dissolution of the normal ego in order to extricate it from a false reality. He leaves out our need for human contact. His is a lonely journey into an impersonal

7 *Ibid.*, p. 118.
8 R.D. Laing, *The Divided Self* (Baltimore, 1965), p. 39.

void. For unfortunately, he seems to have overlooked the *fact* of schizoid experience—that experience where one feels devoid of a core at the center of one's being. That ego weakness and subsequent masquerade of personality—akin to D.W. Winnicott's "false self" and Karen Horney's "idealized self"—are surely not simply products of a corrupt society, as Laing maintains, but rather must result from a failure in the the mothering process and a lack of mutuality in the earliest processes of maturation—human limitations which may occur in any form of society. The "mothering one"—in Harry Stack Sullivan's words—fails to reflect back to the infant a sense of its own person, and thus the "I am" experience never jells.[9] Without this immediate sense of being a person (a sense that is written large in the Old Testament scholars' translation of Yahweh as I AM THAT I AM), there can be no ontological security. Such unintegreation of self grows into disintegration of self; such lack of relation of one's psyche and one's soma grows into depersonalization. The center of gravity of consciousness transfers from the kernel of a person to the shell; individuality, instead of residing in oneself, turns into a technique. One lives, as Winnicott says, an "as if" existence: encased in a false shell, one behaves only *as if* one were a real person.

Winnicott suggests a different route to the transcendent in his analysis of creativity.[10] He sees creativity as a way of putting oneself into the world, not as a way of producing creations. This way one experiences both self and reality. Creativity is nurtured by the playing which occurs in the intermediate space between a mother and child, that space of paradox where the child is purposively nonpurposive in its activities, where the mother is present but not intrusive. She makes environmental provision for trusting acceptance of her child's unrelated thought-sequences. In this intimate space, the mother reflects back the summation and

9 The references are to D.W. Winnicott, *Collected Papers: Through Paediatrics to Psycho-analysis* (London, 1958); Karen Horney, *Neurosis and Human Growth* (New York, 1950); Harry Stack Sullivan, *Interpersonal Theory of Psychiatry* (New York, 1968).

10 See D.W. Winnicott, *Playing and Reality* (London, 1971), Chapters III and IV.

reverberation of these experiences and that reflection together with her response provides the basis on which her child's individuality can come together and exist as a unit. The child becomes a discrete being, an expression of "I AM, I am alive, I am myself . . . "[11]

Through such a grasp of an "I am" experience, a person feels his being mingled with Being itself. A loss of self brings with it a loss of God. In both, the realities of value, presence, and goodness are just there, without utilitarian purpose. They are there simply because they *are*. They do not need to be justified by products which they may produce. Similarly, a person cannot and need not be justified either. His sense of self comes down to a sense of creative being, not a measuring of his self in terms of created things. Winnicott reports one of his patients as saying "People use God like an analyst—someone to be there while you're playing.[12]

What begins to take shape in Winnicott's thought as a sense of the transcendent as a life lived creatively and imbued with value, is carried further in the thought of Edith Weigert, a psychoanalyst with existentialist associations. The goal of psychotherapy is creativity, she asserts.[13] The therapist sees his patients as people with their own restrictions and distorted adaptations, and envisions their future development of their full potential. Empathy between patient and therapist is not enough to meet this task; the therapist must inspire the patient to imagine his own creative goal of self-actualization, to put into play his own capacities to integrate traditional ideals and his own new and chosen commitments.

Weigert sees the road to health as a progression toward an autonomous morality in which a person comes to accept his destiny, endures his inevitable suffering and anxieties "with the trust in resources that transcend past and present conflicts, beyond the pleasure and pain in the direction toward a creative

11 *Ibid.*, p. 56.
12 *Ibid.*, p. 62.
13 See Edith Weigert, "The Goal of Creativity in Psychotherapy," *The Courage to Love* (New Haven, 1970).

integration."[14] She evokes in her psychotherapeutic concerns the same sense of transcendent being that Heidegger probes in his philosophic writings. Man must not flee or flinch from his being as it is "thrown" into the world. Knowing he will die, man must dare to care for his world and for others, forging his life through "authentic" choices. Only by exercising his intentionality can man rise to his true destiny as a "shepherd of being," as Heidegger puts it, now not a victim, but an active guardian of his own existence.[15]

These words call to mind those of Victor Frankl in *The Doctor and the Soul,* where he emphasizes the three levels of value through which man can choose to activate meaning in his life.[16] The first level consists of those values that can be actualized by doing something, by creating; the second level is made up of those values that accrue to us when we consent to experience something, when we live an experience through to its completion. The third level of value depends on what attitude we adopt when faced with unavoidable suffering. Even when confronted with something unalterable, we are still able to choose how we will react and how we will make it part of ourselves. Thus human life can be fulfilled not only in creating and enjoying, but also in suffering. Frankl calls this urge to find value even in suffering man's "will-to-meaning." It is a drive toward spiritual development, toward consciousness of reality, and toward a clear and significant relationship with it. If left unfulfilled this will-to-meaning produces a peculiar kind of neurosis, characterized by loss of meaning and even rudimentary interest in being alive. One falls into an "existential vacuum."[17]

C.G. Jung carries this notion even further in his discussion of what is for him the psyche's religious function. This is an autonomous drive toward relation of the "personal ego," the center of consciousness, to a larger center of the whole psyche,

---

14 *Ibid.,* p. 107.
15 *Ibid.,* p. 84.
16 See Victor Frankl, *The Doctor and the Soul* (New York, 1965).
17 See Victor Frankl, *Psychotherapy and Existentialism* (New York, 1968).

conscious and unconscious, that Jung calls the "Self." The Self
transcends but does not abrogate the more personal concerns of
the ego. Indeed Jung produces evidence that there seems to be a
motion from the side of the Self toward an open relationship of
ego to Self. Many images thrown up to consciousness when the
Self is "constellated" are God-images, that is numinous symbols
that act to reconcile the opposing factions within the psyche and
evoke from the person experiencing them responses of awe, fear,
reverence, and attentive devotion. Jung does not equate these
images with God as He is in Himself, but nevertheless concludes
that such images and the responses they evoke are clear evidence
of the psyche's experience of what theologians call God. Indeed,
writes Jung, man has "the dignity of a creature endowed with, and
conscious of a relationship to Deity. The soul must contain in
itself the faculty of relation to God."[18]

A person's experience of this religious function feels like an
inner, autonomous urge driving one to complete oneself, to
enlarge consciousness, to take account of unconscious images,
symbols, and "purposes." In fact, one often feels summoned, even
compelled toward the slow and arduous work of building up a
whole and genuinely individual self that includes one's personal
concerns but is no longer centered upon those concerns. Jung
draws parallels between this kind of individual experience and
ancient religious notions of vocation.[19] Like Abraham, one is
called from the familiar homeland to follow the voice of God
wherever it may lead. One is called away from childish identi-
fications with lusts for power and self-gratification. One is
summoned to differentiate oneself from identification with
collective conventions, from family tradition, and stereotyped
roles. One is called by an inner "voice"—a voice that may even
conflict with a traditional superego conscience—to become an

18 C.G. Jung, *Psychology and Alchemy, Collected Works,* Vol. XII (New York,
1967, p. 10. See also "The Relations Between Ego and the Unconscious," *Two Essays on
Analytical Psychology, Collected Works,* Vol. VII (New York, 1966).

19 See "The Development of the Personality," in C.G. Jung, *The Development of the
Personality, Collected Works,* Vol. XVII (New York, 1954).

individual, a unique being who knows both the good and bad in himself. One learns that one can find oneself only by looking beyond ego perspectives to a larger center of being that commands both allegiance and devotion. Many people, Jung contends, fall into neurosis because they either ignore this kind of summons or run away from it. One really has only two choices—willingly to respond to one's destiny, or unwillingly to be dragged there through neurosis or psychosis. For Jung, the suffering that neurosis brings is the price one pays for refusing to suffer legitimately. And such suffering is never really cured until the patient recovers a religious orientation to reality.[20]

Jung calls the journey to the Self the process of individuation. It must not be confused with a simple individualism, for individuation is based on a detailed seeing, seeing, beyond the ego's needs and wishes, seeing how relative needs and wishes are in the larger psychic universe. One develops an active, conversant relationship to the whole psyche and to its unconscious dimension, recognizing the psyche as an objective fact, not as a mere personal possession.[21] To see this objective psyche working within the bounds of one's particular being is to be made aware of the forces of Being itself, working through one's personal life, trying in some way to realize themselves in the textures and fabric of a personal existence. One also comes to see that others have the same kind of inner life. This forges a bond between oneself and others; indeed one often discovers for the first time the otherness of the psyche in meetings and encounters with specific "other" persons. One then gradually discerns, through all the events of one's life, a theme that gathers everything one is and has been into a story, one's *own* story, one's *own* myth, lived *sub specie aeternitatis*. In such a way does general life become repersonalized and a particular life becomes remythologized. Worn-out symbols

---

[20] C.G. Jung, *Modern Man in Search of a Soul,* translated by W.S. Dell and C.F. Baynes (New York, 1933), p. 225.

[21] See C.G. Jung, "Conscious, Unconscious, and Individuation," and "A Study in the Process of Individuation," in *The Archetypes and the Collective Unconscious, Collected Works,* Vol. IX:I (New York, 1959).

revive when correlated to the raw stuff of personal experience. Religious injunctions take on compelling fascination as they are now seen, in their connection to day-to-day life.

One example of the many Jung offers to illustrate the process of individuation is a retelling of the parable of the sheep and the goats.[22] Christ welcomes the elect into heaven because they visited him when he was sick, clothed him when he was naked, gave him food and drink when he was hungry and thirsty, and came to succor him when he was in prison. When the elect ask in surprise when it was in fact that they performed such services for him, Jesus answers that insofar as they did this to "the least of the brethren" they did it for him. Jung then asks, but what if we ourselves are the least of the brethren? What if we scorn some part of ourselves as the very lowest portion of humanity? This inner neglected neighbor, a composite of all that we despise in ourselves, is also the place where Christ meets us. We need then to show special kindness to this rejected side of our own psyche. Moreover, by compassionating this side of our own psyche, a side that presents itself to us as a real "other," we also feed compassion into the world of other persons. What Augustine put so succinctly—*non quod dabet quod non habet*, one cannot give what one does not have—Jung documents empirically through the observation of psychic behavior. We cannot give genuine compassion to others if we fail to feel it and give it also to ourselves.

Jung himself understands his approach to depth psychology as performing a function for Christianity. It may help men see the connection between the sacred truths and their own psyches.[23] We do not then need new religious truths but rather to reconnect to the old ones, in order to rediscover them and find in them unguessed depths. To do this we must go down into the darkness of psychic experience, into the places of sickness and hurt to all that is despised and rejected of men. We must go inward in a way that is also a going outward. Because the psyche is objective, it

---

22 C.G. Jung, *Modern Man in Search of a Soul,* pp. 235-36.
23 C.G. Jung, *Psychology and Alchemy,* p. 13.

does not live within us any more than it does outside us. It *is*, much like Heidegger's notion of transcendent being, much like Winnicott's sense of value as an appreciation of what exists. It is not a product or a producer of products. Thus attention to the depths of the psyche draws us into the open outside world as much as it draws us down into the darkness of personal experience. It pulls us toward other people and involvement in their lives as much as it withdraws us from them into pondering the images of a dream or the fantasies that rise from meditation.

Through attention to the psyche as someting objective, Jung shows us a way through and beyond the divisions of thought into categories of subjective and objective, inner and outer experience, "us and them," good and evil. The psyche encompasses all these opposites because it is only through the experiences of the psyche that we apprehend anything at all. For the psyche mirrors in its own life all the divisions and oppositions that we meet in life. Then, by working on the reconciliation of those oppositions, through conscious adaptation of some symbols that emerge from our own individual experience of the unconscious and others that arise from the collective unconscious in the traditional terms of religion, literature, art, and science, we may be brought in touch with the collective neuroses of our time and discover in them hidden impulses toward growth and fulfillment of being.

One particular area in which Jung's approach is especially helpful is that area of primary religious experience with which we began this essay. For Jung, it is precisely through the receiving and meditating upon these raw primitive apprehensions of being, these religious moments that come to all of us when we are suddenly stunned by a new insight, overcome by the gift of someone's love, or thrown into fear by a nightmare, that we may find living connection with the traditions of dogma and symbol contained in organized religion. This kind of rough experience of the touch of God—or at least what feels to each of us as something grand enough, fearsome enough, powerful and awesome enough to be called God—is amplified through contact with the history of religious experience and imagery. Gradually we may then build a bridge from our private, personal, religious moments to the grander reaches of tradition through which God has made himself known. This experience is burningly alive; its vitality can feed the great traditions of religious symbolism, kindling them anew so that they in turn may shed light on our own dark perceivings. The narrowness of our personal experience is thus stretched and deepened through its connection with all the recorded human experience of God.

What Jung has probed so deeply in his own researches—the psychological side of religious experience—is mirrored in a number of outward, collective developments of our time. More and more psychoanalytical work moves across the boundaries of the disciplines. Erik Erikson applies the methods of ego psychology to such historical figures as Luther and Gandhi to create psycho-historical biographies that probe the effects of these individuals on their times.[24] Others like Geza Roheim and R.J. Lifton have applied the techniques and perceptions of history, sociology, and anthropology to psychological themes, Roheim with particular distinction.[25]

The most important interdisciplinary group to emerge in recent years is, I think, that of Pastoral Counseling. Those who follow its procedures receive both thorough theological training and training in the theories and clinical practice of psychotherapy. They are thus equipped both to deal with the immediate problems of psychological stress and to bring to bear on their patients' and parishioners' lives a concern with value and meaning that transcends past and present conflicts, providing a basis for hope and a willingness to shed the secondary gains of neurotic patterns. Pastoral Counselors recognize and are equipped to deal with the central importance of those primitive religious moments that, in Jung's terms, are often the times when individuals feel directly

24 See Erik Erikson, *Young Man Luther: A Study in Psychoanalysis and History* (New York, 1958), and *Gandhi's Truth: On the Origins of Militant Nonviolence* (New York, 1969).

25 See Geza Roheim, *The Origin and Function of Culture* (New York, 1943), *The Eternal Ones of the Dream* (New York, 1945), *Psychanalysis and Anthropology* (New York, 1950); see R.J. Lifton, *Woman in America* (New York, 1965), *Death in Life: Survivors of Hiroshima* (New York, 1968).

summoned to venture into the unknown of the unconscious, to risk engaging in an authentic life, and to discard those camouflages and deceits we all practice in order, in Heidegger's words, to flee from being.

We cannot conclude this article without brief mention of the direct effect of depth psychology upon Judeo-Christian tradition itself. Depth psychology has moved to humanize religion, to point out clearly that religious commitment must be alive if it is not to have a deadly effect on the souls and relationships of the members of its community. Freud clearly exposes the cant and hypocrisy that religion may disguise, the neurotic distortions that religious performances may baptize. What keeps religious sensibilities lively is a keen sense of the unknown as it intimately touches each of us, of the vital mystery bound up in symbols and conveyed in rituals, that if entered into must expand personal being through living contact with the divine. Thus a major impact of the depth psychology movement on religion is to reveal God as He works in our own personal depths, coming up, so to speak, from below as well as down from above, in dreams, fantasies, and encounters with other persons, through events and neuroses and psychoses just as immediately and urgently as through Scripture and tradition.

The religious task confronting depth psychology is consciously to correlate these psychological experiences to religious tradition. Some authors have made significant beginnings; I will list a few: Erich Fromm's *Dogma of Christ,* Morton Kelsey's and John Sanford's investigations of dreams in relation to Scripture and religious meditation, Wilfred Daim's correlation of the salvific aspects of psychoanalysis with Catholic tradition, Josef Gold-brunner's reinterpretation of holiness as wholeness, my own discussion of the similar focus on sexual symbol of Jung's analytical psychology and Christian theology, Victor White's investigations of the similarities and differences in Jung's thought and theological tradition on issues of revelation, the Trinity, the understanding of evil, Erich Neumann's meditations on the impact of the discovery of the unconscious on the theory and practice of ethics.[26]

Depth psychology has also underlined again the importance of the relationship between persons for the formation of a healthy self and the development of the capacity to endure and enjoy religious experience. There must be a sturdy ego available to integrate numinous events; that ego is nurtured by human exchanges that emphasize mutuality. Erikson offers a psychological interpretation of the Golden Rule, stressing that one can best love oneself only if one at the same time touches off urges toward self-fulfillment in the other.[27] Self and other thrive in mutuality, and wither when isolated or opposed. We end where we began, asserting that in the future depth psychology will by necessity focus more concretely on God because it brings clinical evidence for what Christians have known for centuries, that without a sense of life's purpose, without a felt relation to transcendent meaning, without consciousness that one is a creature endowed with capacities as well as needs, a longing as well as a necessity to relate to God, the soul and the psyche perish.

A SELECT BIBLIOGRAHY

Daim, Wilfred, *Depth Psychology and Salvation.* Translated by Kurt F. Reinhardt. New York: Frederick Ungar, 1963.

Erikson, Erik, *Young Man Luther: A Study in Psychoanalysis and History.* New York: Norton, 1958.

_____, *Insight and Responsibility.* New York: Norton, 1964.

_____, *Gandhi's Truth: On the Origins of Militant Nonviolence.* New York: Norton, 1969.

---

26 The references are to Erich Fromm, *Dogma of Christ* (New York, 1963); Morton T. Kelsey, *Dreams, The Dark Speech of the Spirit: A Christian Interpretation* (New York, 1968); John Sanford, *God's Forgotten Language* (New York, 1968); Wilfried Daim, *Depth Psychology and Salvation* (New York, 1963); Joseph Goldbrunner, *Holiness is Wholeness* (Southbend, 1963); Ann Belford Ulanov, *The Feminine, In Jungian Psychology and in Christian Theology* (Evanston, 1971); Victor White, *God and the Unconscious* (New York, 1961); Erich Neumann, *Depth Psychology and a New Ethic* (New York, 1970).

27 See Erik Erikson, *Insight and Responsibility* (New York, 1964).

Frankl, Victor, *The Doctor and the Soul*. New York: Knopf, 1965.

―――, *Psychotherapy and Existentialism*. New York: Clanon, 1968.

Freud, Sigmund, *The Future of an Illusion*. Translated by W.D. Robson-Scott. New York: Livewright, 1953.

―――, *Totem and Taboo*. Translated by James Strachey. New York: Norton, 1950.

―――, *Moses and Monotheism*. Translated by Katerine Jones. New York: Vintage, 1962.

―――, *Civilization and Its Discontents*. Translated by Joan Riviere. London: Hogarth, 1955.

Fromm, Erich, *The Dogma of Christ*. New York: Holt, Rinehart & Winston, 1963.

Goldbrunner, Joseph, *Holiness is Wholeness*. Notre Dame, Indiana: University of Notre Dame Press, 1964.

Horney, K., *Neurosis and Human Growth*. New York: Norton, 1950.

Jung, C.G., *Two Essays in Analytical Psychology*. Translated by R.F.C. Hull, vol. 7 of *The Collected Works*. New York: Pantheon, 1953.

―――, *The Archetypes and the Collective Unconscious*. Translated by R.F.C. Hull, vol. 9:1 of *The Collected Works*. New York: Pantheon, 1959.

―――, *Psychology and Alchemy*. Translated by R.F.C. Hull, vol. 12 of *The Collected Works*. New York: Pantheon, 1953.

―――, *The Development of the Personality*. Translated by R.F.C. Hull, vol. 17 of *The Collected Works*. New York: Pantheon, 1954.

―――, *Modern Man in Search of a Soul*. Translated by W.S. Dell and Cary F. Baynes. New York: Harcourt Brace, 1933.

Kelsey, M.T., *Dreams, The Dark Speech of the Spirit: A Christian Interpretation*. New York: Doubleday, 1968.

Laing, R.D., *The Politics of Experience*. New York: Pantheon, 1967.

Lifton, R.J., *Women in America*. Boston, Massachusetts: Houghton Mifflin, 1965.

―――, *History and Human Survival*. New York: Vintage, 1971.

Lynd, H.M., *On Shame and the Search for Identity*. London: Routledge and Kegan Paul, 1958.

Menninger, Karl, *The Vital Balance*. New York: Viking, 1963.

Neumann, Erich, *Depth Psychology and a New Ethic*. Translated by Eugene Rolfe. New York: Putnam, 1970.

Reik, Theodore, *Myth and Guilt*. New York: George Braziller, 1957.

Ricoeur, Paul, *Freud and Philosophy: An Essay on Interpretation*. Translated by Denis Savage. New Haven, Connecticut: Yale University Press, 1970.

Roheim, Geza, *The Origin and Function of Culture*. New York: Anchor, 1971.

_____, *The Eternal Ones of the Dream*. New York: International Universities Press, 1945.

_____, *Psychoanalysis and Anthropology*. New York: International Universities Press, 1950.

Sanford, J., *God's Forgotten Language*. New York: J.B. Lippincott, 1968.

Sullivan, H.S., *The Interpersonal Theory of Psychiatry*. New York: Norton, 1953.

Ulanov, A.B., *The Feminine in Jungian Psychology and in Christian Theology*. Evanston, Indiana: Northwestern University Press, 1971.

_____ and Ulanov, Barry, *Religon and the Unconscious*. Philadelphia: Westminister Press, 1975.

Weigert, Edith, *The Courage to Love*. New Haven, Connecticut: Yale University Press, 1970.

White, Victor, *God and the Unconscious*. Chicago: Henry Regnery, 1953.

Winnicott, D.W., *Collected Papers: Through Paediatrics to Psychoanalysis*. New York: Basic Books, 1958.

Art

CHAPTER XXXV

UNIVERSAL THOUGHT AND THE ARTS
IN MODERN TIME

Andrew Osze *

Parallel to the diverse wars among nations throughout the past three centuries a quite different war was also going on: a war between the idealistic and materialistic philosophies. As we now know, this struggle was different not just because it brooked no truce, but because in one way or another the two sides drafted every man, woman and child for the front lines. The conflict also differed in that the opposing forces did not represent the interests, the religious or political concepts, of parties or persons within one or another nation, but the inner duality of each human being—a dichotomy of the rational and irrational.

From man's latent duality the materialists fabricated an "unmasked" duality, classifying people in two groups: the "intelligent" and the "superstitious." It was a war waged both publicly (through books, newspapers, scientific and literary groups) and deep in men's souls. Like some new plague it swept Europe then America, reaching all continents by the first quarter of the twentieth century. And since human perceptivity, by contrast with the quantum leaps of science, tended to lag—while faith in the highest values sank into passivity, favoring defensive self-critique to taking a stand—the rationalists forged ahead year

*Well known Sculptor and Professor of Art, New York, U.S.A. Born 1909 in Hungary. His work represents 62 statues, drawings, mosaics and glass windows in museums, churches and plazas of various countries. His articles on art and literature are published in the magazines of Hungary, Brazil and U.S.A. He has taught in 1962-1964 at Escuela de Bellas Artes, Cusco, Academia del Museo de Arte and at the Catholic University of Lima, Peru, sent there by an American Foundation; he was also granted a fellowship to Italy in 1947-1949.

by year. In the inner life of the masses the positive and negative values more and more lost their metaphysical significance; and since each individual remained alone in his war, his mostly never too strong idealism faced in materialism a force which beyond a certain point seemed almost suicidal to challenge. Not to speak of the appealing social programs of the materialists, before which the gates opened of themselves.

These blows always caught the idealists by surprise. And hardly had they recovered from one when fresh ones fell. In their naivete they kept thinking that newer and worse ones could not come, were amazed at the brashness of the "wicked," and wondered at God's patience. They deemed the danger surrounding them a ficticious danger, having no inkling of its import and potential; they thought they were defending their religion but primarily were defending their conservatism. In this way—badly representing their own interests—they proved persistently incapable of even recognizing their opportunities. Thus understandably the situation on both sides grew more and more vehement, the attitudes more entrenched. In short, the conservatives grew more conservative, the revolutionaries more revolutionary.

In this conflict the artists for a long time, nearly two hundred years, lived as a matter of course in "no man's land." Both sides let him do so, and artists instinctively felt they must dwell there: they saw that the two foes, the idealists and the materialists, each had their positive and negative sides; also that the difference between them lay not in their positive but exclusively in their negative aspects. The positive side in both cases comprised the essence which was likewise the essence of their endeavors and their art. Here we already touch on our present view that everyone is religious who has a goal. Thus every materialist philosophy is too, insofar as it is humanist, a child born of the interaction of many religious cultures. In both the idealist and materialist philosophies humanism is at once the vessel preserving the essence and the essence filling the vessel. The men of art, rather feeling than comprehending this more and more brutally evolving clash in the world, with intuitive wisdom cautiously oriented themselves, seeking to defend their spiritual independence.

In this most artists were successful until the practicioners of the materialist philosophies coarsely intervened, demanding total allegiance. This came to pass because the artists, as they gained a closer acquaintance with these practitioners of materialist philosophies had perceived their spiritual deficiencies. Alarm bells sounded within them: they felt that their independence, their inner life was threatened. And to avoid a collision, in the 1908-1930 period there was a great turn, lest it be said of them that the artists are reactionary, almost from one day to the next they broke with their artistic traditions, yet did not bow to the Party either. In their despairing, orphaned confusion they created "styles" that perhaps were even farther from the "socialist realism" the Party demanded than the most recondite styles of the Christian eras. This so far is the Russian part of early twentieth century developments.

In Italy at about that time the search for a way out took a quite different direction. What in Russia was primarily a political, in Italy was mainly a philosophical stand. Mayakovski, Blok, and D'Annunzio, Marinetti best exemplify the difference between the two types. D'Annunzio and Marinetti never believed in things they later would have had to be fatefully disillusioned with.

Before Mayakovski and D'Annunzio, and in small numbers in their time and afterwards (but all the more clearly illuming the situation), came artists seeking a solution in an entirely different way. They did not swear by political possibilities, but introspectively sensing the deeper interrelationships of phenomena, pursued a single path of development. They lived, as it were, in the catacombs, independent and orphaned; contemporaneously experiencing man's problems from his deepest roots to the stars. In their lifetime they knocked about, misunderstood, and, after death, shorn of their true significance, were assigned to a non-existent Olympus. Shall we give a few names? Mozart, Van Gogh, Rilke . . .

This was the situation till the first quarter of the twentieth century. The ever more chronic deterioration in spiritual life from the baroque period to our days has been recognized by every conscientious cultural historian. Nor would there be any quarrel with those who, generation after generation, gave the diagnoses. The trouble always stems from those who do not heed their "seers," who seriously scarcely ever let their more objective, spiritually oriented "pioneers" have their say.

The situation was further worsened by the "modern" uninhibited commerce in art. Parisian art dealers, running low on paintings and sculptures by the classic artists, began to feature living artists at their auctions—at first just one or two. Then, using proven business psychology, they began publicizing these names, having their own men bid such works higher and higher, using "amenable" art historians and journalists to promote what were then purely commercial goals. When that attempt succeeded, and the progressives took modern art under their wing, meanwhile the dealers brain trust, seeking new markets beyond the impoverished European museums, recruited newly rich Americans. Through the most diverse means they persuaded them to become art collectors, patrons, to establish museums, and finally of course to buy works by the artists they had enthroned. The dealers by now were pushing not just one or two, but fifteen or sixteen artists, so as to be able to satisfy all tastes. By around 1930, through this simple idea the commerce in art already had grown into a world network, an organization at once commercial and political; and as such in its business aspect immoral, in its political aspirations one-sided.

On the business side this organization was not immoral because it only worked with fifteen or sixteen artists (a dealer has the right to work with as many as he pleases) or because their propaganda proclaimed these artists immortals in their lifetime, but because they would not allow the other artists to get ahead. They had many ways of barring from "free enterprise" those who would increase their work, it is easier to deal with fifteen or sixteen artists than two hundred, disturb their politico-cultural aims, and one day perhaps unmask their one-sided speculation.

With their propaganda apparatus they were able to perpetuate the artificial atmosphere they needed for their work, in which their "chosen" became the true artists, the artists who really count, and in which those they would not recognize became misty figures shorn of their significance somewhere on the periphery of society.

This development of affairs I would ascribe to two main factors: the first being the anti-metaphysical stand of the "progressives," which is aggravated by the fact that their self-assured "modernism" always seems to smell of money: outwardly they display a sort of romanticism which within is mixed with greed. The other factor involves the fateful spiritual anemia of the greater part of society which by now seemed bent on insulating itself from life's primal elements.

As already noted above, this art commerce had expanded into a "global network," representing both a business and a political interest. The planners, participants and implementers of this group are without exception "progressive," that is men who from "conviction" actually rather defending their momentary interests represent that side of the unending political chain reaction where their upbringing, the circumstances, that is their one-sidedness, have brought them.

And what, we now ask, was the other side representing the idealist philosophies, the man of sense, the instinctively more careful artist, doing while this "perfect" crime against mankind, unique in history, was being committed? Let us briefly examine why it could have succeeded.

Since the idealist philosophies, spearheaded by the churches, were incapable of assessing the danger that threatened their position, they restricted themselves to just a sort of naive defensive action. At the same time when the liberal press was boldly promoting "utilitarian" values, conservative circles, led by the churches, viewed almost impassively the proponents of solid and needed reforms. While condoning the "restless nature" of the somewhat "obstreperous," they did not know how to deal with the louder voices: those they identified with the devil. That was the time of Promethean, Luciferian, Satanic poses: the heroic age of modern romanticism.

The representatives of idealist philosophies, instead of assuming full responsibility, instead of clarifying present and future possibilities, anxiously defended their traditions and in their already mentioned naivete also defended obvious past errors. The "progressive" trends, perceiving the weaknesses of the opposite camp, pressed their ideas more and more boldly. While the taste of the churches and their adherents tended towards false-sweet plaster saints and all sorts of art shop kitsch as they almost completely ushered out of their thought and lives true modern art, the "progressives" fervently promoted the maximal new-type artistic productions. That the "progressives," led by the brain trust, took a wrong turn, by now is no longer in question. In our era 19th century romanticism, which one might still deem unified, broke into many many small sects, in to ever more fatefully sterile little romanticisms. Up until this turn of events, the artist had been the spiritual pioneer of the community, the authentic sensor of the intuitive world. Whether understood or not, he was the revered symbol of faith in the future, of the potential of evolution latent in life itself. New things mostly had sprung from older values, as a critique of their outworn segments. But what the materialists represented was a sharp break, plus the utter rejection of Christianity, not just of its mistakes, but its eternal parts, too. This also was a romantic attitude. Of course all this was realized step by step. At the start of our century Jesus was still the first socialist. By now, depicting or writing about Jesus is deemed a sure sign of reaction. Here we should mention the name of George Rouault: through his works on religious themes, or more properly his spiritual stand, he rates among those exceptions who in the first half of our century were not willing to "throw out the baby with the bath water." One or two other exemplars of this type seeking objectivity were Edvard Munch, Wilhelm Lehmbruck, Giorgio de Chirico. The take-over of the "progressives" occurred after the end of World War II. The great culture centers were in their hands, they gave fame (i.e. publicity), bread (meaning perhaps millions) to their "chosen;" they globally organized the snobs (especially the affluent ones), they delivered the "masses" (meaning those of limited means) to the excesses of tenth-rate dealers in art. Within a generation they finished off folk art, the instinctive good taste of villagers and town dwellers; they drove into "voluntary" exile or suicide the artists who sought something else than what they approved or who could not preserve the independence that was to form their future.

Recently one of New York City's best known art critics, speaking on a TV program about the situation of the artists, declared that in New York they do not buy a picture because it is beautiful but because the artist, the creator of the work, is on the clique's list. But he did not mention the fact, which evidently did not even occur to him, that to get on the clique's list is not even just a "matter of luck." The worth of such pronouncements is in that they indicate what lies behind appearances. According to appearances the works of the clique's favorites have a value beyond debate, their stock quotations are good, stable; they will outlive the representatives of styles appealing to future buyers (whom they also finance moreover with the devilish plan that after their passing they may refer again and again to the stable value of their "wares." This is their portion. And what lies behind the facade? In the public there is ever more inner dissatisfaction. And even among the "progressives" there is by now an ulcerous internal self-contradiction.

Culture and politics make a strange mix, if indeed two such diametrically opposed worlds can be melded. In my view their relationship might rather be compared with every type of ill-starred marriage: each is in love with a different aim. Culture, once having emerged from infancy, knows no compromise—it is conscience personified. It is possible to misuse it, but he who abuses it cannot escape the consequences. Materialist lexicons thus define art: Art is a skill. Would art then really be just the skill of a craft? No! Art in essence is revelation, and in the form of its appearance assumes a skill which in its elementary form (in the opinion of most pedagogues) exists in everyone and in its advanced state in the achievements which artistic genius can realize.

The conceit of the "progressives" became a hot bed for the most varied types and levels of romanticism: to learn of all things but form no attachment to any; art is just amusement while politics is the defense of open or covert interests etc. How tragi-comical this form of life is begins to grow clearer and clearer in our days: tragic, because it has managed to eliminate meta-physics from culture almost entirely; comical because this result does not equate with any sort of release, but corresponds to the void produced in the human soul by the extirpation of the primal world of metaphysics.

In the twentieth century the plight of the (intuitively or consciously) well-oriented artists grew most critical; they had to bring a new conscience to the new crassness, new perspectives to the new darkness, while defending their creativity without the backing of church or society. Never was artist-prophet so beyond the pale, "such a voice in the wilderness," not just in exemplifying bereft Christian thought, but even if among the "chosen" of the social political clique. Here, to differentiatie between the fate of the "chosen" and the bypassed, we should clarify briefly the nature of the latters' "anti-sociality," enquiring also about the degree to which it existed, if at all. When we are aware that the abused citizen, the so-called "bourgeois," is a child of the same civilization as the artist, poet, thinker, mirroring well or badly the "conscience of the world," when we realize that all are products of the past, with a difference favoring the true artist, who by virtue of his sensitivity and critical acumen lives not just in the present but for the future, we gain a clear view of individual destiny as linked to the destiny of mankind. We then see that "progressive" and "bourgeois" are in pretty much the same cul-de-sac, each victim to his own blindness, to whatever demagoguery best serves his selfish ends.

In the old cultures the spiritual needs of the artist and community comprised an organic whole. The process of in-culcating the good and the beautiful through fear in the primitive cultures, through inspiration in the more advanced, was always the same as regards the basic questions of existence: the hours of faith and doubt glowed with an identical quality and purpose.

In the past even the petty bourgeois respected art's high achievements. At present he hardly knows how to approach it. Exposed to every sort of bad influence, distracted, uncentered, he is but a faint unconscious facsimile of his own former worth. He has lost his identity and become a number among the "masses."

And the "progressives" whom mankind has to thank for all this begin to feel from their "point of vantage" that somewhere an error has "slipped into their calculations," but being themselves also in essence "petty bourgeois" of the rebellious sort, they understandably believe that in their "world-redeeming apparatus" there can only be minor errors.

In the clash between the two mutually exclusive philosophies, the idealistic (which was more and more withdrawing into inner immigration) and the ever bolder "saber rattling" materialistic, we may consider as the first report from the front these lines of Kierkegaard, written in the 1840's: "Modern man has lost his freshness, originality; he has become dependent, his emotional world has shallowed, dried out." From the 1850's on, we find more and more similar pronouncements in the works of the truly great thinkers. How much the situation has deteriorated since Kierkegaard's time only he does not see who will not see. While Kierkegaard sounds the alarm in one town, Tolstoy and Dostoevsky alert every town and village on two continents. And the result? Let us not get ahead of our story.

Romanticism in art and thought is a sect of universal thought from the eighteenth through the twentieth centuries. Since the disappearance of the baroque outlook, with the exception of the spiritual efforts of a few unusual individuals, the spiritual and political currents, isms and individual styles have all been born of romanticism. Impressionism, expressionism, surrealism, neo-realism, neo-classicism; neo-surrealism, neo-neo-expressionism, abstract expressionism, neo-neo-this-and-that, pop art, op art, and in the newest edition Land Art and cybernetic art, all are products of a world viewpoint that has rejected universal thought. Whether admittedly or not these are romantic: resolute attempts, searches for a way out, young exhibitionism. Actually they are more gaspings for breath than trends. Their life span mostly is not much longer than that of a pair of medium grade nylon stockings. And their true value is always in proportion to the amount of their nostalgia to get back in the mainstream, and in the degree to which this romantic picture of the world, as *ersatz* religion, can substitute for other types of metaphysical values within them.

After Kierkegaard, Tolstoy, Dostoevsky, since religious conservatism could not defend universal thought in a timely way,
Nietzsche's day had to come. Is it not strange that in the face of
materialism an "atheist" took up the struggle. Nietzsche was a
metaphysician denying metaphysics, and as a "pagan" was one of
the most spiritual men of his age. He only sought to "re-evaluate"
life's ancient symbols, not to discard them, as the schools of
conservative philosophy claimed. Nietzsche sought to mint afresh
the no longer effective like symbols that had become cliches. The
demand for a true picture of man, for youth, beauty and purity,
both physical and spiritual, was a poet-philosopher's vision. He
was thoroughly misunderstood by those who thought the human
ideal in *Beyond Good and Evil* immoral and interpreted his
pronouncement, "God is dead" to mean that Nietzsche was
denying universal thought, God. Nietzsche was a great poet and as
such was aware of the meaning of metaphysics; that was exactly
why he declared war on "anti-aristocratic" materialism, the
philosophy of the "masses." He thought then that materialism was
the religion of the people. By now we know that peoples can only
accept the various socialisms on a secondary level. We also know
that, after the modern artists of the turn of the century, the
ordinary people recognized the socialist leaders as modern types of
the petty bourgeois. So that if Ortega y Gasset had not been a
scholar living in an ivory tower, instead of *The Revolt of the
Masses* he might, in the light of the situation, have titled his book,
The Destruction of the Masses (i.e. peoples).

It is not easy to comprehend and sort out Nietzsche's play of
symbols, but I aver that the last fifty years have not produced a
new spirit with concepts like his. Sartre and many related spirits of
smaller or greater significance have only put a thin slice of
Nietzsche's cake on their plate. That was all their talents allowed.
And the metaphysicians of the age at best nibbled now and then,
continually in debt as regards a true appreciation of Nietzsche. In
Nietzsche's world there were many mistakes, he exaggerated many
things, but we can't shrug him off as a lunatic or schismatic.
Nietzsche, directly or indirectly, was called upon to arouse in us a
nostalgia for the Grecian and Christian outlook, more precisely

universal thought. If we regard certain portions of his philosophy, he was not a Christian, yet he certainly was if we sense the true significance of his concepts in the light of the perspectives of our spiritual rebirth. If we understand the relationship between art and philosophy, if we know that art in its awareness now precedes now follows the vistas of philosophy, then we also know the resuscitating effect of art on thought, on faith; we also know that the great poets are great metaphysicians too, and *vice versa.* Approaching the question from the negative side, we know how second and third rate art always was in eras unfavorable to metaphysics. At the start of this article we noted that the relationship between culture and politics, as history teaches, can only be satisfying on the surface, and only temporarily. A key reason seems to be that our culture, deep in our instincts, is able to work with possibilities of perception which still cannot appear to our conscious mind. Visionary self-criticism (as we might call this internal process) often as the result of decades of centuries of work becomes consciously critical of a society embodying a certain philosophy. Well the artist, in my view even ahead of the philosophers, is the most precise "instrument" for evaluating this process. He skirmishes with the problems of the present, justly re-evaluating the past again and again, he seeks to enlist it in defense of his vision, and, beyond this constant ardor for truth, seeks to approach possibilities which, beyond a certain point, renders "timely" and alive not just today's but tomorrow's existence. So, understandably culture and politics, art and ideology (the latter an echo of mundane history) can only be linked temporarily. And so long as they are linked, depending on the fateful nature of the link, for that longer or shorter time politics is a clog on culture; in realist civilizations regard for the essence of art, as compared to maximum realization in other eras, becomes a tenth-rate question, and, viewing the picture as a whole, culture becomes a reflex culture.

I must admit that this study of mine holds a challenge. At one and the same time I accuse the "progressive" and idealist sectors: both sides have been equally guilty in the spiritual impoverishment of the masses. The overweening vitality of the "progressives," countered by the other side's passivity, its inability to take a stand attuned to the times, together are responsible, each in different ways, for the tragedy of our era, that crime of the century, whereby the war between them has brought low the peoples' primal emotional world. Much as a house or tree on the battlefield is swirled to fiery destruction, from one moment to the next man became a number, the people just masses. In short, human existence with its rationality and irrationality has fled into a void whence one day it will either be able to make a new start toward life's proper evaluation, again taking up the "cross" of man's primal ideals, now fled to the innermost recesses of his being, or else, in the light of new possibilities, may chart an opposite course leading to spiritual disintegration.

Now let us put the question: does such a thing as an absolute materialist exist? When we observe men of a materialist cast, we see how counterproductive the ignoring of an ingrained impalpable essence of their being can be. Were they not at the same time to be pitied, their sentimentalism and cynicism which masks their pain would make them ridiculous. And if we study artists, poets and writers of a materialist bent, we find them qualitatively second or third rate to the degree thay have accepted the ideas of the "enlightenment." Man cannot crawl out of his skin, and his innate irrationalism, whether accepted or rejected, persists as a force within him. Accepted, it augments our options in that vein; while rejected, it puts us to the test in ever more deceptive guises. Spiritually a man can choose between two tasks: to follow his vision, sharpening his perception of the unfathomable, or else to squander his gifts, rejecting ever worsening possibilities until all life's choices wither away.

All cultures have comprised questioning artists, poets, writers, along with the romantics, but before the age of enlightenment the questioning was reverent, the romanticism was a proportionate part of the whole poetic concept; thoughts and feelings had wings, evolutionary modes formed a whole with all their parts. Today's romanticists are marked by superficiality, rising and falling under the aegis of random ideas when they no longer can galvanize as conveyors of ersatz religion. Among the "progressives" and their artist prototypes romanticism has achieved a preponderance unparalleled in history; though by now this impoverishing, soul-draining trend seems to have reached its final stage. The age-old moral aesthetic fibre of the "masses," now moribund, like a cut down forest can only be renewed from the roots. Meanwhile the forest killers, giving up the primal concept, losing their responsiveness to life's colorful fullness, have grown so one-sided, so self-demeaning, so blind to outlook and experience, that their future seems quite hopeless. Their chance of redemption appears to shrivel up before our eyes. This is how the intellectuals' liberation from the "yoke of transcendental ideals" looks. Bergson, were he still alive, could supplement his observations with new data: he could see the consequences of what he had warned about and his era failed to heed—"we can never arrive at intuition through the intellect." In our day he already could have seen what fatal results abuse of the intellect brings.

What good aspects can we find? Well if the era of materialist philosophies, the 18th and 19th centuries, could produce so many exceptions, brilliant seekers of synthesis the rationalists could not vie with, surely also there must be such among us, assuming their immortal destiny, building bridges to the future like their forebears. If the 19th century could give the world Van Gogh's shining purity, beauty's fresh religious content, mankind's new testament, with Gauguin's poetic scorn of civilization, with Tolstoy's poetic realism; and if the early 20th century could give us a Rilke, a Stephan George, a T.S. Eliot, to pick a few names, then conceivably the rest of our century will also bring its harvest. And once certain events have transpired, assuredly that Force which secretly molds our lives will crystallize the truly redeemable portion of the "age of enlightenment" exemplified by such seekers of truth.

When one has come to know, in some degree, the premises of human existence, its irrational and rational duality, and the limits to nature's "conquest," one perceives that nature either defends or avenges herself: it is not only civilization that sweeps away ancient "naive," "barbarian" cultures, but, the deeper cognitions also dethrone and survive "romantic decay" (Hegel). The key question of our age is the same as in all past eras: it can choose or reject, but cannot escape responsibility for that choice. Our technological civilization, too, has been digging its own grave. For anyone who fails to see this—let us be harsh and speak the judgment of the future—the new synthesis, which follows anarchy as its critique, the new spring, the faith of the catacombs, cannot provide fresh options.

The bankruptcy of the "age of enlightenment" is not the synthesis seeker's. The man of talent can trust in his inspiration, which tomorrow may be able to focus his inner resources so that, alongside the technical aplomb of his age, he may take a spiritual stand leading to a richer life in the light of the ever newer goals of universal thought.

* * *

The following list of names aims simply to give the reader a few illustrative examples to go with the study above, and may serve to highlight the proper appraisal of the problems of our century. This list touches on the various artist types of our era, naturally without attempting any all-inclusive encyclopedic approach, which would hardly be feasible here.

Archipenco, Alexander. Sculptor, Russian, 1888-1919. Out and out "modern" at the start of his career; most poetic later in certain works upon his "conversion" succeeded in creating a synthesis between intuition and intellect.

Arp, Jean. Sculptor, French, 1887-   . Like Brancusi, he favors elemental forms, so that his works could almost be the work of any sea. But while Brancusi is often figurative, he is non-figurative, "abstract," without demanding further horizons of development. He is one of the most typical intellectual of our century.

Barlach, Ernst. Sculptor, German, 1870-1938. Expanded the bounds of baroque sculpture under the aegis of the turn of the century's deep humanism. His dramatic force is unique in the 20th century.

Braque, George. Painter, French, 1882-1963. Influenced first by Van Gogh and Cezanne, he then turned his back on his inheritance, seeking to be "modern" at all costs. Thus his canvases became the battleground between his ambition and his sub-conscious, with now his human essence now his "modernity" seeming to win out.

Brancusi, Antoine. Sculptor, Rumanian, 1876-1957. Cubist, neo-primitive; has deeper worth as cubist. His neo-primitivism, Negro plastic experience, is understandably superficial, following one of the fatal fashions of the day. Even so, his intellect bears the stamp of the universal. Had certain things not disturbed his development, his significance would be more complete.

Calder, Alexander. Sculptor, American, 1898- . Non-figurative; his successive stages comprise the exploitation *ad infinitum* of one or another raw sculptural fancy; the inter-connection of his phases are not newer and newer stages of organic development, but more a form of intellectual maneuver.

Chagall, Marc. Painter, Russian, 1887- . A post impres-sionist-expressionist who keeps repeating and varying certain truly deep Russian experiences of his; and with so fresh a "bloom" that each newer work seems like the first of its genre rather than a self-repetition. This technical *tour de force* stems from his industrial art concept. He cannot draw, borrows his colors from Gothic church windows.

Chirico, George. Painter, Italian, 1888- . Expressionist-surrealist; an echo of Greek and Christian metaphysics in the 20th century. Towards modern civilization his stance is now nostalgic, now panic-stricken. He can be utterly sincere, convincing, but also at times theatrical, amateurish.

Csontvary-Koszta, Tivadar. Painter, Hungarian, 1853-1919. Expressionist; infused with faith, devotion, even when un-disciplined. A wild saint of universal thought; at once a mystic and a modern in the deepest sense of the word.

Dali, Salvador. Painter, Spanish, 1904- . Surrealist; viewing his works we can never know who stands behind them: an artist seeking his way, or a mountebank; he seems at once deep and superficial. His public appearances in no way denote a resolute, profound artist.

Despiau, Charles. Sculptor, French, 1874-1946. An artist of inner discipline, his style marking the transition between Rodin and Maillol; a spirit far less ambitious than Rodin, more intimate than Maillol.

Giacometti, Alberto. Sculptor-painter, Swiss, 1901- Cubist-expressionist; in his self-searching period he was much more of a sculptor than today. Now his characteristic figures are examples of the "anti-sculpture" school. Their tragic content fails to convince; in the form of their appearance they repeat a sculptural cliche. What he really has to say is most expressively, significantly realized in his paintings.

Gauguin, Paul. Painter, French, 1848-1903. Post-impressionist-expressionist; hostile to civilization, his nostalgia for nature makes him one of the well-oriented conscientious witnesses to his age. For him modernity is not a goal, but a way, a new tool, a new possibility, the synthesis of a discovered reality and ideal. Hence derives his modernity's moderation and strength.

Kandinski, Vassil. Painter, Russian, 1866-1944. A realist-cubist, abstract painter; an intellectual who has quite lost his footing. Despite his perpetual "rebirths" he is cold and on a single plane. In all his works I sense the fear of an aerialist.

Klee, Paul. Painter, Russian, 1879-1940. An abstract-expressionist; by contrast to Mondrian, Klee leans to soft colors and looser composition. Though his work is free of a certain confusing intent, he is none the less poetic. He is an auspicious link to universal thought, for his romanticism is not materialistically weighted.

Kolbe, George. Sculptor, German, 1877-1947. In transition between the classic and romantic, he is marked by nostalgic idealism. A sculptor of gentle beauty.

Laurens, Henri. Sculptor, French, 1881-1954. One of the most extreme artists of the so-called secession period. His modernity is strained, his problems not always resolved. Hence the often discomfitting restlessness that gives his work a hysterical effect. His partiality for industrial art forms brings mixed reactions.

Lechmbruck, Wilhelm. Sculptor, German, 1881-1919. Expressionist; Kolbe-type phenomenon, but more modern in the serious sense of the word: a curious mixture of the truly beautiful and a sort of noble tartness. Undoubtedly one of those few whom the future can take as a starting point.

Lichtenstein, Roy. Painter, American, 1923-   . His pictures are cheap, blown-up magazine illustration type vignettes, at once the "glorification" and cynical put-down of shallow, petty bourgeois idealism. A marriage of the spiritual bankruptcy of the "progressive" and non-progressive.

Lipschitz, Jacques. Sculptor, French, 1891-   . An early pioneer of the secession, inextricably bound up with the style-romanticizing of Laurens, Gabo, Chauvin etc.

Matisse, Henri. Painter, French, 1869-1954. Post impressionist; after Rodin's highly idealized bourgeois world, Matisse represents the burgher's materialistic romanticism. His simplicity is never deep; hence the "uninhibitedness" that so characterizes him.

Nevelson, Louise. Sculptress, American, 1909-   . Abstract; she tacks together her reliefs with turn-of-the-century battered furniture. Each of her works is a romantic evocation of mortality. Technically she seems always "out of breath," spiritually one-dimensional. From her creations it is only one step to accepting a half-rotted, soiled mattress as a work of art.

Miro, Joan. Painter, Spanish, 1893-   . He paints ovaries of various living creatures enlarged a million times along with the carnival of his imagined monsters. His world is at once childlike and satanic. With his romantic microscope he has proven to be one of the most successful generals of twentieth century materialism.

Moholy-Nagy. Painter-sculptor, 1895-1946. One of the most radical pioneers of intellectualism, and simultaneously its culmination. It is as if not human hands but a machine had created his works; he has so "succeeded" in eliminating feeling from his mock machines, that this no longer has even a tragic effect; as though one were viewing a blank sheet of paper, an "empty canvas," the "clothes" of Andersen's fairy tale king.

Mondrian, Piet. Painter, Dutch, 1872-1944. Constructivist; his strongly decorative colors enclosed in black iron-work frames bring us "calm" objective-seeming portrayals of depersonalized man and art.

Moore, Henry. Sculptor, English, 1898-   . Behind many many masks (styles) lies always the same naturalist spirit. His periods and trend changes contradict each other: his modernism serves not his message but his ambition. His humanism is appealing; but his concepts do not run deep. His works have an aura of theatrics.

Munch, Edvard. Painter, German, 1863-1944. One of the true greats of 20th century modern art. His expressionism is both prophetic and universal. His achievements are bench marks of our organic spiritual growth.

Naray, Aurel. Painter, Hungarian, 1883-1948. Post impressionist-expressionist; one of the most significant protagonists of Christian thought in the first half of the 20th century. His art is characterized by depth, courage and originality, not in the romantic but in the true sense of the word.

Picasso, Pablo. Painter, Spanish, 1881-   . After the works of his blue period under the influence of Toulouse-Lautrec and Puvis de Chavannes each new period is a distorted, tart echo or caricature of one or another old culture without meaning to be! Behind his accomplishments we see the spiritual inheritance of the 19th century in a dance macabre, the romanticism and cynicism of a materialist.

Pollock, Jackson. Painter, American, 1912-1956. An abstract naturalist; his colors are tasteful, his rhythms ingenious, echoing the atmosphere of tangled weeds and grasses or burnished multi-colored slabs of marble. His spiritual orientation scarcely exceeds the value level of a textile designer.

Smith, David. Sculptor, American, 1906-1965. Neo-cubist; he is the sculptor of fixed form combinations in an imagined void, situations of balance impossible under normal conditions. Beyond doubt the experiment is interesting, certainly to the extent of one cycle. It shows modifications of man's "irrealistic" and realistic concepts.

Roualt, George. Painter, French, 1871-1958. Expressionist;

essentially his spiritual orientation is among the most serene. Brilliance and pain characterize his art. The thick-thin contours enveloping the objects in his pictures are a painterly utilization of the effect of the lead framework in gothic windows.

Utrillo, Maurice. Painter, French, 1883-1955. The eternal echo of one of Van Gogh's gentle hours; yet individual in the deepest sense, for with his own pantheistic melancholy he managed to transmute the glow of his master into a new synthesis.

Vasarely, Victor. Painter, Hungarian, 1908-   . Abstract; his pictures are vibrating arabesques in a certain sense symbolic, in another sense anti-spiritual; hence our feeling that this is rather industrial art than art. And the fact that, as is generally known, so many of his works are produced factory-style (he employs many artists) shows that Vasarely is satisfied with more and more mechanical results.

A SELECT BIBLIOGRAPHY

Barzun, Jacques, *The Use and Abuse of Art.* Princeton, New Jersey: Princeton University Press, 1973.

_____, *Classik Romantik and Modern.* Garden City, New York: Doubleday, 1961.

Jaspers, Karl, *Die geistige Situation unserer Zeit.* Berlin: Gruyter, 1931.

Kramer, Hilton, "Alberto Giacometti's Moral Heroism," *New York Times,* January 18, 1976.

_____, "The Poetic Fables of Marc Chagall," *New York Times,* June 21, 1975.

Spengler, Oswald, *Der Untergang des Abendlandes.* 2 vols. München: Beck, 1922-1923.

Part Four
Specific Problems

PRELIMINARY REMARKS

In the seemingly endless list of questions concerning God's existence and nature, some specific issues emerge as salient. Such is the problem of causality, and such are the problems of suffering and immutability of God. These subjects are only broached here; an elaboration of even the extant investigations would require volumes.

We add to this section an inquiry into natural religion and hope. We particularly cherish the former essay, since Professor Stephen C. Pepper died shortly after having submitted it.

CHAPTER XXXVI

ON THE QUESTION OF A RATIONAL RELIGION
Stephen C. Pepper*

In recent times, a large number of persons in civilized countries have set themselves outside the membership of orthodox religions. They call themselves free thinkers, agnostics, or atheists. The reason is easy to see. It comes mainly from the great progress and success of the sciences in their rational handling of human problems, and the marked contrast of attitude between the experimental methods of science with hypothetical conclusions seeking further and further confirmation, in contrast to the dogmatic attitude of religion demanding implicit faith and unquestionable belief in its rituals and creeds. Science is aimed at intellectual satisfaction, religion rather at emotional security.

What turns the free thinkers away from religion is doubt about the capacity of religion to offer any genuine security. For what can guarantee security in fact for man other than beliefs supported by factual evidence, beliefs an intelligent man can respect as being based on evidences of observation and experiment and logical consistency? If religion depended solely on emotion, there would be no problem. But a problem does arise because the orthodox civilized religions also make a cognitive appeal—to a supreme authority transmitted by priests, or a sacred book, or miracles that can only be divinely interpreted, or emotional experiences with an indubitable feeling of certainty for the truth of the word and the divine presence intuitively (even perhaps visually) revealed. And much stress is laid upon the emotional efficacy of religious belief and the feeling of security it brings, whatever the facts may be.

*(1891-1972) Professor Emeritus of Philosophy at the University of California, Berkeley, California, U.S.A. Deceased shortly after having submitted this article for publication.

Most people in a civilized society with an established religion are born into a church, and do not give much attention to the rational credibility of their creed and ritual. They are well aware of the inconvenience of religious doubt in their society. They are sensible to the many emotional amenities of their church—the social life, the aesthetic surroundings in music and visual art, and the written word, and the often very skilful emotional ministrations of the priests in times of suffering and bereavment. The church also when working effectively supports the moral tone of the community. And in its finest fruition can spread an atmosphere of love over a community that can be felt as the love of God incarnate.

And yet with all these accruing emotional values, an orthodox religion, different from art, cannot rest secure on its emotional assets solely. The creed must be ultimately and implicitly believed, or the whole structure is shaken. A religion suspected as false or fraudulent is no longer real, no longer sincerely and convincingly felt.

In the established orthodox religions of civilized cultures, the central dogma that must be believed is its conception of God, or some corresponding cosmic state such as the Buddhist nirvana. Consequently if we are considering the possibility of a rational religion, we must look for a credible conception of a cosmic state or set of principles that can be reasonably identified with a conception of God. This is not a fantastic idea. As a matter of fact the orthodox creeds of civilized religions are themselves embedded in cosmic theories, on which they depend in part for the supposed stability of their creeds.

Some years ago I made a study of the world theories that have been prominent in the history of occidental philosophy, and called the book, *World Hypotheses.* I chose the term hypotheses on purpose to lift the results out of the level of dogma. These results can consequently give us just the sort of cosmic conceptions that might function as concepts of God for a rational man whose religion (if he chose to have one) would lie outside the commitments required for a dogmatic orthodox creed.

I found four such hypotheses which characterized the four principal separate schools of philosophy in occidental culture. Each of them was based on a distinct paradigm or root metaphor (as I called it) taken from common experience. These were first, formism (or Platonism) based on the far-reaching principle of similarity by which objects may be defined and classified. The second I called mechanism (often referred to as naturalism) based most simply on the principle of push and pull, developing soon into the complex conception of a physical machine, whether mechanical or electromagnetic, stressing effective causal relations in space and time. The third was organicism (or Hegelian idealism), which was based on the principle of coherence and dynamic integration, culminating in the conception of the organic whole, in which every part is needed for the functioning of every other part in a complete harmonious totality. The fourth was contextualism (or Pragmatism), associated with the writings of William James, Charles Peirce, and John Dewey.

Each one of these yields conceptions that can be identified with God as a means of instituting a form of rational religion—conceptions, which, as a matter of fact have been utilized by their respective philosophical movements as *the* proper interpretation of religion. For formism, the conception of God becomes inevitably associated with the realm of essences which are the universal characteristics by which classes of existing things become identified and ordered in the cosmic organization of things. These essences organize into hierarchies. They are themselves eternal beyond the exigencies of change which is restricted to the objects they characterize. All existing things thus look up to the essences for their forms of fulfilment. And the form of all forms at the top of the hierarchy of all essences is the form of Being or Good as the culmination of all other fulfilments. Aristotle enunciated this highest refinement of the formistic conception of God. It has had a long history, and was taken up as the rational formulation of part of the dogma of the Catholic church through the work of St. Thomas Aquinas.

I should perhaps state at this point that every one of these world hypotheses has been promulgated by most of its overenthusiastic exponents as something based on indubitable data, or self-evident principles, or even infallible authority. However, they do not suffer a bit by being relieved of these trappings, and presented as just empirical hypotheses open to confirmation by the evidence that supports them. Indeed, they are in an even stronger position by not having to strain to establish their cognitive certainty, when all they need for reasonable belief is a probability of considerable adequacy. Besides, with four such relatively adequate hypotheses in our philosophical heritage, it is qualitatively unlikely that any one of them contains the whole truth. More likely it is that each is contributing something relevant.

Mechanism (or spatio-temporal naturalism), often called materialism, strikes one first as a strange place to expect a conception of God, suitable for a rational religion. But in Spinoza we have it held in high esteem. True, the materialists are notorious skeptics of religion, often parading their science-based atheism with an irritating air of superiority. For concepts of the natural-sciences have been the troublesome hurdles for orthodox religion to cope with. Most orthodox religions originated from an animistic background and carry along a good deal of the mythologies of primitive religion. Animism is itself an ancient cosmic theory explaining things on the analogy of human actions, motives, and emotions, and even of human shapes. It is the theory that believes in ghosts and spirits and mythical ancestors and hero gods. The evidences of science has been devastating to such beliefs.

Yet many scientists wish to retain a religious foothold. And many have set up as their conception of God the laws determining the structure of nature, which are regarded as unchanging. If the structure of nature, the great machine, is regarded as the work of God, God himself being a transcendent first cause or continuing imminent cause, then we have a typical deistic conception which many have found easy to accept. It affords a bridge away from animistic dogma. The trouble is that such a God outside the cosmic machine is nothing more than a washed out, dehumanized spirit. Besides, the argument for a first cause is not convincing, and the concept is unnecessary. Spinoza was the man who handled the problem with most dignity. God for him is the substance of all things with a spacial mechanical aspect and a corresponding mental aspect and possibly other aspects not known to man. But man lives in the modes of the physical and mental aspects. His mental emotion may sometimes obscure his cognitive awareness of God which would in its ultimate form be expressible in terms of a self-consistent deductive symbolic system. On the ethical side man preserves himself in God by seeking satisfaction harmonious to His being—maximizing his own satisfactions, in short, in relation to those of other men, and indeed the whole world, for the glory of God.

This sort of naturalistic theory of God could easily be brought up to date. And, in fact, it can be found, after a fashion, in S. Alexander's, *Space, Time and Deity.*

As for organicism, that world theory is just made for a pantheistic theory of God. It can be taken over bodily into any liberal religious sect, and so it has been by many Unitarians and Humanists. Ralph Waldo Emerson can be named as one of the earliest Unitarians to do this.

But I am particularly interested in the religious potentialities of contextualism—and in that particular development out of it which I have called selectivism, and exposed in *Concept and Quality.* The interesting peculiarity of this conception of God is that it yields a changing God. Traditionally, God is conceived of as unchanging and eternal. Probably it was felt that only so can man be assured of the security he seeks in God. In this conception the security comes from what might be called man's companionship with God. God and man are pursuing the same ends and they can be helpful to each other.

Let me indicate briefly some of the principal features of contextualism. The first is that of change or process permeating all reality. The root metaphor is that of the occurrence of some historic event in a man's or a group's life. It could be well represented as someone's complete purposive achievement. Let us say it is the lighting of a campfire in the woods preparatory to cooking a catch of trout. If this event is most fully and vividly described it will be in qualitative terms of the sensations and impulses and satisfactions felt by the person building the fire. There was the realization of the need for a fire, an impulse to fulfil the need by an action, then an anticipatory idea of the burning fire that would satisfy the need. This then becomes the goal of the purpose. But to attain this goal, wood must be gathered, and kindling and matches as means to get the fire going. So the total purposive act spreads out as an initial impulse based on a need, followed by a succession of instrumental acts causally inter-connected as means for the attainment of the final goal of the burning fire. The total act spreads over a definite duration, with a beginning and an end and intermediate acts arranged in a causal order.

The outstanding features of such an act are (1) a limited temporal duration enclosing the act, (2) ordered change within the act, (3) an initial impulse from a need requiring the fire as a definite goal for its satisfaction, (4) the anticipatory idea of the fire as a goal and ideas of the means needed to reach it, and (5) the actual acts performed in gathering the means, and finally (6) the satisfaction in the attainment of the fire as the goal of the act.

Such an act is felt by the person performing it as an experience full of changing qualities of sensations, images, tensions, anticipa-tions with future references and final satisfaction, all bound together within the total purposive structure. Such an event is not a succession of disconnected atoms, but is an integral pattern. Nor is the duration enfolding it a succession of disconnected instants, but is a continuous time span. Moreover this time span as experienced has a past, present, and future constantly there as the event moves along. The person's attention span spreads over a duration of some seconds of clock time. This is known as the 'specious present' and is a conspicuous feature of a contextualistic description of reality.

Now I can make the decisive point which distinguishes contextualism from any other relatively adequate world theory. This is the hypothesis that cosmic reality is limited to what actually goes on in the durations of such events as this. When the fire is lighted, the event of the lighting the fire is over and gone and no longer a part of cosmic actuality. A new event has taken its place—the cooking of the fish. The reader may ask what is so astonishing about that? What would you expect? That is just what the contextualist says too. But none of the theories taken up before would let that hypothesis go unchallenged. For the Platonist, the essences are still there in reality. For the mechanist the atoms and electrons still go on and the great spacetime container never changes. And for the organicist the coherent ultimate totality of the universe is never disturbed by limited appearances within the Absolute.

The contextualist is simply insisting upon taking experience as it appears. Since events have limited durations, that is the limit of their actuality. And why seek to deny or circumvent this obvious fact? For him the part after the event ceases to be present is really past and does not actually exist at all, and the future for events not yet actually present likewise does not exist yet. Only the present is in actual existence. However, this actual cosmic present has a certain width to it. It is not the infinitesimal moment of clock time that splits the present at the imaginary line between the seconds before and after. The actual felt qualitative present has an observable width. One can appreciate it in reading a printed sentence. The span of attention spreads over a number of words, or a whole phrase. The earlier words in the duration of the phrase are moving out of the actual present, and the later words are coming in. Only by having the pattern of the phrase all in a present duration could the meaning of the sentence be understood. Similarly with the appreciation of a melody. As a mere succession of separate notes the line and pattern of a musical phrase could never be grasped. It is grasped, however, because it is perceived and felt as actually present as a whole in a duration of several moments of width in terms of clock time. This actual present is the total width of the actual cosmic present for the world hypothesis of contextualism. How wide is it? Wide enough to pass along the patterns of one slab or wave of duration into the next. One cosmic period passes on its patterns of action to the next. And some of these may be in a process of change. This is what makes actual change cosmically possible and actual creation.

Contextualism is the philosophy of creativity *par excellence.*

For not only has this cosmic wave of actuality an efficient width, but also great breadth and depth. Every structured event like the achievement of building a fire is in the context of other events. The fire event was just one of a number of other purposive events for setting up a camp, all going on simultaneously. There were furthermore all sorts of animal and chemical events going on in the woods and soil in what we call the environment of the fire. The width of the simultaneous context actually goes out beyond the woods to the society from which the boys come and so on over the whole surface of the earth and even out to the starry galaxies (if we can trust the word of astronomers). But some of these contexts are much nearer than others in their causal bearing on each other's patterns. And this is important because these causal contacts often require an adaptation of some patterns to others. And they may also yield satisfactions and frustrations. Whence the values of adaptation and satisfaction become cosmic occurrences.

But not only are there these contexts in the width of the cosmic durations of events, there are also contexts in depth. These are best known through the natural sciences as the levels of nature. The fire-building event, as a matter of fact, was based on and embedded in the personality structure of the boy building the fire. It was a capacity of that boy's character that he could carry out that rather complex purposive achievement. The boy's personality actually contained many other such dispositions partly inherited, partly learned. These when not in action acquire their actuality from the living tissues and open paths of a brain structure that maintains its steady states through the metabolism of the organism. These may be considered as organic cell structures. But these in turn maintain their steady states through continuous selective actions of chemical molecules, which in turn are patterns of atoms, and so on down to the sub-atomic elements and the mysteries (at least to the common man today) of quantum mechanics. All these levels of adaptive activity maintaining their respective patterns of steady states lie within a cosmic wave or slab of duration. It is from this great depth of constant patterning that the constancy of actuality attains its remarkable reliability for human and animal prediction and adaptation. And these are all contexts in depth for higher levels that rely upon the lower for their continuity.

Just one more thing needs to be emphasized so that it is not lost from sight in the conclusion we are coming to in the contextualistic identification of God. That is, that for the contextualist every bit of the structure of contexts (we may call them "systems" to introduce a common contemporary expression) is conceived for its actuality in completely qualitative terms. Remember, we described the fire-making achievement in purely qualitative terms. Now, a behaviorist psychologist, for simple experimental manipulation, could, and usually does, convert all these qualitative terms into behavior terms. Among other conveniences, this makes it easy, when greater detail is wanted for certain observations, to offer refined descriptions of the behavior level in terms of physiological concepts. And this may lead on down to a desire to get some details described in chemical terms, or even electromagnetic physical terms. In the course of this progress in scientific refinements, the original experienced qualitative description of the boy's fire-building activity is left far, far behind.

Now it is the contention of the contextualist in contrast to the mechanist to maintain that the ultimate cosmic facts are those described in qualitative terms. If pressed very hard, the contextualist asserts that the formulas and language of the natural scientist when they leave contact with qualitative experience, are just *operations*, symbolic tools, by which they can make predictions from one island of high level qualitative experience to another, and that they are in no manner or degree revelatory of the nature of cosmic entities possibly existing at the lower levels. But others, who perhaps should not be called contextualists but, say, selectivists, like myself, do maintain that these scientific formulas are to a considerable degree revelatory. Otherwise (if they had no correspondence at all to actual cosmic processes), how could they be such extraordinarily reliable 'instruments' of prediction? Moreover, at levels where the symbolic formulas can be checked against the qualitative patterns as in behavioristic descriptions of actual qualitative actions or architectural plans against actual qualitatively perceived buildings, the formulae provide both the operations to be performed to attain their objects and they check in correspondence with the objects attained. Thus the directions given in the plan of a building to find a door in the middle of the first floor of the facade measuring x by y will be perceptually found by following those directions in the completed building at that corresponding location with precisely corresponding measurements in inches tested by a steel tape. The truth of the formula consists not only in the success of the operation in leading you to the predicted object, but also in the correspondence of the relevant symbols to the qualities of the object designated.

Hence this sort of a contextualist will infer by analogy and extrapolation that formulas that are predictively successful for levels of nature below the range of human sense discrimination, will also be referring to qualitative patterns that cannot be even remotely pictured but can be legitimately surmised. Thus a man born blind, though he cannot remotely imagine the hues of colors corresponding to electromagnetic vibrations, can nevertheless surmise their actual existence by analogy with qualitative tones he can hear in correspondence with air vibrations. And thus, to repeat the conclusion earlier stated, the selectivistic contextualist conceives all the patterns of the cosmic wave of actuality as being actually through and through qualitative, and by no means to be confused with the abstract symbols of the chemists and physicists.

It is this concrete fully qualified totality of contexts that the selectivistic contextualist identifies as the cosmic God. Or he may prefer to identify God only with the positive value features in it. Henry Wieman, the most noted theological exponent of this theory identifies God with the creative aspect of experience. When a man in adapting to his environment creatively enhances his environment, the being of God is thereby increased. And God and man have done this in cooperation with each other. It is an act of love. But as a man fails in creativity and yields to frustration and pain and hate he diminishes himself and God and introduces evil.

Suffering and blocking of desires may not be conducive to greater creative vividness and achievement. Contextualism is a theory in which negative values can actually be sought in order to augment the overall value.

The theory is notorious for its encouragement of struggle as a way to higher creative achievement. Difficulty often increases the potential achievement. God, then, for Wieman is the actuality of creative achievement in the total wave of cosmic duration. Men as personalities are systems of dispositions prepared for action in the vast field of other systems in their context, all dynamically making selections for their improvement or stability.

God is the totality of this continuous dynamic movement of actuality from one present duration into a next. He may be conceived of as either this dynamic totality, or as the positive creative aspects of it (as opposed to the blocked and frustrating aspects) in the way Wieman conceives God. In either inter-pretation, this is a pantheistic conception. Every man and all qualitative systems are in God, and God is in them. And all are continually striving for creative achievement on their level. The overall value is adaptation and increasing satisfaction within the process. The circumstances determine whether this can be mutual or must be one-sided. In this way the activity of God (as the total texture and context) for any act can be either sustaining or disciplinary. It is a guiding activity in either case. And the activity comes out of the person guided as well as out of his adapting environment. The world, in short, is not hostile but cooperative even when it is frustrating.

However, for this view there is no great terminal triumph—in the manner of the Hegelian Absolute. There may be many triumphs along the path of a man's life. And each is socially mingled with other men's lives in the contextual disposition of encompassing social structures. And when a man dies (as we say) his personality just dissolves and mingles with the systems that supported him during his personal selective activity. His influence (as we say) lives on in the dispositions he contributed to other systems. In other words, dynamic systems, including men's personalities are born in creative acts out of God and having achieved their potentialities return again into God. And so the actuality of things is constantly replenished.

This contextualistic or selectivistic conception of God is the most recent and the least fully developed of rational religions. It is important in adding an aspect of God not stressed by other relatively adequate conceptions. It has been carried along furthest in consistency by Henry Wieman. There is a background for it in Dewey's ethical meliorism. Whitehead in his theory of God comes close to supporting such a conception of the actuality of God but overspreads it with an ultimate consummation of God in what is almost an Hegelian Absolute.

Thus there are rational interpretations of God which men, repelled by the irrational features of the orthodox religions, could use as the basis of rational religions. In fact, these have been so used, not only by nonorthodox groups but even by liberal groups still regarding themselves as sects of the orthodox religions—like the Unitarians.

It cannot be denied, however, that many deeply religious men will not find themselves drawn to these rational conceptions. They in their turn will be repelled by the very rationality of them. They will seem cold, distant, reserved, entirely lacking in the warmth and comfort and inner security of a God to whom one can pray and worship—a God of love and hope and charity and grace—or even the reverse, a God to fear, the almighty God of righteousness, omnipresent, omniscient, and indubitable.

These are some of the irrational features. But perhaps a rational man should not ignore these features, but should face them, realizing what large numbers of his citizens cannot resist them. Perhaps he should carry his rationality one step further and consider what sort of irrational religion could be devised that would suit these people and yet not expose society to the dangers of irrational religious fanaticism. On Plato's suggestion, what sort of lies (myths) can the wise rational guardian of society devise to keep the irrational passions from breaking out in terror and violence? The danger is not unreal. But Plato's suggestion could well prove a cure worse than the disease. For it leads to the enormous risk of destroying the credibility of authority in society.

The best solution seems to be the paradoxical one prevalent in most democratic societies—that of complete religious freedom in a society in which there is also complete separation of religion and state. The dogmas of the several religions keep each other in check, and the absence of a state religion blocks any accusation of favoritism.

So, a rational man can in a democratic society leave the irrational religions pretty much to their own, and either join an existing rational religious group, or work up such a group among his friends. Or he may be content to be just privately an agnostic, free from religious encumbrances. Yet he may wonder occasionally if there is something he is missing. If so, he would probably conclude that it must have to do with the mystic experience.

Second to the concept of God, and, perhaps not second but first, we find the mystic feature peculiar to religion. It infiltrates almost all religions, even the primitive ones. It is an irrational feature, to be sure, but differs from the myths of animism and magic in being an actual observable fact. Though rare in most persons' lives, it is common among mankind as a whole, and its main characteristics are about the same from whatever race or culture it is reported. It is all-absorbing, ecstatic, seems to be a cognition of the perfection of reality, and convinces one that he will believe in it forever. It is much like another common fact every man will have had (unless most unfortunate), the great experience of falling completely in love. This also is all-absorbing, ecstatic, a feeling of the indubitable perfection of its object, with a love that will never, never cease. Indeed, the mystic experience may be a peculiar kind of falling in love—a sublimated love. If so, we know what to think of it. It is one of the most elevated experiences in the world. An experience to be spread out as much as possible. It brings warmth and sympathy into all who come within its sphere. Thus, others looking at two lovers feel a warm response themselves. They also recall the ecstasy and the feeling of the perfection of the loved one and conviction that it could never change and that they would love forever, and that the whole world should inevitably agree with them. But having lived through it they also know those cognitive beliefs were emotionally exaggerated, though the emotional joy may remain long treasured. So, with the religious mystic experience. It is a wonderful thing to have had. And there is no uniting power in the world stronger than love.

But its cosmic message in rendering all else unreal is not one a rational man can accept without criticism. He will ask for the corrobarative evidence and will not be content to confine himself to that one experience in a world full of many other compelling and fascinating experiences. He will have enough critical judgment to realize that a *feeling* of indubitability is no guarantee of the *truth* of the intuition. So, the rational man will accept the one demonstrable insight of the mystic—namely the healing and uniting power of love. But he will remain skeptical about its cosmic message. It does not provide a relatively adequate world hypothesis.

So, in sum, we are assured that rational religions can be developed—indeed actually have been.

Just let me add one final comment on the relation of belief and commitment to rational religion. As we know, the great advantage of a rational religion is that an intelligent man can accept it without embarrassment from the sort of evidence used to support it. For the evidence comes from relatively adequate world hypotheses with which the religious tenets are compatible. It follows that cognitive belief in a rational religion is never entirely incorrigible. It might seem to follow that a person could not ever give his full commitment to such a religion. This, however, is not true. One can be fully committed to policies and decisions based on hypotheses that cannot themselves be regarded as certain. On the hypothesis that there is some probability of rain, one may fully commit himself to the decision to take an umbrella. Similarly, we may fully commit ourselves to one of a number of alternative rational religions as the one most compatible to our temperament and circumstances. And this decision may help to give a constancy and consistency to our way of living. In short, a rational religion that can be theoretically justified only as a probable belief can consistently be given full practical commitment as a way of life. But, of course, a commitment to an irrational belief would be an unreasonable commitment.

A SELECT BIBLIOGRAPHY*

1. Writings of Stephen Coburn Pepper

(a) Books

Modern Color. Cambridge, Massachusetts: Harvard University Press, 1923.
Problem of Substance: Lectures 1926-1927. Berkeley: University of California Press, 1927. (Pepper joint editor with G. Adams and J. Loewenberg)
Aesthetic Quality: A Contextualistic Theory of Beauty. New York: Charles Scribner's and Sons, 1938.
World Hypothesis: A Study in Evidence. Berkeley, California: University of California Press, 1942.
Digest of Purposive Values. Berkeley, California: University of California Press, 1947.
The Basic Criticism in the Arts. Cambridge, Massachusetts: Harvard University Press, 1949.
Principles of Art Appreciation. New York: Harcourt, Brace and Co., 1949.
The Work of Art. Bloomington, Indiana: University of Indiana Press, 1955.
George Berkeley: Lectures Delivered before the Philosophical Union of the University of California. Berkeley, California: University of California Press, 1957. (Pepper joint editor with Karl Aschenmenner and Benson Mates)
Sources of Value. Berkeley, California: University of California Press, 1958.
Ethics. New York: Appleton-Century-Crofts, Inc., 1960.
Concept and Quality: A World Hypothesis. LaSalle, Illinois: Open Court Press, 1967.

(b) Articles

"The Art of Delight and the Art of Relief," *Philosophy and Phenomenological Research,* 9 (1949), pp. 480-486.

*Compiled by Robert Hall, Department of Philosophy, St. John's University, New York, U.S.A.

"Value and Value Judgments," *Journal of Philosophy*, 46 (1949), pp. 429-434.

"Further Considerations on the Aesthetic Work of Art," *Journal of Philosophy*, 49 (1952), pp. 274-279.

"On Professor Jarrett's Question about the Aesthetic Object," *Journal of Philosophy*, 49 (1952), pp. 633-641.

"The Concept of 'Fusion' in Dewey's Aesthetic Theory," *Journal of Aesthetics and Art Criticism*, 12 (1953), pp. 169-176.

"Natural Norms in Ethics," *Journal of Philosophy*, 53 (1956), pp. 9-15.

"A Neutral Identity Theory," *Dimensions of Mind* (ed. Sidney Hook. New York: New York University Press, 1960).

"Sanctions Versus Reasons for Value Judgments," *Ethics*, 70 (1960), 109-117.

"A Proposal for a World Hypothesis," *Monist*, 47 (1962), pp. 267-286.

"Evaluative Definitions in Art and their Sanctions," *Journal of Aesthetics and Art Criticism*, 21 (1963), pp. 201-208.

"On the Relation of Philosophy to Art," *Revue Internationale Philosophie*, 18 (1964), pp. 183-192.

"Controlled Experimentation in Criticism," *Journal of Aesthetics and Art Criticism*, 23 (1964), pp. 133-38.

"An Essay on the Essay: An Aesthetic Appreciation!" *New Scholasticism*, 41 (1967), pp. 295-311.

"Autobiography of an Aesthetics," *Journal of Aesthetics and Art Criticism*, 28 (1969), pp. 275-286.

"Survival Value," *Journal of Value Inquiry*, 3 (1969), pp. 180-186.

"A Dynamic View of Perception," *Philosophy and Phenomenological Research*, 32 (1971), pp. 42-46.

"On the Uses of Symbolism in Sculpture and Painting," *Philosophy East and West*, 19 (1969), pp. 265-278.

"The Case for Systems Philosophy," *Metaphilosophy*, 3 (1972), pp. 151-153.

(c) Prefaces

Lawrence, Nathaniel, *Whitehead's Philosophical Development*. Berkeley, California: University of California Press, 1956.

Ushenko, Andrew, *Dynamics of Art*. Bloomington, Indiana: University of Indiana Press, 1953.

————, *The Field Theory of Meaning*. Ann Arbor, Michigan: University of Michigan Press, 1958.

2. Studies

Berall, Nathan, "A Note on Professor Pepper's Aesthetic Object," *Journal of Philosophy,* 48 (1951), pp. 750-54.

Edel, Abraham, "Science and Value: Some Reflections on Pepper," *Review of Metaphysics,* 14 (1960), pp. 134-58.

Heyl, Bernard, "Relativism and Objectivity in Pepper's Theory of Criticism," *Journal of Aesthetics and Art Criticism,* 18, (1960), pp. 378-92.

Jarrett, James, "More on Professor Pepper's Theory of the Aesthetic Object," *Journal of Philosophy,* 49 (1952), pp. 475-78.

Henze, Donald, "A Reply to Professor's Pepper Stand," *Journal of Philosophy,* 52 (1955), pp. 433-39.

Kahn, S.J., "Critical Judgment and Professor Pepper's 'Eclectism'," *Journal of Aesthetics and Art Criticism,* 9 (1950), pp. 46-50.

CHAPTER XXXVII

CAUSALITY IN OUR CENTURY

Augustin Riska*

In our century the perennial problem of causality took on dimensions which, though new, are nevertheless not entirely isolated from their philosophical traditions. The great philosophers of the past who shaped the theory of causality in a most significant way are still highly respected, at least by serious students of the field. On the other hand, a growing number of the systematic treatises on causality or its certain aspects, exhibit the efforts of many contemporary authors to deal with this traditional issue by utilizing current conceptual tools which were often a *terra ignota* to previous generations of philosophers and scientists. In particular, physical theories such as quantum mechanics and the theory of relativity have motivated an increasing interest in the problems of causality and determination. However, these revolutions in physics were not the only source of innovation. Rapid developments in modern formal logic, equipped with mathematical techniques, and the achievements of the theory of probability and statistics offer a powerful apparatus by virtue of which the old problems could be reformulated and new horizons opened. Furthermore, the new science of cybernetics, the theory of information, the behavioral sciences, biology, and several other disciplines, have considerably enhanced and intensified the study of causality.[1]

---

*Associate Professor of Philosophy at St. John's University, New York, U.S.A.

1 See Mario Bunge, *Causality: The Place of the Causal Principle in Modern Science.* No serious scholar in the field of causation can ignore this impressive work which is written from sound realistic positions and keeps a balance between vital traditions and our new vistas. See below, A Select Bibliography.

Now, in order to rectify the whole picture, credit must also be given to new philosophical pathways in the field of causality, since, after all, this field has always been a genuine part of the philosopher's domain. Besides philosophy of physics and applied logic, the major philosophical disciplines—metaphysics, epistemology, and ethics—are continuously occupied with the crucial questions of causation, determinism, indeterminism and free will. Aristotle, St. Thomas, Descartes, Leibniz, Spinoza, Hume, Newton, Galileo, Kant, J.S. Mill, Comte, and other acknowledged leading figures in the theory of causality, have formed an undisputable core of our present heritage which tacitly challenges any attempt to reset the theory of causality or, more radically, to dismiss it entirely. New voices, however, have been raised, establishing themselves in this respect as well, extending the ranks of the classical personalities. Although it may be too early to judge them, philosophers such as B. Russell, E. Mach, P. Frank, M. Schlick, P. Duhem, H. Poincare, E. Meyerson, H. Reichenbach, R. Carnap, K. Popper, A. Pap, H. Feigl, F. Waismann, C.D. Broad, F.P. Ramsey, L. Wittgenstein, E. Nagel, on the one hand, and H. Bergson, M. Heidegger, N. von Hartmann, E. Cassirer, R. Ingarden, H. Kelsen, J. Piaget, etc., on the other, have considerably increased our knowledge of what this puzzling "causality" is, or ought to be. And we must also include in this scene such philosophically inclined physicists as A. Einstein, M. Planck, N. Bohr, W. Heisenberg, M. Born, P.W. Bridgman, P.A.M. Dirac, L. de Broglie, D. Bohm, and others.

A contemporary student of causality may, however, be tempted to approach this problem from the two interconnected perspectives which have been distinguished in our century: linguistic and logical.

(1) Through the *linguistic* perspective, causality is viewed as being guaranteed by relevant linguistic expressions which describe, analyze, or construct the causal situation, causal relation (connection), or whatever can be characterized by the adjective "causal." As can be expected, controversies within the current philosophy of language and linguistic theory considerably affect the actual linguistic approach to the problem of causality. The

adherents of the use of constructed, *formalized* languages usually try to remove the ambiguity and vagueness of the colloquial or traditional philosophical discourse on causality. They may talk about causality in either laudatory, or derogatory terms, but in both cases, they are aware of the importance of explicitly stating the vocabulary, syntactic and semantic rules of the language to be used. On the other hand, the *ordinary* language analysts, dominating the British philosophical scene, would rather stick to the colloquial language—however plastic and ambiguous—in order to grasp the contextual usage of the expressions which seem to deal with causal situations of all sorts. Of course, there are various intermediary positions, too. A close scrutiny of all kinds of such applied linguistic practices may, surprisingly or not, reveal the traditional roots of the discussions on causality, stemming from Hume, J.S. Mill, common-sense realism, Aristotle, etc. Nevertheless, although the subject matter is old, the linguistic perspectives are new, attacking the cause—effect dichotomy *via* the varieties of its linguistic representations, and not only through the traditional pathways of conceptual analysis, or the analysis of relevant objects, properties and events.

(2) *Logical* aspects of causation have always attracted the attention of its investigators. In particular, the cause—effect relation has often been linked, even reduced, to the relation between sufficient reason and consequence, thus paying debt to the universal success of deductive logic. However, as Kant justly observed, the traditional formal logic, originating in Aristotle, had been in a state of stagnation and therefore could not be too helpful in tackling any of the serious problems. If this critique of logic was justified in the 18th century, it is positively wrong concerning the fruitful applications of modern formal logic which is, nevertheless, but an expanded continuation of the Aristotelian, Stoic and medieval traditions. Among other things, modern formal logic can handle the notion of relation which was overlooked in the traditional logic. Now relations are represented as binary and, in general, n-ary predicates studied in the predicate (quantificational) logic. Obviously, since the causal relation is a highly distinguishing factor in any causal situation, the apparatus of

predicate logic lends itself to studying the properties of the causal relation (connection, nexus) in their logical articulation. However, as a predicate is incomplete without its arguments, variables or constants, so the causal relation, represented by certain predicates, is incomplete without its members, i.e., without *cause* and *effect*. Thus, two questions can be posed:

(i) What are the members of the causal relation?

(ii) What is the causal relation itself?

Although the answers to question (ii) are of crucial importance, we cannot do well without considering and settling problem complex (i). If we begin with (i), a large body of preliminary insights into causality is presupposed. In other words, the mere posing of problem (i) suggests that we already seem to know much about causation, in both the historical and systematic sense. In fact, various metaphysical or epistemological assumptions might have molded our choice and usage of linguistic and logical devices required for handling the issue. Even if we operate merely on the level of uninterpreted symbols (calculi), we still expect that some semantic steps will be added; thus interpreting the apparent *flatus voci* by their intended meaning. In the case of variables, the specification of their values is guaranteed by the postulated universe of discourse (i.e., the universal class of entities over which the variable ranges). As known from Quine's notion of ontological commitment, or R.M. Martin's notion of ontic involvement,[2] the syntactic category of a bound variable, which can be found in many languages, is accompanied by a kind of 'formal ontology.' Such a formal ontology underlies the semantic interpretation of symbols belonging to other syntactic categories as well, and here we may feel that there is only a small step to be done in the direction of an "informal" ontology or metaphysics.

Indeed, the linguistic expressions representing causes and effects may be endowed with different basic meanings, in accordance with the ontology (whether formal, or "informal" one) chosen.

---

2 Willard V. Quine, *From a Logical Point of View*, 2nd ed. (New York: Harper and Row, 1961), pp. 8-11, 44. Richard M. Martin, *Belief, Existence, and Meaning* (New York: New York University Press, 1969), pp. 17, 30. According to these notions, "to be is to be a value of a bound variable of the system in question."

From the historical standpoint, the following formal-ontological frames have been employed for establishing the general forms of causes and effects:

a) the combination of object and attribute (property);

b) a relation between two or more objects (i.e., a relational network);

c) event or state of affairs;

d) change or process.

This classification is by no means complete and, moreover, it is overlapping. But it reflects the main trends in giving answers to our problem (i). Case (a) is dominantly Aristotelian and parallels the subject-predicate logic, i.e. the subject-predicate structure of any statement, including what could be called a "causal statement" (here a statement referring to either cause, or effect, not to the whole causal situation). The hegemony of this type of logic was certainly embodied in causal discourses for many centuries. Formulations like "The object a causes (produces, etc.) another object b," or, "The attribute P causes (brings about, etc.) the attribute Q," would then be rather elliptical, with a tacit understanding that the missing link (attribute, in the first case; object, in the second) must be supplemented to tell the entire story. Then the complete structure of a causal situation is given, for instance, by: "The object a with an attribute P causes (produces, etc.) the object b with an attribute Q."[3] Obviously, it is not excluded that sometimes the objects a and b are identical; in which case P and Q are attributes of one and the same object. Here the word "object" does not refer only to physical things, but encompasses anything distinguishable, which possesses, or can possess, certain attributes. Needless to say, the controversial notions of substance and essential attributes should be re-considered in this context as well.

Although the so-called causal universals are to be treated in connection with problems (ii), the object-attribute structure of

---

3 Formally, "Pa causes Qb," where the meaning of the word "causes" remains to be specified by settling our problems (ii).

causes and effects also brings forth topics connected with singularity or generality. As a matter of fact, any classification of terms referring to objects and/or attributes[4] must considerably influence the discussions of causal situations; since, for instance, a concrete term (name) may play a significantly different role in a causal context than an abstract one. Even more striking may be a distinction made between an empty term (referring to no existing object) and non-empty term; or the polarity: finite object—infinite object; etc.

As to these subtleties, let us now disregard them and move to the case (b). However, before we proceed further, it is to be stated that the main force behind the instances of case (a) was the Aristotelian idea of the efficient (external) cause. If Bunge is right, this type of cause has actually dominated the modern discussion of causality, leading to the omission of Aristotle's material and formal causes and to a reluctant, re-evaluated acceptance of the final cause.[5]

Case (b) exhibits causes and effects as relational networks based on the above extended concept of predicate. This modern expansion of predicates could find its counterpart in the extended notion of attribute; thus introducing relational attributes as well. Besides terminological uniformity, cases (a) and (b) would then become either identical, or one would encompass the other. A representative sample of such a general causal structure could be given as follows: "The relation R between the objects a, b, c causes the relation S between the objects e, f."[6] When the monadic predicates are technically allowed to represent one-membered relations, the case (a) is actually subsumed under (b). Also an expansion of the relations to infinitely many membered ones is only a matter of technical procedures.

Events or states of affairs are the most serious rivals of the object-attribute approach to causes and effects. Therefore, case (c)

4 Such as the classification elaborated by J.S. Mill, *A System of Logic*, Bk. I, Chapters II-III.
5 Mario Bunge, *Causality*, pp. 32-33, 226.
6 Formally, "$R(a,b,c)$ causes $S(e,f)$," where R is a triadic and S a binary relation.

has been well established in the theoretical and practical treatment of causality. Here the causes and effects consist of events or states of affairs which can, of course, be considered as being simple or complex. If a single event is regarded as being complex, then its inner structure amounts to that of our case (a), or, in a generalized version, to that of case (b). It appears to be more common that a single event (state of affairs) is not analyzed into its components, but taken as an unanalyzed whole. Then a complex event is built in a similar way as the molecular sentences in the truth-functional logic; by a combination of simple events, which could be characterized as events that do not contain other events as their proper components. Moreover, both simple and complex events could be considered as possible values of event variables.[7] However, a cause is rarely given as a single event, but rather as a set of events which may be, according to previous remarks, either simple or complex. Such a set of events resembles a set of premises of deductive inference and, no doubt, this is one of the points which were responsible for the historical attempts to treat cause as a sufficient reason leading to the effect as a deductive consequence of the former.[8] Also the possibility of joining conjunctively all the premises of a deductive inference into a single (however long) premise may find its analogue in combining all the events of which a cause consists, into a single one—a complex cause. Of course, there is a problem concerning the possible operations that could combine events in a similar way as the conjunction joins sentences. This question can be answered only by an elaborated theory or logic of events.

When speaking about events or states of affairs, the distinction drawn between actual and possible events (states of affairs) discloses philosophical problems of extraordinary significance. Apart from the metaphysical issues, the logical aspects of modalities come the fore. Needless to say, without considering

---

7   In extensional first-order logic, events (states of affairs) could be treated as the referents of sentences; on par with Truth and Falsity, or instead of the Fregean referents.

8   Mario Bunge, *Causality*, pp. 226 ff. To day we draw a stricter distinction between causal relation and causal inference.

possible causes (which contain possible events), the causal relation would be limited merely to actually observed cases—a drastic restriction which must undermine any causal universality, whether inductive or not. Therefore the various proposals for the treatment of counterfactuals and subjunctive conditionals[9] are, in such an important way, connected with the modern theory of causation.

Our last case, case (d), focuses on change or process as being the backbone of a causal relation. Change is either a dynamic kind of event, which could reduce the case (d) to (c), or it can be detected by comparing a specific effect with its cause. Such a comparison should show what happened to the object or event occuring in the cause after we found it in the corresponding effect. This 'method of difference' can refer to either objects and their properties, case (a), or to relational networks, case (b), by inquiring into the presence or absence of the features involved.

The notion of change is tightly connected with two other issues: 1. *action* (both the process and the result of it) as performed by a human agent; 2. *spatio-temporal parameters.* The concept of action has accompanied any rudimentary theory of causation, and the idea of a product, made by a producer responsible for it, has vigorously affected the conception of the external, and, in part, final cause. On the other hand, the spatio-temporal parameters are necessary for setting the change into a proper framework. In fact, spatial and temporal characteristics can be treated as distinguished properties of objects or events which may significantly determine any causal situation. Spatial (and also temporal) contiguity between the cause and the effect, just as temporal precedence or antecedence of the cause before the effect, as D. Hume and J.S. Mill stated them, became classical normative maxims imposed upon any causal relation.[10] We shall

9 See an extensive literature on this topic, which was triggered by the original contributions of Nelson Goodman, Roderick Chisholm, and others. The last word in this field is the book written by David Lewis, *Counterfactuals,* Cambridge, Massachusetts: Harvard University Press, 1973.

10 This does not mean that these maxims are undisputable.

discuss these issues later, when dealing with the causal relation itself.

Let us now proceed to the group of problems (ii). Here we are concerned, not with the members of causal relation, i.e., with cause and effect, but with the relation (connection) which they bear. In other words, if the whole causal relation is represented by a formula 'x C y', where the left member 'x' stands for cause and the right member 'y' for effect, our attention is turned just to the meaning of the symbol 'C' which stands for the causal relation itself. Linguistically, this relation can be represented in various ways and by different phrases. However, any philosophical theory of causation tries to abstract from these linguistic (and con-ceptual) varieties what they have in common—the assumed basic properties of the causal relation (whether in the descriptive, or normative sense). There is a stock of, let us say, informal properties of causality which have been detected in the historical process of investigating the concept of causation. In addition to them, the causal relation C can be described merely formally, as being irreflexive, asymmetrical and transitive.[11]

In his comprehensive treatment of causality, M. Bunge noticed the following "informal" characteristics of causality:

a)	constant conjunction	b)	contiguity
c)	antecedence	d)	invariable succession
e)	linearity	f)	unidirectionality
g)	externality	h)	necessary production (efficacy)[12]

Constant conjunction states that whenever cause occurs, the effect occurs as well, and vice versa. But, it cannot be interpreted as the usual logical conjunction, which holds for any pair, or larger complexes, of sentences, provided that all the sentences are true.

---

11 As such, the causal relation is only one member of the entire family of relations which possess the same formal properties. Hence, it is necessary to distinguish it from this family by adding the properties which make the causal relation unique.

12 Mario Bunge, *Causality*, passim.

Moreover, conjunction, in the logical sense, displays symmetry; a property which can hardly be expected from causality.[13] This conjunction disregards temporal ordering, and relevance between the conjuncts. But, as the anti-Humean example of the regular succession of night and day exhibits, even bringing the missing factors into the game does not solve the problem. In spite of all these shortcomings, the idea of a constant conjunction remains as a partial characteristic of the causal bond; since the pairs of causes and effects occur together, in the proper order, making us wonder what glues them together.

Contiguity is to day less popular, howsoever Hume used to emphasize it. Transitivity of causality enables the causal chains to act with intermediate links interfering between, perhaps remote, causes and effects. Because of these indirect bonds, causes and effects may be quite legitimate without being contiguous in space or time. Thus, a cause need not touch its corresponding effect if we do not take into account a possible accumulation of all causes leading to the effect in question. Such a cumulative cause could be contiguous with the effect in question, but the very idea would also be self-destructive; since one might ask why should this cumulation stop just before it reaches our effect and not swallow the "effect" as well? This threat of an infinite progress is analogous to that of an infinite regress. Otherwise, our notions of space and time have also changed considerably together with the mathematical techniques dealing with the puzzle of continuity.

Antecedence or *precedence* in time, as J.S. Mill stated it, used to be accepted as a natural property of causality; for an assumption that the effect may precede the cause has been dismissed as incompatible with common sense. Discussions on the reversibility of time have, however, somewhat undermined this steadfast conviction. Further, while antecedence is a property expected of the Aristotelian notion of an efficient (external)

---

13 Hegelian "interactionists" could accept such a property of causation. Here cause and effect would be co-existent and mutually acting on each other. An interesting contribution to this view is Czeslaw Znamierowski, "Causal Nexus," *Studia Philosophica*, III (1939-1946); Cracoviae et Posnaniae, 1948), pp. 449-465.

cause, it ceases to play a dominant role in considering the notion of a final cause or teleological explanation.

Antecedence is often combined with the previous property—contiguity—but this combination is not necessary, as can be seen from the following view of B. Russell: " . . . if there are causes at all, they must be separated by a finite interval of time from their effects and thus cause their effects after they have ceased to exist."[14] Here Russell, who is a warrior against causality and an advocate of the notion of function, explicitly denies the requirement of a temporal contiguity, and, on the contrary, inserts a finite interval of time between cause and effect. Whatever happens during the duration of this time gap in which the cause exists no more and the effect does not yet take place, in Russell's view, the cause precedes the effect. This actually is a prevailing view, although dependent upon the theory of time employed.

Invariable succession is closely connected with all foregoing properties. The word "invariable" is almost synonymous with the phrase "constant conjunction," and the meaning of the word "succession" suggests the idea of a temporal relatedness in which something is earlier (cause) and something later (effect). The paradigm example of the invariable, uniform or regular succession of night and day, shows how vulnerable this requirement is. Furthermore, there is a problem as to whether our knowledge of the legitimate invariable succession is based on *a priori* grounds or whether it is a result of empirical, i.e. *a posteriori,* procedures. The traditional Kantian problem could be discussed at this point, together with the principle of induction and the principle of causality, which should somehow regulate the "behavior" of the regular succession.

Another approach which belongs to this category is that via the notion of *condition.* As J.S. Mill states, "if there be any meaning which confessedly belongs to the term necessity, it is *uncondi-tionalness . . .* we may define, therefore, the cause of a

---

14 Bertrand Russell, "On the Notion of Cause," p. 393; see also pp. 389-391, where an explanation is given.

phenomenon to be the antecedent, or the concurrence of antecedents, on which it is invariably and *unconditionally* consequent."[15] This additional qualification of invariable succession was used by Mill in order to defend causality against the destructive force of the night and day example. Here unconditionality means that once all the conditions amounting to a cause are present, whatever be the other circumstances, the effect *must* occur and nothing can prevent it from happening. In other words, if a complex, sufficient condition (cause) is completely present, nothing can stop it from producing its effect; so that the effect is dependent only on the sufficient condition in question (cause), and, being unconditioned by anything else, "follows" the cause of necessity. This is a sophisticated approach, but we may still be dissatisfied at leaving open the question, "What makes the cause operate of necessity?"

The approach to causality via conditionality is otherwise responsible for the deduction pattern of causal explanation. That is, if cause is identified with a sufficient condition, and the latter is in turn regarded as sufficient reason, then the effect is a necessary consequent of the sufficient reason (condition, cause). Nevertheless, true causal statements (laws and their instances) are not logically true statements, in the sense that their negations are self-contradictory. In modern terms, true causal statements do not hold in all possible worlds (models) but only in some of them (obviously, relativized to a given system). This contention does not preclude successful participation of true causal statements in deductively valid arguments. In this regard, true causal statements are not different from any other true premises of deductively valid arguments. It appears that true causal statements alone are not sufficient grounds for deducing logically necessary consequences. However, there is certain necessity by which the effect-statements follow from the cause-statements. This causal necessity is hidden in a causal law which accompanies such a transition from a specific cause to a specific effect. However, what is a causal law? Does it

15 J.S. Mill, *A System of Logic*, p. 222.

possess a probabilistic weight given by an inductive evidence? Or, is it a synthetic *a priori* statement?

Deductive patterns of causal explanation thus tacitly assume causal laws as given and justified by other means (e.g., inductive). Thus, causality is not explained away by showing a deductively valid argument (or argument-schema) which takes care of one of its instances.

Another property of causality—*linearity*—is often represented by appropriate geometrical diagrams, such as chains consisting of links.[16] Whether the causes and effects—the links of causal chains—are regarded as simple or complex, the idea of linearity, as M. Bunge justly remarks, reflects the methodological necessity of isolating connected events (or facts, or whatever else) from the whole system. Bunge is right when he contends that "if causal chains are valid in limited contexts, it is because they constitute a rough reflection of reality, that is, because there *is* in the real world something vaguely resembling the causal chain."[17] On the other hand, he is also aware of the limitations of this artificial isolation, and, in this respect, seems to share N.R. Hanson's objection against the notion of causal chains and his "spider's web" imagery. Otherwise, linearity does not shed too much light on the necessity of the causal nexus. Linearity helps one in grasping the entire causal context in a simplified, visible representation, displaying one of the basic formal properties of causality—its transitivity. The idea of necessity may enter the field of investigations in considering the first cause (prime mover) which is the first link of the richest metaphysical causal chain, or, negatively, in considering the infinite regress without any first cause whatsoever.

Unidirectionality of causality is connected with its asymmetric nature, i.e., the effect cannot "cause" its cause. Here the problem of temporal ordering is present as well, so that previous con-

16 An interesting probabilistic, quantitative explication of the causal chains and causal nets has been given in I.J. Good, "A Causal Calculus (1)," *British Journal for the Philosophy of Science*, (1960), pp. 305-318.

17 Mario Bunge, *Causality*, p. 134

siderations regarding antecedence, contiguity, time-gap must be reviewed at this point. As a matter of fact, the direction and irreversibility of the time flow determines the direction of causal (cause—effect) chains. However, when causality is regarded as symmetrical (as the Hegelian partisans of a general "inter-actionism" could claim), it will not be unidirectional but polydirectional instead. Yet this latter view is rather devious and it may reduce the problem of temporal relationship between cause and effect to that of simultaneity, or at least partial simultaneity. The obvious argument raised here is that if the cause ceases to exist, then it actually cannot affect its effect, and vice versa. Thus, at least partial, co-existence (simultaneity) of the "cause" and the "effect" is necessary for making them work on each other. But then the words "cause" and "effect" could be replaced by a phrase "interacting factor," for instance, and one might wonder what would remain from a "normal" theory of causation at all. Moreover, the simultaneity of cause and effect may well lead to the identity of all causes and effects whatsoever, and therefore to neo-Eleatic attacks on the reality of time and change.[18]

Externality of cause as to its effects stems, according to Bunge, from the Aristotelian notion of efficient cause. Otherwise, there is usually no precise definition of externality and apparently an appeal to intuitive understanding of the notion is assumed. To make the discussions about external and internal properties, relations, etc., more lucid, we might be forced to adopt some clear-cut logical or, say, topological, devices such as the boundaries between classes (sets) or structures, or perhaps boundaries between parts and wholes. Then the talk of extrinsic and intrinsic determinants, and so forth, could become much more reasonable than it usually is. But even this correction would not change externality into a really significant factor in elucidating causal necessity.

The remaining property—*necessary production*—should save causality and point its dynamic and active character. According to this property, the effect not only happens, appearing after the occurence of the cause, but it is actively produced by the cause; and it cannot happen that the cause, once present, would fail to produce its effect. This magic formula seems to contain the entire essence of causality and it also seems to fit well into all kinds of dynamic, process philosophies. Nonetheless, when a deep grasp of the causal mechanism is at stake, we cannot achieve too much with mere metaphorical formulations which have been the beloved of romantic philosophers of all sorts.

The activity of cause upon its effect suggests a consideration of how much "energy" the cause "loses" in producing its effect. As is known, maxims like *"causa aequat effectum"* had preceded the explicit formulations of the principle of conservation of energy, being perhaps their philosophical forerunners. These maxims were supported by the powerful notions of sufficient reason and all-embracing deductivism, which were discussed in the above paragraph concerning the role of conditions in explaining causality. In this light, the content of the effect would already be contained in (or equal to) its cause, and thus the cause would only unfold its content, submitting it, fully or partly, to its effect (and so forth). This idea is well known and points back to the dilemma: *prima causa,* or infinite regress. More surprising is another alternative, that supports so well the idea of emergent novelties, according to which the effect may contain more than its cause. If this alternative holds, then the cause may really creatively produce its effect, rather than unfold its own content. But the apparent novelty in the effect could arise because of a narrow causal explanation which had identified a partial cause with the whole cause. This epistemological (in principle) defect, projected to the ontological level, might be responsible for creating the "effect-creation," and thus an irrational residue, as E. Meyerson called it.

These controversial notions of production and novelty may be efficient in ontological and epistemological discourses, but they must terrify a logician who wants to translate them into his own conceptual network. To encompass such a goal, a neat deductive edifice would be out of order. Furthermore, the content-gap between cause and effect would differ from the so-called induction-gap, in that the content-gap is observed in each particular instance of the causal relation, whereas the induction-gap arises out of the uncertainty of whether or not the next (and further) observed case will be the same as all the previous ones. However, when the logician is not bothered by all these subtle problems, he may still be content with a constant conjunction and linear regular succession appearing between the cause and the effect, whatever the relations between their contents may be. Again, from such a deliberate truncation of the notions of cause and effect it is only a small step to replacing causality by functionalism. A more serious approach to the problem of production and novelty may, on the other hand, require a careful scrutiny of elliptical (incomplete, hidden) causes, as well as a consideration of potentialities, possibilities, infinite sets of properties and states of affairs, etc.

Many foregoing remarks and criticisms might appear as representing the purely negative portion of my study. Indeed, the key notion of *causal necessity* has remained obscure. As stated before, causal necessity is not to be identified with either logical necessity (analyticity) or a mere universal law.[19] The property of causal necessity should be ascribed to certain premisses of "causal" inferences, presumably to so-called universal causal statements. Such linguistic (or, at the best, conceptual) treatment of the causal necessity is compatible with the contemporary attitude toward the notions of truth, falsity, probability, etc., but it may lack the power of grasping what is actually the necessity attached to the relation C. To meet this challenge, one may contend that the necessary (or other) properties of the causal relation C can be viewed (or perhaps simulated) through the corresponding properties assigned to the symbol 'C'. However, this linguistic or conceptual procedure cannot be satisfactory. One feels that the concern with the causal relation C precedes any postulation

19 Frank P. Ramsey's subtle analyses of these problems can be regarded as classics in this area. See his "General Propositions and Causality," and "Causal Qualities," both in *The Foundations of Mathematics* (London: Routledge and Kegan Paul, 1931), pp. 237-255, 260-262.

imposed upon, or revolving around, the symbol 'C'. The reversal of this process may be useful as a methodological device, but at the same time harmful in the ontological respect. Yet, it is very important to set the relevant ontological considerations into an adequate, up-to-date linguistic or conceptual framework.

In the contemporary literature on the subject one can find numerous examples of treating the causal relation in the new way. Some authors try to apply certain kind of modal logics, struggling, in general, with the problem of conditionals or implication;[20] others employ a probabilistic approach,[21] or even a sort of causal algebra.[22] Most of these attempts are too technical and cannot be handled in the context of this study. However, a serious student of causation, causal universals or laws, causal explanations, etc., should carefully look at the important technical trials, in order to keep pace with the current investigations and avoid an anachronous, old-fashioned treatment of the issues in question. Obviously, a critical attitude is an indispensable tool, as a safeguard against empty fashion or novelty at any price.

Yet, one thing appears to be certain: causality, the important philosophical category required for answering the pressing "why?" questions in all areas of human knowledge, has survived many vicious attacks, and has fared better in this century than in previous centuries.

* * *

Concerning the theme "Causation and the Problem of God in Contemporary Philosophy," the elaboration of which would properly fit into the context of this anthology, it can only be stated that the present methodological study is a necessary

---

20 A.W. Burks, "The Logic of Causal Propositions," *Mind*, (1951), pp. 363-382; Stanislaw Jaskowski, "On the Modal and Causal Functions in Symbolic Logic," *Studia Philosophica*, (1951), pp. 71-92.

21 Patrick Suppes, *A Probabilistic Theory of Causality*, also I.J. Good, *op. cit.*

22 Patrick Suppes, *op. cit.*, Chp. IV. Zoltan Domotor, "Causal Models and Space-Time Geometries," *Synthese*, (1972), pp. 5-57, is an excellent review of various technical approaches to the problem of causality.

prerequisite but not a sufficient ground for an efficient treatment of such an important topic. At the same time, a hope should be expressed that the open field, left by the logician, but entered into by a metaphysician or theologian, will be successfully explored— with the help of the new logician's tools and considerations.

No doubt that here the philosopher faces a fathomless sea of heavy and intricate issues some of which were implicitly outlined in the context of the present study (such as the dictum "causa aequat effectum," or another scholastic maxim: "causa cessante cessat effectus"). In order to tackle such questions, one must be deeply concerned with the distinction between primary and secondary causes, as well as with the concepts of infinity, continuity, actuality, existence, *causa sui*, creation out of nothing, and so like. But this is a program which, both in the systematic and historical aspects, goes far beyond the possibilities of this essay.

A SELECT BIBLIOGRAPHY

Aquinas, St. Thomas, *Summa Theologiae*. Tr. by Fathers of the English Dominican Province. 24 vols. London: Burns Oates & Washbourne, n.d.

Aristotle, *Metaphysics*. Tr. by H. Tredennick. 2 vols. Cambridge, Massachusetts: Harvard University Press, 1947.

————, *Physics*, in *Works*, ed. by W.D. Ross. 2 vols. Oxford: Clarendon Press, 1930.

Bohm, David, *Causality and Chance in Modern Physics*. London: Routledge & Kegan Paul, 1957.

Born, Max, *The Natural Philosophy of Cause and Chance*. 2nd ed. Oxford: Clarendon Press, 1951.

Braithwaite, Richard B., "The Idea of Necessary Connection," *Mind*, 36 (1927), pp. 467-477; 37 (1928), pp. 62-72.

Broad, C.D., *Induction, Probability, and Causation: Selected Papers*. Dordrecht, Holland: D. Reidel, 1968.

Bunge, Mario, *Causality: The Place of the Causal Principle in Modern Science*. Cambridge, Massachusetts: Harvard University Press, 1959.

Carnap, Rudolf, "Dreidimensionalität des Raumes und Kausalität: Eine Untersuchungen über den logischen Zusammerhang zweier

Fiktionen," *Annalen der Philosophie und philosophischen Kritik* (Leipzig), 4 (1924), pp. 105-130.

Cassirer, Ernst, *Determinism and Indeterminism in Modern Physics: Historical and Systematic Studies of the Problem of Causality.* New Haven, Connecticut: Yale University Press, 1957.

Davidson, Donald, "Actions, Reasons, and Causes," *Journal of Philosophy*, LX (1963), pp. 685-700.

Donceel, J., "Causality and Evolution: A Survey of Some Neo-Scholastic Theories," *New Scholasticism*, 39 (1965), pp. 295-315.

Downing, P.B., "Subjunctive Conditionals, Time Order and Causation," *Proceedings of the Aristotelian Society*, 59 (1959), pp. 125-140.

Ducasse, C.J., *Truth, Knowledge and Causation.* New York: Humanities Press, 1968.

Feigl, Herbert, "Notes on Causality," *Readings in the Philosophy of Science*, ed. by H. Feigl and M. Brodbeck. New York: Appleton-Century-Crofts, 1953, pp. 408-418.

Frank, Philipp, *Philosophy of Science.* Englewood Cliffs, New Jersey: Prentice-Hall, 1957.

Galileo, Galilei, *Opera*, 20 vols. Florence: Edizione Nazionale, 1890-1909.

Gilson, Etienne, "Avicenne et les origines de la notion de cause efficiente," *Atti del XII Congresso Internazionale di Filosofia*, 9, Florence, 1960, pp. 121-130.

Goodman, Nelson, *Fact, Fiction, and Forecast.* Cambridge, Massachusetts: Harvard University Press, 1955.

Grünbaum, Adolf, "Causality and the Science of Human Behavior," *American Scientist*, 40 (1952), pp. 665-676.

Hanson, Norwood R., "Causal Chains," *Mind*, 64 (1955), pp. 289-311.

Hart, H.L.A. and Honore, A.M., *Causation in the Law.* Oxford: Clarendon Press, 1959.

Hartmann, Nicolai von, *Neue Wege der Ontologie.* 3rd ed. Stuttgart: Kohlhammer Verlag, 1949.

Hartshorne, Charles, "Causal Necessities: An Alternative to Hume," *Philosophical Review*, 63 (1954), pp. 479-499.

Hume, David, *A Treatise of Human Nature.* 2 vols. New York: Dutton, 1911.

Ingarden, Roman, "Quelques remarques sur la relation de causalité," *Studia Philosophica*, 3 (1948), pp. 157-166.

Kelsen, Hans, "Causality and Retribution," *Philosophy of Science*, 8 (1941), pp. 533-556.

Leibniz, Gottfried W. von, *Philosophical Papers and Letters.* Tr. and ed. by L.E. Loemker. Chicago: University of Chicago Press, 1956, 2 vols.

Lenzen, Victor, *Causality in Natural Science.* Springfield, Illinois: C.C. Thomas, 1954.

Lerner, Daniel (ed.), *Cause and Effect.* The Hayden Colloquium on Scientific Method and Concept. New York: The Free Press, 1965 (contributions by R.A. Dahl, L.S. Feuer, A. Kaplan, D. Lerner, E. Mayr, E. Nagel, T. Parsons, P.A. Samuelson and H.A. Simon).

Maritain, Jacques, *A Preface to Metaphysics: Seven Lectures on Being,* New York: Sheed and Ward, 1958.

Meyerson, Emile, "Hegel, Hamilton, Hamelin et le concept de cause," *Essais,* Paris: Vrin, 1936.

———, *Identity and Reality,* tr. K. Loewenberg. New York: Dover, 1962.

Mill, John Stuart, *A System of Logic.* London: Longmans, Green, 1952. First published in 1843.

Piaget, Jean, *The Child's Conception of Physical Causality.* London: Routledge and Kegan Paul, 1965.

Reichenbach, Hans, *The Rise of Scientific Philosophy.* Berkeley, California: University of California Press, 1951.

Russell, Bertrand, "On the Notion of Cause," *Proceedings of the Aristotelian Society,* 13 (1913), pp. 1-26.

———, "On the Notion of Cause," in *Readings in the Philosophy of Science,* ed. by H. Feigl and M. Brodbeck. New York: Appleton-Century-Crofts, 1953, pp. 387-407.

———, *Human Knowledge: Its Scope and Limits.* London: Allen and Unwin, 1948.

Schlick, Moritz, "Causality in Everyday Life and in Recent Science," *Readings in Philosophical Analysis,* ed. by H. Feigl and W. Sellars. New York: Appleton-Century-Crofts, 1949.

Sellars, Wilfrid, "Counterfactuals, Dispositions, and the Causal Modalities," *Minnesota Studies in the Philosophy of Science,* II, ed. by H. Feigl *et al.,* Minneapolis, Minnesota: University of Minnesota Press, 1958, pp. 225-308.

Suppes, Patrick, *A Probabilistic Theory of Causality.* New York: Humanities Press, 1970.

Waismann, Friedrich, "The Decline and Fall of Causality," *Turning Points in Physics,* ed. by Crombie, Amsterdam, 1959.

Wartofsky, Marx W., *Conceptual Foundations of Scientific Thought.* New York: The Macmillan Comp., 1968.

CHAPTER XXXVIII

GOD'S EXISTENCE AND
THE EVIL OF SUFFERING

*Andrzei Woznicki**

The problems of God's existence and the presence of evil in this world involve several philosophical issues and include all the basic themes of theodicy. Vindicating the justice of God's permitting the presence of evil in the world entails three main questions: 1. God's perfections themselves, 2. the divine creation of the world, and 3. the ultimate purpose of all created things. The presence of evil in a world which was created by God challenges His attributes, His Essence, and Existence itself. If God is the most perfect Being, then why did He permit evil to exist? If God created the world then is God also the cause of evil? If God in creating the world had some purpose to achieve, then is there any value in the existence of evil in the world?

These questions are also the basic issues at hand in the traditional proofs of the existence of God; the ontological, which is based on the notion of the most perfect idea of God; the cosmological, which is grounded on the notion of divine causality; and the teleological, which points to the ultimate destiny of the created world.

In view of this connection between the question of God's existence and the possibility of challenging God's existence by the fact of evil in the world, the theodectic resolution of *scandalum mali* can be challenged in regards to the Divine attributes, essence and existence. This challenge is based on God's Immanent

*Associate Professor of Philosophy at the University of San Francisco, San Francisco, California, U.S.A.

Activations in the Created World, and Transcendent Directivity of the Created World.

The ambiguity of the coexistence of goodness and evil in the world is still less bearable when innocent and righteous people suffer evil. In this situation there is apparently genuine and justifiable ground to doubt whether God is benevolent and whether He exists at all. Although the question of vindicating God from responsibility of tolerating the evil, or of causing innocent creatures and righteous people to suffer, has been discussed previously by both ancient and medieval masters, the contemporary approach to this problem has a more existential significance than an ontological one. A presentation of the contemporary approach to the affliction of innocent people might center itself on the punishment of a righteous man as elaborated by J. Royce and the suffering of innocent children as presented by Dostoyevsky on one hand, and contemporary nihilism as forecasted by Nietzsche with its *theologia diaboli* of Sartre on the other hand.

1. Divine Immanence and the Traumatic Consciousness of the Absurdity of Human Suffering

Man conceptualizes God as the most perfect Being Who is Absolute and Necessary in His essence and Unlimited and Unsurpassable in His existence. Understood in this way, the perfectibility of God indicates that in God there is no real distinction or separation between His essence and His existence. This conception defines God as an all-encompassing Reality, independent and immune from any imperfections; this means specifically that God is immune from evil.

The human experience of God as the Most Perfect and Highest Being indicates that God's own perfection excludes evil, not only in God Himself, but in all of His creative activations. The reason for this is that an Absolute, Necessary, Unlimited and Unsurpassable God is not and cannot be related to any other beings upon which He could depend, nor could His creation be less than a manifestation of His essence and existence. In other words, since

God's own perfection consists in ontological identity of His essence and His existence, there cannot be in God any lack in His Being, i.e., nothingness. Moreover, since God's essence and existence constitute absolute identity, God in His creative activations transcends the possibility of falling away from His ultimate design or in achieving the final purpose of His creativity. In the order of divine activity then, the relationship between God and all His created beings can be only unilateral: namely, that of the created to the Creator, and not *vice versa*. It follows that the unilateral relationship of created beings to God consists in not having necessary beingness, but in their contingency, their limited essences and existences. As such, they find themselves in the constant possibility of evil, i.e. lack of permanent fulfillment of their beingness.

God's creativity in causing creatures to exist out of nothingness is only virtually distinct from His own nature, and as such, results in some created thing outside Himself that must have a specific purpose. Fellini in his film *La Strada* makes Il Matto say to Gelsomina that even a little pebble has some purpose. But, since God's creative act is only virtually distinct from His own nature, the process of creation is nothing but a manifestation of God Himself: *productio rei ex nihilo sui et subiecti* is also *emanatio quaedam* of God (St. Thomas). Consequently, God can be judged according to the way He creates and executes the world.

In view of the unilateral relationship of created things to God, we can only know the results and effects of the Divine creative activation and not God Himself as the Creator. The results of God's creative activation, however, reveal that in the world created by God there is not only goodness but evil as well. Therefore man perceives a metaphysical ambiguity as to the very nature of God. On one hand the goodness of the created world attests to the benevolence of God, but on the other hand, the overwhelming presence of evil in the world indicates that the results of God's creative activations are not desirable.

(a) Divine and Human Suffering according to Josiah Royce

The presence of moral evil in the form of the suffering of a righteous person assails the logic of our mind, and even seems to contradict God's existence. The reason for this is that the just man is, as in the description of the biblical Job, honest and sincere in his life, simplehearted and righteous to others, and pious and devout to God Himself. Moreover, the punishment of a righteous person calls God's existence and perfection into question because it denies not only any Divine creativity, but also any motives for personal improvement of God's created beings. Finally, if the just man *already* shows his goodness and willingness to follow God in all and everything, then suffering evil in such a person seems to be useless since he already has achieved a certain level of perfectibility as a creature.

The interrogations into the problems of the suffering of a righteous man lead us to several questions about God's existence and His Attributes: how can we explain the punishment and suffering of a just person? Even if there would be any ultimately beneficial reason, either for him or for another, for the suffering of a righteous man, is there any sufficient reason to suffer, and, if so, how can one know it? Why is the suffering of evil afflicted on the innocent man who already is following God's will?

One of the classical works which directly deals with the question of suffering of righteous man is Josiah Royce's treatise, "The Problem of Job," published in the book *Studies on Good and Evil*.

The philosophical approach to the question of the suffering of a righteous man can be formulated in several ways, and could take the following form of dialectical reasoning: If God, as Almighty, can do whatever He wants to do; and if God, in His Omniscience, can foresee everything, then God by His Omnipotence could direct a just man to his ultimate destiny without unnecessary suffering, especially in view of the fact that such suffering will be oblivious to God anyway. (See what is said in the Bible while Job was being afflicted.)

Royce proposes to solve these dilemmas by accepting an idealistic dialectic of creative co-existence between contingent and necessary Being according to the principle that God is present in/through you. He is Absolute Being, so You are one with God; you are part of his life in the way you share with Him being. Now, if there is no essential difference of kind between contingency and necessity of being, then man can share God's perfections. But in view of this premise, Royce resolves that in man's suffering, God is suffering too: *"your sufferings are God's sufferings."*

The question then of the suffering of an innocent person takes on a new form, namely: "Why does God suffer?" Royce argues that since God is present in suffering in the world, and it is posited that "his world is the best possible world," then it is clear that it is everlastingly perfected by God's presence in the world, not only as a sufferer, but as triumphant Goodness as well.

The resolution of the problem consists then in the dialectical tension of goodness and evil itself "which falls directly within the familiar and momentous as well as too much neglected philosophy." Royce insists that the terms "g o o d" and "e v i l" cannot be taken apart from each other: "We forget the experiences from which the words have been abstracted." Since goodness and evil are mutually intertwined we can define goodness only in terms of evil, not in terms of innocence or righteousness. Since there is ontological priority of goodness against evil, then we are obliged to improve goodness in ourselves by "the removal of evil from the world." Evil then is *not* an illusion, but a real, necessary condition for improving the best of all possible world. The only difference between good and evil consists in a difference between divine and human perception. What God sees in unity, we can only see in fragments.

In solving the question of evil, in this way, Royce advocates not only a hierarchy of various interests and different impulses, but presupposes an orderly harmony which both justifies and resolves any conflicts of value which can happen. In view of this order of goodness and evil, Royce would not only justify the presence of evil as being consistent with the perfection of the world, but also advocates the necessity of the evil for that perfection. Consequently Royce is arriving at the solution of Job's problem by addressing himself to the biblical patriarch, telling him that his suffering does not separate him from God because his suffering is also his God's suffering. Royce also excludes the possibility of preventing suffering in God and man because he predicts that the ultimately good will finally come in the process of activating goodness in the world by triumphing over evil. And, although it is God's triumph over evil and not man's, Royce answered that since man sees fragmentarily "his truth as through a glass darkly," he fails to realize that God's truth or triumph is man's as well. In order to triumph with God over evil man must subordinate it as much as possible, and in this way he becomes "the minister of God's triumph."

Royce's idealistic solution to evil assumes an inner tension between primary and secondary experiences of goodness and evil, based on satisfaction and dissatisfaction, and as a result of this inner tension man "comes to love his own hates, and hates his own loves ... " Now, the view of man's mutual interchangeability of experiences of goodness and evil is, according to Royce, based on a variety of "impulsions and interests" and not on ontological motives and causes. Although admitting with Royce that "there are good and bad states of tension," the question still remains: can those states of tension be justified when resolved into some higher form of harmony? The only motive power of justifying the experienced tension between good and evil which Royce can offer consists in "the form, rather than the mere content of life," and in this way he subordinates evil to goodness.

But Royce's proposed solution to the evil of the suffering of an innocent and righteous man is, as he admits himself, not exclusive but inclusive in God's creative activations for the betterment of the best of all possible worlds. As such, it finds itself in an immanent order of God's presence as *Creator,* but does not resolve the transcendent character of God's creative activation as such. For even if we would accept with Royce that "God here sorrows not with, but in your sorrow," then to whom should the triumph over evil be ultimately attributed? If God rather than righteous man suffers unnecessarily; and if man rather than God, is not necessary to the resolution of the evil of man's suffering, then both the evil and the triumph over evil would need to have another power other than from God or man. Royce admits that the ultimate triumph over evil would be God's, and it is the sufferer's fault that he does not and cannot share the triumph over evil with God. But even if the sufferer could share with God the triumph over evil, the priority still would be with God and not man. One can also reason that when God's will is man's will, then man's willing an evil would be God's will, and in the situation of sinners God's will cannot share the divine triumph in the sinner's damnation.

Whatever Royce can say for the justification of evil as understood as a manifestation of God's ultimate triumph over evil, the suffering of a just person is not resolved, because even if man is "the minister of God's triumph," the main question of "why" and "what" is not revealed.

The fallacy of Royce's theory that evil does not negate the perfection of God on the ground that not God but man as free agent may fail, consists in the fact that if God can be justified in allowing the suffering of a just person, what are the reasons for such an evil to exist if God's own perfection is immune from evil both from within and from without, because otherwise He would not be Being but would only have Being. And, if by evil we understand lack of being, or nothingness, then God's existence would not be self-contained and self-sufficient as such. Consequently, if we find the locus of evil in God's creative actions in the world, then God is the ultimate cause of the evil.

Admitting for the sake of argument that God is the cause of the suffering of a righteous person, one may suggest that He causes such evil either directly or indirectly. If God would be the cause of suffering of a just person directly, then he is unmerciful and as such malevolent in his creative activation in the world. But if God allows the evil to be experienced by a just person indirectly, for instance through the devil, then either God is impotent, or God is unable to restrain the power of the devil, and consequently makes the devil equal to Himself. In either way the divine and demonic power in the world would be mutually intertwined and the suffering of a just person would be without any logical explanation, and the person involved would find himself in a helpless situation, unable to judge whether to accept or refuse the evil.

(b) Suffering of Innocent Children and Human Freedom in Dostoyevsky

The argument against God's existence on the ground of the suffering of innocent children can be formulated in the following way: if God exists and if He does allow innocent children to suffer evil, then He does not deserve to exist, and therefore does not exist. This line of reasoning which Dostoyevsky ascribes to his rebellious heroes like Ivan, in the novel *The Brothers Karamazov,* is based on a polarity of human existence between the needs of his body and the wants of his spirit. On one hand, Ivan finds himself enjoying "the thirst for life in me," but on the other hand he realizes the demonic character in him. Ivan is fully aware that the demonic power in his mind is only one side of him, and although he realizes that the demonic power in him does not have superhuman reality in a form of a devil, nevertheless he wants desperately to believe in the devil's existence, because then "not he but his devil will take the consequences of evil and suffering."

In a dialectical tension between his belief and disbelief in the devil's existence, Ivan is tortured in his conscience. Now, if there is conscience, there must be Law; but if there is Law, then there must be punishment for those who transgress the Law. In order to avoid the torture of one's own conscience and punishment for breaking the Law, man must negate his own conscience, because only man without conscience may justly avoid punishment by it. But Ivan has "the stings of conscience" and therefore he is unable to avoid suffering by his guilty feelings, or to transcend guilty conscience.

Refusing both virtue and suffering as irrational Ivan turns to his intellect, and in searching for a resolution of evil he experiences a new dilemma: either to accept the world in which evil is present and to reject God the Creator, or *vice versa.* For Ivan, the world is material and sensual and therefore also irrational, and consequently he must detach himself from the world by rejecting it entirely. In his intellectual venture into the resolution of evil, Ivan wants to realize platonic perfection by repressing the world of senses and by re-creating the world of his spirit. In other words,

Ivan wants to realize divinity by rejecting the needs of his body and its material urges.

The greatest evil of this world is the fact that little children suffer, because due to their age they cannot be guilty; they are innocent.

The evil of suffering of innocent children without any justification leads Ivan to conclude that there is no justice in the world. Now, if the injustice of suffering children is inherent in the world, then Ivan must reject not so much God Himself, but His world. The evil of the suffering of innocent children as a case study of evil leads Ivan to reject the world created by God, because its evil is not only inherent by the fact of being *in* the world, but also it is a property *of* the world itself.

Not being bound by "logic of life" man is in regard to his existential needs and demands absolutely free in determining his human nature. Human freedom however, is not r e a l freedom, because there is evil in the world, and man cannot escape from it. The absurdity of human freedom does not consist in fearing death and loving life as such, but in the fact that "man loves life because he loves suffering." But in order to overcome love of suffering, man must find a freedom which would make man indifferent to both: to life and death, to joy and pain, to goodness and evil. However, since "God is the pain of the fear of death," one ought to become god himself and in this way conquer the evil in the world by establishing a new human reality. Kirillov in *The Possessed* believes that there is a possibility of overcoming evil suffering if there really is no eternal life, but only the present one. Now, in order to overcome evil man must do two things: first he must convince himself that everything is good, because only in this way man can exercise his real freedom without any fear or restrictions; and second, he must prove the possibility of becoming sovereign only and exclusively to his own 'free-self-will,' and in this way realize his own divinity as a man-God.

The fallacy of Kirillov seems to lie in the fact that human existence being finite and limited in its 'free-self-will' is not and cannot be compatible with infinite and unlimited God himself. Now, the real freedom of man cannot resolve evil by deification of the human being but by subordination of man to God. The true dichotomy between God-man and man-God can, according to Dostoyevsky, consist (as interpreted by Nicholas Berdyaev) in choosing "either freedom with suffering or containment without freedom." For Dostoyevsky freedom is the very foundation on which any justification of God and man could be based. But only in divine love can the alleged dichotomy between good and evil in the world be resolved. In conclusion one can say with Berdyaev that Dostoyevsky's inner struggle with God and freedom leads to liberation from evil by accepting suffering as redemptive power.

As shown by Dostoyevsky, human freedom is both a creative and destructive power. It can be creative if based on Divine Love through which man directs himself towards self-realization by subordination to God. Human freedom can however, be a destructive force if its power is used by man for 'self-independence' as a 'being-who-in-self-perfection-wants-to-rely-only-on-his-own-free-self-will.' Human freedom is then creative when based on goodness and destructive when grounded on evil.

The decisive motive power of choosing between freedom of goodness with God and freedom of evil against God is, according to Dostoyevsky, man's conscience.

2. Divine Transcendence and the Ecstatic Fascination with Evil

The philosophical principle of intelligiblity says that whatever is, is, and is as it is, and can be known as it is, either objectively from without, or subjectively from within the human mind. In Kant's philosophy the principle of intelligibility can lead neither to objective nor subjective truth. It has been limited to the realm of phenomena, whereas the noumenal world of reality remains completely unknown. But, if the intelligibility of reality is limited to the realm of phenomena only, as given in sense-intuition, then not only transcendental knowledge is impossible, but also the immanent world of external things cannot be known as such, because the mind does not depend on the object, but the object depends on the mind. However, since Kant reduces intelligibility of reality to phenomena in sense-intuition within the human mind only, then theoretical reason depends on an *a-priori* reasoning and the practical reason can ascribe any laws to nature only as pure postulates. Consequently the human mind is neutral towards both objective and subjective truth.

In view of the dialectical tension between theoretical and practical reason, the question of God's existence and the problem of evil in the world cannot be satisfactorily solved in Kant's philosophy. Theoretical reason cannot prove God's existence, because God is noumenon and as such is unknown to us. But, since God as noumenon cannot be known by theoretical reason, then the question of God's existence can be accepted by practical reason only as a postulate, i.e. as principle of a categorical imperative of man's morality. As a result of this dialectical tension between theoretical and practical reason, Kant changed the problem of God's immanence from the order of knowing to the order of doing.

Although Kant did not intend to eliminate the metaphysical question of God's existence, nevertheless both his *Critiques* undermine the confidence of the human mind to prove God's existence, and therefore they created in the consciousness of the contemporary man a doubt about the ultimate possibility of resolving the question of goodness and evil on one hand, and the problems of God's existence on the other hand. Generally speaking *Kritik der reinen Vernunft* actually kills God, and *Kritik der praktische Vernunft* did not factually prove the necessity of God's existence. After reading Kant's *Kritik der reinen Vernunft*, Heinrich Heine declares the death of God: "Do I hear the sound of the bell? Get down on your knees. Man is bringing the last Sacraments to the dying God."

Heine's declaration of the dying God as a consequence of the *Kritik der reinen Vernunft* became even more evident in *Kritik der praktische Vernunft*, where God's existence became, according to Heine, "a pure invention." As a matter of fact, Kant convinced his readers that God's existence is necessary for man's life and moral behavior rather than as the real Being independent from human existence. However, since God's existence is only a postulate of the practical reason and not reality as such, then wouldn't it be better to change the question of the necessity of God's existence to the question of the necessity of justifying man's existence as self-independent being?

The question of evil as afflicting Divine Essence can be approached both by contrasting God's immanent presence in the world with man's creative activity in shaping human reality, and by opposing God's transcendent activation with human existence as a free being. The analysis of evil as afflicting Divine Essence would be based in the first case on the spiritual crisis of contemporary world, and in the second case on the impossibility of resolving evil by man's freedom alone.

(a) Nietzschean Proclamation of God's Death as the Origin of Contemporary Nihilism

In his *Die Fröhliche Wissenschaft,* Nietzsche declares through the madman that God is dead: "Where is God? . . . I will tell you. We killed him, you and I. We are all murderers." Now, Nietzsche tries to prove the proclamation of God's death on the ground of the Kantian doctrine of *Ding an sich.* But if God as *Ding an sich* cannot be known, then God cannot be known, and then God does not exist for us.

The proclamation of God's death did not arise in Nietzsche from his conviction in the non-existence of God, but was an act of will to replace Him and to declare man as a new god. In other words, by killing God Nietzsche wants to substitute for Him man, who would elevate himself to superman by "transvaluation of all values" through the Will to Power. The Will to Power is, according to Nietzsche, the very essence of all reality and as such also the very causality of everything which happens in this world. The Will to Power is also for Nietzsche the ultimate principle of self-realization of man, and as such the only justification of man's claim to become super-human without any supernatural force including God himself. Nietzsche realizes however that by being deprived of the benevolent guidance of God, man is by necessity oriented toward evil. The reason for this evil is the greatest strength of man in becoming superhuman. Moreover, evil is the only consolation of man for both the strength which arises from it and the possibility for using it in becoming super-human. In self-realization man must be able not only to do evil, but also to become evil. Now, in doing the highest evil and therefore becoming also the greatest super-human, man is marked with the deepest suffering. As a matter of fact, the greater the man, the greater the suffering.

However, although he accepts suffering as the most distinct mark of being human, Nietzsche nevertheless declares suffering as meaningless and senseless. Proclaiming Will to Power as the sole force for self-realization, Nietzsche realizes that his Dionysian world is dialectically split between 'the eternally-self-creating' and the 'eternally-self-destructing' world. But since the Will to Power is a universal force of all reality, the split between the 'eternally-self-creating-and-self-destructing-world' projects itself into the dialectical tension in human will as well: between the Will to Create and the Will to Destroy, the Will to Life and the Will to Annihilate. In the dialectical tension then between the Will for Being and Will for Non-Being there is, according to Nietzsche, the superiority of the Will for Non-Being over and against the Will for Being.

When we take under consideration, however, that the Will to Power is also the ultimate principle of transvaluation of all values, then in the dialectical tension of human will man experiences both: goodness and evil. But, since the Nietzschean proposition to resolve human existence consists in going beyond goodness and evil, then his postulate of the Will to Power as an ultimate force for liberation of man becomes self-mocking illusion and deception. In addition, Nietzsche realizes that the 'eternally-self-creating-and-self-destructing-world' is without any goal and directions, and man's Will to Power is by the same token deprived of any criteria whatsoever.

Nietzsche realized that the denial of God's existence will lead the contemporary man to the absolute nihilism which Nietzsche himself already experienced to the very end and has seen it behind himself, under himself and beyond himself. Experiencing evil and suffering thoroughly, Nietzsche proclaims a new gospel of the future which would lead to establishing "nihilistic religion." Now, this nihilistic religion is searching for a new order of values, and defining the highest one by developing the instinct for *decadence.* But since the ultimate principle of reality is the Will to Power, then the instinct for decadence is nothing but a manifestation of individual will. However, being a manifestation of the Will to Power, the instinct for decadence is based on an act of someone's own will. But Nietzsche, as the most perfect nihilist, admits that the act of Will is illusion, because there is no Will but only *Willens-Punktuationen,* through which man's Will to Power is able to improve itself or to be lost. Thus Nietzsche's logic of nihilism ends in the logic of the illusive Will to Power.

The underlining principle of nihilism is, according to Nietzsche, the Lust for Destruction which ends in the decline of any values, meanings and aspirations of man. Now, the prophesied nihilism of Nietzsche will come to a full realization in the contemporary absurdist philosophers who not only negate God but also aim at a total annihilation of man. The Nietzschean Will to Power as a manifestation of man's independency will, for Sartre, become the very basis of human existence. The old God becomes replaced by man and Sartre searches for the sources of divinity in man and attempts to find them in existential freedom.

(b) "Theologia Diaboli" and "Iustificatio Mali" in Sartrian Existentialism

'To exist' for Sartre does not mean being, because being is nothing but 'thing-in-itself' *(l'être en soi).* 'To exist' means 'to-be-for-itself' *(l'être pour soi).* But 'to-be-for-itself' requires self-possession, belonging of someone to himself. This is realized only in such a being which possesses consciousness, because 'to-be-for-itself' requires the ability to transcend 'to-be-in-itself.' But transcending my 'being-in-itself,' 'I-the-being-for-itself' am an ontological emptiness, because I never can be what I am, and I belong to myself in respect to that what never can be myself as such, i.e. as 'being-in-itself.' Consequently I experience my existence as an alienation from being, or as a desire for being which I am not.

But being able to transcend 'being-in-itself' of myself, I am identified with my own freedom. I am condemned to be free, because I am free for nothing, both in regards to being and becoming. I am free because my freedom has no goal to be achieved. Now, even if there were a goal to be achieved then it would be 'being-in-itself' and not 'for-myself,' namely essence and not existence. But since man's existence precedes his essence, I am doomed to constantly create my essence in order to negate it. As a matter of fact, in the dialectical tension between my existence and essence, I am 'being-who-finds-itself-in-suspension-between-being-in-itself-and-being-for-myself.'

The character of suspense of human existence between 'being-in-itself' and 'for-itself' indicates the need for security. This ontological need for existential security Sartre tries to find in attributing absolute character to human freedom. To be in suspension means that human existence is always in the process of changing, through which man shapes not only his past and present, but also his future. Now, in the moment of death, man ceases to be 'being-for-itself' and reaches the state of 'being-in-itself.' Freedom then is the very essence of man's life as a 'being-for-itself,' and while dissipating his own existence in/through death, man reaches the ultimate destiny of human being as a 'being-in-itself.' Now, between *l'etre en soi* and *l'etre pour soi* there is an unbridged gap. It means there is nothing which could be in common with each other, because there are two distinct entities. Being in its state of *en soi* my entity is completed and fulfilled, and being in its state of *pour soi* my existence is not completed and always imperfect. For this reason *l'être en soi* is lacking freedom and *l'être pour soi* is nothing but freedom itself. Consequently man's being, although having freedom in himself, is nevertheless diminished "une décompression d'être."

Being diminished, incomplete, divided between *en-soi* and *pour-soi,* man wants to do two things: to realize *l'être en soi* and to preserve himself as *l'être pour soi.* Consequently man tries to combine the fullness of being and fullness of consciousness.

Therefore the aim of man is to become "l'être-en-soi-pour-soi," namely God. The notion of "l'en-soi-pour-soi" is a contradiction in terms, which leads man to struggle for his own existence without any hope for a final resolution. In self realization man cannot hope also for an ultimate solution of his existence through God. God is a contradiction in terms as well, because if God were absolutely fulfilled and perfect being he would be *l'être en-soi* and as such deprived of consciousness. On the other hand, if God had consciousness and personal being, He would be *l'être-pour-soi* and consequently be condemned to futility of existence. Consequently not only God but man also is a contradiction in terms and human freedom is existential futility.

The basic fact of man's existence consists in his solitude and loneliness. Loneliness is the very structure of human existence, because of the consciousness and inevitability of death. Being alone means constant absence of being and this absence of being which makes us alone as deprived of our own being condemns us to prison. Now, if our existence is a prison, as being condemned to being alone, then everyone must commit crimes in order to remain alone. Human existence becomes a jungle in which every man has a right to kill and destroy.

Loneliness as the ontological condition for man's freedom leads Sartre to conclude that human existence is subject to suffering; Sartre speaking of Genet said; "It is in suffering alone that he can feel himself to be free, because it is the only feeling which comes from within himself . . . " Now, in suffering human existence undergoes transformation through which man experiences his freedom from 'being-in-itself' to 'being-for-itself' by "wishing that his actions be effects of an absolute will which draws its motive from itself alone and not from the world." Suffering an evil then is not necessarily a destructive force but a creative power in the resolution of human existence as an absolute freedom and an unlimited independency. In this way Sartre's *philosophia entis* becomes *theologia diaboli*. Consequently it is not theodetic *iustificatio Dei*, but *iustificatio mali* that is the ultimate purpose of Sartrian existentialism; this would lead to an apology for all crimes and a proclamation of evil under every form.

Atheistic existentialism is then helpless in confronting the tragedy of human existence and cannot deliver man from his imprisonment. The main difficulty of the atheistic existentialism stems from rejection of transcendency. Charles du Bois writes: "Rejecting transcendency we leave ourselves open to the danger of deification of man. This is the basic problem of today's life. At the basis of atheistic existentialism lies a rejection of being and acceptance of nihilism: 'abversio ab ente conversio ad nihilem'."

Concluding Remarks

The world as created by God is as if it were created *in* God, by being in unity *with* His immanent and transcendent presence both from within and without. Now, taking into consideration the existential condition of man as a contingent being, his relationship with God is possible only by living in accordance and harmony with himself. But in establishing the relationship between God and his creation two divine approaches can be established: descension movement of God to the created world by His immanent activation, and ascension movement of the created world to God by His transcendent attraction. The former movement being internal and inherent of God in the world consists of His being present in the world, and the latter movement being external of the world in regard to God is being above the world. This mutual relationship between God and His creation St. Thomas expresses as follows: God's creative activation is so immanent in this world that He is actually absolutely transcendent to any created things.

The ontological fallacy of the alleged incongruity between God's existence and the presence of evil in the world consists mainly in recognizing God's immanency and transcendency as conceived in the spatio-temporal order of our human experience of divinity. The divine transcendency should not be understood either in quantitative geometrical terms of space and time or in terms of qualitative endurance of human existence. Referring to the tension between divine immanency and transcendency, Jaspers concludes that the very notion of transcendency indicates that, although never becoming the world itself as proposed by pantheistic systems like Spinoza's, it speaks nevertheless as if it were through the world, and yet remaining beyond it. But, if the contingent world does not constitute a reality of its own, in a sense of being independent from God the Creator, then it points to the Being which exists of necessity, and directs *beyond* the contingent one by transcending it.

Now, being both immanently and transcendently present in the world, God is not and cannot partake in the suffering of evil, because both the immanent and transcendent activation of God are positive in nature and creative in character. Moreover, being in the process of becoming, the created beings suffer evil for the ultimate completion of their beingness by going beyond the state of their imperfection. Ontologically speaking, the presence of evil and suffering is not offensive to God's existence, but the very condition of divine immanent and transcendent activation in leading the created beings to their final state of "to be."

However, phenomenologically speaking, one may insist that God by creating beings in/with their contingency is, at least, indirectly the origin and initiator of the suffering of evil, because, why did He not create beings in their final perfection in the first place? But if we take under consideration the fact that divine creative activation is positive not only in nature but in its character as well, then the evil arising from the contingency of created beings cannot be evaluated in the order of being as such, but only in the order of becoming. Now, in the order of becoming, the evil of suffering can be either destructive or constructive.

The search for the original meaning of the experience of evil consists then not as much in logical or rational explanation of the very presence of evil in the world, but in phenomenological deciphering of one's own existential experience. In other words, by suffering evil one experiences only one's own existential condition (André Malreaux). Consequently if suffering is experienced destructively, then not God but man should be blamed for it, because, due to his imperfection he does not follow always the creative character of divine activation. Now being able to explain the presence of evil in the world either logically or rationally, it becomes consequently for man a mystery of the destruction of the claim of being in its totality, according to Nietzsche's proclamation that if there were a God, then how could I resign myself not to be one.

The presence of evil, however, remains a mystery as long as man conceives himself as absolutely deprived by God-the Creator of any possibility of overcoming it. Yet, by the act of creation God manifests His love for the created things through the very fact of bringing them up from nothingness, communicating and diffusing His divine goodness. The attribute of Divine Love then prevents the ultimate supremacy of evil over goodness, because if God is Love, and if He creates the world, and if He creates the world as a manifestation of Himself, then there exists a possibility of overcoming evil. Otherwise God would be impotent and by the same token He would be contradicting Himself as the Creator.

A SELECT BIBLIOGRAPHY

1. General Studies

Buber, Martin, *Images of Good and Evil,* translation by Michael Bullock. London: Routledge and Keegan Paul, 1952.

Conche, M., "La souffrance des enfants comme mal absolu," *L'homme et son prochain* (Paris: Presses Universitaires, 1956), pp. 145-148.

Hildebrand, Dietrich von, *The Nature of Good and Evil.* New York: McKay, 1952.

Journet, C., *The Meaning of Evil,* translation by M. Barry. London: Geoffrey Chapman, 1963.

Krapiec, Miecislas Albert, *Pourquoi le Mal? Reflexions philosophiques,* translation by Genevieve Roussel. Paris: Edition du Dialogue, 1967.

Lavelle, Louis, *Le Mal et la Souffrance.* Paris: Plon, 1947.

Maritain, Jacques, *Court traité de l'existence et de l'existant.* Paris: Hartmann, 1947.

Scheller, Max, *Le sens de la souffrance.* Paris: Aubier, 1936.

Siwek, P., *The Philosophy of Evil.* New York: Ronald Press, 1951.

Vernaux, Roger, *Problèmes et Mystères du Mal.* Paris: La Colombe, 1956.

2. Evil and Morality in J. Royce

Aronson, Moses Judah, *La Philosophie Morale de Josiah Royce.* Paris: Librairie Felix Alcan, 1927.

Fuss, Peter, *The Moral Philosophy of Josiah Royce.* Cambridge, Massachusetts: Harvard University Press, 1965.

Mahowald, Mary Briody, *An Idealistic Pragmatism.* The Hague, Holland: Martinus Nijhoff, 1972.

Marcel, Gabriel, *La Métaphysique de Royce.* Paris: Aubier, 1945.

3. Suffering and Freedom in F. Dostoyevsky

Berdyaev, Nicholas, *Dostoevsky.* Cleveland, Ohio: World Publishing Co., 1962.

Gibson, Alexander Boyce, *The Religion of Dostoevsky.* Philadelphia, Pennsylvania: Westminster Press, 1974.

Guardini, R., *L'universe religieux de Dostoievskij,* translated by H. Englemann and I. Girard. Paris: Edition du Seuil, 1947.

Rowe, William W., *Dostoevsky: Child and Man in His Works.* New York: New York University Press, 1968.

Shestov, L., *La Philosophie de la Tragedie–Dostoiewskij et Nietzsche,* translated by B. de Schloezer. Paris: J. Schiffrin, 1926.

4. Death of God and Nihilism in Nietzsche

Baroni, Christophe, "Dieu est-il mort? De Nietzsche à Jung," *Syntheses,* 224-235 (1965), pp. 328-343.

Biser, Eugen, "Die Proklamation von Gottes Tod. Nietzsches Parabel 'Der Tolle Mensch im Licht der Textgeschichte," *Hochland,* 56 (1963-1964), pp. 137-152.

Brocker, Walter, "Nietzsche und der Europäische Nihilismus," *Zeitschrift für philosophische Forschung,* 3 (1949), pp. 161-177.

Buber, Martin, *Eclipse of God.* New York: Harper & Row, 1952.

Flam, Leopold, "Nietzsche et le nihilisme," *La Revue de l'Université de Bruxelles,* 12 (1959-1960), pp. 90-102.

Granier, Jean, "La critique nietzscheenne du Dieu de la métaphysique," *Revue des Sciences Philosophiques et Théologiques,* 52 (July, 1968), pp. 389-407.

Jaspers, Karl, *Nietzsche.* Berlin: W. de Gruyter, 1936.

Löwith, Karl, *Kierkegaard und Nietzsche oder philosophische und theologische Uberwindung des Nihilismus.* Frankfurt a.M.: V. Klostermann, 1933.

Schrey, H.H., "Die Überwindung des Nihilismus bei Kierkegaard und Nietzsche," *Zeitschrift für systematische Theologie,* 21 (1950), pp. 50-68.

Sefler, George, "Nietzsche and Dostoevsky on the Meaning of Suffering," *Religious Humanism,* 4 (Fall, 1970), pp. 145-150.

5. Human Existence, Freedom and God in J.P. Sartre

Arntz, Joseph T.C., "L'athéisme au nom de l'homme? L'athéisme de Sartre et de Merleau-Ponty," *Concilium,* 16 (1966), pp. 59-64.

Blondel, Maurice, "The Inconsistency of Jean-Paul Sartre's Logic," *The Thomist,* 10 (Oct., 1947), pp. 393-397.

Descoqs, P., "L'athéisme de J.P. Sartre," *Revue de Philosophie,* (1946), pp. 39-89.

Duméry, Henry, "L'athéisme sartrien," *Esprit,* 18 (February 1950), pp. 240-252.

Ecole, Jean, "Das Gottesproblem in der Philosophie Sartres," *Wissenschaft und Weltbild,* 10 (1957), pp. 265-276.

Haug, Wolfgang Fritz, *Jean-Paul Sartre und die Konstruktion des Absurden.* Frankfurt a.M.: Suhrkamp Verlag, 1966.

Heinemann, Frederick H., "Theologia Diaboli," *The Hibbert Journal,* 52 (October 1953), pp. 65-72.

Jolivet, Régis, *Sartre ou la théologie de l'absurde.* Paris: Fayard, 1965.

Möller, Joseph, *Absurdes Sein? Eine Auseinandersetzung mit der Ontologie J-P Sartres.* Stuttgart: Kohlhammer, 1959.

Rideau, Emile, "Un humanisme social athée: Jean-Paul Sartre et le christianisme," *Nouvelle Revue théologique,* (December 1963), pp. 1039-1062.

Schrag, Calvin O., *Existence and Freedom: Towards an Ontology of Human Finitude.* Evanston, Illinois: Northwestern University Press, 1961.

Wyschogrod, Michael, "Sartre, Freedom and the Unconscious," *Review of Existential Psychology and Psychiatry,* 1 (Fall, 1961), pp. 1179-1186.

CHAPTER XXXIX

THE GOD—WORLD RELATIONSHIP

*Paul Surlis**

1. Traditional Teaching

The immutability of God is axiomatic in scholastic philosophy and natural theology. It is also an article of faith from the 4th Lateran and First Vatican Councils (D428, 1782). Mutability was excluded from God in Catholic thought because change in the intrinsic being of God would mean loss of some perfection or acquisition of a new one with consequent denial of absolute perfection to God. And only an infinitely perfect God is worthy of worship and an adequate ground for faith and hope. As a corollary from the immutability of God, Augustine, Aquinas and Catholic thought generally, deduced that all relationships from God to the universe are purely mental while relationships from the universe toward God are *real.*

The reality of the relationship between God and the universe, it was held, would make God dependent to some degree on creation and all such forms of dependence were absolutely to be avoided. God as subsistent being could not acquire a new accidental relation and so St. Thomas put the matter thus: "God's temporal relations to creatures are in Him only because of our way of thinking about Him but the opposite relation of creatures to Him are realities in creatures" (1, 13, 7 ad 4). Creation and Incarnation—to take paradigmatic examples—did not involve change in God because the divine decree in each instance was eternal and identical with the divine essence and hence always unchanging. The only change involved was in the terms of the divine decrees,

*Associate Professor of Theology at St. John's University, New York, U.S.A.

the created universe and the assumed human nature of Christ respectively.

2. Difficulties with Traditional View

In the manner described briefly above metaphysical coherence was observed but it would appear at an enormous price. If God as Pure Act remains unchanged by Creation or the Incarnation then no very relentless logic is required to argue that if He is unchanged then He is *unaffected* also. And if God is unaffected by Creation presumably He remains unaffected by its fate and so to the conclusion that He is *indifferent* to human struggle and suffering, indeed to the entire scheme of things.

The attempt to preserve the absolute perfection of God was successful but at the expense of the significance of history and time. How far the *perfection* of God was preserved is, of course, utterly questionable. The common sense objection that to be unmoved by the fate of the created universe is unworthy of God is surely valid. And the Incarnation always mattered, it was said, because it showed supreme concern. But the doctrine of the immutability of God remained undislodged and meaning and significance were salvaged for the universe and its history by the expedient of having recourse to the divine will decreeing that they should matter. Thus it may be argued an ultimate voluntarism was seen to ground the very order of things and God, though remote and unconcerned, was mightily susceptible to being regarded as capricious and cruel for creating a world where suffering abounds when He might have decreed it otherwise.

3. Voluntarism Accentuating Problems

Obviously, Christian piety with its biblically inspired conviction that God enters into relationships of love, mercy and forgiveness with his creatures, seems to have been unimpeded by the metaphysics and dogma which would classify all divine-human relationships as of the mind only *(aliquid rationis)*. Even though the instinct of piety is sound and reflects a view of God essential to faith, it would appear that at the systematic level a meta-physical view of God which precluded change in Him or any real relationship between Him and the universe was given precedence over faith. This is surely an instance where there is not merely distinction but conflict between the *substance* of the faith on the one hand and the *manner of its expression* on the other. Indeed, it may be argued that a consequence of the foregoing was a profound ambivalence in thought, especially with reference to the problems of evil and suffering and efforts to formulate a theodicy. It should be borne in mind that the mysteries of evil and suffering serve only to focus the entire problem more sharply, because the problem encompasses the significance of the entire created order, and is not limited to the existence of evil and the difficulties it raises.

4. Evil, Suffering and the Will of God

It is clear that the mystery of evil and the paradox of suffering are rendered more acute for the Christian who professes belief in a God who is both all-loving and all-powerful. An all-loving God would put an end to evil and suffering unless he were unable to in which case He is no longer all-powerful. While an all-powerful God who does not put an end to suffering scarcely deserves the name God according to the classical formulation of the dilemma. But is there not in this very manner of formulating the problem merely a sharpening of voluntaristic assumptions? The idea seems to be that the conditions obtaining in the universe are arbitrarily chosen by God—but ultimately for good reasons—so the Christian would be compelled to argue.

The problem of evil is posed in essence with the suffering of one innocent child. However, there is no gainsaying the fact that increasingly frequent manifestations of gigantic, catastrophic evil, all forms of violence, the physical and psychic suffering caused by happenstance or deliberately inflicted, all create in our time an unprecedented awareness of the challenge posed to faith in God. For many whose faith is eroded by whatever modern form in which the classical dilemma—He cannot or He will not—is posed, it may not be untrue to say that the God of metaphysics is being appealed to against the Christian faith. Christian apologists have always recognized that there is no entirely satisfactory answer to the mystery of evil, that the best response is to tackle existing evils out of compassion, motivated by love and in the conviction that all suffering may be redeemed and redeeming in union with the sufferings of Christ. According to the daring thought of St. Paul a residue of suffering remains to be filled up in the members of the faithful who constitute a mystical unity with Christ. Even in the face of the most agonizingly capricious evil and suffering the true believer does not surrender his faith in the omnipotence or love of God on the one hand, nor in human freedom and responsibility on the other. But appeal is so quickly and frequently made to the 'will of God' when questions are pressed that one suspects voluntaristic assumptions remain unrecognized both in the topic under discussion and in theories of miracles, the atonement, *and* natural law to take random examples from diverse areas all of which are viewed according to the more general theory one holds on the God-world relationship.

5. A Real Relationship Affirmed

How is God related to the world? That He is involved in and affected by human history (and even minor events in the cosmos like the fall of the sparrow), is the clear message of the Bible. Scholastic theology appealed to scattered biblical texts to affirm the unchanging nature of God (e.g. Mal. 3:6 "For I am the Lord, and I change not;" James 1:17 "With whom there is no change nor shadow of alteration"). But other texts could be culled from the Bible which attest to God's changes of mind and mood. However, the proof-text approach appears no more relevant in this discussion than in any other. The upshot of the Biblical (non-systematic) evidence favors the view that God was experienced as a free, personal agent, active in human affairs; a God transcendent where human images and concepts are concerned and so presumably transcending the human categories of change and immutability, but this approach was not explored in theology.

Scholastic metaphysics retained the concept of the immutability of God, correctly it would seem, in view of preserving infinite perfection as among God's most essential attributes. But concepts suggesting contraries in God or any form of mutability or dependence were strained off as "mixed perfections" unworthy of the Infinite Being. The results was a God for whom the theatre of history did not appear to matter in any ultimate way.

If today we reject the God-world relationship traditionally described as non-real, and if we are unwilling to adopt an explanation which would identify 'all that is' with God (pantheism) what is the alternative? That there is an alternative is being affirmed by many today. And while it would be wrong to claim a consensus where none exists, it does appear that a few significant authors espouse on this issue a modified form of pantheism which is referred to as panentheism.[1]

6. Panentheism

The term *panentheism* is chosen to designate a model of the God-world relationship that falls somewhere between classical theism with its monarchical model and dualism. The monarchical model, as Macquarrie calls it,[2] stresses God's transcendence over, and priority to, the world: God affects the world but He remains unaffected by it. Dualism asserts that God and the world are independent and opposed realities.[3] The model designated by the word 'panentheism' is more organic. The transcendence of God is not abandoned but it is qualified. God and the world are seen as 'distinguishable but not separable within an organic whole which

---

[1] For a concise account of the meaning of the term as used here see K. Rahner and H. Vorgrimler "Panentheism," *Theological Dictionary* (New York: Herder & Herder, 1965), pp. 333-334.

[2] John Macquarrie, *Thinking About God* (New York: Harper and Row, 1975), pp. 110 ff.

[3] There is much latent dualism in theoretical aspects of Christian thought and a corresponding practical Manichaeism in Christian conviction but that cannot concern us here.

embraces both of them.'[4] In the God-world relationship stress is placed on intimacy and *reciprocity* of relationship.

As Rahner expresses it according to panentheism 'the all' is not identified with God but is rather said to be *in* God, not, however, spatially but as an inner modification of his being.[5] The events of history affect God not because he is ontologically dependent on them but because by a free and gracious act he deigned in creation not merely to sustain all things in being but to submit to change in his own being, change dependent on the outcome of history.

In this view the *risk* of creation is not for man alone, it exists for God also. The world is still viewed as having been created out of nothing. It is distinct from God. It is not absorbed into the divine being and yet the created order may be spoken of as being within God and, in a manner, determinative of his being. In other words it would be candidly admitted that God who remains immutable is *also* subject to change because of his free decision to be so.

It should be noted that there is no question of asserting that God, incomplete in his essence, is coming to perfection through creation's development. And insofar as change and mutability are affirmed of God it is insofar as they do not imply *imperfection* in God. No less than did classical theism must we affirm the infinite perfection of God.

7. *The Trinitarian Analogy*

Walter E. Stokes in his philosophical revision of the God-world relationship has argued—correctly—that the denial of a real relationship between God and this world is made with constant appeal to God's *nature* and the consequences that would follow if God in his *nature* were to be essentially ordered to this world. Stokes observes that this emphasis on nature indicates that inadequate attention was paid to a theory of relation proper to

---

4 Macquarrie, *op. cit.,* p. 111.
5 K. Rahner and H. Vorgrimler, *ibid.*

person in the traditional approach. Stokes locates God's real relationship to the world in his personal, free and loving decision to create and such a personal relation, Stokes argues, 'detracts only from a conception of God as a necessary nature in the Greek conception of the term, not at all from God's perfection as a personal being.'[6]

Similarly, on the analogy of the doctrine of the Trinity which affirms that God transcends both oneness and multiplicity, may we not assert that God is at once pure act and pure potency, necessary and contingent, eternal and in time, absolute and related to all reality? But to speak thus without self-contradiction it seems necessary to utilize the distinction favored for example, by Rahner who has expressed the view that God who is immutable in himself may undergo change in what is other than himself. That Rahner, in the context to which we refer, is thinking of change-in-God must not be overlooked.[7] The 'word became flesh,' Rahner reminds us, is the central affirmation of Christianity and this event, this becoming, is that of God himself. Rahner writes, too, of the death of Jesus as the *death of God.* He states that only half the truth is being expressed if the death of Jesus is predicated only of the human nature leaving God unaffected.[8] On the one hand it is affirmed that God, being immutable, cannot die or have a history and yet with these statements one must co-affirm that it is God who has a destiny, through the Incarnation, in what-is-other-than-himself. There is a dialectic at work here and the principles of identity and non-contradiction cede to a higher principle which can contain the tension of opposition. At all events, the 'Word became flesh' is a statement of faith which takes precedence over ontology. Insofar as ontology and metaphysics are inescapable, even in theology, they must be used to *express* the substance of the faith but not allowed to *determine* it.

[6] Walter E. Stokes, "Is God Really Related to This World?" *Proceedings of the American Catholic Philosophical Association* (Washington, 1965), pp. 145-151; see pp. 149-150.

[7] K. Rahner, *Theological Investigations* (Baltimore: Helicon, 1966), Vol. IV, pp. 113-114.

[8] K. Rahner, "Jesus Christ," *Sacramentum Mundi* (Burns & Oates, 1969), Vol. III, p. 207.

8. The Incarnation

The Incarnation teaches us that immutability, which is not eliminated, is a characteristic of God in spite of which he can truly become something else. But this possibility is not an imperfection or deficiency in God; rather, it indicates to us the summit of his perfection which would be less than it is if, as well as being infinite, God could not become less than he always is.

Jürgen Moltmann in *The Crucified God* also asserts the primacy of faith over metaphysics.[9] And, however much one may disagree with his staurocentric doctrine of the Trinity, (the crucifixion is an event between the Father and the Son from which proceeds the Spirit), one can only approve of his intention to give all Christian statements about God, creation and sin, their focal point in the crucified Christ rather than in metaphysical or moral categories.[10] Moltmann, too, affirms the necessity of maintaining a relationship between the divine and the human in the Incarnation and crucifixion which is more than merely dialectical as this leaves both the divine and the human unaffected in deference to the traditional exposition of the immutability of God which Moltmann (following Althaus) places in question.[11]

Undoubtedly, some traditions of Christian thought will be more at home with the Cross in the heart of God than others. But doctrines of divine compassion and true involvement in human relationships are common to all major Christian pieties.

In passing we may note that this insistence of the precedence of faith over ontology when the faith is being systematically articulated can only redound to the advantage of philosophy as Trinitarian influence on the concepts of 'nature' and 'person' testifies.

Of far greater value is the conjunction of the unsearchable mystery of God Himself and the mysteries of human suffering and death. There can no longer be any facile rejection of God in the

---

9   J. Moltmann, *The Crucified God*. New York: Harper and Row, 1974.
10 *Ibid.,* p. 204.
11 *Ibid.,* p. 206.

name of suffering as if God observed pain with Olympian detachment and subjected man to the trials and tribulations of this universe for the good of his soul. The human mind would balk, however, at the thought of God *overcome* by suffering and so to preserve the divine basis for the virtue of hope we continue to speak of divine immutability. But, because we can speak of the all-powerful God subjecting himself (for reasons we cannot fathom but which must incline us to take ever more seriously the meaning and the threat of evil), by free and gracious decision to historical events so that history may be said to be 'in God' who is affected by its outcome—because this is so the model of God which has hitherto obtained is being altered. And not only the model of God but the model of man whose free behavior matters not just *before* God but *for* God.

Conclusion

To revert to the terminology with which we began we may assert that relationships between the universe and God are reciprocal. The Incarnation which is a truth of faith teaches Greek metaphysics that the God of Christian faith empties Himself because He is committed to a universe where the values of freedom and love are so eminently worthwhile that the all-free and all-loving God co-suffers with man so that man may be free to love. The mysteries of evil and suffering are not eliminated but, hopefully, all suspicion of capricious imposition is removed from God and the moral commitment to value is given a new significance.

A SELECT BIBLIOGRAPHY

Collins, James, *God in Modern Philosophy*. Chicago: Henry Regnery Co., 1959.

Donceel, Joseph, "Second Thoughts on the Nature of God," *Thought,* Vol. XLVI, pp. 346-370.

Fackenheim, E.L., *The Religious Dimension in Hegel's Thought*. Bloomington, Indiana: Indiana University Press, 1968.

Hartshorne, C. and Reese, W.L., *Philosophers Speak of God.* Chicago: University of Chicago Press, 1963.

Hick, John, *Evil and The God of Love.* Landon: The Macmillan Co., 1966.

Küng, Hans, *Menschwerdung Gottes.* Freiburg: Herder, 1970.

———, *On Being A Christian.* New York: Doubleday, 1976.

Macquarrie, John, *Principles of Christian Theology.* London: SCM Press, 1966.

Roth, Robert J. (ed.), *God Knowable and Unknowable.* New York: Fordham University Press, 1973.

Schoonenberg, P., *Man and Sin.* Notre Dame, Indiana: University of Notre Dame Press, 1965.

Stokes, Walter E., "Is God Really Related to this World?" *Proceedings of the American Catholic Philosophical Association.* Washington, D.C.: Catholic University Press, 1965.

Taylor, Michael J. (ed.), *The Mystery of Suffering and Death.* New York: Alba House, 1973.

CHAPTER LX

A CONTEMPORARY JEWISH VIEW OF
SUFFERING AND GOD

Leonard W. Stern *

Judaism in the time span of the last two centuries, designated
the Modern Jewish Period, has not been greatly concerned with
the problem of good and evil. Modern Jewish thinkers from the
time of Moses Mendelssohn (1729-1786) until almost our own time
have not generally dwelled upon the question how does a good
God permit evil and wanton destruction to occur.[1]

Much of modern Jewish thought and preaching simply stated
the Biblical presentation that God has set before the individual
both good and evil.

I have set before thee life and death, the blessing and the curse
therefore choose life that thou mayest live, thou and thy seed.[2]

The emphasis is on the responsibility of the individual to build
as good and as meaningful a world as possible. Man in this view is
often perceived as a co-worker with God who participates in the
work of creation which is renewed daily.[3] In a recent anthology of
writings by modern Jewish thinkers there is no essay devoted to
the religious issue of good and evil.[4]

It is primarily since the Holocaust 1939-1945, the destruction

*Assistant Professor of Theology at St. John's University, New York, U.S.A.

1 Rotenstreich, Nathan, *Jewish Philosophy in Modern Times*. See Index pp.
275-282.

2 Deuteronomy 31:19b.

3 Stern, M., *Daily Prayer Book,* p. 43.

4 Noveck, Simon, *Contemporary Jewish Thought*. Clinton, Massachusetts: The
Colonial Press, 1969.

of 6,000,000 Jews in Europe, that the issue of theodicy is dramatically raised. Regarding this event we can raise the riddle of God and evil as follows:

> If God is unlimited in power and goodness why is there so much *prima facie* gratuitous evil in the world.[5]

Auschwitz is the single word that relates the Jew to the recognition of the *prima facie* gratuitous evil in the world. Auschwitz symbolizes the systematic destruction of a third of world Jewry by a civilized country with the active or tacit approval of many other civilized and so called advanced countries.

The name Auschwitz conjures up for the Jew images of the (Jewish) world destroyed not once, not tenfold, not a hundredfold, not a thousandfold, but of a world destroyed over and over six million times for no reason or purpose. (Auschwitz was the name of one of the death camps in which almost 2,000,000 Jews were persecuted and killed in two years.) A modern historian has written:

> The horror and the magnitude of this hellish operation, instituted at the command of the Nazi rulers, carried out by seemingly civilized human beings, mock any description.[6]

Auschwitz has stirred the emotions and has challenged the traditional religious roots of Judaism and perhaps (from a Jewish perspective) the religious roots of Christianity. Pope John XXIII composed the following penitential prayer shortly before his death on June 3, 1963:

> We now acknowledge that for many, many centuries blindness had covered our eyes, so that we no longer see the beauty of thy chosen people and no longer recognize in its face the

---

5 Madden and Hare, *Evil and the Concept of God,* p. 3.
6 Keller, Werner, *Diaspora,* p. 433.

features of our first born brother. We acknowledge that the mark of Cain is upon our brow. For centuries Abel lay low in blood and tears because we forgot thy love. Forgive us the curse that we wrongfully pronounced upon the name of the Jews . . . [7]

Leo Baeck, a rabbi, a teacher, a scholar, and a survivor of the Holocaust wrote about the Nazi terror as follows:

But soon other voices sounded forth out of Europe striving to submerge all else, voices that served untruthfulness, that praised crime and jeered at righteousness. States disregarded their duties of faithfulness toward their citizens. Houses of prayer in which faith, righteousness and justice had been proclaimed were burned to the ground . . . and those that committed this knew what they committed. And the powers which practiced every crime, created the readiness for new crimes . . . [8]

Richard Rubenstein in this book *After Auschwitz* confronts the problem of faith in the contemporary world. He states that it is not the physical sciences which challege a personal God, but rather the social sciences and literature which depicts the limitations of faith and the inevitable tragedies of human existence. Rubenstein sees not nature as an impediment to belief but the evil that man has committed. He wrote:

The real objections against a personal or theistic God come from the irreconcilability of the claim of God's perfection with the hideous human evil tolerated by such a God.[9]

It was the Holocaust, symbolized by Auschwitz, which challenged and threatened the faith of the Jew and yet in the years immediately after this period of destruction there was little

7 *Ibid.*, p. IX (not numbered).
8 Baeck, Leo, *The People Israel*, pp. 385-386.
9 Rubenstein, Richard L., *After Auschwitz*, p. 86.

involvement with the religious issues raised by the Holocaust. The
first response of the American Jew was to deepen his own religious
identity. He became affiliated with the synagogue and built new
ones in the suburban communities which grew up after the Second
World War.[10] The involvement of the Jew was in affirming his
Jewishness. In more recent times, especially in the last ten years,
there has been a new found interest in the religious issues. Perhaps
the enormity of the crime against the Jew, against civilization,
could only gradually be experienced and even admitted. To open
one's mind, one's heart, and one's soul was to risk being consumed
by the forces of rejection, alienation and destruction.

Elie Wiesel, a modern novelist, in a popular article evokes the
pain of the contemporary Jew through the name that has become
synonymous with infamy and degradation. He begins the article
with the words Auschwitz 1944.[11] The former 'rosh yeshiva,' a
religious leader of a religious academy, who is incarcerated in a
concentration camp is talking with another inmate. The rabbi
expresses his pity for the former Jews who had converted to
Christianity but whose conversion was not recognized by Hitler.
His new found discipline asks him if he can tell what is the
meaning of suffering for the Jew in the concentration camp. The
rabbi responds that suffering always elicits questions.[12]

Wiesel then presents the values of Judaism that he had learned.
He declares that the Jew has to live his religion and has to define
himself and his religious faith. It is necessary to serve God by
witnessing for man even while declaring God's right to judge man.
He also relates that he learned that man could not set in
opposition God and creation.[13] Wiesel indicates that one of the
perplexities of Auschwitz is that the Jew after the Holocaust could
too easily define himself not by conformity to a Jewish way of life
and not by committment but simply by declaring that he is
Jewish.[14]

10 *Ibid.*, p. 90.
11 National Geographic Society, *Great Religions of the World*, p. 173.
12 *Ibid.*
13 *Ibid.*, p. 177.
14 *Ibid.*, p. 186.

Emil Fackenheim also expresses his conviction that the Jew must survive as Jew otherwise he presents Hitler with posthumous victories in achieving the destruction of the Jewish people. It is a religious issue for the Jews to survive, to remember the victims of Auschwitz through memory and the continuation of his religion. The Jew must not despair and remove himself from doing battle against the forces of evil and he may not despair of the God of Israel even if it is necessary for the religious Jew to define his relationship with God in new forms.[15]

Fackenheim considers Jewish survival a holy task whether survival by the Jewish community or by the Jewish secular community. He states that the Jew is under a holy obligation to survive in order to tell the tale of Auschwitz. He relates the struggle of the modern state of Israel to the battle against Auschwitz or evil which he declares is still raging. He sees a form of anti-Semitism in the willingness of many nations to accept the right of many people (including the Arabs) to exist, while requiring that the Jew earn that same right of existence. This aspect of anti-Semitism, which today must be viewed more than ever as a force for destruction, is further emphasized by insisting that other nations not engage in wars of aggression while declaring Israel an aggressor even when it fights wars simply to survive. The destruction, past and present, that is symbolized for the Jew by the word Auschwitz elevates existence for the Jew to the supreme value. Fackenheim believes that the Jew has too long willingly accepted suffering, destruction and martyrdom. He believes that after the destruction that the Jew has experienced, he, the Jew, must climb down from the cross not only to reaffirm his ancient rejection of an ancient Christian view but more to reject any Jewish involvement with willing or tacit acceptance of martyrdom.[16]

Fackenheim then relates the challenge to the secular and to the religious Jew to the significance of Sinai for each group. Sinai

---

15 Fackenheim, Emil, *God's Presence in History,* p. 84-88.
16 *Ibid.,* pp. 86-87.

symbolized the offering of the covenant by God to the Jewish people and the acceptance of the covenant by the Jews. The infamy of Auschwitz has secularized religious Judaism and commands the religious Jew to wrestle with his God in however revolutionary ways. It also challenges the secular Jew to spiritualize his framework by insisting that he not cut off his secular present from his religious past.[17]

Martin Buber was concerned with the problem of evil and suffering during the early period of Nazism. Buber in considering the problem of evil and the inability of man to perceive the Holy One Blessed Be He, discusses this issue in the *"Eclipse of God."* He states that an eclipse of the sun does not eliminate the reality of the sun but is the result of an obstruction between the eye and the object.[18] Buber rejects Sartre's declaration that God is dead, that He spoke to man in the past but that now He is silent or dead.[19] Rather Buber relates to Isaiah's teaching tht the living God is both a self-revealing and a self-concealing God.[20] Buber teaches that through the I-Thou relationship we become open to man and to God. An attitude of openness establishes and interpersonal relationship and enables mankind to reject the self-centered attitude.[21] It leads us to use our energies toward the achievement of a goal. It is only through our acts that we become real and participate in God's creation of the world. Evil exists and requires man to act in conjunction with the will of God, in concert with our conversations with God expressed in the needs of the situation, and given form by the performance of deeds required by those needs.[22] Buber taught that man must respond to the voice of God as one responds to the voice of a friend. This voice for Buber involves the mystical relationship between the individual and God. Buber rejects solitary meditation as a means of

17 *Ibid.,* pp. 88-89.
18 Buber, Martin, *Eclipse of God,* p. 23.
19 *Ibid.,* p. 66.
20 Isaiah 45:15b, Verily, Thou art a God that hidest Thyself O God of Israel, the Saviour.
21 Agus, Jacob B., *Modern Philosophies of Judaism,* pp. 268-269.
22 *Ibid.,* pp. 272-273.

experiencing God. He teaches that only through love for the other do we love God.[23]

Abraham Joshua Heschel is concerned not only with man's relationship to God but also with God's search for man. Man's search for God is not only of significance to man, but also to God who has chosen man to serve Him. Heschel declares that faith comes out of awe, out of the willingness to answer the challenge of God. Heschel states that the essence of Jewish religious thinking is not in attaining a concept of God but in articulating memories when His Presence illuminated our lives. The world of faith is one to which the individual must return and respond. Heschel has taught us that spiritual events are real and causes creative events to occur since He communicates His will to the mind of man.[24]

Heschel says that man derives his dignity from being created in the likeness of God. In Judaism it is taught that there is an inextricable bond between the holy and the good and man must strive to be holy before he can be good. The Jew must worship regardless of his mood because it is God's will that he pray and that he believe.[25] It is through the observance of the mitzvot (commandments and religious acts) that the Jew maintains his relationship with his God. In performing the mitzvot, the Jew acknowledges God's concern with the fulfillment of His will.[26]

Heschel in his last book, *A Passion for Truth,* contrasts two individuals important in Chasidic Judaism, Rabbi Israel the son of Eliezer better known as the Baal Shem Tov (The Master of the Good Name) c. 1690-1760 and the Reb Menahem Mendel of Kotz also known as the Kotzker (Rebbe). The Baal Shem Tov, the founder of the movement, declared that everyone is precious to God and that God could be found in everyone and everywhere (even, he would have taught, in the concentration camps).[27] Everyone he regarded as having divine worth and his concern and love reached out to all people. The Baal Shem Tov brought to the

---

23 *Ibid.,* p. 277.
24 Heschel, Abraham Joshua, *God in Search of Man,* pp. 136-143.
25 Heschel, Abraham Joshua, *Man's Quest for God,* pp. 94-98.
26 *Ibid.,* pp. 94-114.
27 Heschel, Abraham Joshua, *A Passion for Truth,* pp. 28-29.

Jew and to Judaism a new spirit, a spirit expressed with joy, love, song, and fervor even in a time of pain and trouble. It was as if he brought not only the message to the people but as if he brought God himself.[28]

The Kotzker Rebbe taught that the individual must serve God not because he so desired but rather despite himself—because he did not want to serve Him.[29] He had a preoccupation with man's evil and with the evil in the world. He believed that man's will is often confused and physical pleasures and material comforts cause man to deceive himself. The Kotzker Rebbe was concerned with the abyss which separated man from God and he sought to point to the bridges that could lead across it to God.[30] He was disturbed by the willingness of man to accept the status quo with its attendant evils which makes him an accomplice to the evil. Although this Rebbe could not have anticipated the holocaust that befell his people he recognized the capacity for evil, based upon lies, which makes possible the demonic in our world.[31] The holocaust was based upon the lie that the Jew is responsible for all the social wrongs in the world and that by destroying him the problems would be solved.[32]

Through this work Heschel also relates to the destruction at Auschwitz. Auschwitz challenges Heschel to live in both awe and consternation, in fervor and in horror. He is aware of the need to be concerned with mercy as well as with the remembrance of the evil of which man is capable. There was for Heschel the tension between exaltation and dismay, between affirmation and denial.[33] Thus for Heschel the joy of life, the value of the individual, and the meaning of religious fervor, was balanced by the recognition of the separation of man from God and from religion; he also recognized that people of high esteem and of average position are

28 *Ibid.*, p. 7.
29 *Ibid.*, p. 29.
30 *Ibid.*, p. 30.
31 *Ibid.*, p. 317.
32 *Ibid.*, p. 321.
33 *Ibid.*, XIV.

willing to accept and even to perform evil and destructive works. Heschel would not only require man (or lead man) to experience, declare, and teach God's love for man and man's obligation to God; he would also insist that his deeds be authentic acts of truth, righteousness, and committment to God.[34]

The issue of good and evil, of suffering and destruction, of faith and hope were given new immediacy and poignance through the literary works of Eli Wiesel. Wiesel, a survivor of Auschwitz, questions the meaning of Auschwitz and destruction in his many novels and writings. He challenges God and in his very challenge he affirms Him. His unwillingness to accept suffering and destruction as God's will and yet his constant search for the meaning of life raises the confrontation to a religious experience. He draws upon the classical midrashic tradition of examining the problem and the issues from all aspects through parables in an attempt to refine, define, and redefine the concepts. He would remind both man and God of the covenant and of the dual relationship.

Wiesel is concerned with the capacity for evil which man has revealed through the Holocaust. He is aware that evil and destruction have debased and not ennobled man. He is concerned with the irrationality of man. Wiesel presents us with the difficulty of man's life, of the lies he lives, of the falseness of which he is capable and which he must accept. Through his writings he enables us to see ourselves and to accompany him as he seeks his faith. He causes and demands that we remember those who were persecuted and killed. We find a fascination with the destruction but also a struggle for faith and for religious affirmation.

Wiesel, a journalist, a writer, has become for many modern Jews the theologian. He brings the message of life and the meaning of memory. He leads his reader to experience pain and rejection but he also indicates a path to life. Wiesel denies only to open a path to affirmation, and affirms and yet gives us no peace by causing us to remember the evil and destruction of which man is capable. He challenges belief and yet recites the Kaddish, the memorial prayer,

34 *Ibid.*, pp. 24-30.

aware that it is an affirmation of God's goodness.[35] He requires man to wrestle with his God and yet he strives after Him. When he or his characters find no meaning in life they go to the Chasidic rebbe. When the faith of the rebbe is challenged by the survivors of Auschwitz and they speak of the impossibility of faith after the events of the Holocaust, the rebbe declares that the response to Auschwitz must be belief and faith in God.

Richard Rubenstein, who was one of the first contemporary Jewish thinkers to raise Auschwitz as a religious issue, rejects a personal theistic faith. Yet he leds others to faith. In his book, *The Religious Imagination,* he discusses the rabbinic view of freedom. An affirmation of a theistic God in Judaism rejects the view of a religious theism as the enemy of human freedom. The rabbinic tradition was based on the religious convictions of the rabbis that God created the world and that nothing happened independent of His will. Yet the rabbinic tradition also conceives of God granting a degree of free choice to His creatures. The individual is under an obligation to fulfill his nature by fulfilling God's will. To perceive the God of theism as consistent with human freedom requires viewing the act of creation, however limited and circumscribed, as a gift rather than as an impediment. The rabbis conceived of man endowed with a limited degree of freedom which required the study and application of Torah which contained God's instruction for the Jewish people.[36]

Auschwitz confronts the modern Jew with the problem of affirming his faith in spite of the evil and suffering he has experienced. Louis Jacobs in his book *Faith* reminds us that evil and suffering are obstacles to man's belief in God.[37] The problem of evil raises the question of the necessity for suffering and evil. It is difficult to accept suffering and evil as having been created by a good and all-powerful God. If God tolerates evil, is He all-good or must He tolerate evil because He is not all-powerful? The Jewish tradition requires recognizing the problem of evil and still living by

---

35 Weisel, Elie, *The Gates of the Forest* (New York: Avon), p. 223.
36 Rubenstein, Richard L., *The Religious Imagination,* pp. 138-150.
37 Jacobs, Louis, *Faith,* p. 113.

faith. Evil is viewed as a prerequisite for man to make moral choices and for the good to be realized. This is the cost for a world in which man can and must strive for moral values. Modern man, like Job, can see part of the path which enables him to live by faith. In the Jewish tradition it is incumbent upon him to pursue righteousness and to wage battle against evil.[38]

Auschwitz for the modern Jew symbolizes the evil that man must confront, this evil that threatens to destroy the community and the individual. The modern Jew confronts the problem of living with his faith in a world which has witnessed ever greater weapons of destruction. The answer of the Jew to Auschwitz is to survive as a Jew individually and collectively. The answer of the Jew to Auschwitz is to remember his past, to memorialize his martyrs to declare his faith through his committment to his people, and to struggle against evil. This is the meaning of the central and core prayer of Judaism in which the Jew declares his faith individually and collectively. This is the meaning of the term Israel in the prayer Hear O Israel, the Lord is our God, the Lord is one. Israel refers here to both the individual Jew and the total Jewish community.

After Auschwitz the Jew realizes that more than ever he must affirm his belief in God even while he recognizes the evil that exists in the world. We would memorialize those Jews who died with faith in their hearts by affirming our own faith. We express our belief and our sense of awe in the words of the following prayer:

The greatness of the Eternal One surpasses our understanding and yet at times we feel His nearness.

Overwhelmed by awe and wonder as we behold the signs of His presence, still we feel within us a kinship with the divine.

---

38 *Ibid.,* pp. 113-125.

As so we turn to You, O God, looking at the world about us, and inward to the world within us, there to find You, and from Your presence gain life and strength.[39]

A SELECT BIBLIOGRAPHY

Agus, Jacob B., *Modern Philosophies of Judaism*. New York: Behrman's Jewish Book House, 1941.

Baeck, Leo, *This People Israel*. Translated by Albert Friedländer. New York: Holt, Rinehart, and Winston, 1965.

Borowitz, Eugene B., *A New Jewish Theology in the Making*. Philadelphia: Westminister Press, 1968.

Buber, Martin, *Daniel*. New York: Holt, Rinehart and Winston, 1964.

_____, *Eclipse of God*. New York: Harper and Row, 1952.

_____, *Good and Evil*. New York: Charles Scribner's Sons, 1953.

Central Conference of American Rabbis, *Gates of Prayer for Weekdays*. New York: 790 Madison Ave., 1975.

Fackenheim, Emil L., *God's Presence in History*. New York: New York University Press, 1970.

_____, *Quest for Past and Present*. Bloomington, Indiana: Indiana University Press, 1968.

Friedlander, Albert H., *Out of the Whirlwind*. New York: Union of American Hebrew Congregation, 1967.

Glenn, Paul J., *Theodicy*. St. Louis, Missouri: B. Herdor Book Company, 1939.

Gordis, Robert, *Poets, Prophets and Sages: Essays in Biblical Interpretations*. Bloomington, Indiana: Indiana University Press, 1971.

Heath, Thomas R., *In Face of Anguish*, New York: Sheed and Ward, 1966.

Heschel, Abraham Joshua, *A Passion for Truth*. New York: Farrar, Strauss and Giroux, 1973.

_____, *God in Search of Man*. New York: Harper and Row, Harper Torchbooks, 1966.

_____, *Man's Quest for God*. New York: Scribner, 1954.

Jacobs, Louis, *Faith*. London: Vallentine, Mitchell, 1968.

Keller, Werner, *Diaspora*, New York: Harcourt & Brace World, 1963.

Lookstein, Joseph H., *Faith and Destiny of Man*. New York: Bloch Publishing Company, 1967.

Madden, Edward H. and Hare, Peter H., *Evil and the Concept of God*. Springfield, Illinois: Charles C. Thomas, 1968.

---

[39] Central Conference of American Rabbis, *Gates of Prayer for Weekdays*, p. 28.

Noveck, Simon, *Contemporary Jewish Thought.* Clinton, Massachusetts: The Colonial Press, 1969.

Plotkin, Frederick S., *Judaism and Tragic Theology.* New York: Schocken, 1973.

Rotenstreich, Nathan, *Jewish Philosophy in Modern Times, From Mendelssohn to Rosenzweig.* New York: Holt, Rinehart and Winston, 1968.

Rubenstein, Richard L., *The Religious Imagination.* Indianapolis Indiana: The Bobbs Merrill Company, 1968.

Soper, Edmond Davison. *The Religions of Mankind.* 3rd ed., Nashville. Tennessee: Abingdon Press, 1966.

Stern, M., *Daily Paper Book.* New York: Star Hebrew Book Co., 1931.

Wiesel, Elie, *The Accident.* New York: Avon, 1970.

_____, *Beggar in Jerusalem.* New York: Avon, 1971.

_____, *Dawn.* New York: Avon, 1971.

_____, *The Gates of the Forest.* New York: Avon, 1970.

_____, *The Jews of Silence.* New York: Holt, Rinehart and Winston, 1966.

_____, *Legends of Our Time.* New York: Avon, 1972.

_____, *Night.* New York: Avon, 1972.

_____, *One Generation After.* New York: Avon, 1971.

_____, *The Oath.* New York: Avon, 1973.

_____, *The Town Beyond the Wall.* New York: Avon, 1969.

CHAPTER XLI

HOPE AND THE PRESENT INSTANT

Anna-Teresa Tymieniecka *

When everything fails, when the present is nothing but the shipwreck of our tenaciously carried on endeavors, when our life-situation seems to stifle in germ our most ardent aspirations or leaves no place for the working out of our plans, when earthquake, plague and disease threaten our existence, still we always hope. What is *hope* that it may brave the elements, surpass social conditioning and disregard life itself? We often say: "As long as there is life, there is hope."

And yet, is it not hope that is the ultimate target of contemporary literature in its attempt to reach beyond constraints to the freedom of man? It seems that *freeing* man from all the cultural, social and anthropological entanglements, which compose his natural life conditions, would free him also from hope; would set him free not only from the artifacts of civilization but also from the futility of his natural inclinations and expectations: his natural finiteness.

In fact, it is as reasonable to see hope bound to life as it is to see it ultimately related to freedom. It is from the framework of the first that we have to unravel its meaning, arriving ultimately at the significance of the second.

But it is from within man's temporal, inexorably fleeting nature and his innermost struggle to find this unique, personal foothold within the flux, to give significance to his existence, that hope takes its role and meaning.

*Professor of Philosophy, The World Institute for Advanced Phenomenological Research and Learning, Belmont, Massachusetts, U.S.A.

While all hope surges to serve the temporal finiteness of man, only one kind, *Hope par excellence,* achieves its completion.

What is hope?

According to a set of essential elements of experience, we differentiate as hope:

(1) *Expectation,* the basic feature of the temporality of human consciousness and condition of psychic life (its constituents are: intention, anticipation, wish, desire, etc.);

(2) *Hope,* the regulative ideal of psychic life. The hope of earthly or eternal happiness, promising the fulfillment of the nostalgia for the infinite, the perfect and the beautiful that the finiteness of life leaves unsatisfied.

(3) *Hope* as the faith and assurance that the anonymous, inexorable fleetingness of life will be redeemed in the accomplishment of an unique *destiny,* briefly, hope as the fulfillment of the spiritual destiny of the soul.

(4) *Hope* as the completion of the temporal in the *imminent transcending instant.*

In whatever form we experience it, hope is a complex psychic act. As such it is surging within the stream of consciousness at a specific instant of the present. We experience it as carrying us beyond this stream of the immediately experienced present into a nearer undefinable future. We experience it as an expansion of our actual experience into something that is not given yet, but anticipated: an objective. The objective of hope is not present in concrete experience but only appears imaginatively, at a distance, meant to be actually given in some future. But as Bergson has justly remarked, although it is given as a mere possibility, it neither appears in a clearcut form of an ideal object nor in any precise form. In other words, the objective of hope as the terminal of the act does not, like the object of perception or memory crystallize into a single, precise object; the act of hope projects its intentions as a wide spread of variations upon one theme, none of which is intended in particular but all vaguely outlined and glimmering together in their respective nuances. Due to this spread the objective of hope lends to experience a lived radiating expansion. While memory, perception and imagination terminate in a precise object, strictly determined and reposing in itself with sharp contours distinguishing it in the field of actual experience, the act of hope in all its variations carries us from the *present* field of consciousness into an *anticipated* present in which its objective is supposed to be actualized. This latter appears as a range of possibles each radiating upon the others the respective attractiveness of its specific features. Thus the objective of hope is richer than any of its possible actualizations, which, should one occur, would have to be a clear-cut particular instance singled out from all of them and excluding all the others—consequently, losing all its attractiveness which appears at the horizon of expectation.

In fact, sensory perception does not consist of one singular instance which gives us the perceived object, e.g., a tree or a table, its 'image.' Rather, it is the result of a series of perceptual glances, each containing only an aspect of the object being focused upon and also an indication of some other aspect to be completed in further glimpses. Sensory perception has an anticipatory element. Without the fact that each glimpse contains an indication of the anticipations to be actualized, we could never continue the series of perceptual glimpses and arrive at a synthetic act which yields the complete perceived object.

But in perception the anticipation contained in each glimpse is a concrete indication of the instances to come and belongs to the unfolding of the present instance, that is to the same segment of the one spacious present. None of the specific acts of intending carries us beyond it; to the contrary, the unfolding of the series itself gives to the lived experience the temporal unity of the present. It is in the nature of the intended object that all the anticipatory elements of the intentions meet in view of presenting it *right there,* in its *immediate appearance.* This immediate appearance punctuates the lived present itself by captivating our attention. When it passes out of the focus of attention a new experience establishes a new lived present.

In imagination we also complete the first outlined form to some degree in a temporal line. In fact, we may leave it for the time being and take it up at another time at will. But in the intentional act of imagining a thing there is no indication of a future stage at which this should occur. In this way the act of imagination and its constructive process are temporally free.

It is the specific feature of hope that the act in which we experience it, which occurs within a given lived present intends a state of affairs to occur in a *different* present than itself; furthermore it possesses also a specific relation to imagination, to will and to our emotional system of experience.

In fact, like all experience, hope emerges from a specific situation; but unlike sensory perception for which a specific psycho-physical situation is a determinant, or unlike memory and imagination in which it is the *continuity* of the cognitive or constitutive progress of our psychic life that is determining (e.g., we remember only what we have already known); it is within the associative system of the cognitive process that instances of memory occur even if they are stimulated by emotional impulses. Hope emerges quite clearly from the emotional situation. It is the situation created by the present that falls short of our desires, the avenues of its dynamism being to narrow for our spontaneous expansion, the prospects it offers for the fulfillment of our aspirations, dreams and innermost longings being imperfect or fallacious, or our longings remaining out of tune with its tendencies and orientation. Or, becoming critical, it might be that the present opposes, eradicates, challenges and dwarfs our attempts and prospects for the immediate fulfillment of our desires and aims. Thus, clearly, it is from the incompleteness felt in the present or from emotional distress, disappointment, dissatisfaction, delusion or discontentment, that hope emerges. It opens a perspective beyond the narrow limits of the present. It alleviates distress, discounting its causes to a passing value; it makes us rise again from disaster, promising that all can be made up again and it remedies by serenity the frustrations of life.

Indeed, among the basic features of the act of hope,

differentiating it from the cognitive acts, are: firstly, that it is not a part of our cognitive automatism of operations, organizing and making intelligible felt experience, but that it is, on the contrary, meant to expand our horizon of felt experience beyond the limits of the present. Secondly, its dynamism surges from the fact that our spontaneous willful acts are counteracted, encounter obstacles or fall short of their aim. So much for its source. As for its specific character, it primordially complements our emotional deficiencies, alleviates our stresses, frustrations and failures, and thus restores the equilibrium of our innermost personal life. It complements, in the guise of potential fulfillment, of illusory completion that we find in our innermost strivings of the present only haphazardly scattered, sketched or altogether denied, thus escaping our hold. Indeed each and every individual existence even if advancing in a most harmonious interplay of forces with the world and through an unhampered and favorably stimulated unfolding from within, does not consist in the present alone. To the contrary, each and every segment of the lived present, of the actual field of experience, as poignant as it might be and apparently absorbing of all our attention, remains always incomplete. Presently accomplished tasks, actualized projects and fulfilled wishes remain like the relation of a fragment to the total project in which our being visualizes itself.

Never accomplished, each particular achievement drops from us lifelessly and leaves us empty. Our habits which seemingly make our being become automatized responses of this dimension which has lost contact with its vital source. The human being is at each instant filled with new incoming experience, like a skeleton clad with new, ever changing cloth, like an instrument activised with ever new infusing forces and energies coming and going, never to be counted upon. Can man in this flux, his only power seeming to lie in organizing it, identify himself with anything relatively consistent? Can he find anything that is his *very own,* absolutely present now and here, but this net of intentions, aspirations, desires, wishes, plans and expectations? On the contrary, it seems that each actual concrete field of experience swims in the undetermined horizon of the whole project yet to come. For example, we live not only in the satisfaction of good school grades received at the end of *this* trimester but in the prospective joy or grief to be caused by those to come at the end of the school year. Our momentary disappointment with our present poor results in research is already alleviated by the prospect of the ulterior improvement. Our happiness in communion with the beloved being is enhanced by the faith in its continuity, which might in fact break at any instant and never be retrieved again. Without the expansion, which the fragmentary experience of the present finds in the anticipated glimmering completion expected as the corollary, as an answer to our innermost tendencies and desires, we would not have accomplished the measure of equilibrium and of equipoise, which is indispensable for our existence. In our youth, carried by the dynamism of action and creation, we tend to disregard the lived present and to see ourselves in our future. Only in our middle years do we suddenly realize that projects fail us: neither do we ever actualize them completely, nor do we keep them faithfully. In fact, we play with them according to circumstances, like throwing a ball in the air and catching it. We realize that the real *us,* our *real* life, which in our onward *élan* we always postponed till the future date when "all our dreams would be realized," once they failed, was lived by us all the way through in *every concrete present.* We realize the whole perspective of hope was merely the emotional completion and the emotional expansion of the fragmentary immediate moment. Without it our tendencies would find no rest and would drift in all directions blindly and restlessly, whereas our real being has to be maintained in an equipoise between gains and losses, between victories and defeats, accomplishments and failures, desires and contentments, exercise and rest. We discover that hope in all its features, in its radiating, expanding and enriching function as an imminent promise, does not consist or depend upon the realization of its objectives. With all the halucinatory attraction that they may exercise upon us, luring us to strive for, they *are not real* and never will be in any future. Their essential function is to enhance and complete the *present* experience.

Yet hope fulfills this function in various ways at different levels of human existence; thus it appears in various types.

1. Expectation

The nature of man in its dynamic progress is essentially a matter of his conscious functions. Although life itself in its simplest forms indicates more emphasis upon organic articulations and processes than upon self-awareness, we see, on the one hand, that the most primitive forms of life in their receptivity, sensitivity and reactivity, exemplify the simplest forms of intentionality, that is, of a self-activated orientation and directness towards something else instead of being totally self-consuming like the operations within brute, inorganic matter. This self-activated directness is at the same time articulated and organized towards an aim. The aim is survival. On the other hand, the more we advance in the study of life, the more we see emphasized the role of the brain, of the nervous system, in sum the conscious or intentional organization of all the vital, organic functions over these organic functions considered in themselves (e.g., the function of the heart as a pump, etc.) as was the case in earlier science.

It appears, in fact, that not far from the view of the scholastics, consciousness in its various degrees of awareness enters extensively, as the factor of articulation and organization, into all directly inspectable human functions mentally and physically. To temporality as the basic feature of consciousness is to be brought the essence of the complete human being. We emerge in this world and progressively unfold all our faculties by recognizing them in our growing awareness of the world and of ourselves. The same awareness makes us develop ourselves within a world of our own and acknowledge progressively the successive stages of our development: the natural ascending stages of growth, of youth, maturity and the descending stages of decay. We may in a conscious act retain for an instant a fixed image of ourselves, like the image of our first youth, of our childhood or manhood, but we cannot stop for an instant the actual progress of our course. Our being is fleeting in its totality and each instant of the present, as soon as it occurs, is irretrievably receding from the focus of attention into the adumbrating shadows of the past.

It is through our conscious operations extending as far as our bodily motions and organic functioning that we unfold our being in this marvelous specifically human way of living in the present experience while we unfold it. We construct a world around us in this extraordinary way of making within us a lived, *personally* experienced universe which is ourselves. We identify ourselves with the course we follow through the whole gamut of conscious acts culminating in self-awareness that, instead of being simply totally absorbed in this stream of experience through which we consciously exist, we grasp it synthetically in its three phases of the imminent present, the past into which it sinks, and the future towards which it tends.

But contrary to Bergson, we cannot say that it is the work of memory, as the most significant, the fundamental principle of the conscious life, to differentiate mind from matter, or the conscious life of higher animals from the mere vital subsistence of the lower ones. Certainly, memory by bringing about the synthetic grasp of the whole unfolding of man's experience and thus establishing a basis for continuity among the dispersed segments, allows for a purposive or teleological self-orientation of this course or at least the establishing of its meaningful interconnectedness. Thus understood the function of memory may be fundamental for man who is always in a dynamic progress and does not ever stop for a rest, remaining always unfinished, changeable and radically unidentifiable with anything concrete, fixed or distinctively delineated. He is in fact what he is as much in his virtualities, which have not yet unfolded, as in those which have and thus he may take an unforseeable turn in his development.

And yet for man who at the core of his being is spread upon the temporal pattern, with its narrow span of the poignantly absorbing but instantaneously vanishing presents, and past-presents progressively sinking into oblivion or the future, which is not yet there, but which as an undertermined and unforseeable illusory co-presence is the perspective of the present itself; it is this orientation of the underlying dynamism of his processional nature towards the future that is most fundamental.

In fact, the complete structure of man's consciousness in its vital role of expanding, promoting and articulating life is from the throng of the basic stream from which the conscious, intentional acts surge up to their most minute organization, oriented towards this future, which is not there, which might never come, but which is co-present as the foundation of the process of the unfolding.

Contemporary psychiatry has much insisted upon the role of the dimension of future in general in conscious life. But what is the distinctive role of *expectation* as a *mode of consciousness* differentiated from basic forms of *intention, anticipation* and from spontaneous *passions* like desire, which will also transport us from our status in the here and now towards this not yet present?

In fact, the basic intentional nature of consciousness, which consists of a stream of conscious acts, each surging from its depth as already oriented towards something, towards an object, is at its fundamental level constructed with an orientation towards the future. As I mentioned, at the primordial cognitive level of sensory experience, individual acts as fragmentary glimpses in the specific present of the field of consciousness, are already related in their structure to a temporal series; they are not self-sufficient and next to clearly filled out qualities they contain vaguely delineated or empty spaces and thus indicate a complement to come. That is, from one present instance there is a bridge towards the next to continue it. It is due to the element of anticipation within the act itself that we are guided towards the next one to satisfy this anticipation: (e.g., of seeing the back of an apple, of which only the front appeared in the first glimpse; the front with a part of the side in the second, and with a part of the top in the third; each of them anticipating the appearance of the next). Thus the serial structure of perception is already grounded in anticipation of the *next* present, anticipation which was not satisfied in the already *given* present.

But is the complete set up of our natural life above this fundamental structure of the basic cognitive experience not structured in a comparable way? Was it not said that to be a child means to live constantly beyond yourself? Is all the training and

teaching through all the stages of childhood not always expecting
and prompting child to become what he is not yet; learn what he
does not know yet; do of what he is not yet capable; and
understand what he cannot yet comprehend? Had we followed
some of the naturalistic trends in education waiting until a child is
'ready' for something to come out of him "naturally," we would,
in the first place, not allow him to advance further in his
development than beyond that of a human animal. But even then
is not a child essentially always living in advance of himself? While
crawling does he not already anticipate standing up straight and is
he not prompted to the effort to do it, imagining himself doing
so? Is not the whole curve of our route aiming in its progress at
fragmentary accomplishments at each stage, based upon the
structuring of the acts so that none of them becomes an aim in
itself, none gives us rest, but all, each anticipating the incoming
one, occur as instances of a functional series? In infancy we are a
child to be, in childhood we are already a project of an adolescent,
in adolescence a draft of an adult, which in reality we might never
become. It is from this anticipatory nature of our functions that
we draw both the continuity with the past and the stimulus
towards the future. This anticipatory structure is the vehicle of the
purposes of nature, it is the condition through which the life
progress of the individual being is accomplished.

At the more specifically individual level of the psychic life we
witness an analogical situation. Most important of all, not only the
cognitive functions of consciousness like perception, imagination,
memory, reflection, the purely speculative level of intelligence,
etc., but also our personal world and existence which derive their
impetus, substance, and personal significance from the vibrating
pulp of emotions, are also roots in this structure. They are the
pulp of our individual feelings insofar as they are united and
organized by the sweeping impetus of passions that give the tone,
the fragrance, the felt quality and the orientation to lived
experience.

Desires, ambitions, wishes, aspirations, activate or put out of
play our faculties and talents; they lead us to develop habits
serving their purposes, to forge qualities of heart and attitudes of

will like courage, perseverance, stubbornness and tenacity. Finally, they set into an outline the course of action, mobilizing all our routine functions towards accomplishment of aims and purposes. In fact, due to them our individual life never rests, or reposes in the given present. We live the experience of the present already in view of the expectations which the future is meant to fulfill. The individual psychic life in all its radiating dynamism is never concentrated or enclosed within the present experience but expands into the future by expectations. Without this expansion the personal life would be truncated at each point. Each and every psychic act is in itself incomplete, only a fragment of a plan, of a scheme or of a project to be accomplished. We devise the meaning of the present from the expectations which prolong it. From them it derives its relative completeness and its significance to satisfy us for the time being by establishing the equipoise between the desire and its absent target.

As psychiatry has observed, we feel alive insofar as we expect, as we expand in our feeling the narrow and limited present experience into vast perspectives of an illusory future. Strangely enough, inasmuch as this horizon of expectations is necessary for the dynamism of life—and we see how with the vanishing range of expectations the life dynamism shrinks and vanishes—it is also the limit of our personal freedom. In fact, we could say with contemporary literature that man, as the product of a specific civilization and society from which he has borrowed all the forms of life, as a member as well as a person, of expression, behavior and ways of thinking, but even those of feeling since it is the society which impressed upon him its moulds, is in all this not "his own self." But, even there where we would believe that we are most intimately ourselves, namely in our desires, aspirations and ambitions, we could say with Beckett and Camus that the aims which we believe to be our inner-most strivings are the anonymous forms which humanity has forged and that we just borrow indolently and blindly and *play* with them like pebbles, but deep down they are all the same.

Going further it could be said that these arbitrary forms, which express nothing significant and uniquely personal, are nothing more than the vehicles of nature oriented towards natural survival. Thus we would be from our very origin moulded as a standard being and when we arrived at self-awareness we would find ourselves to be chained by the social forms of civilization as well as by those of nature itself. Both are contingent, lasting only as long as the life they serve.

Camus' man, in order to become himself, has to detach himself not only from all the natural attachments of feeling higher or lower, of tendencies, of beliefs and ideals, but also from all preference, ambition, aspiration and expectation. This poses "freedom" against life. In fact Camus' hero discovers freedom from life in a fulgurating "happiness" surpassing the concrete experience of hope only at the prospect of his imminent death. However, with an absurd inconsistency, which must have escaped the author, he reaches this state only when after an existence of pure vegetal passivity, he is provoked into an outburst of rage galvanizing in him all the passion so far stultified. Is there any stronger act affirming life?

2. Hope as the Regulative Ideal

Camus' stranger, freed from all natural expectation, is also totally indifferent towards the transnatural hope of salvation, of redemption, of life in immortality.

Hope of happiness, justice and redemption emerge also from the emotive substance of consciousness. It surges within us in response to our nostalgias, longings and higher strivings which are perpetually disabused by the finiteness of life and of our own being. Longing for the beautiful and good, for justice and love, and feeling an urgency to satisfy our thirst for it we find only limited, imperfect, deceptive instances which fall short of our thirst. Can we remain with this dissatisfaction? Would not the acceptance of the failure spoil the texture of our life and of the meaning of man's endeavors? Is this thirst, which already contains a taste for the perfectly beautiful, just, infinitely merciful and comprehending (which makes us already feel it and be it in part) not an evidence that it *should* be found, if not in the present experience then in another present to come? How could we live with the nostalgias, the fulfillment of which means a real completion of life, if they are radically denied us? Would life itself not lose its higher aim? Finally, are these higher longings and innermost strivings precisely the ones which unfold into aspirations, dreams and ideals, raising natural limited existence to a higher level of spirit?

The experience of the present might not give them a concrete satisfactory answer. They may be dwarfed an infinite number of times by each successive one. We might finally discover the finiteness of human life and our own finiteness, which means that our possibilities to accomplish them are limited. We might conclude that nothing in life itself can ever answer to their standards and yet could we altogether banish them from our orbit? If we did, we would be condemning ourselves to the narrow limits of nature, depriving ourselves from all the higher dimensions of existence, making our own being shrink instead of expand, becoming dull instead of radiant. Thus we *hope*. We pursue relations that break while seeking the true and lasting friendship and love that we *hope* to find. We compose awkward and empty verses seeking the perfect verse we *hope* to create. It is hope that gives light, joy and assurance to the dull, uncertain and doubtful present. It is on the wings of our higher aspirations that we unfold our spirit and it is hope that completes the broken, unfinished, missing, fragmentary odds and ends. It compensates for want of radiance, perfection, and beauty. It is hope which opens the infinite dimension for our nostalgias and thus allows us this exalted existence for which we feel the urge.

And when we discover the finiteness of life, the congenital incapacity of man to stand still, to remain, to open himself completely, to receive and bring anything into completion in his limited frame; when we discover the impossibility of satisfying our innermost urges for the infinite and perfect, for the true and the absolute in this framework of nature, we do not give up but *hope* to be redeemed from it some day. We hope to exchange this for another eternal and perfect existence. We convert our earthly expectations into transnatural hope.

Both hopes of earthly happiness and of transnatural felicity respond to our innermost nostalgias. They complete the lacking concrete feelings, they expand the limited present into imaginary infinitude, they lift it to a higher imaginary dimension. They are obviously meant for the sake of the present.

But is it not the present that is the core of life? Is it not in the concrete, vibrating present that we enact our being, that we unfold our organic being from germ towards its *telos* intended by nature? Is it not in the present that we lead the moral struggle forging our moral being? Is it not in the present that we discover our virtualities, our hidden strivings, that we fight to unravel our true self, our own meaning of life and our *authentic destiny?* Indeed it is in the present that we have to realize this destiny, and if there is the question of redemption, it is also only in the present that there could be the chance to accomplish it.

In short, as much as the concrete present life might always escape any serious responsibility with which we would like to invest it; as much as, consequently, we would like to treat it lightly and transpose all the weight to the side of infinity, perfection and absolute that we imagine so poignantly in response to our longing; if we escape life we abandon all. For hope of the absolute, of the all-comforting love, of a complete understanding, total redemption from the finiteness, is meant for *this life.* What sense would it make to establish a world falling short of all essentials for a truly meaningful existence, and allowing for it only after it is finished? What sort of comedy would creation then be?

If creation is meaningful, if the human finiteness in its play with the absolute makes sense, the game of redemption would have to be played right here. It is here that we would have to struggle, seek, develop and accomplish it.

But how do we lift ourselves from the natural turpitude of passive endurance? How do we not succumb under pain, suffering, disappointment, and discouragement? In short, how do we lift our hearts, and courage, and ignite our energies in order to struggle for the higher existence, for the transcending of the automatism of nature which enslaves us to its purposes? Again hope as a reservoir of ideals for all higher completions of life urges us to courage, lifts us up, enlivens the atrophied energies, wakes us from the lethargy, completes the voids and thus regulates our struggle.

Thus hope emerges from life and serves the orbit of life in all its higher spiritual dimensions. The spirtualized and mystical images of infinite love, communion with the undivided and one which makes us feel transported above the finite orbit of nature into which our spiritual effusions of love and happiness flow, respond to our deepest urges; final outposts of our human faculties, they are meant to alleviate life and invigorate our truly spiritual resources to realize their aims. But these images of eternal happiness even in themselves do not promise us anything in a transnatural future. They have no anticipatory links beyond the closed system of the finite human being. They might be his ultimate regulative ideals for the earthly existence but they do not have wings other than imaginary ones to transport us any further. Their dynamic resources stem from life itself. With all the ties and expectations of the natural being suspended, with the complete dispossession of the mystic, we see, both in the case of John of the Cross and St. Thérèse of Lisieux, that in the dark night of the senses which normally gives the light of natural knowledge, all knowledge and imagination vanish and with them faith and hope. They are both meant for the creature with its full endowment; not beyond.

And are the images which hope of redemption offers us anything else but artifacts we have construed in analogy to the here and now experienced situation? Is the eternal happiness we covet not the exalted image of the human happiness we experience in various limited ways?

Should this mean that hope, as the answer to our higher and deeper strivings beyond this function, is only luring us with futile imaginings? That certainly is not right, but what is obvious is that it does not project us directly beyond the finiteness of life and nature; that it does not, consequently, have a representational value of any reality; that the "truth" it contains is to be evaluated only indirectly with respect to its function and *not* its promise. The future promises nothing but illusions.

Neither does it mean that the promise of eternal life is vain.

But, as Furipises Choir proclaims, hope is the goddess of illusion.

3. Hope in the Fulfillment of the Transnatural Destiny of the Soul

Time carries everything away, says St. Augustine and it is sharply expressed in the myth of Chronos devouring his own children. Our own being, essentially temporal, flees away at the completion of the actual experience of each present instant till all is spent from our initial reservoir of forces and virtualities, and till our network of expansive radiation in plans, projects and expectations vanishes in an unavoidable death. It is due partly to our self-absorption in the present, partly to the ever-expanding expectations that we live as if life would last forever, and are unable to face our death. How can we face death which is our last expectation with no range of possibilities to choose from, but definitely final? In fact, the dynamic nature of man expanding in ever new expectations seems to give us in the present the reach into the future thus giving us an illusion of power, of domination, or at least of a grasp of the change itself. In close scrutiny we may even see that all of our concerns in life express surreptitiously the tendency to conjure the fleetingness of life, the unsatiable voracity of time. We crave to install some lasting footholds within the contingent flux. Our institutions, professions, family devotions, great causes, creative endeavors all ultimately aim at conjuring the vanishing existence. All ultimately fail. No great accomplishment will outlast humanity, which is itself in flux and in a temporal unfolding.

And yet we do not stop to seek a point of reference that would conjure the fleetingness and give it a lasting significance. If everything comes to be and then vanishes without a system of references that would punctuate a difference between such a course of things and another, between such a development of our being and all the others which we could have undertaken, between the haphazard outcome of the play of circumbiant forces and an accomplishment due to our labor in which our innermost tendencies and nostalgias have the upper hand over the natural play of circumstances and our survival, then, indeed, human life would be a cruel delusion of all these deepest longings which make the true fabric of our human substance.

But what if within the cyclic course of our natural existence we find not only nostalgias and strivings for values which nature cannot actualize, but also a foothold for their accomplishment? Camus' stranger is not, in fact, a complete man. He let himself drift along the temporal sequence of his being. He did not struggle, did not seek, consequently did not reveal to himself either his higher strivings or his deeper virtualities. What if he had understood the true finiteness of life, which does not consist in a total resignation to follow the natural course of things, but on the contrary, releases the higher aspirations to overcome it within ourselves? Total submission to contingency of nature is the acceptance of a total defeat; total resignation is the death of the spirit.

It seems, indeed, that there is something which we might have bypassed and which is precisely what life is about: our "trans-natural" destiny. Had there not been within ourselves virtualities of an order not reducible to nature itself, with its physiologico-psychic regulations, and serving other purposes than cyclic growth, we could consider our existence meaningless, like that of a flower, and our longings unfulfilled. But in our quest, reaching the borderline of finiteness of life, we may dig into ourselves and discover a voice to be consulted, discover an impulse towards an inner path to follow, a line of inward growth to unfold in which all the vanishing love, hate, desires, struggles, dis-appointments, joys and exultations may be salvaged from total oblivion. They may become significant insofar as they convey our deepest commitment to the role they played in forging our personal, inward, spiritual destiny. Like death, we never have our destiny in front of us. Never can we face it directly since it is never present, but in the segment of the outline already accomplished; we work at it by trial and error, not knowing where it will lead us; unlike the course of nature which is advancing automatically, we advance making deliberate choices to justify that in which we have nothing but the subjective, inner voice. Yet we feel that *we are on the way*. It is the only thing that matters: *to be on the way*. By each step of scrutiny we discover significance in what, in the perspective of helpless finiteness, seemed meaningless. In reference to this the meanderings of the outline—in which we forge our own inward progress—the flat, dull, contours of events, beings and relations, come to their full dimensions. They radiate new lights and generate signs pointing our further turns to take. All doors which were closed to our empirical quest now open to our scrutiny in a different dimension and we have only to choose which one to enter.

Freed from the rules and regulations of the natural path of life—since to engage upon the route of an inward destiny means to be inwardly disengaged from the purposive life routeine—do we enter nto a new slavery? Sartre wants to show us in the *Flies* how Orestes after having freed himself from all the constraints of his nature, from conventions, from the fear and expectation of an universal religion, social morality (even the seemingly unalienable filial ties in killing his own mother), stays denuded from all ambition, aspiration and in fact from all future. But his freedom from constraints and his freedom from earthly prospects, desires, and projects means at the same time a *vacuum* in which he cannot take any advantage of it. That is, having equated *all* our aspirations and strivings with the natural ones, and having disposed of them, the man of Sartre and Camus has only the negative freedom not to be constrained in his action, but lacks the positive freedom to act, to exercise his powers. If our forces and powers are only those of nature, then, indeed, having lost objectives for their possible application, death is the only act which remains to be accomplished. Certainly, if freedom from contingent ties, ambition and inclinations would mean freedom from all projects and aspirations then life would be not only of no use—it would not even be possible.

And yet there is also a positive side of freedom: to exercise our forces, to act, to unfold our virtual potencies. If we look into ourselves, we discover that the natural dynamism of growth is not the only spontaneity which moves us. When we enter from within the quest after the true meaning of our existence, we find that there are aspirations other than those prompting the course of life.

Forging our destiny we find at each and every step of our quest that we must deliberately decide upon one out of many choices possible which lie outside of the automatized routine of the choices of the current life. We discover the freedom to act which releases all our inner moral and spiritual forces towards a unique, special and personal end. We have the freedom to choose this end or to deny it. At every step we have the freedom to acknowledge the inner voice, to interpret it in one way or another, or to remain deaf to it. No doubt we are inclined in our choice towards some direction, but the inclination does not come any more from the anonymous tendencies of nature or from haphazard coincidences of the social situation. They express our innermost being, our most intimately personal source.

We have the freedom to decide what we want to become in our unique way. We have the freedom to follow our own intimate inclinations and to unfold a spontaneous route of creation from our intimately personal resources. In brief, we have the freedom to pull ourselves from the anonymous individuality of nature into a personal and unique destiny. Our freedom is neither altogether blind, nor restricted by luring images. We have *Hope.*

And yet at this level are the images, the expectations and the anticipations of our natural set-up altogether useless? Once we have seen through their relative, limited significance are they still an obstacle and a chain? Or on the contrary, how could we exist in our inner dimension without having the outer? We could not release this subterranean stream without a soil from which to wring it out. Nature is to be neither rejected nor neglected! To the contrary, once we have freed ourselves from its original hold and pursue a personal, uniquely original course in the midst of its anonymous operations, each trifle, otherwise most insignificant, takes on a meaning. Nothing can be neglected anymore as a passing item to be forgotten. From the monotonous and flat surface our existence rises into a pluridimensional fulgurating wealth, in which we dig to find our way, endowing it with meaning. All enters into our great game in the new roles and functions which we discover for it.

In short, to pursue the spiritual destiny means to carry on the

struggle between the finiteness of our very being, of life, of the
world and our longing to transcend it. It consists in conjuring the
fleetingness of our contingent temporal existence, that of a
product of nature by creation of a transnatural course of growth,
corresponding to our higher strivings, which transcends the laws
and the pattern of contingency. It means to unfold a different
route, which although it forges our inward being in a temporal
succession, does not give in to the devouring temporality of nature
but is the creative unfolding of our higher, transnatural telos.

And yet, it is only within contingent nature that we may
accomplish it. We need all our natural resources, expectations and
hopes to carry it on. We need its spontaneity and forces for the
pursuit and the struggle itself. We need the bowels of nature and
the world as the very medium and battlefield. It is within
contingency itself that we may unfold and gain this great game of
"redemption."

But is this spontaneity we unfold within enough to bring us
through this blind, confused, dark maze of the pulsating world? In
our quest we feel constantly at the point of loss and the absence
of assurance and comfort. Are we not beyond the certitudes of
opinion, universal beliefs of mankind and laws of reason? Are we
not the only ones to decide upon our very own evidence and
conviction?

All on our own we still have Hope. We have no anticipation of
events to follow, expectation of satisfactions and fulfillment of
our desires, or images of infinite and perfect perspectives to exalt
our being, to expand our existence, and to ignite our latent
enthusiasms. We only *hope* that on our way, we will arrive at its
terminal; our existence will not vanish as a futile segment of
haphazard games of nature, society, culture, or cosmic forces; we
will arrive at the culminating point of our quest, accomplishing
our route. Our struggles will not be in vain. Life will be redeemed
in the final accomplishment of our destiny.

Thérèse of Lisieux, after having despoiled herself of all natural,
contingent attachments, inclinations, strivings and expectations
has also lost the natural spontaneity for life, faith and hope. The
images of the Infinite, Perfect and Absolute have vanished at the

borderline of the finiteness and left her without any comfort in the midst of darkness. Then she discovers the *destiny* which she has accomplished and a new hope surges that her life will not be in vain; she will leave the testimony of a route to be followed which conjures the finiteness of existence. Other beings may redeem their contingency from the devouring time.

She has discovered Hope: the finite aim of life being consummated in the accomplishment of the transnatural destiny. Death is no more a doom, a menace to avert our eyes from. It is the point of destination, the time of harvest.

Thus hope counteracts the dread of the finality of Death. To the inevitable end, which always appears to us as an untimely doom—putting a sharp limit to our natural expansiveness that seems to never subdue or reach a definitive stage—it juxtaposes the completion of a destiny to which nothing more should or could be added; after the completion of which life would be superfluous and vain. Since we progress in the darkness, no guidelines or constraints of everyday concerns hamper our *personal freedom;* having nothing but ourselves as its guide and system of reference, it is hope which reconciles the anguish of the futility of life with our innermost urge for truth and validity by assuring that nothing is in vain in the work of redemption. And yet has our personal freedom no light of its own?

4. Hope as the Completion of the Temporal in the Transcendence

Did we not by this tortuous way come back from where we started and reach back towards the re-evaluation and re-appreciation of the present? What a paradox: it is certainly because of its essential narrowness, apparent haphazardness and incompleteness that we reach beyond it by our hopes. But is it not from its wealth of the ever-fluctuating and never adequately graspable elements of experience of ourselves and the world, ever renewing, reshaping in an infinite array of forms, qualities, nuances of the life texture radiating in all directions, infinitely suggestive, evocative, inspiring our imagination, feelings, wishes, in short is it not due to this ever freshly exploding, transforming and transient existence, the contingent nature of things and ourselves that we may unfold all our virtualities and in the midst of it conceive, outline and forge the lasting substance of our being? For what other purpose after all would the whole game of finiteness and transcendence, the game of redemption as patterned in the creative design be meant for, and be aimed at? What else could be the meaning of human freedom?

Is it not in this contingent world that Christ had to accomplish the work of redemption? Is it not to work for it that He has taught us? The contingent world is all we have; all mystics agree that we cannot have a conception of anything beyond it. Yet the question of transcendence lies at the heart of contingency. We cannot after Christ's message content ourselves with living according to the law or with leading "a good life" in the "divine presence" and thus cooperating with the work of creation. We seek to transcend in an imminent way, but once on the way, in the dark, when the tread constantly vanishes from sight and menaces to break, when there is no help, no guarantee, no support, where do we turn? What evidence will lift our heart when hope is nebulous, lost from sight, buried in the dull misery of the present instant? In fact, when our spontaneity is almost extinguished by the cold and hard blows of triviality, our hope cannot lift itself from the ground and project a faith into a work, which lies undone, into a being, who lies inert and paralyzed.

In our radical loneliness, left completely to our own judgment with nowhere to turn because all doors remain closed, all our little joys dull, our tasks meaningless, could we ever pull ourselves together again and rise from the bottom of oblivion unless . . . *How could we stand loneliness unless we believed in the communion of souls?!*

It might happen that unexpectedly, at an incalculable instant we might discover within another man traces of his having preceded us on the road. It might occur that for an instant we will "communicate" with another man our innermost concern and the uncertainty we share. We might also attempt to "communicate" to others our plight and thirst for truth in creative work, thus revealing it to ourselves. Is it not communication alone that makes us emerge again from the inertia of our own matter and the chaotic opacity of the human world? But of what does this communication consist? How long may the circumstances, which allow it, last? How long do we have courage, feeling of purpose, and strength of commitment to struggle for it, counteracting all the spontaneous forces of the circumambient world and our own unstable, fluctuating nature to preserve it, to keep it alive? What is the meaning of the instant of human communion?

We have found that all hope completes the present by expanding it into what is not yet there and letting it be lived as if it were. Thereby hope makes us surpass effectively the narrow limits of the contingent present; it amplifies, gives a deeper perspective and activates our experience. But all types of hope we have so far discussed surpassed the narrowness of the present along the temporal spread, along the stretch of life-expectations and in its modes direct or derived. The effective fulguration of hope is crystallized in the images which it proposes to us. Our imagination is meant to serve the purpose of this life and closing its virtualities upon it; what else could we imagine than what belongs to the equipment of natural, life-promoting forces?

And yet what we long after is to surpass, to transcend the narrowness of life, to transcend the finiteness of man. If that could be accomplished at all, it could not be by the expansion of successive presents. It is not in an ever-advancing postponement, in an illusory future, made according to the pattern "now and after" over which we have no hold, which is nothing but the present play of illusion that this could be done. Neither could we redeem the vicissitudes of temporality in a nontemporal stage, within an "after" that would not be anymore temporal since, then, with the vanished finite, contingent, developing nature of man, all our actual aims, means, stimuli and occasions would vanish.

Yet it might happen that when all seems lost—when the only and unique friend has lost faith in us, denied us and left us abandoned, then what hope could we nurture? What could we expect if the objects of expectations were rejected beforehand? What could we imagine about eternal happiness, if its paradigm in the human heart were denied us? What could we know about the ultimate Divine mercy, understanding, solicitude, compassion and tenderness if we did not live it in man? First of all what could remain valid for us within ourselves, such that we could rely upon, hold on to, if in our absolute trust and abandon, and faith, we were denied, rejected and dissolved within another heart?

Yet, even when all seems to be lost—all the laborious search for the destiny swept away from the scene—a dark wall enclosing us from all sides, then it might happen that our empty eyes instead of reflecting against the wall will be drawn into a perspective opening before them; that instead of stopping at the usual facade of the self-enclosed moulds of nature and culture shaped being, representing nothing but a concrete temporal instance of the vast shaping scheme of civilization, we are bedazzled by a sudden revalation of an inward sphere to this outward shell, uniquely itself, uncomparable and unprecedented. Instead of a specific instance of virtualities culturally determined and responding to the social situation of the moment, restrained to it in its significance, in this intensity of the instant, the inward eye opens upon and sinks into an infinite depth. Perspectives, as if outlined by myriads of rays, which usually scattered about, each of them confined to a narrow frame of one being, now open, gathered all in the unique intensity of the instant within one human universe, the ALL.

Instead of always missing our aim, and retreating discouraged into our own shell, we encounter, as Leibniz would say "a monad," a soul who unlike all the others which reflect the universe each from their single point of view—their particular perspective—reflects the universe in all its avenues to be followed in the essence of creation. From our narrow frame we are transported beyond the succession of time and the present situation. The world, the universe of man, its thin and dull surface seems like a base relief from the flatness of the present moment raised into infinitely expanding dimensions into which our shrunk, mutilated and despoiled self sinks as in the endless abundance of Being. From the neutral dullness of everyday existence our own inert, muted, deafened being expands into a luminous, radiating sphere. All the bits spread over the succession of becoming, scattered over the whole surface and thus deprived of the inward force flowing together into the personal universe of man, as if it were the spirit of the human heart that it is all about.

What does it matter that such a perfect instant, which like "a day of spring in the middle of winter" reaches beyond the cycle of time, the sum total of human nostalgias, expectations, dreams, and illusions finding their fulfillment in the present instant gathering the past and future, the holocaust of one total experience, may be *rarissime?* Is it not there, in the human communion that we find the redemption of the fleetingness of time? We discover that although hopes projecting us into the future will never become real, they are not altogether futile; they exalt our spirit for the right cause, the fulfillment of which is initiated right *now,* right *here* in the present instant.

In fact, how can such an encounter, such an instant communion between two men be possible? Each of them having originated and developed his being in a different temporal sequence within different anthropological and social systems, along different lines, their original authentic being lost in this mould of contingency, how could they ever pierce through it? How, in this opaque maze in which each attempt at communication seems to be necessarily at cross-purposes since the human universe is split into an infinite amount of self-encapsuled individual worlds, solitary islands upon an unchartable sea, could two souls ever meet in the purity of their inward truth? In this infinitely complex array of the ever-evolving, forming themselves and blurring their contours, could it ever be planned that two souls would ever meet? Each follows its own trajectory; each closes itself to the others in its specific way.

The occasion is truly extraordinary. In the absolute density, as a focus of an infinite array of coincidences, unifying the disparate temporal series, phases of future and past united, this *imminent* present instant transcends the limits of contingency itself. The fulguration of the imminent instant responds to what we desperately long for; it fills all the voids opened by our innermost longing; it lifts our heart in a new *HOPE, the authentic hope making us feel that nothing is in vain.* What does it matter that this moment might not last, might never come again? That the vicissitudes of life, fluctuations of our being, anxiety and fear might destroy in germ this unique communion of the souls?

But was it not in such an unique instant that redemption itself, that Christ in person came to us when we were abject, denied and lost, abandoned by the only friend who had our absolute trust when we were agonizing through the period of Christian hope? In this effervescence of our whole being responding and flown into our deepest longing after the absolute, the beautiful, the elevated, the perfect, having found its terminal within another human universe were we not, for once, totally free? Could we ever again feel deserted and lost in the battlefield? We do not need to seek approvals in an illusory future; we are free to pursue our road and we know that nothing is in vain.

Let time make all the ravages. Let it carry away all illusion and all expectation; let it cut short all attachments and all bonds; let it divide and put asunder the closest knits running through our heart; let it destroy youth, beauty, health and life itself. We have the present instant, which may surge imminently in all the dimensions of existence allowing us in the act of HOPE to consummate the completion of freedom.

Happiness, beauty, and personal truth unfold in the succession of finite instants. *Carpe Diem!*

A SELECT BIBLIOGRAPHY*

Bloch, Ernst, *Das Prinzip Hoffnung.* Frankfurt am Main: Suhrkamp, 1967.

Boros, Ladislaus, *Living in Hope.* Tr. by W.J. O'Hara. New York: Herder and Herder, 1970.

Braaten, Carl, E., *The Future of God: The Revolutionary Dynamics of Hope.* New York: Harper and Row, 1969.

Cousin, Ewert, H. (ed.), *Hope and the Future of Man.* Philadelphia: Fortress Press, 1972.

Edmaier, Alois, *Horizonte der Hoffnung: Eine Philosophische Studie.* Regensburg: Pustet, 1968.

Ellul, Jacques, *L'esperance oubliée.* Paris: Gallimard, 1972.

Fackre, Gabriel, *The Rainbow Sign: Christian Futurity.* Grand Rapids, Mich.: W.B. Eerdmans Pub. Co., 1969.

Fromm, Erich, *The Revolution of Hope: Toward a Humanized Technology.* New York: Harper and Row, 1968.

Marcel, Gabriel, *Homo Viator: Introduction to a Metaphysic of Hope.* Tr. by Emma Crauford. Chicago: Regnery, 1951.

Moltmann, Jurgen, *Theology of Hope.* New York: Harper and Row, 1967.

Sherman, Franklin (ed.), *Christian Hope and the Future of Humanity.* Minneapolis: Augsburg Publishing House, 1969.

Whelan, Joseph, P. (ed.), *The God Experience: Essays in Hope.* New York: Newman Press, 1971.

*Compiled by Harold Pemberton, St. John's University, Jamaica, New York, U.S.A.

Index

INDEX

Reichelt, K.L., 155, 161-162, 173, 180.
Reichenbach, H., 1020.
Reik, T., 941, 955.
Reinhardt, K., 954.
Reischauer, E., 80, 296.
Renckens, H., 378.
René, F., 482.
Reverdin, O., 387.
Richard, R.L., 811.
Richards, A., 32, 39-40, 47.
Richardson, A., 811.
Richardson, W.J., 773.
Ricoeur, P., 881, 955.
Rideau, E., 1041.
Rievaulx de, A., 426.
Rilke, R.M., 961, 971.
Ringer, G., 680.
Ringer, V., 680.
Ringgren, H., 378.
Riska, A., x, 1001.
Rist, J., 795, 797.
Ritter, C., 402, 407-409, 413.
Riviere, J., 941.
Roberts, A., 413.
Robin, L., 387, 389, 402, 406-407.
Robinson, E.A., 933.
Robinson, J.A., 724.
Robinson, J.A.T., 486, 777, 794, 811.
Robinson, J.M., 773.
Robinson, N., 848.
Robinson, S., 760.
Robson-Scott, W.D., 941.
Rochefoucauld la, F., 588.
Rodriguez, O., 584.
Roheim, G., 952, 955-956.
Rolfe, E., 955.
Rolfes, E., 417, 442.
Root, H.E., 591, 603, 611.
Rosmini, A., 689.
Ross, F.H., 295.

Ross, W.D., 391, 393, 396, 403, 406, 418, 420, 423, 426, 439, 442, 1018.
Rosthal, R., 680.
Rotenstreich, N., 1052, 1065.
Roth, R.J., 1052.
Rotwein, E., 611.
Rouault, G., 964, 976.
Rowan, J.P., viii, 385, 439.
Rowe, W.W., 1040.
Rowley, H.H., 347, 350, 361, 363.
Royce, J., 1022-1027, 1039-1040.
Rubenstein, R., 780, 794, 811, 1055, 1062, 1065.
Rumi, A., 67-68, 574.
Russell, B., 277, 397, 550, 573, 807-808, 1002, 1011, 1020.
Rylaarsdam, J.C., 315.

Sabara, 213.
Sabellius, 788.
Samuel, V.C., 508, 513, 519.
Samuelson, P.A., 1020.
Sandmel, S., 351.
Sanford, J., 953-954, 956.
Sangharakshita, B., 164-165, 180.
Sankara, R., 186, 190-191, 196-211, 217-218, 230, 238, 244, 277.
Sankaracarya, A., 213.
Sansom, G.B., 297.
Sanson, H., 585.
Sarkan, Z., 516.
Sastri, S.S., 213.
Sartre, J.P., xi, 8-9, 485, 533, 757, 770, 794-795, 807, 851-863, 968, 1022, 1034-1037, 1041, 1058.
Saul, 358.
Saunders, E.D., 296.
Savage, D., 955.